Praise for H. W. Brands'

Traitor to His Class

"Brands is something of a rare breed. . . . This volume shows the precision and attention to detail that one would expect from a scholar and, at the same time, reads like a novel. . . . [It] will appeal to the expert and the general reader alike." —*The Christian Science Monitor*

"Fresh, approachable, evenhanded." —*The Boston Globe*

"H. W. Brands has accomplished a remarkable feat in this terrific work. As if he were creating characters in a novel, he has brought to vivid life the central figures in his story—FDR, Eleanor, Sara Roosevelt, Winston Churchill, and the inner circle in the White House—while at the same time providing a fresh understanding of the rich historical context for their thoughts and actions at every step along the way."
—Doris Kearns Goodwin, Pulitzer Prize–winning historian and author of *Team of Rivals*

"An easy-to-read portrait of a towering figure in American history."
—*St. Louis Post-Dispatch*

"Brilliantly executed. . . . Lean, with no fatty padding or sermonizing. Brands is resolutely evenhanded in his treatment of FDR, and he makes no attempt to persuade his readers of FDR's virtues or lack thereof."
—*The Dallas Morning News*

"H. W. Brands is a master at finding the essence of an important American life, telling its story grippingly and showing us why it is important to our own generation. With *Traitor to His Class*, he has surpassed even his own high standard. This judicious and compelling work is the first major one-volume biography written by an historian too young to have lived in Franklin Roosevelt's time. It deserves a wide audience, especially among those younger Americans who need to be told why we all owe so much to FDR."
—Michael Beschloss, author of *Presidential Courage* and *The Conquerors*

H. W. Brands

Traitor to His Class

H. W. Brands is the Dickson Allen Anderson Centennial
Professor of History at the University of Texas at Austin.
The author of *Andrew Jackson*, *Lone Star Nation*, and *The
Age of Gold*, he was a finalist for the Pulitzer Prize for bi-
ography for *The First American: The Life and Times of
Benjamin Franklin*. He lives in Austin, Texas.

www.hwbrands.com

Traitor to His Class

❖ The ❖

PRIVILEGED LIFE *and* RADICAL PRESIDENCY

of FRANKLIN DELANO ROOSEVELT

H. W. BRANDS

ANCHOR BOOKS

A Division of Random House, Inc.

New York

FIRST ANCHOR BOOKS EDITION, SEPTEMBER 2009

Copyright © 2008 by H. W. Brands

All rights reserved. Published in the United States by Anchor Books,
a division of Random House, Inc., New York, and in Canada
by Random House of Canada Limited, Toronto.
Originally published in hardcover in the United States by Doubleday,
a division of Random House, Inc., New York, in 2008.

Anchor Books and colophon are registered trademarks of
Random House, Inc.

All photographs are courtesy of the Franklin Delano Roosevelt Library,
except for "With Hoover en route to the Capitol" and "Signing
the Social Security Act," which are courtesy of the Library of Congress.

The Library of Congress has cataloged the Doubleday edition as follows:
Brands, H. W.
Traitor to his class : the privileged life and radical presidency of
Franklin Delano Roosevelt /
H. W. Brands.—1st ed.
p. cm.
Includes bibliographical references and index.
1. Roosevelt, Franklin D. (Franklin Delano), 1882–1945.   2. Presidents—United States—
Biography.   3. United States—Politics and government—1933–1945.   I.   Title.
E807.B735 2008
973.917092—dc22 [B]
2008015164

Anchor ISBN: 978-0-307-27794-7

Author photograph © Barton Wilder
Book design by Elizabeth Rendfleisch

www.anchorbooks.com

Printed in the United States of America
11th Printing

CONTENTS

Prologue

Franklin Roosevelt's Sunday morning began as most of his Sundays began: with a cigarette and the Sunday papers in bed. He wasn't a regular churchgoer, confining his attendance mainly to special occasions: weddings, funerals, his three inaugurations. In his youth and young adulthood he had often spent Sundays on the golf course, but his golfing days were long over, to his lasting regret. This Sunday morning—the first Sunday of December 1941—he read about himself in the papers. The *New York Times* gave him the top head, explaining how he had sent a personal appeal for peace to the Japanese emperor. Neither the *Times* nor the *Washington Post*, which provided similar coverage, included the substance of his appeal, as he had directed the State Department to release only the fact of his having approached the emperor. This way he got credit for his efforts on behalf of peace without having to acknowledge how hopeless those efforts were. The papers put the burden of warmongering on Japan; the government in Tokyo declared that its "patience" with the Western powers was at an end. Heavy movements of Japanese troops in occupied Indochina—movements about which Roosevelt had quietly released corroborating information—suggested an imminent thrust against Thailand or Malaya.

Sharing the headlines with the prospect of war in the Pacific was the reality of war in the Atlantic and Europe. The German offensive against the Soviet Union, begun the previous June, seemed to have stalled just short of Moscow. Temperatures of twenty below zero were punishing the German attackers, searing their flesh and freezing their crankcases. The Germans were forced to find shelter from the cold; the front apparently had locked into place for the winter. On the Atlantic, the British had just sunk a German commerce raider, or so they claimed. The report from the war zone was sketchy and unconfirmed. The admiralty in London volunteered that its cruiser *Dorsetshire* had declined to look for survivors, as it feared German submarines in the area.

Roosevelt supposed he'd get the details from Winston Churchill. The president and the prime minister shared a love of the sea, and Churchill, since assuming his current office eighteen months ago, had made a point of apprising Roosevelt of aspects of the naval war kept secret from others outside the British government. Churchill and Roosevelt wrote each other several times a week; they spoke by telephone less often but still regularly.

An inside account of the war was the least the prime minister could provide, as Roosevelt was furnishing Churchill and the British the arms and equipment that kept their struggle against Germany alive. Until now Roosevelt had left the actual fighting to the British, but he made certain they got what they needed to remain in the battle.

The situation might change at any moment, though, the Sunday papers implied. The Navy Department—which was to say, Roosevelt—had just ordered the seizure of Finnish vessels in American ports, on the ground that Finland had become a de facto member of the Axis alliance. Navy secretary Frank Knox, reporting to Congress on the war readiness of the American fleet, assured the legislators that it was "second to none." Yet it still wasn't strong enough, Knox said. "The international situation is such that we must arm as rapidly as possible to meet our naval defense requirements simultaneously in both oceans against any possible combination of powers concerting against us."

Roosevelt read these remarks with satisfaction. The president had long prided himself on clever appointments, but no appointment had tickled him more than his tapping of Knox, a Republican from the stronghold of American isolationism, Chicago. By reaching out to the Republicans—not once but twice: at the same time that he chose Knox, Roosevelt named Republican Henry Stimson secretary of war—the president signaled a desire for a bipartisan foreign policy. By picking a Chicagoan, Roosevelt poked a finger in the eye of the arch-isolationist *Chicago Tribune,* a poke that hurt the more as Knox was the publisher of the rival *Chicago Daily News.*

Roosevelt might have chuckled to himself again, reflecting on how he had cut the ground from under the isolationists, one square foot at a time; but the recent developments were no laughing matter. Four years had passed since his "quarantine" speech in Chicago, which had warned against German and Japanese aggression. The strength of the isolationists had prevented him from following up at that time, or for many months thereafter. But by reiterating his message again and again—and with the help of Hitler and the Japanese, who repeatedly proved him right—he gradually brought the American people around to his way of thinking. He persuaded Congress to amend America's neutrality laws and to let the democracies purchase American weapons for use against the fascists. He sent American destroyers to Britain to keep the sea lanes open. His greatest coup was Lend-Lease, the program that made America the armory of the anti-fascist alliance.

He had done everything but ask Congress to declare war. The Sunday papers thought this final step might come soon. He knew more than the papers did, and he thought so, too.

❖   ❖   ❖

$\mathcal{B}$UT THERE WAS something he didn't know, or even imagine. Roosevelt was still reading the papers when an American minesweeper on a predawn patrol two miles off the southern coast of the Hawaiian island of Oahu, near the entrance to Pearl Harbor, spotted what looked like a periscope. No American submarines were supposed to be in the area, and the minesweeper reported the sighting to its backup, the destroyer *Ward.* The report provoked little alarm, partly because Hawaii was so far from Japan and partly because Pearl Harbor's shallow bottom seemed sufficient protection against enemy subs. Some officers on the *Ward* questioned the sighting; eyes play tricks in the dark. Perhaps there *was* an American sub in the area; this wouldn't have been the first time overzealous security or a simple screwup had prevented information from reaching the patrols. In any event, the *Ward* responded slowly to the asserted sighting and spent most of the next two hours cruising the area and discovering nothing.

While the desultory search continued off Oahu, Roosevelt in Washington pondered the latest diplomatic correspondence. American experts had cracked Japan's code more than a year earlier; since then Roosevelt had been secretly reading over the shoulder of the Japanese ambassador. Yesterday evening— Saturday, December 6—he had read a long message from Tokyo to the Japanese embassy. The message answered an ultimatum from Roosevelt, coming after many weeks of negotiations with the Japanese, in which the president insisted that Japan give up the territory it had seized in Southeast Asia and disavow designs on more. The Saturday message from Tokyo left no doubt that the Japanese government rejected the president's ultimatum.

"This means war," Roosevelt told Harry Hopkins, his closest adviser and constant companion these days. Hopkins agreed. Hopkins added that since war had become unavoidable, there would be advantages to striking the first blow.

Roosevelt shook his head. "We can't do that," he said. "We are a democracy and a peaceful people." He paused. "We have a good record."

But there was something strange about the Saturday message. The introduction explained that it contained fourteen parts, yet only thirteen were included. The final part had been withheld until this morning, Sunday. A courier brought it to the White House just before ten o'clock. Roosevelt read it quickly. It said what anyone could have inferred from the previous parts: that Japan was breaking off the negotiations with the United States. The Japanese ambassador was instructed to deliver this news to the State Department at one o'clock that afternoon. The precision of the instruction was unusual. Why one o'clock? The most probable answer appeared to be that the delivery would coincide with the expected Japanese attack against Thailand or Malaya.

At six o'clock Hawaiian time—eleven o'clock in Washington—a task force of six Japanese aircraft carriers turned into a stiff wind three hundred miles north of Oahu. The ships and their four hundred warplanes constituted the most powerful naval strike force ever assembled till then—a fact that made it all the more remarkable that the carriers had managed to slip away from Japan and steam for eleven days toward Hawaii undetected by American intelligence or reconnaissance. Nor did any Americans see or hear the wave after wave of torpedo planes, bombers, and fighters the carriers launched into the predawn sky. The planes formed into assigned groups and headed south.

Roosevelt frequently took lunch at his desk in the Oval Office, and he did so this Sunday. Hopkins joined him. They were eating and discussing the crisis in the Pacific and the war in Europe when a radar station on the north shore of Oahu detected signals on its screens unlike anything the operators had ever observed. Radar was a new technology, introduced in Hawaii only months before. The operators were novices, and their screens had often been blank. But suddenly the screens lit up, indicating scores of aircraft approaching Oahu from the north. One of the operators telephoned headquarters. The duty officer there told him not to worry. A reinforcement squadron of American bombers was expected from California; the headquarters officer assumed that these were the aircraft on the north shore radar screens.

Roosevelt and Hopkins had finished eating when the first wave of Japanese planes approached Pearl Harbor. Roosevelt had a mental image of Pearl, as he had visited the naval base early in his presidency. But it had grown tremendously in the seven years since then. It boasted one of the largest dry-docks in the world, a rail yard with locomotives and cars that moved freight between the berthed vessels and various warehouses, a factory complex that could fabricate anything needed to maintain or repair a ship, tank farms with fuel enough for extended campaigns across the Pacific, a midharbor naval air station on Ford Island to defend the base and the ships, a naval hospital to treat the sick and wounded, barracks for the enlisted men and civilian personnel, and other support facilities along the harbor and in the surrounding area.

But the heart of Pearl Harbor was "Battleship Row," on the east side of Ford Island, where seven of America's greatest warships were moored this Sunday morning. An eighth was in the drydock. These vessels, the pride of America's Pacific fleet, embodied a generation of efforts to secure America's national interest in the western ocean. Their construction had begun on the Navy Department watch of Franklin Roosevelt, who as assistant navy secretary from 1913 to 1920 had employed every means of patriotic persuasion, bureaucratic guile, and political finesse to augment America's naval power. The *Arizona,* the *Oklahoma,* the *Tennessee,* and the *Nevada,* now gleaming in the Sunday morning sun, were his babies, and no father was ever prouder.

All was calm aboard the battleships as the Japanese planes approached the base. The sailors and civilians on the ships and ground initially mistook the planes for American aircraft. When the sirens wailed a warning, most within earshot assumed it was another drill. But as the Japanese fighters screamed low over the airfield, strafing the runways and the American planes on the tarmac, the reality of the assault became unmistakable. Some Americans on the ground thought they could almost reach out and touch the rising sun painted on the wings of the Japanese aircraft, so low did the fighters descend; others, with a different angle, could peer into the faces of the Japanese pilots through the cockpit windows as the planes tore by.

The Japanese fighters suppressed any defensive reaction by American aircraft, guaranteeing the attackers control of the air. The Japanese bombers and torpedo planes concentrated on the primary targets of the operation: the American battleships. The torpedo planes approached low and flat, dropping their munitions into the open water beside Battleship Row. The torpedo warheads contained a quarter ton of high explosives each, and the torpedoes' guidance systems had been specially calibrated for Pearl's shallow waters. The American crewmen aboard the battleships saw the torpedo planes approaching; they watched the torpedoes splash into the water; they followed the trails from the propellers as the torpedoes closed in on the ships. With the ships motionless and moored, and the surprise complete, there was nothing the seamen could do to prevent the underwater missiles from finding their targets. The *California* took two torpedo hits, the *West Virginia* six, the *Arizona* one, the *Nevada* one, the *Utah* two. The *Oklahoma* suffered the most grievously from the torpedo barrage. Five torpedoes blasted gaping holes in its exposed port side; it swiftly took on water, rolled over, and sank. More than four hundred officers and men were killed by the explosions, by the fires the torpedoes touched off, or by drowning.

The destruction from below the surface of the harbor was complemented by the Japanese bombers' attacks from high overhead. Dive bombers climbed two miles into the sky to gain potential energy for their bombing runs; the Americans on the ground and ships heard their rising whine long before the planes burst through the scattered clouds and released their munitions upon the ships and the facilities on shore. Conventional bombers dropped their payloads from a few thousand feet in elevation; what those on the ground and ships first heard of these was the whistling of the armor-piercing bombs as gravity sucked them down. The misses were more obvious at first than the hits; geysers of water spewed into the air from the physical impact of the errant bombs. The ones that hit their targets disappeared into the holes they punched in the decks, hatches, and gun turrets of the vessels. Only when they had plumbed the depths of the ships did they detonate, and even then the overburden of steel muffled and shrouded their explosions.

But the explosions were more destructive for being contained. Nearly all the battleships sustained severe bomb damage; by far the worst befell the *Arizona*. Several bombs set it afire and triggered a massive secondary explosion that split its deck and burst its hull. More than a thousand seamen died in the fires and blast, and the vessel settled on the harbor bottom, its superstructure still burning ferociously above the waterline.

❖ ❖ ❖

ROOSEVELT HAD FINISHED lunch by now. He received a call from the State Department informing him that the Japanese ambassador had postponed his visit until two o'clock. The president was pondering this new wrinkle when the Oval Office phone rang again. It was Frank Knox, who said the Navy Department had received a radio report from Oahu, where the American commander was advising all stations that an air raid was under way. "This is no drill!" the commander emphasized.

Harry Hopkins reacted the way nearly every other knowledgeable person did on hearing the report. "There must be some mistake," Hopkins said. "Surely Japan would not attack in Honolulu."

Roosevelt was as astonished as Hopkins. He had expected an attack on Thailand or Malaya, conceivably the Philippines. But not Hawaii. Hawaii was too far from Japan, too far from the Dutch East Indies, whose oil was the chief object of Japan's southward expansion, and too well defended.

Yet the president listened calmly to the news. Now that he thought about it, the very improbability of an attack on Pearl Harbor must have made it appealing to the Japanese, who had a history of doing the unexpected. He assumed that the American forces at Pearl would acquit themselves well.

If the report from Hawaii *was* true, Roosevelt thought, it made his job easier. He had been prepared to ask Congress for a war declaration in response to a Japanese attack against Southeast Asia. He had believed he could get a declaration, but because that region meant little to most Americans, he knew he would have to work at it. Now that American territory had been attacked, he would hardly have to ask.

He called the State Department, where the Japanese ambassador and an associate had just arrived for the ambassador's postponed meeting. Roosevelt spoke with Cordell Hull, the secretary of state. "There's a report that the Japanese have attacked Pearl Harbor," Roosevelt said.

"Has the report been confirmed?" Hull asked.

"No."

Hull agreed with Roosevelt that the report was probably true, but he didn't mention it in his meeting with the two Japanese diplomats. By now the timing of the original appointment was obvious: it had been intended to coincide with the onset of war between Japan and the United States. The postponement remained a mystery. The Japanese diplomats said nothing of the events in Hawaii, but the secretary's knowledge of the Pearl Harbor attack colored his response to the note the diplomats handed him, the intercepted version of which he had read previously. "In all my fifty years of public service," Hull said, letting his anger rise as he spoke, "I have never seen a document that was more crowded with infamous falsehoods and distortions—infamous falsehoods and distortions on a scale so huge that I never imagined until today that any government was capable of uttering them." He ordered the Japanese diplomats from his office.

❖ ❖ ❖

THE BOMBING AND strafing continued for more than an hour and a half.
Many of the Japanese bombers made multiple passes before dropping their
ordnance, as the broken clouds and then the heavy smoke blocked their view
of their targets. The fighters crisscrossed the area, too, in their case to ma-
chine-gun sailors in the water, soldiers and civilians fleeing burning buildings,
and aircraft and facilities they had missed or not aimed at before. The Americans now returned the fire, with modest success. Anti-aircraft guns brought
down two dozen of the more than three hundred attacking planes. As the
Japanese planes crashed to earth and sea, their hurtling wreckage added to the
destruction.

By quarter to ten, the last of the Japanese planes ran out of bombs and ammunition and turned away to the north. Their pilots looked back and down
upon a remarkable morning's work. The placid scene of resting power that
had greeted their approach had become a burning, bloody chaos; the core of
America's mighty Pacific fleet was a ruin of twisted steel, flaming oil, floating
bodies, and battered pride.

❖ ❖ ❖

ROOSEVELT NOW KNEW that the initial reports were accurate, as he had
expected. What he hadn't expected, and what shocked him far more than he
let on, was how much damage the attack did. The initial notice had suggested
a raid, but this was far more than a raid. It was a major strike with potentially
strategic implications. And the American defenders had been caught inexplicably unready. The news from Hawaii remained incomplete, but each additional report revealed an unfolding debacle.

At three o'clock Washington time, as the Japanese planes were clearing
Oahu's north shore en route to their rendezvous with their carriers, Roosevelt
convened a meeting of his principal diplomatic and military advisers. Cordell
Hull, Frank Knox, and Henry Stimson were there, along with Admiral Harold
Stark, the chief of naval operations, and General George Marshall, the army
chief of staff. The mood was grim but determined. For months all had expected war; now all exhibited a certain relief that it had finally come. All were
stunned by the manner in which the fighting had commenced; all anticipated
a long and difficult, though ultimately successful, struggle.

Roosevelt asked Marshall about the disposition of the army in the Pacific and particularly of the army's air forces in the Philippines. Marshall said he had ordered Douglas MacArthur, the commanding general in Manila, to take every precautionary measure. The president directed that the Japanese embassy in Washington and Japan's consulates in other cities be protected against vigilante violence and that Japanese citizens in the United States be placed under surveillance. He rejected a military cordon around the White House but ordered Stimson and Knox to safeguard America's arsenals, private munitions factories, and key bridges.

Roosevelt told the group he would go to Congress the next day. Cordell Hull recommended a detailed description of Japan's history of aggression in Asia and the Pacific. Roosevelt rejected the advice. His statement would be succinct, he said. The only thing that mattered at the moment was that Japan had attacked America and killed many Americans.

As the group dispersed to carry out his orders, Roosevelt dealt with messages and queries that arrived by phone, cable, and courier. Winston Churchill called from England. "Mr. President, what's this about Japan?" the prime minister asked.

"It's quite true," Roosevelt answered. "They have attacked us at Pearl Harbor. We are all in the same boat now."

"This certainly simplifies things," Churchill said.

During the course of the afternoon, new information detailed the disaster in Hawaii. Five battleships had been sunk or were on fire and sinking. Several other vessels had been destroyed or seriously damaged. More than a hundred aircraft had been blasted beyond repair. More than two thousand sailors and soldiers had been killed, and more than a thousand others wounded. Late in the afternoon, word arrived that Japanese planes had attacked American bases in the Philippines and, despite Marshall's warning to MacArthur, inflicted heavy damage.

Calls came from the Justice and Treasury departments, where officials needed guidance on how to respond to the apparent state of war with Japan. Press secretary Stephen Early ran in and out of the Oval Office, relaying information from the president to reporters. Harry Hopkins recommended a meeting of the full cabinet and a presidential briefing of the congressional leadership. Roosevelt summoned Grace Tully, his personal secretary, and dictated a draft of the message he would deliver to Congress the next day.

The cabinet gathered at half past eight in the Oval Office. The department secretaries crowded around the president's desk, feeling the weight of history on their shoulders. Roosevelt reinforced the feeling by describing the session as the most important cabinet meeting since Lincoln had convened his secretaries at the beginning of the Civil War.

Roosevelt read the group the draft of his message to Congress. Hull complained that it was too short and unspecific. The president ignored him.

At nine-thirty the congressional leaders arrived. Roosevelt explained the situation in the Pacific. He formally requested the opportunity to speak to Congress the next day. A time was set: half past noon. The lawmakers asked whether the president would seek a war declaration. He said he hadn't decided.

They didn't believe him, and he didn't expect them to. He realized that if he acknowledged a decision for war, the news would be all over Washington within minutes of the legislators' leaving, and all over the world within hours. He didn't want to preempt himself or slight Congress.

The lawmakers were ready to declare war even without a presidential request. Tom Connally of Texas emerged from the White House demanding vengeance against the Japanese. "Japan started this war in treachery," Connally said. "We will end it in victory." Warren Austin of Vermont considered war a foregone conclusion. "Of course it's war," Austin said. "I can't see any other sequel." Harry Byrd of Virginia vowed to "wipe Japan off the map."

Even the isolationists supported war. Robert Taft of Ohio characterized a war declaration as necessary and inevitable. Arthur Vandenberg of Michigan had previously charged Roosevelt with trying to take America to war and had criticized him harshly. "But when war comes to us," Vandenberg now said, "I stand for the swiftest and most invincible answer." New York's Hamilton Fish promised to address America from the floor of the House of Representatives and urge the people to unite behind the president. "And if there is a call for troops," Fish said, "I expect to offer my services to a combat division."

❖   ❖   ❖

THE AMERICAN PEOPLE reacted more slowly. Most had followed the growing crisis in Asia with varying degrees of concern but also with the knowledge that previous crises had come and gone without entangling America directly. Most had expected that this crisis too would pass. The small number paying the closest attention had, with Roosevelt, supposed that the Japanese would attack somewhere; with Roosevelt nearly all of these imagined the blow would fall on Thailand or Malaya. Almost no one considered Hawaii a likely target.

The news from Pearl Harbor shocked the nation. The first reports reached Seattle and San Francisco as churches were emptying from morning services; congregants shared the ill tidings in shocked whispers. The news caught Kansas farm families sitting down to midday dinner; fathers and mothers looked at their teenage sons and suddenly saw soldiers about to be sent overseas. The news arrived in Chicago at halftime of a football game between the Chicago Bears and the crosstown Cardinals and made the game seem suddenly unimportant. The news halted tourists in Manhattan's Times Square, where they huddled against the December chill to read the sobering bulletins crawling along the headline tickers. In Boston the local CBS radio affiliate interrupted its review of the year's top stories to break the story that outdid them all.

For the rest of that day and through the night, Americans listened and waited. They listened to their radios to learn the extent of the damage. How many ships had been lost? How many servicemen killed? They waited to hear what the disaster meant. Would it be war? Surely yes, but what kind of war? War against whom? Japan, of course, but Germany as well? War for how long? To what end?

Their questions extended to the person who would provide them the beginning of answers. All knew the aspect Roosevelt presented to the public. How could they *not* know the face and voice of the man who had served longer than any other president in American history? Yet few professed, and none convincingly, to fathom the mind and heart, the motives and inspirations, that lay beneath and behind this familiar presence.

Not that people didn't form opinions—strong opinions. His enemies excoriated him as a communist and damned him for disregarding property rights and violating the canons of the capitalist marketplace. The wealthy denounced him for having betrayed the class of his birth. *Time* magazine devoted a lead article to the "burning bitterness" the better-off felt for Roosevelt. "Regardless of party and regardless of region," the Henry Luce weekly asserted, "today, with few exceptions, members of the so-called Upper Class frankly hate Franklin Roosevelt." Their hatred was heightened by their confusion as they reflected on Roosevelt's apostasy. Why did he do it? What could have converted this scion of privilege into a radical critic of the established order?

Roosevelt's friends were no less mystified. They applauded his boundless energy, his unsinkable optimism, his bold willingness to employ the engines of government to tackle the social and human consequences of the worst industrial depression the nation had ever experienced. But they too wondered at the sources of his governing philosophy. What traumas or epiphanies had transformed a Hudson Valley patrician into a champion of the common people of America? Those on the inside scratched their heads, and sometimes tore their hair, at his leadership style, which set aides against aides, cabinet secretaries against cabinet secretaries, and the Democratic party against itself. After more than eight years they remained astonished at his ability to make visitors to the White House come away thinking he had agreed with whatever they had told him, without in fact his agreeing to anything.

Mostly they marveled at the calm he exuded at the eye of one storm after another. The signature line of his first inaugural address—that the only thing America had to fear was fear itself—had seemed a rhetorical flourish when inserted into the text, a brave but essentially empty effort to calm the country at the most dangerous moment of its worst financial crisis. But once those words were spoken, in his steady, confident tenor, and after they flashed across the radio waves to every neighborhood, village, and hamlet in the country, they magically acquired a substance that soothed the worst of the fears and allowed the president and Congress to pull the financial system back from the brink.

The insiders knew something of the source of his confidence. They knew how his golden youth of wealth, travel, and athletic vitality had segued into a charmed young adulthood of political preference and rapid advance—and how the brilliant career had been cut short, apparently, by a devastating attack of polio. Crushed by despair, he had clawed his way back to hope; struck down physically, he gradually regained his feet. He reentered the political arena, a fuller man for what he had lost, a deeper soul for what he suffered. His touch with the people seemed surer than ever, his voice more convincing. The people responded effusively, electing him governor of New York twice, then president overwhelmingly. They applauded his performance on their behalf and reelected him by a still larger margin. And after another four years they defied historical precedent and conventional wisdom to reelect him again. It was a record to imbue anyone with confidence.

Yet much of the mystery remained. He was gregarious, genuinely enjoying spirited conversation and the company of others. But the substance of the conversations flowed in one direction; though he talked a lot, he gave nothing away. Not even his wife—his companion and ally of thirty-six years—professed to know his mind. He rarely read books other than dime mysteries, so his tastes in reading furnished few clues. He kept no diary. His letters were singularly opaque. He spoke with journalists more often than any president in

American history, yet though his remarks treated policy in detail, they revealed little of the policy maker. His speeches evinced his devotion to democracy, to fair treatment of ordinary people, and to American national security, and did so with passion and eloquence. But the wellsprings of that devotion, the source of that passion, remained hidden. He seemed to like it that way.

❖   ❖   ❖

ℛOOSEVELT LEFT THE White House at noon on Monday, December 8, for the mile-and-a-quarter drive to the Capitol. His Secret Service contingent, mustered to maximum strength and tuned to a quivering degree of suspicion, scowled at the masses that lined both sides of Pennsylvania Avenue. After yesterday, who knew what form the enemy might take? The scores of thousands, however, registered only support for the president. They cheered, not lustily, not even enthusiastically, but with a strangely moving somberness.

His car pulled close to the rear entrance of the House chamber. In his early days in politics he would leap from his car at every opportunity to shake hands and kiss babies. Now he had to be lifted into a wheelchair and rolled to the speaker's room. He waited there until half past twelve, when, with the further help of strong arms and the heavy steel braces that locked his knees into place, he shuffled the several feet to the dais.

He gripped the lectern to steady himself, and let the room fall quiet. Immediately before him, on his left, sat the nine justices of the Supreme Court, their black robes more appropriate today than usual. To his right were the ten cabinet secretaries. Eighty-two senators sat behind the justices and the secretaries; the other fourteen members of the upper house were still hurrying back from the out-of-town locations where the stunning news had caught them. Three hundred eighty-nine members of the House of Representatives filled the seats behind the senators, demoted to the rear despite being the regular tenants of the chamber. Hundreds of visitors packed the galleries.

As he looked out on the expectant faces, Roosevelt remembered another audience, gathered half a decade earlier, to which he had declared that the current generation of Americans had a rendezvous with destiny. He had been thinking then of the challenges facing the country at home: a gravely disordered economy, a society showing years of strain. He had been calling his compatriots to figurative arms against the opponents of the changes he deemed essential to America's political and social development. The changes had commenced during his first term and had dramatically altered Americans' expectations of their government. He intended for the changes to continue and to become a permanent part of the American moral landscape.

But now he summoned his fellow citizens to literal arms. In a manner not even he could have guessed, as a result of events he couldn't have foreseen, his prediction of a special role for his generation of Americans had acquired a new and far broader significance. To them, as to no generation before them, had been entrusted the fate of the world. On them rested the hope of humanity, the belief in personal freedom and national self-government.

He took a breath. In a few seconds he would lead Americans across the threshold of a future radically different from anything they or their forebears had ever known. Some in his audience appreciated the magnitude of the task they were about to undertake; all understood the gravity of the moment.

The chamber was quiet. The nation listened.

"Yesterday, December 7, 1941," he began, "a date which will live in infamy . . ."

PART I

Swimming to Health

1882 ✣ 1928

1.

WARREN DELANO SPOILED ALL HIS CHILDREN BUT SARA ESPECIALLY. Delano was a New Bedforder who, like some others of that intrepid seaport, became a China merchant, which in the mid-nineteenth century meant he dealt in opium. He amassed a fortune in the East and retired to a handsome estate on the Hudson River where Sara was born in 1854. Yet the Panic of 1857 caught Delano out, and he found himself on the verge of ruin. He returned to China, redoubled his energies, and sold more opium than ever. He fetched his family from America and settled them in Hong Kong, where they lived in Oriental opulence. Seven-year-old Sara found the experience at once overwhelming and mundane: overwhelming in its initial foreignness, mundane in the way everything attached to family eventually becomes for children.

Her worldly education continued when the family returned home. Though legal, the opium trade wasn't respectable, and after Delano decided he'd accumulated enough to weather future downturns, he worked himself away from the business. The family took various routes home. Sara sailed with a brother and sister to Singapore and then Egypt, where the Suez Canal was under construction. They visited France and England before crossing the Atlantic to America. Along the way—if not earlier—she discovered that travel agreed with her, and during the next decade she returned to China and France, lived in Germany, and transited the completed Suez Canal.

By the time she finally resettled into life along the Hudson, she felt herself a person apart. Few of her neighbors had seen so much of the world; almost none of her contemporaries had partaken of such exotic experiences. She might not have said she was too good for the neighborhood—but her father said it on her behalf. Warren Delano took special pains to protect his daughter from the young men of the Hudson Valley. The military academy at West Point comprised the closest collection of bachelor males; the cadets found Sara, who had grown into a tall, slender, self-composed beauty, most enchanting. They came courting, only to be rebuffed by Sara's father, who understood that West Point, which provided a free education to young men clever and pushy enough to win the approval of their states' elected officials, appealed to the ambitious but impecunious among the nation's emerging manhood—precisely the sort from whom Sara should be protected.

Warren Delano had other suspicions of his daughter's suitors. As a staunch Republican he distrusted individuals of the opposite persuasion. "I will not say that all Democrats are horse thieves," he declared in a moment of magnanimity. "But it would seem that all horse thieves are Democrats." One young man was vetoed on account of his red hair.

Sara seemed not to resent or resist her father's intrusion into her love life. On the contrary, because she idolized him she accepted the high standards he set for her suitors. Years slipped past and she remained unattached to any save him. By the time she reached twenty-five she was well on the way to spinsterhood, a fate she viewed with outward equanimity.

But one day she accepted a dinner invitation from an old friend. During her peripatetic childhood Sara had lived in New York City for a time and become close to Anna Roosevelt, called Bamie (pronounced "Bammie"; also called Bye), the older sister of Theodore Roosevelt, the future president. Brilliant but afflicted by a spinal ailment, Bamie was, like Sara, a spinster-in-progress, and her widowed mother hosted a party for her and her sister, Corinne.

Mrs. Roosevelt was playing matchmaker that evening and had also invited James Roosevelt, a fifth cousin of Bamie, once removed. The Roosevelts had nothing against distant cousins marrying, as events would reveal, and Mrs. Roosevelt may have been thinking of pairing Bamie with James. But James saw only Sara. "He never took his eyes off of her and kept talking to her the whole time," Mrs. Roosevelt recalled.

A Delano-Roosevelt match wasn't an obvious one. James was fifty-one and Sara twenty-five. James had a son—James Jr., called Rosy—just six months older than Sara. And James was a Democrat.

Yet if James was old enough to be Sara's father, that stood him well in the eyes of Sara's actual father. Warren Delano had done business with James Roosevelt's partners and knew James from clubs they had in common. James's years promised stability in a relationship; James's wealth allayed concerns about fortune seeking. As for his politics, a series of visits by James to the Delano home opened Warren's eyes. "James Roosevelt is the first person who has made me realize that a Democrat can be a gentleman," he said later, still marveling at the thought.

For Sara's part, she saw in James Roosevelt things she hadn't seen in her youthful suitors. Her father was her model of what a man ought to be; James approached the model as closely as any man could and be plausibly marriageable. In 1880 Sigmund Freud was still a student at the University of Vienna and had yet to loose his theories of psychosexual development on the world; but Sara's friends didn't require Freud to tell them that much of what attracted her to James Roosevelt was his resemblance to the only man she had ever loved and admired. Perhaps Sara herself saw this, too.

In any case, when James Roosevelt requested of Warren Delano permission to marry his daughter, and Delano assented, Sara accepted the proposal with pleasure. A huge wedding would have been planned had James not been a widower; as it was, the prospect of the Roosevelt-Delano nuptials set dollar signs gleaming in the eyes of dressmakers, florists, coachmen, and caterers up and down the Hudson Valley. James's son, Rosy, had recently married Helen Astor, the daughter of high-society czarina Mrs. William Astor. (The dimensions of the Astor ballroom established the numerical limit of Ward McAllister's celebrated "four hundred.") Meanwhile on the Delano side, Sara's uncle Franklin Delano had married William Astor's sister. A merger of the Roosevelt and Delano clans, under the kindly gaze of the Astors, promised to be a memorable event indeed. But Sara's aunt Sarah Delano, for whom she was named, minus a letter, died amid the planning, and out of respect the ceremony was greatly simplified. A mere hundred guests witnessed the exchange of vows at the Delano home in October 1880. The couple departed that afternoon for the short carriage ride to Springwood, James Roosevelt's estate at Hyde Park. A month later the honeymoon began in earnest when the newlyweds left for Europe on a grand tour that lasted most of a year.

❖   ❖   ❖

Sara DOTED ON her husband but even more on the son she gave him. Fittingly for one who would end his life as the arbiter of Europe's fate, Franklin Delano Roosevelt was conceived on the Continent, perhaps in Paris, where James's father and dozens of Delanos met the honeymooners and occupied an entire floor of the Hôtel du Rhin. The couple returned home in plenty of time to ready themselves and the Hyde Park house for its new occupant. "At a quarter to nine my Sallie had a splendid large baby boy," James Roosevelt wrote in the family diary for January 30, 1882. "He weighs 10 lbs. without clothes."

From the beginning Sara asserted herself regarding her son. James Roosevelt wished to name the boy Isaac, after his paternal grandfather. Sara vetoed the idea. She doubtless didn't say as much to her husband, but her actions revealed that she considered the boy more a Delano than a Roosevelt, and the names she chose reflected her view. She initially thought to name her son Warren Delano, after her father. But her brother had just buried a young son named Warren and, upon Sara's inquiry, informed her that he couldn't endure the idea of another child of the family, so close in age to his lost boy, carrying the same name. Consequently Sara turned to her favorite uncle, Franklin Delano, who was childless and now delighted to have a namesake.

The christening of Franklin Delano Roosevelt took place at the St. James Episcopal Chapel in Hyde Park. The godmother was Eleanor Blodgett, a longtime friend of Sara's. There were two godfathers: Sara's brother-in-law Will Forbes and Elliott Roosevelt, Theodore's younger brother. Theodore might have seemed the more obvious choice between the two Roosevelt brothers, being the older and by most measures the more responsible. But Sara liked the charmingly troubled Elliott better than the earnest Theodore, and in any case she didn't expect her son's second godfather to play much role beyond the christening.

Franklin's infancy was unremarkable in certain respects. Weaned at twelve months, walking at sixteen, he was neither precocious nor slow. His first words were "Mama" and "Papa," apparently in that order; he added "Mamie" for the nurse who tended to the less appealing aspects of child rearing. Nurses and nannies weren't unusual among families of even modest means in New York in the Gilded Age; the millions of immigrants who poured into America during the latter half of the nineteenth century included hundreds of thousands of girls and young women willing to work for little money and remain till they found husbands. Helen McRorie, Franklin's nurse, had more experience than most in her occupation; Sara insisted on the best. And Helen had more help than most nurses. James and Sara Roosevelt employed several servants: a housekeeper named Elspeth McEachern (called Tiddle by young Franklin and thereafter by the rest of the family), a cook, a butler, a gardener, a horseman, multiple maids, and casual laborers as the work required. James Roosevelt was a gentleman farmer, which meant that the actual farming at Springwood was done by the hired men.

Sara bore James no other children, almost certainly, considering the ease with which she conceived Franklin, by her choice. Consequently Franklin grew up without live-in siblings, half brother Rosy, Sara's contemporary, having long since left home. But he never lacked for people about the house. In fact, in keeping with upper-class custom in America at the time, he saw more of the help than he did of his parents. Sara and James refused to let the responsibilities of parenthood impinge on their active social lives. They entertained their Hudson Valley neighbors and were entertained in turn. They dropped down to New York City, sometimes taking Franklin—and his nurse—and sometimes leaving them home. Franklin naturally was included on the regular summer visits to Sara's ancestral home near New Bedford; she insisted that he learn to cherish his Delano roots.

In his adulthood, hearers would sometimes wonder where Franklin Roosevelt got his accent. He didn't sound like a New Yorker, not even a Hudson Valley Knickerbocker. He didn't sound like a New Englander, despite the summers spent among the Delanos. He *did* sound rich, but this was as much a matter of tone and timbre—the self-confidence of one who expected the world to treat him well—as of pronunciation. And most other rich Americans sounded little like Roosevelt.

He sounded vaguely British, which made sense in terms of his upbringing. As a child and youth, Franklin Roosevelt spent almost as much time in Britain and continental Europe as in America. Before his fifteenth birthday he traveled eight times to Europe; each visit lasted months, and the eight together accounted for years of the period of his life when he was mastering language. His closest companions during much of this time were the Ulster natives Mamie and Tiddle, which perhaps intensified the British influence on his patterns of speech.

The trips started early. Franklin wasn't yet three, in the fall of 1884, when James, Sara, Franklin, Mamie, and Tiddle crossed the Atlantic to England, where Franklin, Mamie, and Tiddle remained—at Tunbridge Wells—while James and Sara proceeded to France and Germany. After several weeks at various spas, Franklin's parents came back to England and the family spent the winter there. They didn't return to America until the spring, more than half a year after embarking.

Subsequent journeys followed a similar pattern. James, already suffering from the heart ailment that would kill him, found particular relief at the spa at Bad Nauheim, north of Frankfurt. His and Sara's visits to Nauheim became annual affairs, and until Franklin went off to school, at the advanced age of fourteen, he often accompanied his father and mother. He spent enough time in Germany to acquire moderate proficiency in the language—a facility he put to good use decades later. Like his mother and her generation of Delanos, he became as comfortable at sea as on land and as familiar with the countries of Europe as with his own.

❖ ❖ ❖

FASHION IS OFTEN cruel, but few fashions ever blighted so many lives as the one precipitated in America by the 1886 publication of *Little Lord Fauntleroy*, a novel for children and especially their mothers by Frances Hodgson Burnett. The English-born Burnett spun a story of an American boy who discovers that he is really an English earl and has to learn to play the part. The story prompted American mothers to imagine similar strokes of fortune touching their offspring and to dress their lads in readiness. Velvet suits with lace collars became the uniform of the scions of the aspiring classes; barbers despaired as the boys' locks were allowed to grow past the ears to the nape and shoulders. The fact that real earls-in-waiting and barons-to-be didn't dress this way had scant effect on the phenomenon in America, which like most fashions assumed a life of its own. Compounding the trauma for the victims was the simultaneous emergence of comparatively convenient photographic technology, which meant that their moments of mortification were frozen in silver gel for posterity.

Photographs from Franklin Roosevelt's fourth year show him in full Fauntleroy regalia. In one a wool cap perches atop his auburn locks, and patent boots keep the wind from his shins. In another his hair falls uncovered across his shoulders and down his back, and a silk sash wraps his waist. He appears happy, with a blooming cheek, a steady gaze, and a nose remarkably well defined for a child so young.

Nor did he have any reason not to be happy. He was the center of the universe, as far as he knew. No siblings intruded upon his consciousness—Rosy visited but might as well have been of another generation. Several adults, starting with his parents but including the hired staff, apparently had nothing better to do than to meet his needs and indulge his whims. The world afforded ceaseless entertainment: pony and buggy and sleigh rides, tobogganing on the slopes above the Hudson, journeys by train and steamship to exciting cities and countries, stays in fine hotels and fancy houses.

Neither did his Eden tarnish with age. He avoided the typical childhood trial of starting school by the simple expedient of not attending school till he was a teenager. His parents engaged tutors to teach him his letters and numbers and the other prerequisites for a genteel existence. He rarely clashed with other children, for he spent most of his time among adults.

In one respect he may have been cared for *too* well. Most children in the nineteenth century, like most children for millennia past, were exposed to all manner of microbes at an early age. Many died of infant and childhood illnesses, but those who survived developed robust immune systems, able to cope with the mundane infections they subsequently encountered. Franklin Roosevelt, by virtue of his comparative isolation, missed out on some of this tempering. Not for years would the consequences become apparent, but when they did, they would be devastating.

Among his childhood toys were boats: model boats at first but eventually the genuine article. His mother and uncle told tales of the China trade and their round-the-world voyages on clipper ships; during the summer visits to New Bedford he haunted the wharves, clambered about the old whalers, and heard the wizened harpooners talk of their personal Ahabs and Moby Dicks. When he was nine his father purchased a sailing yacht (with auxiliary engine), the fifty-foot *Half Moon,* which Franklin immediately adopted as his own.

The vessel sailed out of New York harbor but coasted up to New Bedford and on around Cape Cod to the Gulf of Maine. At the north end of the gulf, where the estuary of the St. Croix River meets the Bay of Fundy, in Canadian waters but barely a mile from Maine, it dropped anchor at Campobello Island. In the 1880s a group of land developers began promoting the island as a summer getaway for wealthy Americans. The attraction was the weather—pleasantly cool even in the hottest August—but also the isolation. Summer was the unhealthy season in America's burgeoning cities. Cholera and yellow fever weren't quite the scourges they had been, chiefly due to improved sanitation, but these and other maladies still struck with frightening frequency. And even outside the cities, malaria laid thousands low in the steamy months of the year.

The James Roosevelts discovered Campobello Island the year after Franklin was born. Friends recommended it, James and Sara and Franklin visited it, and James and Sara decided to build a cottage there. Upon its completion, months at Campobello became a summer ritual for the family.

A central part of that ritual was sailing. Franklin crewed for his father until he was tall enough to see over the tiller, at which point he often took the helm. The winds in the Bay of Fundy could be daunting, even in summer, and the tides, among the highest in the world, challenged the sharpest sailor. Franklin thrived on the tests.

Sailing and the sea absorbed him. He consumed books about boats and the feats of great mariners. He doodled sloops and ketches in the margins of the work he did for his tutors; his earliest surviving letter to his mother—

doubtless the first he wrote, as Sara saved everything—included a remarkably evocative rendering of three vessels under sail. He could scarcely contain his excitement while waiting for the *Half Moon* to be delivered. "Papa is going to buy a cutter that will go by naphtha"—for the auxiliary engine—"and we are going to sail in it at Campobello," he wrote his aunt in the spring of 1891. When the family traveled to Germany that summer, he apprised his cousins of his favorite activities: "On this paper is a picture of the big lake on which we row, and Papa got me a great big boat and I sail it every day."

❖   ❖   ❖

ENDICOTT PEABODY WAS an American-born, English-schooled Episcopalian priest and the walking, breathing embodiment of the manly Christian virtues as they were understood in America of the Victorian age. He excelled at sports, especially boxing, and had faced down rowdies from his first pulpit, in Tombstone, Arizona Territory. (He arrived not long after the infamous 1881 gunfight at the OK Corral, in which the Earp brothers and Doc Holliday exchanged lethal fire with Ike and Billy Clanton and their friends.) Besides improving his boxing skills, Peabody's Arizona experience revealed a knack for fundraising; he frequented the saloons of the town in a successful effort to persuade the patrons to contribute to the construction of a proper church for the frontier diocese.

Upon his return to the East, he devoted this talent to the fulfillment of a long-standing dream to establish an American school for young men that would reproduce the best of English private education. It helped Peabody's cause that his family was rich and well connected. His father was a partner of J. P. Morgan's father, and his brother had married into the Lawrence family of Massachusetts. The Lawrences summered at Campobello with the James Roosevelts, to whom they described Peabody's plan for a boys' school. James Roosevelt was impressed by the board of trustees Peabody had put together, starting with Morgan. Sara Roosevelt took note that the most distinguished families of New York and Boston were enrolling their sons for admission, years before the boys would be old enough to enter the school. Lest Franklin lose out, she put his name on the list.

By the time Franklin arrived, in September 1896, Peabody's vision had taken fair shape. The school was located thirty-five miles north of Boston, above the Nashua River and two miles from Groton village, which was just visible from the higher parts of the hundred-acre campus. The school's handful of structures included a classroom building, a chapel, a gymnasium, a boathouse, and the most recent addition, the Hundred House, opened in 1891 as a dormitory for the hundred boys of the school. Students typically entered at age twelve and remained for six years, but because Sara couldn't part with Franklin so young, he didn't enter till fourteen, when he joined the students of the third "form," or year.

His early months at Groton marked the first time he'd been away from his family circle for long, and he was predictably homesick. "Thanks very much for your letters," he wrote his parents in late September. "The more the better." He discovered that the other boys received edible delicacies from home. "Could you send me some grapes or other small fruit? It would be very nice." He described his daily routine, focusing on athletics, which constituted an obsession at Groton. Every boy played every sport, or tried to. The masters—the teachers—were likewise expected to play, following Peabody's continuing vigorous example. Autumn being football season, Franklin leaped onto the gridiron. "I played football today on the 4th twenty-two (7th eleven)," he explained in his initial letter home. "I play right halfback or fullback." He was no standout, being light and not especially fast. But he was as determined as any of the boys, and he took pride in his battlefield wounds. "I managed to dislocate my fourth finger in a small football game," he recounted. "I have not been able to play since, in consequence, but I shall begin again tomorrow."

James and Sara naturally wished to know how their son's studies proceeded. "I am all right in Latin, Greek, Science, and French; a little rusty in Algebra but not more so than the others," he wrote. This was reassuring to his parents, but even more to Franklin. Much as in sports, the boy who hadn't been around other boys didn't know how he compared intellectually with his contemporaries. Not surprisingly, given his age and the Groton ethos, his status on the field mattered more to him than his standing in the classroom. But parents who paid Groton's tuition expected academic progress reports, which Endicott Peabody religiously provided. Franklin's first-month report showed an average of 7.79 (out of 10), with the highest marks for algebra (9.75) and English literature (8.5) and the lowest for Greek (6.75) and history (7.33). The grade report also covered personal habits; Franklin rated a perfect 10 for punctuality and 9.68 for decorum. His class rank was fourth (of nineteen). This satisfied Endicott Peabody, who summarized Franklin's performance: "Very good. He strikes me as an intelligent and faithful scholar and a good boy."

❖ ❖ ❖

FRANKLIN ROOSEVELT SPENT four years at Peabody's school, during which time his adult personality gradually emerged. Of course, it was the premise of Endicott Peabody's pedagogy that the adult personality didn't merely *emerge* during the Groton years but was significantly *shaped* by the Groton experience. This belief informed every aspect of Groton life, from the rigorous living conditions to the regimented daily routine. Like the other boys, Franklin was assigned a Hundred House cubicle, a space of sixty square feet containing a bed, a dresser, and a chair. The walls of the cubicle were taller than the tallest boy but stopped well short of the ceiling, thereby affording each inmate some privacy but not too much. A few hooks on the walls held what clothes didn't fit in the dresser, but the total storage capacity was meager, requiring the boys to choose between winter clothes and lighter gear for their kit on hand. An early cold snap could leave them shivering in linen; an unseasonable warm spell had them sweating in wool.

A communal lavatory adjoined the dormitory. Most American homes at this time didn't have piped hot water, and neither did Groton. Cold water— plenty of it—was an essential part of the routine, with each boy being required to take a cold shower every morning, for purposes of hygiene and to calm youthful spirits. In early fall and late spring, the temperature of the water could be almost comfortable, but when snow covered the hill and ice sheeted the rivers and ponds, the morning shower was decidedly bracing.

After showers and dressing, the boys filed to the dining hall for 7:30 break-fast. Chapel followed at 8:15, and then classes from 8:30 till noon. A substantial meal fueled the young scholars for two more classes, which were followed by a vigorous afternoon of organized athletics. Supper revived them sufficiently for another chapel service and for study hall, at the end of which the Reverend and Mrs. Peabody bade each boy good night, and all retired.

The regimen of the school was designed to instill self-discipline and build character. In the case of Franklin Roosevelt it definitely introduced him to a more spartan lifestyle than he had encountered before. The buildings were barely heated; during cold weather the boys wore heavy coats even indoors. On one occasion a winter gale blew open a transom in the dormitory during the night; Franklin and the other boys awoke beneath snowdrifts on their bed-clothes. In spring the discomfort came from the opposite end of the thermometer. "Today is *broiling*, and *five* boys fainted in church this a.m.," Franklin wrote his parents during a particularly warm stretch.

Groton introduced Franklin to something else he hadn't encountered: regular outbreaks of disease. A hundred boys living close together provided a festering ground for all manner of contagions. Most were fairly innocuous: colds, influenza ("grippe"), mumps, pink eye, earaches, assorted intestinal disturbances. But other afflictions occasioned greater concern. Symptoms of scarlet fever triggered the immediate quarantine of the patients; on the occasions when this failed to stem the spread, classes were canceled and the students sent home. (A standard precaution against the import of illness from outside the school was the requirement that students bring a certificate of good health upon return from vacations.) Whooping cough could be severe or mild, but it was so common that the school sometimes ignored outbreaks and let the sufferers—including Franklin Roosevelt during the spring of his junior year—walk around whooping.

Franklin was neither sicker nor healthier than most of his classmates. The school doctor examined the boys regularly, recording their growth, muscular development, and vital signs. For reasons he didn't explain, the physician concluded that Roosevelt had a "weak heart" and consequently should refrain from exerting himself excessively. The patient rejected the diagnosis. "I told him that he was a liar (not quite in those words)," he wrote his parents. And he blithely ignored the advice, engaging in every athletic activity imaginable—and a few, including a handball derivative called "fives," unimagined by any save Endicott Peabody and his fellow Grotonians. Roosevelt received his share of whatever infections were going around. Sara sent him regular supplies of cod liver oil—a good source of vitamin D, although this particular aspect of its prophylactic powers wasn't known at the time—and insisted that he take it. But he still succumbed to scarlet fever, whooping cough, mumps, flu, colds, and sundry other maladies.

❖   ❖   ❖

SARA'S SOLICITUDE reflected not merely the concern any mother feels for her child but also Sara's understanding that the Roosevelts weren't the most robust of physical specimens. Franklin's father, James, continued to decline during Franklin's teenage years; during the autumn of 1900 James's condition grew alarming. Sara arranged for the two of them to winter in South Carolina, but he became too sick to travel. She regularly informed Franklin of his father's condition; Franklin responded with worried remonstrance. *"Make Papa rest,"* he wrote in mid-November. When James rallied, Franklin took excessive encouragement. "I am so glad Papa is really better," he remarked the day after Thanksgiving. "I only hope he will be absolutely well again in a few days."

Probably Sara wasn't telling Franklin the whole story; she must have known a full recovery was impossible. And in fact this rally gave way to a relapse. "I am too distressed about Papa and cannot understand why he does not improve more quickly," Roosevelt wrote in early December. Only days later he received word to hurry to New York City, where James was staying at a hotel between visits to his doctors. On December 8, 1900, Franklin's father died.

Franklin remained with his mother throughout the holidays. And during the following year he observed a sort of mourning by using stationery bordered in black. But otherwise his father's passing appeared to affect him fairly little. He had never known his father except as an old man, and one who was often sick. In many respects James was more a grandfather than a father to his younger son. An eagerly athletic boy like Franklin had difficulty seeing himself in James.

The chief emotional effect of James's death was to reinforce the bond between Franklin and Sara. Always her only son, Franklin now became the only man in her life. She doted on him as never before; without James to care for at Hyde Park, she rented a house in Boston during winters to be closer to him. James left Franklin a modest inheritance, but the bulk of the estate went to Sara. Sara supported Franklin and did so in what she judged his best interests. But it was *her* judgment, not his, that counted. And she no longer had to heed James's opinion in the matter.

Even as his father's death made Franklin more dependent on Sara financially, it also made him feel more responsible for Sara emotionally. Until now James had provided an outlet for Sara's emotions; with James gone that function fell entirely to Franklin. He grew solicitous of her in ways he hadn't been before; when she became upset he was the one who soothed her. The bond between mother and son, already strong, grew stronger.

2.

$\mathcal{F}$RANKLIN GRADUATED FROM GROTON IN THE SPRING OF 1900 AND enrolled that fall at Harvard, down the road in Cambridge. At the beginning of the twentieth century, Harvard aspired to intellectual eminence, but social standing still counted for more among the undergraduates than academic achievement. Boys from wealthy families inhabited the "Gold Coast" along Mt. Auburn Street, living in large apartments, dining in expensive eating houses, and gathering in exclusive clubs. Boys from poorer families lived across Massachusetts Avenue in the drab, crowded dormitories of the Yard. The two castes mingled in the lecture halls, but outside the classrooms they rarely encountered each other.

Roosevelt, naturally, was a Gold Coaster. He lived at Westmorly Court, a prime property, in a four-room apartment he shared with Lathrop Brown, another Grotonian. "The sitting room is large enough for two desks, and the bedrooms and bath light and airy," he wrote home. "The ceilings are very high." The suite was bare when Roosevelt arrived. "The rooms look as if struck by sheet lightning, the sitting room having the chairs and tables but no curtains or carpets. . . . The bed is in place in my room, and it looks inhabitable, but one trunk is the sole piece of furniture of Lathrop's room." The apartment perked up when Sara sent carpet and curtains, and Roosevelt and Brown put pictures on the walls. A rented piano completed the décor and provided a focus for entertaining.

Roosevelt's circle widened at Harvard. "On Monday I went to a 'Beer Night' in a Senior's room," he noted. "It is a regular institution by which a senior has a few of his classmen and about 20 Freshmen in to his room in order to get them acquainted with each other." Sports played a socializing role at Harvard as they had at Groton, and Roosevelt threw himself into the games. He was realistic about his prospects for football. "There are still over 100 candidates"— or about a quarter of the freshman class—"for the '04 team, and I shan't make it, but possibly a scrub team." The scrubs were where he wound up, yet he enjoyed the distinction of being elected captain of one of the eight scrub squads. "It is the only one composed wholly of Freshmen, and I am the only Freshman captain."

He joined the school newspaper. Like the football team, the *Crimson* required tryouts; cub reporters who made the grade could hope to rise to editorial ranks. Roosevelt discovered in himself a certain flair for reporting. He wrote easily, and he could talk his way into information that eluded his rivals. His first weeks at Harvard were the last weeks of the 1900 presidential campaign; the campaign evoked great interest on the Harvard campus, with most of the students, doubtless following the lead of their fathers, supporting Republicans William McKinley and Theodore Roosevelt against Democrats William Jennings Bryan and Adlai Stevenson. "Last night there was a grand torch-light Republican parade of Harvard and the Massachusetts Institute of Technology," Franklin wrote home. Franklin joined the Republicans for the festivities. "We wore red caps and gowns and marched by classes into Boston and through all the principal streets, about eight miles in all. The crowds to see it were huge all along the route, and we were dead tired at the end."

Amid the excitement of the marching, Roosevelt didn't neglect his reportorial duties. Harvard's own president, Charles Eliot, spoke loudly and often for good government, but in the current contest he had declined to endorse either McKinley or Bryan. *Crimson* rules forbade first-year reporters from interviewing Eliot, but Roosevelt, feigning ignorance, buttonholed the Harvard president anyway. Caught by surprise, Eliot blurted out his preference, and the *Crimson* carried Roosevelt's scoop under the headline "President Eliot Declares for McKinley." The story won Roosevelt a coveted spot on the regular staff.

The position brought greater responsibility. "I am working about six hours a day on it alone, and it is quite a strain," he told Sara. His hard work was rewarded during the autumn of his sophomore year when he was elected to the editorial board. The choice reflected his peers' assessment of his talents as a journalist, and perhaps the persuasive skills that would make him an effective campaigner when he turned politician. It also revealed the appreciation of his classmates that he could afford the job. One responsibility of the editors was to treat the staff to dinner and related diversion. To celebrate their election, Franklin and four other new men threw a lavish dinner, followed by an evening at the theater. "Great fun, speeches, songs, etc.," he reported to Sara.

❖ ❖ ❖

$\mathcal{R}$oosevelt's family connections grew even more valuable when Theodore Roosevelt became president upon McKinley's assassination in September 1901. Having a cousin as governor had been a mark of distinction for Franklin; having a vice president perhaps more so (yet not necessarily, given the low esteem in which vice presidents were held in those days). But having a president in the family was truly impressive. Whether Cousin Theodore's ascent to the apex of American politics contributed to Franklin's election as a *Crimson* editor is impossible to know. It certainly lent luster to the family name. Yet Franklin's diligence and flair had marked him for months, and Theodore's inauguration probably only made a logical choice easier.

Franklin didn't wait long to capitalize on Theodore's new office. Alice Roosevelt, Theodore's daughter by his deceased first wife, turned eighteen in February 1902; the occasion required that she be formally presented to society. Edith Roosevelt, the First Lady, hosted a White House debut, the first of its kind at the executive mansion and the most lavish ball there since the days of Dolley Madison almost a century before. Alice was queen of the night, with a very large court. "Three hundred beautiful and beautifully gowned young women and a body of smart young men almost as numerous practically made up the party," the *New York Times* reported. A handful of adults were present; these conspicuously did not include the president, who at Edith's urging or Alice's insistence left the stage to his daughter. "The White House was filled with young people," the *Times* reporter wrote, "and they enjoyed themselves after the manner of young people. The state apartments had been turned over to them, with no other injunction put upon them than that they would incur the great displeasure of the President if they did not make a jolly night of it. They appeared to heed this injunction."

The guests included several Roosevelts. Franklin rode the train down from Boston on the Friday morning of the ball, took tea with one set of family friends and dinner with another. "Then to the dance, which was most glorious fun," he told his mother. "From start to finish it was glorious. . . . We left at 2 a.m. and I slept till 12 on Saturday." That afternoon he visited the new— as of 1897—home of the Library of Congress. A White House tea followed, again hosted by Edith, with Alice once more the center of attention and her father still absent. "All most interesting," Franklin recorded. On Saturday night he attended a reception given by the Austrian ambassador, and he mingled with numerous members of the diplomatic corps. Sunday brought more of the same. "On the whole it was one of the most interesting and enjoyable three days I have ever had," Franklin wrote Sara.

❖　❖　❖

THIS WAS SAYING a lot, for Franklin Roosevelt enjoyed nearly all his college days. "On Saturday I went to Beverly to the Beals, played golf that day, and on Sunday went to the Sohier's camp on a neighboring lake for the day, returning here Monday a.m.," he wrote from Cambridge on a Wednesday in October of his junior year. "Now (11 p.m.) I am just back from a dinner of the Massachusetts Republican Club, of 1,000 people, at which Secretary Shaw of the Treasury and Senator Lodge made most interesting addresses. Mr. Beal gave me the ticket, and it was the chance of a lifetime." Perhaps Mr. Beal, the father of one of Roosevelt's Harvard classmates, wished to make a Republican out of his son's friend; perhaps he simply wanted to do a favor for the budding journalist.

Roosevelt joined several of the clubs that ruled Harvard's extracurricular universe. The Porcellian Club, the most exclusive, snubbed him, for reasons he never learned. A black ball—literally—from any of the sixteen members sufficed to bar a prospective new member; Roosevelt received at least one in the critical vote. The rejection stung, the more so since Cousin Ted had been a Porcellian member. Later—during the First World War—Franklin remarked that his rejection was the "greatest disappointment of my life." This may have revealed a lingering hurt; it also reflected the minor character of his failures till then. While he was at Harvard he certainly didn't appear to dwell on his exclusion from the single stuffiest of the clubs but rather made do quite well with others. He was chosen for Alpha Delta Phi, known as the "Fly Club," of which he became librarian; the Institute of 1770; the Signet Literary Society; the Memorial Society, which served as keeper of Harvard history and traditions; and Hasty Pudding, the student theatrical group.

He didn't exactly ignore his studies. His courses included a full round of English, history, and government, as well as the odd philosophy and fine arts class. He passed them all, without distinction. And because he had taken several college-level courses at Groton, he completed the requirements for his bachelor's degree by the end of his third year.

But he didn't dream for a minute of skipping his fourth year, which he expected to be his time of social glory. In the autumn of his third year he was elected assistant managing editor of the *Crimson,* and in the spring managing editor. He could reasonably anticipate, given the paper's traditions, making president, or editor in chief, in his fourth year, if he stayed in school. When he took his summer vacation in 1903 in Europe, on a tour of the Swiss Alps, he carried along the previous year's editorials and read them with an eye to doing better. His preparation paid off on his return, when he was indeed elevated to the top post.

The editor of the *Crimson* wasn't, by virtue of his office, as prominent on campus as the football captain or the stroke oar of the crew team, but he was a big man nonetheless. He certainly had a voice no other student possessed. In that era the editor wrote all the editorials (later he would share the job with an editorial board). Roosevelt took advantage of his forum to pass judgment on Harvard football, chiding the student body for insufficient support and the team for uninspired play. His latter comments provoked an angry reaction from team members. "I am glad to say the effect has been just what was wanted; it has stirred up the team by making them angry, and they are playing all the harder for it," he congratulated himself. He weighed in on politics, urging his fellow students to join the Political Club, and the Political Club to get practical. "With such a large city as Boston close at hand, it would be easy to send in parties, under the guidance of some experienced man, which in one day could learn more than through the means of lectures." He publicized a series of political talks, explaining that "the committee in New York which has selected the speakers hope that by arousing sufficient interest men may be induced to enter New York politics upon leaving college."

The paper almost monopolized his time, but not quite. He played golf during the week and on Saturday afternoons shouted for the football team. "I was one of three cheer leaders in the Brown game, and felt like a d—— f——, waving my arms and legs before several thousand amused spectators," he told his mother, with poorly disguised delight. "It is a dirty job; one gets chiefly ridicule. But some poor devil has to suffer, and one can't refuse." He attended the Bachelors' Ball in Boston—"which was very exclusive, very animated, and rather tipsy," he remarked. "I got back at 6." He went to the wedding of a fraternity brother and took upon himself the task of introducing his classmates to the mother of the bride. "Mrs. Kay was much impressed by his *savoir faire,*" the grateful groom recalled. "His charm and ease of manner were apparent in those early days."

❖   ❖   ❖

ELEANOR ROOSEVELT WAS a Roosevelt before she married Franklin Roosevelt. Her father was Elliott Roosevelt, Theodore's brother. Alice Roosevelt
was a cousin. Her mother was Anna Hall Roosevelt—"one of the most beautiful women I have ever seen," Eleanor wrote, many years after her mother
died. Coming from another child of another mother, such a comment might
have required discount for the bias of the excessively close. In Eleanor's case,
any discount must have been in the opposite direction, for she was not close
to her mother and never identified with her in any way. Her mother was beautiful; she herself was not—certainly not by her own reckoning. And her
mother inhabited a world that never warmed to Eleanor, nor Eleanor to it.
"My mother belonged to that New York City society which thought itself all-
important," Eleanor said. "In that society you were kind to the poor; you did
not neglect your philanthropic duties in whatever community you lived; you
assisted the hospitals and did something for the needy. You accepted invitations to dine and to dance with the right people only; you lived where you
would be in their midst. You thought seriously about your children's education; you read the books that everybody read; you were familiar with good literature. In short, you conformed to the conventional pattern."

Eleanor's father inhabited Anna's society but was not really of it, which
may have been why Eleanor identified much more strongly with him. Or it
may have been the flaws in Elliott Roosevelt's character. Elliott was the more
attractive and engaging of the two Roosevelt boys, with blond hair, handsome
features, and a winning personality. But there was a crack in his character, and
in the repeated poundings of sibling competition with the older and more
ambitious Theodore, it opened wider and wider. Their parents sent Elliott off
to Texas in his teens to recuperate from a nervous breakdown; when the boys'
father died soon after, Elliott employed his inheritance to fund a round-the-
world tour. He hunted tigers in India and other beasts elsewhere, finally gaining an edge on his brother, who had yet to bag anything larger than a bear. He
brought home heads, hides, and an exotic reputation, which helped sweep
Anna Hall, in full bloom at nineteen, off her feet and to the altar. He loved her
madly but badly, being already addicted to alcohol and becoming addicted to
the opiates he ingested for pain following a riding accident that shattered his
leg. He squandered what remained of his fortune and got a servant girl preg-

nant; she threatened a public scandal and had to be bought off by Theodore and the family.

The sordid details were kept from Eleanor, who knew only that her father loved her with a strange desperation. He needed Eleanor, for Eleanor loved him as Anna never could. Eleanor made no demands, held him to no standards. Eleanor forgave his absences—in sanatoriums and hospitals, often, drying out—and greeted him more ardently the longer he was gone. "Though he was so little with us, my father dominated all this period of my life," she remembered. "Subconsciously I must have been waiting always for his visits. They were irregular, and he rarely sent word before he arrived, but never was I in the house, even in my room two long flights of stairs above the entrance door, that I did not hear his voice the minute he entered the front door. Walking down stairs was far too slow. I slid down the banisters and usually catapulted into his arms before his hat was hung up." There was no other man for Eleanor—not when she was a girl, and not when she was a young woman. "He dominated my life as long as he lived, and was the love of my life for many years after he died."

His importance to her grew even as his presence diminished. When Eleanor was eight, Anna died of diphtheria. Elliott came home for his wife's final days, and he broke the news to Eleanor. "He was dressed all in black, looking very sad," she remembered. "He held out his arms and gathered me to him. In a little while he began to talk, to explain to me that my mother was gone, that she had been all the world to him, and now he had only my brothers and myself, that my brothers were very young, and that he and I must keep close together." He said that he had to leave and that the children would stay with their mother's parents. But he would return. "Some day I would make a home for him again. We would travel together and do many things which he painted as interesting and pleasant. . . . Somehow it was always he and I. I did not understand whether my brothers were to be our children or whether he felt that they would be at school. . . . There started a feeling that day which never left me—that he and I were very close together, and some day would have a life of our own together."

The promised day never came. Elliott spiraled downward after Anna's death. He drank more heavily than ever and consorted with women of ill repute. Even Theodore, who had hardened his heart against his brother's sins, pitied him, more or less. "Poor fellow!" he declared after learning that Elliott had crashed a carriage into a lamp post and injured his head. "If only he could have died instead of Anna!"

Elliott's end came soon enough. Seized by a fit of delirium tremens, he thrashed about uncontrollably, tried to leap out a window, sweated and foamed, and finally collapsed in a fatal heart attack.

Eleanor refused to credit the news when she heard it. Since moving in with her grandparents, who had exhausted their tenderness on their own children and had none left for Eleanor or her brothers, she had perfected a habit of retreating into a world of fantasy when things went wrong. This defense made her seem strange and sullen to adults and other children, but it shielded her from disappointment when her father didn't come as promised, when her grandmother scolded her for behavior she didn't realize was wrong, or when the servants took out their own frustrations on her, knowing she was too timid to report them. The word of her father's death arrived just before her tenth birthday. "I simply refused to believe it," she remembered. "And while I wept long and went to bed still weeping, I finally went to sleep and began the next day living in my dream world as usual." Her grandmother decreed that the children not attend the funeral. "So I had no tangible thing to make death real to me. From that time on, I knew that my father was dead, and yet I lived with him more closely, probably, than I had when he was alive."

Her early teens were deeply troubled. She was lonely, physically fearful, and yet stubborn. By her later admission, she lied as a matter of course, which simply elicited harsher responses from her grandmother. For reasons best known to herself, Mrs. Hall refused to let Eleanor visit her Roosevelt relatives more than once or twice a year. Perhaps she thought the demons that had hounded Elliott to his death lived in the Roosevelt closets; perhaps she thought Eleanor's cousin Alice, who was just eight months older than Eleanor but already displayed a wild streak, was an evil influence. Yet the distance didn't prevent Eleanor from idolizing Alice, who seemed "so much more sophisticated and grown-up that I was in great awe of her."

The other Roosevelts were mostly nice. Aunt Corinne, Elliott's and Theodore's sister, threw Christmas parties for the youngsters of the clan. Eleanor attended, with a mixture of anticipation and dread. She liked seeing people her own age, but she was awkward and shy. She couldn't dance, and her clothes were horribly out of fashion. Yet a certain boy seemed not to notice. "I still remember my gratitude at one of these parties to my cousin Franklin Roosevelt when he came and asked me to dance with him."

Thoughts of Franklin helped tide her through difficult days. The Halls grew harder and harder to live with. Besides her stern and narrow-minded grandmother, Eleanor had to endure some uncles who were undeniably alcoholic and potentially abusive. For protection—presumably before the fact but possibly after—her grandmother or an aunt installed three heavy locks on Eleanor's bedroom door. A girlfriend who spent the night asked Eleanor what the locks were for. "To keep my uncles out," she replied.

Life took a turn for the better when, at fifteen, she became old enough to attend boarding school. Her Hall aunts transported her to England and deposited her at Allenswood, a school for girls just south of London. Where none of the students had parents at hand, the orphaned Eleanor no longer felt uniquely alone. In fact she had one distinct advantage over most of the other girls. Her first nurse had been French, and with her mother constantly socializing and her father frequently gone, she had learned French before she learned English. The Allenswood headmistress, Mademoiselle Marie Souvestre, insisted that the girls speak French. "It was quite easy for me," Eleanor wrote. "But for many of the English girls who had had very little French beforehand, it was a terrible effort."

In her seventy years Marie Souvestre had developed decided notions of propriety and pedagogy. The girls got three baths a week; any more would have elicited queries as to how one became so dirty. Their beds and dressers were inspected daily; a drawer out of order could result in the contents being cast across the floor. The morning constitutional, a brisk walk about the town common, took place in rain, sleet, or snow. The school had nominal central heating but none of the girls could feel it. Field hockey was required; bruises to arms, legs, and heads were expected.

Yet Eleanor grew to love Marie Souvestre. In the first place, as a Frenchwoman among the English, the headmistress favored her few American students. In the second place, she flouted orthodoxy. She was an atheist who couldn't imagine a God being bothered with the pettiness of human affairs. Religion, she said, was a crutch for the weak. Eleanor had never heard anything so radical. "Mlle. Souvestre shocked me into thinking," she said.

Marie Souvestre made Eleanor sit opposite her at meals, and gave her portions of the special dishes she sometimes ordered prepared for herself. When guests came to the school—including Beatrice Chamberlain, the sister of future prime minister Neville Chamberlain—Eleanor was introduced, and she participated in the conversations they had with the headmistress.

Marie Souvestre sometimes took Eleanor with her for holidays. On one trip they traveled by train from Marseilles, ticketed to Pisa. But when the conductor announced the station at Alassio, their plans suddenly changed. "I am going to get off," she told Eleanor. Eleanor grabbed their bags and they tumbled out. Souvestre explained, as they stood alone on the platform with night falling, that she had a friend in Alassio. "Besides," she said, "the Mediterranean is a very lovely blue at night, and the sky with the stars coming out is nice to watch from the beach." As it happened, her friend was away, and they spent the night in a damp room that caused Souvestre to catch cold. But they saw the stars rise over the sea, and she deemed the discomfort well worth it. "I had learned a valuable lesson," Eleanor recalled. "Never again would I be the rigid little person I had been heretofore."

At eighteen Eleanor's idyll ended and she returned to America. Her debut into New York society was "utter agony." She felt too tall and ungainly. She knew few of the girls and fewer of the boys. She still couldn't dance. The mirror condemned her as visibly inferior to the other Hall women. "I knew I was the first girl in my mother's family who was not a belle, and though I never acknowledged it to any of them at that time, I was deeply ashamed."

❖   ❖   ❖

$\mathcal{F}$OR THIS REASON she responded to Franklin's overtures with skepticism, albeit grateful skepticism. She had encountered Franklin a few times since the dance where he plucked her from among the wallflowers. On a visit home from Allenswood she had been traveling by train up the Hudson toward her grandmother's house when he walked past her in the coach car. He stopped and they chatted, and he invited her to say hello to Sara in the Pullman car. Sara was pleasant but proper. Nothing came of this encounter.

After Eleanor returned from England for good, she saw more of Franklin. They moved in the same circle and went to the same parties and receptions. In January 1903 Eleanor attended Franklin's twenty-first birthday party. During the subsequent months they saw each other several times, sporadically at first, then more often. One day he dropped by a settlement house on Rivington Street in Manhattan's Lower East Side where she did volunteer work with immigrant children. "All the little girls were tremendously interested," she remembered, "and the next time they gathered around me demanding to know if he was my 'feller.' "

He wasn't yet. Franklin moved cautiously in courting Eleanor. He required time to discover his heart; he also worried what his mother would think. He had dated other girls, including a seventeen-year-old named Alice Sohier with whom he grew sufficiently serious that her parents sent her to Europe to chill the romance. The strategy worked, and the relationship faded. Franklin never told Sara about it. Sara made no secret of her belief that young people lost their minds when they heeded their hearts. Franklin must finish college and get well started on a career before even thinking about a serious relationship.

Such was her reasoning on the subject; her emotions were no less strong. He was the man in her life, and she wasn't one to share. Eventually, of course, he'd have to marry. She wanted grandchildren. But there was plenty of time for that.

She didn't tell Franklin all this; she didn't have to. Her tone of voice when he discussed girlfriends said more than enough. As a result he simply stopped speaking of girls with her. For many months he disguised his growing attachment to Eleanor. The fact that they were kin made the deception easier, as their appearance at many of the same events was taken as a matter of course.

Consequently Sara was astonished when Franklin informed her at Thanksgiving 1903 that he and Eleanor intended to marry. He had proposed to Eleanor the previous weekend, and she had accepted at once. He wanted to delay telling Sara, but Eleanor urged him to speak out. "I never want her to feel she has been deceived," Eleanor wrote him. "Don't be angry with me, Franklin, for saying this, and of course you must do as you think best." He accepted the advice and told Sara at the Delano Thanksgiving dinner. "Franklin gave me quite a startling announcement," Sara remarked in her diary that night.

But she kept her composure, determined to attack this unwelcome development obliquely. Franklin was planning to visit Eleanor in New York; Sara insisted on joining him. The three would have a good conversation, she said. Sara allayed Eleanor's fears that she would reject the engagement outright, instead simply counseling patience. They mustn't rush into anything. Eleanor was relieved. "Dearest Cousin Sally," she explained to Sara, "I must write you and thank you for being so good to me yesterday. I know just how you feel and how hard it must be, but I do so want you to learn to love me a little. You must know that I will always try to do what you wish." Franklin sent his mother similar thoughts from Harvard. "Dearest Mama," he said, "I know what pain I must have caused you, and you know I wouldn't do it if I really could have helped it." But he could *not* help it; he loved Eleanor. "I know my mind, have known it for a long time. . . . Result: I am the happiest man just now in the world; likewise the luckiest." He added reassurance that Eleanor would never come between them. "Dear Mummy, you know that nothing can ever change what we have been and always will be to each other."

Without apparent difficulty Sara persuaded the couple to postpone any public announcement of their engagement. This left her free to try to undo what young love had done, without the world being any wiser. She scheduled a six-week Caribbean cruise and, despite the demands of Franklin's newspaper work during his final semester at college, insisted that he join her. If distance alone didn't diminish his ardor for Eleanor, she calculated, he might meet another girl. He did meet other girls, and some older women too. But he didn't forget Eleanor, and he returned to New York more devoted than ever. Sara then applied to Joseph Choate, a longtime friend and the current American ambassador to Britain, to take Franklin to London as his private secretary. Choate said he'd like to help but already had a secretary.

Eleanor found Sara's sabotage attempts irksome, yet she held her tongue and pen. She wished Franklin would assert himself more forcefully on her behalf, but when he didn't she declined to be provoked. Precisely what she communicated to him is impossible to reconstruct; she later burned their courtship correspondence. But clearly she didn't deliver any ultimatums or throw any tantrums. She was too much in love.

Why she loved Franklin so, she probably couldn't have said. Obviously there was chemistry between the twenty-one-year-old man and the nineteen-year-old woman. But beyond the physical attraction, Franklin doubtless signified to Eleanor things she had lost or never experienced. The Delanos were daunting as individuals, yet they stuck together in a way that Eleanor's own family never had. "They were a clan," Eleanor wrote. "And if misfortune befell one of them, the others rallied at once. . . . The Delanos might disapprove of one another, and if so, they were not slow to express their disapproval, but let someone outside as much as hint at criticism, and the clan was ready to tear him limb from limb." The thought of having the clan at her back doubtless appealed to Eleanor.

At one level or another, Franklin must have seemed a replacement for her lost father. A certain physical resemblance existed, and it was complemented by Franklin's charm and easy social grace, which matched Eleanor's memories of her father. But whatever the likeness, Eleanor had been searching for a strong male figure since her father died—in fact, since before that, if she was being honest with herself. Just how strong Franklin truly was, she couldn't say. But she was willing to take a chance on him.

Franklin had his own reasons for loving Eleanor. In the first place, she was better-looking than she let on. Alice Roosevelt, who rarely had a kind word for anyone, remarked of Eleanor, "She was always making herself out to be an ugly duckling, but she was really rather attractive. Tall, rather coltish-looking, with masses of pale, gold hair rippling to below her waist, and really lovely blue eyes." Of course Alice, being Alice, couldn't stop there. She felt compelled to add, "It's true that her chin went in a bit, which wouldn't have been so noticeable if only her hateful grandmother had fixed her teeth."

Beyond her appearance, Eleanor was intelligent and more thoughtful than most of the girls Franklin encountered at parties and mixers. She spoke French better than he did, she had lived abroad, and she had experienced aspects of life that made his own sheltered existence seem mundane. That her uncle was the president of the United States didn't diminish her appeal. Franklin remained far from knowing what his future held, but it was difficult to imagine that having in-laws in the White House would hurt his prospects, no matter what he attempted.

❖   ❖   ❖

Yet those White House in-laws—in particular Theodore Roosevelt—made the wedding itself problematic. In the autumn of 1904 Sara acknowledged defeat in her effort to prevent the marriage of Franklin and Eleanor, and she permitted the engagement to be announced. A date was set for the wedding, then reset and reset again. The problem now wasn't Sara but Theodore, who would stand in for Eleanor's deceased father. The president, after winning election in November 1904, had to be reinaugurated, and he had to accommodate all the other demands on the time of the nation's head of state and head of government. Finally an opening came into view: March 17, when Theodore could stroke the pride of New York's Irish Americans in the morning by reviewing the annual St. Patrick's Day parade and tend to the family matters in the afternoon.

The ceremony was held at the brownstone of Eleanor's cousin Susie Parish on East Seventy-sixth Street. From the bride's perspective it was a fiasco. After McKinley's assassination the Secret Service took no chances on losing another president, and it threw a cordon around the entire neighborhood. Wedding guests were stopped and interrogated; all were delayed by the tangles the president's presence created in the traffic of the Upper East Side. Many fumingly reached their destination only after the ceremony ended.

Endicott Peabody, officiating at the request of Franklin and Sara, asked who gave the bride away. Theodore answered loudly, "*I* do." Eleanor and Franklin exchanged vows, rings, and kisses. Theodore congratulated the groom with a joke that soon made the rounds: "Well, Franklin, there's nothing like keeping the name in the family!"

At this point a door that connected Susie Parish's house to the matching house of her mother next door was thrown open, and the wedding party was introduced to the larger crowd at the reception. Theodore, who could never resist an audience, strode forward and hypnotized the guests in his usual fashion. Years later, Eleanor recalled the moment distinctly: "Those closest to us did take time to wish us well, but the great majority of the guests were far more interested in the thought of being able to see and listen to the President; and in a very short time this young married couple were standing alone." Eleanor of course said nothing, although she surely hoped that her new husband would speak up. But he was as smitten as the rest. "I cannot remember that even Franklin seemed to mind."

How she felt beyond that, she didn't say. But the experience couldn't have eased her lifelong insecurities, and if she thought she saw her future in the sight of her husband drawn irresistibly toward politics, in preference to her, she could have been forgiven.

3.

ℱRANKLIN ROOSEVELT PROBABLY COULDN'T HAVE IDENTIFIED PRE-
cisely when he began to model himself on Cousin Ted—or Uncle Ted, as the
president became upon Franklin's marriage to Eleanor. Perhaps it was during
one of Franklin's visits to the Roosevelt White House, as the younger man
looked around and imagined himself living there. Perhaps it was at the wedding, when Franklin experienced the magnetic attraction of political power.
Doubtless Sara suggested, likely often, that if one Roosevelt could reach the
pinnacle of American politics, another Roosevelt could, too.

Whatever its origin, Franklin's emulation of Theodore shaped his personal
and professional life for decades, and it manifested itself soon after his wedding. Theodore had gone from Harvard to Columbia Law School. Franklin
did the same. Theodore had found law school dull and dropped out before
finishing. So did Franklin—although in his case he took and passed the New
York bar exam, something Theodore never accomplished. Columbia president
Nicholas Murray Butler later chided Franklin Roosevelt for not completing
his degree. "You will never be able to call yourself an intellectual until you
come back to Columbia and pass your law exams," Butler said. Roosevelt answered with a laugh: "That just shows how unimportant the law really is."

His job search began in the obvious places: the clubs, dining rooms, and sa-
lons of those he knew socially. Lewis Ledyard was commodore of the New
York Yacht Club, besides being a leading partner in one of the most powerful
law firms on Wall Street. Edmund Baylies was a partner in the same firm, in
addition to being a member of the Yacht Club and the Knickerbocker Club
and president of the Seamen's Church Institute, a charitable organization.
Franklin knew both men from the Yacht Club, of which he was a member, and
he knew Baylies from the Knickerbocker, to which he also belonged, and the
Seamen's Institute, on whose board of directors he served. Baylies and Ledyard
thought Roosevelt promising, and they offered him the equivalent of an ap-

prenticeship. For a year he would work without pay. If he did well he would be placed on a small salary and on the track that led to partnership.

Roosevelt commenced his legal career with a conspicuous lack of gravity. He printed cards for the occasion:

FRANKLIN D. ROOSEVELT
COUNSELOR AT LAW
54 WALL STREET
NEW YORK

I beg to call your attention to my unexcelled facilities for carrying on every description of legal business. Unpaid bills a specialty. Briefs on the liquor question furnished free to ladies. Race suicides cheerfully prosecuted. Small dogs chloroformed without charge. Babies raised under advice of expert grandmother etc., etc.

The principals of the firm, by contrast, took their calling quite seriously. When Roosevelt arrived, Carter, Ledyard & Milburn was up to its cufflinks and cravats in the signature antitrust suit of the era, with John Milburn personally serving as counsel to John D. Rockefeller's Standard Oil Company, then under indictment by Theodore Roosevelt's Justice Department. Lewis Ledyard represented J. P. Morgan and the United States Steel Corporation, the giant trust Morgan had created in 1901, which continued to swallow its competitors under Ledyard's legal guidance. Three decades later Franklin Roosevelt would consider big business, and the lawyers who defended the great firms, to be his mortal enemies, but at the outset of his career he entertained no such prejudices. On the contrary, Carter, Ledyard & Milburn seemed everything a young man in his position could ask for.

An apprenticeship was appropriate, for academic legal education in those days strongly favored theory over practice. Roosevelt discovered that Columbia had prepared him hardly at all for the day-to-day work of a lawyer. He had never been inside a courtroom and didn't know the first thing about trying a case. "I went to a big law office in New York," he explained afterward, regarding his hiring by Carter Ledyard. "And somebody the day after I got there said, 'Go up and answer the calendar call in the supreme court"—the New York supreme court—"tomorrow morning. We have such and such a case on.'" Roosevelt had to confess that he had no idea how to do what was being asked. "Then the next day somebody gave me a deed of transfer of some land. He said, 'Take it up to the county clerk's office.' I had never been in a county clerk's office. And there I was, theoretically a full-fledged lawyer."

Those just ahead of Roosevelt in the firm's hierarchy gradually filled him in on what Columbia had failed to teach him. They introduced him to the procedures and personnel of the New York courts. He caught on sufficiently that the firm appointed him managing clerk in charge of municipal litigation. He mainly pushed paper but in the process gained an appreciation for how the law affected the lives of those caught in its coils. He was assigned some minor cases of his own and learned to bargain with opposing counsel in order to settle cases before they reached trial. His heart wasn't always on the side of his clients, typically big corporations being sued by plaintiffs and lawyers with far inferior resources. One story remembered of Roosevelt had him haggling with a plaintiff's lawyer over a claim for damages. The lawyer asked for $300; Roosevelt refused. The lawyer asked for $150; Roosevelt again refused. Roosevelt finally visited the lawyer's apartment. The lawyer was not at home, but his mother was, and she explained that the family was in dire straits. The condition of the apartment confirmed her remarks. Roosevelt wrote a note to the lawyer: "I would be glad to settle this case for thirty-five dollars. I cannot get myself to honestly believe that it is worth a cent more, probably less. Enclosed is a small personal check which I am sure you will not return until you are well out of these temporary difficulties." The check was for $150. "I wept," the lawyer said. "Six months later I paid him back."

Away from work Roosevelt mingled with the people an up-and-coming member of the New York elite should know. He sailed at the Yacht Club and lunched at the Knickerbocker. He golfed in Westchester County when staying in the city, and on Dutchess County courses when at Hyde Park. By all appearances he was making a successful start on a life of respectable ease and moderate good service to the institutions upholding the status quo of capitalist America.

❖ ❖ ❖

ELEANOR ROOSEVELT WORKED hard at her marriage, trying to be a loving wife to Franklin and a devoted daughter to Sara. Neither task came easily. Sara's presence had hovered over the newlyweds' ship as they steamed to Britain on their honeymoon, and it tracked them across the Continent. Franklin still felt the responsibility for his mother's happiness he had inherited upon his father's death—a responsibility Sara did nothing to diminish. Now

Eleanor, partly from a desire to become one of the Delano clan, and partly, no doubt, from considerations of self-defense, committed herself to being the daughter her mother-in-law had never had. "Dearest Mama . . . ," she wrote Sara, who had arranged the details of the journey, "Thank you so much, dear, for everything you did for us. You are always just the sweetest, dearest Mama to your children, and I shall look forward to our next long evening together, when I shall want to be kissed all the time."

Not a week passed that Sara didn't receive multiple letters from the new-lyweds—long letters relating all but the most intimate details of the honey-moon. From London to Paris to Venice to St. Moritz and down the Rhine the travelers proceeded, informing Sara of their progress—and being informed, in turn, of Sara's progress preparing the house they would live in upon their re-turn. It was on East Thirty-sixth Street, just three blocks from Sara's own house. Franklin gave not the slightest hint of wanting to provide for Eleanor himself; on the contrary he wrote his mother, "We are so glad that it is really through you that we get the house. . . . It is so good that you take all the trou-ble for us." He closed this letter with words that may have revealed more than he intended: "Ever your loving infants."

Besides tending to Sara back home, Franklin and Eleanor visited many cousins, uncles, aunts, and family friends and acquaintances scattered about Britain and France. They saw the Whitelaw Reids in London, where Reid was now the American ambassador. They had lunch with Sidney and Beatrice Webb ("They write books on sociology," Franklin said of the Fabian couple) and tea with Beatrice Chamberlain. They stayed with some Delanos in Paris and traveled for a time with Bob Ferguson, a British Rough Rider comrade of Theodore Roosevelt's. Eleanor caught up with old teachers at Allenswood, un-fortunately not including Marie Souvestre, who had recently died.

Especially in England they were treated like aristocracy on account of their last name. "We were ushered into the royal suite, one flight up, front, price $1,000 a day—a sitting room 40 ft. by 30 ft., a double bedroom, another ditto and a bath," Franklin wrote from London. "Our breath was so taken away that we couldn't even protest and are now saying, 'Damn the expense, wot's the odds'!"

The final weeks of the honeymoon coincided with Theodore Roosevelt's successful mediation of the Russo-Japanese War, for which he would be awarded the Nobel Peace Prize. "Everyone is talking about Cousin Theodore, saying that he is the most prominent figure of present-day history," Franklin wrote, with vicarious pride. He told Sara they would be home soon. "You know how we long to see our Mummy again."

Eleanor found the voyage home difficult. She wasn't the sailor her husband was, and she sorely feared disappointing him. The outbound journey had been suspiciously easy, with fair weather and calm seas the entire way. But the return was a trial, despite conditions hardly more severe. On landing she learned the reason: she was pregnant. "It was quite a relief," she wrote. She had worried not simply about being unable to keep up with Franklin as a traveler. "Little idiot that I was, I had been seriously troubled for fear that I would never have any children and my husband would therefore be much disappointed."

Aside from the morning sickness, the pregnancy went smoothly. She suffered the ordinary first-baby jitters, magnified in her case by not previously having spent time with infants. "I had never had any interest in dolls or little children, and I knew absolutely nothing about handling or feeding a baby." The nurse she hired to assist her turned out to be no help. The woman was young and scarcely more experienced than Eleanor. "She knew a considerable amount about babies' diseases, but her inexperience made this knowledge almost a menace, for she was constantly looking for obscure illnesses and never expected that a well fed and well cared for baby would move along in a normal manner." Yet Eleanor was too timid to complain. "For years I was afraid of my nurses, . . . who ordered me around quite as much as they ordered the children."

Sara offered assistance but on her own terms. She set up Eleanor and Franklin's first house, and when their family outgrew that she built them another, on East Sixty-fifth Street—adjacent to her own new house, with rooms that opened into the matching rooms of her house. Eleanor had no say in the design or decorating of her house. She might have asserted herself but didn't. As a result she felt the independence she had learned from Marie Souvestre slipping away. "I was growing very dependent on my mother-in-law, requiring her help on almost every subject, and never thought of asking for anything which I felt would not meet with her approval." In later years she reflected on Sara: "She is a very strong character, but because of her marriage to an older man she disciplined herself into gladly living his life and enjoying his belongings, and as a result I think she felt that young people should cater to older people. She gave great devotion to her own family and longed for their love and affection in return. She was somewhat jealous, because of her love, of anything which she felt might mean a really deep attachment outside of the family circle."

Eleanor was usually charitable in her assessment of others' motives, and she may have given her mother-in-law more benefit of the doubt than Sara deserved. But whatever the wellsprings of Sara's omnipresence in the lives of Eleanor and Franklin, it ultimately provoked a breakdown. "I did not know what was the matter with me," Eleanor wrote, "but I remember that a few weeks after we moved into the new house in East 65th Street I sat in front of my dressing table and wept, and when my bewildered young husband asked me what on earth was the matter with me, I said I did not like to live in a house which was not in any way mine, one that I had done nothing about and which did not represent the way I wanted to live."

If Franklin ever felt Sara's presence to be a burden, he didn't say so. And doubtless her demands weighed less on him, who had outlets beyond the household for his energies and emotions, than they did on Eleanor, who could never escape her mother-in-law. Yet whatever his own perception of Sara, he offered little sympathy to Eleanor. "He thought I was quite mad and told me so gently, and said I would feel different in a little while," Eleanor recalled. Then he left her to cry alone.

❖　❖　❖

THERE WERE OTHER occasions for tears. The first baby, Anna Eleanor, born in 1906, was followed by a son, James, in 1907, and a second son, Franklin Jr., in 1909. Franklin Jr. was the biggest of Eleanor's babies and appeared the most robust. His parents and grandmother fussed over all three and took the standard precaution among the well-to-do of clearing out of the city during the unhealthy summer season. They typically sojourned at Hyde Park before heading to Campobello. Eleanor would take the children by train; Franklin would gather a group of male friends and sail up the coast in the *Half Moon II,* the successor to his father's boat, which had been destroyed when the naphtha tank exploded. Eleanor never quite understood the appeal of these boys' weeks out. "They always told me what delicious things they had had to eat on the boat. Apparently their idea of perfection was a combination of sausages, syrup and pancakes for every meal, varied occasionally by lobster or scrambled eggs. My husband was the cook as well as the captain, and was very proud of his prowess."

Franklin was an accomplished sailor, but even the best boatmen meet trouble now and then. Some of Eleanor's cousins, the Parishes, were coming to Campobello to visit, and Franklin and Eleanor sailed the mile to Eastport to greet the evening train. On the return the compass light failed, and Franklin replaced it with a lantern. Meanwhile a thick fog set in, requiring Franklin to navigate by compass alone. The crossing took longer than usual, but at first he attributed the delay to the slow speed he was keeping on account of the fog. Suddenly a passenger in the bow shouted "Hard aport!" and Franklin veered over just in time to miss crashing into a dock at the village of Lubec, far off course. Mystified and chagrined, he recharted the course. A few minutes later another warning call came from the bow, and Franklin had to maneuver frantically to keep the boat from grounding on a small island he hadn't expected. More confused than ever, he checked the compass, then rechecked it, before finally realizing that the lantern was made of steel that was deranging the compass. He removed the lantern and thereafter read the compass by match light, and eventually brought all to safety. "Never again were we able to induce Mrs. Parish to attempt a trip to Campobello," Eleanor recalled.

The summer of 1908 proved an exception to the Hyde Park–Campobello routine. One-year-old James had contracted pneumonia that spring, and Eleanor was leery of subjecting him to the chill and damp of the Bay of Fundy. Besides, she wanted to stay close to regular medical care. So the family rented a house at Seabright, on the New Jersey coast. The quarters were cramped by comparison with what they were used to, but James recovered in the sun and salt air.

The following year Franklin Jr. was the one who caused the greatest concern. The family stopped at Hyde Park en route back from Campobello to New York City. Eleanor and Franklin went ahead to the city, only to learn that the three children had caught the flu. Little Franklin, just six months old, was the worst off. Eleanor fetched a doctor from New York and returned to Hyde Park; the doctor declared that the baby's heart had been affected and insisted that he be taken to a hospital in New York. Hospital care in such a case consisted of little more than watchful waiting, and though cause for hope appeared now and again, the baby died in early November.

Franklin was saddened, but Eleanor was consumed with self-reproach. "I felt he had been left too much to the nurse and I knew too little about him, and that in some way I must be to blame. I even felt that I had not cared enough about him. . . . I made myself and all those around me most unhappy during that winter. I was even a little bitter at my poor young husband who occasionally tried to make me see how idiotically I was behaving."

4.

$\mathcal{T}$HOSE WHO KNEW FRANKLIN PROFESSIONALLY DURING THIS PERIOD—
in particular his fellow law clerks, with whom he spent hours every day, sharing confidences and dreams—realized he wasn't long for the law. "I remember
him saying with engaging frankness that he wasn't going to practice law forever," Grenville Clark recollected years later. "He intended to run for office at
the first opportunity. . . . He wanted to be and thought he had a very real
chance to be president." Roosevelt sketched the route, which drew liberally on
the experience of his kinsman in the White House. "I remember that he described very accurately the steps which he thought could lead to this goal,"
Clark continued. "They were: first, a seat in the State Assembly, then an appointment as Assistant Secretary of the Navy . . . and finally the governorship
of New York. 'Anyone who is governor of New York has a good chance to be
President with any luck' are about his words that stick in my memory." Roosevelt said all this most matter-of-factly, in a way that compelled respect if not
outright admiration for his audacity. "I do not recall that even then, in 1907,
any of us deprecated his ambition or even smiled at it as we might perhaps
have done. It seemed proper and sincere; and moreover, as he put it, entirely
reasonable."

It was a stretch even so. Simply entering politics was unusual for one of
Roosevelt's class. Theodore Roosevelt had shocked his family and friends by
taking the plunge a quarter century earlier; a godfatherly type told him that
politics was grubby, low, and rough, and its practitioners were not those with
whom gentlemen associated. "I answered that if this were so it merely meant
that the people I knew did not belong to the governing class," Theodore Roosevelt recalled. "I intended to be one of the governing class." Franklin did, too,
following Theodore's example.

Yet Franklin's course was, if anything, harder than Theodore's had been.
Theodore's people were Republicans, the relatively respectable party in New

York. Franklin's folks were Democrats, the party of Tammany Hall. Defection appears never to have occurred to Franklin; consequently any political career he commenced would have to struggle against, surrender to, or otherwise take account of the most storied and arguably the most corrupt political machine in America.

To be sure, Tammany Hall had mellowed somewhat since the days of Boss William Marcy Tweed, who bilked the city of millions in the aftermath of the Civil War. Tweed eventually died in jail, an object lesson in the wages of corruption. But the source of the corruption—the wellsprings of the cesspool, so to speak—remained. In fact they flowed more strongly than ever as America continued to industrialize and to attract immigrants by the several hundred thousand per year. The immigrants arrived in need of homes, jobs, education, and the myriad other goods and services required to make a new life in a strange land. Relatives and friends from the old countries supplied some of the needs, but being mostly poor themselves, they could do only so much. Government, as government, had yet to conceive its role as providing social services. Consequently the machines—headed by the bosses, staffed by precinct captains, and manned by regiments of ward heelers—found their niche acting as the immigrants' sponsors and protectors. They helped the newcomers locate housing and employment; they furnished food and clothing if these ran short; they interceded with police and judges when youthful enthusiasm got out of hand or want drove men to desperate deeds. In return they asked only for loyalty at election time. And they usually got it.

The more thoughtful, or merely more sophistic, of the bosses formulated a philosophy of the machines as agents of democracy. "Consider the problem which every democratic system has to solve," Richard Croker, Tammany's chief at the turn of the century, told journalist William Stead. "Government, we say, of the people, by the people, and for the people. The aim is to interest as many of the citizens as possible in the work—which is not an easy work, and has many difficulties and disappointments—of governing the state or the city." Government officials had to appeal to the needs and desires of citizens. In New York, citizens were often immigrants. "We have thousands upon thousands of men who are alien born, who have no ties connecting them with the city or the state," Croker said. "They do not speak our language, they do not know our laws. They are the raw material with which we have to build up the state." Tammany took upon its shoulders the building. It welcomed the newcomers and made them Americans. "Who else would do it if we did not?" Croker conceded that certain of Tammany's tactics couldn't stand close scrutiny. But he refused to apologize for them. "If we go down into the gutter, it is because there are men in the gutter."

Croker's logic wouldn't be lost on Franklin Roosevelt, once Roosevelt turned to politics. But it largely eluded New York voters in 1901, when Croker and Tammany were ousted in favor of a reformist slate led by Columbia University president Seth Low. Tammany beat a tactical retreat and reconstituted itself under the leadership of Charles Murphy, who by 1910 dominated the Democrats not only of New York City but of New York state.

❖ ❖ ❖

*I*T WAS CHARLES MURPHY whom Roosevelt confronted when he decided to run for the state senate that year. Roosevelt had intended to aim lower, for the state assembly. When the Democrats of Dutchess County heard that he was interested in politics—and that even while living in New York City he had maintained his voting residence in Hyde Park—they approached him eagerly. The Roosevelt name was the most famous in American political life; in fact, with Theodore Roosevelt just then completing a post-presidential grand tour of Europe, it might have been the most famous political name in the world. Beyond the candidate's family celebrity, a Franklin Roosevelt campaign would be self-financed—or at least financed by the candidate's mother—which was no small consideration for a county organization strapped for funds. Finally, Dutchess County, like most of the rest of upstate New York, was historically Republican. Any candidate would be a long shot, and if Franklin Roosevelt flubbed his chance little would be lost.

Yet there was reason for hope. The national Republicans had taken to feuding since Theodore Roosevelt left office, with the party's conservatives striving to reclaim control of the GOP and the party's progressives struggling to maintain the momentum they had achieved under the Rough Rider. The split in the Republicans afforded hope to Democrats all across the country, including upstate New York. In Dutchess County, assemblyman and former lieutenant governor Lewis Chanler, who had hinted at retirement, became sufficiently encouraged by his prospects to announce at the last minute for re-election. This prompted the county's Democratic committee, meeting in early October, to nominate Roosevelt for the state senate rather than the assembly.

The switch was a stroke of luck, but whether good luck or bad wasn't immediately apparent. A senate seat was a bigger prize than a spot in the assembly, but for precisely this reason the Republicans would contest the senate election more vigorously. Yet Roosevelt was rarely inclined to second-guess fate, and he didn't do so now. "I thank you heartily for the honor you have done me," he told the nominating convention, in what amounted to his maiden speech as a candidate. "But even more do I thank you for giving me an opportunity to advance the cause of good government under the banner of the Democratic party."

The voters of Roosevelt's senate district knew his name, but they didn't know him. And with only a month between the nomination and the election, he had to work hard and travel fast to introduce himself to them. New York's rural voters still expected candidates to visit them by train or horse and buggy, if the candidates visited them at all. Roosevelt laid out a map of the three counties his district comprised and determined that he'd never cover them all the old way. And so he hired a big, gaudy red, open-topped Maxwell automobile. He hoisted flags from the rear of the car and enlisted the company of Congressman Richard Connell, a rare successful Democrat in upstate New York, and they roared from town to town and village to village. They met farmers on the road who were as intrigued by the car as by its passengers. But whatever the reason they stopped, Roosevelt leaped out to shake their hands, ask them what they wanted from their state government, and promise to represent them to the best of his ability.

His prepared speeches stressed honest government and fair treatment of farmers. Yet mostly they revealed an attractive young man. "Humboldt, the great traveler, once said: 'You can tell the character of the people in a house by looking at the outside,' " he informed a small crowd at the public library in Pleasant Valley, not far from Poughkeepsie. "This is even more true of a community. And I think I can truthfully say that of all the villages of Dutchess County—and I have been in pretty nearly every one—there are very few that appear as favorably as Pleasant Valley." Before this race Roosevelt had no particular reason to think he'd like, or be good at, campaigning. But he discovered he loved it and had a gift. He told jokes on himself. "I'm not Teddy," he reminded one audience—by way of reminding them that he *was* a Roosevelt. While the crowd laughed, he continued, "A little shaver said to me the other day that he knew I wasn't Teddy. I asked him why, and he replied, 'Because you don't show your teeth.' " But Franklin did say "Bully," just like Teddy, and, in conscious echo of Theodore's Square Deal, which called for government efficiency and an even hand between business and labor, he declared, "I am running squarely on the issue of honesty and economy and efficiency in our state senate." That his opponent was a protégé of a longtime Republican foe of Uncle Ted reinforced the family connection.

Roosevelt's listeners responded with surprising enthusiasm. The twenty-eight-year-old candidate had no special qualifications for office; he brought no compelling new ideas to the campaign; he had little in common with most of the voters of his district; he utterly lacked elective experience. But he had that something—that sincerity, that charisma—that caused people to respond. And when voters went to the polls on November 8, they elected Franklin Roosevelt to the New York senate by a margin of 1,440 votes out of 30,000 cast.

The victory wasn't wholly personal; it was a good day for Democrats as a party. They captured both houses of the New York legislature, and the federal House of Representatives. In neighboring New Jersey, another Democratic first-timer, Princeton University president Woodrow Wilson, won the Garden State governorship.

All the same, it was a fine start for Roosevelt's political career. Not even Uncle Ted, whose first victory had been in a race for a state assembly seat, had done better.

❖ ❖ ❖

FRANKLIN ROOSEVELT ARRIVED in Albany as the majority Democrats were deciding who should replace Republican senator Chauncey Depew in Washington. Depew had served two terms in the Senate and hadn't done poorly for New York. If his fate had been up to the voters of New York, he probably would have continued in office. But in those days before the Seventeenth Amendment he answered to the legislature, not the voters, and the Democrats weren't about to waste their upset victory on returning a Republican to Washington.

Among the New York Democrats, the strongest element was the Tammany delegation, which took its orders from Charles Murphy. The Tammany boss decreed that William Sheehan—"Blue-Eyed Billy"—should become New York's next senator. Sheehan, a former lieutenant governor who had subsequently made a fortune in transport and utilities, with Tammany's help and to Tammany's benefit, wasn't markedly less qualified than many of those who held seats in the Senate, but his candidacy caught the force of the rising progressive headwind. Near the top of the list of progressive must-fixes was the method of electing senators. Reliance on the legislatures seemed anachronistic eighty years after the nation's embrace of democracy; it allowed machines like Tammany to frustrate the will of the people. For a decade progressives had demanded the popular election of senators. But till the Constitution could be amended to that effect, they waged their antiboss battles within the state-houses.

The current round of the contest in New York began on January 1, 1911, when Franklin Roosevelt and the rest of the lawmakers swore their oath of office. Among the freshmen, Roosevelt attracted the greatest attention. "His patronymic had gone before him," a feature writer the *New York Times* sent to Albany to profile the Democratic Roosevelt explained. "Those who looked closely at the lawmaker behind Desk 26 saw a young man with the finely chiseled face of a Roman patrician, only with a ruddier glow of health upon it. He is tall and lithe. With his handsome face and his form of supple strength he could make a fortune on the stage." During the campaign some New Yorkers had imagined a closer family relation between Franklin and Theodore Roosevelt than actually existed; the *Times* writer set the matter straight. He also suggested a difference in style between the former president and the novice state senator. "It is safe to predict that the African jungle never will resound with the crack of Franklin D. Roosevelt's rifle. The thought of the hartebeest and the wildebeest, the mobile springbok and the deceitful dig-dig does not set the blood tingling in his veins. As far as he is concerned, the roaring lion may pursue unmolested its prey until such time as it shall lie down with the lamb."

Yet one beast drew the fire of the new senator. "Only if you should happen to say 'Tiger!' you will find that Franklin D. Roosevelt believes there is good hunting nearer home," the *Times* asserted. The tiger was the mascot of Tammany Hall, and Roosevelt, as a bearer of that famously combative and progressive name, had a symbolic rifle thrust into his hand whether he wished it or not.

In fact he relished the fight. Roosevelt's political philosophy was largely inchoate at the beginning of his career. He couldn't have convincingly explained where he stood on half the issues that confronted legislators at that time. But his upbringing had caused him to value honesty in government; the example of Uncle Ted pushed him toward progressivism; and his emerging political instincts told him he'd be noticed if he bearded the Tammany tiger. Besides, he didn't like being told what to do. This only child of an indulgent mother had never experienced the weight of discipline, and he didn't propose to shoulder it now.

Yet discipline was precisely what was expected of Democrats in Albany. In the matter of selecting a senator, the party traditionally operated as a bloc.

The candidate of the party caucus was, ipso facto, the candidate of all the Democrats in the legislature. Because Tammany controlled a majority of the Democrats in the legislature, Charles Murphy's choice for senator would carry the caucus, and because the Democrats constituted a majority in the legislature, Murphy's candidate would win the election.

There was one loophole. Innocently or otherwise, Roosevelt asked Alfred E. Smith, a Tammany man more approachable than some of Murphy's followers, just how tightly party rules bound the members. Smith replied that if Roosevelt attended the party caucus, his vote for the caucus candidate would be required. But if he didn't attend, he could vote his conscience. Roosevelt noted Smith's forthrightness and thanked him for it—and proceeded to boycott the caucus.

If that had been the extent of his rebellion, Murphy would have shrugged. Yet Roosevelt, on account of being a Roosevelt, was in the spotlight, and his independence prompted concern among the Tammany leadership. "Big Tim" Sullivan, a Murphy crony, inquired whether this new Roosevelt was really kin to the Rough Rider; informed that he was, Sullivan remarked, "Well, if we've caught a Roosevelt, we'd better take him down and drop him off the dock. The Roosevelts run true to form, and this kid is likely to do for us what the Colonel is going to do for the Republican party: split it wide open."

Tammany's worries intensified when Roosevelt's boycott of the caucus spread. Roosevelt wasn't the only progressive in Albany, and twenty other Democrats joined him in pledging to resist Murphy's dictation. They proposed, as an alternative to Sheehan, Edward M. Shepard, a reformer from Brooklyn. Partly on account of his famous name, but equally by virtue of his wealth, Roosevelt emerged as the leader of the rebels. Few of the legislators could afford to rent houses in Albany; most took rooms in hotels. Roosevelt was one of the rare renters, and the large house he and Eleanor leased on State Street near the Capitol became a third home for the insurgents. "The men arrived sometime during the morning," Eleanor recalled. "They went up to the Senate, cast their votes, ate their lunch, and during the afternoon were back at our house for smoking and talk in the library. They went out again for supper, and returned and spent the entire evening." Their presence ultimately created problems for Eleanor and the children. "One morning the nurse came to me and announced that the children were slowly choking to death in their room because the fumes of the cigars which had been smoked downstairs for months had permeated the bedroom above." Yet rather than evict the smokers, Eleanor moved the children.

Roosevelt initially ducked the label of leader of the insurgency. "Leader?" he responded to a question. "I should not claim that title. There really is no leader." He similarly denied any attempt to split or otherwise weaken the Democratic party. "This is not a split in the party, or even a fight in the party. We are merely a group of men who are taking a rational view of a situation that is not very difficult to size up, and acting in accordance with that view. . . . I am a Democrat first, last, and all the time."

But he didn't deny opposing bossism and fighting for honest democracy. "The control by Tammany Hall of the state Democracy will stand under present conditions as an insurmountable obstacle in the way of party success," he said. "This fight involves a much bigger question than whether Shepard or Sheehan shall go to the United States Senate." Taking a deep breath, till he became quite full of himself, Roosevelt asserted, "The election of Mr. Sheehan would mean disaster to the Democratic party not only in the state but in the nation."

Whether or not it affected the nation, the Roosevelt insurgency did draw the attention of the national press. Since the Tweed scandals of the 1870s, everyone in America knew of Tammany Hall; to those many outsiders who looked on Gotham as Gomorrah, Tammany equaled bossism at its most corrupt. The efforts of a new Roosevelt—and one rather more photogenic than Theodore—to tame the Tammany tiger made the best copy since the colonel had assaulted San Juan Hill in the Spanish-American War. Paper after paper across the country carried pictures of Roosevelt and reports of his rebellion against Boss Murphy; editor after editor endorsed his struggle. The *Cleveland Plain Dealer* reminded readers of Theodore Roosevelt's valiant campaigns against corruption and declared, "Franklin D. Roosevelt is beginning his public career fully as auspiciously. . . . If none of the colonel's sons turn out to be fit objects for popular admiration, may it not be possible that this rising star may continue the Roosevelt dynasty?"

❖ ❖ ❖

Yet Tammany was wily and determined. New York legislators, like nearly all state legislators then and after, required incomes beyond what they received for their lawmaking service. A handful, like Roosevelt, were financially independent; the others operated farms or businesses or pursued professions. Several of the insurgents had contracts with the state or with businesses dependent to a greater or lesser degree on the goodwill of Tammany Hall. As the boycott of Sheehan proceeded, these vulnerable ones found themselves pinched where it hurt. Contracts were canceled, loans called, mortgages foreclosed. Roosevelt bravely promised to make the victims whole. "Some of us have means, and we intend to stand by the men who are voting for principle," he declared. "We shall see to it that they are protected in the discharge of their public duty. They shall not suffer because they are faithful to the people." Just *how* he proposed to do this, he didn't say. His own means—and Sara's—rendered him impervious to Tammany's economic counterattack, but they didn't stretch far enough to cover all his allies.

Tammany unveiled other weapons. Sheehan was Irish, as were Murphy and many of Tammany's most loyal supporters. Old-stock Americans of such pedigrees as Roosevelt's often looked down on the Irish, especially the destitute refugees of the Great Famine of the 1840s and their heirs. Though in his case inaccurate, imputations of anti-Irish feeling in Roosevelt's opposition to Sheehan and Tammany weren't implausible. From allegations of anti-Irishism to charges of anti-Catholicism was a short step, which Tammany's rumormongers readily made.

Roosevelt denied the rumors vigorously. "This is absolutely untrue!" he shouted. "We do not ask and do not care from what stock a man may have sprung or what his religious beliefs may be. All we ask is that he be a fit man for United States Senator." He pointed out that the insurgents included a number of Irishmen and Catholics. Yet his denials simply gave the accusations a larger audience, as Tammany reckoned they would.

Roosevelt fumblingly counterattacked. He alleged that Sheehan was in bed with Thomas Fortune Ryan, an infamous speculator who, with Tammany's help, had managed to monopolize rail transport in much of New York City. Or if Sheehan wasn't in bed with Ryan, at least he was in church with Ryan: Roosevelt asserted that the two attended the same ten o'clock mass at St. Patrick's Cathedral. It was a silly charge—hundreds of worshipers attended the same service—and Roosevelt soon let it drop.

But he held his ground otherwise. The insurgency wasn't going away, he declared. "The Sheehan men can keep up the struggle as long as they choose. They will find that we can stand it as long as they can. They must be aware, however, that the longer they keep up the battle the worse it is for the Democratic Party."

Murphy eventually agreed. He invited Roosevelt to his hotel suite. The day happened to be Roosevelt's twenty-ninth birthday, and the Tammany boss exuded good cheer. He met Roosevelt with what Roosevelt afterward characterized to reporters as a "delightful smile," and he conducted the interview with respect and friendliness. "I know I can't make you change your mind unless you want to change it," he told Roosevelt (again by Roosevelt's account). "Is there any chance of you and the other twenty men coming around to vote for Sheehan?" Roosevelt responded, "No, Mr. Murphy. . . . In the first place, we believe a great many of our Democratic constituents don't want him to be the United States senator, and in the second place, he is altogether too closely connected with the traction trust in New York City." In Roosevelt's version, Murphy said he accepted this reasoning. He intimated that he had chosen Sheehan more from a sense of personal obligation than from conviction that he was the best man for the job. He told Roosevelt that if the insurgents were dead set against Sheehan and could never vote for him, then he—Roosevelt—should tell Sheehan this to his face, and explain why. Presumably, once Sheehan realized he couldn't be elected, he would withdraw and save the party further embarrassment.

Roosevelt inferred from the session that Murphy was weakening. He proceeded to his house on State Street to enlist Eleanor's further support. "My husband came home and announced that the gentleman he was fighting against would be with us for luncheon the next day," she recalled. "After luncheon I was to entertain 'Blue Eyed Billy' Sheehan's wife while my husband talked to him in his study. Lunch was not so bad, for I had my husband to carry the burden of the conversation, but after lunch we two women sat and talked about the weather and anything else inconsequential that we could think of, while both of us knew quite well that behind the door of my husband's study a really important fight was going on."

The issue wasn't settled that day. Sheehan left as determined as ever; Roosevelt stood equally firm. "Mr. Sheehan is delightful personally," he told reporters. "But that is one thing; the senatorship fight is another."

Yet as the impasse continued, it obstructed the work of the legislature, and Tammany and the Democratic regulars feared that after years of Republican control of the state, they were frittering away an opportunity that might not recur soon. Murphy quietly decided to cut his losses. His support of Sheehan grew less and less conspicuous, until the candidate got the message and decided at the end of February to withdraw. Albany watchers anticipated a quick compromise, that the real work of the legislature might begin.

But Roosevelt wasn't through. He and his fellow insurgents rejected the substitutes Murphy suggested, one after another until more than a dozen had been vetoed. Roosevelt, publicly reconsidering his earlier promise of loyalty to the Democrats, hinted that if he couldn't work with Tammany and Murphy he might strike a bargain with Republican boss William Barnes. Murphy responded with his own overtures to Barnes.

Meanwhile Tammany's sapping operations against the insurgency began to tell. One by one Roosevelt's allies weakened and sought an end to the battle. A stroke of misfortune improved the chances for compromise when the Capitol caught fire in late March and burned badly. Already weary and now displaced, the legislators as a body grew anxious for a solution. Murphy proposed a new candidate, Judge James Aloysius O'Gorman. Before ascending the bench O'Gorman had been a Tammany leader, or sachem, but since then he had earned a reputation for independence of mind and integrity of decision. The choice saved face for both sides in the long struggle: Murphy could point to O'Gorman's early political career, Roosevelt to his recent judicial service.

All that remained was to negotiate the details of the settlement. Roosevelt insisted on amnesty for himself and the insurgents: no reprisals from the Democratic leadership for their display of conscience. Al Smith and another Tammanyite, Robert Wagner, conveyed Murphy's assurances on this issue. While Roosevelt and a hard core of the insurgents made a final point by refusing to attend the caucus that nominated O'Gorman, they sent word that they would vote for the judge in the legislature.

Roosevelt proclaimed a victory for principle. "We have followed the dictates of our consciences and have done our duty as we saw it," he declared. But he was also happy to claim a personal triumph, one suggesting that the pressmen's parallels to combative Uncle Ted weren't without basis. "I have just come from Albany and the close of a long fight which lasted sixty-four rounds," he told an audience at the annual dinner of the Young Men's Christian Association in New York City the next day. "At the end of it was a free-for-all. Some got battered, but you can see by me that there were few scratches on the insurgents."

5.

𝓡oosevelt's rivals often lamented the luck that blessed his career at crucial moments. He wouldn't have denied that fortune smiled on him, and he knew from no less an authority than Uncle Ted that luck could make all the difference between success and failure at the apex of public life. "As regards the extraordinary prizes, the element of luck is *the* determining factor," Theodore wrote his eldest son, Ted, who was Franklin's near contemporary. Franklin didn't read this letter, but he certainly heard the sentiment from Theodore, who often acknowledged that his brilliant success owed to two remarkable strokes of luck: his own good luck in surviving his heroics at San Juan Hill and McKinley's bad luck in being assassinated. Had the dice been weighted ever so slightly differently, the world would scarcely have heard of Theodore Roosevelt.

Franklin's initial good fortune had been to run his first race for office as the New York Republican party was fracturing between the progressives and the standpatters. The window for Dutchess County Democrats opened just long enough for him to step through, and it began closing almost at once. The 1911 elections for the New York assembly restored the Republican majority to the lower chamber, and the 1912 elections threatened to do the same to the senate. Roosevelt had reason to anticipate retirement from office.

But smiling fate intervened once more—assisted by none other than Uncle Ted. Republican progressives warned the Rough Rider that everything he had accomplished in the White House would be imperiled by another four years of his protégé, William Howard Taft. Rested after his safari and world tour, and restless after three years out of power, TR declared himself a candidate for the Republican nomination for president in 1912. This Roosevelt insurgency garnered incomparably more attention than Franklin's fight with Boss Murphy, but it recapitulated the same themes. TR denounced the Taft machine as corrupt and unconcerned with ordinary Americans; the welfare of the people required a fresh blast of democracy. Several states by this time held preference primaries; Roosevelt trounced Taft in most of these, including one held in Taft's home state of Ohio. But Republican party rules left the majority of the votes at the national convention in Chicago in the hands of the regulars, who rebuffed Roosevelt to renominate Taft. Roosevelt thereupon bolted the convention, trailing a large portion of the party behind him. This insurgent column reorganized under the banner of the Progressive party (nicknamed Bull Moose for TR's characterization of his rude good health) and girded for combat. "We stand at Armageddon, and we battle for the Lord," Roosevelt proclaimed.

Indirectly they battled for the Democrats, as anyone not blinded by emotion could see. Since the 1850s the Democrats had elected precisely one president (Grover Cleveland, albeit twice). Sixty years after the industrial revolution began transforming American life, the party of Jefferson and Jackson had yet to come to terms with the political meaning of that revolution. The South dominated Democratic congressional politics; southern senators and congressmen sat on important committees and protected the interests of their states and districts. But the South sorely handicapped the party in presidential politics. The blatantly racist politics of the South alienated voters elsewhere, putting southern presidential hopefuls in an impossible bind. To win a name in the South required repeatedly playing the race card, but doing so effectively disqualified one for president.

The Democrats might have mitigated their southern burden by embracing the Democratic machines of the urban North. Yet the notorious corruption of Tammany Hall and its counterparts in other cities caused their favorites credibility problems of their own when seeking higher office. Even had the machines been exemplars of integrity, the cities, with their large and growing immigrant populations, seemed so foreign to rural voters that the graduates of city politics had scant appeal beyond the boroughs. It merely compounded the problem that rural districts were constitutionally overrepresented in most state legislatures, and the rural states in the federal electoral college.

If some charismatic figure could build a bridge between the two pillars of the party—between the South and the cities—the Democrats might again elect presidents as they had before the Civil War. Till then their only hope lay in a civil war among the Republicans.

This was precisely what Theodore Roosevelt's defection in the summer of 1912 touched off and what enabled the Democrats to envision reoccupying the White House. Since the turn of the century, Democratic conventions had been pro forma affairs, with candidates vying for the dubious privilege of losing, often badly, to the Republican nominee. This time the contest was genuinely bitter because the prize was real.

❖ ❖ ❖

$\mathcal{I}$N THE EARLY summer of 1912 Franklin and Eleanor embarked on what amounted to a second honeymoon. They left the children with the nurse, nanny, and servants, and headed for the Southwest. They crossed the Mississippi on a Louisiana train ferry that handled several cars at a time. No bridge yet spanned the lower Mississippi, partly because the river was so wide but also because the floods that periodically inundated the land on either side of the river would have played havoc with any but the sturdiest approaches and abutments. In fact, a flood that surged downstream in 1912 nearly prevented Franklin and Eleanor from getting across; theirs was the last train ferried over for several days.

They traversed western Louisiana and the entire width of Texas, exiting the train at Deming in southern New Mexico. Bob Ferguson, the British Rough Rider, and his wife, Isabella, had moved from Scotland to New Mexico on account of the tuberculosis that was slowly taking Bob's life. As with other diseases incurable by contemporary medicine—a large category in the second decade of the twentieth century—treatment consisted of transporting the patient to an environment as supportive as possible of the patient's immune system. For tuberculosis patients this meant somewhere high and dry. Davos, Switzerland, was famous for its tuberculosis sanatoriums; Bob Ferguson, the cavalryman, preferred the American West. He and Isabella were building a home in the mountains of New Mexico; meanwhile they and their children kept house in a tent.

Eleanor had never been camping, and the visit to the Fergusons opened her eyes to its possibilities. She was amazed at how well the Ferguson children adapted to their new surroundings and regimen. "My city ideas had to be rapidly adjusted when I saw them eating pork and beans and all kinds of canned food which would have been considered absolute death to children of their age in eastern surroundings," she remembered. She had read about cowboys and heard Uncle Ted tell of his experiences among the cattlemen of Dakota. Now she encountered the hardy breed herself. All were polite, but Isabella informed her that courtesy sometimes concealed darker currents. "Last week I thought I had a really good boy to do the work," Isabella told Eleanor.

"But I found he was wanted for the murder of his brother, so I had to let him go to jail."

❖ ❖ ❖

FRANKLIN AND ELEANOR timed their return east to allow Franklin to attend the Democratic national convention in Baltimore. Two candidates had distanced the field during the primary season: Champ (shortened from James Beauchamp) Clark of Missouri and Woodrow Wilson of New Jersey. Clark, a nine-term congressman and the current speaker of the House, appealed to party conservatives; Wilson, the Princeton president who had become New Jersey's governor, wore the progressive mantle. Some of the same issues that were splitting the Republicans threatened to divide the Democrats, but two factors seemed certain to prevent a full-blown schism. First, because the Democrats lacked an incumbent, the progressive challenge couldn't well be construed as lese majesty, as it was among the Republicans. Second, because the Democrats had been exiled so long from the White House and appeared doomed, under normal circumstances, to wander the wilderness for decades longer, they were desperate to take advantage of the opportunity of Theodore Roosevelt's rebellion.

Franklin Roosevelt had liked Woodrow Wilson's style from the moment the professor had first taken on the New Jersey establishment. After accepting the endorsement of Democratic boss James Smith in the 1910 campaign, Wilson proceeded as governor to topple Smith from power. Smith and his lieutenants cried foul, but other members of the machine sued for peace, on Wilson's terms. Roosevelt was impressed that a liberal could be so cunning.

He first met Wilson personally in late 1911, traveling to Trenton to pay his respects and indulge his curiosity. Wilson asked what support a progressive presidential candidate might expect in New York. Roosevelt offered his own backing and said other progressives would join him. Wilson inquired what, precisely, this meant; Roosevelt conceded that it might not mean much. New York Democrats operated under a unit rule at national conventions; they all voted with the majority. And because Boss Murphy, who despised New Jersey progressives almost as much as he detested the New York variety, controlled the majority, the prospects for Wilson weren't good.

Yet Wilson took the long view. Murphy might win the early rounds, but if the progressives went to the people, they couldn't help triumphing. Perhaps 1912 was their year; perhaps they'd have to wait. But their cause would prevail. Wilson, a devout Calvinist and predestinarian, was certain of that.

His confidence was catching, and Roosevelt enlisted with a group of New York Democrats for Wilson. His anti-Tammany reputation preceded him, and he soon was named chairman of the group's executive committee. He solicited donations for Wilson—money that funded speakers, articles, and advertisements on behalf of the New Jersey governor. And when the Democrats convened at Baltimore, following the crack-up of the Republicans at Chicago, he headed an unofficial New York delegation committed to Wilson.

Inside the convention hall, Champ Clark led the early balloting, to no one's surprise. But the Democrats' two-thirds rule for nominations—adopted in the early days of national conventions, to enforce party discipline—prevented Clark from claiming victory. And with each ballot that failed to put him over the top, his candidacy lost momentum.

The break occurred on the fourteenth ballot. William Jennings Bryan, the Democrats' three-time nominee and, despite his three defeats, still the hero of the southern and western wings of the party, rose to announce that he was switching his vote from Clark to Wilson. He explained his decision as a rebuke to Charles Murphy and boss rule; he said that he'd support Wilson only so long as Murphy did not.

But the explanation was lost in the pandemonium that followed the announcement of the switch. A brawl broke out between Clark delegates and Wilson men. One Clark delegate was heard to mutter, in Bryan's direction, "By God, somebody ought to assassinate him."

Roosevelt's role at the convention consisted chiefly of offering moral support to Wilson. He disappointed some onlookers who, hearing that "Roosevelt is coming," expected Theodore and found only Franklin. But he let out to reporters that he had spoken with Kermit Roosevelt, Theodore's son, who related that his father, in Franklin's words, was "praying for Clark." The story appeared in the papers, as Franklin intended, and bolstered Wilson's prospects. At a crucial early moment, when a faction of Clark men tried to stampede the convention by staging a noisy demonstration for the Missourian, Franklin Roosevelt led an even louder counter-cheering squad for Wilson. Throughout the convention he took every opportunity to introduce himself around, making a widely, if not deeply, favorable impression.

And he applauded the convention's outcome, when it finally occurred. "Wilson nominated this afternoon," he wired to Eleanor, who had taken the children to Campobello. "All my plans vague. Splendid triumph."

❖ ❖ ❖

*T*HOUGH VAGUE, Roosevelt's plans weren't unconsidered. He traveled from Baltimore to Sea Girt, New Jersey, where Wilson, in line with tradition, had kept his distance from the convention and where, while taking the salt air, he was simultaneously measuring the temperature of various elements of the party. With Taft and Theodore Roosevelt dividing the Republican vote, Wilson could count on New York's bloc of electors, the largest in the country. But he couldn't count on the post-inaugural cooperation of New York's congressional delegation unless Charles Murphy fell from power. By one line of reasoning, in fact, Murphy was more dangerous than ever, for the Republican rift at the top of the ballot would make almost any down-ballot Democratic slate of candidates easy victors. Murphy wouldn't have to appease the progressives but could pack his people onto the Wilson bandwagon, whether they agreed with Wilson or not. Wilson doubtless realized it already, but Roosevelt reminded him that the true battle for New York would be fought not at the polls in November but at the Democrats' nominating convention in October.

Wilson accordingly blessed Roosevelt's strategy of building up a pro-Wilson, anti-Tammany organization of Democrats. This group, calling itself the Empire State Democracy, gathered at the Hotel Astor in Manhattan in late July to indict Murphy politically on multiple charges of misfeasance, malfeasance, and nonfeasance. "In imbecility, in greed, and in suspected partnership in violence," the new group's manifesto asserted, "the small clique claiming control of the party organization has been bound to abhorrent criminal forces, to predatory special interests, to favored corrupt contractors, and to unscrupulous patronage-mongers. . . . The patriotism of self-respecting men requires, and true party loyalty demands, that at whatever cost that bondage shall be broken by the rank and file."

Roosevelt endorsed the Empire State manifesto but supplied his own interpretation. "They refer to us as 'irregular,' " he said of Murphy and his henchmen. They were wrong. "We are the regulars. The system, Tammany, has prevented the Democrats from having control in New York for sixteen years." The time had come to restore the Democrats—the real Democrats, which was to say the ordinary, honest people of New York—to their rightful place in charge of their own destiny. "This is the year to go ahead and strike, and we've got the club."

To the surprise of many progressives, their declaration of war against Tammany prompted Murphy to seek a truce. He offered to let the Tammany dele-gates at the state convention vote their consciences, and he accepted the nom-ination of a moderately progressive candidate for governor in place of the incumbent regular. Finally, he acquiesced in the renomination, by a unanimous vote of the nominating committee, of Franklin Roosevelt for state senator.

As things transpired, Murphy's retreat was tactical rather than strategic, and Tammany survived the 1912 campaign season as it had survived every other season for more than a century. All the same, Roosevelt could plausibly claim credit for another victory over the forces of bossism and corruption.

❖ ❖ ❖

$\mathcal{H}$AD THE 1912 presidential campaign been designed expressly for the pur-pose of educating Franklin Roosevelt in competing theories of government power, it could hardly have unfolded more enlighteningly. William Howard Taft, the conservative among the three presidential candidates, believed that government ought generally to defer to the wisdom of the marketplace. Taft's Justice Department prosecuted certain industrial monopolies, including Rockefeller's Standard Oil Company, which was dismantled by order of the Supreme Court. But by and large Taft trusted Adam Smith's invisible hand to promote the interests of the nation and produce the greatest good for the greatest number of the American people.

Theodore Roosevelt and Woodrow Wilson were far less enamored of the capitalist status quo. Each believed that capitalism was running away with democracy, that the invisible hand was strangling economic opportunity and holding millions of Americans in thrall to corporate greed. Each endorsed the progressive idea that government must intervene in the marketplace on behalf of the private sector's victims.

But they differed sharply on the nature of the intervention. Theodore Roo-sevelt contended that the optimal riposte to the power of corporations was the power of the people, as exercised through government. In a widely reprinted speech he outlined what he called the "New Nationalism," a philos-ophy premised on the belief that combination—the establishment of ever-bigger corporate entities—was an ineluctable fact of modern economic life. "Combinations in industry are the result of an imperative economic law which cannot be repealed by political legislation," Roosevelt asserted. This being so, political wisdom consisted in controlling rather than dismantling the combi-nations. "The effort at prohibiting all combination has substantially failed.

The way out lies, not in attempting to prevent such combinations, but in completely controlling them in the interest of the public welfare." The federal government, with powers enhanced for the purpose, was the single body competent to bring the great corporations to heel.

Woodrow Wilson took less comfort in big government. As a professor Wilson had studied government historically, and he became convinced that government operated better as a policeman of the economy than as its overseer. He concurred with Theodore Roosevelt that the fundamental problem of American life was the excessive power of corporate capital. "The inventive genius and initiative of the American people," he said, "is being held back by the fact that our industrial field is so controlled that new entries, newcomers, new adventurers, independent men, are feared, and if they will not go partners in the game with those already in control of it, they will be excluded." The function of government ought to be to level the field among the industrial and commercial contestants. But where Theodore Roosevelt proposed to accomplish this by expanding the power of government, Wilson advocated reducing the power of business. "What I am interested in is laws that will give the little man a start, that will give him a chance to show these fellows that he has brains enough to compete with them and can presently make his local market a national market and his national market a world market." Wilson's "New Freedom" would break up the trusts, restore the conditions of competition that had prevailed in the nineteenth century, and then let the little man have his day.

Franklin Roosevelt had special reason to follow the arguments of Colonel Roosevelt and Professor Wilson. Franklin Roosevelt was a progressive, but his progressivism remained amorphous on most subjects not directly related to the politics of New York state. He could learn directly from the contest between the New Nationalism and the New Freedom as theories of governance; he could also learn indirectly, by observing how American voters responded to the competing versions of progressivism. Moreover, he had a personal stake in the fight. He had committed publicly to Wilson, and his career stood to advance if Wilson won. At the same time, having modeled himself on Theodore Roosevelt, he couldn't help wondering whether this part of Uncle Ted's career would be worth emulating, too.

Unfortunately for Franklin Roosevelt's political education, the meaning of the 1912 campaign was confused by the three-way nature of the race, and never more than on election day. Wilson received 6.3 million votes, to 4.1 million for Roosevelt and 3.5 million for Taft. Translated into electors, the result gave Wilson 435 against 88 for Roosevelt and 8 for Taft. Obviously progressivism had won, but how much of Wilson's popular vote reflected simple Democratic loyalty, as opposed to endorsement of his small-government progressivism over TR's big-government version and Taft's comfort with the status quo, was impossible to determine. Equally puzzling was how long the distinction would persist in practice, once the campaign faded into memory.

❖ ❖ ❖

FRANKLIN ROOSEVELT'S IMMEDIATE memories of the campaign were clouded by an illness that afflicted him during its final weeks. Following his convention-shortened vacation at Campobello, he and Eleanor cruised down the coast to New York, where they planned to meet friends for an evening on the city. But he felt weak and feverish and had to beg off. The next day he was worse. Eleanor called a doctor, who was mystified at the patient's symptoms. "No one could understand what was the matter with him," Eleanor recalled. She nursed Franklin for several days, till she started feeling poorly herself. She summoned the doctor back, and he diagnosed her illness as typhoid fever. Franklin had had typhoid as a child, which was why no one thought to test him for it. But in fact he had contracted it again, and though Eleanor's infection burned itself out fairly quickly, his reinfection kept him bedridden for weeks.

While Eleanor and the doctor reasoned backward to figure out how she and Franklin had contracted the water-borne disease—she eventually identified a pitcher of water on the boat from Campobello; they had taken care not to drink the water but had rinsed their toothbrushes in it—Franklin wrestled with the problem of conducting his reelection campaign from his sickbed. Heretofore his style had been intensely personal and physical. He had insisted on meeting as many constituents as possible, pumping their hands, patting the heads of their children, and doing whatever else he could to diminish the patina of inherited wealth that still clung to him. Now that he was an invalid, if only temporarily, he had to adopt an alternative plan.

Luckily he had help. Louis McHenry Howe was a Hoosier by birth, the son of one of Indianapolis's most prominent families. But the Panic of 1873 bankrupted his father and forced the family to seek refuge with relatives in Saratoga Springs, New York, where Louis grew up. He became a reporter and then, for a time, editor and owner of the *Saratoga Sun*. He developed a passion for politics and might have entered the arena himself if not for an off-putting appearance—Howe described his own face as "one of the four ugliest" in New

York state, and even Eleanor Roosevelt, who learned to love him dearly, called him a "gnome-like looking little man"—and an impatience with posers and fools. Instead he sought a candidate he could devote himself to, a man who could serve as the vehicle for his intelligence and ambition. Likely figures were few in Albany, but when Franklin Roosevelt arrived in 1911, Howe decided he qualified.

Roosevelt's acuity in judging character would prove to be one of his greatest gifts; his first important verdict—in the case of Louis Howe—was perhaps the most insightful of all. Many people couldn't stand Howe. Beyond his unprepossessing physiognomy were personal habits that repelled the fastidious. He rarely changed his suit, which was chronically covered with ash from the cigarettes he never stopped smoking. His wicked sense of humor impaled friends nearly as often as it skewered enemies. But Roosevelt managed to see past Howe's idiosyncrasies to his distinctive gifts. Howe understood New York state politics as almost no one else did. He knew where Tammany buried the bodies (metaphorically, for the most part). In an age before scientific polling, he had an uncanny feel for public opinion. And Roosevelt liked him—liked his irreverence, liked his passion for politics, liked his capacity for intrigue.

Howe recognized this, and during the summer of 1912, when the newspaper business was slow, he appealed to Roosevelt for work. "If you can connect me with a job during this campaign," he wrote, "for heaven's sake help me out." Roosevelt threw him some small assignments, and then, after being hit by typhoid, hired him to manage his reelection campaign.

Howe delivered a virtuoso performance. He drafted letters from Roosevelt to all the important constituencies in his district. In Roosevelt's name he asked farmers for advice on strengthening agriculture. He consulted commercial fishermen on how to conserve the shad run. He assured apple growers that their crops would be fairly measured and marketed. He declared Roosevelt's support for woman suffrage. On one occasion he drafted a full-page newspaper advertisement specifying the Roosevelt platform; upon its completion he sent Roosevelt a proof, with a note: "As I have pledged you in it, I thought you might like to know casually what kind of a mess I was getting you into." Howe traveled the district in Roosevelt's stead, reminding audiences that Roosevelt had faced down Tammany and contending that such integrity ought to earn him the support of all honorable Hudson Valley voters, Republicans as well as Democrats.

In late October the strategy seemed to be working. One of Roosevelt's Hyde Park neighbors told him, "I have talked quietly with a number of Republicans and think I can safely promise you 35 or 40 who did not vote for you before are willing to do so now on the good showing you made in Albany against the Murphy ring."

The strategy was still working on election day. Roosevelt received 15,590 votes to 13,889 for his Republican opponent. "My husband was reelected thanks to Louis Howe," Eleanor explained simply.

6.

$\mathcal{R}$OOSEVELT HAD FELT COMPELLED TO DEFEND HIS STATE SENATE SEAT in order to maintain his political credibility, but he was hoping less for a return to Albany than for an assignment to Washington. He may or may not have appreciated that genuinely reforming New York politics—definitively defeating Tammany Hall—would require a much larger reorganization of the national political economy than could be accomplished from the New York senate. Yet he certainly understood that a stint in Washington, as part of a Wilson administration, would do far more for his career than another two years in Albany.

He had reason to think he might be in line for a federal appointment. The sixteen years since Grover Cleveland had left office constituted almost a lifetime in politics, with the result that the new administration would have to look to Democrats as green as Roosevelt to fill the scores of appointive positions in the various cabinet offices. The Democrats were especially weak on naval affairs, having surrendered that issue to the Republicans about the time sail gave way to steam. Franklin Roosevelt had never served in the navy, but his practical knowledge of the sea outstripped that of nearly every other Democrat of comparable political promise and ambition.

Josephus Daniels, Wilson's choice for secretary of the navy, thought so. "As I entered the Willard Hotel on the morning of Wilson's inauguration, I ran into Franklin Roosevelt," Daniels remembered. "He was bubbling over with enthusiasm at the incoming of a Democratic administration and keen as a boy to take in the inauguration ceremonies." Roosevelt knew that Daniels had been nominated for secretary, and he offered congratulations. Daniels thanked him and then asked if Roosevelt would like to come to the Navy Department as assistant secretary. "His face beamed his pleasure. 'How would I like it? I'd like it bully well. It would please me better than anything in the world. I'd be glad to be connected with the new administration. All my life I

have loved ships and have been a student of the navy, and the assistant secretaryship is the one place, above all others, I would love to hold.' " Daniels
explained that he hadn't asked Wilson about the appointment and would
have to make some inquiries. But he wanted to check with Roosevelt first, to
see if he wanted the job.

Daniels became Roosevelt's first political sponsor. A North Carolinian by
birth, a lawyer by education, a newspaperman by profession, a Grover Cleveland Democrat by inheritance, a Bryan Democrat by conviction, and a progressive Democrat by political necessity, Daniels had boosted Wilson early in
the pages of the Raleigh *News & Observer* and later as a member of the Democratic national executive committee. Upon Wilson's victory he fell in line for
a cabinet post. In part because Daniels's father had been a shipbuilder, for the
Confederacy among other clients, but mostly because the more senior positions had gone to supporters with greater claims—William Jennings Bryan, for
example, became secretary of state—Wilson assigned him the Navy Department.

Daniels knew nothing about naval administration per se and little enough
about administration on any large scale. He visited the departing navy secretary, George Meyer, who offered advice. "In the Navy Department there is no
chief of staff, and nothing important is done which does not go over the desk
of the secretary," Meyer said. He urged Daniels to maintain this system, and he
warned against those who wanted to change it. "You will find that in the navy
there are officers who wish to have an organization like that in the army or of
some foreign navy." To accede would be a grave mistake and must be resisted.

Daniels was just the person to stand up to the admirals and their allies, in
particular the corporations that did business with the navy. "Daniels was one
of the few living men who had the exact combination of qualities needed to
grapple with the navy as it was in 1913," an observer remarked. "He had no
personal friends in the navy, and he had the Puritan's conscience and stubbornness. He entered the department with a profound suspicion that whatever
an admiral told him was wrong, and that every corporation with a capitaliza-
tion of more than $100,000 was inherently evil. In nine cases out of ten, his for-
mula was correct: the navy was packed at the top with dead wood, and with
politics all the way through, and the steel, coal and other big industries were
accustomed to dealing with it on their own terms. With all that, he had sound
judgment of men coupled with an innate affection for a rebel."

Daniels hadn't known Franklin Roosevelt long, but what he'd seen convinced him that Roosevelt would make a fine deputy. They met at the Balti-

more convention, where Daniels controlled the passes for newspaper correspondents. Roosevelt arrived with several upstate New York editors in tow.
"He was in a gay mood, and I thought he was as handsome a figure of an attractive young man as I had ever seen," Daniels remembered. Daniels handed
over the passes and struck up a conversation. "At that convention Franklin and
I became friends—a case of love at first sight—for when men are attracted to
each other there is born a feeling that Mexicans call 'simpática,' a word that has
no counterpart in English. A lasting friendship was born."

After the election and their inauguration day encounter at the Willard,
Daniels went to Wilson for permission to make Roosevelt his assistant. Daniels
knew that Wilson sought geographic balance in his administration, and he
pointed out that a New Yorker would nicely complement a North Carolinian
at the Navy Department. He mentioned Roosevelt's sailing background and
added that he was "our kind of liberal." Wilson agreed at once. "Send the nomination over," the president said.

Even as he did so, Daniels interviewed New York's senators regarding Roosevelt. Democrat James O'Gorman, by custom of the upper house, could block
a Democratic appointment from his home state. But O'Gorman had only
praise for the man whose insurgency had resulted in his election. New York's
senior senator, Republican Elihu Root, lacked a veto, being from the opposition party, yet he appreciated Daniels's courtesy in consulting him. Root knew
Theodore Roosevelt well, having sponsored him for New York governor in
1898 and served as his secretary of war, and he had strong opinions about the
Roosevelts. As Daniels recalled: "When I told him that the President had in
mind naming Franklin Roosevelt as assistant secretary, a queer look came on
his face. 'You know the Roosevelts, don't you?' he asked. 'Whenever a Roosevelt rides, he wishes to ride in front. . . . They like to have their own way.' "
Daniels assured Root he could handle Franklin Roosevelt. "I told the Senator
that I would hate to have an assistant who did not have a mind of his own. I
told him I wanted an assistant who would help pull the load and I had no fear
of a strong man as assistant secretary. I would wish no other kind."

Roosevelt's nomination sailed through the Senate, and he moved into his
office—the same one Uncle Ted had occupied—in the State, War, and Navy
Building just west of the White House. One day not long after his installation,
he and Daniels posed for photographers on an upper-floor porch looking
down on the executive mansion. The prints came back, and Daniels showed
the best one to Roosevelt.

"Franklin," he asked, "why are you grinning from ear to ear, looking as pleased as if the world were yours, while I, satisfied and happy, have no such smile on my face?"

Roosevelt seemed surprised at the question and offered no answer except that he always tried to look good in pictures.

"I will tell you," Daniels continued. "We are both looking down on the White House and you are saying to yourself, being a New Yorker, 'Some day I will be living in that house'—while I, being from the South, know I must be satisfied with no such ambition."

❖   ❖   ❖

$\mathcal{P}$ARTLY BECAUSE HE had his eye on the White House, Roosevelt cultivated the navy brass more carefully than Daniels did. The admirals appreciated that he plumped for more and better ships whenever possible. Since its establishment in 1900, the general board of the navy had contended that America's enlarged world role required a bigger fleet. The board was chaired in 1913 by George Dewey, the hero of the Manila Bay battle that opened the Spanish-American War, and America's most distinguished naval officer, and it proposed an aggressive building program of four battleships, sixteen destroyers, and two submarines each year for the next several years. Josephus Daniels respected Dewey, but he didn't hesitate to cut the board's request by half when he presented his budget recommendations to Congress.

Roosevelt took care not to contradict his boss directly, but he made plain that he thought Dewey rather than Daniels had the better sense of what American security required. Skeptics in Congress and around the country suggested that smaller ships, designed for coastal defense, would meet the nation's needs; Roosevelt rejected this argument as woefully short-sighted. "Invasion is not what this country has to fear," he said. "In time of war, would we be content like the turtle to withdraw into our own shell and see an enemy supersede us in every outlying part, usurp our commerce, and destroy our influence as a nation throughout the world?" Of course not. "Yet this will happen just as surely as we can be sure of anything human if an enemy of the United States obtains control of the seas." America's vital interests spanned the globe, and America's power had to span it too. "Our national defense must extend all over the western hemisphere, must go out a thousand miles into the sea, must embrace the Philippines and over the seas wherever our commerce may be." American vessels must be state of the art. "Dreadnoughts are what we need," Roosevelt declared. Dreadnoughts were the most powerful battleships of the day. "The policy of our Congress ought to be to buy and build dreadnoughts until our Navy is comparable to any other in the world."

To a later generation, one accustomed to American military preeminence, Roosevelt's proposed standard—"comparable to any other in the world"— would appear unexceptionable. But in the second decade of the twentieth century it was radical to the point of revolutionary. For a century Britannia had ruled the waves, insisting on a navy the equal of her principal competitors' combined. Not even Dewey's general board advocated challenging Britain's supremacy. But partly because Roosevelt saw farther than the seventy-six-year-old Dewey, whose strategic vision was dimming, and partly because he wanted to make a name for himself, the assistant secretary staked out an extreme position on naval construction.

He strove to claim credit for each step taken toward his goal. In March 1914 he hammered the first bolt, a ceremonial silver fastener, into the keel of a new dreadnought being constructed at the Brooklyn navy yard. The ship was designated Number 39 during construction; it would be christened as the U.S.S. *Arizona.* The keel laying had been scheduled to start earlier, but Roosevelt ordered its postponement till he could arrive. "It was an impressive moment," a reporter explained. "And there was none in the throng who did not realize that the banging of the hammer meant the actual beginning of construction of the biggest ship ever built in New York."

Besides displaying his concern for American security, Roosevelt's hammering signified his appreciation of the importance of the Navy Department as an employer. For the crowd at the Brooklyn yard, the new battleship represented thousands of jobs and millions of dollars in wages. These meant a great deal to those who received them and scarcely less to those who dispensed them. Of such were political loyalties fashioned. Roosevelt hadn't been a year in his post, and already he was showing a gift for the art of government spending. He suffered no pangs of conscience that the navy provided jobs; dreadnoughts weren't pork barrels. All the same, when the jobs were being handed out, he insisted on reminding the recipients, and their voting friends and kin, that they had him to thank.

But delivering jobs made him, in effect, an employer, with all the potential for upsetting labor that being an employer entailed. Many of the shipyards were unionized, requiring Roosevelt to deal with the union leaders, who were hardly the kind of people he had grown up with or met at Groton and Harvard. Most of them saw him as a college boy who could be cowed or a bureaucrat who might be ignored, but hardly as an ally in their struggle for higher wages and better working conditions for their members and more power for themselves.

Yet Roosevelt surprised them, as he surprised many others in his career. He afterward explained his Navy Department initiation into labor relations:

> I had not been there more than about a week when a delegation from the Brooklyn navy yard came down and said, "Mr. Roosevelt"—they had not started to call me Frank; they did in about another week—"there is one thing that we want you to do. You know, you, as assistant secretary of the navy, have charge of all labor matters." I said, "That is fine; I did not know it." "Will you do something to change the present method of working out the wage scale paid in the navy yard?" I said, "Fine. How is it done?" "Well," they said, "do it yourself." I said, "Why, hasn't it been done by the assistant secretary in the past?" "No, it has been done by the officers." And they went on to tell me how unjustly the wage scales in all of the navy yards on both coasts and on the Gulf of Mexico had been arranged each year by a special board of naval officers. After I had been there about three days longer, I think, I got Joe Daniels to sign an order making it the duty of the assistant secretary to fix the wage scale each year.

But the assistant secretary didn't fix the wage scale by himself. The naval board continued to meet and make its recommendations; these reflected the view of the admirals and embodied, to a more or less obvious degree, the disdain the braided classes felt for the toilers who strained with wrench and riveter. The workers felt particular resentment at the refusal of the board to take sufficient account of local costs of living in determining the wage scales.

Roosevelt couldn't work magic with the wages. Congress set the department's overall budget, and more money for workers meant less for ships and naval operations. Besides, the admirals had powerful friends on Capitol Hill and were astute at protecting what they had come to consider theirs. Yet Roosevelt made clear to the labor leaders—the ones who soon called him Frank—that his door was always open. And with a shamelessness that would have been infuriating had he not been so personally charming, he took credit when wages went up and dodged blame when they didn't. He attended hearings where workers aired their grievances, and though he couched any encouragement in reminders that regardless of what he proposed, Congress would ultimately dispose, his warm handshake and reassuring smile let the workers know he was on their side. Daniels, who didn't mind delivering bad news, acquiesced in Roosevelt's arrangement and let his assistant be gone when that bad news reached the workers. "Take what is offered," one labor leader counseled his negotiators, regarding a parley with Daniels. "And go after the rest when Mr. Roosevelt returns."

It helped matters that Roosevelt's years at the Navy Department were a flush time for American shipyards. His relentless calls for a bigger navy contributed to the building boom, but the great events of world affairs—in particular the First World War—contributed much more. All the same, it was with substantial and not entirely unwarranted pride that Roosevelt was able to boast, after the fact, that during his seven and a half years at the Navy Department labor relations had been productive and smooth. "We did not have one single major dispute—no strike, walk-out, or serious trouble in all of the navy yards all over the United States."

$\mathcal{H}$ENRY ADAMS HAD BEEN YOUNG ONCE, ELEANOR ROOSEVELT AS-
sumed. It was hard to know for sure. Adams lived across Lafayette Square from
the White House, in the home he had built two generations earlier beside that
of John Hay, his longtime friend and fellow ironist. Though Hay died a decade
before Eleanor and Franklin arrived in Washington, Adams remained at his
post, guarding the republic against the shenanigans of the transients at both
ends of Pennsylvania Avenue. The old-timers in the capital, the ones who
stayed from Congress to Congress and administration to administration,
called themselves "cave dwellers"; Henry Adams in 1913 was the senior
troglodyte. "He was pointed out to us as a leaf-frail old man in a Victoria,
drawn by one horse which looked as if it had made the whole trip with him
from his boyhood," Jonathan Daniels, Josephus's son, remarked. For fifty years
since the 1860s, when it had become clear that the nation had nothing to offer
Adams by way of office or authority comparable to that which it had bestowed
on his great-grandfather and grandfather, presidents John Adams and John
Quincy Adams, he had muttered into his tea against the trend of public affairs. "The progress of evolution from President Washington to President
Grant was alone evidence enough to upset Darwin," Adams wrote. He hadn't
approved of Theodore Roosevelt, whom he dismissed as "pure act." Woodrow
Wilson appeared somewhat more thoughtful, but Adams could never bring
himself to trust a Democrat or a native southerner. On an afternoon when
Eleanor and Franklin Roosevelt came for lunch, Franklin was discussing a
matter of pressing importance for the administration. "Mr. Adams looked at
him rather fiercely," Eleanor recalled, "and said: 'Young man, I have lived in
this house many years and seen the occupants of that White House come and
go, and nothing that you minor officials or the occupant of that house can do
will affect the history of the world for long!' "

Adams tolerated dogs better than humans, and after Eleanor one day caught him playing with a Scottish terrier she thought she detected a soft heart behind his cynical façade. But other aspects of life in Washington remained mysterious to her. Not that she lacked counsel. On learning that Franklin would be joining the Navy Department, Theodore Roosevelt sent a special message to Eleanor via Franklin. "I do hope she will be particularly nice to the naval officers' wives," Theodore wrote. "They have a pretty hard time, with very little money to get along on, and yet a position to keep up, and everything that can properly be done to make things pleasant for them should be done." Aunt Anna, who had astonished the whole family by finally marrying at the age of forty, offered similar advice. Her husband was a retired rear admiral, William Cowles, who educated her to the challenges of navy life, especially for the officers' spouses. "You can do a great deal to make life pleasant for them when they are in Washington," Anna told Eleanor. "And that is what you should do."

Eleanor certainly tried. During the early weeks in the capital she religiously traced the circuit of official Washington. On Mondays she called on the wives of the justices of the Supreme Court. On Tuesdays she saw the spouses of members of the House of Representatives, starting with the New York delegation but gradually including the other states. On Wednesdays she covered the cabinet, on Thursdays the Senate, on Fridays the diplomatic corps. When she was lucky the wives in question were not at home; many were making their own rounds. Eleanor left her card. To those who were in she recited what soon sounded like a jingle in her own ears: "I am Mrs. Franklin D. Roosevelt. My husband has just come as Assistant Secretary of the Navy."

That first spring flew by, till she made her escape to Campobello with the children. She wasn't surprised to discover that the Navy Department claimed more of Franklin's time than the legislature at Albany had, or that he was delighted that it did. He shared his enthusiasm for his work in his letters. After a strategy session aboard the presidential yacht *Sylph*—which landsman Wilson regularly lent to his subordinates—Franklin could hardly contain himself. "I have never had such an interesting conversation on that kind of a trip," he wrote Eleanor. "We covered every country on the globe!" But offsetting her happiness that his responsibilities engaged his passion was the disappointment she felt each time he postponed his own journey north.

When he did come she wasn't entirely pleased he had. He celebrated the Fourth of July by ordering the battleship *North Dakota* to join the festivities at nearby Eastport, Maine. The townsfolk were thrilled, but Eleanor was aghast to learn that she was expected to entertain the officers. She survived the week-end's picnics and parties yet could manage no more than a grim smile when Franklin jokingly promised that in the future he'd never dispatch anything larger than a destroyer to the vicinity of Campobello.

His joke was serious, as Eleanor discovered when Franklin subsequently arrived aboard the destroyer *Flusser,* following an inspection voyage in adjacent waters. The skipper was William Halsey, a young navy lieutenant. "Unlike most Assistant Secretaries of the Navy (and Secretaries, for that matter), he was almost a professional sailorman," Halsey wrote of Roosevelt years later. "I did not know this then. All I had been told was that he had had some experience in small boats. So when he asked me to transit the strait between Campobello and the mainland, and offered to pilot us himself, I gave him the conn (steering control) but stood close by. The fact that a white-flanneled yachtsman can sail a catboat out to a buoy and back is no guarantee that he can handle a high-speed destroyer in narrow waters. A destroyer's bow may point directly down the channel, yet she is not necessarily on a safe course. She pivots around a point near her bridge structure, which means that two-thirds of her length is aft of the pivot, and that her stern will swing in twice the arc of her bow." Yet the amateur pilot proved his mettle. "As Mr. Roosevelt made his first turn, I saw him look aft and check the swing of our stern. My worries were over; he knew his business."

In the autumn of 1913 Eleanor and Franklin settled into a house they rented from Anna and William Cowles at 1733 N Street. The residence had been called the Little White House during Theodore's presidency, in recognition of the amount of time TR spent there consulting his sister, who was widely considered one of the sharpest political analysts in Washington. The name lingered, and more than a few observers supposed that Franklin Roosevelt was planning to move from the Little White House to the real thing. He brushed off such suggestions by pointing out that the location, just six blocks from the Navy Department, was most convenient for a busy public servant. The small backyard with roses climbing an arbor provided the children a place to play and Franklin and Eleanor to sit in the moments they found together.

Eleanor discovered that domestic issues were more complicated in Washington than in New York. She unthinkingly imported her favorite servants, who happened to be white, only to be informed by the keepers of the capital culture that in Washington, as elsewhere in the South, servants were black. To confuse the issue by employing white servants risked blurring the color line essential to southern life. Eleanor eventually swapped her white servants for black ones, even as she wondered that so much depended—in the minds of her new neighbors, at any rate—on so little.

❖ ❖ ❖

THE CULTURAL CONSERVATISM of the capital extended beyond the race question. Despite the progressivism of the era and of the Wilson administration, women in Washington were essentially confined to traditional roles. "Nearly all the women at that time were the slaves of the Washington social system," Eleanor wrote. They supported their husbands and raised their children, and counted themselves lucky to do so. Two women alone, of Eleanor's acquaintance, challenged the status quo. One was Martha Peters, the wife of a Massachusetts congressman and the sister of William Phillips, the assistant secretary of state. Her rebellion was primarily negative; she opted out of the calling-card circuit.

The other was Alice Roosevelt Longworth. Alice's White House wedding to Congressman Nicholas Longworth had been a brilliant occasion, either because of or despite the presence of her father, who stole the show even more thoroughly than he had at the wedding of Franklin and Eleanor. But the Longworth-Roosevelt marriage hadn't gone well. Nick drank copiously and philandered notoriously, humiliating and outraging Alice. She contemplated divorce but learned that her father and stepmother wouldn't stand for it. "Although they didn't quite lock me up," she recalled, "they exercised considerable pressure to get me to reconsider." So she took her pleasures elsewhere. She made her home a salon where the mildly disreputable might gather and gossip. She herself was a marvelous mimic and spared no one. Her imitation of Helen Taft amused even friends of the Republican First Lady, although it prompted Edith Roosevelt to urge her to watch her step. "Remember for Nick's sake to be really careful what you say," Edith warned. "People are only too ready to take up and repeat the most trivial remarks."

Careful was the last thing Alice chose to be. If her actions reflected poorly on Nick, she judged, it was no more than he deserved. Eleanor Roosevelt, observing her cousin, was at once appalled and attracted by such independence, which was far beyond anything she could muster at this stage. "I was perfectly certain," Eleanor remembered, "that I had nothing to offer of an individual nature and that my only chance of doing my duty as the wife of a public official was to do exactly as the majority of women were doing, perhaps to be a little more meticulous about it than some of the others were."

As a public wife Eleanor began to entertain. She couldn't enter the all-male clubs—the Chevy Chase and Metropolitan—where Franklin golfed and drank with his friends and those he hoped would become his friends. James Roosevelt recalled caddying for his father on Sunday mornings; the attraction was the twenty-five-cent pay and the excuse to skip church. One regular Roosevelt links partner was Republican senator—and future president—Warren G. Harding. "All I remember about Harding was that he seemed amiable and that Father enjoyed golfing with him," James said.

Eleanor wouldn't have joined Franklin's clubs even if she could have; she remained shy and retiring. It was an effort for her merely to open her house to the friends and acquaintances he brought home from work. But Sunday gatherings became semiregular. Eleanor served scrambled eggs and cold cuts to William Phillips of the State Department; Franklin Lane, the secretary of the interior; Adolph Miller, a Lane aide who transferred to the staff of the new Federal Reserve Board; and their wives. They all found Franklin delightful in a middleweight way. "I knew him then as a brilliant, lovable, and somewhat happy-go-lucky friend," Phillips remembered of Roosevelt. "The qualities that made him great matured later." As for Eleanor, she was appealing in an unassuming manner. "She seemed to be a little remote, or it may have been that Franklin claimed the attention, leaving her somewhat in the background," Phillips explained. "She was essentially domestic, and her interest in public affairs was centered in her husband's career rather than in any thought of a career of her own."

Yet Eleanor had her moments and her methods. Phillips recalled sharing breakfast with Franklin and Eleanor one morning. She asked Franklin if he had received a letter from a particular person.

"Yes," he answered, continuing to drink his coffee.

"Have you answered it, dear?" she inquired.

"No," he said, still drinking.

"Don't you think you should answer it?"

"Yes."

"Don't you think you should answer it now?"

"Yes."

Phillips concluded the story: "And he answered it then and there. I gathered that the letter might never have received a reply without the watchful eye of his wife."

❖ ❖ ❖

As much as Roosevelt relished life in the nation's capital, he realized that Washington was a wasteland of elective politics. No one was ever elected senator or governor or president from the federal district; every viable candidate had a base in his home state. With this in mind, Roosevelt spent as much energy worrying about the affairs of New York as about those of the Navy Department, and he took few steps in his capacity as assistant secretary without weighing their effects on politics back home.

His first avenue of influence was patronage. As a large employer, the Navy Department could function much like one of the urban machines, bestowing jobs on supporters in the same way that Boss Murphy and Tammany Hall did. The process was complicated by civil service rules, which limited firings and complicated hirings. But Roosevelt managed to install allies and their friends in navy yards and other places of employment about New York. He simultaneously expanded his reach beyond the navy. He ingratiated himself with Daniel Roper, his counterpart in the Post Office Department, who allowed Roosevelt to identify worthy recipients of postmasterships. With his knack for self-promotion, Roosevelt soon claimed—discreetly, since much of what he was doing violated the spirit if not the letter of the civil service laws—that anyone who wanted a federal job or contract in New York needed to talk to Franklin Roosevelt.

He might have been even more assertive had Wilson not refused to alienate Tammany Hall. As a progressive, Wilson regarded Tammany with distaste, but as a practical politician—far more practical than most people knew—he appreciated that he couldn't carry New York without Tammany. In this regard, Wilson's interests differed from those of Roosevelt, who had won his reputation attacking Murphy and who had to remain on the offensive if he wished to return to elective politics.

The difference became apparent during the summer and early autumn of 1914. Roosevelt hadn't held the assistant secretaryship for even eighteen months, but he itched to proceed on his path to the White House. Uncle Ted had moved on after fourteen months; time was passing. Besides, the career benefits of a bureaucratic job diminished dramatically over time; eventually the refusals and rejections that formed an inevitable part of the bureaucrat's life piled up till they were all anyone remembered. Roosevelt's charm might postpone the day of reckoning but couldn't forestall it forever.

Consequently Roosevelt decided to make a run for the Senate. The 1914 elections would be the first under the provisions of the Seventeenth Amendment, which finally let voters themselves, rather than the state legislatures, choose senators. That same year New York joined the ranks of progressive-minded states in selecting its Senate nominees by primary election. Between them, primaries and the direct election of senators dealt a double blow to bosses, pushing Charles Murphy and his ilk to the edge of extinction.

Or so the progressives hoped. In fact the bosses proved more resourceful than their opponents expected. After Roosevelt had Louis Howe launch a trial balloon in early 1914, he tried to persuade Wilson to take a public anti-Tammany stand. The president demurred and indicated that other officials of the executive branch should follow his lead. "My judgment is that it would be best if members of the administration should use as much influence as possible but say as little as possible in the politics of their several states," Wilson wrote Roosevelt.

Wilson's directive might have determined the issue for an assistant secretary of lesser ambition. And indeed for a time Roosevelt kept quiet. He had been mentioned, by Howe among others, for governor as well as for senator, and he kept denying interest in the former office long enough to convince those who might have pushed his candidacy that he really didn't want it. When a final attempt by some supporters to win an endorsement from Wilson fell short, Roosevelt issued a definitive denial. "To repeat what I have now said more than half a dozen times, I am not a candidate for nomination for Governor of New York," he told reporters.

But only three weeks later, to the surprise of many who knew him, including Howe, he declared his candidacy for the Senate. "My senses have not yet left me," he assured Howe, who was fairly certain they had.

Somehow Roosevelt had gotten the impression Wilson wanted him to run. William G. McAdoo said so, Roosevelt told Josephus Daniels, and McAdoo, Wilson's Treasury secretary and son-in-law, should have known. Daniels cautioned Roosevelt, predicting he'd have a hard time against the Tammany candidate in the primary and perhaps a harder time against the Republican nominee in the general election. Daniels urged Roosevelt to check with Wilson before making a decision.

Roosevelt declined the advice and ignored the discouragement. Perhaps he exaggerated what McAdoo had actually said; perhaps he feared that if he asked Wilson directly, the president would tell him to stay out of the race. Perhaps he hoped to force Wilson's hand in the contest. But Wilson kept aloof, and when Tammany tapped James Gerard, a machine man yet one respectable enough to have won Wilson's nomination to be ambassador to Germany, Roosevelt realized he'd been outflanked. Roosevelt initially hoped Gerard would decline the endorsement, as the war in Europe had just begun and the ambassador presumably wouldn't want to vacate his post. Gerard accepted the Tammany endorsement but remained in Berlin during the primary campaign, leaving Roosevelt to flail against an absent opponent.

He did so energetically. He visited navy yards, courting the union vote. He motored across the rural districts, reaching out to farmers. He wrapped himself in the mantle of the administration, although the mantle slipped whenever Gerard's supporters rejoined that the president had refused to choose between these two members of his administration. He denied disrupting the party, even as he criticized Boss Murphy. A reporter asked what kind of Democrat he considered himself to be. "I am a regular organization Democrat of Dutchess County, a New York State Democrat, and a National Democrat," he answered. "I am not an anti-Tammany Democrat, but, in this campaign, as in many others, I have taken a consistent position against the control of the Democracy of this state by Charles Francis Murphy, believing that he is a handicap to our Democracy."

The primary contest resulted in the worst defeat Roosevelt would ever suffer. Gerard received 210,000 votes to his 77,000. As Murphy and Tammany gloated, Roosevelt put on his bravest smile and congratulated the winner. "Will make an active campaign for you," he added, "if you declare unalterable opposition to Murphy's leadership and all he stands for." Gerard saw no reason to make such a declaration, logically deeming Murphy's support more valuable than Roosevelt's. Roosevelt affirmed Democratic regularity but sat on the sidelines as Republican James Wadsworth buried Gerard in the general election.

8.

ELEANOR REMEMBERED HER FATHER BY NAMING HER THIRD SON FOR him, and of all the Roosevelt children Elliott took the greatest interest in family history. It was Elliott who, inquiring after the cause of his grandfather's premature death, was told by his mother that her father had suffered from a brain tumor for which alcohol offered the only pain relief. Whether or not he believed this version—which almost certainly wasn't true, given the etiology of alcoholism and brain tumors—he reported it without comment in the memoir he wrote as an old man.

He reported much else, with extended comment. His first memories were of life in Washington while his father was the assistant secretary of the navy. He remembered what a dashing figure his father cut as he came down to breakfast each morning dressed in a starched high collar, an expensive English-tailored suit that hung impeccably on his lanky frame, and polished leather shoes purchased straight from London. His father was always a bit behind schedule but was never the least concerned on account of it. "Good morning, Babs," he would say to Elliott's mother, who had been up for hours. He would kiss her on the cheek and then turn to the children. "Good morning, chicks—how are we all today?" He would kiss them too. As he sat down, Eleanor would ring a silver bell, which signaled the servants that the master of the house required his morning meal.

Elliott recalled his father as the model of cheerfulness, despite the demands his office placed on him. "He invariably woke in a high good humor, ready and eager to tackle anything the day might bring," Elliott wrote. "I do not remember a breakfast time when there wasn't a smile on his lips and in his eyes." As he inquired of Eleanor and the children what their day might hold or mentioned something on his own calendar, he appeared oblivious to the passage of time. Not so Eleanor, who constantly checked the clock to ensure the punctual departure of her husband and the school-bound children.

Typically the doorbell would ring before Franklin finished his coffee. A servant would answer, and Louis Howe, who had become Franklin's chief aide at the Navy Department, would be shown in. "Good morning, Boss. Good morning, Mrs. Roosevelt," Howe would say. Franklin and Eleanor would smile in response—he with true warmth, she out of politeness. "Mother made no pretense that she liked him," Elliott said of Howe. "She felt somehow excluded from the intimacy he and Father shared, the affectionate bantering that went on between them, the secrets they kept exclusively to themselves." She also found Howe's manner crude and his hygiene deficient. But she smiled nonetheless. "Would you care for some breakfast, Mr. Howe?" she would say. "No, thank you," he would answer, "but I would like some coffee, please."

Howe survived on caffeine and nicotine, and on the adrenaline stimulated by proximity to power. The combination kept his weight a bit above one hundred pounds and his lungs in a chronic state of rebellion. "Don't you think you should see a doctor about your cough?" Eleanor would inquire as he hacked across her breakfast table. He would respond, "It's an old friend. I once saw a doctor in Albany who gave me two months to live. That was nearly ten years ago."

Franklin would finish his breakfast and Howe his coffee. Franklin would kiss Eleanor and the children again, grab his hat—a felt bowler in winter, a straw boater in summer—and head out the door. Elliott, summoning testimony, memory, and imagination, recalled the fifteen-minute journey to the Navy Department:

> He must have loved striding down Connecticut Avenue every weekday morning with Louis hurrying along at his side, the two of them looking uncannily like Don Quixote and Sancho setting out to battle with giants. Government girls on their way to their typewriters turned their heads to watch. Society gossips rated Father to be among the handsomest men in town, long-muscled, superbly fit from weekend exercise. His good friend Nigel Law, Third Secretary at the British Embassy, who had arrived aboard the *Lusitania* in November, 1914, thought that he was "the most attractive man whom it was my good fortune to meet during my four years in America."

❖   ❖   ❖

Had Roosevelt won election to the Senate, he would have had to alter his daily route to the office. As it was, he stuck to Connecticut Avenue, turning the heads of the office girls on that street. He also turned the head of a young woman he passed on the stair of his own house. Lucy Mercer's father was descended from the Carrolls of Maryland, the most distinguished Catholic family in America, with roots in Lord Baltimore's colony and a signature—Charles Carroll's—on the Declaration of Independence. Carroll Mercer, Lucy's father, characterized his occupation as "gentleman" on her birth certificate. Lucy's mother, Minnie Tunis, was generally considered the most beautiful woman in Washington and was, by virtue of a large inheritance, one of the richest. Her virtues ended about there, in the thinking of the straitlaced, for after a first marriage turned sour she divorced her husband to marry Carroll Mercer. They celebrated by living in grand style, having two daughters, and squandering most of their money. Carroll Mercer fought beside Theodore Roosevelt at San Juan Hill and came home to relocate his family to one of the comparatively modest row houses on N Street, just off Connecticut Avenue. Not long thereafter he himself moved out, leaving Minnie to rear Lucy and her sister. She accomplished the task by various means, including the kindness of other gentlemen entranced by her charms. The gossips raised a racket but couldn't negate the effect of the beauty of Minnie and the girls, who grew up to be as attractive as their mother. The net result for Lucy, who turned twenty-two the month after the Franklin Roosevelts arrived in Washington, was that she required a job yet considered herself above most ordinary labor. Eleanor Roosevelt, for her part, felt the need for a guide through the social intricacies of the capital. Anna Cowles had known the Mercers in better days; most likely Anna was the one who suggested Lucy to Eleanor.

At first Lucy seemed a godsend. "She and Mother worked together in the living room," Elliott recalled. "There was no other space available. Lucy would curl herself gracefully on the carpet, spreading out for sorting the letters, cards, bills and invitations that flowed in, prompted by Mother's calls. Lucy was gay, smiling, and relaxed. We children welcomed the days she came to work." With confident efficiency, Lucy answered the letters, acknowledged the cards, and paid the bills. Even Sara Roosevelt, to whom criticism came more naturally than praise, was smitten. "She is so sweet and attractive, and adores you, Eleanor," Sara wrote her daughter-in-law.

Eleanor appreciated the help but had difficulty warming to Lucy. Eleanor had always been insecure about her looks, and bearing six children—Elliott, a second Franklin Jr., and John, after Anna, James, and the deceased first Franklin Jr.—in ten years hadn't added to her confidence. Franklin grew more handsome with each passing year; she felt old and ugly. Lucy's presence made her feel worse. And Lucy possessed a sparkle, a joie de vivre, that matched Franklin's ebullience but contrasted sharply to Eleanor's somberness. Before long Eleanor couldn't help detecting an enthusiasm in Franklin's hellos to Lucy she hadn't heard for years in his greetings to her.

She couldn't complain to Franklin without feeling petty. But she begrudged more than ever the weeks he stayed in Washington while she tended the children at Campobello. And when he postponed his departure from the capital, and then postponed it again, she found herself doubting his excuses. "I will wire you tomorrow or Tuesday whether I can go up next Sunday or the following," he wrote on a Sunday in July 1914. He added, as if to assuage her unspoken doubts, "I have dined at home almost every evening." Three days later he apologized that "it may be impossible to get off this Sunday as J. D. may go to Raleigh." Roosevelt went on to say that work was consuming him. "I have been as usual going every second, at the office till 7:30 last night. . . . Dined here alone." Eleanor didn't object to Franklin's devotion to his duties, but she couldn't help wondering: Was it his work he found so compelling, or Lucy?

She felt that she was losing him, and she didn't know how to respond. Every close relationship she had ever experienced had ended disastrously—in abandonment or premature death. She didn't know that love could weather crisis, didn't know how to fight for what she valued. As he drifted away, she gradually closed herself off, seeking to recapture the emotional self-sufficiency she had found to be her only refuge as a child.

❖   ❖   ❖

THE MORE SHE WITHDREW, the easier it was for him to rationalize his behavior. Eleanor seems never to have enjoyed the physical aspects of marital love; her daughter, Anna, later recalled her saying, just before Anna married, that sex was "an ordeal to be borne." Franklin had long set his heart on six children, following the lead of Uncle Ted; after her sixth child, Eleanor may have decided enough was enough. Had she enjoyed sex she and Franklin might have employed one of the methods of contraception then available; since she didn't enjoy it, she may have employed the most basic method of all. Perhaps she articulated an embargo against intimacy; perhaps she simply let Franklin know, by her lack of interest, that she wanted nothing more of it.

Her coolness might have come as a disappointment to Franklin; it might, alternatively, have provided an excuse for him to do what he was tempted to do anyway. Washington had always been hard on family life, from the earliest days of the republic when travel was difficult and most members of Congress left their wives at home. Women plying the oldest profession had spotted an opportunity and found enough patrons among the members to maintain a lively trade. The growth of the executive branch during and after the Civil War increased the permanent population of government officials, but Congress still came and went, as, at greater intervals, did those executive branch employees not protected by the civil service reforms. The result, even during the second decade of the twentieth century, was that life in Washington reflected a peculiar transience among the governing classes. In the swirl of receptions and dinners, existing attachments frayed and new ones readily formed.

A man on the make like Franklin Roosevelt didn't have to look far to find models of infidelity—not far at all. Nick Longworth's extramarital adventures grew more notorious with each passing month. Alice knew of the affairs but ignored them till one evening she discovered Nick and her close friend Cissy Patterson coupled on the floor of her bathroom. Alice was surprised, though less about Nick than about Cissy, who was supposed to be having an affair with Senator William Borah. After a memorable tryst between Cissy and Borah at one of Alice's parties, Alice's maid recovered some distinctive hairpins from the floor of the library. Alice sent them to Cissy with a note: "I believe they are yours." Cissy answered, "And if you look up in the chandelier, you might find my panties."

Alice decided that two (or more) could play that game, and she pursued Borah. The "stallion from Idaho," as he was known around Washington, reciprocated her interest, and their affair soon stoked the gossip engines of the capital. "Everybody called her 'Aurora Borah Alice,' " Hope Miller, a member of Alice's set matter-of-factly recalled many years later. Eventually Alice became pregnant. Most of her acquaintances assumed Borah was the father—including Nick, who vetoed Alice's initial choice of a name for the baby girl. Alice, in perhaps her most brilliantly malicious stroke of humor, wanted to name the child Deborah. Nick drew the line. He would raise the baby, he said, and in the event doted on her far more than Alice did. But he wouldn't have a child under his roof named "de Borah." Alice settled for Paulina.

What Franklin Roosevelt made of all this is impossible to say. By the time the most scandalous parts became known, he was in no position to comment on other people's affairs. But he doubtless told himself that flirtations were the norm among Washington's summer bachelors, and if women found him attractive, who was he to push them away? Hostesses were happy for Lucy Mercer to fill Eleanor's empty place at dinner; Lucy's social antecedents, not to mention her manners and looks, were such as to elevate the tone at almost any table. When the flirtation began to turn more serious is equally hard to say. Perhaps it did so gradually, perhaps with a swiftness that took the lovers' breath away. But whether sudden or slow, Franklin's attachment to Lucy eventually overtook his love for Eleanor.

The affair was a secret chiefly from those who weren't supposed to know. Alice Roosevelt caught on early. "Lucy was beautiful, charming, and an absolutely delightful creature," she recalled. "I would see her out driving with Franklin, and I would say things like, 'I saw you out driving with someone very attractive indeed, Franklin. Your hands were on the wheel, but your eyes were on her.' And he would say, 'Yes, she is lovely, isn't she?' " Alice encouraged the affair, for her own complicated reasons. "He deserved a good time. He was married to Eleanor," she said later. Alice probably felt that Franklin's affair in some way excused her own. On at least one occasion she appears to have taunted Eleanor by saying she had a secret that ought to interest her. But Eleanor, wishing neither to give Alice the satisfaction she obviously coveted nor to have her own fears confirmed, declined to be enticed into asking what Alice's secret was.

Yet the secret—or half secret—took a toll on Franklin and Eleanor's immediate family. Elliott afterward wrote of a "vague hostility" that suffused the household. He was a young child then; perhaps he recalled things accurately, or perhaps he imputed later feelings to the earlier time. Quoting his mother's published recollection regarding the same period, that "there was a sense of impending disaster hanging over all of us," Elliott remarked that readers naturally assumed she was talking about the troubled state of world affairs. "But by 'all of us' she meant not the country at large but her family. She was talking about trouble much closer to home." Speaking for himself, Elliott adopted language of a later era in describing a "cold war" between his parents.

Franklin and Eleanor fought—not directly over Franklin's affair, which remained unspoken, but over other matters. She blamed him when he didn't arrive at Campobello on schedule. She accused him of ignoring her letters. "You never answer a question, and nothing I ask for appears!" She insulted Lucy gratuitously by trying to pay her for volunteer work. She gloated in the knowledge that her insult had hit the mark. "She is evidently quite cross with me!" she wrote Franklin. Finally, after another period of procrastination in his departure from Washington for Campobello, she delivered what appears to have been an ultimatum. "I *count* on seeing you the 26th," she wrote. "My threat was no idle one!" Elliott, reading this letter later, had little difficulty discerning its meaning. "There was no mystery," he said. "She threatened to leave him."

Meanwhile Eleanor did something she hadn't done since the early years of the marriage: she consciously cultivated Sara. Perhaps Eleanor understood that an explosion was imminent and wanted to protect herself—and her children—against it. Perhaps she guessed that Sara would take her side, at least this once. "I miss you and so do the children," Eleanor wrote her mother-in-law in a typical letter from the period. "As the years go on, I realize how lucky we are to have you, and I wish we could always be together. Very few mothers I know mean as much to their daughters as you do to me." A few weeks later she declared, "I wish you were always here! There are always so many things I want to talk over and ask you about, and letters are not very satisfactory, are they?"

9.

$\mathcal{F}$RANKLIN ROOSEVELT WASN'T ALONE IN NOT SEEING A EUROPEAN war coming. Americans made Woodrow Wilson their president with only the vaguest notion of where he stood on world affairs. "It would be the irony of fate if my administration had to deal chiefly with foreign affairs," Wilson remarked confidentially just before his inauguration. As a professor of government and history, Wilson had studied European affairs for decades and, with most experts, had come to the conclusion that a major war in Europe was nearly impossible. Border scrapes—the international equivalent of barroom scuffles—would occur, but none of the great powers had any incentive to burn the bar down. Even if a big war somehow got started, it couldn't last long, for the powers would run out of the money required to keep modern armies in the field.

This reassuring logic began to unravel in the summer of 1914, when Serbian terrorists calling themselves the "Black Hand" killed the next in line to the throne of the dual monarchy of Austria-Hungary. The terrorists were almost ludicrously inept; the bomb they tossed at the car of Franz Ferdinand bounced off without igniting, and most of the plotters were arrested. Only by the dumbest luck did one of those not arrested find himself face-to-face with the archduke later that day, and this time he couldn't miss. Gavrilo Princip's bullets killed Franz and his wife, Sophie, and triggered a slow-motion cascade of diplomatic protests as Austria demanded of Serbia the right to investigate the murder, Russia warned Austria not to pressure Serbia, Germany told Russia to leave Austria alone, and France and Britain threatened Germany over Russia. Each protest prompted the armies of the countries involved to prepare for war. At first the preparations were chiefly demonstrative: to lend weight to what the ambassadors were telling the foreign ministers. But the reciprocal mobilizations developed a dynamic of their own. Any reasonably efficient army can mobilize to go to war on a given day, but no army can maintain war readiness for long. As the Russians, Germans, French, and British approached peak readiness, each feared the consequences of standing down first. The Germans, loathing the Russians and disdaining the French, decided to strike rather than step back. Germany declared war on Russia on August 1, 1914, and on France on August 3. The first general European conflict since Napoleon began.

Americans watched in hypnotized horror as Europe went over the brink. They thanked God for having dug the Atlantic Ocean so wide and deep and congratulated their ancestors for having evinced the foresight to leave that lunatic continent. Hardly an American man or woman registered disapproval when Wilson, following the precedent of George Washington at the outbreak of the previous round of Europe's attempted self-destruction, declared American neutrality. Again following General Washington, who in his farewell address had warned his compatriots against excessive emotional attachment to foreign countries, Wilson urged Americans to be "impartial in thought as well as in action."

❖   ❖   ❖

*U*NTIL 1914 Theodore Roosevelt had been a good loser regarding his defeat at Wilson's hands two years before. The people had spoken, and anyway the prize he lost to Wilson was no more than he had held before. The outbreak of war in Europe, however, changed things entirely. TR knew enough history to realize that the European conflict afforded the statesmen of the world, including the American president, the opportunity to transform international affairs—and to win reputations of truly historic proportions. Roosevelt was proud of the record he had compiled in the White House from 1901 to 1909, but he knew it would never vault him into the pantheon of American politics—into the company of such towering figures as Washington and Lincoln, who had led the country through war. Though he had received much criticism for his assertion that "no triumph of peace is quite so great as the supreme triumphs of war," he still stood by every word. And now it galled him to think that Wilson, who had never served under arms, who didn't know a mortar from a howitzer or a destroyer from a dreadnought, and who had defeated him in 1912 only because the Republican regulars immorally denied him the nomination, was the president to enjoy this rare chance at historical greatness. Roosevelt gnashed his teeth and cursed the unfairness of it all.

Franklin Roosevelt didn't communicate directly with Theodore these days. As one of the most visible members of the Wilson administration, Franklin had to exercise care not to consort conspicuously with the enemy. Theodore understood. "Now, Sara," he wrote Franklin's mother in response to an invitation to him and Edith to stay at Hyde Park while visiting the Hudson Valley, "I am very doubtful, from Franklin's standpoint, whether it is wise that we do so. . . . I shall be in the middle of a tour in which I am attacking the Administration, and I think it might well be an error, from Franklin's standpoint, if we stayed with you. . . . I hope you understand, dear Sally, that it is the exact truth to say that I am only thinking of Franklin's interest."

The outbreak of the European war diminished what little discouragement Franklin felt at the failure of his halfhearted bid for the Democratic nomination for the Senate that year. A post with a peacetime navy could be enjoyable, especially for a sailor like Roosevelt, but it didn't do much for a man's reputation after the initial benefits of the appointment wore off. A job with a wartime navy was another matter. Roosevelt didn't know whether the United States would enter the European war, but he had to prepare for that possibility. The opponents of American intervention, currently led by President Wilson, were invoking George Washington; Franklin Roosevelt could cite the father of his country, too, about preparation for war being the best preventive.

Doing so meant drawing farther from Josephus Daniels and the pacifist wing of the administration. Daniels and Secretary of State Bryan believed, General Washington notwithstanding, that preparing for war made war more likely. Bryan resisted efforts to upgrade the army, while Daniels denied that the European war demanded any acceleration of the Navy Department's construction program. The navy's general board was still recommending four new battleships a year; Daniels again told the House naval affairs committee that two were plenty.

Members of the House committee, who generally found the arguments of the career admirals more persuasive than those of the North Carolina newspaperman, summoned Franklin Roosevelt for a third opinion. They had reason to believe he would bolster the admirals' case, for he had just produced a detailed estimate of navy readiness that declared the service singularly unready. Scores of American ships were in reserve rather than on active duty. "That is to say, they have on board only from 25 percent to 50 percent of the crews necessary to man them in case of war," Roosevelt explained. Dozens more were even less ready—"manned by from 10 percent to 20 percent of their regular complements, just enough to prevent them from rusting to pieces." Still more were "hopelessly out of date." To remedy the shortfall in readiness required a major infusion of personnel. Roosevelt said the navy needed eighteen thousand enlisted men to bring all existing vessels into war-fighting trim. The additional ships currently under construction would demand still more—a thousand men each, for example, for the new battleships *Oklahoma* and *Nevada.*

Roosevelt's report was a work of political art as much as a statement of policy. It didn't exactly contradict Daniels, who had focused on the construction of ships rather than the enlistment of sailors. But its essential thrust was in the opposite direction, for whether the navy lacked metal or men, it was, in Roosevelt's view, far less ready for use than Daniels let on.

Roosevelt recognized the danger his borderline insubordination involved. Sending Eleanor a copy of the report, he declared, "The enclosed is the truth, and even if it gets me into trouble I am perfectly prepared to stand by it. The country needs the truth about the Army and the Navy instead of the soft mush about everlasting peace which so many statesmen are handing out to a gullible public."

In his appearance before the House committee, Roosevelt did stand by his report. A correspondent covering the hearings explained, "Mr. Roosevelt impressed the committee by his promptness in answering questions and by his candor." Afterward Roosevelt himself thought he had done well. Describing the hearings as "really great fun and not so much of a strain," he told Sara: "I was able to get in my own views without particular embarrassment to the Secretary."

The House committee invited him to return. Members wanted to know where the United States ranked among the naval powers of the world. Roosevelt responded with what must have seemed an obscure formula, named for the German naval strategist Otto Kretschmer, that involved tonnage, armor, gun size, and speed. After a certainly intentional eye-glazing exposition of the Kretschmer formula, Roosevelt revealed that the United States ranked third, far behind Britain, a bit behind Germany, and comfortably ahead of France.

Committeemen pressed him on the readiness of the fleet. He noted a difference between theory and practice. The Navy Department's theory was that a ship in reserve could leave port within twenty-four hours and start fighting at once; the practice was rather different. "A battleship in reserve could go to sea tomorrow," Roosevelt said. "But it would take three months to shake her down. Two-thirds of her crew would be new to the ship and would have to fit themselves to her." When a committee member asked why more ships weren't kept in commission, ready to fight, Roosevelt answered, "It is a necessity as a matter of economy that all our ships should not be in commission all the time. No navy does that—except that of one country." Roosevelt's listeners perhaps expected him to identify Britain as the perpetually ready power; he got a laugh when he explained that it was Haiti. "She has two gunboats, and they are in commission all the year around."

The hearing went smoothly for Roosevelt until members delved into his apparent difference with Secretary Daniels regarding manpower. Again Roosevelt carefully avoided prescribing policy, but he didn't retreat from his earlier description. If anything, the situation seemed to have gotten worse. "We are from 30,000 to 50,000 men short of the needs of the navy as laid down in the confidential war plans of the War College," he informed the committee.

❖ ❖ ❖

UNTIL THE SPRING of 1915 the debate over the size and strength of the navy was, if not quite academic, less than immediately consequential. The fighting among the major belligerents had stagnated in the mud of northern France, with neither the Germans, on one hand, nor the French and British, on the other, able to break the murderous deadlock imposed by the momentary advantage in armaments defenders held over attackers. Trench warfare claimed lives in numbers no one had imagined just months before, but the front lines barely moved.

So the belligerents turned to naval warfare to secure the mastery both sides were denied on land. The British blockaded Germany with surface ships; the Germans reciprocated with submarines. The latter were slow and unarmored; they attacked effectively only without warning. And when their torpedoes struck their targets, the U-boats lacked the capacity to rescue survivors.

Americans understood the situation but appreciated its import only after a German submarine sank the British liner *Lusitania*. The British had exploited the Germans' reluctance to target passenger ships, by transporting munitions aboard the liners. Notices from the German government warning Americans to stay off British vessels traversing the war zone were published in American papers; one such notice appeared in New York papers on the day the *Lusitania* left New York, bound for Liverpool. But the passengers ignored the warning as disinformation, assuming, in any event, that the swift liner could outrun the U-boats. This assumption proved tragically mistaken when, on May 7, 1915, a German torpedo boat blasted a hole in the *Lusitania*'s hull, triggering a secondary, internal explosion that sent the vessel to the bottom just off the southern coast of Ireland, with the loss of nearly 1,200 lives, 128 of them American.

This first direct blow against the American people sorely tested the Wilson administration's neutrality policy. The policy was already under strain from a different direction. Just weeks into the war the French government, aware that its cash reserves couldn't sustain a protracted conflict, had asked J. P. Morgan & Company to float French bonds in the United States. Secretary of State Bryan vehemently opposed the bond sale, on the ground that it would erode American neutrality more surely than any other action. Wilson initially accepted Bryan's argument and vetoed the loan. But when the French modified the request, asking simply for credits toward the purchase of American goods, Wilson gave his approval. He added that he would approve credits requested by the other warring powers as well.

Though neutral in form, Wilson's credit policy favored France and Britain in practice. Those countries were better connected to American markets than Germany; combined with Britain's naval superiority, which allowed a more effective blockade of Germany than Germany could impose against Britain, the New York–London–Paris financial connections funneled American money far more freely to France and Britain than any analogous connections did to Germany and Austria-Hungary. Yet even the American credits couldn't keep the French and British armies provisioned, and in the spring of 1915 French and British officials applied for unrestricted loans. Without the loans, they said, their war effort would collapse, with disastrous consequences for democracy in Europe—and for the economic health of the United States. They persuaded Robert Lansing, Bryan's second at the State Department. "The result would be restriction of outputs, industrial depression, idle capital and idle labor, numerous failures, financial demoralization, and general unrest and suffering among the laboring classes," Lansing wrote Wilson regarding a refusal to approve the loans. The president, not wishing to hazard such a result, let the loans proceed.

The *Lusitania* sinking made Wilson's decision easier, although not at first. American papers reacted with understandable outrage at the mass killing of Americans; editors thundered that Germany must be chastised. Wilson initially resisted the tide of opinion. "There is such a thing as a man being too proud to fight," the president declared. But when this evoked an even louder outcry—how could America be "too proud" to avenge its dead citizens?—he adopted a stronger position. He filed a protest with the German government demanding that Berlin alter its submarine policy and provide guarantees against another such attack. After Germany responded unsatisfactorily, Wilson sharpened his warning. He declared that persistence in Germany's submarine

policy would constitute an "unpardonable offense" against American sovereignty and that he would be forced to interpret any future incident similar to
the *Lusitania* sinking as "deliberately unfriendly" to the United States.

This was too much for William Jennings Bryan, and almost too much for
Josephus Daniels. The secretary of state complained that Wilson's policy put
America on the path toward war; a single torpedo fired by a hot-headed or
fog-blinded German U-boat captain could drag the United States into the
maelstrom that was consuming Europe. To underscore his objection, Bryan resigned. Daniels supported Bryan, although not to the extent of surrendering
his job.

❖ ❖ ❖

FRANKLIN ROOSEVELT OBSERVED the fight within the administration at
first hand, taking mental notes on the subject of wartime leadership. He in-
terjected where he could. The Anglophilia he and most members of America's
upper class exhibited to one degree or another influenced his attitude toward
the European war, and he felt himself drawn toward Britain's side even before
the *Lusitania* sinking. "Today Sir C. Spring Rice lunched with me," he wrote
Eleanor in early 1915, referring to the British ambassador, who had been the
best man at Uncle Ted's wedding to Edith and was now cultivating the younger
Roosevelt. "Von Bernstorff"—the German ambassador—"was at the next
table, trying to hear what we were talking about! Springy and Von B. would kill
each other if they had a chance!" The tension of the high-stakes diplomacy
delighted Roosevelt, who added mischievously, "I just *know* I shall do some
awful unneutral thing before I get through!"

His neutrality diminished further amid the *Lusitania* crisis. If he wished
to keep his job—and, with war looming, he definitely did—he couldn't be as
vocal as Uncle Ted, who was taxing Wilson and Bryan loudly for not breaking
relations with Germany. But Franklin railed in private against Bryan and
Daniels. "These are the hectic days, all right!" he wrote Eleanor. "What d' y'
think of W. Jay B.? It's all too long to write about, but I can only say I'm dis-
gusted clear through!" To Bryan's credit, in Roosevelt's eyes, the secretary of
state finally had the dignity to get out of the way when he could no longer
support policies the president deemed essential to American security. Not so
Daniels, who continued to obstruct from within. "J. D. will *not* resign!" Roosevelt declared indignantly.

To the president, Roosevelt offered encouragement. Bryan's departure was a heavy political blow, as Bryan intended it to be. The now-former secretary of state knew his constituency, and he recognized that all those farmers were leery of getting dragged into Europe's war. Wilson's personal attraction for this crucial part of the Democratic coalition was essentially nil; without Bryan he'd have great difficulty keeping the Democrats together. Roosevelt realized that other voices counted more with Wilson than his, but he tendered support all the same. "I wanted to tell you simply that you have been in my thoughts during these days and that I realize to the full all that you have had to go through," he wrote the president. "I need not repeat to you my own entire loyalty and devotion—that I hope you know. But I feel most strongly that the Nation approves and sustains your course and that it is *American* in the highest sense."

Wilson appreciated the gesture. Roosevelt's letter "touched me very much," the president replied. "I thank you for it with all my heart. Such messages make the performance of duty worth while, because, after all, the people who are nearest are those whose judgment we most value and most need to be supported by."

❖ ❖ ❖

Wilson required the support especially as the 1916 election approached. Nearly all the Republicans who had followed Theodore Roosevelt out of the party in 1912 were following him back in, and the arithmetic of American national politics increasingly re-summed toward the Republican majority that had characterized the country since McKinley beat Bryan in 1896. In his favor with voters, Wilson could count certain domestic accomplishments: the creation of the Federal Reserve system, the establishment of the Federal Trade Commission, a downward revision of the tariff. He could also hope that voters worried by the war in Europe would want to stick with the leader they knew. Whether these would outweigh the institutional Republican edge in the electoral college was the central question.

Wilson trod carefully, particularly on matters relating to the war. Ever more he believed that a German victory would endanger the United States in a way a British and French victory wouldn't. Germany had started the war; Germany's autocratic government both reflected and amplified what Wilson and many others perceived to be an inherent aggressiveness in the German people. In early 1916 Wilson quietly sent Edward House, his informal intimate, to Britain to test the waters of cooperation. House and British foreign secretary

Edward Grey initialed a memorandum of understanding to the effect that the United States would propose a peace conference and that if Germany refused to participate, America would probably enter the war on the side of Britain and France. The House-Grey memo didn't bind the United States to anything, but it made clear that Wilson himself had abandoned the moral neutrality he had urged on his compatriots not two years before.

Yet he didn't trumpet the abandonment. In fact he stressed just the opposite: that he had kept the United States out of war. This became the theme of his reelection campaign, to which Franklin Roosevelt contributed his expected share. Roosevelt ignored for the moment his differences with Daniels and Wilson and berated the Republicans for hindering the president's efforts to prepare the country for whatever might befall it. "Every minute of time taken up in perfectly futile and useless argument about mistakes in the past slows up construction that much," he told the Navy League. "Worse than that, it blinds and befogs the public as to the real situation and the imperative necessity for prompt action." Employing an image he would use in similar circumstances more than two decades later, Roosevelt demanded, "How would you expect the public to be convinced that a dangerous fire was in progress, requiring every citizen's aid for its extinguishment, if they saw the members of the volunteer fire department stop in their headlong rush towards the conflagration and indulge in a slanging match as to who was responsible for the rotten hose or the lack of water at the fire a week ago?"

Roosevelt's efforts and those of other Democrats almost weren't enough. The early returns on election night told heavily for Wilson's Republican opponent, Charles Evans Hughes. Wilson went to bed thinking the race was lost; Roosevelt stayed up to tell friends he might have to return to the practice of law. Things looked grim the next morning; newspapers reported Hughes the victor. But as the ballots in the West were tallied, Wilson's prospects improved. "The most extraordinary day of my life," Roosevelt wrote Eleanor at noon. "Wilson may be elected after all." The counting proceeded with nerve-rending slowness. "Another day of the most wild uncertainty," Roosevelt recorded on the Thursday after the Tuesday election. "Returns, after conflicting, have been coming in every hour from Cal., N.M., N.D., Minn., and N.H." If Wilson won enough of these, he might barely squeak past Hughes.

This was just what happened. Wilson wound up with 9.1 million votes to Hughes's 8.5 million, and 277 electoral votes to Hughes's 254. Less than 4,000 votes ultimately separated the two candidates in California, whose thirteen electors gave Wilson his margin of victory.

❖ ❖ ❖

WILSON'S TRIUMPH SPARED Roosevelt a return to the private sector; it also freed the president to deal more forthrightly with the German threat. At the end of 1916 the United States was the great imponderable in the European equation. The front in France had scarcely moved for two years, despite casualties on both sides that numbered in the millions. American money and provisions kept the British and French fighting, but not fighting so well as to defeat the Germans. Yet Germany was weakening under the strain of the British blockade, and Berlin realized it couldn't hold out forever. To break the deadlock, the German government decided to rescind all restrictions on its submarine commanders. The Germans understood that the new policy would bring the United States into the war, but they were willing to gamble that a cutoff of American resupply to the British and French, combined with a major German offensive in France, would compel the Western allies to sue for peace before American troops could reach the battlefield in meaningful numbers. Accordingly, in January 1917 Berlin announced that it would begin sinking all ships—passenger liners and freighters, neutral vessels and enemy—in the waters around Britain.

Wilson might have responded to the German announcement with a request of Congress for a war declaration. Instead he simply handed Bernstorff his passport and severed diplomatic ties with Germany. Perhaps the president still hoped that war might be averted; perhaps he wished to move slowly enough toward war that even the most reluctant Americans could keep pace. When Albert Burleson, the postmaster general, suggested at a cabinet meeting that public opinion could force his hand, Wilson replied, "I want to do right, whether popular or not." Whatever his reasons, Wilson waited until American ships actually started going down—in late March—before approaching Congress.

His hesitance paid off in a manner he couldn't have anticipated. While the world waited on Wilson, revolutionaries in Russia toppled the czar. Nicholas II had always been the odd man out in the anti-German alliance; his autocratic regime, more reactionary even than those of Germany and Austria-Hungary, prevented the British and French from proclaiming theirs a war for liberal values. The unrepresentative character of the Russian government gave Wilson pause in weighing intervention; the American president insisted on fighting for principle, and he couldn't discern any principles he and Nicholas shared. Consequently, the overthrow of the czar in March 1918 (February by the unreformed Russian Orthodox calendar) and the proclamation of a provisional government committed to republican rule came as a tremendous relief to Wilson, removing the last impediment to a clear-conscienced embrace of American belligerence.

The Zimmermann telegram was a bonus. In hopes of distracting the Americans, Berlin tried to lure Mexico to its side, promising the Mexican government a restoration of territories Mexico had lost to the United States in the 1840s, in exchange for Mexican support against the Americans. The German foreign minister, Arthur Zimmermann, made this astonishing offer in a January 1917 telegram that also called on Mexico to help persuade Japan to jump from Britain's side in the war to Germany's. British agents intercepted the telegram, deciphered and translated it, and in February delivered it to the U.S. government, fully aware of the impact it would have on American public opinion. The inevitable anti-German reaction, combined with Berlin's submarine campaign, eliminated what little remained of sympathy for the German cause.

On April 2, 1917, Wilson addressed a joint session of Congress. The president retraced Germany's increasingly egregious violations of American neutrality, contending that these more than justified a declaration of war. Yet he made plain that in his judgment war was not simply a response to injuries past and present but an instrument for ensuring a better future. "The world must be made safe for democracy," Wilson said. "Its peace must be planted upon the tested foundations of political liberty."

Congress might have granted Wilson's request for a war declaration at once, but the sweep of his idealism took some of the lawmakers aback. They debated the matter, and though the ultimate vote was overwhelmingly in favor, it required two days to achieve. All the same, when Wilson signed the war declaration on April 6, he knew he had the backing of the great majority of the American people.

❖   ❖   ❖

As a student of executive leadership, Franklin Roosevelt couldn't help admiring Wilson's mastery in allowing support for war to build. Americans in August 1914 had recoiled in horror from the very thought of intervention; now, in April 1917, their representatives voted 455 to 56 in favor of war. Roosevelt had never stopped thinking that he himself might be president one day, and despite the impatience he had vented over American unpreparedness, he had to admit that Wilson had accomplished a remarkable feat, one any future president could hardly improve upon.

When he thought of himself as a future president, Roosevelt returned to the script he had mapped out a decade earlier. The stage directions now called for him to resign from the Navy Department to enlist in the active military. That was what Uncle Ted had done at the comparable moment in 1898, and Franklin knew enough of history and politics to realize that it was the Rough Rider, not the former assistant secretary, who went on to become governor, vice president, and president.

Roosevelt considered following the script. He made noises about seeking active duty. But he soon decided against it. In the first place, men whose opinions he valued told him he would be crazy, even derelict, to leave Washington, where his actions in the Navy Department might materially influence the outcome of the war, to serve in the trenches or on some ship, where his actions couldn't matter beyond the reach of his rifle or the view from his bridge. "Franklin Roosevelt should, under no circumstances, think of leaving the Navy Department," Leonard Wood, TR's commanding officer in Cuba, told a mutual friend, for Franklin's benefit. "It would be a public calamity to have him leave at the present time."

In the second place, the present war was a different beast than Uncle Ted's war. A day's fighting by a few thousand troops in front of Santiago largely determined the result of the contest with Spain; after nearly three years of bloodletting by several million troops, the outcome of the European war remained in the balance. Even if Franklin hadn't already appreciated how drastically war had changed between 1898 and 1917, he would have learned the lesson very quickly from Theodore's experience when he tried to reprise his Rough Rider role. TR began raising a division of volunteers, only to have his actions vetoed by Wilson, who explained that this war required regular, disciplined troops, not the volunteer, freelancing units of the Spanish-American War. Wilson was playing politics, ensuring that his Republican rival not become a hero again. But he was also being sincere. Any war directed by progressives must be orderly, impersonal, and scientific.

Finally, and perhaps most significantly, Franklin's decision to depart from the Roosevelt script showed that despite sharing a name and some superficial traits, he was a different kind of man than Uncle Ted. Theodore, too, had been told that abandoning the Navy Department for the cavalry would be irresponsible, but he refused to listen. He couldn't help himself. Since childhood he had been obsessed with strength, with manliness, with the military. He had tested himself in every way imaginable—on the athletic field, in the pursuit of dangerous animals, on the political stump—except for the one way that mattered most to him: on the field of battle. He was too much the patriot and the politician to have admitted it, but he almost certainly would have preferred performing heroically in a losing national cause to doing nothing distinguished in a victory.

Franklin Roosevelt labored under no such obsession. He was ambitious, but he lacked his cousin's insatiable need to be moving, doing, testing, confronting. Theodore understood the demons that had driven his brother Elliott to drink and dissolution, because he sometimes felt them closing in on him. What a later generation would call depression ran in Theodore's branch of the Roosevelt family, as the self-destructive behavior of Elliott and various other kinsfolk demonstrated. Theodore refused to let the demons catch him. "Black care rarely sits behind a rider whose pace is fast enough," he wrote, revising Horace. His whole exhausting life was, among other things, a race against that black care.

Franklin Roosevelt knew nothing of that sort of inner struggle—at least not in 1917. His thirty-five years on earth had been as blessed as any man could wish. His family wealth and connections, the love and devotion of his parents, his good looks and natural charm made life easy. He waltzed from triumph to triumph, scarcely breaking a sweat. The principal complaint against him was precisely that success came so easily. No one disliked him; this was nearly impossible. But it wasn't difficult to envy him, and enviously call him shallow for never having supped at disappointment or drunk of despair.

And so, in his shallowness—or innocence or simple well-adjustment—he decided not to risk becoming cannon fodder to scratch a psychic itch that wasn't even his own. He stayed at the Navy Department, determined to ensure that the American fleet did its part to secure the victory he, with Wilson now and so many others, considered essential to the survival of democracy.

10.

$\mathcal{B}$UT IF HE WASN'T GOING TO CHARGE UP THE FRENCH EQUIVALENT of San Juan Hill, he could still apply his considerable energy—his share of the Roosevelt zest—to assaulting the hills at hand. The Battle of the Atlantic had begun for the United States even before the American war declaration, when German U-boats started sinking American merchant vessels. Roosevelt snatched up the gage and determined to punish the German fleet.

This was no small task. For strategic and political reasons, the British had declined to share with a neutral American government the extent of the damage German submarines were doing to British and French shipping. Once the United States entered the war, Roosevelt and other administration officials were shocked to be told that the Germans were sinking nearly a million tons per month. At this rate, the German gamble—on strangling Britain and France before American power came to bear—might well succeed. The first priority, the one on which the war currently hung, was to counter the U-boats.

Opinions differed on the best defense against the submarines. The admirals of the British and American navies preferred a steady-as-she-goes policy of fighting the U-boats with the ships and tactics at hand. Destroyers were the anti-submarine vessels of choice; they could escort convoys of troop transports and freighters, keeping the prowlers away and killing them when they got too close. This approach risked little; it also promised relatively little beyond what it was already accomplishing. The entry of the United States into the war increased the number of available destroyers but didn't offer any radical solution to the submarine problem. Britain's admirals were especially conservative; skeptics accused them of putting the safety of the British navy before the security of the British empire.

Those skeptics included Franklin Roosevelt. In time the world would discover that Roosevelt's reflexive response to emergency was action. Many other men, many other leaders, liked to ponder their options carefully before acting;

Roosevelt typically acted first and pondered later. In part this approach revealed an activist temperament; he was a doer rather than a thinker. In part it
followed from a belief that in a crisis almost any action was better than none
and that errors, which were inevitable in any case, could be corrected as easily on the run as standing still.

To the status quo thinking of the admirals, Roosevelt riposted two novel-
ties. The first involved small patrol boats that could increase the number of
eyeballs searching for enemy submarines. Only a few shipyards produced the
big steel ships that formed the backbone of the American navy, but scores of
builders could turn out lesser wooden craft. Roosevelt envisioned hundreds of
the patrol vessels, in two models: 110-footers with three engines, and 50-footers
with single engines. The admirals looked askance at even the larger of the
boats, fearing they'd steal resources and attention from the real ships; they dismissed the smaller ones as flotsam beneath the dignity of any blue-water man.

Josephus Daniels for once allied with the admirals, primarily because he
distrusted the profit motive of the boat-builders more than he doubted the
bureaucratic self-seeking of the gold braids. He didn't prevent Roosevelt from
fighting for the patrol boats, but he frowned on the whole business. "How
much of that sort of junk shall we buy?" he wrote in his diary after a typically
vigorous Roosevelt appeal. The answer to Daniels's question was several hundred of the patrol boats, which Congress—sensitive to the needs of those many
small boat-builders—seconded Roosevelt in declaring essential to the war effort.

Roosevelt's other novelty was even more controversial. To his sailor's eye,
the German success with submarines was almost inexplicable. Germany is
hardly landlocked, but its seafront affords it access only to the Baltic and North
seas, which *are* geographically constrained. The British and French navies
seemed to have fairly well blocked up the Strait of Dover with mines, nets, and
patrols, preventing the U-boats from skirting Britain's southern shore en route
to the open Atlantic. Roosevelt reasoned that if the British and the Americans
could do the same to the broader channel between Scotland and southern
Norway, the submarines would be stymied. Those caught within the North
Sea blockade would be unable to get out; those stuck outside would starve for
want of fuel and ammunition.

The idea wasn't original with Roosevelt. The British had considered it before the Americans entered the war, only to reject it as infeasible. Too many
mines were required, the water was too deep for successful mooring, and no
mining project so ambitious had ever been attempted, let alone accomplished.

Yet Roosevelt pushed forward on what he called his "pet hobby," convinced that answers would turn up if sufficient intelligence and money were applied. He argued that a few hundred million dollars would purchase sufficient mines and nets to close the northern outlet of the North Sea to all but the boldest and luckiest of U-boat captains. The British and Americans didn't have to stop every sub; merely by lengthening the odds against safe passage they could tip the balance in the war of the sea.

Roosevelt's initial efforts went nowhere. London continued to resist the mine blockade—or mine barrage, as it was formally called—as a waste of limited resources. The technical difficulties remained overwhelming. "Project has previously been considered and abandoned," the British admiralty curtly declared.

The situation changed during the summer of 1917. As Roosevelt had anticipated, the war brought out the best in American ingenuity. An inventor named Ralph Browne visited Roosevelt's office with blueprints for an antisubmarine weapon he called the "Browne Submerged Gun." Roosevelt doubted the efficacy of the weapon as a whole, but the trigger mechanism looked promising. Long wires dangled from surface floats; when anything metal—the hull of a submarine, for instance—touched the wires, it closed an electrical circuit and detonated the gun. Substitute a mine for the gun, Roosevelt reasoned, and suddenly closing the North Sea became much more feasible.

Roosevelt repitched the barrage, first to Daniels, who liked the idea, and then to Wilson. "I am very sorry to bother you," Roosevelt wrote the president disingenuously, before telling him what he ought to do to get the project moving. "Some one person in whom you have confidence should be given the order and the necessary authority to execute the plan without delay. . . . He, working with an Englishman clothed with the same orders and authority, will succeed if success is possible." The project ought to receive the highest priority. "This is a bigger matter than sending destroyers abroad or a division of battleships, or building a bunch of new destroyers—it is vital to the winning of the war."

Wilson was intrigued. The president had long believed that "shutting up the hornets in their nest," as he put it, made more sense than chasing them one by one across the open ocean. He gave Daniels the floor at a cabinet meeting the next day and let the navy secretary present the case for the barrage. "I told W. W. it was very difficult but was the only plan possible to shut off the submarines," Daniels wrote in his diary. "It might cut off ½ and that would be important. Very costly and difficult, but all things are possible." Wilson weighed the matter and gave his approval. With the American president aboard, the British dropped their opposition.

Roosevelt hurled himself into the project. He had anticipated Wilson's approval and arranged to purchase a hundred thousand of the new firing mechanisms; these had to be fitted to the same number of mines, which themselves had to be manufactured. Orders went out to several hundred contractors for steel, high explosives, wire and cable, electrical circuitry, railcars to move the raw materials to assembly plants and from the plants to seaports, ships to carry the equipment across the Atlantic, and other ships to position the mines. New procedures for mine laying, in waters up to six hundred feet deep, in weather as foul as anywhere on the seven seas, had to be devised on the spot. Gradually the entire chain of fabrication, delivery, and placement took shape, and during the summer and autumn of 1918 the intrepid mine layers slipped seventy thousand mines beneath the surface of the North Sea. (The mine layers had to be intrepid, as the underwater bombs had a habit of detonating spontaneously while being laid.) They would have deployed that many again had the war's end not terminated the project.

The effect of the barrage on the outcome of the conflict was hard to determine. Though it was never completed, it killed four U-boats for certain, and possibly four more. This was a small fraction of the total number of German submarines sunk. Yet Admiral William Sims, for one, called the mine barrage "exceedingly important" in ending the war. "That submarines frequently crossed it is true," he said. "There was no expectation, when the enterprise was started, that it would absolutely shut the U-boats in the North Sea. But its influence in breaking down the German morale must have been great." Sims considered what the submarine crews experienced in approaching the minefield. "The width of this barrage ranged from fifteen to thirty-five miles; it took from one to three hours for a submarine to cross this area on the surface and from two to six hours under the surface. Not every square foot, it is true, had been mined . . . but nobody knew where these openings were, or where a single mine was located. The officers and crews knew only that at any moment an explosion might send them to eternity. A strain of this sort is serious enough if it lasts only a few minutes; imagine being kept in this state of mind anywhere from one to six hours!"

Roosevelt, applying similar logic, later claimed for the North Sea barrage a large part of the credit for the discontent that culminated in the mutiny of the German navy at the end of the war. As a prime mover of the barrage, Roosevelt had cause to exaggerate its influence. And he probably did exaggerate. But whether the effect was large or small, it was clearly positive. And Roosevelt could definitely take credit for that. "If Roosevelt had not been there, the North Sea barrage would never have been laid down," Admiral Frederic Harris explained.

❖ ❖ ❖

For all his efforts on behalf of the mine barrage, Roosevelt spent less time fighting the Battle of the Atlantic than various skirmishes of the Potomac. The struggle against Germany drew Americans together, but it hardly eliminated differences of opinion among them. Some initially supposed that since maritime troubles had drawn the United States into the war, American participation might be confined to the high seas. When the Wilson administration made clear that this was not to be so, that American soldiers would join the French and British in the trenches of the western front, and that many of these soldiers would be conscripts, even members of Wilson's own party complained. "In the estimation of Missourians," Champ Clark declared, "there is precious little difference between a conscript and a convict." But Congress went along with the administration, authorizing a draft and otherwise mobilizing the country for war.

Many of the progressives, judging themselves lovers of peace, had assumed they would be the wrong sorts of people to run a war. Wilson told Josephus Daniels in 1914, "Every reform we have won will be lost if we go into this war." But to their surprise, and in some cases to their dismay, the progressives discovered that they were the ideal war administrators. The reformist temperament in American life has always hidden a coercive streak: if people won't shape up voluntarily, they should be encouraged, even compelled, to do so. American abolitionists didn't rely on persuasion to free the slaves; they fought a civil war. American prohibitionists didn't merely denounce demon rum; they outlawed it—in several states by 1917, and very shortly in the country as a whole.

Upon American entry into the war, Wilsonian progressivism turned coercive overnight. The draft was the first triumph of coercion over voluntarism—although the president, unwilling to acknowledge what he and Congress were doing, denied that conscription was coercive. He called it simply "selection from a nation which has volunteered in mass." As additional coercions followed, neither the president nor other members of the administration bothered to disguise them. The War Industries Board mobilized American industry behind the war effort, replacing Adam Smith's invisible hand with the plainly visible hands of federal officials who directed the operation of major parts of the nation's economy. Before the war ended, the government essentially seized the American railroad industry and ran the rails from Washington. The Committee on Public Information marshaled American opinion, enlisting hundreds of professional writers and tens of thousands of "four-minute men": fast-talking speakers whose job was to keep support for the war at what one CPI directive called "white heat." The Espionage and Sedition Acts directly forbade any obstruction of the war effort, even by mere words. Eugene Debs, the socialist leader, was arrested for denouncing the draft, convicted, and sent to prison—where he remained in November 1920, when he received nearly a million votes for president.

Franklin Roosevelt didn't write any of the laws or larger regulations of the period, but he observed their effects, approved of most of them, and participated in the implementation of some. He enlisted his own publicist, the American novelist Winston Churchill, to spur the sluggards in the Navy Department, including Josephus Daniels at times, to swifter action. (In later years, after the British Winston Churchill came to figure in Roosevelt's life, a certain retrospective confusion of the two Churchills inevitably occurred.) Roosevelt fed Churchill information that Churchill used in magazine articles, to frequently good—in Roosevelt's opinion—effect.

As part of his effort to increase the number of patrol boats, Roosevelt encouraged his yachting friends to sell or donate their vessels to the navy. Many did so willingly, but others refused or demanded exorbitant payment. Roosevelt denounced such ingrates as impediments to the war effort. Congress agreed, concluding that if the bodies of ordinary Americans could be drafted, so could the yachts of the wealthy. The legislature gave Roosevelt authority to seize the vessels, which he did with obvious pleasure. His personal contribution to the program was the *Half Moon II,* which joined the navy during the summer of 1917.

✧   ✧   ✧

ANOTHER ROOSEVELT CONTRIBUTION was more frivolous. The *New York Times* ran an article about efforts to conserve food, according to guidelines issued by the federal Food Administration. The story featured Eleanor Roosevelt, who explained what she, her family, and their servants were doing to cut

back. "Making the ten servants help me do my saving has not only been possible but highly profitable," she said. "Since I have started following the home-
card instructions, prices have risen but my bills are no larger."

Franklin winced on reading the piece and twitted Eleanor. "I am proud to
be the husband of the Originator, Discoverer, and Inventor of the New Household Economy for Millionaires!" he wrote. "Please have a photo taken showing the family, the ten cooperating servants, the scraps saved from the table,
and the hand book. I will have it published in the Sunday Times."

Eleanor didn't think the incident funny at all. "I'd like to crawl away for
shame," she wrote Franklin.

❖   ❖   ❖

In the summer of 1918 Roosevelt traveled to the front. The German gamble of the previous year had failed as the Americans and British improved their
convoy techniques on the Atlantic and the German ground offensive stalled in
the mud of northern France. The Germans tried again the following spring
and drove to within artillery range of Paris. But they could get no closer, and
with each passing month more American troops arrived—green troops, but
well equipped and backed by America's unequaled economic power.

Roosevelt's presence was incidental to the combat, but it was essential to his
political future. He had chosen not to fight, but he couldn't miss the fighting.
Already he imagined how he would present himself after the war: as one who
had seen the carnage, who understood what war did to a country and a people. It wouldn't be the same as having fought, but it was something.

His excuse for making the trip was that the navy had dozens of installations in France and Britain, and the marines—that proudest branch of navy
warriors—were playing a pivotal role at the front. Roosevelt argued to Josephus Daniels that the Navy Department needed to dispatch a representative to
the battle zone to inspect the men and facilities. The secretary was too essential in Washington to be gone the several weeks a proper tour would require;
the assistant secretary must go. Daniels assented.

Roosevelt left Brooklyn on July 9 aboard the *Dyer*, a new destroyer. In
calmer times the navy gave new vessels thorough shakedown cruises before
putting them into service; amid the press of the war the *Dyer*'s crew shook her
down on the crossing to Europe. "It is pretty rough," Roosevelt wrote on the
third day, in a journal he kept of the trip. "Even the troop ships roll and
pitch. . . . One has to hang on all the time, never moving without taking hold

with one hand before letting go with the other. Much of the crockery smashed; we cannot eat at the table even with racks, have to sit braced on the transom and hold the plate with one hand."

To avoid attracting German submarines, the ships of the convoy darkened their lamps at night. From the *Dyer*'s position at the starboard quarter of the convoy, Roosevelt could just discern the "great black lightless masses" of the vessels; he pronounced the effect "very weird." The fourth day began with a call to battle stations. Roosevelt raced to the bridge. "The lookout in the foretop had reported a vessel ahead, quickly reporting another and another and another until we began to wonder if we had run into the whole German fleet," he recorded, catching his breath. Closer inspection revealed something less threatening but by no means reassuring. A twenty-eight-ship convoy of American merchantmen out of Norfolk was crossing the path of Roosevelt's convoy from south to north. Had the encounter occurred many minutes earlier there likely would have been blood on the water. "We would have run through them in the dark at eighteen knots and some bad smash-up would almost surely have followed." Convoy schedules and routes were carefully arranged to prevent such collisions, but mishaps occurred. Roosevelt made a note to improve the scheduling procedure.

Northeast of the Azores the convoy entered the active submarine zone. A predawn alert sent Roosevelt hurtling out of bed. "This is the second time I have sprinted for the bridge in pajamas and bare feet. I realized my costume today and apologized to Poteet"—the *Dyer*'s captain—"before descending, but he said it made an excellent and distinctive uniform for a flag officer as long as the Secretary of the Navy does not try to change it to the old-fashioned night-gown and carpet slippers." Roosevelt's regular attire was distinctive enough. "I wish I could travel all the way in my destroyer costume—my own invention—khaki riding trousers, golf stockings, flannel shirt, and leather coat. It does not soil or catch in things!"

The *Dyer* landed at Portsmouth and Roosevelt proceeded to London, where the British admiralty put him up at the Ritz. The next morning he met with Sir Eric Geddes, the First Lord of the Admiralty. They talked of the joint Anglo-American antisubmarine efforts, and Geddes informed him of a new British program to fit certain warships with flat decks for launching and catching airplanes. The concept was experimental but promising, Geddes said.

Roosevelt spent two fascinating hours with British naval intelligence officers. "Their intelligence department is far more developed than ours," he concluded. "This is because it is a much more integral part of their Office of Operations." He determined to remedy the problem once back in Washington.

He conversed at length with George V. "The King has a nice smile and a very open, quick and cordial way of greeting one. He is not as short as I had expected, and I think his face is stronger than photographs make it appear." The interview ran half an hour over the scheduled fifteen minutes. "He was a delightfully easy person to talk to, and we got going so well that part of the time we were both talking at the same time."

Roosevelt met with Prime Minister David Lloyd George, who impressed him with his "tremendous vitality." Lloyd George in peacetime had polarized British politics; in wartime he taught Roosevelt—and others—a valuable political lesson. "The Conservatives who used to despise him as a demagogue, the Liberals who used to fear him as a radical, and most of the Labor people who now look on him as a reactionary, may hate him just as much as ever and be unwilling after the war to trust reconstruction to his hands. But they will stand by him just as long as his administration keeps the winning of the war as its only political aim."

Roosevelt addressed the Anglo-American Luncheon Club, and attended a dinner gathering of the British imperial war ministers, where he was introduced to Britain's Lord Curzon, Canada's Sir Robert Borden, and South Africa's General Jan Smuts, each of whom greatly impressed him. "A really historic occasion," Roosevelt called it. He also met Winston Spencer Churchill, who did not impress him—at least not enough for him to mention Churchill in his journal of the trip. Churchill reciprocated the neglect, forgetting the meeting until he was reminded of it by Roosevelt decades later.

❖ ❖ ❖

On July 31 Roosevelt left London for France. He crossed the Channel and landed at Dunkirk, which anchored the British presence in France. "I had no idea that the British were sending in so many supplies through this place," he wrote. The Germans were fully aware of Dunkirk's importance and had been blasting it with artillery for three years, and more recently with airplane-delivered bombs. "There is not a whole house left in this place. . . . I did not see one pane of glass in the town, and almost every house-front is pock-marked by fragments of shell."

Roosevelt's party drove to Calais, where German planes had been trying out new, very large bombs, weighing more than a thousand pounds. "These have smashed things up over a large radius," he wrote. "I saw a spot where one had landed in the middle of a street—about six houses on each side of the street were completely wrecked by it and many people killed."

In Paris, Roosevelt met French prime minister Georges Clemenceau. "I knew at once I was in the presence of the greatest civilian in France," Roosevelt recorded. "He did not wait for me to advance to meet him at his desk, and there was no formality such as one generally meets. He almost ran forward to meet me and shook hands as if he meant it, grabbed me by the arm and walked me over to his desk and sat me down about two inches away. He is only 77 years old, and people say he is getting younger every day. He started off with no polite remarks because they were unnecessary, asked me three or four definite questions about our naval production and what I thought of the effect of the submarine campaign on the troop transportation." Roosevelt's answers satisfied Clemenceau, who turned to the current state of the fighting. "He jumped up, took me over to a big map with all the latest troop movements and showed me the latest report from General Degoutte, covering progress north of Château-Thierry up to one hour before."

Roosevelt had never been so close to wartime command, and he was mesmerized. "He launched into a hair-raising description of the horrors left by the Boche in his retreat—civilian population carried off, smashing of furniture, slashing of paintings, burning of houses—and he said, 'These things I have seen myself,' for the wonderful old man leaves his office almost every Saturday in a high-powered car, dashes to some part of the front, cheered by troops everywhere he passes, visits a Corps Commander, travels all night, goes up a good deal closer to the actual battle line than the officers like, keeps it up all day Sunday, and motors back in time to be at his desk on Monday morning."

Clemenceau paused, as if to let Roosevelt catch up. "Then, still standing, he said: 'Do not think that the Germans have stopped fighting or that they are not fighting well. We are driving them back and will keep them going back because we are fighting better, and every Frenchman and every American is fighting better because he knows he is fighting for the right and that it can prevail only by breaking the German Army by force of arms.' He spoke of an episode he had seen while following just behind the advance—a Poilu and a Boche still standing partly buried in a shell hole, clinched in each other's arms, their rifles abandoned, and the Poilu and the Boche were in the act of trying to bite each other to death when a shell had killed both. And as he told me this he grabbed me by both shoulders and shook me with a grip of steel to illustrate his words, thrusting his teeth toward my neck."

❖ ❖ ❖

$\mathcal{I}$N MID-JULY the German army had tested the troops of the American Expeditionary Forces in the Second Battle of the Marne. For three days the Germans pressed forward, but on July 18 the Americans retaliated furiously at Château-Thierry with a coordinated artillery and infantry counterattack. They forced the Germans to yield the ground just taken and, more significantly, demonstrated that the Americans could fight effectively. With ten thousand Americans pouring into France every week, Château-Thierry signaled the beginning of the end for Germany.

Roosevelt approached the Marne in early August. Soldiers clogged the road: French reinforcements heading into battle, German prisoners being led away. This was Roosevelt's first sight of the enemy. "They did not impress me as being physically unfit, but there is an awful contrast between the amount of intelligence in their faces compared with the French Poilus." From Meaux to Château-Thierry, civilian French refugees brought traffic nearly to a standstill. They had fled the German onslaught; now they were returning to their homes, or what they hoped would still be their homes. "They went with big carts drawn by a cow or an ox and a calf trotting behind, bedding, chickens, household goods, and children, and sometimes a grandmother, piled on top, all of them taking it perfectly calmly, remembering always their good fortune in having got away before the arrival of the Boche, ready to start in again even from the ground up, but constantly impressing upon their children what the Boche has done to northern France in these four years."

On reaching Château-Thierry, Roosevelt was struck by the failure of the French, who had retaken the town ten days earlier, to rebuild any of the bridges over the Marne. Soldiers, animals, and vehicles had to cross on rickety floating bridges. The problem appeared to be a shortage of steel. Roosevelt jotted another note to himself: "Forethought in providing bridge steel would have made a better record."

Roosevelt toured the battlefield. He was no military expert, but as he surveyed the ground he began to grasp what the fighting there had been like. "We walked to the edge of the woods and looked east. No wonder this was the key to the salient. In front the ground, while rolling, was in general lower and more open, and even a civilian's eye could see that the few wooded higher points could be turned without offering half the defensive strength of the jungle we were about to enter." Immediately beyond lay the makeshift graves of German soldiers, whose unclaimed bodies had been interred beneath humble wooden crosses. Farther on were graves with slightly different crosses marking fallen Frenchmen and Americans. The ground itself was frozen into angry billows tossed up by the exploding artillery shells. Merely walking across the battlefield was a physical and emotional ordeal. "We had to thread our way past water-filled shell holes and thence up the steep slope over outcropping rocks, over-turned boulders, downed trees, hastily improvised shelter pits, rusty bayonets, broken guns, emergency ration tins, hand grenades, discarded overcoats, rain-stained love letters, crawling lines of ants, and many little mounds, some wholly unmarked, some with a rifle stuck bayonet down in the earth, some with a hel-met, and some, too, with a whittled cross or wrapping paper hung over it and in a pencil scrawl an American name."

Though the sensory impact of the battlefield was overwhelming—"the smell of dead horses is not only evident but very horrid," Roosevelt wrote—he insisted on pushing closer to the active fighting. "We drove into Fère-en-Tardenois and met here the artery of communications for this sector: camions, artillery, and moving troops filled the road in both directions, but the stream never stopped. We turned sharply north just as a series of exploding shells fol-lowed by little white puffs indicated a Hun plane, probably doing photo-graphic work." They passed large piles of live shells dumped by the Germans in their haste to retreat; in one place a circle of felled trees, their broken crowns pointing away from a crater at their center, showed where another such dump had been before it exploded. Roosevelt's party crossed a small stream and en-tered the shattered village of Mareuil. "Just as we were descending from the motors, a loud explosion went off very close by. Some of the party jumped perceptibly, realizing that we were within easy range of the Hun artillery. It was, however, only one of our own 155s so cleverly camouflaged in a tree just off the road that we had not noticed its presence." Roosevelt insisted on ex-amining this gun and some others, and he fired one of the 155s against German positions far over the horizon.

The next day Roosevelt drove to Verdun, the site of the tremendous 1916 siege and battle. Shell holes still pocked the road, which construction crews worked to repair. Villages along the way had been blasted beyond restoration. "All this was nothing, however, to the sight that met our eyes when we looked down over the town. Great gaps showed where buildings had once stood. De-tached and jagged walls were everywhere, and of the houses still standing not one roof remained intact. It was a scene of colossal destruction." The town re-mained within reach of German artillery, and so its garrison of four thousand troops huddled in tunnels sixty feet beneath the ancient citadel at the town's highest point.

Roosevelt toured the tunnels and shared lunch with the commandant and his staff, who showed him about the town afterward. "The first thing that met our eyes on one of the walls was the memorable original signboard which was posted near the entrance to the citadel during the siege, and on which the thousands of troops going forward to hold the line read the words which, for the French people, will sum up for all time their great watchword of four years: 'Ils ne passeront pas.' "

Roosevelt's party crossed the Meuse River to the battlefield itself. They were given helmets and gas masks, just in case. Nowhere had the fighting been more violent than here, but at first it didn't show. "There were no gashes on these hills, no trenches, no tree trunks, no heaps of ruins—nothing but brown earth for miles upon miles." Closer inspection, however, revealed that the monotony was the result of shelling so intense that it obliterated all preexisting features of the terrain. "When you look at the ground immediately about you, you realize that this earth has been churned by shells, and churned again. You see no complete shell holes, for one runs into another, and trench systems and forts and roads have been swallowed up in brown chaos."

❖ ❖ ❖

ROOSEVELT'S EXPERIENCE in France shaped his perceptions of war and added to his mental album of lessons for an aspiring president. It also made him decide to resign from the Navy Department and seek active service. The war was winding down, but he might get in a few licks before it ended. Neither the president nor anyone else could criticize him for leaving his post; he had done his duty in Washington, and with distinction. He had a right to fight.

His plan was to return to France as part of a naval artillery unit—a battleship battery mounted on railcars. Such an assignment might not be the stuff of heroism, but it would allow him to see action. With luck he might be decorated, even lightly wounded. A president-in-the-making couldn't ask for more.

Roosevelt's excitement at this prospective turn in his career caused him to ignore the first twinges of illness as he raced around tying up the loose ends from his inspection tour. He told himself he could catch up on his rest on the ship home. He climbed the gangway under his own power but collapsed in his cabin, more debilitated than he had realized. The pandemic of influenza that was starting its sweep around the world—it would kill more than fifty million before it burned out—had infected many of the soldiers Roosevelt had mingled with, and it followed him aboard the *Leviathan*. Quite possibly he suffered a touch of the flu himself; if so, his case was one of the mild ones. Of greater concern was a bad case of pneumonia. Both his lungs began to fill with fluid, and though he coughed incessantly, he couldn't clear them. Doctors in those days had no medication for pneumonia; rest, liquids, and ample nourishment were the standard prescription. Roosevelt received all of these, but his immune system had been compromised, and he struggled simply to hold his ground.

He was confined to bed the whole voyage to America. A wireless message from the ship alerted the Navy Department that the assistant secretary was ill; the *Leviathan* should be met by orderlies with a stretcher. The department relayed the news to Eleanor, who shared it with Sara, and both women came to the dock in New York. Sara directed the orderlies to her house on Sixty-fifth Street. Roosevelt's condition stabilized there, but his recovery proceeded slowly. He relocated to Hyde Park; not for a month was he on his feet and ready to return to work.

He delivered the report of his inspection tour to Daniels and prepared to offer his resignation to the president. He visited the White House armed with arguments he thought Wilson wouldn't be able to resist. The one thing he hadn't counted on was the first objection the president raised: that the war was about to end. Wilson revealed in confidence that the Germans were suing for peace. Long before Roosevelt could reach the front, the fighting would be over.

This news elated the world as soon as it was made public, but it left Roosevelt ambivalent. Though he shared the relief that the bloodletting was over, by now he really wanted to see action. With decent luck, there would never be such a war again. Yet this meant that there would be no comparable chance for the peculiar distinction that comes with military service. Other men—other politicians—would be able to tell their war stories and display their ribbons and medals. At such moments Roosevelt would have to remain silent.

❖   ❖   ❖

HE HAD ANOTHER, more personal reason for regretting not being able to return to the front. Roosevelt's inspection tour in France and Britain gave Lucy Mercer reason to write him regularly for the first time. The Delanos tended to be collectors, and Roosevelt, like his mother, never threw a letter away. On his return to America, his luggage contained Lucy's letters. He had intended to unpack his bags himself, but the pneumonia that prostrated him left his kit in other hands. While he drifted in and out of consciousness, Eleanor unpacked her husband's suitcases and found the letters.

"The bottom dropped out of my own particular world," she told her friend Joseph Lash years later. "And I faced myself, my surroundings, my world, honestly for the first time." Her comment was revealing, especially the part about honesty, which indicated that Lucy's letters, while a shock, weren't a surprise. They simply compelled her to acknowledge what she had implicitly denied till now: that her husband loved another woman.

What to do? That was the question for Eleanor—as for so many other wounded spouses throughout history. Should she leave or stay? To leave would free her from a situation that had grown emotionally intolerable. In an era that gravely disapproved of divorce, it would be humiliating, but perhaps no more humiliating than what she had been through, facing the snickers and suggestive glances of those who knew what she now had to acknowledge. Leaving would also expose the children to the opprobrium of the broken home. They wouldn't starve—her own inheritance, Sara's concern for her grandchildren, and the courts of New York would see to that. But they would grow up marked by disgrace, which to Eleanor's way of thinking would be almost as bad as starving. Leaving might well ruin Franklin too. What divorced man had succeeded in politics? None that Eleanor had heard of. Nor had any made a respectable reputation in law or business. Franklin's fate wasn't her first consideration at this point, but, if only for the sake of the children, she couldn't ignore it. Anyway, she didn't stop loving him just because he had wounded her.

Yet to stay was scarcely more appealing. Could she ever trust him again? Could she ever trust herself? She had been rescued from her childhood insecurities by his love, but now, after she had painstakingly come to believe in herself, she discovered she hadn't been rescued at all. The knowledge was devastating.

She couldn't decide alone. She had to consult Sara, whose meddling had been a cause for resentment but whose intense concern suddenly seemed a source of strength. She and Sara and Franklin met in the only suitable place for such an interview: the great library in the house at Hyde Park. What was said there was never recorded. But Alice Roosevelt Longworth later told of a comment by Corinne Roosevelt Robinson, her and Eleanor's aunt. "Always remember, Alice," Corinne said, "that Eleanor offered Franklin his freedom."

If Eleanor did, Franklin must have pondered accepting it. Some months earlier, when the strain on the marriage had become intense, the possibility of divorce apparently arose in another conversation with Eleanor and Sara. He said something that prompted Sara, in a follow-up letter to him and Eleanor, to lecture him on his duties to family and tradition. "One can be as democratic as one likes, but if we love our own, and if we love our neighbor, we owe a great example," Sara wrote. "Do not say that I *misunderstood*. I understood perfectly. But I cannot believe that my precious Franklin really feels as he expressed himself."

Now, at the moment of crisis, Sara summoned arguments more powerful than appeals to family honor. "If divorce were the answer, she would cut off Father's money as punishment for his offense," Elliott Roosevelt wrote, relating the version accepted by the children. Franklin's own inheritance might support him, but it wouldn't sustain two households. As a working lawyer or business executive he might manage to provide for Eleanor and the children, as well as for himself, but he would have to abandon his political hopes—which in any case would be shattered by the divorce.

Additional reasons were adduced against divorce, including the fact that Lucy was a Catholic. This presumably precluded marriage to a divorced man. But the Catholicism in Lucy's family didn't run deep, as her parents' breakup demonstrated. She might well have chosen Franklin over orthodoxy, had matters come to that.

They didn't. If Franklin had indeed been tempted to follow his heart out of his marriage to Eleanor, he decided upon Sara's ultimatum to follow his ambition back in. Eleanor insisted that he promise never to see Lucy again. He couldn't possibly object, and he gave the required pledge. The children, who were better placed than anyone else to know, inferred an additional condition: that she and Franklin would never resume conjugal relations. Not for years would the younger children appreciate the significance of their parents' separate bedrooms. But none of the five ever detected a breach in the emotional wall the separation raised in the middle of their family.

11.

$\mathcal{I}$N THE AUTUMN OF 1918, ON THE EVE OF THE ALLIED VICTORY IN THE war, Woodrow Wilson committed the greatest blunder of his presidency. He should have known better, if any president should have, for he had studied politics his whole adult life. Had he been advising a president other than himself, he would have warned against making congressional elections a referendum on the administration's war policies. He would have predicted a sixth-year slippage in party support, for it was the norm among second-term presidents as the inevitable accumulation of bent and broken promises took its toll. And he most definitely would have argued against urging voters to put foreign affairs first as they selected their congressmen. Voters had never done so in the past; it tempted fate to ask them to alter historic habits.

But hubris had set in. As the end of the war hove into sight, Wilson looked to the peace conference that would follow. For Wilson the war had always been about the peace; an unsatisfactory settlement, he believed, would render all the carnage, all the expense, all the compromises with principle wasted. He had decided to attend the peace conference himself, and to bolster his position he called on the American people to rally behind him. "If you have approved of my leadership and wish me to continue to be your unembarrassed spokesman in affairs at home and abroad," he said, "I earnestly beg that you will express yourselves unmistakably to that effect by returning a Democratic majority to both the Senate and the House of Representatives."

He knew he was taking a chance. His closest advisers, including his wife, told him so. But he couldn't help himself. He needed the vote of confidence, the better to speak at the peace conference for humanity, as he intended to do. Predestinarian that he was, he may have believed that God wouldn't let him down.

But the American people did. They handed not one but both houses of Congress to the Republicans. Wilson wasn't simply repudiated; he was delivered over to his enemies. Any treaty he brought home from Paris would have to win the approval of two-thirds of the Senate, a formidable standard under the best of circumstances but one made suddenly more daunting by the presence of Henry Cabot Lodge at the Senate door. Lodge would chair the foreign relations committee, which would examine the treaty, conduct hearings, and report its findings to the full Senate. Lodge opposed Wilson politically and despised him personally; he dismissed Wilson's literary productions with the comment that while they might suit Princeton they would never have passed muster at Harvard, Lodge's school. Lodge's dark eyes and Van Dyke beard had always given him a slightly sinister aspect; now, in the malevolent satisfaction of his and the Republicans' victory, he seemed likely to be downright Mephisthophelean toward anything the president returned with from Paris.

❖   ❖   ❖

FRANKLIN ROOSEVELT SAW the disaster approaching but was helpless to prevent it. If the president wouldn't listen to his intimates, he certainly wouldn't heed an assistant secretary. Fortunately for Roosevelt, no one could blame the debacle on him. The lingering effects of the pneumonia—perhaps compounded by the emotional stress of his confrontation with Eleanor over Lucy—allowed him to beg off from campaigning for the Democrats that season. When the roof fell in on the president, none of the debris hit Roosevelt.

At least not at once. The wounded Wilson set off for Paris in January, and when he arrived, Roosevelt was there to greet him. Roosevelt had hoped to return to France to fight; instead he oversaw the denouement of the fighting. The U.S. navy's large wartime presence in Britain and France required liquidating; Roosevelt got the assignment.

Eleanor accompanied him. Ordinarily she wouldn't have, as he was on government business, and spouses typically stayed behind. But after his pneumonia he still needed a nurse or the equivalent, and Eleanor filled the part. In light of what had transpired between them the last few months, she may have considered herself equally his chaperone. This, obviously, wasn't for public consumption.

The voyage was uneventful. Walter Camp, the Yale coach who essentially invented American football, had taken his philosophy of physical training to Washington during the war, leading government officials in calisthenics each morning to clear their heads and ready them for a hard day at their desks.

Franklin Roosevelt was one of Camp's prize specimens—"a beautifully built young man, with the long muscles of the athlete," Camp observed. Having contributed his part toward winning the war, Camp now determined to help secure the peace by similar attention to the mind-body connection. He joined Roosevelt's France-bound American contingent and drilled the travelers on the deck of the *George Washington*. Roosevelt again bent and stretched in the front row, doubtless happy for the physical release the exercise afforded. When the others headed for their staterooms and showers, Roosevelt hit the shuffleboard and quoits courts. Occasionally he reviewed his papers, sitting beside Eleanor, who slogged her way through Henry Adams's dismal autobiography. "Very interesting, but sad to have had so much and yet find it so little," she remarked.

The most important development of the eight days of the voyage occurred not on the ship but on the shore of Long Island Sound. Theodore Roosevelt had been in and out of the hospital, but in the year of the flu pandemic so had tens of thousands of other Americans. His various maladies made him uncomfortable, yet none seemed likely to kill him. And so, when he died in his sleep on January 6, 1919, the loss took America by surprise. "The old lion is dead," his son Archie cabled the other sons. Franklin and Eleanor got the word by wireless aboard the *George Washington*. "We were shocked by the news of Uncle Ted's death," Eleanor wrote Sara. "Another big figure gone from our nation, and I fear the last years were for him full of disappointment."

Franklin Roosevelt didn't comment directly on his cousin's passing. Perhaps he reflected on ambition's—and life's—ultimate end; perhaps he wondered whether he would be remembered and mourned as widely at his own death as Theodore was being remembered now. He may have felt a certain relief at the prospect of no longer being the "other Roosevelt," the one in the Rough Rider president's shadow.

Whatever musings Theodore's death evoked, they dissipated soon after Franklin and Eleanor reached France. January 1919 was a glorious time to be an American in Paris, and especially to be associated with Woodrow Wilson. The people of France knew nothing of Wilson's political setback at home, or if they knew they ignored it in their ecstatic welcome to the American president. Banners awaited his docking at Brest, bearing the message "Hail the Champion of the Rights of Man." Two million Parisians lined the Champs Elysée to pay Wilson homage; three divisions of French troops struggled to keep the crowds from lifting him bodily from his carriage and hoisting him on their shoulders. "I saw Foch pass, Clemenceau pass, Lloyd George, generals, returning troops," an American newsman remarked. "But Wilson heard from his carriage something different, inhuman—or superhuman."

Franklin and Eleanor absorbed the excitement. "I never saw anything like Paris," Eleanor wrote Sara. "It is full beyond belief, and one sees many celebrities and all one's friends! People wander the streets unable to find a bed, and the prices are worse than New York for everything."

The thrill of being at the center of the world while the statesmen of the great powers negotiated humanity's future doubtless eased, or perhaps simply disguised, the personal tension between Franklin and Eleanor. The relaxation, or distraction, continued as Franklin took Eleanor to visit some of the battlefields. Because the fighting had halted under an armistice rather than a surrender, the front technically remained a war zone, and most women, including wives of assistant secretaries, weren't allowed. But Roosevelt ignored the ban, and before anyone acted to enforce it, Eleanor's observation of the battle sites was, as Franklin told Sara, "a fait accompli."

Franklin's official business focused on selling American assets to the French government. The navy's ships, of course, could be sailed home, but bases and other immovable infrastructure would have to be left in place. Or so the French supposed, and they offered the American government a pittance in payment for the facilities. Roosevelt, in one noteworthy instance, informed them that they were wrong. The wireless station at Bordeaux appeared quite permanent to most observers, but when the French made what Roosevelt deemed an insulting offer, he ordered the American personnel to prepare to dismantle it. The navy would ship it home, he told his French counterparts. The French government quickly recalculated and the next day improved its offer substantially. Roosevelt was delighted and shared his pleasure with Eleanor. She passed the good news to Sara: "This is a big success but don't mention it!"

Other successes were smaller. Roosevelt visited a fort held by U.S. marines at Ehrenbreitstein in the occupied German Rhineland; seeing no American flag above the battlements, he demanded of the commandant to know why. The officer said he didn't want to offend the Germans. Roosevelt indignantly returned to Paris and informed General Pershing that this would never do. "The German people ought to know for all time that Ehrenbreitstein flew the American flag during the occupation," he declared. Pershing agreed, and soon Old Glory was snapping in the German breeze.

Within a month Roosevelt completed most of what needed doing. He might have stayed longer, but Eleanor wanted to get back to the children, and he wished to share a sea voyage with Wilson, who was returning to America to sign legislation and tend to other pressing executive business before resuming his seat at the peace conference. The president had been far too busy with Lloyd George, Clemenceau, and Italy's Vittorio Orlando to have time for his assistant navy secretary at Paris, but Roosevelt hoped that aboard the *George Washington* they might speak.

And so they did, albeit not as confidentially as Roosevelt would have preferred. Wilson invited Franklin and Eleanor to lunch with him, Mrs. Wilson, and a few other distinguished passengers. Never one for small talk, Wilson launched into an impassioned defense of the League of Nations, the centerpiece of his plans for the postwar settlement. "The United States must go in, or it will break the heart of the world," he told the group, "for she is the only nation that all feel is disinterested and all trust." Eleanor thought this statement sufficiently noteworthy that she recorded it verbatim. Something else Wilson said also caught her attention, and doubtless Franklin's too. "He said he had read no papers since the beginning of the war, that Mr. Tumulty"—Joseph P. Tumulty, Wilson's private secretary—"clipped them all for him, giving him only important news and editorials." Eleanor wondered at handing a secretary such implicit power. "This is too much to leave to any man," she remarked in her diary.

❖ ❖ ❖

THE FIGHT FOR the League of Nations dominated American politics from the spring of 1919 through the autumn of 1920, and it commenced upon the *George Washington*'s landing in Boston. The destination had originally been New York, the vessel's home port, but Wilson decided to take the fight to Henry Cabot Lodge's turf. Boston held a parade for Wilson, which suggested that not all of New England, or even of the Bay State, stood behind Lodge. Roosevelt rode in the parade, and he joined Wilson for lunch with Massachusetts governor Calvin Coolidge. He sat on the platform at Mechanics Hall while Wilson summoned America to enlist with him in a mission devoted to the highest ideals of democracy. A peace not based on ideals would be unworthy of the American people, Wilson said, and would not last. The president declined to mention his principal antagonist by name, but everyone knew he was speaking of Lodge in warning of the fate that would befall those who opposed the League. "Any man who resists the present tides that run in the world," Wilson declared, shaking a long, accusing finger, "will find himself

thrown upon a shore so high and barren that it will seem as if he had been separated from his human kind forever."

Roosevelt's opinion of the League of Nations at this point is unclear. Nothing in his past—and not much in his future—suggested an affinity for the
kind of impassioned idealism that informed Wilson's vision of the League.
Roosevelt was more the pragmatist than the idealist, more the tinkerer than the
true believer. He also realized that the League had become a monomania with
Wilson. The president could justify any compromise at Paris, any political tactic at home, that would deliver the League and secure American membership
therein. Roosevelt would never get so passionate about anything. Monomania
wasn't in his nature. He was a politician, not an ideologue; he served people,
not causes.

❖   ❖   ❖

WILSON, AFTER RETURNING to Paris, got his League incorporated into the
Treaty of Versailles, signed in that suburb of the French capital in June 1919.
The compromises the president made to win the support of Britain, France,
and Italy for the League disconcerted some Americans, who wondered what
had happened to self-determination and other principles Wilson had cham-
pioned before and during the war. The charter of the League, in particular the
war-triggering clauses of article 10, which pledged the United States to defend
the sovereignty and security of fellow League members, by military force if
necessary, disturbed many others, who feared that America's independence
would thereby be infringed. But Wilson was proud of his handiwork, and he
brought the treaty home and personally delivered it to the Senate in July. Lodge
met him at the door of the upper chamber and asked if he could carry the
document inside. Wilson clutched it tightly, glared at Lodge, and said, "Not
on your life."

The treaty might have provoked a searching debate over the role of the
United States in world affairs. For brief moments it did elicit serious discussion. But it became so entangled in the partisan wrangling of Republicans and
Democrats, and so enmeshed in the private animosity of Wilson and Lodge,
that the larger issues often faded from view. Lodge insisted on reading all
eighty thousand words of the treaty aloud, with stentorian slowness, reckoning that American interest in Europe would diminish the farther the war
slipped into the past. The greater part of a year already separated the armistice
from the present; Lodge could reasonably expect to delay a final vote on the

treaty till the peace had lasted longer than the war itself—at least the part of the war Americans participated in. It wasn't inconceivable that the elections of 1920 would be fought over Wilson's precious League. Lodge certainly hoped so. The foreign relations chairman scheduled hearings; everyone, it seemed, with an interest or an opinion was invited to testify.

Wilson endured Lodge's siege for two months before mounting a counteroffensive. The Republicans controlled Congress, but the president might appeal to the American people. In 1919 radio remained a wireless substitute for telegraphy; it had yet to become a broadcast medium. Consequently, for Wilson to reach the American people required that he travel to where they lived. He left Washington in September, intending to circle the country by train. He started preaching the League gospel in Ohio, then continued across Indiana to Missouri. He warned of the day of judgment should the Senate reject the treaty and the League. "There will come some time," he said in St. Louis, "in the vengeful Providence of God, another struggle in which not a few hundred thousand fine men from America will have to die, but as many millions as are necessary to accomplish the final freedom of the world." He spoke in Montana and Idaho and Washington and drew crowds at every stop. A reporter traveling with Wilson thought the tour was going quite well for the president. "It seems a safe assertion that the ten states through which he has passed believe with him that the Treaty of Peace should be ratified without delay," the newsman wrote, "and that they are willing to have the United States enter a League of Nations."

Wilson swung south into Oregon and California, and then east to Colorado. At Pueblo, he gave the speech of his life. "There is one thing that the American people always rise to and extend their hand to, and that is the truth of justice and of liberty and of peace," he said. "We have accepted that truth, and we are going to be led by it, and it is going to lead us, and through us the world, out into pastures of quietness and peace such as the world never dreamed of before."

He might have won the country to his cause. But on the threshold of victory, Wilson fell silent. The Pueblo speech, after weeks on the road, wore him out. He suffered from chronic hypertension, and the stress of the tour triggered what seems to have been a minor stroke. His doctor, traveling with him, had feared such an attack, and he immediately canceled the rest of the tour. The president's train sped east to Washington, where Wilson summoned the strength to walk through Union Station and smile at the supporters who greeted him there. But a major stroke felled him at the White House. "He looked as if he were dead," the White House usher recalled. "There was not a sign of life."

For weeks he lay in a sickroom, shielded from the outside world by his wife, his doctor, and his secretary, who together conspired to conceal the extent of his disability. The administration drifted rudderless; not even Wilson's cabinet secretaries knew his true condition.

❖ ❖ ❖

THE ASSISTANT SECRETARIES knew even less. Having decided, before Wilson told him of the impending armistice, to leave the Navy Department, Roosevelt had difficulty summoning enthusiasm for his old job, which grew dreary in the aftermath of the war. "Things have been so quiet here as to be almost terrifying," he wrote Josephus Daniels in April 1919. "Literally nothing has happened outside of the routine work." The routine was painful when it wasn't boring. Roosevelt battled with bureau chiefs over the disposition of a shrinking budget, chose which thousands of workers to lay off from navy yards, determined which hundreds of ships to mothball or scrap, and explained to a hostile Congress how the navy had spent its wartime millions. A controversy developed over the award of contracts to supply the navy with oil; political allies of those who did not receive contracts alleged favoritism toward those who did. Another row resulted from the refusal of Secretary Daniels to approve all the ribbons and medals Admiral Sims thought his men deserved; Sims responded by blasting the Navy Department for criminal negligence in the prosecution of the war. The Republican Senate happily probed the charges, conducting three months of hearings in the spring of 1920. The indictment didn't stick, but the investigation exhausted the civilian personnel of the Navy Department, including Roosevelt, who in the process found more reason to admire Daniels and less to respect Sims and the admirals.

He pondered how to get out of office gracefully. The Wilson administration was hemorrhaging talent as its end approached, with cabinet secretaries and their underlings leaving for law firms, investment banks, corporate boards, and the other posts in the private sector where public servants recouped— or simply couped—their fortunes following stints in Washington. Some of the incorrigibly political plotted campaigns for elective office in 1920, but sober Democrats estimated their party's chances that year as slim to minuscule. Prudence counseled letting the Republicans have their day.

Wilson's stroke and the consequent paralysis of the administration accelerated the rush to the door. In November 1919 the Versailles treaty came up for a vote in the Senate. Lodge had attached several reservations to the treaty. These were either honest attempts to fix what Lodge and other critics considered wrong with the treaty or cynical efforts to sabotage it; Lodge let senators draw their own conclusions. When Wilson, communicating uncertainly through his wife, ordered the Senate Democrats to reject the treaty-plus-reservations, it fell short of even a simple majority, with Democrats supplying most of the negative votes. Lodge then allowed a vote on the unencumbered treaty. It failed by a similar margin, although now the Republicans were mostly responsible. Lodge might thereupon have declared the treaty rejected. But he liked the issue enough to let it linger over the winter. In March 1920 the treaty came to a final vote. Reservations had been reattached, and Wilson, more feeble than ever, again attempted a veto. This time several Democrats disobeyed the president and voted in favor. Yet it still fell seven votes shy of the necessary margin, with 49 in favor, 35 against.

The failure of the treaty left the administration dead in the water, and more of Roosevelt's colleagues clambered off. For months he himself had been plotting his escape. "I wish it were possible for me, now that the war is over, to return to something a little more lucrative than this position," he told an acquaintance. He sounded out two attorney friends, Grenville Emmet and Langdon Marvin, about opening a New York law practice. The three agreed on terms of a partnership, to be called Emmet, Marvin & Roosevelt. Emmet and Marvin laid the groundwork; Roosevelt would join them at his first opportunity to leave the administration without embarrassing either himself or the president.

$\mathcal{B}$Y THE SUMMER OF THEIR EIGHTH YEAR IN OCCUPANCY OF THE White House, the Democrats held no hope of extending their lease beyond March 1921. A whole litany of issues, besides the Treaty of Versailles, split the country in the wake of the war. The economic readjustment was wrenching, as strikes idled hundreds of factories and hundreds of thousands of workers, price rises pinched tens of millions of households, and markets in stocks, bonds, and commodities alternately sizzled and fizzled as the global economy reintegrated the recently warring national economies. The war had commenced a transformation of American race relations, with African Americans migrating from the farms of the South to the cities and factories of the North. The migrants encountered suspicion and hostility, which turned bloody during and after the war in Chicago, New York, Omaha, and East St. Louis, Illinois. But the migrants kept coming, intent on sharing some of the prosperity and personal freedom that had long eluded them in the segregated South. Though the Wilson administration didn't overtly encourage the violence, it implicitly legitimated the hostility by extending the Jim Crow system to the federal workforce. Since the end of Reconstruction, the federal government had stood by while the states gutted the Constitution's ostensible guarantees of equal rights for African Americans; now Washington joined the evisceration.

Other issues bled the country metaphorically. Decades of preaching, praying, keg smashing, and still wrecking culminated in the 1919 ratification of the Eighteenth Amendment, which prohibited the production and distribution of intoxicating beverages. The drys hadn't won over the wets, and it wasn't even clear they outnumbered them. But because the wets were concentrated in the cities, which were underrepresented in the politics of ratification (as in state and national politics generally), the drys dictated policy. The Eighteenth Amendment split the country not merely in terms of taste in beverages but also along lines of class and wealth. The amendment said nothing about possession of alcohol or its personal consumption; those persons rich enough to stock wine cellars and liquor closets ahead of January 16, 1920, the day on which the Volstead Act, the enforcing statute, took effect, could tipple to their gullets' content.

Another amendment promised, or threatened, to be no less revolutionary. For three-quarters of a century—or about as long as Susan B. Anthony lived—feminists had agitated for the vote for women. Their efforts finally paid off during the Progressive era, in part because the progressives assumed that old-stock middle-class—and presumptively progressive-minded—women would vote in larger numbers than their ethnic working-class sisters. But until the experiment actually took place—that is, before the federal elections of 1920, the first to which the Nineteenth Amendment applied—no one could say for sure. The only certain thing was that for every statistical person (not always a woman) convinced that female voting was a boon to democracy, there was some substantial fraction of another person (not always a man) who remained skeptical, if not flatly opposed. The professional pols, those who prided themselves on heeding experience rather than theory, were at a particular loss, as their experience encompassed nothing quite like this radical expansion of the electorate.

Beyond the realm of constitutionalism were persons and groups who defined radicalism rather differently. The Russian revolution, which had proceeded from its moderate first stage of early 1917 to the Bolshevik triumph of the following autumn, had invigorated socialists, communists, syndicalists, anarchists, and nihilists around the world. Not many of any of these groups but the socialists inhabited the United States, yet the specter of communism frightened American officials and voters—the former anticipating a favorable response from the latter—into undertaking a campaign of suppression of radical thought and practice. The wartime Espionage and Sedition Acts remained in force after the armistice, and Wilson's Justice Department, under the leadership of Attorney General A. Mitchell Palmer, launched a series of raids on leftist organizations during the winter of 1919–20. The Palmer raids and the ensuing "red scare" turned up a modest number of actual communists, a larger number of sympathizers, and an undetermined collection of hapless drop-ins who suffered from bad timing in being present when the G-men swooped through. Thousands were jailed; hundreds of immigrants were deported. The Palmer raids encouraged private vigilante action against labor organizers, particularly the "Wobblies" of the Industrial Workers of the World, some of whom suffered gruesome treatment at the hands of self-appointed defenders of American security and respectability.

The threat of domestic revolution was largely a figment of fevered imaginations or, in some cases, cynical political calculation. But it wasn't woven of utterly whole cloth. Police intercepted dozens of mail bombs addressed to prominent capitalists and public officials; explosive devices they didn't detect blew the front off Attorney General Palmer's Washington home and killed dozens and wounded hundreds in the heart of Wall Street.

The Palmer house bombing might have injured, or even killed, Franklin and Eleanor Roosevelt had their luck been a little worse. After outgrowing Anna Cowles's N Street house, the Roosevelt family had moved to R Street, across from the attorney general's residence. On the night of the bombing Franklin and Eleanor had just walked past the Palmer house, returning from a dinner engagement, when the bomb detonated. "I went over to the Attorney General's immediately after the explosion," Roosevelt explained to the police, "and was very much gratified to find that no one had been injured despite the terrific wreckage of the front of the house." Rubble was strewn all along the street; among the debris that landed on the Roosevelt doorstep was a body fragment, evidently from the bomber.

❖   ❖   ❖

WHEN THE POLITICAL parties gathered in the summer of 1920 to choose their nominees for president, the angry, fearful mood of the country permeated both conventions. The Republicans, deprived of Theodore Roosevelt, deadlocked between General Leonard Wood and Illinois governor Frank Lowden before settling—in what became the proverbial smoke-filled room of Chicago's Blackstone Hotel—on a handsome nonentity, first-term senator Warren G. Harding of Ohio. Shrewd minds among the Republicans questioned the Harding nomination, pointing out that no sitting senator had ever won the White House. Shrewder minds said not to worry. No one in America knew who Harding was, let alone that he sat in the Senate. If a controversial record of legislation was the issue, Harding posed little problem, as he had missed two-thirds of the roll call votes during his five years in office.

The Democrats, meeting in San Francisco, had a more difficult time choosing a candidate. To begin with, they were Democrats, which meant they—still—awkwardly straddled the gap between the multiethnic (and increasingly multiracial) cities of the North and the fiercely segregationist white South. And they—still—labored under the two-thirds rule, which dictated marathon conventions and nominees notable chiefly for being the last men standing. Finally, their titular leader, Woodrow Wilson, who might have provided direction to the delegates, was confined to his sickroom, shrouded in silence. The president was said to nurse delusions of a third term; besides demonstrating how far gone he truly was, this report prevented prospective successors from mounting vigorous campaigns. Former Treasury secretary William McAdoo cast himself as the heir to Wilson, but his failure to win Wilson's endorsement—despite being the president's kin—undercut his claim. Attorney General Palmer hoped his stern treatment of subversives would work in his favor; it did among rural conservatives but left liberals cold and labor hostile.

As the front-runners failed to reach the two-thirds elevation of the nomination mountain, party leaders looked for a compromise candidate. James M. Cox had the merits of being a governor, which showed off executive ability better than holding a cabinet post or a Senate seat; of being from Ohio, which grew presidents the way Iowa grew corn; of being a wet, which attracted city dwellers; and of not being associated with Wilson, which appealed to an increasing portion of the party as time passed.

Franklin Roosevelt had little to do with Cox's emergence as the convention favorite. Roosevelt attended the convention as a New York delegate but one whose reputation by now largely transcended New York state politics. This was a mixed blessing. Since his failed attempt to win the Democratic nomination for Senate in 1914, Roosevelt had considered making other races: for New York governor in 1918 and for governor or senator in 1920. But one thing and then another kept him out, not least the lack of a groundswell beneath him. His single significant accomplishment of the period in New York politics was a truce with Tammany Hall. In the spirit of wartime unity, Roosevelt addressed the Society of Tammany's annual Independence Day celebration in July 1917. The appearance raised eyebrows, as the *New York Times* observed in reminding readers that Roosevelt, "although a Democrat, has been unsparing in his denunciation of Tammany." Who proposed the truce is unclear. Roosevelt intimated that Tammany came to him, although he hardly gloated. The *Times* reported that Roosevelt got a laugh "by remarking that the member of Tammany who invited him declared that if Tammany could stand it to have him, he could stand it to come." He proceeded to give an innocuously patriotic speech, lauding the war effort and summoning all Democrats to pull together.

The good feeling persisted during the following years. Roosevelt endorsed Tammany's Al Smith for governor in 1918 and supported Smith after he carried the election. At San Francisco in 1920 he associated conspicuously with Boss Murphy, and after Tammany's Bourke Cochran proposed Smith for president as New York's favorite son, Roosevelt leaped up and gave a rousing seconding speech.

The purpose of the New Yorkers' San Francisco performance—as all interested parties appreciated—was less to promote Smith than to boost Roosevelt. Smith's national prospects in 1920 were nil, but Roosevelt's were realistic. Some loose talkers had pushed Roosevelt for president; he dismissed the suggestion as absurd—even as he milked it for publicity. But he didn't dismiss pre-convention rumors that he might be considered for vice president. A Roosevelt nomination for number two made real sense. The kind of gray personage the party might well settle on for president would definitely benefit from the sparkle and dash the comparatively young, undeniably attractive Roosevelt would bring to a national campaign. And the further the presidential nominee stood from Wilson, the more the ticket would need a Wilsonian in the second slot for balance. Democratic progressivism, like the Democratic president, might be ailing, but it wasn't dead. If the party didn't wish for its progressives to sulk on the sidelines, it needed to give them reason to turn out. Roosevelt might be just that reason.

Things transpired in San Francisco according to the New York script. Roosevelt's speech for Smith explicitly asserted the unity of New York Democrats behind the governor but implicitly promised that a New Yorker anywhere on the ticket would produce a New York majority for the Democrats in November. As Cox crept past McAdoo in the balloting for president, the availability of Roosevelt as a balancer quelled the complaints of the party's progressives. Cox finally prevailed at the forty-fourth ballot and promptly let out that Roosevelt would be quite acceptable as a running mate. In those days the parties had more autonomy in choosing vice presidential candidates than they would later, but a good word from the presidential nominee never hurt. The party approved Roosevelt by acclamation.

❖   ❖   ❖

THEODORE ROOSEVELT HAD been forty-one upon receiving the Republican nomination for vice president in 1900. Franklin Roosevelt was thirty-eight when the Democrats did him the comparable honor in 1920. Yet if Franklin was ahead of Uncle Ted's pace in one respect, he was behind him in others. He hadn't become a military hero. Nor had he been elected governor of New York. Perhaps most significantly, where the McKinley-Roosevelt ticket of 1900 had a very good chance of winning—and in fact won quite easily—the Cox-Roosevelt ticket of 1920 had no chance at all.

Roosevelt wasn't the one to admit it. On the contrary, he threw himself whole-heartedly into the campaign. His apparent enthusiasm benefited from the absence of scientific polling of voters, which wouldn't arrive until the mid-1930s. Candidates and their managers sounded out editors around the country, sampled incoming correspondence, and consulted tea leaves and entrails to divine how their tickets were faring. Wishful thinking often filled the large gaps in the intelligence, so that candidates could convince themselves right up to the moment of an electoral deluge that their prospects were sunny.

Roosevelt probably didn't believe that he and Cox could win, but he behaved as though he did. His acceptance speech—delivered, according to custom, not at the convention but weeks later, at his home—identified him as a root-and-branch Wilsonian. Some question initially surrounded the stance of the Cox ticket regarding the League of Nations, given the controversy the League had elicited and the defeat it had suffered. Cox and Roosevelt met with Wilson, to receive the president's blessing and affirm their Democratic solidarity. "As we came in sight of the portico, we saw the President in a wheel chair, his left shoulder covered with a shawl which concealed his left arm, which was paralyzed," Roosevelt recounted later. "The Governor"—Cox—"said to me, 'He is a very sick man.' " Cox approached Wilson and offered his hand. Wilson wearily raised his eyes and spoke in a low, weak voice. "Thank you for coming," he said. "I am very glad you came." Roosevelt was startled by Wilson's feebleness; Cox was moved to tears. After some small talk, Cox told Wilson, "Mr. President, we are going to be a million per cent with you and your Administration, and that means the League of Nations." Wilson, whose gaze had fallen, looked up again. "I am very grateful," he said, almost inaudibly. "I am very grateful." Cox and Roosevelt passed through the president's office on the way out. Cox called for a piece of paper and sat down at a writing table. "There he wrote the statement that committed us to making the League the paramount issue of the campaign," Roosevelt remembered. "It was one of the most impressive scenes I have ever witnessed."

Roosevelt perhaps embellished the interview with Wilson in the recounting, but the upshot of the session—that he and Cox would fight their campaign on the League of Nations—was true enough. In his speech accepting the vice presidential nomination, Roosevelt embraced a Wilsonian, internationalist view of America's global role. "Modern civilization has become so complex and the lives of civilized men so interwoven with the lives of other men in other countries as to make it impossible to be in this world and not of it," he declared. The war had stirred noble emotions in Americans; these must not be allowed to expire without issue. "To the cry of the French at Verdun: 'They shall not pass'; to the cheer of our men in the Argonne: 'We shall go through'; we must add this: 'It shall not occur again.' " Critics alleged that the League was airy and impractical. Roosevelt didn't deny that the League was inspired by idealism, but he rejected most vehemently that it was impractical. "The League of Nations is a practical solution of a practical situation." It was not perfect, but neither had the Constitution of 1787 been perfect. The League had been assailed as anti-national, which was taken to mean that it was anti-American. "It is not anti-national. It is anti-war." For Americans to reject the League would be to turn their backs on their own values. They must not do so. "This is our hour of test. . . . We must go forward or flounder."

❖ ❖ ❖

As Roosevelt spoke from the Hyde Park porch, Eleanor and Sara sat close by, listening. Sara had silently suffered all morning as the throngs of news reporters, party functionaries, well-wishers, and curious passersby trampled her lawn, bruised her flowers, and generally did violence to the decorum that, at her insistence, had always characterized her home. If not for her pride in Franklin and her appreciation that the country was finally recognizing his remarkable talents, she would have called the sheriff and had them all removed.

Eleanor's concerns were less for propriety and the property and more for the privacy of herself and her family. Franklin had been a public figure for a decade, but the attention he received as state senator and then assistant navy secretary was nothing like this. He was suddenly a national figure—which meant that she was, too, whether she liked it or not. He hadn't asked her whether he ought to accept the nomination; her first news on the subject was a telegram to Campobello from Josephus Daniels in San Francisco: "It would have done your heart good to have seen the spontaneous and enthusiastic tribute paid when Franklin was nominated unanimously for vice president today. Accept my congratulations."

Eleanor wasn't sure congratulations were in order. "I was glad for my husband," she wrote later. "But it never occurred to me to be much excited." She understood that Franklin's career came first and that her job was to adjust to it. She accepted this arrangement, almost fatalistically. "I carried on the children's lives and my own as calmly as could be, and while I was always a part of the public aspect of our lives, still I felt detached and objective, as though I were looking at someone else's life."

The campaign required more of Eleanor than any of Franklin's public endeavors thus far. He embarked in mid-August on a monthlong train tour across the country, during which he spoke several times a day to audiences large and small, pre-organized and spontaneous. He reiterated the necessity of American membership in the League of Nations; on the domestic side he promised to extend the progressive reforms of the Wilson administration.

Candidates' wives didn't always accompany their husbands on political tours. Some simply refused; others pleaded responsibilities at home. But Eleanor's sense of duty—and perhaps her lingering suspicions of her husband's fidelity—prompted her to join him. It was hard service and largely thankless. She was the sole woman in the entourage, and the men didn't know what to make of her. Politics had been and essentially remained a male sport; the candidates, their assistants, and the reporters who covered them made rolling smokers and running card games out of the whistle-stop tours. Franklin acted much more like one of the boys than like her husband. "He had speeches to write, letters to answer, and policies to discuss," she said. "In the evenings, after they got back to the train, all the men sat together in the end of the car and discussed the experiences of the day from their various points of view." The smoking and drinking and especially the gambling offended Eleanor. "I was still a Puritan . . . and was at times very much annoyed with my husband."

Franklin was too busy to notice her annoyance, or perhaps he simply didn't care enough to address it. But Louis Howe noticed and cared. The vice presidential nomination had given Roosevelt the excuse he needed to quit his Navy Department post; Howe, who required a regular income, stayed on. Yet he took a leave of absence for the campaign, and he assigned himself the task of educating Eleanor in the nuances of national politics. She was dubious and distant at first, not least because she realized that Howe and Franklin shared a bond she and Franklin didn't. "I resented this intimacy," she conceded later. She continued to think Howe slovenly and uncouth. "He not only neglected his clothes, but gave the impression at times that cleanliness was not of particular interest to him."

But neither her resentment nor her distaste put Howe off. He artfully drew her into the campaign by showing her drafts of speeches and soliciting her reactions. "I was flattered, and before long I found myself discussing a wide range of subjects. I began to be able to understand some of our newspaper brethren and to look upon them as friends instead of enemies." She came to realize that they were as bored by the repetitiveness of the campaign as she was. The ice melted, and they started making faces at her from the back of the crowds, hoping to get her to giggle during some especially solemn part of one of her husband's speeches. When she would accompany Franklin through crowds and women would exclaim over his good looks, the boys from the campaign car—not realizing how close to the bone they were cutting—would teasingly ask if she was jealous.

She never became an enthusiast campaigner for her husband. "I still think campaign trips by anyone except the presidential candidates themselves are of little value," she wrote years later. But she began to view politics itself as more interesting than she had thought, and in that regard came to view her husband in a different light than before.

❖   ❖   ❖

SOME VOTERS REASSESSED Roosevelt, too, but they weren't nearly numerous enough to overcome the Democrats' deficiencies that season. The ticket of Cox and Roosevelt started the campaign far behind that of Harding and Calvin Coolidge, and if the Democrats closed the gap the improvement wasn't noticeable. The election results told the grimmest tale in the history of the Democratic party. Harding and Coolidge trounced Cox and Roosevelt by 16 million to 9 million in the popular balloting and 404 to 127 in the electoral vote. The congressional elections completed the massacre, with the Republicans establishing a dominance in both houses they hadn't enjoyed since Reconstruction.

James Cox never recovered from the debacle; his campaign with Roosevelt was his last. But the crack-up scarcely touched Roosevelt. American voters don't hold vice presidential candidates accountable for the failure of their tickets; blame rises to the top. Positively, the campaign gave Roosevelt a national platform and allowed him to find his national voice. It furnished voters the opportunity to size him up and imagine him as president. On this scale he compared favorably with the man who won. If voters could envision Warren Harding as president, they could certainly envision Franklin Roosevelt.

Besides, had Cox won, Roosevelt would have receded into the nether world still occupied by vice presidents in the days before they became their party's presumptive next nominees. (A second lightning strike on behalf of a Vice President Roosevelt appeared improbable. Cox was hale—he lived to be eighty-seven—and he wasn't the type to attract assassins.) With Cox's defeat, Roosevelt emerged as one of his party's leading men.

All that was required was patience. Of this Roosevelt possessed enough. A few weeks after the election he wrote to Stephen Early, a reporter who had joined the campaign team as Roosevelt's advance publicist. "I want to have a talk with you about the situation in general," Roosevelt said. The immediate future was dark, but things would turn around. "Thank the Lord we are both comparatively youthful."

13.

Roosevelt's remanding to the private sector was a personal shock, even though by the time it occurred it was no surprise. Having forsaken the law for politics a decade earlier, on account of the tedium of the counselor's craft, he hardly thrilled to return to the world of wills, contracts, and lawsuits. He softened the blow by finagling a second job, beyond his law partnership with Grenville Emmet and Langdon Marvin, as the New York representative of the Fidelity & Deposit Company, a Baltimore-based seller of surety bonds. Roosevelt knew little about surety bonds except that they guaranteed contracts, but he knew something about sailing, which appealed to the Fidelity & Deposit chairman, Van Lear Black, who hired him, and he knew much about government, which was the principal reason Black and the Fidelity board made him a vice president and agreed to pay him $25,000 a year for part-time work. Roosevelt's responsibilities were vague, but Black and the board reckoned that Roosevelt's Washington connections would serve the company well, one way or another.

In January 1921 Black and Fidelity threw a dinner for their new colleague at Delmonico's; among the guests were some of the most powerful men of American industry, finance, and government: Edward Stettinius of United States Steel, Owen D. Young of General Electric, Daniel Willard of the Baltimore & Ohio Railroad, William P. G. Harding of the Federal Reserve, Judge Augustus N. Hand of the U.S. District Court for New York, Van Lear Black himself. Fed chairman Harding gave the keynote address of the evening, touring the horizon of international finance and urging his listeners to be optimistic but responsible in pursuing their opportunities as America and the world completed the conversion from war to peace. Roosevelt spoke briefly, thanking Black and Fidelity for hosting the dinner, expressing gratitude to the guests for coming, and relating anecdotes of government in Washington. By evening's end, Roosevelt appeared positioned to become a full-fledged member of the postwar capitalist class in America, a post-progressive generation that recognized that business and government need not be adversaries, as often in the past, but could be partners, to the benefit of all concerned. "Never have I imagined a more delightful or a more delicious dinner," he wrote Black afterward.

But residual obligations—leftovers from the Navy Department—delayed Roosevelt's transition to his new career. The Republican sweep in the 1920 elections had disposed and empowered the GOP to dredge up muck to throw against the Democrats, and during the spring and summer of 1921 a special subcommittee of the Senate naval affairs committee probed allegations of misbehavior among enlisted men and navy investigators at a Newport training facility. The charges were stale—two years old—but sordidly spectacular. Their essence was that the navy had sent agents among the Newport trainees to investigate immoral and illegal behavior, which in that time and place included homosexual activity. The agents were said to have entrapped young men by soliciting sodomy. The charges may or may not have been true; the line between legitimate investigation and illegitimate entrapment, especially in consensual activities, has always been difficult to draw and enforce. But needless to say, suggestions that innocent boys might have been lured into acts that most of American society considered unspeakable, by agents of the government no less, was profoundly disturbing—and politically explosive.

For Roosevelt, the more personally germane issue was whether, assuming the entrapment had occurred, he had authorized it. The majority report of the Senate subcommittee asserted that he did. The report, a massive work of fifteen volumes and six thousand pages, blindsided Roosevelt, who thought he had received a promise from the subcommittee to let him review its findings before they were made public. But he learned, only just before the fact, that the report was about to be released. He interrupted the family's summer vacation at Campobello to race to Washington to try to forestall the release. Although the Republicans on the subcommittee insisted on going ahead, they allowed him a few hours to examine the report before the press got copies, so that while he wasn't able to influence either the conclusions of the report or the language in which they were couched, he did manage to release his own independent rebuttal, which appeared in the same news stories as the report itself.

The report condemned Roosevelt in the strongest language possible—language, in fact, that was too strong for the newspaper accounts. "Lay Navy Scandal to F. D. Roosevelt," the main headline of the *New York Times* said of the subcommittee's conclusions. "Details Are Unprintable." Yet the essence of the allegations was clear enough. Roosevelt must have known of the entrapment and authorized it, the report said; or if he didn't know, he was "most derelict in the performance of his duty." The whole affair was "deplorable, disgraceful, and unnatural," not to mention "absolutely indefensible and to be most severely condemned."

Roosevelt rejected the report in language equally categorical. He alleged a "clear breach of faith" on the part of the Republican majority in not letting him answer the charges before they were made public. He accused the Republicans of a "premeditated and unfair purpose of seeking what they mistakenly believe to be a partisan political advantage." He denied knowing anything about the details of the Newport investigation, ridiculing the very notion that while overseeing the affairs of a navy of hundreds of ships and hundreds of thousands of men, he had the time to supervise a small office of a dozen employees. The Republicans were the ones who had engaged in shameful behavior. "I accuse them of deliberate falsification of evidence, of perversion of facts, of misstatements of the record, and of a deliberate attempt to deceive." The American people knew better than to fall for such partisan slander. "This business of using the Navy as a football of politics is going to stop. People everywhere are tired of partisan discussion of dead history."

❖   ❖   ❖

MAYBE THEY WERE. Roosevelt's reputation didn't appear to have been damaged by the report, which must have seemed to most honest observers as a late, low blow. But the events surrounding its release—his rush to Washington in the heat of midsummer, his frantic reading of the report and his drafting of the rebuttal, the worry the whole affair caused him—taxed Roosevelt's constitution more than he realized. "I thought he looked quite tired when he left," his Washington secretary, Marguerite LeHand—called Missy—wrote Eleanor following her boss's departure back north. Yet Roosevelt was reluctant to acknowledge fatigue, at least when politics or public duty called, and en route to Campobello he stopped at a Boy Scout camp on the Hudson. The Boy Scout Foundation of Greater New York was one of his many worthy causes, and he was currently president. Reporters covered the camp outing, which involved much waving of flags, marching, and reaffirming of the mission of the scouts. Photographers made a visual record for the papers and for posterity. One picture showed Roosevelt leading a procession; his eyes drooped a bit but his posture, as always, was athletically straight and tall.

Roosevelt generally reasoned, often rightly, that the fatigue he most often suffered was of the mental and psychological kind. His favored cure was fatigue of the physical kind, in particular the weariness of body that comes from sustained exertion of muscle and bone and that pushes aside the cares of office. He administered the cure to himself on his return to Campobello in early August 1921. Arriving aboard the yacht of Van Lear Black, which he piloted through the final tricky passage of the Bay of Fundy, he took Black fishing the next day; for hours he baited hooks, rigged tackle, identified the gathering grounds of the wily cod, and played the tireless host to his new employer. At one point he unusually lost his footing and slipped from the boat into the bay. "I'd never felt anything so cold as that water," he recalled later. "I hardly went under, hardly wet my head, because I still had hold of the side. . . . But the water was so cold it seemed paralyzing." This sensation was odd, given that Roosevelt had been in that same water innumerable times before. He chalked it up to the heat of the August sun and of the boat's engine, which had caused him to sweat profusely. He gave it little more thought.

A few days later he took Eleanor and the children sailing aboard the *Vireo*, the craft he had purchased to succeed his war donation, the *Half Moon II*. Just as his father had taught him to sail, so now he showed his own sons the ropes. They seemed apt pupils, and the outing went well. On the home leg someone spotted smoke over an uninhabited island in the bay. Forest fires were common enough in the area that neighborhood protocol demanded that whoever noticed one should try to put it out. The Roosevelts landed on the island and attacked the blaze with fir boughs Roosevelt cut for the purpose. The work was hot and strenuous and lasted hours; by the time the flames had been beaten into submission, father and family were soaked with sweat, begrimed with dust and soot, and exhausted from head to toe. They reembarked from the island and reached home around four. Roosevelt thought a swim would be a cleansing, bracing end to the day. The children liked a pond on the other side of Campobello Island, not least because its water was several degrees warmer than that of the bay. Eleanor excused herself, but Franklin led the young ones at a jog across the island. The lake washed them and refreshed the kids, but it didn't give Roosevelt the lift he'd been expecting. And so he plunged into the bay, hoping its fifty-degree water would have its usual tonic effect. This did help, and though he still felt a little sluggish on emerging, he headed the troops on a quick march back to the house.

By the time they arrived a more profound weariness was setting in. Too spent to change out of his swimming suit, Roosevelt sat down to read the mail.

He eventually felt a chill and, with considerable effort, made his way upstairs to bed. He assumed he was catching cold and crawled under the covers to warm up and rest. He told Eleanor to serve the children dinner without him.

His symptoms the next day suggested something besides a cold. He had a fever and found it difficult to move his left leg. He initially attributed the leg problem to a strain or slight tear of a muscle, and he managed to hobble about well enough to shave. But then his right leg began balking, too, and he had to return to bed.

Eleanor sent for Dr. E. H. Bennett of nearby Lubec. Bennett had known the family for years and had ministered to their minor bumps, bruises, and infections with the calming touch of the small-town general practitioner. He crossed over to Campobello, examined Roosevelt, and pronounced the illness a cold. The patient should stay in bed and let time work its healing.

Eleanor accepted the advice with ambivalence. She had seen Franklin with colds, and they weren't anything like this. Yet Bennett was the doctor, and he had treated many more colds than she had observed. All the same, she remained by Franklin's side while the children went off on a camping trip previously planned for the whole family.

She grew more worried almost at once. Franklin's symptoms steadily worsened. His back ached badly; his legs became numb and then completely immobile; the paralysis began to creep up his torso. Even his arms and hands started to go limp. He discovered he couldn't hold a pen to write.

Bennett belatedly recognized his misdiagnosis and the need to consult an expert. Fortunately August was a good month to fall sick on the Maine coast, as much of the northeastern medical establishment vacationed there. Louis Howe had brought his family to Campobello to join the Roosevelt holiday; now he escorted Bennett back to the doctor's mainland office, and the two began calling around for a specialist. They turned up William W. Keen, an elderly Philadelphia surgeon vacationing at Bar Harbor, who agreed to come over and examine Roosevelt. Howe knew that Keen had been part of a team of surgeons that secretly removed a tumor from the mouth of Grover Cleveland during the summer of 1893. The secrecy had been important, in that Congress was locked in a fight over the nation's money supply, with advocates of a gold standard battling proponents of silver. Cleveland preferred gold, but his vice president, Adlai Stevenson, liked silver, and the merest hint of weakness on the gold side—such as cancer in the president—might precipitate a financial panic. A Philadelphia paper got wind of the story within weeks, yet the White House denied it, and the doctors, including Keen, maintained their silence for decades. Howe was already worrying about the career ramifications for Roosevelt of a serious illness, and he took comfort in Keen's ability to keep a secret.

Keen concluded that the patient's most serious symptoms—the back pain and paralysis—resulted from a blood clot pressing upon the spinal cord. The fever was the consequence of an unrelated infection that would diminish on its own. Meanwhile Howe, Eleanor, and anyone else who could be mustered into service ought to massage Roosevelt's legs, to enhance the blood circulation there and maintain muscle tone until the clot dissolved.

Accordingly Roosevelt's wife and his political man Friday took turns kneading his legs. The procedure was painful, for although the legs had lost their ability to move, they had regained their sense of touch, which in fact had grown more acute. But Roosevelt gritted his teeth and told Eleanor and Howe to continue.

The therapy yielded no positive result. The paralysis grew worse. Roosevelt lost control of his bladder and bowels, requiring Eleanor and Howe to treat him like an invalid. His fever intensified, and so did the pain. By the end of the fifth day since the onset of the symptoms, he was almost delirious.

But this was the worst. The next day his fever diminished and the pain began to dull, from a knifelike stabbing to a chronic ache. Roosevelt's mind gradually cleared, and he and the others focused on what seemed a slight improvement in his muscle control. "We thought yesterday he moved his toes on one foot a little better," Eleanor wrote Franklin's half brother, Rosy.

Louis Howe knew from his own childhood illness the emotional dangers of false encouragement, and while Eleanor and Franklin seized on signs of recovery, he looked for evidence of continuing affliction. He wrote to Franklin's uncle Fred Delano for help enlisting medical opinion more expert and current than that of the bucolic Bennett and the octogenarian Keen. Delano consulted specialists in New York and Boston, who, on the basis of Roosevelt's reported symptoms, suspected infantile paralysis, as poliomyelitis was commonly called. They recommended Robert W. Lovett of Boston, the country's leading authority on polio. Lovett had an office in Newport, Rhode Island, and he agreed to travel north.

Lovett required only a brief examination of Roosevelt to determine that his illness was indeed polio. Lovett had seen far worse cases, and he knew that patients tended to improve as the inflammation that accompanied the first infection abated. A complete recovery for Roosevelt was not out of the question, he said. But the massages must stop, as they risked damage to the muscles and caused the patient needless pain. Warm baths would be helpful, not merely to soothe the pain but to facilitate muscle movement that would forestall atrophy. "He can do so much more under water with his legs," Lovett said. Yet Lovett had seen enough of polio to realize that pain and atrophy were only part of the problem. "There is likely to be mental depression," he warned.

❖   ❖   ❖

THE MEMBERS OF the Roosevelt household responded variously to Lovett's diagnosis. Eleanor thought first of the children. Not for nothing was the disease called infantile paralysis; it typically struck the young. This largely explained why Bennett and Keen missed the diagnosis; adult-onset polio was very rare. The rareness exacerbated Eleanor's alarm, for if the present strain was virulent enough to fell Franklin, she reasoned, the children must be even more vulnerable. Lovett reassured her. Though considerable uncertainty still surrounded polio's mode of transmission, he assumed that if the children were going to be exposed, they already had been and would by now have manifested symptoms.

Lovett's words reassured Eleanor, though for weeks she watched the children covertly for any sign of fever, any indication of muscle weakness. By the end of that time she had discovered a new role for herself with respect to her husband. From the start of their relationship, she had often felt herself the needier of the two. She was much less self-confident than Franklin; she was much more dependent on his love and esteem than he was on hers. Over several years she had slowly convinced herself of the reality of his love and had come to accept herself as worthy of it—only to have her conviction and self-perception shattered by the discovery of his affair with Lucy Mercer. She and Franklin stayed together for the children and for Franklin's future, but she had never regained the feeling that she meant anything essential to him. She had expected that she never would.

But now, suddenly, he needed her, in a very fundamental way. He needed her to thread the catheter into his urethra and to do so with care and skill, to avoid pain and prevent an infection of the kind that often shortened the lives of bedridden patients. He needed her to sponge-bathe him, to dress him, to lift him from his bed to his wheelchair, to manage his finances, to do the hundred things he realized, day by day, that he could no longer do. She discovered within herself resources she hadn't known she possessed. She became an able nurse, adept with catheters, thermometers, and several forms of physical therapy. She sharpened her management skills, taking over direction of the family economy. She shouldered much of his part of the parenting burden, becoming half a father in addition to remaining a full mother.

In all of her new responsibilities she found a purpose she hadn't known before. Her husband needed her, really needed her. Did he *love* her? That was a harder question. Did *she* love *him*? Equally difficult. But he needed her, and she liked the feeling. It was a beginning—or, more precisely, a new beginning.

❖ ❖ ❖

*L*OUIS HOWE'S RESPONSE to Roosevelt's illness was similar, in certain respects, to Eleanor's. Howe hadn't known quite what to do with himself as Roosevelt segued from public office to the private sector. Almost a decade earlier Howe had hitched his wagon to Roosevelt's star, and then proceeded to promote that star in every way possible. He still intended that Roosevelt should be president someday, and he be Roosevelt's chief adviser. But the 1920 election delayed the unfolding of Howe's design, forcing Roosevelt into the private sector and Howe himself to find new work. The Navy Department let him remain through the transition to the Harding administration, then thanked him for his eight years' service and sent him on his way. Roosevelt offered to bring him to Fidelity & Deposit, as his assistant. Howe accepted the offer with reservations, being unfamiliar with the bonding business and uncertain where his relationship with Roosevelt was headed.

Roosevelt's illness changed everything. From the moment Howe heard the diagnosis of polio, he recognized his new calling, as the agent of Roosevelt's recovery. Physical recovery would be welcome, of course, but Howe was most concerned with Roosevelt's political recovery. A politician didn't need to walk; he needed to think—and plan and coax and cajole and threaten. He didn't need legs; he needed only a sound head. Perhaps, in retrospect, Howe now let himself imagine that Roosevelt's very athleticism had served him poorly as a politician, making him appear a lightweight beside those men who devoted themselves entirely to the governing arts. Perhaps Howe perceived the polio as leveling the ground between himself and Roosevelt. Howe's small stature and compromised health had always left him at a physical disadvantage to Roosevelt; Howe now stood taller than Roosevelt and enjoyed the edge in mobility. Moreover, Howe could command Roosevelt's attention as never previously; henceforth when they sat down to plot out Roosevelt's future, Howe could be sure the boss wouldn't bounce away for a sail or a round of golf.

And at some level Howe must have appreciated that Roosevelt's disability guaranteed his—Howe's—indispensability. Roosevelt had first leaned heavily on Howe during his reelection campaign of 1912, when typhoid fever had prostrated him and he had no one else to turn to. Howe had proved his mettle sufficiently for Roosevelt to take him to Washington and the Navy Department. But as Roosevelt's career advanced, he attracted other men prepared to devote themselves to his future, and by the time he joined the national ticket in 1920 he had his pick of political suitors. It certainly occurred to Howe that he might be jilted—if gently, as Roosevelt was a gentleman. The polio fairly precluded such a separation. The summer suitors would find other prospects; Roosevelt would have to rely on Howe, just as in 1912. Only this time the reliance would be long-term, perhaps permanent.

Howe never articulated this thinking, at least not in any form that survived. Perhaps he never laid it out completely in his own mind. He certainly didn't explain to Eleanor or Franklin what he was up to. He simply made himself useful—finding and transporting doctors, keeping reporters and other nosy people at bay, reassuring Eleanor and Roosevelt himself. "Thank heavens," Eleanor wrote of Howe amid the worst of Franklin's physical crisis. "He has been the greatest help."

❖   ❖   ❖

SARA ROOSEVELT WAS nearing the end of her annual European vacation when Franklin became ill. Eleanor didn't inform her of her son's condition. "I have decided to say nothing," she told Rosy. "No letter can reach her now, and it would simply mean worry all the way home." Eleanor sincerely wished to spare Sara helpless fretting, but she probably had an additional motive. Eleanor knew her mother-in-law well enough to realize that she would attempt to assume charge of Franklin's recuperation. Eleanor wouldn't be able to resist Sara's influence entirely, if only from financial considerations. Franklin would be unable to work for some extended period, and already it was apparent that his medical care would be costly. Not long after William Keen left Campobello, the eminent doctor sent his bill "for $600!," as Eleanor wrote in amazement. But Eleanor, who had been fighting Sara over Franklin ever since the young lovers first told her of their relationship, had no intention of surrendering her husband at this late date. Maybe she had learned it from Louis Howe, perhaps she intuited it on her own, but Eleanor understood that knowledge is the prerequisite to power, and she determined to maintain control of knowledge of Franklin's condition as long as she could.

Of course Sara had to be informed eventually. Her ship was scheduled to arrive in New York at the end of August; a few days before it docked Eleanor wrote: "Dearest Mama, . . . Franklin has been quite ill and so can't go down to meet you on Tuesday." She offered nothing more in explanation and sent the note to Rosy, who greeted his stepmother's boat in Franklin's stead and delivered Eleanor's message.

The very lack of details in Eleanor's message must have tipped Sara to the seriousness of her son's condition; her sensitivity on anything touching Franklin was exquisite. Whatever she guessed, Rosy and Fred Delano, who also met the boat, supplied the facts as soon as it docked. Sara naturally felt terribly for Franklin—for his present and future pain, for his loss of mobility, for the blow to self-esteem of one whose identity had been closely connected to his physicality. But much as for Eleanor and Louis Howe, the polio gave Sara cause to lay a new claim on Franklin. She had never shared her son gracefully—not with Eleanor, not with the world at large. Her fondest hope had been for him to ease into the role his father had vacated, as the seigneur of Springwood. He had chosen politics instead. Now Sara assumed that politics was out of the question—or at least she hoped it would be. Franklin would retire to Hyde Park; what else could he do? "He is a cripple," one family friend wrote to another. "Will he ever be anything else?" Sara didn't have to hear such sentiments to know how common they were; she felt them herself. Perhaps she congratulated herself on maintaining control of the family money. Since he couldn't work, he would have no choice but to honor her wishes and come home.

❖   ❖   ❖

*T*HE OBJECT OF the unspoken competition had little thought at first for the plans or feelings of Eleanor, Sara, and Howe. Dr. Lovett had been right; depression was a real threat. Franklin Roosevelt had experienced occasional disappointment, as at his snub by the Porcellians at Harvard, and sadness, upon the death of his father and the first Franklin Jr. But he had never been really unhappy, a fact that reflected both his innate temperament and his life circumstances. Roosevelt's temperament tilted toward the sunny side of any street, and his circumstances had been such as to shield him from most of what other people typically became unhappy about. Life had been very good to Franklin Roosevelt, and he knew it.

But suddenly life wasn't so good. As his fever diminished and his head cleared, and as he learned the cause of his symptoms, he came to realize that paraplegia would be his lot for some considerable time, perhaps forever. His days of effortless physical grace had been cut short by an unlikely twist of evil luck. For the children's sake he tried to put up a brave front, but his anger, fear, and frustration sometimes burst through. He exploded without warning during one visit by Bennett, startling Eleanor and taking even the doctor aback. For days and weeks he wondered what to make of himself, wondered whether life was worth living, whether all he had worked toward was suddenly and forever beyond his reach. The doctor's prescription simply made things worse. Almost never had Roosevelt felt himself the victim of inexorable fate; on those comparatively rare occasions when things went wrong in his life, his natural reaction was to fight back, to launch a counteroffensive. But Dr. Lovett, the polio expert, told him *not* to do anything. Aside from the warm baths, he must simply rest: no massage, no attempts to move about, nothing that fatigued him at all. A harsher sentence for an activist personality was difficult to imagine; no wonder he was frustrated and depressed.

Yet his moment of self-pity passed—at least as far as Roosevelt let others see. The mindset of the Victorian era in which Roosevelt grew up had its quirks and foibles, but one of its virtues was its employment of outward denial as a coping strategy. Males of Roosevelt's generation—and to some extent the females too—were expected to meet misfortune with a stiff upper lip and a sturdy smile, to deny that anything serious was wrong and to soldier forward. Doubtless for certain persons in particular circumstances this approach was counterproductive, but in many other cases it was a perfectly reasonable response to conditions beyond the ability of the sufferer to control. Fate was more capricious then, or so it seemed. Disease struck unexpectedly, often inexplicably, in that era of relative medical ignorance. Hurricanes, tornadoes, and blizzards ravaged unprepared populations in the days before scientific forecasting. Financial panics plunged nations into chaos at a time when neither economists nor policy makers understood how industrial economies really worked. When everyone was a victim at one point or another, no one won sympathy by wearing victimhood as a badge. Get over it, get on with life, might have been the motto of the era.

It became Roosevelt's modus operandi. It didn't keep him from thinking about what he had lost; it didn't prevent his cursing his luck when the pain in his legs left him lying awake at night. Never had his future been so darkly unknowable. Would he be a cripple for life? What would people think of him? Could he ever be intimate with a woman again? How could he run for office if he couldn't even walk?

As Fauntleroy

At the helm on the Bay of Fundy

With James Roosevelt

Harvard man

Newlyweds

Looking to the White House with
Josephus Daniels

At the Brooklyn
navy yard to lay the
keel of the *Arizona*

With Uncle Ted

For vice president, with James Cox

The family in 1920: Roosevelt, Sara, Eleanor; Elliott, Franklin Jr., John, Anna, James

*H*ydrotherapy

*W*ith Elliott and the giant fish in Florida

With Missy LeHand at Warm Springs

Madison Square Garden, 1924

When Al Smith
was an ally

With Howe and Farley at the Chicago convention, 1932

But when morning came he pushed back the demons of despair. The Roosevelts refused to be weak in public. The Delanos refused even more adamantly. By the time Sara reached his bedside, her son had mastered his emotions sufficiently to treat his illness almost as a lark. Dr. Bennett and Eleanor were in the room when Sara entered. "I am glad you are back, Mummy," he said with a smile. "I got up this party for you!" Sara afterward wrote to her sister of the "happy, cheerful attitude" Franklin maintained. During one examination by Bennett, Sara noted from outside the door of Franklin's room: "I can hear them all laughing."

❖   ❖   ❖

$\mathcal{R}$OOSEVELT'S ILLNESS extended his stay at Campobello much longer than he had expected, and by mid-September he was eager to get off the island and back to civilization. This was no easy matter. The isolation of Campobello had enabled Louis Howe to hold the press at a distance, but it also complicated Roosevelt's returning to New York without alerting the world to his condition. Walking or riding from the dock at Eastport to the train station was typically a public act, conducted in full view of whoever happened to be around. Because Roosevelt—still considered one of the most eligible Democrats in the country—had been out of sight for more than a month, the local stringers for the major papers mounted a stakeout as the summer season drew to a close.

Howe weighed various tricks for distracting the newsmen, before resorting to simple prevarication. He announced that Roosevelt's boat would be arriving at a certain hour and invited reporters to be present. Then he whisked Roosevelt—carried to and from the boat on a stretcher by several islanders well paid to keep their mouths shut—into the dock ahead of schedule and onto a private railcar before the reporters realized they had been fooled.

The ruse bought Howe time, but only a little. The reporters immediately realized that Roosevelt had something to hide, and the stakeout shifted down the line to New York. On September 16 the city's papers had the story. "F. D. Roosevelt Ill of Poliomyelitis," the front page of the *New York Times* declared. Yet Howe still managed to control the story and put it in the most favorable light. The regular Roosevelt family physician, George Draper, declared, on the basis of Howe's testimony and his own cursory examination of Roosevelt at the Presbyterian Hospital, that the patient was much improved. "I cannot say how long Mr. Roosevelt will be kept in the hospital," Draper told reporters. "But you can say definitely that he will not be crippled. No one need have any fear of permanent injury from this attack." Roosevelt himself—which was to say, Howe—declared through the hospital's superintendent that he had had a "comfortable trip" and was feeling "very well."

The news that one of the most prominent men in the country had contracted polio triggered an outbreak of concern in New York and elsewhere regarding the disease. Authorities immediately sought to put the Roosevelt case in perspective. The director of New York City's infectious disease bureau, Dr. Louis Harris, reported that the city had experienced 269 cases in the previous year, of which slightly less than one-fifth had been fatal. The cases were more numerous than in recent years, but not so much more, Harris hastened to explain, as to constitute an epidemic. Additionally, although the late summer and early fall—the current period—was the time when the incidence of polio peaked, it always declined with the onset of cool weather. Folk wisdom asserted that the countryside was safer than the city; Harris said this was not true. In fact, in a substantial fraction of the reported cases, the infection seemed to have occurred outside the city. Residents were advised to remain calm, conduct themselves sensibly, and avoid crowds. How this last bit of advice was to be followed in the nation's largest city, Harris declined to say.

❖   ❖   ❖

OTHER REACTIONS TO the news of Roosevelt's illness were more personal. Within days Roosevelt began receiving letters from polio victims relating their own stories, offering encouragement, and generally expressing solidarity with a famous man who shared, at least in this one respect, their fate. "Fellow Sufferer," wrote a Minneapolis woman. "Through the enclosed clipping"—a piece about Roosevelt—"I have just learned the pretty and truthful name of that which I have suffered for eleven years." (The news accounts popularized, in many locales for the first time, the label poliomyelitis in place of infantile paralysis.) This woman explained that she walked with a cane, although she allowed this was common enough for one of her age: "only 87½ years old."

Roosevelt was touched by the woman's sympathy and good humor. He thanked her for her kind thoughts and added that he hoped to be as lucky as she. "If I could feel assured that time could treat me so lightly as to leave me at eighty-seven and half years with all my vigor, powers, and only a cane required," he wrote, "I would consider that my future was very bright indeed."

Additional letters arrived from old friends and associates. Walter Camp

picked up on the positive tone of the press coverage. "This is just a line to assure you how glad all your old friends were to get reports that you are coming
along all right," Camp wrote Roosevelt. He recalled the exercise sessions during the war and said he hoped "to repeat the old days when Delano, McAdoo,
Davis, and you formed my 'Flying Squadron' and we 'double-quicked' in Potomac Park!"

Answering Camp required all the appearance of optimism Roosevelt could
summon. The mere mention of those days when he had been Camp's prize
physical specimen drove home yet again how much he had lost. And though
Roosevelt encouraged Howe and his doctors to portray his condition in the
most positive light, he knew they were stretching the truth shamelessly. Yet he
set his jaw, clamped the smile on his face, and dictated a reply—since his hands
remained too weak to manipulate a pen. He told Camp how well he remembered the sessions in Potomac Park. He added, "I can assure you that if I could
get up this afternoon and join with Messrs. McAdoo, Davis, and Delano in a
sprint for the record, I would consider it the greatest joy in the world. However, the doctors are most encouraging, and I have been given every reason to
expect that my somewhat rebellious legs will permit me to join in another
course of training sometime in the future."

❖   ❖   ❖

*D*ID HE BELIEVE IT? This was a critical question as his recovery began. To
display optimism to the world was one thing; to actually expect improvement
was something else. Patient histories showed that polio victims benefited from
physical therapy: from moving their legs under their own remaining power,
often in water; from having their legs moved by nurses, therapists, and anyone
else willing to lend a hand; and from walking as best they could on crutches,
braces, and supporting arms. The cause of their paraplegia was neurological—
damage to the nerves that initiated and controlled muscle movement—but
the consequences were muscular, as the leg muscles atrophied from lack of
use; circulatory, from the lack of assistance those muscles had supplied to the
heart in pumping blood about the body; and skeletal, when the large bones of
the legs and hips lost calcium from lack of weight-bearing stress. Sometimes,
or so experience suggested, the damaged nerves recovered to a certain degree,
and the physical therapy contributed to the recovery, with the patients re-
gaining partial or in rare cases nearly full use of their legs. But even where the
nerves were permanently affected, the physical therapy helped forestall the

secondary symptoms, which complicated the paralysis, leading to general decline and sometimes premature death.

The secret to consistent physical therapy was hope. To every person who contracted the disease—very young infants perhaps excluded—the disability came as a severe psychological blow. Dr. Lovett had encountered this often enough to consider the depression he had predicted for Roosevelt part of the disease itself. Most patients regained their emotional equilibrium sooner or later, but those who managed to view their altered circumstances with hope were more likely to stick to the regimen of therapy required to make any substantial degree of physical recovery possible.

Roosevelt gave every outward impression of hope. He spoke consistently of believing that he would get better, and he frequently pointed to improvements in this or that measure of muscular control. Yet the improvements were often less than he claimed, which suggests some degree of deception—perhaps deception of himself as much as of others.

Whatever his true feelings, he certainly *acted* as though he expected to improve. Rarely had a patient exhibited greater diligence toward recovery than Roosevelt. He undertook his therapy, after Lovett gave his approval, with a zeal that shortly worried the doctor. Lovett had discovered that certain patients overdid their therapy, from denial of the extent of their injuries or impatience at the slowness of their recovery. Roosevelt's overwork probably reflected a bit of both, and Lovett and George Draper, the New York doctor, felt obliged to slow him down. Yet caution entailed hazards of its own, for it might convey discouragement. Finding the balance was extremely difficult—and tremendously important. "The psychological factor in his management is paramount," Draper wrote. "He has such courage, such ambition, and yet at the same time such an extraordinarily sensitive emotional mechanism, that it will take all the skill which we can muster to lead him successfully to a recognition of what he really faces without crushing him."

Draper, who directed the day-to-day treatment, and Lovett, who consulted from Boston, handled Roosevelt gently, indulging his optimism to a greater degree than they might have with patients less determined or less famous. They knew that Roosevelt's chances of walking again were very small. But little was to be gained by sharing this knowledge with the patient, as long as his ignorance didn't cause him to injure himself further. So they quietly kept watch and let him dream about getting back on his feet.

14.

THE AUTUMN OF 1921 AND THE FOLLOWING WINTER PASSED SLOWLY but swiftly, in the paradoxical manner that clocks creep but calendar pages fall away for the under-occupied ill. Roosevelt remained in Manhattan to be close to Dr. Draper and his therapists and to the children, who attended school in the city, except for James, who had graduated to Groton. Friends and former associates dropped by to visit; Roosevelt greeted them with a hearty good cheer that often took them aback. Josephus Daniels wasn't sure what to expect of his old assistant, who had once skipped across the decks of rolling ships with a nonchalance that worried even the tars. Daniels's uncertainty showed as he approached Roosevelt's bed, and it prompted a characteristic reaction. "He hauled off and gave me a blow that caused me nearly to lose my balance," Daniels remembered. "He said, 'You thought you were coming to see an invalid, but I can knock you out in any bout.' " Roosevelt wasn't always so physical with guests, but with those who had known him in public life and whose opinion mattered to his future in politics, he took pains—sometimes literally—to prove that he was no less forceful, no less able to stand up for friends and against enemies, than he had ever been.

He kept touch with the outside world to the extent he could. By personal conferences at his home and by telephone, telegraph, and letter, he conducted various business of the New York office of Fidelity & Deposit. By similar means he communicated with leaders of the state and national Democratic party, consulting on policies, on personnel, on past and future campaigns. In every case his object was to reclaim as much of his old life as possible.

In February 1922 he was fitted for leg braces. These heavy steel traps clamped about his shins and thighs and connected to leather belts that encased his hips and torso; when the hinges at his knees were locked into place, the devices could support his weight in an upright posture—once he learned how to balance himself. This task, for one who hadn't stood at all for six months and who lacked the stabilizing forces supplied to most people by the muscles of their feet and legs was tricky and arduous. Yet Roosevelt, with the help of his therapists and the encouragement of Eleanor, Louis Howe, the children, and Sara, eventually mastered it.

Far more daunting was learning to walk in the braces, or rather to lurch forward, step by ungainly step. Because his hip and thigh muscles didn't have the strength and coordination to swing the braces, he had to employ the muscles of his abdomen and lower back. He would prop himself on two crutches and one leg while, with a lean and a twisting heave of his pelvis, he threw the other leg forward. After months of strenuous practice he managed to develop a kind of rhythm, which made his gait resemble a walk in tempo if in little else. Yet he never became really stable, and he kept to his wheelchair except when something extraordinary dictated that he stand.

❖   ❖   ❖

SARA WAS RIGHT in one thing about her son's affliction: he would be more comfortable physically at Hyde Park than he was in the house on East Sixty-fifth Street. The Manhattan residence had easily accommodated the Roosevelt family when the children were younger and smaller, but as they grew they needed more space. And now the house had to accommodate Franklin's live-in nurse, in addition to the regular staff of servants.

Louis Howe also required a room, having decided to move in with his boss. Two years earlier Eleanor wouldn't have tolerated Howe's permanent presence under her roof. But the bond that had developed between them during the 1920 campaign grew stronger under the strain of Franklin's illness. Eleanor, moreover, understood the importance of a positive outlook in her husband's recuperation, and she appreciated that the hours he spent with Howe, re-fighting old political battles and plotting new ones, did him more good than any medication or physical therapy.

Unfortunately, neither Howe's hygiene nor his manners had improved. He smoked constantly and ubiquitously—at breakfast, in the parlor, on the stairs—till every room reeked of smoke and ashes covered the carpets and the furniture. Franklin smoked, too, but at least he was housebroken. Howe wore the same suit day after day till Eleanor insisted that he change it. He puzzled and irritated the children, who wondered how this interloper had horned his way into the family and what kind of person abandoned his own wife and children—who lived in Poughkeepsie, where Howe visited them on week-ends—to take up residence with another family.

Anna Roosevelt, now fifteen, felt Howe's presence most acutely. He displaced her from the large bedroom on the third floor she thought should be hers. She carried her complaints to Sara, whose negative opinion of Howe—that "dirty, ugly little man," she called him—was no secret to anyone in the family. Sara naturally sided with Anna. "Granny, with a good insight into my adolescent nature, started telling me that it was inexcusable that I, the only daughter of the family, should have a tiny bedroom in the back of the house while Louis enjoyed a large, sunny front bedroom with his own private bath," Anna recalled. "Granny's needling finally took root. At her instigation, I went to Mother one evening and demanded a switch in rooms."

Eleanor later remembered this period as the "most trying winter of my life." She told Anna that the whole family had to make sacrifices. She herself didn't have a bedroom at all but slept in one of the younger boy's rooms and dressed in Franklin's bathroom. Yet she understood that more was involved than living arrangements—and that Sara was using Anna for her own purposes. "Because of constant outside influences," Eleanor recalled, "the situation grew in her"—Anna's—"mind to a point where she felt that I did not care for her and was not giving her any consideration." Franklin's patience on the subject was understandably limited, which didn't help matters. "There were times at the dinner table when she would annoy her father so much that he would be severe with her and a scene would ensue. Then she would burst into tears and retire sobbing to her room."

Eleanor held things together as long as she could. But one day, not especially more trying than most others of that period, she suddenly found herself weeping uncontrollably. "I could not think why I was sobbing, nor could I stop," she wrote. Elliott arrived home from school, saw his mother in a state in which he had never observed her, and fled in alarm. Franklin Jr. and John, to whom she had been reading, wandered away mystified. Louis Howe heard her sobs and gallantly tried to console her; failing, he too abandoned the field. "I sat on the sofa in the sitting room and sobbed and sobbed." After a long while she crossed through one of the passageways connecting the house to Sara's, which was empty following Sara's move to Hyde Park for the season. She splashed herself with cold water and eventually calmed down. "That is the one and only time I ever remember in my entire life having gone to pieces," she recollected decades later.

❖ ❖ ❖

THE STRESSES CHANGED but didn't noticeably diminish during the spring of 1922, when the family followed Sara to Hyde Park. Sara had readied the house for Franklin's arrival, adding ramps where a step or two would have stymied him, retuning the elevator added during her husband's final illness, and instructing the servants on the care of an invalid—which was how she viewed her son. Beyond the concern of any mother for her child, she hoped to show Franklin how much more pleasant life could be at Hyde Park, away from the noise and dirt of the city, in a house large enough to accommodate his shrunken world, among people who respected him for what he was rather than what he did.

At Hyde Park, Sara reclaimed some of the primacy in Franklin's life she had lost to Eleanor. Springwood was *her* home; she would have a hand in all that happened there. Eleanor might be Franklin's wife, but at Springwood she would be Sara's guest. And guests had certain duties, among them deference to their hosts.

For the most part Eleanor didn't challenge Sara's claims. She appreciated that Sara—and Sara's servants—shouldered much of the burden of Franklin's physical care. She had never liked to manage a house; at Springwood she didn't have to. The children, besides, were making ever greater demands of her, especially now that Franklin could no longer do much of what he had done before. "I became conscious of the fact that I had two young boys who had to learn to do the things that boys must do—swim and ride and camp," she wrote. Because her own experience out of doors was quite limited, she had to teach herself as she taught them. It wasn't easy. "I had no confidence in my ability to do physical things at this time. I could go into the water with the boys, but I could not swim. It began to dawn upon me that if these two youngest boys were going to have a normal existence without a father to do these things with them, I would have to become a good deal more companionable and more of an all-around person than I had ever been before."

Her renaissance began behind the wheel of one of Sara's cars. After a minor mishap some years earlier, Eleanor had left the driving to others. But camping trips and kindred adventures required the personal mobility cars increasingly provided, and she determined to master the motor arts. Early outings went poorly. She smacked a stone gatepost, and later, en route to a picnic, rolled the car, with children aboard, backward off the road, down a sharp decline, and into a tree. "It was pure luck I did not overturn the car and seriously injure someone," she confessed. But gradually she tamed the unruly vehicle, and the family drives grew less exciting, to general relief.

❖ ❖ ❖

SOMETHING ELSE discouraged Eleanor from competing with Sara. Since discovering Franklin's affair with Lucy Mercer, Eleanor had self-consciously cultivated interests of her own. The needs of the children initially limited the time she could devote to her interests, but as they grew older she found herself freer. The campaign of 1920 had attuned her to politics in a way that came naturally to most Roosevelts but heretofore not to her. She joined the League of Women Voters and the Women's City Club of New York, and met women who provided role models for the person she increasingly wanted to be: confident, independent, useful. She learned to type and write shorthand. She studied cooking—not actually to put food on her family's table but for the satisfaction of knowing she *could* do so if the supply of servants ever failed.

At first her name meant more than her talents to the organizations she joined. In the early 1920s, following Theodore's death and Franklin's national race, the Roosevelt name was the most valuable political property in America. And with the enfranchisement of women, a woman bearing the Roosevelt name was doubly useful to political and other organizations that hoped to catch the public eye. In the spring of 1922, the executive secretary of the women's division of the New York Democratic party, Nancy Cook, called to ask Eleanor to speak at a party fund-raiser. Eleanor initially demurred, disliking to speak before audiences and in any event wondering what she would say. But Franklin urged her to reconsider, doubtless thinking the experience would both broaden her horizons and defend the trademark on the family name. Louis Howe seconded the urging, from similar mixed motives, and he offered to help with the speechwriting and with tips on delivery. Eleanor let herself be persuaded, for Franklin's sake and her own.

She spoke briefly at first, and poorly. "I had a very bad habit, because I was nervous, of laughing when there was nothing to laugh at," she remembered. Howe, who sat in the back of her audiences, recorded her titters and pointed them out to her afterward. He gave her a rule for speaking she never forgot: "Have something you want to say, say it, and sit down." She followed his advice and gradually got better.

❖   ❖   ❖

THE FIRST ANNIVERSARY of the onset of Franklin's illness found him at Hyde Park, stubbornly optimistic regarding his long-term prognosis but increasingly impatient with his lack of short-term progress. The paralysis had settled into his legs, leaving his hands, arms, and shoulders free and mobile. His arms and shoulders were growing stronger than they had been before his attack, as they now carried much of the weight his legs had borne. On his crutches they provided both support and locomotion; in his bed they pulled him up and about via bars and straps above his mattress; around the house they propelled him by wheelchair and, on occasion, across the floor on his rear end. His arms and shoulders grew stronger still from an exercise designed for his legs. On the Springwood lawn, at the suggestion of another polio sufferer, he had a set of parallel bars constructed waist-high, just far enough off the ground that his feet could touch while his arms held most of his weight. He would move along the bars, willing his unbraced legs to walk, while his arms and shoulders did the actual work against gravity.

He took up swimming as therapy. At first he merely sat in the pond by the spring house, for the hydraulic massage its waters provided. But the water was cold, and to ward off its chill he would paddle around. In time a neighbor, one of the Astors, offered use of his heated indoor pool, which allowed Roosevelt to linger in the water. "The legs work wonderfully in the water, and I need nothing to keep myself afloat," he informed Dr. Draper.

Yet all the therapy and all his determination failed to produce what he really wanted: stronger legs. His legs weren't getting worse, but after a year they weren't getting better. His mobility was improving, but that was compensation—stronger arms, greater skill with his braces and crutches—rather than recovery. And even his mobility improved in distressingly small increments. He set for himself the goal of walking, on braces and crutches, from the house down the two-hundred-yard driveway to the road. Each day he struggled a bit farther before his arms gave out and he sank, exhausted, to the ground.

❖   ❖   ❖

FOR A MAN of affairs, a world traveler since birth, Springwood soon seemed a prison. Another reason Eleanor didn't bother fighting Sara's plan to reclaim her son was that she knew Franklin would never consent to the confined life his mother intended for him. After a long summer in Hyde Park, he returned to Manhattan. He remained a vice president of Fidelity & Deposit, although he hadn't been to the office in more than a year. He decided to pay his employer a call.

In that era, paraplegics weren't expected to venture into the world, and the world made little accommodation for them or anyone else who couldn't walk, climb stairs, step up and down curbs, mount train platforms, and get in and out of automobiles. The mere sight of a cripple—the common term and conception—who wasn't begging for coins could often draw crowds. Roosevelt attracted a curious audience upon his return to the Fidelity & Deposit office on lower Broadway. The ride downtown was no problem; a chauffeur guided the family Buick. This driver had been chosen, as well, for his strength of limb, for after the car pulled up to the door of the building, he had to manhandle Roosevelt from the back seat to a standing position and lock his braces straight. They had rehearsed the routine at home, but any opening performance is always fraught with uncertainty, and in this case a gust of autumn wind flipped Roosevelt's hat to the street. The driver couldn't retrieve it without dropping Roosevelt; while they debated what to do, a helpful passerby picked it up and put it back on Roosevelt's head. Roosevelt laughed his thanks to the stranger, even as the sweat that soaked his shirt and coat betrayed his anxiety.

Inside the building, the marble floor, polished to a gleaming smoothness that made transit easy for everyone else, challenged Roosevelt's advance. He had never practiced with crutches on such a surface, and their rubber tips struggled for a grip. With a grim smile and the driver's help he got almost to the elevator before the crutches slipped and he tumbled heavily to the stone floor.

Again he put on a brave face. He laughed as though he were romping with his children on the floor of his bedroom, and he nonchalantly accepted the offer of two sturdy young fellows who, together with the driver, stood him up again and deposited him bodily in the elevator. The rest of the outing passed unremarkably. "A grand and glorious occasion," was how he described the luncheon his boss, Van Lear Black, hosted for him that day. But not for months did he return to the office, and rarely during the rest of his life would he allow himself to be placed in a position to suffer such an embarrassing pratfall.

❖   ❖   ❖

*H*EALTH RESORTS IN America had never developed the following their European counterparts enjoyed, which was why James Roosevelt, Franklin's father, had traveled to Germany every year. Part of their failure to catch on was the underdeveloped state of American medicine, compared with that of Europe. It was the doctors as much as the waters that drew the infirm to Bad Nauheim in Germany, Baden in Switzerland, and Spa in Belgium (which gave its name to the species). Another part of the failure resulted from the underdeveloped state of the American economy. Medical tourism was expensive, and the number of Americans who could afford to travel and spend weeks or months to regain or improve their health was comparatively small.

Yet a few places earned names for themselves and profits for their proprietors. Saratoga Springs had attracted the infirm for decades before Louis Howe's parents took him there in the 1870s. Stafford Springs, Connecticut, and Berkeley Springs, Virginia, boasted longer histories; Blue Licks, Kentucky, and Hot Springs, Arkansas, made do with shorter résumés.

A warm springs near Pine Mountain, Georgia, had enticed human visitors for centuries, perhaps millennia. The indigenous peoples and later the first white settlers ascribed healing powers to the soothing, mineral-laden waters. As early as the 1830s the springs were being touted as a destination for cure seekers; by the late nineteenth century the traffic to the area had grown large enough to cause one Charles Davis to build a three-hundred-room hotel, the Meriwether Inn. The resort included tennis and bowling facilities, a dance hall, and a shooting range, in addition to the swimming pool that captured the healing waters for the convenience of the guests. But it was Davis's misfortune to open the resort in time for the depression of the 1890s, which cut deeply into discretionary spending on such items as health vacations. Davis lacked the money to maintain the place through the hard times, and as the nineteenth century ended it was falling into disrepair.

Franklin Roosevelt paid no attention to Warm Springs until he contracted polio, but as his rehabilitation stalled he became intrigued by reports of the Georgia spa. He and Eleanor traveled south to investigate. "The old hotel with its piazzas called to mind the southern belles of Civil War days," Eleanor related. "The outdoor swimming pool was the one really fine thing about the place." The pool was all Franklin saw, and at the first opportunity he shed his clothes and lowered himself in. "I spent over an hour in the pool this a.m.," he wrote Sara. "It is really wonderful and will I think do great good."

The water's secret was its warmth and unusual density. Like most warm springs, this one drew its heat from deep below the surface. The rains that fell on Pine Mountain, above the resort, filtered through crevices in the granite down to depths where the crust retained some of the heat of its magmatic origin. Reaching an impervious layer, the warm water ran along this layer till the layer breached the surface several miles from Pine Mountain and water gushed forth at the rate of several hundreds of gallons a minute—more after unusually rainy seasons, less following drought. Besides transferring heat from the depths to the surface, the water transported large quantities of dissolved minerals. Water laced with minerals is denser than fresh water and supports with unusual force whatever is immersed in it. Swimmers discover they can't sink even if they try; persons who walk and otherwise exercise in the water can do so almost effortlessly.

Between the warmth and the buoyancy of the Warm Springs waters, Roosevelt found he could pad and paddle about the pool there for hours. Most of the initial positive effect was psychological; not surprisingly for one eager to be cured, he attributed his new stamina to improvement in his leg muscles rather than to the lighter load they were carrying. But even after he discounted for the water's effect, he could hope that the extended exercise it allowed would, in time, rebuild his withered muscles. "The doctor says it takes three weeks to show effects," Roosevelt told Sara. Even if it took three months, or three years, he felt, it would be time and effort well spent.

Almost immediately Roosevelt adopted Warm Springs as his second home. "The cottage is delightful and very comfortable, and with Roy and Mary"—staff on loan from the proprietors—"we shall be most comfortable," he informed Sara. Roosevelt made friends with the neighbors at once. Thomas Loyless had edited the *Atlanta Constitution* till the Ku Klux Klan, experiencing a revival in the 1920s, forced him and his liberal voice from the paper; he retreated to the mountains near Warm Springs, where Roosevelt got to know him and his wife. "We have gone motoring with Mr. and Mrs. Loyless and have seen the country pretty thoroughly," Roosevelt informed Eleanor after she had returned to New York. "I like him ever so much, and she is nice but not broad in her interests. But she chatters away to Missy"—Missy LeHand, who had come south with Franklin and Eleanor to handle Franklin's correspondence—"on the back seat, and I hear an occasional yes or no from Missy to prove she is not sleeping."

Eleanor was less entranced by Warm Springs, which was one reason she had excused herself after helping her husband settle in. "I remember the first house we lived in, and my surprise that I could look through the cracks and see daylight," she said of the cottage Franklin found delightful. The mode of living in backwoods Georgia was more rustic than she was used to. She described her "perfect horror" at learning that chickens for dinner had to be purchased live.

"At Hyde Park there were chickens in the farm yard, but that was a mile away from the house and I didn't hear them being killed. In Warm Springs they ran around in our yard, until the cooks wrung their necks amid much squawking and put them in the pot. Somehow I didn't enjoy eating them."

Yet Eleanor learned to like the neighbors. Her side of the Roosevelt family had a connection to the Warm Springs area. Eleanor's Grandmother Mittie— Theodore Roosevelt's mother—was Martha Bulloch by birth; besides possessing uncles and cousins who fought for the Confederacy during the Civil War, Mittie had relatives for whom the town of Bullochville, adjacent to Warm Springs, was named. Eleanor never knew Mittie, who died the year Eleanor was born, but she and Theodore's children spent many hours with Mittie's sister, Anna Bulloch Gracie, who regaled them with stories of the antebellum South. "She had made me feel that life in the South must be gracious and easy and charming," Eleanor remembered. The reality of southern life around Warm Springs in the 1920s was rather different. "For many, many people life in the South was hard and poor and ugly," Eleanor noted of her initial visit. The experience affected her deeply; like her husband she had a habit of filing observations away for future reference. The trials of the South made her appreciate the kindness the neighbors showed her and Franklin. "Hardly a day passed that something was not brought to our door—wood for the fireplace, or a chicken, or flowers. Frequently the flowers came arranged in an old silver bowl or china vase that was a priceless family possession, and I would worry until the flowers faded and the container was returned to its owner."

As Eleanor realized, it was Franklin, the celebrity visitor, the neighbors were most interested in. If one important, wealthy northerner had come to Warm Springs, others might follow, to the economic benefit of the town and county. "On Wednesday the people of Warm Springs are giving me a supper and reception in the Town Hall," Franklin wrote Sara. "And on Friday evening, our last day, I am to go to Manchester, five miles away, for another supper and speech. I think every organization and town in Georgia has asked me to some kind of a party. . . . Missy spends most of her time keeping up a huge and constant local correspondence."

❖　❖　❖

*D*URING THE MID-1920s Roosevelt divided his time among Warm Springs, Hyde Park, and the Florida coast, where he cruised aboard a houseboat he purchased with a friend. The *Larooco* became a vacation home and office combined. Missy LeHand lived on board, managing Roosevelt's paperwork and serving as his all-purpose assistant. Louis Howe traveled down from New York to apprise the boss of political developments and spike the Florida punch with his mordant wit. Howe dictated the bylaws of the logbook to Missy, who typed them for the record:

> This Logbook must be entirely accurate and truthful. In putting down weights and numbers of fish, however, the following tables may be used:
> 2 oz. make 1 logbook pound.
> 5 logbook pounds make "a large fish."
> 2 "large fish" make "a record day's catch."
> 2 inches make 1 logbook foot.
> 2 logbook feet make "big as a whale."
> Anything above "whale" size may be described as an "icthyosaurus."
> (Note: In describing fish that got away, all these measures may be doubled. It is also permitted, when over 30 seconds are required to pull in a fish, to say, "After half an hour's hard fighting . . .")

When the spirits of the guests required fortifying—generally just as the sun was passing over the figurative yardarm—Roosevelt brought out the grog. In public Roosevelt was a proper dry, keeping well within the bounds of the Eighteenth Amendment and the Volstead Act. In private he was a merry wet, drawing on his private stash to serve drinks to guests at Hyde Park and, in southern Florida, capitalizing on that region's proximity to Cuba and the rum-runners who plied the Florida Strait.

Roosevelt's guests included college classmates, professional acquaintances, and friends of friends. Wives occasionally joined their husbands, affording Missy female company. "Resourcefulness and good humor weighed heavily with him in a man," Elliott Roosevelt noted regarding his father's choice of houseboat guests. "In a woman, he looked for warmth of spirit and physical attractiveness." Frances de Rham, a spark from Franklin's pre-Eleanor days, qualified on both counts, as did Cynthia Mosley, whose husband, Oswald Mosley, had yet to make himself notorious as Hitler's principal British apologist.

❖   ❖   ❖

ELEANOR RARELY came aboard. She didn't fish or play cards, and she much preferred the company of her own friends. Two in particular satisfied her need for stimulation and affection. Nancy Cook, of the women's division of the New York Democratic committee, had first been attracted to Eleanor by her family name, but before long a friendship blossomed and Eleanor was inviting Cook for weekends at Hyde Park. Cook was as irreverent and stubborn as Eleanor, at this stage, was proper and uncertain; Eleanor soon adopted Cook as her role model. To underscore the identification, Eleanor ordered matching tweed knickerbocker suits for the two of them.

The third vertex of Eleanor's triangle was Marion Dickerman, Nancy Cook's longtime domestic partner. Younger and quieter than Cook, Dickerman provided a steadiness Eleanor found appealing. Together Cook and Dickerman drew Eleanor deeper into politics of a progressive, even radical nature. Eleanor began consorting with feminists, trade unionists, and socialists. Dickerman had run for the New York state assembly against the conservative Republican speaker, who branded her a man-hating Bolshevik; she lost, but narrowly. She subsequently accepted a position as dean of New Jersey State College, yet her reputation for radicalism followed her. To Eleanor it added to her appeal.

The three women worked together and often played together. In the summer of 1925 they embarked on a road trip from Manhattan to Maine by a circuitous route. Eleanor brought Franklin Jr. and John, one of their cousins, and a friend of John's. The plan was to camp along the way. Automobile campers often paid farmers for the right to pitch tents in a fallow field, but when Eleanor inquired of one farmer whether they might stay on his place, he eyed the three women suspiciously. "Where are your husbands?" he demanded. "Mine is not with me," Eleanor answered, "and the others don't have husbands." The farmer snorted, "I don't want women of that kind." He told them to move along.

The trip tested everyone's patience. Cook and Dickerman weren't used to small boys and found their antics unpleasant. The young Roosevelts didn't like their mother's friends and let her know it. Franklin Jr. tried to cut down a tree with an ax and nearly lopped off his foot. Johnny and his friend wandered away in Quebec City and turned up only after thoroughly frightening Eleanor and annoying her companions further. The car crashed into a ditch and later a lumber wagon. By the time they reached Campobello the travelers couldn't bear the thought of another mile in the big Buick; they summoned Dickerman's sister and had her drive it away.

Yet the friendship among Eleanor, Nancy, and Marion survived and in fact grew stronger. Spurred toward personal independence by Nancy and Marion, Eleanor determined to build a house for the three of them on the property at Hyde Park. Franklin endorsed the idea, knowing how Sara cramped Eleanor's style in the main house and how Eleanor's friends irritated Sara. Franklin pointed out that he owned part of the property, having purchased a tract along the Val Kill, a creek two miles from the main house, on which the group often picnicked. As Dickerman told the story, Eleanor was lamenting, late in the summer of 1924, that the season would end, Sara would close up Springwood, and the good times on the Val Kill would cease. Franklin responded, "But aren't you girls silly? This isn't Mother's land. I bought this acreage myself. And why shouldn't you three have a cottage here of your own, so you could come and go as you please?" The Val Kill idea took shape that autumn, and the cottage was built the following summer. For Nancy and Marion it provided a permanent home; the couple lived there till 1947. Eleanor came and went, according primarily to the needs of her children. By now her marriage to Franklin placed almost no demands on her; he scarcely figured in her considerations of where to spend her time.

Franklin called the Val Kill house the "Honeymoon Cottage." How fully he intended the analogy is unclear, but the place certainly provided an idyllic escape of the kind associated with honeymoons. Eleanor embroidered the trio's initials—"E.M.N."—on the linen; friends provided monogrammed gifts of the sort newlyweds typically receive. Franklin himself furnished various items, including a book entitled *Little Marion's Pilgrimage,* which he presented on the occasion, as he put it, "of the opening of the Love Nest on the Val-Kill."

Val Kill became a world unto itself. The group pooled resources to build a furniture factory for Nancy, the artisan of the three. The factory produced replicas of traditional American designs, preserving a part of the nation's heritage, as the three conceived it, while providing employment for craftsmen whose livelihoods were threatened by industrialization. "She wanted to use methods employed by our ancestors," Eleanor said of Nancy's plan, "and see whether she could find a market for furniture which, though the first processes were done by machinery, would be largely handmade and therefore expensive."

The Val Kill partnership expanded into other areas. Eleanor edited a newspaper, the *Women's Democratic News,* while Marion implemented her theories of education as principal of the Todhunter School for girls, which the trio eventually purchased from the British woman who had founded it. Eleanor joined Marion in attempting to bring the real world to the classroom, and vice versa. She taught courses in literature, history, and current events and led field trips to New York, where the students visited City Hall and sat in on trials in the courts. "This made the government of the city something real and alive, rather than just so many words in a text book," she afterward explained.

15.

*W*ITH FRANKLIN AND ELEANOR FASHIONING THEIR SEPARATE LIVES, the children struggled to find their own niches. Anna experienced the greatest difficulty. Sara still employed Anna against Eleanor, constantly reminding her that her mother was neglecting her in favor of Louis Howe and now her new women friends. Sara insisted that Anna come out as a debutante at eighteen, despite Franklin's apathy and Eleanor's ambivalence. Eleanor might have sided with Anna, who detested the debutante crowd and all it entailed, but she declined to pick another fight with Sara, and the old, insecure part of her secretly wondered whether Sara wasn't right to introduce Anna to high society. "I was *informed* that I had to come out in society," Anna remembered. "And I *died*. . . . I *wasn't* going to come out. And Granny said, 'You *are*.' And I went to Mother, and she said, 'You *must*.' " Anna knew better than to appeal to Franklin. "Father you couldn't draw into this. He'd just say, 'That's up to Granny and Mother. You settle all this with them.' I couldn't go to Father on this. He wouldn't give me the time of day."

Not that Anna wasn't complicit in certain of Sara's schemes. After an unsuccessful attempt at college—as Harvard didn't admit women, she chose Cornell—Anna found love, or something approximating it. Her brother Elliott detected a secondary agenda. "Sis was in a hurry to marry, to escape the cold war which promised no armistice between Granny and Mother, Mother and Father," Elliott wrote (amid the real Cold War of the 1970s). Anna brought her beau to Hyde Park for Christmas. Curtis Dall was a stockbroker and a Princeton grad, twenty-nine years old and excessively proud, in the estimation of Elliott and James. The Roosevelt boys invited him to a pickup game of hockey—"to knock some of the starch out," Elliott said. "We tripped him. Blood was streaming from a cut made by a skate slicing into his chin, when Sis took him into the house, raging at us for damaging her beloved." The blood had dried but Anna's anger toward the whole family still burned when she and Dall were married in 1926. Sara insinuated herself into the affair by buying a lavish apartment for the newlyweds—behind Eleanor and Franklin's back. When her gift was discovered, Sara pleaded the best intentions. "Eleanor dear, I am very sorry that I hurt you," she wrote. "I did not think I could be nasty or mean, and I fear I had too good an opinion of myself." She had simply wanted to surprise Eleanor and Franklin, who of course couldn't afford to give the newlyweds such a useful present. "I love you, dear, too much to ever want to hurt you," Sara said. If she had made them angry—"well, I must just bear it."

✣　✣　✣

THE ROOSEVELT BOYS had less to do with Eleanor and more with Franklin, albeit not much more. "In the summer of 1926 Father, for the first and only time in his life, took a major, positive, forceful action to guide and prepare me for the sort of rude world in which I eventually would have to live," James recalled. As the eldest son, James had been the first to leave home for boarding school—Groton, of course. He had lived away during the whole period since his father contracted polio. He joined the family for summers at Hyde Park, but as his final year at Groton concluded, Franklin decreed that he should take a job outside the family circle. Franklin inquired among his associates and found James a job at a paper mill in a frontier region of Quebec, near the town of Desbiens. He sent instructions ahead that the son of Franklin Roosevelt was not to be shown any special consideration. These proved unnecessary, as James discovered on arrival. "None of the lumberjacks in Desbiens . . . had the faintest idea who Franklin Roosevelt was," James recalled. "And if they had, they could not have cared less."

James learned to appreciate that summer's experience but only after the fact. The long days of muscle-straining work—sorting logs, shoveling chips, heaving pulp, stacking paper—wore him down and toughened him up, and convinced him that his father was a heartless brute. "I remember staying mad at Father almost every moment of the summer." He nursed his anger in silence. "I wrote no letters at all to either of my parents." The one merit he detected in his exile was that it was so far out of the way that there was nothing on which to spend his minimal wages—eighteen cents per hour and keep. By the time he returned to civilization he'd amassed enough to purchase a car. And when he did return, he went to see not his father at Hyde Park but his grandmother at Campobello. "Granny made much over me, as she never had approved of sending me up to that awful place." Eventually, just before heading to Harvard, James visited Franklin at Hyde Park. Like his siblings, James craved his father's approval, and he kept his dissatisfaction over his summer experience to himself. "I was too proud to tell him how much I had disliked it." But Franklin figured it out, and he never sent the younger boys to such a rigorous finishing school.

Elliott, the second (surviving) son, rebelled more openly, as second sons often do. He couldn't stand Groton, after he got there, and at every opportunity told his parents so. As graduation approached he vowed he would never go to Harvard, no matter what anyone said or did. Franklin decided that a western trip would do the boy good, and he arranged for him to spend the summer on a ranch in Wyoming. But Elliott disappeared en route, and for two months no one in the family heard a word of his whereabouts. Franklin appeared unconcerned, but Eleanor grew more and more worried. For weeks she suffered in silence, until her maternal fears got the better of her stoicism. "Franklin, we must do something about finding this boy," she said. Roosevelt called the New York state police, who wired their counterparts in Wyoming, who located Elliott on a different ranch than the one Franklin had made the arrangements with. The foreman who had agreed to hire Elliott had taken a new job on a neighboring ranch, and Elliott required some time to find him. With the calculating thoughtlessness of the teenage rebel, he neglected to inform his parents of the switch. Their letters to him gathered dust for months at the old ranch; when Elliott finally wrote back, his chief concern was that Franklin and Eleanor might have made him look bad to his friends. "I suppose you told everybody how terrible I was. . . . I suppose there is no use in asking you to keep my defects and faults quiet."

Yet there were moments of filial satisfaction. James and Elliott took turns keeping their father company in Florida. James enjoyed the visits, in part because his father treated him as one of the gang. James fished with Franklin and his friends, talked politics with Franklin and friends, and probably drank with Franklin and friends. (Both were subsequently silent on this point. James did say he sat out the poker games Franklin and friends played daily.) On one occasion James joined Franklin for lunch with William Jennings Bryan, who currently devoted his persuasive powers to promoting Florida real estate to northern tourists.

Elliott, being younger and more resentful, fit less readily into Franklin's crowd. But Elliott liked to fish, and one day's exploit furnished the stuff of family legend. "Last night we caught the record fish of all time!" Franklin recorded in the ship's log.

Elliott had put out a shark hook baited with half a ladyfish, and about 8 o'clock we noticed the line was out in the middle of the creek. It seemed caught on a rock and we got the rowboat and cleared it. It then ran under *Larooco,* and with E. and Roy and John and the Capt. pulling on it, we finally brought a perfectly enormous Jewfish along side. We could just get his mouth out of the water and put in two other hooks and a gaff. Then Roy shot him about eight times through the head with my revolver. As he seemed fairly dead we hoisted him on the davit, which threatened to snap off at any moment. He was over seven feet long, over five feet around, and his jaw opened eighteen inches. We put him on the hand scale this morning, which registers up to 400 pounds. He weighed more than this, as he was only two-thirds out of water, so we figure his weight at between 450 and 500 lbs.

❖   ❖   ❖

DURING ROOSEVELT'S first visit to Warm Springs, two reporters from Atlanta caught wind of his presence there and wrote an article entitled "Swimming Back to Health," which was picked up by papers around the country. The article piqued interest in the curative powers of the Warm Springs waters, and in April 1925, during Roosevelt's second visit, a steady trickle of polio patients began arriving. The owners of the Meriwether Inn eyed the visitors skeptically. It wasn't obvious they could pay their way, and they had an unsettling effect on the other guests. As the cause and mode of transmission of polio remained a mystery, fathers and mothers didn't have to be paranoid or callous to fear that their children might be harmed by swimming with persons who obviously had contracted the disease. When these guests began cutting their vacations short, the management understandably grew concerned.

Roosevelt unexpectedly found himself the advocate for his fellow sufferers. The owners might contemplate putting the other polio victims back on the train and sending them away, but they couldn't do so to one of Roosevelt's stature—and with him on the premises they couldn't do it to the others either. Roosevelt resolved the problem, for the time being, by persuading the management to dig a separate pool, some distance below the main pool. Here he took his own exercise, and he encouraged the others to join him. And lest the regular guests have to meet the polio victims in the halls of the hotel, Roosevelt arranged for them to stay in some of the abandoned cottages about the resort.

They quickly came to appreciate him, and then to love him, for his efforts on their behalf. He reciprocated the fond feeling. He was delighted to hear them call him "Dr. Roosevelt" and flattered by the attention they paid as he showed them exercises that had worked for him. Some of these he had learned from Dr. Lovett; others he invented himself. One man didn't know how to swim when he arrived; Roosevelt taught him the basic arm strokes, and soon the fellow was bobbing about with the rest of the group. Two ladies were quite rotund and consequently buoyant; Roosevelt had to struggle to get their feet to the bottom of the pool, so that they could practice walking in the water. He would push one knee down till the foot hit bottom, then reach for the other knee—only to watch the first knee shoot back to the surface. Great effort on his part and intense concentration on theirs were required to succeed in planting both feet on the pool bottom at once.

The resort had no resident physician, and certainly no polio specialist. None of the new guests had Roosevelt's advantage of advanced—for that era—polio care, and they were eager to hear what he could tell them of the disease they shared. He had Missy LeHand help him prepare a series of charts showing the human musculature and indicating which muscles were affected by polio and therefore needed special exercise. He answered their questions, assisted them in locating specialists near their homes, and charmed them with his natural optimism.

The experience boosted Roosevelt's spirits as much as theirs, and as much as anything he had done since contracting the disease. To some degree his positive attitude reflected his comparative physical advantage over several of the others; self-pity appeared particularly out of place when others were much worse off. To some degree it reflected the actual improvement he felt in his condition. His half brother, Rosy, now in his late sixties, had suffered a knee injury; Franklin wrote him a letter of concern and appended a status report: "My own knees are really gaining a lot of strength. This exercising in warm water seems to be far and away the best thing, and I think you will be delighted with the progress I have made."

✣　✣　✣

*A*s Roosevelt led the exercises in the pool, as he answered the questions at the water's edge, as he felt the spirits of the group rise on the mutual encouragement each offered to all, an unexpected vision took shape in his mind's eye. His conversations with the resort's management and his observations of the other guests convinced him that Warm Springs would never become a satisfactory facility for polio victims unless it was owned and operated by someone sympathetic to their plight. Roosevelts and especially Delanos had invested in less worthy ventures; Franklin now determined to put his money where his heart lay, and purchase the resort. As owner he would have the freedom to implement what he had learned in his own rehabilitation and to assist others—doctors and patients, working together—in devising new treatments.

By early 1926 he was talking openly of his plan. "I had a nice visit from Charles Peabody"—the brother of the principal owner—"and it looks as if I have bought Warm Springs," he wrote Sara. He was deliberately trying to shock his mother; he hadn't yet bought the place, but he was letting her know he intended to, regardless of the opposition he was sure she would raise. "I want you to take a great interest in it," he continued, "for I feel you can help me with many suggestions, and the place properly run will not only do a great deal of good but will prove financially successful."

Sara was indeed leery; so was Eleanor. Though Franklin and Eleanor's activities and circles of friends continued to diverge, their finances remained intertwined. They had enough for daily expenses, but James was in college and the younger boys, if perhaps not the rebellious Elliott, would follow. Eleanor wasn't sure where the money would come from. "I know how you love creative work," she wrote Franklin. "My only feeling is that Georgia is somewhat distant for you to keep in touch with what is really a big undertaking. One cannot, it seems to me, have vital interests in widely divided places." Yet she conceded that her caution might be excessive. "I'm old and rather overwhelmed by what there is to do in one place. . . . Don't be discouraged by me; I have great confidence in your extraordinary interest and enthusiasm."

She had reason to worry. Franklin was talking of sinking $200,000, or two-thirds of his net worth, into the property. Renovations would run through additional tens of thousands before the place began to attract the kind of clientele that might actually make it pay.

He went forward all the same. In April 1926 he announced his purchase of the resort; shortly thereafter he spelled out the improvements he planned and the results he anticipated. "The first thing to be done concerning the curative powers of the spring waters will be to conduct some experiments under able physicians," he told reporters. "This summer we expect to bring a limited number of patients to Warm Springs who will receive treatment under the direction of a staff of physicians. The physicians then can tell definitely the value of the warm waters." Roosevelt said he expected the experiments to be an "unqualified success," which would justify the construction of a sanitarium.

Though polio rehabilitation would be the focus of the first phase of the resort's redevelopment, Roosevelt's broader plan was much more ambitious. He described for the reporters a year-round facility catering to persons with plenty of money to spend on rest and outdoor recreation. He said that he had already engaged Donald Ross, the St. Andrews–bred Scotsman who built the finest golf courses of his generation, to carve a championship facility out of the forest on Pine Mountain. A three-thousand-acre shooting preserve would entice visitors partial to the thrill of the hunt. Riding trails—safely distant from the shooting preserve—would allow guests to gallop, trot, or walk their steeds over hill and dale. A stocked lake would bring out the Izaak Walton in visitors.

Roosevelt discreetly but clearly explained that the polio sanitarium would be separate from the larger resort facilities. He didn't say so explicitly, but it was also clear that he hoped the revenues from the larger facility would underwrite the polio portion. Roosevelt's model for the larger facility was premised on the sale of memberships to the golf club and of home sites in what he called the "cottage colony" that would grow up around the golf course. Roosevelt expected the members and guests to be of two kinds: northerners who came south for the winter and returned home in the spring, and southerners who headed for the hills during the summer. Borrowing a page from experienced promoters, Roosevelt assured reporters that enthusiasm was high, without revealing details. The list of prospective members included "some of the best people in the South and some of the best people in the North," he said. "When this list grows a little larger we will be ready to announce the names of the first members."

As Roosevelt expected, the mere fact of his purchase of Warm Springs assured the resort much positive publicity. From Atlanta to New York articles and editorials recounted the sale, his plans, and the positive impact the new ownership would have on a region bedeviled by poverty and lack of opportunity. "The waters of Warm Springs have been pronounced equal in some respects to the most famous health waters of Germany and Austria," the *Atlanta Constitution* declared. "There is good reason to believe, therefore, that this resort, under the direction of one so able financially to develop it, and whose heart is so closely wedded to it, will become one of the great attractions of Georgia, and of marked economic value to the state."

In conjunction with the unveiling of his plans for the resort, Roosevelt organized the Georgia Warm Springs Foundation, which was chartered in New York in January 1927. The foundation's purpose was to institutionalize Roosevelt's dream while capturing the tax advantages available to nonprofit or-

ganizations. In time the foundation would buy out Roosevelt's ownership, re-
paying his investment—and thereby enabling Eleanor to breathe easier regarding the children's education. In the shorter term it enabled Roosevelt to
dun his friends on behalf of his cause, but in the foundation's name rather
than his own. Edsel Ford, the son of the automaker, on visiting Warm Springs
became an early donor. "Mrs. Ford and I are deeply impressed with the wonderful work which is being carried out here at Warm Springs and we would like
to do something towards the development," Ford wrote. "I am sending here-
with a check for twenty-five thousand dollars which I hope you will accept for
the Foundation with our best wishes for its complete success."

The evolution of Roosevelt from politician to entrepreneur and healer impressed observers all the more. Following the announcement of a program to
bring cash-short polio victims, at foundation expense, to Warm Springs, the
Atlanta Constitution hailed the moving spirit of the enterprise as "Roosevelt
the Reliever." Applauding his "sympathetic and splendid philanthropy," the
paper went on to predict, "It will be one of the superb blessings to humanity
if Mr. Roosevelt and his associates shall succeed in demonstrating that our
Georgia Warm Springs is the 'pool of Siloam' to many thousands of the sufferers from the dread affliction that so deadens the limbs, spines, and even the
brains of human creatures."

❖   ❖   ❖

ROOSEVELT GREW AT Warm Springs in ways he couldn't have anticipated.
Besides being Dr. Roosevelt to the patients, whose numbers expanded with
each passing month, he was "the Boss" to the hundreds of men and women
who worked on the grounds, built the golf course and the cottages, dug the
pools, and tended the cows and chickens and corn and soybeans on the farm
he purchased adjoining the resort. (But not cotton. "We'll grow no cotton," he
declared, convinced that cotton contributed to the exhaustion of soil and the
cycle of debt that trapped so many southern farmers). He was the dynamo of
the Warm Springs Foundation, the phone caller and letter writer who hit up
everyone he could think of for contributions to the worthiest cause he knew.
He was the irresistible embodiment of polio, who hurried to Atlanta when he
learned the American Orthopedic Association was meeting there and, against
the scientifically skeptical inclinations of the distinguished doctors, persuaded
them to send a team to Warm Springs to examine the facility and the thera-
peutic powers of the water.

He was also the face of the outside world to many of his Georgia neighbors. Tom Bradshaw, the Warm Springs village blacksmith, explained that he could rig a Model T with pulleys and levers to let a person drive with his hands and arms alone. Roosevelt laughed with pleasure at the thought, and laughed even louder each time he got in the car and tooled along the roads of Meriwether County. He shouted and waved at the men, women, and children he passed; he stopped to chat, to commiserate regarding the woeful price of crops, and to share a jar of moonshine when the revenuers weren't looking. Some of those he encountered had never seen a Northerner; almost none had ever met a wealthy Yankee who treated them with such honest good cheer.

He charmed them all. He put the "polios"—as he and they called themselves—at ease with his matter-of-factness toward his disability. He led them in jokes, sometimes at the expense of the able-bodied guests. The young male assistants who propelled the wheelchairs about the grounds he dubbed "push boys"; he struggled to suppress his mirth when some of the push boys, pretending paralysis, lowered themselves into the waters of a fountain that graced the front lawn of the resort and leaped out, proclaiming a miraculous cure, to the astonishment of gullible visitors. He played poker with all comers, taking the money of polios and able-bodies alike.

He held court in a cottage built to his specifications. Shortly after unveiling his master plan for the resort, he contracted for the construction of one of the first new cottages, for himself. Ground was broken in the autumn of 1926; the house was ready for occupation by the following February. Eleanor and Missy traveled to Atlanta to purchase a stove and refrigerator for the place; they collaborated on other touches to lend the feel of home. (Rarely did the two spend much time together, especially without Roosevelt. One wonders what they talked about on their Atlanta trip; neither ever said.)

Missy, who served as Roosevelt's hostess, became more indispensable with each passing year. Her cottage was one of the next ones built. The full nature of Roosevelt's relationship to Missy inspired quiet conjecture then and somewhat less-guarded guesses since. Elliott Roosevelt assumed they were lovers and had been at least since their days in Florida. Elliott contended that their intimacy "was treated as a simple fact of life aboard the *Larooco*." He continued: "Everyone in the closely knit inner circle of Father's friends accepted it as a matter of course." As for his own reaction: "I remember being only mildly stirred to see him with Missy on his lap as he sat in a brown wicker chair in the main stateroom, holding her in his sun-browned arms, whose clasp we children knew so well. When Sis and Jimmy on occasion witnessed much the same scene, they had a similar reaction, as I learned when we spoke afterward. It was not in Father to be secretive or devious in his dealings with us. He made no attempt to conceal his feelings about Missy."

Elliott explained that during this period his father regained feeling in his legs, with positive consequences for his overall mental and physical state. "Except for the braces," Roosevelt declared, in a letter Elliott quoted, "I have never been in better health in my life." Elliott elaborated: "There was an additional reason, besides the return of sensation in his legs, for his mood of exhilaration. One of the innumerable medical reports on his general well-being stated explicitly: 'No symptoms of *impotentia coeundi.*' " The obvious implication, to Elliott at least, was that Missy made Roosevelt feel like a man again.

❖   ❖   ❖

THE WARM SPRINGS experience broadened Roosevelt as nothing else could have. For years afterward he credited his experience in Georgia with providing insight into this aspect or that of politics, economics, or the American dream. "It was way back in 1924 that I began to learn economics at Warm Springs," he recalled on a visit to Georgia as president, to dedicate a schoolhouse.

> Here is how it happened. One day while I was sitting on the porch of the little cottage in which I lived, a very young man came up to the porch and said, "May I speak with you, Mr. Roosevelt?" And I said, "Yes."
>
> He came up to the porch, and he asked if I would come over to such and such a town not very far away from here and deliver the diplomas at the commencement exercises of the school.
>
> I said, "Yes," and then I asked, "Are you the president of the graduating class?" He said, "No, I am principal of the school."
>
> I said, "How old are you?" He said, "Nineteen years."
>
> I said, "Have you been to college?" He answered, "I had my freshman year at the University of Georgia."
>
> I said, "Do you figure on going through and getting a degree?" He said, "Yes, sir, I will be teaching school every other year and going to college every other year on the proceeds."
>
> I said, "How much are they paying you?" And the principal of that school said, "They are very generous. They are paying me three hundred dollars a year."

Well, that started me thinking. Three hundred dollars a year for the principal of the school. That meant that the three ladies who were teaching under him were getting less than three hundred dollars a year. I said to myself, "Why do they have to pay that low scale of wages?"

At that particular time one of the banks in Warm Springs closed its doors. At the same time one of the stores in Warm Springs folded up. I began realizing that the community didn't have any purchasing power. There were a good many reasons for that. One reason was five cent cotton. You know what five cent cotton, six cent cotton, seven cent cotton meant to the South. Here was a very large part of the nation that was completely at the mercy of people outside of the South, who were dependent on national conditions and on world conditions over which they had absolutely no control. The South was starving on five and six and seven cent cotton. It could not build schools and it could not pay teachers.

Roosevelt concluded this story by saying that he then began to see the economy of the country as a whole. He had read about low crop prices, but he had never witnessed in firsthand, personal terms what they meant for those honest, struggling farmers who were compelled to accept them. The cost to the present was the poverty, illness, and despair that seemed endemic to much of the South; the cost to the future was the failure of the underfunded schools to educate the children and end the cycle of poverty.

Roosevelt told another story that elaborated his point. On his first visit to Warm Springs he had been jolted to consciousness in the middle of the night by the sound of a train rumbling through the village and blasting its whistle across the slope of Pine Mountain. He lay awake for some time afterward, pondering various subjects but mostly muttering about his interrupted sleep. "So I went down to the station and said to the stationmaster, 'What is that train that makes so much noise, and why does it have to whistle at half past one in the morning?' 'Oh,' he said, 'the fireman has a girl in town.' " Roosevelt asked what the train carried and where it was bound. "That is the milk train for Florida," the stationmaster said. Roosevelt assumed the milk came from Georgia or perhaps Alabama. He was surprised to be told that, no, it came from Wisconsin and Minnesota. Later he went to the village store to purchase a sack of apples. He had seen apples growing in the southern Appalachians and assumed he'd get some of those. But the local store carried no such local produce; the only apples the storekeeper stocked came from Oregon and Washington. He encountered a similar situation with beef. He couldn't find any local meat, only cuts sliced and dressed in Chicago and Omaha. The lesson he drew was the same one as in his school tale: southern troubles weren't the South's alone but manifestations of national difficulties. Solutions must be similarly national.

Doubtless Roosevelt's Warm Springs stories improved in the telling. Like many another moralist—and Roosevelt's stories invariably had a moral—Roosevelt dealt in truths deeper than surface detail. And the moral of his own Warm Springs story was that it connected him emotionally to the plain people of the South and, through them, to the ordinary people of America. Southern poverty wasn't *news* to Roosevelt; as an intelligent and well-read person, he had long known that the lot of southern farmers was a hard one. Nor had he been unaware, theoretically, that the problems of the South—and of other regions, for that matter—were tied to the condition of the national economy. But for the first time he *felt* what poverty meant to those who lived it daily.

Beyond improving his grasp of economics, Roosevelt's time at Warm Springs—and his overall experience of polio—made him better able to empathize with victims of misfortune generally. No one could suffer such an arbitrary blow of fate without becoming better attuned to others who suffered similarly. Capricious calamity isn't part of the American dream, which promises success to those who strive diligently toward reasonable goals. Other cultures have allowed greater scope for accident or the whims of the gods, but fatalism never caught on in America. Yet sometimes bad things *do* happen to people through no fault of their own. Roosevelt now understood this in a way he hadn't before.

Polio certainly helped people sympathize with *him* as they hadn't previously. Roosevelt's first four decades gave ordinary Americans little to identify with in him. His patrician background, mannerisms, and accent would have made him an ideal candidate for president in the age of Washington, Jefferson, and Madison, when ordinary Americans expected their leaders to stand above them. But the age of deference had ended with the election of Andrew Jackson; after that candidates for president needed to display a common touch if they hoped to win the people's confidence. Though some candidates faked it, the most successful were those whose bond with the people was genuine. Comparatively few Americans had suffered the specific disabilities associated with polio, but all had suffered in one way or another. And in their suffering they now could identify with Franklin Roosevelt.

16.

$\mathcal{N}$OT EVEN ROOSEVELT'S WORST RIVALS WOULD HAVE SAID THAT HIS contracting polio was anything but a misfortune. Yet some could have complained that if a Democrat with presidential ambitions *had* to come down with the disease, he couldn't have chosen a better time than the early 1920s. The decade after the World War was a wilderness period for the Democrats. The Republicans remained the nation's majority party, chiefly by virtue of their success in delivering on the promises of the economic revolution of the late nineteenth and early twentieth centuries. The Republican coalition combined nearly all the business interests of the country and added sufficient numbers of urban workers and midwestern farmers to lock up the White House and Congress. Against this coalition the Democrats arrayed nothing nearly so unified but rather the tired dualism of city bosses and southern gentry, with western mavericks shouting from the sideline. Pulled three ways at once, the Democrats went nowhere.

Roosevelt reentered the political lists gingerly. Following the shellacking he and James Cox suffered in 1920, he had no choice but to return to New York state politics, if he intended a political future. His eight years in Washington had weakened his position with the state party, and to maintain his electability he needed to restore his base. If he still wanted to be president—which he did, though the polio complicated the timing and logistics—he had to be able to count on New York's support. Aside from Wilson, whose capture of the White House owed chiefly to the Republicans' split in 1912, the only president the Democrats had elected since the Civil War was a New Yorker, Grover Cleveland. Roosevelt might have a chance of repeating Cleveland's accomplishment but only if he had the strong support of his home state.

With Louis Howe's help he communicated with the Democratic leaders in New York. He wrote letters to party officials around the state, urging them to keep the faith in the present dark hour for Democrats. The letters let Roosevelt preserve his political visibility even as they obscured his physical visibility, for in his letters he consistently minimized the severity of his illness and maximized the extent of his recovery. The strategy succeeded well enough that Tammany Hall spoke of nominating him for governor in 1922, on a ticket that included Al Smith for senator. Roosevelt let the talk continue for several months before acknowledging that he wasn't ready for a race just yet.

But he could help determine who *did* run. Smith had been elected governor in 1918, defying that year's Republican trend, and he had nearly been reelected in 1920, despite the Republican landslide in the rest of the country. Yet Smith didn't want to be governor again. He had taken a job with the United States Trucking Company and was, in the words of one of his Tammany Hall associates, "making big money for the first time in his life." Smith was happy to consider a Senate nomination, since the part-time work of Congress would have allowed him to keep his private-sector job. But the governorship was full-time, as he knew from experience. For this reason he had been one of the strongest supporters of the Roosevelt-Smith ticket for governor and senator.

When Roosevelt begged off, the pressure on Smith to make another run for governor intensified. If Smith declined, the nomination might well go to William Randolph Hearst, which was the last thing Tammany wanted. Hearst's ambitions were as large as Roosevelt's, and his family fortune—accumulated by his late father, George Hearst, the most successful miner in American history—was many times greater. After helping to provoke the Spanish-American War in 1898, the populist press lord advanced far enough in politics to win election to the House of Representatives in 1902 and 1904. His bid for the Democratic nomination for president in 1904 failed, and he subsequently wandered off to splinter parties. But he returned to the Democrats in time to criticize Al Smith's governorship and threaten a takeover of the party in 1922. Most of Tammany despised Hearst and would quickly have squelched his ambitions had he been an ordinary politician. But his fortune and his newspapers made him a formidable antagonist. Fear of Hearst, as much as love of Roosevelt, inspired the Tammany groundswell for the latter; when Roosevelt withdrew from consideration, Tammany turned in desperation to Smith.

The Tammany chieftains looked to Roosevelt to persuade Smith of his duty to state and party. Roosevelt responded with an open letter to Smith. "In every county the chief topic of political conversation is, 'Will Al Smith accept if he is nominated?' " Roosevelt declared. "Already unauthorized agents are saying that you will not accept, and many are being deceived and beginning to lose interest as a result." This would be a shame, in fact a tragedy. Roosevelt reminded Smith—that is, the readers of this open letter—that he had compiled a distinguished record as governor and that he had run a million votes ahead of the national Democratic ticket in 1920. "Many candidates for office are strong by virtue of promises of what they will some day do. You are strong by virtue of what you have done." Without citing specifics—of which he had none—Roosevelt asserted confidently that voters were tiring of the Republicans and were eager to return good Democrats to office. "You represent the hope of what might be called the 'average citizen.' " Roosevelt acknowledged that family considerations inclined Smith to seek financial security. "I am in the same boat myself," he said. "Yet this call to further service must come first. Some day your children will be even prouder of you for making this sacrifice than they are now."

Roosevelt's letter flushed Smith into the open, where he had no choice but to agree to accept an offered nomination. And it stymied Hearst, who lacked any comparable endorsement. "It appears to have rather punctured the Hearst boom," Roosevelt remarked happily. Roosevelt wasn't ready to declare victory, though. Hearst had money and could generate headlines at will. "Eternal vigilance is necessary in politics," Roosevelt said, "Al will not be nominated until the votes are actually cast in the convention."

Roosevelt labored to see that the votes were cast for Smith. He hosted a Hyde Park reception for Smith, who, after two years as governor, didn't have to be introduced to Roosevelt's Dutchess County neighbors but who nonetheless benefited from being seen with a local boy. Roosevelt passed up the state Democratic convention, on grounds of health, but sent Louis Howe and Eleanor—this being the first time the state party allowed women to serve as voting delegates. Smith easily won the nomination for governor, leaving Hearst to hope to land the party's nod for senator. Yet Smith blocked that avenue by vowing to withdraw from the governor's race if the convention nominated Hearst for senator. Smith tried to talk Roosevelt into accepting the Senate nomination, both to drive the nails into Hearst's coffin and to turn out a large Democratic vote in the general election. Roosevelt declined, citing the same reasons of health as before.

But on the whole he felt pleased with the results of the convention. The fact that his name kept popping up for office revealed that the Democrats still admired him, disability or no. And they still listened to him, which was no less gratifying. "I had quite a tussle in New York to keep our friend Hearst off the ticket and to get Al Smith to run," he wrote a friend, "but the thing went through in fine shape."

❖ ❖ ❖

ROOSEVELT COULDN'T CLAIM credit when Smith won the general election six weeks later. America's transition from war to peace occurred less smoothly than the Republicans in 1920 had intimated it would under their wise guidance. As the demand for agricultural and industrial products fell off after the armistice, farmers and manufacturers found themselves overplanted, overinvested, and overstaffed. Meanwhile the removal of wartime controls allowed wages and prices to seek their own level for the first time in years. The result was a roller-coaster ride for the economy, which plunged in 1919, rose in 1920 (in time for the elections), and plunged again in 1921 and 1922. The latter drop made the Republicans vulnerable, especially in states like New York, where Prohibition added to voters' dissatisfaction. The Eighteenth Amendment was as unpopular in New York City as in most other urban areas, and New Yorkers didn't hesitate to vent their displeasure at those they considered responsible, namely the Republicans. The result was a thumping victory for the wet Democrat Smith and renewed hope among Democrats generally that as New York went in 1922, so the nation might go before long.

Roosevelt imagined, on his best days in the months that followed, that he would be the one leading the party to victory. Not long after the election he wrote to James Cox of the "very successful summer" he had spent at Hyde Park. "The combination of warm weather, fresh air, and swimming has done me a world of good. . . . The legs are really coming along finely, and when I am in swimming work perfectly. This shows that the muscles are all there, only require further strengthening. I am still on crutches but get about quite spryly."

Yet when his physical progress failed to keep pace with his hopes, he recognized that his political comeback would have to wait a while longer, and he rededicated himself to the advancement of the Democratic party as a whole. The party needed his help, badly. During the 1920s the Democrats' paralysis grew worse than ever. The current source of the trouble, or at least its most obvious manifestation, was the Ku Klux Klan. The twentieth-century Klan was an ecumenical update of its Reconstruction-era predecessor; it targeted not only African Americans but Catholics, Jews, immigrants, feminists, communists, and anyone else who challenged its members' narrow notions of conservative values. The modern Klan spread far beyond the Old South, planting active chapters in such previously unlikely locales as Indiana and Oregon. The Klan tipped political races in several states and was influential in getting Congress to pass the first comprehensive immigration control measure, in 1924. A Klan parade down Pennsylvania Avenue in Washington in 1925 featured thousands of hooded, white-sheeted members.

The rise of the Klan complicated the politics of the Democratic party, aggravating the divisions among the party's eastern, southern, and western wings. The eastern Democrats, who embodied the machine politics of the big cities, were conservative economically, being generally supportive of banks and other big business; friendly to immigrants, on whom they had depended politically for decades; and wet, urging repeal of the Eighteenth Amendment. The southern Democrats were the heirs of the post-Reconstruction "Redeemers" and were the current strongest column in the Klan. They looked on New York as the source of most evil in America, with Wall Street and the Lower East Side haunting their dreams about equally, the former on account of its control of the nation's commerce, the latter for furnishing refuge to Catholic and Jewish immigrants. New York was also the home of the speakeasies, which the southern Democrats—dry to the last Baptist—considered dens of iniquity. The West was the wild card in the Democratic deck. The western Democrats numbered many fewer than the Easterners or the Southerners, but they potentially held the balance between those two groups. The Westerners were the party radicals on economic issues, having absorbed the message of Populism during the 1890s and never forgotten it. Western farmers felt the pain of the continuing postwar agricultural slump and demanded relief, relatively undistracted by such other issues as race and immigration. On Prohibition the Westerners were predominantly dry.

Each segment of the party had its champion in 1924. Al Smith was the darling of the Easterners, having lived down his Tammany past to become, in his second term as New York governor, a persuasive spokesman for clean, efficient government. Catholic and wet, Smith symbolized the cosmopolitan tolerance on which the eastern Democrats prided themselves. Oscar Underwood appealed to Southerners by virtue of his Alabama roots and residence. His name on the tariff reduction act of 1913 still reminded southern farmers of his devotion to their cause, as against that of Wall Street—and against many of the eastern Democrats. Yet Underwood hoped to reach the rest of the party, and presumably the rest of the country, by roundly denouncing the Klan. He went so far as to declare the Klan a mortal threat to democracy and the most important issue facing the party, and he demanded that other candidates join him in condemning the organization. William McAdoo, the former Treasury secretary, who had relocated from Washington and New York to California—

for personal reasons, he said, but really to distance himself from Tammany Hall—was the favorite of the West.

Smith, as a Catholic target of Klan vituperation, had no difficulty accepting Underwood's challenge and denouncing the Klan. But McAdoo demurred. Having grown up in Georgia during the era of the first Klan, McAdoo considered the second edition comparatively harmless. Moreover, with Underwood on record as opposing the Klan, parts of the South were suddenly in play. If McAdoo could finesse the Klan issue—neither endorsing the Klan, which could ruin his chances in the nation as a whole, nor repudiating it, which would cost him southern support—he might carry the 1924 convention. On a visit to Georgia he issued a statement regarding the Klan: "I stand four square with respect to this and I stand four square with respect to every other organization on the immutable question of liberty contained in the first amendment of the Constitution of the United States, namely freedom of religious worship, freedom of speech, freedom of the press, and the right of peaceful assembly." A leading Klan official, apparently after communicating privately with McAdoo, applauded this statement as perfectly acceptable to the organization. The Klansman might have gone farther had he not feared that an open endorsement would be used against McAdoo. But the message to the Klan rank and file was clear: McAdoo is with us in spirit.

This was what worried Roosevelt, who would have supported fellow New Yorker Smith anyway but now considered McAdoo's Klan connection a formula for electing Republicans for another six decades. Until the 1920s Roosevelt had never thought deeply or systematically about the future of the Democratic party or its place in American national politics. His first few years in government had been consumed with New York state politics, and during most of his time in the Wilson administration the Democrats had been the ruling party, a condition unconducive to serious reflection about the future. But after the defeat of 1920 Roosevelt turned his mind to long-term strategy. He recognized that Wilson's success had been a fluke, the beneficiary of a Republican rift that probably wouldn't be repeated in Roosevelt's lifetime. The Republicans had been the normal majority party since the Civil War, and if the Democrats hoped to break the GOP's hold on power, they would have to reconfigure and reposition themselves.

As a first step, they needed to decide what to keep and what to reject of their Wilsonian inheritance. Wilson's had been an unusual administration, in that it had begun with an overwhelmingly domestic orientation and ended obsessed with foreign policy—indeed, obsessed with a single item of foreign policy: the League of Nations. Roosevelt understood that any obsession was unhealthy, but he remained committed to the internationalist principles of the League, and he believed that a judicious educational effort by the Democrats could win them support at the expense of isolationist Republicans. "I am not wholly convinced that the country is yet quite ready for a definite stand on our part in favor of immediate entry into the League of Nations," he wrote James Cox in 1922. "That will come in time, but I am convinced we should stand firmly against the isolation policy of Harding's administration."

As a modest first step toward this goal, Roosevelt headed a committee to create an endowment honoring Wilson and the principles of the League. Ill health—first Wilson's and then Roosevelt's—complicated the fund-raising, but by the time Wilson died, in 1924, the Wilson Foundation had collected more than $700,000 and was beginning to sponsor activities relating Wilson's beliefs to current affairs.

More directly, Roosevelt addressed the crux of American skepticism on international affairs: article 10 of the covenant of the League of Nations, which committed signatories to the defense of one another against external aggression. The skeptics contended that this article unconstitutionally stole war-declaring power from Congress and war-making power from the president. Wilson's explanations in 1919 hadn't seriously dented this conception, and subsequent efforts by lesser League advocates hadn't either. Roosevelt knew better than to try; instead he advocated rewriting the offending article. In response to a contest organized by Edward Bok, the longtime editor of *Ladies' Home Journal,* to generate proposals for means of fostering world peace, Roosevelt drafted a plan for an updated and improved version of the League of Nations. Roosevelt's version would be called the "Society of Nations," in recognition, he explained, "that public opinion in the United States is, and will be for some time to come, sufficiently hostile to the present formula of the League of Nations to preclude any use of the old name." The Society's membership would be similar to the League's, except that it would include the United States. Its structure would differ in giving more power to a permanent executive committee, consisting of the five great powers (the United States, Britain, France, Italy, and Japan) and six rotating members. Decisions would be by a two-thirds majority rather than by the unanimity required of the League. "Common sense cannot defend a procedure by which one or two recalcitrant nations could block the will of the great majority," Roosevelt explained. Most significantly for Americans, article 10 of the League covenant would be diluted dramatically. In place of the guarantee that the League would "preserve as against external aggression" the independence and territory of member states, Roosevelt's draft specified that members would "undertake to respect" one another's sovereignty and borders. And in the event of violation, the Society would merely "make recommendations" as to appropriate responses.

In the end Roosevelt declined to enter his League revision plan in Bok's contest. Eleanor had become a member of the committee evaluating the entries, and rather than ask her to recuse herself he simply shelved his plan. Perhaps he had second thoughts about going public with his proposal at a time when any mention of the League risked triggering an isolationist backlash. Yet he mentally filed away his thoughts, as he had been filing away political reflections for years, to await a more propitious time. And when that time arrived he would sponsor a successor to the League that looked very much like his Society of Nations.

Meanwhile he concentrated on issues where he thought progress *was* possible. Though the Harding administration eschewed involvement in European affairs, in matters pertaining to Asia and the Pacific it was less diffident. Charles Evans Hughes, Wilson's adversary in 1916 and now Harding's secretary of state, brought representatives of the leading naval powers to Washington, with an eye toward curtailing an escalating arms race and establishing a framework for security in the Pacific. The Washington Conference opened on Armistice Day 1921; it generated the ordinary effusions of goodwill and, over the next three months, an extraordinary series of treaties pledging the great powers to unprecedentedly self-denying behavior. The United States, Britain, and Japan consented to reduce their navies and to refrain from fortifying their Pacific possessions. They agreed to arbitrate disputes, to respect the status quo in the Pacific, and specifically to honor the territorial integrity of China.

Roosevelt attempted to build on Hughes's accomplishment. In the summer of 1923 he published an article in *Asia* magazine asking, "Shall We Trust Japan?" He answered that Americans should do so and that the Washington Conference gave them reason to believe they could. The Washington system engaged Japan's honor, which Japan's leaders were loath to besmirch. More to the point, the naval limitations largely eliminated Japan's ability to threaten China or shake the status quo. America itself was still more secure. "Even if Japan in 1914 had any false notion that she could threaten us either through Mexico or by direct invasion of the Pacific Coast," Roosevelt said, "it is safe to say that her strategists have now tacitly abandoned such ideas." He added, as one who knew something about positioning ships and other naval assets: "As long as ten years ago naval experts said that a fleet crossing a wide ocean from its home base must of necessity lose from a quarter to a third of its fighting force. If that judgment was true ten years ago, then the principle is even more true today; for the addition of two new dimensions, under water and in the air, to the fighting area has made the protection of the capital ship—super-dreadnought or battle cruiser, the fundamental fighting unit—a much harder task than it was then."

❖   ❖   ❖

On the issue of greatest interest to voters—the health of the economy—the Republicans appeared unbeatable. Farmers continued to suffer from low prices, high debt, and unrealistic hopes of a return to the flush years of the war, but city dwellers—who, according to the 1920 census, for the first time outnumbered their rural compatriots—were doing very well. The hiccups of the postwar transition had given way to a period of robust growth. Consumers spent the piles of money they had saved during the war, when military production had crowded out consumer goods. Topping the lists of must-have items were new cars. "The paramount ambition of the average man a few years ago was to own a home and have a bank account," a small-town banker observed. "The ambition of the same man today is to own a car." Henry Ford's Model T remained the most popular model; in 1920 the Tin Lizzies came off the assembly line at Ford Motor's monster River Rouge plant in Detroit at the rate of one per minute. Half the cars in the world were Fords. A growing part of the other half consisted of the many models gathered under the General Motors umbrella and marketed with uncanny adeptness by GM chief Alfred P. Sloan.

The auto boom echoed in other industries. The steel industry rolled square miles of sheet metal for fenders; the rubber industry tapped whole rain forests to make tires; the glass industry floated and cooled acres of windscreens and side panes. Big Oil was an even bigger winner: the millions of cars required billions of gallons of gasoline. (As a bonus to the petro-men, railroads and ships converted from coal to diesel during this same era.) The road-building industry benefited as the various levels of government discovered that averting mayhem on the highways required constructing wider, smoother, straighter roads than horses and buggies had needed.

The auto boom reshaped American housing. The lifting of the wartime caps on construction would have triggered a modest surge in home building, but the advent of the auto age allowed builders to venture much farther from the centers of cities. New neighborhoods—suburbs—sprang up where truck gardens and orchards had grown. Cheap land translated into lower costs to builders and lower prices to purchasers, who secured mortgages and signed contracts while the carpenters and plumbers were still pounding and fitting away.

The new houses demanded new furniture and new appliances. Electricity for the first time entered the average home, lighting rooms, washing clothes, refrigerating food. Telephones kept families in touch with friends and one another; radios gradually connected households to the wider world of public affairs, music, and sports.

Americans looked out upon the material world that surrounded them and, with the exception of those farmers, accounted it good. No one knew how long the bounty would last; no one ever knew such things. But while it did last, Americans were likely to stick with the party that presided over the prosperity.

❖   ❖   ❖

FOR THIS REASON the Democratic convention of 1924 was something of a charade, having as much to do with auditioning future candidates as with selecting a leader to send against the Republicans. When the delegates gathered at New York's Madison Square Garden, the contest came down to Al Smith and William McAdoo. Oscar Underwood had faded after his rejection of the Klan, and the handful of minor candidates weren't generating appreciable support. McAdoo led, but Smith was closing, partly on account of the Klan controversy but also because of a scandal involving Republicans. In 1922 the *Wall Street Journal* had broken a story relating that Harding's secretary of the interior, Albert Fall, had allowed a private petroleum company to lease the navy's oil reserve at Teapot Dome, Wyoming, without the customary competitive bidding. As the tale unfolded during the next two years, it revealed a web of corruption that reached from Washington to California. Harding appeared honestly surprised and was undeniably distraught. "I have no trouble with my enemies," he told journalist William Allen White. "I can take care of my enemies all right. But my damn friends, my God-damn friends, White, they're the ones that keep me walking the floor nights!" Albert Fall was tried and convicted of taking bribes. Several others joined him in the dock and a few behind bars; a couple escaped justice, or at least prison, by killing themselves. Teapot

Dome entered the vocabulary of American political corruption alongside the Tweed Ring and Crédit Mobilier.

All this delighted the Democrats, with William McAdoo being the signal exception. One of Fall's tempters was Edward Doheny, a Californian who had hired McAdoo as legal counsel, on an annual retainer of $25,000. No one alleged malfeasance in McAdoo, but clearly it was his access to official Washington—rather than his competence as a lawyer, for example—that made him attractive to Doheny. Although McAdoo's Teapot Dome connection didn't prevent his accumulating enough support to roll into the 1924 convention with a lead in committed delegates, it tainted him in the eyes of the uncommitted, who fretted that a McAdoo nomination would deprive the Democrats of the biggest stick they hoped to swing against the Republicans that autumn.

The Smith forces rallied behind their leader and his first lieutenant, Franklin Roosevelt. The death of Charles Murphy had deprived Smith of an obvious campaign manager, and the candidate's eye naturally fell on Roosevelt, who could bring to the Smith campaign a polish and national presence it conspicuously lacked. Roosevelt could write and call influential people Smith didn't know; Roosevelt, the old-stock Protestant, could reassure delegates that a Smith nomination wouldn't hand the party to immigrant Catholics.

For Roosevelt, heading the Smith campaign suited his comeback plans perfectly. He could tell that this wasn't the year to be the Democratic nominee. The Teapot Dome scandals had damaged the Republicans as a group but were sparing the top of the ticket, chiefly because Harding's sudden death in August 1923 had eliminated the man in charge at the time of the influence peddling. Calvin Coolidge, the current occupant of the White House, could believably claim that he had had nothing to do with the whole affair. Roosevelt thought the Democrats should try to keep the scandal before the voters, but he doubted the effort would do much good.

So he focused on the convention. He contrived to break custom and deliver the speech putting Smith's name before the convention. Candidates had typically enlisted the party's most celebrated orators for this function, but times were changing, and with them standards of political speech. Although no one knew it then, the 1924 convention marked William Jennings Bryan's final appearance before the full party; yet even that summer it was clear that the days when successful rhetoric required Bryanic lung power to fill a hall were passing. Electric amplification allowed speakers to lower their voices, to draw listeners into a realm of intimacy denied their pre-Edison forebears. Radio would shortly reveal the full effect of this change, and no one would employ radio more effectively than Franklin Roosevelt. But aspects of the change were already in evidence when Roosevelt addressed the Democratic convention of 1924.

He carefully plotted his path to the dais. Several times he rehearsed his steps, his left arm holding the right arm of his son James, his right arm and shoulder supported by a crutch, his legs cocooned in their steel braces. He taught James the art of the clenched-teeth smile, the seemingly effortless nod of the head accomplished amid great muscular and psychological strain. On the night of his address, when he and James reached the platform, he took his second crutch from his son and turned to a delegate nearby. Motioning with his head toward the speaker's stand, he said, "Go up and shake it, will you?" The delegate hesitated, puzzled. "Shake it!" Roosevelt insisted. "I must know if the speaker's stand will bear my weight."

As the delegate tested the stand's sturdiness, Roosevelt began his solitary final steps forward. Every eye in Madison Square Garden followed his progress; every breath hesitated, awaiting his fall. When he reached the stand the delegates and the visitors in the galleries erupted in sustained applause. Roosevelt smiled and nodded the more, but where another speaker, or Roosevelt himself a few years earlier, would have waved to the thousands clapping and shouting his name, he now didn't dare release his grip on the speaker's stand, either to acknowledge the applause or to wipe the sweat that poured from his face.

Gradually the hall fell quiet. "To meet again so many friends whom I have not seen since the last Democratic national gathering gives me a thrill of pleasure," Roosevelt began. The audience cheered again. He continued to smile, and to grip the stand. The cheering gradually died.

He reintroduced the delegates to Al Smith with a self-deprecating reminder of the Democrats' woes in 1920. "When our national ticket in the state of New York went down to defeat under a plurality of 1,100,000, he lost this state by only 74,000," Roosevelt said. "He got one million more votes than I did—and I take my hat off to him!" McAdoo's supporters were claiming for their candidate the title progressive reformer; Roosevelt countered the claim by citing Smith's record on behalf of the less fortunate:

> He obtained laws prohibiting night work for women and the employment of small children. He secured state pensions for widowed mothers and state aid for the promotion of the health of rural communities. That is progressive!

He has sponsored a practical workmen's compensation law, and has established labor boards to mediate disputes between employer and employee; he was responsible for the best factory laws ever passed in any state. That is progressive!

Under his leadership, cooperative marketing, the extension of state highways built for miles, not votes; diversification of crops and the reforestation of denuded lands have marched hand in hand. That is progressive!

Roosevelt summoned the spirit of the Democrats' progressive former president, only recently deceased, on behalf of Smith's vision. "It was the illustrious Woodrow Wilson, my revered chief and yours, who said, 'The great voice of America does not come from the university. It comes in a murmur from the hills and the woods, from the farms, the factories, and the mills—rolling on and gaining volume until it comes to us from the homes of the common people.' " The common people were the core constituency of the Democrats, and among the common people the dreams of America never flagged. "Four years ago, lying opponents said that the country was tired of ideals—they waged a campaign based on an appeal to prejudice, based on the dragging out of bogies and hobgoblins, the subtle encouragement of false fears." But America had not lost her faith, Roosevelt insisted. "Idealism is of her very heart's blood. Tricked once we have been. Millions of voters are waiting today for the opportunity next November to wreak their vengeance on those deceivers."

Al Smith was the man who would lead them. "He has a power to strike at error and wrongdoing that makes his adversaries quail before him. He has a personality that carries to every hearer not only the sincerity but the righteousness of what he says. He is the Happy Warrior of the political battlefield."

❖   ❖   ❖

*A*s ROOSEVELT FINISHED, the crowd erupted once again. Some were cheering for Smith; all were rooting for Roosevelt. "A noble utterance," conservative journalist Mark Sullivan called the speech. "It will rank as the high point of the present convention and it belongs with the small list of really great convention speeches." The *New York Herald Tribune* described Roosevelt as "the one man whose name would have stampeded the convention were he put in nomination." The *Herald Tribune* added, "He is the only man to whom the contending factions could turn and at the same time save their faces and keep square with the folks at home. . . . From the time Roosevelt made his speech in nomination of Smith, which was the one great speech of the convention, he has been easily the foremost figure on floor or platform." The *New York Evening World* asserted, "No matter whether Governor Smith wins or loses, Franklin D. Roosevelt stands out as the real hero of the Democratic Convention of 1924. Adversity has lifted him above the bickering, the religious bigotry, conflicting personal ambitions and petty sectional prejudices. It has made him the one leader commanding the respect and admiration of delegations from all sections of the land. . . . Roosevelt might be a pathetic, tragic figure but for the fine courage that flashes in his smile. It holds observers enchained."

Roosevelt's reputation for lighthearted courage—many delegates decided *he* was the Happy Warrior, the one the more literate recalled Wordsworth characterizing in the poem that began "Who is the happy warrior? Who is he / That every man in arms should wish to be?"—only increased when the convention got down to the bruising business of choosing a nominee. As most expected, McAdoo led early but lacked the votes to put Smith away. A dozen ballots produced little movement; a dozen more, then another dozen, and another and another left the delegates gasping for air but no closer to a decision. Roosevelt returned to the rostrum after sixty-six ballots to move that Governor Smith be allowed to address the convention in person. This was a breach of tradition so egregious as to require the assent of two-thirds of the delegates; the Smith delegates naturally supported the motion, as did some quaverers on the McAdoo side. But the defections weren't numerous enough to open the convention-hall door to the governor, and the balloting continued with the candidates kept off the premises.

The contest became a battle of attrition, with each side battering and bleeding the other. Smith pulled ahead of McAdoo but couldn't achieve the necessary two-thirds majority. Victory for either side increasingly appeared impossible.

Roosevelt huddled with Smith and, following the ninety-third ballot, again addressed the convention. "I am here to make a brief and very simple statement on behalf of Governor Smith," he told the delegates. "After nearly one hundred ballots it is quite apparent to him and to me that the forces behind him, the leader in the race, and behind Mr. McAdoo, who is second, cannot be amalgamated. For the good of the party Governor Smith authorizes me to say that immediately after Mr. McAdoo withdraws, Governor Smith will withdraw his name."

McAdoo declined the offer, but after six more ballots he released his delegates to vote their judgment of the party's good. A few did so at once, then more and more. The critical break occurred when the women of the California delegation, the most determined of the McAdoo diehards, lowered the flags they had been waving incessantly for their favorite.

The beneficiary of McAdoo's tacit withdrawal, and of Smith's more formal version, was John W. Davis of West Virginia. Davis was known to oppose the Ku Klux Klan and excessively powerful corporate trusts, but otherwise he had left few marks on the public record that anyone could object to. The exhausted delegates fell in line behind his candidacy, and on the 103rd ballot he received the nomination.

❖   ❖   ❖

YET THE REAL beneficiary of that exhausting week was Roosevelt. "The most popular man in the convention was Franklin D. Roosevelt," the New York Times asserted. "Whenever word passed around the floor that Mr. Roosevelt was about to take his seat in the New York delegation, a hush fell over the Garden. On his appearance each time there was a spontaneous burst of applause."

The political insiders agreed. Tom Pendergast, Kansas City's counterpart to the late Charles Murphy, told Ike Dunlap, a Pendergast man who knew Roosevelt, "I met your friend Franklin Roosevelt in New York and had just a few words with him. I want to say this, Dunlap—you know I am seldom carried away or become overly enthusiastic in meeting men of all stations of life, but I want to tell you that had Mr. Roosevelt . . . been physically able to have withstood the campaign, he would have been named by acclamation the first few days of the convention. He has the most magnetic personality of any individual I have ever met, and I predict he will be the candidate on the Democratic ticket in 1928."

17.

ROOSEVELT HEARD THE PRAISE AND PONDERED HOW TO MAKE THE most of it. From the state of the economy and the country he assumed that Americans weren't done with the Republicans yet; a comeback by the Democrats almost certainly would require a stumble by the GOP. But the Democrats would reward their loyalists when that stumble occurred, and Roosevelt positioned himself to be seen as the most loyal son of America's oldest party. He polled Democratic leaders around the country regarding the most promising steps for the party, and he summarized the replies in a published letter to Thomas J. Walsh, the Montana senator who had been permanent chairman of the Democratic national convention in 1920. A consensus had emerged, Roosevelt said, that what the Democrats needed to do was reiterate the essential difference between themselves and the Republicans. "The Democracy must make it clear that it seeks primarily the good of the average citizen through the free rule of the whole electorate, as opposed to the Republican Party, which seeks a mere moneyed prosperity of the nation through the control of government by a self-appointed aristocracy of wealth and of social and economic power." To this end the party needed to put national issues above local concerns. The Democrats had divided themselves by region, with the Easterners advocating one thing, the Southerners another, and the Westerners something else. Roosevelt refrained from specifying the divisive issues, lest he reinforce the division by doing so, but Prohibition and the Klan came quickly to attentive minds. The consequence was that voters had no idea what the party, as a national party, believed or advocated. The remedy, Roosevelt said, was to emphasize what the various elements of the party had in common. To facilitate this he recommended a national meeting of state Democratic leaders, to be held in the spring of 1925 and charged with defining what made Democrats Democrats.

Senator Walsh and other party officials responded positively to Roosevelt's recommendation. But resistance developed precisely where Roosevelt feared it would: among the populists long associated with William Jennings Bryan. The three-time Democratic nominee and former secretary of state had never stopped distrusting the party's eastern business element, and with the emergence of Prohibition as a polarizing issue, he learned to distrust the party's eastern ethnic—that is, wet—element too. Bryan countered Roosevelt's unity plan with suggestions that the Democrats' southern and western wings join forces against the East.

Bryan's opposition conjured fears—and hopes, among Republicans—of a confrontation between Roosevelt and Bryan at the annual Jefferson Day dinner in Washington in April 1925. The event had produced some of the most memorable scenes in American history, including Andrew Jackson's defiant rejection of the secessionism of his own vice president, John C. Calhoun, amid the nullification crisis of Jackson's first term. "Our Federal Union," Jackson had thundered, "it must be preserved!" The rift among the Democrats wasn't quite so deep almost a century later, but Washington quivered with excitement at the thought of a showdown between the crippled champion of liberal unity and the aging lion of agrarian dissent.

It didn't come to that. A showdown was the last thing Roosevelt wanted, and he wrote the organizers of the Jefferson dinner explaining that his physical recovery required a longer stay at Warm Springs that season than he had anticipated. He couched his regrets in typically upbeat fashion, asserting that after another several weeks of therapy he might be able to "throw away" his crutches. Bryan had no such compelling excuse, but he too begged off, simply saying that his calendar was full.

Yet Roosevelt met Bryan nonetheless. He traveled from Warm Springs to Miami, where Bryan was still selling land, to pitch party unity in person. "He was, at first, fearful that a conference, especially a large one, would result in more trouble than good," Roosevelt remarked a short while later. But Roosevelt persisted, and Bryan gradually softened. "After we had talked for over an hour he agreed that if the conference were kept small, as I outlined, it would accomplish very great things." Bryan's stated concern was that Easterners and city dwellers would dominate the party, as they had during the evil days of Grover Cleveland. "But, as I pointed out to him, there are millions of really progressive Democratic voters in these localities who cannot be read out of the Party by making the Democracy a mere combination of the South and the West, and he agreed that the Party policies and Party effort must be made national instead of sectional."

❖ ❖ ❖

$\mathscr{B}$RYAN'S AGREEMENT came too late. Other elements of the party had been happy to let Bryan take the blame for frustrating Democratic unity, but as Bryan's resistance began to melt under the warmth of the Roosevelt sun, they raised objections of their own. Some simply didn't believe that Bryan's conversion to party unity was sincere, suspecting the old man—although he was a mere sixty-five, he seemed to have been around forever—of hoping to lead one last revolt. Others questioned Roosevelt's motives. Was the proposed conference an honest effort to mend the party or a vehicle Roosevelt hoped would carry him to the 1928 nomination?

The objections had the desired effect of delaying Roosevelt's conference, pushing it back into summer of 1925, when the whole idea of a conference exploded amid events neither Roosevelt nor Bryan anticipated. The Tennessee legislature, at the behest of conservative Christians, had recently approved a law forbidding the teaching of evolution in the state's public schools. The American Civil Liberties Union enlisted a young teacher named John Scopes to challenge the law, and the ensuing trial, in the small town of Dayton, attracted the attention of much of the country. Bryan, one of America's best-known Christian fundamentalists, took the witness stand as an authority on the Bible. Scopes's lawyer, celebrated atheist and defense attorney Clarence Darrow, grilled Bryan unmercifully and tied him in logical knots but failed to shake his conviction that the author of Genesis, not Charles Darwin, had got the story of creation right. The Bryan-Darrow confrontation, which was broadcast by radio to a national audience, deepened the rift between traditionalists and progressives in American life, with the former concluding that Bryan had held his ground while the latter thought he was made to look a fool. Scopes was convicted—the verdict was later overturned on a technicality—but the more dramatic, and poignant, conclusion occurred when Bryan suddenly died less than a week later. H. L. Mencken, the acid-penned journalist and social commentator, remarked: "God aimed at Darrow, missed, and hit Bryan instead."

Roosevelt's hopes for a party conference died with Bryan, but his desire to discover common ground on which a national ticket might stand persisted. Al Smith remained the favorite of Democrats' city wing, which grew in numbers and influence with each passing year. Westerners and some Southerners still liked William McAdoo, but after Smith won reelection as New York governor in 1926, by the largest margin in the history of the Empire State, he appeared the odds-on favorite to capture the Democratic nomination for president in 1928.

The only person who potentially blocked his way was Franklin Roosevelt. The longer Smith's lead over McAdoo stretched, the more desperately party strategists asked themselves whether American voters would embrace a wet Catholic and the more attractive Roosevelt looked as an alternative. Roosevelt had most of what made Smith attractive: a strong eastern presence and credibility with the party's urban wing. And he traveled without Smith's heavy baggage, being Protestant and tactfully silent on Prohibition. His physical disability netted out neutrally: what he lost in lack of mobility on the campaign trail he recouped in voter sympathy. The big question was whether he could lead a ticket. Nearly everyone thought he had done well as number two in 1920, but number two wasn't number one.

There was another question: whether Roosevelt wanted the nomination. As often as his friends and supporters urged him to run, he deflected their appeals in favor of Smith. He would have registered greater interest in the 1928 nomination had he thought there was anything in it, but the Republican prosperity continued, causing most political analysts to doubt that voters would be inclined to dump the GOP for the Democracy. Farmers were hurting, but farmers had been hurting for decades without their injury redounding to the Democrats' benefit. The nation's center of gravity now rested in the cities; till something shook the confidence of city dwellers, the Republicans would remain America's party.

Roosevelt said as much in a confidential letter to Josephus Daniels in the summer of 1927. "Strictly between ourselves," Roosevelt wrote, "I am very doubtful whether any Democrat can win in 1928. It will depend somewhat on whether the present undoubted general prosperity of the country continues. You and I may recognize the serious hardships which the farmers in the South and West are laboring under, but the farmers in the South will vote the Democratic ticket anyway, and I do not believe that the farmers of the West will vote the Democratic ticket in sufficient numbers even if they are starving."

So he put his shoulder to the Smith wheel. If Smith by a miracle won, the country would benefit, as Smith, in Roosevelt's view, was far preferable to any Republican. And Roosevelt would get credit for party loyalty, which could only help a Roosevelt run eight years later. (Neither Roosevelt nor Smith even considered a ticket with both men on it, as the Twelfth Amendment effectively bars a single-state ticket.) If Smith lost, Roosevelt would still get the loyalty credit, which he could redeem in four years.

Smith needed help in the area of foreign policy especially. The only foreign policy Tammany pursued was friendly relations with the countries that supplied the immigrants that kept the bosses in power. Such relations were harder to ensure in the age of immigration restriction than they had been during the open-door era prior to 1924, but Tammany men still marched in St. Patrick's Day parades, waved the Italian flag on Columbus Day, and honored as many mother countries as there were ethnic neighborhoods in New York. Smith learned little more about foreign policy in Albany. In a later period governors would venture overseas to drum up foreign business and otherwise represent their states to the world, but in the 1920s such modest drumming as was done remained the province of the federal government.

Roosevelt's extensive personal experience of the world and his long attention to foreign affairs contrasted sharply with Smith's inexperience and inattention, and consequently he was the natural choice both to tutor Smith and to define a Democratic foreign policy for the country. In the summer of 1928 he answered an invitation from the Council on Foreign Relations, a New York association of internationalists, to present what amounted to the Democrats' foreign policy platform.

He made his case cautiously. The popular isolationism that had seized American policy since Wilson's battle with the Senate Republicans over the Treaty of Versailles continued unabated. If anything, the booming economy convinced most Americans that they didn't need the rest of the world, and various unsettling developments abroad made them think they didn't *want* the rest of the world. Mussolini had seized control of Italy, and though a certain fascination with Fascist efficiency emerged among America's business classes, many more Americans wished to have nothing to do with the Duce. The Soviet Union, as Russia's empire was now called, had dropped off the world map, partly because Stalin wanted things that way while he consolidated his grip on the Kremlin and partly because the capitalist democracies, including the United States, were doing all they could to quarantine the Bolshevik infection. China was a mess, having descended into civil war after the long-expected collapse of the Manchu dynasty. Japan was making more ominous noises than ever about establishing an empire in East Asia.

Germany was a looming question mark. The hyperinflation of the immediate postwar period had been brought under control, but the former autocracy's attempt at democracy was failing to inspire confidence in anyone, including Germany's tentative democrats. The gang of thugs and unemployed war veterans who had gathered under the banner of National Socialism had already tried once, in 1923, to topple the German government, and though the leaders had been tossed into jail, they were now back on the streets and in the beer halls, nursing their grievances against democracy, against foreigners, against communists, against Jews, and against the Versailles system. In spirit they weren't much different from the Ku Klux Klan in America, and their revolt against modernity reflected fears not unlike those that inspired Prohibition and the anti-evolution movement. But the Nazis, and especially their leader, Adolf Hitler, were far more ruthless than anyone in the United States—and far more ruthless than anyone outside their movement knew.

Republican officials in Washington kept America's distance from the world. They publicly decried the League of Nations as the antithesis of everything George Washington and the other founders had fought for. On certain low-visibility issues like public health and education, they cooperated quietly with the Geneva-based body, but on anything approaching high politics or diplomacy they continued to shun it. They denied the jurisdiction of the World Court over Americans or American actions, preferring that their country and their countrymen remain, in a technical and sometimes practical sense, outlaws to the rest of the world. They raised America's tariff wall, effectively closing American markets to many foreign goods. And when they finally agreed to reschedule war loans due the United States from foreign debtors, they did so with a conspicuous lack of grace. Calvin Coolidge at first rejected calls for relief of the Europeans' financial distress with a typically terse retort: "They hired the money, didn't they?" The Republican president relented only far enough to put Germany in America's debt, along with Britain and France. The Germans needed money to pay what the Versailles treaty said they owed the British and the French in reparations; the British and French needed the reparations to repay their loans from the United States. Coolidge approved a plan whereby Germany would borrow American money to pay the British and French, who would close the circle by using Germany's payments to service their American loans. The beauty of the plan, from the standpoint of American bankers, was that they would receive interest all the way around.

Beauty of this sort was mostly in the eyes of the participating bankers. To please the much larger group not in the lending trade, the Coolidge administration endorsed the Pact of Paris of 1928, also called the Kellogg-Briand Treaty, after American secretary of state Frank B. Kellogg and French foreign minis-

ter Aristide Briand. On its face, the Paris treaty would revolutionize diplomacy, by the simple expedient of forbidding war. The signatories, eventually
including almost every government in the world, solemnly promised not to resort to war to resolve international disputes. The treaty was gloriously innocuous, containing no provisions for enforcement. Its toothless quality was
reflected in the 85 to 1 vote in its favor in the U.S. Senate.

This was the record Roosevelt assailed in July 1928. He had help in drafting his Democratic manifesto from Sumner Welles, a thirty-five-year-old New
Yorker with roots even deeper in America's upper crust than Roosevelt's, with
similar experiences of school and college at Groton and Harvard, and with an
equally international outlook on American policy. Hamilton Fish Armstrong,
the editor of *Foreign Affairs,* which had been founded six years earlier by the
Council on Foreign Relations to keep the Wilsonian dream alive, helped whip
the argument into final shape.

Roosevelt rejected the go-it-alone attitude of the Republicans, and he denied that it represented America's historic traditions. He walked his readers
through the nineteenth and early twentieth centuries along a path of constructive internationalism. The Monroe Doctrine was a formula for hemispheric peace, he said. Disputes with Britain over Canada's borders and over
Civil War damages were settled by arbitration. The Spanish-American War,
for all the provocation of the *Maine*'s destruction, was "not a war of revenge,
but the offer of a helping hand" to the suffering Cuban people. Annexation of
the Philippines, with an eye toward preparing the Filipinos for self-
government, was a "precursor of the 'Mandate' theory of the League of Nations." The United States had helped organize the Hague tribunal, the
forerunner of the World Court. Theodore Roosevelt had mediated an end to
the Russo-Japanese War.

The World War exemplified America's attachment to internationalist ideals.
Woodrow Wilson led the country into the war not for selfish gain but to uphold the principle of neutral rights. During the war he guided the belligerents
toward a just and equitable peace. "Slowly, through 1917 and 1918," Roosevelt
said, "the American President brought home to the hearts of mankind the
great hope that through an association of nations the world could in the days
to come avoid armed conflict and substitute reason and collective action for
the age-old appeal to the sword." At the Paris conference after the war, Wilson
resisted attempts by Britain and France to base the peace settlement on the
same narrow nationalist designs that had produced the war in the first place.

But then things had gone wrong. The Republican Senate rejected the League of Nations and the internationalist vision it embodied. The Harding administration, Roosevelt asserted, had made a fetish of "caution and small-mindedness" in foreign affairs. The Washington Conference's limits on naval construction should have been the start toward broader arms control, but the Republicans refused to take the next steps, missing an opportunity that might not recur in a lifetime. Their boycott of the World Court flew in the face of common sense and national interest. No less an authority—and card-carrying Republican—than Elihu Root had endorsed the World Court as "the latest institution wrought out by the civilized world's general public opinion against war." But the Coolidge administration, frightened to death that the court might sometime rule in some way against some American, refused to have anything to do with it. The Republicans' handling of debt reorganization was clumsy and off-putting. The Republicans tried to explain away the hostility their policies provoked by asserting that nobody loved a creditor. "True," Roosevelt rejoined, "but every creditor is not a hated creditor. In time of general poverty and retrenchment our Government has seemed greedy. . . . While exacting payment we have by our discriminatory and exorbitant tariff policy made it doubly hard for them to pay."

The fundamental problem was that the Republicans didn't take foreign policy seriously. Republican leaders had failed the American people in a matter of the most critical importance. The situation was grave—but not yet irreversible. "If the leadership is right," Roosevelt said, "or, more truly, if the spirit behind it is great, the United States can regain the world's trust and friendship and become again of service. We can point the way once more to the reducing of armaments; we can cooperate officially and whole-heartedly with every agency that studies and works to relieve the common ills of mankind. . . . It is the spirit, sir, which matters."

❖   ❖   ❖

As the 1928 Democratic convention approached, the groundswell for Smith rose higher and higher. The party went south for the first time since the Civil War, to Houston, where the delegates gathered in Sam Houston Hall. Smith's longtime partner from their Tammany days, Robert Wagner, headed the platform committee; Roosevelt served as Smith's floor manager. To the casual observer Roosevelt looked much recovered from his appearance before the national party in 1924. He dispensed with the crutches and relied on his leg braces, a cane, and son Elliott's arm.

As on that earlier occasion, he gave the speech placing Smith's name before the convention. He lauded Smith's leadership, as revealed by the progressive reforms New York had enacted during Smith's tenure as governor. He noted the overwhelming margin by which Smith had been reelected, and he recounted the confidence Smith continued to inspire among the ordinary people of New York. He spoke of Al Smith the man, asking what was so special about him and supplying the answer:

> It is that quality of soul which makes a man loved by little children, by dumb animals; that quality of soul which makes him a strong help to all those in sorrow or in trouble; that quality which makes him not merely admired but loved by all the people—the quality of sympathetic understanding of the human heart, of real interest in one's fellow men. Instinctively he senses the popular need because he himself has lived through the hardship, the labor, and the sacrifice which must be endured by every man of heroic mold who struggles up to eminence from obscurity and low estate. Between him and the people is that subtle bond which makes him their champion and makes them enthusiastically trust him with their loyalty and their love.

Roosevelt's speech was broadcast by radio around the country. The overwhelming majority of those who heard him that evening had never met Smith and never would. They couldn't tell whether Roosevelt described him accurately or not. But they all felt they learned something about Roosevelt—about what he valued in a man, about the kind of person *he* was.

❖　❖　❖

$\mathscr{T}$HE GENERAL CAMPAIGN of 1928 started mean and grew meaner. After the Democrats chose Smith, the Republicans nominated Herbert Hoover, an Iowa orphan who became a millionaire mining gold and baser minerals, and then an international hero organizing refugee relief during the World War. President Harding had drafted him to be commerce secretary in the early 1920s, and after the administration covered itself in scandal, Hoover was one of the few to emerge untainted. He strongly seconded Coolidge's view that the business of America was business, and when Coolidge announced, with customary succinctness, "I do not choose to run for president in 1928," Republicans looked to the administration's businessman-in-chief to succeed him. Hoover garnered the GOP nomination without difficulty, pledging to extend the prosperity of the current decade into the next.

Hoover was as reassuring to American traditionalists as Al Smith was disconcerting. His Quaker background might have appeared exotic in another year, but compared with Smith's Catholicism it landed Hoover squarely in the Protestant mainstream—especially after Hoover abjured the most distinctive of the Friends' tenets, pacifism. His endorsement of Prohibition was sincere and strong and contrasted sharply with Smith's opposition. Hoover's midwestern roots gave him a grip on the heartland Smith couldn't come close to matching. Hoover stood for the country against the city, and especially against the immigrants and corrupt political machines that characterized the city in the mind of middle America.

Hoover likely would have won even had the Republicans campaigned solely on the prosperity their party had delivered, or at least presided over. But public-opinion polling in the 1920s was immature and inaccurate, and Hoover's advisers had little way of knowing how their candidate stood. The Republicans took no chances, employing every device of speech, print, broadcast, rumor, and innuendo to damage Smith in voters' eyes. They traced his Tammany origins to Boss Tweed of Gilded Age infamy, and they refused to allow that the machine might have mellowed in sixty years. "Tammany is Tammany," declared William Allen White, the Kansas editor who grew famous lambasting the Populists in the 1890s. "And Smith is its prophet." Some Republicans whispered, others shouted, that Smith's support for the repeal of Prohibition reflected a lushness in his personal behavior. The Prohibitionist temperament typically conflated any use of alcohol, or any desire for any use of alcohol, with full-blown alcoholism; when some Republicans reported, credibly, that Smith had sipped from time to time, other Republicans magnified the reports into falling-down drunkenness.

The most virulent assaults centered on Smith's religion. In an era when racism was institutionalized across the South and indulged informally in much of the North, when anti-Semitism went unremarked in clubs, colleges, and corporate boardrooms, and when the Ku Klux Klan paraded boldly down the main street of the nation's capital, anti-Catholicism barely bothered to hide its face. "Shall we have a man in the White House who acknowledges allegiance to the Autocrat on the Tiber, who hates democracy, public schools, Protestant parsonages, individual right, and everything that is essential to independence?" demanded Dr. Charles Luther Fry, a prominent Lutheran divine, addressing a

large group of his co-denominationalists in New York. The anonymous attacks on Smith's religion were still more scurrilous. "To Murder Protestants!
And Destroy American Government! Is the Oath Binding Roman Catholics,"
screamed one handbill. Anti-Catholic lecturers toured the country, some
claiming spuriously to have been priests or nuns before seeing the Protestant
light and describing in lascivious detail what carnal sinning occurred behind
closed doors in the rectories and convents of America, starting with satanic or-
gies and culminating in the murder of the ill-gotten offspring.

Hoover did little to restrain the Republican low-roaders. "I stand for religious tolerance both in act and in spirit," he said. Doubtless he was sincere. But
intolerance was the organizing principle of his party that year. The critical
gains occurred not among Republicans, who would have voted for Hoover
anyway, but among rural Democrats. "The Republican headquarters was the
parlor affair," an Oklahoma Democrat explained of the GOP operations in his
state. "The real place of activity was across the street in the so-called Hoover-
Democrat Headquarters, a combination of Ku Klux and ultra-protestants with
four times the clerical force and activity of the Republican headquarters, and
every item of expense paid by the Republican headquarters, numerous paid
speakers, big and little, constantly speaking all over the state with the most
horrid stories of what the Pope would do to the people of this country."

❖   ❖   ❖

ROOSEVELT HADN'T intended to enter the fight. He left the Houston convention convinced he had done for the Democratic party about all he could
or ought to that season. He wasn't one to get carried away by the inspirational
rhetoric of a convention, even his own, and in any case Louis Howe regularly
reminded him that 1928 was not the Democrats' year. The still-rising economy made the Republicans irresistible. Roosevelt should give a few speeches
on Smith's behalf, Howe said, but otherwise retreat to Warm Springs, continue
his exercises, and prepare for 1932. The boom couldn't last forever.

Roosevelt listened and nodded agreement. And he did retreat to Warm
Springs. But he neglected to sever all communications with the North, and
when the New York Democrats gathered in state convention at Rochester at the
end of September he heard their appeals for him to come to the party's rescue
in the governor's race. He was the only one with the political stature to follow
Smith in Albany, they asserted. Besides, the presidential race was going badly

in New York, especially upstate where the Klan had grown alarmingly strong. Smith wouldn't stand a chance if he couldn't carry his home state and its nation-leading forty-five electoral votes. Roosevelt was the only person who could bring New York voters to their favorite-son senses.

Roosevelt refused to take telephone calls from the Rochester convention or the top officials of the Democratic party. Smith and John Raskob, the chairman of the Democratic National Committee, pleaded with Eleanor, a delegate to the state convention, to intercede with her husband. "They told me how much they wanted him to run, and asked me if I thought it would really injure his health," she remembered. "I said I did not know; that I had been told the doctors felt that if he continued with his exercises and swimming at Warm Springs he might improve." Eleanor's equivocation was all the encouragement Smith and Raskob needed. They assured her they wouldn't do anything to jeopardize Roosevelt's recovery. It would be an easy race, and a relaxed governorship. They then inquired whether there might be other reasons behind Roosevelt's reluctance. She mentioned the $200,000 he had invested in Warm Springs, and by her words or the worried tone in her voice she made Raskob— the party's money man—understand that this wasn't something her husband could treat lightly. Raskob asked whether it would have any effect on Roosevelt's decision in the governor's race if he was relieved of his financial worries. "I told him I was sure it would not," Eleanor wrote. She was less than convincing, as events at once proved.

Smith and Raskob worked Eleanor by turns. She said she never interfered in her husband's politics, and she certainly wouldn't attempt to persuade him to do something he didn't want to do. They said they wouldn't dream of asking her anything of the sort. But would she agree to let them make their own case to him? She allowed she might. Would she get him on the telephone? She said she would try.

Perhaps Roosevelt hadn't decided about the governor's race; perhaps he simply liked being wooed. But as time ran out for the Rochester convention, he made himself deliberately scarce. He motored ten miles to Manchester, Georgia, to give an address. The third-floor auditorium was packed when he got word that Eleanor had been calling the phone at the corner drug store down the street; he kept talking a half hour longer than expected—ironically, lauding Smith to the local Democrats. When he finally finished, he visited the drug store. Eleanor was about to leave Rochester on the late train to New York City, but she managed to get him with a final call. "He told me with evident glee that he had been keeping out of reach all day and would not have answered the telephone if I had not been calling," she wrote afterward. She explained that she had to go and passed the handset to Smith.

Smith spoke, then shouted, into the phone, but the connection was poor and the operator had to interrupt to ask Roosevelt to try using the telephone in the Warm Springs hotel when he got back to the resort. This additional delay made Smith and Raskob even more anxious, not least since the telephone link to Warm Springs was notoriously undependable. Yet when Roosevelt arrived at the hotel and the phone rang, Raskob's voice came through quite well. The Democratic chairman urged Roosevelt to accept the nomination, for the good of the party. Roosevelt balked, citing his commitment to Warm Springs and the Warm Springs Foundation. Raskob responded impatiently: "Damn the Foundation! We'll take care of it."

He passed the phone to Smith. "Take the nomination, Frank," Smith said. He explained that Roosevelt wouldn't have to campaign very hard—just make a few speeches and he'd be sure to be elected. And he could run the governor's office at his convenience. He would have to open the legislature in January, but then he could go back to Warm Springs for a couple of months while the lawmakers moved as slowly as they always did. He could return to Albany toward the end of the session, sign the bills, send the boys home, and be in Georgia again eighteen hours later.

Roosevelt scoffed at this projected schedule. He knew he couldn't govern that way, and he knew Smith wouldn't have been able to, either. "Don't hand me that boloney," he said.

At this point Herbert Lehman came on the line. Lehman was being touted for lieutenant governor, and he said he'd relieve Roosevelt whenever he required a break.

Smith grabbed the phone back. "Frank," he said, "I wasn't going to put this on a personal basis, but I've got to." He said he needed Roosevelt at the top of the state ticket if he—Smith—were to have any chance of winning the national race.

Roosevelt still resisted. He said things weren't as grim as Smith made out. Hoover might still be beaten.

Smith snorted, and stated the question to Roosevelt directly: "If those fellows nominate you tomorrow and adjourn, will you refuse to run?"

This was Roosevelt's final chance to close the door. If he told Smith he would refuse, the governor would have to find someone else. But if he didn't say that—if he simply said nothing—Smith would take his response as a yes and the convention would nominate Roosevelt, leaving him no alternative but to accept.

Maybe Roosevelt was still ambivalent. Maybe he just wanted to squeeze all the advantage out of playing hard to get. He repeated that he wasn't ready to resume public life. He said he couldn't authorize putting his name before the convention. But he didn't declare explicitly that he would repudiate the nomination.

This was what Smith wanted to hear—or not hear. "All right," he said. "I won't ask you any more questions."

The deal was concluded the following day. Roosevelt's name was put into nomination at Rochester. The weary delegates hardly bothered to applaud, and they didn't bother to call the roll. They approved the nomination on a voice vote and departed.

❖ ❖ ❖

"*M*ESS IS NO name for it," Louis Howe telegraphed Roosevelt. "For once I have no advice to give."

Roosevelt's chief political strategist couldn't imagine what had come over his man. They had agreed months before that 1928 was a Republican year. And the reaction to Smith's candidacy simply reinforced the conclusion that this was a good season to be out of politics. Smith would break his sword on the Republican boom and the anti-Catholic, anti-immigrant bigotry, leaving Roosevelt as the most credible Democrat standing. But now Roosevelt had spoiled everything by volunteering for a lost cause. With luck a man might have one chance at the presidency; Howe had been working for nearly two decades to get Roosevelt that chance. And Roosevelt had thrown it away.

For what? For party unity? The Democrats, who daily gave new meaning to the concept of self-destruction, couldn't expect that of anyone. For Al Smith? What had Smith ever done for Roosevelt? For the sake of ambition? Foolish ambition was worse than no ambition at all.

If Howe couldn't understand Roosevelt's motives, Roosevelt himself might have been no wiser. He couldn't have gainsaid Howe's objections, which made perfect political sense. No doubt the smartest thing would have been to do just what Howe advised: lie low for another few years, write the occasional article, deliver thoughtful speeches, do favors for fellow Democrats, and make ready for 1932.

But logic didn't get the last word, not this time. Roosevelt's appearances at the Democratic conventions in 1924 and 1928, and especially the receptions he received there, reminded him how much he loved the game of politics. With those two brief exceptions, he had been out of the game for eight years, and Louis Howe wanted him to stay out another four. He had devoted as much time to his physical recovery as anyone could have, and though he still professed optimism about further improvement, he doubtless realized in his heart that he had gotten back all the leg strength he was going to get. The Warm Springs project was a worthy cause, but other people could manage it.

He was forty-six years old. He knew himself well enough to appreciate his talents. He had a gift for politics—for inspiring people to work with him toward a common civic goal. Polio aside, he was in the prime of life; his gifts wouldn't increase with the passing years. If anything, they would tend to deteriorate. And in a polio survivor they might deteriorate faster than in other persons.

Roosevelt wasn't a gambler. But neither was he a slave to calculation. And in 1928 he cast aside calculation and threw himself into a race smart money said he would lose.

❖   ❖   ❖

*A*T FIRST HE campaigned for Smith, despite the odds against the national ticket. "Smith has burned his bridges behind him," Roosevelt confided to a friend. He did what he could to repair the damage. In a speech at Rochester he praised Smith's policies on education and public health. In Syracuse he cited Smith's contributions to water-power development. In Jamestown he lauded the governor for paving rural roads.

As he warmed to his task, he lashed out at the Republicans—not the ordinary party members, whose votes he courted, but the party leadership, whose record he disdained. "Somewhere in a pigeon-hole of a desk of the Republican leaders of New York State is a large envelope, soiled, worn, bearing a date that goes back twenty-five or thirty years," he told a crowd in Buffalo. "Printed in large letters on this old envelope are the words, 'Promises to labor.' Inside this envelope are a series of sheets dated two years apart and representing the best thought of the best minds of the Republican leaders over a succession of years. Each sheet of promises is practically the duplicate of every other sheet in the envelope. But nowhere in that envelope is a single page bearing the title 'Promises Kept.' "

As he hit his stride he hammered at what had become the central, if unacknowledged, theme of the Republican presidential campaign. "I have just come from the South," he told an audience at Binghamton, which had experienced a rash of Klan activity. "I have seen circulars down there in the Southern states that any man or woman in this audience would be ashamed to have in his home. I have seen circulars that were so unfit for publication that the people who wrote and printed and paid for them ought not to be put in jail, but ought to be put on the first boat and sent away from the United States." Roosevelt tried to shame New York's bigots into better behavior by associating them with their more virulent southern cousins. He told a tale from Dixie:

> Just after I got down to Georgia, an old friend of mine in a small country town, a farmer, came in to see me, and said, "Mr. Roosevelt, I am worried. A lot of my neighbors, all Democrats—we are all Democrats down here—say that they cannot vote for Governor Smith, and I don't know what the reason is. But there must be some good answer. Will you tell me so I can go back and talk to them? They tell me, these neighbors of mine, and they show me printed handbills saying that if Governor Smith becomes president of the United States, the Methodist and Baptist marriages over here among our neighbors will all be void and that their children will be illegitimate.

Roosevelt's audience laughed at the improbability of this assertion. "You may laugh," he continued.

> But they were not laughing. They thought it was true, and they were honest, law-abiding citizens. They did not have the education, the contact, to know better. Oh, I could go on and tell you a thousand stories along that line.

Roosevelt expressed relief—or hope—that New Yorkers weren't so gullible or mean-spirited as to hold a man's religion against him. "I believe that this year we in the state of New York have got beyond those days of prejudice and bigotry."

The campaign lasted barely three weeks, but by its midpoint something curious became apparent, at least to certain observers. Perhaps Roosevelt had intended this all along; perhaps it occurred to him in the act; perhaps he never consciously realized it. But the more he spoke of Al Smith's qualifications for president, the more it sounded as though *he* were running for the White House. In every speech he would start by pointing to Smith's accomplishments as New York governor, but as he portrayed what a progressive federal government might achieve in the future, his passion for the subject grew intensely personal. He sketched what government could do to develop the hydropower resources of the nation, bringing electricity to rural areas and lowering rates in the cities. He explained how the Republicans had persistently blocked such development, diverting resources and profits into the pockets of their friends. He spoke of the need for government to guarantee pensions for the elderly, who too often ended their lives in the poorhouse. "One of the most oppressing things that I have to do on occasion in this state is to visit the county poorhouse," he told a crowd at Rochester. "It just tears my heart to see those old men and women there, more than almost anything that I know." He spoke of the need for stronger labor legislation, to protect workers from excessive hours and to rectify the imbalance between management and workers in strikes and other disputes. The Republicans claimed to be the friends of labor. "How *dare* they say that!" Roosevelt demanded. "How do grown up and ostensibly sane political leaders perjure themselves that way?" He called for government aid to farmers, who had been suffering for years and been neglected by those same Republicans. "I want to see the farmer and his family receive at the end of each year as much for their labor as if they had been working not on a farm, but as skilled workers under the best conditions in any one of our great industries."

As a candidate for governor, Roosevelt couldn't well debate the Republicans on foreign policy. But he came close. He returned to the issue of religion in politics as a way of reminding voters of his experience abroad in the World War—and of what Americans had fought and died for in that war. "I go back in my memory ten years ago, ten years ago this autumn," he said in Buffalo.

I go back to a day in particular when several miles behind the actual line of contact between the two armies I passed through wheat fields, wheat fields with the ripened grain uncut; wheat fields in which there were patches, little patches of color, something in the wheat, and some of those patches wore a dark gray uniform and others of those patches wore an olive drab uniform. As we went through these fields there were American boys carrying stretchers, and on those stretchers were German boys and Austrian boys and American boys being carried to the rear, and somehow in those days people were not asking to what church those German boys or those American boys belonged. Somehow we got into our heads over there and we got into our heads back here that never again would there be any question of a man's religion in the United States of America. . . .

If any man or woman, after thinking of that, can bear in his heart any motive in this year which will lead him to cast his ballot in the interest of intolerance and of a violation of the spirit of the Constitution of the United States, then I say solemnly to that man or woman, "May God have mercy on your miserable soul."

❖ ❖ ❖

*V*OTERS CROWDED Roosevelt's appearances, responding to his vision and urging him on. Smith's advisers were less appreciative. "Tell the candidate that he is not running for President but for Governor," Smith's manager wired Samuel Rosenman, whom Smith had loaned to Roosevelt for assistance with speeches. "And tell him to stick to state issues."

It was too late. On election day the contest for president proved to be a Republican rout. Smith held his own in the cities, but he got trounced in the country, losing by six million votes total. He dropped five states of the old Confederacy and, most embarrassingly, New York, where Hoover's upstate vote outweighed Smith's large majority in New York City. Whether the country voters rejected Smith for being a Catholic, a wet, an advocate of immigrants, a progressive, or simply a Democrat in a time of Republican prosperity was impossible to tell.

But what *was* possible, indeed inescapable, was that leadership in the Democratic party passed from Al Smith to Franklin Roosevelt that day. As the looming disaster for the Democrats had grown apparent in the weeks before the election, Roosevelt's chances of carrying New York appeared slim. The early returns on voting day provided little reason for encouragement. Yet Roosevelt refused to concede to Albert Ottinger, his Republican rival, and as the tallies from certain Republican counties were slow in being reported, he sensed he might have a chance. "I have an idea that some of the boys upstate are up to their old tricks of delaying the vote and stealing as many as they can from us," he told Sam Rosenman. He decided to intervene. He called sheriffs in the tardy counties. "This is Franklin Roosevelt," he said. "I am watching the returns here at the Biltmore Hotel in New York City. The returns from your county are coming in mighty slowly, and I don't like it. I shall look to you, if they are unduly delayed, and I want you personally to see that the ballots are not tampered with. If you need assistance to keep order or to see that the vote is counted right, call me here at this hotel and I shall ask Governor Smith to authorize the state troopers to assist you."

Roosevelt was bluffing. The state troopers lacked the capacity to deal with vote tampering. But the sheriffs probably didn't know that. Whether or not Roosevelt's calls were the cause, the returns started arriving more swiftly. When they were totaled they revealed a Roosevelt victory. The margin was narrow: twenty-five thousand votes out of more than four million cast. Yet it was enough.

PART II

The Soul of the Nation

1929 ❖ 1937

18.

OF THE NEW INDUSTRIES OF THE 1920S, NONE SO CHARACTERIZED THE decade as advertising. Publicizing products had been an aspect of marketing for many years, but during the 1920s advertising took on a life and identity of its own. The American economy had lately crossed the historic divide between the age of scarcity, when the principal problem of economy was producing enough, and the age of surplus, when the problem was producing too much. For the first time in American history—and the first time in human history on such a broad scale—people had to be persuaded to consume all they collectively could produce. This was the challenge of America's "New Era," as its propagandists dubbed it, and it was the mission of advertising. "In the past, wish, want, and desire were the motive forces of economic progress," Herbert Hoover declared to a conference of advertising executives. "Now you have taken over the job of creating desire." Bruce Barton, the high priest of advertising, asserted, "Advertising is the spark plug on the cylinder of mass production. . . . Advertising sustains a system that has made us leaders of the free world: The American Way of Life." Barton didn't claim his craft was beyond reproach; nothing human was. "If advertising sometimes encourages men and women to live beyond their means, so sometimes does matrimony. If advertising is too often tedious, garrulous, and redundant, so is the U.S. Senate." In other words, advertising was as human as love and as American as democracy.

Every modern industry, or at least every successful modern industry, heeded the advertising imperative, with many making products into their own advertisements. "Bathtubs appear in stylish shades," one observer wrote. "Dishpans are no longer plain Cinderellas of fire and ashes; following a wave of the hand by the fairy godmother—style—they now appear resplendent in blues and pinks. . . . Automobiles change with the calendar. Last year's offerings are made social pariahs; only this year's model is desirable until it, in turn, is made out of fashion by next year's style. Furniture, clothing, radios, phonographs, tumble from the fertile minds of scientists and designers and . . . drown the sales possibilities of products that already stagger with infirmity at the age of one year."

The New Era battened on the institutionalized optimism that was advertising's stock-in-trade—on the confidence that this year's products would be better than last year's, that this year's sales would be greater than last year's. Growth had always been the key to success in the American economy, but for most of American history the essential growth was growth in supply; in the age of scarcity, demand took care of itself. The titans of the nineteenth century— John D. Rockefeller, Andrew Carnegie—had focused on production, correctly confident that whatever they produced in oil and steel the American economy would consume. But as the country industrialized more fully, demand became the crux of the economic question, till in the New Era it emerged as the sine qua non of continued prosperity. If demand remained robust, the economy would thrive. If demand flagged, for whatever reason, the economy would slump. And demand depended on confidence: on the conviction, among others, that incomes would rise to support increasing purchases of all the goods the economy could produce.

Confidence could be self-fulfilling. If merchants expected sales to rise, they would expand their inventories by sending larger orders to suppliers, who would hire extra workers and invest in additional plant. The workers, with paycheck-swollen wallets, would become the customers for the merchants' expanded inventories, in a virtuous circle with no obvious end.

Confidence was even more essential in another signature economic activity of the New Era: the buying and selling of securities. Wall Street had been the heart of the nation's financial sector since the mid-nineteenth century, but in the decade after the World War the buying and selling of stocks and bonds became a national obsession. "Wherever one went, one met people who told of their stock market winnings," a broker explained. "At dinner tables, at bridge, on golf links, on trolley cars, in country post offices, in barber shops, in factories and shops of all kinds." A financial reporter, describing a popular form of pooled investing, declared, "Hardly a week now passes but a new investment trust appears on the horizon." Before the war, the stock market had been a province of perhaps half a million investors; during the 1920s the province swelled to country size, comprising some fifteen million men and women who hoped their shares of the booming economy would make them rich. Stories of heretofore improbable success abounded: of the broker's valet who heeded his boss's tips and cleared a quarter million in profit, of the registered nurse whose bedside manner toward her well-informed patients earned her a quick thirty thousand, of the widow who took a flier in copper and landed the cash to pay off her mortgage, of the struggling young man who plunged into Niles-Bement-Pond and resurfaced with enough money to retire in style. The masters of investment became household words and cultural heroes; speculators like Samuel Insull, Jacob Raskob, and Billy Durant took the place on the front pages formerly occupied by industrialists Carnegie, Rockefeller, and Henry Ford. Everyone knew about bulls and bears; the terminology of the stock market infiltrated the larger language. To "sell something short" had originally meant to bet on a fall in price and carried no connotation of the outcome of the bet; during the 1920s, when short sellers consistently lost money—since everything was going up—it came to imply a mistaken judgment of something's value.

Hard figures supported the euphoria that surrounded the stock market. The bull market of the New Era began in 1922 with the Dow Jones industrial average bumbling along below 80; by January 1929 the Dow had hurtled past 300. The future promised to be even brighter than the past. "Business is entering the new year upon a high level of activity and with confidence in the continuance of prosperity," one respected forecaster averred. A prominent banker declared, "All major indications point to a prosperous coming year."

Those indications included the recent election of a president who was every businessman's dream and who embraced the New Era with enthusiasm. "One of the oldest and perhaps the noblest of human aspirations has been the abolition of poverty," Herbert Hoover proclaimed in accepting the Republican nomination. "We in America today are nearer to the final triumph over poverty than ever before in the history of any land. The poorhouse is vanishing from among us. We have not yet reached the goal, but, given a chance to go forward with the policies of the last eight years, we shall soon, with the help of God, be in sight of the day when poverty will be banished from this nation."

As voters overwhelmingly concurred that Hoover—rather than Al Smith—was the man to lead them farther into the New Era, Wall Street jubilantly seconded the opinion. The "Hoover market" of the autumn of 1928 lifted share prices to record levels. And in his inaugural address Hoover promised more of the same. "We have reached a higher degree of comfort and security than ever existed before in the history of the world," he said. "Through liberation from widespread poverty we have reached a higher degree of individual freedom than ever before. . . . We are steadily building a new race—a new civilization great in its own attainments."

❖ ❖ ❖

"IT LOOKS LIKE I will have a man-sized job on my hands for the next two years," Roosevelt wrote Archie Roosevelt, Theodore's son, shortly after the 1928 election. Much of the job would consist of dealing with the Republicans who controlled the New York legislature and who, after the broad Republican sweep, were in a singularly unaccommodating mood. They considered Roosevelt's narrow victory a fluke that would be rectified at the first opportunity and ought to be subverted till then.

Roosevelt addressed the hostile group in his inaugural speech on January 2, 1929. Agriculture remained the conspicuous exception to the boom of the 1920s; farm prices and incomes continued to lag. Roosevelt noted this and called for measures to elevate farm income till rural life became as materially attractive as city life. Hydroelectric power had been a contentious issue in New York state politics for years; the heart of the discord was whether hydropower sites should be developed publicly or transferred to private hands. Roosevelt came down firmly on the side of the former, telling the lawmakers that control of promising sites should "definitely remain in the people." He advocated new laws protecting labor, including a "real eight-hour day and forty-eight-hour week" for women and children (the existing laws were often flouted), the extension of workmen's compensation to cover occupational diseases (and not just accidents), the creation of a board to advise on minimum and equitable wages, the restriction of the use of injunctions by management against unions in labor disputes, and the establishment of an expert commission to advise on old-age security.

The chamber didn't warm while Roosevelt was speaking. He hadn't expected it to, and his conclusion conveyed promise but also a hint of warning. "The verdict on our relationship that I most desire from you," he said, with a bared-teeth smile, "is that I have at least been fair and reasonable and friendly."

The Republican lawmakers filed out of the assembly chamber frowning and proceeded to ignore essentially everything Roosevelt had said. He wasn't surprised; in their position he might have done the same thing. But rather than hector his opponents, he devoted himself to cultivating his allies—or those who might become his allies. No Democrat could expect to govern New York without the aid of Tammany Hall, and though Roosevelt realized he would never enjoy the sidewalk credibility of Al Smith, he reasoned that he might bring Tammany around to his view of the needs of the state. Two weeks after his inauguration he headlined Tammany's annual speakers' bureau dinner. With nary a hint of past enmity, he thanked his "old friends" of Tammany for their support in the recent election. And he called upon the speakers' bureau, in particular, to carry the worthy task forward. "Upon you rests the responsibility for the education of the voter in the aims and principles of the Democracy, not only of the city and the state but of the nation."

Because the theme of the evening was political speaking, Roosevelt offered advice on this essential art. He reminded his listeners that in the early days of the republic, effective oratory had been crucial to political success. "Elections were won or lost, parties were driven out or swept into power entirely as the public speakers on one side or the other proved most able and convincing," Roosevelt said. "It was the golden day of the silver tongue. With rare exceptions, the great public man had also to be classed as a convincing orator." Things had changed as newspapers spread; voters learned to gather their information and take their cues from the daily papers. A powerful pair of lungs and a resonant set of vocal cords didn't hurt the prospective office-holder, yet they were no longer necessary. The best speakers were often not the candidates themselves but the rally men, the functionaries appointed to whip up enthusiasm at gatherings of the party faithful.

The wheel continued to turn. Roosevelt predicted that radio would supplant the press as the primary means of connecting candidates to voters. Or *re*connecting candidates to voters: Roosevelt saw the new technology as a return to earlier forms:

The pendulum is rapidly swinging back to the old condition of things. One can only guess at the figure, but I think it is a conservative estimate to say that whereas five years ago 99 out of 100 took their arguments from the editorials and the news columns of the daily press, today at least half of the voters, sitting at their own fireside, listen to the actual words of the political leaders on both sides and make their decision based on what they hear rather than what they read. I think it is almost safe to say that in reaching their decision as to which party they will support, what is heard over the radio decides as many people as what is printed in the newspapers.

This development was good news for the Democrats, who in most parts of the country had faced a skeptical, often hostile Republican press; it was even better news, though he didn't mention it in his Tammany speech, for Roosevelt himself, who was becoming a master of radio. His mastery faltered on this occasion, though. He didn't personally attend the meeting, held at the Commodore Hotel in Manhattan, but expected to have his voice transmitted from his office in Albany. The technology balked at the last minute, however, and a stand-in, New York supreme court justice William Collins, was summoned to read a telegraphed version of Roosevelt's text.

Roosevelt took to the airwaves more successfully in the months that followed. The Republicans in the legislature refused to budge, obviously intending to sabotage Roosevelt's administration and hoping to elect a governor of their own in 1930. Roosevelt berated them for putting party interests ahead of the welfare of the people. The Republicans had promised sound policies on the development of hydroelectric power, but "not a single move was made by the writers of this platform to put forward any program, sound or unsound," he said. The Republicans had cast themselves as friends of labor, yet when the state labor commission recommended measures to improve the lot of workers, "the Republican leaders decreed the death of these bills and, then going still further, failed to continue the life of the commission." Roosevelt had pressed the lawmakers on maximum-hour legislation, but "the Republican majority refused to allow the bills even to come to a vote."

Roosevelt required time and practice to perfect the form of his radio addresses. Listeners to these early broadcasts thought he sometimes tried to communicate more information than the medium could readily handle. But the overall response was favorable, and he made his radio reports to the people of New York a regular part of his routine as governor.

He discovered something about radio he hadn't realized at first: that it was particularly effective in the hands of the executive branch of government. Since the beginning of the century, political power had been shifting from the legislature to the executive. The trend was especially noticeable in Washington, where Theodore Roosevelt and Woodrow Wilson had made themselves the center of national political attention, but it applied in the states as well. The larger government grew, the greater the power wielded by the person who headed the government, either a governor or the president. At the national level, the emergence of the United States as an international power with global interests elevated the president still further, in that foreign affairs, to a much greater degree than domestic affairs, had always been the peculiar province of the executive.

Radio added a technological boost to the institutional trend toward greater executive power. Any legislature speaks with many voices, an able executive with one. In the nineteenth century, the many voices were often more effective than the one, since no voice carried farther than the physical sound waves generated by the speaker. But radio neutralized the advantage of multiplicity and in fact negated it. Radio allowed the single-voiced executive to communicate with a clarity that reduced the many-throated legislature to relative cacophony. A Roosevelt at the microphone could enter the homes of the millions of his listeners, forging a personal relationship that left even the most powerful legislators at an irretrievable disadvantage. Over time Roosevelt's radio audience would come to feel they knew him as they had known no other executive; it was an aspect of his political genius, amplified by radio and sharpened by experience, that he made them think *he* knew *them*.

❖ ❖ ❖

By the summer of his first year in office Roosevelt had accomplished nothing of note in bending the Republican legislature to his will. The economy remained strong, and neither the leaders of the GOP nor their corporate supporters saw any reason to alter the conservative course that had served them well since the start of the decade. Roosevelt recognized what he was up against. "The business community is not much interested in good government," he told a fellow Democrat. "And it wants the present Republican control to continue just so long as the stock market soars and the new combinations of capital are left undisturbed." Some Democrats had been urging the party to shift to the right, to accommodate the mood of the New Era; Roosevelt preferred to stay the progressive course till the New Era ran out of steam. "Prevailing conditions are bound to come to an end some time," he predicted. "When that time comes, I want to see the Democratic party sanely radical enough to have most of the disgruntled ones turn to it to put us in power again."

He was preaching his radical patience in the summer and early autumn of 1929 as Wall Street bounded along in the seventh year of its bull market. The bounding grew more vigorous by the month; the daily swings of share prices, after averaging in the mid-single digits till mid-decade, had tripled by the end of 1928 and nearly doubled again during 1929. Stock pickers and stock watchers didn't know what to make of it. Joseph Kennedy, one of the most successful of the speculators, thought things had gone too far when he stopped on Wall Street to have his shoes shined and received, in addition, advice to go long in oil and railroads. He determined at once to get out of the market, explaining to his wife that when a bootblack started offering stock tips, there was no room for professionals. Other pros—Bernard Baruch, Owen Young,

David Sarnoff, apparently even Herbert Hoover—likewise liquidated their stock holdings. Baruch told Will Rogers to run for his life. "You're sitting on a volcano," the speculator quietly advised the humorist. "Get as far away as you can."

An assortment of pessimists spoke publicly and loudly. Roger Babson, whose projections had won him a following during the previous years, told the National Business Conference that the sky was about to fall. "A crash is coming which will take in the leading stocks and cause a decline from 60 to 80 points in the Dow Jones barometer," Babson declared at a moment when the Dow stood at 380. "Fair weather cannot always continue. The economic cycle is in progress today, as it was in the past. The Federal Reserve System has put the banks in a strong position, but it has not changed human nature. More people are borrowing and speculating today than ever in our history. Sooner or later a crash is coming, and it may be terrific."

But pessimists had been predicting the end of the bull market for years. Some had been disinterested in their forecasts of doom, while others, notably short-selling speculators, had been hoping to profit from a fall. Either way, they had been wrong. After each downward lurch, the market had resumed its climb, rising higher than before.

This explained the failure of most observers to absorb the full meaning of the events that began to unfold on Wednesday, October 23. Just after midday, for reasons no one could fathom, investors began to shed automobile stocks. Similar sell-offs had occurred many times since the beginning of the bull market, but in this case the selling continued longer than before, and it triggered unusual alarm. That the heaviest selling took place at the end of the day didn't help matters, for it allowed nervous investors to spend the hours after the market closed poring over the ticker tape for signs of the direction stocks would take the next morning.

Market stalwarts professed undiminished confidence. Irving Fisher, a Yale economist, ascribed the recent gyrations to a "lunatic fringe of reckless speculation" and declared that the fundamentals of the market were as sound as ever. Share prices would recover quickly and would regain the "higher plateau" upon which modern efficiencies in production and distribution had rightly placed them. Rumors circulated that the big banks, doubtless assisted by the Federal Reserve, would flood the market with liquidity to ensure that leveraged investors not be caught out.

The jawboning had worked in the past, but this time it failed. Again for reasons no single person could entirely fathom, the market collectively panicked. By the opening bell on Thursday, October 24, the orders to sell were already backlogged beyond the ability of the staff of the stock exchange to process them. The logjam intensified the panic, as investors realized, with prices falling, that each minute that an order went unfulfilled signified that much deeper a loss. The bull market had been built, to an unprecedented degree, on borrowed money, with many lenders free to call in their loans should the value of their collateral—the shares the loans purchased—decline. As the prices fell, the lenders called their loans, forcing the investors to sell. The glut of sell orders depressed the price further, prompting new loan calls, and the virtuous circle that had lifted share prices as the bubble expanded suddenly turned vicious. Market volume broke previous records by 50 percent; the informal "curb market," outside the exchange itself, nearly doubled its previous largest day. The ticker ran hours behind, leaving sellers uncertain how badly they had been wounded. The normally circumspect *New York Times* described Wall Street as a war zone. "Wild-eyed speculators crowded the brokerage offices, awed by the disaster which had overtaken many of them," the paper declared. It proceeded to detect a sign of hope amid the debacle, relating reports of a banker bailout and recounting the assertion of the city's big financial houses that the market remained sound in the face of this "technical" correction. (Thomas Lamont of J. P. Morgan & Co. attributed the falling prices to "air holes" in the market.) The *Times* put particular emphasis on some last-minute buy orders, especially in steel. "The tide had turned," the paper proclaimed.

Other voices joined the hopeful chorus. "We believe that present conditions are favorable for advantageous investment in standard American securities," one large brokerage informed its customers and the broader public. Herbert Hoover called a special press conference to offer his personal reassurance. "The fundamental business of the country, that is, the production and distribution of commodities," the president said, "is on a very sound and prosperous basis."

The bullish rhetoric appeared to pay off on the Friday after what already was being called "Black Thursday." Prices held steady and actually gained a bit on average; volume was healthy but not outlandish. In that era the market operated half-time on Saturdays, and this second day after the debacle proved almost boring. Brokers and the staff of the exchange caught up on their sleep on Sunday; the cleaning crews removed the last signs of the Thursday disaster.

Then on Monday, from causes no more explicable than those of Thursday, the bottom fell out of the market once more. This time blue-chip stocks suffered most grievously, driving the Dow Jones average farther down than it had ever plunged in a single day. The market's hall of fame was transformed into a hall of horror; U.S. Steel lost 17 points, Union Carbide 20, Westinghouse 34, General Electric 47. The liquidation continued on Tuesday, and it took the especially unnerving form of block trading—sales of ten thousand shares, twenty thousand, fifty thousand—which suggested that banks and other financial institutions, far from riding to the rescue of the market, were fleeing. Volume on Bloody Tuesday surpassed that of Black Thursday; by the close of business that day, the Dow had lost 30 percent in less than a week. The broader *New York Times* index fared even worse, plunging 40 percent.

❖   ❖   ❖

WHAT IT ALL MEANT, none could say. If the carnage continued, investors would suffer still more, to their dismay and, in some cases, dissolution. But the investing class, while larger than ever in American history, remained a distinct minority of the American people. Fifteen million men and women owned stock—which meant that seventy million didn't.

The critical question was whether Wall Street's swoon would prostrate the larger economy. Past financial panics had sometimes spilled over into commerce and industry, but sometimes not. The current panic was the worst in American history, but that might simply have been because the bull market that preceded it was the largest and longest in history. With luck—and astute leadership in key parts of the political economy—the damage to the stock market might be contained. If the economy's fundamentals were as sound as Hoover asserted, America's hundreds of thousands of non-financial businesses, and their tens of millions of employees, might be spared the fate of the suffering investor class.

The effect of the stock crash on the broader economy was the most important question facing the country in the late autumn of 1929, but a related question was the effect of the crash, and whatever ensued, on the fortunes of the major political parties. The crash placed Franklin Roosevelt in a delicate position. He had long believed, and had been saying quietly, that the Democrats wouldn't return to power until the bloom fell off the rose of the Republican economy. The stock crash certainly singed the tips of the petals, and it suggested that additional wilting might be in store. Roosevelt the politician—the presidential hopeful—could hardly help thinking that the worse the economic news, the better his prospects of finally following Uncle Ted into the White House. But no politician who aspired to the presidency—and certainly not the governor of the state whose largest city was the capital of the American financial industry—could afford to be caught showing the slightest satisfaction at the misfortunes of investors. Privately, Roosevelt might dream of what the ill tidings portended, but publicly he had to hope the stock market recovered and the damage didn't spread.

In speeches and in comments to the press, Roosevelt adopted the position that the current difficulties confirmed the need for the progressive reforms he had been advocating since the beginning of the decade. He traveled to Chicago in December to address a gathering of Illinois Democrats. His appearance was partly in support of Democratic candidates for the 1930 congressional elections; it was also in the service of his own ambitions, as a test of the western waters for the 1932 presidential race. This, at any rate, was the interpretation the delegates from eighty-two Illinois counties, mostly rural, placed on his appearance, and by the evidence of their lusty chorus of "East side, west side, all around the town," they liked what they saw and heard. Roosevelt reviewed a half century of American history, declaring it an era of unexampled progress "in the liberation of the individual from the drudgery of the daily struggle for existence." Unfortunately, the benefits of progress had not been evenly shared. Agriculture trailed industry, largely because farmers had been denied the benefits of combination that amplified the productivity of manufacturers and because they had suffered from a high tariff and other measures that protected industry at agriculture's expense. Until now the weakness of the farm sector had affected the farm sector almost alone, leaving city dwellers indifferent to their rural compatriots' plight. But such a situation couldn't persist. America was in "a state of unstable equilibrium," Roosevelt asserted. "And nothing can remain in that condition for long." Roosevelt blamed the Republicans for robbing the farmers, and he called on the Democrats to defend them. If the Democrats did so, he predicted, they would be rewarded at the polls.

❖ ❖ ❖

OF COURSE, for Roosevelt to be considered for president in 1932, he had to be reelected as governor in 1930. New York's short cycle had been designed to keep elected officials accountable to voters; in the process it dictated deadlock when one party controlled the legislature and the other party the governorship. Both Roosevelt and the Republicans looked to the 1930 elections to break the deadlock—he with growing confidence, they with mounting trepidation.

The half year after the stock crash revealed that the damage would not be confined to the financial sector. For seven fat years the stock market had risen on the confidence that pervaded the economy as a whole. Market watchers perceived an intimate connection between share prices and business activity. "The stock market and business are more closely allied than at any time in history," the *Wall Street Journal* declared in early 1929. "You cannot have prosperity with a protracted decline in stocks. Neither can you have an advancing market with business on the decline." When written, these words were intended to justify the high prices for stocks; after the stock prices collapsed, they became a prophecy of depression.

The Great Depression of the 1930s was hardly the consequence of the stock crash alone. In certain respects, both resulted from the unstable condition of the larger economy. Agriculture's troubles were well known, but other sectors were not much stronger. A bubble in Florida real estate had burst amid a hurricane in 1926; the escaping pressure flattened much of the residential construction industry. Auto sales had been sluggish for some time; Henry Ford sobered observers by declaring that the industry was substantially overbuilt. Banking labored under its chronic dependence on the confidence of depositors; should anything shake that confidence, even the most responsibly run bank would be at risk.

Nor were the sources of instability confined to America. For decades, but especially since the World War, American finance had been intimately entwined with European finance, rendering American banking houses vulnerable to the missteps and follies of their transatlantic counterparts. Whether mere misstep or full-blown folly, the decision of Britain's chancellor of the exchequer, Winston Churchill, to put Britain back on the gold standard at the prewar exchange rate had the most far-reaching effects. Churchill's decision ignored the fundamental changes the war had wrought in the world economy; it overvalued the pound and undervalued the dollar, making American exports cheap and draining Britain's financial reserves westward across the Atlantic. Benjamin Strong, the governor of New York's Federal Reserve Bank and the de facto leader of the Federal Reserve system, did what he could to rectify the situation, slashing American interest rates and thus making the dollar less attractive to overseas investors. But the lower interest rates fueled the stock speculation that inflated the Wall Street bubble, limiting Strong's ability to counter the pernicious consequences of Churchill's exercise in imperial nostalgia.

Strong watched the bubble grow, with concern but not alarm. He understood the risks but believed that he and the Federal Reserve had the tools to deal with emergent crises on Wall Street. "The very existence of the Federal

Reserve System is a safeguard against anything like a calamity growing out of money rates," he declared. "We have the power to deal with such an emergency instantly by flooding the Street with money." Perhaps the Fed did have the power, but after the untimely death of Strong in 1928, it lacked the nerve. It lowered interest rates modestly after the stock crash, but skittish investors simply interpreted the reduction as a signal that the Fed, too, had lost confidence in stocks and that worse days were coming. They unloaded still more of their stocks. The flood of liquidity Strong had promised never amounted to more than a trickle, and as investors went into hiding, the nation's money supply shrank by as much as one-third. Prices fell commensurately, crushing debtors, who had to repay their obligations with dearer dollars, and discouraging producers from expanding, or even maintaining, output.

America's elected officials did little to alleviate the troubles, and more than a little to aggravate them. Congress and the White House weighed in during the summer of 1930 with the Smoot-Hawley tariff, which tried to protect American jobs and profits by doubling the average duty on imports. "I do not assume the rate structure in this or any other tariff bill is perfect," Hoover said on signing the measure. "But I am convinced that the disposal of the whole question is urgent. . . . This provision is a progressive advance and gives great hope of taking the tariff away from politics, lobbying, and log-rolling." The president asserted that the tariff was "largely directed to the interest of the farmer," and he predicted that farmers would especially benefit. He added the hopeful conclusion that "with returning normal conditions our foreign trade will continue to expand."

Hoover was wrong on all counts, except for his admission that the tariff wasn't perfect. The Smoot-Hawley tariff wasn't progressive but regressive, undoing even more of what the Democrats had accomplished by way of freeing trade during the 1910s. It represented the triumph of politics and lobbying, winning passage over the published objections of hundreds of distinguished economists. The rhetoric of concern for farmers provided the cover for Congress to ratchet up the rates on numerous manufactured goods. Foreign trade did not expand, nor business conditions return to normal; instead the new American tariff triggered a beggar-thy-neighbor economic war among the great powers that impoverished them all and punished American farmers especially.

19.

*A*S THE STOCK MARKET CONTINUED TO SLIDE DURING 1930, AND AS the larger economy began to track Wall Street's downward course, Democratic candidates became more viable than they had been for nearly a generation. The Democrats in 1930 gained control of the House of Representatives for the first time since the World War, and they cut deeply into the Republican majority in the Senate.

And in the state race that everyone was watching, they—or rather Franklin Roosevelt—smashed the Republicans with an authority that gave heart to Democrats nationwide and pause to all Republicans. New York was something of a microcosm of the country as a whole, its upstate farmers suffering from the same low prices as farmers elsewhere, and its urban workers getting laid off in proportions comparable to those of other American cities. Roosevelt registered sympathy but at first accomplished little to ease the pain of his suffering fellow New Yorkers. Yet no one really expected him to do much, in part because of the opposition of the Republicans in the legislature, in part because it didn't occur to people to look to Albany for solutions to what was clearly a national problem. Roosevelt rode the dissatisfaction to victory by the astonishing margin of 730,000 votes, or twice the previous record plurality in New York history.

Roosevelt's triumph was personally satisfying, and it augured important changes in the direction of New York politics. But the larger significance wasn't lost on observers in the Empire State or beyond. "The tremendous vote for Governor Roosevelt was regarded as increasing greatly his chance for the Democratic nomination for President in 1932, for which he is known to be an aspirant," the *New York Times* explained on its front page the morning after the election.

Roosevelt hardly bothered to deny his intentions. For the record he declared that he had his hands full governing New York, but he declined to disavow the efforts of others to put his name forward. And he undertook actions designed to elevate his visibility among voters in the country at large. Some moves were subtle. He employed his powers as governor to direct monies to the construction of the Theodore Roosevelt Hall at the Museum of Natural Science in New York City. More than a decade after the Rough Rider's death, voters could be excused for forgetting that TR had been a Republican nearly all his political life; what stuck in the public mind was the connection between the Roosevelt name and a bold, progressive approach to national problems. Franklin Roosevelt was happy to encourage the connection and remind people that things had been better when a Roosevelt ran the country.

Roosevelt played the other side of the progressive street as well. Woodrow Wilson's star remained in eclipse, but holdover Wilsonians still wielded influence within the Democratic party. Roosevelt reached out to Wilson's old confidant Edward House, a Texan with considerable pull among the Democrats' southern wing. The initial gesture was a simple request for advice. Roosevelt sent Louis Howe to visit House with a draft letter responding to a query from supporters; Howe asked House for help revising and sharpening the reply. House had long looked askance at Roosevelt, and even more so at Howe, but on this occasion he was pleased. "It is a joy to cooperate with him," House wrote Roosevelt regarding Howe. "We never have any arguments and have no difficulty in reaching conclusions satisfactory to us both." House proceeded to promote Roosevelt in Texas and the South, particularly among former supporters of William McAdoo and the late William Jennings Bryan. House's efforts didn't erase all southern suspicions of the New York governor, but they prevented any alternative candidate from gaining traction in Dixie.

Roosevelt worked the West through another proxy. James Farley had been the New York state Democratic chairman before becoming Roosevelt's 1930 campaign manager, and before that he had been Al Smith's fair-haired Irishman. Smith appointed Farley boxing commissioner, a post that earned him sufficient fame that Lucky Strike paid him to endorse its cigarettes. Farley might have become a rival to Louis Howe among Roosevelt's supporters, except that where Howe was a policy man at heart, for whom politics was a means to the end of progressive policy, Farley preferred his politics unsullied. The game was what mattered to him, not the final score. Outsiders often expected Farley to be as brusque as the streets of New York, but in fact he spread the charm of the Irish, adapted to local circumstances, wherever he went. Louis Howe thought he was the ideal person to send west. "He has a wholesome breeziness of manner and a frank and open character which is characteristic of all Westerners," Howe remarked. "In addition, I think he gives a distinct impression of being a very practical and businesslike politician."

The Westerners thought so, too, at least enough to register their advance approval of a Roosevelt candidacy. On an eighteen-state tour that carried him from Lake Superior to Puget Sound and then south to California and back across the Great Basin and Plains to Chicago, Farley talked up Roosevelt and the need for party unity and listened intently to Democratic committee members, state chairmen, newspaper editors, potential delegates, and anyone else who might influence the outcome of the 1932 convention. Some were coy, others forthright. William Howes of South Dakota was both. "Bill was a canny politician who had been in the game for years, usually working hard for the Democratic ticket only to see it go down under a Republican landslide on election day," Farley remembered. "He knew the game backwards and forwards. We sat there for some time exchanging generalities, without disclosing what either of us really had in mind. Just before it was time to go, Bill decided to let me know what he really thought. He plumped his fat fist on the table and growled in a deep voice: 'Farley, I'm damned tired of backing losers. In my opinion, Roosevelt can sweep the country, and I'm going to support him.' "

Similar comments from other Democrats caused Farley to conclude that the West was Roosevelt's for the taking. "I am satisfied, Governor, that the leaders want to be on the bandwagon. . . . There are a lot of Democratic candidates for governor and state offices who believe there is a real chance of winning with you as the nominee, and they feel there is absolutely no hope if anyone else is named."

❖   ❖   ❖

THE EAST WAS another matter. Had Roosevelt been a Republican—or, rather, had the Democratic party operated the way the Republican party did—his approach to the 1932 nomination would have taken the form of a victory parade many months before the convention. But the Democrats' two-thirds rule meant that a determined minority could hope to stall the candidacy even of a person favored by an otherwise overwhelming majority of delegates. The eastern wing of the party included elements opposed to Roosevelt for various reasons. Economic conservatives of the Grover Cleveland school thought him unreliable on fiscal and business issues. Philosophers of the party considered him shallow. Supporters of Al Smith resented the eclipse of their man by his erstwhile protégé.

Smith himself tried to hide his resentment but didn't succeed. In December 1931 Clark Howell, the publisher of the *Atlanta Constitution,* visited Smith at his office in the newly completed Empire State Building. Howell and the *Constitution* had supported Smith at some cost to their credibility in the South, and Howell thought his loyalty had earned him an expectation of candor. "He seemed glad to see me," Howell wrote Roosevelt after the interview with Smith. "For a few minutes we indulged in generalities, and then I got down to business." Howell wanted to know how Smith would respond to a Roosevelt candidacy. "Governor," Howell said, "you hold in the palm of your hand the assurance of an overwhelming Democratic victory next year, or you are in a position where you could jeopardize the present prospect of sure success."

"How?" Smith inquired.

"By your attitude toward Franklin Roosevelt. With your support of him, all opposition to him will vanish, and his nomination will be a mere formality. The country expects you to support him, and it will not believe that you can possibly do otherwise."

"The hell I can't!" Smith burst out. He quickly added, "I do not mean that I will not support him." But he refused to give Roosevelt or anyone else a blank check. "I am for the party first, above any man, and I will support the man who seems best for the party."

Howell explained why he thought Roosevelt was the best man.

"But you speak for the South," Smith replied. "You don't understand the situation up here as I do."

Howell asserted that Roosevelt would sweep the South and probably three-quarters of the states west of the Mississippi.

"But that is not this section," Smith countered.

"With your support it is," Howell responded. He listed the states—New York, Massachusetts, Rhode Island, Connecticut, New Jersey—that Roosevelt could easily carry.

Something was eating at Smith. Howell probed to find out what it was. "Governor," he said, "is there any ground for personal hostility on your part against Roosevelt?"

"No," Smith answered slowly. "He has always been kind to me and my family, and has gone out of his way to be agreeable to us at the mansion at Albany." While saying this, Smith rose from his desk and began pacing. "But, do you know, by God, that he has never consulted me about a damn thing since he has been governor? He has taken bad advice, and from sources not friendly to me. He has ignored me!" Smith suddenly slammed his hand down on the desk. "By God! He invited me to his house before he recently went to Georgia, and did not even mention to me the subject of his candidacy."

Howell explained that Roosevelt wasn't officially a candidate and didn't want to put Smith in the awkward position of having to answer questions about something Roosevelt hadn't yet revealed to the public. Smith refused to be mollified. He complained that Roosevelt's "damn fool friends" were doing him and the party more harm than good. He ended by saying that he was, at the moment, neither for nor against Roosevelt and that he would take his time deciding what to do.

❖ ❖ ❖

W̶HILE ROOSEVELT pondered how to deal with Smith, he confronted the task of governing the largest state in America in the throes of its worst depression in history. His tools were distinctly limited. He had no control over monetary or trade policy and only marginal influence on taxes, and hence could do nothing about the causes of the depression. He was left to deal with its effects. His first priority was relief: government assistance to those left hungry and homeless by the layoffs that continued to spread from shop to shop, factory to factory, industry to industry. Roosevelt's political philosophy, like that of most of his progressive generation, had been shaped by the generally good times of the early decades of the twentieth century, when the chief function of government, in the progressive view, had been to restrain the excesses of American capitalism. Busting trusts, capping rail rates, ensuring the safety of food and drugs, protecting the nation's natural resources: these had been the progressives' priorities. It hardly occurred to the progressives that government someday might have to sustain, rather than restrain, capitalism and to supplement the incomes of large numbers of people caught short by its collapse.

Nor did this fully occur to Roosevelt yet. But the floundering economy caused him to reconsider the purpose of government and to reconfigure his basic philosophy. "What is the state?" he asked a special session of the New York legislature, which he called in the summer of 1931 to address the needs of the swelling population of unemployed. "It is the duly constituted representative of an organized society of human beings, created by them for their mutual protection and well-being." Roosevelt's definition wouldn't have passed muster in any introductory political science class, ignoring those tyrannies and oligarchies that had other aims than the protection and well-being of the people. But he wasn't addressing a political science class, and his description suited his legislative purpose, which was to get the New York senate and assembly to appropriate funds for unemployment relief. "The duty of the state toward the citizens is the duty of the servant to its master. . . . One of these duties of the state is that of caring for those of its citizens who find themselves the victims of such adverse circumstance as makes them unable to obtain even the necessities for mere existence without the aid of others. That responsibility is recognized by every civilized nation."

Here again a picky listener might have taken issue with Roosevelt's formulation. Most of the countries of Western Europe had recognized the responsibility of the state to support the people in time of distress, but the question inspired heated debate in America. In the 1880s Grover Cleveland had vetoed a bill promising government payments to drought-stricken Texas farmers, on the ground that the measure would foster dependence on the government's dole. "Though the people support the government," Cleveland asserted, "the government should not support the people." Cleveland's position remained popular almost fifty years later, and though most Americans had come to accept the idea of government relief for certain natural disasters—hurricanes, floods, earthquakes—many Americans, maybe most, had yet to be convinced that business cycles qualified.

Roosevelt therefore had to exert himself to persuade the New York legislators to act. "The economic depression of the last two years has created social conditions resulting in great physical suffering on the part of many hundreds of thousands of men, women, and children," Roosevelt told the lawmakers. "Unless conditions immediately and greatly change, this will, we fear, be aggravated by cold and hunger during the coming winter." Some observers were looking to the federal government for help. Perhaps the Hoover administration and Congress would act, but even if they did, there was no way of knowing when the help would come. "The State of New York cannot wait," Roosevelt told the lawmakers.

He proposed the creation of a new agency empowered to deliver relief as rapidly as possible to the people who most needed it. The "Temporary Emergency Relief Administration"—soon shortened to TERA—would find or create jobs for the unemployed, and where jobs couldn't be provided it would furnish food, clothing, fuel, and housing to the unemployed. Under no circumstances would cash—a dole—be given to individuals. Beyond this, however, the TERA should be granted "the widest latitude and discretion" in apportioning $20 million in emergency funds.

The Republicans grudgingly gave Roosevelt the money and authority he wanted. He appointed Jesse Straus, of the R. H. Macy department store chain, to head the TERA. Straus understood how large organizations operated and gave the relief agency credibility for care in not wasting taxpayers' money. But he knew little about delivering social services. For this expertise Roosevelt turned to a chain-smoking wraith of a man who headed, ironically, the New York Tuberculosis and Health Association. Harry Hopkins was a prototype of the modern social worker, having caught the progressive spirit at Grinnell College in his home state of Iowa and spun it into a career on New York's Lower East Side, not far from where Eleanor Roosevelt had made an avocation out of similar sentiments. He worked in child welfare and later civilian relief during the World War. Meanwhile he discovered a penchant for politics, of both the labor and partisan varieties. He helped found the American Association of Social Workers in the early 1920s and campaigned for Al Smith for governor and president. In the 1928 campaign he encountered Franklin Roosevelt, who appreciated his passion for social work, his aptitude for politics, and his ability to function on less food and sleep than anyone Roosevelt knew.

Hopkins infused the TERA with his energy and commitment, but the agency hardly dented the distress the sinking economy was visiting upon New York. By the end of 1931 some 1.5 million New Yorkers were out of work and the initial appropriation of $20 million had been spent. Roosevelt returned to the legislature and asked for more money, to be raised by a $30 million bond issue. His measure was submitted to the voters in a referendum and approved.

❖   ❖   ❖

WHILE THE NEW money was being disbursed, Roosevelt acknowledged what political observers had taken for granted at least since his overwhelming reelection in 1930: that he was a candidate for president. "It is the simple duty of any American to serve in public position if called upon," he wrote the secretary of the North Dakota Democratic party in January 1932. Party officials in that state wished to enter Roosevelt in their primary. "I willingly give my consent," he declared, "with full appreciation of the honor that has been done me."

Roosevelt proceeded to explain what his candidacy entailed. In radio addresses and in person he spoke, as he put it, on behalf of the "forgotten man at the bottom of the economic pyramid." For too long, he said, government had operated for the benefit of the wealthy, consigning the poor to the margins of public life. The Hoover administration had responded to the crisis by furnishing aid to big banks and corporations. This approach was characteristic of the Republicans, Roosevelt said, and characteristically wrong. It treated ordinary men and women as secondary to the powerful firms that had long dominated American life. And it certainly hadn't done anything to alleviate the depression, which grew worse with each passing month. Roosevelt advocated "building from the bottom up," as he put it: supplying aid to those who most needed it. He also urged a reduction in the tariff. The Smoot-Hawley impost, far from protecting American industry, had devastated it, as even Republicans should have realized it would. If American factories ran anywhere near capacity, they would produce more than Americans by themselves could consume. "We must sell some goods abroad," Roosevelt asserted. But foreign countries could acquire the dollars to purchase American goods only by selling their products in America. "This foolish tariff of ours makes that impossible." The crisis before the country was far greater than the Hoover administration understood. "We are in the midst of an emergency at least equal to that of war," Roosevelt declared. "Let us mobilize to meet it."

Hoover was an easy target during the spring of 1932. The Reconstruction Finance Corporation, the embodiment of the president's trickle-down approach, had achieved little. Yet Hoover was constrained from taking stronger measures by his own self-help philosophy and by the simple fact that he was president and therefore responsible for American welfare in a way Roosevelt wasn't. Roosevelt, the outsider, could paint the depression in all its grim detail, and even embellish where he thought embellishment would serve his purpose. Hoover had to soft-pedal the country's problems, knowing that a declaration of emergency might frighten people and make conditions even worse than they already were.

Roosevelt recognized his advantage and pushed it hard. "Two weeks ago I said that we were facing an emergency more grave than that of war," he declared at a Jefferson Day dinner in St. Paul, Minnesota. "This I repeat tonight." He may well have been right, but he didn't help matters by reminding Americans how frightened they should be. "A great fear has swept the country," he said. "Normal times lull us into complacency. We become lazy and contented. Then with the coming of economic stress we feel the disturbing hand of fear. This fear spreads to the entire country, and with more or less unity we turn to our common government at Washington."

So Roosevelt said, and so he hoped—at any rate about the turning to Washington. There were plenty of Americans who saw no compelling reason to look to the federal government, who accepted the Republican preference for relative inaction by government and for reliance on the business cycle to restore prosperity, if slowly. Yet Roosevelt could see that their number was shrinking and that the patience of America was wearing thin. His political strategy was based on a belief that America's patience would wear out by November 1932.

In Atlanta in May he offered the clearest view of where he intended to take the country should he be elected president. His commencement address at Oglethorpe University was longer on substance than many such speeches, and the graduates, most wondering how they would find jobs in an economy already oversupplied with workers, listened carefully. "As you have viewed this world of which you are about to become a more active part," Roosevelt said, "I have no doubt that you have been impressed by its chaos, its lack of plan. Perhaps some of you have used stronger language. And stronger language is justified." Lack of planning was the bane of the modern American economy, which regularly produced tremendous waste. Some of the waste was the necessary consequence of technological change, Roosevelt granted. "But much of it, I believe, could have been prevented by greater foresight and by a larger measure of social planning." The depression revealed the extent of the waste. "Raw materials stand unused, factories stand idle, railroad traffic continues to dwindle, merchants sell less and less, while millions of able-bodied men and women, in dire need, are clamoring for the opportunity to work."

Experts and amateurs adduced various causes for the depression, Roosevelt said, and they prescribed remedies that followed from their explanations. Some blamed the business cycle and counseled patience to let the cycle turn further, to renewed prosperity. Others looked backward to the World War and outward to the international economy and advocated rescheduling debts and reparations and manipulating exchange rates and currency flows.

Roosevelt didn't deny that the business cycle and the larger world influenced American affairs, but he urged his listeners to look within the American economy, in particular at the lack of balance between producers and consumers. While corporate profits had soared during the 1920s, wages grew by far less, and farm prices stagnated. The excess profits piled up in the corporate coffers till they spilled into the stock market, with results that became painfully apparent in October 1929. Under a saner system, the benefits of modern technology and the productivity it yielded would have been shared more evenly. "It is well within the inventive capacity of man, who has built up this great social and economic machine capable of satisfying the wants of all, to insure that all who are willing and able to work receive from it at least the necessities of life." Roosevelt didn't quite say that government should be the guarantor of jobs for all those willing and able souls—which was what he was later accused of saying—but he came fairly close. "It is toward that objective that we must move if we are to profit by our recent experience." Nor did Roosevelt suggest specific routes to his goal. These would emerge in the fullness of time.

Yet he did describe what would become the characteristic method of his administration. Unsurprisingly—Roosevelt being a politician, and this being a political speech—he attributed his approach to the genius of the American people. "The country needs—and, unless I mistake its temper, the country demands—bold, persistent experimentation. It is common sense to take a method and try it. If it fails, admit it frankly and try another. But above all, try something."

❖ ❖ ❖

THE CLOSER THE Democratic convention drew, the more inevitable a Roosevelt nomination appeared, and the greater the scrutiny the presumptive nominee experienced. By the early 1930s Walter Lippmann had been the most influential observer of the American political scene for perhaps a decade. He had helped found the *New Republic* in the year Woodrow Wilson entered the White House, and he assisted Wilson in negotiating an end to the World War at Paris in 1919. He was a progressive at heart but considered himself a pragmatist; he also considered himself a shrewder judge of American politics and policy than any American politician or policy maker. From his desk at the *New York Herald Tribune* he offered counsel to parties and voters and handed down verdicts on candidates. In January 1932, following Roosevelt's announcement for president, Lippmann assessed the New York governor.

"The art of carrying water on both shoulders is highly developed in American politics, and Mr. Roosevelt has learned it," Lippmann declared. Roosevelt's feat, Lippmann explained, consisted in attacking and defending the status quo simultaneously, declaring the need for fundamental reforms even while disclaiming any such intent. Lippmann had to admire Roosevelt's ingenuity, but he was at a loss as to what the governor actually stood for. "It is not easy to say with certainty whether his left-wing or right-wing supporters are the more deceived. The reason is that Mr. Roosevelt is a highly impressionable person, without a firm grasp of public affairs and without very strong convictions." Certain of Roosevelt's supporters called him a dangerous enemy of those malign forces that currently afflicted America; Lippmann dismissed such descriptions as laughable. "Franklin D. Roosevelt is an amiable man with many philanthropic influences, but he is not the dangerous enemy of anything. He is too eager to please. The notion, which seems to prevail in the West and South, that Wall Street fears him, is preposterous. . . . Wall Street does not like some of his supporters. Wall Street does not like his vagueness and the uncertainty as to what he does think, but if any Western Progressive thinks that the Governor has challenged directly or indirectly the wealth concentrated in New York City, he is mightily mistaken." Roosevelt's record as governor revealed a penchant for brave words rather than bold deeds. "I doubt whether anyone can point to a single act of his which involved any political risk." The keepers of the status quo needn't worry about Roosevelt. "Franklin D. Roosevelt is no crusader. He is no tribune of the people. He is no enemy of entrenched privilege. He is a pleasant man who, without any important qualifications for the office, would very much like to be President."

❖   ❖   ❖

LIPPMANN'S DISMISSAL encouraged Al Smith to step in front of the Roosevelt train. Smith still smarted at what he considered Roosevelt's flippant treatment of him; he also chafed at his own bad luck in peaking too soon. George Van Schaick, a Smith ally whom Roosevelt had made superintendent of insurance, tried to nudge Smith toward an endorsement of Roosevelt. Smith responded with a litany of complaints against Roosevelt that turned into an angry postmortem of the 1928 campaign. "He became quite heated," Van Schaick said. "He reviewed the campaign against him based largely on his religion and spoke very bitterly of the narrowness and bigotry which had developed in certain sections. He spoke with deepest feeling. . . . He said that having been defeated on such narrow and un-American grounds in 1928, that now in 1932 when it was quite likely an auspicious Democratic year, all should stand aside and give him another chance to overcome the prejudice he had faced in 1928. He said further that FDR should recognize it and not attempt to take the nomination away from him."

Smith wasn't so candid in public, but he adopted a strategy designed to deny Roosevelt the nomination and reclaim it for himself. Two weeks after Roosevelt tossed his hat in the ring, Smith issued a statement:

> If the Democratic National Convention, after careful consideration, should decide it wants me to lead, I will make the fight; but I will not make a pre-convention campaign to secure the support of delegates. By action of the Democratic National Convention of 1928, I am the leader of my party in the

nation. With a full sense of the responsibility thereby imposed, I shall not in advance of the convention either support or oppose the candidacy of any aspirant for the nomination.

It was a shrewd maneuver, one Roosevelt might have admired if it hadn't come at his own expense. Smith, standing on the disputably high ground of a nomination that had proved to be the worst disaster in the Democrats' recent history, absolved himself of endorsing Roosevelt and implicitly invited party conservatives to launch a stop-Roosevelt offensive at the convention. Smith knew perfectly well how the two-thirds rule worked; the opponents of the front-runner merely had to impugn his inevitability and hold out till the convention grew exhausted and desperate. At that point the convention could well turn to one who had carried the banner before. The Happy Warrior might take the field again.

❖   ❖   ❖

ROOSEVELT DETERMINED to forestall such an outcome, by a strategy exactly along the lines of what Walter Lippmann criticized. Anyone could see that the depression had opened the door for the Democratic candidate in the general election; the only thing the candidate had to do was to avoid missing the opening by veering too far to the left or the right. Balance was the key to victory, and if balance required placating both progressives and conservatives, Roosevelt was willing to oblige.

Balance required care and effort, though. On two issues, a Democratic candidate might easily misstep. The first was Prohibition, which wasn't quite as divisive in 1932 as it had been in 1924 and 1928 but still evoked passions. The sentiment in favor of an embargo on alcohol continued to erode with the undeniable failure of the federal government to enforce the law at all thoroughly and with the increasing need of the states for tax revenues to replace what the depression had cost them in sales and income taxes. Yet Prohibition remained symbolically powerful in the rural parts of the country, a last stand against the otherwise irresistible tide of modernity.

Roosevelt initially attempted to straddle the issue. He supported repeal of the Eighteenth Amendment but without vigor or even, for many months, voice. While other Democrats staked out their positions, he kept mum. Walter Lippmann held Roosevelt's silence against him, as further evidence of his lack of leadership. Al Smith was even more annoyed. With the 1932 election approaching, Smith wanted Roosevelt to join him in a cultural war on those who had voted against him four years earlier, with repeal of the Eighteenth Amendment being the test issue. "Why in hell don't he speak out?" Smith demanded of Clark Howell, in the interview with the *Atlanta Constitution* publisher. Smith knew that Roosevelt privately opposed Prohibition. "Now ain't the time for trimming."

That Smith could say such a thing made clear—to Howell and, more significantly, to Roosevelt—why he had lost so badly in 1928 and why he mustn't win the nomination in 1932. Not in sixteen years had the stars been so favorably aligned for Democrats; to risk victory by taking a provocative, party-splitting stance on Prohibition would be the height of folly. The Eighteenth Amendment was as good as dead anyway; the movement for repeal hardly required Roosevelt's support. On the contrary, the good of the party—and of the country, Roosevelt could reasonably extrapolate—required just the trimming that so angered Smith.

Eventually Roosevelt broke his silence on Prohibition. In February 1932 he called for a return of the liquor question to the states, that they might tolerate or continue to prohibit alcohol as they saw fit. This agnostic position, favoring repeal of the federal amendment but allowing states to impose their own bans, placed Roosevelt midway between the wets and the drys. He added a rationale that made his compromise even less controversial: he stressed repeal as a fiscal measure, promising a "large source of additional revenue" to those states that loosened the taps and bungs but taxed what they spouted.

The other issue that threatened to divide the party and derail Roosevelt's advance to the nomination was the appropriate attitude toward the world beyond America's borders. Remnant Wilsonians wanted Roosevelt to reembrace the central teaching of their departed philosopher-president: that America and the world were irretrievably interconnected. In 1932 the Wilsonians were still calling for American membership in the League of Nations, at this point primarily as an acknowledgment of the global, or at least transatlantic, character of the depression and a first step toward discovering international remedies. Roosevelt seemed a natural to join such a call, having been an ardent Wilsonian and currently castigating the Republicans for the economic nationalism behind the Smoot-Hawley tariff. But internationalism raised hackles on the neck of middle America, precisely that portion of the electorate that had abandoned Smith in such hordes in 1928. To woo them back into the party required reassurances from Roosevelt that he wouldn't put the interests of Europeans or other foreigners ahead of American interests.

Roosevelt couldn't easily rewrite the past, and he didn't try. "In common with millions of my fellow countrymen, I worked and spoke, in 1920, in behalf of American participation in a League of Nations," he admitted in early 1932. "For that course I have no apology to make." Had present circumstances recapitulated those of that earlier time, he said, he would be working just as hard for American membership in the League. "But the League of Nations today is not the League conceived by Woodrow Wilson." Roosevelt let listeners imagine that things might have been different if the Republicans hadn't sabotaged Wilson's vision for the League. Had the United States been a member all these years, the League might have evolved more positively. But there was little to be gained by arguing the point. The League was now an instrument for the advancement of the narrow and often nefarious purposes of the European powers. "Therefore I do not favor American participation."

❖   ❖   ❖

HAVING DODGED, as he hoped, the bullets of Prohibition and internationalism, Roosevelt advanced toward the convention. A generation after the progressives had specified primary elections as the ideally democratic way of narrowing candidate fields, the Democratic party chose the delegates to its national convention by a combination of primaries, caucuses, state conventions, and backroom back-scratching. Roosevelt's political labors of the previous decade—his correspondence with state Democratic officials, his cultivation of William Jennings Bryan and Edward House, his convention appearances, his dispatch of Louis Howe and James Farley to consult with southern and western party leaders—had been undertaken with this welter of decision-making in mind, and during the spring and summer of 1932 his efforts paid off. He won an early lead in delegates, and his advantage widened with each passing month.

But he left nothing to chance. He continued to woo southern Democrats especially, hosting events at Warm Springs designed to make this Hudson Valley Dutchman seem a Scots-Irish son of Dixie. He engaged Huey Long, the Louisiana senator, in a good-natured argument about the proper method of eating corn pone with potlikker. "Because I am at least an adopted Georgian, I am deeply stirred by the great controversy," Roosevelt wrote the *Atlanta Constitution*. "I suggest referring the whole subject to the platform committee of the next Democratic National Convention." Yet after Long announced for dunking, Roosevelt couldn't remain silent. "I crumble mine," he declared.

Several weeks before the convention nearly all the South had climbed aboard the Roosevelt bandwagon. Texas and Virginia were the main exceptions, holding out, respectively, for favorite sons John Nance Garner, the speaker of the House, and Harry Byrd, the governor of the Old Dominion. The West was equally enthusiastic, with almost every state but California, where Garner won the primary, pledging for Roosevelt.

Only the East occasioned worry. Al Smith's partisans joined others intent on stopping Roosevelt, and the alliance campaigned hard in New England, where it captured Massachusetts for Smith and split the rest of the region with Roosevelt's forces. Smith's backers fought Roosevelt to a draw in New York.

The result was that Roosevelt entered the Chicago convention with a commanding lead over Smith but not a decisive one, given the party's two-thirds rule. Roosevelt toyed with trying to repeal the rule, which would have allowed a first-ballot victory, but he rejected the idea as suggesting a lack of confidence. He concentrated instead on wooing Garner, whose Texas and California delegates could put Roosevelt over the top.

Garner at first refused to budge. Having attended conventions since the turn of the century, the wily Texan understood that strange things happened once the balloting began. Smith might stymie Roosevelt but be unable to win himself; the convention might turn to Garner in the belief that any Democrat could defeat the wounded Hoover.

The first ballot went as expected. Roosevelt received 666¼ votes, substantially more than half but some hundred shy of two-thirds. The second ballot, which was called at once—as dawn began to break outside the Chicago convention hall—was the crucial one, for it would show movement. If Roosevelt gained ground, he could count on victory. But if he slipped, he might lose everything. Roosevelt stayed away from the convention, as candidates did in that era, but Farley worked the hall on his behalf and secured eleven additional votes. Smith meanwhile lost six votes. Roosevelt's men sighed with relief and encouragement, Smith's with frustration and foreboding.

A third ballot brought Roosevelt five more votes and cost Smith an additional four. At this point Garner had to make a decision. If he held out too long, Roosevelt might win on his own, leaving Garner with nothing to show for his success in Texas and California. But if he threw his support to Roosevelt too soon, he would give up whatever—admittedly slim—chance he had of winning the nomination for himself. His delegates were committed to him for the duration. William McAdoo, the former candidate who now headed the

California delegation, told Sam Rayburn, Garner's floor manager, "We'll vote for Jack Garner until hell freezes over if you say so."

Garner decided not to wait that long. He refused to risk an extended battle that might spoil the Democrats' first good shot at the White House in sixteen years. As he later recalled, "I said to Sam, 'All right, release my delegates and see what you can do. Hell, I'll do anything to see the Democrats win one more national election.' "

Garner's concession proved the difference. The switch of Texas and California prompted other states to follow suit, and on the fourth ballot Franklin Roosevelt received the Democratic nomination.

20.

Rexford Tugwell met Roosevelt at the governor's mansion in Albany, and one of the first things he noticed was the shoes. "Curiously unworn," was how Tugwell described them. This shouldn't have been curious at all. Everyone in New York who cared to know realized that Roosevelt didn't walk. Not everyone appreciated the extent of his disability, which he continued to minimize. But no one had seen him strolling the sidewalks of Albany or Manhattan, and no one expected to see him. A man who didn't walk didn't wear out shoes.

Yet Tugwell still found it curious, for it belied the broader impression of the man. Tugwell taught economics at Columbia University, with a specialty in the business of agriculture. Roosevelt learned about him through Raymond Moley, a Columbia colleague from the political science department who had been advising the governor on prison reform. Roosevelt decided to pick the brains of experts on a variety of subjects important to a prospective president. Moley brought Tugwell up from the city on the afternoon train; they arrived at the mansion in time for dinner.

Eleanor Roosevelt commenced the personal talk. She quickly learned that Tugwell came from Chautauqua County and that his family had been farmers, mostly dairy and fruit. His father had run a business on the side.

Roosevelt pushed the conversation toward public policy. He had long thought that one solution to the unemployment problem was to encourage jobless city dwellers to relocate to the country. What did the professor think?

Tugwell disagreed. Farming was a complex affair, he said. City folks wouldn't know where to start. And country life was different from city life. They would probably be bored and unhappy.

Roosevelt responded—"a little testily," Tugwell thought—that at least they would have something to eat.

Tugwell didn't admit even that. They wouldn't have something to eat unless they could grow it themselves, and most would be unable to do so.

The discussion continued, but Tugwell found himself unable to take his eyes off Roosevelt. As the dinner ended, the governor rolled his wheelchair from the dining table to the living room, talking all the while. Without dropping a syllable or pausing for breath, he transferred himself easily from his wheelchair to the sofa. Tugwell thought the conversation provided a cover, a disguise for his disability. "The talking was calculated," Tugwell recalled. "His crippled legs must have led to the invention of many such diversions, finally becoming unconscious."

The sofa sat low to the floor, and Roosevelt's legs projected high and forward. He occasionally moved them by putting his hands under his knees and shifting them manually. "When he did this, enormous shoulder muscles bunched under his jacket and relaxed smoothly," Tugwell wrote. "It occurred to me that, during the eleven years of his struggle to get back the use of his legs, the rest of his body had really become overdeveloped. I wondered what his jacket size must be. I imagined that if Roosevelt had not worn custom-made clothes, he probably could not have found his size in most stores."

Roosevelt's large head and thick neck matched his shoulders and torso, yet somewhat oddly. Tugwell could understand how the exercises Roosevelt had done for rehabilitation had developed the muscles of his upper body, but he wondered what exercises had enlarged his head. He had seen pictures of the young Roosevelt, the lean athlete. Something of that younger man remained in the figure seated before him—"immobile but still athletic."

Roosevelt's face was as interesting as his body. "It was a mobile and expressive face," Tugwell said. "It might have been an actor's." Tugwell afterward mentioned this to Moley, who agreed. "He said it *was* an actor's, and a professional actor's at that. How did I suppose he'd created and maintained the image of authority?"

Tugwell was taken a bit aback. He asked Moley if the Roosevelt he had spent the evening with wasn't, then, the real Roosevelt.

Moley reflected before answering. His explanation stuck with Tugwell, who recalled it years later:

Yes, he said, in the sense that all this paraphernalia of the governorship had become part of him. It was a real talent; it was a lifetime part that he was playing. . . . He'd figured out what he ought to be like in order to get where he wanted to get and do what he wanted to do, and that was what was on display. Ray added, thoughtfully, that no one would ever see anything else.

Moley had been studying Roosevelt for some time. His sessions with the governor and then presidential candidate had segued from prison reform to politics generally, and he became, with Tugwell, Adolf Berle, and a few others, a member of what the press soon called the Brain Trust. Moley measured Roosevelt as a politician and a man, and what he perceived impressed him, in a complex way. "You ask what he is like," he wrote to his sister, who had inquired about Roosevelt. "That isn't easy to answer, because I haven't had the chance to confirm a lot of fleeting impressions." But those fleeting impressions, confirmed or not, added up to a striking portrait of the man who seemed certain to become America's next president:

> One thing is sure, that the idea people get from his charming manner—that he is soft or flabby in disposition and character—is far from true. When he wants something a lot he can be formidable—when crossed he is hard, stubborn, resourceful, relentless. I used to think on the basis of casual observation that his amiability was 'lord-of-the-manor,' 'good-to-the-peasants' stuff. It isn't that at all. He seems quite naturally warm and friendly—less because he genuinely likes many of the people to whom he is pleasant (although he does like a lot of people of all sorts and varieties) than because he just enjoys the pleasant and engaging role, as a charming woman does. And being a born politician, he measures such qualities in himself by the effect they produce on others. He is wholly conscious of his ability to send callers away happy and glowing and in agreement with him and his ideas. . . .
>
> The stories about his illness and its effect upon him are the bunk. Nobody in public life since T.R. has been so robust, so buoyantly and blatantly healthy as this fellow. He is full of animal spirits and keeps himself and the people around him in a rare good humor with a lot of horseplay. . . . The man's energy and vitality are astonishing. I've been amazed with his interest in things. It skips and bounces through seemingly intricate subjects, and maybe it is my academic training that makes me feel that no one could possibly learn much in such a hit or miss fashion. I don't find that he has read much about economic subjects. What he gets is from talking to people. . . . When he stores away the net of conversation, he never knows what part of what he has kept is what he said himself or what his visitor said.

❖ ❖ ❖

*U*PON LEARNING that he had carried the Democratic convention, Roosevelt announced that he would do something historically unprecedented: he would address the delegates in person. Tradition dictated that the nominee receive official notification, which typically arrived several weeks after the convention, before delivering his acceptance speech. Roosevelt refused to wait that long— or to wait at all. The decisive vote in Chicago concluded at half past ten on Friday night; by seven thirty Saturday morning he was on an airplane flying west. Air travel wasn't a novelty in 1932; Charles Lindbergh's epic crossing of the Atlantic five years earlier had seen to that. But political candidates didn't travel by air, in part because they wanted to stop and make speeches along the way. Roosevelt, however, chose to fly, in order both to signal a break from the past and to get to the convention before the excitement surrounding his nomination diminished.

Bad weather slowed the flying, and while he made his way across Ohio and Indiana the convention nominated John Nance Garner for vice president. Roosevelt had almost no say in the decision. Garner let it be known that after thirty years in the House he would like to retire to the vice presidency, and the transfer suited all concerned: the Texas delegation, as honoring their favorite son; the Californians, as giving the West a presence in a Roosevelt administration; the Roosevelt camp, as the least that could be done for Garner and his southern and western supporters. There was one other consideration, unspoken except among Garner's closest friends. Roosevelt seemed hale enough, but so had Warren Harding before he died. Polio couldn't be beneficial to one's long-term health; Garner might inherit the presidency before four years were out. Perhaps this possibility inspired the words of Alabama congressman John McDuffie, who praised Garner to the convention as a "sturdy and rugged character" and a "real red-blooded he-man." The convention approved Garner unanimously on the first vice presidential ballot.

By the time Roosevelt reached the Chicago Stadium, many of the delegates, including nearly all those pledged to Smith, had departed. But their seats were taken by visitors who voiced their enthusiasm for the nominee when his car finally cleared the heavy traffic from the airport. "As Mr. Roosevelt advanced to the rostrum, the great hall seemed to surge upward, an illusion which accompanied the sight of so many thousands rising simultaneously to their feet," Arthur Krock of the *New York Times* reported. "It was evident that the thousands of people believed they were in the presence, not only of the nominee of the Democratic party, but of the next President of the United States."

The thousands in the stadium, and the millions more across the country who listened to Roosevelt's speech on the radio, heard the nominee embrace the credo of liberalism—proudly, defiantly, confidently. "The Democratic party by tradition and by the continuing logic of history, past and present, is the bearer of liberalism and of progress," Roosevelt declared. He explained that there were two ways of viewing the role of government in matters touching economics and social life. "The first sees to it that a favored few are helped, and hopes that some of their prosperity will leak through, sift through, to labor, to the farmer, to the small business man. That theory belongs to the party of Toryism, and I had hoped that most of the Tories left this country in 1776." But they had not left. Instead they had regathered as Republicans and had administered the lopsided prosperity of the 1920s. Corporate profits had soared but weren't shared. Consumers and workers were forgotten. The imbalance was unsustainable, and it had inevitably produced the stock crash and the depression. "You know the story. Surpluses invested in unnecessary plants became idle. Men lost their jobs. Purchasing power dried up. Banks became frightened and started calling loans. Those who had money were afraid to part with it. Credit contracted. Industry stopped. Commerce declined. And unemployment mounted."

Against the Republicans' approach of every man for himself, Roosevelt posited a Democratic philosophy of all for one another. This had been the essence of liberalism from the beginning; it became even more so under present circumstances. "Never in history have the interests of all the people been so united in a single economic problem," Roosevelt said. The depression was threatening city and country, farmers and workers, debtors and creditors, management and labor. "Danger to one is danger to all." The Republicans, refusing to acknowledge the interconnections, had refused to take ameliorative action; a Democratic administration would rectify the Republicans' failure. "We are going to make the voters understand this year that this nation is not merely a nation of independence, but it is, if we are to survive, bound to be a nation of interdependence."

The Republicans pleaded helplessness against what they described as inexorable laws of economics. "But while they prate of economic laws, men and women are starving. . . . Economic laws are not made by nature. They are made by human beings." Farmers knew this and rightly expected more of government than they were getting; Roosevelt proposed strong action to reduce crop surpluses. Homeowners knew this as they struggled with their monthly payments; Roosevelt promised measures to lower interest rates and prevent foreclosures. Workers knew this in their search for jobs to replace the ones they had lost; Roosevelt declared that the federal government should enter the labor market and hire workers to develop the nation's resources.

As he reached the climax of his speech, Roosevelt asserted that the current troubles wouldn't have been wasted if Americans discovered how to respond.

> Throughout the nation, men and women, forgotten in the political philosophy of the government of the last years look to us here for guidance and for more equitable opportunity to share in the distribution of national wealth. On the farms, in the large metropolitan areas, in the smaller cities and in the villages, millions of our citizens cherish the hope that their old standards of living and of thought have not gone forever. Those millions cannot and shall not hope in vain.
>
> I pledge you, I pledge myself, to a new deal for the American people. Let us all here assembled constitute ourselves prophets of a new order of competence and of courage. This is more than a political campaign. It is a call to arms. Give me your help, not to win votes alone, but to win in this crusade to restore America to its own people.

❖   ❖   ❖

TECHNICALLY SPEAKING, a candidate in 1932 could have waged a national campaign without leaving home. Radio increasingly knitted the nation into a single communications sphere, enabling the candidate to reach almost any interested citizen via the airwaves. But political practice lagged behind technical advance. The national radio networks—two NBC networks, the Blue (which would become ABC) and the Red (NBC); and CBS—covered politics as news and introduced candidates to the voters, but they did so on the networks' terms rather than candidates' or the parties'. The networks also carried advertising: of automobiles, appliances, apparel, real estate, cigarettes, and myriad other goods and services. Yet the general use of radio to advertise candidates—to present the candidates to voters on the candidates' terms—remained in the future. A candidate who wanted to get his message out to voters still needed to get himself out to voters, which meant touring the country.

Whistle-stopping had a mixed history. William Jennings Bryan's western tour in 1896 had failed against William McKinley's front-porch campaign.

James Cox and Franklin Roosevelt had toured in 1920 and lost to the stay-at-home Harding. Silent Cal Coolidge had kept silent and still in Washington while John W. Davis barnstormed and got buried in 1924.

Roosevelt's advisers urged him to avoid a continental campaign. The momentum of events was clearly in his favor; he simply needed to avoid mistakes to capture the White House. And mistakes were easier to avoid in Albany or Hyde Park than in distant locales where the Republicans could lay traps and spring tricks. On the road he would be pestered to speak in detail about his plans and policies, and details, at this stage, would only get him into trouble. Besides, he was governor of New York; he might best demonstrate his fitness for national executive office by tending to the state executive office he currently held. To neglect his current office in the quest for a future office might strike voters as irresponsible.

There was another aspect to the caution, rarely voiced. Roosevelt looked healthy and strong, but he was a polio survivor and a paraplegic. Cross-country travel was strenuous, cross-country political travel even more so. What if Roosevelt became fatigued and stumbled, literally or figuratively? There was the related question of political perceptions. Roosevelt never directly denied his disability, and anyone who followed politics knew about his struggle with polio and its aftereffects. But neither did he trumpet his disability, and he would be asking for the votes of people who had *not* followed politics. At home he could control camera angles and access by reporters; on the road he would be at the mercy of chance and local planners. At a time of national distress, Americans were looking for strength in their leader. Would they accept that a half-paralyzed person could provide such strength?

Roosevelt ignored the advice and flicked away the worries like so much cigarette ash. "I have a streak of Dutch stubbornness in me," he told Jim Farley. "And the Dutch is up this time. I'm going campaigning to the Pacific Coast and discuss every important issue of the campaign."

Dutch stubbornness was part of the story. Another part was the desire of the recovering polio victim to test himself. Could he stand the strain of an extended tour? If he couldn't, better to know now than later, for as difficult as a campaign might be, its stresses would be nothing next to those of the presidency itself. The former assistant navy secretary was familiar with shakedown cruises as they applied to ships; a Pacific Coast tour would serve the same purpose for himself.

And there was something else again. Roosevelt was already thinking past the election to how he would govern. Hoover's continuing failure was a tribute to caution; Roosevelt intended to be the boldest president since Lincoln. A western swing would showcase his boldness and carry his fight against caution and timidity across the continent. For decades the West had been a wild card in American politics, electing everyone from Populists to Progressives to Democrats to Republicans. The West would test Roosevelt's ideas even as it tested his constitution.

He set out in early September. At Topeka he aired his thinking on the farm problem to an audience that included Bryanites, Wilsonians, Hooverists, and the odd Debsian. He reiterated his perception of the seamlessness of American economic life. "Industrial prosperity can reach only artificial and temporary heights, as it did in 1929, if at the same time there is no agricultural prosperity," he said. "This nation cannot endure if it is half boom and half broke." Any effective answer to the farm question must tackle the problem of overproduction, and the federal government should take the lead. "I favor a definite policy looking to the planned use of the land," Roosevelt said. Some acreage would have to be withdrawn from production—voluntarily, to the extent possible. Coercion would be counterproductive. Yet careful planning and cooperative education would yield a policy all could live with and benefit from. The purpose was simple and beyond dispute—"the restoration of agriculture to economic equality with other industries within the United States."

At Salt Lake City, Roosevelt turned from agriculture to industry. Railroads weren't the quintessential mode of transport they had been in Roosevelt's youth; cars, trucks, and buses had eroded the trains' oligopoly of land travel. But the railroad industry remained one of America's largest, and together the rail companies still carried the great bulk of what Americans wanted moved from one place to another. The railroads, however, were in a sad state. Overbuilt during the nineteenth century and never sufficiently thinned, they suffered from their own version of the oversupply that afflicted farmers. Capitalist theory would have let them slug it out, with the weaker ones failing. But the collateral damage would have been as dire as from a similar remedy in agriculture. The railroads employed nearly two million workers; some thirty million Americans owned railroad stock either directly or through savings banks and insurance companies; the entire American population depended on speedy and reliable rail service. The cause of the rail troubles, like the cause of the farm problems, Roosevelt said, was "the entire absence of national planning." The answer, as in farming, was precisely such planning. "The individual railroads should be regarded as parts of a national transportation system."

At Seattle, Roosevelt spoke on the tariff. The workers in Seattle, the great seaport of the Northwest, were among the most militant in the country; many had participated in the general strike of 1919, which began on the docks and in the shipyards before paralyzing the city as a whole. The depression had the Puget Sound district again on edge—an edge Roosevelt sharpened by blaming the Republicans' Smoot-Hawley tariff for disrupting the trade on which Seattle and its hinterland depended. He had to be careful in proposing remedies, for any reduction in American tariffs threatened further damage to American jobs. And so he proposed reciprocal reductions of tariffs, negotiated country by country. "This principle of tariff by negotiation means to deal with each country concerned, on the basis of fair barter," he explained. "If it has something we need, and we have something it needs, a tariff agreement can and should be made." Such an approach would restore trade without jeopardizing American livelihoods. In the process it would ease the international tensions the tariff war had produced.

At Portland, where the mighty Columbia River slowed on its long rush from the Rocky Mountains to the sea, Roosevelt spoke of hydroelectric power. Again he urged a national perspective. "The question of power, of electrical development and distribution, is primarily a national problem," he said. "When the great possessions that belong to all of us—that belong to the nation—are at stake, we are not partisans; we are Americans." Electricity promised great benefits to Americans of all regions and occupations. "It lights our homes, our places of work, and our streets. It turns the wheels of most of our transportation and our factories. . . . It can relieve the drudgery of the housewife and lift the great burden off the shoulders of the hardworking farmer." It could do so, at any rate, if the government ensured that it not become a captive of private interests. Roosevelt didn't propose to dismantle existing private power companies, but he advocated a larger role for government as a regulator of private companies and in some cases their competitor. On a larger scale, the federal government must direct the development of regional watersheds. Critics would cry radicalism, Roosevelt acknowledged. For them he had an answer: "My policy is as radical as American liberty. My policy is as radical as the Constitution."

❖　❖　❖

By THE END of September, with the election still six weeks away, Roosevelt had given voters a fairly comprehensive view of his philosophy of government. He believed that the depression signified a breakdown of the American capitalist system; the system's unfettered competition had run the economy into a deep rut from which the American people could not escape without the intervention of government. Government planners, in a Roosevelt administration, would temper and guide the competition, adding Washington's visible hand to the invisible hand of the marketplace. Roosevelt remained stingy with details of government's guidance, but anyone at all interested in politics realized that a vote for Roosevelt would be a vote for greater government participation in the American political economy.

On one issue Roosevelt was less than candid. As a veteran of Washington and the present chief executive of New York state, he couldn't help but realize that the programs he envisioned would be expensive. Yet he spoke as though he could have his New Deal—the phrase was just beginning to be capitalized— and trim government too. Roosevelt railed at the Republicans for profligacy in government. "We are paying for the cost of our three kinds of government"— federal, state, and local—"$125 a year for every man, woman, and child in the United States, or $625 for the average family of five people," he said. This level of spending was outrageous and couldn't be sustained. Roosevelt condemned the Hoover administration for fiscal mismanagement, and for covering its mismanagement with a string of prevarication. "It started off by saying that it was going to balance the budget," Roosevelt declared. "Fine! Then it said it was balancing the budget. Fine! And finally it said it had balanced the budget. Better yet!" But it hadn't balanced the budget, as the Treasury Department's own report for the most recent quarter made plain. " 'Excess of expenditures over receipts,' " Roosevelt quoted indignantly: " '$402,043,002.' There you are!"

A Roosevelt administration would do much better. It would speak forthrightly, and it would manage the government effectively. "Before any man enters my cabinet," Roosevelt said, "he must give me a two-fold pledge: 1. Absolute loyalty to the Democratic platform, and especially its economy plank"—which promised a balanced budget—"2. Complete cooperation with me looking to economy and reorganization in his department." Lest the message somehow be lost, he reiterated: "I regard reduction in federal spending as one of the most important issues of this campaign. In my opinion, it is the most direct and effective contribution that government can make to business."

❖   ❖   ❖

HERBERT HOOVER was a proud man who despised Franklin Roosevelt for some of the same reasons Al Smith did. Like Smith, Hoover had earned, through hard work and applied intelligence, everything he attained in life. He couldn't see that Roosevelt had earned anything, and with the smugness of the self-made man he assumed Roosevelt was lacking in character and ability. He didn't deny that Roosevelt possessed a certain charisma, but he considered charisma badly overrated—especially when it caused those who came into contact with Roosevelt to fall for the arguments he was making against Hoover's administration.

Hoover initially attempted to ignore Roosevelt's assaults, on the ground that a president had more important things to worry about. Hoover didn't lack for worries during the summer and autumn of 1932. The depression persisted, although Hoover detected signs of economic improvement that were lost on most disinterested observers. Veterans of the World War were demanding early payment of a bonus Congress had promised for their old age. Many of them were unemployed, and they gathered in Washington to register their opinion with the legislature and the administration. In time the "Bonus Army" swelled to twenty thousand, along with many wives and children. Washington, like other cities during the depression, included a large population of homeless people; the arrival of so many more unattached souls made the local authorities nervous. That the vets were skilled with weapons and that some had become radicalized by the collapse of the economy contributed to the concern their presence evoked.

Hoover opposed prepayment of the bonus, contending that the government couldn't afford it, that veterans shouldn't be given special treatment, and that capitulation to pressure would encourage other groups to try similar stunts. The Republican Senate joined him in opposition after the Democratic House voted in favor. The House and the Senate did agree, with Hoover's concurrence, that the federal government should assist in the demobilization of the Bonus Army, by offering to pay to transport the protesters home.

Most accepted the government's offer and departed. But a few thousand, many with no homes to return to, remained where they were on the east bank of the Anacostia River. A separate contingent occupied some government buildings not far from the White House, from which they sallied forth to picket the White House. Hoover, who had displayed coolness and courage directing relief in Europe during the World War, unaccountably took fright at this dismal display by a comparative handful of hoboes. He barricaded himself in the executive mansion and ordered the capital police to clear the squatters from federal property. When the vets resisted, the affair turned violent. Two of the protesters were killed and several policemen were injured. Hoover ordered federal troops to augment the police force.

Command of the military operation fell to General Douglas MacArthur, a decorated World War veteran who had advanced to chief of staff of the army. His aide was Dwight Eisenhower, a major with talent but little opportunity to show it. Eisenhower questioned the necessity of deploying federal soldiers against the protesters, and he advised MacArthur against getting personally involved. "He had no business going down there," Eisenhower recalled later. "I told him it was no place for the chief of staff." But MacArthur was eager to act against what he judged an incipient insurgency. "That mob down there was a bad-looking mob," he told reporters after a reconnaissance of the veterans' camp. "It was animated by the essence of revolution."

Hoover gave his approval. "A considerable part of those remaining are not veterans," the president asserted. "Many are communists and persons with criminal records." The right to petition was a cornerstone of American politics, but other values, notably order and tranquility, were equally essential. "The first obligation of my office is to uphold and defend the Constitution and the authority of the law. This I propose always to do."

MacArthur's units swept through the veterans' camp with bayonets, machine guns, and tanks. The general apparently exceeded Hoover's orders, advancing farther than the president desired and utilizing more force than Hoover wished. But Hoover failed to call him back, and within a short time the Anacostia camp was an empty, smoldering ruin.

The victory, such as it was, came at the cost of scores of casualties, including the death of a small baby, which outraged millions of Americans already disposed to think of Hoover as distant and hard-hearted. Franklin Roosevelt, observing from Albany, shared the outrage even as he understood that he would benefit from it. "Well, Felix," he told Felix Frankfurter, an adjunct member of the Brain Trust, "this will elect me."

❖　❖　❖

THE EPISODE enlightened Roosevelt about Douglas MacArthur. As the real army was routing the Bonus Army, Roosevelt was having lunch with Rex Tugwell. They were discussing farm policy and political matters when a call came from Huey Long in Louisiana. Roosevelt took the call at the table, allowing Tugwell to hear his end of the conversation. Long's loud voice enabled Tugwell to hear the other end as well.

"God damn it, Frank!" Long began. "Who d'you think got you nominated?" Long had supported Roosevelt at the Democratic convention.

"Well, you had a lot to do with it, Huey," Roosevelt answered, declining to add the obvious: that others had had much more to do with it than Long had.

"You sure as hell are forgettin' about it as fast as you can. Here I sit down here and never hear from anybody, and what do I see in the papers? That stuffed shirt Owen Young comes to see you." Young was the chairman of General Electric and a presumed enemy of the populist policies Long favored.

"Oh, I see a lot of people you don't read about," Roosevelt said. "The newspaper boys only write up the ones their editors like."

"We won't even carry these states down here if you don't stop listening to those people," Long shouted into the phone. "You got to turn me loose."

"What do you mean, turn you loose? You don't need anyone to do that. You *are* loose."

"I can't win elections without money. . . . I'll carry this country for you, but I can't do it without money."

"You never needed money before. Why do you need it now?"

"Damn it! You musta been born yesterday. I know where to get money when I'm runnin' for myself. But this ain't the same. I'm runnin' for you; don't you know that? . . . You mind what I tell you. Stop wastin' time seein' those Owen Youngs. Let me come up there. People are goin' to feel a lot better if they see me comin' out of that big house than those crooks that got us into this mess in the first place."

"I'll see you get asked, Huey. You keep your shirt on. It will be all right."

"You ask me up there, Frank. I'll give you some schemes that'll bring in the votes."

The telephone call terminated when Roosevelt hung up, with Long still bellowing down the wire. Roosevelt shook his head in a combination of astonishment and recognition. "You know," he told Tugwell, "that's the second most dangerous man in this country." Before Tugwell could respond, Roosevelt elaborated: "Huey's a whiz on the radio. He screams at people and they love it. He makes them think they belong to some kind of church. He knows there's a promised land, and he'll lead them to it. Everyone will be rich; there will be no more work. And all they have to do is vote the way he says. He'll throw all the wicked Wall Streeters into a pit somewhere and cover it up. Then he and his folks can build their paradise. It's a time for that kind of thing. It's spreading." Roosevelt recognized that he'd have to deal with Long at some point. But he would do so very carefully. "When anyone eats with Huey, it had better be with a good long spoon."

Roosevelt had never spoken so unguardedly to Tugwell, who found this discursion fascinating. Tugwell almost forgot a mental note he had made amid the telephone conversation, but he remembered it as the luncheon ended. "You said Huey was the second most dangerous person, didn't you?" he asked Roosevelt. "Did I hear it the way you said it?"

Roosevelt had been waiting for the question. He smiled. "You heard it all right," he answered. "I meant it. Huey is only *second*. The *first* is Doug MacArthur. You saw how he strutted down Pennsylvania Avenue. You saw that picture of him in the *Times* after the troops chased all those vets out with tear gas and burned their shelters. Did you ever see anyone more self-satisfied? There's a potential Mussolini for you. Right here at home. The head man in the army. That's a perfect position if things get disorderly enough and good citizens work up enough anxiety." Roosevelt explained that he knew MacArthur from the World War. "You've never heard him talk, but I have. He has the most portentous style of anyone I know. He talks in a voice that might come from an oracle's cave. He never doubts and never argues or suggests; he makes pronouncements. What he thinks is final. Besides, he's intelligent, a brilliant soldier like his father before him. He got to be a brigadier in France." Now he saw his opportunity in America. "If all this talk comes to anything—about government going to pieces and not being able to stop the spreading disorder—Doug MacArthur is the man. In his way, he's as much a demagogue as Huey. He has as much ego, too. He thinks he's infallible—if he's always right, all people need to do is to take orders. And if some don't like it, he'll take care of them in his own way."

❖ ❖ ❖

THE BONUS ARMY debacle struck Hoover as another example of the bad luck that had dogged him since taking office. First the stock crash, then the collapse of the economy, and now this. The president felt misused by fate and misunderstood by the American people, who made bitter jokes at his expense. Shantytowns were "Hoovervilles," pockets turned inside out were "Hoover flags." At least one hitchhiker got himself across the country on the strength of a scrawled placard warning "Give me a lift or I'll vote for Hoover."

It didn't help matters that Hoover wasn't a regular politician. He had never run for office before 1928. He had been anointed to succeed Coolidge and been elected without effort. He had never been subjected to the kind of roughing up that typically comes with democratic politics. When, in 1932, Roosevelt landed some stinging blows, he took personal offense.

Hoover couldn't believe that anyone might honestly and knowledgeably differ with him regarding economic theory. His global career in mining, his experience in Europe during the war, and his trade-promoting initiatives as commerce secretary had attuned him to the international aspects of modern economics, and he was mentally and morally convinced that America's depression was principally the result of disturbances abroad. He knew that *he* had done nothing to bring it on, and he deeply resented anything indicating he had. He equally resented suggestions that his policies ignored the ordinary people of America. *His* roots were as ordinary as anyone's, and he never forgot them. Or so he told anyone willing to listen.

He hadn't intended to campaign hard, believing a few speeches urging the electorate to steer a steady course would suffice. But Roosevelt's relentless attacks aroused his combative instincts. And when Republican Maine, which voted in September for Congress and statewide offices (to avoid the cold of November), returned Democrats, the president's complacent illusions evaporated. "It is a catastrophe for us," he said of the Maine result. "The thing for us to do is to carry the fight right to Roosevelt. . . . We have got to crack him every time he opens his mouth."

In a series of speeches he would have considered beneath him just months before, Hoover blasted Roosevelt for attempting to provoke class warfare and for frightening investors who, the president claimed, were poised to return to the markets and revive the economy. Hoover couldn't decide whether Roosevelt was naïve or cynical in blaming American speculators and the Republican administration for the depression—whether Roosevelt simply didn't understand that the depression was an international phenomenon or, understanding, nonetheless chose to make it appear the fault of rich Republicans. The roots of the crisis, the president contended, ran backward to the World War and outward across the Atlantic and Pacific to Europe and Asia. The international debt and reparations tangle had greatly magnified otherwise manageable domestic troubles. Anyone who argued otherwise was a liar or a fool. Hoover charged Roosevelt and the Democrats with constructing a "labyrinth of inaccurate statements," of being "false prophets of a millennium promised through seductive but unworkable and disastrous theories of government." The solution to the depression was not government intervention in the economy but patient adherence to the principles that had constructed the economy in the first place. When October's statistics revealed that nearly a million men had gone back to work in the most recent quarter, Hoover claimed confirmation of the soundness of the administration's policies. "To enter upon a series of deep changes now, to embark upon this inchoate 'new deal' which has been propounded in this campaign would not only undermine and destroy our American system, but it will delay for months and years the possibility of recovery."

Beyond the current quarter, and beyond the present campaign, Americans faced a choice between two visions for their country. "This campaign is more than a contest between two men," Hoover asserted. "It is a contest between two philosophies of government." Hoover characterized his own conservative philosophy as that which had built the nation; it put its faith in the individual and the private sector. He described Roosevelt's philosophy as one that looked to government. In this it was novel and threatening. "You cannot extend the mastery of government over the daily life of a people without somewhere making it master of people's souls and thoughts," Hoover said. Roosevelt talked of the government controlling the economy, as though the government would stop there. It would not. "Economic freedom cannot be sacrificed if political freedom is to be preserved."

❖   ❖   ❖

*J*IM FARLEY ASSERTED, safely after the fact, that he had been confident of the outcome of the 1932 election well in advance. "As the campaign moved down the homestretch . . . ," he said, "it was as certain as anything humanly could be that the American electorate was getting ready for one of those periods of drastic upheaval which result in the 'ins' being tossed out rather unceremoniously while the 'outs' take over the government." The evidence took various forms. "President Hoover was out on the stump frantically endeavoring to regain the magic of his lost prestige. Larger and larger crowds flocked to the Roosevelt rallies to get a glimpse of him, one of the best signs that popular sympathy was running in his direction." Another signal was even more telling. "The 'fence-sitters' and the gentlemen who love to bet on the winner were flocking into headquarters to congratulate me and others on the manner in which the campaign was conducted. There are always large numbers of those folks, whom I once heard described as invincible in victory and invisible in defeat."

Roosevelt could read the signs as well as Farley, and while he shared Farley's confidence he determined to keep the pressure on. He intended not to coast to election but to win in a rout. He was convinced that the country needed a change of direction. He had been convinced of this for a decade—convinced that the capitalist-tilting, status quo policies of the Republicans were unfair to the ordinary people of America and counterproductive to America's abiding national interests. But only now did the country appear to agree. Roosevelt insisted that the agreement be rendered as loudly and clearly as possible.

He wrapped up his campaign where Democrat candidates had finished for decades: at Madison Square Garden, on the Saturday before the election. "Our case has been stated and made," he told the eager throng of party faithful. "In every home, to every individual, in every part of our wide land, full opportunity has been given to hear that case, and to render honest judgment on Tuesday." Roosevelt didn't quite declare victory, but he came close.

> From the time that my airplane touched ground at Chicago up to the present, I have consistently set forth the doctrine of the present-day Democracy. It is the program of a party dedicated to the conviction that every one of our people is entitled to the opportunity to earn a living, and to develop himself to the fullest measure consistent with the rights of his fellow men. You are familiar with that program. You are aware that it has found favor in the sight of the American electorate. . . . Tonight we set the seal upon that program. After Tuesday, we go forward to the great task of its accomplishment.

❖ ❖ ❖

DEMOCRACY DOESN'T delve into voters' minds; it merely counts their votes. Certainly many of those who voted for Roosevelt on November 8, 1932, were drawn to the polls by his vision of an America united by equality of opportunity. Just as certainly, many were driven to the polls by their dissatisfaction with Hoover's management of America's political economy. But there was no way of telling where the balance lay between the two groups—between those who voted for Roosevelt's New Deal and those who voted against Hoover's old one.

The distinction would be crucial, but it wasn't on that day. Roosevelt cast his own ballot at Hyde Park, as he always did, and he traveled to New York to await the returns. Four years earlier, from the same Biltmore Hotel, he had felt obliged to threaten to send the sheriffs to ensure a fair tally in the race that narrowly made him governor; this time a whole army couldn't have halted the landslide that made him president. He beat Hoover by 7 million popular votes (23 million to 16 million), and 413 electoral votes (472 to 59). He carried forty-two of forty-eight states, losing only Pennsylvania, Connecticut, Delaware, Vermont, New Hampshire, and Maine (which came back to the Republicans in the presidential contest, after its earlier defection to the Democrats).

The landslide extended to the congressional races. The Democrats added 97 seats to their existing majority in the House, giving them a margin of 310 to 117. They captured the Senate almost as decisively, by 60 to 35. Overnight the Republicans were transformed from the dominant party in the country to a footnote. Roosevelt and the Democrats, if they could maintain even a semblance of unity, could essentially ignore the party of Lincoln, McKinley, and the first Roosevelt.

This final formulation—the *first* Roosevelt—lingered in Franklin Roosevelt's mind as he prepared to become the second President Roosevelt. "Give my regards to all the family," he told Theodore's son Kermit, who dropped by the Biltmore to offer congratulations. Kermit said he would. "But I don't know how welcome this news is going to be."

21.

"*I* WISH I KNEW WHAT YOU ARE REALLY THINKING AND FEELING," Franklin said to Eleanor on election night. She had congratulated him on his victory, but with less enthusiasm than might have been expected in the next First Lady of the United States.

She declined to enlighten him. "From the personal standpoint, I did not want my husband to be president," she explained afterward. "I realized, however, that it was impossible to keep a man out of public service when that was what he wanted and was undoubtedly well equipped for. It was pure selfishness on my part, and I never mentioned my feelings on the subject to him." She didn't have to. She and Franklin had been together for three decades, and he could sense her misgivings even if he didn't know their precise nature. She was later more forthcoming, although not to him. "As I saw it, this meant the end of any personal life of my own," she said. "I knew what traditionally should lie before me. I had watched Mrs. Theodore Roosevelt and had seen what it meant to be the wife of the president, and I cannot say that I was pleased at the prospect. . . . The turmoil in my heart and mind was rather great that night."

Franklin's election sealed the bargain Eleanor had made with him fourteen years earlier. They had decided against divorce in part to preserve his political career. Now that he had grasped the holy grail of American politics, he could ask no more of her. Had she stepped back, perhaps playing the White House hostess but otherwise leaving politics to him, he could have had no complaint. Most other First Ladies had been retiring; she could have followed their lead.

But she didn't. Instead she became even more active in politics than she had ever been. In the process she revealed the hidden part of her bargain with Franklin—hidden from him for years, and perhaps from herself for some substantial period. In standing by him in public, even as she refused to lie beside him in private, she preserved not only his political career but her own. Politics came naturally to the niece of Theodore Roosevelt, although she didn't awaken to its possibilities until after she had married Franklin and borne him six children. Probably not coincidentally, her political awakening occurred shortly after her bargain with Franklin, in the 1920 campaign in which Louis Howe mentored her. She discovered she liked the thrill of the contest. Her encouragement to Franklin to return from polio to politics was for his benefit but also for hers. Politics added meaning to her life—the meaning of participation in important endeavors and of working toward worthy ends.

Franklin's election as governor had broadened Eleanor politically. A lifelong liberal of the noblesse oblige school, she embarked as New York's First Lady on the same kinds of improving initiatives that had first attracted her to progressivism on Rivington Street. Franklin insisted on visiting various state institutions, to determine whether they were providing value for taxpayer money, but he often discovered on arrival that he couldn't get past the front door, as the buildings that housed the agencies weren't designed for paraplegics. So he would send Eleanor inside. At first he provided lists of items to observe and questions to ask—how many beds there were in each asylum room, whether prison inmates received the food the legislature had appropriated monies for. Soon Eleanor was poking around on her own. "Before the end of our years in Albany," she said without the modesty that sometimes shrouded her accomplishments, "I had become a fairly expert reporter on state institutions."

Roosevelt's election as president expanded her vistas still further. The federal bureaucracy was denser and more elaborate than New York state's; she would have to sharpen her reporting skills to uncover its secrets. But Franklin would need her more than ever, if only because the country was so much bigger than the state and because the demands on a president made a governor appear a part-timer. Eleanor would lose some of the personal independence she had come to cherish, but her compensation would be political influence of a degree wielded by very few.

❖   ❖   ❖

JAMES ROOSEVELT remembered something else about the moment of Franklin's victory. "When we finally got home that night"—to the house on East Sixty-fifth Street—"I helped him into bed, the same bed in which I had seen him, an almost helpless invalid, that first Christmas after his polio attack. He was still Pa, only now he was not just Pa; he was the President-elect of the United States." Yet they talked as father and son, in a way they hadn't talked in years. They spoke for a long time, neither wanting the moment to end. Finally James kissed his father good night.

"You know, Jimmy," Franklin said, "all my life I have been afraid of only one thing—fire. Tonight I think I'm afraid of something else."

"Afraid of what, Pa?"

"I'm just afraid that I may not have the strength to do this job." He paused reflectively. "After you leave me tonight, Jimmy, I am going to pray. I am going to pray that God will help me, that he will give me the strength and the guidance to do this job and to do it right. I hope you will pray for me, too, Jimmy."

Roosevelt rarely talked about religion, his own or others'. Yet Eleanor thought Franklin's religion explained much about his personality and leadership style. His religion was the basis, she said, of his striking self-confidence. It was a "very simple religion," Eleanor observed. "He believed in God and in His guidance. He felt that human beings were given tasks to perform and with those tasks the ability and strength to put them through. He could pray for help and guidance and have faith in his own judgment as a result."

Beyond this basic theology Roosevelt chose not to venture. His reluctance reflected his general aversion to introspection. To think deeply about faith required thinking deeply about the inner life, which Roosevelt hesitated to do. But he kept his distance from religion for other reasons as well. To worship in public demanded that he negotiate the steps and curbs that blocked his access to most public places. He was willing to make the effort on special occasions. But regular attendance at church was more trouble than it was worth, potentially embarrassing to him and definitely distracting to the other congregants.

No less important in guiding him away from religion was the touchiness of the Democrats on the subject. The party included Southern Baptists, Irish Catholics, and East European Jews, in addition to the more mainstream Lutherans, Episcopalians, Presbyterians, and Methodists. Roosevelt had struggled for a decade to draw the different wings of the party together. His election showed he was succeeding. He had no desire to jeopardize his success by raising issues best left to the theologians.

❖   ❖   ❖

HERBERT HOOVER hated Roosevelt during the campaign, and he hated him even more after the election. The lame duck president refused to believe that the landslide for Roosevelt conferred legitimacy on Roosevelt's approach to governance; it simply demonstrated that the American people could be deluded by false promises of an easy return to prosperity. The uptick of the economy before the election allowed Hoover to assert—at the time and afterward—that his patient policies had all but ended the depression, only for the economy to swoon again as a result of Roosevelt's victory, which frightened investors and made them withdraw from the markets once more. Like many other counterfactual claims, Hoover's couldn't be disproved. Decades later the former president would acknowledge certain limitations on his perspective of policy. "My education was that of an engineer," he told an interviewer. "I do not know all the nuances of economics." But in the autumn of 1932 he was convinced that he knew more economics than Roosevelt, and he was determined that his views should guide American policy.

Of most pressing importance during the weeks after the election was a pending loan payment from Britain. The interconnected system of European reparations and loans had continued to creak during the late 1920s, and it was rescued from utter collapse after the onset of the depression only by a twelve-month moratorium on payments among all the major financial powers, including the United States. An Anglo-French-German conference at Lausanne, Switzerland, during the summer of 1932 proposed to extend the suspension of payments but required acceptance by the United States to take effect. Hoover advocated acceptance yet recognized, upon losing the election, that Roosevelt needed to be consulted and, ideally, brought aboard. "I am loath to proceed with recommendations to the Congress until I can have an opportunity to confer with you personally," Hoover wired Roosevelt.

"The President's telegram took us completely by surprise," Ray Moley recalled, referring to the Roosevelt camp. "We could not remember any other case in which an outgoing President, during the interregnum, had asked for the advice and assistance of his successful opponent." The surprise evoked caution, and when Hoover followed up with a telephone call, Roosevelt was wary. Hoover proposed a face-to-face meeting at the White House. "I have a number of things I would like to discuss with you," he said. "And I wonder if you could bring someone with you, because there are a lot of things that ought to be looked into which cannot be decided on the minute."

"Yes, I can bring a secretary," Roosevelt replied. "I hadn't thought of anybody."

"I would like to bring in Ogden Mills, because I would like to give you an outline of what is going on abroad," Hoover said, referring to his Treasury secretary. "I would like to have somebody on your side to start studying these questions. . . . I have a feeling that we have to put up national solidarity."

"That's right," Roosevelt said. For the first time with Hoover, Roosevelt employed his habitual device of suggesting agreement when all he actually intended was to draw his interlocutor out.

Hoover apparently took Roosevelt's verbal nod as assent to the president's call for a united front. He explained that the situation was critical. The Europeans were demanding an answer from the American government to their financial proposal. "Immediate action" was required, Hoover said.

"Yes, that's right," Roosevelt reiterated.

"There are other things that need ironing out with respect to their commitments, but the one definite thing is a note of reply that we should send to them."

"That's right."

The two men arranged to meet a few days hence. Roosevelt would be traveling to Warm Springs for a postelection breather and would stop in Washington. He brought Moley along as his adviser. "When we arrived in Washington on November 22, we found the studied courtesy of the official reception a wry antidote for the warmth of the crowds in the streets," Moley remembered. The last time Roosevelt and Hoover had met was also at the White House, when Hoover the previous April had hosted a reception for a national conference of governors. By design or accident, Hoover had kept the governors and their wives waiting—standing—in the East Room for more than half an hour. Most of the guests managed well enough, but Roosevelt, balanced on his braces, found the wait an ordeal. He said nothing, but Moley and other Roosevelt aides detected a sharper edge in his attacks on the president in campaign speeches in the months that followed.

On this occasion Roosevelt and Moley rode the elevator to the second floor. Hoover was waiting in the Red Room—"grave, dignified, and somewhat uneasy," Moley observed. The president and the president-elect exchanged empty pleasantries before the former turned to the business at hand. "Hoover plunged into a long recital on the debt question," Moley wrote. "He spoke without interruption for nearly an hour. Shyness, at the beginning, seemed to make him fix his eyes on the beautiful seal of the United States woven into the red carpet. After a while he began looking at me as he talked—a circumstance about which I had no more reason to be pleased than the inanimate carpet." Hoover glanced at Roosevelt only intermittently and briefly; Moley read this as evidence of persisting anger at the man who had defeated him. But whatever the delivery of the monologue, its content was impressive. "Before he had finished, it was clear that we were in the presence of the best-informed individual in the country on the question of the debts. His story showed a mastery of detail and a clarity of arrangement that compelled admiration."

But not cooperation, which was what Hoover wanted. The president explained that though the debt and reparation issues were separate—at least from the standpoint of the United States, which had loaned the money to the British and French but had no responsibility for the Versailles reparations settlement—any attempts to resolve the difficulties the two issues raised ought to take place simultaneously. To this end Hoover recommended reconvening the international debt commission that had rescheduled the payments during the 1920s. Hoover's purpose in throwing the conundrum to the debt commission was twofold: to underscore the international aspect of the depression and to mitigate opposition in America to any further rescheduling. Influential members of Congress were already on record as opposing rescheduling, but Hoover thought that by appointing several senators and representatives to the commission he might bring the legislature around. Roosevelt's support would assist his strategy immensely.

Roosevelt wasn't prepared to endorse the president's plan. He agreed that the Europeans ought to be allowed to make their case for rescheduling. "I see no reason why the old legal maxim that a debtor ought to have access to the creditor shouldn't prevail," he said. But then he turned to Moley, who after concurring that the principle of access was sound—"Even a horse trader does that"—predicted that reconvening the debt commission would raise expectations that almost certainly couldn't be met. Better to hold the British and French to the debt payments coming due in December and invite them to make their case for full or partial forgiveness through the regular channels of the State Department.

Roosevelt nodded as Moley spoke—much as he had nodded when Hoover had spoken. But again he was being agreeable rather than agreeing. He hadn't thought the debt question through, and he didn't want to commit himself. Besides, he had serious reservations about going to the debt commission. He recognized that any settlement the commission would recommend would involve forgiveness of at least some of the debt owed the American government. This would be terribly unpopular with Congress. Moreover, turning to an international commission would tend to confirm Hoover's internationalist explanation of the causes of the depression. This was less important now that the election was over, but it still would limit Roosevelt's ability to attack the depression as he saw fit. The New Deal remained in the conceptual stage, with many aspects unformed, but it would certainly entail a fundamental shifting of the balance of power among workers, farmers, and corporations within the American economy. To justify this change, Roosevelt needed to contend that the depression had domestic roots. Finally, Roosevelt was reluctant to tie himself to anything connected to Hoover. If he agreed even to the principle of a debt commission, he would make himself hostage to the recommendations of the commission, which until March 4, 1933, would reflect Hoover's views far more than his own. This was unacceptable.

❖ ❖ ❖

I T WAS UNACCEPTABLE not simply for limiting his freedom of action as he entered the White House but for tying his hands over the longer term. Roosevelt intended much more than reforming the economy; he proposed to reconfigure the American political system. He had been a practicing Democrat for more than two decades, quite long enough to realize how dysfunctional his party was, with its shotgun multiple marriage of country and city, of southern white supremacists and northern ethnics, of Bible-thumping conservatives and agnostic liberals. Roosevelt was a Democrat by birth and convenience but a progressive by conviction and anticipation. He was, moreover, a Roosevelt, whose family name summoned memories of impatience with party and willingness to break old molds in the service of new ideals.

Roosevelt envisioned a realignment of the parties, with himself leading the progressives of both existing parties into a new party not unlike that which Uncle Ted had headed in 1912. "I'll be in the White House for eight years," he told Rex Tugwell during the campaign. "When those years are over, there'll be a Progressive party. It may not be Democratic, but it will be Progressive." This prospect was one reason he had refused to sit on his lead during the campaign, why he continued to press forward long after victory was certain. He wanted to win a personal victory that clearly eclipsed the victory of the Democrats, so that he—rather than the Democrats in Congress—could set the agenda for his presidency. He had yet to reveal just how progressive his policies would be, in part because he hadn't yet decided. But he was certainly more progressive than the southern mules who would try to dominate the Senate, and more progressive than big-business apologists of the party's neo-Cleveland wing.

He was far too canny to tip his hand to any but the most trusted insiders. He certainly didn't inform Hoover, who left their White House meeting thinking Roosevelt had agreed to the calling of the debt commission. Such, at any rate, was what Hoover told Henry Stimson afterward. The secretary of state had expected little from the Hoover-Roosevelt session. "My chief fear is the attitude in which Hoover is approaching the meeting," Stimson recorded in his diary. "He has allowed himself to get so full of distrust of his rival that I think it will go far to prevent a profitable meeting." Hoover's initial reaction after the meeting suggested that Stimson had been too pessimistic. "He told me that they had spent most of their time in educating a very ignorant, and as he expressed it, a well-meaning young man. But they thought they had made some progress. He told me that Roosevelt had promised to come out in favor of the President's and Mills' plan."

In this belief Hoover issued a statement urging Congress to establish the debt commission. Roosevelt responded the next day with a statement of his own, rejecting the commission approach. "My view is that the most convenient and effective contacts can be made through the existing agencies and constituted channels of diplomatic intercourse," Roosevelt said. Nor should the president even consider forgiving any of the debt. "Existing debt agreements are unalterable save by Congressional action."

Hoover was furious—"very much excited," in Stimson's words. The president determined to bulldoze ahead regardless of Roosevelt. Citing the "grave world economic situation," the president announced that he would, on his own authority, appoint a commission to examine the debt question, along with related issues—related in Hoover's mind, at any rate—of currency fluctuations and disarmament. The connection to currencies was obvious enough. The depression had forced several countries off the gold standard, including, most ominously, Britain in 1931. The consequent cheapening of the currencies of the gold-less governments gave their exports an advantage in American markets. The League of Nations had proposed a world economic conference to negotiate an adjustment of currencies, of trade, and of other matters relating to the world economy. Hoover enthusiastically supported the conference, but preparations and complications had pushed its scheduled convening beyond his departure from office. Debt questions were supposed to be excluded from the world conference, at the insistence of the American government, which adopted the position that these were bilateral matters between the United States and its debtors. Many observers considered this stance a charade, for it strained the imagination to think that a conference on world economics could ignore one of the fundamental features of the world economy. But it provided Hoover reason to go ahead with discussions of the debts, to get those out of the way before the conference convened.

The disarmament question related to the economic questions in that arms cost money that most governments found in short supply. If the governments of the great powers—the ones that had agreed to the restrictions of the Washington Conference of the previous decade—could arrange to extend those restrictions, they might all improve their economic prospects without, they hoped, jeopardizing their security.

Hoover's announcement of the appointment of the debt commission was both a response to the developing crisis and an effort to force Roosevelt's hand. "Serious problems have now arisen, and we are bound to recognize and deal with them," Hoover declared. To wait until March 4 would risk irreparable damage to the American economy and that of the broader world. "I propose, therefore, to seek the cooperation of President-elect Roosevelt in the organization of machinery for advancement of consideration of these problems."

As Hoover intended, his announcement put Roosevelt in the uncomfortable position of either acquiescing in the announced policy or defying the president of the United States on a matter declared by the president to be essential to American welfare. Hoover was convinced of the correctness of his position, and he couldn't believe that Roosevelt would risk the opprobrium that would follow a failure to lend a hand in this moment of peril.

He underestimated his rival. Or perhaps he overestimated the regard in which the American people still held him and his judgment. Had Hoover not been so overwhelmingly rejected at the polls, Roosevelt might have hesitated to cross him publicly on a matter of such weight. But Roosevelt recognized that his political authority, if not yet his legal authority, outweighed Hoover's. On the same day that Hoover delivered his message to Congress, Roosevelt telegraphed the White House a rejection of Hoover's approach. "It is my view," he said, "that the questions of disarmament, intergovernmental debts, and permanent economic arrangements will be found to require selective treatment"—in contrast to the unified approach called for by Hoover. A debt commission continued to be a bad idea. The administration might reasonably conduct surveys of the debt question, but "these surveys should be limited to determining facts and exploring possibilities rather than fixing policies binding on the incoming administration." The world economic conference should be kept separate from the debt and disarmament questions. "I recognize, of course, a relationship, but not an identity. Therefore I cannot go along with the thought that the personnel conducting the conversations should be identical." The president's proposal, at bottom, ignored the disparity that still existed between the two men. "It would be unwise for me to accept an apparent joint responsibility with you when, as a matter of constitutional fact, I would be wholly lacking in any authority."

This one sentence summarized what everything came down to. Hoover wanted Roosevelt to share responsibility for policies over which he had no authority, and Roosevelt refused. The problem was inherent in the extended interregnum specified by the Constitution. But it was exacerbated by the distrust between Hoover and Roosevelt. Hoover sincerely believed that the policies Roosevelt espoused would ruin the country; the Republican president hoped to preempt those policies by locking Roosevelt into a framework of international commitments and expectations. Roosevelt naturally resisted. The voters had selected him and rejected Hoover; the president's eleventh-hour efforts amounted, in Roosevelt's view, to nothing less than a subversion of democracy, besides being wrongheaded on their merits.

❖   ❖   ❖

On January 2, 1933, Roosevelt found himself out of a job. Some observers had wondered why Roosevelt didn't resign as governor months earlier, to free himself for the campaign and the transition. Rex Tugwell put the question to Basil O'Connor, a personal and professional friend of Roosevelt's. "The best reason," O'Connor answered, "is that he's poor."

Tugwell expressed surprise, and O'Connor explained. Roosevelt wasn't poor by the standards of ordinary people, but he was poor by the standards of his class. The Roosevelts were an "extravagant family," O'Connor said, and "not one of the lot ever thought of money except to spend it." Sara Roosevelt still held the purse strings, and she didn't hesitate to tighten them when she saw fit. Roosevelt's lifestyle, starting with the ordinary expenses of servants, multiple homes, and travel, and compounded by the extraordinary costs associated with his disability, required a large and constant cash flow. His salary as governor didn't cover the bills, but combined with income from his own portion of his father's estate and from Eleanor's inheritance, and with Sara's dole, it allowed him to get by. To surrender that salary prematurely was too much to ask. O'Connor guessed that when Roosevelt handed over the governorship at the beginning of January 1933, he might have to borrow money to avoid cutbacks in his standard of living. Besides, the governor's job included the governor's mansion, which was a good place from which to run a campaign or direct a transition. The town house in Manhattan was too small, and the estate at Hyde Park too posh. At Hyde Park he'd have credibility problems berating Hoover and the Republican leadership for coddling the rich. The governor's house in Albany wasn't exactly spartan, but it belonged to the people and came with the post to which the people had elected Roosevelt.

Yet on January 2—January 1 being a Sunday—he didn't have a choice. Roosevelt handed the house and the post over to Herbert Lehman. "In taking leave of you, my friends, my neighbors, and my associates, after four years in Albany, I could not fail to have many regrets at the parting," he said. But he would carry his New York experience with him. "To maintain a government of definite action founded on liberal thought has been my aim." So it would continue to be. "The crisis has brought new problems and, at the same time, new possibilities." Roosevelt promised to keep New York in his thoughts while he served the country as a whole. "I shall have a friend in Albany," he declared, looking at Lehman, "and he will have a friend in Washington."

❖   ❖   ❖

ℛOOSEVELT HAD FRIENDS; he also had enemies. This was something comparatively new in his experience. During his first fifty years—he had reached the half-century mark almost simultaneously with his announcement of his candidacy in January 1932—people had sometimes considered him shallow, even supercilious. More than a few had envied his inherited wealth and family connections, although the envy diminished after he contracted polio. A comparative handful had been bruised by his ambition. But almost no one worked up sufficient antipathy to consider him an enemy. He simply wasn't that important.

Things changed with his nomination. During the campaign the Republicans characterized him as a dangerous radical. His "forgotten man" speech gave rise to charges that he was fomenting class warfare. His call for national planning conjured the specter of socialism. Soon the antipathy would escalate into visceral hatred; much of America's upper crust would hiss at "that man" in the White House.

In February 1933 one person carried the hostility to murderous lengths. Roosevelt left Albany following the inauguration of Governor Lehman and headed south. He visited Washington for another unproductive meeting with Hoover and proceeded to Warm Springs, for rest and recreation. En route he toured the Tennessee Valley; at Muscle Shoals in northern Alabama he hinted at great plans he had for harnessing the Tennessee River "from the mountains of Virginia down to the Ohio." After a week at Warm Springs, he traveled to

Florida, where he embarked at Jacksonville on a cruise aboard the yacht of Vincent Astor. The cruise recalled his houseboating days on the *Larooco* and carried Roosevelt and the other passengers to Miami on February 15. He spoke very briefly to the mayor and assembled guests, including the visiting mayor of Chicago, Anton Cermak. Roosevelt praised the fishing while grumbling good-naturedly that he had gained ten pounds in as many days. "That means that among the other duties that I shall have to perform when I get north is taking those ten pounds off."

Among the audience at Miami's Bayfront Park was Giuseppe Zangara, a thirty-three-year-old Italian immigrant. Zangara had arrived in America in 1923, in the last wave of immigration before the restrictions specified by the 1924 reforms took effect. He became a naturalized citizen in 1926; at that point or perhaps earlier, as he started to pick up English, he began employing the English equivalent—Joseph—of his Christian name. According to his own later testimony he had conceived a mortal hatred for the rich and powerful while in his teens in Italy, although resentment toward his father, who had sent him to work at the age of six, seems to have colored his attitude toward authority as well. "Had you tried to kill in Italy?" he was subsequently asked. "Yes, the king," he responded. "Why didn't you kill the king?" "Because I didn't have no chance."

After clearing Ellis Island, Zangara settled in Paterson, New Jersey. He became a bricklayer—a union man—and worked steadily until 1926, by which time he had managed to save $2,500. At some point he developed stomach problems, which, together with his nest egg, prompted him to quit work. Thereafter he never held a regular job. He remained in Paterson during the early years of the depression, which touched him rather less than it did many of his neighbors. But his stomach got worse, and he interpreted its gnawing as a comment on the unfairness of life in a capitalist society. The pain sharpened in cold weather, and during the late autumn of 1932 he traveled to Miami seeking relief.

Yet his suffering continued, and he determined that the only remedy was the assassination of the American president. He would have gone after Hoover immediately, but the cold weather in the North persisted and he decided to wait till spring. At about the time he realized that by spring Hoover would no longer be president, he read in the Miami papers that President-elect Roosevelt was coming to town. His funds were running low, as he had discovered the dog races but not how to pick winners. Yet with eight dollars he purchased a five-shot .32-caliber revolver from a pawn dealer on Miami Avenue.

The newspapers had printed Roosevelt's itinerary in detail, and Zangara met his boat at the dock. But the crowd and the close quarters there prevented him from getting an open shot. So he followed Roosevelt's entourage to Bayfront Park. He waited amid the audience of more than ten thousand, assuming that a man of Roosevelt's importance would speak for a long time. When Roosevelt, speaking into a portable microphone from the rear seat of an open car, finished after less than two minutes, Zangara was caught by surprise. Various dignitaries gathered around Roosevelt's car to shake his hand, wish him well upon his presidency, and perhaps plant the seed of a federal appointment.

Chicago mayor Cermak was closest to Roosevelt when Zangara worked his way to within twenty-five feet of the car. Zangara, a short man, mounted a chair to get a clearer view of the president-elect. He pulled out the pistol and began shooting. The chair wobbled beneath him, and a woman standing nearby grabbed his arm. As a result, his five shots missed Roosevelt. One hit Cermak in the chest, wounding him grievously. Another hit Mrs. Joseph Gill, the wife of the president of Florida Power & Light, also causing serious injury. A third bullet creased the head of William Sinnott, a New York detective traveling with Roosevelt; a fourth nicked the scalp of a Miami resident; the fifth pierced the hand of a visitor from New Jersey.

Roosevelt was startled at the sound of the shots, but otherwise he displayed remarkable composure. "I heard what I thought was a firecracker, then several more," he told reporters afterward. "The man talking with me was pulled back, and the chauffeur started the car." At this point Roosevelt saw blood from one of those wounded. "I looked around and saw Mayor Cermak doubled up, and Mrs. Gill collapsing. Mrs. Gill was at the foot of the bandstand steps. As soon as she was hit she must have got up and started down the steps. She was slumped over at the bottom."

Roosevelt ordered the driver to stop. The driver did so, a short distance from where the car had been. Roosevelt's Secret Service detail countermanded the order, shouting at the driver to proceed, to get the president-elect away from the crowd. The driver hit the gas again. Roosevelt once more told him to stop, to make sure the wounded got to a hospital as quickly as possible. "I saw Mayor Cermak being carried. I motioned to have him put in the back of the car, which would be the first out. He was alive, but I didn't think he was going to last. I put my left arm around him and my hand on his pulse, but I couldn't find any pulse."

Roosevelt ordered the driver to hurry to the nearest hospital. A Miami detective riding on the mudguard of the car looked at Cermak and said he was dying. Roosevelt agreed. But after a few blocks Cermak rallied. He straightened up a bit, and Roosevelt felt a pulse. "I held him all the way to the hospital, and his pulse constantly improved." The car couldn't go fast enough. "That trip to the hospital seemed thirty miles long. I talked to Mayor Cermak nearly all the way. I remember I said, 'Tony, keep quiet—don't move. It won't hurt you if you keep quiet.' "

Cermak was the worst off of the wounded, and while the others were treated and began healing, the mayor hovered near death. In the meantime the authorities interrogated Zangara, who after expending his bullets had made no attempt to flee. The police descended upon him, and he was taken to jail on the nineteenth floor of Miami's high-rise city hall. There the Dade County sheriff, state prosecutors, and agents of the Federal Bureau of Investigation questioned him to determine, most crucially, whether he had acted alone or as part of a conspiracy. "Was anybody with you?" they demanded. "No," he said. "Nobody in Miami?" "No, no place." How had he come to Miami? "By bus." How long had he been there? "Two or three months."

It was to these interrogators that Zangara revealed his animus against the rich and powerful—against "kings and presidents," as he now put it. But he had shot several people besides Roosevelt, the questioners said. Had he intended to kill them too? "No, just him." Had he realized he might hit other people? "No, just him. Just President." Why did he want to kill the president? "Because the President—rich people—capitalists—spoil me when I'm six years old." Did he hate President Roosevelt as a man? "As a man I like him all right." But as a president? "President—always the same bunch."

❖ ❖ ❖

Roosevelt had intended to leave for New York shortly after his Bayfront Park speech. But with Mayor Cermak's life in the balance, he decided to remain in Miami. He stayed at the hospital long enough to learn that Cermak's condition had stabilized and to speak with the other victims and then returned to the Astor yacht in the harbor.

Ray Moley had measured Roosevelt's intellect during the previous year, but he had never observed his courage under—literal—fire. He was most impressed. "Roosevelt's nerve had held absolutely throughout the evening," Moley wrote. "But the real test in such cases comes afterward, when the crowds, to whom nothing but courage can be shown, are gone. The time for the letdown among his intimates was at hand. All of us were prepared, sympathetically, understandingly, for any reaction that might come from Roosevelt now that the tension was over and he was alone with us. For anything, that is, except what happened." Or, rather, what did not happen. "There was nothing—not so much as the twitching of a muscle, the mopping of a brow, or even the hint of false gaiety—to indicate that it wasn't any other evening in any other place. Roosevelt was simply himself—easy, confident, poised, to all appearances unmoved."

The attempted assassination wasn't a total surprise to Roosevelt. As a life-long student of the presidency, he hardly needed reminding that three presidents had fallen to assassins' bullets. Nor could he forget that Uncle Ted had been shot and nearly killed during the campaign of 1912. (As it happened, Theodore's son Kermit had been on the Astor yacht and was with Roosevelt in Miami that day.) "FDR had talked to me once or twice during the campaign about the possibility that someone would try to assassinate him," Moley remarked. "To that extent, I knew, he was prepared for Zangara's attempt."

Moley continued: "But it is one thing to talk philosophically about assassination, and another to face it. And I confess that I have never in my life seen anything more magnificent than Roosevelt's calm that night."

❖　❖　❖

THE WHEELS OF justice moved more swiftly in those days, at least in Florida, than they would later. Zangara was brought to trial five days after the shooting and pleaded guilty to four counts of attempted murder. The lawyers assigned to his defense raised the possibility of an insanity plea, but he refused. "My client has insisted on his guilt," the head of the defense team told the court. "He scoffs at the idea that he may be insane."

Neither was he repentant. "Don't be stingy," he shouted when the judge sentenced him to eighty years in prison. "Give me more—give me one hundred years!" Prior to sentencing, the judge allowed the defendant to be questioned, in order that the court could assess his state of mind. Zangara reiterated his indictment of capitalism. "Capitalism kill me," he said. "My stomach hurt all the time. I kill someone—that makes it fifty-fifty." Asked if he was sorry he had attempted to kill Roosevelt, he replied, "No, no, no—I am only sorry because I did not kill. I am sorry about nothing. Put me in the electric chair."

This possibility remained. At the time of the trial, the other victims were on the road to full recovery, and Cermak seemed out of danger. But the state's attorney reserved the option to retry Zangara for murder in the event Cermak died. (Cermak was well enough to comment on the proceedings. "They certainly mete out justice pretty fast in this state," he said. "If the law could be enforced this swiftly in other states . . . it would have a great tendency to check crime.")

But the trial and sentencing didn't end the investigation into the possibility of a conspiracy. The FBI received numerous reports of links between Zangara and anarchist cells, between Zangara and the Communist party, between Zangara and an organization called the Sons of Italy, and even between Zangara and the Black Hand, the terrorist group behind the 1914 assassination of Archduke Franz Ferdinand, which had touched off the World War. Another angle was that Cermak, rather than Roosevelt, was the real target. By one version of this story, Chicago gangsters were sore at Cermak for cracking down on their illegal operations. By another, they were upset at him for trying to grab a piece of the black market action for himself. Either way, they hired Zangara to eliminate Cermak. The fact that Zangara emphatically denied intending to kill the mayor simply demonstrated how clever the gangsters were.

The FBI pursued the leads in their several directions. The agency examined Zangara's bank records; it tracked his whereabouts in the months and years before the shooting. It followed up alleged sightings of Zangara in unlikely places and examined possible connections between Zangara and persons reported to have spoken especially ill of the incoming president, including one Italian immigrant who pointed at a newspaper photograph of Zangara and muttered, "Damn fool, worthless shot, can't hit anything"—this according to a man who overheard the remarks in a Manhattan barbershop and relayed them to the FBI.

None of the leads survived scrutiny. Meanwhile, however, Cermak took a sudden turn for the worse and died. Zangara was brought to trial again, this time for first-degree murder. He again pleaded guilty, again defiantly. He was sentenced to death, and was executed on March 20. "Lousy capitalists!" he shouted as the straps of the electric chair were tightened around his chest and arms. "All capitalists lousy bunch of crooks!"

❖ ❖ ❖

ROOSEVELT COULD hardly have devised a more dramatic backdrop for his inauguration. The country was in crisis, and the man elected to lead it through its moment of peril narrowly escaped assassination. Hoover added an element of petty bitterness to the drama. Defying tradition, the departing president refused to invite the Roosevelts to dinner the night before the inauguration, substituting an awkward tea. And when Roosevelt tried to end the awkwardness and afford the president a graceful exit from the room, Hoover simply aggravated the discomfort. "Mr. President, as you know, it is rather difficult for me to move in a hurry," Roosevelt said. "It takes me a little while to get up, and I know how busy you must be. So please don't wait for me." Hoover stood up and fixed Roosevelt with a glare. "Mr. Roosevelt, after you have been president for a while, you will learn that the President of the United States waits for no one." He stalked off, leaving his wife to handle the good-byes.

Hoover's mood hadn't improved the next morning. Roosevelt began the long day with a private service at St. John's Episcopal Church, across Lafayette Square from the White House (and just east of where Henry Adams's house, demolished for a hotel a few years earlier, had been). Endicott Peabody, seventy-five years old but still headmaster of the Groton School, conducted the service, which was attended by members of the Roosevelt family and close associates. Roosevelt valued the service for its own sake; he also thought it set a good tone for the first day of his new administration.

At eleven o'clock the car that would carry him to the inaugural ceremonies swung by the Mayflower Hotel, where he and Eleanor had spent the night. Roosevelt took his place in the back seat, and the driver proceeded to the White House to pick up Hoover. The outgoing president took a final look at the mansion but scarcely glanced at Roosevelt as he climbed in. The open car drove up Pennsylvania Avenue to the Capitol, with crowds cheering on either side. Roosevelt initially adopted the respectful posture that the cheers were for the (still) president and declined to acknowledge them. But within blocks the fiction became unsustainable, and he began smiling and waving his top hat at the crowd. The anger radiating from Hoover only intensified.

At the Capitol, Roosevelt let Hoover get out of the car, then took the arm of his son James and entered the Senate side of the building. He observed the swearing-in of the new senators and of John Nance Garner as vice president, and he witnessed the historic adjournment of the last lame duck session of Congress. (The seemingly endless interregnum had prompted approval of the Twentieth Amendment, which shifted presidential inaugurations to January 20 and canceled the post-election meetings of Congress.)

At one o'clock the president-elect and the rest of the inaugural party moved outdoors, to the east steps of the Capitol. A throng of one hundred thousand waited impatiently. Roosevelt's demeanor was uncharacteristically serious.

Arthur Krock was surprised by Roosevelt's somber mood, but he thought it in keeping with the general feeling in Washington. "Though the city was gay with flags and lively with the music of bands and cheers for the marchers in the inaugural parade which followed the oath taking," the New York Times reporter wrote, "the atmosphere which surrounded the change of government in the United States was comparable to that which might be found in a beleaguered capital in wartime."

Roosevelt had been preparing his inaugural address for a week. By his own later account he wrote the initial draft in four hours at Hyde Park on the night of February 27. His longhand sentences were then typed and polished, and reviewed and repolished during the next several days. Roosevelt amended the text by hand up to the last minute and improvised even from the final draft. After taking his oath of office—unusually repeating the words read from the Constitution, by Chief Justice Charles Evans Hughes, rather than saying simply "I do"—the new president turned to the great crowd and, with unsmiling face, declared, "This is a day of national consecration, and I am certain that my fellow Americans expect that on my induction into the presidency I will address them with a candor and a decision which the present situation of our nation impels."

Hoover was standing next to Roosevelt, and his dour expression became a grimace as he anticipated yet another attack on his administration. But Roosevelt proceeded with words of encouragement and hope. "This great nation will endure as it has endured, will revive and will prosper. . . . Let me assert my firm belief that the only thing we have to fear is fear itself—nameless, unreasoning, unjustified terror, which paralyzes needed efforts to convert retreat into advance."

Before long this line about having to fear only fear would be hailed as a landmark of presidential rhetoric. At the time it didn't seem so, not least since it was patently false. Americans had plenty to fear, starting with massive unemployment, widespread hunger, and a collapsing financial system. Yet coming from one who had just survived an assassination attempt, following a decadelong battle with polio, it struck a reassuring tone.

More noticed at the moment was a phrase that corroborated Hoover's grimace and furnished the headlines for the next day's news accounts of the inauguration. Roosevelt assailed the "unscrupulous money changers" of Wall Street as those responsible for America's plight. "Plenty is at our doorstep, but a generous use of it languishes in the very sight of the supply," he said. "Primarily this is because the rulers of the exchange of mankind's goods have failed

through their own stubbornness and their own incompetence." Waxing bib-
lical, Roosevelt declared, at once accusingly and promisingly: "The money
changers have fled from their high seats in the temple of our civilization. We
may now restore that temple to the ancient truths."

Other matters demanded attention. "Our greatest primary task is to put
people to work," Roosevelt said. This task would be accomplished in part "by
direct recruiting by the government itself, treating the task as we would treat
the emergency of a war." It would be aided by a reconfiguration of the American economy. "We must frankly recognize the overbalance of population in
our industrial centers and, by engaging on a national scale in a redistribution,
endeavor to provide a better use of the land for those best fitted for the land."
As means to such a vague end, Roosevelt advanced suggestions that could be
variously interpreted. He called for "definite efforts to raise the values of agricultural products," for "insistence that the federal, state, and local governments
act forthwith on the demand that their cost be drastically reduced," and for "an
adequate but sound currency." On the foreign front he was somewhat clearer:
"Our international trade relations, though vastly important, are, in point of
time and necessity, secondary to the establishment of a sound national economy."

Though Roosevelt's words left listeners uncertain as to what his administration would do, they made plain that the administration would do *something.* "We must act, and act quickly," Roosevelt said. No longer would the
federal government wait for the business cycle to turn and the economy to
correct itself. Roosevelt announced that he would call a special session of Congress. He expected the legislature to rise to the challenge confronting it. But if
Congress failed in its duty, he would take additional steps. "I am prepared
under my constitutional duty to recommend the measures that a stricken nation in the midst of a stricken world may require. . . . I shall not evade the
clear course of duty that will then confront me. I shall ask the Congress for the
one remaining instrument to meet the crisis—broad executive power to wage
a war against the emergency as great as the power that would be given to me
if we were in fact invaded by a foreign foe."

No new president, not even Lincoln amid the secession crisis of 1861, had
spoken so boldly of the power he required and would insist upon. The American people were demanding much, and they deserved all that government
could accomplish for them. "They have asked for discipline and direction
under leadership. They have made me the present instrument of their wishes.
In the spirit of the gift I take it."

22.

Sᴀʀᴀ Rᴏᴏsᴇᴠᴇʟᴛ sᴀᴛ ᴡɪᴛʜ ʜᴇʀ sᴏɴ ᴏɴ ᴛʜᴇ ᴘʟᴀᴛꜰᴏʀᴍ ᴀᴛ ᴛʜᴇ ɪɴᴀᴜ-
guration, beside Eleanor and the children. She observed the ceremony with
the pride any mother would feel on such an occasion, mixed with some stubborn residual conviction that Franklin would have been better off retiring to
Hyde Park after contracting polio. If her thoughts extended beyond her son
and his accomplishments, she might have reflected on the remarkable changes
America had experienced during her lifetime. She wouldn't have put it quite
so, but the country had undergone a capitalist revolution, a thoroughgoing
economic and social transformation in which an agrarian society had given
way to one based on manufacturing; in which land as the predominant form
of property had been eclipsed by bank accounts and corporate shares; in which
small producers had been absorbed, marginalized, or extinguished by giant
enterprises; in which the farmsteads and villages of a rural people had been
overtaken by the cities of an urban nation; in which muscle-powered transport
had fallen far behind the locomotion of steam and internal combustion; in
which handwritten letters as the principal means of communication over distance had been supplanted by telegraph, telephone, and radio; in which a population descended primarily from Northwestern Europeans and West Africans
had been augmented by the arrival of millions from Southern and Eastern
Europe; in which the Protestants who founded America now jostled with
Catholics and Jews; in which material life grew richer but more precarious
and less equal.

The capitalist revolution had triggered, after the turn of the twentieth century, a democratic counterrevolution, as the institutions of government adjusted to the modern terms of economic existence. Progressives led by
Theodore Roosevelt and Woodrow Wilson had tamed the most egregious of
the trusts, curbed the power of the private bankers, established standards of
quality for food and drugs, opened the political process to greater popular

participation, and generally reasserted the principle that even the greatest capitalist entities were ultimately responsible to the American people, acting
through their democratic institutions.

After the World War the balance had shifted again, back in the direction of
capitalism. The business of America, Calvin Coolidge had said, was business,
and business largely had its way. The boom of the 1920s appeared proof of the
efficacy of modern capitalism, which, Herbert Hoover promised, would carry
the country to a new level of enduring prosperity.

The stock market crash had punctured the pretense of the New Era, and the
depression had gone far toward discrediting capitalism. What remained to be
seen—and for Franklin Roosevelt perhaps to help determine—was whether
capitalism's stumble would produce a democratic resurgence. In his campaign
Roosevelt made much of the forgotten man, of the plight of the ordinary people of America, of the interdependence of all classes and occupational groups.
Capitalist individualism—the philosophy of every man for himself—no
longer persuaded. Whether democratic collectivism—the belief that we're all
in this together—could do better was the question of the hour.

It could hardly do worse. The late winter of 1933 was the darkest moment
in American life since the Civil War, which for all the destruction it wreaked
at least was comprehensible to ordinary men and women. The most discouraging aspect of the Great Depression was that it defied common logic. People
went hungry while farmers dumped milk in ditches and left crops standing in
the fields. The thriftiest savers, cautious souls who had shunned the stock market as reckless speculation, saw their carefully tended nest eggs vanish
overnight as banks collapsed. Factories sat idle while millions wanted nothing
more than to go back to work.

The magnitude of the disaster could only be estimated, not least because
the Hoover administration hadn't been eager to quantify the bad news. But the
evidence available to a subsequent generation of historical statisticians indicated that by 1933 the total production of American farms and factories had
fallen by a third, in real terms, since 1929. (The nominal decline was greater but
included a sharp fall in prices as well.) One-quarter of American workers were
unemployed in 1933: twelve million men and women, by the most plausible estimates. Many more were underemployed—working part-time or at jobs beneath their skills and training. Five thousand banks had failed or were failing,
typically leaving their depositors without recourse. The stock market had lost
three-quarters of its value since October 1929, wiping out millions more. Half
a million home mortgages had been foreclosed, rendering the owners at once

bankrupt and homeless. As property values plummeted, property tax receipts shriveled, forcing cities and states to lay off workers or pay them in IOUs.

Hunger scoured the land. Generations accustomed to pulling their own weight often refused to seek organized relief until they were starving; in other locales the relief simply fell short of what was required. Individuals and families hit the road looking for work and shelter; the Hoovervilles that sprang up in every city and many towns were merely the most visible manifestation of the tide of homelessness that swept the country. Young men and women postponed marriage; the nation's birth rate fell by a third.

Old people were particularly vulnerable. Guaranteed pensions were a rarity in the 1930s; workers expected to save for their retirements or work until they died. But bank failures stole their savings, and unemployment their livelihoods. In the human nature of things they were less mobile than the young, often because they were sicker. Some moved in with their children; millions simply suffered alone.

Franklin Roosevelt in March 1933 couldn't know the extent of the calamity; no one could. But if his inaugural address sounded like a war message, it fairly reflected the fact that the depression of the 1930s had done—and was doing— the kind of damage commonly associated with wars. It destroyed lives and livelihoods; it uprooted families and sowed despair; it blighted a whole generation. It cast a grimmer pall over America, and over the American future, than any development of the lifetime of Roosevelt and his generation.

❖   ❖   ❖

At the moment of Roosevelt's inauguration the American banking system verged on dissolution. Banking law in America in the early 1930s was a federal-state hodgepodge. National banks—which was to say, nationally chartered banks; individual bank corporations didn't yet operate across state lines—were controlled by federal law, while state banks followed state laws. Some banks, both national and state, were members of the Federal Reserve system; others were not. As various governors watched banks in their states succumb to "runs"—uncontrolled withdrawal demands by depositors, which frequently ended with the failure of the banks—several pondered the drastic step of declaring "bank holidays," that is, simply closing the banks to business. The idea, or hope, was that the panic would pass: that if depositors were temporarily prevented from withdrawing their funds, they would calm down and decide they really didn't need the money. In fact most neither needed nor really wanted the money. Bank deposits earned interest; cash in a can in the garden or in a shoe box under the bed did not. If the depositors could have been sure their money was safe in the banks, nearly all of them would have been happy to leave it there. With this in mind, the governor of Louisiana declared a state bank holiday in early February. Michigan did the same at midmonth, followed by Maryland, Indiana, Arkansas, and Ohio. At the beginning of March twenty other states closed the doors of their banks. By inauguration day, the American banking system was nearly at a standstill.

The crisis in banking daunted Roosevelt but also afforded him an opportunity. Hoover and the Republicans blamed the new president for the financial paralysis, charging that his attacks on business had sapped the confidence that in ordinary times underwrote the banking system. Some conservatives, apparently including the former president, detected a design in Roosevelt's words and actions; by encouraging the collapse, they said, Roosevelt was paving the way to socialism. Roosevelt had no such plan, as events would soon prove. But the paralysis of the banks left him free to address the problem in almost any way he chose. His first step was to make the de facto national bank holiday official. Inauguration day was a Saturday; on Sunday the banks were all closed anyway; and at one o'clock on Monday morning Roosevelt declared a four-day national bank holiday. From Monday through Thursday, his executive order said, "all banking transactions shall be suspended." In particular, no bank or branch "shall pay out, export, earmark, or permit the withdrawal or transfer in any manner or by any device whatsoever, of any gold or silver coin or bullion or currency or take any action which might facilitate the hoarding thereof."

Roosevelt's closing of the banks was the kind of bold action his inaugural address had promised. Whether it was legal was another matter. He cited a section of the 1917 Trading with the Enemy Act as justification. The act had never been formally repealed, but a body of legal theory held that that law, along with other wartime legislation, had expired upon the signing of the peace treaty with Germany in 1921. (After the Senate rejected Wilson's Treaty of Versailles, the United States had negotiated separate treaties with its wartime adversaries.) Roosevelt solicited the opinion of Thomas Walsh, a Montana senator who was his first choice to be attorney general. Walsh delivered the opinion Roosevelt wanted: that the law was still in effect and that it allowed the president to close the country's banks. But Walsh never had to defend this opinion before a court of law, for he died on March 2 while traveling to Washington for the inauguration.

Had the emergency not seemed so dire, and had the banking system not been paralyzed anyway, Roosevelt surely would have met greater resistance. But even the *Wall Street Journal,* the principal organ of institutional capital, acknowledged that the unprecedented circumstances required strong measures. "A common adversity has much subdued the recalcitrance of groups bent upon self-interest," the paper observed. "All of us the country over are now ready to make sacrifices to a common necessity and to accept realities as we would not have done three months ago."

Moreover, the brief duration of the bank holiday meant that Roosevelt's affront to the corporate sector, if affront it was, would be passing. And it would shortly be submitted to Congress for approval or rejection. Even as Roosevelt closed the banks he acted to reopen Congress, calling the legislature into emergency session. The lawmakers would meet at noon on Thursday, March 9; their first order of business would be banking reform.

The nature of the reform remained to be seen—and to be decided. Hoover and the conspiracy-minded conservatives gave Roosevelt too much credit for foresight and conceptual coherence. Within days it became apparent that the hallmark of Roosevelt's New Deal was improvisation. "I have been so occupied since noon on Saturday that I have not had a chance to prepare any formal remarks," Roosevelt told the annual governors' conference on Monday, March 6. But he extemporized regarding his "four or five main objectives" in closing the banks and calling the legislature into special session. The first objective was to prevent further withdrawals from the banks. The second was "to provide some form of circulating medium for the country in addition to the outstanding currency," so much of which had gone into hiding. A third was to arrange the timely reopening of the banks and their subsequent smooth operation. A fourth—and here he came closest to Hoover's dark forebodings—was to reform the banking system to prevent a repetition of the current crisis. "We want if possible to have a general banking system," Roosevelt explained, "that is to say one covering national banks and state banks, as uniform as possible throughout the country."

❖   ❖   ❖

No competent commander goes to war without able lieutenants. Ray Moley, Rex Tugwell, Adolf Berle, and the other members of the Brain Trust had been indispensable during the campaign, running a kind of graduate seminar for a law school dropout who wanted to be president. Their ideas and words continued to inform Roosevelt's thinking and speeches after the inauguration. But putting the ideas into action required expertise and political heft the professors lacked. Roosevelt had been watching presidents and taking mental notes since Uncle Ted entered the White House; he had seen cabinets go right and cabinets go wrong, watched brilliant ideas languish for lack of support in Congress, witnessed the frustration that followed failure to cultivate those persons who could make or break an administration. He intended a revolution in governance, and he knew enough to start with a strong cabinet.

Yet not too strong. Woodrow Wilson had erred by making William Jennings Bryan his secretary of state. The error was natural: Wilson wanted to appease an important constituency in the Democratic party. And Wilson had no way of knowing a world war was about to break out. Yet having a pacifist for chief diplomat during wartime handcuffed the administration, and Bryan's abrupt departure during the *Lusitania* crisis dealt Wilson's presidency a serious blow.

Roosevelt learned a further lesson from Wilson. The unforgivable failure of Wilson's administration was the president's failure to persuade the Senate to ratify the Versailles treaty. Here again the problem wasn't entirely Wilson's, or at least not within Wilson's control: his sudden incapacity at the climax of the treaty fight left the pro-treaty forces leaderless. But Wilson had prepared the ground for defeat by ignoring the Senate in the negotiation of the treaty and in the formulation of foreign policy generally.

Roosevelt took care to avoid both of Wilson's mistakes in choosing a secretary of state. The leading prospect for the position was Owen Young, the president of General Electric, who had headed the second international debt renegotiation plan of the 1920s and was considered reassuring to both the American business community and the transatlantic financial world. Young had another mark in his favor: amid the efforts by Al Smith to stop Roosevelt's candidacy before the Democratic convention, Young had been mentioned as a compromise candidate. But he took himself out of the running, leaving Roosevelt to sweep to victory.

For such reasons Roosevelt had to consider Young, and to make the considering obvious. He talked about Young with Moley and Berle and Louis Howe, and let them mention the conversations to reporters. But Moley perceived that Roosevelt was never comfortable with the idea of Young as secretary of state. "I got the sense that he didn't feel he could run around in his mental carpet slippers in Young's presence," Moley wrote. Moley overestimated

Roosevelt's need for pajama talk with his cabinet secretaries, but he was right that Roosevelt didn't really want Young. When Young objected that his wife's illness would prevent him from doing justice to the senior position in Roosevelt's cabinet, the president-elect didn't contradict him.

Roosevelt settled instead on Cordell Hull, an eleven-term congressman from Tennessee whom voters in the Volunteer State had elevated to the Senate in 1930. Hull's experience in the Senate offered reassurance that whatever treaties the Roosevelt administration negotiated would receive a fair hearing in the upper house, while the long time it took Hull to reach the Senate suggested a lack of the kind of ambition that might distract or disrupt the administration. "I was really almost thunderstruck," Hull said of being offered the State Department, and his amazement reassured Roosevelt.

In the House and in the Senate, Hull had distinguished himself as an advocate of tariff reduction. This placed him in the mainstream of the Democratic party and promised to keep him busy in the State Department, a prospect that again appealed to Roosevelt, who likewise favored tariff reduction but didn't intend to waste much of his own time and political capital on such a long-term and comparatively thankless project. The only question about Hull was whether he would take the job. In fact he required a month to accept Roosevelt's offer. He explained that the Senate suited him quite well, that foreign policy wasn't his strength, and that Mrs. Hull didn't look forward to the entertaining the wife of a secretary of state was expected to do. Roosevelt waved away Hull's objections, letting him know that the nation needed him at the State Department, that he underestimated his knowledge of foreign affairs, and that Mrs. Hull could stay home if she didn't like fancy dinners. A slightly larger impediment arose when several Democratic senators told Moley that Hull lacked the breadth required of an international statesman. "It's an open secret that he's got only one string to his bow," one of the senators said of Hull's preoccupation with tariffs. "Every time he makes his speech on tariffs, he empties the Senate." When Moley passed this objection along, Roosevelt brushed it aside too. "Tell the senators I'll be glad to have some fine idealism in the State Department," he said.

After State, the most important cabinet position was the Treasury. Here the obvious choice was Carter Glass. The diminutive Virginian reminded some contemporaries of James Madison, others of Alexander Hamilton. Glass had been in Congress as long as Hull and had held a cabinet post as well: Treasury secretary for two years during Wilson's second term. He knew more about money than anyone else in the Democratic party, having helped author the

Federal Reserve Act of 1913 and kept a close eye on the Fed and the currency since.

This expertise was precisely why Roosevelt had to offer Glass the Treasury post, and why Glass ended up not taking it. Glass was a sound-money man, opposing devaluation of the dollar; he was Herbert Hoover's favorite Democrat. By offering Glass the Treasury, Roosevelt got credit for giving Glass's views serious credence. He also made an ally of Glass. But even as Roosevelt informed Glass that he was the best man for the Treasury job, he acknowledged the strength of Glass's counterargument that he could serve the country better in the Senate. When Glass pleaded poor health, Roosevelt let him know he understood about health problems and how they could limit a man's options. The outcome was just what Roosevelt wanted. Glass declined the offer "with fervent good wishes for you and your administration" and a pledge that "I shall ever be ready to serve your administration to the full extent of my capabilities."

Roosevelt settled on William Woodin, a Republican industrialist, director of the Federal Reserve Bank of New York, and trustee of the Warm Springs Foundation who also happened to be a personal friend. Woodin's Wall Street and commercial connections caused informed observers to assume he favored sound money—just as Roosevelt knew they would. But Woodin kept his views to himself—just as Roosevelt knew *he* would. Roosevelt didn't intend to be his own Treasury secretary, but he took comfort in knowing that Woodin wouldn't be overly independent. (He meanwhile got a laugh from Louis Howe's method of casting his vote for the Treasury post. Afraid that word would leak, Howe wired Roosevelt in code: "Prefer a wooden roof to a glass roof over swimming pool." Roosevelt read the message, and then read it again, wondering what Howe was talking about. When he realized it was a comment on the Treasury position—Woodin rather than Glass—he roared with delight.)

The remaining cabinet positions were less central to Roosevelt's immediate plans. Thomas Walsh, the Montana senator, represented an additional nod to the Senate; when Walsh died before the inauguration, Roosevelt had to scramble to find another person for attorney general. Homer Cummings of Connecticut was known to favor Roosevelt's views on important policy matters, having joined the Roosevelt camp long before the convention. Roosevelt had intended for Cummings to be governor general of the Philippines, but upon Walsh's death he reassigned him to the Justice job. Henry A. Wallace had been consulting with Roosevelt for months on agriculture; besides being better versed in the problems facing farmers than just about anyone else in America, the Iowa editor was, like Woodin, a Republican. Roosevelt never forgot that the Republicans remained the majority party in the country; whenever he could bring a Republican aboard without compromising his overall objectives, he was pleased to do so. Wallace got the Agriculture Department.

Harold Ickes landed Interior, which shared with Agriculture the responsibility for America's land-use policies. Roosevelt didn't know Ickes at all; after inviting him for an interview, along with some other candidates for administration posts, Roosevelt looked at a list of their names and called out, "Which one of you is Ikes?"

"Ickes, Mr. President," the Chicago lawyer answered, shortening the first of the two syllables.

"Oh, so that's how you pronounce it."

Ickes was yet another Republican, which counted in his favor, and a progressive, which did, too. Beyond that, Roosevelt found him engaging. "I liked the cut of his jib," he told Moley.

The Labor Department went to Frances Perkins. Roosevelt was determined to nominate the first woman to a cabinet post, and Labor was the likeliest spot, since in those days it included most federal welfare programs. Roosevelt considered Ruth Bryan Owen, the daughter of William Jennings Bryan, for the position but decided on Perkins instead. The selection of either woman was expected to ruffle feathers among union leaders, who had heretofore furnished the secretaries of labor. But New Yorker Perkins was less a stretch than Nebraska native Bryan Owen. Besides, Roosevelt knew Perkins personally and had valued her work as New York's industrial commissioner.

Yet not many other people knew Perkins, and there were many people Perkins didn't know. Ray Moley remembered seeing Perkins and Harold Ickes in Roosevelt's parlor on Sixty-fifth Street. They were clearly strangers to each other. Moley broke the ice. "As you will eventually meet anyhow," he said, "give me the pleasure of introducing the secretary of the interior to the secretary of labor."

❖ ❖ ❖

"GENERALLY SPEAKING, it is an average group of Presidential advisers," Arthur Krock declared of Roosevelt's cabinet. "Its composite trait seems to me to be diligence; brilliance it lacks completely." Roosevelt wouldn't have disagreed. The president didn't want to be overshadowed by his advisers—didn't want them to have or develop independent reputations or constituencies. Some of his motive was simply ego: having reached the top of the greasy pole, he wished for the world to see him as the great man he was convinced he was. But much was political strategy. The progressive revolution he intended would elicit plenty of resistance on its own; for his administration to get caught up in the quarreling that typically occurred when cabinet posts developed into fiefdoms would add unacceptably to his problems.

There was yet another element that contributed to Roosevelt's preference for complaisant cabinet secretaries. To a degree that would become clearer with time, Roosevelt's style of leadership involved setting his subordinates at cross-purposes with one another. The competition that ensued would ensure—or was supposed to ensure—that alternative policies received the fullest airing before Roosevelt himself stepped in and decided which way to go. Sometimes the advisers involved would know that others were on the same task; sometimes they wouldn't until Roosevelt decided against them.

Roosevelt's style of decision-making entailed certain risks. The duplication of effort could waste time and resources. The competition among advisers could fray nerves and ultimately alienate the losers, who might then cause problems for the administration. By concentrating power in Roosevelt's hands, it could overwork him, threatening his health, or overwhelm him, leading to tardy, hastily conceived, or simply bad decisions.

Grace Tully noticed something about Roosevelt's cabinet that may have occurred by accident or perhaps by the president's design. Tully had begun working for Roosevelt in Albany, as assistant to Roosevelt's secretary, Missy LeHand. She followed her bosses to Washington and remained with Roosevelt throughout his presidency. "So far as I was able to judge," Tully said, "no two members of the Roosevelt cabinet were ever real friends. There were the dinners given cabinet members by the President, and there was now and then a poker game held in Harold Ickes' or Henry Morgenthau's house." Morgenthau, Roosevelt's Hudson Valley neighbor, replaced Will Woodin at Treasury after declining health forced Woodin's resignation at the end of 1933. "But beyond these random and infrequent social events, the contacts between cabinet members were largely of an official character."

Much closer personally—to one another and to the president—were Roosevelt's less senior advisers. Louis Howe, having accomplished his life's goal by making Roosevelt president, received the post of president's personal secretary. Of all Roosevelt's official family, Howe was the only one who called him by his given name, and the one who got the first and last words on all matters of substance. Roosevelt put Brain Trusters Moley and Tugwell on the federal payroll, making Moley an assistant to Cordell Hull at the State Department and Tugwell an aide to Henry Wallace at Agriculture. Jim Farley was appointed postmaster general, the traditional slot for campaign managers. The tradition survived from the pre–civil service days of the spoils system, and although the postmaster now had much less patronage to bestow, the practice continued to reflect the fact that neither campaign managers nor postmasters typically had much influence over policy, as opposed to politics.

❖   ❖   ❖

PRESS CONFERENCES had been a feature of White House life since Theodore Roosevelt, feeling sorry for the stringers assigned by their papers to keep an eye on the president's movements and visitors, invited them to come in out of the rain. TR held press sessions irregularly, and he insisted that he not be quoted or, in most cases, even attributed. When he wished to speak as president, he did so through the formal channels of written messages and set speeches.

Press conferences were institutionalized under TR's successors. The typical session with Wilson was something between a lecture and a seminar, with both of which Wilson was familiar from his days as a professor. The World War put a crimp on Wilson's candor, as a slip of the tongue might compromise military secrets or America's position with respect to other countries. Between his concern for confidentiality and the general duress of the war, Wilson suspended his news conferences; after his 1919 stroke they never resumed.

Warren Harding had been a pressman himself and was happy to restore journalists' access to the White House. Yet he too discovered the limits American diplomacy placed on presidential frankness, when he said too much during the Washington Conference. An angry Charles Evans Hughes would have suspended the press conferences again had the matter been his to determine, but Harding resisted, and eventually the president and secretary of state compromised. Harding would answer written questions submitted in advance. This procedure gave him time to prepare answers and if necessary check them with his cabinet secretaries. A further stipulation forbade reporters from revealing which questions the president declined to answer.

Calvin Coolidge kept the requirement of written questions and allowed himself to be quoted in reply, but only with his explicit permission. Herbert Hoover elaborated on this scheme, devising three categories for the information he divulged: written statements that could be quoted and attributed to the president, extemporaneous remarks attributable to "official sources," and sensitive information that must not be cited at all. Hoover's system might have worked had he possessed a more engaging personality or had his perception of presidential responsibility not impelled him to put a uniformly positive gloss on the calamities the country was experiencing. The news corps came to distrust him, and the distrust exacerbated Hoover's reticence. The press conferences grew painful for all concerned.

Roosevelt's relations with the press had always been good, from his days as a state senator to his most recent experiences in Albany and on the campaign trail. More than any president since Theodore Roosevelt, he loved to talk—and even more than TR, he liked to listen to others talk back. Beyond that, his disability, which in another person might have provided an excuse to keep the press at a distance, became for Roosevelt a reason to let the correspondents get close. He didn't stand at a podium in addressing them; he sat behind the desk in his office and let the correspondents gather round. They did so with pleasure, as many as two hundred crowding the room, and the ones in front sometimes being pushed right onto Roosevelt's desk.

At Roosevelt's first session with the reporters, on the morning of March 8, he explained the ground rules. "My hope is that these conferences are going to be merely enlarged versions of the kind of very delightful family conferences I have been holding in Albany for the last four years," he said. "I am told that what I am about to do will become impossible, but I am going to try it anyway." He would eliminate the requirement that questions be in writing, he said, adding, "I see no reason why I should not talk to you ladies and gentlemen off the record just the way I have been doing in Albany and the way I used to do it in the Navy Department down here." Some questions he would decline to answer, for reasons of discretion, policy, or plain ignorance. "There will be a great many questions you will ask about that I don't know enough to answer." Hypotheticals he would reject on principle.

Roosevelt said that he and Stephen Early, whom he had made his principal spokesman, had discussed how they wanted to handle attributions. "Steve and I thought that it was best that street news for use out of here should always be without direct quotations. In other words, I don't want to be directly quoted, with the exception that direct quotations will be given out by Steve in writing." Two other categories of news would be treated differently. "The first is 'background information,' which means any material which can be used by all of you on your own authority and responsibility and must not be attributed

to the White House, because I don't want to have to revive the Ananias Club."
The Ananias Club—named for the early Christian said to have dropped dead
for lying to God—was the exile Theodore Roosevelt imposed on journalists
who broke his reporting rules; some of those present at this first conference
were old enough to remember TR's limbo, as their nervous laughter revealed.

The second category was off-the-record information. This was confidential material intended for only those present at a conference. As sharing of
such information had caused problems under Coolidge and Hoover, Roosevelt
elaborated: "There is one thing I want to say right now on which I think you
will go along with me. I want to ask you not to repeat this 'off the record' confidential information either to your own editors or to associates who are not
here, because there is always the danger that while you people might not violate the rule, somebody may forget to say, 'This is off the record and confidential,' and the other party may use it in a story."

❖ ❖ ❖

$\mathcal{I}$N THE BEST of circumstances Roosevelt's administration might have eased
into its responsibilities—might have had the benefit of the equivalent of a
shakedown cruise. But like the destroyer that carried Roosevelt to Europe in
1918, his administration received its shakedown under full battle conditions.
Roosevelt closed the banks on March 6; he had to figure out how to reopen
them on March 10. The bank holiday would have mitigated the panic by
then—at least he could hope so—but it wouldn't by itself have altered the underlying weaknesses in the banking system. The American banking industry
in 1933 suffered from the same problem that afflicted farming and manufacturing: excess capacity relative to demand. The banking business had boomed
during the 1920s as demand for banking services tracked the surge in the stock
market and business generally. The bust of 1929 and afterward had shrunk the
demand without immediately shrinking the supply.

Another factor contributed to the banks' distress. The failure of the Federal
Reserve to prevent the drastic contraction of the money supply had deprived
the banking system of a large part of its liquidity. As the money dried up, so
did the ability of the banks to meet their depositors' demands. The vicious
circle tightened as the banks' inability to meet demands intensified those very
demands.

The obvious solution was to reduce the supply of bank services, which
meant reducing the number of banks. To some extent this was happening on

its own; the thousands of banks that had failed since the stock crash represented perhaps a third of the preexisting number. Had Roosevelt not cared for the human consequences of the bank failures, he might have allowed the winnowing to continue until supply and demand in bank services achieved a new equilibrium.

But he did care, and Americans cared, which was why he had closed the banks and why he felt compelled to devise some method to reopen the stronger ones while shielding depositors from the consequences of the permanent closure of the weaker. And he had to do it all in a matter of days. The country could survive without banks in much the way a person can survive without water: for a few days and with rapidly increasing distress. Individual wallets and purses emptied; cash drawers and tills ran out; business slowed and then halted. Not even the First Family escaped the effects of the bank closing. Eleanor reported that without new cash she couldn't keep the White House larder stocked.

Much of the work required to reopen the banks took place behind the closed doors of the Treasury and the White House. Will Woodin and Ray Moley met with the governors of the Federal Reserve, with private bankers, with members of Congress, with economists, and with just about anyone else thought to have a large stake or substantial influence in the operation of the nation's banks. Through long days and longer nights they labored, determined to have a bank bill to present to Congress when the special session opened on March 9.

Yet to a surprising extent—to an extent unimaginable in any earlier administration—the discussions of bank reform took place in the plain view of the president's press conferences. Other presidents had treated financial policy as highly confidential; Grover Cleveland's elaborate effort to conceal his oral surgery had been occasioned by his desire to avoid alarming the financial markets. There was good reason for shrouding policy in secret: speculators were ready to leap on the slightest hint of a change in policy. Jay Gould, the most notorious of American speculators, had paid officials of the Grant administration hundreds of thousands of dollars merely to tip him off if any change in policy was imminent during his 1869 attempt to corner the gold market. White House and Treasury officials didn't even have to *say* anything to set the markets tumbling; observers read institutional body language the way poker players read the faces of their opponents, and bet accordingly.

On this account, when Roosevelt commenced his first press conference, on March 8, with a candid discussion of administration thinking on the bank and money question, the reporters listened with astonishment. To be sure, Roosevelt didn't let himself be quoted on the issue, but the information he supplied for background far exceeded anything Hoover or other presidents had provided. The first question put to Roosevelt referred to the bank policy he was expected to announce: "Will you go to Congress or send your message?"

"Send it," Roosevelt replied.

"When will it be available here for us?"

"Judging by the fact that I haven't started to write it, I should say at the last minute possible."

The simple fact that the president hadn't started writing such a momentous document, twenty-four hours before it was due, was news in itself. "Administration in Disarray!" the headlines might have read. Some of the reporters must have been tempted to race for the door, to file their alarming stories at once. But they waited to hear what else Roosevelt had to say. With money in such short supply, various participants and observers were suggesting the use of scrip—essentially IOUs of the kind banks employed among themselves and which were already circulating in places where the banks had been closed for more than a few days. Any advance notice of the administration's thinking on the subject could be extremely valuable, for a decision to employ scrip would devalue the dollar, while a decision not to use it would have the opposite effect.

"Do you favor national scrip or scrip issued by clearing houses?" a clever correspondent asked, before Roosevelt had said anything about scrip at all.

Roosevelt didn't bat an eye. "About Monday, the day before yesterday, a very, very wide use of scrip seemed necessary," he said. "By last night it looked possible to avoid such general use of scrip. But that doesn't mean that scrip will be eliminated by any means. Scrip may be used in many localities pending the working out of a sounder plan and more permanent plan to get additional currency into use."

Reporters who reflected on Roosevelt's answer realized he hadn't given anything away. Scrip might be used; then again it might not be. But the fact that he was willing to discuss the subject freely was seductive. Hoover had treated reporters as adversaries; he met them in the same mood in which many people approach their dentists, and he often seemed as reluctant to open his mouth. Roosevelt, by contrast, brought the journalists into his confidence, making them almost co-conspirators in governing the nation. By accepting his ground rules, they limited what they could write about; for precisely this reason, some reporters deliberately stayed away. But for the great majority he was simply too good a story to pass up.

Roosevelt understood his advantage and played it for all it was worth. He knew he was brilliant in press conferences. His command of policy options was far greater than he had often been given credit for; those long conversations with Moley and the other professors, and with the various experts he had buttonholed over the years, hadn't been for nothing. More important was his ability to break complicated questions down into pieces the ordinary reporter could understand and use. The White House press corps included a few experts on finance and on other specific subjects, but most of its members were generalists, not unlike Roosevelt himself. And in those days journalists rarely boasted advanced degrees, or even undergraduate degrees. They typically learned by watching and listening—again, not unlike Roosevelt.

Roosevelt's self-confidence and personal presence in conducting his news conferences was by itself worth the price of admission. Even within the constraints he placed on what could be reported, each performance was a highwire act. If he put something on the record that should have stayed off, the damage to his administration, and conceivably to the country, could be immense. If he stumbled, even in confidence, he could betray his ignorance to the reporters, losing their respect and damaging himself, perhaps no less severely.

He almost never stumbled. Twice a week, month after month, year after year, he opened the doors and put on his show. The great majority were in his office; others took place at Hyde Park, Warm Springs, or on the road when he was traveling. The performances were typically informative, frequently edifying, always entertaining. Theodore Joslin had worked in the Hoover White House before taking a job with the *Washington Star*; he contrasted his old boss with the new president. "Mr. Hoover always had a smile for the press," Joslin said, giving Hoover some benefit of the doubt. "But he often was restrained. Mr. Roosevelt will wisecrack any day." Yet jokes carried Roosevelt only so far. "The prime difference is in their attitude toward the depression. Mr. Hoover kept his problems to himself. Mr. Roosevelt talks with amazing freedom. There have been times when he has said little of consequence, but he has talked—and remember, that is the one thing the press wants the President to do." As a result, Joslin observed, Roosevelt was "ace high with most of the corps."

❖   ❖   ❖

*T*HE REPORTERS at the March 8 press conference inquired into Roosevelt's position on gold. The banking question was inextricably linked to the money question, in that a surfeit of banks might be also interpreted as a dearth of money. Until his eleventh hour, Hoover had tried to get Roosevelt to commit to defending the American gold standard and thereby the full value of the dollar. Hoover understood what he was asking. "I realize that if these declarations be made by the President-elect," Hoover confided to a fellow Republican, "he will have ratified the whole major program of the Republican Administration; that is, it means the abandonment of 90 percent of the so-called new deal." But Hoover was convinced the New Deal needed to be abandoned, for he believed that Roosevelt's promised agenda was what was destabilizing the financial markets. "Unless this is done, they run a grave danger of precipitating a complete financial debacle." Hoover wrote this letter for the record, and to warn against the nefarious designs of the Democrats. "If it"—the debacle—"is precipitated, the responsibility lies squarely with them, for they have had ample warning—unless, of course, such a debacle is part of the 'new deal.' "

Roosevelt hadn't fought and won the election in order to ratify the very Republican policies he considered responsible for America's distress. He ignored Hoover's entreaties on gold, to the point of refusing to answer Hoover's letters. Whether as a result of his refusal (Hoover's interpretation) or Hoover's policies (Roosevelt's view), the strain on the dollar reached nearly the cataclysmic proportions the lame duck president predicted. During the week before the inauguration hundreds of millions of dollars flowed out of America's banks and hundreds of millions in gold from the federal Treasury. The drain of dollars reflected a loss of confidence that the banks would be able to meet their obligations to repay depositors; the drain of gold a loss of confidence that the government would fulfill its promise to convert dollars to gold. The former was chiefly a domestic problem, as healthy banks were essential to the economies of every city and state; the latter had serious international ramifications, as much of the gold was being withdrawn by foreigners for export to their home countries.

Roosevelt's refusal to join Hoover in declaring for gold naturally led to speculation—figurative and literal—that he would take the United States off the gold standard. At his first press conference he provided the reporters a primer on gold. He read from an article written by "my friend Robey"—journalist, economist, and sometime Brain Truster Ralph Robey—for the *New York Evening Post*. Robey, and now Roosevelt, explained that an effective gold standard had to meet four criteria. First, the dollar (or other unit of currency) must be defined as containing a certain amount of gold of a particular fineness. Second, the government must be committed to coining all the gold delivered to the mint. Third, the government must agree to convert paper dollars to gold upon demand. Fourth, gold must be allowed to move freely into and especially out of the country. By these measures, the United States had an effective gold standard. The gold content of the dollar was defined by law, translating into a gold price of $20.67 per ounce. Dollars were redeemable in gold, and gold could be exported at will.

But—and here the reporters sat up and paid close attention—other countries did not meet the four conditions. "For a good long time, as a matter of actual fact, the United States has been the only country on the gold standard," Roosevelt said. Britain had formally gone off gold in 1931. "France has theoretically been on a gold standard, but nobody in France can go and take a bill to the bank and get gold for it, and as far as imports and exports go in France, it has been government controlled." Switzerland and the Netherlands had similar systems.

Roosevelt seemed to be making a case for taking the United States off gold. No reporter put the question so bluntly—in part because of the way Roosevelt stage-managed his press conferences. As in private conversations, Roosevelt was a master at controlling the direction and flow of comments. The location of the conferences—in his office—was initially explained as a convenience, not least on account of Roosevelt's impaired mobility. But it was equally a calculation, which proved out in practice, that reporters would feel themselves to be his guests and would conduct themselves as such. They rarely asked impertinent questions.

In this instance a reporter broached the subject indirectly. The president had spoken in his inaugural address of a "sound and adequate" currency. Did he care to elaborate?

Roosevelt laughingly corrected him. "I put it the other way around. I said 'adequate but sound.' "

"Can you define what that is?"

"No." This monosyllable revealingly elicited further laughter. Where Hoover would have tensed up, if he had answered the question at all, Roosevelt freely—almost merrily—acknowledged that a central part of his inaugural message consisted of indefinable fluff. "In other words—and I should call this 'off the record' information—you cannot define the thing too closely one way or the other." He allowed himself to say that when the banks were closed, the country had lacked an adequate currency. "There wasn't enough circulating to go around." And he hoped that when the banks reopened, "a great deal of the currency that was withdrawn for one purpose or another will find its way back."

But if it didn't, the administration was prepared to supplement it. Scrip might be employed, or perhaps bank notes issued by the Federal Reserve. "In other words, what you are coming to now really is a managed currency, the adequateness of which will depend on the conditions of the moment. It may expand one week and it may contract another week."

This was real news, for a managed currency was the opposite of one based on gold. The purpose of a gold standard was to prevent mere mortals—that is, politicians—from fiddling with the money supply to suit their short-term purposes. Roosevelt proposed precisely such fiddling.

"Can we use that part—'managed'?" one reporter immediately queried, envisioning his lead and likely headline.

"No, I think not," Roosevelt said.

Yet this was the biggest financial news in years, and so the reporters tried other tacks. "You haven't defined what you think is 'sound.' "

"I don't want to define 'sound' now." But Roosevelt did say—"entirely off the record"—that "in its essence we must not put the government any further in debt."

"When you speak of a managed currency, do you speak of a temporary proposition or a permanent system?"

"It ought to be part of the permanent system—that is off the record. It ought to be part of a permanent system so we don't run into this thing again."

❖ ❖ ❖

AND SO IT BECAME, though not for another month. The immediate challenge was to reopen the banks, which the administration and Congress contrived to do almost on schedule. Woodin, Moley, and several others were still drafting a bank bill as the members of Congress gathered on the morning of Thursday, March 9; the delay compelled Roosevelt to extend the bank holiday "until further proclamation by the President." The extension bought enough time for Congress to receive the bill but not enough for the government's printers to make copies for the members. Undeterred by their own ignorance, they approved it—in the form of a wadded-up newspaper, which served as a proxy for the bank bill itself—within hours. The law retroactively granted Roosevelt authority to close the banks and embargo gold, thereby removing any taint of unconstitutionality from Roosevelt's executive action. Looking forward, the bank bill authorized him to reopen the banks when he saw fit, under the supervision of the comptroller of the currency, and to direct the Federal

Reserve to issue notes that would circulate as money, regardless of the strictures of the gold standard, which remained technically in effect.

Roosevelt signed the bank measure that same Thursday evening. He shortly
announced a timetable for reopening the banks. On Monday the twelve Federal Reserve branch banks would reopen, along with banks in each of those
twelve cities. On Tuesday banks in cities where the bank clearinghouses had
continued to operate—roughly 250 cities altogether—would reopen. On
Wednesday the rest of the country's banks would reopen. The whole schedule,
however, was subject to the oversight of the Treasury, which would bar particularly precarious banks from reopening, lest they quickly fail and threaten
the others.

❖   ❖   ❖

THREE DAYS AFTER signing the bank bill, Roosevelt delivered his first radio
address as president. The term "fireside chat" wasn't yet in general use, but it
would have been appropriate on this late-winter night. A week earlier Roosevelt had said the only thing Americans had to fear was fear itself; now he
served up reassurance along with a basic lesson in economics. "I want to talk
for a few minutes with the people of the United States about banking," he said.
"I want to tell you what has been done in the last few days, why it was done,
and what the next steps are going to be. . . . I know that when you understand
what we in Washington have been about, I shall continue to have your cooperation as fully as I have had your sympathy and help during the past week."

The first part of Roosevelt's lesson explained why banks were so prone to
failure from public loss of nerve. "When you deposit money in a bank, the
bank does not put the money into a safe deposit vault. It invests the money in
many different forms of credit—bonds, commercial paper, mortgages, and
many other kinds of loans. . . . The bank puts your money to work to keep
the wheels of industry and of agriculture turning around." Only a small portion of the deposits remained on hand, to cover the ordinary needs of the public for cash. "The total amount of all the currency in the country is only a small
fraction of the total deposits in all of the banks." What had happened during
the recent panic? "Because of undermined confidence on the part of the public, there was a general rush by a large portion of our population to turn bank
deposits into currency or gold—a rush so great that the soundest banks could
not get enough currency to meet the demand." Once the rush started, it was a
simple matter of arithmetic that the banks would run out of cash.

The bank holiday had been proclaimed to stem the rush. It had done its job. Roosevelt acknowledged the inconvenience the bank closings had caused. But the closings had been necessary to prevent further damage to the banking system. And they had worked. "No sound bank is a dollar worse off than it was when it closed its doors last Monday." The bank holiday, moreover, had given Congress the time to pass legislation to relieve the stress on the banks. Officials of the Treasury Department were examining banks to see which could stand reopening, and the Federal Reserve was printing new currency to supplement the old. "The new currency is being sent out by the Bureau of Engraving and Printing in large volume to every part of the country. It is sound currency because it is backed by actual, good assets"—namely the notes and bonds of the federal government.

The key to the success of the whole program was the cooperation of ordinary Americans. "There is an element in the readjustment of our financial system more important than currency, more important than gold, and that is the confidence of the people. Confidence and courage are the essentials of success in carrying out our plan." Fear had been the enemy; fear remained all that could foil the new system. "Let us unite in banishing fear. We have provided the machinery to restore our financial system. It is up to you to support and make it work. It is your problem no less than it is mine. Together we cannot fail."

23.

LIKE MANY OTHER MEN WHO ASPIRE TO GREATNESS, FRANKLIN ROOsevelt could be incredibly self-centered. Men seldom become great without believing the world revolves around them. If Sara Roosevelt hadn't doted so on her only son, he would have lacked some of the self-confidence that enabled him to think he could overcome his polio and return to the political arena. Whether Sara appreciated this irony—that her very solicitude for her son, articulated over his first four decades of life, was much of what made him ignore her pleas to retire to Hyde Park squiredom for the remainder of his life—is unclear. She never became accustomed to the spectacle of politics, especially when it played out on her front lawn or in her dining room. Huey Long had arrived for lunch during the 1932 campaign and put on his characteristically egregious show. Franklin was compelled to suffer the Louisiana senator in silence, but Sara wasn't. "Granny endured it as long as she could," James Roosevelt remembered, "then, in a stage whisper that could have been heard down at the stables, inquired: '*Who* is that *dreadful* person?' " Sara naturally took pride in her son's elevation to the highest office in the land and even issued a statement upon departing the capital after his inauguration: "I shall leave my son in Washington, confident that he will give all the strength that is in him, to help his country, and I shall be glad if every mother will pray God to help and preserve him."

Yet the realities of public life often disconcerted and wounded her. She felt personally the political attacks on Franklin, and she sometimes found it difficult to reconcile his policies with the culture in which she had grown up and which still surrounded her in the Hudson Valley. She disapproved of Eleanor's involvement in politics, which, notwithstanding the Nineteenth Amendment, Sara considered the province of men. After Franklin's inauguration, Eleanor made a habit of visiting parts of the country most badly hit by the depression.

One news report depicted her in a coal mine in the Appalachians; Sara wrote Franklin a few days afterward, her displeasure oozing from between the bland words: "I hope Eleanor is with you this morning. . . . I see she has emerged from the mine. . . . That is something to be thankful for."

Eleanor valued Franklin's new position more than Sara did. The role of First Lady of the nation didn't differ enormously in kind from that of First Lady of New York, but the scale was much larger. Her first chore was to make a home of the White House, and she discovered that while a staff of eight or ten had sufficed to run the governor's mansion in Albany, three to four times that many maids, butlers, ushers, cooks, gardeners, secretaries, security guards, and chauffeurs were required at the president's house. The expenses were proportionally greater, and much came out of the president's pocket. The federal government paid the wages of the staff, but the president, for reasons most apparent to the Congress that had imposed the practice in the early days of the republic, had to feed them. The president also had to pay for the Christmas parties and bonuses that were perquisites of their jobs. The government footed the bill for state dinners, but personal guests were the responsibility of the president. If Eleanor hadn't heard it from Uncle Ted's side of the family, she soon learned that the presidency drained most incumbents not simply psychologically and physically but financially as well. Eleanor's separate financial accounts shielded her from the losses the presidency imposed on Franklin, but not from the worries they produced.

Had Aunt Edith been speaking to Eleanor, she could have told her about the myriad demands on a First Lady's time. The receptions alone—for dignitaries from other countries, for members of Congress, for governors, for party officials, and for the well-heeled faithful—could wear the strongest woman down. Eleanor felt her feet screaming after only a few such receptions, until one of the members of the honor guard, who knew a bit about standing at attention for long periods, offered the hint to flex her knees ever so slightly now and then. No one would notice and the strain would be much less. Eleanor took the hint, and it worked. But it did nothing for the problem of having to shake hundreds of hands during the average reception, and thousands in the typical week. Here her genes came to the rescue. "I was lucky in having a supple hand, which never ached," she wrote.

People wrote to the president about policy matters; they often wrote to the First Lady about personal issues. Amid the depression, Eleanor received countless letters relating the travails of their authors. Most were sincere, although some were ill conceived. One woman said she wanted a baby and hoped Mrs. Roosevelt could find her one. A follow-up letter arrived shortly saying that once she had the baby, she would need milk for it, and so could Mrs. Roosevelt get her a cow? And to keep the milk cold, she could use an icebox, if that wouldn't be too much bother.

Some letters were patent scams. A young girl wrote that she had been chosen valedictorian of her high school class but didn't have money to buy a dress and so would have to give her speech in her brother's overalls. Could the First Lady help out? The envelope included a page from a mail-order catalogue showing the sorts of dresses that would be appropriate. Eleanor was normally a trusting type, but something about this letter evoked suspicion. She asked one of her staff to inquire about the girl and discovered that she wasn't poor, wasn't valedictorian, and in fact wasn't even graduating. Another con artist intended to write Eleanor asking for money but at the same time wrote to an accomplice who was to act as a character reference if the White House investigated. The letter to the accomplice detailed the story that was being pitched to Eleanor—but, in an evident mix-up of envelopes, this letter went to Eleanor instead, revealing the whole plot.

Certain of Eleanor's burdens she brought on herself. During the 1932 campaign the Associated Press had assigned Lorena Hickok to cover Eleanor. The two became friends and allies, with Eleanor providing Lorena insight into the campaign and Lorena providing perspective on life among the working classes. Hickok pointed out that the depression had been hard on journalists generally but on women journalists in particular. As in other fields, employers often assumed that men supported families and women didn't and therefore that men were more in need of the jobs that remained available. Eleanor determined to do her part for females of the fourth estate by holding press conferences to which women reporters alone were invited. The discrimination appeared harmless or positive at first, when the topics tended to be of minor importance and focused on the social calendar at the White House. But as Eleanor broadened her activities and emerged as a voice for groups otherwise underrepresented within the administration, her comments elicited the interest of the major newspapers' predominantly male political reporters. At the same time, one of the women reporters—Elizabeth May Craig—regularly argued that the solution to unfairness toward women was not unfairness toward men. Eleanor held the line. "I have great respect for her point of view," she said of Craig, "but I never quite agreed on this question." The men stayed out.

❖ ❖ ❖

𝒯HE ROOSEVELT WHITE HOUSE, besides being home to Franklin and Eleanor, was the permanent address, though not the primary domicile, of their two youngest children, Franklin Jr. and John. Franklin Jr. was finishing at Groton and would start at Harvard in the fall; Johnny was two years behind him at Groton and similarly gone from their parents' home most months. But they attended the inauguration and learned firsthand how their father's new job would affect them. Johnny enjoyed the fast life, and on the night of the inauguration went out partying. He returned late and somewhat the worse for his pleasures. The guard at the White House gate didn't know him, and Johnny carried no identification. The guard refused to wake the president or Mrs. Roosevelt for some kid who seemed to be playing a stupid prank, and he put Johnny off till morning, when his parents vouched for his identity. Not many days later Johnny got hungry in the evening. He went to the kitchen and tried to open the refrigerator, only to find it locked. "What kind of a joint is this?" he demanded of his mother. "You not only can't get past the gates, you can't even get into the icebox!"

Elliott Roosevelt remained in revolt against his parents. His first marriage—of an eventual five—was falling apart, and he blamed his father and mother and their lifestyle, and swore to have nothing to do with any of it. He kept his distance from the White House, visiting only when necessary.

Anna Roosevelt Dall's marriage—her first of three—was likewise collapsing; her response was to seek out her parents rather than shun them. She moved into the White House with her two children, who became the daily delight of their grandmother and especially their grandfather. The president began his mornings with breakfast in bed and the morning papers; he refused to receive visitors, even Eleanor, until he was finished. The only exceptions were the grandchildren, who were allowed to bounce on his bed and romp about the room, regardless of the disruption they caused to the president's concentration on matters of national or international importance.

James Roosevelt joined his mother and father and sister in the White House. James had married—for the first of four times—while Roosevelt was governor; his wife, Betsey Cushing, was one of three daughters of Harvey Cushing, America's most famous neurosurgeon. The Cushing girls were celebrated for their beauty and the prominence of the men they married—a group that included, besides James Roosevelt, Vincent Astor (owner of the yacht that had carried Franklin to Florida before the inauguration), William Paley (founder and longtime chairman of CBS), and Jock Whitney (publisher of the *New York Herald Tribune* and eventual American ambassador to Britain). The wedding of James and Betsey recapitulated in certain respects the wedding of Franklin and Eleanor. Franklin stole the show from the bride and groom, who were left standing alone as the guests gathered around the popular New York governor and leading candidate for the presidency.

Franklin's fondness for Betsey doubtless encouraged him to invite James to come live at the White House after the inauguration. James had provided indispensable assistance during the campaign, physically supporting Roosevelt at campaign stops, serving as subliminal proof of his virility, and providing a foil for his jokes. "This is my little boy, Jimmy," Roosevelt would say, laughing, while looking up at his son, who was a couple inches taller than he was. Invariably Roosevelt would add, "I have more hair than he has!"—at which the gradually balding James would merely smile good-naturedly while the crowd applauded his father's cleverness. Roosevelt wanted to keep James around, and so asked him to join the administration in an informal capacity. "It was an ambiguous sort of arrangement," James recalled. "I had no official status, no salary." James weighed the offer carefully. After a slow start on his career, he was finally making some money in the insurance business. He had Betsey and their small child to support. And he had debts from a chronically spendthrift lifestyle. "I was, as usual, pretty much behind the financial eight-ball," he admitted. Roosevelt offered to pay him out of his own pocket, but James thought such an arrangement sounded too much like an allowance, and he turned it down. But he accepted the rest of his father's offer. "I was intoxicated by the excitement of the campaign I had just been through with him, and I was keen to learn more about politics and government. I knew that stirring events were ahead, and nothing could have kept me from taking advantage of the ringside seat he offered me." So the three moved into the White House as the permanent guests of Franklin and Eleanor.

❖ ❖ ❖

*T*HE WHITE HOUSE became the new home of Louis Howe as well. For the man who had labored for twenty years to make Roosevelt president, the election victory was bittersweet. "I guess I've worked myself out of a job," he said half jokingly—but half seriously. Both Howe and Roosevelt knew that without Howe Roosevelt might never have reached the White House. But now that Roosevelt was *in* the White House, Howe's role was unclear. For a time the press delighted in depicting him as the manipulator behind the throne. "Colonel Howe," he was called, in reference to Wilson's éminence grise, Edward House. Howe accepted the plaudits even as he understood that his hold on Roosevelt was weakening. The more powerful Roosevelt became, the more he attracted powerful people to him. Howe might get elbowed aside.

His uncertain health compounded his problems. The respiratory and heart troubles that had afflicted him for years got worse. His mind was as sharp as ever, and his wit as wicked. But he lacked the stamina for the major initiatives that obviously lay ahead. No one told him he was dying; no one had to. And no one knew whether death would come in six months or six years. But it was coming, and Roosevelt would have been foolish to lean too heavily on a reed that was about to break.

Roosevelt wasn't foolish, yet neither was he hard-hearted. Besides, he knew that Howe, even in his diminished state, could provide him something that would be in decreasing supply in the months ahead—and would be the more valuable for its scarcity. Louis Howe was the last person who could call Roosevelt a fool to his face. The only other person who might have done so was Eleanor, but for all the reasons that made their marriage so complicated, she always felt she had to work by indirection. Howe regularly informed Roosevelt he was being pig-headed. He sent subordinates to Roosevelt's office with instructions: "Tell the president to go to hell." On one occasion Roosevelt exasperated Howe and then left to take a swim. "I hope to God you drown!" Howe shouted after him.

There was never any question that Howe would be part of the White House family. Eleanor set aside the Lincoln Bedroom for him, and he moved his meager belongings in. His wife, Grace, had relocated to Fall River, Massachusetts, and become something of a political force in the southern part of the Bay State. She and the children visited Washington occasionally—more frequently as Howe grew sicker—but their lives evolved separately from his.

As a representative of the president, Howe felt obliged to improve his manners and appearance. He still smoked his Sweet Caporals, and he still played the horses. But he brushed the ashes aside when reporters from the major dailies and magazines dropped by for an interview, and he had his suit pressed when a photo with the president was on the schedule. While he felt well enough to get out, he drove around Washington in a big Lincoln sedan equipped with a short-wave radio that filled up the rear seat and allowed him to eavesdrop on conversations momentous and trivial. The Secret Service worried, after the attempt on Roosevelt's life, that persons close to the president might be in danger. Lacking the manpower to guard Howe and the persuasiveness to keep him from his rounds, the agency issued him a revolver for self-defense. The license that accompanied the weapon, identifying Howe as a "special operative," gratified his sense of the absurd.

❖ ❖ ❖

*M*ISSY LEHAND completed the live-in portion of the White House family. She had been with Roosevelt for thirteen years and had abandoned all semblance of a normal life in order to serve him. She was too busy for suitors, too old for many of them, and uninterested anyway. She had followed Roosevelt to Florida, Warm Springs, and Albany, and there was no question that she would move to Washington with him, nor any that she would live in the White House—and be on duty around the clock. Her universe was bounded by her bedroom on the third floor, near the bedrooms of Anna's children, and her office on the first, next to the president's office. She handled Roosevelt's most important correspondence, diverting lesser missives to Grace Tully and other assistants. She drafted many of Roosevelt's replies, instructed merely by a nod of his head or a wave of his hand. She often lunched with Eleanor, leaving Franklin to Howe or official visitors. She frequently attended state dinners. "She is one of the best groomed women in Washington and attractive, with her soft gray hair bringing out the youthful contours of her face," a capital columnist noted. She almost never spoke to the press, partly because she didn't want to, partly because Roosevelt preferred that she not, and partly because she gave reporters nothing they could use. Her rare quoted comments reflected credit upward. "One never seems to be working hard with the Roosevelts because they work so much harder than anybody else," she self-effacingly said.

❖ ❖ ❖

*A*S FOR THE MAN who had brought them all there, he settled into the White House and quickly made himself at home. He knew he would be living there for four years; he hoped for eight. He didn't imagine he would spend the rest of his life there. He shared the public parts of the building with the American people, and the residence with Eleanor, Anna, James, Louis, and the rest of the White House family. But two rooms on the second floor were his private sanctum, open to others only by invitation—with the exception of Louis, who allowed no door to come between him and Franklin.

Frances Perkins remembered the president's bedroom. "A little too large to be cozy, it was not large enough to be impressive," she wrote.

> A heavy dark wardrobe stood against a wall. (There are no closets in the White House and wardrobes are necessary.) A marble mantelpiece of the Victorian type carved with grapes held a collection of miniature pigs—Mexican pigs, Irish pigs, pigs of all kinds, sizes, and colors. Snapshots of children, friends, and expeditions were propped up in back of the pigs. There was an old bureau between the windows, with a plain white towel on top and the things men need for their dressing arrangements. There was an old-fashioned rocking chair, often with a piece of clothing thrown over it.
>
> Then there was the bed—not the kind you would expect a president of the United States to have. Roosevelt used a small, narrow white iron bedstead, the kind one sees in the boy's room of many an American house. It had a thin, hard-looking mattress, a couple of pillows, and an ordinary white seersucker spread. A folded old gray shawl lay at the foot. "Just the right weight," the President once said. "Don't like these great heavy things." An old gray sweater, much the worse for wear, lay close at hand. He wore it over night clothes to keep his shoulders warm when he had a cold.
>
> A white painted table, the kind one often sees in bathrooms, stood beside the bed, with a towel over it and with aspirin, nose drops, a glass of water, stubs of pencils, bits of paper with telephone numbers, addresses, and memoranda to himself, a couple of books, a worn old prayer book, a watch, a package of cigarettes, an ash tray, a couple of telephones, all cluttered together. Hanging on the wall were a few pictures of the children and favorite familiar scenes. And over the door at the opposite end of the room hung a horse's tail. When one asked what that was, he would say, "Why, that's Gloucester's tail." Gloucester, a horse raised by the President's father, had been regarded by the family as one of the finest examples of horseflesh in the world.

Next to the bedroom was Roosevelt's study. John Adams, the building's first resident, had used the oval-shaped room as a parlor; on New Year's Day 1801 he and Abigail hosted a reception for their Washington neighbors and the citizens of the republic. Millard and Abigail Fillmore made the room into a library; Benjamin and Caroline Harrison installed the first White House

Christmas tree there. Roosevelt converted the room into his private study. Its formality softened, and then disappeared, beneath the clutter of books, knick-knacks, and personal treasures that followed him around. He had old friends join him there after hours, and also persons he hoped would become his new friends. Catholics were a vital Democratic constituency; Grace Tully recalled an afternoon with Cardinal Joseph Dougherty of Philadelphia. Roosevelt guessed that Tully, an Irish lass, would like to meet the cardinal, and he invited her to join them. "I'd love to, Mr. President," she responded, "but I'll follow in a few minutes. I must freshen up a bit."

"You're fine as you are, child," Roosevelt said. "Remember, this doesn't call for lipstick. He's a cardinal."

Tully ignored the president's remark. "Why not a dab of lipstick," she remembered asking herself. "Doesn't a cardinal wear red?" By the time she reached the study, the president and the cardinal were engaged in lively conversation. Eleanor and Anna were there, along with Anna's young son Johnny. Tully had heard that the cardinal was stout; in person he was more than stout. "Seated beside the president on a sofa, he was so relaxed that his chest seemed to reach his chin, and his stomach reminded me of a promontory much like the pictures of an outline map in our elementary geographies." Eleanor had the kitchen send up refreshments, which the cardinal obviously enjoyed. "While he talked he drank deeply of his tea and worked steadily at a serving of dainty sandwiches," Tully recalled. "Crumbs began to speckle the promontory of clerical cloth spreading across his ample front. . . . Despite my better intentions, I could not help but recall the legend of beloved St. Francis of Assisi dispensing bread to the birds."

The others noticed, too. Anna was tense throughout the visit, and upon the cardinal's departure she voiced her relief that he had gone.

"Why, Sis," Roosevelt responded, surprised. "I thought the old cardinal was grand."

"So did I," Anna said. But she explained that she was almost sure Johnny was going to come up to her and say, "Mummy, that fat man is spilling tea and crumbs all over his tummy. Shall I tell him?"

❖   ❖   ❖

Guests who came later in the day than Cardinal Dougherty were treated to Roosevelt's famous cocktails. The Democratic landslide of 1932 encouraged

Congress, even before Roosevelt's inauguration, to propose the repeal of Prohibition; the proposal went to the states and became the Twenty-first Amendment. Roosevelt had never taken Prohibition personally, but the repeal allowed him to practice his bartending craft more openly than he had in Florida and at Warm Springs during the 1920s. He liked to make a show of mixing drinks, and the more imbibers the better. His specialties were old-fashioneds, for which he squeezed each drinker's orange personally, and martinis, which Eleanor's brother Hall, on occasional visits to the White House, claimed the president didn't know the first thing about making. Hall, perhaps taking after his and Eleanor's deceased father, liked his martinis much stronger than Roosevelt mixed them. He thought, moreover, that olives were effete, and he flavored his martinis with onions instead.

Roosevelt's guests typically drank what he served them, but the regulars got what they wanted. Grace Tully drank rum during the summer and preferred her old-fashioneds made with scotch rather than bourbon. "I've never heard of such a thing," Roosevelt said when Tully requested the substitution. "It's absolutely sacrilegious." But he poured her the scotch. Harry Hopkins insisted on whiskey sours, which Roosevelt ordered from the kitchen. Henry Morgenthau didn't like his liquor diluted at all. "What does a fellow have to do around her to get a real drink?" he complained. Roosevelt feigned exasperation. "Ring for Lucas and tell him what you want, Henry," the president said. "We want you to be happy."

Roosevelt wasn't as good a bartender as he fancied himself, but his concoctions were generally drinkable. Not always, though. Princess Marthé of Norway visited Washington and brought the president a bottle of aquavit, the fiery staple her compatriots relied on to keep the Scandinavian winter at bay. Some while later Roosevelt asked Tully what she wanted to drink that evening. How about a martini? he suggested. She said that would be fine. Arthur Prettyman, the president's valet, brought the ingredients and Roosevelt mixed them. "This will put hair on your chest," he said, handing her the drink.

Tully took a sip. "Mr. President, that's horrible!" she said. "It will take all the hair *off* your chest," she said.

He tested the drink and whistled at its strength. He looked at the bottle and discovered that Prettyman had brought the aquavit rather than the gin. They laughed, and Tully told the story on her boss for years.

The cocktail hour was sacred as a respite from work. Roosevelt called it the "children's hour"; serious discussion ceased and the talk turned light and even frivolous. Guests who violated the custom were quickly made to appreciate their mistake. Yet Eleanor never caught on—or perhaps she simply refused to honor her husband's preference. She would bring him correspondence she wanted him to read or would raise issues she thought he needed to consider. Sometimes he would put her off, and even when he acquiesced he did so in a way that indicated his annoyance that she was intruding on the scant time he had away from work. She found the experience fruitful enough to bear repeating, but it did nothing good for their personal relationship.

❖   ❖   ❖

Roosevelt's study included a desk by the door to the bedroom. Here he occasionally read but more often worked on his stamp collection. He had acquired his first stamps as a boy, and he added to his inventory each time he and his parents traveled overseas. When friends or relatives wrote home from abroad, he saved the stamps. His circle of philatelic sources expanded gradually as he matured and exponentially after he became president. He inquired of the State Department what it did with the envelopes containing mail from foreign governments and was told that most were thrown away, although the stamp collectors on the department's staff rescued the rare specimens. He indicated that he would like some of the good ones held for himself. Thereafter he received a weekly package from the State Department, delivered by courier each Saturday. He would spend much of that day and often part of the next examining the new items, investigating their origins, and inserting them in his albums. He supplemented these free additions with purchases made through agents and at auctions. His tastes grew more expensive over time, until he decided he'd have to specialize. He chose the Western Hemisphere and devoted himself to the stamps of Central and South America. But dignitaries from all over the world, once apprised that the president liked stamps, would bring him the best of their countries' postal art, and he never turned the gifts down.

When he wasn't working on his stamps, he often played solitaire. He preferred a two-deck variant with ten cards showing. He called it "Spider," for reasons no one could remember. He played by himself, though he enjoyed company while he worked his way through the decks. Missy and Grace sometimes played double solitaire beside him; they would play and chat while he smoked and played silently.

* * *

$\mathcal{R}$OOSEVELT'S WHITE HOUSE day typically began a bit past eight. Arthur Prettyman would bring breakfast and a stack of morning newspapers. Roosevelt scanned the front pages and read the editorials of the papers, which generally included the *New York Times* and *Herald Tribune,* the *Washington Post* and *Times-Herald,* the *Baltimore Sun,* and the *Chicago Tribune.* Later in the day he would peruse clippings compiled for him by the White House staff and still later would examine the major evening papers readily available in the capital: the *New York World-Telegram, Journal American,* and *Sun* and the *Washington Evening Star* and *Daily News.* Most of the time he read the opinions of the editors with the practiced calm of the career politician. Occasionally, however, something struck him as unusually outrageous. "It's a damn lie from start to finish," he would bellow, tearing the offending piece from its page and handing it to Steve Early. The president's press secretary would deal with the matter himself or remind Roosevelt to address the issue at his next press conference, if he hadn't by then thought better of doing so.

Breakfast and the papers required about an hour. At nine thirty Early, Louis Howe, and one or more of the assistants who joined the administration—including, over time, Marvin McIntyre, Edwin "Pa" Watson, Jimmy Roosevelt, and William Hassett—would come in to discuss the day's schedule and any difficulties it might entail. Sometimes a member of the cabinet with a particularly pressing problem would arrive and be shown in. Less frequently the president would receive members of Congress in his bedroom.

The official day began at ten thirty. Roosevelt, having dressed and shaved, would take the elevator to the first floor and be wheeled to the Oval Office. If it was a Friday he would meet with the press. The balance of the morning was typically filled with appointments. Visitors arrived on the quarter hour, but the schedule often fell afoul of Roosevelt's inability to keep his visitors—or, more commonly, himself—from talking too long. Pa Watson or Grace Tully would stand at the door looking cross; Roosevelt would ignore the signal or take it as the excuse to send the visitor along.

Roosevelt's morning lasted until one, when he ate lunch at his desk. If Henrietta Nesbitt, the head of the White House staff and the dictatress of the president's diet, was in a good mood, he would get something he liked, perhaps calf's liver and bacon, or creamed chicken, followed by chocolate pudding or pie. More often he made do with hash and a poached egg.

If it was a Wednesday, the afternoon would include a press conference. The alternation between morning conferences on Friday and afternoon sessions on Wednesday was designed to ensure that neither the morning papers nor the evening papers had a regular advantage in reporting breaking news from the White House. More meetings would ensue—the cabinet typically convened on Thursdays—followed by correspondence in the late afternoon. Quite often Roosevelt would simply sign letters Missy had drafted. When he opted to compose letters himself, Grace would generally take the dictation, as Missy didn't like to. Grace recalled Roosevelt's style:

> When the President was deep in thought during dictation, he would frequently tap his fingers on the arm of his chair. But when his mind was made up on a phrase or a course of action his customary gesture was to stretch out his arms and place his hands flat on the top of his desk. "Now I've got it." That was the gesture of finality. Often while dictating he would push his chair back a bit, grab hold of a trouser leg at the knee, swing the leg over his other knee, and fold his hands. Occasionally he would drop both arms and swing them by his chair while he dictated.

The afternoon's work would end with a swim in the pool constructed in the White House basement with funds from supporters who wanted the president's physical therapy to continue or with a rubdown by the masseur the navy assigned to the president. Roosevelt would meet with Ross McIntire, the White House physician, for symptomatic treatment of his chronic sinus condition.

The cocktail hour came next, followed by dinner. Formal dinners were held in the public rooms on the first floor of the White House; informal dinners took place in the family dining room on the first floor or in the study upstairs. After dinner Roosevelt might prepare a speech or tidy up some additional correspondence. Sometimes he worked on his stamps or watched a movie. His favorite actress was Myrna Loy. He kept his preference in film stars within the White House family, in part because Loy was said to have been the favorite actress as well of John Dillinger, the notorious bank robber who was shot to death in Chicago after leaving a Loy film. Roosevelt tried to get her to visit the White House, but on the one occasion when she did so, he was out of the country. "Well, what was she like?" he asked upon his return.

24.

As AMERICANS TURNED OFF THEIR SETS FOLLOWING ROOSEVELT'S first radio address, they appreciated that their fate was in different hands than it had been in eight days before. The comparative few who could knowledge-ably assess the mechanics of the new banking system understood how little it differed from the old one. The banks remained in private hands. They con-tinued to rely on the confidence of depositors. The government supervision in-volved in the reorganization was modest in scope and temporary in duration. One observer who thought the president should have gone further remarked, "The president drove the money changers out of the Capitol on March 4th, and they were all back on the 9th." Ray Moley, speaking from the inside, thought the result had taken longer but was hardly more earth-shaking. Wearily congratulating himself and Will Woodin—and of course Roosevelt—he asserted, "Capitalism was saved in eight days."

On March 12 that remained to be seen. But what was coming into plain view was that capitalism was under new political management. From the shift-ing tones of the campaign, it had been impossible to tell whether Roosevelt would be the scourge of capitalism or its savior. The evidence of his first eight days suggested that he was more the latter than the former. Alongside the bank bill, Roosevelt sent to Congress a request for authority to slash the federal budget. Shaking his finger at the deficits accumulated and projected by the Hoover administration's budgets—a total of $5 billion by the end of 1934—Roosevelt declared, "With the utmost seriousness I point out to the Congress the profound effect of this fact upon our national economy. It has contributed to the recent collapse of our banking structure. It has accentuated the stagna-tion of the economic life of our people. It has added to the ranks of the un-employed." These evils would continue until drastic economies in government were effected.

Roosevelt's call to cut federal spending was intimately connected to the emergency bank law. The new currency issue was to be based on government bonds, which like everything else in economic life would be less valuable— and in this case less inspiring of the confidence essential to the bank plan—the more of them there were. Roosevelt signaled his purpose in the name he gave to the spending measure: "A Bill to Maintain the Credit of the United States Government."

But Roosevelt contended that economy in government spoke to a larger issue. "Too often in history, liberal governments have been wrecked on the rocks of loose fiscal policy. We must avoid this danger." Putting the government's house in order was the prerequisite to everything else. "National recovery depends upon it." Before long the image of Roosevelt as budget slasher would appear quaintly ironic, even ludicrous. But at the outset of his administration he was deadly earnest, and perfectly plausible. Later generations would equate liberalism with largesse in government, but that was chiefly the legacy of Franklin Roosevelt. Members of Roosevelt's own generation, the children of the Progressive era, were as likely to view government spending with concern as with favor. The progressives complained that government spent too lavishly on business and other private interests, whether directly through subsidies of such endeavors as railroad construction or indirectly via the tariff. Postwar liberals looked askance at the tariff and at the trade-promotion activities of Hoover's Commerce Department, whose very headquarters— "that great marble building which is facetiously called in Washington the 'Temple of Fact Finding,' which cost the people considerably more than the Capitol of the United States," Roosevelt said during the campaign—symbolized the government's care and feeding of capitalism.

In any event, when Roosevelt asked for authority to cut the federal budget, people took him seriously. The primary complaint, in fact, of those who questioned the measure was that he would cut too deeply. Roosevelt contended that the fall in prices since 1929 justified a corresponding decrease in the salaries of government workers, and he requested the authority to cut federal pay by 15 percent—including his own pay, which would fall from ninety thousand dollars per year to seventy-five thousand. Not surprisingly, the thought of smaller salaries alarmed civil servants and political appointees and all of those who depended on them in every village, city, and state of the Union. No less dismayed were the armies of military veterans currently or prospectively on government pensions. Veterans were to American politics after the Civil War and again after the World War what the elderly would be to American politics in later decades (again courtesy of Roosevelt): a well-organized constituency with narrow, clearly articulated interests. After each of the big wars, and to a lesser extent after the Spanish-American War, the vets had persuaded Congress to expand the size of pensions and the ranks of the eligible. Presidents sometimes vetoed the measures—Grover Cleveland in the 1880s, Hoover in 1932—but the veterans always came back.

This was why Roosevelt wanted the power to cut the pensions unilaterally. The president's budget bill was a power grab, but it was a power grab with a purpose and a justification. Roosevelt couldn't expect Congress to stand up to the vets; it hadn't stood up to them in the past. The individual members were too exposed politically. "If you don't support this bill, your successor will," lobbyists for the American Legion, the primary veterans' group, told lawmakers whenever a pension measure came up; and experience proved them right. The president was better able to withstand the pressure, primarily because narrow, single issues rarely determine presidential contests. Roosevelt was willing to take the punishment for cutting pensions.

First, though, he had to get the authority he wanted. The American Legion issued a call to political arms against the president. "Wire your congressmen and senators immediately opposing Congress abdicating its constitutional responsibility by granting to the President authority to repeal or amend existing veterans' laws without approval of Congress," the Legion urged its members. Many thousands responded, prompting their representatives in Congress to denounce the budget bill as unconstitutional and unfair. Gardner Withrow, a Progressive from Wisconsin, reminded his colleagues in the House that spending was the prerogative of the legislature; if Congress gave the president the authority he wanted, the House and Senate might as well "shut the doors of the chambers and go home." John Rankin, the Mississippi Democrat who headed the House committee on veterans' affairs, complained that the government, through the Reconstruction Finance Corporation, found money to coddle capitalists "who ought to be in the penitentiary today"; the least it could do was look after the vets. "This is not the time, nor is it just, to make the veteran bear the bulk of this depression burden," Rankin said. Wright Patman, the author of the 1932 bill to pay the bonus early, thought the president was hauling water for the rich. "The Morgans, Millses, and Mitchells are those who will benefit by such legislation," the Texas Democrat declared.

But the dissenters were a minority. Most members were sufficiently traditional in their economic thinking to believe the budget ought to be balanced and sufficiently fearful of the vets and the postal clerks to be glad for Roosevelt to assume responsibility for cutting their pensions and pay. "It will be exercised in a spirit of justice to all, of sympathy to those who are in need, and of maintaining inviolate the basic welfare of the United States," the president promised. Large majorities in both houses—266 to 138 in the House, 62 to 13 in the Senate—took him at his word.

❖ ❖ ❖

ℛOOSEVELT'S BUDGET victory positioned him, for the moment at least, to the fiscal right of Hoover. Roosevelt would do what Hoover had been unwilling or unable to do. The capitalists could only applaud, if tentatively.

Yet Roosevelt's style was nothing like that of the capitalist-friendly administrations that had gone before. The style of Coolidge and Hoover was institutional and stand-offish; the style of Roosevelt was intensely personal. Roosevelt didn't ask Congress to cut the budget; he asked Congress to let *him* cut the budget. He spoke to the American people directly, asking them to trust *him*. He identified himself with the people when he said, in his Fireside Chat on the banking crisis, "It is your problem no less than it is mine." And he proposed a partnership with the people when he promised, "Together we cannot fail."

Americans responded to the Roosevelt style. As the banks reopened during the week after he spoke, millions of Americans took their money out from under those mattresses and returned it to their banks. Anxious others who had been prevented from withdrawing their deposits only by the bank holiday decided to leave their money where it was. As much as a billion dollars returned to the banks by the end of March, out of a circulation of around $7.5 billion. Gold, too, began flowing back into the banks and the Treasury—more than 600 million dollars in gold coin and gold certificates by month's end—as holders rebalanced their portfolios between the security of gold and the convenience of other forms of money.

The praise for Roosevelt's handling of the crisis was overwhelming. The *Philadelphia Inquirer* cheered Roosevelt's "courageous" action. The *Atlanta Constitution* admired the president's "bold and straight-from-the-shoulder" approach. The *Cleveland Plain Dealer* declared, "Mr. Roosevelt leads, as he was elected to lead. Congress responds. The country responds. The nation and the world applaud." The *Portland Oregonian* saw the president's plan as providing an "impetus toward permanent recovery." The *Wall Street Journal* asserted, "Last week marked an end to three years of a nation's drifting from bad to worse, an end to helpless acceptance of a malign fate. . . . For an explanation of the incredible change which has come over the face of things here in the United States in a single week we must look to the fact that the new Administration in Washington has superbly risen to the occasion." William Randolph Hearst, who had opposed Roosevelt earlier and would oppose him again, for now joined the chorus. "I guess at your next election we will make it unanimous," the press lord said.

Roosevelt might have taken time to savor the praise had the banks and the budget been the sum of the nation's woes. But stanching the hemorrhage of money merely made the less acute symptoms more obvious. The new currency the Federal Reserve had printed and begun to distribute proved largely unnecessary; the bank recovery left most of it languishing in the vaults—where it did nothing to ease the downward pressure on prices that was the most painful aspect of the depression for such price-sensitive groups as farmers. For this reason, among those relatively few observers and pundits who withheld their praise following Roosevelt's bank rescue, the principal complaint was that it left deflation unaddressed. "If this currency results in raising prices out of their present abnormally low stage," the *San Francisco Chronicle* remarked, before events rendered the new notes superfluous, "that will be most welcome. A price increase is the prime factor to lift us out of depression."

Deflation was an economywide problem, but because of their chronic indebtedness it hit farmers the hardest. Roosevelt had long commiserated with farmers, and even before the success of the bank rescue was assured, he turned to the farm question. There were two ways of dealing with low prices. One was to expand the money supply. This strategy was what the Populists and silver Democrats led by William Jennings Bryan had advocated in the 1890s with their call for remonetizing silver. They lost their fight in the election of 1896, and the country had officially embraced the gold standard—after decades of observing a de facto version—in 1900. Some silver-state Westerners still agitated for silver, but the first step in any systematic expansion of the money supply would be the abandonment of the gold standard.

The second way to raise prices for farm products was to curtail the supply. This approach posed problems of its own. There were millions of American farmers, and most prided themselves on their independence of mind; to get them to cooperate in reducing production would be exceedingly difficult. It would be all the more difficult on account of the fact that as much as cooperation might benefit the cooperators, it would benefit non-cooperators even more. The non-cooperators—the farmers who did *not* curtail production while others did—would profit from the higher prices without losing from reduced volume. Economics called such non-cooperators "free riders," and they would ride a poorly designed program all the way to the bank.

The effects of the low farm prices were heart-rending. Hundreds of thousands of farmers couldn't make their mortgage payments; scores of thousands lost their homes along with their sources of livelihood. Tens of thousands took to the roads, hoping for something better somewhere else. Farm tenants—renters—lacked security entirely. Lucky farmers who held on to their farms and lived in those regions that still practiced mixed agriculture could feed themselves from the garden plot and the orchard, but across vast swaths of the Midwest and California, where industrial monoculture had set in decades before, farm babies and children went hungry amid mountains of unsold wheat and unharvested corn.

Often the foreclosed farmers watched in helpless silence as their fields and homes fell under the auctioneer's hammer, but sometimes they protested, on occasion violently. They and their friends would come armed to the auctions, intimidating potential purchasers. Others refused to be evicted, clutching the common-law principle that a man's home is his castle and defying the bank's agent, the tax man, or the new owner to storm it. When they gathered at crossroads stores and in Grange halls they spoke ominously of taking matters into their own hands. Those who recalled their history lessons cited Daniel Shays and the Whiskey Rebels of the eighteenth century.

Roosevelt heard of the helplessness and the militancy both. "Pathetic letters are coming in from the farm women," Henry Wallace reported. "I suppose that the most terrible cases of heart sickness and fear in the United States today are those of a tenant farm family where the rent cannot be paid, where eviction is imminent, and where there is not enough machinery and equipment to make it possible for the family to go on another farm. The situation of these people is even more desperate than that of the unemployed in the cities." John Simpson, the president of the Farmers' Union, wrote Roosevelt not long before the inauguration to explain that the countryside was about to explode. "My candid opinion," Simpson told the president-elect, "is that unless you call a special session of Congress, after the fourth of March, and start a revolution in government affairs, there will be one started in the country. It is just a question whether or not you get one started first."

Whether what Roosevelt had in mind for the farm economy was a revolution or not was a matter of semantics. But the centerpiece of his farm program was a dramatic departure from the unbridled competition among farmers that had fostered the uncontrollable overproduction that currently impoverished them all. Roosevelt intended to impose planning on the farm sector. The essential problem was too many fields and too many farmers; the solution was to reduce the number of both. Taking marginal fields out of production would be the first step; taking marginal farmers out of the business would follow.

But neither step would come easily. As chaotic as the farm sector was economically, it was almost as anarchic politically. Not all wheat farmers thought alike, and they certainly didn't think like cotton farmers or hog raisers or dairymen or apple growers. Farm owners often opposed what benefited farm tenants; farm processors found themselves at odds with farm producers. Each group had its spokesmen, some more persuasive and better connected than others.

Had Roosevelt known agriculture well, he might have imposed a design of his own on farm reform. But though he had long considered himself a friend of the farmer, and even postured as a farmer himself on political occasions, he recognized the limits of his expertise. Besides, for him to take a strong position would prematurely alienate those groups that didn't get what they wanted. Alienation for some would happen inevitably, but the longer it could be delayed, the better the chance of passing a farm bill. Clifford Gregory, the editor of the Chicago-based *Prairie Farmer,* the oldest and arguably most important organ of the farmers, recalled a meeting with then-candidate Roosevelt, who explained the approach he would take. "I am going to call farmers' leaders together," Roosevelt said, "lock them in a room, and tell them not to come out until they have agreed on a plan."

Roosevelt tapped Henry Morgenthau and Rex Tugwell as his liaisons with the farm leaders, who gathered in Washington several weeks after the election. Tugwell described the first steps toward building a consensus: "Things were complicated by each of the farm leaders having a program of his own. This was true also of many agricultural representatives in Congress. . . . They had to make speeches defending their own position, to read their own proposals (many of which were already in bill form, already introduced), but Morgenthau and I sat tight and listened. The general result after two days of this was that they agreed unanimously (though some of them merely came in for political reasons and could hardly be counted on)."

What they agreed on was what became the Agricultural Adjustment Act, albeit with considerably more difficulty than Tugwell anticipated. By the time of Roosevelt's inauguration, planting season had begun in the South, and any measure that aimed to curtail production was almost too late already. Roosevelt reconvened the farm leaders for a one-day session on March 10; they confirmed the essence of their earlier agreement and recommended measures that became the basis for the bill he sent to Congress a few days later. Its essence was "domestic allotment," a scheme for reducing the farm surpluses by paying farmers not to produce oversupplied commodities. To those outside the farm sector the concept seemed bizarrely counterintuitive, but to farmers themselves it made sense. They were to cut production, thereby reducing the crops they would have for sale. Perhaps market prices would rise to offset the reduced volume, but perhaps not. They ought to be paid for taking the risk. The logical alternative to paying farmers not to produce was to *compel* them not to produce. Besides being unconstitutional this was politically impossible. Roosevelt's farm bill would create an agriculture administration, which would do the same kind of culling of agriculture that Roosevelt's bank examiners were doing for banking. The farm administration would determine how much of each commodity America's farmers should produce, and it would establish payment schedules to meet those targets.

Domestic allotment was controversial even among farmers, and in order to get the farm leaders on board it was balanced by other initiatives. For decades farmers had wanted the federal government to purchase surplus crops and market them overseas; such a provision was written into the Roosevelt bill. Farmers pleaded for debt relief, arguing that interest rates that had been reasonable before the depression were killing them now; the Roosevelt program promised help on debt, albeit vaguely.

❖   ❖   ❖

CURTAILING PRODUCTION would tend to raise farm prices, but not as fast or surely as increasing the money supply. Diehard populists like Oklahoma Democrat Elmer Thomas contended that every other effort would be wasted unless the president did something about money. Roosevelt's farm bill passed the House in mere days and by an overwhelming margin—315 to 98. But Thomas stalled its progress in the Senate by proposing an amendment authorizing the president to expand the money supply by remonetizing silver, redefining the relationship between the dollar and gold, or reissuing the kind of fiat currency—"greenbacks"—that had circulated during and after the Civil War.

Roosevelt had known that the money question would come up, but he had hoped to keep it separate from the farm issue. The Thomas amendment made this impossible—as Thomas knew it would. The Oklahoma senator felt an obligation not merely to farmers but to the people of America generally. "No permanent relief is possible until the masses have buying power," he declared. The way to give them buying power was to put money in their hands.

On this point opinions differed—as vigorously as they had since Bryan and McKinley slugged it out over silver in the 1890s. Hoover had lost the election but still garnered 40 percent of the popular vote. Not everyone who voted for him backed the gold standard with his devotion, but neither did everyone who voted for Roosevelt want him to sever the dollar's tie to gold. (The million Americans who together voted for Socialist Norman Thomas or Communist William Foster presumably had less reverence for gold than Republicans or many Democrats, but one could never be sure.)

Elmer Thomas's maneuver compelled Roosevelt to take a position on money sooner than he had intended. Roosevelt accepted the Thomas amendment, noting, however, that it only *authorized* the president to devalue the dollar. It did not *require* him to do so. "Purely discretionary" was how Roosevelt, speaking at a press conference, characterized his prospective power to expand the money supply. The Thomas amendment provided various methods of achieving inflation. "I do not have to use any of them," Roosevelt said.

He wasn't opposed in principle to inflation. On April 5, before the Thomas amendment came to a vote in the Senate, Roosevelt employed his new authority under the banking act to order private possessors of gold to surrender their yellow metal for currency. "The chief purpose of the order," he explained, "is to restore to the country's reserves gold held for hoarding and the withholding of which under existing conditions does not promote the public interest." Roosevelt failed to specify, in the moment, just *how* his gold seizure would serve the public interest; several years later he was more forthcoming. "This order served to prevent the accumulation of private gold hoards in the United States," he said. "It served as a means for further strengthening our banking structure and preventing the possibility of a recurring threat." So far so good, and so innocuous. What followed was more controversial and was what the president kept quiet at the time. "It was the first step also to that complete control of all monetary gold in the United States, which was essential in order to give the government that element of freedom of action which was necessary as the very basis of its monetary goal and objective."

The administration's "monetary goal and objective" proved to be a managed currency, one freed of the constraints of gold. The gold order of April 5 was the first step; Roosevelt's acceptance of the Thomas amendment two weeks later was a second. "Congratulate me. We are off the gold standard," he told his economic advisers. Some of them sighed with relief; others spluttered with indignation. Lewis Douglas, the president's budget director, was among the latter. "This is the end of western civilization," he prophesied, only partly in black jest. Will Woodin lamented, "What's a secretary of the Treasury to do when he's presented with a fait accompli?" Roosevelt explained that his acceptance of the Thomas amendment was tactical. "He said that the reason for the amendment was that unless something of this sort was done immediately, Congress would take the matter in its own hands and legislate mandatory law instead of permissive," James Warburg, an adviser to Woodin, recalled.

Roosevelt may have overstated the hazard of a congressional diktat, but the result of the Thomas amendment, which passed the Senate in slightly revised form, and the House shortly thereafter, was to augment the president's power over the money supply. As an indication of what he would do with the added power, he issued an executive order on April 20 forbidding the export of gold without license from the Treasury. More permanently than anything till now, Roosevelt's embargo cut the dollar adrift from gold. The president subsequently defended this action as "designed for the purpose of gaining for the American dollar freedom—freedom at home from the threat of instability, and freedom abroad for the beginning of a new realignment to the other currencies of the world." But this was a rhetorical cloak, and a thin one at that. The freedom that interested Roosevelt was his own freedom to revalue the dollar in keeping with his broader designs for the political economy as a whole.

The Thomas amendment broke the impasse on the farm bill, to the discomfiture of conservative Republicans. Joseph Martin of Massachusetts thought the bill gave entirely too much power to the administration. "When you send out this army of tax gatherers to tell the farmer what he can plant and what he can sell, you are well on the road to Moscow," Martin declared. Michael Hart of Michigan cited a comment by Rex Tugwell, years earlier, that Russia's experiments in agriculture held lessons for America. Hart rejected the professor's latest brainstorm, the farm bill, saying, "I am not going to follow communism." James Beck of Pennsylvania thought a different country provided an apter analogy. "The only argument in favor of this bill is that it is an emergency proposition," the Republican representative said. "That is a most damnable thing, and in Germany, with the same excuse, they are voting power today to Hitler."

Yet the dissenters were a small minority. The farm bill passed the Senate on a vote of 64 to 20. The measure the president signed on May 12, after reconciliation of the House and Senate versions, created the Agricultural Adjustment Administration, which supervised the domestic allotment program. The fight in the Senate over the money question had pushed the initial implementation of the program well into the growing season and produced precisely what Roosevelt had hoped to avoid: the deliberate destruction of crops and livestock in the name of the new federal program. Roosevelt recognized that paying farmers to do nothing would be controversial enough, but paying them to plow up cotton and kill pigs and pregnant cows, while hunger still threatened the land, could be a public relations disaster. As things happened, the administration weathered the storm, chiefly because farmers were desperate for anything that would relieve their plight. But the AAA never entirely got out from under the cloud that shadowed its birth, and when critics of the New Deal adduced evidence against Roosevelt's programs, they often started with those dead pigs.

25.

$\mathcal{R}$OOSEVELT'S REMARK, DURING THE SUMMER OF 1932, THAT HOOVER'S harsh treatment of the Bonus Army had sealed the president's defeat in the election left something obvious unsaid: that the veterans would be back, to confront Hoover's successor. And so they were, in the spring of 1933. Most had been chastened by their defeat the previous summer; many showed the added strain of another several months of unemployment and hardship. Yet all were hopeful that a new and presumably more compassionate administration would give them a more sympathetic hearing.

The reception Roosevelt gave them differed completely from Hoover's. The president treated them not as potential revolutionaries but as honored guests. He ordered a camp prepared for them across the Potomac in Virginia and is-sued a special executive order to cover the cost of tents, latrines, showers, and mess halls serving three square meals a day. While he declined to meet with them personally—"You know," he said in answer to a press conference ques-tion whether he would visit the camp, "I have been working really day and night; I don't believe I can get off"—he did the next best thing. Eleanor Roo-sevelt had followed the vets' story for months; one afternoon Louis Howe asked her to take him for a drive. He needed to get out of the White House, he said, and a tour through the countryside would do him good. As it hap-pened—as Howe and Roosevelt had arranged—the tour took them to the vets' camp. "I was rather surprised," Eleanor recalled afterward. She was even more surprised when Howe announced that he was going to stay in the car. She must go talk to the vets by herself.

It was a brilliant touch. Ten months earlier Douglas MacArthur had led an armored column against the vets; on this afternoon Eleanor Roosevelt entered the camp alone. "Very hesitatingly, I got out and walked over to where I saw a line-up of men waiting for food," she remembered. "They looked me over curiously, and one of them asked my name and what I wanted. When I said I just wanted to see how they were getting on, they asked me to join them." Word that the First Lady was in camp spread rapidly, and the vets all gathered around. They gave her a tour of the camp, showing it off despite the day's rain and the season's mud. She shared their midday meal in the mess hall and spoke about how she had visited the front in 1919 and witnessed what they and their comrades had been through. "I never want to see another war," she said. "I would like to see fair consideration for everyone, and I shall always be grateful to those who served their country." She led the old soldiers—many of whom in fact were little older than her sons—in songs, including "There's a Long, Long Trail." She utterly disarmed them emotionally. "Good luck!" they shouted as she walked back to the car. "Good-bye and good luck to you!" she answered. One vet remarked afterward, still amazed: "Hoover sent the army; Roosevelt sent his wife."

❖   ❖   ❖

$\mathcal{R}$OOSEVELT ALSO SENT jobs. Eleanor's visit, besides foreshadowing the peculiar effectiveness the Roosevelt team of Franklin and Eleanor would develop, bought the president time to deal with the vets, by means of the New Deal reform that was closest to his heart. On March 14 Ray Moley relayed a query from Frances Perkins regarding a relief issue that had come before the new labor secretary. The president didn't answer the question at once. "Instead, he began to describe an idea to which, he said, he had given a lot of thought and which he'd formulated to his satisfaction only the night before," Moley remembered. "It was the stunning idea of putting an army of young men, recruited from the unemployed, to work in the forests and national parks." Roosevelt directed Moley to outline a program.

Stunning though the idea might have been to Moley, it was hardly original. Various states, including Roosevelt's New York, had put young men to work since the onset of the depression, as had certain foreign countries, including Germany and Italy. The Italian model of human organization was already unsavory and the German version would grow odious before long, but they and the state plans demonstrated what governments could do to mobilize the unemployed toward socially constructive ends. Roosevelt had promised something along these lines during the campaign and been ridiculed by the Republicans for utopian excess. But now that he was president, he moved to implement the concept. He summoned members of his cabinet to meet with congressional leaders; together they conceived a program that would enroll unemployed young men and send them off to the woods.

He shared his thinking with the press. "The idea is to put people to work in the national forests and on other government and state properties on work which would not otherwise be done—in other words, work that does not conflict with existing so-called public works," he said. A reporter asked how many people he had in mind. "On the national forests, the Forestry Bureau says two hundred thousand men," Roosevelt answered. The plan would be much more than make-work, although it would certainly provide employment. In the East, where the unemployment was greatest, nearly all the government timber land was second or third growth. The trees—saplings, in many cases—were small and overcrowded. Roosevelt's army of foresters would thin the stands, yielding cordwood today and lumber in the future. They would also build firebreaks, to keep forest fires from spreading.

Roosevelt mentioned the figure of a dollar a day as the wage the two hundred thousand conservation corpsmen would make. One reporter did some quick estimates. "I can see it will run into many millions of dollars," he said. "You would need half a billion or one billion on this one item." Where did the president propose to find the money?

Roosevelt dodged the question, declining to go into the details of a program that didn't yet exist. But speaking on background, he said, "These people would be people who are today on the dole. They are performing no useful work. Those are the only people we would take—people who are performing absolutely no work at all and just being barely supported by communities and states."

One of the reporters pointed out that most of the national forests were in the West. "That would involve a movement from the centers of population for the men to be put to work in those forests. Is that contemplated?"

In fact it was. Roosevelt had long believed that the American population was poorly distributed, with too many people in the East and too few in the West. He hoped the conservation corps would encourage some of those Easterners to relocate to the West. But such ambitious social engineering was more than he wished to share at the moment. "Haven't got to that yet," he said. "Can't tell you."

On March 21 Roosevelt submitted a bill to Congress. He emphasized that the conservation corps would not interfere with the normal labor markets and would confine itself to work on the public domain. The War and Labor departments would handle the logistics of identifying and enrolling 250,000 young men, training them, and transporting them to their work sites; the Interior and Agriculture departments would direct the actual work. The program would require no new funds at once; unspent public works monies would suffice for several months at least. The corps would benefit the public in several ways, Roosevelt said. It would conserve America's natural resources. It would improve the nation's public lands. Not least, it would strengthen the country's moral resources. "The overwhelming majority of unemployed Americans, who are now walking the streets and receiving private or public relief, would infinitely prefer to work," the president asserted. "We can take a vast army of these unemployed out into healthful surroundings. We can eliminate, to some extent at least, the threat that enforced idleness brings to spiritual and moral stability."

Not everyone bought into Roosevelt's vision. Most Republicans disliked anything that gave the Democratic president more power, and though none went so far as to predict that the corpsmen would become Roosevelt's equivalent of Mussolini's Black Shirts, they distrusted and resented the creation of a large class of impressionable young people dependent on the administration for a living. The Mussolini comparison, ironically, was left to the Democrats, including William Green, the president of the American Federation of Labor, who said the president's program smacked "of fascism, of Hitlerism, and in some respects of sovietism." Green told a joint session of the House and Senate labor committees that he objected to the dollar-a-day wage as undermining everything that organized labor had been struggling for. On a more philosophical level, he distrusted the military overtones of the president's scheme. "Labor is deeply apprehensive of this plan," Green said. "It dislikes the regimentation of these men in the army. Labor is always jealous of its rights to voluntary action."

Roosevelt didn't wish to get into a fight with Green, as organized labor was a critical Democratic constituency. But neither did he intend to let such a statement go unanswered. A reporter asked if the president cared to comment on the negative reaction from labor. "No, because I might seem to be answering Bill Green," Roosevelt said. "I will tell you, if you will write it in such a way that it does not appear as an answer to Bill Green. You might take it just for background." The reporters lowered their pens and listened. "In the first place, they all talk about military control and militarization, but that is just utter rubbish," Roosevelt said. "The camps will be run just like those in any other big project—Boulder Dam or anything like that. Obviously you have to have some form of policing. In other words, you cannot allow a man in a dormitory to get up in the middle of the night and blow a bugle." This drew the desired laugh. "You have got to have order, just perfectly normal order that you would have in any kind of big job. That is so much for the military end."

As to the conservation corps disrupting the labor market, Roosevelt said, nothing could be more ridiculous. "This is not competition, because these fellows have no chance to get a job at the present time, and 250,000 men, as Arthur Brisbane"—a Hearst columnist—"pointed out this morning in his column, is a mere drop in the bucket. It is just a little step toward the relieving of 12 million people, but it is a practical step." Regarding the wage rate: "To be sure, they are to be paid only a dollar a day, but it costs the government another dollar a day to take care of them. . . . A two-dollar-a-day wage for that type of work would probably be higher in a great many places than what labor is actually paid." That really *would* disrupt the labor market. Roosevelt cited his own experience as an employer of unskilled workers in Georgia. "In 1929 their pay was about $1.50 or $1.75 a day with no quarters, no food, no clothing." And wages had fallen considerably since 1929.

The Senate approved Roosevelt's conservation corps bill on a voice vote after cursory debate. The House spent longer with it, largely because of labor's opposition. Representatives proposed various amendments; one that stuck was sponsored by Oscar De Priest of Illinois, who in 1928 had become the first African American elected to the House in three decades. De Priest specified that the conservation corps must not discriminate on account of race, color, or creed. Almost no one else would have sponsored such an amendment, but De Priest having done so, few wished to go on record as opposing it. The amended bill passed the House and was reconciled with the Senate's version, and on March 31 Roosevelt signed the law creating the Civilian Conservation Corps.

❖ ❖ ❖

*T*HE ROOTS OF the Securities Act of 1933 lay in the same progressive soil that motivated much else about the New Deal. Samuel Untermyer had come to national prominence as the antagonist of J. P. Morgan in the 1912 Pujo Committee hearings into the money trust. Untermyer, as counsel to the committee, probed, prodded, and embarrassed the great financier, who refused to admit not simply wrongdoing but almost any doing at all, on grounds that his private business was none of Untermyer's or the public's business. Morgan left the hearings in a huff, sailed for Europe on his annual art-buying vacation, and dropped dead in Italy. While the art sellers mourned, Morgan's friends blamed Untermyer for overtaxing Morgan's delicate constitution. Whatever the link, Morgan's passing cleared the way for the Federal Reserve Act of 1913, which transferred effective control of the money supply from the big bankers to the federal government.

The Republican administrations of the 1920s had predictably little use for Untermyer, but the return of the Democrats found him, at seventy-five, as eager as ever to bring the barons of Wall Street to account. Roosevelt knew Untermyer, but it was Ray Moley who enlisted his services shortly after the election. Precisely what Roosevelt wanted Moley and Untermyer to do was as uncertain as much else about the early New Deal. Unlike banking and farming, the securities business was hardly in crisis in 1933. In the doldrums, yes, but Wall Street's crisis had occurred in the six months starting in October 1929. Consequently there was no pressing need for emergency legislation. All the same, Roosevelt and the Democrats had railed against the speculators and profiteers of the stock exchange for so long that they felt compelled to do something to rein them in, even if they weren't currently threatening to break away.

So popular was the idea of restraining Wall Street that multiple groups set to work on the project. At least two of the groups worked for Roosevelt. Besides Moley and Untermyer, Roosevelt commissioned Commerce Secretary Daniel Roper and Attorney General Homer Cummings to get up some legislation, with the assistance of Huston Thompson, another old Wilsonian. The two administration groups worked in parallel and in ignorance of each other till an embarrassing moment of recognition in March. Moley thought Roosevelt had simply forgotten about him and Untermyer when he put Roper and Thompson on the case; more likely Roosevelt let Moley draw that conclusion lest he be offended. In fact Roosevelt wanted to see who had the better ideas.

The ideas differed sharply. Untermyer, whose legal career reached well back into the nineteenth century, recalled when Republican justices had invalidated the most innocuous efforts to restrain business. Eyeing the current makeup of the Supreme Court, he feared that efforts to regulate the securities industry might be similarly tossed out. For this reason he aimed to put the regulators in the Post Office, which had an irrefutable federal mandate. He argued that securities were marketed and delivered via the mails and on this account could be regulated. Roper and Thompson thought the Post Office scheme silly. What did the postmaster general know about Wall Street besides the addresses of the big firms doing business there? Thompson had run the Federal Trade Commission and was perfectly comfortable with the exercise of federal power. But Thompson, and Roper too, knew much less about the securities business and securities law than Untermyer, and their information deficiency became apparent in the imprecision of their arguments.

Roosevelt brought the disputants together and told them to work out their differences. Moley found the experience painful. "The peace conference in the President's study was a frost," Moley remembered. "Old Untermyer felt, and showed, a cold contempt for Thompson's work. Thompson, in self-defense perhaps, kept shooting at the Achilles heel of Untermyer's—the Post Office idea. Untermyer then got on his high horse. Not only was the Thompson bill a mess, but his own was perfect. And that, he wished it understood, included the Post Office idea." Moley despaired, concluding that reconciliation was hopeless. But Roosevelt laughed off his pessimism. He had Thompson incorporate some of Untermyer's suggestions into a revised bill he could send to Congress at once, and he kept aside the rest of Untermyer's plan for subsequent use.

The heart of the bill Roosevelt sent up was a novel concept in the American securities industry. "The big objective is to restore the old idea that a person who uses other people's money does so in a fiduciary capacity," Roosevelt explained in a press conference on March 29. "A person who works in either a stock or a commodity exchange is acting as the agent for other people." This being so, the agent had a responsibility to be as honest and forthcoming as possible. Roosevelt proposed a new standard for the securities trade, what he called "caveat vendor." The common-law principle of caveat emptor allowed sellers to get off too easily. "Let the seller beware as well as the buyer," the president said. "There is a definite, positive burden on the seller for the first time to tell the truth." Roosevelt insisted that he wasn't requiring omniscience, nor was he banning speculation. He gave an example: "If a company is organized to develop a gold mine, and it has got what it and the engineers honestly believe to be a perfectly good speculation, and it is not over-capitalized, there is no reason why it should not get a license to operate, provided that the public is informed that it is, like most gold-mining operations, a speculative venture." The point was to level the field between those issuing the securities and those buying them.

Roosevelt's proposal sparked an immediate reaction from the financial industry. Most brokers and investment bankers didn't want to be regulated at all and loudly said so. Even those who accepted that some regulation was in-

evitable predicted that the president's concept of caveat vendor would provoke endless litigation. One could easily imagine disappointed investors suing
corporate directors or the underwriting banks if a stock issue failed to meet the
investors' hopes. With the burden of proof now on the sellers, juries would
likely side with the investors.

Further complicating the passage of Roosevelt's bill were competing ideas
percolating through Congress. The members of the pertinent committees in
the Senate and House were barraged with opinions, advice, promises, and
threats from lobbyists and principals of the securities industry. Moreover, after
all the new authority Congress had given the president thus far, many senior
members of the legislature felt they had to draw the line somewhere. Moley,
who tried to push the administration's bill forward, described the experience
as "a tortuous dance on the eggs of congressional prerogative."

The dancing took two months, and it ended only when Roosevelt and the
congressional leaders decided to leave a large part of securities reform until later. But enough of Roosevelt's original design informed the Securities
Act of 1933 that the president was able to say, on signing: "This measure at last
translates some elementary standards of right and wrong into law." The new
act required the registration of securities issues with the Federal Trade
Commission—a responsibility later shifted to the Securities Exchange Commission—and the filing of basic information about the issuing corporation.
Roosevelt acknowledged that the act alone wouldn't guarantee a revival of the
stock market, let alone the larger economy. But a continued absence of the standards the act established would preclude a revival. "Without such an ethical
foundation, economic well-being cannot be achieved."

❖ ❖ ❖

𝒯HE CREATION OF the Tennessee Valley Authority was, in its own way, just
as opportunistic as the passage of the Securities Act, and it took its inspiration
from a progressive as old and battle-hardened as Samuel Untermyer. Republican George Norris of Nebraska had applauded Theodore Roosevelt's smiting
of the trusts and especially his conservation of natural resources, but he refused to follow TR out of the party in 1912. He liked Woodrow Wilson do-
mestically but resisted American intervention in the World War and couldn't
abide the League of Nations. As a Republican, Norris benefited from the GOP
hegemony of the 1920s, but as a progressive he chafed at the direction the leadership was taking the party. He backed Al Smith in 1928 and Franklin Roo-

sevelt in 1932. Meanwhile he campaigned quixotically for the abolition of the electoral college and more successfully for the conversion of Nebraska's bicameral legislature to a single-house model (a transformation that would come to pass in 1934).

Norris might never have adopted the Tennessee Valley as a cause had Henry Ford not tried to build an empire there in the 1920s. Amid the same rush to privatize wartime plants and facilities that yielded the Teapot Dome scandal, the Harding administration advertised to sell a federal munitions factory and hydropower plant at Muscle Shoals, Alabama. The raw material for the explosives was nitrates, which might as readily be made into fertilizer; the power plant could be used to encourage additional industrial development. Ford offered to take control of the Muscle Shoals facility on a lease lasting till the end of the twentieth century.

Norris distrusted Ford and disliked the idea of handing over to private enterprise what had been built at public expense. As chairman of the Senate agriculture committee he launched an investigation that concluded, in Norris's sarcastic words, that Ford's bid for Muscle Shoals would be "the most wonderful real estate speculation since Adam and Eve lost title to the Garden of Eden." He visited Muscle Shoals and, like Roosevelt in rural Georgia, came to know and respect the poor folks of the Tennessee Valley. He envisioned what the Tennessee Valley could become under the sympathetic guidance of a progressive presidential administration.

When that administration arrived, Norris didn't have to be asked twice to put together a program. His vision for what would be called the Tennessee Valley Authority encompassed flood prevention, erosion control, irrigation, reforestation, hydroelectric generation, the retirement of marginal agricultural lands, the encouragement of industry, and the diversification of employment. Nothing so ambitious had ever been undertaken by the federal government, and no one knew just which constitutional principles should guide the drafting of the TVA charter. Norris asked Roosevelt, over a working White House dinner, "What are you going to say when they ask you the political philosophy behind the TVA?" Roosevelt responded with a laugh: "I'll tell them it's neither fish nor fowl, but whatever it is, it will taste awfully good to the people of the Tennessee Valley."

The president monitored the drafting closely, and when differing versions passed by the House and Senate went to conference, he guided the hands of the reconcilers, indicating point by point which parts of each version he preferred. The private power companies that felt threatened by the public competition of the TVA labored mightily to handicap the authority by one restriction and then another; they fought especially to keep the TVA out of the business of transmitting electrical power. The authority might build dams and install generators, the companies' directors conceded grudgingly, but it should sell the electricity to the private sector at the powerhouse door. Only by this means would the public benefit from the competition of the capitalist marketplace. Norris led the struggle against the restrictions on TVA transmission, and Roosevelt backed him, reasoning that private control of transmission would negate whatever efficiencies the government achieved in generation. "It was a glorious fight right up the end," Norris's secretary reported after Norris and Roosevelt won, and the president signed the TVA into existence on May 18.

26.

RAY MOLEY HELPED ROOSEVELT WRITE HIS SECOND FIRESIDE CHAT. Eight weeks into the new administration, the president wished to give the American people a sense of what had been accomplished and an idea of what remained to be done. As they reviewed the text before Roosevelt went on the air, Moley flagged certain passages to ensure that they conveyed what Roosevelt intended. A sentence about a partnership between government and the private sector particularly caught his eye, as it indicated what seemed to be a striking departure in government policy. Moley knew about the dual strains of progressive thinking on the relationship between government and business—about Theodore Roosevelt's tolerance of bigness in business so long as it was matched by bigness in government, and Woodrow Wilson's insistence that smaller was better, in both government and business. The radio text, Moley noted, appeared to place Roosevelt on the side of his uncle. "You realize . . . ," Moley told the president, "that you're taking an enormous step away from the philosophy of equalitarianism and laissez-faire." Moley remembered the reaction: "FDR looked graver than he had been at any moment since the night before his inauguration. And then, when he had been silent a few minutes, he said, 'If that philosophy hadn't proved to be bankrupt, Herbert Hoover would be sitting here right now. I never felt surer of anything in my life than I do of the soundness of this passage.' "

The New Deal was criticized, then and later, for philosophical incoherence, among other shortcomings. The charge wasn't entirely unjustified; much about Roosevelt's program was extemporaneous and experimental. But at its heart the New Deal embodied a well-defined philosophy of American political economy—a concept of the proper relationship between American democracy and American capitalism that was radically at odds with inherited wisdom on the subject. Roosevelt had begun sharing his philosophy with the

American people during the 1932 campaign; he continued the exposition with his May 1933 Fireside Chat.

Roosevelt reminded his listeners of the grave problems America had faced at the time of his inauguration. "The country was dying by inches," he said. Prices had plummeted; jobs had disappeared; commerce had shriveled; banks were collapsing; mortgages were being foreclosed; lives were being ruined. The administration had faced two alternatives. The first was to let things work themselves out—to let prices find a new level on their own, to let the strongest banks survive and the rest go under, to let foreclosures proceed and the ousted homeowners scramble for other lodging or make do on the street. This was the course recommended by orthodox economic theory, Roosevelt said. But it was not the one he had chosen. "Such a policy was too much to ask the American people to bear. It involved not only a further loss of homes, farms, savings, and wages, but also a loss of spiritual values"—in particular the values of decency and fair play that made democracy possible.

He had chosen a different path. The fundamental problem of the depression, he explained, was an excess of capacity. "The people of this country have been erroneously encouraged to believe that they could keep on increasing the output of farm and factory indefinitely and that some magician would find ways and means for that increased output to be consumed with reasonable profit to the producer." But there was no magician, and output couldn't continue to grow unchecked. The old days of devil-take-the-hindmost competition must end. Planning—by government officials working closely with representatives of agriculture and industry—was essential.

Roosevelt had heard the criticism of planning, and he anticipated more. Most of it, he said, was foolishly or willfully ignorant. Charges that planning amounted to government control of industry were "wholly wrong." Planning was a form of partnership between government and the private sector in which the government helped businesses do what they ought to do, and even wanted to do, but couldn't do on their own. Roosevelt cited an example from the cotton textile industry. Most textile makers—perhaps 90 percent—were good corporate citizens, willing to put the interests of the community above their own narrow concerns. Among such companies agreements not to slash wages or engage in cutthroat competition were possible. "But what good is such an agreement," Roosevelt asked, "if the other ten percent of cotton manufacturers pay starvation wages, require long hours, employ children in their mills, and turn out burdensome surpluses?" This was where the government could step in. "Government ought to have the right, after surveying and planning for an industry, to prevent, with the assistance of the overwhelming majority of that industry, unfair practices and to enforce this agreement." Enforcement might require a modification or suspension of current antitrust laws and so ought to be handled carefully. "But these laws were never intended to encourage the kind of unfair competition that results in long hours, starvation wages, and overproduction." Preventing such outcomes was simply prudent policy—and it was the essence of the philosophy of the New Deal.

❖   ❖   ❖

ℛOOSEVELT'S VISION of a planned economy inspired the boldest initiative of the early New Deal. What became the National Recovery Administration began with an effort to aid railroads. This was fitting, in that railroads had been responsible for the rise of industry in America, and railroads had been the first sector of the economy to attract the regulative oversight of government. For decades the states and then the federal government had tried to keep the railroads healthy, but not too healthy. The railroads were the nation's largest employers, having millions of workers on their payrolls. They were the nation's largest income-producing investment, furnishing dividends to individuals and families, directly and via investment trusts, all across the country. They were the nation's most important means of transportation, tying communities large and small into a single net. And they were the nation's most chronically troubled industrial sector, suffering bouts of bankruptcies every decade or so. The states and the federal government had subsidized railroad construction during the nineteenth century; the federal government, especially, had regulated railroad operations during the twentieth century. Only rarely had the government bailed out failing railroads. The roads didn't garner much sympathy among the general public, on account of their great size and their history of flouting the public interest. "The public be damned!" railroad magnate William Vanderbilt had said, and the public was often happy to return the favor. After the onset of the depression, Hoover's Reconstruction Finance Corporation had floated loans to the railroads—an effort that secured the future of neither the roads nor Hoover.

Roosevelt had little love for the railroads, but he couldn't ignore their plight. Dozens of railroads had gone into receivership by the time he took office; dividends were down by two-thirds. The roads had laid off more than 700,000 workers and had reduced or suspended service to thousands of communities. As bad as the economy already was, if the railroads sank further they would drag the broader economy still deeper into the pit. And until the railroads recovered, a general recovery would be almost out of the question.

There were other reasons for focusing on railroads, among the major industries. Roosevelt talked of broad-gauged government planning for the economy, but he had never actually attempted it. The railroads provided a place to start—a place to learn what worked and what didn't. The railroads, moreover, engaged in interstate commerce, which brought them under the constitutional purview of the federal government. The Supreme Court, which was dominated by conservative justices appointed by Republican presidents, might challenge government planning for other industrial sectors, but it would be hard-pressed to toss out legislation regarding railroads.

Yet events conspired to blur Roosevelt's focus on the railroads and to bring other sectors under the planning penumbra. Since the start of the depression, advocates of labor had suggested reducing the work week as a means of keeping people on payrolls. Presumably a company would employ a third more workers at thirty hours a week than it did at forty. But such could only be presumed, since workers were reluctant to see their paychecks cut in line with the reduction in their hours worked. The result, from management's point of view, was that forty workers working thirty hours were likely to cost more than thirty workers working forty hours. Beyond this was the traditional resistance of owners and managers to any restraint on their freedom to run their businesses as they saw fit.

Nonetheless Hugo Black of Alabama introduced a thirty-hour bill in the Senate, and it promised to sweep all before it. Organized labor got behind the bill, with the American Federation of Labor threatening a general strike if it wasn't enacted.

Roosevelt recognized the flaws in the thirty-hour concept, including the added labor costs to businesses that were often only a heartbeat from bankruptcy already, the difficulty of applying it to seasonal industries in which demand for labor varied from month to month, and the dubious constitutionality of the government's stepping so egregiously between employers and employees. The Black bill proposed to get around the constitutionality issue by invoking the commerce clause of the Constitution and applying the thirty-hour rule only to companies that dealt in goods crossing state lines. Whether this device would withstand judicial scrutiny remained to be tested. Roosevelt wasn't at all sure that it would, and he didn't want to be the one making the test.

More fundamentally, Roosevelt's understanding of the operations of a capitalist economy made him think a thirty-hour mandate was foolish and probably counterproductive. As much as Roosevelt favored economic planning, he didn't think federal bureaucrats could do it alone—and still less did he think Congress was equipped for the job. The planners ought to include representatives of all those parties who would have to carry out the plans—owners, managers, workers, distributors.

Roosevelt urged the Senate to reconsider, but he couldn't derail the thirty-hour bill, which rolled through the upper chamber by a large margin. The president's only hope, it seemed, of heading off a similar success in the House was to get out in front of the whole issue of industrial planning, by something more sweeping than railroad reform.

As he prepared to do so, he reflected on his prior experience in the federal government. He recalled how America had mobilized during the World War and how the federal government had guided industry during that conflict. Wilson's War Industries Board had apportioned production, orchestrated distribution, and otherwise directed the operation of the industrial economy. Though particular actions of the war board struck certain individuals and groups as unfair, arbitrary, or even irrational, on the whole its contribution to surmounting the crisis of the war was remembered favorably—even fondly, as the depression persisted. To many Americans at the time of Roosevelt's inauguration, the war board offered a model for government leadership in the current crisis.

Robert Wagner, Roosevelt's old colleague from the New York senate, wasn't averse to the war board model, but he thought it didn't give enough weight to the interests of workers. A federal senator since 1927, Wagner began drafting legislation for a national industrial board. Meanwhile Ray Moley lined up the Brookings Institution, a think tank with roots in the Progressive era and headquarters not far from the White House, to examine alternative paths to national economic planning. The commerce and labor departments likewise got in on the planning act, as did various outsiders who hoped to contribute to what promised—or threatened—to become the biggest expansion of government authority in decades.

Roosevelt, as was becoming his habit, let the different groups work away, saving his political capital for such decisions as couldn't be made at a lower level. He weighed in periodically, as when he told reporters at an April press conference a story. "There was a certain little sweater factory in a little town—I won't even give you the location of it—where they normally employed only about 200 people. It was the only industry in town. The owners of the little sweater factory and the employees had always been on exceedingly good terms." But the depression had curtailed demand for sweaters, leaving this factory and its competitors overstaffed. "So the owners and the employees got together and talked the situation over. They only had about six weeks' work in the whole past year, and all the other factories in the country had about the same kind of work—about six weeks out of the year. Well, the result was the population in this little town was practically starving to death. So they got together and decided that the thing they wanted to do was work, even though it would be at much reduced pay. So they figured out that if they could cut their wages 33 percent they could cut the cost of making these sweaters by the same amount, and in that way undersell every other sweater factory." This was what they did. Their marketing agent, armed with the new price sheet, traveled to New York and filled his sales book with orders that would have gone to the company's competitors. The result was a boom for the company, which now had enough work for three shifts a day.

The lesson Roosevelt drew was not the one many of the reporters must have expected. He didn't praise the company and its workers for ingenuity and the shared willingness to sacrifice; instead he argued that the story revealed what was wrong with the current system. The sweater company's policy was "bad business in all ways." It was bad for the company's workers, who were working harder than ever for less pay than before. It was bad for the sweater industry generally, because it forced several competitors out of business, with dire effects on their employees. It was bad for the morale of the region.

The solution to this problem and similar ones lay partly in the direction of the thirty-hour bill. The basic question, Roosevelt said, was "whether we can work out some kind of plan that will distribute the volume of consumption in a given industry over the whole industry." The goal should be not to concentrate production in a small part of the industry—the lone sweater company, so to speak—but to share production among many firms. "We want to spread it out."

Roosevelt sought allies in the business community for his planning concept. Somewhat surprisingly the U.S. Chamber of Commerce, the foremost business lobby in America, had signaled its approval of government planning of the economy. The chamber normally wanted to keep the government at a distance, but the depression had hit its members so hard that they were willing to countenance almost anything to get the economy moving again. The chamber held a dinner at the Washington Auditorium; Roosevelt arrived after the dishes had been cleared. He patted himself on the back for a "slight but definite upturn in most industries" in the two months since his inauguration, and he expressed hope that a recent uptick in commodity prices would benefit farmers directly and workers indirectly, as rising prices translated into more jobs.

But the president had come this night not to report what the captains of industry—"who represent, in all probability, the majority of the employers of the nation," Roosevelt said—could read for themselves in the papers. He came instead to request their cooperation in the task the administration had undertaken. He asked them to refrain from further wage cuts and in fact to raise wages as prices rose. This was only fair. "It is a simple fact that the average of the wage scale of the nation has gone down during the past four years more rapidly than the cost of living," he said. "It is essential, as a matter of national justice, that the wage scale should be brought back to meet the cost of living and that this process should begin now and not later."

A second request involved "bringing order out of chaos," as Roosevelt put it. "You and I acknowledge the existence of unfair methods of competition, of cut-throat prices, and of general chaos. You and I agree that this condition must be rectified and that order must be restored." The government could lead the restoration, but it couldn't put the economy back together alone. "The attainment of that objective depends upon your willingness to cooperate with one another to this end, and also your willingness to cooperate with your government." Roosevelt didn't give the moguls time to reflect on whether the government was actually theirs; instead he put words in their mouths. "In almost every industry an overwhelming majority of the units of the industry are wholly willing to work together to prevent overproduction, to prevent unfair wages, to eliminate improper working conditions. In the past, success in attaining these objectives"—that is, the objectives Roosevelt ascribed to the business leaders—"has been prevented by a small minority of units in many industries. I can assure you that you will have the cooperation of your government in bringing these minorities to understand that their unfair practices are contrary to a sound public policy."

Here Roosevelt *was* accurately summarizing what the business leaders were thinking, and it was what he was counting on to convince the capitalists of the wisdom of his ideas on planning. Roosevelt wouldn't admit it, and he might not have fully appreciated it at the outset, but industrial planning constituted, at bottom, a cartelization of America's major industries, with the federal government acting as a non-profit partner. Big government would join with big business and perhaps big labor to prop up prices, apportion markets, and prevent small operators from undercutting the deal.

A third request was somewhat broader. Roosevelt scanned the business crowd carefully, as if to peer into the hearts beneath the dinner jackets of the guests. It was human nature, he said, to view problems from the perspective of one's own self or company. But the economic crisis had revealed the bankruptcy of this approach.

> It is ultimately of little avail to any of you to be temporarily prosperous while others are permanently depressed. I ask that you translate your welfare into the welfare of the whole, that you view recovery in terms of the nation rather than in terms of a particular industry, that you have the vision to lay aside special and selfish interests, to think of and act for a well-rounded national recovery.

The hall rang with applause. "The president's speech was received with an enthusiasm which can hardly be overemphasized," the business correspondent of the *New York Times* observed. Roosevelt had chosen his audience well. Some, no doubt, were moved by his appeal to a higher, national vision of prosperity, but the line that really got their attention and approval was the one about the government cooperating with corporations against the unfair business practices of their competitors. For decades the government had opposed efforts by big business to prevent smaller companies from spoiling the market by competing too hard; Roosevelt appeared to be saying that the government not only would drop its opposition but would actively join the effort to suppress the spoilers. The government would be more than a member of the cartel; it would be the cartel's police force. No wonder the moguls put down their cigars to cheer the president.

❖   ❖   ❖

𝒲INNING THE SUPPORT of business turned out to be the easy part. Keeping the various intellectuals, bureaucrats, and members of Congress marching in more or less the same direction was harder. Roosevelt let the several groups working on planning proceed, guessing that many of the differences among their proposals would work themselves out before he had to step in and that a modest degree of confusion might actually work in his favor. "We're fiddling along with more legislation than any one man or any legislative body can accurately digest," Hiram Johnson, Theodore Roosevelt's running mate in 1912 and currently a Republican senator from California, wrote his sons. Johnson remained progressive enough to wish the president well. "I am still in the mood of trying anything that may be suggested, and the country is still in the mood, in my opinion, of following Roosevelt in anything he desires." Other members echoed Johnson's view. "This is the president's special session of Congress," a Texas representative declared. "He is the Moses who is leading us out of the wilderness."

The modern Moses had problems akin to those of the original. The closer the promised land loomed, the more restive his followers grew. The rise in prices prompted investors to return to the stock market; in the several weeks after April 1 stocks rose by half. At this point the depression had last longer than any in recorded American history, and it stood to reason—and to Wall Street's hopes—that the hard times had just about run their course. The innovations the president proposed might be unnecessary, even counterproductive. Roosevelt's critics gained traction with each day's rise in the market. "How much longer are we going to continue this delegation of power?" Republican senator Lester Dickinson of Iowa asked. "When are we going to learn our lesson?" William Borah of Idaho declared of the president, "No man can execute all the powers we have given to him." Even Roosevelt's allies began to complain. Henry Ashurst of Arizona, the chairman of the Senate judiciary committee, asserted, "Those senators have read history upside down, or have not read it at all, who do not realize that when you grant power it will not be used as you expect it to be used."

"There is a revolt in the air in the Congress," Hiram Johnson remarked in early June. "Men have followed him upstairs without question or criticism. Some individuals have been mute concerning their most cherished ideas in order that they might contribute what little they could in aid of the President's efforts in this economic crisis. These men have about reached the limit of their endurance." Johnson visited Roosevelt with a delegation from Congress and witnessed the president himself becoming testy. "He is losing a little of his astounding and remarkable poise, and I rather think a bit of his good nature," Johnson said. "He wants us out of the way."

He did indeed. What came to be called the Hundred Days had never been scheduled for that length, or any length. Roosevelt originally thought the special session should conduct a week or two's business, dealing with matters that simply couldn't wait until the regular session began the following January, and then recess, perhaps to return for another week or so in the fall. But members of Congress didn't want to leave and then come back, and consequently Roosevelt thought to let them stay on, perhaps until the end of April or the beginning of May. Yet when the lawmakers proved so amenable to his various suggestions, he kept sending more, and more ambitious, measures, which stretched the session toward the hundred-day mark.

The onset of hot weather, though, in the era before indoor cooling, had always signaled the time to adjourn. A confrontational president might use the heat to extort favors from Congress; Roosevelt had watched Wilson do precisely this in 1913. But a president with Congress on his side typically humored the legislators' desire to escape. Roosevelt accordingly urged the senators and representatives to wrap up their debates and pass the bills before them, that he might sign the bills and they all go home.

They did so, with greater haste in some instances than in others. The industrial planning bill showed the fingerprints of its many authors; it was, in Moley's words, "by now a thorough hodge-podge of provisions designed to give the country temporary economic stimulation and provisions designed to lay the groundwork for permanent business-government partnership and planning." The temporary stimulation took the form of a $3.3 billion appropriation for public works, directed by a Public Works Administration and intended to provide jobs for the unemployed. The groundwork for business-government partnership in planning was the provision for industrial codes that would encourage businesses to cooperate with one another and with labor rather than to continue the free-for-all that had prostrated so many of them.

"In my Inaugural I laid down the simple proposition that nobody is going to starve in this country," Roosevelt said on signing the National Industrial Recovery Act on June 16. "It seems to me to be equally plain that no business which depends for existence on paying less than living wages to its workers has any right to continue in this country." This was a radical—even revolutionary—statement, arrogating to government the responsibility for determining which businesses should exist and which not. Heretofore the government had let the market make that determination. Roosevelt elaborated on the new dispensation:

Throughout industry, the change from starvation wages and starvation employment to living wages and sustained employment can, in large part, be made by an industrial covenant to which all employers shall subscribe. It is greatly to their interest to do this, because decent living, widely spread among our 125,000,000 people, eventually means the opening up to industry of the richest market which the world has known. It is the only way to utilize the so-called excess capacity of our industrial plants.

The "industrial covenants" were the heart of Roosevelt's new order, and they would begin, he said, with a "great spontaneous cooperation" to rehire millions of workers. "The idea is simply for employers to hire more men to do the existing work by reducing the work-hours of each man's week and at the same time paying a living wage for the shorter week." This wasn't Roosevelt's idea; it was the hostage he had given to the thirty-hour forces in Congress to get the bill he wanted. Roosevelt, like most successful politicians, had a knack for convincing himself of the truth of what served his purposes, but even he almost choked on the phrase "great spontaneous cooperation." There might be cooperation, and he hoped it would be great, but he knew it wouldn't be spontaneous. If spontaneity had been possible, the law he had just signed wouldn't have been necessary.

Roosevelt fiddled the truth on other aspects of the law. He explained that the wage-lifting efforts of any single business, acting alone, would fail. "But if *all* employers in each trade now band themselves faithfully in these modern guilds, without exception, and agree to act together and at once, none will be hurt, and millions of workers, so long deprived of the right to earn their bread in the sweat of their labor, can raise their heads again." Aside from the archaic language of "guilds"—the American steel industry, the most powerful industry in the world, a guild?—Roosevelt's assertion that no one would be hurt was demonstrably false. The companies that were undercutting the market would be hurt; they weren't engaged in their current behavior for the pleasure of it. Then there were consumers, who benefited from the competition among producers. *They* would suffer from the rise in prices the rise in wages would entail.

"Many good men voted this new charter with misgivings," Roosevelt conceded, in the closest he ventured to an admission of the law's imperfections. But he quickly added, "I do not share these doubts." The reason he didn't—or said he didn't—was his experience of the World War. "I had part in the great cooperation of 1917 and 1918, and it is my faith that we can count on our industry once more to join in our general purpose to lift this new threat, and to do it without taking any advantage of the public trust which has this day been reposed without stint in the good faith and high purpose of American business."

Those who were following Roosevelt's argument must have been scratching their heads at this logical turn. American business had done very little during the previous few years to cause Americans—Democrats especially—to repose trust in its good faith and high purpose. Roosevelt himself had been elected by railing against American business. Moreover, the premise of the new law was that business couldn't be trusted to act in the public interest without the strong arm of government to enforce acceptable behavior. His analogy to the country's experience during the World War was problematic, to say the least. The war had been expected to be—and proved to be—brief; no one intended the wartime regimentation of industry to last more than a year or two. Even then, when the regimentation ended and government controls were lifted, the economy suffered severe inflation and labor unrest that made many Americans wonder whether the whole effort had been worth it. Roosevelt's audience had to wonder—because he didn't say—whether the new system of "industrial covenants" was to be temporary or permanent. If the former, it might be tolerable. If the latter—all bets were off.

Roosevelt plunged forward. He challenged industry to earn the trust the American people, acting through himself and Congress, were reposing in it. Taking a term from the war era, he warned against "slacker" firms—those that put private interest ahead of the general welfare. Nor was the potential for selfishness confined to single firms. "We can imagine such a thing as a slacker industry." The American people would be watching.

He challenged labor to do its part. An essential aspect of the new law was section 7a, which greatly facilitated the organizing of labor in many industries. This section alone marked a radical shift in the relationship of the government to industry, for until now government had been either hostile or neutral toward labor's long struggle to achieve a semblance of parity with management. But with favor came responsibility. "This is not a law to foment discord"—strikes and other forms of labor protest—"and it will not be executed as such. This is a time for mutual confidence and help."

He challenged the American people. "There is no power in America that can force against the public will such action as we require. But there is no group in America that can withstand the force of an aroused public opinion. This great cooperation can succeed only if those who bravely go forward to restore jobs have aggressive public support and those who lag are made to feel the full weight of public disapproval."

❖   ❖   ❖

WITH THIS MESSAGE Roosevelt rang down the curtain on the special session. He sent the legislators back to their states and districts with his thanks for their "sincere and whole-hearted cooperation" and his congratulations for proving "that our form of government can rise to an emergency and can carry through a broad program in record time."

The program was definitely broad. Congress in the Hundred Days approved fifteen major pieces of legislation, including the Banking Act, which was supplemented at the end of the session by the Glass-Steagall Act, a measure reorganizing the banking system and providing a degree of deposit insurance; the Economy Act, which allowed Roosevelt to rein in spending; the law establishing the Civilian Conservation Corps, which was already enrolling and training scores of thousands of young men; the Securities Act, with its requirements for fuller disclosure of stock issues; the Agricultural Adjustment Act, which made government the guarantor of the health of the nation's farm industry; the measure creating the Tennessee Valley Authority, as a development agency in its own right and a yardstick for electrical power production; and the National Industrial Recovery Act, which put government in charge of industrial planning and pumped billions of dollars into public works. Other laws provided emergency relief to the poor and jobless, debt relief to farmers, and mortgage relief to home owners. On the authority delegated by Congress—either in 1917 or in 1933—Roosevelt took the United States off the gold standard, undoing sixty years of American monetary policy.

It was a breathtaking record, and many members of Congress were convinced they'd need the full six months before the legislature reconvened simply to catch their breath. It was a record, as well, that placed more power—and more responsibility—in the hands of Roosevelt than any peacetime president had ever wielded or borne. "Now that Congress has gone and left him with the framework of an entirely new government system, the President must see that its cogs and shafts work reciprocally," Arthur Krock observed. "The front wheels of the government engine cannot be permitted to revolve more swiftly than the rear wheels if the vehicle is to get where it is bound. Each administrator must see to it that his assistants pursue a certain policy, and the policy of each group must mesh as a general plan. In the most powerful nation of the world, with 130 millions of people to be dealt with, the labor is Herculean. It is more than that, for the strong man of mythology was pretty dumb. It is Olympian."

Whether Roosevelt had the stuff of an Olympian remained to be determined. Many of those who had known him before his inauguration and who watched him during the Hundred Days expressed amazement at how much larger he now seemed. Norman Davis and Raymond Fosdick had worked with Roosevelt in the Wilson administration; Davis told Fosdick, after a visit to the White House: "Ray, that fellow in there is not the fellow we used to know. There's been a miracle here." Fosdick agreed. "There *had* been a miracle, an intellectual and spiritual metamorphosis induced by adversity and triumph," he recounted later.

> Those lonely years of struggle when, as he told me once, his sole, determined purpose was to move his big toe, had done something to his character— something fine and strong which brought him courage and bold confidence, a depth of penetration and a new self-control. From now on he feared nothing, and he faced the problems of his generation not only with level eyes but with sympathy and imagination.

Fosdick afterward recalled a formal dinner at the White House. Roosevelt shuffled down the long passage from the state dining room to the East Room, where the guests were gathered.

> He used a cane and hung heavily on the arm of an aide; and his walk was the slow, painful, contorted shuffle of paralysis. As he approached the door the Marine Band played "Hail to the Chief," and in a flash I realized with a lump in my throat that this apparently broken man was indeed the chief—with the capacity and magnetism of great leadership, and bearing on his face and in his handsome eyes the mark of confidence and power.

Ray Moley had his own interpretation of the Hundred Days. "None of us close to FDR lived normal lives," Moley said of the period. "Confusion, haste, the dread of making mistakes, the consciousness of responsibility for the economic well-being of millions of people made mortal inroads on the health of some of us, like Will Woodin and Joe Robinson"—the Senate majority leader—"and left the rest of us ready to snap at our own images in the mirror." Only the president appeared exempt. "Roosevelt preserved the air of a man who'd found a happy way of life. From March 4th, when he had reviewed his three-and-a-half-hour inaugural parade with every evidence of real enjoyment while Woodin wrestled with the question of how to open the banks, until

June 16th, when Congress adjourned, I saw him lose his poise, self-confidence, and good humor but once." This was in the fight over the budget, when an influential Republican refused compromise. "But for the rest, he was the ebullient, easy, calm man pictured in the Sunday rotogravure sections. This phenomenon, which had seemed remarkable enough during the campaign and banking crisis, now began to take on the appearance of the miraculous. I had, fleetingly, the illusion that Roosevelt had no nerves at all." Roosevelt astonished Moley with his ability to turn from work to play, and back, with neither pause nor self-consciousness.

> What began as a social encounter—say a swim in the White House pool, complete with splashings and duckings—would, with bewildering suddenness, be interrupted by a series of questions on the progress of the railroad legislation. What began as a serious evening's discussion on the guarantee of bank deposits (which FDR distrusted), and whether or not the administration should get behind the Glass bank bill in view of the fact that Glass had accepted the guarantee of deposits to get support for the rest of the bill, would, long before a decision had been reached, become a leisurely night at home: FDR would be working on his stamp collection and start telling anecdotes of his Wilson days; Mrs. Roosevelt would wander in and out to call his attention to passages in a book that she was reading; the sweet-faced Missy LeHand and Grace Tully would appear with photographs for him to sign; Louis would stick his head in and ask wryly if he'd be breaking into this "important conference" if he told us the story of what he had said to Harold Ickes that morning.

Moley thought Roosevelt's ability to shift so easily between work and pleasure was one secret of his tirelessness. There were others. "He had the successful executive's ability to keep his mind clear of details once he had decided on a principle of action, together with a perfect faith that somehow, someone would always be around to take care of details satisfactorily." Moley noted that the details in question could be quite substantial: whether the CCC should enroll a quarter- or a half-million men, whether the federal budget should be cut by four hundred million or five hundred million dollars. "He had the faculty of emerging from three hours of fifteen-minute interviews exhilarated, where another man would be done in." This wasn't because, like Calvin Coolidge, he didn't talk back to his visitors. "FDR enjoyed himself for just the opposite reason. His visitors didn't talk back to him. They couldn't. It was he who called the conversational turns, he who would discourse at length on this or that, he who would catch and hold and visibly delight the caller."

Moley would change his views regarding Roosevelt's policies. But he never lost his admiration for the man's remarkable gifts, including the ability to treat the weightiest subjects with ease and laughter. "In short, he was like the fairy-story prince who didn't know how to shudder. Not even the realization that he was playing nine-pins with the skulls and thighbones of economic orthodoxy seemed to worry him."

$\mathcal{D}$URING THE 1932 CAMPAIGN AND THE TRANSITION THAT FOLLOWED, when Roosevelt had cast scorn on Hoover's argument that the causes of the depression lay overseas, he knew he was exaggerating and oversimplifying. He had reasons for doing so, some good and others dubious. The good reasons were that a new president had to start somewhere in tackling the depression and that domestic causes were more amenable to presidential influence than international ones. The foremost dubious reason was that without such exaggeration he might not have become the new president. Roosevelt was neither the first nor the last presidential candidate to convince himself America needed him more than abstract truth did.

Roosevelt's polio had curtailed his foreign travel; an emergency trip to Europe in 1931, undertaken upon learning that Sara had contracted pneumonia while on vacation, constituted his only overseas journey in nearly fifteen years. But if he had ventured widely he would have seen disturbing signs that the structure of the peace crafted at Paris after the World War was collapsing. Germany had been humiliated by the war-guilt provision of the Versailles treaty and burdened by the open-ended reparations payments, but it hadn't been crushed; the result was that Germany's postwar experiment in democracy was almost guaranteed to fail and that Germans would blame their troubles on the Versailles system. The National Socialists certainly did so during the 1920s, under their strangely charismatic and brilliantly shrewd leader, Adolf Hitler. German Communists clumped the Versailles system with a broader critique of international capitalism and bourgeois democracy and squared off to fight the Nazis for control of the German government. As the depression set in, destroying such prosperity as the Germans had managed to achieve under the reparations-and-debt regime, the Communists gained support among the German people. The Soviet Union, the Communists said, was surviving the depression quite well; its socialist political economy should serve as a model for Germany's own. The millions in Germany's soup lines found the argument appealing and leaned left. Germany's business and propertied classes found the argument appalling and leaned right; having to choose, as they saw it, between the Nazis and the Communists, they sided with the former. In January 1933—just as Roosevelt was interviewing potential cabinet secretaries—banker Kurt von Schroeder invited Hitler to his Cologne home, where he promised the support of his friends and associates in exchange for Hitler's pledge to leave their business interests untouched. A short while later Hitler, as head of the now-majority Nazi party, was asked by President Paul von Hindenburg to form a government.

Americans had difficulty taking Hitler seriously. *Time* magazine devoted five amused pages to his accession. "Last week, on the biggest morning of his life," Henry Luce's weekly reported in early February 1933, "this pudgy, stoop-shouldered, tooth-brush-mustached but magnetic little man bounded out of bed after four hours sleep, soaped his soft flesh with cold water, shaved with cold water, put on his always neat but never smart clothes and braced himself for the third of his historic encounters" with Hindenburg. The first had occurred the previous August, when Hindenburg had treated Hitler contemptuously. " 'With what power, Herr Hitler,' growled Old Paul, 'do you seek to be made Chancellor?' " *Time* reported. " 'Precisely the same power that Mussolini exercised after his March on Rome!' chirped cheeky Adolf. . . . 'So!' bristled Der Reichspräsident with the air of a Prussian schoolmaster about to squelch an urchin. 'Let me tell you, Herr Hitler, if you don't behave, I'll rap your fingers!' " The subsequent months were as unkind to Hindenburg and Hitler's rivals as they were to Herbert Hoover, and by January the German president had been forced to accept Hitler as chancellor. But Henry Luce still found the little man and his program mildly ludicrous. He described the "beer-soused Bavarians" who had backed Hitler's rise to power, labeled the Nazi party "fantastic" (in the sense of embodying Hitler's fantasies), and declared of the Nazi agenda: "Its program consists of stentorian appeals to every form of German prejudice. Essentially Nationalists and patrioteers, the Nazis insert 'Socialist' into their party's name simply as a lure to discontented workers. . . . Today it is no exaggeration to state that the Nazi Party is pledged to so many things that it is pledged to nothing. . . . In so far as it has a doctrine, National Socialism promises the bulk of the German people whatever they want."

The snickering didn't last long. Within the month of Hitler's takeover—and just days before Roosevelt's inauguration—the Nazis burned the Reichstag, the German parliament building. They blamed the Communists convincingly

enough that the government and the German people went along with legislation outlawing the Communist party. On March 5, the day Roosevelt closed
the banks in the United States, new German elections gave Hitler's coalition a
majority, which proceeded at once to award the chancellor near-dictatorial
powers. In a first flexing, Hitler launched a national boycott of Jewish businesses and Jews in the professions.

Even so, in 1933 Japan appeared more threatening than Germany. Roosevelt
had been to Germany several times, and though, like most other Americans,
he found National Socialism puzzling, at least he understood the frame of reference within which the Nazis operated. Japan, by comparison, was a cipher.
Roosevelt knew what other educated Americans knew: that Japan had modernized during the late nineteenth century by adopting Western technology,
that Japan had employed its Western technology against China and then Russia in the long-standing contest for control of Korea and Manchuria, that
Japan had fought on the side of the Allied powers during the World War, that
Japan had joined the Washington Conference protocols on naval arms limitations. Roosevelt also knew that the Japanese had taken offense at various actions by the Western powers over the years. But he didn't know—and almost
no one else in the West knew, either—how much of the offense was honestly
felt and how much was diplomatic melodrama. Were the Japanese *really* upset
at the United States because Theodore Roosevelt persuaded their government
to accept a reasonable settlement of the Russo-Japanese War? Did American
restrictions on immigration sting as badly as some Japanese spokesmen—
including the Japanese ambassador to the United States, who warned of "grave
consequences" for U.S.-Japanese relations—claimed? Did the refusal of the
Paris peace conference to embrace racial equality truly wound the Japanese
psyche? Did the lesser tonnage allowed the Japanese navy at the Washington
Conference matter to ordinary Japanese?

All Roosevelt could do was ask himself what he would have done in the
place of Japan's leaders. He was a politician; they were politicians, after their
fashion. He interpreted the world, for political purposes, in a way that served
his interests; he supposed they did, too. He would have cited—and perhaps exaggerated—American sensitivities in explaining to other governments what he
could and couldn't do; he imagined Japanese leaders did the same.

Yet certain aspects of Japanese policy were undeniable. In September 1931,
at the behest of the nationalist military officers who increasingly dominated
Japanese foreign policy, Japanese troops guarding a railroad across Manchuria
claimed they had been attacked by Chinese bandits at Mukden. The Japanese

army responded by occupying the rest of Manchuria, converting China's northeasternmost province—and the one richest in resources essential to industrial development—into a Japanese puppet state called Manchukuo. The speed of the occupation made obvious that it had been planned in advance and that the whole affair had been staged.

The hijacking of Manchuria marked a resumption of the struggle for East Asia. The Japanese apparently guessed that the Western powers, absorbed as they were in their own economic troubles, would do little to hinder their expansion. The West proved Tokyo correct. The League of Nations discussed the affair interminably, and the United States—which was to say, the Hoover administration—merely refused to recognize the independence of Manchukuo. The American policy did not prevent Japan from exploiting the people and resources of Manchuria, but it was better than nothing. Or so Hoover hoped.

Days before Roosevelt's inauguration, the League of Nations finally acted on the Manchurian question. Although the United States remained outside the League, all the members but one voted to adopt America's non-recognition policy as the League's own. Japan should leave Manchuria and return it to China. The sole dissenter to the League vote was Japan, which declared that it would never leave Manchuria—Manchukuo—but would leave the League at once. China was a "fiction," the Japanese delegate to the League snorted on his way out the door. By this time Japanese troops controlled the entire region north of the Great Wall, which hadn't kept out invaders when it was built and didn't seem likely to keep them out now. China—whether fictional or real— lay open to further depredation.

❖   ❖   ❖

ROOSEVELT REALIZED that sooner or later he would have to deal with the Nazis and the Japanese. Yet he hoped to postpone that day as long as possible, the better to focus on reviving the American economy. Another aspect of foreign policy, however, was related intrinsically to his revival plans and couldn't be so easily kicked down the road. The major trading nations were pushing harder than ever for the international economic conference, which, they hoped, would coordinate efforts to fight the depression. The United States, with the world's largest economy as well as the biggest balance of credits to debts, was the obvious linchpin of any such conference. Yet many Americans were skittish, partly because the conference was being organized under the auspices of the League of Nations but mostly because any conference would almost certainly pressure the United States, as the great creditor, to forgive or reduce the debts it was owed. Franklin Roosevelt, as a candidate and then as president-elect, had promised support for the conference in general terms without committing himself to anything in particular.

As president he was in no greater hurry to sign on to the conference scheme, which was shaping up as a comprehensive approach to debt, reparations, tariffs, and exchange rates. Roosevelt's dance card was full with his domestic reforms; the international conference would have to wait.

But it wouldn't wait forever. One foreign leader after another trooped to Washington to tell him so. Ramsay MacDonald, the British prime minister, arrived in mid-April. Roosevelt didn't expect much from MacDonald, a socialist (that is Laborite) who, "as everyone knew," according to Ray Moley, "was merely a front for as hard-boiled a Conservative Government as England had had for many years." Yet MacDonald *was* the prime minister, and Roosevelt judged him "a man of liberal ideas" who might serve as a vehicle for knocking some sense into the "special-privilege people" who controlled the Conservative party. Whether on his own or at the behest of his Tory backers, MacDonald adopted the Hooverian view that international cooperation was essential to any effort to relieve the depression. The prime minister took a political chance coming to Washington. Recent trends to the contrary notwithstanding, the British still fancied themselves the arbiters of the world's economic fate. The fact remained that the sun never set on the British empire, and so long as it didn't, British governments could pretend to British voters that London somehow kept it aloft. Never before had a British prime minister traveled hat in hand to the former American colonies; if MacDonald returned to Britain without some commitment by Roosevelt to a constructive policy, his government would suffer severe embarrassment.

The talks went less well than MacDonald hoped. Roosevelt surrounded himself with advisers, including Cordell Hull, the secretary of state; Ray Moley, Hull's deputy but in fact Roosevelt's inside man at the State Department; and Herbert Feis, Hull's own economic adviser. Key Pittman, the Democratic chairman of the Senate foreign relations committee, who favored high tariffs and a return to silver currency in some form, sat in as Roosevelt's witness to Congress that the president wasn't selling American interests out to the wily Brits. MacDonald couldn't break through Roosevelt's screen of defenders, and the talks yielded nothing of substance. "It was never the purpose of the present discussions to conclude definitive agreements," a joint communiqué asserted blandly. "They were designed to explore and to map out the territory to be covered."

The French came calling next. The position of Édouard Herriot was even more problematic than that of MacDonald, for though he had thrice been premier, at the time of his visit he was between leadership posts. Nor did he represent what seemed to be a broad current of French thinking on economic issues. But Roosevelt had known him for years, and the acquaintance prompted the French government to send him over.

Herriot wanted to talk about debts; in particular he wanted Roosevelt to offer a reduction in what France was expected to pay. Roosevelt refused, albeit politely. He explained that Congress had taken a firm stand against reducing the foreign debts; consequently his options were limited. He noted, by way of giving Herriot some hope, that President Hoover had refused even to discuss the debt issue with the French (or the others in arrears), but now he—Roosevelt—was talking with Monsieur Herriot about that very subject. As additional encouragement, he told Herriot that if France made good on the payment that was due in December, he would ask Congress for the power to renegotiate the debts. Because Herriot was an old friend, he wasn't surprised when Roosevelt illustrated his position on the debts with a homey example. He described a landlord who rented a house to another man. The renter ran into difficulty and was late with a payment. The landlord was sympathetic. "Pay as much as you can, but remain in possession of the house," he said. Roosevelt's precise point wasn't clear—France could hardly be evicted from its own country—but the tone was encouraging.

After Herriot left Washington the line merely grew longer. The Canadian prime minister was followed by the Italian finance minister, who gave way to the Chinese finance minister, who passed the arriving Mexican finance minister. The vice governor of the Bank of Japan came after a personal envoy from the German government and representatives of various rank from Argentina, Chile, and Brazil. Simultaneous conversations took place between officials of the State Department and their counterparts from foreign governments, until more than fifty countries had filed through the American executive branch. But despite the diligence the diplomats devoted to the exercises, and for all the sincerity they attempted to convey, most of those involved suspected that they were wasting their time. Until Roosevelt tipped his hand, the discussions among the lower downs didn't really matter.

❖ ❖ ❖

*H*E GAVE A HINT in May. The London economic conference would be one of two international extravaganzas that season. A disarmament conference had been at work in Geneva since the previous year, and it remained in session. One reason the conference continued, despite minimal progress, was that disarmament is never simple. The other reason was that Germany's new government was demanding the right to rearm. Hitler and the Nazis contended that the Versailles settlement was unfair and unrealistic; as a sovereign nation, they said, Germany ought to be able to defend itself. Britain and France refused, recalling what the Germans had done with their weapons the last time they possessed them. Britain's MacDonald and France's Herriot, on their visits to Washington, implored Roosevelt to stand by them in resisting Hitler's demands.

Roosevelt responded by sending a message to most of the world's governments urging their cooperation in ensuring the success of both the London economic conference and the Geneva disarmament conference. Together, he said, the conferences would go far toward determining the fate of humanity for a generation to come. In his message Roosevelt called for the entire elimination of offensive weapons. Nations armed, he said, for two reasons: "first, the desire, disclosed or hidden, on the part of governments to enlarge their territories at the expense of a sister nation; . . . second, the fear of nations that they will be invaded." Roosevelt asserted that the governments intending aggression were few but had an effect far beyond their numbers. The majority of countries retained weapons because they feared attack. Their fear was justified, in that military technology had lately given an advantage to attackers. The solution, Roosevelt said, was to banish offensive weapons. "Defenses automatically will become impregnable, and the frontiers and independence of every nation will become secure." The goal for the Geneva disarmament conference, therefore, must be "the complete elimination of all offensive weapons." This was the test of international good faith—this and cooperation at the London economic conference. "If any strong nation refuses to join with genuine sincerity in these concerted efforts for political and economic peace, the one at Geneva and the other at London, progress can be obstructed and ultimately blocked." The world would be watching, and it would hold the non-cooperators to account.

❖ ❖ ❖

*H*ITLER DIDN'T realize how ironic Roosevelt's words, especially those about the London economic conference, would seem before long. The German chancellor was scheduled to deliver a major speech to the Reichstag the next day, and most observers expected more of the anti-Versailles vitriol that had brought him to power. Already Americans realized that Hitler was one to watch, and American radio stations announced that they would carry his speech.

Roosevelt tuned in at the White House. Leaning close to a radio in his office and recalling what he had learned of the German language in his youth, he provided a running translation of Hitler's speech for Louis Howe and Ray Moley. The president heard both less and more than he had anticipated. That Hitler blamed Germany's current troubles on the postwar settlement was no surprise. "All problems at present causing unrest are founded on the shortcomings of the peace treaty," Hitler asserted. "The idea of rendering useful service to other peoples by destroying economically a people of 65,000,000 is so absurd that nobody can dare today openly to expound it." But Germany wasn't the sole sufferer from the ill-begotten pact, Hitler said; the artificial arrangements imposed on European trade and investment by the Versailles system had so crippled Europe's economy as to be directly responsible for the depression that ravaged the region.

Some of Hitler's listeners—perhaps even Roosevelt—expected the chancellor to declare that the Versailles system might be overturned by force. His earlier speeches and writings had revealed no reluctance to threaten armed action to achieve his goals for Germany. But on this day he abjured the use of force. "No new European war could replace the present unsatisfactory conditions by something better," he said. "On the contrary—new wars, new sacrifices, new uncertainties, new economic distress would result." At the end of that road lay "a Europe sinking into communistic chaos."

Hitler surprised Roosevelt further by praising the president's disarmament message. "For President Roosevelt's proposal, the German government is indebted with warm thanks," the chancellor said. "It is ready immediately to endorse this method of remedying the international crisis because it, too, believes that without a solution of the disarmament question no enduring economic recovery is possible." The president's proposal for eliminating offensive weapons and renouncing aggression was brilliant and wise, and Germany would support it wholeheartedly. Hitler reminded the Reichstag—and Roosevelt and the rest of the world beyond Berlin—that the Versailles treaty committed even the victors of the war to work toward disarmament. If those countries lived up to their commitments, they would have Germany's full cooperation.

"If, however"—and here Hitler got to the part Roosevelt was waiting for—"the others are not willing to carry out the disarmament provisions under the Versailles treaty, which is equally binding upon them, then Germany must at least insist on its claim to equality." The natural edge in Hitler's voice sharpened and his high pitch rose further as he avowed his determination to defend Germany's rights. Germany would not submit to anything that perpetuated the inferior status imposed on it at Versailles. Should the other powers attempt to keep Germany down, they would have themselves to blame for what followed. "Responsibility for the political and economic consequences—the chaos that such an attempt would lead Europe into—would fall on those who resorted to such means against a people who are doing nothing to harm the world."

❖   ❖   ❖

THE LEAGUE OF NATIONS organizing committee for the London economic conference invited sixty-seven nations—essentially every independent country it could think of, as well as India and a few other important dependencies. Sixty-six arrived in mid-June 1933 (Panama pleaded poverty and declined to attend). The delegates met in the London Geological Museum and were seated alphabetically by their countries' names in French. The conference was the first of its kind, and one of the most august meetings in world history to that date. Switzerland sent its head of state (President Edmund Schulthess), while eight countries were represented by their heads of government, twenty by their foreign ministers, and the rest by their finance ministers, central bankers, or other officials. Roosevelt dispatched his foreign minister, Secretary of State Cordell Hull. James Cox, Roosevelt's partner in defeat from 1920, would be Hull's deputy.

The centrality of the Americans to the conference was indicated by the fact that its commencement had been delayed to let Roosevelt clear the most pressing part of his domestic agenda before turning to international economic matters. (The conference might have been pushed back even further if not for the

British grouse season. Ramsay MacDonald informed Roosevelt on his visit to Washington that if the conference was still meeting in the fall when the bird shooting started, the British delegates would absent themselves en masse.) Having waited for the Americans—while the world economy remained in chaos—the conference naturally expected much of them.

Cordell Hull expected much of the Americans, too. "If we are to succeed," the secretary of state told the delegates, "narrow and self-defeating selfishness must be banished from every human heart within this council chamber." The gathered nations must put the welfare of the world before the welfare of single countries. "If, which God forbid, any nation should obstruct and wreck this great conference with the short-sighted notion that some of its favored interests might temporarily profit while thus indefinitely delaying aid for the distressed in every country, that nation will merit the execration of mankind." Woe to the isolationist, who failed to appreciate the interconnectedness of the calamities visiting the peoples of the world. "For him no panic has an international character, cause, or cure," Hull said sarcastically. "He credulously believes that the present depression just happened to come upon all the countries at the same time, and that despite demonstrated failure to do so since 1929, each by its own local program can at will restore full prosperity."

"I felt almost physically ill," Ray Moley wrote in response to Hull's address. The secretary of state was describing the position Roosevelt had staked out in the campaign and had never relinquished. Strangely, Roosevelt appeared willing for Hull to speak as he did. The president had read Hull's speech in advance and had suggested that certain passages be toned down. But otherwise he let Hull excoriate the very attitude he—Roosevelt—had made a central part of his approach to foreign policy.

The heart of the matter was whether the American government would cooperate with the governments of the other major powers to restore the international economic order the depression had thrown into disarray. A comprehensive solution would have involved debts and reparations, tariffs, and exchange rates. As poorly as the American economy was performing, the United States remained the strongest country in the world in terms of its overall production and balance of payments. What the conference almost unanimously wanted was for the United States to employ its strength to lift some of the burden of the depression off the rest of the world.

Roosevelt was willing to take certain steps in that direction. With other Democrats he had long decried the high-tariff policy of the Republicans, and he believed that the tariff wars of the last few years had done much to make the current situation worse. In his talks with France's Herriot and the other foreign visitors he proposed a tariff truce—participating countries would agree not to raise their tariffs further—as a first step toward tariff reduction and a restoration of trade. But, on his own account and because he knew members of Congress were watching, he refused to engage in anything like unilateral tariff disarmament. As president, he had to protect American producers.

Political considerations figured even more importantly in his refusal to write down the debts. Roosevelt was enough the realist to recognize that if the governments that owed America money weren't given relief, they might simply default. The United States would have little recourse in that event. In the past, unrequited creditors had occasionally seized customhouses or removable assets, but the days of gunboat diplomacy were over. In any event France was hardly Egypt or Nicaragua. Yet though the financial outcome would be the same, default would have fewer political repercussions for Roosevelt than forgiveness. The former would be blamed on ungrateful foreigners, the latter on the president himself.

The tariff and debt questions loomed over the London conference, but monetary exchange rates were the rub of the meeting (which was formally called the International Monetary and Economic Conference). As long as the governments of the major trading powers had stuck to the gold standard, it prevented them from manipulating their currencies to gain an edge over one another. But with gold falling by the wayside, the governments could avert a currency war only by some kind of international agreement—which was precisely the objective of the London conference. Everyone expected the United States to insist on a devaluation of the dollar, to make American goods cheaper in foreign markets; most believed a moderate degree of devaluation to be justifiable, inevitable, or both. But the important thing was to write the devaluation into some kind of international agreement that other countries could bank on—literally and figuratively—in charting their own courses.

Hull's statement to the conference suggested that the American administration was willing to participate in such an agreement. Yet simultaneous noises from Washington cast into question Hull's ability to speak for the administration. Early reports from London that an agreement on currency stabilization was near prompted the administration to issue a denial. "Such reports cannot be founded in fact," Treasury Secretary Woodin declared. "Any agreement on this subject will be reached in Washington, not elsewhere."

The striking thing about this statement was not its content but its tone. Of course the president would make the final decision about any accord negotiated in London. But for the administration to belabor this fact in language so stark suggested that its delegates in London were negotiating either blindly or in bad faith.

Or that the president was playing a deep game. Roosevelt was not attending the London conference, but he bargained as hard as anyone who did attend. By keeping the Europeans off balance, he hoped to preserve his options and enhance the likelihood of achieving what he considered success. He revealed a little of his thinking at a press conference the day after Woodin's broadside went out. The president, cautioning reporters that he was speaking "absolutely off the record," ticked off three considerations regarding the reports of discrepancy between the views of the American delegation in London and those of the administration in Washington. "In the first place, our people over there obviously could not conclude any kind of an agreement without submitting it back here to the State Department and to me. That is perfectly clear." The second point was equally clear. "That is that they"—Hull and the delegation in London—"have not communicated with us in any shape, manner, or form." The reason this second point required stressing, though Roosevelt naturally didn't say so, was that it wasn't true. The president was getting regular reports from Hull via William Phillips at the State Department. But though the reporters might have guessed at this connection, they couldn't confirm it, and he continued shamelessly: "Therefore, the third point is equally clear, and that is that they have entered into absolutely no agreement on the other side, tentative or otherwise." How he would have known this if he hadn't received any communication from London might have puzzled the reporters, but none pressed him on the matter.

Roosevelt brought the reporters into his confidence, or appeared to do so. "The reason I say this has to be strictly off the record," he said, "is because it looks to me a little bit as if some of our friends belonging to the other nations in London are trying to spread around the idea that we have entered into some kind of an agreement, and then, if it does not go through, try to put the blame for a failure to stabilize on us. . . . I don't think it would be above some people to do just that very thing."

A reporter asked, "Inasmuch as they are using propaganda of this sort, don't you think there should be some kind of reaction?" Presumably the reporter meant a reaction from the president himself, as opposed to Woodin's statement.

"No, I am just wising you to it," Roosevelt replied.

"Can we use this stuff ourselves?"

"No, just keep it in the back of your heads."

Roosevelt had another reason for speaking off the record, beyond his desire to keep his options open. The money markets were rife with speculation as to what the London conference would produce, and the slightest leak of the president's intentions could send the dollar spiking upward or plunging down against the pound and other currencies.

Given that he was speaking off the record anyway, the reporters asked what Roosevelt considered an acceptable stabilization agreement.

Rather than respond, even off the record, he obfuscated. "Oh, my Lord, it would take me two hours, and then neither one of us would know," he said.

A reporter tried another approach. "Is the administration willing to enter into some sort of a stabilization agreement?"

"That sort of question again is too uncertain," Roosevelt said. "It depends on what kind of a stabilization agreement and where it was and what it was."

❖   ❖   ❖

ROOSEVELT'S REFUSAL to commit to a stabilization plan provoked consternation in Europe. The French eyed the Americans with the darkest suspicion. *Le Monde* assailed the "permanent lack of accord" among the Americans and said that the United States should suspend its participation in the conference until the administration "decides on a monetary policy." The Germans were almost as skeptical. "The Americans are getting themselves disliked at the World Economic Conference," one German paper asserted. "They embarrass the whole work of the conference." Another German daily declared, "As it appears now, the Rooseveltian policy looks like a soap bubble that ought to burst just as soon as the failure of the London conference raises again the waves of general distrust and carries them toward the shores of the New World." Even members of the American delegation pleaded for guidance. "If you love us at all," James Cox cabled Roosevelt in late June, "don't give us another week like this one."

To calm the waters Roosevelt sent Ray Moley to London. The same reporters and editorialists who had noted the divergence between Cordell Hull's views and the opinions previously articulated by the president concluded that Moley was going to London to chastise Hull or at least to impose the president's views on the American delegation and perhaps the conference.

Moley didn't want to go. The cloud already over the conference boded ill for its outcome. Nor did the mood in Washington give much hope. Prices had been rising steadily since March, and nearly everyone associated with the administration thought this a promising development that ought to be allowed to continue. An agreement in London to stabilize the dollar (and other currencies) would cut it short. Moley had spoken with Hugh Johnson, who would head the newly established National Recovery Administration, before leaving Washington. Johnson's job was to establish codes for American industry, codes that would specify wages and prices for hundreds—eventually tens of thousands—of goods and services. "I want to ask you one simple question," Moley said to Johnson. "As head of the NRA, what is your feeling about a possible agreement to stabilize?" Johnson responded, "All right, here's my answer: An agreement to stabilize now on the lines your boy friends in London are suggesting would bust to hell and gone the prices we're sweating to raise." Johnson allowed that stabilization would make sense at some opportune moment. "But that moment isn't now." Comparable conversations with officials of the Agricultural Adjustment Administration, the NRA's rural counterpart, elicited similar responses.

What did the president think? Roosevelt experienced the international pressure for stabilization more directly than Johnson, but he was scarcely more inclined to short-circuit what looked to be the best hope for America's swift recovery. He told Moley he could accept an agreement of some sort, provided it allowed sufficient flexibility for prices to rise further. "If nothing else can be worked out, I'd even consider stabilizing at a middle point of $4.15"—the dollar price of the British pound—"with a high and low of $4.25 and $4.05." The president continued:

I'm not crazy about it, but I think I'd go that far. The essential thing is that you impress on the delegation and the others that my primary objective is to raise the world price level. Tell them what our American recovery program is doing to raise prices, relieve debtors, and increase purchasing power. If other nations will go along and work in our direction, as they said they would when they were in Washington, then we can cooperate. If they won't, then there's nothing to cooperate about.

❖   ❖   ❖

MOLEY SAILED for Europe on June 21 and arrived in London a week later. His appearance was much anticipated, despite Roosevelt's efforts to play it down. For the record, Moley was a "liaison officer" between the president and the American delegation, but the record, in this case, wasn't persuasive. "Few are so credulous as to be deceived by the official explanations of Professor Moley's trip," the *New York Times* editorialized. Moley was going to London to crack the American delegation into line and deliver the president's decision. And none too soon. "It is time to drop polite pretenses and have the truth bluntly stated," the *Times* said.

The assumption that Moley was bearing Roosevelt's version of truth, and that this version would allow the world to begin its ascent from the depths of the depression, caused the conference members to hold their breath at Moley's approach. "Moley's reception in London was surpassed only by those given to kings," Hull remembered, his jealousy still showing after fifteen years. Delegations of high officials, newspapermen, and others, their emotions aroused, hurried down to Plymouth to meet Moley and vie with one another in paying him tribute." In London Moley called on Hull, as was the secretary of state's due. But the press ignored Hull in favor of the president's personal envoy. "He appeared as the only person among the Americans whom they had the slightest interest in seeing," Hull said. "During the few days that followed, prime ministers and other top officials of governments flocked after Moley as if he were the Pied Piper. I continued to keep in the background as if I were the most insignificant individual hanging about the conference."

Moley appreciated the attention even while he understood that it wasn't for him, but rather for what he was thought to represent. What he did *not* understand was that Roosevelt, despite what he had said before Moley's departure, hadn't made up his mind about the conference. The favorable news for the American economy continued. The dollar fell further against the pound; a week after Roosevelt told Moley he'd accept stabilization at $4.15, the price topped $4.40. Roosevelt would have been punishing American producers—the very farmers, manufacturers, and workers he was trying to help with the agriculture administration and the NRA—to accept the deal he suggested to Moley. The more he thought about it, and the more he watched the money markets, the less appealing an explicit stabilization formula appeared. To accept a stabilization scheme—a system of fixed exchange rates—would handcuff the American economy to those of Britain and France. Under current circumstances, this seemed a doubtful bargain.

Moreover, it would handcuff *him*. The whole thrust of the Hundred Days was to free the president to manage the American economy as he saw fit. Vigorous leadership—*his* vigorous leadership—was necessary to deal with the emergency, Roosevelt believed. Congress had granted him scope to exercise that leadership at home. To accept a stabilization scheme abroad would undermine much of what he had done during the last three months. He had talked the British and French along, acting the good economic ally but postponing a decision on exchange rates till he had finished with Congress and got the New Deal well started. Now that Congress had adjourned and the New Deal was in motion, he thought seriously about stabilization for the first time. He decided he didn't like it.

On July 3 he announced his decision. To prevent any further confusion, he spoke in his own voice and in the most straightforward, even shocking, language. The idea that exchange rates could restore prosperity—the consensus of the London conference—was a "specious fallacy," he said. Nations must look inward rather than outward. "The sound internal economic system of a nation is a greater factor in its well-being than the price of its currency." For the conference to hold recovery hostage to a delusion of fixed exchange rates would be "a catastrophe amounting to a world tragedy."

❖ ❖ ❖

$\mathcal{R}$OOSEVELT'S MESSAGE blew up the London conference. "A Manifesto of Anarchy," the *Manchester Guardian* headlined it. The *London Daily Express* declared, "America is the bonfire boy of the world. She lights a fire which might have been a beacon, then runs away to watch it burn itself out." The official complaints were more circumspect but hardly less forceful. Ramsay MacDonald, speaking for Britain, Georges Bonnet for France, and Guido Jung for Italy told Hull they had been double-crossed. "All stated very clearly that your yesterday's message was entirely inconsistent with what you had said in Washington," the secretary of state cabled Roosevelt.

When Moley met with MacDonald, the prime minister was a wreck. "I have rarely seen a man more distraught than he was that morning," Moley wrote. "He turned a grief-stricken face to me as I came in, and he cried out, 'This doesn't sound like the man I spent so many hours with in Washington. This sounds like a different man. I don't understand.' " MacDonald declared that the conference was finished, murdered by Roosevelt. "And then, with a curious kind of petulance, he began to speak of what the conference meant to him. For years he had dreamed of such a conference. Its successful outcome, he'd hoped, would be the crowning achievement of his long career. 'The shadows,' he said, were already 'descending' around him."

MacDonald never recovered from the failure of the London conference, which sputtered along for a few more weeks before the delegates acknowledged its hopelessness and gave up. Roosevelt denied responsibility. A reporter asked, just after Roosevelt dropped his bombshell, if the administration would change its policy if the conference appeared to be "going on the rocks." "Don't put it that way," Roosevelt responded. "We don't think it is going on the rocks."

Yet he refused to change course as the craft hit bottom. When the conference ultimately adjourned in early August, Roosevelt blithely attributed the delegates' departure to that British passion for grouse. A reporter, evidently thinking of a vacation, laughingly said America ought to import some grouse. "We have enough grousing in this country," Roosevelt rejoined with an even heartier laugh. He added—"literally and strictly and entirely in the family and off the record"—that one of the contributors to the failure of the conference— "don't put this down"—was "the Continental and London press. It was rotten, absolutely rotten, and they gave us a dirty deal from the time we left here until we got home. . . . The whole press just ganged us from the start to the finish. And their press were told what to say by their governments. And of course the French press is owned by anybody that will buy it. And there you are. It was a rotten situation."

Ray Moley was another casualty of Roosevelt's bomb throwing. The president's reversal embarrassed Moley badly. Cordell Hull shed no tears for his assistant. "That piss-ant Moley," Hull called him. "Here he curled up at my feet and let me stroke his head like a hunting dog, and then he goes and bites me in the ass!" Hull complained to Roosevelt about Moley's habit of communicating to the president behind his back. Hull got hold of one secret message, a cable in which Moley asserted to Roosevelt that Key Pittman was the "only member of delegation able intellectually and aggressively to present your ideas to the conference." Hull had known that Moley looked down on him, but this was too much, as he made clear to Roosevelt.

The president had hired Hull not for his intellect but for his loyalty and his ability to get along with Congress. Forced to choose between Moley and Hull, the president took the part of the secretary. He transferred Moley, who, recognizing the move for what it portended, resigned from the administration. "There has been a unanimous sigh of relief from everybody in the Department," Sumner Welles, the undersecretary of state, wrote. A journalist who had followed the Hull-Moley story from the start observed, "Hull's gaunt figure and downcast eyes are enough to move one to tears, until one remembers the stiletto protruding from Moley's back."

28.

WHEN *TIME* NAMED HUGH JOHNSON ITS "MAN OF THE YEAR" IN December 1933, Franklin Roosevelt could have been forgiven for feeling slighted. Roosevelt was the architect of the National Recovery Administration, Johnson merely its executor. But the president had to admit that Johnson's biography made better copy than his own, and he was happy for the lightning the NRA attracted to strike elsewhere than the White House.

Johnson grew up among the Plains Indians and homesteaders of Kansas and Oklahoma. He attended West Point with Douglas MacArthur and chased Pancho Villa across northern Mexico with John Pershing and George Patton. A certain flair for administration called him to the attention of his superiors, and upon American entry into the World War he was handed the job of directing the military draft. America's most recent draft—during the Civil War—had provoked murderous riots; Johnson's draft went blessedly smoothly. His secret was the marshaling of public opinion behind the draft. "If public opinion in such a country as this could not be persuaded to support a war, this country could not support that war," he explained.

Franklin Roosevelt watched Johnson from down the hall at the State-War-Navy building and made a mental note. Johnson moved on to the War Industries Board, where—by now a brigadier general—he teamed up with Bernard Baruch to commandeer American industry. "I went away with one outstanding lesson burned into my brain," Johnson said afterward: "Government emergency operations are entirely different from routine governmental operations." And coordination of economic activity was crucial. "Lack of it is so dangerous that it may completely frustrate the almost unlimited power of this country."

Johnson retired to private industry and better pay after the war, only to reconnect with Baruch in time to campaign for Roosevelt in 1932. The three men reminisced about their common experience in the World War, and they discussed how to apply it to the depression. "If industry can thus act as a unit for the purposes of war," Johnson said, "why cannot it also act as a unit for the purposes of peace?"

Even before the National Industrial Recovery Act created the National Recovery Administration, Roosevelt floated Johnson's name as the man who would head the NRA, to test the reaction of the press and the public. Whoever headed the NRA would be extraordinarily powerful, the czar of the American economy. In 1932 Johnson had written and printed for friends a blueprint for an American dictatorship. How serious it was supposed to be became a point of contention. Johnson's script was framed as a proclamation by "Muscleinny, dictator pro tem," which suggested a certain tongue-in-cheekiness. But the thrust of the argument was sober enough. Johnson called the depression a "ridiculous if ghastly paradox" and declared that the solution was "singleness of control and immediate action." He proceeded to lay out a program of emergency powers granted by Congress to the president that looked eerily like the agenda of the Hundred Days. With critics already calling Roosevelt a dictator, the last thing he needed was to nominate someone seen as an acolyte of the Duce.

Roosevelt also wanted to gauge how Johnson would react to the prospect of wielding power. "I think he's a good number-three man, maybe a number-two man," Bernard Baruch told Frances Perkins, the labor secretary, in words intended for Roosevelt. "But he's not a number-one man. He's dangerous and unstable. He gets nervous and sometimes goes away for days without notice. I'm fond of him, but do tell the President to be careful."

Roosevelt took Baruch's warning to heart. Rather than give Johnson control of both agencies created by the National Industrial Recovery Act—the NRA and the Public Works Administration—Roosevelt decided to split responsibility and give the PWA to Harold Ickes at the Interior Department. He casually informed Johnson of the decision at a cabinet meeting. Johnson didn't handle surprises well, and on this occasion he turned various shades of purple. "I don't see why," he spluttered. "I don't see why." Roosevelt pretended not to notice and moved on to other business. But as the meeting adjourned, he summoned Frances Perkins. "Stick with Hugh," he said. "Keep him sweet. Don't let him explode." Perkins caught up with Johnson as they left the room. "He's ruined me," Johnson muttered.

Yet Roosevelt had measured Johnson accurately. After Perkins drove the general around Washington for a few hours, to calm him down and shield him from reporters, he accepted Roosevelt's truncated offer. Even so, his inner turmoil surfaced in the comment he made to the press when his appointment became official. "It will be red fire at first and dead cats afterward," Johnson said. "This is just like mounting the guillotine on the infinitesimal gamble that the ax won't work."

Johnson's tenure went surprisingly well at the start. Or perhaps it wasn't surprising, in that the contributors to the codes that were the first order of NRA business were desperate for anything that would ease their pain. Johnson's world was divided into three parts. The NRA recognized industry, labor, and consumers as the keys to recovery; in each sector of the economy, the three groups were convened to contribute to the codes that would govern their behavior and interaction. Johnson started with cotton textiles, in part because of its particularly dire condition, in part because Roosevelt had made it a symbol of cutthroat competition during the campaign, and in part because a group of mill owners had come to Roosevelt asking him to rescue them from themselves. Johnson's business background gave him a credibility with manufacturers most other New Dealers lacked; mill owners who worried about Roosevelt's "professors" found Johnson's straight talk reassuring.

The basic plan for the code making was simple enough. Industry was invited to initiate things by submitting a proposal for a code—that is, for a schedule of production, wages, and prices. This proposal was submitted to representatives of workers and consumers, who would challenge the parts they found unfair or unworkable. With the help of NRA officials expert in that sector—and with timely intervention by Johnson and occasional jawboning by Roosevelt himself—the three groups would hammer out a compromise. The president would sign the code with a flourish, congratulate the parties on work well done, and urge them to carry their spirit of cooperation forward into the implementation of the code.

Textiles fit the pattern perfectly, and within three weeks of the creation of the NRA Roosevelt signed the textile code into law. The president applauded the signatories for their cooperation and good will, and he expressed particular pride that the code abolished child labor in the textile industry. "After years of fruitless effort and discussion, this ancient atrocity went out in a day, because this law permits employers to do by agreement that which none of them could do separately and live in competition." The textile industry had often been criticized—by Roosevelt, among others—as being the most backward of businesses. Suddenly, with the guidance of government, it vaulted to the forefront of industrial enlightenment, becoming "a leader of a new thing in economics and government."

❖   ❖   ❖

How new this "new thing" was sparked vigorous debate. In certain respects the New Deal was structurally conservative, shoring up the capitalist system as the capitalists themselves might have done had they been able. Roosevelt's rescue of the banks fell into this conservative category; his timely assistance allowed the banks to resume business essentially as they had conducted it before the crisis began.

In other respects, though, the New Deal was structurally radical, and in none more radical than in industrial policy. The NRA entailed a breathtaking extension of federal involvement in the American economy. Never in peacetime—and only once, and temporarily, in war—had Washington taken upon itself the responsibility of organizing industry, of making decisions on hiring, production, distribution, and pricing that heretofore had been left to companies and individuals. Not surprisingly, Roosevelt soft-pedaled the revolutionary nature of what he was attempting. In late July 1933, two weeks after signing the textile code, Roosevelt went on the radio to explain the NRA's mission and methods. He stressed the spirit of cooperation that had brought capital and labor together, and he called for more of the same. "I am now asking the cooperation that comes from opinion and from conscience," the president said. Opinion and conscience were the only instruments the government would use in its efforts to revive the economy. "But we shall use them to the limit," he added significantly, "to protect the willing from the laggard and to make the plan succeed."

As Roosevelt's words intimated, the revolution he had in mind was partly structural but equally psychological. The NRA codes would create new institutional relationships among owners, workers, and consumers, but these relationships would be fruitful and durable only if they were accompanied by a change in mindset among the parties to the codes. For decades American capitalism had been premised on competition—on the self-interest Adam Smith had identified as the motive force of the marketplace. Roosevelt was asking the erstwhile competitors to cease their struggle and cooperate. Their aim should not be individual self-interest but the common interest of themselves collectively and of the American people at large.

His model, as he had stated repeatedly, was taken from the nation's experience during the World War. He cited that model in his radio address, when he introduced an emblem—a blue eagle—that would signify participation in the NRA programs. "In war, in the gloom of night attack, soldiers wear a bright badge on their shoulders to be sure that comrades do not fire on comrades," he said. The same principle applied now. "We have provided a badge of honor for this purpose, a simple design with a legend, 'We do our part.' " Roosevelt asserted that Americans could seize their destiny, as they had done during the war. "I have no sympathy with the professional economists who insist that things must run their course and that human agencies can have no influence on economic ills. . . . But I do have faith, and retain faith, in the strength of the common purpose, and in the strength of unified action taken by the American people."

❖   ❖   ❖

$\mathcal{E}$VENTS APPEARED TO confirm Roosevelt's faith during the rest of the summer. The administration targeted ten industries as essential to economic recovery. Besides textiles, these were coal, oil, steel, autos, lumber, garments, construction, wholesale trade, and retail trade. The last four entailed so many firms of such diverse natures that their codes were put on hold for the time being, in order to focus on the first six. The administration's success in textiles led Johnson and the codifiers to turn hopefully to coal and the others.

The coal question had vexed the American political economy for decades. In the 1870s industrial terrorists called Molly Maguires had murdered foremen and other representatives of ownership. The owners retaliated by hiring private spies to infiltrate the workers' communities and turn miner against miner. The pendulum swung in the workers' favor during the Progressive era, when Theodore Roosevelt took the miners' side against a particularly arrogant group of owners. The subsequent generation had accomplished little to alleviate the harsh feelings between the two sides, and the onset of the depression simply made matters worse. "There were, on both sides, the scars of bloodshed in old battles," Johnson remarked, after trying to negotiate a truce. "They recognized the hopelessness of their condition, but there was too much bitter history in the background for them even to confer. They frankly said there was no hope of composition on any national plan." Nor was the divide between the miners and the owners the only one that mattered. The coal industry included hundreds of small operators who didn't trust one another and definitely didn't trust the large concerns. Before Johnson could even approach the unions, he had to persuade the owners to agree on a code proposal.

The annual convention of the coal owners was winding down at Chicago on the day Roosevelt signed the National Industrial Recovery Act. Johnson seized an army plane for a flight from Washington, having called ahead and urged the owners not to disperse before he could make his pitch. "The plane got away on reports of good weather over the Alleghenies," Johnson remembered, "and with the aid of a miniature staff we began at once on the plane to try to prepare a presentation to the convention. It was a task so engrossing that nobody even looked out the window for an hour." When they did, they suddenly lost interest in their paperwork. "My hair rose on end," Johnson said. "Wet wisps of mist were floating and waving by like washing on a clothes line on a windy day. Just as I raised my eyes, one of these ethereal union-suits flapped its legs up and disclosed that we were headed into a mountain not a hundred yards away, with no sight of its top and no idea of what lay on left, right, or bottom." The plane had lost radio contact with the ground and had wandered off course. The pilot couldn't tell where they were or which way to go. Fuel was running low by the time they identified Johnstown (in part by the persisting evidence of the great flood of 1889), forty miles off course. They reached Pittsburgh on empty tanks, grateful to be back on terra firma but more anxious than ever—now that the imminent peril to life and limb had passed—to keep the coal men from leaving Chicago. Johnson drove to a Pittsburgh radio station, which fashioned a link to the convention hall in Chicago. But the effort failed. His impromptu message was garbled and incoherent, and the meeting broke up with the owners no closer to cooperation.

Yet Johnson persisted. He managed to get enough of the owners to sit down with the union leaders to create a passable quorum, and he let them air their ancient grievances. He mostly avoided taking sides, but when one party or the other seemed stuck on an emotional point he employed certain phrases he had learned from army mule skinners in the Mexican campaign. "You do not get a dozen warring districts which have never known peace in our lifetime, and the labor in all these districts, together with each other and with their employees to agree for the first time in history by suavity and slickness or by reading economic lectures by a professor," he explained after the fact.

Johnson kept Roosevelt apprised of the progress of the talks, but the president avoided direct involvement. Feelings were certain to be bruised before the code took final shape, and Roosevelt wanted to be sure that the injured blamed Johnson and not him. Reporters asked how a particular phase of the talks had gone; Roosevelt replied: "It must have been amusing—this is strictly off the record. Apparently Johnson got Pinchot"—Gifford Pinchot, Theodore Roosevelt's conservation mentor and currently governor of Pennsylvania—

"in one hotel, and Lewis"—John L. Lewis, president of the United Mine Workers—"in another, and locked them in. And he got the vice president of the Steel Corporation"—U.S. Steel, which controlled huge coal fields in addition to being the biggest steel company in the world—"in a third hotel, and locked him in and kept them all there. And, at the psychological moment, he would bring two out and get them together, and then the other two, and get them together, and work them around. Hugh Johnson has done a swell job on this."

❖   ❖   ❖

JOHNSON'S EVENTUAL success with the coal men—"a pretty tough baby," he called the coal code at the signing ceremony—might have been expected to serve as a precedent for other major codes. Roosevelt hoped it would, and to some extent it did. But each industry had its own history, problems, and grievances. The American oil industry was particularly troubled, and never more than during the 1930s. The first American oil boom had occurred in western Pennsylvania after Edwin Drake struck the slippery stuff near Titusville in 1859. The black-gold rush that followed was brought under comparative control only when John D. Rockefeller perfected his Standard Oil monopoly in the 1870s. A second boom developed in Texas and along the Gulf Coast after the 1901 blow-in at Spindletop, near Beaumont. This surge rose higher than the first, driving and being driven by the technological shift from steam power to internal combustion.

The third oil boom burst forth amid the Great Depression. Drillers in East Texas struck oil a year after the stock market crash, and during the next several months they and the thousands who raced to the region to exploit the find ascertained that this field dwarfed anything discovered in America previously. But far from being a bonanza, the East Texas boom nearly destroyed the American oil industry. The oil flooded the market and caused prices to collapse, making oil, at times, cheaper than water in the oil regions. Simple capitalist competition explained some of the overproduction, but the rest resulted from the peculiarities of geology and of petroleum law. An oil field can be likened to an oversized ice cream soda with many straws and sippers. The more that goes out one straw, the less there is for everyone else. And the "rule of capture," a common-law principle that dated from the Saxon days in England, where it applied to water rights, and that had been applied to oil law by the Supreme Court in the 1880s, awarded ownership to whoever pumped the oil from the ground, regardless of where that oil originated. The resulting overproduction not only ravaged prices in the short term but threatened the long-term productivity of the fields, in that too rapid depletion could disrupt the fluid mechanisms that caused the oil to flow in the first place.

The situation was one that cried out for the guiding hand of government. The Texas Railroad Commission made a start, having inherited—or seized, depending on one's point of view—responsibility over oil in the state during the days when oil typically traveled by rail. The railroad commission contrived to ration production among the various leaseholders and nudge prices upward. Yet the arrangement was tenuous, despite Governor Ross Sterling's dispatch of the Texas national guard and the Texas Rangers to the oil fields to catch and punish cheaters, and the oil men looked to Washington for additional help just as the NRA's Blue Eagle was being hatched.

Compared with textiles, an industry with hundreds of products, and coal, with its long history of murderous labor relations, the oil business was straightforward; the essence of any code would be caps on production. Yet these would have to be flexible, given the volatility of demand, both foreign and domestic, for oil. The solution, embodied in the NRA code established during the summer of 1933, was for the secretary of the interior, Harold Ickes, to act as national oil director, each month apportioning production among the several oil states. In his first order, issued in early September, Ickes mandated that the country's production be slashed by 300,000 barrels. This order overturned not merely the market mechanisms of capitalism as they applied to oil but also the Supreme Court decision grafting the rule of capture onto the oil industry.

The oil men weren't accustomed to such decisiveness from Washington. Some resisted, contending that the government ought to guarantee prices rather than restrict output. "If you do not give us price regulations," an official of Standard Oil of California declared, "you can make codes from now to doomsday and you will get nowhere." But others were grateful for anything that might save the industry from itself. When prices, which had fallen to four cents a barrel in East Texas that spring, began climbing toward the glorious figure of a dollar, they looked upon Franklin Roosevelt and his New Deal with a fondness they never would have anticipated only a few years before.

❖   ❖   ❖

The auto code suffered from a boycott by Henry Ford. Thirty years earlier, Ford had been a populist hero, building cars for the masses. Ten years after that, he had been the most enlightened of employers, paying his employees five dollars a day at a time when the industry standard was scarcely half as much and putting the American economy on the high-wage, high-productivity path that buried forever—or at least until the Great Depression set in—Karl Marx's prediction about the inevitable immiseration of the working class.

But time and the automobile industry had passed Ford by. Other companies caught on to the secrets of the assembly line, and his Model T looked increasingly stodgy beside the sleek new models put out each year by General Motors. Ford himself grew cranky. His *Dearborn Independent* blamed international Jewry for the problems that afflicted the planet, and he began to see enemies everywhere. He planted spies in his own factories to forestall unionization, and he loudly proclaimed his right to run his company on his terms.

Not surprisingly, this attitude didn't lend itself to the cooperation the NRA codes required. Hugh Johnson had worked with Ford during the war and had found him as public-spirited as any industrialist. Johnson hoped Ford might be brought around again. But he recognized Ford's touchiness, and so he approached the old man, who turned seventy that summer, carefully and surreptitiously. He left his Washington office after work one day, boarded the fastest plane in the army's air force, arrived in Dearborn, spoke with Ford for a few hours, and returned to Washington to be at his desk when the office opened the next morning. None but those actually involved knew anything about the meeting.

Johnson believed things had gone well with Ford. "I thought that he said that he would support what I was doing to the limit and even beyond," Johnson recalled. Ford Motor representatives joined the negotiations on the automobile code and seemed as amenable to a coordinated policy as the representatives from General Motors and the other companies. But at the last minute they pulled out, obviously on orders from Ford himself.

Johnson flew to Michigan once more. This time he talked to Ford's son, Edsel, who seemed upset about the whole affair. He wanted to help but couldn't get around his father's phobia about unions. He told Johnson that Ford Motor would sign the code if the government could assure the company that it wouldn't have to recognize the auto workers' union. Because this was an essential part of the pact, and in keeping with one of the premises of the New Deal, Johnson rejected the offer.

Johnson thereupon applied the kind of moral pressure that was supposed to be a hallmark of the NRA. Ford's refusal to join the auto code was a matter

of public record, even if Johnson's conversations with the company's principals were not. A reporter approached Johnson regarding what the NRA intended to do about Ford. "General," the newsman asked, "how long will Ford
have before you take steps?"

"I do not know," Johnson said—neither confirming nor denying that he
was considering steps.

"Before you crack down on him?" the reporter pressed. "Will you crack
down on him?"

"I think maybe the American people will crack down on him when the
Blue Eagle is on other cars and he does not have one."

"In other words, you will not give it to him if he does not sign?"

"Of course not."

Johnson and Roosevelt generally spoke and acted as though compliance
with the NRA were voluntary. This wasn't entirely true, as Johnson's implicit
appeal to American consumers to boycott Ford revealed. And the administration's leverage went further than that. Another reporter asked if government
agencies would divest themselves of the Fords and Lincolns in their auto fleets.
Johnson said they would not. "There would be no point in getting rid of those
that they have," he said, before adding significantly: "But they won't get any
more. The government has signified its intentions of buying only from those
industries which display the Blue Eagle."

Reporters asked Roosevelt at the president's next press conference whether
Johnson's position reflected that of the White House. Would the administration countenance a boycott against Ford? Roosevelt didn't want to pick a fight
with Ford or to be seen as taking sides in a code dispute. He selected his words
with care. "I don't think he has put it quite that way," Roosevelt replied. "I
think he put it entirely in the negative way instead of the positive way. In other
words, raising the question as to whether—not any suggestion from topside of
a boycott, but as to whether people actually would, of their own volition, buy
a car that did not have NRA on it. That is a very different thing."

"Just a suggestion?"

"No, not a suggestion. It is just asking a hypothetical question."

It wasn't hypothetical at all. Johnson had raised the issue of a consumer
boycott, and though Roosevelt danced around it, he enforced Johnson's threat
to halt purchases of Ford products. After the auto code took effect among the
other manufacturers, and among auto dealers across the country, Ford continued to resist Johnson's effort to get him to join. A reporter queried Roosevelt: "Can you tell us anything about that controversy?"

"I have not had any part in it at all, except what I read," the president answered. But Congress had banned government purchase of noncompliant products, and he was bound to enforce the law. "We have got to eliminate the purchase of Ford cars," Roosevelt said.

❖   ❖   ❖

As BOLD AS the NRA was in conception, it was more audacious in action. By the autumn of 1933 the major codes were in place and the principal industries were adjusting to their demands. The Blue Eagle was the symbol of the new regime of planned and guided capitalism, and Hugh Johnson was its embodiment. On his good days Johnson reveled in the authority, even as he maintained sufficient savvy to deny he wielded it. "I want to avoid even the smallest semblance of czarism," he asserted. "It is industrial *self*-government I am interested in. The function of this act"—the Recovery Act—"is not to run out and control an industry, but for that industry to come to this table and offer its ideas as to what it thinks should be done." Johnson contrasted the NRA to its farming counterpart, the Agricultural Adjustment Administration, at least as he perceived the two agencies. "AAA thinks that government should run business. NRA thinks that business should run itself under government supervision."

Johnson provided that supervision, and considerable moral support as well. Johnson launched the Blue Eagle with all the propaganda resources of the federal government. In press releases, pamphlets, fliers, newspaper columns, and radio broadcasts, he summoned the American people to the great struggle of their generation. He targeted women particularly. "Women do 80 percent of our buying," he told an audience in St. Louis. "It is they who can put the Blue Eagle on everything that moves in trade or commerce. . . . When every American housewife understands that the Blue Eagle on everything that she permits to come into her home is a symbol of its restoration to security, may God have mercy on the man or group of men who attempt to trifle with this bird." Johnson followed the president's lead in likening the current crisis to war, and he cited some precedents of his own. "Those who are not with us are against us," he said. "And the way to show that you are a part of this great army of the New Deal is to insist on this symbol of solidarity exactly as Peter of the Keys drew a fish on the sand as a countersign, and Peter the Hermit exacted the cross on the baldric of every good man and true." Johnson entreated Americans to purchase products and services bearing the Blue Eagle and to

purchase them in quantities not seen for years. He acknowledged the counterintuitive character of this recommendation; in hard times the prudent
householder normally kept the purse strings tight. Such an approach might
have made sense when the economy was in free fall, but now it would be fatal
to the nation's recovery. "Unpainted houses, cracked shoes many times half-
soled, shiny pants, rattling automobiles, dyed dresses, refurbished wardrobes—
all these badges of unselfish husbandry must now be replaced if this plan is to
have a fair chance to do what we hope for it," Johnson said. "We must shake
ourselves out of this four-year-old idea of doing without against a rainy day,
and we must do that overnight. . . . Buy! Buy now! Buy within prudence everything you need and have so long denied yourselves. It is the key to the whole
situation."

In the spirit of a wartime rally—or perhaps one of Peter the Hermit's religious crusades—Johnson organized a Blue Eagle parade in New York City. For
weeks Johnson's subordinates at the NRA negotiated with city officials, securing permits, enlisting law enforcement, ensuring access and egress for
emergency vehicles, and publicizing the event to all within commuting distance of Manhattan. Pledge lists were circulated; over a million consumers in
the city promised to patronize only businesses that flew the Blue Eagle. On
the day of the parade the army of the Blue Eagle swamped the New York transit system. "Swollen by streams of passengers from every transit line in the city,
a vast lake of humanity overflowed the grass plots and concrete plazas of
Washington Square yesterday, and broke in a white surf of banners against the
encircling hotels and housefronts," an eyewitness asserted. "They were dressmakers, mechanics, office boys, clerks, and chorus girls—workers all of them,
ready to hike four miles for the President and the NRA." The parade had been
scheduled to start at half past one; it got off late when the crush of participants prevented Johnson and the other distinguished guests from reaching
the start on time. But then away they went. "Neatly canalized, the lake became
a broad river of humanity flowing between human dikes," a journalist
recorded. "The crowds lining the streets pressed forward for a better view, pa-
trolmen grew red in the face, and the horses of mounted policemen pranced
dangerously near the toes of onlookers." The throng was widely accounted to
be the largest in the history of New York, numbering upwards of a quarter
million.

Johnson stood for hours on a reviewing stand; as the marchers went by
he recognized familiar faces and was tempted to wave. But seeing the
massed cameras on the street below the stand, calculating the angle at which

they would take their pictures, and realizing that any careless gesture would be interpreted by NRA critics as a Fascist salute, he generally nodded and kept his arm low. His caution failed. *Time* ran a picture showing an arm protruding Mussolini-like from Johnson's shoulder. "But it wasn't my arm on that photograph," Johnson complained afterward. Maybe not. Yet Johnson's explanation sounded even more implausible. "I think it was the arm of Mayor O'Brien, who stood beside me, which had been faked onto my body."

The *New York Times,* which had been skeptical of much relating to Roosevelt's program, offered a mixed review of the day's events. "There have been more brilliant processions," the editors asserted.

This one had little color or variety. It was for the most part a monotony of the commonplace. But it had all the more promise for that. It was democracy's answer out of its daily life to the challenge of the years of depression. The resolute feet that went marching on till midnight were indicative of the spirit—employers and employees marching side by side. But it is the days after that will count, when one has to march alone without the visible association of others in the same effort.

❖   ❖   ❖

ROOSEVELT DIDN'T attend the Blue Eagle rally, leaving the Mussolini comparisons to Johnson. But he did some public relations work of his own. At a press conference the day of the rally, he conducted an impromptu seminar in economics for the reporters. Johnson had been saying that the NRA had accomplished 25 percent of its program; the correspondents wanted to know if the president agreed with this assessment. Roosevelt didn't wish to differ with his NRA chief publicly, but neither did he intend to raise unrealistic expectations. "This is off the record," he said. "Perhaps those figures are true—I don't know, so far as putting people back to work goes. . . . This program is part of a very big project we are engaged in. We can't accomplish it in six months or even a year. . . . But we are making very definite progress." Roosevelt apologized for not having hard figures, which were difficult to come by on certain key aspects of the economy. Yet he reiterated that things were moving in the right direction, if slowly, all across the board. "Wheat isn't high enough, cotton isn't high enough. There aren't nearly enough people back at work. But they are going back, and we hope that as time goes on, week after week, we are going to have not only more people back at work, but we are going to have higher farm prices."

The president did have some figures that bolstered his claim to overall improvement. Current estimates from the Department of Agriculture placed 1933 gross farm income at $6.1 billion, up from $5.1 billion in 1932. This was a big increase, although more work remained. The dream of farmers was the price level that had prevailed before the World War. Whether or not Roosevelt considered a return to this level realistic, he typically spoke as though he did. "If we take the prewar level of 100—this is actual farm prices—they were down to 50 in March of this year," he explained. "And they are back now to about 66⅔. In other words, they have gone about a third of the way back." Administration policy aimed to continue to close the gap.

The White House seminar continued three days later. The Blue Eagle parade had put the NRA on the front pages of all the papers, and the reporters had numerous questions for Roosevelt. One involved the Labor Department's cost of living index, on which various wage codes were based. Some people judged it out of date; what did the president think?

Roosevelt agreed. "I have been dissatisfied with the index that they have been using right along," he said. The Labor Department was working on changing it. "For example, one of the items that they figure on in fixing up this cost index is high-buttoned ladies' shoes. I am told by the girls that they don't make them any more. What they are trying to do in the Department of Labor is to get the index to represent more nearly the things the average family has to buy to live on."

Another question involved section 7a of the Recovery Act, governing the rights of labor. The language of the section was broadly favorable to workers but vague:

> Employees shall have the right to organize and bargain collectively through representatives of their own choosing. . . . No employee and no one seeking employment shall be required as a condition of employment to join any company union or to refrain from joining, organizing, or assisting a labor organization of his own choosing. . . . Employers shall comply with the maximum hours of labor, minimum rates of pay, and other conditions of employment, approved or prescribed by the President.

Yet the act specified no sanctions in the event employers violated its provisions, and it left considerable room for interpretation. Management was interpreting it narrowly, labor broadly. "Do you want to say anything on that?" a reporter asked Roosevelt.

"I suppose I will have to, but will have to do it off the record," the president replied. He knew he couldn't dodge the issue entirely, but the vagueness of section 7a had been deliberate and he didn't want to commit himself to anything before he absolutely had to. "I read it over last night," he said of the section. "It looks pretty clear." But he declined to expound that clarity, preferring obfuscation instead. "It provides for collective bargaining when you come to the necessary interpretation of it. That interpretation should arise from, or be caused by, some specific case. And then you would have to interpret that specific case in the light of Article 7a, instead of putting down a hypothetical interpretation which again would have to be interpreted in the light of a given case."

The reporters weren't satisfied with this runaround. They pushed Roosevelt to say something more concrete.

"There are a great many interpretations which people have tried to make, and no two ever agree on the actual interpretation of the language," he said, as unhelpfully as before. "So I am standing on 7a."

Could they put *that* on the record?, the reporters asked.

"I tell you what—suppose you put it this way, as background: that the White House feels that Article 7a is very plain English and that the interpretation of Article 7a will come about when specific cases arise requiring an interpretation, and until such cases arise it doesn't seem advisable to the president that people should make hypothetical interpretations. Let it go at that."

❖   ❖   ❖

*J*OHN L. LEWIS had his own interpretation of section 7a. Lewis was two years older than Roosevelt, having been born in Iowa in 1880; somewhat shorter, though with an even larger, more impressive head; substantially heavier, as befit a man who represented the brawn of the laboring classes; equally willing to illustrate a point with an anecdote, often embellished and dramatically acted out; better read, or at least more likely to season his stories with Shakespeare and allusions to Eastern mythology; no less charismatic, both up close and before crowds; and wholly as pleased with himself when the center of attention. "He who tooteth not his own horn," Lewis often said, typically between toots, "the same shall not be tooted."

Lewis inherited the mining instinct from his Welsh mining forebears, and he worked the coal mines of the Ohio Valley till he was thirty. He enlisted in the United Mine Workers and rose to become president of the union about the time Warren Harding became president of the United States. Harding and his Republican successors weren't friendly to organized labor, and in the shakeout from the wartime boom, the miners were hit by the falling rubble. The onset of the depression compounded their woes; by 1933 the ranks of the UMW had dwindled to 100,000, from 400,000 in 1920.

Through most of that period, Lewis retained the fundamental faith in capitalism that long distinguished the labor movement in America from its counterparts in Europe. He expected and desired that workers remain workers and owners owners. He voted Republican right through the election of 1932. But when Roosevelt defeated Hoover and when the New Deal promised to make life better for organized labor, he discovered merit in the Roosevelt approach. He roundly applauded the National Industrial Recovery Act, especially section 7a. "From the standpoint of human welfare and economic freedom," he said, "we are convinced that there has been no legal instrument comparable with it since President Lincoln's Emancipation Proclamation." Lewis yielded nothing to Roosevelt or Hugh Johnson in propaganda prowess; the UMW at once launched an organizing campaign that appealed to the same patriotic emotions as the Blue Eagle parades and rallies. "The President wants you to unionize!" spokesmen for the UMW told miners across the coal belt. "It is unpatriotic to refuse to unionize. Here is your union. Never mind about the dues now. Just join up!" A broadside that circulated among the hills of Kentucky put the matter forcefully: "The United States Government has said LABOR MUST ORGANIZE. . . . Forget about injunctions, yellow dog contracts, black lists, and fear of dismissal. The employers cannot and will not dare to go to the Government for privileges if it can be shown that they have denied the right of organization to their employees. ALL WORKERS ARE FULLY PROTECTED IF THEY DESIRE TO JOIN A UNION."

Lewis took this attitude to the negotiations over the coal code. Patrick Hurley, the Republican secretary of war responsible for the orders that sent Douglas MacArthur against the Bonus Army in 1932, represented some of the mine operators. Hurley's heartland upbringing matched Lewis's; he proudly expatiated on his boyhood in Indian Territory and his hardscrabble youth on the frontier. He added, for Lewis's benefit, that he had once worked in the mines and had carried the union card of the UMW. Lewis watched Hurley carefully from beneath his shaggy eyebrows. He raised himself to his full height, threw his head back, and declaimed what seemed to be congratulations. "It is a matter of pride to a member of the United Mine Workers to see a man of that organization go out into the highways and byways of national politics and make a name for himself that is recognized throughout the country," Lewis said. His gaze turned to a glare as he continued: "But it is a matter of sorrow and regret to see a man betray the union of his youth"—and Lewis here brought Hurley's fellow management representatives into his frowning view—"for thirty lousy pieces of silver." Hurley leaped to his feet and rushed toward Lewis, angrily insisting that he retract the slander he had just uttered. Lewis stood fast, as though to let Hurley's outburst break upon his rugged form. In a calm voice he told the chair of the meeting: "Strike out 'thirty pieces of silver.' Let it stand: 'betray the union of his youth.' "

The coal operators—and other employers—were forced to accept the language of section 7a and to see its principles written into the industrial codes. But they weren't without recourse. Despite its apparent curbs on company unions, many employers turned to just such alternative organizations and encouraged workers to join them. Some of the enticements were illusory, but others were real: higher wages, broader benefits, better working conditions. To workers accustomed to little but hostility from management, the company unions marked a signal improvement.

This was precisely what bothered Lewis, William Green of the American Federation of Labor, and other labor leaders. The company unions gave workers something, but not nearly what Lewis and Green thought the workers ought to receive and what they thought the workers would get under independent unions like the UMW and those affiliated with the AFL. In the several months following passage of the Recovery Act, company unions sprang up by the hundreds. The independent unions naturally complained, and many launched strikes to preempt the company unions, to resist their spread, or to register disapproval of the whole scheme. Meanwhile they appealed to the Roosevelt administration and to Congress to strengthen the guarantees they believed section 7a had accorded them.

❖   ❖   ❖

The NRA was the most radical and potentially the most important of the New Deal programs, but the Civilian Conservation Corps was the closest to Roosevelt's heart. It was also the one that promised to have the most immediate impact on the unemployment rate in America, a fact that intensified his affection for it. The stated goal of the CCC was to put a quarter million men to work within a few months; nothing so ambitious had ever been attempted by government in America. The nearest parallels were the raising of armies for war, which accounted for Roosevelt's decision to enlist the War Department, despite early opposition from the military brass. The officers complained that their line was warfare, not social work. But when the commander in chief insisted, and when Congress supplied the money to ensure that the civilian corps did not steal resources from the military corps, the army came around.

Besides the War Department, Roosevelt recruited the Departments of Interior and Agriculture to construct the camps and supervise the projects the men would undertake. Meanwhile he kept a close eye on the whole affair. "I want *personally* to check on the location and scope of the camps, assign work to be done, etc.," he wrote on an organizational chart he devised for the corps. This was a bad idea, as soon became apparent. Amid the myriad other demands on his time, Roosevelt couldn't keep up with the creation of the hundreds, then thousands, of CCC camps. At first the corps' director, Robert Fechner, humored Roosevelt and sent the president each request. But after the backlog at the White House started crimping the work on the ground, Fechner exercised greater authority of his own.

Neither Fechner nor Roosevelt—nor anyone else, for that matter—realized what the government was getting into with the CCC. The head of Agriculture's Forest Service bravely promised to build the requisite camps—some thirteen hundred in the first wave—by midsummer, only to discover that his agency had nowhere near the requisite administrative and logistic capacity. Reluctantly he and Fechner leaned more heavily on the army, which, even more reluctantly, shouldered a larger share of the burden. The target population of the corps was unemployed young males from the cities, but they were soon supplemented by some twenty thousand "local experienced men"—lumberjacks, hunting guides, and the like. Dual necessity inspired this expansion: city boys who didn't know a penknife from a Pulaski would have been lost, literally and figuratively, in the forests, and the loggers and guides would have been angry at being excluded from work they were particularly competent to do. "It is clearly impossible to import into forest regions non-residents even from within the same state, and have peace there unless local unemployed laborers, accustomed to making their living in the woods in that very place, are given fair consideration as concerns their own means of livelihood," a letter to Roosevelt from Fechner and other interested parties asserted. The loggers, in particular, were a rough bunch. Should they be excluded they might burn down the camps or the forests or both.

Considerations of a slightly different sort caused Roosevelt to expand the purview of the corps to include American Indians. Poverty had been a severe problem on reservations and in the surrounding regions since the nineteenth century, and the drought that afflicted large swaths of the Plains deepened the misery. The drought simultaneously aggravated erosion, making the reservation districts suitable for the kind of restorative work that was part of the corps' raison d'être. The requisite changes were made in the recruitment schedules, and nearly fifteen thousand Indians were added to the ranks of the conservationist workforce.

Another contingent came from the Bonus Army. Eleanor Roosevelt had charmed the veterans personally, but what disbanded the group definitively was the promise of inclusion in the conservation corps. This required some stretching of the corps mandate, as most of the vets were beyond the age limit of twenty-five years, and many were married, also in contravention of CCC practice. But smart politics and simple justice suggested that exceptions were in order, and Roosevelt issued an executive order authorizing the enlistment of twenty-five thousand vets. Some grumbled that the thirty-dollar monthly wage wasn't what they had hoped for. But considering their alternatives, many judged the offer a bargain and donned the uniform of the CCC.

The vets found much about corps life familiar. Work days began with six o'clock reveille. The young men turned out of their cots in the tents that served as initial shelter, arranged in neat rows along paths lined with gravel. A first order of business in most camps was building wooden barracks to replace the tents; thereafter the men slept in bunks. A cold shower or splash constituted the morning ablutions, which were followed by a half hour's calisthenics and other exercise. (Whether Roosevelt, in personally approving this part of the program, grew wistful at thoughts of Walter Camp's wartime regimen is impossible to know.) Breakfast was served at seven and consisted of lumber-camp fare in substantial, if not Paul Bunyan-esque, proportions. Ham and eggs, hot cereal and stewed prunes, milk and coffee fueled the bodies for the morning's work in the woods.

Roll call and inspection followed breakfast, and by eight the men were off to the job sites. If these were close to camp, they hefted their tools and walked; if farther, they piled into trucks and were driven. They cleared brush, built trails, and planted trees—hundreds of trees, thousands of trees, eventually millions of trees. At noon they broke for lunch, which was delivered to the site if they weren't within walking distance of the mess hall. In the hall the meal was often hot; in the woods it typically consisted of sandwiches, more coffee, and pie. Work resumed and lasted till four, when the men returned to the camp. The hour before dinner was their own, to read any mail that might have come, write letters, play baseball or football, or do whatever else young men do in the absence of young women and alcohol. Some camps had libraries stocked with magazines and popular books; mobile libraries served those camps without fixed facilities.

All day the men wore work clothes, typically denim jeans and work shirts. For dinner they donned dress uniforms: olive drab supplied by the army. Eventually Roosevelt designed a dress uniform specifically for the CCC: forest green shirts and slacks. Dinner was even heartier than breakfast or lunch; the men downed beefsteaks, potatoes, bread, vegetables, fruit, milk, coffee, cake, and pie. An early measure of the success of the program was the muscle and bone the young men added to their frames. According to CCC statistics, the average enrollee arrived weighing 147 pounds and standing 5 feet 8¼ inches tall, at twenty years of age. This was below the norm for healthy, well-fed young men of that era, and it reflected the poverty most of the enrollees had experienced during adolescence. Within a month or two, the typical corpsman had put on ten or twelve pounds; many added height as well, though this naturally took longer.

Roosevelt remarked on the healthy growth when he toured CCC camps in August 1933. The president traversed the Shenandoah Valley west of Washington, stopping at five camps below the Blue Ridge. Someone in the corps had suggested that Roosevelt visit a model camp; he vetoed this plan in favor of examining several examples of the real thing. The five camps were a fair cross-section of the CCC in action. Each camp contained about two hundred men. Some of the camps were on public property; others were on private land. The men were clearing downed trees and dead wood, as a precaution against fire, and extending trails and improving roads. They were most proud of the stone guard walls they had built along the Blue Ridge Skyline Drive, where the pavement ran dangerously close to sheer cliffs.

Roosevelt rode in an open car beneath the hot Virginia sun. As he arrived at each camp, the men lined up in their army dress for inspection. They remained at attention till he gave the nod to their commander, who told them to break ranks—at which point they mobbed the president's car to shake his hand. At one camp he ate lunch, attacking his fried steak, mashed potatoes, string beans, lettuce-and-tomato salad, and apple cobbler, washed down with iced tea, with almost as much gusto as the men did. "I wish I could spend a couple of months here myself," he declared. "The only difference between us is that I am told you men have put on an average of twelve pounds each. I am trying to lose twelve pounds." At another camp a self-proclaimed "Hillbilly Band" serenaded the president with "Turkey in the Straw." At a third camp the corpsmen built a bonfire and burned an effigy of "Old Man Depression."

For Roosevelt, the mission of the conservation corps had as much to do with conserving human resources as with saving America's forests. He concluded his tour of the Virginia camps with the comment that he hoped the CCC camps all over the country were as inspiring as these. "All you have to do is look at the boys themselves to see that the camps are a success," he said.

29.

ELEANOR ROOSEVELT VISITED CCC CAMPS, TOO, BUT USUALLY WITH-
out her husband. She spent few days with Franklin—and of course no nights.
She filled her calendar with her own activities, her own causes, her own companions. Being First Lady could sometimes be exciting. Amelia Earhart came
to Washington and took Eleanor flying. "It was like being on top of the world!"
Eleanor exclaimed. Being First Lady could also be a chore. She naturally hired
a housekeeper to run the executive mansion; Henrietta Nesbitt received the
job because Eleanor knew and liked her from Hyde Park, where she had operated a small tea house. The appointment was a disaster. The meals at the
White House became notorious for the terrible food: leathery meat, watery
soup, unrecognizable vegetables, cheap wine. Guests shared horror stories;
Franklin complained. But Eleanor professed not to notice, and Mrs. Nesbitt
stayed on. Certain of those who knew of the personal tension between Eleanor
and Franklin surmised that Mrs. Nesbitt was, in a subtle and perhaps unconscious way, Eleanor's instrument for asserting control over her husband in one
area of their relationship where she could.

More commonly she simply struck out on her own. She continued her
press conferences and began speaking on the radio. Her six-minute weekly
broadcasts weren't publicized as a counterpart to Franklin's Fireside Chats,
nor did she intend them as such. But inevitably some observers interpreted
them that way. Eleanor's broadcasts clearly differed from Franklin's in one crucial respect: she was paid for them. The three-thousand-dollar weekly fee
struck many people, including Eleanor, as exorbitant. "No one is worth $500
a minute," she admitted. But the fee was what the sponsor, the Johns-Manville
corporation, a manufacturer of building materials, was willing to pay, and
Eleanor arranged for the funds to be transferred to the American Friends Service Committee. She wrote a monthly column for *Woman's Home Companion*,
for which she received a thousand dollars per month. She tried, in her radio

broadcasts and her column, to avoid topics that might embarrass Franklin. She skirted politics, at least at first, and concentrated on matters of domestic and maternal interest.

She traveled frequently, often in the company of Lorena Hickok, the reporter from the 1932 campaign. Hick, as she was called, had had to fight her way into the male preserve of political reporting. She swapped lewd stories with the boys on the beat and shared the booze that eased the boredom of waiting for news to break. She covered the Lindbergh kidnapping case for the Associated Press, crawling through snowdrifts around the Lindbergh house in response to a rumor that the baby had been retrieved. The AP put her on to Eleanor Roosevelt in 1932, an assignment that cost Hickok her objectivity and eventually—after her editor learned that she was letting Eleanor read her stories before she filed them—her job. Eleanor thereupon found her a position with Harry Hopkins, who headed the administration's relief program. Yet she made time to travel with Eleanor, and the two became close friends.

Eleanor usually traveled in her official role as First Lady, giving the requisite interviews and speeches. Occasionally, though, she tried to retrieve the private life she had enjoyed before her husband became so famous. In the summer of 1933 she and Hick took a road trip to Quebec and around the Gaspé Peninsula. She left the Secret Service at home, to the agents' displeasure. "They predicted that we'd be kidnapped," Hickok remembered. The abduction and killing of the Lindbergh baby had shocked the nation the year before, and law enforcement was on high alert. Hickok and Eleanor laughed. "The idea of anyone trying to kidnap two women, one nearly six feet tall"—Eleanor—"and the other weighing close to two hundred pounds"—Hickok—"seemed funny," Hickok said. Eleanor chuckled: "Where would they hide us? They certainly couldn't cram us into the trunk of a car!" The trip went well and inconspicuously. Eleanor wasn't as recognizable as she would become, and to many of the people they encountered they were simply two women on a holiday. Others apparently recognized Eleanor but left her alone. "They're all Republicans up here," she explained to Hickok in New Hampshire.

Subsequent vacations were less satisfactory. Franklin Roosevelt declared 1934 to be "National Parks Year," and Eleanor decided to tour the West with Hickok. At Yosemite she insisted that they ride horses among the mountain peaks; she found the experience exhilarating, but Hickok, who avoided exercise whenever possible, gasped and strained at the altitude and the effort. "How could you do this to me?" Hickok complained. "You'll manage," Eleanor responded.

Hickok recuperated on the drive from Yosemite to San Francisco, where she had arranged for them to stay in a small, previously quiet hotel. The owner was surprised to learn that the second member of Hickok's party was the president's wife, yet he maintained his aplomb and their secret. One member of the hotel staff, however, was less discreet, and when the women returned from dinner the lobby was overflowing with reporters. Flashbulbs popped; questions were shouted at Eleanor. She refused to answer, beyond declaring, "I'm here on a vacation. I'd like to be left alone." But San Francisco was ruined for them. Reporters and photographers followed them all around the city the next day. They had intended to remain longer but decided to leave at once.

They drove north into Oregon, stopping at Bend, a small town on the east side of the Cascades. The news of their approach had preceded them, and the manager of their hotel said some people wanted to meet them. Eleanor begged off. "We're tired," she said. "We have to leave very early tomorrow morning." Dinner was quiet, and the two watched the sun set over the snow-capped mountains. But as they exited the dining room they encountered a large crowd, headed by the mayor. Eleanor sent Hickok along and, as politely as possible, shook the required hands.

Half an hour later she extricated herself. She went upstairs and slammed the door—"something I'd never known her to do before, nor did I ever know her to do it since that night," Hickok remembered. Eleanor sat down on the bed.

On either cheek was a red spot. They used to appear that way when she was annoyed.

"Franklin was right!" she said.

"What do you mean?" I asked her.

"Franklin said I'd never get away with it," she replied. "And I can't."

She was silent for a moment. Then she sighed and added: "From now on I shall travel as I'm supposed to travel, as the President's wife, and try to do what is expected of me." Then she added defiantly: "But there's one thing I will not do. I will not have a Secret Service man following me about. *Never!*"

If the western trip failed as a getaway, it confirmed the bond between Eleanor and Hickok. Eleanor remained attached to Franklin by complex ties of affection, obligation, and ambition, but deeper emotions gradually connected her to Hick. "I've been wondering what I really want for my declining years," she wrote Hick in the spring of 1934. She had attended a conference on aging and the problems old people in America sometimes confronted. "I hope you and I together have enough to make it gracious and attractive." She reflected on the future, and her thoughts included Hick more often than they did Franklin. "Someday we'll lead a leisurely life and write—so we can take our work with us and do all the things we want to do."

Hickok had difficulty waiting. "And now I am going to bed—to try to dream about you," she wrote when they were apart. She counted the moments till they would be together again.

> Only 8 more days. 24 hours from now it will be only 7 more—just a week. I've been trying to bring back your face to remember just *how* you look! Funny how even the dearest face will fade away in time. Most clearly I remember your eyes, with a kind of teasing smile in them, and the feeling of that soft spot just northeast of the corner of your mouth against my lips.

Eleanor reciprocated. She told Hick how she had been helping some friends set up a house and had fallen asleep beside one of them in a big double bed. "Only I wished it was you," she wrote. She regularly reassured Hick, who often seemed the needier of the two emotionally. "Love is a queer thing," Eleanor wrote. "It hurts one but it gives one so much more in return!" She, too, wished for their separation to end. "Someday we will do lots of work together! I love you deeply, tenderly and my arms feel very empty."

❖   ❖   ❖

*H*UEY LONG'S AMBITIONS as a young man weren't much different from Franklin Roosevelt's. He told the woman he would marry that he intended to enter politics at the state level, advance to governor, then run for national office, eventually president. That such ambitions seemed natural for Roosevelt, a scion of the New York gentry, but excessive for Long, a child of back-country Louisiana, accounted for much of Long's resentment against Roosevelt.

Until the 1920s Long's ambitions and resentments remained hidden from most of the country. He made a minor stir by attacking Standard Oil from his seat on the Louisiana commission that regulated the petroleum industry in the state, and he ran third for governor in 1924. But he learned from his defeat and in 1928, even as Roosevelt was squeaking to victory in the race for New York governor, Long barged into the governor's house in Baton Rouge by the largest margin in Louisiana history. His politics were populist; his slogan— "Every man a king, but no one wears a crown"—was borrowed from William Jennings Bryan. Yet Long was no Bryan. The essential sweetness that even

Bryan's opponents noted in the Nebraskan was utterly missing in the Kingfish, as he called himself. The journalist A. J. Liebling said that Long's complexion was "the color of a sunburn coming on"; in truth it wasn't sunburn so much as indignation, on behalf of himself and those he professed to speak for. Long toured the Cajun districts of his state and doffed his hat beneath the boughs of the Evangeline Oak. "It is here under this oak where Evangeline waited for her lover, Gabriel, who never came," he said to the dirt farmers gathered round.

> Evangeline is not the only one who has waited here in disappointment. Where are the schools that you have waited for your children to have, that have never come? Where are the roads and the highways that you send your money to build, that are no nearer now than ever before? Where are the institutions to care for the sick and disabled? Evangeline wept bitter tears in her disappointment, but it lasted through only one lifetime. Your tears in this country, around this oak, have lasted for generations. Give me the chance to dry the eyes of those who still weep here!

Long rammed laws through the legislature, bypassing the formerly powerful and trampling the toes of the wealthy. He bent some rules in the process, and the bending allowed his enemies to mount an effort to impeach him. Punches were thrown in the state house of representatives; blood was drawn. Long looked to the senate for support, persuading a core of senators to announce for acquittal even before the charges were fully aired. He lived to fight another day, with different tactics than before. "I used to try to get things done by saying 'please,' " he said (to the puzzlement of those many who had never heard the word pass his lips). "That didn't work, and now I'm a dynamiter."

Louisiana law forbade Long from succeeding himself as governor in 1932, and so, before his term was half finished, he plotted how to take his high-explosive act elsewhere. He ran for the U.S. Senate in 1930 and won but declined to assume his seat until he could arrange the election of a minion as his replacement for governor. Oscar Allen fit the bill perfectly, demonstrating not the slightest independence. "A leaf once blew in the window of Allen's office and fell on his desk," Long's brother Earl said. "Allen signed it."

The Great Depression hit Louisiana harder than most states. Long hit back with methods not dissimilar to those Roosevelt would employ at the national level. He poured money into public works, building bridges by the score and paving roads by the thousands of miles. He hatched a plan to curtail cotton production by means of a cotton holiday: a concerted refusal by southern farmers to plant a cotton crop in 1932. The holiday never happened, because of Long's in-ability to secure the support of other cotton states, but it softened up the oppo-sition to the less drastic crop restrictions Roosevelt's AAA would introduce. It also allowed Long to cast himself as the champion of poor folks all across the South. "You are the Moses of the cotton farmer," one of those farmers told him.

Long sided with Roosevelt in 1932, albeit ungraciously. "I don't like your son of a bitch," he told an emissary from the Roosevelt camp. "But I'll be for him." In public Long played the loyal Democrat, and he won votes for the Roo-sevelt ticket in the districts where he stumped for it—all the while expanding his own voter base. His salvos against the citadel of privilege amazed even hardened journalists. "Seven motor trucks and Senator Long's private auto-mobile composed the campaign caravan," one reporter wrote. "Two of the trucks were the specially designed and built sound trucks developed by him. . . . Each is equipped with four amplifying horns. Inside the vehicle body are the loudspeaker panels, an attachment for playing phonograph records, several folding chairs, a folding table, a pitcher and glasses." One of the sound trucks would arrive at a rally half an hour before Long was scheduled to speak. It would play music and draw a crowd. Long's car would pull up, and the sen-ator would leap out. By no means were all of his listeners starving; many drove in their own cars, clogging the roads for miles around. But soon he'd have them believing the wolf was at the very door.

> Think of it, my friends! In 1930 there were 540 men in Wall Street who made $100,000,000 more than all the wheat farmers and all the cotton farmers and all the cane farmers of this country put together! Millions and millions and millions of farmers in this country, and yet 540 men in Wall Street made $100,000,000 more than all those millions of farmers! And you people won-der why your belly's flat up against your backbone!

Long stuck with Roosevelt only until the latter's inauguration. He chal-lenged the president on the emergency banking bill, complaining that it did more for bank owners than for bank depositors. He joined the cry against Roosevelt on the budget act. He deplored the industrial codes of the NRA as capitulation to capital. "I want to stay on good terms with the administration," he declared unpersuasively, "and I am going to do so if it is possible, but I do not have to."

Roosevelt initially ignored Long's criticism, even after Long followed the president onto the airwaves with radio chats of his own—although in Long's case the chats tended to be rants. In June 1933, however, Roosevelt decided to put Long in his place. He invited the senator for a visit. "It was a morning appointment," James Farley remembered. "The day was hot, and Huey came charging into the White House in his usual breezy and jaunty manner. He was nattily dressed in light summer clothes and wore a sailor straw hat with a bright-colored band." The conversation commenced innocuously but grew warm when Long claimed credit for Roosevelt's nomination at Chicago. Farley, who thought *he* had had something to do with the convention's decision, pointed out that Long's Louisiana delegation had been seated only with the assistance of then-Governor Roosevelt. The tone sharpened the more. "Huey had come in with a chip on his shoulder, and although his words were courteous enough, it was obvious from his attitude that he was there for the purpose of testing the mettle of the President." Long conspicuously kept his hat on during the conversation. "At first I thought it was an oversight," Farley said, "but soon realized it was deliberate." Farley couldn't decide whether to call the senator on his discourtesy or keep quiet. The president silently warned him off. "I glanced at Roosevelt and saw that he was perfectly aware of what was taking place and, furthermore, was enjoying it immensely. . . . He had a broad smile on his face which never changed for a moment, not even when Huey leaned over to tap him on the knee or elbow with the straw hat to emphasize one of his finer points, a trick which Huey pulled not once but several times." Marvin McIntyre, Roosevelt's appointment secretary, missed Roosevelt's cue. "I saw McIntyre standing there with his teeth clenched and I thought for a moment that he was going to walk over and pull the hat off Huey's head." Long finally got the message and took the hat off.

Long had arrived hoping to receive assurance that he would be consulted in the awarding of federal patronage in Louisiana. He left with nothing. "What the hell is the use of coming down to see this fellow?" he complained to Farley on the way out. "I can't win any decision over him." Nor did he win any appointments. As the jobs went to his rivals in Louisiana, his anger mounted. He tried to block federal funds spent in Louisiana by his enemies, and when he was chastised by Interior Secretary Ickes, he summoned reporters to read them his bill of particulars against the New Deal. He urged the newsmen to wire his message north. "While you are at it, pay them my further respects up there in Washington. Tell them they can go to hell."

Roosevelt's opposition wounded Long briefly. The Roosevelt forces in Louisiana mobilized against the Long alliance, while the senator himself spun momentarily out of control. A drunken incident involving a crowded public bathroom and Long's urine soaking the trousers of another man resulted in a black eye for Long, physically and politically. Northeastern papers tut-tutted the southern bumpkin; some southern papers did, too. Long looked to be down, perhaps for the count.

But he regained his feet with a program—or rather a promise—that threatened to suck the air right out of the New Deal. Long's Share Our Wealth plan proposed a radical redistribution of American wealth. A draconianly progressive wealth tax, rising to confiscation on fortunes above $8 million, would fund a guaranteed income for every family in America, as well as pensions for the elderly, aid to schools, and additional public works. "God invited us all to come and eat and drink all we wanted," Long asserted. "He smiled on our land and we grew crops of plenty to eat and wear. He showed us in the earth the iron and other things to make everything we wanted. He unfolded to us the secrets of science so that our work might be easy. God called: 'Come to my feast.' " But a greedy few had elbowed everyone else aside. "Rockefeller, Morgan, and their crowd stepped up and took enough for 120 million people, and left only enough for 5 million for all the other 125 million to eat. And so many millions must go hungry and without these good things God gave us unless we call on them to put some of it back." By Long's reckoning, the wealthiest 2 percent of Americans owned 60 percent of the wealth; this imbalance explained much of the country's current predicament. Equity and efficiency pointed in the same direction: toward a sharing of America's wealth. The rich hoarded their wealth, causing the current depression. The poor would spend this wealth, reviving the engines of prosperity.

Long's plan had problems, starting with its arithmetic. There simply weren't enough rich people to provide the incomes he promised. But this didn't prevent the concept from catching on. Share Our Wealth clubs sprouted all over the country. By early 1935 Long boasted of some twenty-seven thousand chapters and seven million adherents. No one took these numbers at face value, but even discounted for Kingfish hyperbole, they signified a large and growing demand for measures more radical than anything Roosevelt had contemplated thus far.

❖   ❖   ❖

Huey Long was better at tapping popular passions than Roosevelt, but he wasn't as good as Charles Coughlin, in part because Coughlin wasn't at first so obviously political. In fact Coughlin wasn't obviously anything, except exceedingly good at radio, better even than Roosevelt. Coughlin was called the "Radio Priest" because, not long after taking charge of a struggling parish in suburban Detroit, he talked a local station manager—like Coughlin, an Irish Catholic—into giving him air time to raise money and combat the noxious preachments of the Ku Klux Klan. Coughlin proved to be a radio prodigy, with "a voice of such mellow richness," author and fan Wallace Stegner said, "such manly, heart-warming, confidential intimacy, such emotional and ingratiating charm, that anyone tuning past it on the radio dial almost automatically returned to hear it again. . . . It was a voice made for promises."

At first it promised merely heaven: eternal bliss to those who embraced the Gospels and the teachings of the Church and contributed to the Shrine of the Little Flower, as he called his parish church. But not long after the start of the depression Coughlin's sermons turned political. Radio stations across the industrial Midwest had begun carrying Coughlin's program; no part of the country suffered more painfully from the collapse of American manufacturing. Catholic theology was broad enough to embrace both defenders of the status quo and advocates of social change; Coughlin sided at first with the latter. He backed Roosevelt for president in 1932, although, as he explained to the candidate, he couldn't deliver a formal endorsement without violating his clerical neutrality. But after Roosevelt's election and inauguration he declared, "The New Deal is Christ's deal," and he treated the president as the best friend America's poor had ever had.

He also treated the president as his own best friend, annoying those who truly were close to Roosevelt. Marvin McIntyre got almost as testy at Coughlin as he did at Huey Long, notwithstanding McIntyre's engrained respect for the Roman collar. But Roosevelt told his people to be nice to Coughlin, and he encouraged the priest to continue to forward helpful suggestions.

In time, though, Coughlin caught on that his suggestions weren't being taken seriously. The last thing Roosevelt needed was more advice on money, but this was precisely what Coughlin made his primary cause. Coughlin insisted on devaluing the dollar by raising the price of gold, which accorded with Roosevelt's plans, and by remonetizing silver, which didn't. Coughlin became to silver in the 1930s what William Jennings Bryan had been in the 1890s, except that Coughlin, while praising silver's benefits for ordinary people, was speculating in silver futures for himself. In the spring of 1934 the administration published a list of large purchasers of silver futures; the general point of the publication was to demonstrate that the demand for silver money was less than disinterested. Whether anyone in the White House initially realized that the list included Coughlin's personal secretary is unclear, but the 500,000 forward ounces she bought—on her own account, she unconvincingly claimed—seemed solid evidence that Coughlin had reasons less lofty than the popular welfare for praising the white metal.

Coughlin probably didn't need the embarrassment of the silver scandal to turn openly against Roosevelt, but the incident added a personal element to his animus. Though his priestly vows presumably prevented a run for office in his own name, he organized what he called the National Union for Social Justice, which advocated policies more advanced, from a vaguely social-justice perspective, than those of the New Deal. Coughlin's radio program promoted the organization to its millions of listeners; Coughlin complemented his broadcasts with rallies that made the National Union look increasingly like a third party.

* * *

*P*RECISELY BECAUSE his ambitions were less patent than Long's or Coughlin's, Francis Townsend posed a greater threat to Roosevelt than either the Kingfish or the Radio Priest. Dr. Townsend didn't start practicing medicine till he was in his mid-thirties; he didn't leave South Dakota for Southern California till he was past fifty; he didn't find his true calling—political agitation—till he was pushing retirement. And retirement was precisely what he began pushing in 1934, when he and a Texas promoter named Robert Clements formed Old Age Revolving Pensions, Ltd. Their brainstorm was pensions with a twist: the federal government should pay two hundred dollars per month to every American over sixty, on the strict condition that the recipients retire from work and spend the money as it came in. The spending was what inspired the "revolving" label, and it would, according to the Townsend Plan, underwrite the whole program by forcing the money to recirculate, thereby reviving the economy. A sales tax would provide the direct funding, but in a larger sense the plan would fund itself, through the prosperity it would restore. The jobs released by those sexagenarians currently working would furnish immediate benefits to the younger men and women who moved into them.

The mathematics of the Townsend Plan were as dubious as those of Long's wealth-sharing scheme; eminent critics noted that more than half the country's output would be diverted to less than a tenth of the population. "Dr. Townsend's error lies in forgetting the simple truth that someone must produce the wealth which is consumed by the non-producers, be they infants, old

people, sick people, the unemployed, the idle rich, or the criminal classes,"
Walter Lippmann explained. "If Dr. Townsend's medicine were a good remedy,
the more people the country could find to support in idleness, the better off
it would be." Townsend was unimpressed by Lippmann's logic and unfazed by
his criticism. "My plan is too simple to be comprehended by great minds like
Mr. Lippmann's," he said.

Equally unimpressed were the tens of millions of men and women who
joined the tens of thousands of Townsend Clubs around the country and who
put their signatures to a petition Townsend circulated, calling on Congress to
enact his plan. "The zeal of those promoting the plan is evangelical, almost fa-
natic," conservative columnist Mark Sullivan observed. "The pressure on Congress is much greater than was ever brought by veterans for the bonus. . . .
Promoters of the bill say it is supported by ten million persons over 60, ten million more who have dependents over 60, and twenty million more who expect
to become 60 some time—and to whom the plan looks good. That would be
about all the voters there are." Sullivan exaggerated for effect—but the effect
wasn't lost on members of Congress. Oregon Republican William Ekwall captured the spirit in the House when he declared, "About 120,000 people in my
district have signed a Townsend petition. When I first heard of this I laughed
at it. Then I got the smile off my face. It's like a punching bag—you can't dodge
it. If we don't pass it this session we'll have to meet it when we get back home."

❖   ❖   ❖

By the autumn of 1934 it seemed that everyone was promoting a plan to
end the depression. Upton Sinclair, the muckraking journalist from the days
of Theodore Roosevelt, had, like Townsend, moved to California, where the
same passion that had inspired *The Jungle*, his exposé of the meatpacking industry—which was supposed to drive America to socialism rather than vege-
tarianism—gave rise to EPIC, short for "End Poverty in California." Sinclair's
plan aimed to turn the means of production in the state over to the producers. The state would supply land to the landless and factories to the jobless. It
would also print pseudo-money that could be spent only on items grown or
manufactured within EPIC's pseudo-economy. To publicize his plan, Sinclair
announced his candidacy for California governor. Or perhaps the point of his
plan was to publicize his candidacy; either way, the plan and the candidacy
garnered great publicity. In the Democratic primary Sinclair trounced the
mainstream candidate and polled more votes than the incumbent governor

did in the Republican primary. Veteran observers of California politics, even while scratching their heads trying to understand the EPIC phenomenon, saw little to prevent Sinclair from sweeping into the governor's house in November. Sinclair requested a conference with Roosevelt, which Roosevelt declined, leaving Sinclair to proclaim his revelation on his own. "Capitalism has served its time and is passing from the face of the earth," he said. "A new system must be found to take its place."

❖ ❖ ❖

IT WASN'T AN accident that land-transferring socialism took hold in California. Though nicknamed for its mining past, the Golden State lived or died on agriculture, and in the mid-1930s it was on the verge of dying. The same problems of overproduction that vexed farmers elsewhere existed in California, but they were exacerbated by the historic tendency of Americans in other parts of the country to look west for solutions to their problems. During the depression no part of the country suffered more than the Great Plains, where a host of evils beset farmers who hadn't been prosperous to begin with. Excessive optimism during the homestead era of the late nineteenth century had led to the settlement of districts that couldn't really support the communities planted upon them; modern technology permitted the plowing of vast swaths of grassland that never should have been broken and turned; unprecedented demand during the World War had driven prices to unsustainable levels. Prices fell after the war, weakening the economies of the Plains states. They fell further with the onset of the depression.

Then the rains ceased. Farmers hadn't lived on the Plains long enough to know that drought was part of the recurrent climate pattern in that region (the aboriginal peoples knew, which was why they didn't try to farm there). Some farmers attributed the drought to bad luck, others to the wrath of God. The wrathful explanation seemed the more persuasive when hot winds blew across the parched, torn earth and lifted tons of topsoil high into the air, building battlements of brown, churning dust five thousand feet tall and fifty miles long that blotted out the sun and choked humans and livestock as the wave of airborne topsoil rolled across villages, towns, and cities.

Lorena Hickok encountered a dust storm on the northern Plains. Harry Hopkins had put her to work reporting on the lives of ordinary Americans, in order to determine where federal relief was needed most. "When I got up at 7:30 this morning, the sky seemed to be clear," she wrote from South Dakota.

But you couldn't see the sun! There was a queer brown haze—only right above was the sky clear. And the wind was blowing a gale. It kept on blowing, harder and harder. And the haze kept mounting in the sky. By the time we had finished breakfast and were ready to start out, about 9, the sun was only a lighter spot in the dust that filled the sky like a brown fog. We drove only a few miles and had to turn back. It got worse and worse, rapidly. You couldn't see a foot ahead by the time we got back, and we had a time getting back! It was like driving through a fog, only worse, for there was that damnable wind. It seemed as though the car would be blown right off the road any minute. When we stopped, we had to put on the emergency brake. It was a truly terrifying experience. We were being whirled off into space in a vast, impenetrable cloud of brown dust.

They had the street lights on when we finally groped our way back into town. They stayed on the rest of the day. By noon the sun wasn't even a light spot in the sky any more. You couldn't see it at all. It was so dark, and the dust was so thick that you couldn't see across the street. I was lying on the bed reading the paper and glanced up—the window looked black, just as it does at night. I was terrified, for a moment. It seemed like the end of the world.

Farming became impossible in the Dust Bowl, as a large swath of the Plains was soon called. Farm families left the region by the tens of thousands, fleeing to California. They didn't know what they would find there, but they were certain it couldn't be worse than what they were leaving. Their journey became a social and human epic, a tale of tragedy and courage immortalized in John Steinbeck's *Grapes of Wrath* and similar works; their experience contributed to the political EPIC of Upton Sinclair after their arrival added to the glut of agricultural workers in California. Some of the migrants turned militant, joining the Communist party or at least following the Communists out on strike in the Salinas and Imperial valleys. But a larger number found Sinclair's promise of land to the landless more appealing. Democratic socialism they could stomach, revolutionary communism probably not.

❖ ❖ ❖

HARRY BRIDGES ARRIVED in the United States from Australia shortly after the World War. He joined the radical Industrial Workers of the World as the Wobblies' never-promising fortunes faded amid the postwar crackdown on leftists, but he soon jumped ship for the San Francisco local of the International Longshoremen's Association. From the standpoint of steady work, this was another bad move, for the ILA had been shunned by the dock owners since a wrenching strike at the war's end. Bridges was blacklisted, making him more radical than ever. Whether or not he formally joined the Communist party became a matter of later dispute, but he didn't disguise his belief that the Marxists had it right on the inevitability of class struggle between workers and owners. A dock strike in San Francisco in July 1934 turned lethally violent when the owners imported strikebreakers and the strikers resisted. The police opened fire, killing two strikers. Bridges's charisma and pugnacity had propelled him to leadership among the dockers, and in the wake of the killings he attempted to extend his reach by calling a general strike of all workers in the city. General strikes in other countries had often foreshadowed revolution, and this one got off to a promising start. For nearly a week the city was paralyzed, its docks closed, its cable cars still, its warehouses silent. The summer fog off the ocean rolled down streets vacant of traffic and almost empty of pedestrians. Eventually the spell broke, and the workers drifted back to their jobs. But rarely had labor shown such strength, and never in American history had the possibility of a working-class revolution loomed so large.

Militant unionists mobilized similarly in Minneapolis. The Teamsters played the role in the Twin Cities that the longshoremen filled at the Golden Gate; the conflict the Teamsters provoked—or suffered, depending on one's point of view—was even bloodier than that in San Francisco. Police fire killed two and wounded more than sixty. Governor Floyd Olson, no lackey of capital, was so alarmed that he imposed martial law lest the violence escalate or Minneapolis follow San Francisco into a general strike.

The labor violence spread still further east as the summer faded. Textile workers in New England complained that mill owners weren't honoring their commitments to the cotton code of the NRA; when the owners ignored the complaints the workers struck. Sympathizers in several eastern states joined the stoppage, and vandals and arsonists soon jumped in. Again the police entered the fray; again blood flowed in the gutters. "A few hundred funerals," a textile trade paper editorialized, "will have a quieting influence."

* * *

ROOSEVELT WOULD HAVE been forced to comment on the strikes had he not spent the month of the worst of the fighting incommunicado. At the beginning of July he embarked on the first two-ocean cruise ever undertaken by a president. His ship was the *Houston,* one of the new class of American cruisers. At six hundred feet in length and a mere sixty-five feet abeam, it sliced through the seas as swiftly as any vessel afloat. "Her quoted speed is 30 knots, but her officers smile when they say it," a reporter covering the voyage explained. Roosevelt chose the *Houston* for its speed but also for the fact that as a fleet flagship the vessel had quarters for an admiral—or a president—in addition to those for its own commander. The crew painted and polished the ship and rearranged a few things for his convenience. A space on deck was cleared so he could view films and newsreels when the evening was calm. Otherwise Roosevelt insisted on experiencing the ship in the same manner as its officers and men. They would be sailing through steamy weather and sultry seas; his cabin was to be ventilated but not cooled. "There is no such luxury as air-conditioning aboard, and no one denies that when the sun beats down on a steel ship it generates heat," the reporter remarked.

Roosevelt's voyage had several objectives. Not the least was simple rest and relaxation. Salt air had always invigorated his mind and body, and he expected it would invigorate him now. Presidential holidays on land presented problems of logistics and security; on board the *Houston* these largely disappeared. Roosevelt wanted to visit some of America's strategic overseas possessions, particularly Puerto Rico, the Panama Canal Zone, and Hawaii. He wished to be the first American president to traverse the Panama Canal.

He also desired to lend a personal touch to his foreign policy toward Latin America. For the century since the announcement of the Monroe Doctrine in 1823, the United States had treated Latin America as its peculiar sphere of influence. This had never sat well with most Latin Americans, who interpreted America's seizure of half of Mexico in the 1840s, its invasion of Cuba in 1898, its annexation of Puerto Rico in 1899, and its occupation of several Central American and Caribbean countries during the first quarter of the twentieth century as evidence of Yankee arrogance and hostility toward self-determination south of the Rio Grande. By the late 1920s the American policy had begun to appear counterproductive even to Washington, and Herbert Hoover quietly charted a new course.

But it was left to Franklin Roosevelt to proclaim the new approach publicly. "In the field of world policy," he declared in his inaugural address, "I would dedicate this nation to the policy of the good neighbor—the neighbor who resolutely respects himself and, because he does so, respects the rights of others." There was more to this statement than improving relations with Latin America; Roosevelt intended it as a condemnation of Japan's treatment of China and a warning to Germany not to defy its treaty commitments to the rest of Europe. Yet the very demands of broader American interests made improving relations with Latin America the more imperative. Roosevelt sent Cordell Hull to Montevideo, where the secretary of state added America's signature to a statement denying the right of any country in the hemisphere to intervene in the affairs of any other country. As such intervention was a prerogative Theodore Roosevelt had claimed for the United States vis-à-vis Latin America, Franklin Roosevelt's declaration, in December 1933, that "the definite policy of the United States from now on is one opposed to armed intervention" assumed special significance.

Six months later Roosevelt complemented his friendly words with a presidential visit to Latin America. In Haiti, where American marines had been stationed since Woodrow Wilson's first term, he pledged to withdraw the troops and turn control of the country over to the Haitian government. In Colombia he proclaimed a new era in hemispheric relations, one characterized by fair play and justice. In Panama he congratulated the people of that country for their role in constructing the great canal through which the *Houston* passed, and he expressed hope that the partnership would continue.

From Panama the *Houston* steamed west to Hawaii. The governor of the territory threw a giant luau; sixty thousand people turned out to honor the president. Roosevelt ate poi and pineapple and applauded the hula dancers; he took particular note of construction on the naval facility at Pearl Harbor. The president's motorcade rolled past the machine shops and warehouses that fitted and repaired the Pacific fleet and past the tank farm where the navy stored the oil that fueled the ships' mighty engines. He saw the giant drydock that had collapsed mysteriously while under construction but that had been completed and now serviced the navy's largest vessels. He gazed upward at the eight-hundred-foot radio masts that allowed Pearl to communicate with vessels far at sea and was told that even more powerful facilities were being built across the island. He drove by the hospital and other medical facilities and toured the submarine base, where he reviewed the seamen and the civilian personnel. A flyover by eighty warplanes—fighters and bombers—concluded the review.

Roosevelt applauded the pilots, the seamen, and everyone else at Pearl. "They constitute an integral part of our national defense," he declared.

❖ ❖ ❖

$\mathcal{B}$Y THE TIME Roosevelt returned to the West Coast, the dock strikes had ended. The timing wasn't accidental. He could have come home earlier to deal with the strikes, and some in the administration thought he should. But Roosevelt saw little to be gained. As Louis Howe explained to Frances Perkins, who was wondering whether Roosevelt should sail to San Francisco upon the outbreak of the general strike in that city: "It will put the president right in the middle of an obligation to settle whatever is wrong out there. He's in no position to do that. . . . He shouldn't do it anyway." Roosevelt agreed, and kept away.

His eventual return coincided with the start of the 1934 congressional races. Incumbent presidents' parties typically suffer at the midterm, especially following such overwhelming victories as Roosevelt and the Democrats won in 1932. Rarely do such candidates and parties live up to the hopes that bore them into office, and voters make them pay for the disappointment. The remarkable popular reaction to the promises and programs of Huey Long, Father Coughlin, Francis Townsend, and Upton Sinclair, and the radical agitation among industrial workers, revealed the deep desire of millions of Americans for more than Roosevelt and the Democrats were currently delivering. On the single issue that mattered more to Americans than any other—the state of the economy—Roosevelt didn't have much to offer. The promising signs of the spring and summer of 1933 had given way to a brief drop, which had been followed by another stretch of recovery. From October 1933 to March 1934 the *New York Times* index of economic activity rose by nearly 20 percent. But the growth stalled, and for the rest of the year the economy stagnated. As a whole, 1934 proved better than 1933, but production remained far below what it had been in 1929. The New Deal had alleviated America's despair, but it hadn't ended the depression.

Roosevelt nonetheless determined to make the elections a referendum on the New Deal. As he traveled east from Portland, he stopped in the Columbia Gorge at the construction site of the Bonneville Dam. He praised the engineers and workers for their magnificent efforts, and, while not mentioning Upton Sinclair's land-redistribution program directly, he pointed out that the electricity and the irrigation provided by the Bonneville Dam and other dams on the Columbia would yield much the same result as Sinclair's scheme. At Glacier National Park he lauded the accomplishments of the young men of the CCC in improving the park and improving themselves. At Green Bay he praised Wisconsin's senators, Republican Robert La Follette Jr. and Democrat Francis Ryan Duffy—"both old friends of mine"—for their bipartisan support of the New Deal.

Arriving in Hyde Park at the end of August, Roosevelt rounded out the campaign with his most sweeping defense of the New Deal. He ticked off the achievements of the administration in rescuing the banks, cleaning up the stock market, boosting farm prices, rationalizing industry, protecting workers, employing the jobless, and generally restoring hope. He acknowledged that some of the new programs were expensive. But the alternative would have been more expensive. "No country, however rich, can afford the waste of its human resources." Certain critics said strong measures had been necessary but were no longer needed. "Now that these people are coming out of their storm cellars," Roosevelt scoffed, "they forget that there ever was a storm." Conservatives complained that the New Deal eroded individual liberty. Liberty was indeed the issue, the president said, but liberty meant more than letting the rich and powerful do whatever they would. "I am not for a return to that definition of liberty under which for many years a free people were being gradually regimented into the service of the privileged few. I prefer and I am sure you prefer that broader definition of liberty under which we are moving forward to greater freedom, to greater security for the average man than he has ever known before in the history of America."

Roosevelt's strategy of converting the congressional elections into a personal referendum succeeded brilliantly. John Nance Garner, a veteran of many campaigns, had asserted that if the Republicans won no more than three dozen seats in the House, the administration would be justified in declaring the result a victory. The Republicans not only did not win three dozen seats but *lost* thirteen seats, leaving them outnumbered by the Democrats by more than three to one. In the Senate the GOP surrendered nine seats to the Democrats. The state races reflected the national trend; Republicans wound up in control of the governor's mansions in a mere seven of the forty-eight states.

As the experts recovered from their shock, they unanimously agreed on a single explanation for the Democratic victories: Roosevelt. "He has been all but crowned by the people," Republican William Allen White glumly acknowledged.

30.

SOCIAL SECURITY HAD A DOZEN FATHERS IN AMERICA AND ONE MOTHER. Frances Perkins became Roosevelt's lieutenant for social security by virtue of being secretary of labor, a social worker, and a woman. As secretary of labor she oversaw America's labor force, which, to her way of thinking and Roosevelt's, required assistance when its members were temporarily without jobs, were disabled, or were retired. As a social worker she had long experience dealing with the less fortunate among the American people. As a woman (and a mother) she was presumed to have a sensibility withheld from some of her male colleagues.

American progressives had been talking up unemployment insurance and old-age pensions since before the World War. Roosevelt had signed on to this dual version of social security during the 1920s, endorsing it for New York during his time as governor. The Democratic party embraced the concept in its 1932 platform. But different people had different ideas as to how it should be effected. Some thought the burden should fall on business; others relied on government. Some believed the states should take the lead; others looked to Washington. Some advocated focusing on the most vulnerable groups of workers and their dependents; others adopted a more inclusive view.

Roosevelt thought bigger than most. "There is no reason why everybody in the United States should not be covered," he told Perkins. "I see no reason why every child, from the day he is born, shouldn't be a member of the social security system. When he begins to grow up, he should know he will have old-age benefits direct from the insurance system to which he will belong all his life. If he is out of work, he gets a benefit. If he is sick or crippled, he gets a benefit."

Roosevelt wanted a system that was simple and ubiquitous—"so simple that everybody will understand it," he said. "The system ought to be operated through the post offices. Just simple and natural—nothing elaborate or alarming about it. . . . And there is no reason why just the industrial workers should get the benefit of this. Everybody ought to be in on it—the farmer and his wife and his family." Roosevelt thought postmen could double as social security agents, especially in the countryside. "The rural free delivery carrier ought to bring papers to the door and pick them up after they are filled out. The rural free delivery carrier ought to give each child his social insurance number and his policy or whatever takes the place of a policy. The rural free delivery carrier ought to be the one who picks up the claim of the man who is unemployed, or of the lady who wants old-age insurance benefits."

Leaning back in his chair, imagining the smiles on the faces of those women, children, and old people, the president concluded: "I don't see why not. I don't see why not. Cradle to the grave—from the cradle to the grave they ought to be in a social insurance system."

Perkins believed Roosevelt was dreaming. "I felt sure that the political climate was not right for such a universal approach," she recalled. Not only would it contradict the individualism and self-sufficiency on which Americans had long prided themselves, it would break the budget. The most feasible plans linked contributions to payments: what individuals would receive, during periods of unemployment or in old age, would be tied to what they contributed, during periods of work. But building up the reserve fund to sustain the payments would take time. In the interim, somebody else would have to cover the costs.

Roosevelt rejected Perkins's caution. He acknowledged that the program would be deflationary, at least at first, in that it would take money out of circulation through the taxes that supported it. "We can't help that," he said. "We have to get it started or it will never start." Yet he told Perkins to trim where she could, starting with staffing the conceptual development of the program. "Be economical. Borrow people around the government from different bureaus. Don't go outside any more than you are obliged to."

The serious planning began in the summer of 1934. Under the authority of the National Industrial Recovery Act, Roosevelt created a Committee on Economic Security, broadly charged with studying problems relating to the security of individuals and with proposing solutions to those problems. Perkins headed the committee. "We borrowed from every department," Perkins remembered: "economists, analysts, lawyers, clerical and stenographic workers, statistical experts, and equipment." Harry Hopkins kicked in $125,000 from his relief budget to cover operating expenses. The committee considered several basic questions. Should the program concentrate on temporary troubles like unemployment and workplace injuries? Should it deal with longer-term challenges like permanent disabilities? Should it emphasize normal and fore-seeable developments, in particular retirement? Should medical insurance be part of the package? Should social security be a federal program or a federal-state partnership? Should it be funded by workers, by business, or by general tax revenues? Should payments be based on need or on worker contributions?

The committee examined various models. Other countries had established social security systems years or decades earlier; these shed light on how par-ticular aspects of unemployment compensation, disability insurance, and pen-sion programs operated in practice. In the United States, Wisconsin had established an unemployment compensation program in 1932; many Wiscon-sinites thought it could serve as a template for a national program.

The committee heard testimony from numerous groups. Business leaders feared that a tax on business would simply prolong the depression. Labor lead-ers liked the general concept of social security, but some worried that it would weaken unions by causing workers to look to government rather than to the unions for their welfare. Townsendites and other advocates for the elderly wanted to ensure that pension payments were high enough to meet the needs of retired people.

Roosevelt let the committee do its work but provided guidance at key mo-ments. Perkins called a conference at Washington's Mayflower Hotel in No-vember 1934, to which two hundred industry leaders, labor officials, and academic experts were invited. Roosevelt received the group at the White House and offered his opinions as to what a system of social security ought to encompass. "Unemployment insurance will be in the program," he said definitively. He contended that the program ought to be a federal-state col-laboration, allowing experimentation by the separate states but affording guarantees only the federal government could provide. Unemployment in-surance should be funded by workplace contributions rather than general taxes; workers would pay for what they received. "It is not charity." Old-age pensions, too, should be based on "insurance principles"—that is, on specific contributions by individual workers. Some committee members advocated including health insurance under the social security umbrella. Roosevelt agreed that illness was "a very serious matter for many families with and with-out incomes," but he remarked that health insurance might be added to the package "later on."

Two problems, related to each other, proved the most refractory in devel-oping the social security concept. The first had to do with funding. If pen-sions were funded entirely by contributions, workers already near retirement would receive pitifully small amounts. Some contribution from general revenues almost certainly would be necessary for the first several years of the program.

The second problem involved the constitutionality of the program. Whether the federal government could compel workers and business to contribute to a social security plan had never been tested. Roosevelt's worries on this point pushed him toward the federal-state collaboration. As Perkins noted, "If the federal aspects of the law were declared unconstitutional, in the federal-state system we would at least have state laws which could be upheld legally."

Perkins took some encouragement on both issues from a personal encounter with Harlan Fiske Stone. The secretary of labor and the Supreme Court justice found themselves at a reception together; Perkins described what her committee was up to but added that she worried about the constitutionality of the program it would propose. "Your court tells us what the Constitution permits," she said in a statement that was also a question. Stone replied softly, "The taxing power of the federal government, my dear—the taxing power is sufficient for everything you want and need."

Roosevelt resisted applying the general taxing power to social security. As often as the committee contended that taxes were necessary, the president responded, "Ah, but this is the same old dole under another name." When the committee recommended funding part of the program with deferred taxes—that is, by increasing the current deficit and letting future generations pay the cost—he declared, "It is almost dishonest to build up an accumulated deficit. . . . We can't do that. We can't sell the United States short in 1980 anymore than in 1935."

Yet the demand for a tax-funded system mounted. Roosevelt knew that Huey Long's Share Our Wealth scheme and Francis Townsend's revolving pension plan were fiscal folly, but he also knew that they were political magic. Looking to the elections of 1936, he determined that the administration had to come up with a program that would provide pensions soon enough and large enough to satisfy at least some of the redistributionists. "We have to have it," he told Perkins. "The Congress can't stand the pressure of the Townsend Plan unless we have a real old-age insurance system."

The need to get social security up and running compelled Roosevelt to accept a funding scheme that combined individual contributions with initial receipts from general revenues. In defending this compromise to a critic who complained that the contributional aspect of the program, embodied in payroll taxes, did nothing to rectify economic inequality, the president ex-plained, "I guess you're right on the economics. But those taxes were never a problem of economics. They are politics all the way through. We put those pay-roll contributions there so as to give the contributors a legal, moral, and polit-ical right to collect their pensions and their unemployment benefits. With those taxes in there, no damn politician can ever scrap my social security program."

✻   ✻   ✻

$\mathcal{I}$N JANUARY 1935 four bills were introduced in Congress displaying various aspects of Roosevelt's design for social security. A more fastidious president might have insisted that his allies on Capitol Hill speak with a single voice. But Roosevelt refused to preempt those lawmakers who wanted to see their names on what might be the most important piece of legislation in a decade. "You will hurt Bob Doughton's feelings," he told Perkins, by way of explain-ing what would happen if she told the North Carolina Democrat not to in-troduce a bill bearing his own name. Roosevelt's politeness was pragmatic as well. Doughton chaired the House ways and means committee; his enthusi-astic support would be essential to the success of social security both now, in the authorization stage, and later, in appropriations. Besides, Roosevelt reck-oned that multiple targets would be harder for the enemies of social security to hit.

The hostile fire commenced immediately. The National Association of Manufacturers called social security the first step toward "ultimate socialistic control of life and industry." Alfred P. Sloan, the chairman of General Motors, declared, "Industry has every reason to be alarmed at the social, economic, and financial implications. . . . The dangers are manifest." Republican repre-sentative John Taber of New York confused Congress with the world but nonetheless made plain his profound alarm: "Never in the history of the world has any measure been brought in here so insidiously designed as to prevent business recovery, to enslave workers, and to prevent any possibility of the em-ployers providing work for the people." Taber's Republican and New York col-league James Wadsworth asserted ominously, "This bill opens the door and invites the entrance into the political field of a power so vast, so powerful as to threaten the integrity of our institutions and to pull the pillars of the tem-ple down upon the heads of our descendants." Daniel Reed, yet another GOP representative from Roosevelt's home state, waxed wroth more succinctly: "The lash of the dictator will be felt."

Roosevelt let his enemies rage. The 1934 elections had made him in-vulnerable, for the time being at least. And most of the senators and repre-sentatives interpreted the pressure from Townsend and Long just as he anticipated. After the competing bills were amalgamated in each chamber, the resulting measures passed the House on a vote of 371 to 33 and the Senate by 76 to 6. Reconciliation required additional heavy lifting, but on August 14, 1935, Roosevelt signed the Social Security Act into law. The measure estab-lished a system of unemployment insurance, support for dependent children, and old-age pensions. Life would never be without risks, Roosevelt explained at the signing, but the government could reduce the uncertainty. "We have tried to frame a law which will give some measure of protection to the aver-age citizen and to his family against the loss of a job and against poverty-ridden old age." Congress should be proud of itself. "If the Senate and the House of Representatives in this long and arduous session had done nothing more than pass this bill, the session would be regarded as historic for all time."

❖ ❖ ❖

Lorena Hickok recorded the experience of the most destitute during the depression, and she explained what happened when a person in New York City applied for relief:

You go first to a schoolhouse in your neighborhood designated as a precinct home relief office. If you are the kind of person the government really should be interested in helping, you go there only as the last resort. You have used up all your resources and have strained the generosity of your relatives and friends to the breaking point. Your credit is gone. You couldn't charge a nickel's worth at the grocery store. You owe several months' rent. The land-lord has lost his patience and is threatening to throw you out. Maybe you've already gone through an eviction or two. . . . The chances are you've been hungry for some time. And now there's no food in the house. You've simply got to do something.

If your children happen to attend the school where you must go to apply for relief, it just makes it that much tougher. It's true, of course, that you don't use the same entrance, that the chances are against your running into them or any of their playmates—but you don't know that.

There will be a policeman around—maybe several. A lot more would be there inside of three minutes if you caused any commotion. The Commissioner of Public Welfare feels that serious riots have been prevented by locating each Home Relief Station within a short distance of a police station. . . . If you get by the policeman—and some people, I have been told, take one look at him, lose their courage, and turn around and go home—you have to tell some man at the door what you're there for. If you've got any pride, it hurts. And maybe he isn't any too patient. He's on relief himself, perhaps totally unqualified temperamentally for the job and worried about how he's going to make ends meet if he doesn't get his paycheck next week. . . .

You go into a room filled with people. Up at the front are a line of makeshift desks, where interviewers are taking down the stories of relief applicants. You sit down on a bench in the back of the room. And there you wait, wondering if they're going to make you sell the radio, which wouldn't bring in enough to feed the family two days. . . . Eventually you get your turn. Maybe the questions aren't so bad, but you hate answering them just the same. If the person asking the questions were sympathetic and tactful, qualified by experience and temperament for the job, it might not be so bad. But the person asking those questions is just another victim of the depression like yourself. . . . Possibly he hates the job—and hates you because you're part of it. . . .

Finally you get out—and go home and wait.

What you waited for was word that Harry Hopkins had enough money to keep the wolf from your door for another month. As Roosevelt's relief director, Hopkins headed first the Federal Emergency Relief Administration and later the Civil Works Administration. The president's charge to Hopkins was to get money to state and local relief agencies as quickly as possible. "Action had to be immediate," Roosevelt explained later. Congress provided Hopkins with $500 million, and Hopkins made a fast start spending it, disbursing $5 million in his first two hours on the job. "The half-billion dollars for direct relief of states won't last a month if Harry L. Hopkins, new relief administrator, maintains the pace he set yesterday," the *Washington Post* reported the morning after Hopkins began.

Hopkins soon became a symbol of the New Deal, ministering to the poorest and most unfortunate victims of the depression. He and those he gathered around him—"they were young, thin, overworked-looking, and tremendously alive," a newcomer to the cadre wrote of the Hopkins crowd—tried to give work to the jobless in exchange for the aid they dispensed, but the work was secondary and sometimes nonexistent. Either way, the program was controversial. When the jobs didn't appear, the workers were on the dole, which was bad for their morale and for the politics of relief. When the jobs did develop, they were often patently make-work, which was almost as bad.

Though Hopkins spent swiftly, he didn't spend lightly. "It takes a lot of nerve to put your signature down on a piece of paper when it means that the government of the United States is going to pay out a million dollars to the unemployed in Chicago," he explained. "It takes decision, because you'll have to decide whether Chicago needs that money more than New York City or Los Angeles. You can't care very much what people are going to say because when you're handling other people's money whatever you do is always wrong. If you try to hold down wages, you'll be accused of union-busting and of grinding down the poor; if you pay a decent wage, you'll be competing with private industry and pampering a lot of no-accounts."

To help determine whether Chicago needed money more than New York, Hopkins relied on reports from agents he sent into the field. Lorena Hickok was one of the best. Hickok covered the country from east to west and north to south. In the coal valleys of West Virginia she learned that the greatest need was for hospitals. "There is not in the state a single city or county hospital with free clinics or free beds," she wrote Hopkins. The endemic poverty of the people of the region had deepened amid the depression. "Some of them have been starving for eight years. I was told there are children in West Virginia who have never tasted milk." The malnutrition magnified the chronic diseases of miners and their kin, and the maladies of the poor in general. "I heard of whole families having tuberculosis in some of the mining camps. There are the usual elements of typhoid. . . . Dysentery is so common that nobody says much about it. 'We begin losing our babies with dysentery in September,' one investigator remarked casually. Diphtheria was beginning to break out in Logan and Mingo counties when I was there."

In Kentucky Hickok found the same problems and some others. "They are a curiously appealing people," she said of the mountaineers of the eastern part of the state.

They all carry guns and shoot each other. And yet they never think of robbing people. I cannot for the life of me understand why they don't go down and raid the Blue Grass country. . . . They shoot each other, and yet there is in them a great deal of gentleness. Toward their children, for instance. And you hear about them stories like this: Relief in Kentucky having been none too adequate in the matter of clothing, most of them are scantily clad. An investigator visiting one of their villages back up in the mountains in Clay county a few weeks ago noticed that all the men and boys, as they passed one cabin, pulled their caps down over their eyes. When asked why, they told him: "Well, you see, the women folks in that thar place hain't got no clothes at all. Even their rags is clean wore out and gone."

Adequate clothing was a problem in North Dakota too. Hickok described one farmer, no poorer than many on the Northern Plains. " 'Everything I own I have on my back,' he said. He then explained that, having no underwear, he was wearing two pairs of overalls and two very ragged denim jackets. His shoes were so far gone that I wondered how he kept them on his feet." Hickok was visiting in October; already the north wind nipped bare and lightly covered flesh. She and her companions walked about a farm house, shivering themselves in their thick coats and jackets. "When we came out to get into the car, we found it full of farmers, with all the windows closed. They apologized and said they had crawled in there to keep warm."

❖ ❖ ❖

ROOSEVELT DISLIKED relief as much as many of the recipients did. He acknowledged its necessity in the early days of his administration, but he never beat down his nagging concern that it demoralized its recipients and risked making the temporarily unemployed permanently unemployable. For this reason he determined to phase out relief in favor of jobs—private jobs if possible, government jobs if necessary.

The federal jobs program had been divided since 1933 between the fiefdoms of Harold Ickes and Harry Hopkins. Different philosophies drove the two men. Ickes, heading the Interior Department's Public Works Administration, thought like a businessman, insisting on value for money. He contended that federal projects should prime the pump of the private economy and then liquidate themselves. He preferred spending money on equipment to spending money on workers, as the former would stimulate employment among equipment manufacturers and strengthen the private sector, with long-term benefits for the whole economy. Hopkins, by contrast, thought like a social worker. His goal was to put as many people on the job as possible. What those people produced was less important than the fact that they received a paycheck. Their pay would benefit them at once and benefit the larger economy as they spent it on food, clothes, housing, and other necessities.

The competing philosophies produced confusion in the administration of the relief programs and bruises among the administrators. Ickes, the older of the two, constantly felt put upon. "I worked every Sunday and every holiday, Christmas included," he recalled with martyred pride. "I signed all of the public works contracts myself. I must have signed, at first, at least 5,000, each one in triplicate. My desk used to be piled so high with stuff for signature that it was appalling. I was working beyond human endurance."

Hopkins considered Ickes a plodder who simply didn't understand the crisis the country faced. "All day planning the work program, which would be a great deal easier if Ickes would play ball," he recorded in his diary in May 1935. "But he is stubborn and righteous, which is a hard combination. He is also the 'great resigner'—anything doesn't go his way, threatens to quit. He bores me."

Ickes thought Hopkins a spendthrift. "It is becoming ever clearer that Hopkins is dominating this program," Ickes said of relief in June 1935. "And this domination will mean thousands of inconsequential make-believe projects in all parts of the country."

Administrative harmony and economic efficiency should have suggested that Roosevelt decide between his two relief administrators and their competing philosophies. But he didn't. His refusal reflected his chronic difficulty letting subordinates go, but it also revealed his desire to play both sides of the street on the politics of relief. For those who wanted proof that the government's relief dollars weren't being wasted on meaningless projects, he pointed to the accomplishments of Ickes and the PWA, including the construction of the Bonneville Dam, the electrification of the Pennsylvania Railroad from Washington to New York, and the building of thousands of new schools, hundreds of hospitals, dozens of airports. To those who put more value on the number of jobs the government created, he cited Harry Hopkins, the FERA and CWA, and the 4.2 million Americans Hopkins put to work.

In the spring of 1935, as Roosevelt pondered how to expand the public works program, he had to decide who would handle the enlarged task. "Ickes is a good administrator, but often too slow," Roosevelt mused. "Harry gets things done. I am going to give this job to Harry." But not to Harry alone. The president appointed Hopkins head of a new agency, the Works Progress Administration, with charge of disbursing new federal job funds. Meanwhile Roosevelt made Ickes a member of the committee that oversaw allotments to the WPA. Ickes accepted the arrangement with comparative grace. "Hopkins will fly off on tangents unless he is watched," Ickes remarked.

But Ickes and the committee couldn't keep Hopkins grounded. Expanding on the fine print in the WPA charter, Hopkins launched numerous projects on his own authority. Before long he was encroaching on the territory of Ickes and the PWA. (It was at this point, if not before, that Ickes developed the conviction that Hopkins had chosen the name of his new agency to create deliberate confusion with the PWA.) Nominally the PWA was assigned all construction projects that cost over $25,000, but Hopkins defeated this provision by breaking large bids into several small contracts. And Hopkins was simply the more effective infighter. Hugh Johnson observed admiringly of Hopkins: "He has a mind like a razor, a tongue like a skinning knife, a temper like a Tartar, and a sufficient vocabulary of parlor profanity—words kosher enough to get by the censor but acid enough to make a mule-skinner jealous."

Hopkins, moreover, had imagination Ickes lacked. While the great majority of WPA money went to build roads, bridges, schools, libraries, parks, and other uncontroversial facilities, Hopkins spent substantial sums putting writers and artists to work. The Federal Writers' Project employed several thousand journalists, novelists, and poets to gather memories and news clips into oral histories, local histories, and guidebooks to the forty-eight states. The Federal Theater Project enlisted playwrights, directors, and actors to carry the dramatic arts to communities that often hadn't received them. Similar visual art and music projects did much the same for the artists and audiences involved.

Hopkins's projects provoked controversy. Some of the fuss focused on the mere idea of underwriting artists and intellectuals. Hopkins dismissed this part of the criticism with a wave of his cigarette. "Hell," he said, "they've got to eat just like other people." He had more trouble with the complaint that many of the productions, especially by the theater group, displayed a liberal-to-radical bias. He could explain that artists tended left and that to dictate content to artists would constitute censorship. But conservatives, already annoyed at subsidizing eggheads, didn't buy his disclaimers.

Ickes continued to have his own reasons for resenting Hopkins. Nearly every week the WPA encroached further into the territory of the PWA. "We voted millions upon millions of dollars for Hopkins, absolutely blind," Ickes recorded after one cabinet meeting. By contrast, PWA projects encountered close scrutiny—"with Hopkins exercising what amounts to a veto power," Ickes grumbled. Roosevelt appeared oblivious to what was happening. "Hopkins seems to sing a siren song for him."

At temper's end, Ickes confronted Roosevelt and declared that Hopkins was deliberately driving the PWA out of existence. "I never thought I would talk to a president of the United States the way I talked to President Roosevelt last night," Ickes recorded. Roosevelt told him to calm down. He did, for a time. But the problem festered.

It came to a head at a cabinet meeting in the spring of 1936. Congress was considering the budget for the coming fiscal year; Roosevelt warned Ickes not to air his grievances against Hopkins in front of the Senate appropriations committee. "It was clear as day that the President was spanking me hard before the full cabinet," Ickes noted. That afternoon he submitted a letter of resignation.

Roosevelt didn't reply. Ickes had previously arranged a lunch meeting with the president for the following noon. Hearing nothing from the White House regarding his letter, he wondered whether the meeting was still on. He called Missy LeHand. Yes, she said, the president was expecting him. And yes, the president had read the interior secretary's letter.

Ickes didn't know what to think as he entered Roosevelt's office. A slight smile, but nothing more, crossed the president's face. Silently he presented Ickes a handwritten memorandum:

The White House
Washington

Dear Harold—
    1. P.W.A. is not "repudiated."
    2. P.W.A. is not "ended."
    3. I did not "make it impossible for you to go before the committee."
    4. I have not indicated lack of confidence.
    5. I have *full* confidence in you.
    6. You and I have the same big objectives.
    7. You are needed, to carry on a big common task.
    8. Resignation *not* accepted!

Your affectionate friend,
Franklin D. Roosevelt

The two men ate lunch, and Ickes went back to work.

$\mathcal{A}$s ESSENTIAL AS THE NATIONAL RECOVERY ADMINISTRATION seemed to Roosevelt and to many of those who participated in crafting its codes, the reconstruction agency was never loved. Businesses chafed at its restrictions and cheated when they could. Labor alleged that the codes favored management and restricted the right to strike. Consumers, who valued the NRA least of all, complained that they paid dearly for the benefits to business and labor. The unspoken secret of the Great Depression was that for those workers who kept their jobs—in other words, for three out of four workers, even at the worst of the long slump—life wasn't especially uncomfortable. Low prices meant that dollars stretched farther than before. A fundamental purpose of the NRA was to raise prices; to the extent that it achieved its purpose, it hurt consumers. This was one reason Hugh Johnson and the NRA spent such effort on moral suasion, for consumers' material interests lay precisely in patronizing those companies that undercut the price-fixing aspects of the industrial codes.

Lorena Hickok had rooted for the NRA from the start. But her honesty as a reporter compelled her to acknowledge its shortcomings. "Oh, I've kidded myself right along, trying to believe that the codes were working, at least in the big industries—that the textile people, for instance, were complying probably to the extent of 60 percent," she wrote Hopkins in the spring of 1934. "But I wonder. I'll bet you right now that 99 percent of American big businessmen are trying to beat them and succeeding. And the little fellows aren't even pretending to live up to them. They can't. The whole damned outfit are simply grabbing everything they can for themselves out of improved business stimulated by Government priming and public confidence in the President. They're not contributing anything."

The perception of wide-scale cheating encouraged critics who had questioned the advisability or feasibility of the NRA from the outset. William Randolph Hearst lashed the program as "absolute state socialism" and contended that the initials really signified "No Recovery Allowed." Walter Lippmann asserted, "The excessive centralization and the dictatorial spirit are producing a revulsion of feeling against bureaucratic control of American economic life."

Hugh Johnson answered the critics, most vigorously. "Men have died and worms have eaten them, but not from paying human labor thirty cents an hour," he declared. On a separate occasion he likened the recalcitrant to mobsters. "Al Capone was a poor ignorant Sicilian piker next to those rugged individualists who wanted to prolong the dark ages of human relations." Johnson turned to the Bible to castigate code-cheaters. "We all know the possibility of an Iscariot in every Twelve," he said. "Even Judas survived for a season—and then hanged himself for shame."

The president couldn't fault Johnson's enthusiasm, but the NRA chief's behavior became a problem. His drinking may or may not have contributed to his evocative phrasing, but it was no secret among the Washington press corps, who conducted a Johnson self-destruction watch. His assistant, Frances Robinson, had to cover his lapses increasingly often, explaining why her boss was absent or looked so dreadful. He clung to her—figuratively and perhaps otherwise. Meaning to be complimentary, he described her as more than a secretary, which naturally prompted questions regarding how much more. When Johnson complained that these questions were "hitting below the belt," the speculation simply increased.

Roosevelt finally concluded that Johnson had to go. He took the step reluctantly, fully aware, as Arthur Krock put it, that Johnson was the "complete and perfect buffer"—the one who could be counted on to distract the critics of the president and his closest advisers by saying something outrageous. "When the air around them seemed full of missiles, the General would come along with an incendiary speech to a public audience or a colorful string of threats to a group of stubborn businessmen," Krock explained. But by the autumn of 1934 Johnson's erratic behavior became too much of a distraction, and Roosevelt let him know he had to resign.

It was a tearful parting. Two thousand people jammed the auditorium of the Commerce Department where Johnson bade his farewell. Some were NRA loyalists wishing to hear their chief's final words; many were voyeurs wondering if Johnson would detonate going out the door. The thrill seekers were disappointed. Johnson lavished praise on the NRA staff: "You can treasure in your hearts your part in as great a social advance as has occurred on this earth since a gaunt and dusty Jew in Palestine declared, as a new principle in human

relationship, 'The kingdom of heaven is within you.' " He had expected to out-
live his usefulness; the only thing left was to exit gracefully. "The last words of
Madame Butterfly, engraved on the haft of her samurai dagger, express my
philosophy about this whole business: 'Con onor muore chi non puo serbar
vita con onore.' Which means roughly: 'To die with honor when you can no
longer live with honor.' "

Johnson's departure solved Roosevelt's immediate NRA problem but not
the deeper question of industrial planning. From the start there had been confusion as to how long this shotgun partnership of government, business, and
labor was supposed to last. Was it an emergency measure, to be phased out as
the economy revived? Or was it a long-term undertaking, a permanent transformation of the American political economy? Roosevelt and the drafters of
the Recovery Act deliberately fudged the issue by giving the NRA a two-year
charter. Two years had seemed an eternity in the frantic atmosphere of the
Hundred Days, and it calmed critics who wondered what would become of
American free enterprise. But twenty-four months wasn't long at all in terms
of industrial planning, and the uncertainty about the NRA's future undermined its effectiveness. Businesses that didn't like it could hope to drag their
heels till it expired, and the friction made the expiration more likely.

The NRA's defenders predicted baneful consequences should the agency
die. Ray Moley, no longer on the administration's payroll but still a supporter
of the New Deal, declared that there was no returning to the bad old days of
unbridled competition. "We must keep the NRA going," he said. "Industrial
laissez-faire is unthinkable." The AFL's William Green concurred. "It is unthinkable on the part of labor that we should go back, after having taken such
a forward step in economic planning," the union boss asserted. John L. Lewis
and the United Mine Workers remained convinced that the NRA was essential to the welfare of the working classes; the UMW journal called the agency's
establishment "the greatest victory for labor that ever was achieved."

Roosevelt recognized the liabilities the administration incurred by keeping
the NRA alive, but he judged these smaller than the costs to the country of
letting it die. "We must continue to protect children, to enforce minimum
wages, to prevent excessive hours, to safeguard, define and enforce collective
bargaining," he told a Fireside Chat audience shortly before the NRA's charter
was due to expire. He contrasted the current public attitude with the mood
that had existed when he took office, when "individual self-interest and group
selfishness were paramount in public thinking." The mindset of the nation
had changed. "More and more people, because of clearer thinking and a bet-

ter understanding, are considering the whole rather than a mere part relating to one section, or to one crop, or to one industry." This was a major advance for democracy. The work must continue, and so must the NRA.

❖   ❖   ❖

Charles Evans Hughes interpreted things differently. Hughes had come within a whisker of being the last bearded president; his narrow, delayed defeat by Woodrow Wilson in 1916 kept the progressive movement alive for another few years and kept Franklin Roosevelt's career on track. Hughes's work as secretary of state during the 1920s—as well as an earlier stint as associate justice of the Supreme Court, from which he had resigned to run for president—recommended him to Herbert Hoover, who appointed him chief justice in 1930.

The NRA was destined to come before Hughes and the high court. For more than a century the court had been ruling on the extent to which government might legitimately interject itself in the workings of the economy. The Marshall court of the early nineteenth century had defined the nature of contracts and defended the commerce clause of the Constitution against state intrusion; the Republican court of the late nineteenth century had limited the applicability of antitrust legislation. During the Progressive era the court reversed itself on antitrust—mandating the breakup of Standard Oil, for instance—and delineated the degree to which the government might limit working hours in the interest of workers' health and welfare. The strongest and most persuasive voice on the Progressive-era court in favor of letting government look out for workers was Louis Brandeis, appointed by Wilson in 1916 and ever since an advocate of judicial experimentation in tempering the excesses of capitalism. Although Brandeis was personally skeptical of big government, he believed that the courts ought normally to defer to the legislature in matters of political economy. By trial and error Congress could discover the optimal balance between public welfare and private interest.

The NRA was the grandest experiment in political economy Brandeis, Hughes, or any of the other justices had ever encountered. Even the drafters of the Recovery Act worried about its constitutionality. Two issues were most problematic: whether the federal government could intrude so egregiously upon the private sector as the NRA codes allowed, and whether the intrusion, if constitutional, should be directed by the legislative branch or the executive. The case that tested the NRA arose in Brooklyn, where the Schechter brothers

bought and sold chickens. The poultry business presented formidable obsta-
cles to the NRA code makers, comprising thousands of small firms operating
at the intersection of agriculture and commerce. But eventually a code was
pieced together, and Roosevelt approved it in April 1934. Schechter Poultry,
like many other small operators, considered the constraints of the code illegitimate and oppressive. The Schechters refused to accept the code and went
about their affairs much as before. Their competitors complained, forcing the
government to take note. Had the Schechters' violations involved only maximum hours and minimum wages, they might not have attracted the attention
they did, but the brothers were alleged to have broken a rule about what constituted a healthy chicken fit for human consumption. Selling sick chickens
was sure to make these small businessmen less sympathetic as defendants, and
the feds moved in and arrested them.

They were convicted at trial, and an appeals court upheld the conviction.
The Supreme Court, which was looking for a test of the NRA, agreed to review
the case. Everyone understood the momentousness of the proceedings. If the
NRA was sustained, Roosevelt's grand experiment in government planning for
the economy could go forward; if it was struck down, the country would be
thrown back on the rules and expectations of the Hoover era. Donald Richberg,
the acting chairman of the National Industrial Recovery Board, special assistant
to the attorney general, and a seasoned Supreme Court lawyer, took a chair on
the government's side and presented the case for the NRA. "The NRA law was
enacted for the purpose of checking the progressive destruction of industry, to
make possible an orderly advance by industry instead of a disorderly retreat,"
he said. The depression had provoked a disastrous collapse in demand and
prices, with catastrophic effects on wages and employment. Congress had wisely
stepped in, under the authority granted it by the commerce clause of the Constitution. Critics of the NRA complained that the industrial codes often involved
price fixing, which injured consumers and violated at least the spirit of antitrust
laws; Richberg explained that price fixing wasn't involved in the poultry code or
the current case. The fixing of wages and hours *was* involved, but Richberg contended that such action was necessary to restore order to the poultry industry—
as it was necessary in other industries. If Congress could not stop the "vicious
cycle of wage-cutting," Richberg declared, "then it is impotent indeed."

Joseph Heller, speaking for the Schechters and all the opponents of the
NRA, didn't challenge Richberg and the government on the broad questions
of government planning for the economy, but he did question whether the
commerce clause applied in the present case. Congress was authorized to reg-

ulate interstate commerce, Heller told the justices, but the Schechters did business only in New York. To be sure, some of the chickens they purchased were hatched elsewhere, but by the time the Schechters acquired them they were naturalized New Yorkers, in effect.

To illustrate the picayune character of the poultry code, Heller noted that one of the violations charged against the Schechters was their failure to observe the standards of "straight killing." He paused to let the justices inquire what straight killing was. A court reporter described Heller's answer: "He went into a long, detailed, and at times excited description of the process that sent the usually solemn justices into gales of laughter. One after another took the cue and prodded him with questions until it was entirely clear that 'you have got to put your hand into the coop and take out whichever chicken comes to you first.' " This was to prevent the chicken grabber from favoring one customer over another.

"And it was for that your client was convicted?" Associate Justice James McReynolds asked.

"Yes, and fined $5,000 and given three months in jail," Heller replied. Heller went on to explain that if a customer wished to purchase half a crate of chickens, he had to divide the crate physically in half and take whatever chickens happened to be in that half. Associate Justice George Sutherland asked what would happen if the chickens all huddled into the other half. Heller conceded that that would be a puzzler. "The court joined in the laughter that followed," the reporter wrote.

Heller's fellow counsel, Frederick Wood, seized the moment of levity to reiterate the defense's contention that the poultry code pushed the commerce clause too far. If the government's argument was upheld, Wood asserted, the commerce clause would become "destructive of our dual system of government and subversive of our political, social, and economic institutions under the Constitution."

The justices weren't laughing—and neither was the Roosevelt administration—when the court delivered its judgment in the Schechter case. By a unanimous vote the court struck down the poultry code and the NRA-supporting arguments on which it rested. Charles Evans Hughes, writing for the court, acknowledged that government authority might expand during emergencies. "Extraordinary conditions may call for extraordinary remedies," the chief justice said. But the Constitution imposed limits on government, even in emergencies. "Extraordinary conditions do not create or enlarge constitutional power." Hughes rejected the government's contention that the poultry codes were intrinsically concerned with interstate commerce. He drew a distinction between activities directly related to interstate commerce and those, like the Schechters', only indirectly related. If the commerce clause was stretched as far as the government proposed, the chief justice declared, there would be few constraints on federal power. "For all practical purposes we should have a completely centralized government."

Hughes's coup de grace against the NRA was a blow at the president himself. The primary complaint of Roosevelt's opponents during the Hundred Days had been that he was gathering too much power to himself: that the executive branch was usurping the authority of the legislature, albeit with the legislature's own approval. This was the fundamental finding of Hughes and the eight associate justices in the Schechter case. The Constitution vested federal legislative authority in Congress, and in Congress alone, Hughes said. "Congress is not permitted to abdicate or to transfer to others the essential legislative functions." Congress had from time to time legitimately authorized the executive branch, working through the Federal Trade Commission and other agencies, to determine fair trade practices. But the NRA codes went far beyond the FTC rules and, in any event, explicitly superseded those rules. "The code-making authority thus conferred," Hughes concluded for the court, "is an unconstitutional delegation of legislative power."

❖   ❖   ❖

THE COURT'S VERDICT against the NRA, and especially the unanimity of the decision, dealt a mortal blow to the New Deal, at least as originally configured. Roosevelt had made industrial planning the centerpiece of his economic policy; the Schechter result negated the premises on which the planning rested. Conceivably Congress could have overseen code writing similar to that of the NRA. But only conceivably, for in the real world of politics, no code with any teeth could have passed muster with the legislature, which would have been lobbied to paralysis by the interested parties. If there were to be codes at all, they would have to be the work of the executive branch. And the Supreme Court now said this was unconstitutional.

Had the decision been close—by a vote of 5 to 4 or even 6 to 3—Roosevelt might have hoped for a reversal before he left office. Several of the justices were nearing retirement, or so he could reasonably expect. He would replace them with men more attuned to his philosophy of government, and all would be well. But the decisiveness of the defeat—even Louis Brandeis voted against the government—made clear that the problem ran deeper than the personnel of the court.

The rejection of the NRA cast the entire framework of American industrial relations into chaos. The seven hundred codes were presumptively illegitimate; the twenty million workers whose pay and conditions the codes covered were thrown back on the mercies of a capitalist marketplace that had treated them badly since the start of the depression. At the time of the Schechter decision, the Justice Department was prosecuting some four hundred cases of code violations. The court's action compelled Roosevelt to drop the charges and abandon the prosecutions.

The Schechter decision was handed down on Monday, May 27. That same day the Supreme Court, by equally unanimous votes, demolished two other pillars of the New Deal. The decision in *Louisville Bank v. Radford* overturned the law that furnished mortgage relief to debt-strapped farmers. The verdict in *Humphrey's Executor v. United States* disallowed Roosevelt's removal of a member of the Federal Trade Commission and thereby severely constrained his ability to bring government agencies into line with his policies.

Black Monday, as Roosevelt's supporters remembered the day of the conservative trifecta, seemed to halt the New Deal in its tracks. The conservatives had contended from the start that the extraordinary delegation of power to the president was not merely unwise but unconstitutional. They had lacked the votes in Congress to prevent it, but now they found the votes where they mattered more, in the Supreme Court. What made the anti–New Deal decisions so frustrating for Roosevelt was that they followed by mere months the New Deal's ratification by the public, in the elections of 1934.

❖ ❖ ❖

Roosevelt's favorite president was Andrew Jackson—an odd preference in one regard but natural in another. Jackson's hard-luck boyhood and orphaned youth could scarcely have differed more from Roosevelt's privileged upbringing, and the battlefield victories that made Jackson famous lacked any counterparts on Roosevelt's résumé. Yet Jackson brought democracy to the White House and governed as the first truly popular president, beloved of the ordinary people of America and devoted to their defense and welfare; and Roosevelt could conceive of no higher goal for himself than confirming democracy and serving ordinary Americans.

The Jacksonian model gained even greater appeal for Roosevelt after Black

Monday. Jackson was famous for treating Supreme Court decisions as advisory at best. Jackson vetoed as unconstitutional a bill rechartering the Bank of the United States, despite a previous decision by John Marshall's court specifically affirming the bank's constitutionality. The fight over the bank became a centerpiece of Jackson's second administration, prompting Old Hickory to vow to his vice president: "The Bank, Mr. Van Buren, is trying to kill me. *But I will kill it!*" When the high court rejected Jackson's Indian policy in a controversial case involving the Cherokees and Georgia, Jackson reportedly declared, "John Marshall has delivered his opinion; now let him enforce it."

In each case Jackson believed that Marshall, the last holdout of the discredited Federalist party, was denying the American people their democratic right to discover new solutions to the problems that vexed them. Roosevelt felt the same way about Hughes and the conservative court of the 1930s. Roosevelt noted that the American people had upheld Jackson against the court, and he hoped the American people would do the same for him.

But he had to tread carefully. In Jackson's day the doctrine of judicial supremacy had yet to take hold. Credible opinions differed as to whether the Supreme Court spoke for the government as a whole or simply for the judicial branch. By the 1930s the question had been fairly well settled, in favor of the former. The decisions of the Supreme Court were construed as the law of the broader view. Roosevelt couldn't defy the court as openly as Jackson had done and expect to get away with it. He would have to move obliquely.

In a meeting of the cabinet in June 1935 he noted the advantages of lying low. "His theory is that we ought to accept the opinion of the Supreme Court," Harold Ickes recorded in his diary after the meeting, "letting credit or blame rest where it belongs in that respect." Roosevelt wanted Americans to know that he needed their cooperation, that he was not "a magician who can pull rabbit after rabbit out of the hat." Roosevelt didn't like the outcome of the recent cases, but he recognized the advantages of blaming the Supreme Court for frustrating the will of the people. "He is not at all averse to the Supreme Court declaring one New Deal statute after another unconstitutional," Ickes noted after a subsequent cabinet session. "He believes that the Court will find itself pretty far out on a limb before it is through."

❖ ❖ ❖

*M*EANWHILE ROOSEVELT addressed a more imminent threat. Huey Long's Share Our Wealth clubs continued to beguile millions of Americans, and the

Kingfish was making convincing noises about running for president in 1936. The Social Security Act dealt with part of Roosevelt's Long problem, but the insurance approach to old-age pensions that rendered Social Security politically palatable left unaddressed the class resentment that stoked much of the Long craze. Roosevelt sallied into the class war with a sweeping proposal to shift a much larger part of the tax burden onto the wealthy.

"Wealth in the modern world does not come merely from individual effort," he explained in a message to Congress in June 1935. "The individual does not create the product of his industry with his own hands; he utilizes the many processes and forces of mass production to meet the demands of a national and international market." If anyone in American history could be called self-made, it was Andrew Carnegie; yet even Carnegie had acknowledged his debt to his fellows. "Where wealth accrues honorably," Roosevelt quoted the steel-maker, "the people are always silent partners." The wealthy therefore had a particular obligation to contribute to the maintenance of society. Roosevelt explained how they might fulfill this obligation, in three government-assisted steps.

The first was a sharply progressive inheritance tax. The transfer of great wealth from generation to generation was "not consistent with the ideals and sentiments of the American people," Roosevelt said. The inheritance tax he now proposed would enhance social equality even as it reduced the national debt.

Roosevelt's second recommendation was a substantial increase in the marginal tax rates on high incomes. The principle of graduation currently stopped at $1 million, with the result that although a worker with an income of $6,000 paid a marginal rate twice that of a worker making $4,000, an investor making $5 million paid no greater rate than one making $1 million. This arrangement had negative consequences for federal revenues, and even worse results for American morale. To remedy the situation, Roosevelt advocated "very high taxes" on large incomes.

Roosevelt's third recommendation paralleled his second but applied to corporations rather than individuals. Corporate profits, even more than individual incomes, owed much to government and to society at large, the president said. Government created corporations through charters; government protected corporations through systems of laws; society furnished corporations their labor and their customers. As with individuals, some corporations benefited more than others, and large corporations benefited most of all. Equity dictated that large corporations pay more than small ones. At present corporate profits were taxed at a uniform rate. Roosevelt recommended reducing the rate on smaller corporations by a quarter and increasing the rate on the largest by the same amount.

Roosevelt's tax message "burst on most of Congress and the public like a bombshell," according to Arthur Krock. There were cheers in the House of Representatives when the message was read, and cold silence in the Senate. Only Huey Long broke the chill in the upper chamber. "I just want to say 'Amen,' " he declared for the record, even while calculating what the message meant for his own prospects.

Long wasn't the only one making that calculation. Roosevelt's tax plan was widely interpreted as an effort to steal Long's thunder. "For the time being he has silenced Huey and taken him into camp," the *Los Angeles Times* remarked, in an editorial similar to those in many other papers. "However hard it comes, the Kingfish must perforce applaud." Yet Roosevelt's tax plan was far from popular across the whole country. Editorialists, including many otherwise sympathetic to administration policies, worried about its consequences. "President Roosevelt made a political masterstroke, even though its immediate effect may be to slow down recovery," the *Kansas City Star* declared. Other papers were less kind. "It will aggravate fear and uncertainty in the very quarters where the administration needs support in its re-employment efforts," the *Boston Herald* predicted. The *Chicago Tribune* asserted, "The stability of a great office has been lost while its holder scrambles for the support of the least stable element of our population in competition with men known as the leaders of the lunatic fringe." The *San Francisco Chronicle* remarked, "Coming at this time, after the President's defeat before the Supreme Court on his unconstitutional NRA program, the action has the ugly look of a reprisal by a man checked in his course but determined to have his way."

Appearances aside, there was some question how determined Roosevelt was to get his tax proposal put into law. He hadn't consulted the obvious members of Congress ahead of time. If anything, he went out of his way to keep them ignorant. "Pat Harrison's going to be so surprised he'll have kittens on the spot," Roosevelt said of the chairman of the Senate finance committee. Harrison's House counterpart, Robert Doughton, rejected the philosophy beneath the president's tax scheme. "I don't subscribe to the soak-the-rich idea at all," the ways and means chairman said. The speaker of the House, Joseph Byrns, was equally surprised and no more enthusiastic. The president's tax proposal would go on the "ought" list, rather than the "must" list, he explained. Doughton, who would have more to say about the proposal's timing than anyone else, concurred. "If we don't get to it this session, the committee can spend some time on it in the fall."

Roosevelt himself didn't seem to be pushing the tax plan. No sooner had he tossed his grenade into the Capitol than he left Washington. Franklin Jr. was rowing on the junior varsity crew for Harvard, which was about to compete against Yale. Roosevelt took the train to New London, Connecticut, for the race, and then spent a long weekend at Hyde Park. By the time he returned to Washington whatever momentum his message had given to the equalitarian forces in Congress had largely dissipated.

Roosevelt's strategy gradually became apparent. He had no intention of pressing his tax plan on Congress in the current session. He knew Washington well enough to understand that tax codes aren't rewritten in weeks, and certainly not in the heat of the summer. His purpose was political rather than fiscal. He wanted to demonstrate to the followers of Huey Long that two could play the share-our-wealth game. Perhaps he would pursue his tax code in the next session of Congress, perhaps he wouldn't. He would be guided by circumstances at that point. In the meantime he had made a statement, which was all he intended at present.

❖　❖　❖

In the summer of 1935 it was impossible to know which way the American political economy was headed. Congress was expanding the New Deal, by means of Social Security and the WPA, even as the Supreme Court was contracting it. The president was proposing a drastic revision of the tax code, but he wasn't exerting himself on its behalf. There had always been an ad hoc quality to Roosevelt's policies, but now the ad hockery was resembling caprice. Was the New Deal ending or just beginning?

Particular groups especially wanted to know. Roy M. Howard, the chairman of the board of the Roosevelt-friendly Scripps-Howard newspaper chain, sent the president a warning. "That certain elements of business have been growing more hostile to your Administration is a fact too obvious to be classed as news," Howard wrote in an open letter to the White House. "So long as this hostility emanated from financial racketeers, public exploiters, and the sinister forces spawned by special privilege, it was of slight importance. No crook loves a cop." But the criticism had lately changed. "Throughout the country many business men who once gave you sincere support are now not merely hostile, they are frightened." They feared that the president was promoting a tax code "that aims at revenue rather than revenue." Their misgivings were bad for the administration and worse for the country. "There can be no real recovery until the fears of business have been allayed through the granting of a breathing spell to industry, and a recess from further experimentation."

Roosevelt gave Howard what he wanted. The New Deal had been a response to a national emergency, he said. Dramatic action, on a broad front, had been necessary. "This basic program, however, has now reached substantial completion and the 'breathing spell' of which you speak is here—very decidedly so."

Roosevelt's reassurance sent the stock market sharply upward. The *New York Times* index touched its highest level in half a decade. A veteran reporter covering the reaction to the president's message explained: "The statement that his basic program had 'reached substantial completion' was hailed as highly constructive."

❖   ❖   ❖

ON A SLOW afternoon near the end of the congressional session of 1935, Huey Long amused his Senate colleagues and reporters by recounting what he described as a plot to assassinate him. Two of his supporters, he said, had been staying in a New Orleans hotel when they chanced to hear voices in the next room. Whether the voices were unusually loud or Long's friends singularly acute of hearing, the senator didn't explain. But the gist of the discussion was that Long would be murdered. Long didn't appear to take the threat seriously; in fact he treated it as a joke. Those present at Long's recounting couldn't decide whether the senator was telling the truth, exaggerating for effect, or pulling their legs entirely.

A month later they remembered his words. On the evening of September 8, Long was walking out of the chamber of the Louisiana House of Representatives in Baton Rouge, where he had been giving orders to local operatives regarding legislation that would consolidate his hold on Louisiana, presumably in readiness for a run for president the following year. A young Baton Rouge physician, Carl Weiss, the son-in-law of one of the leaders of the anti-Long forces in Louisiana, approached the senator beneath the capitol rotunda, pulled a pistol, and shot him in the abdomen. Long's bodyguards, members of the Louisiana state police, instantly returned the fire, pumping dozens of bullets into Weiss and killing him on the spot. Long survived the shooting itself, the ambulance trip to the hospital, and multiple transfusions of blood, but the damage to his colon and kidney was too great and he died in the early morning of September 10.

Roosevelt issued the requisite statement of dismay and regret. Privately he was relieved at not having to factor Long into his strategy for 1936. Jim Farley, the administration's vote counter, predicted that if Long had lived he would have polled six million votes for president on a third-party ticket. "I always laughed Huey off, but I did not feel that way about him," Farley told Harold Ickes. "He was good for that many votes."

32.

$\mathcal{W}$HEN RAY MOLEY AND OTHERS NOTED THE CHANGE THAT SEEMED TO have come over Roosevelt during the Hundred Days—his greater confidence, his presence, his comfort with power—they were not speaking of foreign affairs. Roosevelt's boldness in domestic matters was balanced by a diffidence regarding the world beyond American borders. If anything, he appeared to have regressed: from the assertive assistant navy secretary who thought he knew better than Wilson what American security required to a president who scuttled the London economic conference for fear it would complicate his plans to alleviate the depression at home. Roosevelt weighed every action on the diplomatic front for its domestic effects; if an important constituency seemed likely to complain, he moved with care, if he moved at all.

Yet certain issues had to be addressed. Woodrow Wilson's policy of ostracizing the revolutionary regime in Russia had been popular at the outset, reflecting at once Americans' fear of the radical politics of the Bolsheviks, the offense most took at the official atheism of the Soviet government, and the damage a few suffered at the repudiation by the communist government of debts incurred by its czarist predecessor. But the ostracism failed to modify Moscow's behavior, and after the Red Scare waned, after American religion survived its distant exposure to Soviet atheism, and after the depression compelled nearly every other country to repudiate its debts to America, the nonrecognition policy appeared increasingly anachronistic. Worse than that, it became counterproductive. American business groups, desperate for markets, agitated for the opportunity to export to Russia. American strategic thinkers, worried about Japan and Germany, hoped to employ Russia as a counterweight to the west of the former and the east of the latter.

Roosevelt leaned toward recognition from the start of his presidency. As harsh as he could be toward certain business groups when it suited his political purposes, he fully understood that exports benefited all classes in America. And, without thinking too specifically about it, he concurred in the belief that an American-Russian rapprochement might give pause to aggressors in Central Europe and East Asia.

From a personal standpoint, Roosevelt had confidence in his diplomatic skills. He didn't openly boast of his expertise in foreign affairs, although he knew more about the world abroad than any president before him, with the debatable exception of John Quincy Adams. But he was certain he could handle any foreign leader he encountered. He may have been wrong, at least at this stage of his career. Yet having dealt with the likes of Charles Murphy, Herbert Hoover, and Huey Long, Roosevelt couldn't imagine that Joseph Stalin would be much more of a challenge.

Even so, he proceeded with caution. Political conservatives had largely abandoned their opposition to Russia; in the opinion of Scripps-Howard publisher Roy Howard, "The menace of Bolshevism in the United States is about as great as the menace of sunstroke in Greenland or chilblains in the Sahara." But American Catholics continued to fret that recognition would signal acquiescence in the suppression of religion in Russia.

Roosevelt invited the leader of the Catholic opposition, Father Edmund Walsh, to the White House. Walsh taught foreign policy at Georgetown University (where the School of Foreign Service would be named for him), and he prided himself on his imperviousness to flattery and political charm. He drew a sharp line against recognition and determined to defend it. Recognition of Moscow would amount to the "canonization of impudence," Walsh said. "You cannot make a treaty with that evil trinity of negations: anti-social, anti-Christian, anti-American." But he couldn't resist Roosevelt. "Leave it to me, Father," the president said. "I am a good horse dealer." With what Walsh later described as "that disarming assurance so characteristic of his technique in dealing with others," Roosevelt convinced Walsh that American interests—and the interests of Christianity and society—were in good hands. Walsh left the meeting having agreed to suspend his campaign against recognition and to encourage other opponents to do the same.

Roosevelt still had to deal with the horses—the Soviets—themselves. Though he knew nothing in detail about the inner workings of the Kremlin, he had to assume, simply as a politician, that there must be forces in Russia that would oppose a rapprochement with the United States for political reasons of their own. He therefore chose to proceed with caution, lest an overture from Washington be rebuffed, to the detriment of American prestige and the embarrassment of his administration.

He orchestrated a meeting in Treasury Secretary Henry Morgenthau's office between the State Department's William Bullitt and Boris Skvirsky, Moscow's unofficial envoy to Washington. Skvirsky appeared first. Morgenthau told him Bullitt would arrive shortly with a draft note. "His face lit up with a big smile," Morgenthau remembered.

> Bullitt made his entry on the stage as arranged by the president himself, sat down, and said to Skvirsky, "I have a piece of paper in my hand unsigned. This document can be made into an invitation for your country to send representatives over here to discuss the relationship between our two countries. We wish you to telegraph the contents of this piece of paper by your most confidential code, and learn if it is acceptable to your people."

If it was acceptable, Bullitt explained, President Roosevelt would sign the note. If it was not, Skvirsky must never speak of the offer or even of the meeting. Still holding the note, Bullitt demanded that Skvirsky give his word of honor to do as required. The Russian promised he would.

"Does this mean recognition?" he asked.

"What more can you expect than to have your representative sit down with the president of the United States?" Bullitt answered.

The representative who sat down with Roosevelt was Maxim Litvinov, an old Bolshevik currently serving as Stalin's foreign minister. Litvinov was among the more cosmopolitan of the Bolsheviks, having lived in London for ten years before the October Revolution and taken an English wife. But he could be stubborn in dealing with Western governments. "Litvinov and I continued to argue for two hours on the subject of debts and claims," Bullitt informed Roosevelt after one session. Litvinov insisted that the American claims against the Soviet government were grossly exaggerated, and he refused to budge from what Bullitt characterized as an "absurd" figure of $50 million. As Litvinov headed for the White House, Bullitt urged the president: "I think you should endeavor forcibly to get him to fix at least $100 million as the lower limit."

Roosevelt, having determined that recognition would serve American interests, decided not to quibble much over the price. He offered $75 million, which Litvinov accepted. After the State Department worked out various details, the deed was done. "I trust that the relations now established between our peoples may forever remain normal and friendly," Roosevelt said to Litvinov with a handshake, "and that our nations henceforth may cooperate for their mutual benefit and for the preservation of the peace of the world."

⁂

*H*IS DEFTNESS IN recognizing Russia made Roosevelt think he could accomplish something similar with the World Court. American adherence to the international tribunal should have been uncontroversial. For years the national platforms of both the Democrats and the Republicans had endorsed membership. The American Bar Association recommended joining, as did the American Legion, American labor unions, teachers' associations, most newspapers, many state legislatures, and hundreds of other organizations ranging the spectrum from the radically pacifist to the soberly pragmatic. The World Court was an arm of the League of Nations, but it didn't share the principal drawback—in American eyes—of the League: the ability to order member nations to engage in collective security measures. If anything, membership in the World Court would enhance America's freedom of action by protecting the interests of Americans from legal challenges by foreigners. Only the willfully obstinate, one would have thought, could oppose such a worthy goal.

This was certainly what Roosevelt thought. But having encountered plenty of willful obstinacy during his years in politics, he moved carefully. At a press conference early in the Hundred Days, a reporter inquired whether he would ask the Senate to take up membership in the World Court. The president declined to respond. "Not even off the record," he said.

His caution persisted through the following year and past the 1934 elections, whose heartening results gave him courage to move forward. The Democrats now controlled five more votes than the sixty-four needed to ratify a treaty of adherence to the World Court, and the president assumed that this margin, combined with his prestige and the broad popular support for membership, as measured by numerous polls, would enable him to carry the day. In January 1935 he put the matter to the Senate. "The movement to make international justice practicable and serviceable is not subject to partisan considerations," he declared. The growing turmoil in foreign affairs rendered American participation in a central institution promoting justice and stability essential. "At this period in international relationships, when every act is of moment to the future of world peace, the United States has an opportunity once more to throw its weight into the scale in favor of peace."

Roosevelt expected some reaction, but nothing like what he got. Charles Coughlin, then at the height of his broadcast influence, immediately mobilized his listeners against the World Court. "I appeal to every solid American who loves democracy, who loves the United States, who loves the truth, to stand four square back of those tried and true senators of long experience in their hopeless yet honest fight to keep America safe for Americans and not the hunting ground of international plutocrats," the radio priest implored. "Today, whether you can afford it or not, send your senator a telegram telling him to vote 'no' on our entrance into the World Court."

Coughlin's listeners responded, flooding the Senate with more messages than the local offices of Western Union and Postal Telegraph had ever handled. Meanwhile the Hearst papers hammered on the World Court as unable to preserve peace and unwilling to protect Americans. The onslaught of naysaying reinforced the convictions of outright opponents of the court in the Senate and pushed several fence-sitters into opposition.

Recalling Wilson's failure with the Senate over the League, Roosevelt tactically accepted a reservation offered by Republican Arthur Vandenberg of Michigan reaffirming America's noninvolvement in the affairs of Europe. The measure had little to do with the World Court, but it satisfied a certain element of the isolationists. Roosevelt initially balked at another addendum, which would require him to return to the Senate for two-thirds approval before presenting a case to the court. "From the strictly constitutional standpoint," he told reporters on background, "that is a definite limitation of the constitutional prerogatives of the executive which cannot be of any effect." But he eventually swallowed his scruples and accepted this provision too.

Each concession simply encouraged the opponents. One by one they announced their undying hostility to the World Court, however hedged by reservations. Roosevelt countered by enlisting adherents to speak out in favor. The night before the climactic vote, Eleanor Roosevelt took to the air in an unusually direct effort to influence a political decision. "I am speaking to you tonight as a citizen and as a woman deeply interested in this question," she explained. A great deal had been said on both sides of the issue, but much of it was irrelevant.

> The only real question before us now is whether we want to throw the weight of the United States behind cooperative efforts of nations to develop international law and apply it to the settlement of disputes, or whether we despair of any substitute for war. . . . It seems to me that we, the strongest nation

in the world, can not be afraid to take this step, to make this gesture. . . . Is it really the spirit of our country, men and women, young and old, that they are afraid to join the World Court? I cannot believe it.

Whatever the feelings of the men and women of America, thirty-six senators voted against the court, killing Roosevelt's hopes of easing his country toward a share of responsibility for world order. The defeat was a major embarrassment for the administration. In public Roosevelt kept his temper. "Any comment to make on the World Court?" a reporter asked. "Only this," Roosevelt answered: "That I am very grateful to Senator Robinson for the very able and honorable fight which he conducted, and to the others who supported the World Court." In private he aired his anger. "As to the 36 gentlemen who voted against the principle of a World Court," he wrote majority leader Robinson, "I am inclined to think that if they ever get to Heaven they will be doing a great deal of apologizing—that is if God is against war, and I think He is."

❧   ❧   ❧

*H*IS TROUBLES WITH Congress over foreign policy were just beginning. In 1934 the Senate had appointed a special committee to investigate connections between the arms industry and American intervention in the World War. Gerald Nye of North Dakota headed the committee. Nye was a Republican but of the agrarian-radical, business-distrusting type; he had made a name for himself investigating the Teapot Dome scandal and showing how the oil industry had corrupted the Republican administration of Warren Harding. Now, in an expression of bipartisan fair-mindedness, he sought to reveal how the munitions industry had corrupted the Democratic administration of Woodrow Wilson—and led American foreign policy disastrously astray. That the current Democratic president had been a key figure in Wilson's Navy Department, a major purchaser of munitions, lent interest to the investigation, as did the increasingly obvious parallels between world events of the 1910s and those of the 1930s.

The Nye committee held hearings and gathered evidence. The witnesses and the evidence revealed that American arms makers had profited enormously from the World War, as had American bankers, whom Nye added to the list of targets of his probing. Nye had no doubt, as he made clear in numerous statements, that the financial interests of the armsmongers and the money men had been decisive in propelling the United States to war. A whole "merchant of death" literature sprang up around the Nye investigations and extended the committee's findings up to the present. The committee itself eventually published a report condemning the still-standard practices of the weapons industry as "highly unethical, a discredit to American business, and an unavoidable reflection upon those American governmental agencies which have unwittingly aided in the transactions so contaminated."

The "unwitting" disclaimer was the price of unanimity in the bipartisan report; in fact Nye and many others were convinced that certain American officials were wholly witting in their pernicious activities. And the forward thrust of the report indicated quite plainly the desire of Nye and the committee to shape the foreign policy debate of the mid-1930s. The depression constituted the foreground of the debate; while millions of Americans suffered at home, most of their compatriots had difficulty summoning enthusiasm for crusades on behalf of sufferers elsewhere. The downward-spiraling condition of international affairs formed the background of the debate. Mussolini, after crushing democracy in Italy, was provoking a dispute with Ethiopia over that country's border with Italian East Africa. Ethiopia sought calm, but the Italian dictator escalated the affair by sending troops to the frontier and ranting about Italian honor. Meanwhile Hitler revealed that Germany had built an air force, in violation of the Versailles treaty, and was reinstituting conscription, toward the goal of creating a half-million-man army. As if his actions didn't speak loudly enough, the Nazi leader declared the Versailles system dead. The Japanese continued to consolidate their hold on Manchuria and to speak of an Asian version of the Monroe Doctrine, by which they meant that Japan ought to dominate East Asia the way the United States dominated the Americas and that other countries ought to keep out, as other countries generally kept out of the Western Hemisphere.

Americans watched in alarm, but alarm alleviated by satisfaction that the oceans to America's east and west remained almost as wide as ever. The overwhelming response among the American people was that the United States ought to stay out of other people's troubles. Convinced pacifists held this view on principle; the much larger group that didn't reject military action altogether contended that nothing on the horizon threatened the United States directly or would threaten it unless American leaders foolishly let the nation be drawn in. In April 1935 college students across the country staged a "peace strike," dropping their books and abandoning their classrooms to insist that America eschew war. "Abolish the ROTC!" demanded the signs of strikers at the City College of New York. "Build Schools, Not Battleships!" Albert Einstein endorsed the movement toward world peace, writing in the *Daily Princetonian* that "the creation of the deeply felt good-will is the first important step to attain that goal." Reinhold Niebuhr of the Union Theological Seminary proposed a clerical boycott of war, urging his fellow ministers to refuse to serve as chaplains in the event of war's outbreak.

Congress echoed the calls for peace. Advocates of legislation to ensure America's noninvolvement in future wars clamored to put their names on neutrality measures. Most looked backward to view the road ahead. Recalling—with the help of the Nye committee hearings—how Wilson's neutrality of August 1914 had become America's belligerence of April 1917, the neutralists demanded not simply that the United States remain impartial between the two sides in a war but that Americans abandon their long-standing insistence on trading with the two sides. The weapons trade was forbidden in all the neutrality proposals; particular versions would have jettisoned American loans, American travel on belligerent vessels, or American exports not carried in foreign ships.

Roosevelt didn't want to have to deal with neutrality legislation. This was the season of Social Security and the WPA, not to mention the Supreme Court's initial assault on the New Deal. But the world pressed in. "These are without doubt the most hair-trigger times the world has gone through in your lifetime or mine," Roosevelt wrote Breckinridge Long, the American ambassador to Italy, in early March. "I do not even exclude June and July 1914, because at that time there was economic and social stability, with only the loom of a war by governments in accordance with preconceived ideas and prognostications. Today there is not one element alone but three."

In public Roosevelt downplayed the threat to peace. His domestic agenda came first, and in any event he knew he'd have trouble restraining the neutralists once he acknowledged the danger abroad.

His diffidence momentarily spared him controversy, but it led to an appearance of drift. "No one today knows what is the foreign policy of our Government," Key Pittman, Democratic chairman of the Senate foreign relations committee, wrote Roosevelt. "Are we going to participate in European affairs, or are we going to keep out of them? Are we going to enforce treaties, or are we going to abandon them? Are we going to be innocent lambs and simply generous in our international trade, or are we going to be horse traders?"

Roosevelt didn't enlighten Pittman or anyone else. As the neutralists in Congress pressed toward passage of a neutrality law, Roosevelt refused to say whether he would support or oppose such a measure. Even off the record he tried to have it both ways. "We do want and ought to have some additional neutrality legislation," he told reporters, "but we are faced with a legislative situation at the end of the session. Therefore I said to Bill Phillips"—the undersecretary of state—"this morning, I said: 'I am perfectly willing, if we can get an agreement on neutrality legislation, so long as it does not block the adjournment of Congress.' " Given Roosevelt's ambitions for domestic legislation, this tepid endorsement was tantamount to saying he hoped the neutrality bill would disappear.

It didn't. Roosevelt got the domestic laws he wanted and a neutrality law he didn't want. The measure he received from Congress mandated that in the event of war Americans would be prohibited from shipping "arms, ammunition, or implements of war" to the belligerents. Roosevelt's halfhearted opposition had succeeded in getting a certain executive discretion written into the neutrality bill: the president would determine what constituted "implements of war" and whether a state of war in fact existed. Even after winning this concession, Roosevelt toyed with the idea of a veto, but in the end he chose not to fight the clear trend of public and congressional opinion. He put the best face on things in signing the neutrality law. "I have approved this Joint Resolution because it was intended as an expression of the fixed desire of the Government and the people of the United States to avoid any action which might involve us in war," he said. "The purpose is wholly excellent, and this Joint Resolution will to a considerable degree serve that end." In the next breath, though, he warned that conditions might change and require a new approach. "History is filled with unforeseeable situations that call for some flexibility of action."

❖ ❖ ❖

HAROLD ICKES'S COMBATIVENESS often caused Roosevelt problems. The interior secretary's running feud with Harry Hopkins roiled Washington, complicated public works policy, and afforded reporters embarrassing glimpses of the administration's dirty linen. But Ickes's feistiness sometimes served a purpose. In December 1935 Ickes accepted an invitation to address the Town Hall forum of Detroit. The event began inauspiciously. Ickes had taken the overnight train from Washington but hadn't slept well; he arrived bleary and worn. The auditorium was actually a movie theater in the Fisher Building, an ornately expensive structure underwritten by pre-depression profits from the company the seven Fisher brothers had founded to make auto bodies for Detroit's car manufacturers. The lights in the theater didn't work or simply weren't turned on. "It was a curious experience talking into a dark cave," Ickes recorded in his diary. Nor was the audience friendly. "It was a well-fed, well-dressed, prosperous crowd, mainly Republican, I should judge."

The audience got no friendlier as Ickes blasted the opponents of the administration as narrow-minded men who "either possess great wealth themselves or are little brothers of the rich who abase themselves before wealth in the hands of others." American democracy found itself challenged by a "cruelly ruthless exploiting class looking to a return to power that will make it possible for them to grow even richer while the masses become poorer and poorer." These exploiters branded the New Deal a step toward communism. They were lying and knew it, Ickes said. "Communism is merely a convenient bugaboo. It is the Fascist-minded men of America who are the real enemies of our institutions through their solidarity and their ability and willingness to turn the wealth of America against the welfare of America."

Roosevelt was in Warm Springs when Ickes spoke; he returned to Washington a week later. "Whether or not he read anything about my Detroit speech, he did not indicate," Ickes recorded after meeting with the president. In fact Roosevelt did know about the speech, but he preferred to act as though he didn't, partly because praise went to Ickes's head and partly because Roosevelt didn't want to be held responsible for Ickes's particular choice of words.

Yet he endorsed Ickes's combative approach, for he had determined to wage a fighting campaign for reelection. Events hardly dictated this choice. The depression hadn't ended, but production, employment, and the stock market were all substantially higher than when he had taken office. More significant from a political standpoint, the national mood was decidedly more hopeful. The reforms of 1935 had pushed the demagogues to the margins, where they still shouted, indeed louder than ever, but precisely because the popular ear had turned away. Roosevelt might have coasted to reelection on a feel-good platform of positive achievement and encouraging prospects.

But he didn't. Instead of political peace he brought the sword. The opponents of the New Deal were not simply mistaken, he asserted; they were malign. Their motives reflected not a different view of democracy but a rejection of democracy itself. "In March 1933, I appealed to the Congress of the United States and to the people of the United States in a new effort to restore power to those to whom it rightfully belonged," he declared in January 1936, in what was billed as his annual message but which simultaneously served to kick off his reelection campaign. Congress and the people had responded by establishing a fresh relationship between the American government and the American people. "Our aim was to build upon essentially democratic institutions, seeking all the while the adjustment of burdens, the help of the needy, the protection of the weak." Sad to say—although Roosevelt didn't sound sad saying it—not everyone had embraced the new dispensation. The agents of organized greed had opposed it. They had briefly admitted their failure in the wake of the 1932 election and fled the scene of their crimes. But they were back. "They seek the restoration of their selfish power."

Roosevelt did not identify these evil men by name—lest, perhaps, they defend themselves against his allegations. But he painted their actions in lurid detail. "They steal the livery of great national constitutional ideals to serve discredited special interests. . . . They engage in vast propaganda to spread fear and discord among the people. . . . They would gang up against the people's liberties." They despised democracy, wishing to impose rule by the rich and few. "Autocrats in smaller things, they seek autocracy in bigger things." Roosevelt challenged these enemies of the people to state openly what they believed. They cast aspersions on the New Deal, suggesting that it had retarded recovery. If this was their conviction, if they wanted to repeal the signature measures sponsored by the administration and approved by Congress, let them assert as much, that there be an open debate. Roosevelt welcomed the challenge.

> Shall we say to the farmer, "The prices for your products are in part restored. Now go and hoe your own row"? . . . Shall we say to the needy unemployed, "Your problem is a local one"? . . . Shall we say to the children who have worked all day in the factories, "Child labor is a local issue and so are your starvation wages"? . . . Shall we say to the unemployed and the aged, "Social security lies not within the province of the federal government; you must seek relief elsewhere"?

Merely asking these questions, Roosevelt suggested, would give the lie to the claims of the enemies of democracy. "Our resplendent economic autocracy does not want to return to that individualism of which they prate, even though the advantages under that system went to the ruthless and the strong." Rather they wished to capture the instruments of power the New Deal had created. "In the hands of a people's government this power is wholesome and proper. But in the hands of political puppets of an economic autocracy such power would provide shackles for the liberties of the people. Give them their way and they will take the course of every autocracy of the past—power for themselves, enslavement for the public."

It was an astonishing performance. Presidents typically employed a higher tone in delivering their annual messages; Roosevelt's was a campaign broadside, and an incendiary one at that. He had guaranteed the largest possible audience by delivering it in the evening, so that Americans could hear it live on the radio (and in so doing completed the conversion of the written annual message into the prime-time spectacle of the State of the Union address). By branding his opponents as enemies of the people, Roosevelt came disturbingly close to the demagoguery not only of Father Coughlin and the late Huey Long but also of the fascists of Europe. To be sure, he intended nothing like the Nazi purges, but by declaring class war in America, he polarized politics as American politics hadn't been polarized since the Populist era.

The surprising aspect of Roosevelt's performance was that it was fundamentally nonpartisan. In fact, the striking thing about the campaign of 1936 was how little it had to do with parties. Roosevelt remained a progressive, although by now liberal was the more common identifier for his philosophy. And he understood that progressivism, or liberalism, transcended party lines. There weren't enough Democrats in the country to have cast all those pro–New Deal votes in the 1934 elections; Republicans had defected in large numbers. Nor by any means were all Democrats liberals. Conservatives controlled the party in the South; to these were added some wealthy Democrats from other regions who were more conservative than many Republicans.

Roosevelt occasionally dreamed of building a new party, one not bound by the prejudices and alliances of the Democratic past. But in his waking hours he settled for reconstructing the coalition on which Democratic power had been based. He was a Democratic president, and he led the Democrats into the campaign. But even to Democratic audiences he emphasized that the true struggle was larger than any party. Five days after his State of the Union speech, he addressed the Democrats by radio on the occasion of their annual Jackson Day dinners. "I speak tonight to this Democratic meeting, to these Democratic meetings throughout the nation, in the same language as if I were addressing a Republican gathering, a Progressive gathering, an Independent gathering, a Farmer-Labor gathering, a gathering of business men or a gathering of workers or farmers," he said. "There is nothing that I say here tonight that does not apply to every citizen in the country no matter what his or her political affiliations may be."

Again he raised the battle flag. "We are at peace with the world, but the fight goes on," he said. "Our frontiers of today are economic, not geographic. Our enemies of today are the forces of privilege and greed within our own borders." Andrew Jackson provided the model and the inspiration for the contemporary struggle. "Jackson sought social justice; Jackson fought for human rights in his many battles to protect the people against autocratic or oligarchic aggression." Jackson's enemies, the autocrats and oligarchs, had resisted him with all the weapons of propaganda and intimidation at their disposal. "But the people of his day were not deceived. They loved him for the enemies he had made." Roosevelt cast himself as the modern Jackson in summoning all men and women of good faith to join his battle against the narrow, selfish interests: "the small minority of business men and financiers against whom you and I will continue to wage war."

❖　❖　❖

AL SMITH COULDN'T stand it any longer. The former governor and presidential candidate had kept his differences with Roosevelt to himself, out of loyalty to the Democratic party if not regard for his former protégé. Not that he wasn't tempted to go public—by certain other Democrats. During the summer of 1934 John Raskob organized members of Wall Street's Democratic minority to pronounce against the New Deal. The group called itself the American Liberty League, and it was joined by various Republicans. Raskob asked Smith, for whom he had done numerous financial favors, to join, and Smith did. For several months more Smith's attachment to the Democratic party continued to outweigh his concerns about the direction in which Roosevelt was taking it, but after Roosevelt launched his scorched-earth campaign against wealth and conservatism, Smith decided to fight back.

The Liberty League gathered at Washington's Mayflower Hotel in late January 1936, a few weeks after Roosevelt's Jackson Day speech. "The listeners in the dining room, who numbered 2,000 in the aggregate, represented, either through principals or attorneys, a large portion of the capitalistic wealth of the country," a reporter at the dinner observed. Smith commenced his remarks by reaffirming his party loyalties. "I was born in the Democratic party and expect to die in it," he said. "It is not easy for me to stand up here tonight and talk to the American people"—his speech, too, was being broadcast by radio—"against a Democratic administration. . . . It hurts me." But it had to be done. The president had crossed the line of political discourse by arraying class against class. "It has been freely predicted that if we were ever to have civil strife again in this country it would come from the appeal to the passions and prejudices that come from the demagogues who would incite one class of our people against the other." The president was attempting to do precisely that.

Smith blamed Roosevelt for ignoring the Democratic platform on which he had been elected in 1932. Where was the balanced budget? Where the reduction in federal spending the platform promised? The platform had pledged to lighten the burden of government upon private enterprise; what had been the reality? "NRA! A vast octopus set up by government that wound its arms all around the business of the country, paralyzed big business and choked little business to death."

To this point in his talk, Smith's critique of Roosevelt was standard conservative fare. But as he warmed to his task, Smith's indictment grew feverish. The New Deal was socialism in poor disguise, he said. "The young Brain Trusters caught the Socialists in swimming and they ran away with their clothes. Now, it is all right with me if they want to disguise themselves as Karl Marx or Lenin or any of the rest of that bunch, but I won't stand for their allowing them to march under the banner of Jackson or Cleveland." The choice was plain, at least to Smith. "There can be only one capital, Washington or Moscow. There can be only one atmosphere of government, the clear, pure, fresh air of free America, or the foul breath of communistic Russia. There can be only one flag, the Stars and Stripes or the flag of the godless Union of the Soviets. There can be only one national anthem, the 'Star Spangled Banner' or the 'Internationale.'"

❖   ❖   ❖

As the Republicans looked toward the 1936 election, they had to decide how much distance to put between themselves and the New Deal. Almost none of the GOP leaders liked Roosevelt's reforms in principle, but more than a few acknowledged the popularity of certain of them—and if the leaders hadn't recognized it on their own, the defections in the Republican ranks would have clued them. William Borah—Alice Roosevelt's paramour, Woodrow Wilson's foe, and the voice of Republican pragmatism at this point—put the matter concisely. "Unless the Republican party is delivered from its reactionary leadership and reorganized in accord with its one-time liberal principles," the Idaho senator said, "it will die like the Whig party, of sheer political cowardice." The people were demanding change, and the Republican party wasn't giving it to them. "They are offered the Constitution. But the people can't eat the Constitution."

Alfred M. Landon agreed. The Kansas governor was the sole survivor among Republican governors of the Democratic tidal wave of 1934. Kansas had always been a curious state politically, from its territorial birth in the blood of the slavery crisis, through the Populist passions of the Gilded Age, and on to the Ku Klux Klan battles of the 1920s. Alf Landon jumped into politics from the oil fields of southeastern Kansas, running for governor in 1932 on a platform of fiscal retrenchment and defeating the Democratic incumbent when a quack doctor, John "Goat Glands" Brinkley, siphoned off some of the rejuvenationist vote.

Though often called the "Kansas Coolidge" for his reluctance to waste either money or words, Landon wasn't entirely averse to progressive ideas. He had voted the Progressive ticket in 1924, favoring La Follette over the real Coolidge. In his inaugural address as governor he sounded a good deal like Franklin Roosevelt. "Our problems have been intensified by the great industrial plutocracy we have built since the last depression of 1893," he said. "I do not believe the Jeffersonian theory that the best government is the one that governs the least can be applied today. I think that as civilization becomes more complex, government power must increase."

Many Republicans had difficulty swallowing Landon's latitudinarianism; others realized that something like it was the party's only plausible hope of challenging Roosevelt and the New Deal. The governor skipped the primaries that preceded the 1936 convention. "My fixed purpose," he explained, "is to keep the party in the best possible shape to win the election." Landon appreciated that unity was the GOP's only hope against Roosevelt. William Borah and Herbert Hoover were battling for the party's soul and perhaps for its presidential nomination. Borah strove to liberalize the party, Hoover to maintain its conservative character. Landon left the fighting to the others, judging that his best chance was to promise to do much of what Roosevelt was doing, only better. "We cannot go back to the days before this depression," he said. "We must go forward, facing our new problems."

Landon's strategy made sense to most Republicans. The strategists among the GOP leadership decided that they needed to bridge the gap between the industrial states of the East and the farm states of the West; midwesterner Landon seemed their likeliest bet. Borah faded, and while Hoover hoped for a draft, especially after the party leaders agreed to let him address the convention at Cleveland, the speech did him more harm than good. The Hoover of

1936 looked too much like the Hoover of 1932, and the delegates decided not to risk a rematch of the earlier race. Landon won on the first ballot, acting as though the nomination had sought him rather than the reverse. To lend verisimilitude to this fiction, he rejected Roosevelt's example from four years earlier and stayed personally away from the convention. Yet he issued a statement from the executive mansion in Topeka that he intended to wage "one of the most aggressive campaigns the Republican party has seen in many years."

❖ ❖ ❖

*R*OOSEVELT'S RENOMINATION by the Democrats was a foregone conclusion, as was his appearance at the Philadelphia convention to accept the nomination. His speech tolled the same warnings he had been making for months, with a twist appropriate to the convention's setting in the birthplace of American freedom. He denounced the "economic royalists" of the Republican era as the moral descendants of King George III. These "privileged princes" had created a "new despotism" and fastened it upon the American people. The election of 1932 had been the equivalent of the battles of Lexington and Concord, and the New Deal was the analogue to the Declaration of Independence. Roosevelt didn't claim infallibility for his program; administrations and presidents made mistakes.

> But the immortal Dante tells us that divine justice weighs the sins of the cold-blooded and the sins of the warm-hearted in different scales. Better the occasional faults of a government that lives in a spirit of charity than the consistent omissions of a government frozen in the ice of its own indifference. There is a mysterious cycle in human events. To some generations much is given. Of other generations much is expected. This generation of Americans has a rendezvous with destiny.

Roosevelt kept up the drumbeat during the autumn campaign. He reminded voters of what he had confronted on taking office: the hunger, the homelessness, the fear. He lampooned those conservatives who had been happy for the government to save their bank accounts but now criticized it for the very regulations that kept them whole. He ridiculed charges that the administration wasted money on relief. "Of course we spent money," he said. "It went to put needy men and women without jobs to work."

He concluded the campaign, as usual, at New York's Madison Square Garden. Twenty thousand supporters crowded the building. Eleanor, Anna, and Sara joined him on the platform. With sarcasm honed through months of repetition, he heaped derision on those who had driven America to the brink of disaster. "Nine crazy years at the ticker and three long years in the breadlines!" he pronounced. "Nine mad years of mirage and three long years of despair!" The enemies of the people now strove to regain their power by discrediting what the administration, with the support of the people, had accomplished to undo their folly. The administration had frustrated them, and their frustration redoubled their fury. "They are unanimous in their hate for me," Roosevelt said. "And I welcome their hatred."

The crowd erupted. They cheered and stamped their feet so long that Roosevelt had to ask them to be quiet. Gradually they calmed down.

"I should like to have it said of my first administration that in it the forces of selfishness and of lust for power met their match."

Another outburst, longer and louder than before. Roosevelt paused for the shouters to fall silent.

"I should like to have it said of my second administration that in it these forces met their master."

The twenty thousand exploded in delirious enthusiasm. Their thunder rolled around the hall. The band struck up "Happy Days Are Here Again." Roosevelt beamed defiantly.

❖ ❖ ❖

*I*N 1936 in New York state, gambling on presidential elections was legal, common, and regularly reported in the newspapers. As Americans trooped to vote that November, the published odds favored Roosevelt's reelection by 3 to 1. A widely noted straw poll organized by the *Literary Digest* was forecasting a large Landon victory, but the bookies rejected the forecast, as did the brokers on Wall Street, where the wagering was 9 to 5 in favor of Roosevelt. "Betting commissioners recalled yesterday that the only time the favorite in the presidential election lost was in the Wilson-Hughes contest in 1916," the *New York Times* gaming correspondent noted.

The Roosevelt camp was confident. Jim Farley, who had conducted a poll of his own, rounded out the campaign with a memo to the candidate. "I am sending you by special messenger a book which will contain copies of letters from leaders in every state," Farley wrote, referring to Democratic officeholders, campaign directors, and other influential party members. The letters supported a prediction Farley had made earlier, which had seemed quite bold at the time. "I am still definitely of the opinion that you will carry every state but two—Maine and Vermont."

Farley got it exactly right. Roosevelt's 28 million votes constituted nearly 61 percent of the popular tally, the largest portion in American history till then (and the second-largest ever, surpassed only, and narrowly, by Lyndon Johnson in 1964). The president won forty-six states and 523 electoral votes to Landon's two states and 8 electoral votes. Asked to comment on the outcome, Farley told reporters that the Republican adage that as Maine went, so went the nation, would have to be revised. "As Maine goes," Farley chortled, "so goes Vermont."

33.

"THE PRESIDENT SEEMED VERY HAPPY YESTERDAY," HAROLD ICKES wrote in his diary on November 7, 1936. "He talked a lot about the election and its implications. He spoke of the fact that he has now an absolutely free hand." Roosevelt and the cabinet pondered how the administration might exercise its new freedom. "There was a good deal of discussion about the Supreme Court," Ickes recorded. "I think the President is getting ready to move on that issue." The solicitor general, Stanley Reed, filling in for the absent attorney general, Homer Cummings, noted that Justice Harlan Fiske Stone was ailing. Roosevelt responded, laughingly, that Stone might be sick but Justice McReynolds would still be rendering reactionary opinions when he was 105 years old. Roosevelt nonetheless instructed Reed to proceed as quickly as possible with pending government cases that touched on the constitutionality of the New Deal. "He expects this legislation to be declared unconstitutional," Ickes remarked, "and evidently looks to that as a background for an appeal to the people over the head of the Court."

❖ ❖ ❖

INAUGURATION DAY 1937 came six weeks earlier than inauguration days past, as a result of the Twentieth Amendment, and the weather was as foul as winter could be in Washington. A cold rain drenched the crowds that began gathering around the Capitol and along Pennsylvania Avenue at dawn. The inaugural committee prepared to move the ceremony indoors but consulted with Roosevelt before making the final decision. The president asked whether the crowds were already in place outdoors. Informed that they were, he declared, "If they can take it, I can."

Roosevelt arrived at the Capitol a few minutes before noon. A half hour later he stepped to the speaker's stand, holding the arm of James. The rain beat down harder than ever, swirling about the rostrum, soaking the president's bare head and streaming down his face. From time to time he wiped the water from his forehead and cheeks; he read his speech through rain-spattered spectacles. The previous four years had constituted a revolution in Americans' moral and political understanding, he said. "We have always known that heedless self-interest was bad morals; we know now that it is bad economics." In the past four years, the people of America had enhanced the power of popular government and reined in the powers of private autocracy. "They have been challenged and beaten." But much work remained.

> In this nation I see tens of millions of its citizens—a substantial part of its whole population—who at this very moment are denied the greater part of what the very lowest standards of today call the necessities of life. I see millions of families trying to live on incomes so meager that the pall of family disaster hangs over them day by day. . . . I see one-third of a nation ill-housed, ill-clad, ill-nourished.

The president remarked this point not in discouragement but in hope. As much as Americans had achieved so far, that much and more could they yet achieve.

> We are determined to make every American citizen the subject of his country's interest and concern. . . . The test of our progress is not whether we add more to the abundance of those who have much; it is whether we provide enough for those who have too little.

Roosevelt, with Eleanor at his side and the rain still pouring down, rode from the Capitol to the White House in an open car. His silk hat collapsed around his ears long before the limousine covered the mile and a half; Eleanor's wool hat fared only slightly better. He remained exposed to the elements for another ninety minutes reviewing the inaugural parade. He came in from the storm only in time to greet the three thousand guests at the White House reception.

*   *   *

MISSING FROM THE soggy celebration—missing from a Roosevelt victory for the first time in a quarter century—was the person more responsible for those victories than any besides Roosevelt himself. Louis Howe's health had declined relentlessly during Roosevelt's first term, till he became effectively bedridden. But the president insisted that he remain at the White House, a member of the family. He ensured that Howe be treated with respect by everyone in the administration, even after Howe's laboring lungs and faltering heart so constrained his activity as to render his advice uninformed and irrelevant.

Howe conserved his energies for a few pet projects. The CCC he shared with Roosevelt, boasting to all who would listen how "he and Franklin" had planned the conservation corps for years before it became part of the New Deal. He toured the camps with the president when the journeys weren't too arduous, and he took undisguised delight when, with Roosevelt's quiet complicity, the young men at various camps named their principal thoroughfares "Louis McHenry Howe Boulevard."

He shared a project of a different sort with Eleanor. A special bond linked Eleanor and Howe, namely Franklin, who needed them less than they each needed him and who needed them still less the more he grew into the presidency. Yet this only strengthened the connection between the First Lady and the First Assistant. Howe had made a political wife out of Eleanor during the 1920 campaign, and he made a politician out of her after the 1932 election. He applauded her press conferences, and he abetted the political turn they took as time went on. Eleanor nominally ruled out political questions, but she defined politics so narrowly as to rule in much that really was political. She condemned sweatshops and child labor and called for higher salaries for teachers. She lamented the isolationism that tied America's hands as the world grew uglier and more violent. She took pains to state that she didn't speak for her husband, but both she and Franklin let reporters infer that she said what he might have said had party and congressional politics not constrained him. "Sometimes I say things which I thoroughly understand are likely to cause unfavorable comment in some quarters," she explained at one session. "Perhaps you newspaper women"—she still barred the men from her conferences—"think I should keep them off the record. What you don't understand is that perhaps I am making these statements on purpose to arouse controversy and thereby get the topics talked about and so get people to thinking about them."

She gave speeches around the country and fielded questions germane, inane, and sometimes intrusive. "Do you think your husband's illness has affected his mentality?" a listener inquired in Akron. "I'm glad that question was asked," she responded softly, while the audience squirmed. "The answer is yes. Anyone who has gone through great suffering is bound to have a greater sympathy and understanding of the problems of mankind." The audience stood and applauded loudly.

She commenced a newspaper column that supplanted her radio broadcasts and magazine writing. "My Day" ran six times a week and was syndicated by United Features across the country. Designed to give readers a glimpse into the daily life of the First Lady, it also gave them a glimpse of her mind and heart. She again avoided the overtly political, but her preferences—for humanity, decency, equality—informed nearly every piece.

She consented to interviews that revealed more of her life than any First Lady had ever revealed. Cissy Patterson—of the romp on the floor of Alice Roosevelt's house—had taken up writing features for the *Washington Herald*. Noting that Eleanor had become a model for many American women, Patterson asked where she had acquired her ability to move through "these cram-crowded days" with a "sure, serene, and blithe spirit." Was she really so calm? "You are never angry, for instance?"

"Oh, no," Eleanor answered. "I really don't get angry. . . . You see, I try to understand people."

"But when you were young, were you free like this? So free—so free of yourself?"

"No. When I was young I was very self-conscious."

How the change, then? Surely it was a struggle.

"Little by little, as life developed, I faced each problem as it came along. As my activities and work broadened and reached out, I never tried to shirk. I tried never to evade an issue. When I found I had something to do, I just did it. I don't know. . . ."

Patterson tried putting words in Eleanor's mouth. The First Lady was "a complete extrovert, of course."

Eleanor refused to be drawn. She took control of the interview without another word. "She just glanced up over her knitting needles, with those clever grey eyes of hers," Patterson recounted. For her readers' benefit, Patterson concluded, "Mrs. Roosevelt has solved the problem of living better than any woman I have ever known."

Louis Howe rooted her on. "Eleanor, if you want to be president in 1940, tell me now so I can start getting things ready," he said, only half jokingly. She didn't want to be president, but she did want to do some of the things she thought a president ought to do. She read Lorena Hickok's reports from West Virginia and nearly wept at the tribulations of the poor folks there. She urged Franklin to include money for a homesteading experiment designed to make unemployed coal miners and their families self-sufficient. Franklin needed little urging, having thought and talked of such things since the mid-1920s. He arranged for $25 million to be added to the outlay for relief to get the experiment started. The federal government would purchase land for a small number of villages, where it would build houses and barns and workshops in which the inhabitants would pursue a life balanced between farm and city, between the old and the new. They would grow crops to eat and sell and would manufacture furniture and other light products to use and sell.

Richard Arthur's farm, near Morgantown, West Virginia, became the site of Arthurdale, one of the first of the experimental communities. Eleanor provided the energy to effect the conversion; Louis Howe pulled the levers of government to make her energy most efficient. The task was considerable, as the government had never engaged in the like and no one knew where the authority resided.

Howe claimed the authority, speaking in the name of the president, and the project moved forward in fits and starts. Howe had no experience building homes, and in his hurry he managed to order pre-built structures that didn't fit the foundations that had been poured for them. They lacked insulation and were unsuited to winter in the West Virginia mountains. Eleanor wanted the homes to be examples of modern convenience, but making them so threatened to break the project's budget. "The cost of the thing is shocking," Harold Ickes wrote. Roosevelt had put the Arthurdale project in the Interior Department, and Ickes had to contend with both Eleanor and Howe. "It worries me more than anything else in my whole Department," he moaned.

Eleanor considered the cost overruns a forgivable flaw in a noble experiment. She knew perfectly well that the entire budget of the Subsistence Homestead Program, as the administrative parent of Arthurdale was called, was less than Harry Hopkins spent in a slow week. She was consequently pleased when Franklin transferred the program from Ickes's bailiwick to Hopkins's. And she contended that if the concept of modern homesteading could be proven to work in principle, the costs would come down with repetition.

The economic costs, that is. The political costs remained high. The opponents of the New Deal castigated Arthurdale as a communist plot, akin to the collectivization campaign then under way in the Soviet Union. Coal companies looked askance at anything that diminished their workforce. Firms that produced items that competed with Arthurdale's current or prospective output complained of the government subsidies the Arthurdale shops received.

Eleanor ignored the carping and carried on. But she couldn't ignore the excessive costs. She invested many thousands of dollars of her own money into the project and dunned friends to invest as well. "Mr. Baruch has given me 'carte blanche,' " she wrote with pleasure after receiving a check from Bernard Baruch, "and says that anything which I want I am to do with the money which he has given us, and that he will stand by for another year."

In time Arthurdale emerged as a vibrantly attractive community. More than a hundred permanent houses of various designs replaced Louis Howe's prefabrications. The community farm produced vegetables, fruit, eggs, chickens, and milk. Like the community store, it was organized as a cooperative, with residents pooling their labor and sharing the revenues. A community school instructed children who otherwise would have terminated their education years earlier. Practical arts supplemented book learning. "Over in the school shop you will find a surveying transit that the high school boys made, including the drawing of the leveling glass, and there is a telephone set made by the girls," a visitor in the spring of 1935 explained. "There are radio sets and amplifier, a testing meter reclaimed from the junk pile and put in order after two weeks' work, and other apparatus all made by the shop students."

❖   ❖   ❖

LOUIS HOWE NEVER saw it. By the beginning of 1935 he had become so weak he couldn't leave his bedroom. An oxygen tent helped him breathe, but it couldn't cure him of the tobacco habit that exacerbated his symptoms. His condition grew so dire that his daughter, visiting her father at the White House in March, telegraphed home: "No hope beyond twenty-four hours." But Howe wasn't ready to let go. He woke up and demanded, "Why in hell doesn't somebody give me a cigarette?" His wife, Grace, who had long since learned to live without her husband, joined the death watch at the White House. In August he had to be moved to the Naval Hospital. Roosevelt ordered a special telephone line installed so Howe could remain in contact. The president visited regularly; he and his oldest adviser laid plans for the 1936 campaign.

In flashes Howe could be his old self. "As he talked, with dry twists of humor, the hospital atmosphere faded quite away," a reporter allowed into his room explained. "Howe, in pajamas gaily striped, made it clear that there was the busy office of the President's Number One Secretary." He ordered newspapers and other sources of political intelligence brought to his bed; he drew organization charts, sketched political pamphlets, suggested topics for campaign speeches.

But before the campaign was well under way, he realized he wouldn't see its end. "Franklin is on his own now," he said. He died on April 18, 1936.

Roosevelt ordered a state funeral for his friend. He and Eleanor accompanied the body to Fall River, where, amid the rotten snow and bare branches of the Massachusetts April, they laid Louis Howe to rest.

❖ ❖ ❖

JOHN L. LEWIS considered himself as responsible as anyone else for Roosevelt's overwhelming reelection victory. The mine workers' chief had thrown the manpower and money of the union behind Roosevelt, contributing half a million dollars and thousands of volunteers who walked the working-class neighborhoods of America's industrial cities urging the residents to get to the polls and mark their ballots for Roosevelt and the Democrats.

Lewis, in supporting Roosevelt, was registering thanks for past favors and soliciting future ones. With the judicial overthrow of the NRA, the guarantees to labor of section 7a evaporated. In their place Congress had approved the Wagner Act, which reaffirmed labor's right to organize and established the National Labor Relations Board to secure that right. The NLRB would oversee workplace elections for union representation, levy penalties for unfair labor practices, and intercede between management and labor when bargaining broke down. Roosevelt could claim little credit for the act, which rightly went to his old colleague from the New York senate, Robert Wagner, but he happily endorsed its aims. "By assuring the employees the right of collective bargaining it fosters the development of the employment contract on a sound and equitable basis," the president said. "By preventing practices which tend to destroy the independence of labor, it seeks, for every worker within its scope, that freedom of choice and action which is justly his."

But the Wagner Act provided merely the framework for organizing labor; labor itself had to do the heavy lifting. Lewis took the lead, after an acrimonious split between his United Mine Workers and the American Federation of Labor. For decades the AFL had represented the aristocracy of labor, the skilled workers who were difficult to replace and therefore easy to organize. Unskilled workers remained largely unorganized. Lewis had made a start organizing the unskilled of the mining industry, and he hoped to extend his success to other industries. When the AFL leadership refused to sanction his strategy, he led a walkout—punching a recalcitrant AFL man on the way to the door.

Lewis's new group, the Committee for Industrial Organization (soon to become the Congress for Industrial Organization), targeted two industries—steel and autos—above all. The steel industry had been the graveyard of industrial organization since the infamous Homestead strike of 1892; a sequel in 1919 confirmed the dubious distinction. The U.S. Steel Corporation earned its nickname, Big Steel, by employing over 200,000 men and producing more steel than the second-largest steel-producing *country* in the world (Germany). Smaller by comparison—but still larger than most national steel industries—were the handful of firms collectively called Little Steel.

Despite their size and power, Lewis had reason to believe Big and Little Steel were vulnerable. The modest revival of the economy since 1933 had caused the companies to rehire workers, increase production, and anticipate profits for the first time in years. If Lewis and the CIO—working through a subsidiary called the Steel Workers Organizing Committee, or SWOC—could crimp the supply of workers, they could threaten production and jeopardize profits. The companies would be forced to accept the principle of industrial unionism.

Similar reasoning inspired efforts to organize the automobile industry. The oligopoly of Detroit's Big Three—General Motors, Ford, and Chrysler—was even more complete than that of Big and Little Steel. The automakers had been equally tenacious in resisting broad-gauged unionization. Ford Motor was especially ruthless in spying on, beating up, and blacklisting any workers who dared to spread the union word on company grounds. Wives of autoworkers frightened their children into good behavior by saying that Harry Bennett, Ford's head union buster, would come after them if they didn't behave.

For this reason efforts to organize autos were shrouded in secrecy until a fateful afternoon in late December 1936. On that day the United Auto Workers seized General Motors' Fisher Body Plant Number One in Flint, Michigan. Their technique was simple: they sat down in place and locked the doors. The tactic was shrewd: Fisher One contained the dies on which a large portion of GM's car bodies were fashioned. By stopping work there and by preventing the company's men from entering the plant, the UAW put its hand around the throat of GM production.

The sit-down strike suffered from the minor flaw of being illegal. The workers were trespassers, and naturally the company appealed to the Michigan authorities to remove them. Ten years earlier, or twenty or thirty or forty, those authorities almost certainly would have complied. But the governor of

Michigan, Frank Murphy, was a liberal Democrat, a friend of Franklin Roosevelt, and an ally of organized labor. "I'm not going down in history as Bloody Murphy!" he responded to those demanding he bring in the National Guard. "If I send those soldiers right in on the men, there'd be no telling how many would be killed."

In previous strikes when state officials had hesitated to protect company property, management had taken its case to Washington, where Republican presidents—and such conservative Democrats as Grover Cleveland—had ordered the dispatch of federal troops. But Roosevelt refused to intervene. "What law are they breaking?" the president asked rhetorically of Frances Perkins. "The law of trespass, and that is about the only law that could be invoked. And what do you do when a man trespasses on your property? Sure, you order him off. . . . But shooting it out and killing a lot of people because they have violated the law of trespass somehow offends me. I just don't see it as the answer. The punishment doesn't fit the crime."

Roosevelt rationed his public statements. "Have you anything to say about this automobile strike?" he was asked at a press conference in January 1937, when the sit-down had stretched into its fourth week.

"I think that, in the interests of peace, there come moments when statements, conversations, and headlines are not in order."

"Do you plan to intervene in the automobile strike?" another newsman queried.

"I think I have already answered the question."

"Did you read Mr. John L. Lewis's statement?" Lewis had promised the support of the CIO in a "fight to the finish" with General Motors.

"I have already answered the question," Roosevelt replied.

"May that one sentence be directly quoted?"

"Yes."

So it was, in all the nation's papers the next day. The president's one-liner was generally read as a rebuke to Lewis, who hoped for better from the president he had helped elect. But Roosevelt's mere neutrality revealed the sea change that had occurred in labor relations in America. Even a neutral federal government was far more than labor had grown to expect.

Lewis carried on without the president. After GM's lawyers persuaded Michigan courts to issue injunctions against the strikers, Governor Murphy told Lewis he had no choice but to enforce the injunctions. Lewis responded with his usual theatricality. "I shall order the men to disregard your order, to stand fast," he told Murphy. "I shall then walk up to the largest window in the plant, open it, divest myself of my outer raiment, remove my shirt, and bare my bosom. Then, when you order your troops to fire, mine will be the first breast that those bullets will strike! And as my body falls from that window to the ground, you listen to the voice of your grandfather"—Lewis knew that Murphy's grandfather had been executed for insurrection in Ireland—"as he whispers in your ear, 'Frank, are you sure you are doing the right thing?' "

It didn't come to that. The management of GM had no more desire for a bloodbath than Murphy did. After seven years of depression, capitalism was in poor enough repute as it was; to add manslaughter to the indictment against it would have been disastrous. The company extended feelers to the workers' representatives.

Roosevelt nudged things along. After a briefing from Frances Perkins on the status of the negotiations, he placed a call to William Knudsen, the GM chief. "I know you have been through a lot, Bill, and I want to tell you that I feel sorry for you," he said. "Miss Perkins has told me about the situation and what you are discussing, and I have just called up to say I hope very much indeed that you go through with this and that your people will meet a committee." Knudsen hid whatever surprise he felt at receiving the president's call and responded in what Roosevelt took as a positive tone. The president reinforced the car man's cooperation. "Fine, fine, Bill," he said. "Thank you very much, Bill. That's good."

Six weeks into the strike, GM accepted the United Auto Workers as the bargaining agent for the employees in the striking factories. John L. Lewis characteristically took credit. A touch of flu constrained his eloquence, but he managed to call the agreement "another milestone on labor's march." A GM spokesman said simply, "Let us have peace and make automobiles."

The conquest of steel came harder. Big Steel took a lesson from Big Auto's experience, and rather than risk a sit-down strike of its own, U.S. Steel bowed to Lewis's demand that the SWOC be recognized as the representatives of the steel workers. The company moreover gave the workers a raise and made the forty-hour week standard.

But Little Steel resisted, largely to avoid being sucked under in Big Steel's wake. Big Steel might pay the workers more and still profit; Little Steel might not. Thomas Girdler of Republic Steel responded to the CIO's success in enrolling workers at U.S. Steel—three hundred thousand within sixty days of Big Steel's surrender—by branding the CIO's organizers communists. The undeniable fact that more than a few CIO members were indeed card-carrying Communists lent plausibility to the charge, but what made Girdler's opposition more formidable was the weaponry—shotguns, tear gas grenades, billy clubs—he provided to Republic's security guards. On Memorial Day 1937 Girdler's four hundred guards squared off against some thousand strikers and supporters at Republic's South Chicago plant. Police joined the guards as the strikers approached the plant, and a bloody riot ensued. At least ten persons were killed and several dozen injured.

The Chicago violence mirrored trouble elsewhere. Police mortally shot three men outside a CIO office in Masillon, Ohio. Two steelworkers died in fighting at Youngstown. The governor of Pennsylvania declared martial law to forestall bloodshed at Johnstown.

Labor leaders called on Roosevelt to condemn the heavy-handedness of the police and the corporate enforcers. The business classes insisted that he speak out against labor's excesses. He did both, after a fashion. In a press conference in late June a reporter inquired of his reaction to the recent struggles between labor and management. "I think I can put it this way," he answered. "Charlie Taft"—the son of President William Howard Taft and chairman of a mediation board that had failed to achieve a settlement between steelworkers and management—"and I agree that in the nation, as a whole, in regard to the recent strike episodes, the majority of people are saying just one thing, 'A plague on both your houses.'"

"Could you interpret that a little bit, Mr. President?" the reporter followed up.

"There is the old dunce cap," Roosevelt answered, irritated at being pressed. "Isn't that perfectly clear? It ought to be."

"Is that your opinion?"

"It is what we agreed."

"The majority of Americans?"

"That is what Charlie Taft and I agreed was the general feeling in the country."

"What are you going to do about the plague, Mr. President?"

"I think that covers it all right. . . . You can use that direct if you want. 'A plague on both your houses'—that is what we agreed to."

Unsupported by the president, the strike against Little Steel petered out. "Though not as yet officially called off, the strike is lost," a sympathetic journalist wrote in the *Nation* in midsummer 1937. "To deny it is plain silly." This reporter, and other observers, blamed the harsh tactics of Little Steel, the complicity of state authorities, and the inexperience of the strike leaders in dealing with the steel industry.

John L. Lewis blamed Roosevelt. "It ill behooves one who has supped at labor's table and who has been sheltered in labor's house," the CIO chief said, "to curse with equal fervor and fine impartiality both labor and its adversaries when they become locked in deadly embrace."

❖ ❖ ❖

Roosevelt might have been willing to take a stronger stand on the strikes had he not been embroiled, during this same period, in the biggest mess of his presidency. The trouble, entirely of his own making, began in another news conference, shrouded in greater secrecy than usual. As the reporters filed into his office on February 5, 1937, Roosevelt sat silently behind his desk. "All in," the assistant controlling entrance declared, closing and blocking the door. The correspondents knew Roosevelt had come from a special meeting of the Democratic congressional leadership and another of the cabinet. They didn't know the topic of those meetings.

Roosevelt looked about the room, scanning his audience with greater care than usual. "I have a somewhat important matter to take up with you today," he said. "And I am asking that this message of today"—he held up a sheaf of papers—"be held in very strict confidence until the message is released. . . . Copies will be given to you as you go out, and don't anybody go out until that time."

He laughed, less heartily than was his custom. The reporters laughed with him, uncertainly. One joked, "We brought our lunches." Roosevelt replied, "I'm glad you did."

"As you know," the president continued, "for a long time the subject of constitutionality of laws has been discussed. And for a good many months now I have been working with a small group in going into what I have thought of as the fundamentals of the subject rather than those particular details which make the headlines." He again observed the audience, to catch their reaction. None said a word; all listened intently, most taking notes.

Roosevelt produced a letter from the attorney general describing the increasing workload on the federal courts and the mounting delays this had produced. "More than fifty thousand pending cases, exclusive of bankruptcy proceedings, overhang the federal dockets—a constant menace to the orderly processes of justice," Roosevelt read. "It is an intolerable situation and we should make shift to amend it." The attorney general recommended creating new judgeships at the district and circuit level. But this action, he said, should be part of a comprehensive overhaul of the federal judiciary.

The president now turned to a message of his own, which, as he explained, he would deliver to Congress in less than an hour. Partly reading, partly extemporizing, Roosevelt covered the main points. He explained how the role of the federal courts and judges had evolved during the decades since independence. "For example, from the beginning, over repeated protests to President Washington, the justices of the Supreme Court were required to 'ride circuit' and, as circuit justices, to hold trials throughout the length and breadth of the land—a practice which endured over a century." Roosevelt put down his papers and looked out above his glasses. "I might add that riding circuit in those days meant riding on horseback. It might be called a pre–horse and buggy era." This joke on himself—his references to the pre–New Deal era as the age of horse and buggy in Republican politics had become a cliché—elicited the laughter he expected. "That is not in the message," he added, to more laughter.

He returned to his text. He noted that the composition of the federal courts had been in frequent flux since 1789. The Supreme Court, for instance, had been established with six members; it shrank to five in 1801; it expanded to seven in 1807; it grew to nine in 1837 and ten in 1863; it fell back to seven in 1866; it returned to nine in 1869.

By now it was clear where Roosevelt was going, and the reporters sat absolutely still, listening intently for the first airing of what certainly would be a radical proposal. "At the present time the Supreme Court is laboring under a heavy burden," the president declared. The workload was clogging the channels of justice. The high court was compelled to decline to hear the great majority of the cases presented to it. Part of the problem—not simply for the Supreme Court but for the federal courts in general—was the inadequate numbers of judges. But part involved the fact that the judges held office for life. "This brings forward the question of aged or infirm judges—a subject of delicacy and yet one which requires frank discussion," Roosevelt said. Until 1869, federal judges had received no pensions. As their modest salaries left little for saving, most judges had had no alternative to working "to the very edge of the grave." Roosevelt looked up. "I am talking about 1869," he said, to laughter. Congress in 1869 had passed a pension law making it possible for judges to retire with financial dignity. But many didn't retire, preferring to remain on the job. The legislators who had drafted the pension law were surprised. "It was then proposed that when a judge refused to retire upon reaching the age of seventy, an additional judge should be appointed to assist in the work of the court." The proposal passed the House but failed in the Senate. The situation festered until 1919, when a new law was passed providing that the president could appoint additional district and circuit judges upon determining that incumbent judges over seventy were unable to discharge their duties on account of mental or physical impairment. But this law had proved ineffective, for the obvious reason. "No president should be asked to determine the ability or disability of any particular judge," Roosevelt observed.

The problem remained. It was more subtle than most people realized. Modern jurisprudence involved immense complexities, Roosevelt said. Judges had to be at the top of their game. And they had to be sensitive to changing social, economic, and scientific conditions. Older judges sometimes couldn't keep up. "Little by little, new facts become blurred through old glasses fitted, as it were, for the needs of another generation; older men, assuming that the scene is the same as it was in the past, cease to explore or inquire into the present or the future." This truth was recognized in most areas of employment, by the government no less than in private industry. Civil servants had to retire at seventy. Military and naval officers had to retire at sixty-four. Several states required judges to retire at specific ages. Federal judges, almost alone, were exempt, to the detriment of their performance. Roosevelt proposed to remedy the situation by "a constant and systematic addition of younger blood," which would "vitalize the courts and better equip them to recognize and apply the essential concepts of justice in the light of the needs and the facts of an ever-changing world."

Roosevelt recommended that Congress pass legislation "providing for the appointment of additional judges in all federal courts, without exception, where there are incumbent judges of retirement age who do not choose to retire or to resign." Though Roosevelt deliberately didn't emphasize it, the journalists in the room understood that his phrase "without exception" contained the sum of his proposal: he intended to alter the makeup of the Supreme Court. Some of the reporters doubtless looked to the door, instinctively wanting to be the first to file this stunning story. But the door remained closed and guarded.

Roosevelt continued: "If an elder judge is not in fact incapacitated, only good can come from the presence of an additional judge in the crowded state of the dockets. If the capacity of an elder judge is in fact impaired, the appointment of an additional judge is indispensable. This seems to be a truth which cannot be contradicted." His recommendation raised no issue of constitutional law. No judge or justice would be compelled to resign. In fact, those who remained on the court beyond retirement age would be able to do so more easily—that is, with less workload and strain—than at present. The nation would benefit from their wisdom and experience.

Roosevelt grew more specific in describing his proposal. When a federal judge who had served ten years reached the age of seventy years and six months and did not retire, the president would nominate an additional judge to that jurist's court. The nominations would require the consent of the Senate, just as at present. In the case of the Supreme Court, the high tribunal would never have more than fifteen justices.

Roosevelt wrapped up the session. "That is about all in the act. The rest is technical. And that is all the news."

A reporter asked whether he would read the message himself or have it delivered.

"It will be read in about half an hour."

"Mr. President, this question is for background, but is this intended to take care of cases where the appointee has lost mental capacity to resign?" Nervous laughter rippled among the reporters.

"That is all," Roosevelt said.

"Was that the reason for the special cabinet meeting?"

"Yes."

"Can you tell us what the reaction was this morning?"

"There was no discussion."

❖   ❖   ❖

THERE WAS A great deal of discussion after Roosevelt's proposal was read to Congress. In fact, nothing he ever said or did provoked such an outpouring. Newspapers around the country weighed in at once, nearly all negatively. The *Hartford Courant* lamented the "disguise of sophistry" under which Roosevelt forwarded his plan. The *Baltimore Sun* asserted, "To put it conservatively, Mr. Roosevelt has been disingenuous with the people." The *Des Moines Register* warned, "No matter how great and good a man may be, executive aggrandizement is not safe for democracy." The *New York Herald Tribune* predicted that the president's scheme would "end the American state as it has existed throughout the long years of its life." The *Los Angeles Times* called Roosevelt's plan "a program of almost devilish ingenuity," one aimed at "making Congress and the Chief Executive the masters of the nation instead of its servants." The *San Francisco Chronicle* described the president's message as "an open declaration of war on the Supreme Court." The *Chronicle* went on to say, "By his own choice, Mr. Roosevelt's second political honeymoon is over. He has raised an issue which he knows will invoke an opposition as implacable as is his own purpose. On it he invites a fight to the finish. Inevitably he will get it."

Other organizations and individuals delivered similar verdicts. Church groups condemned the proposal as putting religious freedoms at risk. State bar associations deemed it an attack on the rule of law. A former president of the American Bar Association labeled the court-reform plan a "shortcut to dictatorship." The Women's Press Club voted a resolution opposing it. Columnist Dorothy Parker declared, "If the American people accept this last audacity of the President without letting out a yell to high heaven, they have ceased to be jealous of their liberties and are ripe for ruin." Amos Pinchot, a Progressive partner of Theodore Roosevelt from 1912, published an open letter to Congress asserting, "If Congress passes this bill, or any bill like it, it will have taken a long and perhaps irrevocable step into dictatorship. . . . The duty of Congress now, its one great chance for service, is to keep Mr. Roosevelt from destroying democracy and setting up personal government in its place."

Congress heard its duty from many others besides Pinchot. Letters and telegrams flooded into the Capitol mailroom by the hundreds of thousands. No one kept a tally, but the overwhelming sentiment was clearly against Roosevelt's plan. Maury Maverick, a Democratic congressman and Roosevelt loyalist from Texas, conceded the point in explaining it away. "All that this uproar in the mailbags means is that the *Literary Digest* voters are trying to conduct another election," Maverick said.

The response of most of the other legislators was more subdued yet no less significant. Democratic leaders were miffed that the president hadn't consulted them ahead of taking such a momentous step. He merely informed them in the meeting the day he sent the message up. The lawmakers understood Roosevelt's reasoning—he knew they would try to talk him out of his proposal—but this simply made matters worse. Kentucky senator Alben W. Barkley complained that Roosevelt was a "poor quarterback" on the court plan. "He didn't give us the signals in advance of the play." House judiciary committee chairman Hatton Summers, whose support would be essential to the president's proposal, told fellow Texan John Nance Garner and others in the vice president's car, en route from the White House meeting back to the Capitol, "Boys, here's where I cash in."

The Democratic rank and file were hardly more enthusiastic. Congressman Edward Cox of Georgia reflected the shock and disappointment of many in his party. "Living within the presence of the fine things which the president has accomplished, it is difficult to withhold from him a power which he wants," Cox said. "But his recommendation that the membership of the Supreme Court be increased from nine to fifteen, thereby enabling him, through willing appointees, to change the meaning of our basic laws and our whole system of government, asks for something which no man in all this world ought to enjoy. The recommendation constitutes the most terrible threat to constitutional government that has arisen in the entire history of the country."

Recognizing, after the fact, the need to bring the Democratic leadership around, Roosevelt invited several influential senators to the White House. The meeting simply made the battle lines clearer. Carter Glass of Virginia called the court plan "frightful." Edward Burke of Nebraska said, "I would rather be right than agree with the president," and vowed to use "every bit of energy I possess to defeat the proposal." Burton Wheeler of Montana, who had supported Roosevelt on the substance of nearly all his reforms, drew the line at this attack on the Supreme Court. "The usurpation of the legislative functions by the courts should be stopped," Wheeler said. "But to give to the executive the power to control the judiciary is not giving the law-making power back to that branch of the government to which it rightfully belongs, but rather is increasing the danger inherent in the concentration of power in any one branch of the government."

Unsupported in Congress, Roosevelt turned to the people. He had always known the people would be his best bet. He had waited until after the 1936 election precisely to have the people at his back. His appeals to the memory of Andrew Jackson had been made with the people in mind. They understood democracy; they had supported the New Deal; they would rally to him now. All that was necessary was for him to frame the issue in terms the people could understand.

Naturally he took to the radio, in a Fireside Chat on March 9. "I am reminded of that evening in March, four years ago, when I made my first radio report to you," he said. The country had been in crisis, but Congress and the executive branch had moved swiftly. The economic recovery that ensued, and that continued, demonstrated how prudent and effective the New Deal measures had been. Yet they hadn't gone unchallenged. The Supreme Court had reversed some of the most important reforms, and it narrowly circumscribed others. Roosevelt likened the American government to a three-horse team, consisting of Congress, the presidency, and the courts. "Two of the horses are pulling in unison today; the third is not." Critics of court reform contended that the president was trying to drive the team. He was not, because he wasn't the driver. "It is the American people themselves who are in the driver's seat. . . . It is the American people themselves who expect the third horse to pull in unison with the other two."

The judicial branch, the Supreme Court in particular, was the one pulling in the wrong direction, against democracy and the will of the people, Roosevelt said. It had gone beyond the Constitution in doing so. The people's representatives in Congress had passed laws to protect the people and secure their prosperity, but the court had struck them down. The recovery program of the administration was in jeopardy, but so was the very structure of American democracy. The people must respond, on their own behalf and on behalf of democracy. "We must take action to save the Constitution from the court and the court from itself."

Critics had labeled the administration's proposal an effort to "pack" the court, Roosevelt said.

> If by that phrase "packing the court" it is charged that I wish to place on the bench spineless puppets who would disregard the law and would decide specific cases as I wished them to be decided, I make this answer: that no president fit for his office would appoint, and no Senate of honorable men fit for their office would confirm, that kind of appointees to the Supreme Court.
>
> But if by that phrase the charge is made that I would appoint and the Senate would confirm justices worthy to sit beside present members of the court who understand those modern conditions, that I will appoint justices who will not undertake to override the judgment of the Congress on legislative policy, that I will appoint justices who will act as justices and not as legislators—if the appointment of such justices can be called "packing the Courts," then I say that I and with me the vast majority of the American people favor doing just that thing—now.

❖ ❖ ❖

𝒯OR ONCE THE Roosevelt wizardry failed. The American people were unmoved by the president's appeal. George Gallup had begun conducting public opinion surveys just as the New Deal was being born; not long after Roosevelt unveiled his court plan, the pollster asked people what they thought of it. A majority disapproved, and the majority grew—from 51 percent to 59 percent—the more voters heard and thought about it. No less significantly, the polling revealed that the unpopularity of the court plan was damaging voters' regard for Roosevelt himself. In February, before he announced his court plan, the president had received a favorable rating from 65 percent of respondents; this number slid to 60 percent amid the furor over the court. *Fortune* magazine asked voters if they would support Roosevelt for a third term. The portion answering positively fell from 53 percent to 45 percent.

Heretofore Roosevelt had been able to count on popular support when Congress hesitated, and that popular support had typically caused Congress to fall in line. Now the dynamic worked in reverse: the popular disaffection with Roosevelt's court plan gave courage to those senators and representatives who opposed it. They stood firm and refused to reconsider.

Yet Roosevelt's effort wasn't without avail. Perhaps Owen Roberts would have changed his mind about the constitutionality of certain New Deal legislation even without the sword of Roosevelt's reform plan hanging over the court's head. Evidence indicates that the conversion of the associate justice, who had voted against the New Deal previously, began before Roosevelt revealed his reform design. But the conversion certainly occurred after the 1936 electoral landslide, which got the attention of all the justices. In any event, the Supreme Court decided in *West Coast Hotel v. Parrish*, on March 29, 1937, that a Washington state minimum wage law was constitutional. The vote was 5 to 4, and the fifth vote was that of Roberts, who had voted the opposite way in a nearly identical case from New York just the previous session.

Roberts's reversal, which brought the court and therefore the Constitution to the side of the New Deal, amounted to "the greatest constitutional somersault in history," in the words of an amazed but approving Maury Maverick. "Owen Roberts, one single human being, had amended the Constitution of the United States by nodding his head instead of shaking it," the Texas congressman continued. "The lives of millions were changed by this nod." The identity of the punster who called Roberts's conversion "the switch in time that saved nine" has been lost to memory, but the formula stuck, for it captured both the change on the court and the fact that the change deprived Roosevelt of his reason for reforming the court. A follow-on decision in April, by the same five-justice majority, upholding the Wagner Act, confirmed the change and further eroded Roosevelt's argument for adding justices.

The president let the court plan die, to the immense relief of most of his party. But the whole affair cast him in an unfavorable light. In presenting the plan he tried to cloak his real motives and fooled no one. In failing to get the reform through Congress, he cost himself the invincibility that had seemed to surround him since March 1933 and that the 1936 election had only intensified.

The irony of the court scheme was that the very effort by which Roosevelt secured the New Deal judicially ruined his chances of expanding the New Deal politically. Conservatives had been waiting for the clever Roosevelt to outfox himself; merely months into his second term, he seemed to have done just that. No one was ready to write him off, but few expected anything truly original or consequential from the rest of his presidency.

PART III

The Fate of the World

1937 ❖ 1945

34.

AND THEN EVENTS RODE TO HIS RESCUE. NOT AT ONCE, AND NOT IN the way Roosevelt or anyone else would have wished, but in such fashion as to allow a subtle and canny leader to make the most of them.

If Roosevelt's first term was all about domestic policy, his second term centered increasingly on foreign affairs. This played to his strength, to a degree most Americans only gradually appreciated. Roosevelt's first-term allergy to foreign policy was topical rather than systemic; he kept clear of the world not because he lacked strong views but because he realized his views weren't generally shared. As a convinced democrat he could tell himself he had no business leading the American people where the people weren't willing to go; as a career Democrat he remembered how Woodrow Wilson's presidency had wrecked upon the shoals of Americans' aversion to foreign entanglements. He determined not to repeat Wilson's mistake.

In 1937 foreign affairs polarized American politics more strongly than ever. Unlike the fights over the New Deal, the struggle between the international-ists and the isolationists blurred party and ideological lines, pitting Democrats against Democrats, Republicans against Republicans, liberals against liberals, conservatives against conservatives. Valid arguments, historical and contemporary, were adduced on both sides of the debate. The internationalists contended that the lesson of the World War was that Europe's troubles became America's, sooner or later, and that the thugs of the world would never behave till the responsible nations, including the United States, compelled them. The isolationists countered that the lesson of the war was that Europe was a sink-hole for idealism and a graveyard for American youth; they asserted that the Europeans could handle their criminal elements themselves and would do so if made to know the Americans were *not* coming to their rescue. As for Asia, the isolationists saw little threat to the United States from Japanese expansion into China. Some thought the Japanese might actually improve the neighborhood by forcing China to modernize, much as Japan had modernized under pressure from the West two generations before. The internationalists countered that Japan was upsetting the balance of power in the Far East, besides brutalizing all who fell under its sway.

Roosevelt's views tended strongly—albeit not uniformly—internationalist, but his governing coalition contained many isolationists, and he didn't want to jeopardize the New Deal over the problems of other countries. His torpedoing of the London economic conference was isolationist in effect if not in explanation, and it won him favor with the America-firsters in his party and among the Republicans. His endorsement of the World Court lost him much of that favor, while his acquiescence in the neutrality law had a neutral effect.

He might have attempted to maintain his balance between the two sides if the fascists hadn't forced the issue. Mussolini, after blustering against Ethiopia for months, ordered an assault on the East African kingdom. The mismatch between the opposing armies shocked even jaded war reporters; when Emperor Haile Selassie's criers shouted "Up with your spears!" to his subjects, the criers weren't speaking metaphorically. Against the defenders' spears, the Italian invaders threw modern tanks and fighter airplanes. The Ethiopian state was crushed under the fascist jackboots.

About the time Addis Ababa fell, a second front opened in the fascists' war on civilization. The Spanish republic had been struggling for years, challenged by reactionaries in the army and others dissatisfied with leftward trends in Spanish affairs. In July 1936 General Francisco Franco led the army in a revolt against the government. What was intended as a coup stalled and then metastasized as the government refused to give way. The Spanish civil war pitted the center and left of Spanish politics against the right, with the former, calling themselves Loyalists, comprising republicans, socialists, and communists, and the latter, the Nationalists, including monarchists, militarists, Catholic clergy, and fascists. The conflict grew more complicated as foreigners joined the fray. Some came as volunteers, mostly supporting the Loyalists; others came under orders from their home governments. Italy sent infantry and armored units to bolster the Nationalists; Germany contributed transport planes, bombers, and crews to the Nationalist cause. The Soviet Union countered these with contributions of planes, other weapons, and military advisers to the Loyalists. Most Americans sympathized with the Loyalists; as many as three thousand enlisted in the Abraham Lincoln Brigade of foreign fighters. But few Americans wanted the United States government to get involved.

Neither did Roosevelt. Shortly after the Spanish war began, the president traveled to Chautauqua, New York, to address that community's venerable gathering of summer self-improvers. "I have seen war," he said, referring to his 1918 tour of France. "I have seen blood running from the wounded. . . . I have seen children starving. . . . I hate war." Roosevelt said he couldn't prevent war, but he could register America's strong disapproval. "I can at least make clear that the conscience of America revolts against war and that any nation which provokes war forfeits the sympathy of the people of the United States."

The Spanish war escalated during the spring of 1937. In April German warplanes in support of the Nationalists bombed the Basque town of Guernica in northern Spain. The attack killed hundreds and leveled most of the town, and foreshadowed a new phase in the evolution of warfare: strategic bombing for the purpose of destroying the morale of civilian populations. German officials later acknowledged what seemed obvious at the time: that the Nazis were testing their air force for potential use against more challenging targets. Between that ominous prospect and the immediate revulsion against the fascist cause, Guernica became a symbol—immortalized by Pablo Picasso—of civilization under siege by the forces of organized violence. "At 2 A.M. today, when the writer visited the town, the whole of it was a horrible sight, flaming from end to end," a front-page article in the *New York Times* declared. "The reflection of the flames could be seen in the clouds of smoke above the mountains from ten miles away. Throughout the night houses were falling, until the streets were long heaps of red, impenetrable ruins." The article continued:

> In the form of its execution and the scale of the destruction it wrought, no less than in the selection of its objective, the raid on Guernica is unparalleled in military history. Guernica was not a military objective. A factory producing war material that lay outside the town was untouched. Two barracks on the outskirts containing small forces were untouched. The town was not near the lines. The objective of the bombardment seemingly was demoralization of the civilian population and destruction of the cradle of the Basque race.

The reaction in America was immediate. Religious groups staged protests. The pastor of the Park Avenue Episcopal Church in New York called for a world-wide strike of mothers against the murder of the children of Guernica. A petition signed by scores of clerics, educators, lawmakers, corporate officers, and union officials condemned "the unspeakable crime of war on women and children, waged with a brutality and callousness unparalleled in modern times." In Congress, William Borah, whose clarion voice seldom rang out across the Senate chamber anymore, summoned his old energy and indignation. "Here fascism presents to the world its masterpiece," Borah said of Guernica. "It has hung upon the wall of civilization a painting that will never come down—never fade out of the memories of men." The destruction of Guernica, the Idaho Republican asserted, was "the most revolting instance of mass massacre of modern times."

Yet the anger offered little guidance for action. Some of the protesters advocated American aid to the beleaguered Loyalists. Others urged invoking the neutrality law against Germany and Italy. Still others held that the United States should withdraw more deeply into its isolationist shell.

Roosevelt did invoke the neutrality law against Spain, forbidding the shipment of American arms and ammunition to that country's government. But he declined to include Germany or Italy in the embargo, contending that since Spain didn't consider itself at war with those countries, neither should the United States. Moreover, to invoke the law against Germany and Italy, on grounds of their intervention in the Spanish struggle, would logically require invoking it against the Soviet Union and France, which were aiding the Loyalists. Besides entangling the United States in Europe's affairs to a far greater degree than Roosevelt was willing to hazard, such a move might actually harm the Loyalists.

❖   ❖   ❖

A THIRD FRONT in the fascist war of conquest erupted halfway around the world during the summer of 1937. Japanese troops tangled with Chinese soldiers at the Marco Polo Bridge outside Peiping (later Beijing). The Japanese magnified the clash into an excuse to occupy Peiping and thrust south into the Chinese heartland. By autumn the fighting had grown into a full-scale war between Japan and China. As in the case of the Spanish war, Americans had little difficulty distinguishing the aggressors from the victims in the Sino-Japanese war. Their sympathies went out to the Chinese.

What else would go out to the Chinese was the question Roosevelt had to wrestle with. To invoke the neutrality law and embargo weapons to both sides would favor the Japanese, whose military-industrial base was far better developed than China's. Yet *not* to invoke the law in what patently was a war would violate the law's spirit and risk embroiling the United States in the East Asian conflict. Neither China nor Japan had chosen officially to declare their conflict a war, leaving the president room for discretion.

He measured domestic opinion during an October visit to Chicago. The visit started promisingly. Tens of thousands of Roosevelt's supporters lined the route of his motorcade down Jackson Boulevard and fell in line behind the president's car as it moved up Michigan Avenue. Airplanes circled overhead; boats on the Chicago River and Lake Michigan whistled and blared their greetings.

But the cheering stopped and the audience listened, many in hostile silence, as the president described the turbulent condition of world affairs. "The present reign of terror and international lawlessness began a few years ago," Roosevelt explained. It had grown steadily worse as fascist aggressors, without bothering to declare war, wreaked havoc on the blameless. "Civilians, including vast numbers of women and children, are being ruthlessly murdered with bombs from the air. . . . Innocent peoples, innocent nations, are being cruelly sacrificed to a greed for power and supremacy." Until now the violence afflicted only countries separated by wide oceans from America, and isolationists contended that it would remain a distant threat. But they deluded themselves, Roosevelt said. Should the violence continue, every part of the world would suffer. "Let no one imagine that America will escape, that America may expect mercy, that this western hemisphere will not be attacked." One course only could avert disaster. "The peace-loving nations must make a concerted effort to uphold laws and principles on which alone peace can rest secure." Roosevelt likened the wave of lawlessness to a medical contagion. "When an epidemic of physical disease starts to spread, the community approves and joins in a quarantine of the patients in order to protect the health of the community against the spread of the disease."

Roosevelt didn't specify what he meant by a quarantine. In fact, lest his audience—in Chicago and beyond—think he was advocating military action, he stressed the opposite. "It is my determination to pursue a policy of peace. It is my determination to adopt every practicable measure to avoid involvement in war." Yet a desire for peace wasn't enough. "There must be positive endeavors to preserve peace."

❖ ❖ ❖

ROOSEVELT HAD WANTED to get the attention of the country, and by the evidence of the press reaction, he succeeded. The tenor of the reaction—in particular to his mention of a "quarantine"—varied dramatically. The isolationist *Chicago Tribune* was deeply skeptical. "Japan will not easily be beaten to her knees," the *Tribune* warned, "and the threat of a boycott may only serve to inflame the patriotic ardor of the Japanese." The *Oregonian,* speaking for many on the West Coast, asserted that the interests of the other great powers in China were larger than the interests of the United States; those other powers ought to take the lead in chastising Japan. The *Baltimore Sun* adopted a different view, calling the speech "an admirable restatement of the principles of international morality." The *Washington Post* read it as a rejoinder to the isolationists. "The forces now fighting intolerable aggression, whether in the case of the Chinese at Shanghai or the Spaniards defending Madrid, are neither cowards nor weaklings," the *Post* said. "With the assurance that the United States has not forgotten all moral standards in its ostrich hunt for security, the strength of their resistance will be redoubled."

The ambivalence afforded Roosevelt little guidance. "Do you care to amplify your remarks at Chicago, especially where you referred to a possible quarantine?" a reporter asked him at a news conference the next day.

"No," Roosevelt answered, obviously uncomfortable.

The correspondents pressed him to say something.

"I can only talk really completely off the record," the president said.

What did the president mean by a quarantine? a reporter asked. "As I interpreted it, you were speaking of something more than moral indignation. . . . Is anything contemplated?"

"No. Just the speech itself."

Economic sanctions?

"Not necessarily. Look, 'sanctions' is a terrible word. They are out the window."

What, then?

"I can't tell you what the methods will be. We are looking for some way to peace."

Would there be a conference of the opponents of fascism?

"No. Conferences are out the window. You never get anywhere with a conference."

Roosevelt wished he had never raised the issue of a quarantine. "It is a terrible thing," he told speechwriter Sam Rosenman, "to look over your shoulder when you are trying to lead, and to find no one there."

35.

JOHN MAYNARD KEYNES THOUGHT ROOSEVELT SHOULD HAVE THE benefit of the best economic thinking in the world, which was why the English economist had written the American president in the aftermath of the Hundred Days. Keynes critiqued certain aspects of the New Deal even as he offered encouragement and a lesson in the theory of employment and money he was then developing. "You have made yourself the trustee for those in every country who seek to mend the evils of our condition by reasoned experiment within the framework of the existing social system," Keynes said. "If you fail, rational change will be gravely prejudiced throughout the world, leaving orthodoxy and revolution to fight it out. But if you succeed, new and bolder methods will be tried everywhere, and we may date the first chapter of a new economic era from your accession to office."

Keynes described Roosevelt's leadership task as comprising economic recovery and institutional reform. The latter could wait; in fact it *ought* to wait. "Haste will be injurious, and wisdom of long-range purpose is more necessary than immediate achievement." Recovery came first. In this realm the president had got some things right but others wrong. His administration should have paid more attention to increasing the purchasing power of consumers. "In the economic system of the modern world, output is primarily produced for sale; and the volume of output depends on the amount of purchasing power." A depression was, by definition, a shortfall of demand; the remedy to a depression must come in one of three forms. Individuals could be induced to spend more, businesses could be persuaded to spend more, or government could decide to spend more. In a depression the first two sources of spending—individuals and businesses—typically failed. "It is, therefore, only from the third factor"—government—"that we can expect the initial major impulse."

Roosevelt had read Keynes's letter and filed it away. His view of Keynes coincided with his view of most other academic economists, which was that they didn't understand how policy was made in the real world of politics. In any case, by the time Keynes wrote—in December 1933—the economy appeared to be recovering. The president saw no reason to jeopardize the recovery to suit the notions of an English intellectual.

Roosevelt had occasion to dust off Keynes's letter in the autumn of 1937. At the very moment when he was trying to nudge Americans toward greater responsibility for world peace, the American economy was falling off a cliff. The 1937 plunge wasn't as deep as the dive that followed the stock crash of 1929, but it was swifter and, because it came after four years of improvement, more disheartening. Industrial activity in early 1937 had finally topped that of 1929, while unemployment had diminished to less than 15 percent. Relief rolls were down and were scheduled to shrink further as Roosevelt's determination to end relief in favor of jobs shaped the new laws of that season. As long as unemployment, a lagging indicator of the economy as a whole, remained in double digits, it would have been impolitic for Roosevelt to declare the depression ended. Yet it wasn't unreasonable for him to think in such terms.

Then, for no good reason anyone could discern, the recovery suddenly lurched into reverse. The stock market collapsed, with the Dow Jones average plunging from 190 in August to 115 in October. Wealth vanished more rapidly than at the worst of the 1929 crash. Corporate profits plummeted by four-fifths. Steel production fell by three-quarters. Unsold autos jammed factory and dealer lots. As the furnaces were banked and the assembly lines shut down, two million people lost their jobs, crowding back onto the relief rolls Roosevelt had hoped to render obsolete.

The "Roosevelt recession," as the president's critics alliteratively labeled it (when they weren't calling it the "Democratic depression"), reopened nearly every aspect of the debate that had surrounded the New Deal from its inception. Republicans and other conservatives naturally blamed the government's intrusion into the private sector. No depression in American history had lasted so long, they correctly noted, and none had witnessed such overweening ambition on the part of government. Ergo, the ambition had prolonged the depression. "Right in the midst of good business, we have a loss of billions of dollars to thrifty folk," asserted Bruce Barton, the ad man, who was now running for Congress on the Republican ticket. "There is only one reason: politics and the threat of more politics. . . . There is no possible explanation of the present fear and loss except one: too many politicians monkeying too much."

A person didn't have to be campaigning for office or to consider incumbents monkeys to credit at least some of Barton's argument. The very flexibility on which Roosevelt prided himself had the perverse effect of rendering investors unable to make reasoned judgments about where to put their money. Lammot du Pont, the current spokesman of the famous family, explained the view from Wall Street:

> Uncertainty rules the tax situation, the labor situation, the monetary situation, and practically every legal condition under which industry must operate. Are taxes to go higher, lower, or stay where they are? We don't know. Is labor to be union or non-union? . . . Are we to have inflation or deflation, more government spending or less? . . . Are new restrictions to be placed on capital, new limits on profits? . . . It is impossible even to guess at the answers.

Nor was it only conservatives who held this opinion. Adolf Berle, of the original Brain Trust, conceded the capitalists' argument. "Practically no business group in the country has escaped investigation or other attack in the last five years," Berle said. "Irrespective of their deserts, the result has been shattered morale. We have not, in the absence of a large Government ownership program, any class or group to whom we may turn for economic leadership. It is, therefore, necessary to make that group pull itself together." Henry Morgenthau argued a similar case. The Treasury secretary had advocated deficit reduction from the beginning, contending that a balanced budget would do more for the economy, by boosting business morale, than almost anything else the administration could do. The nosedive of 1937 strengthened his case. "We are headed right into another depression," he told the president. Morgenthau granted, for tactical purposes if no other, that federal deficits had been acceptable during the president's first term, to deal with the emergency. But conditions had changed. "The domestic problems which face us today are essentially different from those which faced us four years ago. . . . We want to see private business expand. We believe that much of the remaining unemployment will disappear as private capital funds are increasingly employed. . . . We believe that one of the most important ways of achieving these ends at this time is to continue progress toward a balance of the federal budget."

A competing faction within the administration asserted that Berle and Morgenthau had it all wrong. These younger New Dealers were a cadre of lawyers, economists, and other ambitious fellows who had come to Washington to take part in Roosevelt's reformation of the American political economy. Thomas Corcoran, nominally counsel to the Reconstruction Finance Corporation but actually an adviser with broad portfolio, was their unofficial leader; Benjamin Cohen, Isador Lubin, Leon Henderson, and Jerome Frank were Tommy the Cork's lieutenants. These "janizaries," as their critics called them, lived for their jobs, talking politics and economics from early morning at work till late at night over drinks in Corcoran's Georgetown home. They had experience in neither elective politics nor practical business, but they professed to tell the politicians and the businessmen what to do. They were often clever enough to get away with it. Their mindset was that of the progressives of a generation before: they blamed big capital for the economy's woes, and they looked to government—that is, to the agencies they themselves staffed—to make the profiteers mend their irresponsible ways.

Their diagnosis of the 1937 slump was just the opposite of Morgenthau's. They pointed out that the federal budget that year was closer to balance than any since the New Deal's start, on account of reductions in relief spending and increases in taxes, particularly the payroll taxes that funded the new Social Security system. The ergo for them was that the declining deficit had caused the recession. Their prescription was to expand the deficit so that government spending would provide what private spending did not.

The young New Dealers bolstered their arguments with the economic theories of John Maynard Keynes. The British economist published his magnum opus, *The General Theory of Employment, Interest, and Money,* in 1936. The work involved intricate analysis of all manner of economic and monetary policies, but for political practitioners the moral was that government ought to intervene, energetically and forthrightly, when the private sector failed. As the moral pertained to the 1937 recession, the federal government should increase the deficit as a countercyclical correction to the shortfall in private consumption.

Keynes couldn't expect Roosevelt to read his whole book, which even for economists was heavy slogging. So he summarized its main points in another letter. Consumption, Keynes told Roosevelt, was the key to recovery. Private consumption languished—this was the essence of the recession—and therefore public consumption must expand. In particular the government must spend more—much more—than it took in, so that the deficit would put money in the hands of people who would spend it again, in their turn. The people who received the money must be the poor and middling, not the rich; ordinary farmers and workers, not powerful business owners. Ordinary peo-

ple spent their incomes, from necessity; the rich might sit on the money, depriving it of its multiplier value.

Keynes didn't suggest that Roosevelt write off the rich and the business
classes. The cooperation of business would ultimately be essential in sustain-
ing any recovery. But the economist urged the president to treat the capitalists
with caution.

> Businessmen have a different set of delusions from politicians and need,
> therefore, different handling. They are, however, much milder than politi-
> cians, at the same time allured and terrified by the glare of publicity, easily
> persuaded to be "patriots," perplexed, bemused, indeed terrified, yet only too
> anxious to take a cheerful view, vain perhaps but very unsure of themselves,
> pathetically responsive to a kind word. You could do anything you liked with
> them, if you would treat them (even the big ones) not as wolves and tigers but
> as domestic animals by nature, even though they have been badly brought up
> and not trained as you would wish. It is a mistake to think that they are more
> *immoral* than politicians. If you work them into the surly, obstinate, terrified
> mood of which domestic animals, wrongly handled, are so capable, the na-
> tion's burdens will not get carried to market, and in the end public opinion
> will veer their way.

❖ ❖ ❖

BETWEEN THE FISCAL conservatism of Morgenthau and the budget hawks
and the liberalism of the junior New Dealers, with the unsolicited kibitzing of
Keynes on the side, Roosevelt had to chart a course for the American economy.
His head and his past were on the side of the budget cutters; his instincts had
always been to trim government spending. But his heart and his politics were
on the side of the spenders. He resented the failure of investors—many of
whom came from backgrounds similar to his own—to acknowledge their debt
to the community at large and their obligation to repay it. And he appreciated
that fat capitalists made easy targets.

The October 1937 edition of the Fireside Chats came a week after Roosevelt's Chicago speech on quarantining aggression. He touched briefly, and
vaguely, on the themes of that earlier speech, but most of his talk treated the
domestic economy, in particular the role of business in triggering the current
recession. Roosevelt didn't target all businessmen; as when he attacked Republicans, he distinguished the evil few from the virtuous many. The former,

besides withholding investment funds, had been spreading malicious stories about government, thereby undermining the democratic faith of the latter. "Most business men, big and little, know that their government neither wants to put them out of business nor to prevent them from earning a decent profit," the president said. "In spite of the alarms of a few who seek to regain control of American life, most business men, big and little, know that their government is trying to make property more secure than ever before by giving every family a real chance to have a property stake in the nation." Roosevelt echoed his salvos of the 1936 campaign when he blamed "private monopolies and financial oligarchies" for endangering American prosperity by refusing to lower unconscionably high prices. On Wall Street, not in Washington, should Americans seek the villains in the current recession. The government was doing everything it could to undo the harm the business barons had done. "We are already studying how to strengthen our antitrust laws in order to end monopoly, not to hurt but to free legitimate business."

Roosevelt extended the attack in his annual message to Congress, delivered at the beginning of 1938. The recession had worsened with the winter; the prospects of recovery had retreated commensurately. More than ever the American future required the cooperation of honest businesses and their resources, Roosevelt said. "Capital is essential." And capital could expect to be rewarded. "Reasonable earnings on capital are essential." But capital, for its own sake and that of the country, must not overreach. "Misuse of the powers of capital or selfish suspension of the employment of capital must be ended, or the capitalistic system will destroy itself through its own abuses." Roosevelt identified the worst of the abuses: "tax avoidance . . . security manipulations . . . price rigging . . . collusive bidding . . . unfair competition . . . intimidation of local or state government." Most of these practices resulted from excessive concentration of corporate power in the hands of a very few firms, whose directors belligerently asserted their right to employ their property as they saw fit. Roosevelt didn't deny the right, but he linked it to responsibility. "The man who seeks freedom from such responsibility in the name of individual liberty is either fooling himself or trying to cheat his fellow men. He wants to eat the fruits of orderly society without paying for them."

❖ ❖ ❖

BLAMING GREEDY CAPITALISTS might be a political strategy, but it wasn't an economic policy. Roosevelt had to decide whether to cut spending or expand it. At first he leaned toward Morgenthau, hoping that the back of the depression had been broken and that the current difficulties were fleeting. If this was so, he was willing for government's role to diminish. In October 1937 he met with congressional leaders and declared his intention of balancing the budget by fiscal 1939. "The President told them with a real 'burr' in his voice," Morgenthau recorded in his diary, "that he expected to balance the budget, that he wanted enough money to balance the budget, that he expected to keep expenditures down so he could balance the budget, and that if any committee passed an appropriation over and above his estimates he would immediately serve notice on that committee that they must find the additional revenue."

Within a week of this meeting, however, the stock market lurched down again, suffering the single day's biggest loss in six years. Even Morgenthau was shaken, calling the sell-off "an hysteria resembling a mob in a theater fire." When the market didn't recover, and as the effects of the dive rippled into the larger economy, Roosevelt reconsidered his devotion to a balanced budget. He called a cabinet meeting to consider his options. None appeared new or particularly effective. "I am sick and tired," he said, "of being told by the cabinet, by Henry, and by everybody else for the last two weeks what's the matter with the country, and nobody suggests what I should do."

After a long silence, Morgenthau spoke up. "You must do something to reassure business," the Treasury secretary said.

"You want me to turn on the old record," Roosevelt replied.

"What business wants to know is this: Are we headed toward state socialism, or are we going to continue on a capitalistic basis?"

"I have told them that again and again."

"Tell them for the fifteenth time. That's what they want to know."

Jim Farley echoed: "That's what they want to know." The president should explain that he was going to cut the cost of government.

"All right, Jim," Roosevelt answered. "I will turn on the old record."

Morgenthau left the meeting encouraged. "This is the first time that the cabinet had ever talked on a man-to-man basis with the President and that we did not sit back and either talk trivialities or listen to him," Morgenthau recorded.

Yet the more Roosevelt thought about the recession, the angrier he grew at the greedy capitalists. In a telephone conversation he told Morgenthau that a "wise old bird" had informed him that big business was behind the recession, self-consciously sabotaging the economy in order to force the administration to back away from reform.

Morgenthau inquired who the owl was. Some were better informed than others, he said.

"It is not necessary for you to know," Roosevelt responded.

Morgenthau, surmising that the owl was the president himself, anticipated a change in course. It came in stages. The Treasury secretary was scheduled to speak to an audience that would include business bigwigs; he wanted to tell them that a balanced budget was still the administration's goal. He showed his draft to Roosevelt, who read Morgenthau's words: "This administration is going to do everything possible to promote a continuation of recovery and to balance the budget through cutting expenditures. But I wish to emphasize that in no event will this administration allow anyone to starve." The latter sentence was already a concession to the spenders in the administration. Yet it wasn't enough for Roosevelt. He appended an additional promise: "Nor will it abandon its broad purpose to protect the weak, to give human security, and to seek a wider distribution of our national wealth."

Morgenthau choked. "If you want to sound like Huey Long," he told the president, "I don't." But he gave the speech, with Roosevelt's coda. And it convinced no one in the business community that the administration was serious about reducing the deficit—for the good reason that the administration, regardless of what Morgenthau wanted, was not serious. Each week brought worse news about the economy. In December the Labor Department calculated that nearly two million people had lost their jobs since September. Government economists predicted that another million would be laid off by the middle of January. This was no financial stumble but a broad economic collapse. The early months of 1938 seemed eerily like the start of 1933. Hunger once more threatened millions; tent cities sprang up anew—and might have been called Rooseveltvilles if the term hadn't been so awkward. The federal capacity to provide relief had been deliberately reduced the previous summer; it could not re-expand fast enough to cover the growing need. Sixty thousand men and women went without food for a week in Cleveland when local agencies couldn't make up for the federal shortfall. Chicago closed down its relief offices lest they be crushed by the burden of those who descended upon them.

The acuteness of the emergency created a consensus in the administration that strong measures had to be taken. Even Morgenthau, calling the rate of decline "something terrible," advocated an increase in relief spending. "If $250 million will stop this downward spiral, it's cheap," he said. Roosevelt agreed.

He called the money-committee chairmen from Congress to the White House and requested the quarter billion.

Yet the deeper issue remained. What was the meaning of the New Deal? Was it a stopgap program to get the private sector back on its feet and then fade away? Or was it a permanent reorientation of the political economy, with government guiding business forever?

Roosevelt refused to decide definitively. But as the economy continued to languish, he let the radical New Dealers speak their minds as if on the administration's behalf. Robert Jackson, a janizary who headed the Justice Department's antitrust division, declared that the downturn had been caused by a "strike" of the capitalists against the people. "Certain groups of big business have now seized upon a recession in our prosperity to liquidate the New Deal and to throw off all governmental interference with their incorporated initiative and their aristocratic anarchy," Jackson said. The monopolists were cynically disingenuous in blaming the government for the slump. "The only just criticism that can be made of the economic operations of the New Deal is that it set out a breakfast for the canary and let the cat steal it."

Harold Ickes was older than the janizaries, but he yielded nothing to them in his disdain for big capital. America's economic troubles, Ickes proclaimed, were the fault of "the sixty families who have brought the rest of the business men of the United States under the terror of their domination." Their malign efforts were nothing new. "It is the old struggle between the power of money and the power of the democratic instinct." But the stakes were higher than ever. "Big business fascism" was closer than most Americans realized. "We say that Germany isn't Germany any more. Italy isn't Italy any more. . . . Should we be getting ready to say 'America isn't America any more'?"

Roosevelt kept quiet, still pondering his options. "As I see it," Morgenthau remarked at a lunch in March 1938, "what you are doing now is just treading water."

"Absolutely," Roosevelt replied.

But when the stock market dove again a week later, with no improvement in the broader economy, Roosevelt decided to take on big capital himself. He ordered Jackson at Justice to prepare antitrust suits against the most obvious monopolists. "Get plenty strong," the president said. "We're going into training for the heavyweight championship."

And he finally decided between the retrenchers and the expansionists. Several of the latter followed the president to Warm Springs, where he was taking his spring vacation. Morgenthau considered such blatant advocacy beneath him, and he soon regretted his hauteur. "They just stampeded him," the Treasury secretary moaned. "He was completely stampeded. They stampeded him like cattle." Morgenthau underestimated the president's intellectual autonomy, but he accurately assessed the result of the lobbying.

Roosevelt unveiled his decision in a Fireside Chat in April. He said that after much deliberation he had determined that the public interest required the federal government to make "definite additions to the purchasing power of the nation." These would take the form, primarily, of increases to public works: $1 billion for permanent improvements to buildings and the like in the states, counties, and cities; $300 million for slum clearance; $100 million for highways; $37 million for flood control and reclamation; $25 million for improvements to federal buildings.

This spending was intended to promote prosperity, but it had a larger goal: the survival of democracy. "Democracy has disappeared in several other great nations," Roosevelt said, "not because the people of those nations disliked democracy, but because they had grown tired of unemployment and insecurity, of seeing their children hungry while they sat helpless in the face of government confusion and government weakness." Forced to choose between voting and eating, desperate people chose the latter. Americans had a justified faith in their own democratic institutions, but the health of these institutions required a collective effort to secure the material needs of the ordinary citizens of the country. "The very soundness of our democratic institutions depends on the determination of our government to give employment to idle men." For the first time—but not for the last—Roosevelt described the New Deal as a bulwark of American defense.

> The people of America are in agreement in defending their liberties at any cost, and the first line of that defense lies in the protection of economic security. Your government, seeking to protect democracy, must prove that government is stronger than the forces of business depression.

❖ ❖ ❖

THE LINK BETWEEN prosperity and democracy—between economic security at home and the security of American institutions and values in a world of troubles—came naturally in the spring of 1938. The war in China had escalated till it touched Americans. In December 1937 an American gunboat, the

Panay, patrolling the Yangtze River in accord with treaties between the United States and China, suffered attack by Japanese warplanes near Nanking. The presence of the *Panay* and its purpose in being there were no surprise to the Japanese, who had been informed by the vessel's commander of its location and its mission of evacuating American nationals from the zone of the fighting. But for reasons that escaped the commander and his men, more than a dozen Japanese planes bombed and strafed the craft, killing three Americans, wounding eleven others, and sending the vessel to the river bottom.

Roosevelt responded at once with indignation. "Please tell the Japanese Ambassador," he directed Cordell Hull:

1. That the President is deeply shocked and concerned by the news of indiscriminate bombing of American and other non-Chinese vessels on the Yangtze, and that he requests that the Emperor be so advised.

2. That all the facts are being assembled and will shortly be presented to the Japanese Government.

3. That in the meantime it is hoped the Japanese Government will be considering definitely for presentation to this Government:

a. Full expressions of regret and proffer of full compensation.

b. Methods guaranteeing against a repetition of any similar attack in the future.

Roosevelt's insistence that the Japanese emperor be advised of the American president's shock and concern was more than diplomatic protocol. During this period, American officials never quite knew where decisions in Tokyo were being made. The emperor, of course, was the head of the Japanese state, but whether he was the head of the Japanese government was unclear. Roosevelt feared that if the militarists behind the war in China had their way with Japan's foreign policy, the United States would have no choice but to confront them with force. His hope, consequently, for averting conflict was that the militarists would *not* have their way. If the emperor learned how seriously the United States took the attack on the *Panay*, perhaps he would rein in the generals.

Roosevelt never discovered whether the emperor got his message. Japanese officials informed the State Department that the attack had been an unhappy mistake. "This was the lamest of lame excuses," Hull later remarked, and it grew lamer as additional evidence arrived showing that Japanese patrol boats had machine-gunned survivors fleeing the sinking *Panay*. The secretary of state was convinced that the attack was a warning to the United States not to get involved in Japan's fight with China.

Roosevelt agreed, although the question remained as to *who* was giving the warning. The Japanese government conveyed its "profound apology" and agreed to Roosevelt's other conditions, including reparations and assurances against similar incidents in the future. Whether this would bind the "wild, runaway, half-insane men," as Hull described the leaders of the Japanese army on the Yangtze, was another matter.

Roosevelt had to prepare for the possibility that it wouldn't. He didn't want to take military action against Japan, in part because the U.S. navy currently lacked the ability to project American power against Japan in China and in part because he knew he had almost no support in Congress for such action. The isolationist bloc remained solid; its leaders decried as "jingoism" any suggestion of a stern response to the gunboat sinking. "If Japan has accepted responsibility and apologizes, there is not much more that the United States can do," Democrat Elbert Thomas of Utah told the Senate. "You can't go to war with a nation which admits it was wrong." Thomas's Republican colleague from Nevada, Pat McCarran, asserted, "We should have been out of China long ago."

Consequently Roosevelt explored other means of influencing Japan's conduct. He asked Morgenthau to ascertain the executive's legal authority to seize Japanese assets in the United States. If the president lacked legal authority, the Treasury secretary was to determine whether the assets could be seized extralegally and whether the Japanese could do anything about it. "After all," Roosevelt told the cabinet, "if Italy and Japan have evolved a technique of fighting without declaring war, why can't we develop a similar one?"

❖   ❖   ❖

MORGENTHAU'S EFFORTS bore fruit that would be harvested only later. With Tokyo giving every indication of making good on its promise to prevent future attacks, Roosevelt lost what leverage he might have had to budge the isolationists.

In any event, he wasn't ready to start a fight in Congress, for he had a fight on his hands already. The conservative opposition to Roosevelt's domestic program intensified during the spring and summer of 1938. His allies in Congress had sponsored a measure designed to put a floor under wages and a ceiling over hours, but the bill bogged down in conference when corporate executives claimed it would ruin their businesses, besides violating their freedom of contract. Southern conservatives—Democrats to a man—backed business on this one, asserting that the administration's bill would deny their region its competitive advantage and trample their cherished states' rights. With great effort Roosevelt's allies managed to get a bill passed, one that mandated a forty-cent minimum wage and a forty-hour standard week, but it included so many exemptions and loopholes as to cast the whole enterprise into question. Amid the deliberations, liberal Democrat Martin Dies of Texas proposed an amendment in meaningful jest: "Within ninety days after the appointment of the Administrator, she shall report to Congress whether anyone is subject to this bill." The amendment failed but the question remained. The bill's one worthy accomplishment was banning child labor in interstate commerce. After signing the measure, Roosevelt put down the pen and declared, "That's that," referring to child labor but also to his near-term hopes for broader workplace reform.

The president met similar resistance on taxes. Business-sympathetic Democrats joined Republicans in blaming high taxes for the recession and sought to reduce them, especially those that targeted capital gains and undistributed profits. Roosevelt opposed the reduction, still deeming business, not business taxes, responsible for the slump. But he couldn't keep his legislative forces in line, and the lawmakers approved a tax bill with the provisions he disliked. He refused to sign the bill, saying it undermined the principle of progressivity in taxation by taxing small profits and large profits at the same rate. "That, my friends, is not right," he declared. Yet because the Treasury needed a tax measure, he let the bill become law without his signature. He promised to revisit the tax issue when the new Congress convened after the 1938 elections.

❖ ❖ ❖

THE CONSERVATIVE REVOLT caused Roosevelt to wonder whether the entire New Deal was at risk. The southern Democrats had always been reluctant reformers, and with the president presumably a lame duck their reluctance had become defiance. It was hardly inconceivable that a Republican president, elected in 1940, would forge an alliance with the conservative southern Democrats and dismantle the New Deal bit by bit—or all at once.

Roosevelt might have retreated in order to consolidate his position. He could have given the conservatives enough of what they wanted on peripheral issues like minimum wages to ensure support for such central programs as Social Security. He could have turned the New Deal in a cautiously moderate direction.

But the president chose a different path. Convinced of both the correctness of his vision for America and the continuing potency of his personal charm, he took the fight to the conservatives. He declared war within his own party. During the late winter and spring of 1938 he directed his most trusted assistants, including his son James, who had taken over some of Louis Howe's responsibilities, and Harry Hopkins, who was becoming the president's all-purpose fixer, to identify Democratic primaries where administration support might tip the balance between pro– and anti–New Deal candidates. The White House operatives focused on the South, where conservative opposition was strongest and where segregationist politics guaranteed the general-election victory of whichever candidate won the Democratic primary. They scored an early victory in May in Florida when James Roosevelt proclaimed the administration's support for Claude Pepper, a New Deal liberal, and Pepper went on to trounce his primary opponent, an outspoken anti–New Dealer.

The president himself kept aloof till the primary season heated up at the start of the summer. In late June he took his campaign to the air. "There will be many clashes between two schools of thought, generally classified as liberal and conservative," he told a Fireside Chat audience. The liberal school was able to recognize that the novel conditions of modern life necessitated new remedies and ways of thinking; the conservatives were not. The conservative school wanted government to ignore modern problems. "It believes that individual initiative and private philanthropy will solve them—that we ought to repeal many of the things we have done and go back, for instance, to the old gold standard, or stop all this business of old age pensions and unemployment insurance, or repeal the Securities and Exchange Act, or let monopolies thrive unchecked—return, in effect, to the kind of government we had in the twenties." The question was whether voters would agree with this reactionary position. Roosevelt thought they should not, and, to illustrate his point, he told a story he said came from China. "Two Chinese coolies were arguing heatedly in the midst of a crowd. A stranger expressed surprise that no blows were being struck. His Chinese friend replied: 'The man who strikes first admits that his ideas have given out.'" Americans ought to take the lesson. "I know that neither in the summer primaries nor in the November elections will the American voters fail to spot the candidate whose ideas have given out."

It was a risky strategy, causing Roosevelt's most seasoned political advisers to groan. "The Boss has stirred up a hornet's nest," John Nance Garner observed. "The feeling is becoming intensely bitter. It's downright unhealthy." Jim Farley told the president directly, "Boss, I think you're foolish."

Roosevelt appreciated the risk he was taking. He remembered how Wilson's appeal for a vote of confidence in the war effort had backfired in 1918; his current appeal for a vote of confidence in the New Deal might backfire, too. He understood that second-term presidents often suffer from voters' sixth-year itch and that congressional elections often turn on local, idiosyncratic issues. But he considered the stakes sufficiently high to warrant the risk, and he plunged ahead. He toured the country, stopping in states and districts with close races pitting his allies against his enemies. In Louisville he endorsed Alben Barkley over the Kentucky senator's conservative opponent. In Oklahoma City he told an audience that Senator Elmer Thomas had been "of enormous help to me and to the administration," and he castigated Thomas's rival as a perennial naysayer.

In Georgia the "purge," as Roosevelt's opponents and much of the press were calling it, grew the most personal. Walter George was a three-term senator who was as solidly planted in the upper chamber as a person could be. He feared neither Republicans nor Democratic presidents. He disdained most aspects of the New Deal, and he didn't hesitate to vote his disdain. Yet Roosevelt bearded the old lion in his Barnesville den. Speaking to George's face—and the faces of Governor E. D. Rivers and Georgia's other senator, Richard Russell— Roosevelt reminded his listeners that he was an adoptive son of their state. He said he had nothing against Senator George as an individual. "He is, and I hope always will be, my personal friend. He is beyond question, beyond any possible question, a gentleman and a scholar." But he was wrong politically. "On most public questions he and I do not speak the same language." Roosevelt explained that as a Democratic president he needed the cooperation of Democrats in Congress to carry out the people's will. "That is one of the essentials of a party form of government. It has been going on in this country for nearly a century and a half." Roosevelt put two questions to Georgia Democrats as they approached the primary. Was their candidate a fighter for the broad objectives of the party and the administration? And did he honestly believe in those objectives? "I regret that in the case of my friend, Senator George, I cannot honestly answer either of these questions in the affirmative."

Roosevelt wasted his breath. Georgia voters rejected his advice and returned George to the Senate. South Carolina voters did the same for Cotton Ed Smith after Roosevelt visited the Palmetto State. Maryland voters reelected Millard Tydings over Roosevelt's opposition.

The president suffered a shellacking that season beyond the failure of his purge. The Republicans picked up eight seats in the Senate and eighty-one in the House. They netted a gain of thirteen governorships, winning with Harold Stassen in Minnesota and John Bricker in Ohio and barely losing with Thomas Dewey in New York, where Roosevelt's protégé Herbert Lehman clung to office by the thinnest of margins. The Democrats still held the balance in both houses of Congress, but the purge's failure predictably emboldened southern conservatives in their defiance of the White House. "It's time to stop feeling sorry for the Republicans," Jim Farley grumbled.

36.

"THERE WERE ONLY TWO PEOPLE WHO STOOD UP TO FRANKLIN," Eleanor remarked years later to Henry Morgenthau. "You and Louis."

"No, you are wrong," Morgenthau replied. "There were three—Louis, myself, and Eleanor Roosevelt."

The question of who stood up to Franklin became more critical the longer Roosevelt remained in office. Howe, Morgenthau, and obviously Eleanor had known Roosevelt for many years before he became president. They appreciated the growth in his stature and power, but they never lost touch with the ordinary man he had been—and the ordinary man he still was beneath the trappings of office. But Howe died, and Eleanor spent more and more of her time on her own causes: her travels, her lectures, her column. Morgenthau stayed in daily contact with Roosevelt, but his influence was diluted by the many others who laid claim to the president's time and energy. And nearly all these others knew Roosevelt only as president—as the man who, among other things, could advance or retard their careers, who could bestow or withhold favors.

Harry Hopkins was one of these, and he was conspicuously excluded by Eleanor and Morgenthau from the short list of persons who stood up to Franklin. Eleanor couldn't decide what she thought about Hopkins. Her heart went out to him when his wife died of cancer in 1937, leaving him bereft and solely responsible for their five-year-old daughter, Diana. Hopkins himself had been diagnosed with cancer, and while doctors, on removing a large part of his stomach, thought they had got it all, no one could be sure. "Just before Christmas in 1938 Mrs. Roosevelt came to our house in Georgetown to see me," Hopkins later wrote Diana.

At that time I was feeling none too well. I had seen a great deal of Mrs. Roosevelt during the previous six months, and the day she came out she told me she thought I seemed to be disturbed about something, and wondered if it was a feeling that something might happen to me and that there was no proper provision for you. She told me that she had been thinking about it a good deal and wanted me to know that she would like for me to provide in my will that she, Mrs. Roosevelt, be made your guardian.

Hopkins knew the story of Eleanor's own orphanhood, and he doubtless guessed that her experience had sensitized her to Diana's situation. He gratefully accepted the offer.

Yet he realized it was much more about Diana than about him. After taking some pains to bring Hopkins into the inner circle of the White House family, Eleanor began to wish she hadn't. His actions as czar of relief stole headlines she thought should have been Franklin's. And when he attracted criticism she resented the bad light he brought on the administration. Conservatives repeated endlessly a statement attributed to Hopkins that he forever denied having made but that seemed to summarize the Hopkins attitude toward relief and politics: "We shall tax and tax, and spend and spend, and elect and elect." At every opportunity the conservatives slapped him down. In 1937, amid the uproar provoked by Roosevelt's court-packing plan, the House of Representatives wrote a rider into the relief appropriations bill, cutting Hopkins's salary from $12,000 to $10,000. "This was pure spite," the *Baltimore Sun* asserted, "for what is a saving of $2,000 a year in a job like that? But while the business has no monetary significance, it is highly significant as revealing the emotional state of members. They must hate Hopkins with a frantic hatred when they are driven to do as childish a thing as cutting $2,000 off his salary to express their anger and resentment."

It was spite, to be sure, but there was something else. After the 1936 election, political handicappers predictably looked to the 1940 race. Most assumed that Roosevelt would be tempted to try for a third term but that, like every one of his predecessors who had felt the temptation, he would resist it. Presumably he would cast his support to a candidate committed to preserving and perhaps extending the New Deal. Vice President Garner was too conservative, besides being a Southerner. Various otherwise likely senators and governors had looked askance at significant parts of the Roosevelt reforms. In effect, only the loyalists were left. Of these, Hopkins was the most loyal and arguably the most able. Hopkins mentally worked through the process of elimination and began to fancy himself presidential material.

Roosevelt didn't discourage him. In the spring of 1938 he invited Hopkins to the White House for a chat. The conversation commenced with Roosevelt venting the anger he still felt at the conservatives on the Supreme Court. He explained that it had long been tradition for the chief justice, at the start of each autumn session of the court, to call the White House to inform the president that the court had convened. The president would then invite the justices over for a visit. Justice Hughes had been careful to follow the tradition for the first three years of Roosevelt's presidency, but he had failed to do so in 1936. Roosevelt took this lapse as a conscious affront. "And remember," he told Hopkins, "this was six months before the court fight started."

Roosevelt mused about appointments to the court before sidling around to the question of his own successor. He didn't disqualify himself for 1940, but he described his "personal disinclination" to run again and explained that Eleanor definitely didn't want him to run. He said the family finances required the replenishment a former president might accomplish but a sitting president could not. Hyde Park was costing his mother more than she was earning in interest and dividends from the family trust.

Roosevelt listed several possible candidates for the Democratic nomination, only to explain why each wouldn't do. Cordell Hull was too old. Harold Ickes was too crotchety. Henry Wallace and Frank Murphy lacked broad constituencies. Jim Farley wanted the nomination as much as anyone, but Roosevelt judged him the "most dangerous" of the plausible prospects because of his growing disenchantment with the New Deal and his weak understanding of foreign affairs.

Roosevelt finally came around to Hopkins. The president noted the fact of Hopkins's divorce, which would upset Catholics and some others. But his second marriage had turned out well—before his wife's recent death—and other candidates had survived worse scandals. Grover Cleveland had fathered a son out of wedlock, had owned up, and had been elected twice. A larger question was Hopkins's health. Campaigning for president was a trying job, being president more trying still. Hopkins seemed to be healthy enough now, but voters would wonder whether he could stand the strain. Yet Roosevelt remarked that he himself had neutralized the presidential health question as it applied to him; on balance it needn't disqualify Hopkins.

Roosevelt and Hopkins were the only persons present at this meeting. The sole record was Hopkins's notes, jotted down afterward, which ended with the phrase "assurances and hopes." Roosevelt never spoke so unguardedly to Hopkins again on the subject of a possible successor. Perhaps he was as sincere as

Hopkins apparently thought he was; perhaps he was thinking out loud. Perhaps Hopkins, like so many others who fell under Roosevelt's spell, heard more than Roosevelt actually said.

In any case, Hopkins gave the impression, even without saying anything explicitly, of having the inside track to the nomination, which didn't endear him to others around the president. Hopkins encouraged—goaded, some said—Roosevelt to attempt the purge of the Democratic conservatives; when the effort backfired, Hopkins's critics were happy to hand him the blame. Hopkins's colleagues from the early days of the administration remembered how he told them to ignore politics. "We're here to implement a policy," he had said. But as the presidency loomed in his mind's eye, politics rose alongside it. He grew impatient at the "goddam New Dealers" for their excessive spending, conveniently ignoring that he had taught them most of what they knew on the subject.

Meanwhile he left Eleanor behind. "Here was Harry who was Mother's protégé to start with," Anna Roosevelt remembered, "and suddenly Harry became Father's protégé." Eleanor tried to mask her hurt at what she interpreted as Hopkins's betrayal, as she always tried to mask her hurt. But the mask occasionally slipped. She feigned illness as an excuse to hole up in a small apartment she kept on East Eleventh Street in New York. To one friend, however, she related the cause of her distress. "I haven't been ill at all," she told Esther Lape. "Something happened to me. I haven't gotten used to people who say they care for me but are only interested in getting to Franklin. But there was one person of whom I thought this was not true, that his affection was for me. I found this was not true, and I couldn't take it."

❖   ❖   ❖

$\mathcal{P}$RESIDENTS OFTEN TURN to foreign affairs when their domestic agendas stall. Roosevelt might have felt relief at reverting to diplomacy in the autumn of 1938 had the diplomacy of that season not been so uniformly disheartening. The civil war in Spain ground forward to an increasingly inevitable victory for the fascists. Ethiopia struggled for breath beneath the treads of the Italian tanks. Japan continued its brutalization of China. Hitler flaunted his scorn for international opinion more flagrantly than ever.

Congress meanwhile tightened the strictures on Roosevelt's conduct of foreign policy. The Neutrality Act of 1935 had been modified in 1936, extending the president's discretion as to whether a state of war existed but requiring him, in the event of war, to caution Americans against travel on belligerent vessels, and forbidding American loans to belligerents. A subsequent revision, in 1937, directly banned travel on belligerent ships and encouraged the president to require that belligerent purchases of American goods—other than weapons, which continued to be embargoed—be carried away in non-American ships. In each case the experience of the World War motivated the legislators. The travel ban was intended to avert another *Lusitania;* the cash-and-carry provision was to prevent the emergence of an American financial stake in the victory of one side or the other and to keep belligerent warships from attacking American merchant vessels.

Roosevelt would have preferred complete freedom in formulating American policy toward foreign wars, but so long as he maintained the right to determine when a war existed, he saw little reason to expend political capital against the isolationists. They were fighting the last war, which had been duly declared by all participants. He prepared to fight the next war, which, by recent and continuing evidence, might well not be. From Roosevelt's perspective, the critical question wasn't what American law would allow but what American public opinion would tolerate. With the public on his side, Roosevelt could outflank the isolationists; without the public, any victory over the isolationists would be empty.

Briefly it appeared that the isolationists might mobilize public opinion against the president. Louis Ludlow was a moderate Democrat but a radical democrat, besides being an Indiana isolationist. He hatched a plan to put war to a popular vote and succeeded so far with his scheme as to get Congress to consider a constitutional amendment writing it into the supreme law of the land. In the angry aftermath of the *Panay* sinking, the Ludlow bill was reported out of committee, where the administration's allies had contained it for months, and was put on the schedule for a floor vote. Roosevelt watched the water rise beneath the measure, hoping it would ebb on its own. When it didn't, but threatened to swamp the administration, he issued a stern warning. The proposed amendment, he said, would "cripple any President in his conduct of our foreign relations" and would "encourage other nations to believe that they could violate American rights with impunity." Roosevelt credited the sincerity of the sponsors in their desire to keep the United States out of war. But they were misguided. "It would have the opposite effect."

Roosevelt's harsh words frightened dozens of Democrats into deciding against the amendment, and it failed. But by asserting his primacy in foreign policy, Roosevelt increased the political stakes for himself of whatever followed.

As it happened, those stakes were increasing for reasons independent of the contest between the legislature and the executive in America. For many years Hitler had agitated for the absorption of his Austrian homeland into the German empire; after taking control in Berlin he directed a campaign of sabotage against the Austrian government. The 1934 assassination of the Austrian chancellor was followed by terrorist attacks on other Austrian officials and institutions. In March 1938 Hitler threatened to invade Austria unless the government agreed to *Anschluss,* or union, with Germany. After the cowed government agreed, he invaded anyway, on grounds that the two countries were now one and therefore that the invasion wasn't really an invasion.

Roosevelt viewed the developments in Central Europe with impotent alarm. Privately he described the Nazis and their ilk as "international gangsters," and his first thought after the takeover of Austria was to issue a condemnation from the White House. But given the strength of isolationist sentiment in Congress, he realized that there was nothing he could do to reverse Hitler's coup and that American condemnation followed by American inaction would simply discredit the United States as a nation and himself as president. He let Cordell Hull issue a statement expressing America's "serious concern" and left it at that.

Roosevelt might have done more had other countries come to Austria's aid. But the French and British had been even more traumatized by the World War than the Americans had, and though an American-style isolationism wasn't an option for them—Germany and Italy were simply too close at hand— appeasement was. Before long appeasement would become the most vile label anyone could hang around a diplomat's neck, but in 1938 it was a politically defensible policy. Neville Chamberlain, the British prime minister and the foremost apostle of appeasement, was willing to go to almost any length to avert a repetition of the carnage of the war. If the Austrians wouldn't defend themselves against Hitler, Chamberlain saw little reason for the British to do so. Psychology and politics aside, Chamberlain appreciated that Britain wasn't militarily ready for a war with Germany. In a year or two it might be. Whatever bought time, therefore, improved Britain's chances of dealing successfully with the German tyrant.

Roosevelt found it convenient to follow Britain's lead. The isolationists wouldn't let him get out in front of London; his own concern at Germany's growing power wouldn't let him fall far behind. Roosevelt's imitative policy persisted through the summer of 1938 as Hitler put pressure on the government of Czechoslovakia. A postwar godchild of Wilson's, carved out of the defeated Austro-Hungarian empire, Czechoslovakia exemplified both the lofty principle of self-determination and the complex practice of creating new states from the wreckage of old ones. The portion of Czechoslovakia that bordered Germany contained three million Germans; like Austria, this region—called the Sudetenland—included some honest advocates of a "greater Germany," some opportunistic Nazi sympathizers, and many people simply hoping to survive the near future without another war. Hitler initially called for autonomy within Czechoslovakia for the Sudeten Germans, but he escalated by September to demand annexation of the region to the German reich.

His ultimatum put the French and British in a bind. France had a treaty with Czechoslovakia nominally guaranteeing Czechoslovakia's security, but most French citizens had no desire to fight Germany over the borders of a country that hadn't existed twenty years earlier. Britain was even less enthusiastic, lacking both the formal commitment of a treaty and the geographic adjacency that always made Germany loom larger to the French than to the British. Yet even Chamberlain had to worry that Hitler's appetite for conquest would grow with the eating.

Roosevelt shared the worry. The president hadn't figured out what to make of Hitler. He couldn't tell how much of Hitler's bombast was sincere and how much was cynical. He didn't know, at any given point, whether Hitler was bluffing or serious. He couldn't say whether Hitler wanted the fruits of war or war itself. He hoped the German people possessed the sense to turn from Hitler to someone more reasonable, but he had no idea if they would. In other words, he knew as much, and as little, about Hitler's motives and plans as anyone outside Hitler's inner circle—or perhaps Hitler's head—knew.

The president admitted he was operating in the dark. "You cannot get news," he told reporters, off the record, as the Czech crisis intensified. "The fellows covering that situation—there is no way in which they can get the dope, the plain facts. . . . While our State Department dispatches are not as wild as the newspaper stories, they are darned near, and that is saying a lot." Roosevelt wanted the French and the British to stand up to Hitler, but not if that would lead to war—and definitely not if it required any commitment from the United States.

The president at first let Cordell Hull speak for the administration. The secretary of state called in the German ambassador to warn confidentially but pointedly where Berlin's actions were leading. The path of "force, militarism, and territorial aggression," Hull said, could easily provoke a general conflict that would make the last war look tame. "There will scarcely be left a trace of the people who brought it on or those against whom it was waged." In public, though, Hull confined himself to generalities. He observed the tenth anniversary of the Kellogg-Briand Treaty by remarking on the "great tragedy of today," namely that the spirit of that antiwar covenant was being lost. "In certain parts of the world strife and conflict are bringing untold misery to millions, and in other parts the idea of warfare is being actually glorified."

The British and French had hoped for more from the United States and may even have expected it. The French ambassador asked Hull whether the president was communicating secretly with the Germans or the Czechs.

He wasn't. As controversial as public diplomacy could be while the isolationists held the balance of effective power in Congress, its explosive potential was nothing next to that of secret diplomacy. Roosevelt had to assume that any secret initiative of his would leak and that when it did the isolationists would grow stronger than ever.

Accordingly, when the crisis reached the point where he had to take action of some sort, he did so in full view of the public. By mid-September Hitler had worked himself and the German people into a war frenzy; Nazi tanks and infantry massed along the border separating German territory from Czech Sudetenland. The Czech government, in contrast to the Austrian government, refused to yield to Hitler's demands. War in the heart of Europe loomed.

Britain's Chamberlain, determined not to give up on peace, flew to the rescue, or tried to. The prime minister was in his seventieth year and had never been on a plane. But he stowed his misgivings in his briefcase, armed himself with an umbrella against the German rain, and flew off to meet the Nazi dictator. An interview at Berchtesgaden yielded a formula for Sudeten self-determination that appalled the Czech government and left Hitler only slightly more satisfied. But the plan saved sufficient face that Britain and France forced it on the Czechs, who were made to understand that they could expect no help from either country if they resisted.

Yet Hitler wasn't appeased. He had wanted war, and Chamberlain's arrangement deprived him of a promising pretext. After muttering to himself for a few days, he declared that the Sudeten Germans must be protected by the troops of the German reich. Once again war clouds boiled above the mountains of Moravia.

At this point Roosevelt weighed in. The president circulated a memo to the governments of Germany, Czechoslovakia, Britain, and France declaring the peace of Europe to be in "immediate danger." An outbreak of war would be disastrous, he said. "The lives of millions of men, women and children in every country involved will most certainly be lost under circumstances of unspeakable horror. The economic system of every country involved is certain to be shattered." Claiming to speak as an honest broker—"The United States has no political entanglements. It is caught in no mesh of hatred"—the president called on all parties to keep talking till they found a solution. "So long as negotiations continue, differences may be reconciled. Once they are broken off reason is banished and force asserts itself."

It was an utterly vacuous statement, as Roosevelt realized. But it was the best he could do. Even without the pressure from the isolationists—even had Roosevelt been a free agent in the matter—he wouldn't have done much more than he did. America's strategic interest in Czechoslovakia's borders was nil, and Roosevelt's political interest was scarcely greater. It was easier to argue that the mapmakers had got things wrong in dissecting the Hapsburg empire than to say that the United States should become involved in a Central European fight. Perhaps Hitler would have to be dealt with at some point, but America could find a more compelling set of circumstances.

As much as anything, Roosevelt's memo was written for the record. He wrote again for the record after Hitler answered his appeal with a wordy defense of Berlin's position. The Czech government was the problem, Hitler said, not the German government or the long-suffering Sudeten Germans. And the Czech government must bear the blame if the negotiations failed, as appeared likely. "It does not rest with the German Government, but with the Czechoslovakian Government alone, to decide, whether it wants peace or war."

Roosevelt replied to Hitler as one statesman to another. "The world asks of us who at this moment are heads of nations the supreme capacity to achieve the destinies of nations without forcing upon them, as a price, the mutilation and death of millions of citizens," the president stated. "History, and the souls of every man, woman, and child whose lives will be lost in the threatened war, will hold all of us accountable." Yet Roosevelt was even less forthcoming regarding a role for America than in his earlier message. "The Government of the United States has no political involvements in Europe, and will assume no obligations in the conduct of the present negotiations."

Roosevelt's diffidence left Chamberlain to rescue the peace—at Czechoslovakia's cost. The British prime minister flew to Munich, where he met with Hitler and French premier Édouard Daladier, as well as Italy's Mussolini, who joined the negotiations at Hitler's behest. Chamberlain and Daladier gave Hitler the Sudetenland. He gave them his word that the Sudetenland was all he wanted.

❖   ❖   ❖

THE MUNICH ACCORD won the democracies time—during which Hitler turned his aggressiveness in another direction. The November murder of a minor German diplomat in Paris by a man identified as a Polish Jew provided the pretext for a rampage against everything Jewish in Germany. Nazi gangs looted and burned Jewish businesses, homes, and synagogues in hundreds of cities, towns, and villages and terrorized Jews, thousands of whom were arrested. Jews were expelled from Munich. Previous outbreaks of anti-Jewish violence, though obviously sanctioned and orchestrated by the ruling party, had typically been attributed to Communists or criminal elements; in this case the regime didn't bother to deny its imprimatur. "The justified and understandable anger of the German people over the cowardly Jewish murder of a German diplomat in Paris found extensive expression during last night," the Nazi propaganda minister, Joseph Goebbels, asserted. "In numerous cities and towns of the Reich, retaliatory action has been undertaken against Jewish buildings and businesses." Goebbels, applauding the "healthy instincts" that had given rise to the violence, went on to say that additional chastisement was in store for the Jews. "A final answer to the Jewish assassination in Paris will be given to Jewry by way of legislation and ordinance." A series of decrees soon followed proclaiming the purpose of effecting the "liquidation of the Jews" and the "elimination of Jews from German economic life." A fine of one billion marks was levied on the Jewish people collectively; immediate repair of the damage to Jewish property was required, at the owners' expense; insurance payments for the property damage were confiscated by the government; Jews were barred from operating most businesses or holding responsible positions in German corporations; Jews were forbidden to patronize theaters, dance halls, and other places of public recreation.

This latest pogrom elicited protests from governments and other groups across Europe and North America. Roosevelt declared that the news from Germany had "deeply shocked" American public opinion. "I myself could scarcely believe that such things could occur in a twentieth-century civilization." To underscore his concern, Roosevelt recalled the American ambassador from Berlin.

More quietly Roosevelt examined methods to alleviate the plight of German Jews. The immigration quotas from Germany had been filled, but some ten to fifteen thousand German Jews were in the United States on visitors' visas. If they returned home, they would suffer the same treatment as Jews who had never left. "I don't know, from the point of view of humanity, that we have a right to put them on a ship and send them back to Germany under the present conditions," Roosevelt mused to reporters. He possessed the authority to extend the visitors' visas for six months, and he chose to exercise it. Congress theoretically could override the president's decision, but the legislature wasn't in session. "They will be allowed to stay in this country under the six months' extension," Roosevelt said, "because I cannot, in any decent humanity, throw them out."

A reporter asked if the president intended to extend the extension when the six months ended.

"Yes," he said.

"And on and on?"

"I think so."

Fifteen thousand was a very small number given the scope of the tragedy befalling the Jews, but it was the best Roosevelt could do at the moment. The isolationists in Congress were as leery of saving European Jewry as they were of challenging fascism; at the core of the isolationist philosophy was the belief that the problems of other countries and peoples were for those other countries and peoples to solve. Even for the fifteen thousand, Roosevelt had to reassure the skeptics that the refugees would not be eligible for citizenship. He explained that their numbers wouldn't grow, since the German government had stopped issuing passports to Jews. And he said that he wouldn't ask Congress to raise the immigration quota. Revealing perhaps more than he intended, Roosevelt concluded his remarks on the refugees with a sigh. "It is a very difficult problem," he said.

❖ ❖ ❖

FOREIGN POLICY GOT no easier during the following months. In January 1939 Roosevelt for the first time opened his State of the Union address with a discussion of international affairs. "A war which threatened to envelop the world in flames has been averted," he said, referring to the Czech crisis. "But it has become increasingly clear that world peace is not assured. All about us rage undeclared wars, military and economic. All about us grow more deadly armaments, military and economic. All about us are threats of new aggression, military and economic." Never had Roosevelt spoken so forthrightly about the threat to America and its values.

> Storms from abroad directly challenge three institutions indispensable to Americans, now as always. The first is religion. It is the source of the other two—democracy and international good faith. Religion, by teaching man his relationship to God, gives the individual a sense of his own dignity and teaches him to respect himself by respecting his neighbors. Democracy, the practice of self-government, is a covenant among free men to respect the rights and liberties of their fellows. International good faith, a sister of democracy, springs from the will of civilized nations of men to respect the rights and liberties of other nations of men. In a modern civilization, all three—religion, democracy and international good faith—complement and support each other.

Roosevelt wasn't ready to challenge the isolationists directly. He proposed no military action against the foes of religion, democracy, and international good faith. But as he had suggested in his quarantine speech fifteen months earlier, he said there were methods short of war for dealing with aggression. At a minimum, America should avoid actions that encouraged aggressors. The neutrality law embodied a noble sentiment, but it operated erratically and sometimes to the benefit of aggressors. This deficiency should be rectified.

The president pushed harder in the area of armaments. Citing the "old, old lesson that probability of attack is mightily decreased by the assurance of an ever ready defense," he asked Congress for $525 million in new money for defense. The army would receive $450 million and the navy $65 million, with $10 million for the training of civilian air pilots. Two-thirds of the army's share, or $300 million, would be used to purchase airplanes—there being, at this time, no separate air force. Roosevelt took pains to assert that preparation for war did not imply intention for war. His request for appropriations did not "remotely intimate" that he had "any thought" of engaging in another war on European soil, he said. Even so, prudence required preparing for the worst.

Roosevelt's arms request was still pending when Hitler again bolstered the president's argument for a stouter defense. In March 1939 the Nazi dictator decided that the Sudetenland wasn't enough of Czechoslovakia for Germany and imposed a German protectorate over the Czech portions of the country. Some observers interpreted this step as more of the same bullying as before;

others perceived a difference, in that for the first time Hitler was annexing *non*-German territories to the reich. Either way, the action belied Hitler's Munich promise to aggress no more, and it put Europe and the world on notice that Germany's appetite remained unsated.

Roosevelt and his advisers drew the same conclusion. "No one here has any illusions that the German Napoleonic machine will not extend itself almost indefinitely," Adolf Berle remarked after meeting with the president and top officials of the State Department. Berle went on to describe the administration's conundrum regarding Hitler.

> 1. Whatever we do, we shall have to go alone. Neither France nor Britain can be trusted; they are frightened and unfrank. This is particularly true of the British government.
>
> 2. Any move we make will be the first move in a constant irritating policy which will lead to a modified state of war.
>
> 3. In the event the European situation does explode, we are then in the war in any event.
>
> 4. There is no use merely irritating. Unless we are prepared to knock out the principal, I do not see that we gain much.

As he had before, Roosevelt let others in the administration take the lead in responding to Hitler's latest outrage. The White House kept quiet while the State Department issued the administration's formal protest. Yet even this came cloaked in generalities, mentioning neither Hitler nor Germany and touching but lightly on Czechoslovakia. "Acts of wanton lawlessness and of arbitrary force are threatening world peace and the very structure of modern civilization," the State Department memo asserted.

Reporters naturally inquired whether Roosevelt had anything to add. Not on the specific subject of Czechoslovakia, he said. A newsman took his hint. "Mr. President," he asked, "do you want a revision of the neutrality legislation this session?"

"Put the question a little differently," Roosevelt prompted. "Do we need legislation on neutrality at this session? The answer is: Yes." But he did not elaborate.

Roosevelt's reluctance was politically calculated. In private he was getting "madder and madder," Harold Ickes observed. The president ordered administrative measures—ones not requiring congressional approval—to punish Germany and prevent its benefiting from the dismemberment of Czechoslovakia. He imposed new duties on imports from Germany and suspended special trade arrangements with Czechoslovakia lest Germany sneak its own exports into America under Czech labels.

In April Roosevelt took a bolder step than any he had attempted before. He sent simultaneous public messages to Hitler and Mussolini urging them to commit their governments to peaceful resolution of difficulties with other countries. "Hundreds of millions of human beings are living today in constant fear of a new war," he said. Each week brought a new threat. "If such threats continue, it seems inevitable that much of the world must become involved in common ruin." Recent events were especially ominous. "Three nations in Europe and one in Africa have seen their independent existence terminated. A vast territory in another independent nation of the Far East has been occupied by a neighboring state. . . . This situation must end in catastrophe unless a more rational way of guiding events is found." The governments of Germany and Italy had repeatedly declared that they desired peace. If this was true, Germany and Italy shouldn't object to making their desires specific. Roosevelt asked for promises that Germany and Italy would not attack other countries; he listed thirty-one by name. He offered to serve as an intermediary with those countries, which would be expected to offer reciprocal pledges of non-aggression. Once the process of guaranteeing got under way, the United States would undertake an additional leadership role in the realms of disarmament and freer trade—the former to ease the crushing burden of defense, the latter to ensure access of all countries to necessary supplies and markets.

Roosevelt explained that the American government offered these proposals "not through selfishness or fear or weakness." It spoke, rather, from a sincere desire to spare the world new conflict. He hoped the governments of Germany and Italy would respond in kind. "Heads of great governments in this hour are literally responsible for the fate of humanity in the coming years. . . . History will hold them accountable."

Roosevelt didn't really expect a positive response. Words hadn't halted Hitler and Mussolini before, and words probably wouldn't halt them now. But he needed to speak out, if only for the record. The president concluded an Easter vacation in Georgia with a grim farewell. "My friends of Warm Springs," he said, "I have had a fine holiday here with you all. I'll be back in the fall if we do not have a war."

Hitler reacted about as Roosevelt anticipated. The German dictator took the president's message to the Reichstag and used it as a prop in another diatribe against the Versailles system and the iniquitous constraints it placed on German prosperity. "Mr. Roosevelt!" Hitler sneered. "The vastness of your nation and the immense wealth of your country allows you to feel responsible for the history of the whole world and for the history of all nations." Germany had neither such luxury nor such pretensions. "In this state there are roughly 140 people to each square kilometer, not 15 as in America. The fertility of our country cannot be compared with that of yours. We lack numerous minerals which nature has placed at your disposal in unlimited quantities." Hitler rejected as ridiculous Roosevelt's assertion that the German government owed something to the world. "I cannot feel myself responsible for the fate of the world, as this world took no interest in the pitiful state of my own people. I have regarded myself as called upon by Providence to serve my own people alone and to deliver them from their frightful misery."

❖   ❖   ❖

WHILE FRANKLIN ROOSEVELT's appeal to the fascist conscience of Germany and Italy was failing, Eleanor Roosevelt's appeal to the democratic conscience of America fared better. During the same week of April 1939 that the president sent his message to Hitler and Mussolini, Marian Anderson sang on the steps of the Lincoln Memorial, and Eleanor Roosevelt was largely responsible.

For all his expressed concern for the downtrodden, Franklin Roosevelt had done little for African Americans as African Americans. To be sure, they enlisted in the CCC and took jobs with the PWA and WPA. And black farmers received benefits from the AAA, although because the crop-support payments went to landowners rather than tenants, and because blacks tended to be tenants, blacks received less from the agriculture agency than their numbers would have indicated. Yet Roosevelt left the most obvious source of black inequality—the Jim Crow system of segregation—untouched. The reason for his hands-off attitude was politically unassailable: southern Democrats would have revolted even more violently against the New Deal had it attacked segregation. Roosevelt judged that civil rights reform must await a more enlightened time and probably another administration.

Eleanor acknowledged fewer political constraints. She made a point of visiting black homes on her tours of the rural South, and she invited African American leaders to the White House to discuss methods of addressing black problems. Walter White, the head of the National Association for the Advancement of Colored People, became a regular correspondent. White pointed out that NRA codes for the South typically included a lower wage for blacks than whites; Eleanor put White in touch with Donald Richberg, Hugh Johnson's successor at the NRA. Though the wage differentials didn't disappear, White and the NAACP discovered they had an ally in the White House.

But not the one they really wanted. A priority for African American leaders during the 1930s—as for decades—was a federal anti-lynching law. Eleanor arranged for White to discuss the measure with the president, and she prepared him by relating objections her husband had raised when she had brought up the bill over dinner. By the time White entered the president's office, he was ready. "Joe Robinson tells me the bill is unconstitutional," Roosevelt said. White adduced evidence suggesting that the Senate majority leader was wrong. Roosevelt offered another objection; White countered again. After a couple more thrusts and parries, the president grew annoyed. "Somebody's been priming you," he said. "Was it my wife?" White, not wishing to implicate Eleanor, kept still.

Roosevelt granted that justice might favor the anti-lynching law. But politics didn't. "I did not choose the tools with which I must work," he said. Southerners, by virtue of their seniority in Congress, controlled the most important committees in the House and Senate. "If I come out for the anti-lynching bill now, they will block every bill I ask Congress to pass. . . . I just can't take the risk."

Because he couldn't, or wouldn't, the anti-lynching bill failed. "I'm sorry about the bill," Eleanor wrote White. "Of course, all of us are going on fighting, and the only thing we can do is hope we have better luck next time."

Roosevelt often tolerated his wife's political causes with indifference or even resigned humor, but he was genuinely irritated at the encouragement she had given White to press an issue that threatened real harm to the New Deal coalition. "Walter White for some time has been writing and telegraphing the President," press secretary Steve Early wrote in a memo intended for Eleanor's eyes. "Frankly, some of his messages to the President have been decidedly insulting."

Eleanor fired back. She conceded that White perhaps had an obsession with lynching. But he had reason. "If I were colored," she said, "I think I should have about the same obsession that he has."

Roosevelt let the White matter drop—and Eleanor opened a new front in the civil rights campaign. She brought African American contralto Marian Anderson to the White House for a recital. The evening went splendidly; Anderson's voice was in top form, and few persons thought twice about the politics of the matter.

But when Howard University tried to arrange a performance by Anderson at Constitution Hall, the reaction was decidedly different. Washington in the 1930s suffered from a lack of facilities for any large indoor event. The deficiency had become drenchingly obvious at Roosevelt's second inauguration, prompting Harold Ickes to propose the construction of an auditorium to render such presidential heroics—or theatrics—unnecessary. "I pointed out that it was absurd that the capital of the richest country in the world should be the only one in any of the leading countries that lacked a proper public auditorium," Ickes recalled. But no action had been taken, and Constitution Hall remained the largest venue. Yet it wasn't a public space, being controlled by the Daughters of the American Revolution. The Daughters refused permission for the Anderson performance, despite regularly granting permission for white speakers and singers to use the hall.

The ban provoked complaints from groups and individuals more attuned to equal rights than the Daughters. Eleanor Roosevelt, a formerly proud Daughter, resigned in public protest. "The question is, if you belong to an organization and disapprove of an action which is typical of a policy, should you resign or is it better to work for a changed point of view within the organization?" she wrote in her column. In other cases of disagreement, she had often chosen to work from within. But now she couldn't. The affront to equality was too great. "To remain as a member implies approval of that action, and therefore I am resigning."

She didn't leave it at that. She encouraged Walter White and Anderson's manager, Sol Hurok, to approach Harold Ickes about a concert on government property. Ickes responded enthusiastically and took the matter to Roosevelt, who told him to go ahead. The concert was held on Easter Sunday afternoon. A special stage was constructed at the foot of the Lincoln Memorial, on the side facing the Washington Monument. The crowd was estimated at seventy-five thousand, with blacks and whites represented about equally. They stretched far down either side of the reflecting pool, and loudspeakers projected Anderson's voice for all to hear. The major radio networks broadcast the performance across the country.

Ickes introduced Anderson, giving the DAR the back of his hand. "There are those, even in this great capital of our democratic republic, who are either too timid or too indifferent to lift up the light that Jefferson and Lincoln carried aloft," the interior secretary said. "In this great auditorium under the sky, all of us are free. When God gave us this wonderful outdoors, and the sun, the moon, and the stars, He made no distinction of race, creed, or color."

Anderson commenced with "America," in her own oblique riposte to the Daughters. She segued to a love aria from *La Favorita* and then "Ave Maria" by Schubert. "She sang with her eyes closed, effortlessly and without gestures, as enchantment settled on the notables up front and on the multitude out beyond," the music critic of the *Washington Post* observed. Anderson concluded with four spirituals, culminating in "Nobody Knows the Trouble I've Seen." At the end of the performance the audience erupted into applause lasting several minutes and crowded toward Anderson with such excitement that she had to be hustled up into the memorial proper, to take shelter beside the Emancipator himself.

Eleanor stayed away, lest her presence further provoke the bigots and detract from the moment. But Walter White acknowledged her role. "Thanks in large measure to you," the NAACP director declared, "the Marian Anderson concert on Sunday was one of the most thrilling experiences of our time."

37.

*U*NDER THE CIRCUMSTANCES, ROOSEVELT WAS HAPPY FOR THE DIS-
traction. He was pressing for repeal of the neutrality law but wasn't making
much headway. Key Pittman, the Nevada Democrat who headed the Senate
foreign relations committee, had introduced another revision of the law, eliminating the mandatory arms embargo and putting all foreign trade on a cash-
and-carry footing. Roosevelt liked the former provision but not the latter.
"While the cash-and-carry plan works all right in the Atlantic," he said, "it
works all wrong in the Pacific." Britain and France had the money and ships
to purchase and fetch American supplies, but China was short of both.

The isolationists stood firm. "Roosevelt wants to fight for any little thing,"
a suspicious Hiram Johnson told his son, and the California Republican judged
it the responsibility of Congress to see that the president couldn't. The Senate
foreign relations committee leaned toward easing the restrictions on the president, but when Pittman held hearings on the neutrality law, the testimony
simply splintered the administration's allies. "We have eighteen members present at this hearing, and so far we have eighteen bills," Pittman told Roosevelt.

Roosevelt invited committee members to the White House, where he and
Cordell Hull argued that an arms embargo would make war more likely by
diminishing the usable influence of the United States. As a concession Roosevelt said he could tolerate a cash-and-carry amendment. He added—and
indeed emphasized—that he had no intention of sending American troops to
Europe in the event of a war there.

He resorted to extraneous inducements as well. Nevada's Pittman had lobbied for the silver interests of his state almost since the Populist era; Roosevelt
persuaded the Senate to boost silver subsidies. He took comparable care of
other legislators.

When even this strategy failed, he brought the leaders of both parties in
the Senate, along with Vice President Garner, back to the White House. "It was

a desperate effort," Hull acknowledged, "but both the President and I felt we had to make one last, supreme attempt to prevail on the Senate leaders to recognize fully and clearly the perils to our own nation that were just ahead if war should come to Europe."

Roosevelt opened the meeting with criticism of Gerald Nye, the arch-isolationist, and suggested that if Nye could be circumvented the arms embargo might be lifted.

William Borah interrupted. "There are others, Mr. President," the Idaho Republican asserted.

"What did you say, Senator Borah?" Roosevelt asked.

"There are others, Mr. President." Borah asserted his own opposition to repeal of the embargo, and he said the president was exaggerating the likelihood of war in Europe.

Roosevelt turned to Hull. "Cordell, what do you think about the possibility of danger ahead?"

"If Senator Borah could only see some of the cables coming to the State Department about the extremely dangerous outlook in the international situation, I feel satisfied he would moderate his views."

Borah snorted. "I have my own sources of information," he said. "And on several occasions I've found them more reliable than the State Department."

Hull grew hot. "Never in my experience had I found it nearly so difficult to restrain myself and refrain from a spontaneous explosion," he recalled. "I knew from masses of official facts that piled high on one another at the State Department that Borah was everlastingly wrong." He said almost as much to Borah's face: "I scarcely know what to think about anything in the light of the complacent way Senator Borah has brushed aside the whole mass of facts we have at the State Department, which completely disprove his theory that there will be no war."

Whether the others present agreed with Borah or with Hull on the danger of war, the senators backed Borah on the politics of neutrality. Roosevelt polled the group, and to a man they said the arms embargo could not be repealed. "Well, Captain," Garner told Roosevelt, "we may as well face the facts. You haven't got the votes, and that's all there is to it."

❖   ❖   ❖

PERHAPS HIS DEFEAT on the arms embargo inclined the president to indulge himself at congressional expense when the opportunity arose. The same session of the legislature that refused to untie his hands on foreign policy provided him a minor victory on government reorganization—in particular by authorizing the establishment of an administrative office for the federal judiciary. Amid the thunder out of Europe and Asia and the fight for control of foreign policy, almost no one paid any attention to the measure. But Roosevelt did, and he made the country pay attention, too.

"Today, August 7, 1939, deserves special recognition," the president declared upon signing the judiciary bill, "because it marks the final objective of the comprehensive proposal for judicial reorganization which I made to the Congress on February 5, 1937." Other Democrats groaned that the president was reminding the country of the court-packing debacle, but Roosevelt, still stinging from that embarrassing defeat, insisted on raising it. And he insisted that it wasn't a defeat after all. He reiterated several parts of the reform bill that had been lost in the furor over the issue of additional justices, and he congratulated himself for their successful incorporation in subsequent measures.

But these were the filler of his court-reorganization scheme, as everyone knew. The nut of the matter was the hostility of the Supreme Court to New Deal legislation. "Measures of social and economic reform were being impeded or defeated by narrow interpretations of the Constitution," Roosevelt recalled, "and by the assumption on the part of the Supreme Court of legislative powers which properly belonged to the Congress." On this point his victory was sweetest. "It is true that the precise method which I recommended, was not adopted, but the objective, as every person in the United States knows today, was achieved. The results are not even open to dispute."

He was right. The Supreme Court's reversals in the spring of 1937, upholding the constitutionality of the Wagner Act and other pro-labor legislation, had been followed by the retirement of Associate Justice Willis Van Devanter. Roosevelt nominated Alabama senator Hugo Black to replace the conservative Van Devanter, and although Black's nomination evoked protests over his former membership in the Ku Klux Klan, his Senate connections and Roosevelt's stature sufficed to win Black the approval of the upper house. Roosevelt got another nomination in 1938 and two more in 1939, by which time the court was more Roosevelt's than Charles Evans Hughes's. Conservatives admitted as much by their cries of complaint. Roosevelt relished the distress. "Attacks recently made on the Supreme Court itself by ultraconservative members of the bar indicate how fully our liberal ideas have already prevailed," he said in his August 1939 signing statement. Speaking at a press conference the next day, he added: "I think it is very important to stress the fact that out of the seven objectives—and they are all very, very important objectives—six were obtained by legislation, and the seventh by the opinions and decisions of the Supreme Court itself."

"A thousand per cent," a reporter remarked. "It is a good batting average, Mr. President."

Roosevelt nodded his head and smiled.

❖   ❖   ❖

THE SAME REPORTER, Richard Harkness, asked what the president thought about the refusal of Congress to repeal the arms embargo. Roosevelt interrupted: "Don't, for Heaven's sake, say 'The Congress,' but a substantially unanimous Republican minority in both Houses, both the House and Senate, plus about twenty per cent, twenty-two per cent of the House and twenty-five per cent of the Senate."

Roosevelt's point, of course, was that the isolationists were a minority, albeit one that had managed to stymie the administration. He went on to assert another point. "They made a bet," he said, referring to the isolationists' prediction that there would not be a war in Europe.

> They bet the nation, made a large wager with the nation, which may affect, if they lose it, about a billion and a half human beings. Now, that is pretty important. They have said, "There will be no war until sufficiently long after we come back in January so that we can take care of things after we come back." I sincerely hope they are right. But if they are not right and we have another serious international crisis they have tied my hands, and I have practically no power to make an American effort to prevent such a war from breaking out. Now that is a pretty serious responsibility.

It grew more serious—very much more serious—within weeks. For two decades the principal enemy of the German National Socialists had been the German Communists and their ideological kin in other countries. The Communists had provided the foil for the Nazis, the specter they conjured to elicit the support of German industrialists and bankers. In time the German Communists—intimidated, assassinated, or incarcerated—lost credibility as a threat, and the Nazis turned to the Jews. But foreign Communists continued to stir the fascist blood, which flowed hot in the Spanish civil war. By the time the Spanish conflict ended, with a fascist victory in early 1937, the Nazis appeared primed to take on the Bolsheviks directly.

For their part the Bolsheviks—which was to say, the Communists of the Soviet Union—had tried to stiffen the spine of the democracies against the Nazis. Whatever Roosevelt's intentions in offering recognition to the Soviet Union in 1933, Stalin had accepted the American president's conditions in the hope, however vague and distant, of outflanking the Germans. That same year the Soviet government ratified a nonaggression treaty with France. In 1934, not long after Germany walked out of the League of Nations, the Soviet Union walked in, to enhance its international respectability and its prospects of linking up with the Western Europeans. In 1935 Stalin ordered the Comintern, the ostensibly independent but obviously subservient (to Moscow) international congress of Communist parties, to support the "Popular Front," a tactical alliance of the Communist parties of the Western democracies with Socialists and other anti-fascist groups. In 1938 Stalin strove to steel the Western democracies against Hitler's demands on Czechoslovakia, offering military assistance to the Czechs and lobbying for a seat at the table in Munich.

But the West rebuffed his overtures, accounting them as cynical as they certainly were. Yet cynical or not, they were more substantial than anything Czechoslovakia was getting from the West, and their rejection by the democracies caused Stalin to reconsider his strategy. The Popular Front failed to warm up the West, where many conservatives—among others—still spoke of communism as being a greater threat than fascism and openly endorsed a strategy of provoking a fight between the two authoritarian ideologies, the better to destroy both. Stalin's cynicism took a new direction as he pondered an ideological truce with Hitler, perhaps embodied in a nonaggression pact.

Hitler found his own path to the same destination. The Nazi leader had never considered Poland's borders any more legitimate than those of Czechoslovakia, in that the resurrected Polish state contained territory taken from the second German reich after the World War. The Polish Corridor, separating East Prussia from the rest of Germany, was an especial abomination. The plains of Poland meanwhile offered the "lebensraum," or living space, for which Hitler had lusted since composing *Mein Kampf* in the early 1920s. Almost incessantly the Nazi government and its propaganda machine conducted a psychological war against the Poles. Yet Hitler reasonably assumed that any German military thrust into Poland would provoke a Soviet response, perhaps drawing Germany into a war it wasn't ready to fight.

Hitler may or may not have been as cynical as Stalin, but he was at least as shrewd. He took note when Stalin fired his cosmopolitan (and Jewish) foreign minister, Maxim Litvinov, and replaced him with the provincial (and ethnic Russian) Vyacheslav Molotov. And he responded positively when, in August 1939, Stalin suggested the possibility of a nonaggression pact.

The deal was concluded in short order. On August 22 Berlin stunned the world by announcing that Foreign Minister Joachim von Ribbentrop would travel to Moscow to sign the agreement. Special editions of German papers carried the news, extolling as a masterstroke what would have been accounted treason just weeks before. Ribbentrop was the author of the 1937 Anti-Comintern Pact, marrying Germany and Japan in everlasting enmity to the Soviet Union; now Ribbentrop was being feted in the very homeland of the Bolshevik beast.

❖   ❖   ❖

"I*T IS STILL* too early to judge the implications of this new coup," the *New York Times* remarked on the day of the announcement, echoing a sentiment shared by observers across the planet. "But one immediate significance revealed itself when German quarters spread the rumor that Herr Hitler was also determined to force a solution this week of the German-Polish conflict. . . . A German solution will be sought by diplomacy if possible; if not, by the German Army."

Roosevelt did what he could to encourage the diplomatic solution. Hitler had never responded—other than in his scathing Reichstag speech—to the president's letter of the previous April urging a promise of nonaggression against Germany's neighbors. At a loss as to what else to do, Roosevelt wrote another letter. "I am again addressing myself to you with the hope that the war which impends, and the consequent disaster to all peoples everywhere, may yet be averted," he told Hitler. Without presuming to judge between the claims of Germany and Poland, Roosevelt called upon the German government—and the Polish government: he wrote a similar letter to Poland's president—to engage in direct negotiations, to submit their dispute to arbitration, or to appoint an impartial mediator. "I appeal to you in the name of the people of the United States, and I believe in the name of peace-loving men and women everywhere, to agree to the solution of the controversies existing between your government and that of Poland through the adoption of one of the alternative methods I have proposed."

Poland predictably accepted Roosevelt's offer. Hitler, equally predictably, ignored it. The dictator likewise brushed aside efforts by Britain and France for a diplomatic solution to the crisis. He delivered an ultimatum to the Polish government that, if accepted, would have dismembered the Polish state. But even this demand wasn't serious, for rather than await a reply, he gave his army the order to march. On September 1, a million German troops poured east, and the second European war in a generation began.

❖   ❖   ❖

"IT IS AN eerie experience walking through a darkened London," Kathleen Kennedy wrote.

> You literally feel your way, and with groping finger make sudden contact with a lamp post against which leans a steel-helmeted figure with his gas mask slung at his side. You cross the road in obedience to little green crosses winking in the murk above your head. You pause to watch the few cars, which with blackened lamps move through the streets. With but a glimmer you trace their ghostly progress. You look, and see no more, the scintillating signs of Piccadilly and Leicester Square, the glittering announcements of smokes and soaps. Gone are the gaily-lit hotels and nightclubs; now in their place are somber buildings surrounded by sandbags. You wander through Kensington Garden in search of beauty and solitude and find only trenches and groups of ghostly figures working sound machines and searchlights to locate the enemy. Gone from the parks are the soapbox orators and the nightly strollers. But yet the moon shines through and one can see new beauties in the silent, deserted city of London. It is a new London, a London that looks like Barcelona before the bombs fell.

Kathleen Kennedy was the nineteen-year-old daughter of Joseph P. Kennedy, the American ambassador to Britain. Joe Kennedy was an odd choice for the post, being Irish by descent and a bootlegger and stock market speculator by profession. His Irish blood inclined him to think ill of the British, while his bootlegging and speculation caused many respectable Democrats to think ill of *him*. But he had opened his wallet to Franklin Roosevelt in 1932 and was rewarded with appointment as founding chairman of the Securities and Exchange Commission. More than a few observers wondered that Roosevelt had set this fox to guard the henhouse, but the appointment paid off with high marks for both Kennedy and the SEC. Kennedy endeared himself further to Roosevelt by taking on Father Coughlin and demonstrating that the radio priest didn't command the allegiance of all American Catholics. Kennedy revealed a soft spot for fascism during the Spanish civil war, when he reminded Roosevelt that American Catholics wanted no truck with the Communist-backed Loyalists. Roosevelt didn't want to intervene in Spain, either, although for different reasons, and in 1938 he sent Kennedy to London as American ambassador.

The Court of St. James's was the stuffiest assignment for any American diplomat, and it gratified Roosevelt's sense of humor to think of Kennedy causing the toffs to choke on their toddies. Yet Kennedy got on famously with the government of Neville Chamberlain, in fact becoming the prime minister's staunchest defender against those who criticized his policy of appeasement. And when the policy apparently failed—when the war began in 1939—he continued to defend it, saying that it hadn't failed at all but bought Britain precious time. "It is a terrible thing to contemplate," he wrote in his diary on September 3, the day Britain and France declared war on Germany for its invasion of Poland, "but the war will prove to the world what a great service Chamberlain did to the world and especially for Britain." If the prime minister had let Hitler start a war at the time of the Munich conference, Kennedy said, he would not have had public opinion behind him. "A great many people in England and especially in the dominions were not at all convinced that Hitler's demands on Sudetenland were not fairly reasonable." Moreover, Britain might have had to go to war alone, as France wasn't eager to fight. Finally, Britain had been utterly unready for war. "England's condition to meet an air raid attack was almost pathetic. They couldn't have licked a good police force attack in the air. Anti-aircraft guns and organization was pathetic. The Germans would have come over and slaughtered the people."

England's anti-aircraft capacity still left much to be desired, which was why Kathleen Kennedy and her siblings had to stumble about in the dark of blacked-out London. "Joe returned from an exploring trip with a very swollen, black eye," she wrote of her eldest brother. "No one believed his story of walking into a lamp post until we read in the next morning's paper of hundreds bumping into trees, falling on the curb, and being hit by autos with such results as broken legs, fractures, even death. Thus now one hears tap, tap, tap, not of machine guns but of umbrellas and canes as Londoners feel their way homeward."

Kathleen's comments were for herself and her family; her father's were for Roosevelt. "High Government officials are depressed beyond words that it has become necessary for the United States to revert to its old Neutrality Law," the ambassador wrote. Chamberlain and the others wanted the opportunity to purchase American equipment, on a cash-and-carry basis. But they felt Washington was letting them down. "America has talked a lot about her sympathies but, when called on for action, has only given assistance to Britain's enemies." All the same, London would continue to look to Washington and would lay plans accordingly. "The English are going to think of every way of maintaining favorable public opinion in the United States, figuring that sooner or later they can obtain real help from America."

Kennedy warned against trusting Britain's capacity to tend to anything but its self-interest, however sweet its words might be. "As long as we are out of the war and the possibility is still present that we might ever come in, England will be as considerate as she can not to upset us too much. Because of course she wants to drag us in." Kennedy related a story from his days in business. Charles Schwab, the steel man, had told him during the First World War that labor always seemed to get the better of negotiations with management. "I asked him why, and he said, 'Joe, because that's their problem 365 days of the year.' " The British were in a similar position with respect to the United States, Kennedy told Roosevelt. "It is their problem now twenty-four hours a day."

❖   ❖   ❖

$\mathcal{R}$OOSEVELT RARELY confined himself to a single view on any subject, and for a counterpoint to Kennedy's warnings about Britain he cultivated the current incarnation of John Bull himself. Roosevelt and Winston Churchill had communicated only once since their 1918 encounter, and only in one direction. In 1933 Churchill sent Roosevelt a copy of his biography of Marlborough—a Churchill ancestor—containing an inscription endorsing the New Deal: "With earnest best wishes for the success of the greatest crusade of modern times." This sentiment might have read oddly, coming from a Tory, but Churchill's politics were unpredictable on various subjects other than the British empire, which he defended with unwavering determination. Churchill had been railing against Hitler for years and decrying the appeasement policies of Chamberlain only slightly less long; as those policies came a cropper with the German invasion of Poland, Churchill appeared a possible, even likely, successor to Chamberlain. The prime minister felt obliged to bring Churchill into the cabinet, as First Lord of the Admiralty, a position he had held during the First World War.

Churchill's appointment provided Roosevelt a pretext for striking up a correspondence. "It is because you and I occupied similar positions in the World War that I want you to know how glad I am that you are back again in the Admiralty," Roosevelt wrote Churchill on September 11, 1939. "Your problems are, I realize, complicated by new factors, but the essential is not very different. . . . I shall at all times welcome it if you will keep me in touch personally with anything you want me to know about." The president invited Churchill to bypass the normal channels of the American State Department and the British Foreign Office. "You can always send sealed letters through your pouch or my pouch." (Lest this invitation cause trouble with Chamberlain, Roosevelt wrote the prime minister on the same day: "I hope you will at all times feel free to write me personally and outside of diplomatic procedure about any problems as they arise.")

Roosevelt's letter to Churchill arrived in early October, the mails having been slowed by the outbreak of the war and the concern it raised for the security of shipping. Churchill responded almost at once with a telephone call taking Roosevelt at his word that he would welcome personal exchanges. The American naval attaché in Berlin had been informed by a German admiral that the British were planning to blow up an American passenger ship, the *Iroquois,* sailing from Ireland to America with more than five hundred Americans evacuating the war zone and to try to pin responsibility on the Germans. The attaché reported the information to Washington, where the administration queried British officials, who naturally threw the blame—for disinformation—back on the Germans. Churchill raised the subject in his telephone conversation with Roosevelt. He warned the president that the Germans might be intending to destroy the ship themselves and blame the British. The danger from submarines was nonexistent in the part of the Atlantic the *Iroquois* had reached. "The only method can be a time-bomb planted at Queenstown," Churchill said. "We think this not inconceivable." Churchill went on to urge Roosevelt to publicize the German deception. "Full exposure" of all the facts known to the American government, he said, was the "only way of frustrating the plot." Action was "urgent."

Roosevelt realized that Churchill had his own agenda in speaking as he did. Publicity was by no means the only way of frustrating the German plot, if indeed there was a plot. A search of the *Iroquois* would do quite well and would be necessary in any event. But Roosevelt followed Churchill's advice in publicizing the threat. The inconclusiveness of the intelligence left many newspaper readers puzzled but nonetheless made the point the president most wanted made: that the European war posed a danger to Americans.

❖   ❖   ❖

THE TIMING WAS crucial, for Roosevelt was in the thick of a battle of his own, to repeal the arms embargo. He had observed the final descent to war with a feeling of helpless irresponsibility. At a news conference just hours after the German troops invaded Poland, he began to redeem the credit he had accumulated with the press during the previous six years. He explained how he had learned of the invasion just before three o'clock that morning and how William Hassett, his assistant, had immediately informed the press associations. "I do not believe at this particular time of this very critical period in the world's history," he added, "that there is anything which I can say, except to ask for full cooperation of the press throughout the country in sticking as closely as possible to facts. Of course that will be the best thing for our own nation, and, I think, for civilization." Roosevelt noted that rumors often flew faster than facts during moments of crisis. He urged the reporters to take care before repeating whatever they had heard. "It is a very simple thing to check either with the State Department, or any other department concerned, or with the White House." He provided a current example. "The secretary of state called me up about fifteen minutes ago, before I came over here, and said there was a report out—I do not know whether it was printed or not, but if it was printed it would be a pity—that we had sent out a general order for all American merchant ships to return to American ports." The report was not true, and it wasn't especially damaging. But it did sow confusion and in some cases alarm. Roosevelt added, "I do not think there is anything else I can tell you about that you do not know already." Yet he agreed to answer questions.

"I think probably what is uppermost in the minds of all the American people today is, 'Can we stay out?' " a reporter asked. "Would you like to make any comment at this time on that situation?"

"Only this, that I not only sincerely hope so, but I believe we can; and that every effort will be made by the administration so to do."

"May we make that a direct quote?"

"Yes."

The president reiterated his position when he took to the airwaves two days later, after Britain and France had declared war on Germany. In one of his most succinct Fireside Chats, Roosevelt explained that until that very morning he had "hoped against hope that some miracle would prevent a devastating war in Europe and bring to an end the invasion of Poland by Germany." But such was not to be. He reminded his listeners of his efforts to preserve the peace. And he affirmed that he was as determined as ever to keep the United States at peace. "Let no man or woman thoughtlessly or falsely talk of America sending its armies to European fields. At this moment there is being prepared a proclamation of American neutrality. This would have been done even if there had been no neutrality statute on the books, for this proclamation is in accordance with international law and in accordance with American policy."

All the same, Americans must recognize the danger to their country.

> You must master at the outset a simple but unalterable fact in modern foreign relations between nations. When peace has been broken anywhere, the peace of all countries everywhere is in danger. It is easy for you and for me to shrug our shoulders and to say that conflicts taking place thousands of miles from the continental United States, and, indeed, thousands of miles from the whole American hemisphere, do not seriously affect the Americas—and that all the United States has to do is to ignore them and go about its own business. Passionately though we may desire detachment, we are forced to realize that every word that comes through the air, every ship that sails the sea, every battle that is fought, does affect the American future.

For this reason, the kind of neutrality Roosevelt proclaimed was not the sort Wilson had requested a generation earlier. "This nation will remain a neutral nation, but I cannot ask that every American remain neutral in thought as well. Even a neutral has a right to take account of facts. Even a neutral cannot be asked to close his mind or his conscience."

❖   ❖   ❖

AFTER THE STRUGGLE with Congress that summer, there was no doubt that Roosevelt would invoke the arms embargo, which he did on September 5, in accord with the neutrality law of 1937. And after his statement to the American people, there was no doubt he would try to persuade Congress to revise the neutrality law and repeal the arms embargo. "I hope and believe that we shall repeal the embargo within the next month," Roosevelt wrote Neville Chamberlain.

The president called a special session of Congress, and when the lawmakers convened on September 21 a message from Roosevelt awaited them. Special sessions devoted to foreign affairs were rare in American history, convened primarily when a president asked for a declaration of war. Roosevelt assured the legislators, and the American people, that nothing could be farther from his mind. The question was: how to stay out of war? The president reminded the lawmakers that he had asked them to repeal the arms embargo only three months earlier, and they had refused. He reminded them that he had been warning of just such an outbreak of war as had recently occurred. He reminded them that he had said that a legislatively mandated neutrality might have an unneutral effect and thereby facilitate aggression. He reminded them that America's historic neutrality had been a matter of executive policy rather than legislative mandate.

This historic position, he said, should be the goal, at least with respect to weapons. Congress should repeal the embargo provisions of the 1937 act. "They are, in my opinion, most vitally dangerous to American neutrality, American security and, above all, American peace." The embargo blindly failed to distinguish between aggressors and their victims, encouraging the former and preventing the latter from purchasing the requisites of their defense. Roosevelt allowed that certain parts of the neutrality law might remain as currently written or even be strengthened. American ships might be barred from traveling in war zones. American citizens might be prevented from sailing on belligerent ships. Foreign purchases might be required to be cash-and-carry. He would leave to Congress how to handle such provisions.

But the arms embargo must be repealed. The critics would contend, as they had contended for years, that repeal would move the United States closer to war. They were as wrong now as they had always been. "It offers far greater safeguards than we now possess or have ever possessed, to protect American lives and property from danger. It is a positive program for giving safety. . . . There lies the road to peace!"

The isolationists disagreed, but the outbreak of the war, after Borah and the others had dismissed the prospect, enhanced Roosevelt's reputation for diplomatic prescience and put the isolationists on the defensive. Public opinion swung to the president's side. A Gallup poll showed a solid majority of Americans supporting repeal of the arms embargo; the only group opposing repeal, and that by a small margin, was German-born immigrants.

The Gallup poll showed something else. While 95 percent of respondents wanted the United States to stay out of the war, 84 percent wanted Britain and

France to defeat Germany. "In other words," George Gallup explained, "the surveys point unmistakably to the fact that the present debate over changing the neutrality act—both in Congress and throughout the country—cannot be regarded as solely a debate on 'pure' neutrality. To a great many Americans the issue is simply one of helping England and France, without going to war ourselves."

The isolationists dug in. They held rallies in several cities, demanding genuine neutrality and excoriating Roosevelt and the British and French for endangering it. Charles Lindbergh, the isolationists' celebrity, claimed to be even-handed between the belligerents, but his language echoed themes being trumpeted by the Nazis. America's link to Europe, Lindbergh said, was "a bond of race and not of political ideology." The aviator explained: "It is the European race we must preserve; political progress will follow. Racial strength is vital; politics, a luxury. If the white race is ever seriously threatened, it may then be time for us to take our part in its protection, to fight side by side with the English, French and Germans, but not with one against the other for our mutual destruction." Lindbergh was willing to accept a modification of the arms embargo suggested by Herbert Hoover, one allowing the sale of defensive weapons but forbidding the export of offensive arms. "For the benefit of Western civilization we should continue our embargo on offensive armaments," Lindbergh declared.

Roosevelt recognized that he had the isolationists at a disadvantage on the arms embargo. And having said his piece, he brought forward other advocates of repeal. The White House produced military experts who dismissed the distinction between offensive and defensive weapons. Fighter planes could shoot down enemy bombers, they said, but they could also support advancing tanks. Even bombers could be defensive if used against an invading army or to preempt an air attack.

As the isolationists grew desperate, they lashed out at Roosevelt more vehemently than ever. One isolationist senator, Democrat Joel Bennett Clark of Missouri, reported that the president had attended an Episcopal service at which the priest asked God to preserve King George of England against his enemies. "I certainly do not want to impose the duty on the president of the United States of getting up and walking out of the church during the prayer," Clark said, perhaps not reflecting on Roosevelt's difficulty in walking under any circumstances. "But the news of it went out to the civilized world; and, after the incident, to have the president have his picture taken with the pastor, glancing at this prayer book which had been presented by the King and Queen, does not add anything to our general reputation for impartiality and neutrality." Several isolationists predicted that the campaign for embargo repeal was the opening round of the 1940 presidential campaign. Whether or not the United States actually went to war, Roosevelt would cast himself as commander in chief and urge Americans not to change leaders amid a crisis.

The isolationists realized they were fighting a losing battle. "You can't lick a steamroller," Charles W. Tobey, a Republican senator from New Hampshire, lamented. On the decisive votes, Roosevelt prevailed by wide margins: 63 to 30 in the Senate, 243 to 181 in the House. The president reiterated that the measure was intended to preserve America's peace, not threaten it. "I am very glad that the bill has restored the historic position of the neutrality of the United States," he said.

❖ ❖ ❖

ROOSEVELT'S VICTORY brought joy to Britain. "The repeal of the arms embargo, which has been so anxiously awaited in this country, is not only an assurance that we and our French Allies may draw on the great reservoir of American resources," Neville Chamberlain wrote Roosevelt. "It is also a profound moral encouragement to us in the struggle in which we are engaged. . . . I am convinced that it will have a devastating effect on German morale."

Repeal brought joy to particular groups in America as well. The same edition of the New York Times that bannered the congressional turnaround tucked a two-inch article on an inside page. "Los Angeles aircraft manufacturers looked forward tonight to the greatest boom in the history of their industry as a result of the arms embargo repeal," the paper's California correspondent noted. "Douglas, Lockheed and North American, the principal factories here, hold more than $110,000,000 worth of foreign and domestic orders, and expect them to be doubled."

At the time the war in Europe began, the depression in America was nearly a decade old. Nine million men and women remained unemployed, and the nation's output was still below its 1929 level. Thousands of factories were idle or half staffed; mines produced at far below capacity; ships, barges, and trains begged for traffic. The arms embargo hadn't figured centrally in stifling growth, but its lifting, combined with the anticipated demand by the American military for armaments, brought new hope to American heavy industry. The aircraft sector responded first, from an expectation that this war, to a greater degree than any before, would be fought in and from the skies. Yet if

the war lasted, everything associated with fighting—trucks, tanks, ships, rifles, bullets, boots, blankets, uniforms, foodstuffs—would be in tremendous
demand. Such was the lesson, at any rate, of the First World War, which had
set the American economy humming. Such was the hope of American manufacturers, American workers, and American farmers as the war in Europe
commenced.

Roosevelt encouraged the hope, which had double meaning for him. Precisely when he determined to try for a third term is unclear. He never revealed
his thinking on the subject. Perhaps there was no single moment of decision.
Perhaps the possibility of doing what no other president had done took shape
in his unconscious mind and emerged only slowly in his consciousness. But at
some level, unconscious or otherwise, he weighed his options and their relative merits. To retire would free him of the strain of executive responsibility.
Four years as governor and eight years as president made for a long time in
charge. His personal constitution seemed to be standing the strain fairly well,
but the machinery would start creaking sooner or later.

But what would he retire to? His memoirs, perhaps, which doubtless would
earn him a sizable advance and allow him to bolster the family finances. Yet he
had never written more than twenty pages in his life. His stamp collection?
That was a mindless diversion from work, not anything to pursue for its own
sake. The Warm Springs Foundation? It was thriving without him. To a genteel life at Hyde Park? There he would be back under his mother's roof and his
mother's attempted domination. Sara was grudgingly pleased that he had become president, but she wasn't inordinately impressed. And Hyde Park was
her home before it was his. He had gone into politics partly to get away from
Sara, and he had returned to politics after polio to stay away from her. He
would be fifty-nine a week and a half after leaving the White House in 1941, if
he did leave then. The thought of moving back in with his mother scarcely inspired him.

Neither did the thought of retiring to a life with Eleanor. The life they currently shared revolved almost entirely around politics. The children were
adults and had lives of their own. The rationale of holding the marriage together for their sake had vanished. They had given Franklin and Eleanor several grandchildren, but even persons far more devoted to domesticity than
Franklin and Eleanor didn't find grandchildren sufficient grounds for sus-
taining a loveless marriage.

The love indeed had gone out of the marriage. A certain fondness survived—a remnant warmth resulting from long familiarity, shared experiences,

and similar values. But if Eleanor's thoughts tarried more than briefly on her husband's happiness—or his unhappiness, his frustration, his satisfaction, his fear, his anger—she didn't reveal them to him. And if he wondered, in his odd idle moment, how she was faring—or even where she was, on those very many days when she wasn't in Washington—he didn't let on.

Retire? As at so many other junctures in his career, Roosevelt looked to Uncle Ted—and what he saw disposed him to remain in the arena. Theodore hadn't known what to do with himself after the presidency. He frantically slaughtered the wildlife of the African veld on a year-long safari, but even the blood of the lions and elephants hadn't slaked his ambition, and he returned to politics, only to be rebuffed by the party he had led. He again sought release in physical action: an ill-conceived expedition to the darkest heart of the Amazon. He nearly died, and the experience ruined his health permanently. He became a bitter partisan, reviling Wilson in language he would have considered seditious had the attacks been leveled against him when he was president. Franklin's personality differed from Theodore's, and Franklin knew it. But the Rough Rider's final decade didn't speak well for voluntary retirement from the presidency.

Nor did the experience of other recent presidents. In Franklin's adulthood, only Theodore Roosevelt, Wilson, and Coolidge left the White House other than by death or defeat. Wilson was broken in health and spirit during his last eighteen months in office, and he never recovered. Coolidge's retirement was graceful enough, but Roosevelt didn't consider Silent Cal a role model for much of anything. Besides, even the quiet confines of rural Vermont proved more than Coolidge could handle; he expired before the term he chose not to run for did.

There was another reason not to retire. Although Roosevelt lacked the organized understanding of history possessed by Uncle Ted, he knew what made for greatness in American history, if only because he had seen how the same knowledge in Theodore had eaten away at the Colonel's soul during the First World War. Theodore knew—and Franklin learned—that presidential greatness required rising to a historic challenge. George Washington was accounted great for leading America to independence in the Revolutionary War. Abraham Lincoln was reckoned great for having held the country together during the Civil War. The war that broke out in Europe in 1914 had presented Wilson with the opportunity for comparable greatness. Theodore Roosevelt recognized this, and the recognition, combined with the knowledge that he, not Wilson, would have been the one to benefit from the opportunity had the Republican nomination in 1912 not been stolen by the Taft forces, rankled him mercilessly. The fact that Wilson, at war's end, fumbled the opportunity rankled him the more.

Franklin Roosevelt knew the story well, having observed it from the unique position of being at once inside the Wilson administration and inside the Roosevelt family. And he understood that the war that was now beginning in Europe afforded him an opportunity at least comparable to what Theodore had coveted and Wilson mishandled. He himself had had one historic opportunity to rise to greatness—and he had fallen short. In public he was politician enough to proclaim the successes of the New Deal in treating the symptoms of the Great Depression; in private he was honest enough to recognize the New Deal's central failure—to end the depression itself.

But now fate threw him another opportunity, one that might allow him to remedy his failure even as it gave him the chance to write his name in bold letters across the history of the world. Whether as peacemaker or warmaker, the American president at this moment of crisis would hold the balance of global power in his hands. The United States had tipped the balance in the First World War but then retreated from responsibility for the result. It could tip the balance again—and it certainly would, if Franklin Roosevelt was in command. The stakes were higher than ever. Not merely Europe but Asia was at risk. And the challenge was more profound than ever. Fascism threatened the very existence of democracy. The freedoms on which America had been established might survive or they might be extinguished. Whether it was the one or the other could well rest with the man who held the American presidency during the next few years. A side effect of the fighting abroad would almost certainly be the recovery of the American economy. Whoever was president at the time would get the credit.

Such a chance at greatness had been given to no president in American history. It was an opportunity the like of which few persons in the long course of human history had ever faced.

Retire? Hardly.

38.

"$\mathcal{H}$ITLER IS TALLER THAN I JUDGED FROM HIS PHOTOGRAPHS," SUM-ner Welles wrote Roosevelt from Berlin.

> He has, in real life, none of the somewhat effeminate appearance of which he has been accused. He looked in excellent physical condition and in good training. His color was good, and while his eyes were tired, they were clear. He was dignified both in speech and movement, and there was not the slightest impression of the comic effect from moustache and hair which one sees in his caricatures. His voice in conversation is low and well modulated. It had only once, in our hour and a half's conversation, the raucous stridency which is heard in his speeches—and it was only at that moment that his features lost their composure and that his eyes lost their decidedly "gemütlich" look. He spoke with clarity and precision, and always in a beautiful German, of which I could follow every word, although Dr. Schmidt of course interpreted, at times inaccurately.

Roosevelt had sent Welles to Germany to size up Hitler and the Nazi leadership. The undersecretary of state's public charge was to listen and observe. "This visit is solely for the purpose of advising the President and the Secretary of State as to present conditions in Europe," Roosevelt told the press in February 1940. "Mr. Welles will, of course, be authorized to make no proposals or commitments in the name of the Government of the United States." Privately Roosevelt authorized Welles to go further: to see if the good offices of the American president might induce the Germans to call off their war before engaging Britain and France directly. The odds appeared slim; Hitler could not step back without losing face. But it was worth a try. If it worked, it would be a brilliant stroke, benefiting millions of Europeans, saving the United States from possible involvement in the conflict, and almost certainly bringing a second Nobel Peace Prize to the Roosevelt family.

The president's efforts to downplay the Welles mission failed; the undersecretary's approach aroused "the greatest interest in the highest government circles here," according to the American chargé d'affaires in Berlin, Alexander Kirk. German leaders had no illusions that Welles was simply gathering facts; they assumed he was attempting, on Roosevelt's behalf, to compel Germany to abandon the causes that had guided its policies for the last three years. They determined to resist anything of the kind.

"The Minister received me at the door, glacially and without the semblance of a smile or a word of greeting," Welles wrote Roosevelt after a session with Foreign Minister Ribbentrop. "I expressed my pleasure at being afforded the opportunity of talking with him, and spoke in English, since I knew that he spoke English fluently, having passed, as a wine salesman, several years in England, and four years in the United States and Canada. The Minister looked at me icily and barked at the famous Dr. Schmidt, the official interpreter, who stood behind him: 'Interpret.' "

Welles explained that President Roosevelt had authorized him "to ascertain whether there existed a possibility of the establishment of a sound and permanent peace in Europe." The American government was not interested in anything temporary or precarious. Whatever the foreign minister cared to disclose would be for the president's ears only.

"Ribbentrop then commenced to speak and never stopped, except to request the interpreter from time to time to translate the preceding portion of his discourse, for more than two hours," Welles wrote Roosevelt. "The Minister, who is a good-looking man of some fifty years with notably haggard features and grey hair, sat with his arms extended on the sides of his chair and his eyes continuously closed. He evidently envisioned himself as the Delphic Oracle." The sum of the oracle's message was that Germany had no quarrel with the United States and that no aspect of its foreign policy impinged on America's legitimate interests. The hostile attitude the Roosevelt administration had adopted toward Germany came therefore as a mystery to German leaders, himself included. "He could only assume that lying propaganda had had a preponderant influence."

In his account to Roosevelt, Welles said he had felt obliged to hold his tongue and not respond to Ribbentrop. "He was so obviously aggressive, so evidently laboring under a violent mental and emotional strain, that it seemed to me probable that if I replied at this juncture with what I intended to say, violent polemics would presumably ensue."

Ribbentrop didn't require the encouragement. He angrily lectured Welles on the course of Germany's European diplomacy, explaining how the Führer had sought good relations, particularly with England, but had been rebuffed. "Time and again England had not only repulsed his overtures with scorn— and the German word 'Hohn' came out like the hiss of a snake—but had with craft and guile done her utmost to prevent the German people from once more assuming their rightful place in the family of nations." The English had provoked the current war by goading the Polish government to unreasonable demands. The German government knew this for a fact. "It had incontrovertible proof that England had incited the Poles to determine upon war against Germany," Welles reported Ribbentrop as saying. "And it had incontrovertible proof that statesmen of countries not in the slightest degree connected with the issues involved had urged the Polish government to make no concession of any nature to Germany."

"Here the Minister paused and looked pointedly at me," Welles recounted. Ribbentrop seemed to be adding the United States to the list of agents provocateurs. Welles said nothing.

German patience had been pressed to the limit, Ribbentrop continued. "The Poles had undertaken every kind of cruel repression against the German minority in Poland." The torture and the mutilation inflicted on the Germans were "unbelievable." The foreign minister offered to provide Welles with photographic and documentary evidence. "Finally Germany, to protect Germans in Poland, and as means of self-defense against Polish mobilization, had been forced to take military action." At which point, for no good reason, England and France had declared war on Germany. "Germany would not have declared war on England and France," Ribbentrop asserted.

Looking to the future, the foreign minister described Germany's goals. "Germany wished for nothing more in Europe than what the United States possessed through the Monroe Doctrine in the Western Hemisphere. As a great power she was entitled to the safeguarding of her vital interests." Ribbentrop referred to his time in the United States and said he understood that Americans felt—"quite legitimately"—that the Monroe Doctrine was essential to American security. Accordingly they should understand why Germans felt similarly about their own sphere of interest.

Germany would defend its interests against those who had declared war against it. "Germany was strong and completely confident of victory. She had immense military superiority, and from her eastern and southern neighbors she could obtain the raw materials she required." The German government and people were prepared for a long war, but they believed it would be a short one. The American undersecretary had come to learn of Germany's peace terms. They were simple. The "will on the part of England to destroy Germany" must be "killed once and for all." Unfortunately, there appeared to be no shortcut to that end. "I see no way in which that can be accomplished," Ribbentrop concluded, "except through Germany victory."

The diatribe left Welles exhausted and discouraged. "Ribbentrop has a completely closed mind," the undersecretary wrote Roosevelt. "It struck me as also a very stupid mind. . . . He is clearly without background in international affairs, and he was guilty of a hundred inaccuracies in his presentation of German policy during recent years." Welles mentally tried to wash himself of Ribbentrop's venom as he left the meeting. "I have rarely seen a man I disliked more," he told the president.

❖ ❖ ❖

*H*ITLER, BY COMPARISON, was a sweetheart, at any rate in personal style and tone. Roosevelt valued Welles's report on Ribbentrop as revealing the mindset of the Nazis generally, but the president really wanted to know about Hitler. Not since Napoleon was defeated at Waterloo had a single person held such power of life and death over Europe. If Hitler wanted a continent-wide war, that war would ensue. If he did not, it wouldn't. Roosevelt needed to know what Hitler wanted, and Welles's job was to find out.

The exterior of the building that housed the chancellor's office looked like a factory. "My car drove into a rectangular court with very high blank walls," Welles wrote Roosevelt. "At one end was a flight of broad steps leading into the Chancery. Monumental black nudes flanked the portico to which the steps led. The whole impression of the court was reminiscent of nothing other than a prison courtyard." A company of soldiers gave the Nazi salute as Welles passed. The head of the chancery, Otto Meissner, greeted Welles cordially. The two waited as others entered the building. "We then formed a procession of some twenty couples headed by Meissner and myself, and with very slow and measured tread first traversed a tremendously long red marble hall, of which the walls and floor are both of marble; then up a flight of excessively slippery red marble steps into a gallery which, also of red marble, has windows on one side and tapestries on the other. The gallery is lined on the tapestry side by an interminable series of sofas, each with a table and four chairs in front of them." Off the gallery was a series of drawing rooms; in one of these Welles waited the few minutes until Hitler was ready to receive him.

The chancellor invited Welles to sit beside him and nodded to the under-secretary to speak. Welles reiterated that he came with no proposals. But he went on—"in as eloquent terms as I could command"—that President Roosevelt yet hoped that there might be a basis for a "stable, just, and lasting peace." If statesmanship failed, a "war of annihilation" would ensue. "From such a war as that, who would be the victors? . . . Not only would the belligerents be the losers, but also the neutrals, of which the United States was the most powerful. We as a people now realized fully that such a war must inevitably have the gravest repercussions upon almost every aspect of our national structure."

Hitler answered "very quietly and moderately," Welles related to Roosevelt. But the substance of his response was identical to that of Ribbentrop. He taxed Britain and France for trying to prevent Germany from achieving its rightful place among nations, for provoking the Poles to make unreasonable demands on Germany, and for declaring war on Germany without justification. He asserted that Germany needed resources from beyond its borders simply to survive. He reminded Welles that Germany had existed as an empire half a millennium before Columbus discovered the New World. The German people "had every right to demand that their historical position of a thousand years should be restored to them."

Hitler warned against thinking that a change of government would alter Germany's policies. "I am fully aware that the allied powers believe that a distinction can be made between National Socialism and the German people," he told Welles, speaking simultaneously to Roosevelt.

> There was never a greater mistake. The German people today are united as one man, and I have the support of every German. I can see no hope for the establishment of any lasting peace until the will of England and France to destroy Germany is itself destroyed. I fear that there is no way by which the will to destroy Germany can be itself destroyed, except through a German victory. I believe that German might is such as to ensure the triumph of Germany, but if not, we will all go down together.

Welles tried not to appear shaken by this apocalyptic statement. He replied that it was the belief of the American government that the nations of Europe could find grounds for a stable and lasting peace and that no nation, let alone all of them, would have to "go down."

"Hitler looked at me," Welles wrote Roosevelt, "and remained quiet for a moment or two. He then said, 'I appreciate your sincerity and that of your Government, and I am grateful for your mission. I can assure you that Germany's aim, whether it must come through war or otherwise, is a just peace.' I replied by saying that I would remember the phrase the Chancellor had used."

❖ ❖ ❖

WELLES'S REPORTS WERE as close as Roosevelt ever got to Hitler, and the experience was sobering. Whether the German dictator was a madman was difficult to say, but he certainly was determined. He would have his continental war—Roosevelt essentially abandoned what slim hopes he had entertained of preventing it—and Europe would be put on the rack again.

The agony started in earnest in the spring of 1940. The eerie quiet that had followed the conquest of Poland was abruptly broken in April when Hitler ordered his armies into Norway and Denmark. Next came a German invasion of the Netherlands, Belgium, and Luxembourg, followed in turn by the main event of the fighting season: an all-out assault on France.

"The scene has darkened swiftly," Winston Churchill wrote Roosevelt on May 15. Churchill had just become prime minister, replacing Chamberlain, whose appeasement policy was being torn to shreds by the German panzer divisions. Churchill was by no means the favorite of the Conservative party regulars, but, like Theodore Roosevelt among America's Republicans a generation earlier, he was too popular to be denied.

Churchill had prepared for the premiership by, among other tactics, cultivating Roosevelt. For months he had sent the president detailed accounts of the naval battles between the Royal Navy and the German fleet. Roosevelt responded as Churchill's informants, knowing the American president's passion for the sea, suggested he would. "Ever so many thanks for that tremendously interesting account of the extraordinarily well-fought action of your three cruisers," Roosevelt wrote upon receiving one such report. "I wish much that I could talk things over with you in person—but I am grateful to you for keeping me in touch, as you do."

Churchill intended that the personal connection deepen. "Although I have changed my office," he wrote Roosevelt, "I am sure you would not wish me to discontinue our intimate, private correspondence." With the Germans over-running the Low Countries and thrusting into France, the prime minister described the Allies' predicament and their hopes for American help.

> The enemy have a marked preponderance in the air, and their new technique is making a deep impression upon the French. I think myself the battle on land has only just begun. . . . The small countries are simply smashed up, one by one, like matchwood. . . . We expect to be attacked here ourselves, both from the air and by parachute and airborne troops in the near future, and are getting ready for them. If necessary, we shall continue the war alone, and we are not afraid of that.
>
> But I trust you realize, Mr. President, that the voice and force of the United States may count for nothing if they are withheld too long. You may have a completely subjugated, Nazified Europe established with astonishing swiftness, and the weight may be more than we can bear.

Churchill asked Roosevelt to modify the American position from neutrality to "nonbelligerency," by which he meant the United States would become an ally in all but actual fighting. He pleaded for warships, in particular destroyers to counter the threat from German submarines. The destroyers might merely be loaned, as British shipyards were laying new keels rapidly. "This time next year we shall have plenty," Churchill said. British supply lines could break in the meantime, though, without the additional sub-hunters. He asked for as many aircraft as the United States could spare, at least several hundred. These might also be loaned and might be repaid by planes already being constructed in American factories for the British air force. Similarly for antiaircraft weapons and ammunition—"of which again there will be plenty next year if we are alive to see it." Other materials, raw and finished, were hardly less critical. Britain would pay in kind or cash for them, though not at once. "We shall go on paying dollars for as long as we can, but I should like to feel reasonably sure that when we can pay no more, you will give us the stuff all the same."

Roosevelt responded cautiously. He was far too canny not to realize that Churchill had been wooing him; he intended for the wooing to persist. "I am sure it is unnecessary for me to say that I am most happy to continue our private correspondence," he assured the prime minister. "I am, of course, giving every possible consideration to the suggestions made in your message." But the measures Churchill recommended were beyond his legal authority as president. The destroyer loan was a case in point. "A step of that kind could not be taken except with the specific authorization of Congress, and I am not certain that it would be wise for that suggestion to be made to Congress at this moment." Congress would object that America needed the destroyers itself. And Congress might well be right. Besides, accomplishing the transfer would take at least six or seven weeks, by which time the contest in the Atlantic presumably would have been decided. As for the planes Churchill wanted, these would have to come from the factories, not from America's military inventory. And they would have to be paid for. Roosevelt's silence on Churchill's request for credit indicated that the money must appear up front. "The best of luck to you," Roosevelt closed, in words that must have sounded ironic when Churchill read them.

The prime minister refused to be dissuaded. Every day the news from France grew more dire; every day the threat to Britain increased. "I understand your difficulties, but I am very sorry about the destroyers," the prime minister wrote Roosevelt on May 20. "If they were here in six weeks they would play an invaluable part." The planes he had requested were, if anything, even more crucial. "The battle of France is full of danger to both sides. Though we have taken heavy toll of enemy in the air and are clawing down two or three to one of their planes, they have still a formidable numerical superiority. Our most vital need is therefore the delivery at the earliest possible date of the largest possible number of Curtiss P-40 fighters now in course of delivery to your army."

Churchill tried to impress on Roosevelt the stakes of the current struggle. It was nothing less than life or death for democracy and individual liberty. "Our intention is, whatever happens, to fight on to the end in this Island," he asserted.

Members of the present administration would likely go down during this process should it result adversely, but in no conceivable circumstances will we consent to surrender. If members of the present administration were finished and others came in to parley amid the ruins, you must not be blind to the fact that the sole remaining bargaining counter with Germany would be the fleet, and if this country was left by the United States to its fate, no one would have the right to blame those then responsible if they made the best terms they could for the surviving inhabitants.

Excuse me, Mr. President, putting this nightmare bluntly. Evidently I could not answer for my successors, who in utter despair and helplessness might well have to accommodate themselves to the German will.

Roosevelt, on receiving this message, had to ask whether Churchill was serious. Would the British really surrender their fleet, the instrument of their global greatness these last two centuries? Without a navy Britain would lose its empire, and without its empire Britain would be nothing more than a small island in a cold sea.

Roosevelt couldn't read Churchill's mind. He could ask himself what *he* would have done in similar circumstances. As a navy man he couldn't imagine surrendering the American fleet so long as it had fuel and friendly ports to sail to. And he had difficulty imagining Churchill—who still identified himself in correspondence with Roosevelt as a "former Naval Person"—surrendering the Royal Navy so long as Canada's ports remained beyond the reach of the Nazis. Churchill alluded to his successors; perhaps they wouldn't be as devoted to the fleet as he. But even Chamberlain had seen the light, finally, and was said to be backing Churchill's determined stance.

Roosevelt had to assume that Churchill was exaggerating for effect. He knew *he* would have exaggerated, had he been in Churchill's position. A man didn't reach the top of the greasy pole of politics, in either Britain or America, without learning to tailor his talk to his audience. Even as Churchill held out to Roosevelt the prospect of surrender, he swore to Parliament that he would never surrender—and that neither would England. The last week of May saw the British Expeditionary Force—the army London had sent to France—caught between the German Wehrmacht and the English Channel. For several agonizing days it looked as though the entire force of nearly 200,000 might be captured or destroyed. But desperation, bravery, and fair weather allowed the army's escape through the port of Dunkirk and its evacuation to England, where it lived to fight another day.

On June 4 Churchill vowed that it would keep fighting as long as humanly possible. "Even though large tracts of Europe and many old and famous states have fallen or may fall into the grip of the Gestapo and all the odious apparatus of Nazi rule, we shall not flag or fail," he told the House of Commons.

> We shall go on to the end. We shall fight in France; we shall fight on the seas and oceans; we shall fight with growing confidence and growing strength in the air; we shall defend our island whatever the cost may be. We shall fight on the beaches; we shall fight on the landing grounds; we shall fight in the fields and in the streets; we shall fight in the hills; we shall never surrender. And even if, which I do not for a moment believe, this island or a large part of it were subjugated and starving, then our empire beyond the seas, armed

and guarded by the British fleet, would carry on the struggle, until, in God's good time, the new world, with all its power and might, steps forth to the rescue and liberation of the old.

❖　❖　❖

CHURCHILL'S WORDS were tremendously stirring, but they directly belied Churchill's warning—or threat—that the fleet would be surrendered to the Germans. And what was Roosevelt to make of Churchill's reference to a New World rescue of the Old—"in God's good time"?

Roosevelt had his own timetable. England's crisis coincided with the climax of the primary season in American presidential politics. The isolationists had lost to Roosevelt on the issue of the arms embargo in the autumn of 1939, but their influence revived as the elections of 1940 approached. On the thirteenth anniversary of his famous transatlantic flight, Charles Lindbergh decried what he considered outlandish descriptions of the Nazi threat to the United States. Alarmists spoke as though the Germans were on America's doorstep. They weren't, Lindbergh said, and wouldn't be even if they conquered all of Europe. Assertions of American vulnerability to air raids were simply delusional. "The power of aviation has been greatly underrated in the past," Lindbergh said, speaking as America's aviation expert. "Now we must be careful not to overrate this power in the excitement of reaction." If anything, the rise of air power made America more impregnable than in the past, for it allowed the extension of America's defenses far out to sea. "Great armies must still cross oceans by ship. . . . And no foreign navy will dare to approach within bombing range of our coasts." The demands for intervention were purely political, Lindbergh said. "The only reason that we are in danger of becoming involved in this war is because there are powerful elements in America who desire us to take part. They represent a small minority of the American people, but they control much of the machinery of influence and propaganda. They seize every opportunity to push us closer to the edge." The appropriate answer to their demands was political, as well. "It is time for the underlying character of this country to rise and assert itself, to strike down these elements of personal profit and foreign influence."

Even if Roosevelt had believed Churchill about Britain being on the brink of surrender, he would have moved forward only slowly. To rescue Britain simply to hand the American government over to the isolationists would have been folly. Roosevelt's vision was grander than Churchill's. His view encompassed not merely Europe but Asia, the Pacific as well as the Atlantic. And his time horizon stretched beyond the present moment, beyond the impending election, to the coming decades and generations. Roosevelt wasn't more prone to rationalization than most other politicians in democracies, who have regularly argued to themselves and others that they couldn't accomplish the great things they intended if they didn't get elected. But he wasn't conspicuously less prone, either. He would do what he could to keep England fighting, but until November it wouldn't be nearly what Churchill wanted.

For months Italy had been threatening to enter the war on Germany's side. For months Roosevelt had been trying to prevent Mussolini from taking that step. He wrote the Italian dictator confidentially to warn against a "further extension of the area of hostilities" and delivered his sharpest threat thus far of American intervention: "No man can today predict with assurance, should such a further extension take place, what the ultimate result might be—or foretell what nations, however determined they may today be to remain at peace, might yet eventually find it imperative in their own defense to enter the war."

Mussolini was unmoved. "Italy has never concerned itself with the relations of the American republics with each other and with the United States (thereby respecting the Monroe Doctrine)," he replied, "and might therefore ask for reciprocity with regard to European affairs." A second letter from Roosevelt, in which the president described himself as "a realist" and said that a broader war "would pass beyond the control of heads of state," produced no greater effect. "There are two fundamental motives which cannot escape your spirit of political realism," Mussolini told the president, "and those are that Italy is and intends to remain allied with Germany, and that Italy cannot remain absent at a moment in which the fate of Europe is at stake." After tarrying a bit longer, to let the fate of Europe become that much clearer—which was to say, to let Germany roll across northern France toward Paris—Mussolini declared war on Britain and France.

Roosevelt responded with his strongest public statement yet. "On this tenth day of June, 1940, the hand that held the dagger has struck it into the back of its neighbor," he declared. Roosevelt had been planning for some weeks to address the graduates of the University of Virginia, and he intended his speech to be a riposte to Lindbergh and the isolationists. Mussolini's war declaration, which came just as the president was getting ready to leave Washington for Charlottesville, bolstered his case. The president decried the "obvious delusion that we of the United States can safely permit the United States to become a lone island, a lone island in a world dominated by the philosophy of force." Careful listeners caught the repetition of "lone" and the reference it made to Lindbergh, the "Lone Eagle." An island might be the dream of the isolationists, but they could not be more wrong, Roosevelt said. "Such an island represents to me and to the overwhelming majority of Americans today a helpless nightmare of a people without freedom—the nightmare of a people lodged in prison, handcuffed, hungry, and fed through the bars from day to day by the contemptuous, unpitying masters of other continents." American safety required simultaneous action on two fronts. "We will extend to the opponents of force the material resources of this nation; and, at the same time, we will harness and speed up the use of those resources in order that we ourselves in the Americas may have equipment and training equal to the task of any emergency."

❖   ❖   ❖

AMID THE WORSENING news from the Continent, Roosevelt's promise of aid to the opponents of fascism sounded to Churchill like the peal of salvation. "We all listened to you last night and were fortified by the grand scope of your declaration," the prime minister wrote the president. "Your statement that the material aid of the United States will be given to the Allies in their struggle is a strong encouragement in a dark but not unhopeful hour." Roosevelt's promise encouraged Churchill to renew his request for specific American aid. Airplanes would be required to repel the air assault and possibly amphibious invasion Hitler was sure to direct at England soon. But destroyers were needed even more. "The Italian outrage makes it necessary for us to cope with a much larger number of submarines which may come out into the Atlantic and perhaps be based on Spanish ports. To this the only counter is destroyers." Churchill had previously asked for forty or fifty; now "thirty or forty" would do. "We can fit them very rapidly with our ASCICS"—a version of sub-seeking sonar—"and they will bridge the gap of six months before our war-time new construction comes into play. We will return them or their equivalents to you without fail at six months notice if at any time you need them." Earlier Churchill had spoken as though the fate of Europe would be decided within weeks; his chronology now expanded, but time remained of the essence. "The next six months are vital. If while we have to guard the East Coast against invasion a new heavy German-Italian submarine attack is launched against our commerce, the strain may be beyond our resources, and the ocean traffic by which we live may be strangled. *Not a day should be lost.*"

Churchill's appeal was seconded in the most poignant way from France, where the French army was battling for its life. "For six days and six nights our divisions have been fighting without rest against an army which has a crushing superiority in numbers and material," French premier Paul Reynaud wrote Roosevelt. "Today the enemy is almost at the gates of Paris." The French would never yield, Reynaud vowed. "We shall fight in front of Paris; we shall fight behind Paris; we shall close ourselves in one of our provinces to fight, and if we should be driven out of it we shall establish ourselves in North Africa to continue the fight, and if necessary in our American possessions." Reynaud urged Roosevelt to tell the Americans that France was fighting on their behalf. "Explain all this yourself to your people, to all the citizens of the United States, saying to them that we are determined to sacrifice ourselves in the struggle that we are carrying on for all free men." As the president did so, he should elaborate on what he meant in promising support to the opponents of aggression. "I beseech you to declare publicly that the United States will give the Allies aid and material support by all means short of an expeditionary force. I beseech you to do this before it is too late."

❖   ❖   ❖

ℛoosevelt was touched by the pleas from across the Atlantic; who wouldn't have been? But the brave words of Reynaud and Churchill were belied by the dismal performance of the French and British armies in the field. Reynaud might be a tiger and Churchill a bulldog, but their soldiers were pussycats, at least to judge by the results of their actions. To promise aid to a losing cause would make Roosevelt appear foolish at a moment when cunning was called for. And it might jeopardize American security by squandering resources that would be more effective if kept in American hands.

His Charlottesville speech had had multiple audiences. Roosevelt hoped to encourage the British and French to fight on; their armies continued to be America's first line of defense abroad. He also hoped to counter the isolationists, who remained a potent political force at home. Roosevelt judged that the arguments of Lindbergh and the others were wrong, but he understood that they weren't implausible. The Atlantic was still a formidable barrier to any attack on the United States; reinforced by ships patrolling American waters and planes flying out from American bases, it would allow Americans to repel any invasion Hitler might mount. Of course Roosevelt had to think beyond mere physical security; American prosperity and American values would be at risk in a world dominated by a hostile regime and a vicious ideology. But on this question Roosevelt reaped what he had sown during the first years of his administration. By adopting a nationalist approach to economic recovery, Roosevelt had told the American people, in essence, that the world didn't matter. He had been wrong, as he may have known at the time and certainly figured out later. Yet to admit as much didn't seem prudent.

Hitler's campaign in France proceeded with appalling success. "Our army is now cut into several parts," Reynaud cabled Roosevelt on June 14. "Our divisions are decimated. Generals are commanding battalions." The Germans had entered Paris. The unthinkable was at hand. Only four days after vowing to Roosevelt to fight forever, Reynaud sounded a different note. "At the most tragic hour of its history, France must choose. Will she continue to sacrifice her youth in a hopeless struggle? . . . Or will France ask Hitler for conditions of an armistice?"

The French government hadn't decided, Reynaud told the president. And he appealed to Roosevelt, in terms more desperate than ever, to help it hold on. "The only chance of saving the French nation, vanguard of democracies, and through her to save England, by whose side France could then remain with her powerful navy, is to throw into the balance, this very day, the weight of American power." Reynaud appreciated that the American president couldn't declare war by himself. But he could urge Congress to declare war. And he must do so, at once. "If you cannot give France, in the hours to come, the certainty that the United States will come into the war within a very short time, the fate of the world will change. Then you will see France go under like a drowning man and disappear after having cast a last look toward the land of liberty from which she awaited salvation."

39.

$\mathcal{I}$T WAS TOO LATE. AND IT WAS TOO EARLY. ROOSEVELT LEARNED FROM Churchill that Reynaud had already asked that France be released from its alliance with Britain in order to negotiate a separate peace with Germany. Churchill implored Reynaud to continue the struggle, saying that only Hitler would benefit from an armistice. "He needs this peace in order to destroy us and take a long step forward to world mastery," the prime minister explained to Roosevelt. Churchill seconded Reynaud's final appeal to the American president. "This moment is supremely critical for France," Churchill said. "A declaration that the United States will, if necessary, enter the war might save France. Failing that, in a few days French resistance may have crumbled and we will be left alone."

There would be no such declaration. Roosevelt wasn't ready to take that step. "I am doing everything possible," he said privately, referring to various measures to increase the supply of war material to France and Britain. He probably believed it. But he defined the possible narrowly, and in the context of American politics. "I am not talking very much about it," he continued, "because a certain element of the press, like the Scripps-Howard papers, would undoubtedly pervert it, attack it, and confuse the public mind."

Yet talking about it was precisely what France needed. A straightforward commitment from Roosevelt would mean as much, at the moment, as American arms. Roosevelt refused to oblige, and France went down. On June 21 Hitler received France's representatives in the same railroad car and in the same part of the Compiègne forest where Germany's envoys had signaled their capitulation in November 1918. The next day the French accepted Hitler's terms, which provided for the disarmament of most of the French military and the surrender of the northern three-fifths of the country to German occupation and control. The French were allowed to govern the southern rump of the country and to retain possession of their navy, which in any event had sailed beyond Hitler's reach.

Roosevelt declined to comment on what could be interpreted only as a disaster for democracy and a stunning blow to American security. He left the ill tidings to Cordell Hull to deliver. "These are black days for the human race," the secretary of state intoned. "These are ominous days for us in this country." The forces of evil were rampant in the world. "Never before have these forces flung so powerful a challenge to freedom and civilized progress as they are flinging today. Never before has there been a more desperate need for men and nations who love freedom and cherish the tenets of modern civilization to gather into an unconquerable defensive force every element of their spiritual and moral resources, every ounce of their moral and physical strength."

❖   ❖   ❖

ROOSEVELT WOULD have said more than he did say if the fall of France hadn't coincided with the quadrennial summer season for national political conventions. The Republicans went first, being the challengers, and their convention produced what the editors of the *New York Times* dubbed a "political miracle." Wendell Willkie, a forty-eight-year-old son of Elwood, Indiana, was the darkest of dark horses, a lawyer and businessman who had never sought public office and who hadn't been considered for the presidency until just weeks before the convention. He had entered no primaries, wooed no delegates, hired no professional campaign advisers. He had been a Democrat most of his life, converting to Republicanism only after Roosevelt took the New Deal in what Willkie—with others—perceived as a deliberately anti-business direction. Many Republicans still distrusted his Democratic antecedents. James Watson of Indiana thought forgiveness had gone too far. "If a whore repented and wanted to join the church," Watson said, "I'd personally welcome her and lead her up the aisle to a pew. But by the Eternal, I'd not ask her to lead the choir the first night!"

The one thing that made Willkie acceptable to a nominating majority of the convention—on the sixth ballot—was his internationalist pedigree. To many Republicans the isolationists, including such Senate stalwarts as Arthur Vandenberg of Michigan and Robert Taft of Ohio, had become an embarrassment. Some agreed with Roosevelt that American security required a forward stance on the troubles in Europe, even if they were as vague as he in articulating that conviction. Some simply didn't want to concede to the

Democrats the large and growing portion of the electorate that was tilting internationalist. Willkie had been as forthright as Roosevelt in criticizing the arms embargo; he was even more outspoken than the president in advocating aid to Britain.

Willkie's internationalism was part of what made him such an improbable candidate. He couldn't well criticize Roosevelt's foreign policy, at one of the very few times in American history when foreign policy appeared likely to determine the outcome of a presidential election. He harped on the New Deal, although less on particular programs than on the excessive influence it accorded the federal government. "What I am against is power," Willkie said. "Power ruins anybody that has it. It's the worst corrupting thing in the world."

What went almost without saying was that in criticizing power Willkie was criticizing Roosevelt's run for a third term. The Republican candidate couldn't be explicit because Roosevelt hadn't been renominated yet. In fact he hadn't even announced his candidacy. But he was quietly engineering another nomination. The first step was negative—simply not renouncing a third term as the Democratic convention approached. Roosevelt's silence paralyzed potential rivals within the party, who couldn't declare their own candidacies without breaking with a president of their own party who was doing his best, as most Democrats were willing to acknowledge, to guide the country through dangerous times and who, should he be renominated and reelected, would be able to visit vengeance on the apostates. Southern conservatives who had defied Roosevelt on the New Deal and survived his purge didn't have to worry, but in the Jim Crow era southern conservatives couldn't be elected president and didn't bother to run. All the others had to weigh the risks of taking on a popular president and party leader. "What's the Boss going to do?" John Nance Garner asked Jim Farley in the spring of 1940.

"Your guess is as good as mine," Farley answered. The postmaster general and party chairman coveted the nomination for himself, and he had told friends he would let his name be put to the convention. "I've given up guessing," he said.

Garner eyed Farley closely. "I guess he's going to run," the vice president said.

"It begins to look that way," Farley acknowledged.

"Hell," said Garner, "he's fixed it so nobody else can run."

Roosevelt's second step was to arrange for the convention to be held in Chicago. The Windy City remembered his 1932 nomination and how he had electrified the delegates and the country by flying in to accept the nomination in person. Expectations of presidents and presidential candidates hadn't been the same since, and if Roosevelt was to challenge history in a try for a third term, Chicago was the place for the challenge to be made.

His third step was to orchestrate a draft. He didn't have to do this himself, for as in every administration there were plenty of people hoping for another four years in office. The New Deal had been good to Illinois Democrats and especially to the boss of Chicago's Democratic machine, Edward Kelly, whose men were expected to stampede the convention for Roosevelt. Kelly's affection for Roosevelt was as self-interested as most things the boss did—and as self-interested as the support for Roosevelt displayed by other bosses. "They did not support Roosevelt out of any motive of affection or because of any political issues involved," Edward Flynn, who would succeed Jim Farley as chairman of the Democratic National Committee, recalled. "Rather they knew that opposing him would be harmful to their local organizations. The Roosevelt name would help more than it could hurt, and for that reason these city leaders went along on the third-term candidacy."

The Roosevelt stampede started slowly. Mayor Kelly welcomed the delegates to his city, and when he mentioned the president's name in his opening address the Chicago delegates were supposed to erupt into a mad ovation. But they either misunderstood what was expected or simply missed their cue; the reaction to Kelly's phrase "our beloved President—Franklin Delano Roosevelt" was no more than tepid.

Jim Farley tried to keep it that way. Farley had accepted a job in the front office of the New York Yankees but hadn't begun his duties; his appearance at the convention, as exiting party chairman, was supposed to be his swan song, with the possibility that the delegates would, at the eleventh hour, discover his charms. As it happened, the swan song was "Take Me Out to the Ball Game," played by the convention band at the request of persons unknown. A flustered Farley banged the gavel against the laughter that rolled across the floor of the Chicago Stadium.

Roosevelt kept quiet and mostly out of sight—sailing on the Potomac, weekending in Hyde Park—while the convention conducted its business. Everyone assumed that he would be nominated, but no one seemed to understand how his nomination would occur. Roosevelt's strategy exasperated even some of his oldest associates. "The President's refusal to take anyone, with the possible exception of Harry Hopkins, into his confidence annoyed me," Harold Ickes recorded in his diary. "I have thought for some time that he was overplaying his role of indifference and was displaying too much coyness. It is

all very well for him to try to create the impression generally that he had nothing to do with the third-term movement and was indifferent to it, but I know
that this has not been his state of mind." Ickes had particular reason to be
miffed. He had been the first member of the administration to go public with
support for a third term and for months had waged the fight on his own. "Having declared for him, I persisted, keeping the issue alive, speaking and writing
on the subject, to say nothing of doing a great deal of work." Ickes had made
certain that Roosevelt's name appeared on primary ballots, thereby frustrating Farley and other potential opponents and securing for the president sufficient delegates to control the convention.

Ickes's suspicions notwithstanding, Hopkins evidently didn't know any
more about Roosevelt's intentions than Ickes did. Hopkins's only instruction
from Roosevelt was a handwritten note, addressed to William Bankhead, the
temporary chairman of the convention:

> Dear Will,
>
> When you speak to the Convention on Monday evening will you say
> something for me which I believe ought to be made utterly clear?
>
> You and my other close friends have known and understood that I have
> not today and have never had any wish or purpose to remain in the office of
> the President, or indeed anywhere in public office after next January.
>
> You know and all my friends know that this is a simple and sincere fact.
>
> I want you to repeat this simple and sincere fact to the Convention.

A change of schedule caused the note to be read by Alben Barkley, the permanent chairman of the convention, rather than by Bankhead. But it remained
the sum of Roosevelt's spoken or written advice to his supporters and the rest
of the convention.

Yet Hopkins took it upon himself to organize the pro-Roosevelt forces
in Chicago. They didn't organize easily, given the resentment many veteran
Democrats felt toward Hopkins and the New Dealers. Ickes and Frances
Perkins arrived in Chicago expecting to lead the Roosevelt charge, only to discover that Hopkins had established headquarters already, in the Blackstone
Hotel, and was giving orders as though in the president's name. The effort
nearly backfired, in that many of the delegates found Farley much easier to
work with than Hopkins. Some muttered against Hopkins; others simply
stayed away from the convention, leaving hundreds of seats empty.

The interim result was mass confusion. "Apparently I am not the only one around here who does not know anything," Farley remarked to reporters. Farley was realizing that he had no chance for the nomination, but by now he was worrying that the party would look foolish. He concluded that the only recourse was to keep a sense of humor. "If we can go through this without taking it too seriously, or taking ourselves too seriously," he said, "it will be all right."

The confusion deepened even as it began to be resolved. Amid Senator Barkley's reading of Roosevelt's statement of lack of interest in another nomination, an electronically amplified voice rumbled through the arena, calling, "We want Roosevelt! We want Roosevelt!" The cry was echoed by Mayor Kelly's minions and then spread across the convention floor. A curious reporter traced the mysterious voice to the basement, where a Kelly placeman—the superintendent of sewers, appropriately—commanded the sound system, reading from a printed script.

The spontaneity may have been contrived, but the enthusiasm for Roosevelt was sincere enough, once it got going, and the convention proceeded to renominate him by acclamation. The delegates might have retired in good order and comparatively good feeling had Roosevelt not taken the unusual step of dictating his running mate. In this regard, as in so many others, Roosevelt broke with accepted practice. Conventions still expected to exercise their own prerogative in selecting vice presidential candidates. But Roosevelt wanted to get rid of Garner, who was too close to the southern conservatives he had been trying to purge. Garner wasn't sad to go, yet neither he nor just about anyone else was happy at the replacement Roosevelt named: Henry Wallace, the secretary of agriculture. Harold Ickes and Cordell Hull had each hoped to be named. But neither fitted Roosevelt's specifications. Precisely what those specifications were he never said, but one, presumably, was the potential to be president. Hull came up short. "He goes about looking like an early Christian martyr, and people think that he is wonderful just on the basis of his looks," Roosevelt told Ickes. "However, no one has ever attacked him on the basis of his record, and I regard him as the most vulnerable man we could name." If Roosevelt told Hull why Ickes wouldn't do, the secretary of state declined to record the explanation.

Why Roosevelt chose Wallace was hardly clearer. Perhaps he saw a president in Wallace, but he soon changed his mind, as events would prove. Doubtless he thought the formerly Republican agriculture secretary would appeal to farmers who might be tempted to return to the Republican fold. Quite possibly he liked Wallace because the rest of the party didn't. The animus toward this latecomer to the party was palpable. "Just because the Republicans have nominated an apostate Democrat," one angry delegate told the convention, referring to Willkie, "let us not, for God's sake, nominate an apostate Republican." Frances Perkins put the matter more diplomatically but no less accurately when she recalled, "The party longs to promote its own, and Wallace was not its own." Roosevelt might well have calculated that an unpopular Wallace nomination would leave him free to tap his successor after his reelection.

But the Wallace nomination almost produced a revolt. Ickes, calling it a "damned outrage," threatened to leave the administration and the party; the convention as a whole prepared to nominate its own choice. Only when Roosevelt let out that he was drafting a speech refusing the nomination and would deliver it if the convention rejected Wallace did reality prevail and the delegates decide they would rather have Roosevelt with Wallace than someone other than Roosevelt without Wallace.

❖   ❖   ❖

ELEANOR ROOSEVELT learned for certain that her husband intended a third term at the same time the rest of the world did: during the convention. She hadn't originally liked the idea. "I had luncheon today with Mrs. Roosevelt at the White House," Harry Hopkins wrote in the spring of 1939.

> She asked Diana to come with me, and together with two or three of her friends we lunched out on the porch. After luncheon we went out in the gardens—Mrs. Roosevelt had her knitting—and discussed for three hours the state of the nation.
>
> Mrs. Roosevelt was greatly disturbed about 1940. She is personally anxious not to have the president run again. . . . She feels the President has done his part entirely. . . . She thinks that the causes for which he fought are far greater than any individual person, but that if the New Deal is entirely dependent upon him, it indicates that it hasn't as strong a foundation as she believes it has with the great masses of people. Mrs. Roosevelt is convinced that a great majority of the voters are not only with the President, but with the things he stands for, and that every effort should be made to control the Democratic Convention in 1940, nominate a liberal candidate, and elect him.

Eleanor's feelings on an extension in the White House gradually changed. No liberal candidate emerged except for Roosevelt, who made certain that no such candidate *could* emerge. Eleanor meanwhile reconsidered what a third term would mean for her. On one hand it would lengthen the period of her political juvenility, when she could not speak or write without weighing her words against the wishes and policies of her husband. It would also postpone the reclamation of her private life, which she had all but surrendered after the disastrous West Coast trip with Lorena Hickok. On the other hand, a third term would afford her a continuation of her unique political influence. Eleanor didn't underrate her intelligence or insight, but she appreciated full well the leverage her position as presidential spouse gave to her innate talents. If Franklin retired, she would be much freer than at present, and much less influential.

She followed the proceedings of the convention by radio from the Val-Kill cottage at Hyde Park. She heard Alben Barkley read Franklin's letter to the delegates. She saw the newspaper accounts of disarray among Roosevelt's lieutenants at Chicago, and she received a call from Frances Perkins pleading with her to come and calm things down. She inquired of Franklin whether her presence would be appropriate. "It might be very nice for you to go," he answered. "But I do not think it is in the least necessary."

It wasn't necessary for Roosevelt's renomination, which followed shortly. Yet it seemed, if not strictly necessary, at least strongly advisable as the battle for the vice presidency broke out. Jim Farley added his voice to those urging her to come lest the party fall ignominiously apart. "The situation is not good," Farley said. "I think it desirable, if not essential, that you come." She took a chartered plane to the Chicago air field, where a throng of reporters awaited her at the American Air Lines hangar. "Are you happy about the nomination?" one shouted.

"Happy?" she responded, without the smile expected of a nominee's wife. "I don't know how anyone could be particularly happy about the nomination in the present state of the world. It is a tremendous responsibility to be nominated for the presidency."

"Was the president willing for you to come? Did he wish you well?"

"I don't remember that he wished me well." She smiled now, to soften what she realized sounded harsh. "I suppose, of course, that he was willing for me to come—or I would not have come."

A car whisked her to the convention hall, where she was rushed to the podium to quell the revolt against Roosevelt's selection of Henry Wallace. She stressed the need for party unity, for all to pull behind the president in this hour of world peril. "No man who is a candidate or who is president can carry this situation alone. This is only carried by a united people who love their country and who will live for it to the fullest of their ability, with the highest ideals, with a determination that their party shall be absolutely devoted to the good of the nation as a whole."

Eleanor's statement was just the touch necessary to bring the anti-Wallace factions into line. Perhaps their revolt was chiefly symbolic; perhaps they would have found their own way back into the fold. But with Eleanor lecturing them on the obligation to party and country, they had no choice.

❖ ❖ ❖

ROOSEVELT DECLINED to address the delegates in person. He wished to preserve his air of reluctance but also to make clear that he was answering the call not simply of the Democratic party but of the American people. He had intended to retire after two terms, he asserted by radio. "Eight years in the presidency, following a period of bleak depression, and covering one world crisis after another, would normally entitle any man to the relaxation that comes from honorable retirement." But the world crises mounted, as they had not mounted for generations, culminating in the war that had begun the previous September. Even then, though, he had planned to leave the White House in January 1941. "This fact was well known to my friends, and I think was understood by many citizens."

Roosevelt's friends might have wondered who they were, for none could recall the disclaimers he alluded to. The president left them to their questions. "It soon became evident, however, that such a public statement on my part would be unwise from the point of view of sheer public duty. As President of the United States, it was my clear duty, with the aid of the Congress, to preserve our neutrality, to shape our program of defense, to meet rapid changes, to keep our domestic affairs adjusted to shifting world conditions." Roosevelt's language assumed a more assertive tone. "It was also my obvious duty to maintain to the utmost the influence of this mighty nation in our effort to prevent the spread of war, and to sustain by all legal means those governments threatened by other governments which had rejected the principles of democracy." In this single sentence Roosevelt both framed the election campaign and indicated where he would be leading the country during the next six months—and the four years after that, voters willing.

Americans who disagreed with this interpretation of presidential duty were free to vote against it, Roosevelt said. But they should weigh the risk. "If our Government should pass to other hands next January—untried hands, inexperienced hands—we can merely hope and pray that they will not substitute appeasement, and compromise with those who seek to destroy all democracies everywhere, including here." The fate of nations—of the American nation, to be sure, but of other nations as well—would turn on the current election. Americans confronted one of the great choices of history.

> It is not alone a choice of government by the people versus dictatorship. It is not alone a choice of freedom versus slavery. . . . It is the continuance of civilization as we know it versus the ultimate destruction of all that we have held dear—religion against godlessness; the ideal of justice against the practice of force; moral decency versus the firing squad; courage to speak out, and to act, versus the false lullaby of appeasement.

❖ ❖ ❖

$\mathcal{I}$N JULY 1940 the German Luftwaffe commenced bombing raids against British airfields, naval stations, and cities. The attacks on the military facilities appeared to be intended to weaken British defenses against an impending amphibious assault, the attacks on the cities to weaken British morale. British fliers of the Royal Air Force fended off the German bombers as best they could, but there were simply too many attackers and too many targets for the RAF pilots to handle them all.

The Battle of Britain—as the air contest was called—intensified through August to a September climax, during which the Germans pounded London relentlessly. "The last three nights in London have been simply hell," Joseph Kennedy wrote his wife on September 10.

> Last night I put on my steel helmet and went up on the roof of the Chancery and stayed there until two o'clock in the morning watching the Germans come over in relays every ten minutes and drop bombs, setting terrific fires. You could see the dome of St. Paul's silhouetted against a blazing inferno that the Germans kept adding to from time to time by flying over and dropping more bombs.

Kennedy naturally kept close touch with Churchill, who expressed grave concern that Hitler would follow up the bombings with an invasion. The prime minister determined to redeem Roosevelt's promise to supply the anti-fascist forces—meaning Britain, at this stage—with the materiel they needed to defend themselves. Shortly after Roosevelt accepted renomination by the Democrats, Churchill renewed his plea for weapons. "It has now become most urgent for you to let us have the destroyers, motor boats and flying boats for which we have asked," he said. "The Germans have the whole French coast line from which to launch U-boats, dive-bomber attacks upon our trade and food, and in addition we must be constantly prepared to repel by sea action threatened invasion in the narrow waters." Destroyers were more critical than ever, for in the last ten days the German bombers had sunk or crippled eleven of Britain's destroyers. And they would probably sink or cripple many more. "Destroyers are frightfully vulnerable to air bombing, and yet they must be held in the air bombing area to prevent seaborne invasion." Resupply of the destroyers was imperative. "If we cannot get a substantial reinforcement, the whole fate of the war may be decided by this minor and easily remediable factor."

Churchill, the former naval person, may have realized that a request for ships would resonate more fully with fellow navalist Roosevelt than a request for aircraft or tanks. Or perhaps, like Roosevelt, he simply appreciated the value of ships more than that of planes and tanks. In any event, the American destroyers became the touchstone of Anglo-American diplomacy as the Battle of Britain raged in the skies over the English Channel and England itself. Churchill let pass no opportunity to remind Roosevelt that a comparative handful of ships might make the difference to democracy for generations to come and that the president, by a bold stroke, might make himself a hero forever.

Of course Churchill needed to convince Roosevelt that the ships wouldn't be wasted—that Britain wouldn't go under even after receiving the American assistance. This was no easy task, for with the skies over London raining German bombs, Britain's future was hardly assured. Yet Churchill refused to be discouraged. "He was smoking a cigar when I entered and asked me if I would have a scotch highball and said he would have one," Kennedy recorded after a visit to the prime minister. Fortified by the tobacco and booze, Churchill exuded optimism. "He was confident about everything. He felt that Hitler would invade and soon, but that he would get a terrible reception. In fact the only thing that disturbed him was that Hitler might not invade and Churchill would be in a bad way in that he built up the defenses and army to fight Hitler. He said the British soldiers would probably want their money back, because they won't be satisfied with the show."

Churchill perhaps protested too much to Kennedy, whose pessimism regarding Britain's prospects was no secret. But the prime minister said essentially the same thing to Roosevelt. "I am beginning to feel very hopeful about this war if we can get round the next three or four months," he wrote the president. "The air is holding well. We are hitting that man"—Hitler—"hard in both repelling attacks and in bombing Germany." The crucial question, as before, was the supply of warships. "The loss of destroyers by air attacks may well be so serious as to break down our defence of the food and trade routes across the Pacific." And it put the burden of saving freedom squarely upon Roosevelt. "Mr. President, with great respect I must tell you that in the long history of the world, this is a thing to do now."

Having crossed the Rubicon of a third-term nomination, Roosevelt decided he was ready to cross the Atlantic of closer engagement in the European war. Churchill's words weren't inconsequential; the prime minister's growing hopefulness made an American investment in England's future appear a better bet than it had before. But Roosevelt's own state of mind was at least as significant. He hadn't known what the reaction to his nomination would be. The isolationists, of course, would complain. So would the Republicans and conservative Democrats who had found fault for years. But the crucial element was the broad constituency of ordinary Americans who had been his political base from the beginning. If they took exception to a third term—to his placing himself above George Washington and every other previous president—he would be in trouble. But they didn't take such exception, at least not loudly or in large numbers. They seemed to be accepting his argument that the current world crisis justified an exception to the two-term rule.

Encouraged by this non-reaction, Roosevelt responded to Churchill more positively than in any previous message. "It is my belief that it may be possible to furnish to the British Government as immediate assistance at least fifty destroyers," Roosevelt wrote Churchill. Yet there was a catch, or rather a quid pro quo. "Such assistance, as I am sure you will understand, would only be furnished if the American people and the Congress frankly recognized that in return therefor the national defense and security of the United States would be enhanced." Roosevelt knew that Churchill's reflexive response would be to say that anything that helped Britain defeat the Nazis would enhance American security. But though the president might agree, Congress and the American people would require collateral of a more concrete nature. Roosevelt elaborated:

> It would be necessary, in the event that it proves possible to release the materiel above mentioned, that the British Government find itself able and willing to take the two following steps:

1. Assurance on the part of the Prime Minister that in the event that the waters of Great Britain become untenable for British ships of war, the latter would not be turned over to the Germans or sunk, but would be sent to other parts of the Empire. . . .

2. An agreement on the part of Great Britain that the British Government would authorize the use of Newfoundland, Bermuda, the Bahamas, Jamaica, St. Lucia, Trinidad and British Guiana as naval and air bases by the United States.

Roosevelt explained that the details of the bases agreement needn't be decided at once. As to the assurance regarding the destroyers, the prime minister need make no public announcement; a private pledge to the president would do.

Roosevelt's offer wrapped strategy inside politics and then bundled the package into strategy again. The proposed swap of destroyers for bases made sense strategically: factories in the United States could always build more ships, but ports to base them were in limited supply. Should Britain fall and America have to defend the Western Hemisphere against German assault, the bases—which spanned the western Atlantic from Canada to South America—would be essential.

The deal made even more sense politically. As confident as Roosevelt was becoming regarding a third term, he had no intention of provoking another outburst of isolationism. The deal could be defended as a sharp bargain: as Roosevelt exploiting Britain's extremity to acquire real estate the British would never have surrendered otherwise, in exchange for some out-of-date ships that weren't much good to America anyway.

And the canny politics of the deal would enhance America's security by increasing Roosevelt's room for maneuver. Roosevelt's ego had always been robust, ever since Sara had centered her world, and such of the larger world as the family's ample resources allowed, on her only child. It had grown with each political success, till by now, on the verge of setting a record for presidential longevity, Roosevelt accounted himself at least the equal of America's greatest chief executives. He certainly considered himself more capable of dealing with challenges to American security than Wendell Willkie or Jim Farley or anyone else who had put himself forward as a candidate for president.

And why not? He had been studying the presidency for forty years, practicing the craft for eight. He had been engaged personally in matters touching national security since before the First World War. Could Willkie say that? Could anyone else in America? For that matter, could Hitler match his knowledge of the world? Could Mussolini? Could Stalin? Of the world's current leaders, only Churchill came close to Roosevelt in decades devoted to the strategic arts. And Churchill had been head of his country's government a mere few months. For most of the previous decade—while Roosevelt had been wrestling with the rise of Germany and Japan—Churchill had been a gadfly swatted by elements of his own party as often as by the opposition.

During the summer of 1940 Roosevelt emerged, in his own mind, as the great statesman of the modern era. He realized that it lay in his power to command the heights of international affairs. It would, at any rate, if he did two things: keep Britain fighting and complete his electoral coup. The destroyers-for-bases deal would serve both purposes.

❖ ❖ ❖

CHURCHILL THRILLED at the president's offer. "I need not tell you how cheered I am by your message or how grateful I feel for your untiring efforts to give us all possible help," he wrote Roosevelt. "You know well that the worth of every destroyer that you can spare to us is measured in rubies." Churchill accepted Roosevelt's conditions. The assurance about making sure the ships stayed out of German hands accorded with Churchill's own strong, and oft-stated, inclinations. "We intend to fight this out here to the end, and none of us would ever buy peace by surrendering or scuttling the fleet." Yet Churchill appreciated Roosevelt's willingness not to publicize such a promise. "In any use you may make of this repeated assurance you will please bear in mind the disastrous effect from our point of view and perhaps also from yours of allowing any impression to grow that we regard the conquest of the British Islands and its naval bases as any other than an impossible contingency." As to the bases the president desired, these would present no problem. Churchill, like Roosevelt, was willing to leave the geographical details to a later date. "We can discuss them at leisure."

The details proved to be more difficult than either Churchill or Roosevelt had anticipated. Churchill's political problems were only somewhat less pressing than Roosevelt's; no more than the American president could the British prime minister be seen as giving away assets important to national defense. Churchill proposed treating the transfer of the destroyers and the leasing of naval bases as separate issues. "I had not contemplated anything in the nature of a contract, bargain or sale between us," he wrote Roosevelt. "Our view is that we are two friends helping each other as far as we can." Any acknowledgment of a quid pro quo would create difficulties. "Once this idea is accepted, people will contrast on each side what is given and received. The money value of the arms would be computed and set against the facilities, and some would think one thing about it and some another."

American politics pushed Roosevelt in the other direction. For him, the quid pro quo was essential lest the isolationists be stirred once more into effective action. There was some constitutional question whether the president could transfer American military assets to another country simply on his own authority, but the more important question was the political one of whether he *should* do so. Roosevelt's sensitivity to the politics of the matter was such that he tried to gain Willkie's approval of the deal before he announced it. To some extent this effort was motivated by a sincere desire for bipartisanship in foreign policy. Roosevelt had taken two steps toward bipartisanship by appointing a pair of Republicans to head the cabinet defense departments. Henry Stimson, William Howard Taft's secretary of war and Herbert Hoover's secretary of state, returned, at the age of seventy-two, to the War Department. Frank Knox, the publisher of the *Chicago Daily News* and the Republican candidate for vice president in 1936, took over the Navy Department. Yet bipartisanship was hardly the whole story of the approach to Willkie. Roosevelt reckoned that if Willkie signed on to the destroyer deal, he would give voters even less reason than they already had to swap the incumbent for the challenger. If he refused to accept it, his professed desire to grant Britain all the aid it required would be seen as hollow.

Roosevelt sent William Allen White, Theodore Roosevelt's old admirer and, as the chairman of the self-appointed Committee to Defend America by Aiding the Allies, the leading Republican interventionist, to talk to Willkie. The Republican nominee, doubtless perceiving Roosevelt's game—and with perceptions perhaps sharpened by recollection of Roosevelt's refusal to cooperate with Hoover in 1932—declined to be drawn in.

This simply increased the president's caution. He emphasized the value of the bases to American security, while ignoring the contribution of the destroyers to Britain's defense. In a letter to a skeptic from his own party, Senator David Walsh of Massachusetts, the chairman of the naval affairs committee, Roosevelt related a tale of a run-in with a Dutchess County farmer that may have been apocryphal.

I told him the gist of the proposal, which is, in effect, to buy ninety-nine-year leases from Great Britain for at least seven naval and air bases in British colonial possessions—not including the Dominion of Canada, which is a separate study on my part. The farmer replied somewhat as follows:

"Say, ain't you the Commander-in-Chief? If you are and own fifty muzzle-loadin' rifles of the Civil War period, you would be a chump if you declined to exchange them for seven modern machine guns—wouldn't you?"

Roosevelt continued in his own voice, pleading sincerity and claiming a certain expertise in naval strategy.

> Frankly, my difficulty is that as President and Commander-in-Chief I have no right to think of politics in the sense of being a candidate or desiring votes. You and I know that our weakness in the past has lain in the fact that from Newfoundland to Trinidad our sole protection offshore lies in the three contiguous islands of Porto Rico, St. Thomas, and St. Croix. That, in the nature of modern warfare, is a definite operating handicap. If for fifty ships, which are on their last legs anyway, we can get the right to put in naval and air bases in Newfoundland, the Bahamas, Jamaica, St. Lucia, Trinidad and British Guiana, then our operating deficiency is largely cured.

Roosevelt reminded Walsh that the founder of their party, Thomas Jefferson, had purchased Louisiana under comparable circumstances, while France was beset by England. "He did this without even consulting the Congress. He put the deal through and later on he asked the House Committee on Appropriations to put $15,000,000 into the appropriation bill." The bases in question were no Louisiana, but the transfer was a bargain nonetheless. "The fifty destroyers are the same type of ship which we have been from time to time striking from the naval list and selling for scrap for, I think, $4,000 or $5,000 per destroyer. On that basis, the cost of the right to at least seven naval and air bases is an extremely low one from the point of view of the United States Government—i.e., about $250,000!"

With the press Roosevelt was even more artful. He announced at a news conference that some American naval and military officers were visiting England. "This has nothing to do with destroyers," Roosevelt told the reporters. "But I am initiating, holding conversations with the British government for the acquisition of naval bases and air bases for the defense of the Americas and particularly with relationship to the Panama Canal."

"Did I understand you to say, Mr. President, that they had no relation to destroyers?" a reporter pressed.

"I would not use it," Roosevelt responded opaquely, regarding the information he had just given them. "That is just a little private tip."

The reporters were puzzled. The president was the one who had brought up the destroyers at this session. "This is a matter of destroyers?" one asked.

"It is not a matter of destroyers. That is exactly the point. . . . The emphasis is on the acquisition of the bases—that is the main point—for the protection of this hemisphere. . . . That is all there is to say."

Of course that was *not* all there was to say. Roosevelt recognized belatedly that to deny the connection between the destroyers and the bases would be futile and transparently disingenuous. Yet the formula he ultimately devised was hardly better. He announced a combination gift and trade involving naval and air bases in Newfoundland, Bermuda, the British West Indies, and British Guiana, and American destroyers. "The rights to bases in Newfoundland and Bermuda are gifts—generously given and gladly received," the president explained. "The other bases mentioned have been acquired in exchange for fifty of our over-age destroyers." Roosevelt said nothing more about the ships, stressing instead the defense benefits of the agreement. "The value to the Western Hemisphere of these outposts of security is beyond calculation."

40.

THE FORTUNES OF WAR DECREED THAT BY THE TIME OF ROOSEVELT'S announcement no one seriously disputed that the bases could be valuable to the United States. Germany's bombing of Britain grew ever fiercer; night after night the Luftwaffe turned London into a blazing spectacle. Perhaps the British would survive the Nazi onslaught; perhaps not. But any military regime that could deliver such destruction was one that had to be reckoned with.

Yet Roosevelt's handling of the destroyer-for-bases deal, after his clumsy manipulation of the Democratic convention, reinforced his reputation for dubious maneuvering. The isolationists were the most insistent in asserting that the president was conspiring to take the United States to war against Germany, but one didn't have to be an isolationist to conclude that he wasn't telling all he knew.

Roosevelt's response to the threat from Japan was more straightforward. The war in China, now nearly three years old, had slowed Japan's progress toward what it was calling its "Greater East Asia Co-prosperity Sphere," but the outbreak of war in Europe, by distracting France and Britain, presented Tokyo with temptations to additional expansion it couldn't resist. In June 1940 the Japanese government pressured French Indochina and British Burma, demanding that they close their borders with China—to prevent the anti-Japanese forces in China from receiving outside help—and intimating that if the demand wasn't met military action would follow.

Japan's renewed assertiveness compelled Roosevelt to reconsider his attitude toward Tokyo. During the previous three years Japan seemed to have trapped itself in China, where it could neither defeat the government forces headed by Chiang Kai-shek nor pull back without suffering a grave loss of face and momentum. The stalemate had allowed Roosevelt to concentrate on Europe. But now Japan was on the march again, and the administration must respond.

It was a delicate business, though. To react too strongly would risk a war Americans weren't ready or willing to fight. To react too gently would teach the Japanese militarists that the United States could be treated with impunity.

Roosevelt's first step was a negative one. He refused to renew the commercial treaty that had framed American trade with Japan for decades and that expired in January 1940. The president's purpose was to remind the Japanese of their dependence on the United States for vital raw materials, including oil and scrap iron and steel. Some in the administration wanted him to go further, to an embargo of oil and scrap. But for the time being he preferred to hold this stronger sanction in abeyance.

He complemented the economic nudge with a series of warnings by Cordell Hull to Japanese officials. The Japanese government defended its Asian sphere by invoking the American Monroe Doctrine. Hull rejected the comparison as absurd. "There is no more resemblance between our Monroe Doctrine and the so-called Monroe Doctrine of Japan than there is between black and white," the secretary of state told the Japanese ambassador in Washington. America's doctrine was defensive; Japan's bastardized version was a cover for the most egregious aggression. Hull told the ambassador that the growing chaos in the world had stiffened the resolve of the United States. "The American people have now become thoroughly awakened, aroused, and alert in regard to any threatened injuries to American rights and interests." Their heightened vigilance, Hull added, was a "matter of great gratification to those of us in charge of the foreign affairs of the nation." The secretary directed Joseph Grew in Tokyo to share a sentiment with the Japanese government: "The United States has no aggressive designs, but it will be ready to defend itself against any aggression which may be undertaken against it."

When the warnings produced no positive result, Roosevelt ratcheted things up a notch. In July 1940 he directed that a recent law restricting strategic exports be interpreted to include aviation fuel. Nothing in the interpretation singled out Japan, but the Japanese understood the directive as targeting them, as Roosevelt intended. The Japanese embassy protested that the new rules were "tantamount to an embargo."

Roosevelt squeezed a bit more. In September he added scrap iron and steel to the restricted list. Again, Japan was not mentioned specifically, but the Japanese government, again accurately, denounced the new measure as an "unfriendly act."

The embargoes failed in their broader purpose, though. Japan's aggressive impulses raged unabated. "There cannot be any doubt that the military and other elements in Japan see in the present world situation a golden opportunity to carry their dreams of expansion into effect," Joseph Grew wrote from Tokyo. "The German victories, like strong wine, have gone to their heads." The militarists wanted to grab what they could while the chance persisted. "It has been and is doubtful that the saner heads in and out of the government will be able to control these elements."

❖ ❖ ❖

AMID THE GROWING threats from Germany and Japan, Roosevelt sought to strengthen the American military. In May 1940, as German planes shocked the world into recognizing the destructive potential of airpower, the president called for a dramatic increase in American aircraft production. "I should like to see this nation geared up to the ability to turn out at least 50,000 planes a year," he told Congress. American factories were currently making less than a quarter of this number. He urged a speedup of the army's plans for purchasing tanks, trucks, and artillery. To fund the buildup he asked for nearly one billion dollars in new money.

Two weeks later, as the French folded and the British fled before the Nazi onslaught, Roosevelt requested another billion dollars to prepare the army to train new recruits. "The one most obvious lesson of the present war in Europe is the value of the factor of speed," he said. "There is definite danger in waiting to order the complete equipping and training of armies after a war begins." He also requested authority from Congress to call out the national guard and to bring the army reserve into active service.

After the fall of France the president returned to Congress again, this time asking for five billion new dollars. "The principal lesson of the war up to the present time is that partial defense is inadequate defense," he said. "If the United States is to have any defense, it must have total defense." Roosevelt asserted a goal of acquiring equipment for an army of two million men, with comparable increases in the strength of the navy and the army's air force.

As to where the soldiers would come from, Roosevelt broached a controversial subject. He mentioned "a system of selective training" to ensure that the manpower existed for most effective use of all the new weapons. He declined to specify what he meant by selective training, but other administration officials, including army chief of staff George Marshall, acknowledged that conscription—a draft—was the plan.

A conscription bill was introduced in Congress but bogged down, prompting Roosevelt to put his own shoulder behind it, albeit tentatively. A reporter prodded him at a press conference in early August: "There is a very definite feeling, Mr. President, in congressional circles that you are not very hot about this conscription legislation."

"It depends on which paper you read," Roosevelt responded.

"Well, I read my own, which I believe in."

"I am damned if I do, and I am damned if I do not," Roosevelt rejoined. "I am bound to be criticized whatever I do. Now, on this particular bill, everybody knows that if I were to come out and send up to the Hill a particular measure, what would you boys do, most of you? You would say that the President is 'ordering Congress.' 'Old Mr. Dictator, he is just ordering Congress to pass his bill.' " Roosevelt talked around the subject for several minutes before citing his experience in the Wilson administration. "We figured out pretty well in 1917 that the selective training or selective draft was the fairest and in all ways the most efficient way of conducting a war if we had to go to war. I still think so, and I think a great majority of the people in the country will think so, when they understand it."

Additional circumlocution ended with a reporter's attempt to extract a usable statement. "There is a very quotable sentence right there, if you will permit it," the reporter said.

"What is it?"

"That you are distinctly in favor of a selective training bill—"

"And consider it essential to adequate national defense. Quote that."

Roosevelt's remarks provoked the expected response from the isolationists, who condemned them as another step toward American fascism. Arthur Vandenberg approvingly circulated a letter from former War Secretary Harry Woodring denouncing the conscription bill as a measure "that smacks of totalitarianism." Democrat Burton Wheeler of Montana contended that the compulsory enlistment of Americans ought to require a national referendum. Labor leaders opposed the draft, with the heads of five railroad brotherhoods calling conscription the "very antithesis of freedom." Scores of faculty at the City College of New York signed a petition rejecting conscription.

Yet broader measures of opinion indicated support for Roosevelt and the draft. A survey of papers by the journal *Editor & Publisher* found that 80 percent favored some form of conscription. A Gallup poll revealed that Americans at large supported a draft by a margin of two to one, with comfortable majorities even in traditionally isolationist states of the Midwest.

(Whether registering opposition to the draft, a realistic appraisal of its chances of passage, or other emotions entirely, thousands of young couples flooded marriage license bureaus across the country, in recognition of the fact that the conscription bill would exempt married men. "This is the biggest day we've had this year," the chief clerk in New York City explained. "I hear most couples talking of the proposed draft now pending before Congress. I think it's the reason for this large crowd. . . . We were able to take care of all of them and send everybody home happy.")

Despite the popular support, Roosevelt declined to push any harder for conscription without assurances that his backing wouldn't be used against him. He approached Willkie regarding a joint statement in support of the draft. He wasn't surprised, given Willkie's negative response to his earlier effort on behalf of the destroyers-for-bases deal, when the Republican nominee rebuffed the overture. This didn't prevent him from complaining that Willkie was placing his own interest above that of the country. "He has no desire to co-operate and is merely playing politics," Roosevelt wrote to an ally in Congress.

Shortly thereafter, though, Willkie issued an independent endorsement of the draft, freeing Roosevelt to take the lead on the issue. Critics were advocating postponing a decision till the new year; reporters asked for Roosevelt's reaction. "I am absolutely opposed to the postponement," he said. "It means in these days—and we all know what the world situation is—nearly a year of delay. . . . We cannot afford a year."

With the president, his Republican challenger, and a large majority of the American public behind conscription, not even the isolationists in Congress could stop the bill. In September the legislature approved the first peacetime draft in American history. "America stands at the crossroads of its destiny," Roosevelt said, on signing the measure. "We must and will marshal our great potential strength to fend off war from our shores. We must and will prevent our land from becoming a victim of aggression. Our decision has been made."

❖ ❖ ❖

THE ELECTION OF 1940 should have been one of the most momentous in American history. Franklin Roosevelt was trying to break the oldest taboo in American politics, the one that had always prevented what American democrats—a group that overlapped with American Democrats, but not precisely— had feared: the emergence of a permanent presidency. They knew the power of incumbents and how incumbents could manipulate the political process to their benefit and to the exclusion of challengers. They might well have rewritten the Constitution to forbid third terms if they hadn't assumed that the ghost of George Washington was forbidding enough.

Roosevelt's attempted lese majesty would have provoked a fundamental debate if there hadn't been a war on. The fact of the war, of course, was what provided Roosevelt's political cover. He knew perfectly well there wouldn't be such a debate. At least he wouldn't participate in one, relying on the war as his excuse not to.

The Republicans attempted to force the issue. The party organized a national "No Third Term Day," marked by anti-Roosevelt rallies in hundreds of cities and towns across the country. Willkie, calling Roosevelt "Mr. Third-term Candidate," raised the question at every chance. "If you elect him for a third term, there will be no limit to the imagination of what he has a mandate to do," Willkie told an appreciative audience in Montana. In Syracuse he asserted that Roosevelt, after failing to reorganize the Supreme Court in 1937, had nonetheless packed the court with justices who shared his expansive view of federal power. "Give him another four years and he will fill with his own men not only the Supreme Court but the entire federal judiciary. This is the pattern of dictatorship, the usurpation of power by manufactured emergencies, the circumvention of the legislature, the capture of the courts. . . . These are the last steps on the road to absolute power." After Roosevelt still refused to be drawn, Willkie demanded, "Since he won't discuss the principles of a third term, what does he think about a fourth term?" The president and his supporters were contending that his experience qualified him for extended tenure. If this argument held true, it presumably would be employed again after twelve years, and then after sixteen. "You can pursue that argument on into infinity. You will come to the conclusion that Louis XIV, the worst despot in history, was the best ruler because he served the longest. So I would like to have the third-term candidate enlighten the American people."

Willkie wanted Roosevelt to enlighten the American people about his war plans as well. "Are there any international understandings to put America into the war that we citizens do not know about?" The Republican nominee recounted the Democrats' handling of the First World War, when American boys had fought and died for a dream that bore no resemblance to reality. "We do not want to send our boys over there again. And we do not intend to send them over there again. And if you elect me president, they won't be sent." Willkie challenged Roosevelt to make a similar promise.

This demand got Roosevelt's attention. Polls showed that a double-digit

Roosevelt lead in late September had slipped to six points by the end of October. According to Gallup's interpretation of the peculiar politics of the Democratic party, the race was therefore nearly even. "A lead of 53 percent for the President is actually the equivalent of a neck-and-neck race," George Gallup explained, "because, owing to surplus Democratic majorities in the South, a Democratic President normally requires about 52 percent of the nation to win."

Roosevelt responded with a statement that seemed necessary at the time but that would haunt him later. Speaking at Boston on October 30, he accused the Republicans of "political shenanigans" and Willkie of "unpatriotic misstatement of fact." He praised what the New Deal had done for ordinary Americans and pledged to carry the good work forward. Then, addressing himself specifically to the "mothers and fathers" of America, he declared:

> I have said this before, but I shall say it again and again and again: Your boys are not going to be sent into any foreign wars.

❖   ❖   ❖

ROOSEVELT'S STATEMENT served its immediate purpose. The Willkie tide crested and ebbed, and Roosevelt won his third term by a popular margin of 55 percent to 45 percent, and 449 to 82 in electors.

The campaign left Roosevelt weary. Willkie's badgering had finally persuaded him, just days before the election, to forswear a fourth term, but only obliquely. In a discussion of what he hoped to accomplish in a third term, he had asserted, almost as an aside: "When that term is over, there will be another president." He hadn't mentioned the topic again.

But at the first post-election press conference, a newsman read back Roosevelt's statement and inquired, "Did you definitely mean that?"

Perhaps the campaign had drained his patience. Doubtless the juggling between the contest at home and the wars in Europe and Asia had worn him down. In any event, he responded with uncharacteristic testiness. "Oughtn't you to go back to grade school and learn English?" he snapped at the reporter.

"That was your meaning?"

"Read it. I am not teaching you English. Read it."

"I have read it, sir."

"Read it again."

❖ ❖ ❖

No one was happier at Roosevelt's reelection than Winston Churchill. "I did not think it right for me as a foreigner to express any opinion upon American policies while the election was on," Churchill wrote the president the day after the balloting. "But now I feel you will not mind my saying that I prayed for your success and that I am truly thankful for it." Britain had survived the German bombings, which after their September climax had diminished as the fighter planes of the Royal Air Force inflicted increasing damage on the Luftwaffe. To spare their bombers, the Germans now largely confined their raids to nights. These still spoiled English sleep, but they accomplished less meaningful destruction. And the onset of autumn's nasty weather in the Channel obviated any real threat of invasion until the spring. "We are now entering upon a somber phase of what must evidently be protracted and broadening war," Churchill continued. "Things are afoot which will be remembered as long as the English language is spoken in any quarter of the globe, and in expressing the comfort I feel that the people of the United States have once again cast these great burdens upon you, I must avow my sure faith that the lights by which we steer will bring us safely to anchor."

Roosevelt didn't respond at once. The immediate crisis was over, as Churchill himself acknowledged. The need now was to plan for the longer haul—for the "protracted and broadening war" of the prime minister's description. Having pledged to avoid engagement in foreign wars, Roosevelt intended to keep his distance from Britain. But Britain remained America's best hope, in Roosevelt's view, for precisely such non-engagement. Roosevelt in late 1940 was no more eager for war than the isolationists. Yet their contention that a German victory in Europe would not be cause for alarm, that the United States might defend itself by fighting from American shores, struck Roosevelt as naïve and myopic. Doubtless America *could* defend itself, by itself, in the Western Hemisphere. But the task would be needlessly difficult. As valuable as he had made the bases in Newfoundland, Bermuda, and the West Indies out to be, they were nowhere so valuable a base as Britain, from which bombers might reach the heart of Germany. To retreat to the Western Hemisphere would be to concede control of the Atlantic and its shipping lanes to the Germans. To keep Britain in the war, by contrast, would threaten to bottle the German navy up in the Baltic and North seas.

There was more involved than mere fighting. This war would end, sooner or later. The world would have to be reconstructed. Roosevelt had seen it badly reconstructed once; the result was the current conflict. A reconstruction based on Nazi control of Europe would be far worse. Roosevelt favored democracy over dictatorship for reasons of morality and virtue; how could an American not? But he also believed that democracy was more stable, more peaceful, and more conducive to prosperity—to the prosperity of those living in the democratic countries and to that of their neighbors as well. In a world where fascists flourished, America would know neither peace nor prosperity. Roosevelt couldn't yet see how fascism would be eliminated, but he instinctively understood that it must not be allowed to spread any farther than it already had.

What, then, should be his policy—*America's* policy? It was simple, really: to keep Britain fighting as long and effectively as possible. Every month, every year perhaps, that Britain remained at grips with Germany was a month, a year, during which the United States might remain at peace. As bold as Hitler had proven, he couldn't dream of attacking the United States without defeating Britain first. "Does anyone seriously believe that we need to fear attack anywhere in the Americas while a free Britain remains our most powerful naval neighbor in the Atlantic?" the president asked the American people in a Fireside Chat in December 1940.

> Does anyone seriously believe, on the other hand, that we could rest easy if the Axis powers were our neighbors there? If Great Britain goes down, the Axis powers will control the continents of Europe, Asia, Africa, Australasia, and the high seas—and they will be in a position to bring enormous military and naval resources against this hemisphere. It is no exaggeration to say that all of us, in all the Americas, would be living at the point of a gun—a gun loaded with explosive bullets, economic as well as military.

Isolationists imagined a negotiated peace with Hitler and his accomplices. These "American appeasers," Roosevelt said, should ask the Austrians and the Czechs about negotiating with the Nazis. They should ask the Poles and Belgians and Dutch and Norwegians about the possibility of peace in the vicinity of German fascism. The nature of modern dictatorship was to expand by force. The Axis regimes spoke of a new order, but it was the oldest order in the world: a tyranny of terror and oppression. The British were bravely struggling against this tyranny; America's fate depended on Britain's success. "There is far less chance of the United States getting into war if we do all we can now to support the nations defending themselves against attack by the Axis than if we acquiesce in their defeat, submit tamely to an Axis victory, and wait our turn to be the object of attack in another war later on." London wasn't asking for American soldiers, nor were American soldiers being offered. Any claim to the contrary was a "deliberate untruth." American weapons, not American soldiers, were what was required. Indeed, providing weapons would help ensure that American soldiers *not* go into battle. Roosevelt coined a phrase that would summarize American policy for the following year, and beyond, when he declared: "We must be the great arsenal of democracy."

❖ ❖ ❖

THE POLICY THAT became known as Lend-Lease had multiple purposes. The obvious one was that which Roosevelt identified in his December Fireside Chat: to keep Britain in the war, that the United States might stay out. This part of Roosevelt's aim was perfectly sincere, at least in the short term. Whether it was realistic over time was another question. Quite likely the British, with American weapons and equipment, could hold the Germans at bay, as they had done so far without American help. But it seemed quite *un*likely that the British, even with American arms, could somehow reverse the German victories on the Continent. Roosevelt hadn't decided how long the United States could live with a Nazified Europe, but everything in his public and private statements indicated his belief that the cohabitation couldn't be permanent. At some point, in some way, American power would have to be brought more directly to bear.

Yet even in the near term, becoming the arsenal of democracy would serve purposes other than bolstering Britain. It would allow the expansion of America's defense industry. This would be good for America's own defense, both in deterring attack and in fighting a war should deterrence fail. American businesses and workers would perfect their skills making weapons for export and in the process become ready to build for America's own use if the need arose. "Orders from Great Britain are therefore a tremendous asset to American national defense, because they automatically create additional facilities," Roosevelt told reporters at a December press conference. "I am talking selfishly, from the American point of view—nothing else."

Putting Americans to work building weapons would have broader economic benefits as well. Jobs of any sort remained scarce in America in late 1940; whatever the government could do to find or create jobs would be welcomed. Defense jobs, moreover, were preferable to the kinds of jobs the New Deal had typically provided, in two respects. First, they paid better. Second, they came without the political and psychological baggage of make-work. At this stage Roosevelt didn't expect the defense industry to pull the country out of the depression, but it might well get the process started.

How to fund democracy's arsenal was a question. Would the British pay for the weapons? Would the American government? If the British, would they be required to pay cash, or would they be allowed to borrow? If the American government, would it expect to be reimbursed by the British at some point?

Roosevelt had dealt with these issues before, or at any rate seen them dealt with at close hand. "I remember 1914 very well," he told reporters. Conventional wisdom at the outbreak of the First World War had predicted a short struggle, on the reasoning that the belligerents would run out of cash. "There was the best economic opinion in the world that the continuance of war was absolutely dependent on money in the bank. Well, you know what happened." What happened first was that Americans had put up the money, the Allies had got their weapons, the American economy had boomed, and the Allies had won the war. What happened later was that the war debts poisoned relations between the United States and the Europeans during the decade and a half after the war.

Roosevelt wanted to gain the benefits of war production while preventing the postwar hangover. "What I am trying to do is to eliminate the dollar sign," he said. "Get rid of the silly, foolish old dollar sign." Needless to say, not everyone thought the dollar sign was so silly, but none of the reporters called Roosevelt on it before he provided a better hook for their stories.

Let me give you an illustration: Suppose my neighbor's home catches fire, and I have a length of garden hose four or five hundred feet away. If he can take my garden hose and connect it up with his hydrant, I may help him to put out his fire. Now, what do I do? I don't say to him before that operation, "Neighbor, my garden hose cost me $15; you have to pay me $15 for it." What is the transaction that goes on? I don't want $15—I want my garden hose back after the fire is over. All right. If it goes through the fire all right, intact, without any damage to it, he gives it back to me and thanks me very much for the use of it. But suppose it gets smashed up—holes in it—during the fire; we don't have to have too much formality about it, but I say to him, "I was glad to lend you that hose; I see I can't use it any more, it's all smashed up." He says, "How many feet of it were there?" I tell him, "There were 150 feet of it." He says, "All right, I will replace it." Now, if I get a nice garden hose back, I am in pretty good shape.

The president conceived of something similar regarding aid to Britain.

The thought is that we would take over not all, but a very large number of, future British orders; and when they came off the line, whether they were planes or guns or something else, we would enter into some kind of arrangement for their use by the British on the ground that it was the best thing for American defense, with the understanding that when the show was over, we would get repaid sometime in kind, thereby leaving out the dollar mark in the form of a dollar debt and substituting for it a gentleman's obligation to repay in kind. I think you all get it.

Not all the reporters did get it. Roosevelt had cautioned them about inquiring too closely of a project that was still in the conceptual stage, but one couldn't resist. "Would the title still be in our name?" he asked.

"You have gone and asked a question I told you not to ask," the president replied. "It would take lawyers much better than you or I to answer it."

"Let us leave the legal phase out of it entirely," another reporter asked. "The question I have is whether you think this takes us any more into the war than we are."

"No, not a bit," the president replied.

❖ ❖ ❖

*T*HIS LAST ASSERTION was what provoked all the controversy when the president presented Lend-Lease to Congress in January 1941. He proposed that the legislature underwrite the expansion of American war production facilities and that it appropriate funds to pay for the weapons and supporting equipment the facilities produced. These weapons should be sent to the countries battling aggression, with compensation to be deferred until after the battle was won. Roosevelt again rejected the isolationist assertion that his plan would push the United States closer to war, but more than ever he embraced the cause of those fighting fascism. And for the first time he spoke explicitly of war aims.

In the future days, which we seek to make secure, we look forward to a world founded upon four essential human freedoms.

The first is freedom of speech and expression—everywhere in the world.

The second is freedom of every person to worship God in his own way—everywhere in the world.

The third is freedom from want—which, translated into world terms, means economic understandings which will secure to every nation a healthy peacetime life for its inhabitants—everywhere in the world.

The fourth is freedom from fear—which, translated into world terms, means a world-wide reduction of armaments to such a point and in such a thorough fashion that no nation will be in a position to commit an act of physical aggression against any neighbor—anywhere in the world.

The Lend-Lease bill—introduced in the House with the curious designation, for a bill affirming Anglo-American solidarity, H.R. 1776—evoked the expected response from the isolationists. Several derided the notion that Hitler would threaten the United States even if he conquered Britain. Gerald Nye called the bill a war measure in all but name. "Make no mistake about it," the North Dakota Republican declared of the struggle against the president's proposal. "This is a last-ditch fight. This is our last fight before the question of war itself is raised. If we lose it, war is almost inevitable." Hiram Johnson of California was more succinct: "This bill is war." Republican Robert Taft of Ohio drew laughs from even supporters of the bill when he remarked, "Lending war equipment is a good deal like lending chewing gum—you certainly don't want it back." Wendell Willkie's endorsement of the general idea of Lend-Lease, albeit without reference to a specific bill, prompted the Republican isolationists to remind anyone who would listen that Willkie didn't speak for the Republican party. Democrat Burton Wheeler distanced himself from Willkie differently. "Do not be dismayed because Mr. Willkie, lately of the Commonwealth & Southern, is on the side of Mr. Roosevelt," Wheeler told his isolationist friends. "This puts all the economic royalists on the side of war."

Wheeler went on to lash Lend-Lease as an insult to the American people, an injury to the American Constitution, and an affront to American values. "Never before have the American people been asked or compelled to give so bounteously and so completely of their tax dollars to any foreign nation," Wheeler said. "Never before has the Congress of the United States been asked by any president to violate international law. Never before has this nation resorted to duplicity in the conduct of its foreign affairs. Never before has the United States given to one man the power to strip this nation of its defenses in time of war or peace." Speaking as a skeptic in regard to Roosevelt's domestic policies too, the Montana senator called Lend-Lease another "New Deal AAA foreign policy—plow under every fourth American boy."

Roosevelt took the criticism personally—or at least affected to. He called Wheeler's statement "the most dastardly, unpatriotic thing" he had ever heard. "Quote me on that," he told reporters. "That really is the rottenest thing that has been said in public life in my generation."

Roosevelt had to deal with questioning from within his own administration as well. John Nance Garner wasn't quite out the door; his replacement by Henry Wallace wouldn't be official until January 20. At his final cabinet meeting the vice president made his distrust of Lend-Lease felt. "Garner was there, flushed of face and loud of voice and at least half full of whisky," Harold Ickes recorded.

> We spent a lot of time talking about the lend-lease bill and the question of England's financial ability to pay for more material in this country. Over and over again, in a loud voice and with his customary bad English, Garner kept insisting that he was under the impression from what had been said at Cabinet on previous occasions that the British had plenty of wealth in this country that could be turned into dollars and used to buy munitions. The burden of his song was: "Why, Mr. President, you told us that the British had three or four billion of dollars in this country that could be spent here. The British, per capita, are the richest in the world, and if they care anything about their freedom, they ought to be willing to spend all that they have."

Roosevelt might have ignored Garner but for the fact that the crusty Texan articulated, in his distinctive way, an undercurrent of Anglophobia that still flowed broadly in America. Roosevelt wanted not simply a victory on Lend-Lease but a mandate. The measure would be a vote of confidence in his ability to guide America through the troubles ahead. To silence the skeptics he persuaded Churchill to open Britain's account books to American perusal. "So far as I know," Henry Morgenthau told the House foreign affairs committee, "this is the first time in history that one government has put at the disposal of another figures of this nature." The numbers revealed that the British were indeed strapped, for ready cash if not for illiquid assets. In any event, the whole purpose of Lend-Lease was to put off haggling over just such questions until the military emergency was past.

Churchill provided crucial assistance of another sort. In a radio speech broadcast to America, the prime minister explained that Britain did not want and would not require American troops. "In the last war the United States sent two million men across the Atlantic, but this is not a war of vast armies, hurling immense masses of shells at one another," Churchill said. "We do not need the gallant armies which are forming throughout the American Union. We do not need them this year, nor the next year, nor any year that I can foresee." Roosevelt had sent Churchill part of a poem by Longfellow. "I think this verse applies to you people as it does to us," Roosevelt had written. Churchill now read the verse to the American people:

> Sail on, Oh Ship of State!
> Sail on, Oh Union strong and great!
> Humanity with all its fears,
> With all the hopes of future years,
> Is hanging breathless on thy fate!

The prime minister asked rhetorically what answer he could give to Roosevelt, "this great man, the thrice-chosen head of a nation of 130 million?" The answer was simply this:

> Put your confidence in us. Give us your faith and your blessing, and under Providence all will be well. We shall not fail or falter; we shall not weaken or tire. . . . Give us the tools and we will finish the job.

Equally essential to the success of the Lend-Lease bill was the cooperation of certain members of Congress who hadn't backed the president on other issues. The war in Europe was splintering the opposition to the administration. Since Roosevelt's first term, the anti–New Deal coalition had consisted of Republicans, conservative southern Democrats, and some maverick western Democrats. The war aroused different emotions than the New Deal, and even as many Republicans crossed party lines to join the president, southern Democrats, reflecting the strong patriotic streak of their region, found their way to the president's side. The support of the Southerners was amplified—just as their opposition had been—by their control of the most important committees. After Henry Morgenthau satisfied the pertinent committees regarding the effects of Lend-Lease on American finance, and Cordell Hull, Henry Stimson, and Frank Knox did the same regarding American diplomacy, the American army, and the American navy, respectively, the committees reported the bill favorably to their full houses.

More important than anything, though, was Roosevelt's personal popularity. The 1940 election had demonstrated his appeal to the American people as of November; his actions and words since then had enhanced the widespread feeling that this was the man who should be leading the country through these dangerous times. A poll conducted amid the deliberations over Lend-Lease put the president's approval rating at 71 percent, the highest in the seven-year history of the Gallup organization.

With the stars aligned, Lend-Lease moved steadily, if deliberately, through Congress. An isolationist filibuster was averted. Amendments were added, dropped, revised, and re-added, without materially altering the president's design. The Senate and House passed the measure in early March, the former by a vote of 60 to 31, the latter by 317 to 71.

"Let not the dictators of Europe or Asia doubt our unanimity now," Roosevelt declared. "Yes, the decisions of our democracy may be slowly arrived at. But when that decision is made, it is proclaimed not with the voice of any one man but with the voice of one hundred and thirty millions. It is binding on us all. And the world is no longer left in doubt."

41.

$\mathcal{H}$ARRY HOPKINS ARRIVED IN LONDON MIDWAY THROUGH THE CON-gressional debate over Lend-Lease. Edward R. Murrow, the American jour-nalist who had made his reputation broadcasting news of the German blitz against the British capital, met Hopkins and inquired what brought him to England. "I suppose you could say that I've come here to try to find a way to be a catalytic agent between two prima donnas," Hopkins replied.

One of the prima donnas Hopkins knew as well as anyone did. By early 1941 Hopkins had become Roosevelt's indispensable man. He combined the functions of a civilian chief of staff and a cabinet secretary without portfolio. He had instant access to the president and to whatever passed across the pres-ident's desk. He knew what Roosevelt knew; he often felt what Roosevelt felt, sometimes before Roosevelt did. And he juggled all this without holding any formal title. "The extraordinary fact," Robert Sherwood wrote, "was that the second most important individual in the United States Government during the most critical period of the world's greatest war had no legitimate official position nor even any desk of his own except a card table in his bedroom. However, the bedroom was in the White House."

Hopkins moved into the White House in the spring of 1940. His bedroom—a suite, actually—was located in the southeast corner of the second floor, look-ing out across the lawn to the Washington Monument and the Virginia hills beyond the Potomac. The suite had been a single room during the Civil War, when Abraham Lincoln used it as his study. Hopkins's four-poster bed dis-placed the desk on which the Emancipation Proclamation was signed. More recently the suite had served as quarters for distinguished guests; Britain's George VI slept there during a state visit in 1939. After Hopkins moved in, guests stayed across the hall, in the suite in the northeast corner. On several visits to Washington during the war, Winston Churchill would become quite familiar with Hopkins, as they bumped into each other in the hall every day.

The acquaintance began in January 1941. For some time Roosevelt had been dissatisfied at having to communicate with Churchill through letters and the occasional telephone call. The destroyers-for-bases deal could have been concluded much sooner, he believed, if he had been able to speak with Churchill in person. A comparable thought occurred to him as he laid the groundwork for Lend-Lease and had to estimate Britain's liquid assets and its collateral. "You know," he told Hopkins, "a lot of this could be settled if Churchill and I could just sit down together for a while."

"What's stopping you?" Hopkins rejoined.

"Well, it couldn't be arranged right now." Roosevelt couldn't leave America with his historic third inauguration pending, and he couldn't invite Churchill without seeming to confirm the isolationists' charge that he was selling the country out to England.

"How about me going over, Mr. President?"

Roosevelt initially rejected the idea. Hopkins had charge of the president's speech writing team, among his other duties, and with the annual message and the inaugural address coming up, Roosevelt didn't think he could spare him. Besides, Hopkins would manage the administration's end of the contest for Lend-Lease.

Hopkins responded that the president's regular speech writers—Sam Rosenman and Bob Sherwood—knew their work well enough to get along without supervision. Anyway, Roosevelt always did the final editing himself. As for managing the Lend-Lease bill, Hopkins said he would do as much harm as good with the lawmakers. "They'd never pay any attention to my views, except to vote the other way."

Roosevelt still refused. Yet some weeks later, without informing Hopkins of any change of mind, he announced at a press conference that Hopkins would be traveling to England as his "personal representative."

The reporters knew Hopkins had the president's ear and confidence. "Does Mr. Hopkins have any special mission, Mr. President?" one asked.

"No, no, no!"

"Any title?"

"No, no."

"Will anyone accompany Mr. Hopkins?"

"No, and he will have no powers."

Though Hopkins had lobbied for the mission, the journey almost killed him. He had never fully recovered from his cancer and surgery, and transoceanic air travel, especially during wartime, tested the hardiest constitution. Hopkins flew by Pan American Clipper, a flying boat better known for durability than for speed or comfort. He suffered horribly from motion sickness and had to be guided gently off the plane after it reached England. But he was taken in hand by the British government and made as comfortable as possible in London.

For all Roosevelt's press conference disclaimers, Hopkins had a definite, if somewhat unspecific, mission. "I want to try to get an understanding of Churchill and of the men he sees after midnight," he told Edward Murrow. His first meeting with the prime minister took place not long after his arrival. "Number 10 Downing Street is a bit down at the heels because the Treasury next door has been bombed a bit," Hopkins reported to Roosevelt. "The Prime Minister is no longer permitted to sleep here and I understand sleeps across the street." Brendan Bracken, Churchill's personal assistant, guided Hopkins in.

> Bracken led me to a little dining room in the basement, poured me some sherry, and left me to wait for the Prime Minister. A rotund, smiling, red-faced gentleman appeared, extended a fat but none the less convincing hand and wished me welcome to England. A short black coat, striped trousers, a clear eye, and a mushy voice was the impression of England's leader as he showed me with obvious pride the photography of his beautiful daughter-in-law and grandchild.

Hopkins told Churchill that President Roosevelt would be happy for a chance to meet the prime minister, but only later in the spring, after the Lend-Lease program was safely launched. Churchill reciprocated the feeling. "He talked of remaining as long as two weeks and seemed very anxious to meet the President face to face," Hopkins recounted.

Churchill reflected on the war to date and projected its future course. He said Germany could not invade Britain successfully. "He thinks Hitler may use poison gas," Hopkins related, "but if they do England will reply in kind, killing man for man—'for we too have the deadliest gases in the world'—but under no circumstances will they be used unless the Germans release gas first." The prime minister asserted that air power would determine the outcome of the war. "Churchill said that while Germany's bombers were at the ratio of 2½ to 1"—as against the British—"at the present time, that would soon be reduced to 1½ to 1, and then he felt they could hold their own in the air. Indeed he looks forward, with our help, to mastery in the air, and then Germany with all her armies will be finished. He believes that this war will never see great forces massed against one another."

Hopkins had intended to be in England for a couple weeks; instead he stayed six. Churchill fascinated him. The prime minister held the key to Britain's success, Hopkins told Roosevelt.

> *Churchill* is the government in every sense of the word. He controls the grand strategy and often the details. Labor trusts him. The army, navy, air force are behind him to a man. The politicians and upper crust tend to like him. I cannot emphasize too strongly that he is the one and only person over here with whom you need to have a full meeting of minds.

Hopkins wasn't simply gathering intelligence for Roosevelt; he was also representing Roosevelt to the British. The president, of course, appreciated this part of the mission, and he guessed Hopkins would charm his hosts, in his disarmingly American way, as much as he had charmed Roosevelt. And so he did. From valets to cabinet ministers they praised his unaffected, unassuming approach. "Mr. Hopkins was very genial, considerate—if I may say so, lovable," a waiter at Claridge's Hotel, which Hopkins made his headquarters, remarked. Max Beaverbrook, Churchill's minister of war production, hosted a dinner for Hopkins and invited the London press. "Hopkins rose, looking lean, shy and untidy, grasping the back of his chair," a reporter present recalled.

> His words were private, so no notes were taken. But if it had been possible to record the sentences that came quietly and diffidently from the lips of Harry Hopkins they would have compared well for nobility of expression with the splendid oration which Mr. Roosevelt had delivered two days earlier when he was sworn in for the third time as President of the United States.
>
> Not that Hopkins repeated or even echoed the President's speech. He talked in more intimate terms. Where the President had spoken of America's duty to the world, Hopkins told us how the President and those around him were convinced that America's world duty could be successfully performed only in partnership with Britain. He told us of the anxiety and admiration with which every phase of Britain's lonely struggle was watched from the White House, and of his own emotions as he travelled through our blitzed land. His speech left us with the feeling that although America was not yet in the war, she was marching beside us, and that should we stumble she would

see we did not fall. Above all he convinced us that the President and the men about him blazed with faith in the future of democracy.

❖   ❖   ❖

THE FOREIGN REACTIONS to Lend-Lease varied predictably by country and government. Adolf Hitler scorned the program as desperately ineffectual. "No power and no support coming from any part of the world can change the outcome of this battle in any respect," the German dictator declared. "International finance and plutocracy wants to fight this war to the finish. So the end of this war will, and must, be its destruction." A spokesman for Joseph Stalin interpreted the new development in similarly economic terms: "The war is taking the form of a contest between the world's strongest capitalist industrial machines—a contest for speed, quantity, and quality in the production of weapons."

The prospective recipients of the American aid naturally adopted a more positive view. Churchill declared the program "a new Magna Charta, which not only has regard to the rights and laws upon which a healthy and advancing civilization can alone be erected, but also proclaims, by precept and example, the duty of free men and free nations, wherever they may be, to share the responsibility and burden of enforcing them." Robert Gordon Menzies, the prime minister of Australia, which with the rest of the empire was fighting alongside Britain, said to the Americans, "You are neutral and we are at war, but you have made the whole world understand that the moral and material might of a great neutral country can always be placed behind the belligerent who fights for justice." Jan Christiaan Smuts, the South African prime minister and senior member of Britain's imperial war cabinet, put the matter most succinctly and, arguably, most accurately. "Hitler has at last brought America into the war," Smuts said.

Roosevelt still resisted this characterization but with nothing like the verve of the previous months. The convincing majorities for Lend-Lease demonstrated the willingness of Americans to look the Axis danger in the face. And the language of the Lend-Lease Act revealed Congress's confidence in Roosevelt to guide them against that danger. Entitled "An Act to Promote the Defense of the United States," the measure authorized the president to "sell, transfer title to, exchange, lease, lend, or otherwise dispose of" any defense article to "the government of any country whose defense the President deems vital to the defense of the United States." Not without reason had critics of the bill called it a blank check.

Roosevelt's first move upon passage of the bill was to ask Congress to fill in the blank on the amount line of the check. He sought $7 billion, which had seemed a huge sum only months before but now looked like a mere down payment. In supporting his request, Roosevelt spoke in more belligerent terms than ever. The vote in favor of Lend-Lease, he said, was "the end of any attempts at appeasement in our land, . . . the end of compromise with tyranny and the forces of oppression." The decision to join the struggle required that Americans make sacrifices. "Whether you are in the armed services; whether you are a steel worker or a stevedore; a machinist or a housewife; a farmer or a banker; a storekeeper or a manufacturer—to all of you it will mean sacrifice in behalf of your country and your liberties." Americans would experience the war effort in their daily lives. "You will have to be content with lower profits, lower profits from business because obviously your taxes will be higher. You will have to work longer at your bench, or your plow, or your machine, or your desk." Some Americans might think that since the fighting remained far away, they weren't as deeply involved as those on the front lines. Such an attitude could lead to disaster. "It's an all-out effort—and nothing short of an all-out effort will win."

❖ ❖ ❖

ℛOOSEVELT CONTRIBUTED to the all-out effort by exercising his executive powers to the limit. He created, by presidential fiat, an Office of Price Administration and Civilian Supply, modeled on the executive agencies that commandeered the American economy during the First World War, and a National Defense Mediation Board, to settle strikes that threatened to disrupt war production. He jawboned coal miners and operators in a bituminous dispute to resume mining—"in the interest of national safety." He urged labor and management in general to adopt a wartime mentality. "Our problem is to see to it that there is no idle critical machine in the United States," he said. "The goal should be to work these machines twenty-four hours a day and seven days a week." He requested new funds to allow the National Youth Administration to train defense workers. He seized foreign cargo ships in American ports, where many of them had been caught by the war, on grounds that they were clogging the harbors and could be put to better use by the American merchant marine.

He ordered the secretary of war to supervise a major increase in the production of heavy bombers. "Command of the air by the democracies must and can be achieved," he said.

He kicked off a campaign for the sale of Defense Savings Bonds and Defense Postal Savings Stamps by purchasing the first bond for Eleanor and the first hundred stamps for his grandchildren. He called on Congress to raise taxes to pay for the war effort. "Defense is a national task to which every American must contribute in accordance with his talents and treasure," he wrote Robert Doughton, the chairman of the House ways and means committee.

He redrew the map of the Western Hemisphere, annexing Greenland to greater North America and thereby casting the net of the Monroe Doctrine around that North Atlantic island. He negotiated American basing rights in Greenland with the stranded Danish ambassador. "Under the present circumstances the Government in Denmark cannot, of course, act in respect of its territory in the Western Hemisphere," Roosevelt explained.

He ordered American warships to extend their patrols far out into the Atlantic and protect the Lend-Lease fleet against Germany's disconcertingly successful submarine campaign. But he did so quietly, even deceptively, denying that the patrols were anything like convoys. When reporters pressed him on the matter, he insisted on the difference, though he had difficulty explaining what that difference was. "I think some of you know what a horse looks like," he said. "I think you also know what a cow looks like. If, by calling a cow a horse for a year and a half, you think that that makes the cow a horse, I don't think so."

"Mr. President, can you tell us the difference between a patrol and a convoy?"

"You know the difference between a cow and a horse?"

Roosevelt's spring campaign of war readiness culminated at the end of May with a declaration of unlimited national emergency. "What started as a European war has developed, as the Nazis always intended it should develop, into a world war for world domination," the president told the American people. Those persons who contended that Hitler had no designs beyond Europe were the same ones who had said he had no designs on Czechoslovakia, Poland, Belgium, or France. Yet even if Hitler left the Americas alone, the consequences of Nazi rule elsewhere would destroy the American way of life.

The American laborer would have to compete with slave labor in the rest of the world. Minimum wages, maximum hours? Nonsense! Wages and hours

would be fixed by Hitler. . . . Farm income? What happens to all farm surpluses without any foreign trade? The American farmer would get for his
products exactly what Hitler wanted to give. . . . Even our right of worship
would be threatened. The Nazi world does not recognize any God except
Hitler.

Roosevelt told his radio audience that the central front in the struggle
against fascism had shifted from the air over Britain to the seaways that linked
the Old World to the New. The Battle of the Atlantic extended from the ice
pack around Greenland nearly to Antarctica. German submarines were torpedoing British ships, and even neutral vessels, at an alarming rate. The British
were fighting valiantly, but they weren't winning. The Germans were sinking
ships far faster than the British—even with American help—could replace
them. Until now the United States hadn't taken on the Germans directly, Roosevelt said. Nor would America take them on unless attacked. Yet Americans
must understand what it meant to be attacked in the age of modern warfare.
"Some people seem to think that we are not attacked until bombs actually
drop in the streets of New York or San Francisco or New Orleans or
Chicago. . . . They are simply shutting their eyes to the lesson that we must
learn from the fate of every nation that the Nazis have conquered." Americans
must prepare themselves ahead of the attack. "It would be suicide to wait until
they are in our front yard."

Roosevelt explained that in strengthening American patrols of the Atlantic
he would be guided by two fundamental principles:

> First, we shall actively resist wherever necessary, and with all our re-
> sources, every attempt by Hitler to extend his Nazi domination to the West-
> ern Hemisphere. . . .
>
> Second, from the point of view of strict naval and military necessity, we
> shall give every possible assistance to Britain and to all who, with Britain, are
> resisting Hitlerism or its equivalent with force of arms.

The implementation of these principles demanded the utmost effort by the entire country—hence the declaration of national emergency. "The nation will
expect all individuals and all groups to play their full parts, without stint, and
without selfishness, and without doubt that our democracy will triumphantly
survive."

❖ ❖ ❖

THREE WEEKS LATER the worst-kept secret in modern military history surprised the only person who really needed to know it. The chancelleries, embassies, and intelligence ministries of Western Europe had been buzzing for months with rumors that Hitler was going to double-cross Stalin and attack the Soviet Union. The rumors were plausible enough. No one believed that the Nazi-Soviet non-aggression pact of 1939 had been anything more than a truce of convenience, and almost everyone believed that Hitler, frustrated by his failure to batter the British into surrendering, would be just the type to take out his frustrations on the Russians. The single thing that cast doubt on the rumors was that a German attack on the Soviets would be so stupid. Why would Hitler willingly take on a new enemy—one as large and manpower-rich as Russia—before he had defeated the enemies he already had? But perhaps that was the diabolical genius of the plan: it was so patently stupid that Stalin would never believe Hitler would attempt it.

Plenty of other people believed he would. "From every source at my disposal including some most trustworthy, it looks as if a vast German onslaught on the Russian frontier is imminent," Churchill wrote Roosevelt on June 14. "Not only are the main German armies deployed from Finland to Roumania, but the final arrivals of air and armoured forces are being completed." If true, the rumors foretold a crucial shift in the nature of the war. "Should this new war break out, we shall of course give all encouragement and any help we can spare to the Russians, following the principle that Hitler is the foe we have to beat. I do not expect any class political reactions here and trust that a German-Russian conflict will not cause you any embarrassment."

Embarrassment wasn't the word Roosevelt would have used. When Germany on June 22 did indeed attack the Soviet Union, opening an eastern front in the European war, Hitler went far toward making a prophet of Roosevelt, who had already declared the conflict a world war, provoked by Hitler's insatiable appetite for conquest. But beyond the satisfaction that came from proven prescience, Roosevelt couldn't help fearing that this new development would complicate the strategy he was gradually laying out before the American people. Roosevelt remembered how Wilson had capitalized on the first stage of the Russian revolution of 1917, which toppled the czar and brought Russia—briefly—into the realm of democracy. At the moment of requesting a war declaration, Wilson had been able to say that the purpose of the war was to make the world safe for democracy. Roosevelt had been following Wilson till now, stressing that the most visible victims of fascism had been democracies. By attacking Stalin—by diverting the major part of his army from Western Europe to the East—Hitler lessened the logistical strain on the emerging Anglo-American alliance, but he added to Roosevelt's political burdens. The president only lately had begun to feel that the isolationists were being effectively neutralized; this would give them new life. Should he assert that the United States ought to assist the Soviets—as Churchill clearly wanted America to do—the isolationists' complaint that American resources were propping up British imperialism would be echoed by their outcry that the administration was supporting communism.

Churchill pushed the president harder, and more publicly, in a radio address broadcast in America as well as Britain. "It is not for me to speak of the action of the United States," the prime minister acknowledged. "But this I will say: if Hitler imagines that his attack on Soviet Russia will cause the slightest divergence of aims or slackening of effort in the great democracies who are resolved upon his doom, he is woefully mistaken." Anyone could see that whatever helped Hitler hurt the cause of freedom, and what harmed Hitler served freedom. "The Russian danger is, therefore, our danger and the danger of the United States, just as the cause of any Russian fighting for his hearth and home is the cause of free men and free peoples in every quarter of the globe."

Roosevelt wasn't inclined to be so forthright. He let the State Department weigh in on the relative merits of fascism and communism. Both systems denied fundamental human freedoms, including the right to worship as one's conscience directed, Undersecretary Sumner Welles explained. Yet in wartime choices had to be made. Hitler was on the offensive against democracy; Stalin was not. The conclusion was irresistible: "Any rallying of the forces opposing Hitlerism, from whatever source these forces may spring, will hasten the eventual downfall of the present German leaders and will therefore redound to the benefit of our own defense and security." Even so, Welles declined to say whether the United States would assist the Soviets in their fight against Germany. And he told reporters that Roosevelt hadn't made a decision on the subject.

Welles wasn't exactly lying; Roosevelt had not made a formal decision on aid to Russia. He knew what he intended to do, but he wished to gauge the public reaction before he shared his thinking with the public. The isolationists responded much as he expected. "It's a case of dog-eat-dog," Senator Bennett Clark, a Democrat from Missouri, declared. "Stalin is as bloody-handed as Hitler. I don't think we should help either one. We should tend to our own business, as we should have been doing all along." Harry Truman, Missouri's other senator, also a Democrat, suggested an even-handed—and bloody-handed—approach. "If we see that Germany is winning we ought to help Russia," Truman said. "If Russia is winning we ought to help Germany. . . . Let them kill as many as possible." Truman tilted slightly toward Stalin, however: "I don't want to see Hitler victorious under any circumstances." Robert M. La Follette, the Wisconsin Progressive, predicted that interventionists in America—he didn't identify Roosevelt by name, but he didn't have to—would soon begin "the greatest whitewash act in all history," to make Russia into an acceptable ally. "The American people will be told to forget the purges in Russia by the OGPU, the confiscation of property, the persecution of religion, the invasion of Finland, and the vulture role Stalin played in seizing half of prostrate Poland."

Eight months earlier—before the 1940 election—Roosevelt might have heeded the criticism and stepped back. But when the isolationists' arguments failed to catch on with the broader public, the president moved swiftly to put Russia on the American aid list. He ordered the Treasury to release $40 million in Soviet assets that had been frozen when Moscow and Berlin were de facto allies, and he directed that export licenses be granted to the Kremlin for items previously barred.

"Is the defense of Russia the defense of the United States?" a reporter asked.

Roosevelt declined to answer. But he made clear by his actions that the defense of Russia would *assist* the defense of the United States.

❖ ❖ ❖

FOR TWO DECADES Missy LeHand had scarcely left Roosevelt's side. She served as secretary, gatekeeper, surrogate wife, second mother, adoring partisan, loving friend. She gave up any semblance of a normal life to serve him. He knew it, and he loved her for it. And when she fell ill, typically from overwork and overworry, he suffered from the loss of her steady support and warm companionship.

She had experienced a few breakdowns before but each time had quickly recovered. In June 1941, however, the day before the Germans invaded Russia, she collapsed from a major stroke. Her right side was paralyzed, and she could no longer speak. Roosevelt ensured she was well cared for, and amid the stunning news from Europe and the complications the new twist in the war created for American policy, the president spent time each day at her hospital bedside. He told her stories: about office politics, about Churchill's latest letter or cable, about his troubles with the isolationists. She couldn't reply, and he didn't know how much of what he said she understood. He laughed, in the bluff way he had long laughed at his own infirmity. She couldn't laugh but only cry.

When the doctors at the hospital had done all they could for her, he put her on the train to Warm Springs. He paid for her medical care and rehabilitation, and when it became apparent that she would never recover, he revised his will to ensure her support in the event he died before she did. "I owed her that much," he told James. "She served me so well for so long, and asked so little in return."

*　*　*

 As MISSY's CANDLE flickered, another flame glowed brighter. Since their 1918 parting, Roosevelt and Lucy Mercer had kept their distance from each other. She married a widower, Winthrop Rutherfurd, who was as much older than she was as James Roosevelt had been older than Sara. Lucy was devoted to Rutherfurd, bearing him one child, looking after his five other children, and tending to him as his health eventually failed. But she couldn't help observing the rise of Franklin Roosevelt. They corresponded sporadically. She congratulated him on the birth of his first grandchild—"though I do not know exactly what one's feelings are on that question," she wrote. He asked Missy to get her a ticket to his 1933 inaugural ceremony and to send the White House limousine to fetch her from her sister's house near Dupont Circle. They didn't meet on this day, or at his second or third inaugural ceremony, both of which Lucy likewise attended.

They spoke occasionally by phone. Through Missy and Grace Tully he let the White House operator know that her calls were to be put directly through to him. Sometimes they conversed in French, lest passing ears listen in. They talked of old times and old friends and of the latest news.

Their first personal encounter in over two decades seems to have occurred in June 1941, about the time of Missy's stroke. Lucy's husband had also suffered a stroke, and Lucy traveled to Washington to request the president's help in getting Winthrop admitted to Walter Reed Hospital. The White House log recorded her as "Mrs. Johnson" and indicated that the visit lasted almost two hours.

What the one-time lovers said to each other on this occasion cannot be known. They wrote nothing down, and the White House staff exercised the greatest discretion in keeping the visit quiet. But the meeting lifted for a moment the burdens each carried—his great burdens of state, her more personal burdens—and they agreed to meet again.

❖ ❖ ❖

AMERICAN OFFICIALS expected Japan to exploit the sudden shift in the European war; their only question was how audacious Tokyo would become now that Russia, Japan's historic competitor in Northeast Asia, was fighting for its life against Germany. "There are two groups in Japan," Cordell Hull told Lord Halifax, the British ambassador in Washington. "One is pro-German; the other is a peace group among high officials." The secretary of state explained that his sources asserted that the latter group wanted to turn away from Japan's aggressive policies, to pull Japanese troops out of China, and to prevent a Pacific war. "But I have not taken this too seriously," Hull added.

Roosevelt wasn't taking it too seriously either—although he refused to discount it entirely. As America's involvement in Europe increased, the president sought to maintain America's distance from Asia. Hitler posed a central threat to America, Roosevelt judged; Japan merely a peripheral one. The United States would have to deal with Japan's warlords eventually, but not now. If a peace party, however tentative, existed in Tokyo, American policy ought to help it along.

The peace party seemed to weaken during the summer of 1941. In July Japanese troops occupied southern Indochina. The Japanese ambassador explained to Sumner Welles, filling in for the ailing Hull, that Japan imported a million tons of rice each year from Indochina and that it feared that "de Gaullist French agents" and "Chinese agitators" were fomenting unrest in the region. The move was strictly precautionary.

The ambassador repeated his argument the next day to Roosevelt, who wasn't buying it. The president lectured the ambassador on the patience the United States had shown Japan during the preceding two years. At substantial expense to America's own war effort, the administration had allowed the export of oil products to Japan. Roosevelt was candid as to his motives. "If these oil supplies had been shut off or restricted, the Japanese government and people would have been furnished with an incentive or a pretext for moving down upon the Netherlands East Indies." The United States had sought peace in

Southeast Asia, and it still sought it. But the latest move by Japan, into southern Indochina, created an "exceedingly serious problem" for the United States. The ambassador's contention that it was defensive didn't wash. Surely the Japanese government did not think that any outside power, especially under present circumstances, had designs on Indochina. And as for rice production, the mere occupation by military forces would disrupt the supply chain more than any subversion by alleged foreign agents.

Roosevelt offered to guarantee Japan what it said it wanted from Indochina. He would do "everything within his power" to obtain an international agreement to neutralize Indochina, to prevent Gaullist or Chinese agents from getting a foothold there, and to ensure that Japan received the rice it required. But in exchange Japan must withdraw its forces from the region. Roosevelt added a warning that although Germany might be Japan's ally at the moment, the Japanese would gravely err to put much trust in Berlin. Russia was discovering the depths of German treachery. Hitler, the president said, intended the "complete domination of the world." Japan would not be exempt.

Roosevelt expected little positive response from Tokyo. "I have had no answer yet," he wrote Harry Hopkins a few days later. "When it comes it will probably be unfavorable. But we have at least made one more effort to avoid Japanese expansion."

Roosevelt decided not to wait. On July 26 he took his strongest step thus far: he froze Japanese assets in the United States. The executive order sounded fairly innocuous; its purpose was "to prevent the use of the financial facilities of the United States and trade between Japan and the United States in ways harmful to national defense and American interests." But the effects of the order could be devastating. The American president, without consulting Congress, had declared economic war on Japan.

42.

Joseph Davies had been American ambassador to Moscow during the 1930s. His tolerance for Stalinism was thought by certain of his professional peers to be excessive—some said his memoir, *Mission to Moscow,* should have been titled *Submission to Moscow*—but he had the distinction of being one of the very few Americans who had ever met Stalin personally, and Roosevelt wanted to know whether he thought Stalin and the Russians could survive the German onslaught. "The resistance of the Russian Army has been more effective than was generally expected," Davies replied. Yet the outcome still hung in the balance. Davies supposed the Germans might well conquer White Russia, the Ukraine, and much of Russia proper, perhaps including Moscow. But Stalin could retreat beyond the Urals and carry on the fight from there. Either of two contingencies might prevent such action: an internal revolution that toppled Stalin in favor of a pro-German regime, or a decision by Stalin himself to make peace. Davies thought the former unlikely, given the historic tendency of Russians to rally around "Mother Russia" in time of trouble. The latter would depend on Stalin's assessment of the balance of forces. "Stalin is oriental, coldly realistic, and getting along in years," Davies wrote. "He believes that Russia is surrounded by capitalistic enemies. In '38 and '39 he had no confidence in the good faith of either Britain or France or the capacity of the democracies to be effective against Hitler. He hated and feared Hitler then just as he does now. He was induced to make a pact of nonaggression with Hitler as the best hope he had for preserving peace for Russia." He might do so again.

Such an outcome must be prevented at any cost, Davies said. If it *was* prevented, the results would be most beneficial to America. Hitler had taken a huge chance by invading Russia; for the United States to keep Russia fighting would probably spell his doom. Moreover, cultivating Russia would increase America's leverage with Japan, which would have to worry about its back as it drove farther south. For these reasons, the Russians must not be allowed to think that the likes of Harry Truman spoke for the American government.

> Specifically, I fear that if they get the impression that the United States is only using them, and if sentiment grows and finds expression that the United States is equally a capitalistic enemy, it would be playing directly into the hands of Hitler, and he can be counted upon to use this in his efforts to project either an armistice or peace on the Russian front. . . . Word ought to be gotten to Stalin direct that our attitude is "all out" to beat Hitler.

This was precisely the word Harry Hopkins took to Moscow, on Roosevelt's behalf. The president agreed with Davies—and with Churchill—that necessity mandated cooperation with the communists of Russia against the fascists of Germany. Roosevelt didn't underestimate the differences between the United States and the Soviet Union and between democracy and communism. But Nazi Germany was the great danger of the moment, and Roosevelt believed in dealing with first things first.

"I ask you to treat Mr. Hopkins with the identical confidence you would feel if you were talking directly to me," Roosevelt wrote Stalin, in a letter of introduction Hopkins carried to Moscow in late July 1941. "He will communicate directly to me the views that you express to him and will tell me what you consider are the most pressing individual problems on which we could be of aid."

Hopkins discovered that diplomacy among the Russians was not for the faint of heart—or head or belly. "It was monumental," he wrote of the dinner honoring him on his arrival. "It lasted almost four hours." The food came in course after groaning course, the drink in toast after mind-blurring toast. Hopkins hadn't had much experience with vodka, but he was a quick study. "Vodka has authority. It is nothing for the amateur to trifle with. Drink it as an American or an Englishman takes whiskey neat, and it will tear you apart. The thing to do is to spread a chunk of bread (and good bread it was) with caviar, and, while you are swallowing that, bolt your vodka. Don't play with the stuff. Eat while you're drinking it—something that will act as a shock absorber for it."

Stalin was an acquired taste, as well. He told Hopkins he reciprocated Roosevelt's desire for frank communications, and then he launched into a lecture on political morality. "Mr. Stalin spoke of the necessity of there being a minimum moral standard between all nations," Hopkins wrote Roosevelt. "Without such a minimum moral standard, nations could not co-exist. He stated that the present leaders of Germany knew no such minimum moral standard and that, therefore, they represented an anti-social force in the present world." The Germans thought nothing of signing a treaty one day, breaking it the next, and signing a new and contradictory treaty. "Nations must fulfill their treaty obligations," Stalin said. "Or international society could not exist."

Hopkins didn't know what to make of Stalin's sermonizing. This was the man who murdered his political opponents and liquidated entire classes of people—and now he was complaining of Hitler's lack of integrity? Hopkins was relieved when the talk turned more concrete, to the subject of American aid. "I told Mr. Stalin that the question of aid to the Soviet Union was divided into two parts. First, what would Russia most require that the United States could deliver immediately, and, second, what would be Russia's requirements on the basis of a long war?"

Stalin evidently had given the matter serious thought. In the immediate category he specified twenty thousand anti-aircraft guns, a million rifles, and an unspecified number of large-caliber machine guns. Over the longer term he wanted aviation fuel and aluminum for airplane construction. "Give us anti-aircraft guns and the aluminum and we can fight for three or four years," he said.

At a second meeting—also held in the evening, as Stalin's meetings typically were—Hopkins asked for Stalin's frank assessment of the fighting. Stalin admitted to having been surprised by the German invasion; even till the last moment, he said, he had not believed that Hitler would strike. As a result of his error, many of Russia's 180 divisions had been far from the frontier when the battle began, and the Germans enjoyed an early advantage. But in the month since then, Russia had mobilized another 50 divisions, and expected to muster as many as 350 divisions by the spring of 1942. He guessed that Germany could field 300 divisions. He said he was eager to get as many of his divisions as possible into battle—"because then the troops learn that Germans can be killed and are not supermen." He characterized the morale of the Russian soldiers as "extremely high," acknowledging that this said less about socialism than about patriotism. "They are fighting for their homes and in familiar territory." As for the Germans, they seemed to be tired. German prisoners said they were "sick of war." Even so, the Germans couldn't be counted out. "Stalin repeatedly stated that he did not underrate the German Army," Hopkins wrote Roosevelt. "He stated that their organization was of the very best and that he believed that they had large reserves of food, men, supplies, and fuel." Stalin said that part of the reason the British had failed to stand up to the Germans in 1940 was that they had underrated the Wehrmacht. "He did not propose to do this." He thought the Germans had sufficient fuel, food, and reserves to conduct a winter campaign, but autumn rains would prevent anything more than defensive actions after the beginning of October. By then the Red Army would have dug in. "Mr. Stalin expressed repeatedly his confidence that the Russian lines would hold within 100 kilometers of their present position"—in other words, west of Leningrad, Moscow, and Kiev.

Looking further into the future, Stalin said that it was "inevitable" that the United States would enter the war. "The might of Germany was so great that, even though Russia might defend herself, it would be very difficult for Britain and Russia combined to crush the German military machine." Possibly the mere declaration of war by the United States would break German morale. But more likely the war would be "bitter and long." Stalin said he looked forward to joint operations. "He wanted me to tell the President that he would welcome the American troops on any part of the Russian front, under the complete command of the American army." He also welcomed working with President Roosevelt. "He repeatedly said that the President and the United States had more influence with the common people of the world today than any other force."

Hopkins came away from his meetings most impressed: with the determination of the Russians to defend their territory and with Stalin as a man. "Not once did he repeat himself," Hopkins wrote. "There was no waste of word, gesture, nor mannerism. It was like talking to a perfectly coordinated machine, an intelligent machine." Stalin didn't lack a sense of humor, but it was as controlled as everything about the man. "He laughs often enough, but it's a short laugh, somewhat sardonic, perhaps. There is no small talk in him. His humor is keen, penetrating. He speaks no English, but as he shot rapid Russian at me he ignored his interpreter, looking straight into my eyes as though I understood every word that he uttered." Hopkins spent six hours with Stalin over two meetings. When the second meeting ended, Hopkins's time with the dictator was over. "He said good-bye once, just as only once he said hello. And that was that."

❖   ❖   ❖

During the spring of 1941, as the German emphasis in the war against Britain shifted from the air to the sea, from an attempt to bomb the British into submission to an effort to starve them, German submarines and surface vessels targeted the convoys of ships that carried Lend-Lease provisions from America. Of the German surface vessels the most feared was the *Bismarck,* a great battleship that commenced service in May 1941. Fast, formidably armed, and heavily armored, the *Bismarck* prepared to prowl the North Atlantic, blast the convoys, refuel at sea, and wreak general havoc. The British knew about the *Bismarck* from naval attachés and others who had watched it being built before the war began, and they learned of its mission from messages intercepted and decrypted under the top-secret Ultra program. They sent their best ships, the battleship *Prince of Wales* and the battle cruiser *Hood,* to meet the *Bismarck* and its companion, the *Prinz Eugen,* in the Denmark Strait. But ten minutes into the battle the *Bismarck* put a fifteen-inch shell into the magazine of the *Hood,* touching off a tremendous explosion that split the *Hood* in two and sent the pieces directly to the bottom, with the loss of all but three of its crew of fourteen hundred. The *Prince of Wales,* also damaged, was forced to retreat, allowing the *Bismarck,* itself wounded and leaking fuel, to steam into the open Atlantic.

Churchill, alarmed at the threat the *Bismarck* posed to the lifeline from America and determined to avenge the *Hood*'s destruction, issued a terse order: "Sink the *Bismarck.*" Every available ship and aircraft was summoned to chase the German battleship. Torpedo planes scoured the surface of the sea; after finding the *Bismarck* they skimmed the waves below the effective field of its anti-aircraft guns and launched their single torpedoes before veering aside. The German ship zigzagged sharply to dodge the underwater missiles, but one scored a lucky hit near the vessel's rudder. The steering mechanism jammed, leaving the *Bismarck* to trace a large circle in the ocean. As the British realized the ship's disability, they closed in to deliver the coup de grace. They pounded the *Bismarck* relentlessly with shells and additional torpedoes. The ship's end came on the morning of May 27, when it sank in three miles of water.

The *Prince of Wales* had been repaired by the time Hopkins arrived in London en route home from Moscow. The Russian eating and drinking, the need to be as sharp as Stalin, and the thousands of miles of travel had nearly killed Roosevelt's envoy. "Harry returned dead beat," Churchill informed Roosevelt. Consequently Hopkins was most appreciative when Churchill offered to ferry him across the Atlantic in the finest style and comfort the Royal Navy could offer, aboard the *Prince of Wales.*

The warship was taking the prime minister to meet the American president. Roosevelt had put off seeing Churchill until now, mostly from fear of reviving the isolationists. But with the opening of the Russian front by the Germans and the extension of the Southeast Asian front by the Japanese, Roosevelt decided that the strategic benefits of a conference with Churchill outweighed the political costs.

Yet he shrouded the meeting in secrecy till he was confident of the outcome. He cited security as the reason, and security afforded ample cause for concern. Churchill was fair game for the Germans, and if a torpedo or bomb that killed the British prime minister also dispatched the American president, Churchill's principal supplier, no tears would fall in Berlin. Significantly, though, Churchill wasn't worried about the meeting's becoming known, and he prepared a statement that he and the president were rendezvousing "on board ship somewhere in the Atlantic." But Roosevelt vetoed even this vague announcement. "All that need be said is: 'The Prime Minister is on a short vacation,' " Roosevelt declared. "Any statement now is a direct invitation to the Germans to attack the Prime Minister and his party both going and returning. *When in doubt, say nothing!*"

The warning was wasted. Reporters in London noticed that Churchill's top military advisers had gone missing at the same time the prime minister dropped out of sight. Their counterparts in Washington remarked something similar about America's top brass and the president. British papers surmised publicly that something was afoot. German radio repeated the story before long.

Roosevelt nonetheless plotted an elaborate scheme for losing his newspaper tail. Newfoundland's Placentia Bay, where the United States was constructing one of the bases it had bargained the destroyers for, had been agreed upon as the site for the meeting. "I was faced with a practical problem of extreme difficulty," Roosevelt explained with after-the-fact relish. "I knew that the British prime minister is not constantly accompanied by newspaper men nor camera men, whereas I was always accompanied"—the only exceptions being sea cruises when newspapermen representing the press associations followed the president's vessel on escorting destroyers. To foil the reporters, Roosevelt informed them—or misinformed them—that he would be vacationing aboard the *Potomac* but that in light of the other demands on American defense he couldn't justify bringing a destroyer escort. The reporters would have to stay home.

They bought the story. He traveled by train to New London, Connecticut, where he made a show of boarding the *Potomac*. He stopped at Nonquit, Massachusetts, the next day, for a conspicuous shore visit and an afternoon of fishing in full view of the bathers on the beach. At dusk the *Potomac* steamed off in the direction of the Cape Cod Canal. The deception began as night fell. "At eight o'clock we reversed course," Roosevelt said.

> Going around the south end of Cuddyhunk Island, we anchored in the midst of seven U.S. warships at about 11 p.m., at Menemsha Bight on the western end of Martha's Vineyard. All ships were darkened. At dawn Tuesday, August fifth, the U.S.S. *Potomac* ran along side of the flagship U.S.S. *Augusta* and we transferred my mess crew, provisions, etc.
>
> We found on board Admiral Stark and General Marshall, who joined the *Augusta* via a destroyer from New York late the previous evening. At 6:30 a.m. the U.S.S. *Augusta* and the U.S.S. *Tuscaloosa,* accompanied by five new destroyers, stood out into the open sea. We headed east past Nantucket Shoals Lightship until we were far outside any shallow waters where hostile mines could conceivably be laid. That evening we were 250 miles out in the ocean.

Smiling to himself, Roosevelt prepared for his meeting with Churchill. He knew that Churchill would be asking more than he—Roosevelt—was inclined to give. Churchill wanted commitments: ideally a commitment by the United States to enter the war, but at least a commitment to some specific war aims. American commitments would serve two purposes: they would ease the military burden on Britain, and they would lessen the political strain on Churchill's government. Ordinary politics in Britain had been suspended by the war; Churchill faced no general election in the near term, and he didn't worry much about a no-confidence vote in Parliament. But he had bet his political future on defeating Hitler, and he didn't see how it could be done without American belligerence.

Roosevelt was as leery of commitment as Churchill was eager for it. Roosevelt remembered the Allied secret treaties of the First World War and what an embarrassment they had become for Wilson. Any commitments that emerged from a secret meeting with Churchill would be lumped into a comparably invidious category not only by the isolationists but by the larger group that always worried that American means might be harnessed to British ends. Besides, he had been cultivating American public opinion for months, with all the care he could summon. Americans were moving in the right direction. The slightest misstep could reverse the momentum, with political and military implications he preferred not to contemplate.

Furthermore, Roosevelt had the advantage over Churchill and knew it. He outranked Churchill, to begin with, being a head of state to Churchill's mere head of government. He wouldn't belabor this point or flaunt it, but it was something neither would forget. More important was the matter of American power. Roosevelt wielded instruments of coercion Churchill could only envy. Already American industry was tipping the balance in the anti-fascist struggle. American support for Britain had helped persuade Hitler to redirect his army from west to east. The promise of American support for Russia was steeling Stalin against anything like a second rapprochement with Berlin. American financial power allowed Roosevelt to turn American industry fully toward war without worrying where the money would come from. The name alone of Lend-Lease exemplified the Americans' insouciance regarding cash. A loan, a lease, a gift—all this could be determined later. American military power would complement the country's industrial and financial might, should Washington abandon its proxy policy and enter the war itself. The 130 million Americans were numerous enough to defeat the 70 million Germans, even assuming equivalent arms. But the arms would not be equivalent. American soldiers would have more and probably better weapons than the Germans by the time their armies closed upon each other. A two-front war—should the United States find itself simultaneously fighting Japan (population 75 million)— would slow the Americans somewhat, compelling them to make choices. But the outcome could hardly be questioned.

Finally, there was the moral power the president wielded. America wasn't perfect, but compared with the fascists of Germany and Japan, the communists of Russia, and the imperialists of Britain, Americans looked remarkably benign to the ordinary people of the world. Roosevelt's reputation was especially compelling. He was known as the rich man who stood up for the common man, the president who put down the Big Stick in favor of being a Good Neighbor, the friend of China, the decolonizer of the Philippines (admittedly a work still in progress). Hitler's Germany, Stalin's Russia, even Churchill's Britain—none of these served as a beacon of hope to the oppressed of the world. None provided a model other peoples would freely emulate. Roosevelt's America provided just such a model, and Roosevelt knew it.

❖   ❖   ❖

*H*IS KNOWLEDGE informed the most important achievement of the Atlantic Conference, as it soon came to be called. Roosevelt's *Augusta* and Churchill's *Prince of Wales* reached Placentia Bay on August 9. Churchill, as protocol commanded, prepared to cross to Roosevelt's vessel for the initial visit. Harry Hopkins got there first. The ocean voyage with Churchill had restored him somewhat, and he hastened over to the *Augusta* to greet the president. Between the sessions with Churchill, Hopkins would brief Roosevelt on his Russia trip; for now he sent a note back to Churchill. "I have just talked to the President," he said, "and he is very anxious, after dinner tonight, to invite in the balance of the staff and wants you to talk very informally to them about your general appreciation of the war. . . . I imagine there will be twenty-five people altogether. The President, of course, does not want anything formal about it."

Asking Churchill to speak informally was like asking a lion to hide its mane. After the meal—a modest affair of broiled chicken, spinach omelets, sweet potatoes, cupcakes, and chocolate ice cream—was cleared away, Churchill waxed eloquent about the course of battle till now, extolling the valor of Britain's fliers and seamen, decrying the treachery of the Germans, offering qualified praise for the Russians, wondering at the intentions of Japan.

Roosevelt mostly listened. "I saw Father in a new role," Elliott remembered. Franklin and Eleanor's rebellious son had found his way back to the family as the threat of war increased. Without their knowledge he enlisted in the army air force. Franklin learned of the enlistment when Elliott visited the White House and let himself into the Oval Office, between two of the president's scheduled appointments. "Look, Pop," he said, and handed over his army orders. Years later he remembered Roosevelt's reaction. "He glanced at the piece of paper with my orders on it and looked up with tears in his eyes. . . . He couldn't speak for a moment. Then, 'I'm very proud.' " A few days later, at a Hyde Park dinner, Roosevelt proposed a toast: "To Elliott. He's the first of the family to think seriously enough, and soberly enough, about the threat to America to join his country's armed forces. We're all very proud of him. I'm the proudest."

To show off his soldier son to Churchill, and because he always liked the company of his children, Roosevelt arranged for Elliott to accompany him to Placentia Bay. Elliott sat with Roosevelt and Churchill at the dinner aboard the *Augusta*. He was surprised that his father let others control the conversation. "My experience of him in the past had been that he dominated every gathering he was part of, not because he insisted on it so much as that it always seemed his natural due. But not tonight. Tonight Father listened." And he took in the show. "Churchill reared back in his chair, he slewed his cigar around from cheek to cheek and always at a jaunty angle, he hunched his shoulders forward like a bull, his hands slashed the air expressively, his eyes flashed." His message was that America ought to join the British in the battle against fascism. "The Americans *must* come in at our side. You must come in, if you are to survive."

Roosevelt and the other Americans enjoyed the performance but gave away nothing. "Father listened, intently, seriously, now and then rubbing his eyes, fiddling with his pince-nez, doodling on the tablecloth with a burnt match. But never an aye, nay, or maybe came from the Americans sitting around that smoke-filled saloon."

The next morning the president returned Churchill's call. As it was Sunday, Roosevelt was treated to what he later characterized as a "very remarkable religious service" on the quarterdeck of the *Prince of Wales,* in the shadow of the vessel's great guns. "There was their own ship's complement, with three or four hundred bluejackets and marines from American ships, on the quarterdeck, completely intermingled, first one uniform and then another uniform," Roosevelt said. "The service was conducted by two chaplains, one English and one American, and, as usual, the lesson was read by the captain of the British ship. They had three hymns that everybody took part in, and a little ship's altar was decked with the American flag and the British flag. The officers were all intermingled on the fantail. . . . I think everybody there, officers and enlisted men, felt that it was one of the great historic services. I know I did."

After the service the British and American staffs got down to business. Alexander Cadogan, Churchill's undersecretary for foreign affairs, had come with drafts of parallel statements to be sent by the British and American governments to the Japanese. The heart of the statement Cadogan proposed for Roosevelt was that any further aggression by Japan in the southwestern Pacific would produce a situation in which the American government "would be compelled to take counter measures even though these might lead to war." This was no more than Churchill was prepared to state on behalf of Britain, but it was crucial, from the prime minister's point of view, that Roosevelt be equally forthright. "He did not think that there was much hope left, unless the United States made such a clear-cut declaration, of preventing Japan from expanding further to the south," Sumner Welles recorded of Churchill. "In which event the prevention of war between Great Britain and Japan appeared to be hopeless." The hopelessness followed from the fact that British Malaya and Singapore lay athwart the obvious course of Japanese expansion. "He said in the most emphatic manner that if war did break out between Great Britain and Japan, Japan immediately would be in a position through the use of her large number of cruisers to seize or to destroy all of the British merchant shipping in the Indian Ocean and in the Pacific, and to cut the life-lines between the British Dominions and the British Isles unless the United States herself entered the war." But if the United States joined Britain in threatening hostilities against Japan, Tokyo might pull back.

Roosevelt refused. In the first place, he thought an ultimatum might have just the opposite effect from deterrence. The war party in Japan would employ it to whip up nationalistic feeling and force the government into doing precisely what Roosevelt was warning them against. In the second place, he wasn't ready for war. The American navy required additional preparation, and the army's training program had only begun to produce results. Besides, Roosevelt was still arguing in public that military training was for the purpose of *preventing* American involvement. The last thing he intended to do was issue any war ultimatums.

Instead he issued a broad statement of principles. What came to be called the Atlantic Charter seemed to the British delegation to be hardly more than a press release, the sort of document heads of government agree to when they can't concur on anything substantial. Its eight points constituted Anglo-American war aims, although at Roosevelt's insistence and with Churchill's acquiescence they were awkwardly called "common principles in the national policies of their respective countries on which they base their hopes for a better future for the world." The first point eschewed aggrandizement, territorial or otherwise. The second forswore territorial changes not in accord with the "freely expressed wishes of the peoples concerned." The third affirmed "the right of all peoples to choose the form of government under which they will live." The fourth promised equal terms of trade to all nations, with "due respect" for the "existing obligations" of the United States and Britain. The fifth endorsed improved labor and living standards in all countries. The sixth looked forward, "after the final destruction of the Nazi tyranny," to a peace "which will afford to all nations the means of dwelling in safety within their own boundaries, and which will afford assurance that all the men in all the lands may live out their lives in freedom from fear and want." The seventh supported free travel and commerce across the world's oceans. The eighth called on the nations of the world to disarm, "pending the establishment of a wider and permanent system of general security."

The language of the Atlantic Charter was inelegant but artful—as artful in places as diplomatic prose ever gets. The "existing obligations" disclaimer in the free trade clause exempted the entire British empire, which was based on the exclusionary model of imperial preference. The "wider and permanent system of general security" was Roosevelt's substitute for the "effective international organization" of the British draft. Roosevelt wasn't ready, at this stage, to talk about a new League of Nations, and he was certain the American people weren't ready to hear about it.

All the same, the endorsement of self-determination in points two and three proved revolutionary—so revolutionary that Churchill began qualifying it almost as soon as he got back to England. "At the Atlantic meeting we had in mind, primarily, the restoration of the sovereignty, self-government, and national life of the states and nations of Europe now under the Nazi yoke," he told Parliament. "That is quite a separate problem from the progressive evolution of self-governing institutions in the regions and peoples which owe allegiance to the British Crown."

Many of those peoples didn't think so, which was why they latched onto the Atlantic Charter with the passion they did, and why Roosevelt became their hero. As for the audience whose reaction worried the president more at the moment—members of Congress and the American public—they had different concerns. "Are we any closer to entering the war?" a reporter asked the president at his first news conference upon arriving home.

"I should say no," Roosevelt replied.

"May we quote directly?"

"You can quote indirectly."

❖ ❖ ❖

ONE REASON ROOSEVELT didn't want to be quoted was that he wasn't telling the truth. At least he wasn't telling the reporters, and through them the American public, what he had told Churchill. Or perhaps it was Churchill who bent the story. On his return to England the prime minister reported the Newfoundland meeting to his cabinet. Roosevelt, Churchill said, had laid out a strategy designed to ensure American entry into the fighting. "He would wage war, but not declare it," Churchill explained. "He would become more and more provocative. . . . Everything was to be done to force an 'incident.' . . . He would look for an 'incident' which would justify him in opening hostilities."

Given the way events unfolded, Churchill's assertion rings truer than Roosevelt's denial. But Roosevelt also told Churchill that a request for a war declaration would tie Congress in knots, consuming the whole autumn. He knew what fear, fanned by the isolationists, could do, for even while he and Churchill were meeting at Placentia, the House of Representatives was debating whether to extend the term of service of draftees beyond the twelve months authorized under the Selective Service Act of 1940. The extension had slipped through the Senate, but isolationists in the House were attempting to demagogue the bill to death. Roosevelt warned of the dire consequences of sending the soldiers home. Training and readiness had been necessary in 1940, he declared in a written message, and were even more necessary now. "The danger today is infinitely greater. We are in the midst of a national emergency." To release the troops would compromise America's fundamental security. "We would be taking a grave national risk."

The president's words had the desired effect, barely. On the final day of Roosevelt's meeting with Churchill, the House agreed to the extension by a single vote.

The closeness of the decision explained Roosevelt's reluctance to level with the press and the public about his intentions, and it inspired him to additional efforts to ready Americans for the showdown he considered increasingly inevitable. On September 11 he held a Fireside Chat in which he explained that an American warship, the *Greer,* had been attacked by a German submarine off the coast of Greenland. "She was carrying American mail to Iceland," Roosevelt explained. "She was flying the American flag. Her identity as an American ship was unmistakable."

This was true enough. The ship was indeed carrying mail, it was flying the flag, and its identity was unmistakable—at least to the crew of the British plane the *Greer* was helping hunt and depth-charge the German submarine in question. Roosevelt declined to mention this utterly unneutral, presumptively illegal collaboration, just as he declined to share the conclusion of an internal U.S. navy study that the German submarine commander quite possibly thought he was firing on a British ship.

Roosevelt went on to describe the German attack as "piracy—piracy legally and morally." It was, moreover, "one determined step toward creating a permanent world system based on force, on terror, and on murder." The Nazi threat to America was no longer hypothetical. "The danger is here now." Describing German submarines and raiders as "rattlesnakes of the Atlantic," the president announced a new policy: "If German or Italian vessels of war enter the waters the protection of which is necessary for American defense, they do so at their own peril."

Roosevelt didn't specify what those waters were. But given that he had already claimed the Atlantic clear to Iceland as part of America's defense perimeter, the new approach amounted to a naval war against Germany—ordered by the president, on his authority alone.

"I have no illusions about the gravity of this step," he assured his listeners, in what might have been his frankest statement of the evening. "I have not taken it hurriedly or lightly. It is the result of months and months of constant thought and anxiety. . . . In the protection of your nation and mine it cannot be avoided."

43.

WHETHER THIS STEP WOULD BE FOLLOWED BY ANOTHER DEPENDED, as always for Roosevelt, on the reaction of the public. By now—two years into the European war, four years into the Asian war—Roosevelt could see quite clearly where he thought the United States must go. American democracy must engage fascism directly. Germany's hold on the European continent must be broken; Japan's thrust into China and Southeast Asia must be reversed. And he knew the order in which these tasks must be accomplished. Germany must go down first; Japan could wait. In part this ordering reflected Roosevelt's personal familiarity with Europe; having spent, cumulatively, years of his life in Europe, he could visualize Nazi rule far more easily than he could conjure images of the Japanese occupation of China and Indochina. But it also revealed his understanding of the nature of power. Japan, for all its ambitions, remained a comparatively backward, poor country. Conceivably Japan could subdue Chinese resistance, although this seemed less likely now than ever. Possibly it would capture the resources of the East Indies. But not for decades, if ever, would Japan be more than a regional power. Germany, on the other hand, was almost within artillery range of becoming a global power. If the Germans defeated the Russians, little would stand between Hitler and the oil fields of the Middle East. The Nazis might then sever the British lifeline to India, depriving Britain of most of what made it an empire. Britain itself couldn't hold out for long after that. Whether or not the defeat of Britain included capture of the British navy, Hitler would be in position to build up his own fleet. And whether or not he then assaulted the Western Hemisphere militarily, he would, by his control of Europe, severely damage America economically.

Roosevelt's reasoning caused him to try to provoke a war in the Atlantic even while he attempted to avoid one in the Pacific. As bold a strategist as the president was, he didn't welcome a two-front war. "I simply have not got enough navy to go round," he told Harold Ickes. "And every little episode in the

Pacific means fewer ships in the Atlantic." Germany had to be dealt with first—and the sooner, in fact, the Atlantic war started, the better. If the recent past was any guide, the Japanese might well exploit American engagement with Germany to extend their conquests farther south and west. But once the German question was settled, the United States could deal with Japan.

Roosevelt was pleased to learn that the American people were coming around to his view of the Nazi threat. According to a Gallup poll, 68 percent of Americans endorsed what the papers had taken to calling the president's "shoot on sight" policy toward German warships in the Atlantic. On the broader question of what the United States should do about Hitler, 70 percent said the German dictator must be defeated even if it meant war for the United States. Walter Lippmann, no fan of Roosevelt on many issues, summarized the evolving state of the American mind when he wrote, "After twenty years the American people are emerging from what is undoubtedly the most un-American period in the history of the nation. . . . A cleansing gale has begun to blow across the land and through the corridors and into the musty chambers where, for two decades, Americans have lived so luxuriously"—Lippmann seemed to have forgotten the depression—"but so uneasily, so far beneath themselves. The shock of the World War has unloosed it, but this wind is the very breath of the American spirit itself, proud, confident and sure."

Roosevelt certainly thought so, and, with the rising wind at his back, he pressed American policy forward. On October 9 he called on Congress to repeal the "crippling provisions" of the current neutrality law. One such provision barred American ships from entering belligerent ports; another banned the arming of merchant ships for self-defense. Reversing the former would facilitate deliveries of Lend-Lease supplies; undoing the latter would allow Americans to defend themselves. "The practice of arming merchant ships for civilian defense is an old one," Roosevelt explained. "Through our whole history American merchant vessels have been armed whenever it was considered necessary for their own defense." It was now more necessary than ever. "We are faced not with the old type of pirates but with the modern pirates of the sea who travel beneath the surface or on the surface or in the air destroying defense-less ships without warning." An armed merchantman couldn't prevent a German submarine from firing torpedoes, but it could force that submarine to fire while still submerged and at a distance, giving the merchantman a fighting chance. It couldn't keep German planes from dropping bombs or torpedoes, but it could compel the pilots of those planes to dodge antiaircraft fire.

Roosevelt asserted that he wasn't advocating belligerence. "The revisions which I suggest do not call for a declaration of war any more than the Lend-Lease Act called for a declaration of war." He was simply insisting on Americans' historic right to traverse the seas unmolested. And he took the opportunity to reemphasize the Nazi threat.

> I say to you solemnly that if Hitler's present military plans are brought to successful fulfillment, we Americans shall be forced to fight in defense of our own homes and our own freedom in a war as costly and as devastating as that which now rages on the Russian front. . . . The ultimate fate of the western hemisphere lies in the balance.

Berlin appeared to confirm the president's warning several days later. The shoot-on-sight policy had the predictable effect of making German commanders quicker to fire than before. In mid-October a Lend-Lease convoy came under attack by German submarines. An American destroyer, the *Kearny,* escorting the convoy, replied with a barrage of depth charges. One of the submarines put a torpedo in the *Kearny*'s side, killing eleven of the crew and seriously damaging the vessel, which nonetheless limped into an Iceland port.

"The shooting has started," Roosevelt declared. "And history has recorded who fired the first shot." The war had become personal. "America has been attacked. The U.S.S. *Kearny* is not just a navy ship. She belongs to every man, woman, and child in this nation." The president listed the home states of the eleven sailors killed, before extrapolating: "Hitler's torpedo was directed at every American, whether he lives on our sea coasts or in the innermost part of the country, far from the seas and far from the guns and tanks of the marching hordes of would-be conquerors of the world."

Roosevelt proceeded to drop a bombshell of his own.

> I have in my possession a secret map made in Germany by Hitler's government—by the planners of the new world order. It is a map of South America and a part of Central America, as Hitler proposes to reorganize it. Today in this area there are fourteen separate countries. But the geographical experts of Berlin have ruthlessly obliterated all existing boundary lines; they have divided South America into five vassal states, bringing the whole continent under their domination. And they have also so arranged it that the territory of one of these new puppet states includes the Republic of Panama and our great life line—the Panama Canal. . . .

Your Government has in its possession another document, made in Germany by Hitler's Government. It is a detailed plan, which, for obvious reasons, the Nazis did not wish and do not wish to publicize just yet, but which they are ready to impose, a little later, on a dominated world—if Hitler wins. It is a plan to abolish all existing religions—Catholic, Protestant, Mohammedan, Hindu, Buddhist, and Jewish alike. The property of all churches will be seized by the Reich and its puppets. The cross and all other symbols of religion are to be forbidden. The clergy are to be forever liquidated, silenced under penalty of the concentration camps, where even now so many fearless men are being tortured because they have placed God above Hitler.

The isolationists immediately suspected a forgery. The timing and alleged content of the documents the president described were simply too convenient—too supportive of the administration's agenda. They demanded that he publish the documents.

Roosevelt may have smelled something fishy, too, for he declined the isolationists' demand. The White House pleaded security concerns, but the provenance of the map, in particular, was dubious. Decades later a retired British agent claimed to have drawn the map himself, for the purpose of pulling the United States closer to war with Germany. Roosevelt knew enough of British propaganda tactics from the First World War to know that British forgers were clever. Yet he also knew that none of the skeptics would be able, in the near term, to *dis*prove the veracity of the documents. And they did indeed serve his agenda.

If Roosevelt hoped the *Kearny* would be his *Lusitania,* he was disappointed. No groundswell of support greeted his call for stronger measures. Even the arming of merchant ships seemed a measure too far for those who suspected the president of deliberately provoking incidents on the Atlantic. "If we take this one further step," isolationist Democrat D. Worth Clark of Idaho told the Senate, "our power to resist will be gone. We will be utterly at the mercy of two men, one of them Adolf Hitler and the other Franklin D. Roosevelt." Nor were hard-core isolationists the only ones who held back. Henry Cabot Lodge Jr., the grandson of Wilson's bête noire, had voted for Lend-Lease, conscription, and every one of the president's defense bills, but he drew the line at sending American ships into belligerent ports. "It is one thing to be an arsenal for other countries," the Massachusetts Republican asserted. "It is another thing for our men to be fighting on the battlefield. Measures tending to make us a more effective arsenal should receive support. Those which send us onto the battlefield are still, I believe, to be resisted. If Americans are to be killed in belligerent waters, I fear that we will not be able long to delay the sending of our men to the theaters of this war."

Not even another attack on an American vessel, far more serious than that on the *Kearny,* could convince the skeptics. The *Reuben James* was escorting a convoy off Iceland when a pack of German submarines began firing torpedoes. One hit the American destroyer in the magazine, producing a blast that sheared off the bow and quickly sank the vessel. More than a hundred members of the crew died.

Roosevelt might have taken the incident as the occasion for another stirring speech, or perhaps a diplomatic move against Germany. But he didn't. Instead he waited to assess the public reaction—which, unfortunately for his plans, split along the same lines as before. Administration supporters deemed the sinking of the *Reuben James* further proof of the German menace; Tom Connally of Texas, the chairman of the Senate foreign relations committee, called it "outrageous evidence of the murderous and defiant attitude of the Nazis." But the isolationists contended that the attack revealed why the neutrality law should *not* be revised. "If the losses are going to be this heavy in convoying in our defensive waters," Robert Taft said, "they may be so heavy convoying the rest of the way into British ports that we won't have anything left to defend ourselves with." Gerald Nye said bluntly, "You can't expect to walk into a barroom brawl and hope to stay out of the fight."

The opposition froze Roosevelt in his tracks. He refused to take even the symbolic step of suspending relations with Berlin. A reporter queried him on the subject. "Lots of people who think just as you do on this war issue also think that a continuance of diplomatic relations with Germany is a form of dishonesty," the reporter said. "Would you elaborate your thoughts?"

"Only off the record," Roosevelt responded. "I would have to make it completely off the record."

The reporters listened intently, hoping for some new revelation. All they got was a tepid disclaimer. "We don't want a declared war with Germany because we are acting in defense, self-defense—every action. And to break off diplomatic relations—why, that won't do any good. . . . It might be more useful to keep them the way they are."

Roosevelt's caution reflected his sense that he had enough votes for the changes he wanted in the neutrality law, but only just enough. At a White House conference on November 5, the Democratic congressional leadership told the president that the opposition to the revisions was stubborn and strong. House speaker Sam Rayburn and House majority leader John McCormack suggested that a final push from the president could be crucial. Roosevelt complied by sending a letter for Rayburn and McCormack to read to their colleagues. "Failure to repeal these sections would, of course, cause rejoicing in the Axis nations," the president asserted. "Failure would bolster aggressive steps and intentions in Germany, and in the other well-known aggressor nations under the leadership of Hitler."

The House needed the nudge. An impassioned debate ended in a narrow victory for the president: 212 to 194, with 53 Democrats, including 28 who had sided with the president on the war previously, defecting to the opposition. The result in the Senate was similarly favorable but no more enthusiastic: 50 in favor of revision, 37 against.

"Naturally, the President is pleased with the result," William Hassett, Roosevelt's assistant, told the press. The president wasn't pleased enough to hail the result himself, and he understood that if neutrality revision required this much effort, a war declaration was out of the question for the foreseeable future.

❖ ❖ ❖

ROOSEVELT WAS CERTAIN by now that he knew Hitler's mind, regarding overall strategy if not every tactical twist. He may have read too much into Hitler's intentions for the Western Hemisphere, or he may simply have exaggerated those intentions for political effect. But he doubtless got it right when he spoke of the dependence of the Nazi regime on war and when he concluded that there would be no peace so long as Hitler governed Germany.

Japan, by contrast, remained an enigma to Roosevelt, as to most outside observers. The Japanese prime minister, Prince Konoye, appeared to desire peace, but it was impossible for Roosevelt to tell whether Konoye had any real influence or was simply being used by the militarists to disguise their own predominance. During the late summer and autumn of 1941, while Roosevelt was launching his undeclared war in the Atlantic, he weighed a request from Konoye for a meeting. "Japan and the United States are the last two major powers who hold the key to international peace," the prime minister wrote. "That the two nations should fall into the worst of relations at this time would mean not only a disaster in itself, but also the collapse of world civilization."

Roosevelt wasn't eager for a meeting, not knowing how much of the Japanese government Konoye spoke for. But he was even less eager for a Pacific war, and so he entered into discussions regarding an appropriate date and place. Konoye suggested Hawaii; Roosevelt countered with Alaska, which would require less time for him at sea. Konoye accepted Juneau and asked that the meeting be held as soon as possible—on account, as the Japanese ambassador in Washington put it, "of the efforts of a third country and fifth columnists in Japan, who are now behind a press campaign against the United States, to disturb Japanese-American relations."

The fifth columnists were Konoye's rivals among the military; the third country was Britain, which was indeed hoping to disturb Japanese-American relations. As he had during the Atlantic Conference, Churchill was urging Roosevelt to take a tougher stance against Japan, lest the Japanese attack Britain's Pacific holdings and the United States remain on the sidelines.

Roosevelt wasn't yet ready to risk a Pacific war, but neither was he willing to risk a meeting that might make him look as foolish as Neville Chamberlain had looked after Munich. He strung Konoye along, trying to coax some commitments to better behavior out of the Japanese government before he agreed to sit down with the prime minister. When Konoye couldn't deliver those commitments, the meeting fell through.

Roosevelt immediately began to wonder if he shouldn't have been more accommodating, for Konoye's inability to arrange a meeting with the American president resulted in the collapse of his administration. "It is with great regret and disappointment that my colleagues and I have had to resign owing to the internal political situation, which I may be able to explain to you sometime in the future," Konoye wrote cryptically to American ambassador Joseph Grew. The departing premier went on to express the hope "that you and your government will not be too disappointed or discouraged either by the change of cabinet or by the mere appearance or impression of the new cabinet."

Discouragement wasn't the word for the American reaction; alarm was more accurate. Konoye's replacement was General Hideki Tojo, who had commanded the Kwantung Army, as the legion that enforced Japan's writ in the puppet state of Manchukuo was called. While minister of war in 1940 Tojo had directed the negotiations leading to the Axis alliance with Germany and Italy. His elevation to the premiership signaled—accurately, as events proved—that the military had seized command of Japanese policy once and for all.

Roosevelt guessed as much. The day before Tojo's takeover of the government, he wrote Churchill, "The Jap situation is definitely worse, and I think they are headed north." What Roosevelt meant was that Japan would attack Russia, exploiting Stalin's current preoccupation with Hitler. This prospect wasn't good, since it would complicate the vital task of keeping Russia in the fight against Germany. But it wasn't as bad as it could have been. "In spite of this, you and I will have two months of respite in the Far East."

Tojo's coup occurred between Roosevelt's writing and Churchill's reply. "The Japanese menace . . . ," the British prime minister asserted, "has grown so much sharper in the last few days. . . . Events are now telling their own tale." Yet the latest development simply threw Churchill back on the advice he had given Roosevelt in Newfoundland. "The stronger the action of the United States towards Japan, the greater the chance of preserving peace." To buck up the president, Churchill pledged his country's full support. "Should, however, peace be broken and the United States become at war with Japan, you may be sure that a British declaration of war upon Japan will follow within the hour." As a demonstration of what ought to be done, Churchill dispatched the *Prince of Wales*—"that big ship you inspected," Churchill wrote to Roosevelt, to avoid putting the vessel's name in a cable that might be intercepted—to the British base at Singapore. "This ought to serve as a deterrent on Japan. There is nothing like having something that can catch and kill anything." The prime minister concluded: "The firmer your attitude and ours, the less chance of their taking the plunge."

❖   ❖   ❖

ROOSEVELT'S DIPLOMACY during the weeks that followed was devoted to keeping Japan from taking the plunge. The prospects weren't encouraging. In a cable from Tokyo, Grew noted that the government was whipping up war fever. "Empire Approaches Its Greatest Crisis," the American ambassador quoted a headline in one of the leading newspapers in the Japanese capital. He went on to predict, if the Japanese didn't get their way in the current talks with the United States, "an all-out, do-or-die attempt, actually risking national hara-kiri, to make Japan impervious to economic embargoes abroad rather than to yield to foreign pressure." Grew was exceedingly glum. "This contingency not only is possible but is probable." He added that action by Japan "may come with dangerous and dramatic suddenness."

Grew's pessimism appeared to be confirmed by an intercepted message from Japan's foreign minister, Shigenori Togo, to Ambassador Kichisaburo Nomura in Washington. For some months American and British cryptographers had been able to decode certain Japanese diplomatic cables; the "Magic" intercepts allowed Washington and London to learn what Tokyo was telling its embassies. On November 5, Togo informed Nomura that if a deal with the United States was to be struck it would have to be soon. "Because of various circumstances, it is absolutely necessary that all arrangement for the signing of this agreement be completed by the 25th of this month," Togo said. "I realize that this is a difficult order, but under the circumstances it is an unavoidable one." What Togo did *not* tell Nomura, although the ambassador could infer as much, was that the military was already planning to go to war. November 25 was the date when the decision to strike or to stand down would be made.

Roosevelt and Hull drew the same conclusion from Togo's November 25 deadline. "This, to us, could mean only one thing," Hull wrote. "Japan had already set in motion the wheels of her war machine, and she had decided not to stop short of war with the United States if by November 25 we had not agreed to her demands."

Hull shared this inference with the rest of the cabinet at a meeting on November 7. The secretary of state recounted the recent events and messages and declared, "Relations are extremely critical. We should be on the lookout for a military attack by Japan anywhere at any time." Understandably sobered, the cabinet encouraged the president to prepare the American people.

Armistice Day followed shortly; Roosevelt took the occasion to remind Americans what their country represented in the world. A generation earlier, Americans had gone to war in Europe. The isolationists had since derided that effort, contending that the United States had been deluded by the leaders of Britain and France into doing the Europeans' dirty work. The isolationists, Roosevelt said, were dangerously wrong. Fortunately, most Americans were wiser. "We know that it was, in literal truth, to make the world safe for democracy that we took up arms in 1917," the president asserted. "It was, in simple truth and in literal fact, to make the world habitable for decent and self-respecting men and women that those whom we now remember gave their lives." Americans understood that democracy and decency had to be defended. Roosevelt quoted Alvin York, the much-decorated hero of the First World War: "Liberty and freedom and democracy are so very precious that you do not fight to win them once and stop. You do not do that. Liberty and freedom and democracy are prizes awarded only to those peoples who fight to win them and then keep fighting eternally to hold them." The American people agreed with Sergeant York rather than with the isolationists, Roosevelt said. "They believe that liberty is worth fighting for. And if they are obliged to fight they will fight eternally to hold it."

Despite their pessimism regarding the prospects for Asia and the Pacific, administration officials continued to meet with Japanese diplomats. Ambassador Nomura appeared to Roosevelt and Hull to be an honest professional with a sincere desire to find common ground between his government and America's. This desire may have been what prompted Tojo and Togo to send reinforcement, in the person of Saburo Kurusu, the former Japanese ambassador to Berlin, to Washington. "Kurusu seemed to me the antithesis of Nomura," Hull remembered. "Neither his appearance nor his attitude commanded confidence or respect. I felt from the start that he was deceitful." Hull allowed that Kurusu might strive for an accommodation, but it would be entirely on Japan's terms. And if accommodation failed, Kurusu's mission had a second purpose. "He was to lull us with talk until the moment Japan got ready to strike."

Roosevelt played along. He, too, hoped for an eleventh-hour agreement, although he hardly expected it. His attitude was the American counterpart of Kurusu's: any agreement must be on America's terms. But unlike Kurusu, whose military deadline required him to push for a swift settlement of the outstanding issues between the United States and Japan, Roosevelt was happy to delay. Henry Stimson and Frank Knox had been saying for months that the army and navy needed time to prepare. They continued to say so. Roosevelt sought to give them as much of the time they needed as possible.

Hull met with Kurusu and Nomura almost daily during November; Roosevelt received one or the other about once a week. His themes were firmness and patience. "Nations must think one hundred years ahead, especially during the age through which the world is passing," he told Nomura on November 10. Japan should slow down. It needn't solve its problems all at once. The president said he and Secretary Hull had been working only half a year on the issues Japan considered essential, whereas the Japanese government had been engaged for a decade. Tokyo must let Washington catch up. "Patience is necessary," Roosevelt said.

The president pondered additional measures for gaining time. He jotted a note to Hull sketching a formula for postponing a crisis with Japan for perhaps six months. The American government would offer to ease the economic restrictions on Japan, Roosevelt suggested, and would encourage peace negotiations between Japan and China, if Japan would promise not to send new troops to Indochina and not to declare war on the United States should America enter the European conflict.

Roosevelt knew it was a stretch. He would be asking Japan to abandon its ten-year project of controlling China and to ignore its treaty commitment to Germany in exchange for an easing of restrictions Washington might reimpose at a moment's notice. In fact, the more the president thought about his offer, the less he liked it. The militarists in Tokyo might use it for propaganda purposes and become even more bellicose.

He had just about decided to drop the idea when the Japanese took the matter out of his hands. Kurusu told Roosevelt at a White House meeting that things could explode at any minute. "All the way across the Pacific it is like a powder keg," he asserted. "Some way must be found to adjust the situation." Kurusu nonetheless refused to modify the demands he made on behalf of his government. The Japanese were willing to withdraw their troops from southern Indochina to northern Indochina, he said, and to remove all their troops from Indochina, but only upon "the restoration of peace between Japan and China or the establishment of an equitable peace in the Pacific area." Meanwhile the United States should unfreeze Japan's financial assets, restore the flow of American oil to Japan, and help Japan secure the resources it needed from the Dutch East Indies.

Hull later described the Japanese proposals as "of so preposterous a character that no responsible American official could ever have dreamed of accepting them." Hull was overstating things with the advantage of hindsight, but the Japanese offer did fall seriously short, for it required the United States to accept Japanese hegemony in East Asia—at this point little imagination was required to realize what Tokyo meant by "an equitable peace in the Pacific area." Roosevelt had consistently rejected such an outcome, and he wouldn't accept it now.

On November 25, a Tuesday, the president gathered what he was already calling his "war cabinet" to the White House. Stimson spoke for the War Department, Knox for Navy, and Hull for State. General George Marshall, the army chief of staff, and Admiral Harold Stark, the chief of naval operations, represented the uniformed services. For some weeks the group had been discussing the war in Europe and the Atlantic, and Stimson, for one, anticipated more of the same talk. But Roosevelt "brought up entirely the relations with the Japanese," Stimson recorded in his diary. The secret Japanese deadline had just passed—Tokyo being fourteen hours ahead of Washington—and Roosevelt expected war at any time. "We were likely to be attacked, perhaps next Monday," Stimson paraphrased the president, "for the Japanese are notorious for making an attack without warning, and the question was what we should do. The question was how we should maneuver them into the position of firing the first shot without allowing too much danger to ourselves. It was a difficult proposition."

Stimson's diary would provoke great controversy after the war, when this portion of it was published as part of an investigation into the events leading to American intervention. Given that the Japanese attack Roosevelt predicted did come—at Pearl Harbor—Stimson's account lent credence to charges that Roosevelt deliberately sacrificed the American force there to the Japanese. Roosevelt's defenders would counter that the president's use of the word "we" encompassed the British as well as Americans and that he was thinking of an attack on Singapore or Malaya. Alternatively, Stimson may have transcribed the president's comments carelessly, as his diary entries often reflected haste. More persuasive is the argument that Roosevelt was thinking of an attack on the Philippines. The consensus at the November 25 meeting was that the Japanese would be moving south from Indochina. "Any such expedition to the South as the Japanese were likely to take would be an encirclement of our interests in the Philippines," Stimson's diary continued. Though scheduled for independence in 1946, the Philippines remained American territory. They were lightly defended, partly out of congressional stinginess and partly because they *were* going to become independent. Quite possibly Roosevelt thought a Japanese attack on the Philippines would constitute a sufficient casus belli. Such an attack would not allow, in the words of Stimson's diary, "too much danger to ourselves," and it certainly would get the attention of Congress.

One thing is certain: no one at the November 25 meeting mentioned Hawaii or Pearl Harbor. The thought seems not to have crossed Roosevelt's mind as he increased the diplomatic pressure on Japan. A fresh report, which the president received on November 26, revealed that the Japanese were sending additional troops to Indochina. "He fairly blew up," Stimson recorded. "It was an evidence of bad faith on the part of the Japanese"—that while their emissaries in Washington were ostensibly negotiating a truce, their armies in Asia were expanding the war. The new evidence confirmed Roosevelt's belief that war could no longer be avoided or even much delayed. That same day he delivered his answer to the Japanese proposal. The heart of his message was a one-sentence demand: "The Government of Japan will withdraw all military, naval, air, and police forces from China and from Indochina."

Roosevelt knew this would be as unacceptable to Tojo and his colleagues as their offer was to him. Having fought for ten years to carve out a sphere in China, they were hardly going to abandon their objective so easily. Yet the president thought there was no other reasonable position he could take, even considering the likely consequences. "This seems to me a fair proposition for the Japanese," he wrote Churchill. "But its acceptance or rejection is really a matter of internal Japanese politics. I am not very hopeful, and we must all be prepared for real trouble, possibly soon."

The president called Kurusu and Nomura to the White House. He expressed his disappointment that the Japanese government had not treated the American proposals seriously. "We have been very patient in our dealing with the whole Far Eastern situation," he said. "We are prepared to continue to be patient." But Japan must abandon its aggressive ways. It must withdraw from China, and it ought to reconsider its alliance with Germany. Perhaps the Japanese believed Germany represented the wave of the future. They were mistaken. Germany would fail in its efforts to subjugate Europe, Roosevelt said, if for no other reason than it lacked the manpower to impose its will so broadly. Should the Japanese government follow the path of Hitlerism, it too would fail. "Japan will be the ultimate loser."

The next day Roosevelt left for Warm Springs, for a belated Thanksgiving vacation. He had scarcely arrived when the State Department learned that Tojo was scheduled to give a speech before the most extreme expansionist group in Tokyo. American intelligence had belatedly discovered that the November 25 deadline had been extended to November 29; Hull, upon reading an advance text of Tojo's speech, worried that it might be the signal for an attack. He called Warm Springs and recommended that the president return to Washington.

Roosevelt did so, arriving in time to receive a cable from Churchill. The British were reading the same intercepts as the Americans; the prime minister urged a final joint effort on behalf of Pacific peace. "It seems to me that one important method remains unused in averting war between Japan and our two countries," Churchill wrote on November 30, "namely a plain declaration, secret or public as may be thought best, that any further act of aggression by Japan will lead immediately to the gravest consequences. I realize your constitutional difficulties, but it would be tragic if Japan drifted into war by encroachment without having before her fairly and squarely the dire character of a further aggressive step. . . . Forgive me, my dear friend, for presuming to press such a course upon you, but I am convinced that it might make all the difference and prevent a melancholy extension of the war."

Roosevelt declined Churchill's offer. Having resisted the prime minister's entreaties for eighteen months, he was as reluctant as ever to do anything that smacked of going to war on behalf of the British empire. The Japanese were poised to strike; Roosevelt expected the blow to fall at any moment. The best brains in Washington were predicting an attack against or in the direction of British Southeast Asia. If this occurred, after the United States had issued a joint ultimatum with Britain, an American war declaration would look to all the world—including a great many Americans—like a defense of British imperialism. Nor could the president be sure Congress would approve such a war declaration. If it didn't, Roosevelt would appear an impotent fool.

Roosevelt summoned Nomura and Kurusu to the State Department. Hull was ill again; in his place Sumner Welles read a statement by the president. The statement explained that the president had received reports of Japanese troop movements in southern Indochina. Such movements strongly suggested "further aggression." Citing Germany's history of encroachment upon its neighbors, Roosevelt's statement expressed concern that Japan was preparing an assault against Malaya, Burma, the East Indies, or the Philippines. The president demanded to know Japan's intentions.

❖   ❖   ❖

WHILE ROOSEVELT awaited Japan's reply, the *Chicago Tribune* broke a blockbuster story under banner headlines:

F.D.R.'S WAR PLANS!
GOAL IS 10 MILLION ARMED MEN
HALF TO FIGHT IN A.E.F.

The story, which appeared on Thursday, December 4, was based on a top-secret plan prepared at Roosevelt's request by a joint board of the army and navy. The *Tribune*'s well-connected Washington correspondent, Chesly Manly, had acquired a copy of the plan, which Robert McCormick, the bitterly anti-Roosevelt owner of the *Tribune*, was delighted to publicize. The essence of Manly's four-thousand-word story was that the American military command was already preparing for a European war effort far larger than that of the First World War. "Germany and her European satellites cannot be defeated by the European powers now fighting against her," Manly quoted the secret war plan. "If our European enemies are to be defeated, it will be necessary for the United States to enter the war, and to employ a part of its armed forces offensively in the Eastern Atlantic and in Europe and Africa." This new American

Expeditionary Force would comprise as many as five million soldiers, who would take part in a major offensive against Germany during the summer of 1943.

Reporters naturally questioned the administration as to the veracity of the *Tribune*'s story. Steve Early, speaking for the president, at first refused to confirm or deny the report. But gradually the administration tacitly conceded that the plan was genuine, while asserting that its significance had been exaggerated. Henry Stimson explained that war planners made all sorts of plans; the particular preparations that had been leaked reflected merely one set of contingencies. "They have never constituted an authorized program of the government," Stimson said. Nor did the plan tell the Germans anything the Germans couldn't guess on their own. Even so, the *Tribune* should be ashamed. "The chief evil of their publication is the revelation that there should be among us any group of persons so lacking in appreciation of the danger that confronts the country and so wanting in loyalty and patriotism to their government that they would be willing to take and publish such papers." Harold Ickes had harsher words for the *Tribune,* at least in his diary. "If we had been at war," Ickes said, "this publication would have constituted treason."

Isolationists cited the war plan as further evidence of Roosevelt's duplicity. Even as the president proclaimed his devotion to peace, they said, he was preparing for war. Burton Wheeler demanded a congressional investigation, with witnesses required to testify under oath. Hamilton Fish adopted an attitude of pained astonishment. "I refuse to believe that the President has given his support to any proposal for such an expeditionary force," the New York Republican asserted, in tones that indicated just the opposite: that he *did* believe it. "If we crush the German army, the Russian army will overrun Germany, this country will be left bankrupt and impoverished, and communism will come, bringing chaos and revolution."

The isolationist uproar was still building on Saturday, December 6, when Roosevelt dispatched a letter to Emperor Hirohito. This was an extreme step for an American president, or any other head of government; the emperor, considered divine by the Japanese, didn't receive regular mail. But Japan and America confronted a "deep and far-reaching emergency," Roosevelt said, and extreme steps were required. The president asserted that the escalation of Japanese force levels in Indochina was pushing Southeast Asia toward war. He didn't know whether Hirohito could cancel what was afoot with Japan's military, but he thought the emperor ought to try. "A continuance of such a situation is unthinkable." Roosevelt again called for the evacuation of Japanese troops from Indochina; in exchange he offered to guarantee the neutralization of that French colony. "Both of us," he concluded, "for the sake of the peoples not only of our own great countries but for the sake of humanity in neighboring territories, have a sacred duty to restore traditional amity and prevent further death and destruction in the world."

44.

THE LOOMING PROSPECT OF WAR ADDED NEW RESPONSIBILITIES TO
Eleanor Roosevelt's portfolio, without subtracting any of the old ones. She still
wrote her newspaper column, conducted her press conferences, and broadcast her weekly radio addresses. As part of his declaration of national emergency, Roosevelt had established an Office of Civilian Defense and appointed
New York mayor Fiorello La Guardia to be director. La Guardia asked Eleanor
to become his associate. She initially said no, having enough else to do and remaining leery of taking a paid government post and thereby raising complications for Franklin.

But a pair of deaths in the autumn of 1941 caused her to reconsider. Hall
Roosevelt had been Eleanor's companion during the bleak years after their
parents died. Hall inherited much more of their physical attractiveness than
Eleanor did, but also more of their emotional instability. Decades of excessive
drinking eventually caught up with him, and he came to a slow, agonizing
end. "It has been a hard two weeks," Eleanor wrote a friend shortly after the
death, "and from last Sunday until yesterday morning more harrowing than I
could tell you."

The second death hit Franklin harder than Eleanor. Sara Roosevelt had suffered a stroke in June, and though she still made the annual trip to Campobello, she spent most of her time there confined to her bedroom. Eleanor
visited her mother-in-law while Franklin was meeting with Churchill off Newfoundland; what Eleanor saw didn't afford much hope. "I think she is failing
fast," she wrote of Sara in mid-August. Sara rallied on the news of the Atlantic
Conference, as she took pride in her son's emergence as a leading figure not
just in American politics but in world affairs. She returned to Hyde Park, where
Eleanor helped her settle back in.

For a few days she appeared to be gaining strength, but then she weakened
once more. Eleanor called Franklin and told him to come to Hyde Park as

quickly as possible. He arrived on the morning of September 6, a Saturday. Sara brightened to see him, as she always did when he returned home. He told her of his sessions with Churchill, laughingly describing the slip he had given the press, movingly relating the Sunday service aboard the *Prince of Wales*, seriously recounting the discussions leading to the Atlantic Charter. He did the talking; she was content to listen. After what seemed her best day in weeks, she prepared for bed. Suddenly she fell unconscious. A clot, like that which had caused her stroke, lodged in her pulmonary artery, depriving the brain of oxygen.

Franklin spent the night at her bedside; Eleanor came in and out. The next morning, just before noon, Sara quietly expired. To the astonishment of everyone present, at almost the moment of her death an ancient oak on the property, not far from the house, crashed to the ground. There was no wind, nor had rain softened the ground. Roosevelt gazed at the prone giant, remembering the hours spent playing under its limbs and doubtless reflecting on the fitting moment of its demise.

"The funeral was nice and simple, the casket in the library on the south side and only a spray of Hyde Park flowers on it," Eleanor wrote Anna, who had moved to the West Coast. "We drove to the churchyard and Father stood by the car through the interment service." Franklin had fallen silent upon Sara's death, shutting himself off from his official duties and from as many visitors and well-wishers as he reasonably could. He ordered the road that ran by the estate to be closed lest Sara's final peace—and his sorrow—be disturbed.

To Eleanor he seemed composed, if subdued. "Pa has taken Granny's death very philosophically," Eleanor wrote Anna. Grace Tully saw something different. Roosevelt's secretary was helping her boss sort through Sara's things after the funeral. "She had carefully saved and tagged his christening dress, his first pair of shoes, his baby hair, and some of his childhood toys," Tully recalled. These mementos of his childhood, and this evidence of his mother's loving care, summoned fifty-eight years of mixed feelings to the surface, and for one of the rare times in his life Roosevelt broke down.

Had he been a different man, and Eleanor a different woman, Sara's death might have inaugurated a reconciliation. Sara had come between them from the start of their relationship, and now she was gone. But Franklin turned inward, rather than toward Eleanor. "He never looked toward the grave," one of the few reporters allowed at the funeral noted, "nor did he return an anxious glance cast his way by his wife." He made a gesture in Eleanor's direction afterward, when he said she might take Sara's room in the big house as her own.

"I just can't, and told him so," Eleanor explained to Anna. She couldn't forget all the slights Sara had inflicted upon her, and she couldn't forgive Franklin for waiting this long to put her ahead of his mother. She couldn't risk the kind of rejection she had suffered from every man she had loved, including Franklin. The moment of possibility passed.

James Roosevelt watched his parents struggle with their feelings. He later recounted what the lost opportunity cost his father. "Hyde Park could be only a palliative, not a cure, for the loneliness that was eating inside Father," James said. "Nowhere in the world really was there anyone for him with whom he could unlock his mind and his thoughts. Politics, domestic economy, war strategy, postwar planning he could talk over with dozens of persons. Of what was inside him, of what really drove him, Father talked with no one."

❖　❖　❖

THE DEATHS OF Hall and Sara prompted Eleanor to accept La Guardia's offer of a post in civilian defense. In a world where personal relationships were so fraught and disappointing, duty was a source of comfort. Duty quieted the questions love raised but never answered satisfactorily. During the autumn of 1941 she threw herself into the work of civil defense, devoting evenings and weekends to securing the home front in the event of war. She and some colleagues were working late at the White House on Saturday evening, December 6; before the others departed she took them to bid the president good night. Roosevelt had just dispatched his eleventh-hour appeal to the Japanese emperor. "This son of man has just sent his final message to the Son of God," he grimly joked.

Eleanor turned to the last-minute details for a large luncheon to be held at the White House the next day. The guests were all eager for a chance to break bread with the president. But on Sunday morning Franklin told her that he couldn't spare the time. She wasn't surprised, for he had begged off from numerous events during the previous months. Besides mourning his mother, he had the best excuse anyone could imagine: world peace required his presence elsewhere. There were, moreover, considerations of fatigue. "People naturally wanted to listen to what he had to say," Eleanor remembered. "But the fact that he carried so many secrets in his head made it necessary for him to watch everything he said, which in itself was exhausting." More and more often, Roosevelt simply had a quiet meal in his study with Harry Hopkins or Grace Tully.

He was sharing lunch with Hopkins that Sunday, December 7, when the call from the Navy Department informed him of the attack on Pearl Harbor. He immediately summoned his top military and diplomatic advisers: Stimson, Knox, Marshall, Stark, Hull. They assessed the meaning and consequences of the attack even as updates from Hawaii explained its horrific extent. Marshall and Stark related the orders they had sent to General MacArthur in the Philippines and other American commanders across the Pacific. Roosevelt took a call from Churchill; the prime minister expressed condolences for American losses and good wishes for the struggle ahead.

Roosevelt brought in Grace Tully. "Sit down, Grace," he said. "I'm going before Congress tomorrow. I'd like to dictate my message. It will be short."

Tully was struck by how composed the president seemed. He had been lighting a cigarette when she came in. "He inhaled deeply, then he began in the same calm tone in which he dictated his mail," she remembered. "Only his diction was a little different, as he spoke each word incisively and slowly, carefully specifying each punctuation mark and each paragraph."

The message was indeed short, containing fewer than five hundred words, and it required Roosevelt scarcely longer to dictate than it would to read. The president showed it to Hull, who urged him to add a bill of particulars against Japan. Roosevelt declined. Hopkins suggested a sentence for the end, which Roosevelt accepted.

He ate a quick dinner with Hopkins and Tully and convened the cabinet at eight thirty. He impressed upon the secretaries the gravity of the task before them. At nine he brought in the congressional leadership. He furnished the senators and representatives the latest reports from Hawaii. To a man they insisted on a war declaration.

Additional briefings filled the rest of the evening and spilled beyond midnight. At one o'clock on the morning of December 8 he got into bed. Sleep came slowly. In less than twelve hours he would speak to Congress, to the American people, and to the world. He knew he was right in rejecting Hull's advice for a longer message; at this moment words could be but the faintest echo of the thunder of deeds. He understood that it had long been so when America entered wars. It certainly had been so for the wars of his lifetime. Theodore Roosevelt and the war hawks of 1898 had shouted for war against Spain, but only the destruction of the *Maine* rendered a war declaration possible. Woodrow Wilson had concluded by the beginning of 1917 that democracy could not withstand a German victory in the First World War, but it was only after German U-boats began sinking American merchantmen that he got Congress to agree. In each case the loss of American life and the destruction of American property added a deeply emotional element to the logical arguments about national interest. This addition was crucial, for the American political system didn't respond to logic alone. Franklin Roosevelt had watched TR and Wilson, and learned. His own experience with the isolationists confirmed the lesson. For four years he had warned the nation that fascism posed a grave threat to America's way of life; only now, with the smoke billowing above Pearl Harbor, could Congress concede he was right.

Yet the attack on Pearl Harbor wasn't simply a casus belli; it was a debacle. America's Pacific fleet had been eviscerated by the Japanese bombs and torpedoes; American shipyards would have to work overtime for years to replace the vessels destroyed at Pearl. The lost lives, of course, could never be replaced. Some sort of attack had been necessary to make the isolationists understand the fascist threat, but *this* attack was a disaster.

Roosevelt knew it, and knew he would have to deal with it. But the time for that would come. The task of the moment was to commit the country to the war. Consequently, when the president addressed the legislature at half past noon on December 8, he spoke succinctly. "Yesterday, December 7, 1941, a date which will live in infamy," he said, "the United States of America was suddenly and deliberately attacked by naval and air forces of the empire of Japan." The attack was unprovoked and obviously premeditated. And it was part of a larger aggressive design.

> Yesterday the Japanese Government also launched an attack against Malaya. Last night Japanese forces attacked Hong Kong. Last night Japanese forces attacked Guam. Last night Japanese forces attacked the Philippine Islands. Last night the Japanese attacked Wake Island. And this morning the Japanese attacked Midway Island.

For months Roosevelt had lavished words on the looming threat; now that the threat had taken the form of bombs, torpedoes, and fiery death, he didn't need to. "The facts of yesterday and today speak for themselves." A mere six minutes after he began, he ended:

> Hostilities exist. There is no blinking at the fact that our people, our territory, and our interests are in grave danger. . . . I ask that the Congress declare that since the unprovoked and dastardly attack by Japan on Sunday, December 7, 1941, a state of war has existed between the United States and the Japanese empire.

✢ ✢ ✢

$\mathcal{T}$HE COMBINATION of Roosevelt's words and Japan's actions got the president what he wanted. In 1917 Congress had debated Wilson's war request for four days, and more than fifty members had finally voted against the war declaration. This time there was no debate and almost no opposition. The Senate approved the war resolution twenty-five minutes after Roosevelt finished speaking, the House ten minutes later. The Senate vote was unanimous; in the House the sole dissenter was Republican Jeanette Rankin, who, in her one previous term in Congress, had voted against war in 1917. (Her Montana constituents would respond in 1942 as they had in 1918, retiring her again to private life.)

Roosevelt signed the war resolution at ten minutes past four in a sober ceremony attended by leaders of both parties. He made no further statement and took no questions. His silence reflected his continuing wish to let Japan's crimes speak for themselves, but it also acknowledged the fact that he had no answer to a crucial question on everyone's mind. Did war with Japan mean war with Germany?

More precisely, he had no answer he could share with the American people. Roosevelt had wanted war with Germany; instead he got war with Japan. He still wanted war with Germany, and he expected it. His Magic eavesdroppers had intercepted a cable from Berlin to Tokyo, dated November 29, assuring the Japanese that if they "became engaged in a war against the United States, Germany would of course join in the war immediately." But Roosevelt couldn't share his knowledge without revealing his source, which he definitely would not do.

Anyway, he couldn't be absolutely certain Hitler would fulfill his pledge to Tokyo. The German dictator had lied before. Roosevelt spent the first twenty-four hours after Pearl Harbor making sure Congress declared war on Japan; he spent the next seventy-two hours ensuring that Germany declared war on the United States. On the evening of Tuesday, December 9, the president delivered his first war message to the American people. The central theme of this Fireside Chat was the unity of aggression. "The sudden criminal attacks perpetrated by the Japanese in the Pacific provide the climax of a decade of international immorality," the president said. He traced the ten-year arc of aggression, from Japan's invasion of Manchuria, through Italy's rape of Ethiopia, Germany's serial assaults on Austria, Czechoslovakia, Scandinavia, the Low Countries, France, and Russia, and culminating in Japan's attack at Pearl Harbor. "It is all of one pattern."

Japan had attacked the United States, Roosevelt acknowledged, but Hitler had put the Japanese up to it. "For weeks Germany has been telling Japan that if Japan did not attack the United States, Japan would not share in dividing the spoils with Germany when peace came. She was promised by Germany that if she came in she would receive the complete and perpetual control of the whole of the Pacific area." The Germans and Japanese conducted their military and naval operations according to a single global plan, one that treated any victory for an Axis nation as a victory for all. Japan had struck the United States more openly than Germany and Italy had thus far, but the danger from those countries was no less. "Germany and Italy, regardless of any formal declaration of war, consider themselves at war with the United States at this moment just as much as they consider themselves at war with Britain or Russia." Americans must recognize the global challenge and confront it. "We expect to eliminate the danger from Japan, but it would serve us ill if we accomplished that and found that the rest of the world was dominated by Hitler and Mussolini."

The struggle would test the courage and endurance of the American people. "It will not only be a long war, it will be a hard war," Roosevelt said. The conflict had begun for America in the Pacific, but it would not end there. "The United States can accept no result save victory, final and complete. Not only must the shame of Japanese treachery be wiped out, but the sources of international brutality, wherever they exist, must be absolutely and finally broken."

❖   ❖   ❖

$\mathcal{H}$ITLER DIDN'T SHARE much with Roosevelt, but he accepted the president's conclusion that the struggle between fascism and democracy was a fight to the death. And on December 11 he did precisely what Roosevelt wanted him to do. He notified the American embassy that Germany was declaring war on the United States. "Our patience is ended," Hitler told the Reichstag, by way of explanation. "The American president and his plutocratic clique have always in the past considered us a poor people. They were right! But this poor people wishes to live. . . . It wishes to ensure that it will never again be robbed by the rich nations of the earth, who refuse it its rightful place in the sun."

"The long known and the long expected has thus taken place," Roosevelt asserted in a new message to Congress. This time the president sent his words by courier for the clerks of the Senate and House to read to their chambers, but his relief was palpable nonetheless. After years of warning Americans against the fascist threat, after months of stretching his authority and bending the truth in an effort to educate the American people, even while striving to prevent Hitler from completing his conquest of Europe, Roosevelt would receive his mandate to wage the fight in full earnest. "The forces endeavoring to enslave the entire world now are moving toward this hemisphere," he said. "Never before has there been a greater challenge to life, liberty, and civilization. . . . I therefore request the Congress to recognize a state of war between the United States and Germany."

Not even Montana's Rankin could bring herself to oppose the president (although she did abstain). The Senate voted 88 to 0 for war against Germany, the House 393 to 0. The approving tallies were a bit larger on a companion war declaration against Italy, as straggling members arrived late. The signing ceremony was as subdued as the votes. "I've always heard things came in threes," Roosevelt remarked. "Here they are."

"So we had won after all," Winston Churchill exulted. "The United States was in the war, up to the neck and in to the death."

With Roosevelt the prime minister adopted a slightly less celebratory tone. "Now that we are, as you say, 'in the same boat,' would it not be wise for us to have another conference?" he cabled Roosevelt on December 9. "We could review the whole war plan in the light of reality and new facts, as well as the problems of production and distribution. I feel that all these matters, some of which are causing me concern, can best be settled on the highest executive level. It would also be a very great pleasure to me to meet you again, and the sooner the better."

Roosevelt was willing to meet Churchill, but not at once. He assumed that Churchill's team of soldiers and diplomats had thoroughly prepared an Anglo-American war plan, and he wanted time to develop America's own version. He drafted a reply putting Churchill off. "In August it was easy to agree on obvious main items—Russian aid, Near East aid, and new form Atlantic convoy," he said. "But I question whether situation in Pacific area is yet clear enough to make determination of that character. Delay of even a few weeks might be advantageous."

But before he could send this message shocking news arrived from Southeast Asia. The Japanese attack on British Malaya was no hit-and-run affair, like the raid on Pearl Harbor, but the opening of an amphibious invasion. Britain's naval command dispatched the *Prince of Wales* and the *Repulse,* both recently deployed to Singapore, against the invaders. A Japanese submarine reported their approach, and on the morning of December 10 the Japanese sent a large force of bombers and torpedo planes against the British ships. In a lopsided battle—the British lacked air cover—the *Prince of Wales* and the *Repulse* suffered multiple heavy blows from bombs and torpedoes before capsizing and sinking. Several hundred officers and men went down with their ships.

The news of the sinking stunned British and Americans alike. The Japanese success at Pearl Harbor had been attributed to surprise, but there was nothing surprising—except the outcome—in the attack on the *Prince of Wales* and *Repulse.* Suddenly the Pacific war seemed far more serious than it had just hours before. Roosevelt scrapped his draft message to Churchill and sent another message in its place. "Delighted to have you here at the White House," Roosevelt said. "Naval situation and other matters of strategy require discussion. . . . The news is bad but it will be better."

❖ ❖ ❖

*I*T HADN'T IMPROVED much by the time Churchill arrived. He came by battleship, the newly commissioned *Duke of York,* which conducted its shakedown cruise carrying the prime minister and his advisers west. Like the voyage of Roosevelt to Britain in 1918—aboard a vessel similarly being shaken down—Churchill's transit was alternatively tedious and harrowing. At first it slowed to the speed of the most laggard of its escort, but Churchill's navy minister, Admiral Sir Dudley Pound, grew impatient, declaring that the *Duke of York* was more likely to ram a U-boat than be torpedoed by one. With Churchill's assent Pound gave the order for the ship to cut loose from the escort and dash ahead on its own. The wintry North Atlantic lived up to its reputation; so many waves crashed over the deck of the battleship that Max Beaverbrook groused that he might as well have traveled by submarine.

The American navy and coast guard expected the *Duke of York* to steam up the Potomac to Washington, but Churchill, wishing to speak with Roosevelt as soon as possible, disembarked at Hampton Roads on December 22 and took a plane the rest of the way. He found Roosevelt waiting at Washington's airport. "I clasped his strong hand with comfort and pleasure," Churchill recalled. Darkness had descended over the capital, and the president's car took the two statesmen swiftly to the White House, where an informal dinner awaited them. Roosevelt, as always, mixed the drinks; Churchill imbibed appreciatively. When the dinner was called, the prime minister wheeled the president into the dining room—thinking, by his own recollection, "of Sir Walter Raleigh spreading his cloak before Queen Elizabeth."

Nothing of business had been put on the evening's agenda, but discussion inevitably turned to the war. Several issues demanded resolution. The first entailed strategic priorities, in particular whether the war in Europe and the Atlantic took precedence over the war in Asia and the Pacific. Churchill and his military men thought it did although, after the destruction of the *Prince of Wales* and *Repulse,* with less confidence than before. They recalled that the Americans had concurred in this opinion for several months. But that was before Pearl Harbor, which created a new political dynamic in America. As solicitous as Roosevelt had shown himself to be of American public opinion, Churchill couldn't help worrying that Europe might not loom so large in American strategic thinking as it had.

A related issue involved the nature of Anglo-American collaboration. Both Roosevelt and Churchill remembered the suspicions and outright hostility that had developed during the First World War when British and French generals demanded that American troops be employed as reinforcements in British and French units, under British and French command, and America's generals had refused. The squabbling had diminished the effectiveness of the anti-German coalition and probably prolonged the war. Neither Roosevelt nor Churchill wished to repeat the experience. But how best to prevent it—how most efficiently to coordinate the American and British war efforts—required careful thinking and possibly vigorous discussion.

At a higher level than either military strategy or command coordination was the matter of war aims. During the First World War, Wilson had insisted on America's being an "Associated" power rather than an Allied power; his diffidence reflected his refusal to fight for the imperial purposes that motivated Britain and France. Roosevelt and Churchill had dealt with some of these issues at the Atlantic Conference, but the Atlantic Charter left a great deal unsaid. In any event it committed only the Americans and the British. The anti-Axis ranks included the Soviet Union, China, and several other countries. A statement of purpose on the part of all of them was desirable, almost necessary.

Other questions were logistical. Now that the Americans were themselves fighting, would they be able and willing to continue supplying the recipients of Lend-Lease at the pre–Pearl Harbor level? Assuming agreement on the priority of Europe and the Atlantic, how might American military and naval power be brought most effectively to bear? How soon could American troops start fighting the Nazis? And where?

These last questions inspired much of the table talk that night at dinner. Since June 1940 France had held an anomalous position between Germany and Britain. The Wehrmacht occupied the north and west of the country, while the south was governed by the regime of Marshal Philippe Pétain, headquartered at Vichy. Pétain took care not to provoke Hitler, which meant that his policies were mildly to egregiously collaborationist. But he wasn't a Nazi, and presumably he had the best interests of France at heart. Of greater concern to Roosevelt and Churchill, he controlled what remained of the French fleet and of France's overseas empire, including French North Africa.

Hitler's decision to let Pétain govern Vichy France reflected the reality that there were only so many German troops, and most were currently occupied in Russia. Yet Germany's Russian offensive had stalled for the winter about the time Japan attacked Pearl Harbor, and many observers wondered how long Berlin would tolerate such independence as Vichy exercised.

The question came up at the Roosevelt-Churchill dinner. "There was general agreement that if Hitler was held in Russia he must try something else, and that the most probable line was Spain and Portugal en route to North Africa," Churchill reported to the war cabinet, in the only contemporary account of the evening. "There was general agreement that it was vital to forestall the Germans in North Africa." The emphasis on North Africa indicated the importance of that region for Mediterranean transit, which linked Britain to India, and also the prospect that North Africa would be where American troops would first enter the fight against Germany. "The President said that he was anxious that American land forces should give their support as quickly as possible wherever they could be most helpful, and favoured the idea of a plan to move into North Africa."

Nothing was decided that evening, and Churchill retired to his bedroom on the second floor of the White House, which became his home for the next three weeks. Harry Hopkins was across the hall, and just beyond Hopkins's suite the prime minister directed his support staff to re-create a version of the map room at his command headquarters in London. Roosevelt admired the maps and became a regular visitor; he subsequently ordered the establishment of his own map room downstairs.

The president and the prime minister swapped bedroom visits. Both began their days working in bed, although Roosevelt's day typically commenced earlier than Churchill's. Sometimes Roosevelt would roll into Churchill's room; sometimes Churchill would pad into Roosevelt's. In either case the smoke from Roosevelt's cigarettes would mingle with the heavier fumes of Churchill's cigars, and ashes would fly as each man punctuated his sentences with a jab of his favorite form of tobacco.

Hopkins later dined out on a story of a Roosevelt visit to Churchill's bedroom that caught the prime minister emerging from his bath with not even a towel between his rosy, rotund flesh and the historic atmosphere of the White

House. Roosevelt modestly apologized and started to wheel himself out. Churchill proclaimed that neither apology nor departure was necessary. "The Prime Minister of Great Britain," he said, "has nothing to conceal from the President of the United States."

Robert Sherwood wondered at Hopkins's version and asked Churchill about it. Nonsense, Churchill replied. He never greeted the president without at least a towel. Besides, he said, "I could not possibly have made such a statement as that. The president himself would have been well aware that it was not strictly true."

❖   ❖   ❖

THE DISCUSSIONS became more businesslike with the arrival of the supporting casts. Certain large questions were disposed of readily. Churchill and the British were delighted to discover that however much Pearl Harbor may have jolted the American people, it hadn't swayed the president or the American military from the conviction that Europe was the central theater in the war against the Axis. "Our view remains that Germany is still the prime enemy and her defeat is the key to victory," a paper jointly produced by the American and British chiefs of staff averred. "Once Germany is defeated, the collapse of Italy and the defeat of Japan must follow. . . . Therefore it should be a cardinal principle of A-B"—American-British—"strategy that only the minimum of force necessary for the safeguarding of vital interests in other theaters should be diverted from operations against Germany."

Somewhat thornier was the structure of American-British collaboration. George Marshall would be the quiet hero of America's war before the conflict ended; he started earning his reputation at the Washington conference. "As a result of what I saw in France"—during the First World War—"and from following our own experience, I feel very strongly that the most important consideration is the question of unity of command," Marshall told a meeting of the American and British officers. The group had been talking tactics, and although the discussion had been friendly it hung up on various details. Marshall contended that the hang-ups would recur—and be multiplied for each theater of the war—without unity of command. "I am convinced that there must be one man in command of the entire theater—air, ground, and ships. We cannot manage by cooperation. Human frailties are such that there would be emphatic unwillingness to place portions of troops under another service. If we make a plan for unified command now, it will solve nine-tenths of our troubles."

Marshall's British counterparts weren't so sure, and neither was Churchill. The British guessed that, given America's advantage over Britain in troop numbers and armament, the theater commanders would tend to be American. Sir Charles Portal, the chief of the Royal Air Force, argued that decisions regarding force allocation and similar matters were better made by the "highest authority"—namely the national governments. "When the allocation is decided upon, the directive has been formulated, and the forces allotted, everything else moves smoothly."

Churchill approached the command question in a meeting with Roosevelt. He conceded that unity of command was well and good where there was a "continuous line of battle," as there had been in France during the First World War. But the current situation in the Pacific was different. The scattered condition of the forces and fighting dictated that decisions would have to be made from central headquarters, presumably Washington.

Roosevelt responded that Washington wasn't receiving good intelligence from the Pacific theater. "The reports we are getting from the Far East are very sketchy," he said. A commander on the spot would certainly do better.

Churchill rejoined that a commander on the spot would do worse. "In some cases the troops are separated by a thousand miles," he said. At that distance a commander lacked the personal touch that made theater command advisable. He also lacked the broad perspective a commander based in Washington would have.

At this point in the conversation Max Beaverbrook handed a note to Harry Hopkins. "You should work on Churchill," Beaverbrook's note said. "He is being advised. He is open-minded and needs discussion."

Hopkins took the first opportunity to buttonhole Churchill. "Don't be in a hurry to turn down the proposal," Hopkins said. The prime minister might be pleasantly surprised by the theater commander the president had in mind.

"I was complimented by the choice," Churchill said of Roosevelt's nomination of Sir Archibald Wavell, the commander of British imperial forces in India. But the prime minister wasn't immediately convinced. "It seemed to me that the theatre in which he would act would soon be overrun and the forces which could be placed at his disposal would be destroyed by the Japanese onslaught." Yet after Hopkins orchestrated an informal meeting between Churchill and Marshall, at which the American general reiterated his arguments for unified command with the quiet sincerity that informed all his recommendations, Churchill allowed himself to be persuaded. "It was evident that we must meet the American view," he remarked later.

As part of the same deliberation, the Americans and British decided to establish a Combined Chiefs of Staff, consisting of the joint chiefs of staff of the British and American military establishments or their proxies. The headquarters of the Combined Chiefs would be in Washington. This arrangement favored the American side, in that the American principals would normally be present at Combined Chiefs meetings while their British counterparts would often be represented by deputies. But the headquarters had to be somewhere, and Washington, besides being the capital of the stronger power, was more centrally located between the two major theaters of the war.

Some thought was given to including a Soviet representative on the combined staff. But the possibility was no sooner raised than it was dismissed. Neither Roosevelt nor Churchill knew Stalin, and they saw no reason to let the Soviet dictator in on any more information than was necessary. Besides, they reasoned that the Russians had their hands full battling the Germans. Sending a top general to Washington would take that officer away from where he was needed. Finally, the Soviets weren't at war with Japan, which put them in a different position than the Americans and the British. So the Soviets weren't invited. As matters turned out, Stalin didn't complain.

❖   ❖   ❖

Soviet sensibilities did have to be considered on the issue of war aims. The outline of what the United States and Britain were fighting for had been established at the Atlantic Conference and articulated in the Atlantic Charter. But the war had grown since then, and Roosevelt deemed essential the inclusion of all the nations that, by choice or circumstance, found themselves fighting the Axis. It was Roosevelt who suggested the label "United Nations" for the anti-Axis coalition. And it was Roosevelt who included religious freedom as a principle the United Nations ought to be fighting for.

This was what rubbed the Soviets the wrong way. Maxim Litvinov, the Soviet ambassador to the United States, complained that a religious freedom clause was deliberately provocative. Litvinov allowed that the Soviet government—meaning Stalin, as everyone realized—might accept "freedom of conscience" as a substitute. Roosevelt stood firm, even as he noted that in American practice, dating to Jefferson and the other founders, religious freedom was understood to include the right to embrace no religion at all. Surely Stalin could live with that.

Stalin could, and did. The document that Litvinov signed on behalf of the

Soviet Union—beneath the signatures of Roosevelt and Churchill but above the signatures of T. V. Soong, the Chinese foreign minister, and of the representatives of the other anti-Axis governments—committed the signatory nations to the "common program of purposes and principles . . . known as the Atlantic Charter." The signatories also promised "to defend life, liberty, independence, and religious freedom, and to preserve human rights and justice in their own lands as well as in other lands."

The declaration was less airy regarding military strategy.

(1) Each Government pledges itself to employ its full resources, military or economic, against those members of the Tripartite Pact and its adherents with which such Government is at war.

(2) Each Government pledges itself to cooperate with the Governments signatory hereto and not to make a separate armistice or peace with the enemies.

There was art in the first pledge, in that the signers committed to fight not the entire Axis but only those Axis countries with which they were already at war. Thus Russia didn't declare war on Japan and didn't propose to.

The hard core of the declaration lay in the second pledge, forswearing any separate peace. If this pledge could be believed, the three great powers of the United Nations—as well as the lesser powers—would fight together till Germany was defeated. Each would resist all temptations to strike a deal with Hitler or his successors. They were in the war together until the bitter end.

❖   ❖   ❖

*C*HURCHILL HAD INTENDED to remain in Washington a week and be headed home by the beginning of the new year. But he got on so well with Roosevelt that he extended his visit to three weeks.

At times the relationship threatened to become too cordial for America's good. "Generals Arnold, Eisenhower, and Marshall came in to see me," Henry Stimson wrote in his diary for Christmas Day 1941, "and brought me a rather astonishing memorandum which they had received from the White House concerning a meeting between Churchill and the President and recorded by one of Churchill's assistants." The war secretary was referring to Henry— "Hap"—Arnold, the commander of America's air corps, and Dwight Eisenhower, the operations chief of the general staff, besides the chief of staff.

It reported the President as proposing to discuss the turning over to the British of our proposed reinforcements for MacArthur. This astonishing paper made me extremely angry and, as I went home for lunch and thought it over again, my anger grew until I finally called up Hopkins, told him of the paper and of my anger at it, and I said if that was persisted in, the President would have to take my resignation.

The memorandum in question had been compiled by Leslie Hollis, a brigadier general in the Royal Marines and the secretary of the British chiefs of staff. Roosevelt and Churchill had been discussing the dire peril of the British garrison in Malaya following the sinking of the *Prince of Wales* and *Repulse*. Churchill's military and naval chiefs explained that they were diverting all available units to Singapore in an effort to hold that crucial garrison. Roosevelt remarked that the American reinforcements currently en route to the Philippines via Australia would be unlikely to be able to fight their way to the Philippines in time to relieve Douglas MacArthur. "His view was that these reinforcements should be utilized in whatever manner might best serve the joint cause in the Far East," Hollis recorded, "and in agreement with the Prime Minister he expressed the desire that the United States and British Chiefs of Staff should meet the following day to consider what measures should be taken to give effect to his wishes."

The purpose of Hollis's memo was to inform the American chiefs of the president's commitment; the memo's effect was to alarm Arnold, Eisenhower, and Marshall and infuriate Stimson. The war secretary phoned Harry Hopkins, who said he would check the matter out. In a few minutes he called back and said he had asked Roosevelt, in the presence of Churchill, about the diversion of American reinforcements to Malaya. Roosevelt denied that any commitment had been made, and Churchill supported the president. Stimson was dubious and told Hopkins so. "I then read to him extracts from the paper . . . ," Stimson wrote in his diary, "and he said that they certainly bore out my view."

Roosevelt apparently had realized his mistake even as he denied making it, and Churchill was sufficiently gracious—and farsighted—to cover for him. Nothing more was said about sending the American forces to Singapore, beyond an oblique remark by Roosevelt that evening in a session with Stimson, Marshall, Arnold, Hopkins, and a few others. The president led a review of recent developments. "We discussed various things which were happening and the ways and means of carrying out the campaign in the Far East," Stimson recorded. "Incidentally and as if by aside, he flung out the remark that a paper had been going around which was nonsense and which entirely misrepresented a conference between him and Churchill." Stimson kept quiet—till he got home to his diary. "This incident shows the danger of talking too freely in international matters of such keen importance without the President carefully having his military and naval advisers present. . . . I think he felt he had pretty nearly burned his fingers and had called this subsequent meeting to make up for it. Hopkins told me at the time I talked with him over the telephone that he had told the President that he should be more careful about the formality of his discussions with Churchill."

❖ ❖ ❖

While Hopkins was warning Roosevelt to resist Churchill's charm, the prime minister was testing that charm on the American people. Roosevelt had invited him to speak from the White House balcony the night before Christmas. "This is a strange Christmas Eve," Churchill told the crowd of several hundred gathered in the darkness of the mansion's garden. "Almost the whole world is locked in deadly struggle, and with the most terrible weapons which science can devise the nations advance upon each other." And yet, for a moment, a different mood reigned. "Here, amid all the tumult, we have tonight the peace of the spirit in each cottage home and in every generous heart. Therefore, we may cast aside, for this night at least, the cares and dangers which beset us, and make for the children an evening of happiness in a world of storm."

Two days later Churchill became the first British prime minister to address the American Congress. His rhetorical reputation preceded him; his defiant speeches during the bleak moments of 1940 had stirred the souls even of many who wished to keep America's distance from Britain. Now he was an ally, a comrade-in-arms, and America tuned in—his speech was broadcast by the major radio networks—to hear him speak.

He reminded his audience of his American maternity. "I wish indeed that my mother, whose memory I cherish across the veil of years, could have been here to see me," he said. "By the way, I cannot help reflecting that if my father had been American and my mother British, instead of the other way around, I might have got here on my own." After letting the laughter subside, Churchill continued in the same vein. "In that case, this would not have been the first time you would have heard my voice. In that case I would not have needed any invitation. But if I had it is hardly likely that it would have been unanimous." More laughter. "So perhaps things are better as they are."

He turned serious as he noted that he, like the legislators in front of him, served at the will of the people. This was the glory of democracy, and its strength. "In my country, as in yours, public men are proud to be the servants of the state and would be ashamed to be its masters." And this was what distinguished America and Britain from those that made war against them.

Churchill thanked the members of Congress for the assistance America had provided Britain in its darkest hour. He pledged Britain's assistance to America in the struggle ahead. The contest would be neither swift nor easy. But progress would come. "I think it would be reasonable to hope that the end of 1942 will see us quite definitely in a better position than we are now; and that the year 1943 will enable us to assume the initiative upon an ample scale." Churchill understood that his listeners included more than a few persons who had long discounted the threat fascism posed to democracy. His own country had contained many of similar short sight. Changing their minds had been difficult. "Prodigious hammer blows have been needed to bring us together today." But the hammer blows had done their work. "Here we are together defending all that to free men is dear." Fate had chosen the English-speaking peoples.

> He must indeed have a blind soul who cannot see that some great purpose and design is being worked out here below, of which we have the honor to be the faithful servants. . . . In the days to come the British and American people will for their own safety and for the good of all walk together in majesty, in justice, and in peace.

The speech was a tremendous hit. Alben Barkley, the Senate majority leader, characterized Churchill's comments as "auspicious and impressive." Frederick Van Nuys, a Democratic senator from Indiana, declared, "The speech was a grand résumé not only of past conditions but of what we may expect in the future." Joseph Guffey of Pennsylvania called it "one of the greatest speeches I have ever heard." Even Burton Wheeler, the crusty isolationist, admitted that the address was "clever" and "one which will appeal to the ordinary American," although he added that what America needed at present was "less oratory and more action."

By every measure Churchill's visit was a smashing success for Roosevelt no less than for the prime minister. The two leaders demonstrated that their administrations could work together. Their staff chiefs might argue about this tactic or that, but on the essential elements of strategy they concurred. Germany would be the focus of their countries' combined efforts; Japan would be held at bay. A single commander would direct operations in each theater. The Atlantic Charter would motivate the war effort.

And Roosevelt and Churchill would cooperate as partners and friends. "The last evening of Churchill's visit the President, Churchill, and I had dinner together," Harry Hopkins wrote.

> The President and Churchill reviewed together the work of the past three weeks, and Churchill expressed not only his warm appreciation of the way he and his associates had been treated but his confidence that great steps had been taken towards unification of the prosecution of the war.

The dinner ran long, with neither Roosevelt nor Churchill eager to see the visit end. Ten o'clock was approaching as the prime minister made ready to depart.

> The President and I drove with Churchill to his train to Norfolk, Virginia. A special train had been put on the siding at Sixth Street. The President said goodbye to Churchill in the car, and I walked with him and put him on the train. . . .
> On the way back, the President made it perfectly clear that he too was very pleased with the meetings. There was no question but that he grew genuinely to like Churchill, and I am sure Churchill equally liked the President.

Hopkins had given one of Churchill's aides a small package for Clementine Churchill, the prime minister's wife, whom Hopkins had befriended in London. The package contained a few presents and a brief letter. "You would have been quite proud of your husband on this trip," Hopkins wrote. "He was ever so good natured. I didn't see him take anybody's head off. . . . If he had half as good a time here as the President did having him about the White House, he surely will carry pleasant memories of the past three weeks."

46.

ROOSEVELT GREETED THE NEW YEAR IN 1942 AS THE MOST POWER-ful man in American history. He headed a government stronger and more unified for war than any American government before it. He led a nation with greater capacity for war than any other nation in world history. He stood as first among equals in the most formidable wartime alliance ever gathered.

His political and moral standing was higher than it had ever been. His third election had confirmed his continuing popularity, and the coming of war had demonstrated his prescience. His rhetorical style—in speeches, Fireside Chats, and press conferences—had always been persuasive, but now that the fascists had made him a prophet, his words were more irresistible than ever. He had long spoken for the suffering people of America, staggering under the weight of the depression. Now he spoke for the suffering people of the world, crushed beneath the boot heel of fascism.

No powerful man lacks enemies; even the most persuasive leader leaves some people unconvinced. Pearl Harbor buried isolationism, at least for the moment, but it didn't transform the isolationists into fans of the president. Indeed, it drove some over the edge into conspiracy theories. So conveniently did the pieces of the international puzzle fall into place for Roosevelt after December 7 that the hard-core haters convinced themselves that he had engineered the whole thing. A noisy handful were already alleging that he had consciously allowed the attack on Pearl Harbor as providing a "back door" to the war against Germany. In time the charge would spawn a small library of books and articles claiming to prove Roosevelt's culpability. The charge was plausible from the start, and it gained plausibility with the release, decades later, of the Magic intercepts, which demonstrated that Roosevelt knew war with Japan was coming.

Yet half the world had known war with Japan was coming. What Roosevelt did not know was *where* it was coming. Thailand seemed likely, or Malaya or

Burma. The Philippines was the logical choice if the Japanese decided to attack an American possession directly. But Pearl Harbor seemed beyond their reach. The strongest evidence that Roosevelt did *not* expect an attack on Hawaii was his failure to put the Pacific battleships to sea. It would have been a simple matter to send the big vessels on patrol, leaving a few smaller craft in harbor to absorb the Japanese bombs and torpedoes. This certainly would have provided the casus belli he needed. So also an attack against which the American forces in Hawaii had been warned. In either case Roosevelt could have gone before Congress the next day and delivered precisely the same message he actually presented. And he would not have lost the major part of his Pacific fleet. For Roosevelt, who identified emotionally with the U.S. navy, to have deliberately allowed such destruction was beyond imagination. Or at least it was beyond the imagination of any not blinded by hatred of Roosevelt for other reasons.

Of course he brought the conspiracy theories upon himself. Even his most ardent supporters suspected he had manipulated the truth during the eighteen months before Pearl Harbor. His pledges that the destroyer-for-bases deal and Lend-Lease took America no closer to war rang hollow now. His election-eve promise not to send American boys to fight a foreign war was preserved by the fact that Hawaii wasn't foreign, but it was belied by the near certainty that those boys would be fighting far beyond American soil or even the Western Hemisphere.

With the suspicions swirling about him, Roosevelt had a new task of persuasion, one greater than any he had faced before. The depression had tested his skills of reassurance and inspiration; the war now tested them to a far greater degree. The banking crisis had called for patience; the war called for sacrifice. The New Deal had been born in three months; the war would last three years—if America was lucky. Americans had been required to tighten their belts during the depression; they would have to bury their dead, by the many thousands, during the war.

They would have to work and sacrifice, as they had never worked and sacrificed in their lives. In his first wartime State of the Union address, delivered in early January 1942, Roosevelt spelled out the goals he was setting for the American people. War production would expand dramatically. "In this year, 1942, we shall produce 60,000 planes," he said. "This includes 45,000 combat planes—bombers, dive bombers, pursuit planes. . . . Next year, 1943, we shall produce 125,000 airplanes, including 100,000 combat planes. . . . This year, 1942, we shall produce 45,000 tanks. . . . Next year, 1943, we shall produce 75,000 tanks." Similarly for anti-aircraft guns: 20,000 in 1942 and 35,000 in 1943. For merchant ships: 6 million deadweight tons in 1942 and 10 million in 1943.

Americans would have to sacrifice personally to support this production. "War costs money," Roosevelt said. "So far, we have hardly even begun to pay for it. We have devoted only 15 percent of our national income to national defense. . . . Our war program for the coming fiscal year will cost $56 billion or, in other words, more than half of the estimated annual national income. That means taxes and bonds and bonds and taxes. It means cutting luxuries and other non-essentials. In a word, it means an all-out war by individual effort and family effort in a united country."

The demands of the war would push everything else aside. "Our task is unprecedented, and the time is short. We must strain every existing armament-producing facility to the utmost. We must convert every available plant and tool to war production. That goes all the way from the greatest plants to the smallest—from the huge automobile industry to the village machine shop." Factories would operate twenty-four hours a day, seven days a week, fifty-two weeks a year. "Only this all-out scale of production will hasten the ultimate all-out victory. . . . Lost ground can always be regained, lost time never."

As much as the war would strain Americans physically, it would challenge them mentally and morally. The war would bring bad news; Americans must be ready. "We have already tasted defeat. We may suffer further setbacks. We must face the fact of a hard war, a long war, a bloody war, a costly war."

How long would the war last? "There is only one answer to that. It will end just as soon as we make it end, by our combined efforts, our combined strength, our combined determination to fight through and work through until the end—the end of militarism in Germany and Italy and Japan."

❖   ❖   ❖

To RALLY SUPPORT for the war in general was one thing; to persuade the American people of a particular strategy was something else. The Germany-first strategy developed in the talks with the British was no secret militarily, or at least it was nothing anyone with a modest grasp of geopolitics couldn't figure out unassisted. But it wasn't an obvious strategy politically. America had been attacked in the Pacific, not in Europe. American anger blazed against Japan, not against Germany. For Roosevelt to tell Americans they should ignore Japan for now and defer their vengeance risked confusing the public, deflating the war spirit, and distracting the political system.

But they had to be told, if not all at once. Roosevelt commenced the process in a Fireside Chat on February 23, a Monday. He had hoped to speak on Washington's Birthday, the day before, but in response to pastors' complaints that his radio sermons were competing with their own, he had begun avoiding Sundays. The White House had alerted the press that Roosevelt would be discussing global strategy and suggested that newspapers print maps of the world in that Monday's editions. Hundreds took the suggestion, with the result that when the president went on the air, his listeners were ready for a lesson in global strategy.

"This is a new kind of war," Roosevelt said.

It is different from all other wars of the past, not only in its methods and weapons but also in its geography. It is warfare in terms of every continent, every island, every sea, every air lane in the world. That is the reason why I have asked you to take out and spread before you a map of the whole earth, and to follow with me the references which I shall make to the world-encircling battle lines of this war.

The papers rustled in American homes as Roosevelt walked his listeners around the globe, explaining the significance of each area to American strategy.

Look at your map. Look at the vast area of China, with its millions of fighting men. Look at the vast area of Russia, with its powerful armies and proven military might. Look at the British Isles, Australia, New Zealand, the Dutch Indies, India, the Near East, and the continent of Africa, with their resources of raw materials, and of peoples determined to resist Axis domination. Look too at North America, Central America, and South America.

It is obvious what would happen if all of these great reservoirs of power were cut off from each other either by enemy action or by self-imposed isolation. First, in such a case, we could no longer send aid of any kind to China—to the brave people who, for nearly five years, have withstood Japanese assault, destroyed hundreds of thousands of Japanese soldiers and vast quantities of Japanese war munitions. It is essential that we help China in her magnificent defense and in her inevitable counteroffensive—for that is one important element in the ultimate defeat of Japan.

Second, if we lost communication with the Southwest Pacific, all of that area, including Australia and New Zealand and the Dutch Indies, would fall under Japanese domination. Japan in such a case could release great numbers of ships and men to launch attacks on a large scale against the coasts of the Western Hemisphere—South America and Central America, and North America, including Alaska. At the same time, she could immediately extend her conquests in the other direction toward India, and through the Indian Ocean to Africa, to the Near East, and try to join forces with Germany and Italy.

Third, if we were to stop sending munitions to the British and the Russians in the Mediterranean, in the Persian Gulf, and the Red Sea, we would be helping the Nazis to overrun Turkey, Syria, Iraq, Persia, Egypt and the Suez Canal, the whole coast of North Africa itself, and with that inevitably the whole coast of West Africa—putting Germany within easy striking distance of South America, fifteen hundred miles away.

Fourth, if by such a fatuous policy we ceased to protect the North Atlantic supply line to Britain and to Russia, we would help to cripple the splendid counteroffensive by Russia against the Nazis, and we would help to deprive Britain of essential food supplies and munitions.

This new war was truly a world war, and it would be fought on a world front. On freedom's side, it was being fought by a broad alliance. "The United Nations constitute an association of independent peoples of equal dignity and equal importance," Roosevelt said. All members shared the burdens of war; all shared the same high purposes. "The Atlantic Charter applies not only to the parts of the world that border the Atlantic but to the whole world; disarmament of aggressors, self-determination of nations and peoples, and the four freedoms: freedom of speech, freedom of religion, freedom from want, and freedom from fear."

❖   ❖   ❖

ON THE SAME evening that Roosevelt was conducting his lesson in global strategy, a Japanese submarine surfaced off California near Santa Barbara and lobbed a few shells landward. Quite clearly the purpose was psychological: to steal the president's thunder. The mission succeeded. The same papers that carried Roosevelt's speech included articles about this first attack on the American mainland.

Roosevelt learned a lesson: not to announce major speeches so far in advance. He also detected an opportunity: to impress on Americans the differences between wartime and peacetime. Roosevelt worried from the start about the dissemination of war news. Congress had no sooner declared war on Japan than the president urged caution in repeating reports about the fighting. The initial news from Hawaii had been followed by wild speculation on what the Japanese were up to and where they might strike next. Roosevelt tamped down the rumors by refusing to comment on most of them, but his silence prompted suspicions that the White House knew more than it was saying. A journalist raised the issue at Roosevelt's first wartime news conference. "This is not an impudent question, sir, but it might clear up things," he said. "Do you intend to give the public the benefit of all of the reports you get?"

"I am going to give—all of us are going to give—everything to the public, on two conditions," Roosevelt replied. "The first is that it is accurate. Well, I should think that would seem fairly obvious. And the second is that in giving it out it does not give aid and comfort to the enemy. . . . I should think that those two conditions ought to be put up in every office in Washington."

A reporter remarked sardonically that there was no need to post the rules in government offices. "It is impossible to get any information from any department now," he complained. "They give you the run-around."

"Well, then, you can't assume that the information has conformed to the two conditions."

"You ought to have someone there who can say whether it does conform."

"That has got to be determined by the higher officers—the army and navy."

"But we have been told that these officers have no information—have instructions not to talk on any subject."

"I think that is probably correct."

"Where does that put us?"

"It means that you have got to wait—sit and wait on this information, because you can't determine whether certain information conforms to those two principles. We can't leave that determination in the hands of a third assistant. . . . It has got to come from the top."

A reporter asked Roosevelt to clarify what he meant by a news report giving aid and comfort to the enemy. "Does that mean that no bad news is going to be given out?"

"No, no," the president replied. "It depends on whether the giving out is of aid and comfort to the enemy."

Roosevelt's rules weren't particularly helpful to reporters, as this exchange suggested. Reporters and editors often had to guess as to what would help the enemy and what wouldn't. Yet to a remarkable degree they accorded the president and the administration the benefit of the doubt. Their trust reflected, in varying combinations, their patriotism, their worries about alienating readers, and the respect they had developed for Roosevelt during the previous nine years. Roosevelt's cultivation of the press through hundreds of press conferences had amassed for him a store of goodwill against which he was able to draw during the war. For nearly a decade he had given them story after story, besides providing the best show in Washington. His audience valued his performance.

He continued to cultivate the press after the war began. He restricted information regarding his own movements and whereabouts, to the annoyance of some members of the press corps. And he resolutely enforced, to the extent he could, his two rules of wartime media, especially the one about information that might aid the enemy. But the censoring and repressive hand of government was light compared with its weight in the past. Roosevelt was no First Amendment purist; as on many other subjects, his concerns regarding civil liberties were pragmatic and political rather than ethical. He remembered the Espionage and Sedition Acts of the First World War. He recalled in particular how they had alienated large parts of Wilson's liberal base and contributed to the buildup of pressures that exploded poisonously after the war, dooming Wilson's peace plan and polarizing the country for a decade. Roosevelt was playing a long game, already reckoning how the war should end. He needed the press on his side, and he did what he could to keep it there.

❖   ❖   ❖

*I*N CERTAIN OTHER respects, the Roosevelt touch was far from light. Since the mid-1930s the president had feared the emergence of a fifth column in the United States (at the time, in fact, when this term for domestic disloyalty was being popularized in the Spanish civil war). In August 1936 Roosevelt met with J. Edgar Hoover, the director of the Federal Bureau of Investigation, to discuss "subversive activities in the United States, particularly Fascism and Communism," according to Hoover's memorandum of the meeting. Hoover, again according to his own account, initially demurred, explaining that the FBI's charter confined its investigations to violations of the law. Political activities were off limits. Yet Hoover mentioned a possible way around the stricture. A law left over from the First World War allowed the bureau to respond to requests from the State Department for information. Roosevelt took the suggestion and the next day brought Hoover back to the White House. This time Cordell Hull was present. The secretary of state had even less use for subversives than Roosevelt did, and a saltier vocabulary. "Go ahead and investigate the hell out of those cocksuckers," Hull told Hoover.

The bureau stepped up its surveillance upon the outbreak of the war in Europe, and did so openly. "The Attorney General has been requested by me to instruct the Federal Bureau of Investigation of the Department of Justice to take charge of investigative work in matters relating to espionage, sabotage, and violations of the neutrality regulations," Roosevelt announced on September 6, 1939. The needs of efficiency motivated the president's decision. "This task must be conducted in a comprehensive and effective manner on a national basis, and all information must be carefully sifted out and correlated in order to avoid confusion and irresponsibility." But the centralization of counterespionage also reflected Roosevelt's desire to have direct access to the information the investigators unearthed.

During the next two years the FBI compiled lists of potentially worrisome foreign nationals. The Alien Registration Act of June 1940—often called the Smith Act, for its sponsor in the House of Representatives, Howard Smith of Virginia—loosened the legal reins on the bureau by making a federal crime of advocacy of the overthrow of the American government. Active Communists presumably fell within the scope of the law, as perhaps did closet Nazis and fellow travelers of both the extreme left and the far right. On signing the Smith Act, Roosevelt assured the American people that loyal aliens need have no fear of government. Others had better watch out. "With those aliens who are disloyal and are bent on harm to this country, the government, through its law enforcement agencies, can and will deal vigorously."

The focus on aliens followed the historic practice of most countries during wartime. Governments typically detained enemy aliens on grounds that they posed a prima facie security threat. Normally the aliens were deported to their home countries, but when deportation was inconvenient or impossible, they were sometimes held for the duration of the conflict.

The American government adopted this practice immediately after Pearl Harbor. By December 1941 Hoover and the FBI had identified thousands of Japanese, German, and Italian aliens in the United States; Roosevelt gave the order to round them up. Several thousand were arrested within days—some of the Germans and Italians even before the declarations of war between their home countries and the United States.

The arrests largely quelled public concern about espionage and sabotage as they involved the Germans and Italians. Roosevelt deliberately downplayed the matter. The wartime policy of the FBI, adopted with the president's approval, was to minimize news of the activities of Axis agents, lest the public become aroused. An internal FBI document explained: "There must not be permitted to develop any vigilante system of wartime law enforcement."

Managing passions toward the Japanese, however, proved beyond the capacity of the bureau, and beyond the political will of the president. The surprise attack on Pearl Harbor naturally provoked alarm at the possibility of additional attacks against Americans and American soil. This alarm, combined with the puzzlement that the United States had been caught so unprepared, primed Americans to imagine espionage or sabotage among Japanese nationals living in America. The hoary concept of the "yellow peril" reemerged, coloring attitudes toward anyone of Japanese ancestry. The American intelligence apparatus, having snoozed through Pearl Harbor, grew suddenly insomniac, and like other insomniacs it conjured nightmares from fragments of fact, worst-case scenarios, and whole cloth. Rumors were accepted as truth, or at least as working approximations of truth, by those charged with preventing another Pearl Harbor.

General John DeWitt headed the army's Western Defense Command, with responsibility for the West Coast. Determined not to be California's counterpart to Admiral Husband Kimmel or General Walter Short—two officers already under investigation for failing to defend Pearl Harbor—DeWitt took every report most seriously. Stray radio signals became secret transmissions from Japanese spies to ships offshore. When the signals fell silent, their very silence indicated the insidious guile of the enemy.

The material interests of others inflamed DeWitt's suspicions. For decades the neighbors and economic competitors of the Chinese and Japanese in California and nearby states had resented the Asians' willingness to work long and hard for low wages and modest profit margins; at every opportunity some of those competitors had tried to elbow them aside legally or physically. Pearl Harbor provided a new opportunity, and demands at once arose to drive the Japanese from their homes, their farms, and their businesses. The more forthright didn't disguise their intentions. "We're charged with wanting to get rid of the Japs for selfish reasons," a spokesman for the California Grower-Shipper Vegetable Association said. "We might as well be honest. It's a question of whether the white man lives on the Pacific Coast or the brown man."

Elected officials followed the popular mood and sometimes led it. California's attorney general, Earl Warren, called for the imposition of martial law. "In view of the circumstances, the problem becomes a military problem rather than one in civil government," Warren said. The mayor of Los Angeles demanded the removal of Japanese from the "combat zone," meaning most of the West Coast. Several members of the city council endorsed the mayor's demand.

Pundits joined the calls for removal. Walter Lippmann insisted that security preempted civil liberties. In an essay written from San Francisco and titled "The Fifth Column on the Coast," Lippmann asserted, "The Pacific Coast is in imminent danger of a combined attack from within and from without. . . . It is a fact that the Japanese navy has been reconnoitering the Pacific Coast more or less continually and for a considerable period of time, testing and feeling out the American defenses. It is a fact that communication takes place between the enemy at sea and enemy agents on land." Americans ignored these facts at their peril, Lippmann said. He denied that removal of Japanese Americans from the coastal zone would violate their constitutional rights. "Nobody's constitutional rights include the right to reside and do business on a battlefield. And nobody ought to be on a battlefield who has no good reason for being there. There is plenty of room elsewhere for him to exercise his rights." Westbrook Pegler rarely agreed with Lippmann, but on this subject the outspokenly conservative columnist did. "We are so damned dumb and considerate of the minute Constitutional rights and even of the political feelings and influence of people whom we have every reason to anticipate with preventive action!" Pegler said. "The Japanese in California should be under armed guard to the last man and woman right now, and to hell with habeas corpus until the danger is over."

Confident of public support, DeWitt requested authority to remove the Japanese—including American citizens of Japanese descent—from the West Coast. His request at first divided the Roosevelt administration. Henry Morgenthau thought things were proceeding too fast. "When it comes to suddenly mopping up 150,000 Japanese and putting them behind barbed wire . . . ," the Treasury secretary said, "I want at some time to have caught my breath." Attorney General Francis Biddle initially opposed removal, vowing that "the Department of Justice would not under any circumstances evacuate American citizens."

Henry Stimson was torn. "The second generation Japanese can only be evacuated either as part of a total evacuation, giving access to the areas only by permits," the war secretary wrote in his diary, "or by frankly trying to put them out on the ground that their racial characteristics are such that we cannot understand or trust even the citizen Japanese. This latter is the fact but I am afraid it will make a tremendous hole in our constitutional system to apply it." Yet Stimson, as head of the War Department, had to consider the alternatives. "It is quite within the bounds of possibility that if the Japanese should get naval dominance in the Pacific, they would try an invasion of this country; and if they did, we would have a tough job meeting them." He added, "The people of the United States have made an enormous mistake in underestimating the Japanese." Stimson was determined that this mistake not be repeated, and so he recommended to Roosevelt that DeWitt's evacuation request be approved.

Roosevelt, of course, had the final decision. The president could have overridden Stimson, and perhaps his conscience urged him to. But its urgings were neither loud nor strong, and they had to compete with his political sensibilities. Even less than DeWitt or Stimson could Roosevelt afford another Pearl Harbor, and at a moment of ignorance as to Japan's capabilities, he couldn't say with confidence that the Japanese community in California did *not* harbor spies and saboteurs. During peacetime he was as staunch an advocate as the next person of the principle that individuals should be treated as individuals and not as part of a suspect class, but during wartime he thought this principle might be modified in the larger national interest.

Roosevelt chose not to inquire too deeply into the War Department's reasoning. Stimson sought an interview with Roosevelt to discuss relocation, but the president declined, saying he was busy. This was true enough, given the unprecedented demands on his time, but it also reflected his wish to avoid a face-to-face airing of the issues involved. Stimson had to settle for speaking to Roosevelt by telephone. The president told the war secretary to do what he thought best. John McCloy, Stimson's assistant, recalled Roosevelt saying, "There will probably be some repercussions, but it has got to be dictated by military necessity." Roosevelt added, "Be as reasonable as you can."

On February 19, the president issued Executive Order 9066 asserting that "the successful prosecution of the war requires every possible protection against espionage and against sabotage to national-defense material, national-defense premises, and national-defense utilities" and authorizing the secretary of war "to prescribe military areas in such places and of such extent as he or the appropriate military commanders may determine, from which any or all persons may be excluded." The order did not single out either the West Coast or the Japanese, but it was universally understood to apply peculiarly to that region and those people.

And it was widely applauded, especially when, just four days later, the Japanese submarine shelled the California coast near Santa Barbara. The evacuation began within weeks; ultimately some 110,000 men, women, and children of Japanese descent were removed to internment camps in the desert regions east of the Sierra Nevada and Cascades. Seventy percent of the internees were American citizens. By most evidence, the great majority of those removed had been enthusiastic about living in America before the war began. Some, not surprisingly, had second thoughts in their bleak new homes.

✼ ✼ ✼

AMONG THE BASE motives that inspired the internment of the Japanese Americans was the most basic human motive of all: fear. During the five months after Pearl Harbor—the period when the relocation policy was formulated, approved, and implemented—the armies and navy of imperial Japan appeared invincible. Tokyo's strategy of stunning the Americans and British with lightning blows against Hawaii, the Philippines, Hong Kong, and Malaya and of then driving south to seize the oil of the Dutch East Indies unfolded to perfection. The crippling of the American Pacific fleet prevented Washington from reinforcing General MacArthur in the Philippines. This was just as well, given MacArthur's hopeless condition by the end of the first day of fighting there. Despite his several hours' warning after Pearl Harbor, MacArthur inexplicably allowed his air force to be blasted on the ground by Japanese attackers, leaving Luzon, the main Philippine island, open to invasion by Japanese land forces. The combined American and Philippine army was forced to retreat to the Bataan Peninsula, while MacArthur and his staff holed up on Corregidor, a rock at the entrance to Manila Bay.

MacArthur demanded reinforcements. "The Philippine theater is the locus of victory or defeat," he declared. For the United States to fail to defend the Philippines with every resource at its disposal would be a "fatal mistake."

Roosevelt agreed rhetorically. "The people of the United States will never forget what the people of the Philippine Islands are doing this day and will do in the days to come," he promised. "I give to the people of the Philippines my solemn pledge that their freedom will be redeemed and their independence established and protected. The entire resources, in men and in material, of the United States stand behind that pledge."

But there was something disconcerting to Filipinos about the president's use of the word "redeem," which suggested that Philippine freedom had already been lost. And there was something even more unsettling about the emerging Europe-first strategy, which clearly contradicted Roosevelt's pledge to devote the "entire resources" of the United States to the defense of the Philippines.

Not for the last time, global strategy forced a deferral of promises. MacArthur did not receive his reinforcements, and four decades of short-changing Philippine defense culminated in four months of misery for the islands' defenders. "Our troops have been subsisted on one-half to one-third rations for so long a period that they do not possess the physical strength to endure the strain placed upon the individual in an attack," the American commander on Bataan, Jonathan Wainwright, asserted. In early April the Bataan garrison was compelled to surrender—only to suffer even more grievously on the forced march to prisoner camps and in the camps themselves.

Roosevelt meanwhile ordered MacArthur to leave Corregidor for Australia, to fight another day. MacArthur resisted. "These people are depending on me now," he informed the president. "Any idea that I was being withdrawn for any other purpose than to bring them immediate relief could not be explained." Roosevelt repeated his order, more emphatically than before. MacArthur complied this time, departing in the dead of night by PT boat and dodging Japanese patrols till he reached the southern island of Mindanao, from which he flew to Darwin, Australia. "The President of the United States ordered me to break through the Japanese lines and proceed from Corregidor to Australia for the purpose, as I understand it, of organizing the American offensive against Japan," he told reporters on his arrival. "A primary purpose of this is relief of the Philippines. I came through and I shall return."

As disappointing as the loss of the Philippines was to Americans, it was not nearly as devastating as the loss of Singapore was to the British. For decades British imperial planners had based their strategy for Southeast Asia on the island fortress at the tip of the Malay Peninsula. But like the Americans regarding the Philippines, the British had been distracted by other demands on their resources. The outbreak of the war in Europe additionally deprived Singapore, which by December 1941 possessed but a fraction of its projected strength. The dispatch of the *Repulse* and *Prince of Wales* was supposed to improve the situation; their destruction sank Singapore's hopes with them. Japanese troops drove down the peninsula during January 1942 and captured Singapore and its garrison of seventy thousand in early February.

The fall of Singapore shocked the British like no event of the war thus far. "When I reflect how I have longed and prayed for the entry of the United States into the war, I find it difficult to realize how gravely our British affairs have deteriorated by what has happened since December seven," Churchill wrote Roosevelt. "We have suffered the greatest disaster in our history at Singapore, and other misfortunes will come thick and fast upon us."

He was right. The collapse of Singapore opened Burma and the East Indies to Japanese invasion. Rangoon fell within weeks, enabling Japanese forces to close the Lend-Lease supply line to the beleaguered Chinese government of Chiang Kai-shek. Japanese troops landed on Java and soon controlled that most populous island of the East Indies. Japanese troops occupied the northeastern coast of New Guinea and seized key positions in the various island groups of the southwestern Pacific.

By April 1942 the Japanese empire covered an enormous swath of the earth's surface, from the International Date Line in the east almost to India in the west, and from the North Pacific nearly to Australia. To be sure, much of this was empty ocean—but it was ocean commanded by the Japanese fleet. The Anglo-American strategy had been to contain Japan in the Pacific while concentrating on Germany in Europe. How well the Americans and British would do against Germany remained to be seen. Against Japan they were failing miserably.

❖   ❖   ❖

$\mathscr{P}$ART OF THE problem, Roosevelt thought, was Britain's backward policy in Asia. Indian nationalists had been agitating to eject Britain from India for generations. Their efforts—like the efforts of nationalists in other countries over the decades—took heart from America's traditional and continuing anti-imperialism. Wilson's call for self-determination resonated with Mohandas Gandhi, Jawaharlal Nehru, and other leaders of the nationalist Indian Congress party, who drew on America's Declaration of Independence in writing a similar declaration for India in 1930. Nehru appealed explicitly to Americans for support in articles in *Foreign Affairs* and *Atlantic Monthly,* published as the tide of war was rising a decade later. Britain's declaration of war against Germany in 1939 triggered an outbreak of nonviolent noncooperation in India, partly from resentment that the British imperial government had included India in the war declaration without consulting Indian leaders and partly from hope that Britain's distress would compel London to offer independence— perhaps deliverable at war's end—in exchange for India's assistance against the Axis. The British government was pondering the situation when Churchill took power in the spring of 1940.

Churchill's India problem became Roosevelt's India problem at the time of the Atlantic Conference. The Atlantic Charter's affirmation of the "right of all peoples to choose the form of government under which they will live" seemed to support the position of the Indian nationalists, and Roosevelt's silence in response to Churchill's denials that the charter applied to the British empire encouraged allegations of American hypocrisy. Such allegations were most potent in Asia, where the Japanese had been saying for years that nothing really distinguished American imperialism from the British, French, and Dutch versions.

Roosevelt broached the India issue in his conversations with Churchill in Washington during December 1941 and January 1942. But Churchill rebuffed the president's overtures. "I reacted so strongly and at such length that he never raised it verbally again," Churchill recalled with satisfaction.

Yet the issue didn't disappear. If anything, it grew more pressing after the surrender of Singapore made a Japanese invasion of India suddenly possible. Japan's theater commanders capitalized on their momentum and their country's prestige among Asians by calling on Indian nationalists to embrace the Axis as a means of expelling the British. The Japanese enlisted thousands of Indian troops taken prisoner at Singapore in what would become the pro-Japanese Indian National Army.

Given the collapse of Singapore, Roosevelt had to weigh the prospect that India would put up hardly more of a fight, especially if the Japanese could credibly cast themselves as liberators. Roosevelt didn't like being called a hypocrite any more than most people do, but what really worried him about the Indian situation was the damage it was doing to American prestige and, through American prestige, to American power. America's power was military and economic, but it was also moral. The peoples of the world looked not to Britain and Churchill for hope and guidance but to America and Roosevelt. And Roosevelt intended to keep it that way.

The president knew what a reactionary Churchill was on imperial issues, and he feared that the prime minister's determination to crush the independence movement would get the better of his strategic sense. Besides, the course Churchill had charted might fail on its own terms. By refusing even to consider independence, the prime minister might render independence inevitable— on terms that simultaneously ensured the alienation of India from the Allied cause. Roosevelt understood as well as Churchill that the Indian army was what made Britain a world power. The Royal Navy was important, to be sure. But what allowed Britain to fight far above its weight in international affairs was the Indian army. Without India, Britain would shrink to a mere shadow of its current self. And that shadow wouldn't be of much help to Roosevelt in defeating the Axis.

The president decided to risk Churchill's wrath. "I have given much thought to the problem of India," he wrote the prime minister in March 1942. "As you can well realize, I have felt much diffidence in making any suggestions, and it is a subject which, of course, all of you good people know far more about than I do." But he had to speak his mind. "I have tried to approach the problem from the point of view of history and with a hope that the injection of a new thought to be used in India might be of assistance to you." The president reminded Churchill how the American colonies, upon breaking away from Britain, had established thirteen separate and sovereign governments. The Articles of Confederation had guided the states to victory in the Revolutionary War but had been replaced by the federal Constitution of 1787. "It is merely a thought of mine," Roosevelt said, "to suggest the setting up of what might be called a temporary government in India, headed by a small representative group, covering different castes, occupations, religions, and geographies." This group would be recognized by London as a Dominion government, albeit a temporary one. It would last for the duration of the war and for a year or two afterward. It would give way to a permanent successor, to be established by Indians much as the federal government of the United States had been established by Americans after the Revolutionary War. Roosevelt didn't claim this was a perfect solution, but he thought it offered a path forward. "It might cause the people there to forget hard feelings, to become more loyal to the British Empire, and to stress the danger of Japanese domination." He assured Churchill he didn't wish to impose any solution to the India problem. "It is, strictly speaking, none of my business," he said—before concluding, significantly, "except insofar as it is a part and parcel of the successful fight that you and I are making."

Churchill liked Roosevelt, and he admired the president's gifts of leadership. But he considered him dangerously naïve about issues relating to the British empire. Churchill replied that the president failed to appreciate that the nationalists in India hardly spoke for the whole population. For Britain to grant independence—which Churchill did not for one second propose to do—would be politically immoral as well as militarily imprudent. "We must not on any account break with the Moslems, who represent a hundred million people and the main army elements on which we must rely for the immediate fighting. We have also to consider our duty towards thirty to forty million Untouchables and our treaties with the princes' states of India, perhaps eighty millions." Japan was almost at India's eastern border. "Naturally we do not want to throw India into chaos on the eve of invasion."

Churchill had a point about the Muslims—the "martial races," he often called them—being the backbone of the Indian army. The Congress party was a Hindu league, and the Hindus had never enlisted in the army in large numbers. Yet Roosevelt realized that, as important as India's soldiers were to the Allied war effort, the credibility of the Atlantic Charter was equally important. For Churchill simply to ignore the Indian demands for self-determination risked grave damage to American interests.

In fact Churchill did not simply *ignore* the Indian demands; he punished their authors. During the summer of 1942 Gandhi proclaimed the "Quit India" movement, a campaign of civil disobedience designed to force the British to grant independence. Churchill responded within days by jailing Gandhi, Nehru, and some hundred thousand of the rank and file of the Congress party.

Roosevelt responded to the mass jailing by forwarding to Churchill a letter from Chiang Kai-shek conveying the Chinese leader's dismay at the "disastrous effect" of the British action on pro-Allied morale in Asia. "At all costs the United Nations should demonstrate to the world by their action the sincerity of their professed principle of ensuring freedom and justice for men of all races," Chiang wrote Roosevelt. Over Chiang's words, Roosevelt asked Churchill: "What do you think?"

Churchill thought as little of Chiang's meddling as he had of Roosevelt's. By chance or design, the Quit India campaign nearly coincided with the first anniversary of the Atlantic Charter. The American Office of War Information had indicated its intention of commemorating the occasion with a robust reiteration of the charter's principles. Churchill warned Roosevelt against anything that might create problems for the British government. "Its proposed application to Asia and Africa requires much thought," Churchill asserted. "Great embarrassment would be caused to the defence of India at the present time by such a statement as the Office of War Information has been forecasting." The prime minister expressed confidence that he could rely on the president. "I am sure you will consider my difficulties with the kindness you always show me."

Roosevelt did consider Churchill's difficulties, although kindness had little to do with it. The attitude of Asians counted in Roosevelt's thinking about the world, but the cooperation of Britain counted more. The president ordered the OWI to back off, and he issued an innocuously vague reaffirmation of the Atlantic Charter's general principles. "I am sure you will have no objection to a single line," he wrote Churchill. "It omits wholly anything which would raise questions or controversy."

47.

"I REALIZE HOW THE FALL OF SINGAPORE HAS AFFECTED YOU AND THE British people," Roosevelt wrote Churchill amid the disasters of early 1942. "It gives the back-seat drivers a field day. But no matter how serious our setbacks have been, and I do not for a moment underrate them, we must constantly look forward to the next moves that need to be made to hit the enemy."

How to hit the enemy—this was the question that pushed all others to the rear. The enemy kept hitting America, and not simply in the far Pacific. The formal outbreak of war between the United States and Germany brought the Battle of the Atlantic right up to America's shore. American merchantmen hugged the East Coast and dimmed their running lights for safety, but America's coastal communities negligently left their building lights on, allowing German U-boats to silhouette the vessels against skylines of Miami, Atlantic City, and other urban areas. The ensuing torpedo strikes and sinkings, within easy viewing distance of the beaches, frightened and dismayed Americans. For six months the Germans decimated American transatlantic shipping, destroying nearly four hundred vessels totaling two million tons.

Roosevelt sorely wanted to respond, but he couldn't figure out how. For all that he had prepared America for war prior to Pearl Harbor, much more needed to be done before American forces could engage the Germans or Japan. The administration needed to expand the army dramatically and train and equip the soldiers. It needed to enlarge the navy to defend American shipping and transport the army to where the soldiers would fight. It needed to construct an air force that would cover the ships and soldiers in transit and in combat and destroy the enemy's ability to retaliate. All this was in the works, but it took time. And time wasn't something Roosevelt could wholly count on. America's war effort would never be stronger than the willingness of the American people to make war. After Pearl Harbor they were hot to fight, but with each month that Pearl Harbor receded into the past, their temperature declined. Unless the administration could show progress—unless it could demonstrate that the evil-doers were being punished for their sins—Roosevelt risked the dissipation of the pro-war sentiment he had spent so much time and effort summoning. The autumn would bring elections. Roosevelt wouldn't be on the ballot, but the voters would speak. They would certainly have something to say about the war.

Roosevelt's impatience to hit the enemy prompted a daring raid on Japan's home islands—the riposte, as it were, to Pearl Harbor. The Japanese attack had revealed the feasibility of launching light aircraft from ships, bearing small loads of bombs or torpedoes. But almost no one believed that large bombers with substantial payloads could take off from ships. Lieutenant Colonel James Doolittle of the army air forces was one of the rare optimists, and in early 1942 he proposed to lead a squadron of modified B-25 bombers launched from aircraft carriers against Japan. Roosevelt approved the plan, and on April 1 sixteen B-25s were loaded onto the *Hornet* in San Francisco Bay. The *Hornet* steamed west and rendezvoused north of Hawaii with the *Enterprise,* another carrier, which provided air protection for the *Hornet.* The two ships and their escorts proceeded toward the projected launch point, some six hundred miles east of Japan. But at seven hundred miles they encountered a Japanese patrol boat, which radioed their presence to Japan before being sunk by American fire. Doolittle decided to launch at once lest they lose any more of the element of surprise. The planes got off safely, despite heaving seas, and skimmed the waves single file before fanning out as they crossed the Japanese coast. "Thirteen B-25s effectively bombed Tokyo's oil refineries, oil reservoirs, steel and munitions plants, naval docks and other military objectives," Doolittle reported, in a message forwarded from Hap Arnold to Roosevelt. "One bomber attacked the Mitsubishi airplane factory and other military objectives at Nagoya with incendiary bombs. Two other bombers also attacked Osaka and Kobe with incendiaries. We all took care to avoid bombing schools, hospitals, churches and other non-military objectives." The bombers encountered heavy anti-aircraft fire, barrage balloons, and pursuit from Japanese fighters. Yet they got away, continuing toward China and, in one case, toward Russia. They had hoped to reach friendly territory, but the early launch and other adverse factors caused them to run out of fuel. Most crash-landed, yet only five crewmen were killed. Arnold took pleasure in telling Roosevelt that the American bombs began falling over Tokyo in the middle of a propaganda broadcast by the Japanese government in which a woman speaking in English (one of a type Americans would learn to call "Tokyo Rose") was explaining how secure Japan was from air attack. Of the aftermath of the attack, Arnold added wryly: "With the fifteen planes reported located in East China, one interned in Siberia, and one which the Japanese claim is on exhibition, there is a total of seventeen accounted for—which is one more than we sent over."

The report of the mission put Roosevelt in high spirits, though he declined to confirm details. "How about the story about the bombing of Tokyo?" a reporter asked at the president's next news conference.

"You know occasionally I have a few people in to dinner," Roosevelt replied. "And generally in the middle of dinner some—it isn't an individual, it's just a generic term—some 'sweet young thing' says, 'Mr. President, couldn't you tell us about so and so?' Well, the other night this sweet young thing in the middle of supper said, 'Mr. President, couldn't you tell us about that bombing? Where did those planes start from and go to?' And I said, 'Yes. I think the time has now come to tell you. They came from our new secret base at Shangri-La!' "

The reporters laughed appreciatively.

"And she believed it!"

❖   ❖   ❖

YET THE DOOLITTLE raid, while better than nothing, was a pinprick. It got Tokyo's attention but did nothing to diminish Japan's war-making capacity.

A much bigger blow landed two weeks later. The Japanese, trying to build on their string of victories, sent a task force against Australian-held Port Moresby in New Guinea, hoping to secure the southern flank of their Pacific empire and provide a base for attacks against Australia. American and British intercepts revealed the outlines of the operation, and the American naval command dispatched an aircraft carrier group to block Japan's advance. In the five-day Battle of the Coral Sea, culminating on May 7 and 8, planes from the opposing carrier groups revealed the future of naval warfare by bombing and strafing each other's ships while the vessels themselves never made direct contact. Japan won on points, taking out the American carrier *Lexington* in exchange for a smaller carrier of its own. But the American side claimed both a strategic victory, for repelling Japan's southward advance and keeping the southern sea lanes open, and a moral triumph, by demonstrating that the Japanese weren't invincible after all.

The Americans landed a still heavier blow another month later. The Japanese sent four carriers and seven battleships to seize Midway Island northwest of Hawaii. The broader purpose of the operation was to draw the core of

America's fleet, in particular the carriers that had escaped the attack on Pearl Harbor, into a battle that would decide the fate of the Pacific for years to come. The Battle of Midway did just that, although not as the Japanese intended. As before, American cryptanalysts deciphered the Japanese messages, allowing Chester Nimitz, the American commander, to anticipate the Japanese actions. For four days in early June, planes from each side battered the ships of the other. The Americans had the greater success, and when the smoke cleared the Japanese had lost four carriers and some two hundred aircraft, against one carrier and a hundred planes for the Americans. The Japanese were forced to retreat.

If the Battle of the Coral Sea had slowed Japan's momentum, the Battle of Midway reversed it. The loss of Japan's carriers at Midway did far more damage to Tokyo's ability to project power than the loss of the American battleships at Pearl Harbor had done to America's might. Almost at once the United States gained the naval advantage in the Pacific. Given America's industrial superiority over Japan, the American lead would only grow.

❖   ❖   ❖

*A*ND YET, as satisfying as the naval victories over Japan were, they didn't give Roosevelt what he needed most. Germany remained the primary enemy, and Germany remained beyond reach. Until America took the war to Europe, victory would be a distant dream.

How to get to Europe was the crux of discussion, debate, suspicion, and recrimination among the Allies for more than two years. Roosevelt's military advisers contended that the shortest route was the best. The United States, in concert with Britain, should build up forces in England for a thrust across the Channel to France. Germany would defend France, and the battle would be joined.

Churchill and the British proposed a different strategy. In their thinking, a cross-Channel invasion was too risky. France was too well defended. Better to strike at the Mediterranean underbelly of the Axis. American and British forces should land in North Africa and occupy the southern shore of the Mediterranean, from which they could cross to Italy and eventually drive into Germany from the south. In the meantime, securing the Mediterranean would protect the British position in Egypt and the lifeline to India.

Most of the arguing over where to strike took place between the American and British governments, but an interested third party—and recurrent participant—was the government of the Soviet Union. For Stalin and the Russians, the primary concern was relieving the pressure on the eastern front. Whatever required the Germans to transfer the greatest number of troops away from the East was the best strategy for the Allies. And nothing, in Stalin's view, would draw off more Germans than an Anglo-American invasion of France, as soon as possible. Anything else would hardly be worth the bother.

Roosevelt's position on the second front shifted and wobbled. At times he heeded the cross-Channel counsel of his own advisers, at times the Mediterranean entreaties of Churchill. A president of a different personality and leadership style—a Theodore Roosevelt, for example—might have decided the matter at once and pressed forward with implementation. But Roosevelt left the question open for many months. Some of his hesitation reflected the changing military context, but most revealed his perception that Allied decisions had to come by consensus. Each of the three countries played a different but vital role in the war, giving each of the three leaders, in effect, a veto over important aspects of Allied strategy.

The United States remained the arsenal of democracy—and of communism, in the case of the Soviet Union. By directing supplies to this theater or that, America could shape the course of the war. Given time, the United States would build the most powerful military machine in history, with the capacity to crush almost any foe—but not by itself. America would continue to need its allies, who would supply much of the manpower to wield the weapons, and die in the process.

Britain possessed a formidable navy, a respectable army, and an empire that, though restive in places, still provided London a global reach. Most irreplaceably, Britain would serve as the springboard for the invasion of France, whenever it happened to come.

The Soviet Union's role was to keep Hitler occupied and to kill Germans—lots and lots of Germans. Every German who died on the eastern front was one fewer the Americans and British would have to fight themselves, when their turn came.

Given the complementary nature of these functions, consensus was the only feasible form of Allied decision making. And consensus suited Roosevelt perfectly. He had always preferred to persuade, cajole, and manipulate people rather than to browbeat or intimidate them. His approach had worked with the diverse domestic factions that came together behind the New Deal; Roosevelt assumed it would work with the oddly matched international coalition that was fighting the Axis.

But it drove his advisers to distraction. Stimson and Marshall had gotten a taste of the Roosevelt style in the initial meetings with Churchill at Washington, and they nearly gagged on it. The flavor didn't improve much during the rest of the war. Roosevelt's lieutenants naturally wanted him to make the decisions they thought best for the country, but, failing that, they simply wanted him to *make* decisions. Yet as often as he seemed to make a decision, he would revisit and reconsider it.

❖ ❖ ❖

DURING THE SPRING of 1942 Marshall and the American military chiefs seemed to have won the second-front argument. Roosevelt indicated his preference for an early invasion of France by sending Marshall and Harry Hopkins to London to sell the policy to Churchill. Hopkins carried a note from the president to the prime minister. "What Harry and Geo. Marshall will tell you all about has my heart and *mind* in it," Roosevelt said. "Your people and mine demand the establishment of a front to draw off pressure on the Russians, and these peoples are wise enough to see that the Russians today are killing more Germans and destroying more equipment than you and I put together."

Hopkins and Marshall arrived in England on the morning of April 8 and went straight into a meeting with Churchill. "Marshall presented in broad outlines our proposals to the Prime Minister," Hopkins recorded. Marshall considered the session a remarkable success. "He thought that Churchill went a long way," Hopkins wrote. "He—Marshall—expected far more resistance than he got."

Yet Churchill wasn't convinced. He escorted Marshall and Hopkins to a meeting with Britain's service chiefs. The prime minister applauded the "momentous proposal" the Americans had brought from the president. To such a plan, he said, the British government could only assent. Yet he couldn't help pointing out the complications it would raise for British policy. The great concern at the moment was the threat that German forces thrusting through the Middle East would join up with Japanese forces driving west across the Indian Ocean. To ignore this threat, and to devote excessive manpower and materiel to a premature invasion of Europe, would be a grave mistake. Alan Brooke, the chief of the imperial general staff, seconded Churchill's concern. If the Japanese gained control of the Indian Ocean, Brooke said, the southern supply route to Russia would be lost, with the collapse of Russia itself possibly to follow. Inasmuch as the major purpose of a western front in Europe was to relieve the pressure on the Russians, the proposed operation would be bizarrely misguided.

Hopkins rose to rebut the British reservations. If the American people had their way, he said, the United States would focus its efforts on Japan, which had attacked American forces and territory directly. But the president, on the counsel of his military advisers, had made a basic decision to "direct the force of American arms against Germany." The president had brought the American public around to his way of thinking, and now they wished to fight—"not only on the sea but on land and in the air." And Europe was where such fighting could best be done.

Churchill thanked Hopkins for his forceful statement. The prime minister looked past his own and Brooke's reservations to declare that the British and American governments had achieved "complete unanimity" on general strategy and now could "march ahead together in a noble brotherhood of arms." Planning for a "great campaign for the liberation of Europe" should move forward with the "utmost resolution."

Hopkins and Marshall left the meeting confused. Were they to heed Churchill's assurances or his reservations? They conveyed their confusion to Roosevelt on their return to America. The president determined to stress the positive. "I am delighted with the agreement which was reached between you and your military advisers and Marshall and Hopkins," the president wrote Churchill. "They have reported to me on the unanimity of opinion relative to the proposal which they carried with them. . . . I believe that this move will be very disheartening to Hitler and may well be the wedge by which his downfall will be accomplished."

Roosevelt refused to be diverted by a letter from Churchill himself. The letter affirmed Churchill's "whole-hearted" support for the European operation, but it appended "one broad qualification" relating, as in the London meetings, to the Middle East and Indian Ocean. "It is essential that we should prevent a junction of the Japanese and the Germans," Churchill said. "Consequently, a proportion of our combined resources must, for the moment, be set aside to halt the Japanese advance."

Perhaps Roosevelt believed events of the next few months would prove Churchill's fears of an Axis link across the bottom of Asia as groundless as he thought them to be. Perhaps he relied on his powers of persuasion to bring

Churchill around to an early assault on France. Perhaps he judged that by seizing on Churchill's statement of support for the European operation he could start the machinery required to make the operation happen and that once the machinery kicked into motion there would be no stopping it. In any event, he exuded only encouragement. "I am very heartened at the prospect, and you can be sure that our army will approach the matter with great enthusiasm and vigor," he wrote Churchill. He added, for good measure: "I feel better about the war than at any time in the past two years."

❖ ❖ ❖

IN THE SAME letter, Roosevelt informed Churchill: "I have a cordial message from Stalin telling me he is sending Molotov and a general to visit me."

Stalin, for understandable reasons, became suspicious whenever the Americans and British discussed strategy among themselves, without him or an envoy present. Given that the Americans and British were always talking among themselves—this was what the Combined Chiefs of Staff *did*—Stalin spent most of the war suspicious of Roosevelt and Churchill.

The dithering of the British and Americans over a second front made him even more suspicious. The way to fight Germans was to fight Germans, he believed—the way the Red Army did. Stalin felt particular pressure during the first months of 1942. For almost a year the Russians had carried the burden of the fighting against Germany, and though winter had stalled the Wehrmacht short of Moscow, spring would doubtless bring another offensive. Hitler had taken personal command of the army, which meant that the new drive almost certainly would be more ferocious than the last. Stalin was desperate for anything that would ease the strain, and nothing would accomplish more toward that end than a western front.

Roosevelt assured Stalin that America had Russia's best interests at heart. "I am looking forward to seeing Molotov, and the moment I hear of the route, we shall make preparations to provide immediate transportation," the president wrote. "I do hope Molotov can stay with me in the White House while he is in Washington, but we can make a private home nearby available for him if that is desired."

The visit proved more difficult than Roosevelt expected. Molotov was never cheerful among capitalists, but now he was gloomier than usual as his arrival coincided with the surrender of a Soviet army of 200,000 to the Germans at

Kharkov. For his country's sake, and perhaps for his own, he judged it imperative to bring home a commitment to a second front.

Roosevelt was uncomfortable for different reasons. "His style was cramped," Hopkins observed. The need for interpreters slowed the talks to a crawl, essentially negating what little effect the Roosevelt charm might have had on the Soviet diplomat. And Molotov was simply a hard case, as arrogant ideologically as he was personally humorless.

Molotov's communist ideology afforded him confidence in the ultimate victory of socialism. But between the present and the millennium, he acknowledged, socialism needed help from its capitalist allies. Molotov said that 1942 looked grim and 1943 hardly better. Hitler was preparing a "mighty, crushing blow," which had already begun to fall. The Red Army might not be able to withstand it. "Mr. Molotov therefore put this question frankly," Samuel Cross, a Harvard professor of Slavic languages who sat in on the meeting and took notes, recorded: "Could we undertake such offensive action as would draw off 40 German divisions?" If the answer was yes, Molotov had great confidence. "The war would be decided in 1942." If no, he couldn't predict. A delay of the second front until 1943 would render many things much less certain. "If you postpone your decision," he told Roosevelt, "you will have eventually to bear the brunt of the war, and if Hitler becomes the undisputed master of the continent, next year will undoubtedly be tougher than this one."

Roosevelt answered Molotov by turning to Marshall. "Could we say to Mr. Stalin that we are preparing a second front?" he asked the general.

"Yes," Marshall replied.

According to Cross's notes: "The President then authorized Mr. Molotov to inform Mr. Stalin that we expect the formation of a second front this year."

This was the message Molotov had come to Washington to hear, and though it was followed by several days of discussion in which Roosevelt's advisers appended qualifications and disclaimers, it was the message that informed the joint statement that closed the discussions:

Full understanding was reached with regard to the urgent tasks of creating a second front in Europe in 1942.

The statement left a little room for interpretation. The "full understanding" applied, grammatically speaking, to the "urgent tasks." But to ordinary readers—and to the extraordinary reader in the Kremlin who had sent Molotov to Washington—the operative phrase was "second front in Europe in 1942."

❖ ❖ ❖

$\mathcal{B}$EFORE MOLOTOV LEFT, Roosevelt broached another subject, less pressing but no less important than the second front. He had not discussed this subject in any detail with Churchill, but he wanted to raise it with Stalin, through Molotov. "We know there will be two kinds of postwar settlements," the president said. "First, those among the United Nations, and, second, arrangements for the reconstruction of the other nations with a view to ensuring a more stable form of peace." Regarding the former, Roosevelt suggested that at war's end the Soviet Union and Britain should repay debts incurred under Lend-Lease on a principal-only basis; the United States would waive any interest. Referring to the problems the debts from the First World War had caused, the president said he hoped to prevent similar problems among the Allies after this war. He asked Molotov to present this proposal to Stalin "for the purpose of exploring it without commitments."

Regarding the other nations—Germany, Japan, and Italy—Roosevelt suggested that a peace settlement must start with disarmament and extend to inspection and control of those countries' weapons industries. The president proposed that the senior members of the United Nations—the United States, the Soviet Union, Britain, and China—should police any postwar settlements, serving as "guarantors of eventual peace." Their police actions would extend beyond Germany and Japan. "There are, all over the world, many islands and colonial possessions which ought, for our own safety, to be taken away from weak nations," Roosevelt said.

Molotov cabled Roosevelt's recommendations to Moscow and, before departing, was able to answer that Stalin was "in full accord with the President's ideas on disarmament, inspection, and policing, with the participation of at least Great Britain, the United States, the Soviet Union, and possibly China."

❖ ❖ ❖

$\mathcal{C}$HURCHILL READ THE Roosevelt-Molotov statement with great interest, especially the part about the second front in Europe in 1942. No sooner had Molotov left Washington than the prime minister embarked for the American capital, to make sure Roosevelt didn't mean what he had just said.

Henry Stimson tried to ready Roosevelt for the prime minister's wiles. "May I very briefly recall to your memory the sequence of events which led to and the background which surrounds this problem," the war secretary wrote, perhaps consciously dropping the question mark from what clearly was not intended as a question. During the Anglo-American talks in Washington the previous December, he reminded Roosevelt, both sides had agreed on the value of a second front in 1942. "The one thing Hitler rightly dreaded was a second front. In establishing such a front lay the best hope of keeping the Russian Army in the war and thus ultimately defeating Hitler. To apply the rapidly developing manpower and industrial strength of America promptly to the opening of such a front was manifestly the only way it could be accomplished." These considerations had given rise to Bolero, as the plan for a buildup in Britain preparatory to an invasion of France was called. Bolero would yield benefits even before the invasion took place, Stimson said. "The menace of the establishment of American military power in the British Isles would be immediately evident to Hitler. It at once tended to remove the possibility of a successful invasion of Britain, Hitler's chief and last weapon. It awoke in every German mind the recollections of 1917 and 1918." Recent events—the German advances in Russia, which increased the strain on the Soviet government, and the American victory over Japan at Midway, which diminished the pressure on the United States in the Pacific—rendered Bolero even more advisable. "Under these circumstances, an immense burden of proof rests upon any proposition which may impose the slightest risk of weakening Bolero," Stimson concluded. "No new plan should even be whispered to friend or enemy unless it was so sure of immediate success and so manifestly helpful to Bolero that it could not possibly be taken as evidence of doubt or vacillation in the prosecution of Bolero."

Stimson had the strong support of Marshall. "You are familiar with my view that the decisive theater is Western Europe," the chief of staff wrote Roosevelt. "That is the only place where the concerted effort of our own and the British forces can be brought to bear on the Germans." Any effort by Churchill to divert American forces to the Mediterranean must be resisted. "A large venture in the Middle East would make a decisive American contribution to the campaign in Western Europe out of the question. Therefore, I am opposed to such a project."

Whether Churchill could have overcome the opposition of Stimson and Marshall without help is unclear. On reaching America the prime minister traveled to Hyde Park, where Roosevelt was spending the weekend. Churchill handed the president a memo outlining his concerns about Bolero. German depredations upon Allied shipping in the Atlantic had been especially severe of late; Churchill wondered whether these would disrupt the Bolero buildup. At the least, they must delay things. "We are bound to persevere in the preparation for Bolero, if possible in 1942 but certainly in 1943," he said, in an affirmation that was really a negation. He noted that Bolero thus far was merely an aspiration, while the invasion of France—code-named Sledgehammer—for which Bolero was to be the precursor, was hardly a dream. "No responsible British military authority has so far been able to make a plan for September 1942 which had any chance of success unless the Germans become utterly demoralized, of which there is no likelihood." The Americans weren't any farther along. "Have the American staffs a plan? If so, what is it? What landing craft and shipping are available? Who is the officer prepared to command the enterprise?"

Churchill worried that a premature Channel crossing would fail. He recalled the carnage of the First World War, and especially the debacle at Gallipoli, the botched 1915 invasion of Turkey that he had advocated and helped plan. He feared that an attack on France might become a second Gallipoli and thereby hearten the Germans, demoralize the British, and alienate the Americans. "The British Government would not favour an operation that was certain to lead to disaster, would compromise and expose to Nazi vengeance the French population involved, and would gravely delay the main operation in 1943," Churchill explained to Roosevelt. "We hold strongly to the view that there should be no substantial landing in France this year unless we are going to stay."

It was clear to Churchill that the British and Americans were not prepared to establish a permanent presence in France. This being so, they should think about alternatives to Bolero. "Ought we not be preparing within the general structure of Bolero some other operation by which we may gain positions of advantage and also directly or indirectly to take some of the weight off Russia?"

The other operation was Gymnast, an Anglo-American invasion of French North Africa. Churchill's argument for Gymnast gained sudden and unexpected strength in the middle of the prime minister's visit. On June 21 Erwin Rommel's Afrika Korps captured Tobruk, the last British outpost west of Egypt. With little in Egypt itself to slow a German advance to the Suez Canal, Churchill's nightmare of an Axis connection across the Indian Ocean grew ominously realistic.

"This was one of the heaviest blows I can recall during the war," Churchill wrote afterward. "Not only were its military effects grievous, but it had affected the reputation of the British armies." The garrison at Tobruk had surrendered to a German force half its size. "I did not attempt to hide from the President the shock I had received. It was a bitter moment. Defeat is one thing; disgrace is another."

Only rarely during the war was Roosevelt required to make snap decisions. Typically he had weeks or months to weigh his options. This was one of the rare times. "What can we do to help?" he asked Churchill.

"Give us as many Sherman tanks as you can spare, and ship them to the Middle East as quickly as possible," Churchill said.

Roosevelt sent for Marshall and asked him whether any tanks were available. Marshall replied that the Shermans were just coming off the production lines. The first few hundred had been issued to America's own armored divisions. "It is a terrible thing to take the weapons out of a soldier's hands," Marshall said. But when Roosevelt made plain that he wanted the British to have the tanks, the staff chief didn't object. He volunteered that he could probably find some self-propelled guns as well.

"To complete the story," Churchill recalled, "the Americans were better than their word. Three hundred Sherman tanks, with engines not yet installed, and a hundred self-propelled guns, were put into six of their fastest ships and sent off to the Suez Canal. The ship containing the engines for all the tanks was sunk by a submarine off Bermuda. Without a single word from us, the President and Marshall put a further supply of engines into another fast ship and dispatched it to overtake the convoy. 'A friend in need is a friend indeed.' "

❖   ❖   ❖

An even greater gift was Gymnast. No decision was reached between Bolero and Gymnast during Churchill's visit, but the prime minister's fear for the Suez Canal shifted the balance from the former to the latter. Roosevelt knew perfectly well he couldn't order Bolero to proceed unless Churchill assented; without the British government's enthusiastic support, any operation based in Britain would be doomed from the start. Roosevelt made a calculated decision to humor Churchill, partly from genuine concern for a wartime comrade but partly in the belief the humoring would pay off in the end.

Roosevelt's good humor extended beyond the issue of a second front into an arena of warfare that hadn't existed a few years earlier. A decade before the First World War, Albert Einstein had asserted the equivalence of mass and energy and provided an equation ($E = mc^2$) connecting the two. Several months prior to the Second World War, Otto Hahn observed what Einstein had predicted, when the German chemist split uranium into lighter elements amid a burst of energy. The publication of Hahn's result prompted Einstein, encouraged by fellow physicist Leo Szilard, to write to Roosevelt. In a letter dated August 2, 1939, Einstein explained the recent developments and warned that a determined government could employ them to produce "extremely powerful bombs of a new type." The German government apparently agreed, for it had embargoed exports of uranium from mines in Czechoslovakia. The United States, Einstein told Roosevelt, would be remiss not to commence research in this critical new field.

Roosevelt, impressed by Einstein's reputation and logic, authorized a small program that proceeded slowly but gained momentum, confidence, and scientific support during the next eighteen months. In the autumn of 1941 a committee of the National Academy of Sciences recommended a crash program of atomic development. Roosevelt assented, and the group that would direct what came to be called the Manhattan Project held its inaugural meeting on December 6, 1941.

Meanwhile scientists in Britain began their own atomic effort. The "Directorate of Tube Alloys" pushed forward along lines that paralleled those of the Americans. The work succeeded well enough that Churchill, at the time of his June 1942 visit to Washington, had to decide whether to move from research to production. It was a big step, one he wasn't sure Britain could handle—at least not alone.

He raised the matter with Roosevelt on June 20 at Hyde Park. "Our talks took place after luncheon, in a tiny little room which juts out on the ground floor," Churchill remembered. "The room was dark and shaded from the sun," but it was still, from an English point of view, oppressively warm. "My two American friends"—Hopkins sat in—"did not seem to mind the intense heat." Churchill explained the progress British scientists had made, and how they were convinced a bomb by war's end was feasible. Roosevelt responded that American scientists were proceeding well, too. Churchill proposed an Anglo-American collaboration. "I strongly urged that we should at once pool all our information, work together on equal terms, and share the results, if any, equally between us."

Roosevelt accepted Churchill's offer. Roosevelt wasn't a hard bargainer, generally believing that good will warranted leaving something on the table at the end of a negotiation. In this case it was unclear what any bargaining would be about. The atom bomb project might yield nothing at all. Even if it succeeded, it would produce something no one had ever seen, and no army or air force ever deployed.

The next question was where the production facilities should be located. Yet the question was no sooner asked than it was answered. They couldn't be in Britain, which wholly lacked the fissionable materials bomb making required. Transporting uranium across the Atlantic made little sense given the danger from U-boats and the other demands on Allied shipping. Churchill considered Canada and went so far as to contend, after the fact, that had Roosevelt declined his offer, "we certainly should have gone forward on our own power in Canada."

It didn't come to that. Roosevelt wasn't going to let the bomb building out of the United States. With no publicity, and with nothing committed to paper between them, the president and the prime minister put their two countries into the joint business of developing a bomb that would transform warfare forever.

❖ ❖ ❖

As THE PROSPECTS for an early second front in Europe dwindled, Roosevelt's advisers began to mutter among themselves about reconsidering the Europe-first strategy. They were itching to fight, on grounds strategic, political, and personal. The longer the United States remained on the sidelines, the stronger the Axis grew. The longer the American public had nothing to cheer about, the more likely support for the war would dwindle. And the longer the army's officers remained in their headquarters, as opposed to being on the battlefield, the more distant their chances for distinction and promotion.

Stimson later claimed that the War Department's planning for a Pacific offensive in 1942 was a bluff, intended to push Roosevelt toward a decision in favor of invading France. Perhaps it *was* a bluff, to him. But Marshall, whose sense of professional decorum put him above such ploys, and Admiral Ernest King, whose irascibility was legendary, weren't bluffing. "One thing that might help win this war is to get someone to shoot King," Dwight Eisenhower vented in his diary after a typical session with the admiral. "He's the antithesis of cooperation, a deliberately rude person, which means he's a mental bully." King had an imperial vision of the navy's importance among the services. "The navy wants to take all the islands in the Pacific, have them held by army troops, to become bases for army pursuit and bombers," Eisenhower said. "Then the navy will have a safe place to sail its vessels." But King was a fighter, which appealed to Roosevelt, the more so when King presented what he called "an integrated, general plan of operations" for the Pacific. "We have now—or soon will have—

'strong points' at Samoa, Suva (Fiji), and New Caledonia (also a defended fueling base at Bora Bora, Society Islands)," King informed Roosevelt. "A naval operating base is shortly to be set up at Tongatabu (Tonga Islands) to service our naval forces operating in the South Pacific. Efate (New Hebrides) and Funafuti (Ellice Islands) are projected additional 'strong points.' " Roosevelt located all these places on his map of the South Pacific. "Given the naval forces, air units, and amphibious troops, we can drive northwest from the New Hebrides into the Solomons and the Bismarck Archipelago," King continued. "Such a line of operations will be offensive rather than defensive—and will draw Japanese forces there to oppose it, thus relieving pressure elsewhere."

Roosevelt received King's recommendation in early March; two weeks later he promoted the admiral to chief of naval operations. During April and May, as the likelihood of an early Channel crossing diminished, King contended that any postponement in Europe would free up resources for the Pacific campaign. Roosevelt listened carefully, and in June, on the last day of Churchill's visit to Washington, the president approved the offensive, which would begin with an attack on the obscure island of Guadalcanal in the southern Solomon Islands.

❖   ❖   ❖

CHURCHILL CUT SHORT his visit to return to London to face a censure vote in Parliament. A noisy minority was demanding answers about the military situation in North Africa. Although Churchill was confident of defeating the motion, he judged its mere raising an affront to his leadership, and he determined to crush it. Roosevelt could count votes, even at a transatlantic distance, almost as well as Churchill could, and he too expected the prime minister to survive handily. But he recognized that the prime minister would be distracted till the insurgents were defeated, and in any event he wished to know just how strong Churchill was.

Quite strong, as matters proved. The no-confidence motion was beaten by 475 to 25. "Good for you," Roosevelt congratulated Churchill upon learning the news.

Churchill, heartened by his parliamentary victory, proceeded to drive a stake through the heart of an early second front in Europe. "No responsible British General, Admiral, or Air Marshal is prepared to recommend Sledgehammer as a practicable operation in 1942," he wrote Roosevelt. The invasion itself would be risky, and a beachhead, if established, would be difficult to defend. The mere effort would jeopardize greater plans. "The possibility of mounting a large-scale operation in 1943 would be marred if not ruined." The United States and Britain must shift their attention to North Africa. "Gymnast is by far the best chance for effective relief to the Russian front in 1942. . . . Here is the true second front of 1942."

Roosevelt finally agreed. But he knew his military men did not. He could simply have ordered them to get on board with Gymnast, knowing that Marshall was a good enough soldier to have acquiesced without further complaint and that King had the Pacific campaign to keep him busy. Yet he preferred that they be persuaded, by the same logic that had persuaded him. "You will proceed immediately to London as my personal representatives for the purpose of consultation with appropriate British authorities on the conduct of the war," Roosevelt directed Marshall and King, who would be accompanied by Hopkins. Certain principles ought to inform the London consultation. "We should concentrate our efforts and avoid dispersion. . . . Absolute coordinated use of British and American forces is essential. . . . All available U.S. and British forces should be brought into action as quickly as they can profitably be used. . . . It is of the highest importance that U.S. ground troops be brought into action against the enemy in 1942." For the record, Roosevelt still supported an early western front in Europe. "In regard to 1942, you will carefully investigate the possibility of executing Sledgehammer. Such an operation would definitely sustain Russia this year. It might be the turning point which would save Russia this year." Even so, he didn't rule out alternatives. "If Sledgehammer is finally and definitely out of the picture, I want you to consider the world situation as it exists at that time, and determine upon another place for U.S. troops to fight in 1942."

Having framed the discussions this way, Roosevelt wasn't surprised that they resulted in the abandonment of the early western front. "Marshall and King pushed very hard for Sledgehammer," Hopkins reported after a week in London. But the British stood firmly against it, and Marshall and King reluctantly concluded what Roosevelt already had: that without British support, Sledgehammer simply couldn't go forward.

This left North Africa, as Roosevelt knew it would. And the decision having been arrived at, even if apparently by default, the president was eager to press forward. Roosevelt replied to Hopkins that he wanted to move "full speed ahead" on the North Africa campaign.

48.

"$\mathcal{I}$ SHOULD GREATLY LIKE TO HAVE YOUR AID AND COUNTENANCE IN my talks with Joe," Churchill wrote Roosevelt on August 4. "Would you be able to let Averell come with me? I feel that things would be easier if we all seemed to be together. I have a somewhat raw job."

Joe was Stalin, Averell was Harriman, who had been with Roosevelt at the Atlantic Conference and would become ambassador to Moscow, and the raw job was explaining that there wouldn't be a second front in Europe in 1942. Eight months after the signing of the Declaration of the United Nations, the leaders of the principal members of the alliance had yet to meet. Churchill was traveling to the Middle East, to buck up the troops in Egypt, and he decided to fly on to Moscow. Roosevelt declined to join him. The president considered the United States the first among equals in the Grand Alliance—the armorer of Britain and Russia, the exemplar of democracy— but until American troops got into the fight he would be at a diplomatic disadvantage to Churchill and Stalin, and American interests would suffer accordingly. Yet he wanted a representative at the Churchill-Stalin meetings. So he sent Harriman.

Stalin received the unwelcome news much as Churchill expected. "Stalin took issue at every point with bluntness almost to the point of insult, with such remarks as you can't win wars if you aren't willing to take risks and you mustn't be so afraid of the Germans," Harriman cabled Roosevelt after the initial session. Churchill attempted to mollify Stalin by explaining the rationale for the North African operation. "The Prime Minister drew a picture of a crocodile," Harriman wrote, "and pointed out that it was as well to strike the belly as the snout." Stalin inquired of the details of the proposed operation, displaying what Harriman characterized as a "masterful grasp of its implications." He displayed genuine interest when Churchill described the bombing campaign against Germany already begun by Britain, which the Americans would soon join. "Homes as well as factories should be destroyed," Stalin said. He and the prime minister discussed targets. "Between the two of them they soon destroyed most of the important industrial cities of Germany," Harriman informed Roosevelt.

But Stalin returned to the failure of his allies to fulfill their promise. In a long session that ran far past midnight, he declared that the Anglo-American reversal left Russia in the lurch. "The Soviet Command built their plan of summer and autumn operations calculating on the creation of a second front in Europe in 1942," he said. "It is easy to grasp that the refusal of the government of Great Britain"—Stalin singled out Britain, since Churchill was there, but he spoke to Roosevelt as well—"to create a second front in 1942 in Europe inflicts a moral blow to the whole of the Soviet public opinion." Stalin rejected the Anglo-American argument that 1943 would be better than 1942 for opening a front in France. On the contrary, the Germans had sent all their best troops to Russia, leaving France unguarded. "We are of the opinion, therefore, that it is particularly in 1942 that the creation of a second front in Europe is possible and should be effected."

Roosevelt rejoined from afar. "I am sorry that I could not have joined with you and the Prime Minister," he cabled Stalin. "I am well aware of the urgent necessities of the military situation, particularly as it relates to the situation on the Russian front." The president noted that American forces were engaging the Japanese at Guadalcanal—which, he conceded, didn't do Russia any direct good, in that Russia and Japan were not at war. "I know very well that our real enemy is Germany and that our force and power must be brought against Hitler at the earliest possible moment. You can be sure that this will be done just as soon as it is humanly possible to put together the transportation." Meanwhile, Roosevelt said, the United States would increase its supplies to the Soviet Union, sending a thousand tanks and various other arms, including aircraft, within the month. All the same, he knew that troops were the critical issue. "Believe me when I tell you that we are coming as strongly and as quickly as we possibly can."

❖   ❖   ❖

"EVERYTHING FOR US now turns on hastening Torch," Churchill wrote Roosevelt upon leaving Moscow. Torch was the new name for Gymnast, and it connoted the hopes of the British and Americans to set North Africa on fire, or at least to let it light the way to Europe and eventual victory. The prime minister reiterated the "really grievous disappointment" the Russians felt upon learning that there would be no second front soon, and he judged the North Africa operation, essential on its own terms, to be indispensable in restoring the credibility of Britain and the United States as Russia's allies.

The operation required a commander. Churchill had already broached the subject with Roosevelt, in the context of the broader issue of European command. "It would be agreeable to us if General Marshall were designated for supreme command of Round-up and that in the meantime General Eisenhower should act as his deputy here," the prime minister wrote the president. Round-up was the heir to Sledgehammer, and it designated a second front in 1943 or after. Marshall, as the most forceful advocate of the second front, seemed the obvious choice. Churchill went on to say that Eisenhower could oversee preparations for Torch, which would test American troops and prepare them for Round-up. "As soon as Torch has taken shape, he would command it."

Roosevelt demurred regarding a commander for the invasion of Europe. He didn't think he could spare Marshall, and he didn't have another obvious candidate. In any event, he understood that the decision for North Africa pushed France even farther into the future. Field Marshal Sir John Dill, Churchill's representative on the Combined Chiefs staff in Washington, knew the American military mind as well as anyone. He wrote Churchill on August 1 describing American thinking. "The President has gone to Hyde Park for a rest, but before going he issued orders for full steam ahead on Torch at the earliest possible moment," Dill said. "In the American mind, Round-up in 1943 is excluded by acceptance of Torch." Roosevelt wasn't sharing this view with Stalin, preferring his formula of "we are coming as quickly and powerfully as we possibly can." But it meant that he could wait on choosing a commander for Europe.

For now he was happy to accept Churchill's suggestion of Eisenhower for Torch. Roosevelt didn't know Eisenhower well, but he had implicit faith in the judgment of Marshall, and Marshall liked Eisenhower.

❖ ❖ ❖

"THE ATTACK should be launched at the earliest practicable date," Roosevelt told Churchill of the North African operation. "The date should be consistent with the preparation necessary for an operation with a fair chance of success, and accordingly it should be determined by the Commander-in-Chief"— Eisenhower—"but in no event later than October 30th."

The timing was important for Russian morale—the sooner the better. It was also important to Roosevelt politically. By the end of October the United States would have been at war for eleven months, with little to show for the effort and sacrifice Roosevelt had asked of the American people. And elections would be at hand. The president didn't worry about his own popularity, if only because he wasn't on the ballot. But the Democratic majority in Congress had declined dramatically since 1936, and anything that contributed to voter dissatisfaction might undermine what remained of that majority.

The Republicans treated the war issue with some delicacy, yet not all that much. Wendell Willkie had become Roosevelt's favorite Republican—except for Henry Stimson and Frank Knox—by his support of measures Roosevelt deemed essential to national security. On one occasion Harry Hopkins made a slighting remark about Willkie and provoked "as sharp a reproof" as Robert Sherwood heard Roosevelt utter in the decade they worked together. "Don't ever say anything like that around here again," the president told Hopkins. "Don't even *think* it. You of all people ought to know that we might not have had Lend-Lease or Selective Service or a lot of other things if it hadn't been for Wendell Willkie. He was a godsend to this country when we needed him most." Roosevelt revised his feelings somewhat in September 1942 when Willkie showed up in Moscow and gave a press conference in which he sympathized with the Russian demands for a second front. "They are almost prayerfully anxious for more aid," Willkie said. "They appreciate the help they are getting from us, but do not consider it adequate. The morale value of a second front would be enormous."

Roosevelt affected not to notice. When a reporter sought a reaction to Willkie's comments, the president feigned ignorance.

"You did not know that was going on?" the reporter pressed.

"Oh, I had read some headlines, but I didn't think it was worth reading the stories," Roosevelt said.

The president hadn't planned an extensive political campaign, intending to let his work on the war speak for itself and for the Democrats. But he decided to help with the phrasing. In a Fireside Chat in mid-September he reminded Americans that there were "four main areas of combat" in the war: the Russian front, the Pacific, the Middle East, and Europe. "Various people urge that we concentrate our forces on one or another of these four areas," he said. But most of those people didn't have sufficient information to render valid judgments regarding priorities. "Certain vital military decisions have been made. In due time you will know what these decisions are—and so will our enemies.

I can say now that all of these decisions are directed toward taking the offensive." The president explained that in nine months of war the United States had sent three times as many men overseas as it had during the comparable period of the First World War. "We have done this in spite of greater danger and fewer ships. And every week sees a gain in the actual number of American men and weapons in the fighting areas." The deployments would continue to go forward until America and its allies achieved victory—a victory that would render irrelevant the current talk of one front or another. "This war will finally be won by the coordination of all the armies, navies, and air forces of all of the United Nations operating in unison against our enemies."

Roosevelt complemented this speech and his few others of the campaign with a tour of defense plants. He visited a converted Chrysler factory in Detroit that built tanks, a Ford facility in Willow Run, Michigan, that produced B-24 bombers, an Allis-Chalmers plant in Milwaukee that made ammunition, a Boeing plant in Seattle that assembled B-17s, a Kaiser yard in Portland, Oregon, that constructed cargo ships, an Alcoa smelter in Vancouver, Washington, that turned bauxite into aluminum, and a Higgins yard in New Orleans that churned out landing craft.

Roosevelt's security detail enforced secrecy regarding his movements, which annoyed the press even as it created opportunities for workers at the plants he visited—and at some he didn't visit. It became a fairly common practice for workers arriving home late to claim that the president had dropped by their plant that day. If a spouse expressed surprise, remarking that the local papers had said nothing about a presidential visit, the tardy worker would explain that it was a state secret. On his stop at the Portland Kaiser yard, Roosevelt made a joke of the security that surrounded him. His daughter, Anna, accompanied him and launched a ship, which skidded down the ways into the water. The president rolled forward in his open car, in plain view of newsreel cameras and many thousands of the workers. "You know," he said over the loudspeaker, "I am not supposed to be here today." The crowd laughed appreciatively. But Merriman Smith, a reporter with the United Press syndicate who was detailed to follow the president without knowing where the next stop would be or what he would be able to tell of what he observed, wasn't amused. "Damned if I saw anything to laugh about," Smith said.

Here was the President of the United States making an important public appearance in front of twenty thousand people, yet the newspapers and radio stations had to play like they knew nothing about it. Although three reporters whose normal duty was to send news to thousands of outlets around the world were standing only a few feet from him, the President went on with his joke:

"You are the possessors of a secret which even the newspapers of the United States don't know," he told the shipworkers. "I hope you will keep the secret because I am under military and naval orders, and like the ship that we have just seen go overboard, my motions and movements are supposed to be secret."

Roosevelt knew his actions irked the press. But amid the other demands the war made of him, he was willing to let the reporters fend for themselves. "Quite frankly I regard freedom of the press as one of the world's microscopic problems," he told Steve Early at a moment of particular strain.

❖   ❖   ❖

THERE WAS MORE to the campaign than speeches and inspections of defense plants. The headlong pace of war production was overheating the economy following a decade of chill, and, after two terms of trying to raise prices, Roosevelt found himself having to hold them down. Or perhaps it was Congress that had to do the restraining—the responsibility for prices was a matter of dispute. In April the president had put forward a seven-point program designed, as he stated seven times in the accompanying message to the legislators, "to keep the cost of living from spiraling upward." By September much of the program had been implemented by executive order. The president and the agencies reporting to him had set ceilings on many prices; they had controlled rents; they had established a system of rationing consumer goods; they had issued regulations curbing consumer debt; and they had facilitated the purchase of war bonds. But two points remained: limits on farm prices and higher taxes on incomes. The president was forbidden by existing law from capping farm prices till they reached 110 percent of "parity," the benchmark from the era of the First World War. As for taxes, Congress still wrote the codes.

In a special message to the legislature on September 7, Roosevelt urged the lawmakers to push ahead on these two remaining fronts. He asked for authority to "stabilize the cost of living"—that is, to set maximum prices on farm goods and other as yet uncontrolled items. For the moment he merely asked. But if the legislature refused to grant him authority—the deadline he set was October 1—he would do on his own authority what needed to be done. "Inaction on your part by that date will leave me with an inescapable responsibility to the people of this country to see to it that the war effort is no longer imperiled by threat of economic chaos. . . . I shall accept the responsibility, and I will act."

As for taxes, Roosevelt characterized a tax increase as "one of the most powerful weapons in our fight to stabilize living costs." Raising taxes would reduce Americans' discretionary income and thereby diminish the upward pressure on prices. It would also redistribute the burden of the war. The wealthy were having a wonderful war: profits and dividends were higher than in more than a decade. Roosevelt proposed to eliminate loopholes that let the rich off easily and to boost tax rates sharply at the upper end. "In the higher income brackets, the tax rate should be such as to give the practical equivalent of a top limit on an individual's net income after taxes, approximating $25,000." This was strong stuff, amounting to a confiscatory marginal rate on the highest incomes. But it was no more than what he proposed for corporations. "We must recapture through taxation all wartime profits that are not necessary to maintain efficient all-out war production."

Before the war, Roosevelt had defended similar, albeit less ambitious, measures as promoting economic and social equality. He still emphasized equality, but with a wartime twist. "Such provisions will give assurance that the sacrifices required by war are being equitably shared." Redressing inequality was crucial, now and for the future. "Next to military and naval victory, a victory along this economic front is of paramount importance. Without it our war production program will be hindered. Without it we would be allowing our young men, now risking their lives in the air, on land, and on the sea, to return to an economic mess of our own making."

Roosevelt's ultimatum to Congress won him the price authority he wanted, although the legislators saved a bit of their self-respect by making him wait till just after his deadline had passed. On October 2 he signed the price bill and the next day created the Office of Economic Stabilization, charged with developing and enforcing "a comprehensive national economic policy relating to the control of civilian purchasing power, prices, rents, wages, salaries, profits, rationing, subsidies, and all related matters." It wasn't lost on conservatives that the administration now had greater control of the economy than during the headiest period of the NRA, but under the duress of the war their complaints sounded unpatriotic.

Roosevelt's victory on taxes was even more galling. The president didn't quite get the confiscatory rates he wanted on incomes over $25,000, but he came very close. The Revenue Act of 1942 pushed personal tax rates to a marginal maximum of 88 percent even as it reduced exemptions and nearly tripled the number of people subject to income taxes. A special "Victory Tax" took 5 percent of all incomes over $624, with a portion to be remitted after the war was won.

Roosevelt signed the tax bill without comment, preferring not to remind voters two weeks before the election how deeply the government was dipping into their wallets. But in a Fireside Chat he emphasized that the burden of war was widely shared. "This whole nation of 130,000,000 free men, women, and children is becoming one great fighting force," he said.

> Some of us are fighting the war in airplanes five miles above the continent of Europe or the islands of the Pacific, and some of us are fighting it in mines deep down in the earth of Pennsylvania or Montana. A few of us are decorated with medals for heroic achievement, but all of us can have that deep and permanent inner satisfaction that comes from doing the best we know how, each of us playing an honorable part in the great struggle to save our democratic civilization.

❖ ❖ ❖

The surprising thing about the 1942 elections wasn't that the Democrats lost ground but that they lost as little as they did. Americans had never before been asked to weigh in on a ten-year-old presidency. Given their tendency to tire of incumbents, voters could have been expected to remove members of Roosevelt's party in large numbers. The removals, in fact, were modest. The Democrats lost eight seats in the Senate (the Republicans gained nine, knocking off Nebraska independent George Norris too). But they still controlled the upper house by nineteen seats. The Democratic losses were predictably larger in the House, where Roosevelt's party dropped forty-seven and the Republicans gained forty-five. But here, also, the Democrats still led, by thirteen seats—a slim margin by the standards of the Roosevelt years yet more than enough to control the leadership positions and the agenda.

The Democrats doubtless would have done better had the North African invasion been launched on schedule. But the final preparations lagged, and General Eisenhower refused to be rushed. Roosevelt, to his credit, did nothing to force things along. "When I went in to see Roosevelt and told him about Torch," George Marshall recalled of the prelanding briefings, "he held up his hands in an attitude of prayer and said, 'Please make it before Election Day.' However, when I found we had to have more time and it came afterward, he never said a word. He was very courageous."

Roosevelt awaited reports of the landings at Shangri-La, the new presidential retreat in the Maryland mountains north of Washington. The Secret Service had vetoed the pleasure cruises Roosevelt habitually took aboard the *Potomac* as liable to wartime sabotage or assault. The president himself vetoed the air-conditioning system in the White House, which aggravated his sinus condition. And so he took to the hills during hot weather—and decided he liked them during cooler weather as well. He, Harry Hopkins, Grace Tully, and a few others were amusing themselves on the Saturday evening after election day. Hopkins knew what was afoot; Tully knew *something* was afoot, but not what. "F.D.R. was on edge," she remembered. The others gradually sensed the tension. Roosevelt explained that he was expecting an important call.

Finally the telephone rang. Tully answered it. It was from the War Department. "The Boss's hand shook as he took the telephone from me," she recalled. "He listened intently, said nothing as he heard the full message, then burst out: 'Thank God. Thank God. That sounds grand. Congratulations. Casualties are comparatively light—much below your predictions. Thank God.' "

He put down the phone and turned to the group. "We have landed in North Africa. Casualties are below expectations. We are striking back."

Roosevelt complemented the military operation with messages to the various parties involved. The company commanders distributed a note from the president to the troops. "Upon the outcome depends the freedom of your lives, the freedom of the lives of those you love," Roosevelt declared.

To the people of France, Roosevelt delivered a message in French, broadcast by the BBC. "I speak to you as one who was with your army and navy in France in 1918," he said. "No two nations exist which are more united by historic and mutually friendly ties than the people of France and the United States." American troops had invaded French territory for the sole purpose of defeating France's oppressors. "Do not obstruct, I beg of you, this great purpose. Help us where you are able, my friends, and we shall see again the glorious day when liberty and peace shall reign again on earth. Vive la France éternelle!"

To Marshal Pétain, the Vichy leader, Roosevelt sent a letter. An early draft commenced, "My dear old friend," and described the marshal as the "venerated hero of Verdun." But Churchill, to whom the draft was referred, complained that it was "much too kind," and the phrases were dropped and the tone hardened. Roosevelt justified the Anglo-American invasion on grounds of pre-emptive self-defense, claiming that Germany and Italy were planning to occupy North and West Africa, to the jeopardy of the United States and the United Kingdom. Roosevelt told Pétain that the invading forces were equipped with "massive and adequate weapons of modern warfare" that would be available "for your compatriots in North Africa in our mutual fight against the common enemy." The marshal should join the fight, or at least not hinder it. The United States had only the best intentions toward France. "My clear purpose is to support and aid the French authorities and their administrations. That is the immediate aim of these American armies. I need not tell you that the ultimate and greater aim is the liberation of France and its Empire from the Axis yoke."

Pétain was unpersuaded. "You invoke pretexts which nothing justifies," he replied to Roosevelt. "We are attacked; we shall defend ourselves; this is the order I am giving."

Pétain's position was hardly unreasonable. France remained at Germany's mercy, and the American invasion of North Africa would certainly provoke a German response that would make life more miserable for ordinary French men and women. France as a whole was not ready to throw off the Nazis. Until it was, patience and caution would guide the Vichy government.

❖ ❖ ❖

WHETHER THEY WOULD guide the Vichy officials in North Africa was the critical question—for Roosevelt, for Churchill, and most directly for Eisenhower. The resistance of the French forces in North Africa to the American landings varied from place to place, but Eisenhower, as theater commander, considered it imperative to reduce that resistance however possible. His political agent, Robert Murphy of the American State Department, had sounded out French officers in North Africa and suggested that some might be willing to order their troops to stand down. Admiral Jean Darlan was the ranking French officer in North Africa; after initially declaring the American invasion an egregious blunder, he decided, with Murphy's assistance, that it might be a stepping-stone to political power for himself. He gave the order to cease fire.

What American newspapers dubbed the "Darlan deal" was a bargain of necessity. Darlan wasn't the Americans' first choice to lead the French forces in North Africa. That distinction belonged to General Henri Giraud, who had resisted the German invasion in 1940 until he was captured. He spent the next two years in a prisoner of war camp and then made a spectacular escape. He eluded the Gestapo, which had orders to assassinate him, and he found his way to Gibraltar to offer his services to Eisenhower ahead of the Torch landings. But the French troops in North Africa refused to accept him as their leader, taking their orders instead from Darlan. And they accepted Darlan's orders to cease fire only after the German army, as Pétain had feared, occupied Vichy and the rest of France. The occupation, Darlan told the troops, meant that Pétain was effectively a prisoner and that his orders to resist the invasion were given under duress. But the marshal had sent *him*—Darlan—secret orders authorizing him to act in Pétain's name. Or so Darlan said, and his word sufficed. The deal was done.

The reaction in America astonished Eisenhower and surprised even Roosevelt. The thrust of the complaints was that the United States was collaborating with Nazi collaborators, sacrificing its principles at the very outset of the fighting. Eisenhower defended his actions in a cable to the Combined Chiefs of Staff that was forwarded to Roosevelt. Eisenhower declared that in all of North Africa there was only one man with the stature to secure the cooperation Torch required. "That man is Darlan." If Darlan was repudiated, Eisenhower went on, several bad results would ensue, including a resumption of French resistance, a substantial increase in Allied losses, and a dramatic slowing of the entire operation.

Roosevelt stood by Eisenhower. To reporters he cited what he described as "a nice old proverb of the Balkans that has, as I understand it, the full sanction of the Orthodox Church. . . . It says, 'My children, you are permitted in time of great danger to walk with the devil until you have crossed the bridge.' " To the American people he declared, "I have accepted General Eisenhower's political arrangements made for the time being in North Africa and Western Africa." The arrangement with Darlan had ensured the success of the operation, Roosevelt said. But the president emphasized, and reemphasized, that the arrangement was provisional. "The present temporary arrangement in North and West Africa is only a temporary expedient, justified solely by the stress of battle. The present temporary arrangement has accomplished two military objectives. The first was to save American and British lives on the one hand, and French lives on the other. The second was the vital factor of time. The temporary arrangement has made it possible to avoid a mopping up period in Algiers and Morocco."

The president wrote to Eisenhower directly. "I appreciate fully the difficulties of your military situation," he said. "I am therefore not disposed to in any way question the action you have taken." But the general needed to bear a few things in mind:

> 1. That we do not trust Darlan.
>
> 2. That it is impossible to keep a collaborator of Hitler and one whom we believe to be a fascist in civil power any longer than is absolutely necessary.
>
> 3. His movements should be watched carefully and his communications supervised.

As luck, good and bad, would have it, the Darlan deal faded in importance. The good luck was that of the Allies. The Torch operation proceeded well if not smoothly. The Americans and British expanded their beachheads in Morocco and Algeria and pushed east toward Tunisia. Meanwhile British forces under Bernard Montgomery stunned the Germans at El Alamein in Egypt, winning Britain's first important victory on the ground against Nazi forces and driving Rommel back into the western desert. "This is not the end," Churchill said. "It is not even the beginning to the end. But it is, perhaps, the end of the beginning." Meanwhile on the eastern front, the Red Army commenced a major counterattack against the Germans at Stalingrad.

The bad luck was Darlan's. On December 24 he was assassinated in Algiers by a young man who apparently resented the admiral's recent actions. Churchill later mused on how Darlan's misfortune was his final gift to the Americans and British: "Darlan's murder, however criminal, relieved the Allies of their embarrassment at working with him, and at the same time left them with all the advantages he had been able to bestow during the vital hours of the Allied landings."

49.

"WE HERE ARE ALL HIGHLY GRATIFIED BY THE BRILLIANT SUCCESSES of American and British armed forces in North Africa," Stalin cabled Roosevelt not long after the landings. The Soviet dictator dismissed criticism of the Darlan deal. "It seems to me that the Americans used Darlan not badly in order to facilitate the occupation of Northern and Western Africa," he wrote to Churchill, who shared the letter with Roosevelt. "The military diplomacy must be able to use for military purposes not only Darlan but"—Stalin cited a Russian proverb—"even the Devil himself and his grandma."

Roosevelt hoped to capitalize on the success and good feeling to engage Stalin directly for the first time. "The more I consider our military situation and the necessity for reaching early strategic decisions, the more persuaded I am that you, Churchill and I should have an early meeting," he wrote Stalin on December 2. "I am very anxious to have a talk with you. . . . I can see no other way of reaching the vital strategic decisions which should be made very soon by all of us together. If the right decision is reached, we may, and I believe will, knock Germany out of the war much sooner than we anticipated."

The "right decision" Roosevelt referred to, the one that would "knock Germany out of the war," was one he needed Stalin's help achieving. But he couldn't tell Stalin about it by letter or cable; they must speak in person. Roosevelt hoped to use Stalin to sway Churchill toward a second front in Europe as soon as possible. The president assumed Churchill would find further reasons for delay, for insisting that the Mediterranean was the crucial theater. Roosevelt knew that Stalin favored an immediate second front; together they might force a commitment to Europe out of Churchill.

This was exactly what Churchill feared, and it caused him to push Stalin away. "I think I can tell you in advance what the Soviet view will be," the prime minister wrote Roosevelt. "They will say to us both, 'How many German divisions will you be engaging in the summer of 1943?'" Churchill didn't have a good answer to that question, and he didn't want to be pressed by Roosevelt and Stalin into one that would jeopardize his plans for the Mediterranean.

Stalin was less receptive to a tripartite conference than Roosevelt expected. He didn't like to travel, perhaps partly from the chronic fear dictators have that their enemies will conspire against them in their absence but also, in his particular case at this particular time, because the battle for Stalingrad had reached a critical juncture. Red Army troops had trapped the Germans in the city; victory in the most important battle of the war was in sight. "It is impossible for me to leave the Soviet Union," Stalin wrote Roosevelt. "Front business absolutely prevents it, demanding my constant presence near our troops."

Roosevelt didn't want to appear the supplicant, so he let the matter drop. He settled for another two-way meeting with Churchill. Since the war began, Roosevelt had missed his winter vacations, and the idea of a sunny spot appealed to him. Why not North Africa, which had the additional benefit of being where the fighting was? "I prefer a comfortable oasis to the raft at Tilsit," he wrote Churchill, making a point at once about his holiday preferences and his historical sensibility. The raft at Tilsit referred to an 1807 meeting in the middle of Prussia's Neman River between Napoleon and Russia's Alexander I, which resulted in the de facto division of Europe between France and Russia. Whether Roosevelt intended to imply that he wanted no part in a modern division of Europe—or whether he *did* intend such an outcome, only negotiated in more congenial surroundings—he left for Churchill to divine.

❖ ❖ ❖

THE OASIS TURNED out to be Casablanca, and a holiday mood surrounded the meeting from the start. The conference was code-named Symbol, and Roosevelt played the symbolic angle for a lark. "The aliases from this end will be (a) Don Quixote and (b) Sancho Panza," he wrote Churchill, referring to himself and Hopkins. The prime minister responded in kind. "Should you bring Willkie with you," he joked, "suggest code word Windmill."

The president traveled by plane in mid-January 1943. The trip was his first by air in eleven years, since the lurching ride that had landed him dramatically at the 1932 Democratic convention in Chicago. He remembered at once why he hadn't repeated the Chicago experiment. "I'm not crazy about flying, though it does save time if you have very little," Roosevelt wrote Eleanor en route. "Rather bumpy both days and once or twice last night." To his son John he complained, "I dislike flying the more I do of it!"

Roosevelt's trip to Africa was also the first air journey by a sitting American president and the first presidential crossing of an ocean at war. Not surprisingly, Roosevelt's security team, led by Michael Reilly of the Secret Service, was relieved when the C-54 transport, dubbed the "Sacred Cow," landed and taxied to a stop and the president emerged, gamely smiling and full of political good cheer.

Elliott Roosevelt, by now a lieutenant colonel in the army's air reconnaissance division, greeted his father at the Casablanca air field. The Roosevelt boys came under predictable scrutiny during the war, as the president's critics and some of his friends wondered whether they were receiving special treatment. One Republican congressman, William Lambertson of Kansas, declared that Roosevelt had personally interceded with the War Department to ensure that his sons not be sent to combat zones.

Elliott was the least likely of the four boys to suffer such criticism in silence, and he didn't. He wrote to Representative Fritz Lanham of his home district of Fort Worth, Texas, and requested the opportunity to defend the family's honor. Lanham read Elliott's letter before the House. "Inasmuch as I know that the Congressman"—Lambertson—"could not be referring to me, because I am here with the troops in North Africa," Elliott asserted dryly, "and because I know that my brother Franklin has been on a destroyer in the North Atlantic and still is, there can be only two brothers to whom the gentleman in question refers, my brothers James and John." Neither required defending from the likes of Lambertson, Elliott said, but he was doing so anyway. "The fact that my brother James has won the Navy Cross for gallantry in action"—with the marines in the Pacific—"speaks for itself." John, the youngest, was with the navy's supply corps. "He's been fighting like hell ever since he got in to go on foreign service, and I know that my father or anyone else isn't going to stop him before this show is over." Elliott went on to say, "If the Congressman questions my service, you might tell him that I have spent over two-thirds of my service in the past two years on foreign duty. I've been in every lousy spot the Air Corps can think of to send its men. It's not much fun, I can tell you, especially the butterflies that fly around in your stomach when the German gets the range and lets loose everything he's got at your plane." Elliott asked Lanham to relate these sentiments to the Kansas congressman personally, on his and his brothers' behalf. "Try to explain to him that we, as soldiers, don't care whether or how much he disagrees with the President, but for God's sake let us fight without being stabbed in the back for the sake of politics."

At these words, the members of the House burst into applause. One of the

Republicans requested that the record show that the applause came from both sides of the aisle. Lambertson of Kansas, apparently forewarned, had absented himself.

❖ ❖ ❖

ELLIOTT ACCOMPANIED his father to the villa reserved for the president. "It was quite a place," Elliott recalled. "The living room must have been twenty-eight feet high; it was two stories up, with great French windows that looked out on an extremely handsome garden." Sliding steel curtains, apparently installed recently, could cover the windows against bullets or shrapnel; a swimming pool had been converted to a makeshift air raid shelter. The renovations pleased Mike Reilly; Roosevelt was more impressed, in an ironic way, by the gaudy décor of the master bedroom. He whistled softly, grinned, and observed, "Now all we need is the madame of the house."

Churchill had a villa next door. The prime minister was feeling fuller of himself than usual. "It gave me intense pleasure," he remembered, "to see my great colleague here on conquered or liberated territory which he and I had secured in spite of the advice given him by all his military experts." Those same military experts had accompanied the president or were meeting him in Casablanca, but Churchill was confident they could be beaten into submission once again.

In fact the sessions of the military men were comparatively uncontroversial. Marshall and the Americans still favored France; the British remained focused on the Mediterranean. But with the American presence in North Africa now a fait accompli, the differences were mostly matters of emphasis. And after several days of debate the Combined Chiefs produced a document that laid out Anglo-American priorities for 1943. Topping the list was security of sea communications, on the unchallengeable reasoning that unless the U-boats could be cleared from the Atlantic, or at least their threat reduced dramatically, the logistical buildup required for any major offensive would be in jeopardy. Second was assuring a continuing supply of materiel to the Soviet Union. Russia was by no means out of the woods; a collapse of the Red Army, while hardly anticipated, wouldn't be the strangest thing to happen in the annals of warfare. In third place was the extension of the operations in the Mediterranean. Agreement on this point required some yielding by Marshall and the Americans, but less than might have been expected. The new year had already begun, and by no stretch of the imagination could a major offensive against France be mounted in the few months between the present and the summer fighting season. Realistically, 1944 was the year for the invasion of France; the Combined Chiefs' paper simply formalized the obvious. This was the thrust of the paper's fourth point, which outlined the buildup of Allied forces in Britain during 1943, in preparation for a Channel crossing the following spring. The buildup would include the establishment of heavy bomber units that would be able to reach Germany and win control of the air. The final point of the paper dealt with the Pacific–Far Eastern theater, where the present strategy—of supplying China's army and rolling up Japan's island positions one by one—would continue.

The politics of the conference were more difficult. As the Darlan deal demonstrated, the North African operation had knocked the French question off the shelf where it had been sitting unstably since 1940 and put it back into play. The heart of the question was whether the French were allies or enemies. But because an open, public debate on the issue was impolitic, Roosevelt and Churchill settled for considering *which* of the French might be allies. Darlan's assassination relieved them of the embarrassment their first brush with Vichy entailed, but it didn't remove the temptation to deal with those who had cooperated with the Nazis. Henri Giraud lacked the egregiously collaborationist record of Darlan, but after escaping his prisoner of war camp he had returned to France and supported the Vichy government. He subsequently worked with Eisenhower in Torch and, after the assassination of Darlan, became the American military's candidate for leadership among the anti-German French.

The British candidate was Charles de Gaulle, who despised Vichy and everyone associated with it, including Giraud. He often appeared to despise the Americans, especially after the Darlan deal. He tolerated the British, chiefly because they provided him a refuge and let him act as though he embodied the essence of France. Roosevelt wasn't original when he described de Gaulle as thinking himself some mystical amalgam of Jeanne d'Arc and Clemenceau; the combination occurred to Churchill and Eisenhower, among others. Eisenhower understood why de Gaulle was so widely disliked by his fellow French officers. "At the time of France's surrender in 1940," Eisenhower wrote after the war, "the officers who remained in the Army had accepted the position and orders of their government and had given up the fight. From their viewpoint, if the course chosen by De Gaulle was correct, then every French officer who obeyed the orders of his government was a poltroon. If De Gaulle was a loyal Frenchman they had to regard themselves as cowards."

Churchill grudgingly respected de Gaulle. "I had continuous difficulties and many sharp antagonisms with him," Churchill wrote.

> I knew he was no friend of England. But I always recognized in him the spirit and conception which, across the pages of history, the word 'France' would ever proclaim. I understood and admired, while I resented, his arrogant demeanor. Here he was—a refugee, an exile from his country under sentence of death, in a position entirely dependent upon the good will of Britain, and now of the United States. The Germans had conquered his country. He had no real foothold anywhere. Never mind; he defied all.

De Gaulle defied Churchill when the prime minister attempted to persuade him to join the conference at Casablanca. "De Gaulle is on his high horse," Churchill told Roosevelt at one of their private sessions. "Refuses to come down here. Refuses point blank. . . . He's furious over the methods used to get control in Morocco and Algeria and French West Africa. Jeanne d'Arc complex. And of course now that Ike has set Giraud in charge down here . . ." Churchill shook his head in bafflement.

Roosevelt guessed that there was more to the Churchill–de Gaulle story than the prime minister was letting on. Elliott Roosevelt was present at this late-night meeting, which ended with Churchill agreeing to a recommendation by Roosevelt that de Gaulle be informed that he would lose all Allied support if he didn't come to Casablanca at once. When Churchill retired for the night, Roosevelt asked Elliott to stay, as he felt like talking. "I sat with him while he got into bed, and afterwards kept him up for the time it takes to smoke two or three cigarettes," Elliott recalled. Elliott remarked that Churchill hadn't looked as upset as his words about de Gaulle sounded. "Was I just imagining things, or isn't the P.M. really worried by de Gaulle's pouting?" he asked his father.

"I don't know," Roosevelt replied, laughing. "I hope to find out in the next few days. But I have a strong sneaking suspicion that our friend de Gaulle hasn't come to Africa yet because our friend Winston hasn't chosen to bid him come yet. I am more than partially sure that de Gaulle will do just about anything, at this point, that the Prime Minister and the Foreign Office ask him to do."

"How come?"

"Interests coincide. The English mean to maintain their hold on their colonies. They mean to help the French maintain *their* hold on *their* colonies. Winnie is a great man for the status quo. He even *looks* like the status quo, doesn't he?" Roosevelt remarked that Britain's interest in the Pacific theater was closely related to colonial questions. "Burma—that affects India, and French Indochina, and Indonesia. They're all interrelated. If one gets its freedom, the others will get ideas. That's why Winston's so anxious to keep de Gaulle in his corner. De Gaulle isn't any more interested in seeing a colonial empire disappear than Churchill is."

Elliott asked how Giraud figured in the equation.

"I hear very fine things about him from our State Department people." Robert Murphy was State's, and Eisenhower's, liaison with the French general. "He's sent back reports that indicate Giraud will be just the man to counterbalance de Gaulle."

Elliott expressed surprise that de Gaulle needed counterbalancing. "All the reports we get—you know, in the newspapers and so on—tell of how popular he is, in and out of France."

"It's to the advantage of his backers to keep that idea alive."

"Churchill, you mean? And the English?"

Roosevelt nodded. "De Gaulle is out to achieve one-man government in France. I can't imagine a man I would distrust more. His whole Free French movement is honeycombed with police spies. He has agents spying on his own people. To him, freedom of speech means freedom from criticism—of him."

Elliott thought about this for a moment. As he did, his father yawned. Elliott got up to go. Roosevelt motioned for him to stay. He had more on his mind. "The thing is," Roosevelt said, "the colonial system means war. Exploit the resources of an India, a Burma, a Java; take all the wealth out of those countries, but never put anything back into them, things like education, decent standards of living, minimum health requirements—all you're doing is storing up the kind of trouble that leads to war."

Elliott said he had noticed Churchill's cold glower when India was even mentioned.

"India should be made a commonwealth at once," Roosevelt said. "After a certain number of years—five perhaps, or ten—she should be able to choose whether she wants to remain in the empire or have complete independence." As a commonwealth, India could begin to build the institutions of health and education needed to raise the living standard of her people. "But how can she have these things when Britain is taking all the wealth of her national resources away from her, every year? Every year the Indian people have one thing to look forward to, like death and taxes. Sure as shooting, they have a famine. The season of famine, they call it."

Roosevelt's flight from America had stopped in British Gambia. He had seen and heard only a little of the country, but that little revealed a lot. "At about eight-thirty"—in the morning—"we drove through Bathurst to the airfield. The natives were just getting to work—in rags, glum-looking. . . . They told us the natives would look happier around noon-time, when the sun should have burned off the dew and the chill. I was told the prevailing wage for these men was one and nine—one shilling, nine pence. Less than fifty cents."

"An hour?"

"A *day*! Fifty cents a *day*! Besides which they're given a half-cup of rice. . . . Dirt, disease, very high mortality rate. . . . Life expectancy—you'd never guess what it is. Twenty-six years! These people are treated worse than the livestock. Their cattle live longer!"

Roosevelt asked Elliott, who had been stationed in Algeria, what things were like there. Elliott said it was much the same story. A few people—the white colonials and some favored locals—lived very well, but the vast majority suffered in poverty, disease, and ignorance.

Roosevelt explained what he proposed to do. France would be restored as a world power and then given back her colonies, but only in trust. Each year the French would have to report on the progress their colonies had made.

Elliott asked whom they would report to.

"The organization of the United Nations, when it's been set up. . . . When we've won the war, the four great powers will be responsible for the peace. It's already high time for us to be thinking of the future, building for it. . . . These great powers will have to assume the task of bringing education, raising the standards of living, improving the health conditions of all the backward, depressed colonial areas of the world. And when they've had a chance to reach maturity, they must have the opportunity extended them of independence—after the United Nations as a whole have decided they are prepared for it. If this isn't done, we might as well agree that we're in for another war."

Roosevelt's last cigarette had gone out. Elliott looked at his watch.

"Three-thirty, Pop."

"Yes. Now I *am* tired. Get some sleep yourself, Elliott."

❖ ❖ ❖

THE WEEK PLAYED out much as Roosevelt anticipated. Churchill professed to be urging de Gaulle to come to Casablanca, but the general, he said, was obdurate. Roosevelt meanwhile met with Giraud, who was delighted at the American attention. Giraud spoke no English, and though Roosevelt had an interpreter, Robert Murphy, he made do, for the most part, in Giraud's language. The general emphasized his determination to fight. "No distractions should be permitted to interfere with the conduct of the war," he said. He declared that all he required was American arms. "Only give us the arms. Give us the guns and the tanks and the planes. It is all we need."

Roosevelt asked where the troops to employ the arms would come from.

"We can recruit colonial troops by the tens of thousands!"

Who would train them?

"There are plenty of officers under my command. It constitutes no problem. Only give us the arms!"

Roosevelt tried to get Giraud to address the political problems of the war. The president was thinking ahead to how France would be reconstituted as a great power, and he didn't want to have to rely on de Gaulle. But he got nowhere. "Giraud swept these questions aside," Elliott Roosevelt, present at the meeting, recalled. "He was single-minded." Arms were the general's idée fixe. After Giraud left, Roosevelt shook his head. "I'm afraid we're leaning on a very slender reed," he told Elliott.

Roosevelt's disappointment with Giraud made him want to see de Gaulle all the more. Giraud's focus on fighting and certain other of his comments suggested that he could work with the more political de Gaulle. Roosevelt needled Churchill about de Gaulle over cocktails and meals. Hopkins worked on Churchill as well. The prime minister said he was doing what he could, but de Gaulle was stubborn.

Roosevelt began to wonder whether de Gaulle would ever come. "We delivered our bridegroom, General Giraud, who was most cooperative on the impending marriage and, I am sure, was ready to go through with it on our terms," the president wrote Cordell Hull. "However, our friends could not produce the bride, the temperamental lady de Gaulle. She has got quite snooty about the whole idea and does not want to see either of us, and is showing no intention of getting into bed with Giraud."

But Roosevelt had traveled a long way, and he wasn't going to leave without making every effort to bring de Gaulle to the altar. Henry Stimson, who got the story from Roosevelt upon the president's return to America, related Roosevelt's final effort. Roosevelt and Churchill were talking, and the prime minister registered, or perhaps feigned, exasperation at de Gaulle's refusal to budge from London. "Roosevelt asked whether de Gaulle got any salary and who paid him," Stimson wrote. "Churchill replied that he, Churchill, paid it. Then said the President, 'I should suggest to him that salaries are paid for devoted and obedient service and, if he doesn't come, his salary would be cut off.' De Gaulle came the next day."

Yet he didn't come happily, and his unhappiness showed. He met only briefly with Roosevelt, and in private. No interpreter or note taker was present, although Roosevelt stationed an assistant outside the door, which was kept slightly ajar. De Gaulle, noticing the door and guessing the presence of the note taker, spoke so softly as to be inaudible to Roosevelt's aide. The aide did hear what Roosevelt said. The president defended the Darlan deal, which he knew de Gaulle despised. And he predicted that winning the war would necessitate other compromises. But he said that Giraud had made clear that his sole ambition was to get on with the fighting, until French soil was freed of the enemy. Roosevelt related a bit of American history, explaining how the Civil War had divided the nation for a time but how after the war "the people realized that personal pride and personal prejudices must often be subordinated for the good of the country as a whole." Roosevelt expressed hope that the people and leaders of France would adopt a similar view. "The only course of action that will save France is for all of her loyal sons to unite to defeat the enemy."

The meeting lasted twenty minutes. De Gaulle agreed to nothing—except the one thing Roosevelt wanted most, for now. On the final day of the conference the president managed to get de Gaulle and Giraud to his villa at the same time. Churchill was there, too. "De Gaulle was a little bewildered," Hopkins observed.

> Churchill grunted. But the president went to work on them. . . . De Gaulle finally agreed to a joint statement, and before he could catch his breath, the President suggested a photograph. By this time the garden was full of camera men and war correspondents who had been flown down the day before. I don't know who was the most surprised, the photographers or de Gaulle, when the four of them walked out—or rather the three of them, because the

President was carried to his chair. . . . The President suggested de Gaulle and Giraud shake hands. They stood up and obliged. Some of the camera men missed it, and they did it again.

❖ ❖ ❖

ℛOOSEVELT HAD ONE more trick to play. News of the conference had been blacked out until this final day, and the president wished to give the press corps a story. He arranged a news conference for himself and Churchill, and he commenced with a summary of what had been discussed and decided on. Much was innocuous and predictable, but the news-hungry correspondents scribbled furiously. They thought he had covered all the major topics and was wrapping up when he suddenly added:

> Another point. I think we have all had it in our hearts and our heads before, but I don't think that it has ever been put down on paper by the Prime Minister and myself, and that is the determination that peace can come to the world only by the total elimination of German and Japanese war power.
>
> Some of you Britishers know the old story—we had a general called U. S. Grant. His name was Ulysses Simpson Grant, but in my, and the Prime Minister's, early days he was called "Unconditional Surrender" Grant. The elimination of German, Japanese, and Italian war power means the unconditional surrender by Germany, Italy, and Japan. That means a reasonable assurance of future world peace. It does not mean the destruction of the population of Germany, Italy, or Japan, but it does mean the destruction of the philosophies in those countries which are based on conquest and the subjugation of other people.

Churchill afterward acknowledged "some feeling of surprise" at Roosevelt's unveiling of the policy of unconditional surrender. The policy itself had been in the works for months. It initially arose in American planning the previous May, and it reflected the unsatisfactory denouement of the First World War, which had ended with the German armistice. Roosevelt raised the issue with Churchill at Casablanca, where the prime minister apparently registered some reservations as to whether it ought to apply to Italy, which he—like some of the American planners—thought might be lured away from the Axis by adept diplomacy joined to military duress. Churchill referred the matter to the war cabinet in London, which replied that the surrender policy should not exclude

Italy. As Foreign Secretary Anthony Eden cabled for the cabinet: "Knowledge of all rough stuff coming to them is surely more likely to have desired effect on Italian morale."

But neither the British cabinet nor the prime minister had said anything about making the policy public—hence Churchill's surprise at Roosevelt's doing so without warning. The president's statement left Churchill no choice. "In my speech which followed the President's," Churchill wrote later, "I of course supported him and concurred in what he had said. Any divergence between us, even by omission, would on such an occasion and at such a time have been damaging or even dangerous to our war effort."

❖   ❖   ❖

KEEPING CHURCHILL off balance was a conscious aspect of Roosevelt's strategy. Keeping Stalin off balance came with the territory of the Grand Alliance. As part of their conclusion of the Casablanca conference, Roosevelt and Churchill composed a letter to Stalin. "We have decided the operations which are to be undertaken by American and British forces in the first nine months of 1943," they wrote. "We believe these operations, together with your powerful offensive, may well bring Germany to her knees in 1943. . . . We are in no doubt that our correct strategy is to concentrate on the defeat of Germany, with a view to achieving early and decisive victory in the European theatre." So far so good, Stalin must have thought. But as he read on he saw nothing about an invasion of France. "Our immediate intention is to clear the Axis out of North Africa. . . . We have made the decision to launch a large scale amphibious operation in the Mediterranean at the earliest possible moment. . . . We shall increase the Allied bomber offensive from the U.K. against Germany." The best the British and Americans could offer by way of a second front was the promise of a buildup of forces in Britain and a professed desire "to re-enter the Continent of Europe as soon as practicable."

"I thank you for the information," Stalin replied curtly. Perhaps the Soviet leader felt betrayed; perhaps he thought his allies were reverting to capitalist form. Whatever the case, his displeasure was clear. He reminded the president and prime minister of their earlier promise regarding Germany. "You yourselves set the task of crushing it by opening a second front in Europe in 1943." The Soviet Union awaited fulfillment of this promise. "I should be very obliged to you for information on the concrete operations planned in this respect and on the scheduled time of their realization."

Churchill drafted a joint response. The prime minister explained that the British and Americans expected to complete the conquest of North Africa by the end of April. "When this is accomplished, we intend, in July, or earlier if possible, to attack Italy across the Mediterranean." Roosevelt revised Churchill's draft, not wishing to commit to an invasion of Italy proper, which in any event would anger Stalin the more, as distracting the Allies further from France. Roosevelt's version, which was the one sent to Moscow, said the Americans and British would attack Sicily. Churchill's draft had continued: "We are aiming for August for a heavy operation across the Channel, for which between seventeen and twenty British and U.S. divisions will be available." Roosevelt again revised, keeping the August date but eliminating the commitment to a particular number of divisions, which seemed to him impossible to guarantee. He added a disclaimer: "The timing of this attack must of course be dependent upon the condition of German defensive possibilities across the Channel at that time."

Stalin wasn't mollified in the least. He asked why it would take until April to mop up in North Africa and why until August or later to invade France. The Red Army had closed the ring at Stalingrad and captured some hundred thousand German troops (and nearly two dozen generals). Hitler's army was reeling. "In order to prevent the enemy from recovering, it is highly important, in my opinion, that the blow from the West should not be postponed until the second half of the year, but dealt in the spring or at the beginning of summer."

This time Roosevelt answered by himself. The delay in North Africa, he said, had been caused by "unexpected heavy rains that made the roads extremely difficult for both troops and supplies en route from our landing ports to the front lines and made the fields and mountains impassable." As to the second front: "You may be sure that the American effort will be projected onto the Continent of Europe at as early a date subsequent to success in North Africa as transportation facilities can be provided by our maximum effort." He closed: "We hope that the success of your heroic army, which is an inspiration to us all, will continue."

Stalin rejected Roosevelt's explanation and a similar message from Churchill. His anger seethed from between the lines as he lectured the president on what the Americans and British had promised and repeatedly failed to deliver. "You will recall that you and Mr. Churchill thought it possible to open a second front as early as 1942 or this spring at the latest." No second front had appeared, leaving the burden on the Red Army. "The Soviet troops have fought strenuously all winter and are continuing to do so, while Hitler is taking important measures to rehabilitate and reinforce his army for the spring and summer operations against the U.S.S.R. It is therefore particularly essential for us that the blow from the West be no longer delayed, that it be delivered this spring or in early summer." Stalin concluded ominously: "I must give a most emphatic warning, in the interest of our common cause, of the grave danger with which further delay in opening a second front in France is fraught."

50.

$\mathcal{W}$AS IT A WARNING, OR A THREAT? WAS STALIN SUGGESTING THAT the Red Army might break under unrelieved pressure? Or that the Soviet government might reverse course once more and seek accommodation with Germany? Or was it a political tactic? Was Stalin simply compiling a case to use against the Americans and British at a postwar peace conference? Would Stalin claim the moral high ground for having fought longer and harder than the Anglo-Americans?

While Roosevelt pondered the possibilities, certain matters of domestic governance required his attention—except that nothing after Pearl Harbor was exclusively domestic. For sixty years the United States had closed its borders to nearly all immigration from China. The Chinese Exclusion Act of 1882 reflected the racism and xenophobia of its time, and though the government of China had protested the unfavorable treatment accorded its nationals— in a period when America's borders were open to almost everyone else—its weakness allowed Washington to ignore the complaints. The singularity of Chinese exclusion diminished in the 1920s with the adoption of quotas on immigration generally. China continued to complain during the 1930s, but amid the economic depression and the isolationism of the decade, few in America listened. The onset of the Pacific war changed things. China became an ally and a fellow member of the United Nations. Meanwhile, however, Japan used the issue of Chinese exclusion—which had been broadened to encompass other Asians and extended to a ban preventing Asians resident in the United States from becoming citizens—as a propaganda tool against America. The Atlantic Charter was a sham, Tokyo asserted, in the face of America's ongoing discrimination against Asians.

Roosevelt recognized the damage the hoary policy did to the war effort. As a first step toward rectifying the situation, he directed the drafting of a treaty relinquishing America's extraterritoriality rights in China. Extraterritoriality—the principle that Americans in China were subject to American laws, not Chinese laws—was a vestige of the nineteenth century, when the United States joined Britain and other imperial powers in the system of "unequal treaties" that exploited China's weakness to the advantage of the West. "The abolition of the extraterritorial system in China is a step in line with the expressed desires of the government and the people of the United States," Roosevelt declared in forwarding the new treaty to the Senate. "The spirit reflected by the treaty will, I am sure, be gratifying to the governments and the peoples of all the United Nations." The Senate took the president at his word and approved the pact.

Roosevelt followed up by asking Congress to repeal the Chinese exclusion laws. "Nations, like individuals, make mistakes," the president said. "We must be big enough to acknowledge our mistakes of the past and to correct them. By the repeal of the Chinese Exclusion Laws, we can correct a historic mistake and silence the distorted Japanese propaganda." Repeal would remove the stigma China labored under in American law, and it would allow Chinese nationals their rightful place in the American immigration system. This wasn't saying much, given the pro-European bias of the immigration quotas. Roosevelt himself admitted—in fact boasted, albeit quietly—that the Chinese quota would be "only about 100 immigrants a year." Organized labor needn't worry. "There can be no reasonable apprehension that any such number of immigrants will cause unemployment or provide competition in the search for jobs."

Roosevelt went on to urge the repeal of the law against citizenship for persons of Chinese descent. "It would be additional proof not only that we regard China as a partner in waging war but that we shall regard her as a partner in days of peace." He did not propose to change the citizenship laws as they applied to other Asians, and he acknowledged that the discrepancy would favor China. But China deserved it. "Their great contribution to the cause of decency and freedom entitles them to such preference." Roosevelt didn't detail his big plans for China after the war. Some of the legislators knew what he had in mind; others did not. But again Congress followed the president's lead and repealed the offensive statute.

❖ ❖ ❖

RACE AROSE IN another context during this same period. Eighty years, almost to the week, after race riots convulsed New York City during the Civil

War, race riots erupted in Detroit and Los Angeles. The Detroit riots reflected the strains the wartime economy had placed on the fabric of American social relations and the ambivalent response of Roosevelt and the federal government to those strains. Even before Pearl Harbor, the effects of the approach of war—in the form of the economic revival and the inception of the draft—inspired African American leaders to press for equal treatment for blacks in the military and in the workplace. A. Philip Randolph, the longtime director of the Brotherhood of Sleeping Car Porters, headed the effort. Randolph shrewdly invited Eleanor Roosevelt to the union's annual convention, in Harlem, in 1940. The First Lady was welcomed and granted the opportunity to address the delegates; she reciprocated by arranging a meeting between Randolph and the president.

Roosevelt greeted Randolph, Walter White of the NAACP, and a small group of other black leaders and thanked them for coming. He listened intently as they presented a petition entreating the government to end segregation in the armed services and in defense work. They left, as so many visitors to the White House left, thinking Roosevelt had agreed with them. A short while later, however, even as the president personally asserted that, in federal defense contracts, "workers should not be discriminated against because of age, sex, race or color," a White House spokesman declared that "the policy of the War Department is not to intermingle colored and white enlisted personnel in the same regimental organizations."

Randolph felt betrayed. At least he acted that way. He declared that if the president would not respond to reasoned argument, other forms of persuasion might be necessary. He called for a protest march on Washington by African Americans, to shame the president and the government into doing what was right. Randolph laid the groundwork for the protest during the spring of 1941 and scheduled the march for July 1.

Roosevelt was an egalitarian at heart, if a sometimes paternalistic one, and he might have desegregated the armed forces had politics and the war not constrained him. But he knew that desegregation would antagonize the South and incite those same southern senators and congressmen who had prevented him from taking a stand for civil rights until now. In addition, amid his careful cultivation of popular support for war readiness and ultimate intervention, he opposed anything that distracted the public from the overriding issue of national security. A march by Negroes on Washington, with its white, essentially southern police force, might well result in bloodshed, which was the last thing Roosevelt needed. Finally, he resented anything that smacked of political extortion.

The president talked the matter over with Eleanor. She was in sympathy with Randolph's goals even more than Roosevelt was, but she agreed with her husband that a march would be counterproductive. "I feel very strongly that your group is making a grave mistake at the present time to allow this march to take place," she wrote Randolph. "I feel that if any incident occurs as a result of this, it may engender so much bitterness that it will create in Congress even more solid opposition from certain groups than we have had in the past." When Randolph refused to call off the march, Roosevelt dispatched Eleanor to New York to talk to Randolph and Walter White personally. "Get it stopped," he said.

Eleanor met Randolph and White at New York's City Hall. She repeated her argument that the march could get out of control and provoke a backlash. Randolph threw the responsibility for violence back at her—and her husband. "I replied that there would be no violence unless her husband ordered the police to crack black heads," Randolph recalled. He and White stood firm. Eleanor, with Roosevelt's permission, arranged another meeting of the black leaders with the president.

This session took place two weeks before the scheduled march. Roosevelt asked how many people Randolph and White would bring to Washington. Randolph said one hundred thousand.

Roosevelt looked at Randolph skeptically, then turned to White. "Walter, how many people will *really* march?"

"One hundred thousand, Mr. President," White said.

"You can't bring one hundred thousand Negroes to Washington," Roosevelt responded. "Somebody might get killed."

Not if the president came out and addressed the marchers, Randolph said.

Roosevelt ignored the suggestion. "Call it off," he said, "and we'll talk."

Without explicitly canceling the march, Randolph and White accepted Roosevelt's offer to let them help draft an executive order along the lines they desired. The writing began that day in the Cabinet Room, and it continued for several days thereafter as the various parties likely to be affected registered their objections and support.

A week before the scheduled march, Roosevelt issued the executive order. "I do hereby reaffirm the policy of the United States that there shall be no discrimination in the employment of workers in defense industries or government because of race, creed, color, or national origin," the president said. To enforce the policy he established a Committee on Fair Employment Practice.

The formula worked—for Roosevelt and, to a lesser degree, for Randolph and White. The march was canceled, and the principle of nondiscrimination began to be implemented. The executive order was silent on segregation in the military; as part of the bargain Roosevelt persuaded Randolph and White to leave the soldiers alone.

Roosevelt could compel defense employers not to discriminate, but he couldn't compel white workers and black workers to fraternize in the workplace. Nor could he convince white workers that blacks didn't erode their bargaining power. During the Second World War a second great migration from the South to the North occurred, and the tensions it induced in cities like Detroit mirrored the tensions of the First World War and the first migration. During the summer of 1943 the tension passed the snapping point. On June 20 a large crowd of blacks and whites gathered at Belle Isle, a public park in the Detroit River. The hot weather and the consumption of alcohol by many of the picnickers contributed to a series of scuffles that escalated into concerted violence. Mistaken reports circulated that whites had killed three blacks; blacks responded with random attacks against whites. By late evening the city was out of control, and before federal troops brought order the next day, thirty-four people—twenty-five blacks and nine whites—had been killed.

The riots in Los Angeles revealed a different set of strains. The Immigration Act of 1924 had exempted Mexicans from the quota system because immigration from Mexico had never been large and because employers of Mexican workers—typically commercial farmers in California, Arizona, and Texas—resisted the effort to restrict their work force. As both a cause and a consequence of the open border between the United States and Mexico, the most common pattern of movement was not immigration but migration—a back-and-forth flow of workers from Mexico to the United States during the growing season and from the United States to Mexico during the winter.

Gradually, though, communities of Mexican Americans emerged in Los Angeles and other cities, producing and experiencing the same kinds of stresses that characterized ethnic communities elsewhere. In the barrio of East Los Angeles, many young Mexican Americans distinguished themselves by wearing oversized, elaborately styled "zoot suits," which were an emblem of both ethnic and second-generational identity. The zoot suits also made their wearers easy targets when racial and ethnic tensions emerged during the summer of 1943. In this case the participants were the young Mexican Americans and the mostly white sailors and soldiers from the military facilities in Los Angeles. A series of murders and assaults triggered broader violence, and lurid reporting in the local press kept it going.

A certain civilian-military friction among the young males aggravated the usual mixture of racial and ethnic antagonism. Sailors and soldiers assaulted the zoot suiters, ripping their clothes off and cutting the long hair that completed the look. "We'll destroy every zoot suit in Los Angeles County before this is over," one seaman vowed. Evidence of police favoritism toward the military men prompted the Mexican government to complain, causing the mayor of Los Angeles in turn to tell Mexico City to butt out. "They are Los Angeles youth," Fletcher Bowron asserted, "and the problem is purely a local one." Bowron went on to say, "We are going to see that members of the armed forces are not attacked. At the same time, we expect cooperation from officers of the Army and Navy to the extent that soldiers and sailors do not pile into Los Angeles for the purpose of excitement and adventure and what they might consider a little fun by beating up young men whose appearance they do not like."

Bowron's warning prompted the military to restrict the movements of the soldiers and sailors. Civil and military police stepped up patrols, and the rioting gradually ended. An uneasy calm settled over the city, and Angelenos returned their attention to the war against the Axis.

❖　❖　❖

ROOSEVELT DECLINED to comment on the domestic disturbances. Before the war he would have felt pressure to say something, perhaps to take action. But the war liberated him from all manner of issues he preferred to avoid. With the world in the balance, few could fault him for delegating lesser matters to subordinates.

The fate of the world preoccupied the president during 1943. Roosevelt had hardly returned from Africa when British foreign secretary Eden arrived on his doorstep. Roosevelt didn't know Eden well, except that he seemed quite a different sort from the half-American Churchill. Yet he and Roosevelt got on famously. "Anthony spent three evenings with me," the president informed Churchill midway through Eden's visit. "He is a grand fellow and we are talking everything from Ruthenia to the production of peanuts!" In fact Roosevelt found Eden easier to work with than Churchill, as the president teasingly hinted to the prime minister: "We seem to agree on about 95 percent of all the subjects—not a bad average."

Roosevelt and Eden did indeed range widely, but they spent most of their time envisioning Europe at the war's end. They agreed that Russia would demand changes in the prewar status quo. Eden predicted that Stalin would insist, at the least, on incorporation of the Baltic states into the Soviet Union. Roosevelt concurred, although he remarked that this would provoke "a good deal of resistance in the United States." The president didn't imagine he could prevent Stalin from taking the Baltics. "Realistically," he said, "the Russian armies will be in the Baltic states at the time of the downfall of Germany, and none of us can force them to get out." But Roosevelt didn't intend simply to give the Baltic issue away. "We should use it as a bargaining instrument in getting other concessions from Russia."

Such concessions might involve Poland. Eden and Roosevelt agreed that the Polish question could well be the most difficult to resolve. Poland's boundaries would have to be reconfigured, although neither Roosevelt nor Eden thought geography would be the sticking point. The real problem was the makeup of the postwar Polish state. A Polish government in exile currently operated out of London, and it was even more obstreperous than de Gaulle's Free French. "The Poles are being very difficult about their aspirations," Eden told Roosevelt. "Poland has very large ambitions after the war. . . . Privately they say that Russia will be so weakened and Germany crushed that Poland will emerge as the most powerful state in that part of the world."

Roosevelt acknowledged Poland's desires—and the unlikelihood of their being realized. He couldn't say so publicly, as it would stir up Poles in America, but Poland's fate at the war's end would be decided by the great powers, not by the Poles. And it would be part of a larger settlement with broader goals. "As far as Poland is concerned," Roosevelt said, "the important thing is to set it up in a way that will help maintain the peace of the world."

The Polish question hinged on the German question. And the heart of the German question was whether there would be a single Germany after the war or multiple Germanys. The Russians, Eden supposed, would opt for the multiple versions. "Stalin has a deep-seated distrust of the Germans," Eden said. "He will insist that Germany be broken up into a number of states."

Roosevelt agreed that Germany must be dismembered. Prussia, in particular, must be split off. "The Prussians cannot be permitted to dominate all Germany." But he didn't want to repeat the mistakes of Versailles, in which the victors imposed a settlement that Hitler eventually used against them. "We should encourage the differences and ambitions that will spring up within Germany for a separatist movement and, in effect, approve of a division which represents German public opinion."

To Eden, Roosevelt spoke for the first time at length of his hopes for the international organization that would manage the peace settlement. Churchill had been promoting a European council, with responsibility for regional security. Roosevelt rejected the plan as divisive and distracting. The president favored a single body—emerging from the wartime United Nations—divided into two parts. The larger part would be advisory and would include every independent country that wanted to join. "This body should be world-wide in scope," Roosevelt said. The smaller part, by number of countries, would be where the true power lay. "The real decisions should be made by the United States, Great Britain, Russia, and China, who will be the powers for many years to come that will have to police the world."

Eden agreed that the United Nations should be global in membership. And he didn't dispute the need for guidance by the great powers. But he doubted that China was ready for such a role. He thought the Chinese would probably have to fight a revolution among themselves before their problems were sorted out. In any event, he said, he "did not much like the idea of the Chinese running up and down the Pacific."

But Roosevelt insisted. Some country had to police Asia, and it obviously couldn't be Japan. Moreover, promoting China would yield diplomatic dividends. "China," the president predicted, "in any serious conflict of policy with Russia will undoubtedly line up on our side."

❖   ❖   ❖

THE QUESTION OF who would be lining up with whom played a central role in talks between Roosevelt and Churchill a few weeks later. Yet it wasn't Russia against the West that worried Roosevelt's advisers; it was Roosevelt against them. "I fear it will be the same story over again," Henry Stimson recorded in his diary. "The man from London will arrive with a program of further expansion in the eastern Mediterranean and will have his way with our Chief, and the careful and deliberate plans of our staff will be overridden. I feel very troubled about it."

Stimson and the military men had been working on Roosevelt since Casablanca for a commitment to a particular date for the cross-Channel invasion. "The United States accepts the strategic concept that the war will be won most speedily by first defeating Germany," the American joint chiefs of staff reiterated ahead of Churchill's visit. "Defeating Germany first involves making a determined attack against Germany on the Continent at the earliest practicable date. . . . All proposed operations in Europe should be judged primarily on the basis of the contribution to that end." This was nothing new, of course, but the fact that it had to be restated revealed the concern on the part of Stimson and the chiefs that the president hadn't been convinced—at least not convinced sufficiently to withstand Churchill's arguments in the direction of the Mediterranean.

The talks started promisingly, from Stimson's point of view. Churchill performed as expected. There were no differences of opinion between the British and the Americans, the prime minister said, merely questions of "emphasis and priority." He proceeded to emphasize the Mediterranean, declaring that the immediate objective was to "get Italy out of the war by whatever means might be the best." The defeat of Italy, Churchill predicted, would "cause a chill of loneliness over the German people and might be the beginning of their doom."

Roosevelt responded more forthrightly than Stimson had feared. The president wondered aloud whether the early defeat of Italy would be an unmixed blessing. "Italy might drop into the lap of the United Nations, who would then have the responsibility of supplying the Italian people." He himself, he said, had "always shrunk from the thought of putting large armies in Italy." A major offensive there could easily bog down. "This might result in attrition for the United Nations and play into Germany's hands." At the least, the cost of occupying Italy must be examined before any commitment to an invasion could be made.

Meanwhile, Roosevelt said, preparations for the invasion of France "should begin at once." After two years of talking, the American and British governments should settle on "a concrete plan to be carried out at a certain time." A Channel crossing, the president said, should be "decided upon definitely as an operation for the spring of 1944."

The principals adjourned to let their subordinates fight things out. George Marshall asserted that Italy would suck the life from a second front in France. Any operation "invariably created a vacuum in which it was essential to pour more and more means." An invasion of Italy would commit the British and Americans through 1943 and "virtually all of 1944." Such a commitment would have serious consequences. "It would mean a prolongation of the war in Europe, and thus a delay in the ultimate defeat of Japan, which the people of the United States would not tolerate." Marshall put the matter as directly as he could: "We are now at the crossroads. If we are committed to the Mediterranean . . . it means a prolonged struggle and one which is not acceptable to the United States."

Marshall's navy colleague William Leahy, who held the post of chief of staff to the commander in chief, chimed in to assert that the Pacific could "not be neglected." It was too vital to American strategy. "Immediate action" was necessary to keep China in the war. For this reason, if no other, "the war in Europe must be brought to a rapid decisive close at the earliest possible date."

Leahy's comment gave Alan Brooke an opening for a counterattack. The chief of the British imperial staff fully agreed that the war in Europe must be ended as swiftly as possible. This was why Italy was so essential. "Only by continuing in the Mediterranean can we achieve the maximum diversion of German forces from Russia," Brooke said. Focusing on France would take time, giving the Germans a chance to catch their breath. No major operations would be possible "until 1945 or 1946," far too late to do Russia any good.

Charles Portal, the chief of the British air staff, supported Brooke, declaring that a follow-through in Italy was essential to the success of a Channel crossing. Absent the relief provided by an Italian front, the Red Army might break. The Germans then would be able to send nearly all their troops west to oppose an invasion of France.

For day after day the two sides pounded each other with a verve that, some of the participants must have reflected, ought better have been applied against the Axis. They discussed certain other matters, for diversion almost as much as for anything else. They considered how many bombers might be employed from Britain against targets in Germany and what those targets ought to be. They argued how best to assist China and what balance of blockade, bombardment, and direct assault would be required for the ultimate defeat of Japan. But always they came back to the central question of Italy versus France.

They were still debating when Churchill took his case to the American people, through their elected representatives. Five hundred days had passed, the veteran orator elegantly reminded a joint session of the Senate and House, since he had last addressed them, with "every day a day in which we have toiled and suffered and dared shoulder to shoulder against the cruel and mighty enemy." The fact that Congress had invited him back was a "high mark in my life," Churchill modestly asserted. "It also shows that our partnership has not done so badly."

The prime minister assured his listeners—who included, as before, a national radio audience—that Britain had as large a stake in defeating Japan as America had. "It may not have escaped your attention that I have brought with me to this country and to this conference Field Marshal Wavell and two other commanders in chief from India. Now, they have not traveled all this way simply to concern themselves about improving the health and happiness of the

Mikado of Japan." Churchill pointed out that Britain was already contributing directly to the destruction of Germany by the bombing raids it conducted in concert with the Americans. "Our air offensive is forcing Germany to withdraw an ever-larger proportion of its war-making capacity from the fighting fronts in order to provide protection against the air attacks." He recalled the discouragement he had felt, during his last visit to Washington, when he learned of the fall of Tobruk. "That, indeed, was a dark and bitter hour for me." But the bitterness was eased, almost at once, by gratitude. "I shall never forget the kindness, the delicacy, the true comradeship which our American friends showed me and those with me in such adversity." The Sherman tanks President Roosevelt dispatched to Egypt had been crucial in the campaign to stem the German advance and ultimately reclaim North Africa.

Churchill didn't engage the issue of Italy versus France, at least not directly. But his preference for Italy was well known, and in recounting the glorious victories thus far of American and British arms in the Mediterranean, he left little doubt in the minds of his congressional audience or his radio listeners as to where he thought the next blows should fall. "The enemy is still proud and powerful. He is hard to get at. He still possesses enormous armies, vast resources, and invaluable strategic territory. War is full of mysteries and surprises. A false step, a wrong direction of strategic effort, discord or lassitude among the Allies might soon give the common enemy the power to confront us with new and hideous facts."

❖   ❖   ❖

ℛOOSEVELT HAD ALWAYS known the end game would be the hardest part; he just didn't know it would begin so soon. Churchill's political eloquence proved more than a match for Marshall and Leahy's military reasoning, and the invasion of Italy went forward. In July 1943 an American army under George Patton and a British army under Bernard Montgomery crossed from North Africa to Sicily. A week of fighting brought Patton to within sight of Palermo, the Sicilian capital, which he proposed to take. Patton's immediate superior, British general Harold Alexander, initially authorized the attack but then reversed himself. Patton received the authorization order clearly enough but claimed that the countermand had been garbled in transmission; he plunged ahead and captured the city.

The fall of Palermo precipitated a crisis in the Italian government. Mussolini lost his nerve and then, astonishingly, his job. King Victor Emmanuel, until recently overawed by Mussolini but now fortified by growing restiveness among the dictator's own circle, demanded his resignation. Mussolini meekly consented and was promptly arrested.

The news caught American leaders, like nearly everyone else, by surprise. "Mr. President, what is your reaction to the sudden change in the Italian government?" a reporter inquired of Roosevelt on the afternoon of July 27.

"Reaction?" Roosevelt answered, playing for time.

"Yes, sir."

"I never have reactions. I am much too old." The ensuing laughter bought him another moment.

"Did you have the information that Mussolini would make his exit?" a reporter asked.

"No. No."

"Could you tell us whether there is likely to be any change in our unconditional surrender policy?"

"Oh, I think the secretary of state covered all that pretty well yesterday." In fact Hull had dodged the question, refusing either to reiterate the policy or to say that it had changed.

"Mr. President, if there should be an unconditional surrender, do you think . . ."

"How did you start that sentence? What word?"

"Uh, oh . . ."

More laughter as Roosevelt reminded the group of his oldest rule: "I don't think it's useful for me to go into the details of hypothetical questions."

It was especially not useful given that he himself didn't know what the policy was. Unconditional surrender had been problematic from the start, seeming to handcuff American and British leaders. Yet this was precisely the point, for in tying Roosevelt and Churchill to the mast of the harshest possible anti-Axis policy, it reassured Stalin, who had ample reason—starting with the long history of Anglo-American anti-Bolshevism and continuing through the repeated postponement of the second front—to doubt the steadfastness of his capitalist allies. But the problems with the policy persisted. Did Washington and London really intend to make no distinction among Italians, in the present case, or among Germans, when their time came? Did the deposing of Mussolini make no difference whatsoever?

The Office of War Information, America's propaganda arm, didn't see that anything had changed. Robert Sherwood's agency, reading—metaphorically and almost literally—from the old script, regarded the events in Rome as producing a distinction without a difference. The OWI lambasted Victor Emmanuel as "the moronic little king" and "the Fascist king" in its Voice of America broadcasts. The new head of the Italian government, Marshal Pietro Badoglio, was accounted "a high ranking Fascist."

Reporters immediately inquired whether Roosevelt agreed. Were the OWI broadcasts authorized by the president and the State Department?

"Neither of us," Roosevelt replied. "Nor by Bob Sherwood. And I think Bob Sherwood is raising hell about it now. It ought never to have been done." The reporters scribbled down the president's answer. "Only don't quote me as saying 'raising hell,' " he added.

"The first crack in the Axis has come," Roosevelt told the nation the next day. "The criminal, corrupt, Fascist regime in Italy is going to pieces. The pirate philosophy of the Fascists and the Nazis cannot stand adversity." Roosevelt noted, gloating, that Hitler had not been willing or able to save Mussolini. "In fact, Hitler's troops in Sicily stole the Italians' motor equipment, leaving Italian soldiers so stranded that they had no choice but to surrender." Regarding terms of surrender, the president explained:

Our terms to Italy are still the same as our terms to Germany and Japan—"unconditional surrender." We will have no truck with Fascism in any way, in any shape or manner. We will permit no vestige of Fascism to remain.

Yet this very statement, and those that followed it, hinted that things were neither as simple nor as clear-cut as that two-word slogan suggested. Unconditional surrender applied to the Fascists; did it apply to Italy as a whole? Maybe, maybe not. "Eventually Italy will reconstitute herself," Roosevelt said. "It will be the people of Italy who will do that, choosing their own government in accordance with the basic democratic principles of liberty and equality." The president declined to indicate how long "eventually" would be or to describe the state of government Italy would experience until then. He did declare that the Allies would treat the people of Italy—and the peoples of the other Axis powers, in their turn—fairly and humanely. "It is our determination to restore these conquered peoples to the dignity of human beings, masters of their own fate, entitled to freedom of speech, freedom of religion, freedom from want, and freedom from fear." Roosevelt refused to go beyond this generic reaffirmation of the Atlantic Charter. The present, he said, was not the time to discuss the details of a peace settlement. "Let us win the war first."

❖   ❖   ❖

*I*T WASN'T TOO soon for Americans to discuss among themselves their own postwar future. The sudden collapse of Mussolini's regime, which had ruled Italy for two decades, suggested that fascism might be more brittle than it seemed from the outside and that the war might end more rapidly than anyone had imagined. Roosevelt had put off asking what American society would look like after the war, thinking there was plenty of time for that. Now he offered some hints.

The Four Freedoms, of course, should apply to Americans as well as to people in other countries, and while freedom of speech and freedom of religion were secure enough, freedom from want and freedom from fear required work. All Americans must enjoy these freedoms, Roosevelt said. But the task of guaranteeing them might well begin with assurances to the millions of soldiers, sailors, and airmen who would be demobilized at the conclusion of the fighting. They were making the greatest sacrifice; they deserved the greatest attention.

The president proposed what amounted to a GI bill of rights. First on his list was a mustering-out bonus large enough to cover living expenses for a reasonable period between discharge from the military and the assuming of civilian jobs. Second, unemployment insurance for those unable to find jobs. Third, government funding for further education. Fourth, credit with Social Security for the time spent in the military. Fifth, medical care and rehabilitation for those injured in the service. Sixth, pensions for disabled veterans.

Roosevelt realized he was walking a narrow line, even apart from the ambition and cost of his demobilization program. Talking about policies to be implemented after the war risked distracting Americans from the job at hand. "We still have to knock out Hitler and his gang, and Tojo and his gang," he declared. "We still have to defeat Hitler and Tojo on their own home grounds." If anything, the recent developments should stimulate Americans to greater efforts than ever. "We must pour into this war the entire strength and intelligence and will power of the United States," he concluded. "We shall not settle for less than total victory."

❖   ❖   ❖

*E*ISENHOWER GROANED at Roosevelt's public reaffirmation of unconditional surrender. The policy might make sense to the politicians, but it rendered the army's job more difficult—and more costly in terms of casualties. Eisenhower knew from the Ultra intercepts that Hitler had responded to Mussolini's fall by ordering German troops to Italy. Nazi forces were currently racing from France and Austria into northern Italy toward Rome. Eisenhower hoped to persuade the Italians to turn against the Germans, giving him half a chance to keep the capital from falling into Hitler's hands. But they had to be offered something in exchange for switching sides—some assurance, for example, that occupation by the Allies would be less onerous than occupation by the Germans. If Roosevelt was to be believed, such assurance was precisely what he was forbidden to offer. Unconditional surrender—nothing less.

Yet Eisenhower had reason to think Roosevelt was *not* to be believed. Two days after Roosevelt addressed the nation, the president consulted Churchill on the prospects for Italy. "It seems highly probable that the fall of Mussolini will involve the overthrow of the Fascist regime and that the new government of the King and Badoglio will seek to negotiate a separate arrangement with the Allies for an armistice," Roosevelt wrote. "Should this prove to be the case, it will be necessary for us to make up our minds first of all upon what we want, and secondly upon the measures and conditions required to gain it for us." The overriding goal, as always, was "the destruction of Hitler and Hitlerism." Every advantage that could be wrung out of Italy toward this goal should be exploited. A first such advantage would be control of Italian territory and transportation facilities, for use against the Germans. A second would be control, ideally by surrender, of the Italian fleet. "The surrender of the fleet will liberate powerful British naval forces for service in the Indian Ocean against Japan and will be most agreeable to the United States," Roosevelt said. A third advantage would be the cooperation of the Italian army in fighting the Nazis. How best to attain these advantages was the question. "In our struggle with Hitler and the German army we cannot afford to deny ourselves any assistance that will kill Germans," Roosevelt told Churchill. "The fury of the Italian population may now be turned against the German intruders who have, as they will feel, brought these miseries upon Italy and then come so scantily and grudgingly to her aid. . . . We should stimulate this process."

Churchill worried that Roosevelt was going soft. The prime minister liked the policy of unconditional surrender and thought he and the president ought to stick to it. Eisenhower should sit tight and wait for the Italians to come to him. "It is for their responsible government to ask formally for an armistice on the basis of our principle of unconditional surrender," Churchill said. Eisenhower should not try to make the Italians' fate appear any less harsh than it truly was. "There are great dangers in trying to dish this sort of dose up with jam for the patient." Yet Churchill did accept one Roosevelt recommendation: that Eisenhower refrain from broadcasting any surrender demands. "They would certainly shock the Italian people and would give the Germans full information on which to act."

Roosevelt responded with a poke where he knew Churchill was sensitive. "I told the press today that we have to treat with any person or persons in Italy who can give us, first, disarmament and, second, assurance against chaos," he wrote the prime minister. "I think also that you and I after an armistice comes could say something about self-determination in Italy at the proper time."

The reference to self-determination got Churchill's attention, as Roosevelt knew it would. The prime minister replied that he didn't want the president to get the wrong impression regarding an Italian surrender. "My position is that once Mussolini and the Fascists are gone, I will deal with any Italian authority which can deliver the goods," Churchill wrote. "We have no right to lay undue burdens on our troops." Perhaps some concessions could be offered; quite possibly they would never have to be fulfilled. "It may well be that after the armistice terms have been accepted, both the King and Badoglio will sink under the odium of surrender and that the Crown Prince and a new Prime Minister may be chosen." But as for self-determination: "I should deprecate any pronouncement about self-determination at the present time, beyond what is implicit in the Atlantic Charter." The wrong people might get ideas. "We must be careful not to throw everything into the melting pot."

While Roosevelt and Churchill debated the terms of surrender, their military and diplomatic advisers did the same. The whole process took weeks— which Eisenhower couldn't easily spare. The Allied commander gnashed his teeth and tore what little hair he had left. "Poor Eisenhower is getting pretty harassed," Harold Macmillan, Churchill's political liaison to Eisenhower, remarked. Eisenhower himself longed for the era of sailing ships, when a general in the field had no choice but to act on his own judgment. "In my youthful days I used to read about commanders of armies and envied them what I supposed to be a great freedom in action and decision," he wrote his wife, Mamie. "What a notion!! The demands upon me that must be met make me a slave rather than a master."

Eisenhower grew even more upset when the dithering among the politicians allowed the Germans to get almost to Rome. Badoglio surrendered unconditionally in public, but with private assurances from Eisenhower—tacitly authorized by Roosevelt and Churchill—that leniency would be granted in proportion to Italy's help against the Germans. Eisenhower thereupon broadcast a radio message urging Italy's soldiers to redirect their fire against the Germans.

Roosevelt and Churchill offered similar encouragement from afar. "Now is the time for every Italian to strike his blow," the president and prime minister declared jointly on September 10.

> The liberating armies of the Western world are coming to your rescue. We have very strong forces and are entering at many points. The German terror in Italy will not last long. . . . Strike hard and strike home. Have faith in your future. All will come well.

But all did not come well. The delay allowed the Germans to beat the Americans to Rome. The Germans seized the city, compelling Victor Emmanuel and Badoglio to flee. The prime minister ordered Italy's troops to turn against the Germans, but by the time most of the soldiers got the word, they had been disarmed by the Germans or had disarmed themselves—dropping their guns and packs, shedding their uniforms, and going home.

Eisenhower was angry and disappointed. "We are in for some very tough fighting," he warned the Combined Chiefs.

51.

Nothing revolutionizes the art of war like war itself. Military technology changes slowly during peacetime, as arms makers improve on old designs and experiment with new ones. But until the shells start flying, no one really knows which of the improvements and experiments will stick. Weapons that seemed marginal take center stage; old standbys become obsolete overnight.

The U.S.S. *Iowa* wasn't exactly obsolete in the autumn of 1943, but it contributed far less to America's force projection than its designers had thought it would. When the *Iowa*'s keel was laid in June 1940, battleships were still the state of the naval art, and the *Iowa* was built to be the class of America's battleships. It was nearly nine hundred feet long, with a beam of more than a hundred feet. It boasted nine acres of deck and platform space, and 157 guns, including a main battery of nine 16-inchers. It had two catapults for launching planes, engines that developed over 200,000 horsepower, and a maximum speed of thirty-three knots.

But even before the *Iowa* was commissioned in February 1943, naval combat had passed the battlewagons by. Aircraft carriers were the wave of the present and future, capable of standing off much farther than the battleships and of inflicting much greater damage. The *Iowa* was relegated to a supporting role. Its principal mission during the rest of the war would be to shield American carriers in the Pacific from enemy counterattack.

Yet before it reached the Pacific, it had to cruise to North Africa. Roosevelt's journey to Casablanca in 1942 had cured him of the transatlantic air itch, and when he decided in the autumn of the following year to re-inspect the Mediterranean war zone, he commandeered the *Iowa*. The great ship handled the stormy Atlantic with aplomb. "Heavy following seas were running now, but the *Iowa* rode them comfortably," the navy lieutenant keeping the log of the president's journey recorded on the second day out. But even the *Iowa* had to take precautions. "The seas continued to increase throughout the afternoon, and for a while it was necessary to keep all hands off the top side. One man, R. Uriate (Seaman second class, U.S.N.), suffered slight bruises and a big scare when a wave coming over the main deck caught him and knocked him against a heavy object."

The *Iowa's* skipper, Captain John McCrea, was pleased to show off his vessel's capabilities, especially to such an appreciative observer as Roosevelt. An air defense exercise revealed how the navy had adapted to modern tactics of aerial assault. "Live ammunition was fired from a number of units of the ship's anti-aircraft battery (5-inch, 40 mm. and 20 mm. guns) to demonstrate for the Commander-in-Chief what a veritable curtain of fire a ship of this type can offer as a 'greeting' for enemy planes bent on attacking," the log keeper explained.

Another part of the exercise hadn't been scripted. "During the lull after one round of the series of firings, a moment of extreme tension was brought on by an unexpected explosion, of an underwater nature, in the vicinity of the ship. This explosion was followed by the terse announcement, 'This is not a drill.' " All aboard naturally assumed that a torpedo had exploded, especially as the *Iowa* had sharply altered course just moments before. Indeed a torpedo *had* detonated, but it was friendly rather than enemy fire, for whatever small comfort that was worth. One of the destroyers serving as the *Iowa's* anti-submarine screen had accidentally fired a torpedo in the *Iowa's* direction. The destroyer's captain subsequently explained the mishap as caused by a short circuit in the firing mechanism, probably the result of moisture from the rough seas. In any event, the torpedo's wake was spotted by one of the *Iowa's* lookouts, who warned the bridge, initiating the evasive maneuver that left the torpedo behind. "Had that torpedo hit the *Iowa* in the right spot, with her passenger list of distinguished statesmen, military, naval, and aerial strategists and planners, it could have had untold effect on the outcome of the war and the destiny of our country," the log keeper mused.

Ernest King thought so, too. The gruff navy chief, who was among the distinguished near casualties, was all for sacking the destroyer's captain on the spot. But Roosevelt intervened, explaining that the embarrassment of almost killing several layers of his commanders was punishment enough.

Roosevelt found the voyage invigorating. He interspersed presidential business—meeting with his military and naval advisers, discussing politics and diplomacy with Hopkins, tending to the correspondence that followed him via radio from Washington—with the pleasure of watching the navy go about *its* business. Whenever he could he simply sat on deck. "The President spent more than an hour on the flag bridge during the afternoon, seemingly enjoying the squally weather," the lieutenant recorded.

The closer they got to Africa, the tighter the security drew. An escort aircraft carrier, the *Santee*, provided air cover, with fighter planes scouring the skies around the president's ship. The *Iowa* stopped transmitting Roosevelt's radio messages. Written versions were physically transferred to another vessel and broadcast from many miles away, lest the Germans home in on the radio signals. As the task group approached the Strait of Gibraltar, all ships went to general quarters in readiness for attack. They passed the strait under cover of darkness on the night of November 19, and the *Iowa* anchored just west of Oran the next morning. "Total distance, Hampton Roads, Virginia, to Oran, Algeria, via our route, 3806 miles."

❖ ❖ ❖

ROOSEVELT WAS MET at Oran by Eisenhower and several less senior officers, including Elliott Roosevelt and Franklin Jr. Eisenhower and Franklin Jr. joined Roosevelt for the 650-mile flight to Tunis; Elliott flew in another plane. The president observed the wrecks of the large number of German aircraft that still littered the Tunisian countryside, and he toured the ruins of ancient Carthage. He inspected Elliott's photo reconnaissance squadron, which comprised six thousand American, British, and French fliers and technicians. The next day he visited the battlefields around Tunis, and Eisenhower supplied details of the fighting there. Burned-out American and German tanks attested to the bitterness of the struggle, as did the one American and several German military cemeteries. A camel caravan sauntered by in the distance, the drivers and animals seemingly oblivious to the most recent intrusion on their ancient lifestyle.

To talk with Eisenhower and observe the battle sites was the smaller part of Roosevelt's purpose in returning to Africa. The larger part was to meet a man he had been wrestling with for three years but never encountered personally. Chiang Kai-shek had less of a messiah complex than Charles de Gaulle, perhaps because messiahs have never figured so centrally in Chinese culture as in the cultures of the West. But Chiang was fully as convinced as de Gaulle that he embodied his country, and his actual command of a government and an army—as opposed to de Gaulle's dreams of such command—tended to corroborate his conviction. Yet it was only a tendency, and opinions differed as to

With Hoover en route to the Capitol

With Franklin Jr. and Sara, 1933

With Hopkins

At the wheel at Hyde Park

War against Japan

With Churchill in Washington, December 1941

The handshake: Giraud and de Gaulle

At Casablanca with Hopkins (back left), Harriman (back right), Marshall (front left), and King (front right)

With Stalin at Teheran

With Eisenhower, who has just been informed he will command the invasion of France

With MacArthur,
Nimitz, and Leahy
in Hawaii

One of Yalta's lighter moments

At Hyde Park holding Fala and comforting
a young friend

With Eleanor at Hyde Park

In his element

Warm Springs, April 11, 1945

the degree and quality of Chiang's command, not to mention the character and credibility of the Chinese government and the army.

Roosevelt's liaison to Chiang was General Joseph Stilwell, who despised Chiang. "Vinegar Joe" turned violently acidic in describing the generalissimo, as Chiang styled himself. "Peanut" was Stilwell's private name for Chiang, and the appellation referred only partly to the shape of his shaved head. (Stilwell was mildly more respectful of Roosevelt, whom he called "Frank" in his diary.) Stilwell couldn't decide whether Chiang was more hopeless as a general or as a president. "Peanut is really no dictator," Stilwell remarked with regret. "He issues an order. Everybody bows and says 'sure.' But nobody does anything. He knows all about the smuggling and the rottenness, but he hasn't the power to cure it. . . . Opium traffic in Yunnan still enormous. Guarded by soldiers. Big stocks of hoarded gas, cloth, and other commodities. . . . The Chinese Red Cross is a racket. Stealing and sale of medicines is rampant. . . . Malnutrition and sickness is ruining the army; the higher-ups steal the soldiers' food. A pretty picture."

In fairness to Chiang, the task before him was all but impossible. Beset by the Japanese for a dozen years, beleaguered by indigenous Communists for even longer, Chiang fought a war on two fronts. This was what outraged Stilwell, who argued that Chiang and Mao Zedong, the Communist leader, should bury the hatchet for the duration of the war against Japan. Neither was persuaded; with four thousand years of Chinese history behind them, each took the long view of China's predicament. Japan was a problem of the moment, soon to be vanquished—by the United States if not by the Chinese. The real prize was control of the Chinese government.

Roosevelt's time frame didn't stretch thousands of years, but it did extend into the future, particularly with respect to China. The president flew from Tunis to Cairo, where he met with Chiang and Churchill. The British prime minister thought Roosevelt asked too much of the Chinese leader, and of China. "I was impressed by his calm, reserved, and efficient personality," Churchill afterward wrote of Chiang. But he added that he "did not in those days share in the excessive estimates of Chiang Kai-shek's power or of the future helpfulness of China."

Roosevelt refused to be put off. As he had suggested to Elliott at Casablanca, China was going to be America's postwar counterweight to Russia—and perhaps to Britain as well. At Cairo, Roosevelt affirmed China's membership in what was coming to be called the Big Four. A dinner meeting in Roosevelt's borrowed villa brought the president and Hopkins together with Chiang and

Madame Chiang, the fascinating former Soong May-ling. Madame Chiang was one of three Soong sisters, daughters of an American-educated Methodist minister-entrepreneur and a beautiful, ambitious mother. The eldest of the three girls, Soong Ai-ling, was known as "the one who loves money"; she married the richest man in China. The middle girl, Soong Ching-ling, called "the one who loves China," married Sun Yat-sen, the first president of the Republic of China. The youngest, Soong May-ling, "the one who loves power," married Chiang Kai-shek. In the bargain she persuaded Chiang to give up Buddhism for Christianity. Madame Chiang's mastery of English, which she had perfected at Wellesley College in Massachusetts, her beauty, which seemingly increased as she grew older, and her political astuteness, which hardly ever faltered, made her a favorite among American legislators and a formidable presence in Washington. Roosevelt never refused her a White House interview, and he had great difficulty refusing her requests on behalf of her husband.

At the Cairo dinner Chiang and Madame Chiang got Roosevelt to reiterate his support for China's status as the postwar peer of America, Russia, and Britain. The Chinese minutes of the meeting—apparently the only record made—explained that "President Roosevelt expressed his view that China should take her place as one of the Big Four and participate on an equal footing in the machinery of the Big Four group and in all its decisions." Chiang responded that China would gladly do so.

Roosevelt went on to inquire of Chiang's opinions regarding postwar Japan. Ought the Japanese to be allowed to retain the institution of the emperor? Chiang answered that this question should be left to the Japanese to decide. Roosevelt asserted—again according to the Chinese minutes—that "China should play the leading role in the post-war military occupation of Japan." Chiang again demurred, this time saying that China lacked the wherewithal for such an occupation. "The task should be carried out under the leadership of the United States. . . . China could participate in the task in a supporting capacity should it prove necessary."

❖   ❖   ❖

ROOSEVELT DELIBERATELY kept his Cairo visit short, not wishing to give Stalin additional reason for thinking he and Churchill—and perhaps Chiang—were colluding against Russia. But the visit did include Thanksgiving Day, and the president hosted a dinner for Churchill and his daughter

Sarah, who served as her father's personal assistant; for Elliott Roosevelt, who had rejoined his father in a temporary similar capacity; for Robert Hopkins, who had likewise joined *his* father; and for several others. "Let us make it a family affair," Roosevelt decreed, laughing.

Churchill afterward described the host's bravura performance.

Two enormous turkeys were brought in with all ceremony. The President, propped up high in his chair, carved for all with masterly, indefatigable skill. As we were above twenty, this took a long time, and those who were helped first had finished before the President had cut anything for himself. As I watched the huge platefuls he distributed to the company I feared that he might be left with nothing at all. But he had calculated to a nicety, and I was relieved, when at last the two skeletons were removed, to see him set about his own share. Harry, who had noted my anxiety, said, "We have ample reserves."

Toasts were offered, speeches made. After dinner the group adjourned to the villa's main room, where several of the official meetings had been held. The tables, now empty of papers, were pushed against the walls. A phonograph played dance music. Sarah Churchill, the only woman present, was on her feet all night. "She had her work cut out," her father said, "and so I danced with 'Pa' Watson, Roosevelt's trusted old friend and aide, to the delight of his chief, who watched us from the sofa." Churchill savored the memory. "For a couple of hours we cast care aside. I had never seen the President more gay."

❖   ❖   ❖

The HARD WORK began in Teheran. Roosevelt wouldn't have gone clear to Cairo to meet Chiang, important though he intended for China to be. Cairo was a stop on the way to Teheran, where the most important conference of the war thus far would take place. Stalin had grudgingly agreed to leave the Soviet Union, but only for adjacent Iran. Roosevelt and Churchill, with consciences uneasy over their failure to provide a second front, humored the Soviet leader's comparative immobility.

For several hours out of Cairo, Roosevelt's Sacred Cow seemed a flying carpet. The plane winged east, crossing the Suez Canal at Ismailia before the pilot turned north to give the president a view of what most Americans still called the Holy Land and the inhabitants Palestine. The plane circled Jerusalem, its

roofs shining in the morning sun. Across the desert to Mesopotamia—Iraq—
they flew, traversing the Euphrates and Tigris rivers and spotting Baghdad off
to the south. The pilot found the highway that ran from Abadan to Teheran.
Paralleling the road was the railroad to Russia. "From the air we sighted train
loads and motor convoys loaded with U.S. Lend-Lease supplies, bound from
the Persian Gulf port of Basra to Russia," Roosevelt's log keeper recorded. The
fair weather and clear skies allowed the pilot to follow the road through the
mountain passes rather than climb over the peaks. The plane never exceeded
eight thousand feet in altitude, almost a mile below some of the mountain
tops.

Even before the Sacred Cow landed in Teheran, the skirmishing for position at the conference had begun. Stalin told Averell Harriman of his worry
that the city was too dangerous for the kind of commuting that would be required between the American legation, where President Roosevelt presumably
would stay, and the Russian embassy, where he, Stalin, would be. Teheran had
been under German control until only a few months previous, and the city
almost certainly continued to hide Nazi agents and sympathizers, who might
take advantage of any assassination opportunity. Stalin explained that the
Russian embassy compound was large and commodious; he would be happy
for President Roosevelt to stay there. No such provision was necessary for
Prime Minister Churchill, as the British legation almost adjoined the Soviet
embassy, and in any event the British had a much larger presence in Teheran
than the Americans did.

Roosevelt accepted Stalin's offer, to the dismay of Roosevelt's security team.
The Soviet embassy naturally crawled with Soviet agents, most of whom apparently carried weapons under their coats. Robert Sherwood remembered
the Teheran conference as a "nervous time" for Mike Reilly and his Secret Service men, "who were trained to suspect *everybody* and who did not like to
admit into the President's presence anyone who was armed with as much as a
gold toothpick."

Churchill didn't like Roosevelt's decision either, but he took it with good
grace, to the point of claiming partial credit. By Churchill's account, Soviet
foreign minister Molotov had asserted that Soviet intelligence had uncovered
an active plot to assassinate one or more of the Allied triumvirate. "If anything
like that were to happen," Molotov said, "it could produce a most unfortunate
impression." Speaking for himself, Churchill later wrote: "This could not be denied. I strongly supported Molotov in his appeals to the President to move
forthwith inside the Soviet Embassy. . . . We prevailed upon Mr. Roosevelt to

take this good advice, and next afternoon he moved with his whole staff." If the event in fact unfolded as Churchill remembered, it almost certainly said less about Churchill's powers of persuasion than about Roosevelt's ability to act as though he needed persuading.

❖   ❖   ❖

ROOSEVELT UNSETTLED Churchill a bit more by arranging for his first meeting at Teheran to be with Stalin, alone except for their translators. Roosevelt assumed that the Russians had planted listening devices in the room, but since he was speaking to Stalin he wasn't worried. He supposed the British had *not* been able to bug the room.

"I am glad to see you," Roosevelt said. "I have tried a long time to bring this about."

Stalin took responsibility for the delay, politely but in a manner that reminded Roosevelt of the continuing difference between their two countries with respect to Germany. Stalin said he had been "very occupied because of military matters."

Stalin's style during the Teheran conference contrasted sharply with his practice at home. At least so it seemed to Charles Bohlen, Roosevelt's translator, who had been stationed in Moscow before the war. Bohlen had studied Stalin closely, and he considered him in top form at Teheran. "I reflected on Stalin's fluency and his lack of hesitation in choosing his words," Bohlen recalled.

> There was a kind of texture to his Russian that might be called an accent. His Georgian accent was not particularly noticeable to my ear, although I was subsequently told that some cultured Russians found it irritating. Stalin also seemed to me to be considerate of his interpreter and to be meticulous in observing the length of time that he spoke. He spoke quietly, never raised his voice, and frequently used expressions designed to indicate a certain humbleness of spirit. . . . In Teheran, Stalin used phrases like "in my opinion," "I could be wrong, but I think," and "I believe," with no hint of the arbitrary dictator. I noticed him break from this mold only once, when I approached him from behind with a request from Roosevelt. I had interfered with his study of the Russian text of the final communiqué, and he was tired. Without turning, he snapped over his shoulder, "For God's sake, allow us to finish this work." Then he turned and saw that the interruption came not from a Rus-

sian but from an emissary of the President of the United States. This was the only time I ever saw Stalin embarrassed.

In response to Stalin's remark about being occupied militarily, Roosevelt inquired about the conditions on the battlefront. Stalin said things were not going well. The Red Army had recently lost an important town and was about to lose a crucial railway center. The Germans were bringing up fresh divisions and were increasing the pressure at several points.

But did the initiative not remain with the Russian army? asked Roosevelt.

Stalin said it did, overall. Yet at the moment his troops were unable to mount significant offensive operations, except in the Ukraine.

Roosevelt said he wished it were in his power to compel the removal of thirty or forty German divisions from the Soviet front. This was a principal aim of the United States and Britain, he said, and it would be a subject of conversation in the days to come. But for the moment he wanted to talk about the postwar settlement. He related that he had had an "interesting conversation" with Chiang Kai-shek in Cairo regarding the future of China.

Stalin frowned. "The Chinese have fought very badly," he said. He put the blame on Chiang and his associates, saying the dismal performance of the troops was "the fault of the Chinese leaders."

Roosevelt didn't defend Chiang at this point. Instead he explained how the United States proposed to strengthen China with additional supplies. He let the conversation turn to France, about which Stalin expressed equally vigorous views. General de Gaulle, Stalin said, was "very unreal" in his activities. He acted as though he commanded a great state, when in fact he commanded nothing at all.

Roosevelt agreed. Yet he implied that de Gaulle or someone like him would be essential to reconstructing France after the war. "In the future," the president said, "no Frenchman over forty, and particularly no Frenchman who had ever taken part in the present French government, should be allowed to return to a government position." Roosevelt went on to say that while Churchill believed that France must quickly be reconstructed as a strong nation, he disagreed. "Many years of honest labor will be necessary before France is reestablished," he said. "The first necessity for the French, not only for the government but for the people as well, is to become honest citizens."

Stalin suggested that France ought not to be allowed to reclaim its colonial empire. No Allied blood, for example, should be spilled to restore French rule in Indochina.

Roosevelt said he agreed "one hundred percent." After a century of French rule, the inhabitants of Indochina were worse off than they had been when the French arrived. Roosevelt took this opportunity to re-inject Chiang and China into the conversation. Chiang had said at Cairo that the Indochinese weren't ready for independence. Roosevelt explained that he had replied that perhaps an international trusteeship of some sort could be established, leading to independence within twenty or thirty years.

Stalin said he concurred completely.

Roosevelt extrapolated from Indochina to India, which must receive its independence after the war as well. But he added, by way of warning, that it would "be better not to discuss the question of India with Mr. Churchill."

Stalin agreed that India was a "sore spot" with the British.

Roosevelt said he would like to discuss India further, at a more convenient time. He added in passing that he thought the solution to India's social and economic problems would be reform from the bottom, "somewhat on the Soviet line."

Stalin said the Indian question was complicated by the caste structure of the country. He added, with no apparent enthusiasm: "Reform from the bottom would mean revolution."

The conversation lasted an hour. The president and the marshal were informed that Churchill had arrived. As they went out to meet the prime minister, Roosevelt told Stalin he had enjoyed their informal chat and hoped to repeat it.

❖ ❖ ❖

$\mathcal{I}$N CONTRAST TO the Roosevelt-Stalin tête-à-tête, the three-sided plenary that followed was a full-dress, fully staffed affair. A round table had been brought in, lest a table with straight sides and sharp corners somehow connote precedence among the three contingents. Twelve men sat around the table: Roosevelt, Hopkins, Harriman, and Bohlen for the Americans; Churchill, Anthony Eden, cabinet deputy secretary Lord Ismay, and interpreter Arthur Birse for the British; Stalin, Molotov, Defense Commissar Klimenti Voroshilov, and interpreter V. N. Pavlov for the Russians. George Marshall would have joined Roosevelt, displacing Harriman, but, to the general's lasting chagrin, he misunderstood the schedule and was out touring Teheran while the others gathered.

By common consent, Roosevelt took charge of this first meeting. He strove from the outset to keep it from growing too ponderous. He said that as the youngest of the three present, he ventured to welcome his elders. He added, "We are sitting around this table for the first time as a family, with the one object of winning the war." He explained to Stalin that it had been his and Churchill's practice, at their previous meetings, to be perfectly frank and confidential—"to publish nothing but to speak our minds very freely." He hoped the same practice would apply now. He said the general staffs of the three countries could handle most of the military discussions. "Marshal Stalin, the Prime Minister, and I have many things to discuss pertaining to conditions after the war."

He turned to Churchill, who remarked that the three of them represented "the greatest concentration of power the world has ever seen." Churchill continued: "In our hands here is the possible certainty of shortening the war, the much greater certainty of victories, but the absolute certainty that we hold the happy future of mankind." The prime minister expressed the hope that they might prove themselves worthy of "this God-given opportunity."

Roosevelt nodded, then looked to Stalin. "Perhaps our host would like to say a few words," the president said.

"I take pleasure in welcoming those present," Stalin responded. "I think that history will show that this opportunity has been of tremendous importance. I think the great opportunity which we have and the power which our people have invested in us can be used to take full advantage within the frame of our potential collaboration." He paused to let the translator catch up. "Now let us get down to business," he said.

Roosevelt obliged. He offered a survey of the war and its meaning, starting with the Pacific and with China. He explained that American strategy toward Japan was based, for the present at least, on the principle of attrition: of destroying more Japanese ships and planes than the Japanese could replace. It was essential to this strategy that China continue to tie down the largest part of Japanese resources. "We must definitely keep China actively in the war," he said.

From the Pacific the president moved to Europe. He merely alluded to the delays in opening a second front before reaffirming that the cross-Channel invasion would occur in the late spring of 1944. Weather would prevent anything earlier. "The Channel is such a disagreeable body of water," Roosevelt said, before adding, "No matter how unpleasant that body might be, however, we still want to get across it." (Churchill couldn't help interrupting: "We were very glad it was an unpleasant body of water at one time.")

The projected timetable raised the question of what America and Britain could do in the meantime to ease the burden on the Soviet Union—and it provoked the principal disagreement of the afternoon. Churchill, as always, argued for an operation in the Mediterranean. The British and Americans might push from Rome into the Po Valley, he said, or even strike at Germany from Italy. Perhaps complementarily, a thrust toward the Turkish Straits and the Black Sea would open up new possibilities for provisioning the Soviet Union.

Stalin wasn't buying. He may have suspected the Anglo-Americans of trying to renege again on their second-front promise, or he may have imagined that Churchill was seeking a foothold in Turkey to use against Russia after the war. Either way, he rejected Churchill's plan. He said it would be wrong "to scatter the British and American forces." France was the primary target for their armies, and if they needed something to do while they waited for the Channel to calm, they could attack southern France. "This would be a much better operation than to scatter forces in several areas distant from each other."

Roosevelt let Churchill and Stalin joust a bit before entering the debate on Stalin's side. The marshal's proposal regarding southern France was of "considerable interest," the president said. He thought the military planners should examine it carefully.

Stalin, encouraged, said that the Soviet experience demonstrated the value of launching a major offensive from two directions at once. "The Red Army usually attacks from two directions, forcing the enemy to move his reserves from one front to the other. As the two offensives converge, the power of the whole offensive increases. Such would be the case in simultaneous operations from southern and northern France."

Churchill again objected, but Roosevelt, ignoring him, asserted that the military staffs should set to work at once on the subject of an attack on southern France to precede or accompany the cross-Channel invasion.

❖   ❖   ❖

THE GROUP BROKE long enough to reconvene for dinner. The meal included an "unbelievable quantity of food," according to Bohlen, who had endured many such repasts in Moscow. Cold hors d'oeuvres preceded hot borscht, accompanied by salads, fruits, compotes, various meats, fish, an assortment of wines, and gallons of vodka. Bohlen noticed that Stalin drank very little vodka, preferring wine—"which is understandable when it is remembered that he was born in Georgia, a wine-producing area."

The table talk focused on the future of Europe. Stalin declared that the ruling class of France was "rotten to the core" and deserved to be punished for its collaboration with the Nazis. Even now, he said, the French were actively aiding the Germans. Consequently it would be "not only unjust but dangerous" to rely on France for postwar security. And France should be stripped of its colonial possessions.

Churchill answered that the marshal did the French a disservice. France was a defeated country, he said, and had suffered grievously under the occupation.

Stalin dismissed Churchill's characterization with a sneer. The French hadn't been defeated, he said. They "opened the front" to the German armies. He cited the views of the Vichy ambassador in Moscow as typical of the French ruling classes. The ambassador repeatedly stated that the future of France lay with Nazi Germany and not with Britain or America.

Churchill countered that he could not conceive of a civilized world in which a "flourishing and lively France" did not play a central part.

Stalin waved his hand contemptuously. France was a "charming and pleasant country," he said, but it could not be allowed to play any important role in international affairs after the war.

Roosevelt shifted the subject to postwar Germany. The president offered that the entire Nazi experience must be stricken from German minds. A start might be made by eliminating the word *reich* from the German vocabulary.

Stalin said the president didn't go far enough. The problem wasn't the Nazis but the Germans. They followed the orders of whatever group ruled in Berlin, without questioning the nature of the orders or the legitimacy of those who gave them. Stalin said that he personally had interrogated German prisoners and asked why they had butchered innocent women and children. They had answered simply that they had done what they had been ordered to do. Stalin cited another, earlier example from his own experience. In 1907 he had attended an important meeting of workers in Leipzig. Two hundred German delegates failed to appear because the railroad clerk who was supposed to punch their train tickets didn't show up for work and the German delegates refused to leave the station without the required punch. This mentality of blind obedience to authority, Stalin said, could not be eradicated. Accordingly, German authority—and German power—must be forever constrained. "The Reich itself must be rendered impotent ever again to plunge the world into war." Without getting specific, Stalin recommended a permanent occupation of Germany. "Unless the victorious Allies retain in our hands the strategic positions necessary to prevent a recrudescence of German militarism, we will have failed in our duty."

Stalin seemed to give something back in another comment. He questioned the prudence of unconditional surrender as a stated policy toward Germany. He accepted the principle as military strategy but found it politically wanting. Anti-Hitler Germans, if any remained, would be unlikely to act against the Nazi regime in the face of such an ominously vague formulation. Better, Stalin said, for the Allies to declare what terms they would require at war's end. By making the future concrete, even if unappealing, they would "hasten the day of German capitulation."

❖ ❖ ❖

ROOSEVELT'S PART in the dinner ended suddenly. The president was talking about the Baltic Sea and the need for outside countries to have access to it. Bohlen mistranslated and led Stalin to think the president was demanding access to the Baltic *republics,* which Moscow had annexed to the Soviet Union at the start of the war. The marshal bristled, but the misunderstanding was corrected and the moment passed. Bohlen recalled what happened next:

> Roosevelt was about to say something else when suddenly, in the flick of an eye, he turned green and great drops of sweat began to bead off his face; he put a shaky hand to his forehead. We were all caught by surprise. The President had made no complaint, and none of us had detected any sign of discomfort.

Hopkins, moving quickly, directed that Roosevelt be taken to his room, where Ross McIntire, the navy physician who traveled with the president, examined him. McIntire pronounced the problem to be indigestion.

Roosevelt remained in his room, not returning to dinner. By the next morning he seemed fine. Everyone blamed the borscht, and almost no one thought any more of the incident.

❖ ❖ ❖

THE GERMAN QUESTION recurred throughout the Teheran talks, and it afforded Roosevelt additional opportunity to improve his relationship with Stalin. Roosevelt's move was instinctive, reflecting the sensitivity he had always displayed in social settings, but it was also deliberate, as he explained to

Frances Perkins after the fact. "You know, the Russians are interesting people," he said, in a recollection that smudged some details but captured the essence of the Teheran meeting.

> For the first three days I made absolutely no progress. I couldn't get any personal connection with Stalin, although I had done everything he asked me to do. I had stayed at his Embassy, gone to his dinners, been introduced to his ministers and generals. He was correct, stiff, solemn, not smiling, nothing human to get hold of. I felt pretty discouraged. If it was all going to be official paper work, there was no sense in my having made this long journey which the Russians had wanted. They couldn't come to America or any place in Europe for it. I had come there to accommodate Stalin. I felt pretty discouraged because I thought I was making no personal headway. What we were doing could have been done by the foreign ministers.
>
> I thought it over all night and made up my mind I had to do something desperate. I couldn't stay in Teheran forever. I had to cut through this icy surface so that later I could talk by telephone or letter in a personal way. I had scarcely seen Churchill alone during the conference. I had a feeling that the Russians did not feel right about seeing us conferring together in a language which we understood and they didn't.
>
> On my way to the conference room that morning we caught up with Winston and I had just a moment to say to him, "Winston, I hope you won't be sore at me for what I am going to do." Winston just shifted his cigar and grunted. I must say he behaved very decently afterward.
>
> I began almost as soon as we got into the conference room. I talked privately with Stalin. I didn't say anything that I hadn't said before, but it appeared quite chummy and confidential, enough so that the other Russians joined us to listen.
>
> Still no smile.
>
> Then I said, lifting my hand up to cover a whisper—which of course had to be interpreted—"Winston is cranky this morning. He got up on the wrong side of the bed."
>
> A vague smile passed over Stalin's eyes, and I decided I was on the right track. As soon as I sat down at the conference table, I began to tease Churchill about his Britishness, about John Bull, about his cigars, about his habits. It began to register with Stalin. Winston got red and scowled, and the more he did so, the more Stalin smiled. Finally Stalin broke out into a deep, hearty guffaw, and for the first time in three days I saw light.

He also saw a change in Stalin's behavior toward Churchill, which was one reason Churchill grew so red and scowling. Charles Bohlen summarized a dinner session shortly after the beginning of Roosevelt's ingratiation offensive: "The most notable feature of the dinner was the attitude of Marshal Stalin toward the Prime Minister. Marshal Stalin lost no opportunity to get in a dig at Mr. Churchill. Almost every remark that he addressed to the Prime Minister contained some sharp edge, although the Marshal's manner was entirely friendly." Some of Stalin's jabs were innocuous, the same kind of teasing Roosevelt had initiated. But others had steel at their cold heart. "At one occasion," Bohlen recorded, "he told the Prime Minister that just because Russians are simple people, it was a mistake to believe that they were blind and could not see what was before their eyes."

And what they—or at least Stalin—saw was the old anti-Bolshevism emerging in British policy, beneath what seemed a secret sympathy for Germany. Stalin tested Churchill with a brutal recommendation for the postwar treatment of the Germans. Asserting that the Allies must adopt "really effective measures" to ensure that Germany not rise again, he asserted that two conditions must be met. First, the Allies must retain possession of the "most important strategic points in the world" so that "if Germany moved a muscle she could be rapidly stopped." Second: "At least 50,000 and perhaps 100,000 of the German commanding staff must be physically liquidated."

Churchill objected vigorously to Stalin's second point. "War criminals must pay for their crimes," he conceded, as well as individuals who had committed "barbarous acts." But "the cold-blooded execution of soldiers who had fought for their country" was something he could never countenance.

Roosevelt couldn't tell whether Stalin was serious or simply goading Churchill. The president decided to treat Stalin's proposal—the part about the mass executions—as a joke. He said he couldn't go along with the marshal; the liquidation must be capped at "49,000."

❖   ❖   ❖

𝒯HE MOST SENSITIVE topic at Teheran involved Germany's eastern neighbor. The future of Poland touched each man in a different way. For Stalin, Poland was a security issue. Thrice since the early nineteenth century, twice in Stalin's lifetime, Poland had provided invaders of Russia a running start. Stalin insisted that Poland become a buffer state for the Soviet Union, a shield between Germany and Russia. This implied, although Stalin didn't say so explicitly, a government in Poland that was subservient or at least friendly to Moscow.

For Churchill, Poland was a matter of honor. The German invasion of Poland had precipitated Britain's declaration of war. If the war ended with Poland's having simply traded German masters for Russian, neither Churchill as prime minister nor the British people collectively would be able to hold up their heads again.

The difference between Stalin and Churchill played out in their competing definitions of Poland's future borders and their contradictory visions of Poland's future government. Stalin wanted Poland moved as far west as possible, the better to guarantee Soviet security. Churchill had less concern about Poland's borders, although he couldn't accept a Soviet-Polish frontier that stole a large part of the Polish patrimony. But he wanted the Allies to recognize the Polish government in exile in London. Stalin, as skeptical of Churchill on this issue as on several others, assumed that any Poles London liked would be antagonistic toward the Soviet Union.

Roosevelt appreciated Stalin's security concerns, and he shared Churchill's desire to see Poland free of foreign domination. To these considerations he added one of his own, as he explained to Stalin in another private meeting. He reminded the marshal that the United States would conduct a presidential election in 1944, and he said that though he didn't want to run again, he might feel obliged to if the war was still on. This was where the Polish question came in. "There are six to seven million Americans of Polish extraction," Roosevelt said. "As a practical man I don't wish to lose their vote." He went on to say he appreciated Stalin's concerns about the future of Poland. And he was inclined to agree with him on certain aspects of the Polish question, particularly as they affected borders. But for "political reasons" he had to put off any decisions about Poland, preferably until after November 1944.

Stalin acknowledged that he had wondered about Roosevelt's reticence on Poland. But now that the president had explained, he understood.

❖   ❖   ❖

WHAT MAY HAVE been Roosevelt's most important decision of the war came at Teheran. The commitment to a date for the invasion of France—which by now had acquired the name Overlord—having been made, the Americans and British required a commander. The Americans would be supplying most of the men and materiel; hence Roosevelt would have the choice. Persons close to the question had assumed for many months that the president would choose Marshall. Roosevelt thought Marshall deserved this chance to make history, or at least to be remembered by history. "Ike, you and I know who was the Chief of Staff during the last years of the Civil War," Roosevelt told Eisenhower during the stopover in Algeria en route to Cairo and Teheran. "But practically no one else knows, although names of the field generals— Grant, of course, and Lee, and Jackson, Sherman, Sheridan, and the others— every schoolboy knows them. I hate to think that fifty years from now practically nobody will know who George Marshall was. That is one of the reasons why I want George to have the big command. He is entitled to establish his place in history as a great general."

John Pershing disagreed, at least with the conclusion that Marshall must go to Europe. The octogenarian general, who had been Marshall's mentor and remained America's most distinguished soldier, wrote Roosevelt advising that Marshall stay where he was. "We are engaged in a global war of which the end is still far distant," Pershing explained, "and for the wise and strategical guidance of which we need our most accomplished officer as Chief of Staff. I voice the consensus of informed military opinion in saying that officer is General Marshall. . . . The suggested transfer of General Marshall would be a fundamental and very grave error in our military policy."

Roosevelt replied with characteristic deftness. "My dear General," he wrote, "You are absolutely right about George Marshall—and yet, I think, you are wrong, too!" Marshall was indeed the ideal chief of staff. "But, as you know, the operations for which we are considering him are the biggest that we will conduct in this war." America required him in Europe. "The best way I can express it is to tell you that I want George to be the Pershing of the second World War—and he cannot be that if we keep him here."

But gradually Roosevelt changed his mind. The longer he worked with Marshall, the more he appreciated Marshall's rare gifts. No one else talked back to Roosevelt the way Marshall did; no one stuck so stubbornly to his beliefs in discussions with Churchill and the British brass. Yet no one carried out orders so loyally and efficiently once they were given. And no one embodied soldierly discretion more thoroughly than Marshall. Roosevelt concluded that he had to keep the Virginian close by him on the Potomac.

The only problem was that Marshall wanted the European job. He agreed with Roosevelt that he deserved it, and like Roosevelt he recognized that posterity never remembered desk officers. Saying no to much less worthy persons than Marshall had often caused Roosevelt pain; saying no to Marshall was almost more than he could manage.

During the Cairo conference he sent Harry Hopkins to talk to the general. "Hopkins came to see me Saturday night before dinner and told me the President was in some concern of mind over my appointment as Supreme Commander," Marshall recalled. "I could not tell from Hopkins' statement just what the President's point of view was, and in my reply I merely endeavored to make it clear that I would go along wholeheartedly with whatever decision the President made. He need have no fears regarding my personal reaction." Marshall declined to state his own opinion in the matter.

The next day Roosevelt himself summoned Marshall. "In response to his questions, I made virtually the same reply I made to Hopkins," Marshall said.

> I recall saying that I would not attempt to estimate my capabilities; the President would have to do that; I merely wished to make clear that whatever the decision, I would go along with it wholeheartedly; that the issue was too great for any personal feeling to be considered. I did not discuss the pros and cons of the matter. If I recall, the President stated, in completing our conversation, "I feel I could not sleep at night with you out of the country."

Roosevelt wasn't quite ready to announce a decision. Churchill was deferring to the president on the choice of a commander, but he hadn't fully yielded on the commander's responsibilities. The prime minister remained unconvinced that a single commander would do a better job than the Combined Chiefs in directing the ground, sea, and air forces of the two great powers in the most complicated military operation in history. Marshall and the American chiefs thought they had won this argument ahead of the North African invasion, and they grew exasperated to have to fight it again. But they considered the principle of unified command so important that they were willing to accept a British officer as commander—provided that the British commander be John Dill, who seemed the most capable of the British officers and the one most likely to enjoy the confidence of the American public.

Roosevelt wasn't about to yield the command to a British officer, but the American chiefs' self-denying statement provided him ammunition for use against Churchill. So too did a comment—a question, actually—by Stalin at the second meeting of the principals at Teheran. The American, British, and Russian military staffs had been discussing the progress of their campaigns and their plans for the future, when Stalin politely but sharply asked, "Who will command Overlord?"

"That has not yet been decided," Roosevelt answered.

Stalin shook his head dismissively. The Anglo-Americans still weren't serious, if they hadn't chosen a commander. "Nothing will come of the operation," he said, "unless one man is made responsible not only for the preparation but for the execution of the operation."

Roosevelt realized the time was at hand. The main reason he had traveled all the way to Teheran was to win Stalin's trust. He had made some progress but not enough. Churchill continued to grumble against a unified European command; the prime minister wanted to keep the Mediterranean separate, in part because he thought Roosevelt would choose Marshall, whose hostility to the Mediterranean operations Churchill favored was well known.

To satisfy Stalin, Roosevelt needed to make a decision now. To mollify Churchill, he couldn't choose Marshall. The only other American with the stature for the European command was Eisenhower. Since Roosevelt wanted to keep Marshall in Washington anyway, this settled the matter.

On his return trip from Teheran, Roosevelt stopped in Tunis, where Eisenhower met him. The general climbed into the president's car. "Well, Ike," Roosevelt said, "you are going to command Overlord."

52.

JUST BEFORE LEAVING WASHINGTON FOR CAIRO AND TEHERAN, ROOsevelt had performed a minor miracle. Or perhaps it was more accurate to say he arranged for the performance of a minor miracle, which from his perspective was even better. The Senate approved a resolution sponsored by Tom Connally of Texas endorsing Roosevelt's blueprint for the postwar structure of peace. "Resolved," the measure declared:

> That the Senate recognizes the necessity of there being established at the earliest practicable date a general international organization, based on the principle of the sovereign equality of all peace-loving states, and open to membership by all such states, large and small, for the maintenance of international peace and security.

The endorsement alone was significant; the magnitude of the endorsement—by 85 to 5—was even more significant. One of the dissenters was Hiram Johnson, who had voted against the Treaty of Versailles and didn't see any reason to give Roosevelt what he had denied Wilson. Another was Burton Wheeler, whose isolationism had resurfaced not long after the smoke from Pearl Harbor cleared. But they were the ones isolated now. Nearly everyone else sided with the president.

The victory for the Connally resolution—or "peace resolution," as its proponents managed to get the papers to call it—reflected Roosevelt's success in casting the United Nations as more than a wartime alliance. The alliance would win the war, but it would also constitute the framework for the peace. Perhaps Roosevelt had realized from the start—from the moment he selected the name for the anti-Axis alliance—that by making the United Nations the vehicle of victory rather than something conjured up after the victory had been won, he would grant it a legitimacy in American thinking the League of Nations never enjoyed. Perhaps he was not so prescient and acted simply on intuition. If so, his intuition was uncanny, for it allowed him to win the battle Wilson had lost, even before the battle was joined.

Roosevelt's miracle also reflected his shrewdness in keeping Cordell Hull around. During most of the 1930s the secretary of state had seemed extraneous to American foreign policy, chipping away at American tariffs by means of his reciprocal trade pacts but otherwise having little to do with the conduct of international affairs. Even after the start of the war Hull was often outside the loop of decision, with Roosevelt relying on Hopkins, Sumner Welles, and his own relationship with Churchill in directing American diplomacy. But Roosevelt knew that the time would come when Hull's quarter century of service in Congress and his continued good standing among the senators and representatives would yield crucial benefits.

It was no coincidence that the Senate took up the Connally resolution when it did. Two weeks earlier Hull had traveled to Moscow to meet with his British, Russian, and Chinese counterparts. The quartet of foreign ministers produced a declaration affirming the unconditional surrender policy and proclaiming "the necessity of establishing at the earliest practicable date a general international organization, based on the principle of the sovereign equality of all peace-loving states, and open to membership by all such states, large and small, for the maintenance of international peace and security." Hull's connections on Capitol Hill made it easy for Connally to copy the operative paragraph from the Moscow declaration into his own resolution and for the eighty-five senators to vote in favor. Hull came out an internationalist hero, and Roosevelt got exactly what he wanted, without having to ask for it.

❖ ❖ ❖

ROOSEVELT'S LEADERSHIP style didn't always produce such happy results. Henry Stimson sometimes wished he had never come out of retirement. The war secretary filled his diary with such characterizations of Roosevelt as "the poorest administrator I have ever worked under" and "soft-hearted towards incompetent appointees." In certain instances Roosevelt held the reins too tightly. "He wants to do it all himself," Stimson wrote after he couldn't get an answer out of the White House on a critical matter. Often the president ignored existing channels of authority. "Today the President has constituted an almost innumerable number of new administrative posts, putting at the head of them a lot of inexperienced men appointed largely for personal grounds and who report on their duties directly to the President and have constant and easy access to him."

There was, of course, a method to Roosevelt's madness. As during the days before the war, he insisted that he not become a prisoner of the bureaucracy, which, if given its preferences, might have handed him decisions ready-made. He knew that the risk of imprisonment increased during wartime, as the military expected a deference mere political appointees weren't shown. Yet he considered it even more important to maintain control during wartime. Generals and admirals rarely like to admit that war is a political act, but Roosevelt never forgot it. The war had begun in politics—in the politics of fascism, communism, and democracy—and it would end in politics.

Yet the Roosevelt style exacted a cost. His habit of employing personal envoys irritated Hull, even insulted him. The secretary of state tolerated Hopkins, but only barely, and that because Hopkins worked for the president rather than for the State Department and because Hopkins seemed likely to die any day. Sumner Welles, by contrast, was more than Hull could stand.

Hull disliked Welles personally and despised him professionally. The undersecretary's Groton-Harvard background was as different from Hull's as a man's could be. Hull thought Welles looked down on him, and he wasn't wrong. Hull suspected Welles of undermining him and coveting his job, and he had a point there too.

Roosevelt reassured Hull by saying he didn't want to invest the missions he sent Welles on with the importance they would inevitably acquire if undertaken by the secretary of state. Welles could work more quietly. But the reassurance rarely lasted, and Hull eventually concluded that Roosevelt simply didn't trust him to handle delicate matters. Hull came close at times to demanding that the president choose between him and Welles, but he always pulled back, typically after Roosevelt said or did something to indicate that he was blowing things out of proportion.

Hull lay in wait for the moment Welles would stumble. One such moment had seemed to occur in September 1940. William Bankhead, lately the speaker of the House, had just died, and Roosevelt, wishing to shore up his southern flank, led a group of administration officials to the funeral in Jasper, Alabama. Hull was sick, and Welles assumed his place on the presidential train with Roosevelt, Henry Wallace, assorted cabinet secretaries, and Supreme Court justice Hugo Black. The journey from Washington took twenty hours, most of them hot, and the funeral service itself filled another stifling two. Roosevelt and the rest of the entourage returned to the train for the trip back to Washington.

The president and most of the others retired early that evening, exhausted from the heat and the commotion of the journey. But Welles stayed up, talking and drinking. He kept drinking even after there was no one left to talk to. Finally, far into the morning of the third day out from the capital, he rang for a porter and requested coffee.

When the coffee arrived in Welles's private compartment, the undersecretary was quite drunk. So said the porter later, and so Welles concurred. The porter also said that Welles had propositioned him: had offered him money for sexual relations. The porter rejected Welles's advances and left, shortly telling some of his fellow employees what had happened. Their supervisor heard and informed the railroad's onboard security chief, who told the head of the Secret Service detail assigned to the president. The Secret Service man investigated sufficiently to convince himself of the truth of the porter's tale but then clamped down, insisting that no one say anything, least of all to the press.

The lid held tight, through the 1940 presidential election, only six weeks later, and for another two years after that. But a story like this was impossible to contain forever, especially once rumors wafted to those with an interest in seeing Welles destroyed.

Cordell Hull wasn't the only one who resented Welles. William Bullitt harbored a bitterness still deeper. Bullitt was temperamental, even mercurial. He had served in the Wilson administration but, taking personal affront at a perceived slight, turned against the president to abet the opponents of the League of Nations. He went on to write a bilious account of Wilson's presidency. Roosevelt, for political reasons, had made Bullitt ambassador to France, but after France fell Bullitt had little to do but complain about how little he had to do. A more decisive, bolder, or simply straightforward chief executive would have let Bullitt go, but Roosevelt judged it better to have Bullitt inside the stockade shooting out than outside shooting in. Simply disarming him didn't seem possible. Wilson had tried, and Bullitt had gone over to the opposition. Roosevelt remembered and refused to repeat Wilson's mistake.

Bullitt might well have wanted to take on Roosevelt, but lacking any obvious grounds for doing so, he settled for going after Welles. He disagreed with Welles on various policy issues, but his animus grew personal, as most things did for Bullitt—and as many things did involving Welles, the golden boy of the administration. Bullitt learned of the night on the train, and he began whispering about it around the capital. Drew Pearson, whose "Washington Merry-Go-Round" column specialized in just such gossip, heard the Welles tale but sat on it pending confirmation. Bullitt and Alice Roosevelt Longworth had once been an item; Bullitt made sure the story got to Alice, who had aged without maturing and who detested everything about the New Deal, including its author and his wife—her own kin. Alice added her voice to the anti-Welles murmuring.

If the story had simply been that Welles had made homosexual advances, it might not have threatened the curtain of silence that typically shrouded such matters in Washington in that era. Likewise, if the country had not been at war, Welles's secret could have been safe. But the homosexuality of a diplomat during wartime was presumed to create a security risk, in that the diplomat, with access to confidential information, might be blackmailed. Cordell Hull didn't have to hate Welles to worry that the national interest could be compromised by Welles's continued employment at the State Department. That he *did* hate Welles simply made it easier to indulge Bullitt in Bullitt's vendetta.

Roosevelt tried to separate himself from the whole business as long as he could. He considered Welles something of a protégé, and he enjoyed Welles's company more than that of Hull. He also considered Welles far more capable than Hull. As for Bullitt, he had never trusted him though he sometimes found him useful.

But when Roosevelt heard that Bullitt was spreading stories about Welles, he grew incensed. Bullitt was visiting the Oval Office on State Department business; Roosevelt saw him coming and halted him at the door. "William Bullitt, stand where you are," he said. The president's next words were variously recorded. "You've tried to destroy a fellow human being; get out of here and never come back," one version asserted. Another account was more dramatic. "Saint Peter is at the gate," Roosevelt was said to have declared. "Along comes Sumner Welles, who admits to human error. Saint Peter grants him entrance. Then comes William Bullitt. Saint Peter says: 'William Bullitt, you have betrayed a fellow human being. You can go *down there!*' "

Yet as much as he hated to do it, Roosevelt knew he had to cut Welles off. In August 1943, with the capital gossip growing more lurid, Welles received a call. "The President asked me to see him," Welles wrote his wife the next day. "He said that he had never been angrier in his life at the situation in the State Department, which has now reached an impossible climax." Roosevelt blamed Bullitt directly, for spreading "poison," and Hull indirectly, for not reining Bul-

litt in and for speaking out of turn. "While I don't think he does it deliberately," Roosevelt told Welles, apparently giving the secretary some benefit of
the doubt, "Hull complains about you to every senator and newspaperman he
talks to."

Welles answered that if Hull had ever asked for his resignation, he would
have tendered it at once. "My devotion and affection for the President was the
issue," Welles wrote his wife. "I would never embarrass him, particularly in
wartime. I would resign at once." And indeed he offered to resign, on the spot.

Roosevelt rejected the offer. "I have known you since you were a little boy,
before you went to Groton," he said. "I have seen you develop into what you
now are. I need you for the country. After all, whom have I got? Harry Hopkins is a sick man. I thought he would die when he joined me last week. We are
just moving into the first critical stages of peace talks. You know more about
that than anyone, and you can be of more value than anyone."

Welles said he was touched by the president's loyalty, but he didn't see how
he could continue to work with Hull, who clearly didn't want him around. He
repeated his resignation offer.

Roosevelt again rejected it. Welles responded that he would think the matter over and give the president a decision the following Monday.

That weekend, though, Welles's body broke down. The strain of the situation contributed to a heart attack that didn't kill him but allowed Roosevelt to
accept his resignation without appearing to yield to Bullitt and the scandal-
mongers. The president never forgave Bullitt. He subsequently suggested that
the ambassador might have a future in the politics of Philadelphia, his home
city. Bullitt took the hint and announced for mayor. Roosevelt quietly sent a
message to the Democratic bosses in Pennsylvania: "Cut his throat."

❖ ❖ ❖

THE FIVE WEEKS of Roosevelt's journey to Cairo and Teheran constituted
the longest stretch of his presidency away from the White House. He came
home weary but exhilarated. "I do not remember ever seeing the President
look more satisfied and pleased than he did that morning," Sam Rosenman
wrote of Roosevelt's first day back in the office. "He believed intensely that he
had accomplished what he had set out to do—to bring Russia into cooperation with the Western powers in a formidable organization for the maintenance of peace—and he was glad. . . . He was indeed the 'champ' who had
come back with the prize."

The White House press corps had missed him. And he had missed them. He regaled the reporters with stories of his top-level meetings. "We had an awfully good time—very successful—both in Cairo and Teheran," he said. "We had one banquet where we had dinner in the Russian style. Very good dinner, too. Russian style means a number of toasts, and I counted up to three hundred and sixty-five toasts." The reporters laughed appreciatively. "And we all went away sober. It's a remarkable thing what you can do, if you try." More laughter. "I made one glass of vodka that big"—indicating two fingers—"last for about twenty toasts." Still more laughter.

Roosevelt so enjoyed himself with his regular audience that he broke one of his rules and talked on with a correspondent who lagged behind after the news conference ended and the other reporters had left. His remarks were off the record, but word of them got back to the others. The president had suggested that he no longer liked the label "New Deal" as a description of the administration's approach to domestic affairs. "Would you care to express any opinion to the rest of us?" one of the other reporters inquired at the first opportunity.

"Oh, I supposed somebody would ask that," Roosevelt replied. "I will have to be terribly careful in the future how I talk to people after these press conferences." His voice expressed exasperation, but his subsequent remarks hinted that his stumble was staged. "How did the New Deal come into existence?" he inquired of himself.

There was an awfully sick patient called the United States of America, and it was suffering from a grave internal disorder—awfully sick—all kinds of things had happened to this patient, all internal things. And they sent for the doctor. And it was a long, long process—took several years before those ills, in that particular illness of ten years ago, were remedied. But after a while they were remedied. And on all those ills of 1933, things had to be done to cure the patient internally. And it was done; it took a number of years. . . .

But since then, two years ago, the patient had a very bad accident—not an internal trouble. Two years ago, on the seventh of December, he was in a pretty bad smashup—broke his hip, broke his leg in two or three places, broke a wrist and an arm, and some ribs. And they didn't think he would live, for a while. And then he began to come to. And he has been in charge of a partner of the old doctor. Old Dr. New Deal didn't know "nothing" about legs and arms. He knew a great deal about internal medicine, but nothing about surgery. So he got his partner, who was an orthopedic surgeon, Dr. Win-the-War, to take care of this fellow who had been in this bad accident. And the result is that the patient is back on his feet. He has given up his crutches. He isn't wholly well yet, and he won't be until he wins the war.

❖ ❖ ❖

𝒲HILE REPORTERS explained to their readers how Dr. Win the War had displaced Dr. New Deal, Roosevelt prepared for the latter's return to responsibility for the patient after the war. Most of Roosevelt's State of the Union address of January 1944 dealt with the military situation, recounting past successes and predicting future ones. But the address also included his most comprehensive statement of postwar aims at home, a statement that was the most radical he ever uttered—and indeed more radical than any president before or after ever uttered. Reminding Congress and the radio public of the causes of the war, Roosevelt declared, "We have come to a clear realization of the fact that true individual freedom cannot exist without economic security and independence. . . . People who are hungry and out of a job are the stuff of which dictatorships are made." Asserting that this political and economic truth was "self-evident," Roosevelt proclaimed "a second bill of rights, under which a new basis of security and prosperity can be established for all regardless of station, race, or creed." These rights included:

The right to a useful and remunerative job in the industries or shops or farms or mines of the nation;

The right to earn enough to provide adequate food and clothing and recreation;

The right of every farmer to raise and sell his products at a return which will give him and his family a decent living;

The right of every businessman, large and small, to trade in an atmosphere of freedom from unfair competition and domination by monopolies at home or abroad;

The right of every family to a decent home;

The right to adequate medical care and the opportunity to achieve and enjoy good health;

The right to adequate protection from the economic fears of old age, sickness, accident, and unemployment;

The right to a good education.

Roosevelt reminded his listeners that he had often spoken of the home front and the battle front as being part of a single democratic front. So they would remain when the fighting ceased. "After this war is won we must be prepared to move forward in the implementation of these rights to new goals of human happiness and well-being. . . . Unless there is security here at home there cannot be lasting peace in the world." The president spoke with cold earnestness in warning of a domestic reaction like that which followed the First World War. "If history were to repeat itself and we were to return to the so-called 'normalcy' of the 1920s, then it is certain that even though we shall have conquered our enemies on the battlefields abroad, we shall have yielded to the spirit of fascism here at home."

❖   ❖   ❖

THIS WAS POWERFUL, provocative language of a kind Americans hadn't heard from Roosevelt for years. It reflected, among other things, the confidence he felt after Teheran. "Within the past few weeks, history has been made," he told the American people in his State of the Union address. "And it is far better history for the whole human race than any that we have known, or even dared to hope for, in these tragic times through which we pass." At Cairo and Teheran, he explained, he had discussed the central issues of the war with the leaders of the other major Allied powers. Prime Minister Churchill, of course, was an old friend. "We know and understand each other very well. Indeed, Mr. Churchill has become known and beloved by many millions of Americans." Marshal Stalin and Generalissimo Chiang were new acquaintances. "We had planned to talk to each other across the table at Cairo and Teheran; but we soon found that we were all on the same side of the table." Roosevelt characterized Chiang as "a man of great vision, great courage, and a remarkably keen understanding of the problems of today and tomorrow." As for Stalin:

> To use an American and somewhat ungrammatical colloquialism, I may say that I "got along fine" with Marshal Stalin. He is a man who combines a tremendous, relentless determination with a stalwart good humor. I believe he is truly representative of the heart and soul of Russia; and I believe that we are going to get along very well with him and the Russian people—very well indeed.

Roosevelt revealed that General Eisenhower would command the assault on Europe. "His performances in Africa, in Sicily, and in Italy have been brilliant. He knows by practical and successful experience the way to coordinate air, sea, and land power." Few in the president's radio audience were aware of the debate that had preceded Eisenhower's appointment, and therefore few fully appreciated the concession Roosevelt made in adding: "General Eisenhower gives up his command in the Mediterranean to a British officer whose name is being announced by Mr. Churchill. We now pledge that new commander that our powerful ground, sea, and air forces in the vital Mediterranean area will stand by his side until every objective in that bitter theater is attained."

Roosevelt for the first time publicly tipped his hand regarding the structure he envisioned for postwar peace.

Britain, Russia, China, and the United States and their allies represent more than three-quarters of the total population of the earth. As long as these four nations with great military power stick together in determination to keep the peace there will be no possibility of an aggressor nation arising to start another world war.

Roosevelt realized that a permanent policing role for the United States would arouse the isolationism that had gone dormant since Pearl Harbor but hadn't disappeared. "There have always been cheerful idiots in this country who believed that there would be no more war for us if everybody in America would only return into their homes and lock their front doors behind them," he said. Events had proven them tragically wrong, and the president hoped the lesson would last. "If we are willing to fight for peace now, is it not good logic that we should use force if necessary, in the future, to keep the peace?"

❖   ❖   ❖

ROOSEVELT SPOKE so boldly about an economic bill of rights in part because he was engaged in a struggle for the allegiance of workers, who would benefit the most from his audacious agenda. The wartime wage and price controls functioned better in theory than in practice, and better for management than for labor. Wages were relatively easy to monitor, being far fewer in number than prices, which covered millions of items and whose controls could be evaded by resizing and relabeling. The cost of living advanced steadily during the war, outpacing wage rates. Workers' real incomes increased, but only because of the extra hours of overtime. Union leaders realized that overtime wouldn't last forever and reasonably argued that their members were actually losing ground.

Yet the unions' predicament wasn't entirely bleak. In 1942 the National War Labor Board ruled that in any workplace covered by a union contract new employees must be automatically enrolled in the union unless they specifically opted out during their first weeks on the job. This concession to the unions reflected the labor board's appreciation of the difficulty union organizers were having with the massive influx of workers who knew nothing of the history of organized labor and its struggles; it also reflected the fact that corporate profits were soaring and management as a whole wasn't in a position to complain.

Yet certain managers did complain. Montgomery Ward Company refused to honor the maintenance-of-membership rule, as the NWLB order was called. Attorney General Francis Biddle thereupon led a contingent of armed soldiers into the Chicago headquarters of Montgomery Ward and arrested Sewall Avery, the company president. Biddle's action ignited a storm of protest among conservatives, but it warmed the hearts of union members and most of their leaders.

Not John L. Lewis, though. The mine workers' chief and CIO founder had never forgiven Roosevelt for the president's lack of support in the steel strike, and he was unimpressed by the maintenance-of-membership rule, which didn't provide the UMW anything it didn't already enjoy under the closed-shop—mandatory membership—contract it had negotiated by its own efforts with the mine operators. Lewis refused to be bound by the NWLB directives on wages, and when the miners' contract expired in the spring of 1943, he ordered his men to strike. Half a million miners dropped their tools and headed out of the mines.

Roosevelt responded with a blistering telegram to Lewis, which he read to reporters at a news conference. "These are not mere strikes against employers of this industry to enforce collective bargaining demands," he said of the walkouts. "They are strikes against the United States Government itself." The work stoppage directly threatened the war effort. "The continuance and spread of these strikes would have the same effect on the course of the war as a crippling defeat in the field. . . . Without coal our war industries cannot produce tanks, guns, and ammunition for our armed forces. Without these weapons our sailors on the high seas, and our armies in the field, will be helpless against our enemies."

Roosevelt's telegram was addressed to Lewis, but his message was for the miners themselves. "I am sure that the men who work in the coal mines, whose sons and brothers are in the armed forces, do not want to retard the war effort. . . . Not as President, not as Commander in Chief, but as the friend of the men who work in the coal mines, I appeal to them to resume work immediately, and submit their case to the National War Labor Board for final determination." In the event his friendly appeal didn't suffice, Roosevelt was prepared to take stronger action. "If work at the mines is not resumed by ten o'clock Saturday morning"—May 1, 1943—"I shall use all the power vested in me as President and as Commander in Chief of the Army and Navy to protect the national interest and to prevent further interference with the successful prosecution of the war."

The warning worked, and the strikers returned to the mines. But when the NWLB refused Lewis the two-dollar-a-day wage boost he was demanding, they walked out again. Roosevelt again lambasted Lewis. "The action of the leaders of the United Mine Workers coal miners has been intolerable," he said, "and has rightly stirred up the anger and disapproval of the overwhelming mass of the American people." Roosevelt's verdict on Lewis was widely shared. A poll put Lewis's unpopularity rating at 87 percent; the U.S. Army's journal *Stars and Stripes* cursed, "John L. Lewis, damn your coal-black soul!"

Congress registered its disapproval by passing the Smith-Connally bill, a measure that reversed a decade of pro-labor laws by sharply curtailing the right to strike. The bill went much farther than Roosevelt intended. He had nothing against unions generally, only against Lewis and the UMW leadership. The great majority of workers had patriotically accepted a no-strike policy. "For the entire year of 1942, the time lost by strikes averaged only $5/100$ of 1 percent of the total man-hours worked," Roosevelt said. "That record has never before been equaled in this country. It is as good or better than the record of any of our allies in wartime." For this reason, he said, he was vetoing the Smith-Connally bill.

But Congress overrode the veto, sending a message to other labor leaders not to follow Lewis's lead—and to Roosevelt that he no longer controlled American labor policy.

Railroad workers resisted their lesson. In the autumn of 1943 they locked horns with federal officials who refused the wage increase they thought they deserved. Roosevelt interceded, conferring with the labor leaders, with railroad management, and with the board overseeing the dispute. But his jawboning failed, and the unions prepared to strike.

Roosevelt preempted them. "Railroad strikes by three brotherhoods have been ordered for next Thursday," he told the public on Monday, December 27. "I cannot wait until the last moment to take action to see that the supplies to our fighting men are not interrupted. I am accordingly obliged to take over at once temporary possession and control of the railroads to insure their continued operation. . . . If any employees of the railroads now strike, they will be striking against the Government of the United States."

Roosevelt's seizure of the railroads got him what he wanted in the short term. Hours before his deadline, the unions canceled their strike order. The president had the War Department announce the cancellation; its message explained that the leaders of the three brotherhoods had given assurances that "they and the organizations they represent will take no action which might imperil the successful prosecution of the war."

But the episode infuriated labor. AFL president William Green particularly resented the aspersions cast on the patriotism of the rail workers. George Marshall had declared, albeit not for attribution, that the railroad disputes were lengthening the war and costing thousands of lives. Green learned of Marshall's statement and angrily hurled the allegation back at the government. "I hereby charge that the responsibility for the prolongation of these disputes rests entirely upon bungling, fumbling, and incompetent handling by government officials and agencies," he said.

53.

$\mathcal{I}$N JANUARY 1944 HENRY MORGENTHAU SCHEDULED AN UNUSUAL Sunday meeting with Roosevelt. Morgenthau came not only as Treasury secretary but as Roosevelt's oldest friend in the administration and as a pleader of a special cause. Morgenthau's ancestors were German Jews who had assimilated into mainstream American society. Morgenthau himself had rarely attended synagogue and, by all evidence, never observed Passover. "We Jews of America have found America to be our Zion," Morgenthau's father once said. "I am an American." But during the war the son discovered his Jewish roots when Jewish leaders came to him with evidence that Hitler was systematically trying to exterminate Europe's Jews.

Morgenthau initially hesitated to raise the matter with Roosevelt. He didn't want to presume on their personal friendship, and the plight of Europe's Jews was hardly the responsibility of the American Treasury Department. If any office in the administration was to deal with the issue, it ought to be the State Department. But Cordell Hull wasn't interested, and Breckinridge Long, the assistant secretary to whom Hull referred refugee and related issues, was downright hostile. The State Department had a long history of anti-Semitism that reflected the old-stock Protestant values of the nineteenth-century founders of the American foreign service. Morgenthau concluded that if the fate of the Jews was left to the professional diplomats, there was little hope.

He began looking for an excuse to bring the Jewish question into the Treasury's bailiwick. At the end of 1943 he found one, when the administration received a request to expedite money transfers to refugees from Hitler's war machine. The State Department balked, but Morgenthau, reasoning that anything touching money involved the Treasury, determined to take the matter to Roosevelt. He scheduled a White House meeting.

Roosevelt may have guessed the purpose of the meeting, for others had raised the Jewish question with him. During the summer of 1942 Rabbi

Stephen Wise, the head of the American Jewish Congress, wrote saying that Hitler was trying to annihilate the Jews, as he had threatened to do for years. Wise asked Roosevelt to issue a statement bringing the matter to American and world attention. He said he wanted to read the statement to a Madison Square Garden rally on behalf of the Jews, and he offered language for the president to use. Roosevelt wrote his own words. "Citizens, regardless of religious allegiance, will share in the sorrow of our Jewish fellow-citizens over the savagery of the Nazis against their helpless victims," the president declared. "The Nazis will not succeed in exterminating their victims any more than they will succeed in enslaving mankind. The American people not only sympathize with all victims of Nazi crimes but will hold the perpetrators of these crimes to strict accountability in a day of reckoning which will surely come."

Roosevelt issued similar statements on subsequent occasions, sometimes singling out the Jews as victims of Nazi violence, sometimes not. A month after the Madison Square Garden rally he asserted that new intelligence from Europe revealed that the Nazi occupation of various countries had "taken proportions and forms giving rise to the fear that as the defeat of the enemy countries approaches, the barbaric and unrelenting character of the occupational regime will become more marked and may even lead to the extermination of certain populations." Those persons involved in such crimes would not escape. "The time will come when they shall have to stand in courts of law in the very countries which they are now oppressing and answer for their acts."

In December 1942 Roosevelt brought Stephen Wise back to the White House. The rabbi and several other Jewish leaders delivered a detailed memorandum describing the Nazi extermination program. "Unless action is taken immediately," Wise said, "the Jews of Hitler Europe are doomed." Wise and the others asked for a new statement on behalf of the victims. Roosevelt replied, "Gentlemen, you can prepare the statement. I am sure that you will put the words into it that express my thoughts." He added, "We shall do all in our power to be of service to your people in this tragic moment."

Wise acted at once on the president's offer. The rabbi emerged from the White House meeting to tell reporters that "the President said that he was profoundly shocked to learn that two million Jews had in one way or another perished as a result of Nazi rule and crimes."

Roosevelt followed up with a message of his own—and of America's allies. The president approved a statement by the United Nations condemning the Nazi campaign against the Jews. "From all the occupied countries Jews are being transported in conditions of appalling horror and brutality to Eastern

Europe," the statement declared. "The able-bodied are slowly worked to death in labor camps. The infirm are left to die of exposure and starvation or are deliberately massacred in mass executions. The number of victims of these bloody cruelties is reckoned in many hundreds of thousands of entirely innocent men, women and children." The statement went on to vow that "those responsible for these crimes shall not escape retribution."

Roosevelt kept his door open to the representatives of the Jewish cause. In the summer of 1943 a member of the Polish underground, Jan Karski, who at great personal risk had observed the extermination program in action, carried his eyewitness account to the West. Roosevelt invited him to the White House. Just what Karski told the president is unclear. Karski relayed a message from the Jews of Poland that if the Allies didn't do something to stop the killing, the Jewish community there would "cease to exist." But, according to his later recollection of the meeting, he kept to himself what he had seen with his own eyes. Whatever Karski's words to Roosevelt, the president's reply was succinct: "Tell your nation we shall win the war."

These words didn't satisfy Henry Morgenthau, and when he entered Roosevelt's second-floor study on January 16, 1944, he came armed with a new report detailing the massacres. "One of the greatest crimes in history, the slaughter of the Jewish people in Europe, is continuing unabated," the report began. Roosevelt listened to Morgenthau's summary and scanned the report. He waved aside Morgenthau's assertion that anti-Semitism at the State Department accounted for the lack of interest there in the Jewish troubles, but he accepted Morgenthau's suggestion that responsibility for refugee affairs be moved from State to a special board answerable to the president. The War Refugee Board was assigned to take "all measures within its power to rescue the victims of enemy oppression who are in imminent danger of death and otherwise to afford such victims all possible relief and assistance consistent with the successful prosecution of the war."

Following an order by Hitler to round up the Jews of Hungary, Roosevelt issued his most detailed and scathing condemnation of the Nazi policies:

> In one of the blackest crimes of all history—begun by the Nazis in the day of peace and multiplied by them a hundred times in time of war—the wholesale systematic murder of the Jews of Europe goes on unabated every hour. As a result of the events of the last few days, hundreds of thousands of Jews, who while living under persecution have at least found a haven from death in Hungary and the Balkans, are now threatened with annihilation as Hitler's

forces descend more heavily upon these lands. That these innocent people, who have already survived a decade of Hitler's fury, should perish on the very eve of triumph over the barbarism which their persecution symbolizes, would be a major tragedy.

Roosevelt had already declared that Hitler and his henchmen would be made to answer for their crimes. Now he promised that the reach of Allied justice would extend to those who collaborated with the Nazis. "All who share the guilt shall share the punishment." Roosevelt urged Germans and others to sabotage Hitler's plan. "I ask every German and every man everywhere under Nazi domination to show the world by his action that in his heart he does not share these insane criminal desires. Let him hide these pursued victims, help them to get over their borders, and do what he can to save them from the Nazi hangman. I ask him also to keep watch, and to record the evidence that will one day be used to convict the guilty." Roosevelt pledged that the United States would employ "all means at its command" to assist the escape of Hitler's intended victims, "insofar as the necessity of military operations permits."

This last clause was crucial. Roosevelt remained convinced that the surest way to save the Jews was to win the war as quickly as possible. As it became apparent that a concentration camp at Auschwitz was a centerpiece of the German death machine, some Jewish spokesmen advocated bombing the camp or the rail lines feeding it. The bombing, the advocates argued, would slow the destruction of the Jews and thereby save lives. It would also make a political and moral statement that the Allies knew what was happening at Auschwitz and were trying to stop it.

But there were arguments against the bombing. In the first place, it would certainly kill some of the very people the Allies sought to save. Little imagination was required to predict that Hitler's propagandists would display the bodies of those killed by the bombing and blame the Allies for many more Jewish deaths. Roosevelt was serious about bringing the war criminals to justice, and he didn't want to spoil the evidence of their guilt. In the second place, bombing the camps or the rail lines would require the diversion of scarce resources. American and British bombers were fully employed during 1944 striking targets that contributed to the German war effort. To send planes over Auschwitz might well cost the lives of Allied soldiers. Finally, there was no guarantee bombing the camp would do any good. The rail lines could quickly be rebuilt, and the killing of Jews might be accomplished by other means.

How much of the argument Roosevelt heard, and how fully he participated in it, is unclear. John McCloy, the assistant secretary of war, told a journalist decades later that Harry Hopkins informed him during the summer of 1944 that Roosevelt had been urged by some Jewish leaders to order the bombing but that, in Hopkins's words, "the Boss was not disposed to." Hopkins asked McCloy to staff the request out. McCloy said he had already done so. The air force had rejected the bombing request on cost-benefit grounds. McCloy gave the negative report to Sam Rosenman, and, in McCloy's words, "that was the end of that." McCloy added, in his retrospective interview, that he "never talked" to Roosevelt about the subject.

But McCloy subsequently changed his story. He told Morgenthau's son that he had indeed spoken to Roosevelt about bombing Auschwitz. The president, according to this later version, himself refused the request. He said the bombing would be ineffective and would appear to make the United States complicit in the killings. "We'll be accused of participating in this horrible business," Roosevelt told McCloy.

Which version, if either, is true is impossible to tell. The contemporary record is silent on the subject. What *is* clear is that the bombing did not take place and that it did not take place because Roosevelt did not want it to. He knew bombing was an option, and he could have overridden objections from the War Department, as he had overridden the department regarding the timing of the second front. But he thought bombing would be a mistake. Whether he spoke through Hopkins or McCloy, directly or indirectly, the decision—like every other important decision of the war—was his.

❖   ❖   ❖

ONE REASON ROOSEVELT refused to countenance any distraction from the war against Hitler was that the struggle was reaching a critical phase. "Yesterday on June 4, 1944, Rome fell to American and Allied troops," the president told the country in his only Fireside Chat of the year so far. "The first of the Axis capitals is now in our hands. One up and two to go!" The president dilated on the historical significance of Rome's surrender and on the fact that troops from several of the United Nations—America, Britain, France, Canada, New Zealand, Poland, South Africa—took part in the fighting. He added, "Our victory comes at an excellent time, while our Allied forces are poised for another strike at Western Europe—and while the armies of other Nazi soldiers nervously await our assault."

He could have said more on this last point, but doing so would have betrayed the greatest secret of the Allied war thus far. Roosevelt needed all his skills as an actor to concentrate on the radio script at hand, for he knew that even as he spoke the troops that had been training for the invasion of France were filing into the boats that would ferry them across the Channel. Aircraft loaded with paratroops were winging through the dark toward their drop zones behind the German lines. Within hours the world would know whether the largest amphibious operation in history was a success or a failure. If a success, it would mark the first step toward the liberation of France, and it would signal the beginning of the end of the Third Reich. If a failure, it would devastate Allied morale, perhaps causing Stalin to conclude that the Americans and British were as hapless as they had often seemed faithless. It would give Hitler's regime a new lease on life. Not incidentally, it would mean the end of hope for Europe's Jews.

But Overlord was not a failure. The first waves of American and British soldiers hit the beaches of Normandy after dawn on June 6. At Omaha Beach the Americans suffered heavy casualties, but at several other locations the German resistance was less formidable than Eisenhower, Marshall, and Roosevelt had feared. Within a few hours the heart-clutching phase of uncertainty had passed. The Allies secured a beachhead, and suddenly the sea, which had been their enemy, became their friend. With their control of the air and waves, they could transport attacking troops to the front faster than the Germans could reinforce the defenders. Within two weeks some 600,000 American and British soldiers had landed in Normandy, and the drive toward Paris began.

❖ ❖ ❖

"MY LORD! All smiles, all smiles!"

Roosevelt hadn't slept much after his radio address announcing the fall of Rome. He waited by the phone for word from the War Department that the troops had landed. It came in pieces, but by half past three—Washington time—on the morning of June 6 the news was official. The president received regular updates from then until his afternoon press conference. As the reporters—a record crowd of nearly two hundred—filled the room, he couldn't help noticing how happy they all seemed.

"You don't look like you're so solemn yourself, Mr. President."

"No, I'm not so solemn, I suppose," Roosevelt replied, laughing. "I think this is a very happy conference today."

"Mr. President, how do you feel about the progress of the invasion?"

"Up to schedule. And as the Prime Minister said, 'That's a mouthful.' "
More laughter.

"Mr. President, how long have you known that this was the date?"

"I have known since"—Roosevelt paused for effect—"I would say Teheran, which was last December, that the approximate date would be the end of May or the very first few days of June. And I have known the exact date just within the past few days. And I knew last night, when I was doing that broadcast on Rome, that the troops were actually in the vessels, on the way across."

A reporter asked why, if the decision was made so long ago, the invasion had occurred only now.

"Did you ever cross the English Channel?" the president asked.

"Never been across the English Channel."

"You're very lucky."

"Tide? Is it largely a question of—"

"Roughness in the English Channel, which has always been considered by passengers one of the greatest trials of life, to have to cross the English Channel. And, of course, they have a record of the wind and the sea in the English Channel; and one of the greatly desirable and absolutely essential things is to have relatively small-boat weather, as we call it, to get people actually onto the beach. And such weather doesn't begin much before May."

"Well, was weather the factor, sir, in delaying from the end of May until the first week in June?"

"Yes, yes. After the June date was set, there was only an actual delay of one day."

"Was it timed to come after the fall of Rome?"

"No, because we didn't know when Rome was going to fall."

❖ ❖ ❖

"I THINK WE have these Huns at the top of the toboggan slide, and the full crush of the Russian offensive should put the skids under them," George Marshall wrote Roosevelt a week after D-Day. Marshall almost never employed such informal language with the president, but the success of Overlord and the launch of the biggest Soviet offensive of the war thus far made him feel almost giddy.

Joseph Stalin was more restrained but hardly less optimistic. The Soviet dictator told Averell Harriman—as Harriman related to Roosevelt—that the Anglo-American invasion of France was "an unheard-of achievement, the magnitude of which had never been undertaken in the history of warfare." Writing to Roosevelt directly, Stalin said, "It rejoices all of us and makes us confident of future successes."

Churchill kept his emotions more fully in check. Some of his restraint doubtless reflected his long-standing resistance to the Channel crossing and his concern that things might yet go wrong. But in addition he had to deal with Charles de Gaulle. The French general realized that his homeland was about to be liberated by the American and British armies, and he sought to ensure that he rode at their head. "It is remarkable," Churchill wrote Roosevelt in exasperation, "as he has not a single soldier in the great battle now developing." The prime minister said he was doing all he could with de Gaulle. But if he reached an impasse, he might send the general to Washington. "I think it would be a great pity if you and he did not meet," Churchill asserted wryly. "I do not see why I have all the luck."

Roosevelt smiled as he read the prime minister's lament. "He may visit Washington at the end of this month," the president offered. "But there is no indication yet that he will be helpful in our efforts in the interest of his country."

Roosevelt's offer was an inexpensive gesture, as he knew that de Gaulle wouldn't leave the French theater of operations. Meanwhile the president explained the glad tidings from France to the American people—and tried to keep the tidings from sounding *too* glad. "While I know that the chief interest tonight is centered on the English Channel and on the beaches and farms and the cities of Normandy," he declared in another Fireside Chat, "we should not lose sight of the fact that our armed forces are engaged on other battlefronts all over the world." The situation in Europe, to be sure, was as promising as anyone could hope. "Germany has her back against the wall—in fact three walls at once! In the south, we have broken the German hold on central Italy. . . . On the east, our gallant Soviet allies have driven the enemy back from the lands which were invaded three years ago. . . . And on the west, the hammer blow which struck the coast of France last Tuesday morning, less than a week ago, was the culmination of many months of careful planning and strenuous preparation." Yet it was a long way from Normandy to Berlin. Those months of planning and preparation would be followed by months of fighting and dying. And Tokyo was even farther away, in terms of the time and effort it would take American forces to get there. "We are on the offensive all over the world, bringing the attack to our enemies," Roosevelt said. The attack must continue, to its ultimate global conclusion.

❖ ❖ ❖

$\mathcal{J}$HE REPUBLICANS were in a fix in the summer of 1944 and knew it. The coming presidential election would be a referendum on the war, whether Roosevelt explicitly declared it one or not. And with the war going well, the incumbent would be nearly impossible to beat. Yet the Republicans could look beyond the war and position themselves for that new era.

The leading Republican candidates going into election season were Wendell Willkie and Thomas Dewey. Willkie was a known quantity, with a strong following among international-minded Republicans. But the regulars hadn't liked him in 1940, when Roosevelt seemed at least a little vulnerable, and they liked him even less now, when Roosevelt looked unbeatable. They couldn't imagine letting him lead the party into the postwar era.

Dewey was the fresh face of the GOP. He had won a reputation in New York City during the 1930s prosecuting gangsters and Wall Street manipulators. He lost a close race for governor in 1938, putting a scare into the Democrats, and captured the office in 1942, becoming the first Republican governor in two decades. Dewey was young: if victorious in 1944 he would be, at forty-two, the youngest person ever elected president. He was energetic and handsome. Like the rest of the party, he understood that he was running for the 1948 nomination as much as for the one at hand. Either way he looked a good bet.

The nomination was effectively decided when Dewey trounced Willkie in the Wisconsin primary in April. Willkie had declared the Wisconsin vote a test of his candidacy; when he lost, badly, he withdrew from the race, leaving the field to the New York governor. Dewey was nominated on the first ballot at the Republican convention in Chicago. Taking a page from Roosevelt's biography, he accepted the nomination in person.

The Democrats arrived in Chicago three weeks later. The delegates knew the script—for the first part of the performance. In response to a White House–inspired query from the Democratic National Committee, Roosevelt declared that, if nominated, he would accept the nomination and, if elected, he would serve. "Every one of our sons serving in this war has officers from whom he takes his orders," Roosevelt said. "Such officers have superior officers. The President is the Commander in Chief and he, too, has his superior officer—the people of the United States." The Democratic delegates, standing in for the American people, ordered the president to seek a fourth term.

The scripting of the convention's second act was less obvious. The campaign for the Democratic vice presidential nomination was, in one sense, very much like the campaign for the Republican presidential nomination, in that the campaigners and their advocates were looking beyond Roosevelt. Democratic conservatives had always distrusted—or despised—Henry Wallace, deeming the former secretary of agriculture too liberal on most issues and too erratic on the rest. In 1940 they hadn't been able to organize swiftly enough to block Wallace's nomination, and in any event the looming war and the need for solidarity behind Roosevelt's unprecedented third-term try compelled their acquiescence. But in 1944 they were better organized and even more determined not to risk handing the White House to anyone as closely identified with the New Deal as Wallace.

Roosevelt himself had cooled on Wallace the previous year, when the vice president tangled with Jesse Jones, the secretary of commerce, ostensibly over foreign economic policy but really over the direction of the party. Jones, a conservative Texas businessman, thought Wallace a crackpot. Roosevelt almost agreed at times, when the vice president spouted more of his Christian mysticism than usual. All the same, Roosevelt would have much preferred to keep the quarrel inside the administration. But when Wallace and Jones insisted on speaking out, the president took the highly unusual step of rebuking them in public. Wallace was let to know that if Roosevelt was on the ticket in 1944, he—Wallace—would not be.

As the Democratic delegates gathered in Chicago, the president wrote Samuel Jackson, the permanent chair of the convention:

> The easiest way of putting it is this. I have been associated with Henry Wallace during his past four years as Vice President, for eight years earlier while he was Secretary of Agriculture, and well before that. I like him and I respect him and he is my personal friend. For these reasons I personally would vote for his renomination if I were a delegate to the convention. At the same time I do not wish to appear in any way as dictating to the convention. Obviously the convention must do the deciding.

The phrasing was classic Roosevelt. It appeared to endorse Wallace—a spokesman for the vice president professed to be "very happy" with the president's letter—but in fact it had just the opposite effect. All the regulars remembered how Roosevelt had dictated the selection of Wallace in 1940 by threatening not to run. This time, in leaving the vice presidential nomination up to the convention, Roosevelt implicitly gave Wallace the heave-ho.

He furnished additional guidance. He arranged for Robert Hannegan, the chairman of the Democratic National Committee, to inquire about the preferences of the White House. "You have written me about Harry Truman and Bill Douglas," Roosevelt replied. "I should, of course, be very glad to run with either of them and believe that either one of them would bring real strength to the ticket."

There was less to this response than met the eye. William Douglas was as suspect in conservative Democratic eyes as Henry Wallace. Roosevelt mentioned him simply as a sop to the New Dealers. The double endorsement in fact singled out Truman as the vice presidential nominee—and, in effect, the Democratic heir apparent.

The last of Roosevelt's stage directions was a message to Truman himself. The Missouri senator was in his second term, and though best known as a protégé of the Kansas City Democratic boss, Tom Pendergast, he had lately distinguished himself probing fraud and waste in military procurement. As a midwestern border stater unassociated with the New Deal, Truman was thought to be acceptable to the conservatives and southerners in the party, the ones who were revolting against Wallace.

Truman knew he was being considered, but he balked at putting himself forward until Roosevelt made clear he wanted him on the ticket. The Senate had been the apex of his ambitions. "Hell, I don't want to be president," he told a reporter who said what everyone was thinking: that the vice presidential nomination might well lead to the White House. Besides, he had spent years in the Senate trying to rub off the stain of his Pendergast connections; to join the national ticket would stir up the old stories again.

Hannegan told Truman he had a note from Roosevelt endorsing him. But Hannegan's refusal to let him see it naturally made him suspicious. Hannegan told Truman to come to his suite at the Blackstone Hotel. He placed a call to San Diego, where Roosevelt was inspecting naval installations. Truman could hear Roosevelt's voice on the telephone from across the room.

"Bob, have you got that fellow lined up yet?" the president demanded.

"No," Hannegan replied. "He's the contrariest goddamn mule from Missouri I ever saw."

"Well, you tell him if he wants to break up the Democratic party in the middle of the war, and maybe lose that war, that's up to him!" Roosevelt hung up.

"Oh, shit!" Truman said. He felt trapped—just as others had been trapped by Roosevelt before. "Well, if that's the situation, I'll have to say yes. But why the hell didn't he tell me in the first place?"

The selection proceeded as Roosevelt knew it would. Wallace led on the first ballot, receiving 429½ votes against 319½ for Truman, with the balance scattered among fourteen other candidates. But the votes for Wallace were so many empty gestures, as the second ballot, called immediately, made clear. Truman won in a landslide: 1,100 to 66.

The suddenness of the result caught Truman off guard. He was eating a sandwich on the platform of the convention hall when his victory was announced. Samuel Jackson insisted that he say a few words. Truman put down his sandwich and obliged. "You don't know how very much I appreciate the very great honor which has come to the state of Missouri," he said. "It is also a great responsibility which I am perfectly willing to assume. Nine years and five months ago I came to the Senate. I expect to continue the efforts I have made there to help shorten the war and to win the peace under the great leader, Franklin D. Roosevelt. I don't know what else I can say, except that I accept this great honor with all humility. I thank you." He sat down and finished his sandwich.

❖ ❖ ❖

"*I* SHALL NOT campaign, in the usual sense," Roosevelt said, in accepting the presidential nomination. "In these days of tragic sorrow, I do not consider it fitting. And besides, in these days of global warfare, I shall not be able to find the time." Roosevelt was speaking from his rail car on a siding in Southern California. By the middle of his twelfth year in office, the president seemed to many Democrats almost like God, able to manipulate people and things at long distance. In 1932 he had flown into Chicago to address the delegates, descending from the clouds to deliver the news of the party's rebirth. Now he addressed the delegates from half a continent away. The hall was the same—the cavernous Chicago Stadium. The lights were dimmed, as they had been in 1932. But this time there was no spotlight for the speaker, because there was no speaker. There was only Roosevelt's voice, rumbling through the building's amplification system, booming out of the dark as if from on high. As with most of the president's wartime journeys, this trip to the West Coast had been shrouded in secrecy; no one in the hall knew where he was—Washington? Hyde Park? Cairo?—till he revealed his location in his speech.

"What is the job before us in 1944?" the disembodied voice demanded.

First, to win the war—to win the war fast, to win it overpoweringly. Second, to form worldwide international organizations, and to arrange to use the armed forces of the sovereign nations of the world to make another war impossible within the foreseeable future. And third, to build an economy for our returning veterans and for all Americans—which will provide employment and provide decent standards of living.

The people of the United States will decide this fall whether they wish to turn over this 1944 job—this worldwide job—to inexperienced or immature hands, to those who opposed Lend-Lease and international cooperation against the forces of aggression and tyranny, until they could read the polls of popular sentiment; or whether they wish to leave it to those who saw the danger from abroad, who met it head-on, and who now have seized the offensive and carried the war to its present stages of success. . . .

They will also decide, these people of ours, whether they will entrust the task of postwar reconversion to those who offered the veterans of the last war breadlines and apple-selling and who finally led the American people down to the abyss of 1932; or whether they will leave it to those who rescued American business, agriculture, industry, finance, and labor in 1933, and who have already planned and put through much legislation to help our veterans resume their normal occupations in a well-ordered reconversion process.

The voice rumbled on. None of the listeners dared move, almost as though the omniscience it conveyed would see them, even in the dark. The instructions concluded with words drawn from another era and the final stages of another mortal conflict, spoken by America's secular saint:

With firmness in the right, as God gives us to see the right, let us strive on to finish the work we are in; to bind up the nation's wounds; to care for him who shall have borne the battle, and for his widow, and his orphan, to do all which may achieve and cherish a just and lasting peace among ourselves, and with all nations.

❖   ❖   ❖

No sooner had Roosevelt surfaced in San Diego than he disappeared again. He boarded the cruiser *Baltimore* for a swift passage to Hawaii, to inspect the base where America's war had started and to consult the general who aimed to end it. Since 1942 the war in the Pacific had produced some of the hardest fighting in American military history. The Guadalcanal campaign lasted six months, cost six thousand American lives, and revealed how difficult dislodging the Japanese from their island strongholds would be. In New Guinea the climate and terrain proved as formidable as the enemy; American and Australian troops struggled up and down precipitous ridges drenched in rain and cloaked with impenetrable vegetation. Every species of tropical disease and parasite—malaria, dysentery, typhus, dengue fever, ringworm, jungle rot—attacked the troops from the outside in and the inside out.

Progress was painfully slow, but it was progress still. By the summer of 1944 the Allies had captured positions in the Gilbert and Marshall islands, in addition to the Solomons and New Guinea. American carrier-based planes blasted a Japanese base at Truk in the Carolines. In June at the "Marianas turkey shoot" American fighters destroyed over two hundred Japanese planes while losing but twenty of their own. The securing of airfields on Guam and Tinian in the Marianas brought Japan's home islands within reach of American B-29 bombers. And as the end game in Europe began to unfold, Roosevelt was ready to shift more of his—and America's—attention to the Pacific. This meant talking to Douglas MacArthur.

The president's Pacific tour had other purposes as well. It would boost the morale of the inhabitants of Oahu and honor the memory of the Pearl Harbor dead. It would allow him to review the rank-and-file in Hawaii and Alaska. It would enable him to campaign for president as commander in chief.

Chester Nimitz, the admiral in charge of the major part of the Pacific, had no particular problem with this last aspect of Roosevelt's tour. But MacArthur, the commander for the Southwest Pacific, did. MacArthur was the most political officer of his generation, and yet he was remarkably clumsy every time he ventured near the political arena. He had angled for the 1944 Republican nomination for president but been swatted aside by Dewey. The rejection stung, and now MacArthur took umbrage at being made a prop in Roosevelt's reelection campaign. He cursed the president all the way from his headquarters in Australia to the meeting in Hawaii. "The humiliation of forcing me to leave my command to fly to Honolulu for a political picture-taking junket!" he declared to everyone in earshot on his B-17 from Brisbane. "In all my fighting days I've never before had to turn my back on my assignment."

He made his resentment plain on Roosevelt's arrival. The *Baltimore* lowered the gangway at Pearl Harbor, and Nimitz and dozens of other officers came on board. "One officer was conspicuously absent," Sam Rosenman recalled.

It was General Douglas MacArthur. When Roosevelt asked Nimitz where the General was, there was an embarrassed silence. We learned later that the General had arrived about an hour earlier, but instead of joining the other officers to greet the Commander-in-Chief, he had gone by himself to Fort Shafter.

After we had waited on the *Baltimore* for some time for the General, it was decided that the President and his party would disembark and go to the quarters on shore assigned to them. Just as we were getting ready to go below, a terrific automobile siren was heard, and there raced onto the dock and screeched to a stop a motorcycle escort and the longest open car I have ever seen. In the front was a chauffeur in khaki, and in the back one lone figure—MacArthur.

There were no aides or attendants. The car traveled some distance around the open space and stopped at the gangplank. When the applause of the crowd died down, the General strode rapidly to the gangplank all alone. He dashed up the gangplank, stopped halfway up to acknowledge another ovation, and soon was on deck greeting the President.

Roosevelt refused to respond to MacArthur's unstated challenge, except for a minor poke. "Hello, Doug," he said. "What are you doing with that leather jacket on? It's darn hot today."

MacArthur had never liked the uniforms the regular army wore. While seconded to the Philippine government during the 1930s, he designed for himself the gaudiest field marshal's uniform Eisenhower, then his chief of staff, had ever seen. The nonregulation leather jacket was his latest fashion statement.

"I've just landed from Australia," he told Roosevelt, pointing his corncob pipe at the sky. "It's pretty cold up there."

Roosevelt led the officers on a round of inspections. He visited the wreck of the *Arizona*, lying where it sank in Pearl Harbor. He toured the navy yards and addressed the troops at Schofield Barracks. He had himself rolled through an amputee ward at one of the hospitals, letting the wounded warriors see that their commander in chief couldn't walk. Sam Rosenman had grown accustomed to Roosevelt's disability, but he found the experience deeply moving. "He had known for twenty-three years what it was to be deprived of the use of both legs," Rosenman recalled. "He wanted to display himself and his useless legs to those boys who would have to face the same bitterness. This crippled man on the little wheel chair wanted to show them that it was possible to rise above such physical handicaps." Roosevelt spoke to the young men, one by one, and offered smiling encouragement. But he, too, was touched. "I never saw Roosevelt with tears in his eyes," Rosenman remarked. "That day as he was wheeled out of the hospital he was close to them."

In his tour of the island he traveled in an open vehicle, which unnerved his security team. "Many of the inhabitants were pure Japanese or descended from mixed marriages of Japanese," Rosenman wrote. "Frequently, Admiral Nimitz, General MacArthur, and Admiral Leahy were in the car with him. Following behind in the procession, I could not help thinking how dreadful a toll one well-placed bomb would take. The Secret Service men were worried to distraction."

The president chatted innocuously with MacArthur on their drives around Oahu, but back in the living room of the Waikiki house where he was staying he got down to business. A wall map showed the current disposition of American forces in the Pacific. "Well, Douglas," Roosevelt said, "where do we go from here?"

MacArthur was expecting the question. "Leyte, Mr. President," he said, pointing to the Philippines. "And then Luzon."

At this stage of American strategy in the Pacific, informed opinion split between those who advocated approaching Japan via the Philippines and then Taiwan and those who favored bypassing the Philippines and advancing directly to Taiwan. The army generally favored the former route, and the navy the latter. MacArthur was staking the army's claim—and his own—to the Philippines, and he spent the afternoon trying to bring the president to his side of the argument. He spoke with a fervor that wore Roosevelt out. "Give me an aspirin before I go to bed," Roosevelt remarked to his doctor at the end of the session. "In fact, give me another aspirin to take in the morning. In all my life nobody has ever talked to me the way MacArthur did."

Roosevelt was noncommittal but not discouraging. No decisions were made that week in Hawaii, yet the president gave MacArthur reason for optimism. At a press conference concluding the visit, Roosevelt said he had had "two very successful days" with MacArthur and the other officers, talking about "future plans."

A reporter, bolder than the rest, inquired about those plans. "When General MacArthur was about to leave the Philippines," the reporter observed, "I recall he said something to the general effect that 'I will return.' In view of the setting of this meeting with him, is there anything that you could tell us? Is that true now?"

"We are going to get the Philippines back," Roosevelt said. "And without question General MacArthur will take a part in it." But the president felt obliged to add: "Whether he goes direct or not, I can't say."

The reporter persisted. "Can we say that General MacArthur will return to the Philippines?"

"He was correct the day he left Corregidor, and I told him he was correct."

54.

$\mathcal{F}$OR MOST OF THE WAR ROBERT SHERWOOD SAW ROOSEVELT ON A REG-
ular basis. His duties as a speech writer and then as director of the Office of
War Information made him part of the White House family. But he spent the
first several months of 1944 away from Washington on OWI business, and by
the time he returned he hadn't seen the president in more than half a year. He
paid a visit at first opportunity. "I was shocked by his appearance," Sherwood
recalled. "I had heard that he had lost a lot of weight, but I was unprepared for
the almost ravaged appearance of his face. He had his coat off and his shirt collar seemed several sizes too large for his emaciated neck."

After twenty years on stage, eleven in a continuous run, the old performer
was showing the strain. Since mounting the dais at the Democratic convention
in 1924, Roosevelt had rarely been out of the spotlight and almost never out
of character. The New York governorship and the New Deal presidency allowed intermissions, moments when he could catch his breath and gather
himself. But the war, which began for Roosevelt, if not for America, about 1937,
never stopped, and neither could its American protagonist.

Any war leader would have staggered under the burden. Churchill suffered
a severe case of pneumonia after the Teheran conference; some of his associates weren't sure he'd recover sufficiently to retain the premiership. Stalin's
health was a better-kept secret, but various reports suggested some kind of
nervous breakdown amid the Nazi offensive of 1941.

Yet Roosevelt's burden was greater than those of his Grand Alliance partners. As both head of government and head of state, he combined the roles of
Churchill and King George VI. Churchill boasted that he might be turned out
at any moment, but that possibility was more theoretical than real. The confidence votes weren't even close. And unlike Roosevelt, he didn't have to lead
his party in wartime elections, because Britain's flexible constitution allowed
elections to be suspended for the duration. As for Stalin, he governed by dik-

tat. He didn't have to kiss babies, woo their parents, or cajole their representatives. He didn't shoot his subjects as often as he had during the 1930s, in part
because the Germans were shooting so many that he couldn't afford to waste
the remainder. But everyone remembered the purges and acted accordingly.

The demands of democracy aside, Roosevelt's burden was peculiarly personal. He had determined, not long after contracting polio, that he would deny
its effects on his life and dreams. The sheer physical effort of standing in his
braces, of staggering forward, step by lurching step, of smiling through the
sweat and the clenched hands gripping the lectern for dear life, would have
exhausted anyone. But the emotional effort was at least as great. He couldn't
show his anger at his lost athleticism, his vanished virility, his physical dependence on others. He couldn't be discouraged or despondent. Roosevelts
didn't show their feelings, Delanos even less. And *this* Roosevelt, *this* Delano,
showed his feelings least of all. To allow others inside, to let them see the man
behind the actor, would spoil the effect he had taken such pains to create.

The effect—of the fearless leader, the happy warrior, the father figure on
whom the nation relied—was as central to his own equilibrium as it was to the
country's. His isolation hadn't begun with the polio. He had been emotionally
isolated since boyhood. His close relationships had always been with persons
not his equal. He had no close friends as a boy or young man, no one at Groton or Harvard in whom he genuinely confided. After he entered politics he
had mentors and protégés; as he advanced he lost the mentors and was left
with only protégés and attendants. Louis Howe, Missy LeHand, Harry Hopkins, and the lesser members of the White House family subordinated themselves, their careers, their personal lives to him. After Howe died, none would
talk back to him as Louis had. Missy's stroke deprived him of another, softer
voice. Roosevelt might have confided in his children as they matured, but the
emotional code instilled in him by his father and especially his mother prevented such intimacies.

The result of all this was that the actor never left the stage. By the twelfth
year in the presidential spotlight, the performer's constitution was breaking
down. The first conclusive evidence of incipient failure appeared in March
1944. Ross McIntire, the president's physician, was a navy doctor who specialized in ears, noses, and throats. He received the assignment as presidential
physician because he knew Cary Grayson, Woodrow Wilson's doctor, who was
a friend of Roosevelt's, and because at the time of Roosevelt's first inauguration, sinus complaints were his only chronic medical condition—aside, of
course, from the paraplegia. For decades presidents had been treated by army

or navy doctors, partly on account of the cost saving to the patients, at a time when presidents weren't paid very well, and partly because the president's doctor had to be able to travel with the president on the president's schedule— something few physicians in private practice would have been willing to do. This tradition meant that presidents often didn't receive the best care possible. Military doctors typically weren't at the leading edge of their fields, and the fact that those treating the president were dealing with their commander in chief inhibited their assertiveness. McIntire was no exception to the rule. He was perfectly adequate in treating head colds and other pedestrian maladies, and he was adept at the politics of the navy and of Washington, eventually becoming a vice admiral and the surgeon general of the navy. But he was over his head in treating a patient with chronic complicated illnesses.

To his credit he realized his limitations, albeit belatedly. Roosevelt returned from Teheran in December 1943, having traveled seventeen thousand miles in five weeks. The success of his first meeting with Stalin had boosted his spirits, as did the time he spent aboard ship, but the whole endeavor wore him down. He contracted influenza and spent most of his Hyde Park Christmas holiday coughing and aching. The cough and discomfort persisted into January and February, causing the cancellation of several engagements, including press conferences, which naturally prompted speculation about what was wrong with the president. McIntire finally ordered a full workup in March, bringing in specialists, including Howard Bruenn, a young navy cardiologist. The conditions of Bruenn's consulting reflected navy practice; as a junior officer, he reported to his superior, McIntire, rather than to his patient, Roosevelt.

"He appeared to be very tired, and his face was very gray," Bruenn recalled of his initial examination. "Moving caused considerable breathlessness." The patient coughed frequently. His pulse was seventy-two beats per minute; his blood pressure was 186 over 108. Fluoroscopy and X-rays revealed that the left ventricle of the heart was enlarged and the pulmonary vessels engorged. "Accordingly, a diagnosis was made of hypertension, hypertensive heart disease, and cardiac failure (left ventricle), and acute bronchitis," Bruenn wrote. "These findings and their interpretation were conveyed to Surgeon General McIntire. They had been completely unsuspected up to this time."

This wasn't quite true. McIntire had diagnosed hypertension in Roosevelt in 1937 and again in 1941, although he missed the other maladies. Bruenn proceeded to file a memorandum with McIntire prescribing the standard treatment of that day for such cases: bed rest for a week or two, regular doses of digitalis to ease blood flow through the heart, codeine for the cough, and reduction of dietary salt and gradual weight loss to bring down the blood pressure.

"This memorandum was rejected because of the exigencies and demands on the President," Bruenn wrote. McIntire pointed out the obvious: Roosevelt wasn't a normal patient. He could take the digitalis, he could cut back on his salt, and he could lose weight. But he couldn't stop working, not with a war on. McIntire directed Bruenn to monitor the situation.

The younger doctor did so, examining Roosevelt three or four times a week and ordering electrocardiograms and various other tests. The bronchitis eased, in part as a result of Roosevelt's curtailment of cigarettes, to six per day. But the hypertension worsened. On April 4 his blood pressure was 226 over 118. Roosevelt reported sleeping well and said he felt fine. Yet he was strikingly incurious about his condition. "At no time," Bruenn remembered, "did the President ever comment on the frequency of these visits or question the reason for the electrocardiograms and the other laboratory tests that were performed from time to time; nor did he ever have any questions as to the type and variety of medications that were used."

Roosevelt's lack of curiosity may have reflected the medical ethos of the time, when patients typically deferred to physicians more than they would later. It may have mirrored Roosevelt's preoccupation with his work. With his head full of the war, he would let the doctors worry about his health. It may have indicated a conscious or unconscious act of denial: to refuse to acknowledge that something was gravely amiss. Denial had been his initial strategy for dealing with polio, and in retrospect he couldn't argue with the results. Denial might be the most productive way to deal with a failing heart.

Roosevelt couldn't stop working, but he could take a working vacation. Bernard Baruch volunteered his South Carolina estate, and the president, McIntire, Bruenn, and several members of the White House entourage headed to the Carolina coast. The weather was fair though a bit cool for April. Roosevelt slept late each morning and remained in bed till noon, reading newspapers and answering correspondence. He ate lunch with the group, joined by Baruch and occasional visitors, including Eleanor, Anna, his cousin Daisy Suckley, and military and civilian officials who came down from Washington. After lunch he would nap and in the late afternoon go fishing or for a drive around the plantation. Every day a special plane from the capital brought documents that required signatures; Roosevelt dealt with these before dinner, which began about seven and was the high point of the day. "The conversation was animated, with the President playing the dominant role," Bruenn wrote.

"It ranged from reminiscences with Mr. Baruch over earlier contemporaries and incidents to a discussion of recent and current events."

❖　❖　❖

ONE VISITOR TO Baruch's plantation wasn't recorded in the official log. Roosevelt had continued to see Lucy Mercer Rutherfurd, more frequently following the death of her husband in early 1944. By then Anna was back living at the White House, where she assumed some of the responsibilities of the peripatetic Eleanor and some of the tasks of Missy LeHand. She had to be careful not to confuse the portfolios, especially when Roosevelt one day asked, "What would you think about our inviting an old friend of mine to a few dinners at the White House? This would have to be arranged when your mother is away, and I would have to depend on you to make the arrangements." Anna had learned the story of Lucy years before from Eleanor, and at first she hesitated, out of loyalty to her mother. "It was a terrible decision to have to make," she recalled.

But her love for her father won out. Having come to see him through the eyes of an adult—one who, like him, had been unlucky in love—Anna realized how hungry he was for the kind of companionship that Lucy could provide and that Eleanor couldn't or wouldn't. The First Lady always had an agenda. She rarely met with her husband without bringing up her current causes. These were generally worthy and often underrepresented in the policy circles of the administration, and before the war Roosevelt had been willing for her to push him on such matters. But the war was wearing him down, and he didn't have the energy or time for Eleanor's projects.

For years Missy LeHand had played the second wife, the devoted helpmeet who asked nothing besides the chance to serve the man she loved. But Missy was dying. That he had lost Sara about the time Missy fell ill doubled the blow. From birth Roosevelt had been doted on by at least one woman; now there was none. Anna helped fill the gap, but as a daughter there was only so much she could do.

One thing she did was smuggle Lucy into the White House. A first private dinner was arranged, then several more. Finding evenings when Eleanor was away was easy, given her endless travel schedule. The White House staff and Secret Service agents were discreet. As far as Anna could tell, the meetings consisted of nothing more than dinner and pleasant talk, which eased her conscience. "They were occasions which I welcomed for my father," she said, "because they were light-hearted and gay, affording a few hours of much needed relaxation."

Roosevelt met Lucy outside the White House as well. On fair afternoons he would have himself driven to the home of a mutual friend near Leesburg, Virginia. He and Lucy would visit there, or she would join him in the back seat of the car for a tour of the countryside. In one instance he stopped the presidential train en route from Washington to Hyde Park to visit her at a home she kept in New Jersey. At least once she spent the weekend with him at Shangri-La. And in the spring of 1944, during his month at Baruch's South Carolina estate, Lucy drove over from her winter home at Aiken. Baruch provided the ration coupons to purchase gasoline for the journey.

❖ ❖ ❖

"*I* HAD REALLY a grand time down at Bernie's," Roosevelt wrote Harry Hopkins after returning to Washington. "Slept twelve hours out of the twenty-four, sat in the sun, never lost my temper, and decided to let the world go hang. The interesting thing is the world didn't hang. I have a terrific pile in my basket, but most of the stuff has answered itself."

Howard Bruenn concurred, to a point. "He slept soundly and ate well," Bruenn recorded. The president's spirits and demeanor were much improved. But his blood pressure remained high and in fact got worse, rising to as much as 240 over 130. "He complained of soreness in the back of his neck and a throbbing sensation all through the body." Bruenn and McIntire sent him to bed for two days, and the symptoms subsided.

A new symptom—intermittent abdominal pains—caused McIntire to order X-rays of the gall bladder. When the images revealed gallstones, the president was placed on a low-fat diet of 1,800 calories per day. During the next few months he showed no new symptoms, weathering his journey to California, Hawaii, and Alaska quite well.

But on the return, while giving a speech at a naval facility in Bremerton, Washington, he felt a pressure in his chest that radiated out to both shoulders. The incident lasted perhaps fifteen minutes, and the pressure had disappeared by the time he finished talking. Bruenn checked him for signs of a heart attack but found nothing.

The train journey home was slow and uneventful. Roosevelt stuck to his diet, so well that he shed fifteen pounds. "As usually happens with weight loss of this degree, the President had lost some flesh from his face," Bruenn noted.

"His features had become sharpened and he looked somewhat haggard in place of his normal, robust appearance." Bruenn and McIntire told him he had lost all the weight he needed to lose, and they eased the caloric restrictions on his diet. But he didn't have much appetite, partly because of the blandness of his food, and the weight loss continued.

It was at this point that Robert Sherwood saw him and was shocked at his appearance. Others, too, wondered what was wrong with the president. Rumors circulated, with the election approaching, that the president was gravely ill. "You hear them everywhere you go," journalist Marquis Childs wrote. Childs, a Roosevelt loyalist, refused to believe them. "This is wicked business," he said. "It is the vilest kind of fear campaign." But he knew what drove the campaign. "Some people hate the President so much that the wish is father to the thought that his health is seriously undermined. There is a type of frustrated individual who actually seems to get a malicious pleasure from hinting that he or she has inside information that Roosevelt is suffering from some serious ailment."

The rumors gained sufficient credence that the White House felt obliged to have Ross McIntire refute them. The president's health was "good, very good," Roosevelt's primary doctor declared in September. The president had caught the flu some while earlier, but so had many other people. "He's right back in shape now." When this statement failed to stifle the whispers, McIntire held another press conference. "The President's health is perfectly O.K.," he declared. "There are absolutely no organic difficulties at all." McIntire acknowledged that Roosevelt looked thin, but he said this was by the president's own choice. He had decided to lose some weight, had succeeded, and had become "proud of his flat—repeat f–l–a–t—tummy." McIntire added, "Frankly, I wish he would put on a few pounds."

Roosevelt himself addressed the rumors, at first obliquely. In a radio address from the White House he lamented that the current campaign had been marred by "even more than the usual crop of whisperings and rumorings." Voters almost certainly had not heard the end of them. "As we approach election day, more wicked charges may be made—and probably will—with the hope that someone or somebody will gain momentary advantage. Hysterical last-minute accusations or sensational revelations are trumped up in an attempt to panic the people on election day." But he was confident the people would not be panicked.

The campaign didn't cure what ailed him, but it rekindled his fighting spirit, as campaigns always did. He asked Sherwood if he had listened to any of Dewey's speeches. Sherwood hadn't. "You ought to hear him," Roosevelt said. "He plays the part of the heroic racket-buster in one of those gangster movies. He talks to the people as if they were the jury and I were the villain on trial for his life." The president explained that he himself would be speaking to a Teamsters dinner the next Saturday night. "I expect to have a lot of fun with that one," he said, smiling.

He did have fun. He lambasted the Republicans for callous disregard of the truth. Some were denying that they had ever opposed such popular New Deal measures as Social Security. "Imitation may be the sincerest form of flattery," Roosevelt told the Teamsters, "but I am afraid that in this case it is the most obvious common or garden variety of fraud." Many Republicans were calling him a tyrant. "They have imported the propaganda technique invented by the dictators abroad." The most shameless of the critics said he had left America unready for war. "I doubt whether even Goebbels would have tried that one." Roosevelt's audience grew more indignant with each lash of his tongue. The emotional level was just where he wanted it when he slyly shifted direction.

> These Republican leaders have not been content with attacks on me, or my wife, or on my sons. No, not content with that, they now include my little dog, Fala. Well, of course, I don't resent attacks, and my family doesn't resent attacks, but Fala does resent them. You know, Fala is Scotch, and being a Scottie, as soon as he learned that the Republican fiction writers in Congress and out had concocted a story that I had left him behind on the Aleutian Islands and had sent a destroyer back to find him—at a cost to the taxpayers of two or three, or eight or twenty million dollars—his Scotch soul was furious. He has not been the same dog since. I am accustomed to hearing malicious falsehoods about myself—such as that old, worm-eaten chestnut that I have represented myself as indispensable. But I think I have a right to resent, to object to libelous statements about my dog.

❖   ❖   ❖

THE FALA STORY—replayed endlessly over the radio and in newsreels, with Roosevelt's sarcasm dripping anew each time—disarmed Dewey. Roosevelt delivered a handful of additional addresses in Philadelphia, Chicago, Boston, and New York. The New York address culminated a four-borough tour in an open car amid a cold, driving rain. Most of Roosevelt's companions begged off, but the president didn't want to disappoint the millions of voters who lined the streets, and he wanted to bury the charges that he was on his deathbed. The cheering crowds didn't know that his car periodically darted into garages where he put on dry clothes and took warming shots of brandy.

In early October Al Smith died at the age of seventy. Smith and Roosevelt had been estranged for years, with Smith endorsing Willkie in 1940 after backing Landon in 1936. Smith all but volunteered for service in the Roosevelt administration after Pearl Harbor, yet the president ignored his feelers. Smith's death, however, gave Roosevelt an opportunity to make amends, on his own terms, and to reflect on those better times when Smith had served the Democratic party, and particularly its urban constituencies, well. "Al Smith had qualities of heart and mind and soul which not only endeared him to those who came under the spell of his dynamic presence in personal association, but also made him the idol of the multitude," Roosevelt said. "Frank, friendly and warmhearted, honest as the noonday sun, he had the courage of his convictions, even when his espousal of unpopular causes invited the enmity of powerful adversaries." Those adversaries, of course, had become Roosevelt's own, and Smith's 1928 defeat proved, after the 1929 crash and the ordeal of the Hoover years, to be a badge of Democratic pride. "In a bitter campaign, in which his opponent won, Al Smith made no compromise with honor, honesty, or integrity. In his passing the country loses a true patriot."

Less than a week later, Wendell Willkie died. Smith's passing had not been entirely unexpected, but Willkie's death—by heart attack, following a strep infection, at the age of fifty-two—was a shock. Yet if Smith's death allowed Roosevelt an opportunity to reaffirm his ties to urban Democrats, Willkie's demise let him reach out to internationalist Republicans. Robert Sherwood thought Roosevelt respected Willkie's talent and patriotism so highly that he would not have run for a fourth term if Willkie had won the Republican nomination. But Sherwood himself admitted that this was a "doubly hypothetical surmise," in that the Republican regulars detested Willkie even more than they hated Roosevelt. The president consequently took pleasure in praising the "tremendous courage" of his erstwhile and now deceased opponent. "This courage, which was his dominating trait, prompted him more than once to stand alone and to challenge the wisdom of counsels taken by powerful interests within his own party."

❖   ❖   ❖

*T*wo weeks before the election Douglas MacArthur made good his pledge to return to the Philippines. The president had accepted MacArthur's contention that American strategy and American honor dictated the early liberation of the Philippines, and on October 20 the general splashed ashore on the eastern Philippine island of Leyte. He was in full hero mode. As he stepped into his landing craft, he put a revolver in his pocket. "It's just a precaution, just to make sure that I am never captured alive," he said. He ordered soldiers out of the boats to make room for photographers, and no sooner had he waded through the surf to the sand than he had his signal corps rig a transmitter. "I have returned!" he told the Filipinos and the world. "By the grace of Almighty God, our forces again stand on Philippine soil. . . . Let no heart be faint. Let every arm be steeled. The guidance of Divine God points the way. Follow in his name to the Holy Grail of righteous victory!" To Roosevelt he wrote that the operation was going very well. The Filipinos were reacting "splendidly" to his efforts on their behalf. Victory was in sight. Yet the hero remained humble. "Please excuse this scribble," he told the president, "but at the moment I am on the combat line with no facilities except this field message pad."

Roosevelt responded with a comparable mix of sincerity and theater. "The whole American nation today exults at the news that the gallant men under your command have landed on Philippine soil," he cabled the general. "I know well what this means to you. I know what it cost you to obey my order that you leave Corregidor in February 1942 and proceed to Australia. Since then you have planned and worked and fought with whole-souled devotion for the day when you would return with powerful forces to the Philippine Islands." That day finally had come. "You have the nation's gratitude and the nation's prayers for success."

Additional good news arrived within days, when a U.S. naval force annihilated most of what remained of the Japanese fleet, at the Battle of Leyte Gulf. Four Japanese aircraft carriers, three battleships, eight cruisers, and a dozen destroyers went down with some ten thousand officers and men. The battle closed a chapter of naval warfare; never again would the Japanese fleet venture in force from its home waters.

❖   ❖   ❖

ROOSEVELT COULD HAVE coasted to victory in the election, but he chose to press his advantage. In a radio address delivered before the Foreign Policy Association of New York, he described the present as a crossroads of history for democracy and personal freedom.

The power which this nation has attained—the political, the economic, the military, and above all the moral power—has brought to us the responsibility, and with it the opportunity, for leadership in the community of nations. It is our own best interest, and in the name of peace and humanity, this nation cannot, must not, and will not shirk that responsibility.

Roosevelt's vision of American leadership entailed a radical departure in American diplomacy. He remembered well that American support for the League of Nations had broken over article 10 of the League covenant, pledging members to employ force against aggressors. Yet now he made such a pledge the crux of his election campaign.

The Council of the United Nations must have the power to act quickly and decisively to keep the peace by force, if necessary. A policeman would not be a very effective policeman if, when he saw a felon break into a house, he had to go to the town hall and call a town meeting to issue a warrant before the felon could be arrested. . . . If the world organization is to have any reality at all, our American representative must be endowed in advance by the people themselves, by constitutional means through their representatives in the Congress, with authority to act.

The contrast to the 1940 campaign could hardly have been more dramatic. Then Roosevelt had promised American mothers and fathers that he would not send their sons to fight in foreign wars. Now he promised those same mothers and fathers that he *would* send their sons to do precisely that.

It was a bold move, but not a hugely risky one. In 1940 the isolationists had still been a threat; Roosevelt had had to proceed with caution. Now isolationism was a spent force and internationalism was on the rise. Yet he knew from experience how quickly the American mood could change, which was why he insisted on making the election a referendum on his internationalist vision.

Americans responded by handing Roosevelt a resounding fourth victory. He polled 25.6 million popular votes and 432 electoral votes, against 22 million popular and 99 electoral for Dewey. His popularity reached to the House, where the Democrats reversed their downward trend and gained twenty seats. In the Senate the two parties broke even.

55.

"DEAREST FRANKLIN," ELEANOR WROTE IN EARLY DECEMBER 1944:

> I realize very well that I do not know the reasons why certain things may be necessary nor whether you intend to do them or do not intend to do them. It does, however, make me rather nervous to hear you say that you do not care what Jimmy Dunne thinks because he will do what you tell him to do and that for three years you have carried the State Department and you expect to go on doing it. I am quite sure that Jimmy Dunne is clever enough to tell you that he will do what you want and to allow his subordinates to accomplish things which will get by and which will pretty well come up in the long-time results to what he actually wants to do.

Cordell Hull's uncertain health had finally forced him to resign, after serving longer than any other secretary of state in American history. Roosevelt hadn't chosen a replacement, and Eleanor worried that James Dunne, Hull's assistant, was taking the State Department in an illiberal direction.

Eleanor worried constantly these days, and not simply about the State Department. She was having an eventful, sometimes fulfilling, but often frustrating war. She quit the Office of Civilian Defense after conservatives in Congress vented their displeasure at her causes by cutting funding to the OCD. "I offered a way to get at the president," she observed afterward. She began visiting military hospitals and bases around the country, but when her sons went overseas she determined to follow their example, to the degree a president's spouse could. She traveled to England, where she visited with Churchill and his wife. "One feels that she has had to assume a role because of being in public life, and that the role is now a part of her," she wrote of Clementine Churchill, in words she knew applied to herself as well. "One wonders what she is like underneath." She met with the king, the queen, and assorted lesser royals. She saw the destruction from the German bombs in the Battle of Britain. She toured British and American military facilities and spoke with Eisenhower and his lieutenants. Her matter-of-fact manner impressed everyone she encountered. "Mrs. Roosevelt has been winning golden opinions here from all for her kindness and her unfailing interest in everything we are doing," Churchill informed Roosevelt.

Her journey to England piqued her desire to get closer to the fighting. A Washington appearance by Madame Chiang suggested where Eleanor might go next. Eleanor was initially as smitten by China's First Lady as most people were. She told Franklin what a gentle, sweet character she was. But Madame Chiang's visit coincided with Franklin's troubles with John L. Lewis and the mine workers, and Roosevelt innocently asked her, "What would you do in China with a labor leader like John Lewis?" Eleanor recalled the moment: "She never said a word, but the beautiful, small hand came up very quietly and slid across her throat—a most expressive gesture." Roosevelt afterward inquired mischievously of Eleanor: "Well, how about your gentle and sweet character?" Years later, when Eleanor found other reasons to differ with Madame Chiang, she would say: "Those delicate little petal-like fingers—you could see some poor wretch's neck being wrung."

Madame Chiang's visit provided the impetus for Eleanor to arrange a trip to the Pacific theater. She did so with mixed feelings. "This trip will be attacked as a political gesture," she wrote a friend. "I am so uncertain whether or not I am doing the right thing that I will start with a heavy heart." Her doubts didn't lessen when some of the theater officers made clear that they didn't appreciate her coming. Douglas MacArthur in Australia was even more disrespectful of her than he was of her husband. He wouldn't take the time to speak to her, and he refused her request to get closer to the front, saying he couldn't spare the personnel a woman of her stature required as protection. "This is the kind of thing that seems to me silly," she wrote Franklin. She said she would be happy with a single sergeant as a guide. To a friend she wrote, "I've never been so hedged around with protection in my life. It makes me want to do something reckless when I get home, like making munitions!"

MacArthur handed Eleanor off to Captain Robert White, who at first resented the assignment. He had joined the army to fight the Japanese, not to chauffeur civilians who had no business in the war zone. But his experience with Eleanor changed his mind. "Wherever Mrs. Roosevelt went she wanted to see the things a mother would see," White wrote later.

> She looked at kitchens and saw how food was prepared. When she chatted with the men she said things mothers would say, little things men never think of and couldn't put into words if they did. Her voice was like a mother's, too. Mrs. Roosevelt went through hospital wards by the hundreds. In each she made a point of stopping by each bed, shaking hands, and saying some nice, motherlike thing. Maybe it sounds funny, but she left behind her many a tough battletorn GI blowing his nose and swearing at the cold he had recently picked up.

Eleanor's maternal instincts extended to politics once she returned home. She encouraged her husband to keep the liberal faith, lest the poor and otherwise unfortunate lose out amid the effort to win the war. She tried to persuade him to retain Henry Wallace as vice president, considering Wallace the most reliable of the dwindling number of New Dealers in the administration. "I wrote a column on Wallace but Franklin says I must hold it till after the convention," she told a friend to whom she could air her frustration. "I wish I were free!" At other moments she seemed more eager for a fourth term than Franklin was. "I don't think Pa would really mind defeat," she wrote James. "If elected he'll do his job well I feel sure, and I think he can be kept well to do it, but he does get tired, so I think if he is defeated he'll be content. . . . I am only concerned because Dewey seems to me more and more to show no understanding of the job at home or abroad."

Immediately after the election she challenged Roosevelt to make good on his economic bill of rights. Harry Hopkins recounted a conversation the three of them had, in which Eleanor did most of the talking. "Mrs. Roosevelt urged the President very strongly to keep in the forefront of his mind the domestic situation because she felt there was a real danger of his losing American public opinion in his foreign policy if he failed to follow through on the domestic implications of his campaign promises," Hopkins said. Eleanor stressed full employment—"the organizing of our economic life in such a way as to give everybody a job"—and she told Franklin and Hopkins that they simply had to do more than they were doing. "This was an overwhelming task and she hoped neither the President nor I thought it was settled in any way by making speeches."

❖ ❖ ❖

$\mathcal{R}$OOSEVELT DIDN'T need the reminder that words weren't deeds, but other deeds just then took precedence over his economic bill of rights. The war—both wars, in fact—remained to be won. The distinctness of the conflicts—the one in Europe, the other in the Pacific—became a major issue in American diplomacy during the last months of 1944 and the first months of 1945. The war in Europe was going as well as the Allies could hope. The American and British armies rolled through France during the summer of 1944, with Roosevelt, Churchill, and Eisenhower tactfully letting de Gaulle's Free French army liberate Paris, in support of an uprising by the anti-German resistance there. "Men and women," de Gaulle declared upon entering the capital: "We are here in the Paris that rose to free herself—the Paris oppressed, downtrodden, and martyred, but still Paris—free now, freed by the hands of Frenchmen, the capital of fighting France, of great eternal France."

Roosevelt congratulated de Gaulle and his compatriots, while reminding them that it wasn't just French hands that freed Paris. "We rejoice with the gallant French people at the liberation of their capital," the president said, "and join in the chorus of congratulation to the commanders and fighting men, French and Allied, who have made possible this brilliant presage of total victory."

The Allies pressed east, driving the Germans out of most of Belgium and the Netherlands in September and reaching the Rhine by the end of the month. Optimists, remembering the sudden disintegration of the second German reich at the end of the First World War, spoke of celebrating Christmas in Berlin. But the Germans dug in and launched a ferocious counterattack. The Battle of the Bulge (named for the westward swelling in the front) alarmingly recalled the German successes of 1940. For six weeks from mid-December the Germans threw every unit they could spare into the fight and inflicted the heaviest casualties American forces suffered during the entire war. But the Allied lines ultimately held, and the failed effort exhausted the Germans.

The Soviets meanwhile closed in from the east. The Russians drove the Germans out of the Ukraine and White Russia and fought their way across Poland. The Red Army troops entered East Prussia, some with their own visions of an Orthodox Christmas in Berlin (Stalin having loosened up on religion during the war). But logistics and winter intervened, and the final push awaited the spring of 1945.

In the Pacific the third anniversary of American belligerence found American forces sweeping all before them. MacArthur's troops advanced through the Philippines, reaching the outskirts of Manila by the end of January 1945. A monthlong battle liberated the city, although little remained standing by the time the guns fell silent. In early February American B-29s flying from the Marianas began a firebombing campaign against Japan, which culminated, for the moment, in a three-hundred-plane assault on Tokyo that left the city a blazing ruin.

American scientists and engineers prepared an even more devastating attack. In December 1944 Roosevelt received a briefing on the Manhattan Project from Leslie Groves, the commanding general of the atomic bomb program, and George Marshall. Groves and Marshall explained that the project's scientists and engineers had been pursuing two approaches to an atomic bomb. One approach, relying on the implosion of fissionable material, had appeared promising, in part because it required only a modest amount of the critical substance. Groves had hoped that an implosion bomb might be ready for use by the late spring of 1945. But technical difficulties emerged, necessitating a larger amount of fissionable material, which would require additional months to refine. "We should have sufficient material for the first implosion type bomb sometime in the latter part of July," Groves told Roosevelt. A small number of additional implosion bombs would follow.

The second kind of bomb would produce its explosion by firing part of the fissionable material at the other part. This "gun-type" bomb would produce a much larger blast—the equivalent of ten thousand tons of TNT, as opposed to five hundred tons with the implosion device. The first such bomb, Groves said, should be ready "about 1 August 1945." A second gun-type bomb would not be ready until the end of the year.

Roosevelt listened very carefully to the briefing. He probably didn't fathom all the technical details, but he understood perfectly the crucial matter of timing. The bomb makers weren't offering him anything usable before late July. Roosevelt knew enough about bureaucracies to guess that this was an optimistic forecast. The autumn of 1945 sounded more likely than the summer for the first use of an atomic bomb, assuming the complicated gizmo worked at all. Anything like a campaign of atomic bombing would probably have to wait until 1946 at the earliest.

❖   ❖   ❖

THIS ESTIMATE figured centrally in Roosevelt's thinking as he approached the second meeting of the leaders of the Grand Alliance. He had known since the previous summer that he needed to meet again with Stalin and Churchill to plan the final thrust against Germany, the sequel regarding Japan, and the future of the United Nations. But Stalin refused to leave the Soviet Union just as the war on the eastern front was turning decisively in Russia's favor, and Roosevelt was reluctant to stir up political trouble by traveling to the homeland of communism ahead of the election. Once the election was assured, however, he had Harry Hopkins quietly sound out the Soviet ambassador, Andrei Gromyko, as to where on Soviet soil Stalin would be willing to meet. Hopkins volunteered that the Crimean peninsula might be nice in winter. Stalin responded that the Crimea would be fine. "This was the first indication anyone around the President had that the President would even consider a conference in Russia," Hopkins remembered. "All of the President's close advisers were opposed to his going to Russia; most did not like or trust the Russians anyway and could not understand why the President of the United States should cart himself all over the world to meet Stalin."

But Roosevelt was determined to go. He wanted another opportunity to cultivate Stalin. He wasn't worried, after the election, about the political fallout. And he had never been to that part of Europe. Hopkins thought this last consideration decisive. "His adventurous spirit was forever leading him to go to unusual places," Hopkins said.

Churchill objected loudly. "He says that if we had spent ten years on research we could not have found a worse place than Yalta," Hopkins reported to Roosevelt. But the prime minister was outvoted, and after Roosevelt agreed to a pre-Yalta meeting with Churchill at British-controlled Malta, the prime minister acquiesced.

The Americans soon discovered the cause of Churchill's objections to Yalta. The town had been a health spa in the period when Roosevelt's father visited such places in search of relief from his heart condition. Its sheltered setting, nestled among mountains that kept out the frigid winds from the Ukrainian steppe while letting the low winter sun enter from the southern sky above the Black Sea, made it many degrees warmer than anything nearby. Russian czars built vacation palaces there; the Russian gentry bivouacked in somewhat lesser digs. The neighborhood declined after the execution of the last czar and the flight or extermination of most of the gentry, but the Soviet commissars and their favorites found use for some of the vestiges of the decadent capitalist order. The Livadia palace, constructed by Nicholas II, became to Russian tuberculosis patients under Stalin what Warm Springs was to polio patients under Roosevelt.

The German war was much harder on Yalta than the Soviet revolution had been. German theater commanders established their headquarters at the Livadia palace, but as the Red Army reclaimed the area, the Germans looted and gratuitously ravaged the palace and its environs. With other priorities, the Russian government made no attempt to restore the building, which fell further into disrepair. Rats and larger animals took over, bringing fleas and lice, which in turn brought diseases of various sorts, rendering the erstwhile showcase of the former health spa decidedly unhealthy.

No one thought much of the mess until mid-January 1945, when Roosevelt, Stalin, and Churchill scheduled their conference. Yalta thereupon received a crash rehabilitation. Soviet work crews cleared up the rubble in and around the Livadia. Dachas near Moscow were stripped of their furnishings to replace the pieces stolen or destroyed by the Nazis. Hotel staff were spirited away from other facilities and transported to the Crimea. In an exception to Soviet policy and philosophy, Stalin allowed U.S. navy medical crews to travel to Yalta to fumigate and sanitize the palace, where Roosevelt and the American contingent would be staying.

Roosevelt reached Yalta by sea, air, and land. A sea voyage carried him to Malta, where the British and American military staffs were comparing notes, coordinating plans, and generally prepping for their sessions with their Soviet counterparts. Roosevelt stayed at Malta long enough to have lunch and dinner with Churchill but not long enough to give Stalin more reason to suspect Anglo-American conspiracy. From Malta the Sacred Cow, well guarded by an escort of fighter planes, carried the president to Saki, the airfield nearest to Yalta but still eighty miles away. The road over the mountains to Yalta was endlessly winding and unnervingly narrow; it too was guarded, although perhaps not so well. The war obviously had depleted Russian ranks; many of the roadside guards were young girls.

Roosevelt arrived at night, and Stalin the next morning. Stalin and Molotov stopped by Roosevelt's rooms at the Livadia that afternoon. The three were joined only by their interpreters, Charles Bohlen and V. N. Pavlov. Roosevelt remarked that on the ship coming over he had made a number of bets on whether American forces would reach Manila before Soviet forces got to

Berlin. Stalin laughed and said he hoped the president had put his money on Manila. There was much hard fighting to be done between the Oder, where the eastern front currently ran, and the German capital.

Roosevelt replied that he had seen a sample of German rapacity on the road from Saki. As a result, he was "more bloodthirsty" than he had been the previous year at Teheran. He hoped the marshal would renew his call for "the execution of fifty thousand officers of the German army."

Stalin said everyone was more bloodthirsty than before. The destruction in the Crimea was minor compared with what the Germans had done in the Ukraine. The Germans were "savages and seemed to hate with a sadistic hatred the creative work of human beings," Stalin said. Roosevelt nodded agreement.

The president inquired as to how Stalin had gotten along with de Gaulle, who had visited Moscow several weeks earlier. Stalin said the French general was "unrealistic" about France's postwar role. "France had done little fighting and yet de Gaulle demanded "full rights" with the Americans, British, and Russians.

Roosevelt volunteered to be "indiscreet" with Stalin, saying he wanted to tell the marshal something he wouldn't say in front of Churchill. "The British for two years have had the idea of artificially building up France into a strong power which would have 200,000 troops on the eastern border of France to hold the line for the time required to assemble a strong British army." Roosevelt added, "The British are a peculiar people and wish to have their cake and eat it too."

Stalin asked Roosevelt whether he thought the French should have a zone of occupation in Germany, along with the Americans, Russians, and British.

Roosevelt said a zone for France was "not a bad idea," but it would be given "only out of kindness."

Stalin replied that kindness indeed would be the only reason to give France a sector of Germany.

Roosevelt and Stalin moved from the president's suite to the grand ballroom of the palace, where they were joined by Churchill and various members of their entourages. Stalin asked Roosevelt to open the formal conference, as he had done at Teheran. The president obliged, thanking the marshal for arranging the meeting in such a lovely and historic spot. He expressed his hope and expectation that the three leaders and their parties would get to know one another better during their week together. There was much ground to cover—"the whole map of Europe, in fact." But this afternoon, by agreement, the discussion would focus on the war against Germany.

Roosevelt turned to Stalin, who invited General Alexey Antonov, the deputy chief of the Russian general staff, to review the progress on the eastern front. Antonov provided great detail on the current and prospective operations of the Red Army, all of which appeared promising. They would be even more promising, he said, if the Americans and British would press harder in the west, in particular to prevent the transfer of any German units to the east.

George Marshall responded for the Anglo-Americans. He said the German bulge in the Ardennes, which had caused such concern a month earlier, had been eliminated. The Allied forces had pushed the front back to where it had been, and beyond. The American and British armies were nearing the Rhine, which they would cross in a few places as soon as they got there. But a broad offensive across the river would have to wait until the ice cleared, probably about March 1.

❖   ❖   ❖

*T*HE DISCUSSIONS turned to the settlement that would follow the war. The framework for the postwar United Nations organization had been worked out several months earlier at a conference at Dumbarton Oaks, a wooded estate near the embassy district of Washington. Representatives of the United States, Britain, the Soviet Union, and China had agreed that the organization would consist of a general assembly of most or all of the world's nations, and a security council controlled by the Big Four. Details of membership and voting were left to Roosevelt, Stalin, and Churchill to decide.

The first Yalta dinner—a typical Russian feast, albeit less elaborate than the meals at Teheran, since Roosevelt was the host—avoided business while the food was being served. "Marshal Stalin, the President, and the Prime Minister appeared to be in very good humor throughout," Bohlen observed. "No political or military subjects of any importance were discussed." Only at the end did substance intrude. Stalin reaffirmed his position from Teheran that the three great powers, which had borne the brunt of the war and liberated the smaller victims of Nazi aggression, should have "the unanimous right to preserve the peace of the world." Anything else would insult common sense. "It was ridiculous to believe that Albania would have an equal voice with the three great powers." Russia, Stalin said, would do its part to keep the peace. He was willing to work with the president and the prime minister to safeguard the rights of the smaller powers. But he would "never agree to having any action of any of the great powers submitted to the judgment of the small powers."

Roosevelt concurred. "The peace should be written by the three powers represented at this table," the president said.

Churchill didn't quite contradict Stalin and Roosevelt but recommended letting the lesser countries have their say. Reaching into his bag of proverbs, the prime minister declared, "The eagle should permit the small birds to sing, and care not wherefor they sang."

The fate of Europe provided the theme of the second day's discussions. The three military staffs had drawn a map of proposed occupation zones of Germany, to guide the planning for accepting a German surrender. The map gave an eastern zone, including Berlin, to the Soviet Union, a northwestern zone to Britain, and a southern and southwestern zone to the United States. Roosevelt circulated the map as a basis for discussion among the principals.

Stalin immediately pushed the discussion farther than Roosevelt had intended. The president was speaking of occupation zones, presumably temporary; Stalin said they should be talking about dismemberment, preferably permanent. The question had come up at Teheran, where, Stalin reminded Roosevelt and Churchill, they had concurred in principle that Germany should be broken up. "I would like to know, definitely," Stalin said: "Do we all agree? And if so, what form of dismemberment?" How would the dismembered pieces be governed? "Will each part have its own government?"

Roosevelt tried to slow things down. He said the questions of dismemberment and governance could be decided later, as they grew out of the experience of military occupation.

Churchill offered a middle course. "I think we are all agreed on dismemberment," he said, "but the actual method, the tracing of lines, is much too complicated a matter to settle here in five or six days. It requires very searching examination of geography, history, and economic facts. . . . If asked today, 'How would you divide Germany?,' I would not be able to answer."

Stalin thought Churchill was stalling. Delay could cause serious problems, he said. No one knew how long the war would last. "Events in Germany are developing rapidly toward a catastrophe for them. In view of such rapid events, we should not be without preparation." What would the terms of surrender be? Unconditional surrender had served well as a wartime slogan, but at war's end there would be terms, whether formally announced or not. For example, should the Germans be told that their country was to be dismembered?

Churchill didn't think so. "I see no need to inform the Germans at the time of surrender whether we will dismember them or not," he said. "It is enough to tell them, 'Await our decision as to your future.'"

"I think the Prime Minister's plan not to tell the Germans is risky," Stalin rejoined. To spring dismemberment on the Germans after surrender would put the political onus on the Allies. To include it in the formal surrender document would leave responsibility with the Germans, where it belonged.

Roosevelt sided with Stalin. "It will make it easier if it is in the terms and we tell them," the president said.

Churchill wasn't convinced. Telling the Germans in advance that their country would be divided up would make them fight harder. "Eisenhower doesn't want *that*," Churchill said. "We should not make this public."

Roosevelt didn't think the morale of the Germans was an issue at this late date. "My own feeling is that the people have suffered so much that they are beyond questions of psychological warfare."

Stalin agreed with Churchill on the matter of current confidentiality. "These conditions for the moment are only for us. They should *not* be public until the time of the surrender."

This settled the question for the time being. Roosevelt raised a related question, one he had spoken with Stalin about. Should France receive an occupation zone?

Churchill immediately said yes. "The French want a zone, and I am in favor of granting it to them," he said. "I would gladly give them part of the British zone."

Stalin objected, not only regarding the merits of France's claim, which he continued to dismiss as lacking, but regarding the example it might set. "Would it not be precedent for other states?" More important: "Would it not mean that the French become a fourth power in the control machinery for Germany?" Such an arrangement, he said, was unacceptable.

It wasn't unacceptable to Churchill. The French had occupied Germany earlier, after the First World War. "They do it very well, and would not be lenient," the prime minister asserted. There was another reason for bringing the French in: "We want to see their might grow to help keep Germany down. I do not know how long the United States will remain with us in occupation."

Stalin looked at Roosevelt. He knew, as Churchill knew, that the American role was the crux of the whole discussion of postwar Europe. Would the United States remain committed to European security? Everyone in the room followed Stalin's gaze to Roosevelt. "I should like to know the President's opinion," Stalin said.

Roosevelt certainly had considered the matter, but he hadn't yet articulated an answer. He spoke thoughtfully. "I can get the people and Congress to cooperate fully for peace," he said, "but not to keep an army in Europe a long time. Two years would be the limit."

❖ ❖ ❖

*N*EEDLESS TO SAY, this forecast wasn't included in the communiqué the three leaders issued at the midpoint of the conference. The fact of the Yalta meeting, like that of the previous top-level meetings, had been kept secret from the world. But with Germany on the ropes, Roosevelt, Stalin, and Churchill felt confident enough of their security to issue an interim announcement that they and their advisers were currently meeting "in the Black Sea area." The talks were progressing well. "There is complete agreement for joint military operations in the final phase of the war against Nazi Germany." Discussions of postwar security arrangements had begun. "These discussions will cover joint plans for the occupation and control of Germany, the political and economic problems of liberated Europe, and proposals for the earliest possible establishment of a permanent international organization to maintain peace."

Whether it was wise to raise expectations in this way soon provoked debate. But at the time the communiqué fairly reflected the mood at Yalta. Roosevelt, Stalin, and Churchill had fought through hard times together, and their goal was in sight. They had taken the measure of one another and developed a reciprocal respect. Each put his own country's interests first, but this was as it should be. Nor was it an impediment to peace, for the interests of the United States, Russia, and Britain overlapped sufficiently to allow the three governments to cooperate in the promotion of peace and security after the war. So it appeared, at any rate, at the beginning of February 1945.

The good feeling gave rise to a round of toasts at a dinner hosted by Stalin on February 8. The marshal—whom Bohlen characterized as "in an excellent humor and even in high spirits"—raised his glass to Churchill as "the bravest governmental figure in the world." The world owed the prime minister a debt. "Due in large measure to Mr. Churchill's courage and staunchness, England, when she stood alone, had divided the might of Hitlerite Germany when the rest of Europe was falling flat on its face."

Churchill responded in kind. He praised Marshal Stalin as "the mighty leader of a mighty country, which had taken the full shock of the German war machine, had broken its back, and had driven the tyrants from her soil." Looking ahead, Churchill prophesied, "In peace no less than in war, Marshal Stalin will continue to lead his people from success to success."

Stalin then toasted Roosevelt. Stalin said he himself and Churchill had had relatively simple decisions to make during the war. They had been fighting for their countries' existence. "But there was a third man, whose country had not been seriously threatened with invasion, but who had had perhaps a broader conception of national interest, and even though his country was not directly imperiled had been the chief forger of the instruments which had led to the mobilization of the world against Hitler."

Roosevelt replied that the atmosphere at this dinner was "that of a family," and he believed the same could be said of relations among their countries. "Great changes have occurred in the world during the last three years, and greater changes are to come. . . . Fifty years ago there were vast areas of the world where people had little opportunity and no hope, but much has been accomplished. . . . Our objectives here are to give to every man, woman, and child on earth the possibility of security and well-being."

Stalin raised his glass again. He said it was not so difficult to maintain unity during wartime. The joint desire to defeat the common enemy held the alliance together. "The difficult task comes after the war, when diverse interests tend to divide the allies." But he thought this alliance would meet the test of peace. "It is our duty to see that it does. . . . Our relations in peacetime should be as strong as they have been in war."

Churchill concluded with his trademark orotundity. "We are all standing on the crest of a hill with the glories of future possibilities stretching before us," the prime minister said. "In the modern world the function of leadership is to lead the people out from the forests onto the broad sunlit plains of peace and happiness. This prize is nearer our grasp than anytime before in history, and it would be a tragedy for which history would never forgive us if we let this prize slip from our grasp."

❖   ❖   ❖

THE FRIENDLY FEELING diminished a bit when the discussion turned to two especially sensitive subjects. Stalin insisted that the Ukraine, White Russia (Byelorussia), and perhaps Lithuania be seated in the United Nations general assembly. He didn't pretend that these Soviet "republics" were independent of Moscow; he simply wanted to balance what he presumed would be the pro-

American votes of several Latin American countries and probably the Philippines and the similarly pro-British votes of Canada, Australia, and other members of the Commonwealth. Roosevelt wasn't inclined to deny Stalin's demand, in part because he appreciated its rationale, in part because he didn't want to spoil the good mood at Yalta, and in part because he understood that votes in the assembly wouldn't really matter.

Yet he also understood that explaining any such concession, once he got home, wouldn't be easy. Roosevelt wanted to have things both ways in the United Nations: to keep power in the hands of the Big Four but to create the appearance of equal representation, at least in the general assembly. To rig the voting in the assembly would seem a subversion of international equality.

The president tried to put the issue off until a later date. He launched into a rambling account of the evolution of the British Commonwealth and of the various ways of measuring size and influence in international affairs. But his filibuster failed with Stalin, who patiently heard the president out and then reiterated his original position. The Kremlin eventually got two extra votes in the assembly—not three: Roosevelt did manage to remove Lithuania from the list. What he got in return was Stalin's agreement to support some extra votes for the United States in the assembly, if Washington desired them.

As ticklish as the issue of representation seemed at Yalta, its ramifications were nothing next to those involving Poland. The Polish question had emerged at Teheran but been filed among matters not currently urgent. By Yalta it had become most urgent. The Red Army had liberated Poland from Nazi control; the question now was whether Poland would be liberated from the Red Army. Most Poles demanded that it be, with ample reason. The Soviet government was denying responsibility for the 1940 massacre in the Katyn Forest of many thousands of Polish soldiers and civilians, whose bodies had been found by the Germans in 1943. The Kremlin claimed that the blood was on German hands (as the Kremlin would continue to claim for nearly fifty years). But many Poles knew that the Soviets had done the killing. They also knew that the Red Army had cynically sat across the Vistula River while the Nazis crushed an uprising of resistance forces in Warsaw during the summer of 1944. This time the Polish deaths were counted in the many scores of thousands, and the Russian role, albeit passive, was undeniable.

Two groups of Poles claimed to represent the reviving Polish nation. The self-appointed Polish government in exile in London was bitterly anti-Soviet; the Kremlin-appointed provisional government in Lublin was predictably pro-Soviet. The London Poles had the backing of the British and American governments and the impassioned support of Americans of Polish descent. The Lublin Poles enjoyed the endorsement of Stalin and the Red Army.

The immediate Polish problem at Yalta for Roosevelt, Stalin, and Churchill was to reconcile the two sets of claimants. The larger problem was to balance the desire of the United States and Britain to see democracy planted in Poland against the demand of the Soviet Union to secure its borders against future attack.

"I come from a great distance and therefore have the advantage of a more distant point of view of the problem," Roosevelt said, in raising the Polish question. But his was not a disinterested view, as he readily admitted. "There are six or seven million Poles in the United States." Nearly all of them had strong views on the Polish question. "Opinion in the United States is against recognition of the Lublin government, on the ground that it represents a small portion of the Polish people. What people want is the creation of a government of national unity, to settle their internal differences." Roosevelt suggested the establishment of a council of representatives from the London and Lublin groups, which would oversee the creation of a permanent government and the holding of elections. Yet the president assured Stalin he understood Russia's security concerns. "We want a Poland that will be thoroughly friendly to the Soviet Union for years to come. This is essential."

Churchill joined Roosevelt in advocating a government of national unity. The prime minister reminded Stalin that for the British Poland was a question of honor. Britain had gone to war with Germany over Poland; Britain could accept no less than a postwar Poland that was "free and independent."

Stalin responded that for Russia Poland was "not only a question of honor but also of security." For centuries Poland had been a corridor of attack on Russia. "During the last thirty years our German enemy has passed through this corridor twice. This is because Poland was weak." Stalin proposed that Poland be made strong. "It is not only a question of honor but of life and death for the Soviet state." Roosevelt and Churchill had said they wanted a national unity government for Poland; Stalin doubted that this could be established. The London Poles called the Lublin group "bandits" and "traitors," and "naturally the Lublin government paid the same coin to the London government." Stalin preferred the Lublin group on grounds of their service to the Allied war effort. "As a military man, I must say what I demand of a country liberated by the Red Army. First, there should be peace and quiet in the wake of the army. The men of the Red Army are indifferent as to what kind of government there is in Poland, but they do want one that will maintain order behind the lines."

The Lublin group did that. As for the Londoners, they called themselves resistance fighters, but what they resisted was Poland's liberation. "We have had nothing good from them, but much evil. So far their agents have killed 212 Russian military men. They have attacked supply bases for arms. . . . If they attack the Red Army any more, they will be shot."

❖ ❖ ❖

ℛoosevelt, Churchill, and Stalin eventually reconciled their positions on most issues at Yalta, but the composition of the Polish government formed a persistent stumbling block. Roosevelt appealed to Stalin personally. "I am greatly disturbed that the three great powers do not have a meeting of minds about the political setup in Poland," Roosevelt said in a note to Stalin. "It seems to me that it puts us all in a bad light throughout the world to have you recognizing one government while we and the British are recognizing another. . . . I am sure this state of affairs should not continue, and that if it does it can only lead our people to think there is a breach between us, which is not the case. I am determined that there shall be no breach between ourselves and the Soviet Union. Surely there is a way to reconcile our differences."

Roosevelt suggested one such way. He conceded Stalin's right to worry about the safety of the Red Army as the Soviet troops pushed toward Berlin. "You cannot, and we must not, tolerate any temporary government which will give your armed forces any trouble." But the marshal must take account of the president's political concerns. "You must believe me when I tell you that our people at home look with a critical eye on what they consider a disagreement between us at this vital stage of the war. They, in effect, say that if we cannot get a meeting of minds now, when our armies are converging on the common enemy, how can we get an understanding on even more vital things in the future?"

Roosevelt recommended a meeting of minds via a banging of heads. Stalin had said he would be willing to bring some of the Lublin Poles to Yalta. Roosevelt proposed that he and Churchill prevail on some representatives of the Londoners to come, too. Doubtless recalling the shotgun ceremony between de Gaulle and Giraud, the president imagined the two Polish parties, with appropriate encouragement from their sponsors, agreeing on a provisional government consisting of elements of both sides. "It goes without saying," Roosevelt added—precisely because it did *not* go without saying—"that any interim government which could be formed as a result of our conference with the Poles here would be pledged to the holding of free elections in Poland at the earliest possible date. I know this is completely consistent with your desire to see a new free and democratic Poland emerge from the welter of this war."

Stalin declined to answer this letter. Perhaps his offer to bring the Lubliners hadn't been serious. Perhaps he feared being forced to compromise if the Londoners came. Perhaps he realized the Londoners would rather have met the devil in hell than Stalin at Yalta. The best he would do was allow the Londoners to travel to Moscow at a later date, to talk with the Lubliners.

Stalin realized he held the trump card in his negotiations with Roosevelt. While the president was speaking with Stalin and Churchill, the American chiefs of staff were meeting with their British and Soviet counterparts. The British were open and forthright, as were the Soviets on matters relating to Europe. But the Soviet generals refused even to talk about the other half of America's—and Britain's—war: the conflict with Japan. George Marshall and the American strategists were already laying plans for shifting the focus of American efforts to the Pacific; essential to their planning was knowledge of what the Soviets were going to do against the Japanese. Marshall and the American chiefs envisaged an invasion of the Japanese home islands sometime after the middle of 1945; they earnestly hoped that the Soviet Union would have declared war on Japan by then and would have moved substantial forces from Europe to the Far East. If Soviet units pinned down large parts of the Japanese army, many thousands of American lives would be saved and many months of fighting would be averted. Stalin had declared unspecifically at Teheran that the Soviet Union would join the war against Japan after Germany was defeated. Marshall and the chiefs needed to confirm this commitment and attach a date to it.

The Soviet timetable was the crucial issue for Roosevelt at Yalta—more immediate than voting procedures in the United Nations assembly, more pressing than the makeup of the Polish government. Those were details of the peace; Soviet entry into the conflict against Japan was a matter of the war, which still claimed priority. Roosevelt understood this, which was why he wouldn't push Stalin any harder on Poland. Stalin knew it, which was why *he* stood his ground.

❖ ❖ ❖

*T*HE CONFERENCE ended with a communiqué summarizing the successes of the talks and disguising their failures. The former included close collaboration regarding the final stages of the war in Europe. "Nazi Germany is doomed," the tripartite statement asserted. "The German people will only make the cost of their defeat heavier to themselves by attempting to continue a hopeless resistance." An enigmatically worded pair of sentences explained that the three governments continued to agree on "unconditional surrender terms" toward Germany but that "these terms will not be made known until the final defeat of Germany has been accomplished." The Big Three tipped their hand far enough to say that each of their armies would occupy a zone of Germany and that France would be invited to occupy a zone as well. The communiqué forecast harsh treatment of the Nazi party and the German war machine but said nothing about dismemberment.

On the United Nations, the three governments kicked the matter of representation and voting down the road—specifically, to San Francisco, where a meeting would begin in April to draft a charter of the United Nations organization along the lines established at Dumbarton Oaks. China and France would join the United States, the Soviet Union, and Britain as sponsors.

The Yalta "Declaration on Liberated Europe" reaffirmed "our faith in the principles of the Atlantic Charter" and "our determination to build, in cooperation with other peace-loving nations, a world order under law, dedicated to peace, security, freedom, and the general well-being of all mankind."

Poland rated a section of its own. "We reaffirm our common desire to see established a strong, free, independent and democratic Poland," the communiqué asserted. A provisional government for Poland should be established, including both the Lublin Poles and the London Poles. "This Polish Provisional Government of National Unity shall be pledged to the holding of free and unfettered elections as soon as possible on the basis of universal suffrage and secret ballot."

The communiqué was released from Yalta to an understandably curious world. What was *not* released was more important to Roosevelt than what was. A secret codicil declared:

> The leaders of the three Great Powers—the Soviet Union, the United States of America and Great Britain—have agreed that in two or three months after Germany has surrendered and the war in Europe has terminated, the Soviet Union shall enter into the war against Japan.

56.

"It was the best I could do," Roosevelt told Adolf Berle on his return from Yalta. The Soviet commitment to the war against Japan was vital, allowing American military planners to move ahead confidently, knowing they'd have the help of the Red Army in taking on the Japanese. Stalin's promise of free elections in Poland might prove hard to enforce; Roosevelt was enough of a Democrat to know the means by which his own party prevented free elections in the American South, and he assumed that Stalin was at least as clever as that. But the mere promise was more than Roosevelt could have demanded, given Russia's existing control of Poland. And it was more than Churchill was offering India or the rest of the British empire. Perhaps Roosevelt made too much of personal trust among the leaders of governments, but what was his alternative? The United States couldn't dictate the actions of the Soviet Union. It lacked the manpower and the political will. The only feasible option was to encourage decent behavior by the Kremlin, and the most likely way of doing this was to cultivate the Kremlin's master. "I didn't say it was good," Roosevelt continued, in his Yalta summary to Berle. "I said it was the best I could do."

There was something on Roosevelt's mind the communiqué and codicil didn't address. At one of the Yalta sessions, Stalin alluded to the mortality of the three leaders. They all understood, he said, that as long as they lived, they would not involve their countries in aggressive actions. They had experienced war and would do what was necessary to prevent its repetition. But times, and leaders, would change. "Ten years from now, none of us might be present," Stalin said.

Roosevelt didn't have ten years, and he knew it. He didn't have more than four years, since he certainly couldn't run for president again. He might have much less. At Yalta he carried on through force of will, but he felt his strength ebbing. The 1944 election campaign had revived him, but it also wore him out. He lost his appetite and lost more weight. His doctors removed all restrictions from his diet, and he was fed eggnogs to fatten him up. Yet he didn't respond. "The President has lost ten pounds in the last two to three months and is, I think, rather worried about it," his cousin Daisy Suckley wrote in her diary on Thanksgiving Day. "He looked very thin today, and his aches and pains worry me." At the end of November, Roosevelt went to Warm Springs. His appetite improved, but his weight remained unchanged at 165 pounds. One of his molars became painfully loose and was extracted. He visited with friends and drove about the neighborhood. In early December he took a swim. The warm water seemed to relax him. But on leaving the water his blood pressure was higher than ever: 260 over 150. Though encouraged to eat, he complained that he couldn't taste anything and he lost more weight.

The Christmas holidays saw little improvement. "I had quite a talk with Anna about her father's health," Daisy Suckley wrote. "It is a very difficult problem, and I am entirely convinced that he can *not* keep up the present rate—he will kill himself if he tries." Roosevelt put on the paterfamilias role for a gathering of the grandchildren, but he couldn't maintain the pose. "As the evening wore on, he seemed to me to be terribly tired and to be making an effort even in ordinary conversation."

January brought the inauguration. The war and the president's condition suggested a small ceremony, which was held at the White House rather than the Capitol. The day was cold, with snow on the ground, but Roosevelt insisted on giving his inaugural address without hat or overcoat. His spirits rose on the day's excitement; he was in fine form at the reception that evening.

He remained in good spirits during the long journey to Yalta. The plane ride from Malta to Saki caused him some discomfort, on account of the noise and vibration, but he enjoyed the five-hour car trip from the airport at Saki to Yalta.

His health held up during the conference, despite the enormous pressure attending the talks. On one occasion, however, the tension told. He had been going back and forth with Stalin over Poland, and though he maintained his good humor during the session, he came out drained. "He was obviously greatly fatigued," Howard Bruenn noted. "His color was very poor (gray)." For the first time, Roosevelt exhibited *pulsus alternans,* a regular variability in the amplitude of the pulse indicating failure of the left ventricle. Bruenn was alarmed and ordered that the president's schedule be cut back. Roosevelt saw no visitors before noon, and he took a rest of at least an hour every evening before dinner. His condition stabilized, and the new symptoms went away.

Yet those who saw him daily wondered how long he had left. He appeared "very tired," in Churchill's estimate. "The President seemed placid and frail. I felt that he had a slender contact with life." The most widely circulated photograph from the Crimean conference showed him sitting almost ghostlike between the full-cheeked Churchill and the ruddy Stalin.

The sea journey home allowed time for rest. Roosevelt spent an hour or two on deck every day and enjoyed his contact with the officers and men. The surprise casualty of the voyage was Pa Watson, who died suddenly of a stroke. Watson had been at Roosevelt's right hand for years, and his passing was a blow. "Franklin feels his death very much," Daisy Suckley observed, after he reached America.

❖   ❖   ❖

HE MAY HAVE felt his own death approaching. On his arrival in Washington, Roosevelt threw himself into preparing his report to Congress. He worked a full schedule during the day and often into the night. His appetite failed again, as he complained once more of not being able to taste his food. He lost additional weight and grew more haggard.

His appearance before Congress occasioned further concern. For the first time he addressed the legislators from his wheelchair, for the first time spoke of his disability, and for the first time acknowledged fatigue. "I hope that you will pardon me for this unusual posture of sitting down during the presentation of what I want to say," he began. "But I know that you will realize that it makes it a lot easier for me not to have to carry about ten pounds of steel around on the bottom of my legs; and also because of the fact that I have just completed a fourteen-thousand-mile trip." He looked around the chamber almost wistfully. "It is good to be home. It has been a long journey."

He conceded feeling under the weather. But warming to his audience, he turned his illness into a joke. "I was well the entire time. I was not ill for a second, until I arrived back in Washington, and there I heard all of the rumors which had occurred in my absence."

He let the chuckles subside before turning to the heart of his message. There were two main goals of the Yalta conference, he said. The first was to arrange the defeat of Germany as quickly as possible. The second was to ensure the international cooperation that would render the postwar settlement secure and lasting. Toward both goals, he was pleased to say, the conference had made important progress. "Never before have the major Allies been more closely united, not only in their war aims but also in their peace aims. And they are determined to continue to be united with each other, and with all peace-loving nations, so that the ideal of lasting peace will become a reality."

Roosevelt said nothing about the Soviet commitment to enter the Pacific war. Indeed, to avoid tipping off the Japanese, the president prevaricated. "This conference concerned itself only with the European war and with the political problems of Europe, and not with the Pacific war," he asserted. And he painted the Polish question in brighter colors than he knew it deserved. The Yalta promise of free elections in Poland was an "outstanding example of joint action by the three major Allied powers," he said.

Perhaps he sensed he wouldn't be addressing the legislators again. Perhaps he simply wanted to reiterate the point he had been making since 1937—the lesson he had learned after the last war. He departed from his text to talk from the heart.

> The conference in the Crimea was a turning point, I hope, in our history and therefore in the history of the world. There will soon be presented to the Senate of the United States and to the American people a great decision that will determine the fate of the United States and of the world for generations to come. There can be no middle ground here. We shall have to take the responsibility for world collaboration, or we shall have to bear the responsibility for another world conflict. . . .
>
> For the second time in the lives of most of us, this generation is face to face with the objective of preventing wars. To meet that objective, the nations of the world will either have a plan or they will not. The groundwork of a plan has now been furnished, and has been submitted to humanity for discussion and decision. No plan is perfect. Whatever is adopted at San Francisco will doubtless have to be amended time and again over the years, just as our own Constitution has been. No one can say exactly how long any plan will last. Peace can endure only so long as humanity really insists upon it, and is willing to work for it—and sacrifice for it.
>
> Twenty-five years ago, American fighting men looked to the statesmen of the world to finish the work of peace for which they fought and suffered. We failed them then. We cannot fail them again.

❖   ❖   ❖

UNUSUALLY FOR a Roosevelt speech, his address to Congress read better than it sounded. He hesitated in his presentation and appeared to struggle at times for words. "I did not think it a particularly good speech," the faithful William Hassett conceded. "The President ad-libbed at length—a wretched practice that weakens even a better effort." But Howard Bruenn accepted Roosevelt's explanation that, after departing from his prepared text to lend a personal tone to his comments, he had lost his place coming back.

Yet the symptoms of decline persisted. His color was worse than ever, and he was constantly tired. He agreed to follow Bruenn's advice to go to Warm Springs and rest there as long as necessary for his condition to improve.

William Hassett had watched Roosevelt closely for months. "Tonight had another talk with Howard Bruenn about the President's health," he recorded on March 30.

> I said: "He is slipping away from us, and no earthly power can keep him here."
>
> Bruenn demurred. "Why do you think so?" he asked.
>
> Told him I understood his position—his obligation to save life, not to admit defeat. Then I reminded him that I gave him the same warning when we were here in December. He remembered. I said: "I know you don't want to make the admission, and I have talked this way with no one else save one. To all the staff, to the family, and with the Boss himself I have maintained the bluff; but I am convinced that there is no help for him."
>
> Bruenn very serious. . . . He wanted to know how long I had had this feeling. I told him for a year, but worried particularly because of the Boss's indifference after the Chicago convention—didn't act like a man who cared a damn about the election.

Hassett noted that the Republican tactics in the 1944 campaign had reengaged Roosevelt. "F.D.R. got his Dutch up. That did the trick. He got madder and madder over Dewey's technique." But the improvement didn't last much beyond the election.

> I could not but notice his increasing weariness as I handled his papers with him, particularly at Hyde Park, trip after trip. He was always willing to go through the day's routine, but there was less and less talk about all manner of things—fewer local Hyde Park stories, politics, books, pictures. The old zest was going.
>
> I told Bruenn I had every confidence in his own skill; was satisfied that the Boss was the beneficiary of everything that the healing art can devise. I couldn't suggest anything which should be done differently. But in my opin-

ion the Boss was beyond all human resources. I mentioned his feeble signature—the old boldness of stroke and liberal use of ink gone, signature often ending in a fade-out.

He said that not important. Reluctantly admitted the Boss in a precarious condition, but his condition not hopeless. He could be saved if measures were adopted to rescue him from certain mental strains and emotional influences, which he mentioned.

I told him that his conditions could not be met and added that this talk confirmed my conviction that the Boss is leaving us.

For several days Bruenn seemed the better forecaster. Spring had arrived in Georgia, with warm days and cool nights. Roosevelt responded to the old place, and his appetite and energy returned. He spoke with friends and toured the countryside in his open car. He attended Easter services on April 1. On April 9 he had himself driven the eighty-five miles to Macon, where he met Lucy Rutherfurd and artist Elizabeth Shoumatoff, coming over from Aiken, South Carolina. Shoumatoff had painted his portrait and wanted to paint another. The two women joined Roosevelt and Daisy Suckley for the ride back to Warm Springs. Daisy wished they hadn't gone so far. "The drive was too long," she wrote that evening. "F. was chilly and looked awfully tired all evening."

But Howard Bruenn was quietly encouraged. "His color was much better, and his appetite was very good," the physician wrote on April 10. "He asked for double helpings of food." Roosevelt seemed to be gaining weight, although he wasn't actually weighed. He was sleeping well. He laid plans for a busy weekend, including a barbecue. He attended to the details sufficiently to remark that he had never liked barbecued pork; he told Hassett to request that the manager of the Warm Springs Hotel rustle up the ingredients for Brunswick stew—"preceded by an Old-fashioned cocktail." On a drive about the grounds he encountered reporter Merriman Smith, who was on horseback. "His voice was wonderful and resonant," Smith recalled. "It sounded like the Roosevelt of old. In tones that must have been audible a block away, Roosevelt hailed me with, 'Heigh-o, Silver!' " To Henry Morgenthau, visiting on Treasury business, the president described his intention to open the United Nations conference in San Francisco in two weeks. "I have been offered a beautiful apartment by a lady in the top floor of some hotel, but I am not taking it," he said. "I am going there on my train, and at three o'clock in the afternoon I will appear on the stage in my wheelchair, and I will make the speech. And then they will applaud me, and I will leave and go back on my train. . . . I will be back in Hyde Park on May first."

❖   ❖   ❖

"*I*N THE QUIET beauty of the Georgia spring, like a thief in the night, came the day of the Lord," Hassett wrote on April 12. "Of course I had seen it coming for all too long, but little thought the end so near."

Roosevelt awoke just after nine. Bruenn conducted the morning examination. "He had slept well but complained of a slight headache and some stiffness of the neck," Bruenn noted. "He ascribed this to a soreness of the muscles." Bruenn gave him a light massage, which alleviated the symptoms. "He had a very good morning." Daisy thought Roosevelt seemed better than in many days. "He came in, looking very fine in a double-breasted grey suit and a crimson tie," she wrote in her diary for that day. "His color was good, and he looked smiling and happy and ready for anything."

Hassett saw things differently. "He was in good spirits but did not look well," Hassett recorded. "Color bad; countenance registered great weariness." Hassett left the president's cottage to attend to minor business. The official pouch from Washington was late arriving and didn't reach the compound until after noon. There was a large volume of mail, which Hassett carried up to the president's cottage. "Was shocked at the President's appearance," he wrote. Elizabeth Shoumatoff was sketching Roosevelt, measuring his nose and other features, asking him to turn this way and that and generally—as Hassett interpreted the situation—making a pest of herself. "Altogether too aggressive," Hassett remarked. Roosevelt was being patient, but with effort. "The President looked so fatigued and weary. . . . When I left the cottage, I was fully resolved to ask Bruenn to put an end to this unnecessary hounding of a sick man."

Roosevelt didn't notice Hassett's concern. The president was seated at a table going through the mail. Lucy and Daisy occupied a sofa across the room. Daisy was crocheting; the two women chatted idly between themselves and with Roosevelt. Arthur Prettyman, Roosevelt's longtime valet, and Joe Esperancilla, Prettyman's helper, were putting out lunch. "We have fifteen minutes more to work," the president told Shoumatoff.

Suddenly a strange expression came over his face. His head tilted toward the table, and his hands began to fumble among the letters. Daisy thought he was trying to find something.

I went forward and looked into his face. "Have you dropped your cigarette?" He looked at me with his forehead furrowed in pain and tried to smile. He put his left hand up to the back of his head and said, "I have a terrific pain in the back of my head."

He slumped over and lost consciousness.

Prettyman and Esperancilla carried Roosevelt into his bedroom. Daisy called the Warm Springs operator and told her to locate Bruenn and send him at once. The doctor arrived in ten minutes and found Roosevelt pale, unconscious, and cold, but sweating profusely. His heart rate was 96 beats per minute, and his blood pressure 300 over 190. Mild spasms caused his body to twitch periodically. His right pupil was greatly dilated, suggesting bleeding in the brain. "It was apparent that the President had suffered a massive cerebral hemorrhage," Bruenn recorded. The cardiologist administered papavarine and amylnitrite, to ease the constriction of the blood vessels. He called Ross McIntire in Washington and explained the situation. McIntire immediately phoned another specialist, James Paullin, a consultant to the navy on Roosevelt's case and others, in Atlanta.

Bruenn monitored Roosevelt's condition during the next hour. The president rallied slightly. His color improved and his blood pressure fell to 210 over 110.

But then the left pupil began to dilate. Roosevelt's respiration slowed considerably, and he became cyanotic—his skin began turning blue, starting with the fingertips, from lack of oxygen.

At 3:30, Bruenn noted that Roosevelt's breathing was irregular yet fairly strong. Within the minute, though, the president stopped breathing. He gasped a few times, but then the gasps too ceased. Bruenn listened for a heartbeat but heard nothing. He attempted artificial respiration without effect. He injected Roosevelt with caffeine sodium benzoate in a skeletal muscle, and then adrenalin directly into the heart muscle. Neither restored the heart's action. At this point Dr. Paullin arrived from Atlanta.

But there was nothing he could do, either. At 3:35 Bruenn pronounced Roosevelt dead.

57.

$\mathcal{T}$HE NEWS HIT AMERICA LIKE NOTHING SINCE PEARL HARBOR. THE White House announced the death as rush hour that Thursday evening was beginning on the East Coast. Riders on buses and trolleys heard rumors and stepped off to confirm them; straphangers clambered out of the subway tunnels to ask policemen and passersby if the reports were true. In residential neighborhoods women left dinners cooking on their stoves to meet neighbors at the street corners and share their shock. Restaurants closed early that evening. Some bars did the same; other stayed open to let their patrons drown their sorrow. Concert halls, theaters, and clubs canceled performances. At New York's Stage Door Canteen, the director of *The Seven Lively Arts Show* came on stage during the early performance and signaled for the orchestra to stop playing. "I have a terrible announcement to make," he said. "Out of respect to the memory of the President of the United States, this show cannot go on." The audience had arrived before the tragic news was broadcast, and they looked at one another with puzzled expressions. "The President has just died," the director explained, to gasps throughout the house.

The four major radio networks suspended commercial programming. The New York Stock Exchange announced that it would be closed the next day in the president's honor. Early-season baseball games were canceled. Flags on government buildings dipped to half-staff. Fire departments sounded their alarms in the "four fives," the fireman's requiem. Church bells tolled. Moments of silence—some organized, some spontaneous—were observed on military bases, in government offices, in shops and businesses, at schools.

Men and women wept openly. "No matter what your politics, he was a great man and a good man," a New Yorker declared, wiping the tears from his cheeks. An older gentleman in Washington said he felt "as though I had died myself." A woman in the capital particularly mourned the timing. "If only he could have lived until after Germany falls," she said.

Soldiers took the news especially hard. " 'My God!' was the immediate and almost universal reaction," a journalist with the Third Army in Germany recorded. "Most could say no more." But a few did say more. "I can remember the president ever since I was a little kid," a private first class from Kentucky explained. "America will seem a strange, empty place without his voice talking to the people whenever great events occur. He died fighting for democracy, the same as any soldier." A private with the Seventh Army said, "I couldn't believe such a thing could happen. President Roosevelt was so important to us, I can hardly believe he is gone." An army air forces officer shook his head. "I feel just like we had lost the war," he declared. "That's how bad I feel." A tank sergeant on leave in Paris responded with redoubled determination. He immediately contacted his superior officer and demanded permission to return to the front at once. "I voted for him four times for president," he said. "Since I can't vote for him the fifth time, the least I can do is go back up there and fight for him." This Roosevelt loyalist refused to give the reporter his name, insisting on being identified as "just one of his fighting Joes."

World leaders registered heartfelt admiration for the deceased and concern at what his passing implied. A Chinese government spokesman said that Chiang Kai-shek was "visibly stunned" on hearing of the death. Georges Bidault, the French foreign minister, called it "a great disaster." Charles de Gaulle declared, "I am more shocked than I can say. It is a terrible loss not only for our country and me personally but for all human-kind." Stalin lamented the departure of "the leader in the cause of ensuring the security of the whole world."

In London, Churchill's dismay was revealed in unaccustomed brevity. He addressed Commons:

> The House will have heard, with the deepest sorrow, the grievous news which has come to us from across the Atlantic, which conveys to us the loss of the famous president of the United States, whose friendship for the cause of freedom and for the cause of the weak and poor has won him immortal fame. It is not fitting that we should continue our work this day.

The House thereupon adjourned.

Remembrance took various forms in other countries. France observed a national day of mourning, an honor never before accorded anyone not French. Schools in France spent the day teaching the life and achievements of Franklin Roosevelt. Courts and schools in Italy closed to honor the liberator of Italy

from fascism. Crowds gathered on the streets and in the metro stations of
Moscow, wondering what the news from America meant for Russia. In Scotland 130,000 soccer fans stood bare-headed and silent during a Glasgow match,
mourning the father of Lend-Lease and the architect of the Grand Alliance. A
spokesman for the Mexican government called Roosevelt's death "an irreparable loss, not only to the United States but to the whole world." In Ha-
vana, President Ramón Grau San Martín asserted, "Cuba has lost a great
friend." The prime minister of New Zealand called Roosevelt's death "a colossal loss to mankind." The Australian government issued a statement: "He gave
everything to the cause of freedom and liberty and did not spare himself."

The Axis governments responded ambivalently. The new Japanese prime
minister, Kantaro Suzuki, conveyed his "profound sympathy" to the American people, even while adding, "I must admit Roosevelt's leadership has been
very effective and has been responsible for the Americans' advantageous position today." In Berlin, the Nazi propaganda machine required a day to get its
orders from Joseph Goebbels. But once it did, it applauded the death of the
"war criminal" Roosevelt as a "miracle," on the order of the Führer's survival
of the bombing attempt against his life the previous summer.

❖ ❖ ❖

ELEANOR ROOSEVELT WAS holding her regular press conference that
Thursday morning in Washington. She had been worried about Franklin for
months. "He should gain weight but hates his food," she wrote a friend. "I say
a prayer daily that he may be able to carry on till we have peace and our feet
are set in the right direction." The road to peace, Eleanor judged, ran through
San Francisco, where America would join with the other countries to establish
the permanent structure of international security. At her press conference she
fielded questions implying that the United States could somehow dictate policy to the United Nations. She knew from talking to Franklin about Yalta that
this wasn't so, and she tried to disabuse reporters of the concept. "We will have
to get over the habit of saying what we as a single nation will do," she said.
"When we say 'we' on international questions in the future, we will mean all
the people who have an interest in the question."

That afternoon she was meeting with a State Department adviser to the
delegation the administration was planning to send to San Francisco when
she was summoned to the telephone. Laura Delano was calling from Warm
Springs saying that Franklin had fainted. He was currently in bed and under

Dr. Bruenn's care. Eleanor tactfully closed the meeting and called Ross McIntire. The admiral-doctor tried not to sound alarmed, and he suggested that she proceed with her afternoon schedule but fly with him to Warm Springs afterward. An abrupt cancellation would cause people to talk, perhaps needlessly.

She drove to an annual benefit for a thrift shop run by the Sulgrave Club, near Dupont Circle. She welcomed those attending and urged them to support this worthy cause. She had just finished speaking when a call came from the White House. Steve Early asked her to return to the mansion at once. "I did not even ask why," she remembered. "I knew down in my heart that something dreadful had happened." She apologized to her hosts without sharing her forebodings. "I got into the car and sat with clenched hands all the way to the White House. In my heart of hearts I knew what had happened, but one does not actually formulate these terrible thoughts until they are spoken."

At the White House, Early and McIntire explained that the president had died. Eleanor wasn't surprised, and she maintained her composure. "I am more sorry for the people of the country and the world than I am for us," she said. She thought of the children. Anna was with her and heard the news directly. Eleanor cabled the sad tidings to the boys: Elliott in Europe, and James, Franklin Jr., and John in the Pacific. "Father slept away," she said. "He would expect you to carry on and finish your jobs."

Harry Truman had been summoned to the White House at the same time as Eleanor. The vice president was now shown into the First Lady's sitting room. "Harry," she said, "the President is dead."

Truman, like so many others that day, was stunned. He required a few moments to find words. "Is there anything I can do for you?" he said.

"Is there anything *we* can do for *you*?" she responded. "You are the one in trouble now."

A short while later reporters saw her leave the White House. "Mrs. Roosevelt's tall figure was erect, and her step did not falter," one of them wrote. "A trouper to the last," another remarked.

❖   ❖   ❖

*A*s SOON AS Roosevelt was stricken that afternoon, Lucy Rutherfurd knew she had to get away from Warm Springs at once. A presidential collapse—still more a presidential death, should it come to that—would be huge news. A first question reporters would ask would be who was with the president that

day. People around Roosevelt had been covering up for her—and for him—
for years. She didn't want to make their task any more difficult.

She quickly gathered her things and drove off. She was back in Aiken before Eleanor arrived in Warm Springs from Washington. Whether Eleanor had
an inkling that all wasn't as it seemed or whether she simply asked what the reporters were asking, Laura Delano couldn't lie to her cousin's widow. She said
that Lucy had been with the president in Warm Springs. She went on to say
that Lucy had seen the president several times in Washington, with Anna's assistance.

The revelation was numbing. Eleanor had been preparing herself for bad
news since the war began. "I had schooled myself to believe that some or all of
my sons might be killed, and I had long faced the fact that Franklin might be
killed or die at any time." But she admitted, in her memoirs, that this grim anticipation didn't explain what she felt now. She didn't mention Lucy by name,
but those who knew of the relationship could read between the lines of what
Eleanor did write.

> Perhaps it was that much further back I had had to face certain difficulties
> until I decided to accept the fact that a man must be what he is, life must be
> lived as it is. . . . You cannot live at all if you do not learn to adapt yourself to
> your life as it happens to be. All human beings have failings; all human be-
> ings have temptations and stresses. Men and women who live together
> through long years get to know one another's failings, but they also come to
> know what is worthy of respect and admiration in those they live with and
> in themselves.
>
> If at the end one can say: "This man used to the limit the powers that
> God granted him; he was worthy of love and respect and of the sacrifices of
> many people, made in order that he might achieve what he deemed to be his
> task," then that life has been lived well and there are no regrets.

❖   ❖   ❖

ROOSEVELT HAD planned to go to San Francisco; instead he went home. A
military contingent from Fort Benning drove to Warm Springs to salute the
deceased president and escort the body to the train station. As the flag-draped
casket made its way down Pine Mountain, old-timers wept while the younger
staff and neighbors stared in somber silence. The funeral train pulled out of
the station before noon, commencing the slow journey north.

Across Georgia, the Carolinas, and Virginia, mourners lined the route. Men and women, grandparents and toddlers, white and black, waited in daylight and in the dark to pay their respects to the only president the younger ones had ever known, the president who had made them all feel that the government of their country cared for them. He had given them reassurance during the most frightening phase of the depression, and confidence during the most trying days of the war.

It had been a remarkable accomplishment, reflecting a unique bond between the president and the American people. They put their faith in Roosevelt because *he* put *his* faith in *them*. He believed in democracy—in the capacity of ordinary Americans, exercising their collective judgment, to address the ills that afflicted their society. He refused to rely on the invisible hand of the marketplace, for the compelling reason that during his lifetime the invisible hand had wreaked very visible havoc on millions of unoffending Americans. He refused to accept that government invariably bungled whatever it attempted, and his refusal inspired government efforts that had a tremendous positive effect on millions of marginal farmers, furloughed workers, and struggling merchants—the very people who now lined his train route north.

Did he get everything right? By no means, and he never claimed he did. But he got a great deal right. He caught the banking system in free fall and guided it to a soft landing. He sponsored rules that helped prevent a recurrence of the banking collapse and of the stock market crash that preceded it. The programs his administration formulated furnished jobs and experience to much of a generation of young people. He helped the parents of these young people keep their homes and farms. He showed their grandparents that old age need not be accompanied by poverty. He gave workers a hand in their efforts to rebalance relations between labor and capital.

Beyond everything else, he provided hope. He didn't end the Great Depression, which was too large and complex for any elected official to conquer. But he banished the despair the depression had engendered. He understood intuitively—or perhaps he learned from Uncle Ted and Woodrow Wilson—that the presidency is above all a moral office. A president who speaks to the hopes and dreams of the people can change the nation. Roosevelt did speak to the people's hopes and dreams, and together they changed America.

They changed the world as well. Just as he trusted democracy to reach the right decisions regarding America, so he trusted democracy to reach the right decisions about the rest of the planet, if perhaps more slowly. He concluded, long before most other Americans did, that the United States must take responsibility for the defeat of international aggression. Yet he understood that he was merely president, not a czar, and that until Americans came to share his view any efforts to intervene in the struggles unfolding in Europe and Asia would be worse than wasted. He patiently, and sometimes deceptively, guided American opinion, through public statements and carefully measured actions, until the leader became the led and the country demanded what he had wanted—what he knew the country needed—all along.

His performance during the war was no more perfect than his New Deal policies had been. The fiasco of Pearl Harbor was neither a crime nor a conspiracy, but it was a fiasco nonetheless. The insufficient coordination of America's war production impeded the efforts of the armies of the Grand Alliance. The repeated delays in opening the second front antagonized the Russians and perhaps prolonged the war.

But even more than in domestic matters, he got the big issues right. He held the alliance together. Contemporaries and historians often credited Hitler with providing the cement that kept Americans, British, and Russians working in concert. That assessment wasn't wrong, but it was incomplete. Without Roosevelt to mediate between Churchill and Stalin, to dole out American supplies in sufficient quantities to keep the British and Russians fighting, the alliance might have splintered before the Axis did. Did Stalin trust Roosevelt? Probably not; the Soviet dictator hadn't gotten to where he was by trusting others. But the more important question was whether he trusted Roosevelt's judgment—Roosevelt's judgment of the degree to which American and Russian interests coincided during the war and would continue to coincide after the war. The evidence suggests that Stalin did trust Roosevelt's judgment. He tolerated the backsliding on the second front, and he had little difficulty coming to terms with the president on the fate of Germany.

Did Roosevelt trust Stalin? Probably more than the reverse. But if the president was less cynical than the Soviet strongman, he was no less pragmatic. He understood that Russia could insist on controlling Poland and that there wasn't much he could do about it—because there wasn't much the American people were willing to do about it. Had Roosevelt lived, he would have been obliged to lay out the facts of great-power life to the Poles and their American partisans. Had he lived, he would have had to manage the inevitable loosening of bonds among the Grand Allies. He would have had to face the emotional exhaustion that follows every great sacrifice and the fiscal tightening required to bring means and ends more closely into alignment. He didn't choose the moment of his death, but had he scripted this part of his performance he couldn't have timed his exit better. He left on a high note, before the predictable discord set in.

❖ ❖ ❖

OTHERS HAD EXITED before he did; some stayed longer. Louis Howe, of course, was nearly a decade dead. Missy LeHand had died in the summer of 1944. Harry Hopkins succumbed to cancer the day before what would have been Roosevelt's sixty-fourth birthday, in 1946. Lucy Mercer Rutherfurd died of leukemia in 1948.

Eleanor Roosevelt found her release from the White House personally liberating. Or perhaps it was her release from her marriage, which had constrained her even as her relationship to Franklin provided her a platform she never could have acquired on her own. But by 1945 she held that platform in her own right, and she spent the next seventeen years putting it to good use. She served as an American delegate to the United Nations General Assembly and helped draft the Universal Declaration of Human Rights, which embodied much of what was noble and more than a little of what was unrealistic in her view of the world. She supported Adlai Stevenson in his two unsuccessful campaigns for president. She continued writing and speaking, and prodded the conscience of America far into her eighth decade. "She would rather light a candle than curse the darkness," Stevenson said upon her death in 1962. "And her glow has warmed the world."

❖ ❖ ❖

BY THE TIME she died, the New Deal was almost thirty years old. In its maturity it exercised a hold on American life that would have gratified Roosevelt and appalled his opponents, including those angry, fearful types who had denounced him as a traitor to his class. Its power and durability owed much to a quirk of fate—a large quirk but one unconnected to American domestic politics and policy. If not for the outbreak of war in Europe, Roosevelt would not have run for a third term. If he had not run, the Republicans, campaigning on his second-term troubles, and on his larger failure to restore prosperity, probably would have seized the White House. And they surely would have begun dismantling major parts of the New Deal. The protections to labor would have been vulnerable to a management-friendly executive. The constraints on banks and the stock market would have yielded to the same groups that had resisted them in the first place. Social Security, the centerpiece of Roosevelt's reforms, might have been particularly vulnerable, in that at the end of Roosevelt's second term it had scarcely begun to pay out anything to the great majority of its contributors. For most taxpayers, Social Security as of 1940 was simply a drain on their pocketbooks.

But the war *did* come, Roosevelt *did* run, and the Republicans were barred from the White House for another dozen years. By then Social Security had developed a huge constituency, one so great that Dwight Eisenhower remarked that any president or party would have to be crazy to tamper with the system Roosevelt had created. And so it remained untouchable, except to expand its coverage and increase its benefits—and extend its spirit to such derivative programs as Medicare and Medicaid—into the twenty-first century.

Partly through his own doing, partly through the dice roll of circumstances, Franklin Roosevelt radically altered the landscape of American expectations. The small-government world of the nineteenth and early twentieth centuries was banished forever. Americans demanded more of their government: more services, more safeguards, more security. They got them—along with more taxes, more red tape, more intrusiveness. At times some Americans would wonder whether the cost was worth the benefit. But the skeptics were never convinced enough or numerous enough to turn back the clock and unravel Roosevelt's handiwork. He gave Americans what most of them agreed the country required during the emergency of the depression, and they sufficiently liked what they got that they retained it after prosperity returned. In the generations that followed, as the American economy continued to thrive and as the benefits of America's material fortune rained down on the wealthy even more than on persons of moderate means, the objective and honest of those who had once denounced Roosevelt for class betrayal recognized that, in a decade rife with fascists, militarists, and communists abroad and irresponsible demagogues at home, he was the best thing that could have happened to them.

The transformation Roosevelt wrought in America's world role was no less radical than the change he effected in domestic affairs. America had turned its back on the world during the 1920s, and the depression reinforced Americans' reluctance to think that what happened in Europe and Asia had relevance for them. Roosevelt did little to challenge this view during his first term. But beginning in 1937 he gradually awakened Americans to the dangers of ignoring that wider world and to the necessity of engaging it, for their own sake and others'. So well did he succeed that Americans never seriously reconsidered the conclusions he impressed upon them. In some cases they seemed to have learned Roosevelt's lesson too well, making minor distant troubles imprudently their own. But a lifetime after his death, America remained committed to the principle that had guided his foreign policy: that close involvement with the world was America's responsibility and in America's best interest.

❖ ❖ ❖

HALF A MILLION people greeted the presidential train in Washington and stood in silent tribute as the caisson rolled from Union Station to the White House. Twenty thousand gathered in front of the mansion and refused to go home long after the gates and doors closed behind the procession. A simple funeral service was held in the East Room. Of the boys only Elliott made it to Washington in time to take his place beside Eleanor and Anna. James was en route from the Philippines. He flew ten thousand miles but was delayed by bad weather on the final leg and missed the service by little more than an hour. Eleanor had asked that no flowers be sent, yet they arrived anyway, filling the entire ground floor of the White House and spilling out onto the terraces.

Shortly after the service the casket was returned to the train for an overnight trip to Hyde Park. President Truman, the cabinet secretaries, and the justices of the Supreme Court rode along; a second train carried members of Congress. For the last time Roosevelt ascended the hill from the Hyde Park train station, beside the Hudson, to the big house on the bluff. On a sunny morning with a cold wind he was laid to rest in the hedge-compassed garden between the house and the library he had built to accommodate his papers. A twenty-one-gun salute honored the fallen commander in chief; parade guards of soldiers, sailors, and marines lined the paths and lanes of the estate; warplanes flew in formation overhead; a bugler blew taps. As the body was lowered into the earth the group beside the grave sang "Now the Laborer's Task Is O'er."

But it wasn't quite over yet. At the time Roosevelt died, he was preparing a message to be shared with the country on Jefferson Day. The White House published the message after his death, and it became his benediction and final bow.

"Americans are gathered together this evening in communities all over the country to pay tribute to the living memory of Thomas Jefferson, one of the greatest of all democrats," he said. "And I want to make it clear that I am spelling that word 'democrats' with a small d." Readers imagined Roosevelt pausing to smile, even laugh, as he would have delivered that line. His tone then turned more serious. As important as Jefferson had been in establishing democracy in America, he was equally important in making American democracy a vital element in world affairs. He had purchased Louisiana, sent the navy to punish the Barbary pirates, and held democracy forth as a beacon for other peoples. His legacy of responsibility persisted.

> Today this nation which Jefferson helped so greatly to build is playing a tremendous part in the battle for the rights of man all over the world. Today we are part of the vast Allied force—a force composed of flesh and blood and steel and spirit—which is today destroying the makers of war, the breeders of hatred, in Europe and in Asia. . . . Today we have learned in the agony of war that great power involves great responsibility.

Roosevelt was proud that Americans had accepted their responsibility. And he was confident they would continue to shoulder it in the future. The Nazi regime was crumbling; the warlords of Japan would meet a similar fate.

> But the mere conquest of our enemies is not enough. We must go on to do all in our power to conquer the doubts and the fears, the ignorance and the greed, which made this horror possible. . . . The work, my friends, is peace. More than an end of this war—an end to the beginnings of all wars. Yes, an end, forever, to this impractical, unrealistic settlement of the differences between governments by the mass killing of peoples.

Perhaps, in writing these words in his cottage at Warm Springs, he had had a premonition of his imminent death. Perhaps he simply chose to rework a line that had played well in the past. But in his final statement to the American people, Roosevelt echoed his first statement as their president.

> To all Americans who dedicate themselves with us to the making of an abiding peace, I say: The only limit to our realization of tomorrow will be our doubts of today.

❖　❖　❖

Winston Churchill missed the funeral. The demands of the war prevented a journey to America. But the prime minister had been bracing himself emotionally for the loss of his partner. At the close of the Casablanca conference, Roosevelt made ready to leave. Churchill stopped him. "You cannot go all this way to North Africa without seeing Marrakech," he said. "Let us spend two days there. I must be with you when you see the sunset on the snows of the Atlas Mountains." Roosevelt put off his departure, and he and Churchill drove the hundred and fifty miles across the desert together. They spoke of the war and politics and of the history of the region and the future of the world.

Marrakech was everything Churchill promised. Its lush gardens afforded a respite from the desert, its ancient souks a reminder that life continued amid the war. An American living in the city loaned her villa to the eminent tourists, who arrived just as the sun was setting. The villa had a tower with a view of the mountains and of the city. Churchill climbed the sixty steps; Roosevelt was carried up by strong young men. The two watched the sun go down and saw the dimming light paint the snowy peaks with shifting pastels. Churchill smoked a cigar, Roosevelt a cigarette. "It's the most lovely spot in the whole world," the prime minister sighed.

By now the city had begun to glow, as the lamps in the mosque towers came on. Roosevelt and Churchill descended to a dinner celebrating the successes their countries had shared and the greater victories they expected. The prime minister, the president, and the dozen members of their party ate, drank, and sang far into the night.

The next morning Roosevelt awoke at dawn to board his plane. Churchill refused to let the president drive to the airfield unaccompanied. He put on slippers and robe and the two rode together. They shook hands a final time on the tarmac, and Roosevelt entered the plane.

As the door of the aircraft closed, Churchill turned to the American vice consul, Kenneth Pendar. "Come, Pendar, let's go home," he said. "I don't like to see them take off." The car carrying the prime minister and the diplomat began to pull away. Pendar watched through the rear window as the president's plane gained speed. Churchill couldn't look. "Don't tell me when they take off. It makes me far too nervous." He touched Pendar's arm. "If anything happened to that man, I couldn't stand it. He is the truest friend; he has the farthest vision; he is the greatest man I've ever known."

ACKNOWLEDGMENTS

The author would like to thank the many people who helped make this book possible, including especially Bob Clark and the archival staff at the Franklin Delano Roosevelt Library, Roger Scholl and Bill Thomas at Doubleday, and James D. Hornfischer of Hornfischer Literary Management. Hal Brands and Riley Brands asked impertinent questions and insisted on persuasive answers; my thanks to them, with love.

Sources

The sources for this book, as for most other works of history, fall into two categories: primary sources and secondary sources. The primary sources are those generated by participants and eyewitnesses: their letters, diaries, public statements, memoirs, and the like. The secondary sources are the books and articles produced by historians and others who weren't there when the events recorded occurred.

The chief repository of unpublished primary sources on Roosevelt is the Franklin Delano Roosevelt Library at Hyde Park, New York. Established by Roosevelt himself, the Roosevelt Library set the model for American presidential libraries. It houses the papers of Roosevelt and many of his associates. Documents from this library cited in the text and identified in the notes below are indicated by the abbreviation FDRL.

The published primary sources on Roosevelt's life and presidency are legion. Three published collections of his correspondence have been most important for the writing of this book:

> *FDR: His Personal Letters.* Edited by Elliott Roosevelt et al. 4 volumes. 1947–50.
>
> *Churchill and Roosevelt: The Complete Correspondence.* Edited by Warren F. Kimball. 3 volumes. 1984.
>
> *My Dear Mr. Stalin: The Complete Correspondence between Franklin D. Roosevelt and Joseph V. Stalin.* Edited by Susan Butler. 2005.

Unless otherwise noted, letters identified below come from these collections. Correspondence with Churchill is from the second collection, with Stalin from the third, with other persons from the first. Because these collections are ordered by date, page references have been unnecessary.

Roosevelt's public papers, addresses, press conference transcripts, and other statements can be found in three collections primarily:

> *Public Papers and Addresses of Franklin D. Roosevelt.* 13 volumes. 1938–50.
>
> *Complete Presidential Press Conferences of Franklin D. Roosevelt.* 25 volumes. 1972.
>
> *Public Papers of the Presidents.* Digital collection of the American Presidency Project at the University of California, Santa Barbara: www.presidency.ucsb.edu.

Unless otherwise noted, the Roosevelt statements listed below come from these collections. The third collection contains many of the documents of the first two. It also has audio versions of some of Roosevelt's speeches, including the Fireside Chats. As with the correspondence, these are ordered by date, making further identification superfluous.

Three published collections of government documents have been essential in telling the story of Roosevelt's foreign policy:

Foreign Relations of the United States (FRUS). Various volumes and years.

Peace and War: United States Foreign Policy, 1931–1941. 1943.

Franklin D. Roosevelt and Foreign Affairs. Edited by Edgar D. Nixon. 3 volumes. 1969. (A second series under this title, of facsimiles compiled by Donald B. Schewe and published from 1979 to 1983, adds another 14 volumes.)

The first is the official published record of American foreign relations. The second and third are more specialized.

Roosevelt's family and associates were assiduous and verbose in recording their experiences and their impressions of Roosevelt as a man and as president. The following are the most important of the memoirs, diaries, and collections of letters:

Berle, Adolf A. *Navigating the Rapids, 1918–1971: From the Papers of Adolf A. Berle.* Edited by Beatrice Bishop Berle and Travis Beal Jacobs. 1973.

Churchill, Winston S. *The Second World War.* 6 volumes. 1948–53.

Daniels, Josephus. *The Cabinet Diaries of Josephus Daniels, 1913–1921.* Edited by E. David Cronon. 1963.

Farley, James A. *Behind the Ballots: The Personal History of a Politician.* 1938. Volume 1 of his memoir. *Jim Farley's Story: The Roosevelt Years.* 1948. Volume 2.

Hassett, William D. *Off the Record with F.D.R., 1942–1945.* 1958.

Hickok, Lorena. *One Third of a Nation: Lorena Hickok Reports on the Great Depression.* Edited by Richard Lowitt and Maurine Beasley. 1981.

Hull, Cordell. *The Memoirs of Cordell Hull.* 2 volumes. 1948.

Ickes, Harold L. *The Secret Diary of Harold L. Ickes.* 3 volumes. 1953–54.

Kennedy, Joseph P. *Hostage to Fortune: The Letters of Joseph P. Kennedy.* Edited by Amanda Smith. 2001.

Lash, Joseph P. *Eleanor and Franklin.* 1971.

Lindley, Ernest K. *Franklin D. Roosevelt.* 1931.

Moley, Raymond. *After Seven Years.* 1937.

Morgenthau, Henry Jr. *From the Morgenthau Diaries.* Edited by John Morton Blum. 3 volumes. 1959–67.

Perkins, Frances. *The Roosevelt I Knew.* 1946.

Roosevelt, Eleanor. *This Is My Story.* 1937. Volume 1 of her autobiography. *This I Remember.* 1949. Volume 2. (Referred to as ER.)

Roosevelt, Eleanor, and Anna Roosevelt. *Mother and Daughter: The Letters of Eleanor and Anna Roosevelt.* Edited by Bernard Asbell. 1982.

Roosevelt, Elliott. *As He Saw It.* 1946.

Roosevelt, Elliott, and James Brough. *An Untold Story: The Roosevelts of Hyde Park.* 1973.

Roosevelt, James, and Sidney Shalett. *Affectionately, F.D.R.: A Son's Story of a Lonely Man.* 1959.

Rosenman, Samuel I. *Working with Roosevelt.* 1952.

Sherwood, Robert E. *Roosevelt and Hopkins: An Intimate History.* 1948.

Tugwell, R. G. *The Brains Trust.* 1968.

Tully, Grace. *F.D.R., My Boss.* 1949.

The secondary sources on Roosevelt's life and career constitute nothing less than a library of American history during the late nineteenth century and the first half of the twentieth century. Any comprehensive bibliography of such secondary sources would be far too large to include here. The interested reader may consult Kenneth E. Hendrickson Jr., *The Life and Presidency of Franklin Delano Roosevelt: An Annotated Bibliography*, 3 volumes (2005).

The secondary sources from which direct quotations or specific, hard-to-verify facts have been taken are indicated in the notes. Several secondary works have been especially useful:

Burns, James MacGregor. *Roosevelt.* 2 volumes. 1956–70.

Cook, Blanche Wiesen. *Eleanor Roosevelt.* 2 volumes to date. 1992–.

Dallek, Robert. *Franklin D. Roosevelt and American Foreign Policy, 1932–1945.* 1979.

Davis, Kenneth S. *FDR.* 5 volumes. 1972–2000.

Freidel, Frank. *Franklin D. Roosevelt.* 4 volumes. 1952–73.

Goodwin, Doris Kearns. *No Ordinary Time: Franklin and Eleanor Roosevelt; The Home Front in World War II.* 1994.

Kennedy, David. *Freedom from Fear: The American People in Depression and War, 1929–1945.* 1999.

Leuchtenburg, William E. *Franklin D. Roosevelt and the New Deal, 1932–1940.* 1963.

Schlesinger, Arthur M. Jr. *The Age of Roosevelt.* 3 volumes. 1958–60.

Ward, Geoffrey C. *Before the Trumpet: Young Franklin Roosevelt, 1882–1905.* 1985.

———. *A First-Class Temperament: The Emergence of Franklin Roosevelt.* 1989.

NOTES

PROLOGUE

3   "This means war": Sherwood, 426–27.

7   "There's a report . . . No": Hull, 2:1095.

7   "In all my fifty years of public service": *FRUS: Japan, 1931–1941,* 2:787.

9   "Mr. President, what's this . . . simplifies things": Churchill, 3:605–06.

10   "Japan started this war . . . a combat division": *New York Times,* Dec. 8, 1941.

11   "burning bitterness": *Time,* April 27, 1936.

CHAPTER 1

18   "I will not say": Daniel W. Delano Jr., *Franklin Roosevelt and the Delano Influence* (1946), 164.

18   "He never took his eyes": Rita Halle Kleeman, *Gracious Lady: The Life of Sara Delano Roosevelt* (1935), 101.

18   "James Roosevelt is the first person": Allen Churchill, *The Roosevelts: American Aristocrats* (1966), 155.

19   "At a quarter to nine": Ibid., 156.

23   his earliest surviving letter: *Personal Letters,* 1 (after p. xvi). Unless otherwise noted, letters to and from FDR below can be found in this collection. They are cited simply by date.

24   "Papa is going to buy": To Deborah Delano, April 10, 1891.

24   "On this paper": To Muriel and Warren Robbins, May 30, 1891.

25   "Thanks very much": To Sara and James Roosevelt, Sept. 27, 1896.

25   "I played football": To Sara and James Roosevelt, Sept. 18, 1896.

25   "I managed to dislocate": To Sara and James Roosevelt, Oct. 11, 1896.

25   "I am all right": To Sara and James Roosevelt, Sept. 18, 1896.

25   "Very good": *Personal Letters,* 1 (after p. 32).

27   "Today is *broiling*": To Sara and James Roosevelt, May 13, 1900.

27   "I told him": To Sara and James Roosevelt, April 28, 1899.

28   "*Make Papa rest*": To Sara and James Roosevelt, Nov. 19, 1900.

28   "I am so glad": To Sara and James Roosevelt, Nov. 23, 1900.

28   "I am too distressed": To Sara and James Roosevelt, Dec. 3, 1900.

CHAPTER 2

29   "The sitting room": To Sara and James Roosevelt, Jan. 9, 1900.

29   "The rooms look": To Sara and James Roosevelt, Sept. 25, 1900.

29   "On Monday": To Sara and James Roosevelt, Oct. 19, 1900.

29   "There are still": To Sara and James Roosevelt, Oct. 5, 1900.

30   "It is the only one": To Sara and James Roosevelt, Oct. 19, 1900.

30   "Last night": To Sara and James Roosevelt, Oct. 31, 1900.

30   "President Eliot Declares": Harvard *Crimson,* Oct. 29, 1900, in *Personal Letters,* 1:432n.

30   "Great fun": To Sara Roosevelt, Dec. 8, 1901.

31   "Three hundred beautiful": *New York Times,* Jan. 4, 1902.

31   "Then to the dance": To Sara Roosevelt, Jan. 6, 1902.

32   "On Saturday": To Sara Roosevelt, Oct. 8, 1902.

32   "greatest disappointment of my life": Ward, *Before the Trumpet,* 235–36.

33   "I am glad to say": To Sara Roosevelt, Nov. 6, 1903.

33   "With such a large city": Harvard *Crimson,* Oct. 8, 1903, *Personal Letters,* 1:509.

33   "the committee in New York": Harvard *Crimson,* Jan. 9, 1904, *Personal Letters,* 1:522.

33   "I was one": To Sara Roosevelt, Oct. 26, 1903.

33   "which was very exclusive": To Sara Roosevelt, Jan. 30, 1904.

33   "Mrs. Kay": Note by Herbert Burgess, *Personal Letters,* 1:531.

34   "one of the most beautiful women": ER, 2:3–4.

35   "Though he was . . . our own together": Ibid., 6, 20, 29–30.

35   "Poor fellow!": H. W. Brands, *TR: The Last Romantic* (1997), 259.

36   "I simply refused . . . dance with him": ER, 1:34, 49, 51.

37   "To keep my uncles out": Cook, 1:126, 517n.

37   "It was quite easy . . . into thinking": ER, 1:55, 70–71.

37   "I am going to get off . . . deeply ashamed": Ibid., 81–84, 100–01.

38   "All the little girls": Ibid., 108–09.

38   Alice Sohier: Ward, *Before the Trumpet,* 254.

39   "I never want": From ER, Nov. 24, 1903, FDRL.

39   "Franklin gave me": Sara Roosevelt diary, Nov. 26, 1903, FDRL.

39   "Dearest Cousin Sally": ER to Sara Roosevelt, Dec. 2, 1903.

39   "Dearest Mama": To Sara Roosevelt, Dec. 4, 1903.

40   "They were a clan": ER, 1:122.

40   "She was always": Michael Teague, *Mrs. L: Conversations with Alice Roosevelt Long-worth* (1981), 154.

41   "I do . . . in the family": Cook, 1:166–67.

42   "Those closest": ER, 1:126.

CHAPTER 3

43   "You will never": Horace Coon, *Columbia, Colossus on the Hudson* (1947), 99.

44   "FRANKLIN D. ROOSEVELT": Freidel, 1:82.

44   "I went to a big law office": Remarks, Nov. 3, 1941.

45   "I would be glad to settle": Earle Looker, *This Man Roosevelt* (1932), 51–52.

46   "Dearest Mama": ER to Sara Roosevelt, June 7, 1905.

46   "We are so glad": To Sara Roosevelt, July 22, 1905.

46   "They write books": To Sara Roosevelt, Aug. 30, 1905.

46   "We were ushered": To Sara Roosevelt, June 16, 1905.

46   "Everyone is talking": To Sara Roosevelt, Sept. 7, 1905.

47   "It was quite a relief . . . in a little while": ER, 1:139, 142–46, 152–53.

48   "They always told me . . . I was behaving": Ibid., 143, 147–48, 165.

CHAPTER 4

50   "I remember him": Freidel, 1:86.

50   "I answered": Theodore Roosevelt, *An Autobiography* (1913), 63.

51   "Consider the problem": H. W. Brands, *The Reckless Decade: America in the 1890s* (1995), 108–09.

53   "I thank you": *Poughkeepsie Daily Eagle,* Oct. 7, 1910, in *Personal Letters,* 2:154.

53   "Humboldt the great traveler": Speech notes, *Personal Letters,* 2:157.

53   "I'm not Teddy": Freidel, 1:93.

55   "His patronymic": *New York Times,* Jan. 22, 1911.

56   "Well, if we've caught": Lindley, 78.

56   "The men arrived": ER, 1:174–76.

57   "Leader?": *New York Times,* Jan. 22, 1911.

57   "Franklin D. Roosevelt . . . United States Senator": Freidel, 1:97, 106–07.

58   "The Sheehan men": *New York Times,* Jan. 30, 1911.

59   "delightful smile": Lindley, 92.

59   "My husband": ER, 1:174–75.

59   "Mr. Sheehan": Freidel, 1:109.

60   "We have followed": Ibid., 115.

60   "I have just come": *New York Times,* April 2, 1911.

CHAPTER 5

61   "As regards": Brands, *TR,* 792.

62   "We stand": Ibid., 719.

65   "By God": Michael Kazin, *A Godly Hero: The Life of William Jennings Bryan* (2006), 189.

65   "praying for Clark": Freidel, 1:144.

65   "Wilson nominated": To ER, July 2, 1912.

66   "In imbecility": *New York Times,* July 30, 1912.

66   "They refer to us": Freidel, 1:144.

67   "Combinations in industry": Theodore Roosevelt, *Social Justice and Popular Rule* (1974 reprint of vol. 19 of Memorial Edition of *The Works of Theodore Roosevelt*), 18.

68   "The inventive genius": H. W. Brands, *Woodrow Wilson* (2003), 21–22.

69   "No one could understand": ER, 1:190–91.

69   "one of the four ugliest": Lash, 178.

70   "gnome-like": ER, 1:192.

70   "If you can connect me": Lash, 177.

70   "As I have pledged . . . the Murphy ring": Freidel, 1:151.

71   "My husband was reelected": ER, 1:193.

CHAPTER 6

72   "As I entered": Josephus Daniels, *The Wilson Era: The Years of Peace, 1910–1917* (1944), 124.

73   "In the Navy Department": Ibid., 119.

73   "Daniels was one": Lindley, 117–18.

74   "He was in a gay mood . . . no such ambition": Daniels, *Wilson Era: Years of Peace,* 124–29.

75   to cut the board's request: William J. Williams, "Josephus Daniels and the U.S. Navy's Shipbuilding Program during World War I," *Journal of Military History,* 60 (Jan. 1996), 9.

75   "Invasion is not": Lindley, 120.

75   "Dreadnoughts": Freidel, 1:227.

76   "It was an impressive": *New York Times,* March 17, 1914.

77   "I had not been": Campaign address, Oct. 30, 1928, *Public Papers,* 1:60–61.

78 "Take what is offered": Freidel, 1:203.
78 "We did not have": Campaign address, Oct. 30, 1928, *Public Papers*, 1:61.

CHAPTER 7

79 "He was pointed out": Jonathan Daniels, *The End of Innocence* (1954), 22.
79 "The progress of evolution": Henry Adams, *The Education of Henry Adams* (1999 ed.), 224.
79 "pure act": Brands, *TR*, 419.
79 "Mr. Adams": ER, 1:237.
80 "I do hope": From TR, March 18, 1913, *The Letters of Theodore Roosevelt*, ed. Elting Morison and John M. Blum (1951–54), 7:714.
80 "You can do . . . Assistant Secretary of the Navy": ER, 1:196.
80 "I have never had": To ER, July 29, 1913.
81 "Unlike most . . . his business": William F. Halsey and J. Bryan III, *Admiral Halsey's Story* (1947), 18.
82 "Although they didn't": Teague, *Mrs. L*, 158.
82 "Remember for Nick's sake": Betty Boyd Caroli, *The Roosevelt Women* (1998), 408.
82 "I was perfectly certain": ER, 1:206.
83 "All I remember about Harding": Roosevelt and Shalett, 71–72.
83 "I knew him . . . of his wife": William Phillips, *Ventures in Diplomacy* (1952), 68–70.
85 "My judgment": From Wilson, April 1, 1914, *The Papers of Woodrow Wilson*, ed. Arthur S. Link (1966–92), 29:392.
85 "To repeat": *New York Times*, July 24, 1914.
85 "My senses": Freidel, 1:183.
85 Roosevelt told Josephus Daniels: *Wilson Era: Years of Peace*, 31.
86 "I am a regular organization Democrat": *New York Times*, Sept. 21, 1914.
86 "Will make an active campaign": Ibid., Oct. 26, 1914.

CHAPTER 8

87 "Good morning . . . in America": Roosevelt and Brough, 8–11.
89 "She and Mother": Ibid., 68.
90 "I will wire you": To ER, July 19, 1914.
90 "it may be impossible": To ER, July 22, 1914.
90 "an ordeal to be borne": Cook, 1:536.
91 "I believe": Ralph G. Martin, *Cissy* (1979), 189.
91 "Everybody called": Carol Felsenthal, *Alice Roosevelt Longworth* (1988), 147.
92 "Lucy was beautiful": Teague, *Mrs. L*, 157–58.
92 "vague hostility . . . cold war": Roosevelt and Brough, 6, 79, 115.
92 "You never answer": From ER, July 28, 1917, FDRL.
92 "She is evidently": From ER, Sept. 8, 1917, FDRL.
92 "I *count* on seeing you": From ER, Aug. 15, 1917, FDRL.
93 "There was no mystery": Roosevelt and Brough, 86.
93 "I miss you": ER to Sara Roosevelt, Jan. 22, 1918, FDRL.
93 "I wish you were always here": ER to Sara Roosevelt, undated (Feb. 1918), FDRL.

CHAPTER 9

94 "It would be the irony of fate": Brands, *Woodrow Wilson*, 42.
95 "impartial in thought": Wilson message, Aug. 19, 1914.
95 "no triumph of peace": Brands, *TR*, 317.

96   "Now, Sara": Theodore Roosevelt to Sara Roosevelt, Oct. 2, 1914, *Letters of Theodore Roosevelt*, 8:821.

96   "That is to say": FDR statement, Oct. 21, 1914, *New York Times*, Oct. 22, 1914.

97   "The enclosed": To ER, undated (Oct. 1914), *Personal Letters*, 2:256–57.

97   "Mr. Roosevelt": Lindley, 124.

97   "really great fun": To Sara Roosevelt, undated (Dec. 17, 1914), *Personal Letters*, 2:260–67.

97   "A battleship . . . the War College": FDR testimony, Dec. 16, 1914, *New York Times*, Dec. 17, 1914.

99   "The result": Lansing to Wilson, Sept. 6, 1915, *Papers of Wilson*.

99   "There is such a thing": Wilson address, May 10, 1915, *Papers of Wilson*.

100 "unpardonable offense": Brands, *Wilson*, 61–62.

100 "Today Sir C.": To ER, undated (early 1915), *Personal Letters*, 2:266–67.

100 "These are the hectic days": To ER, undated (June 10, 1915), *Personal Letters*, 2:270–71.

101 "I wanted to tell you": To Wilson, June 9, 1915, *Papers of Wilson*.

101 "touched me very much": From Wilson, June 14, 1915, *Papers of Wilson*.

102 "Every minute": Speech to Navy League, April 13, 1916, FDRL.

102 "The most extraordinary day": To ER, Nov. 8, 1916.

102 "Another day": To ER, Nov. 9, 1916.

103 "I want to do right": Daniels, *Cabinet Diaries*, 118.

104 "The world": Wilson address, April 2, 1917.

105 "Franklin Roosevelt should": Wood quoted in Langdon Marvin to FDR, July 17, 1917, FDRL.

106 "Black care": Sarah Lyons Watts, *Rough Rider in the White House: Theodore Roosevelt and the Politics of Desire* (2003), 56.

CHAPTER 10

108 "How much of that sort of junk": Daniels, *Cabinet Diaries*, 118–21.

109 "pet hobby": FDR report, Oct. 16, 1918, FDRL.

109 "Project has previously": Josephus Daniels, *Our Navy at War* (1922), 131.

109 "I am very sorry": To Wilson, Oct. 29, 1917, with enclosed memo to Daniels, Oct. 29, 1917, *Papers of Wilson*, 44:464–66.

109 "I told W. W.": Daniels, *Cabinet Diaries*, 228–29.

110 "exceedingly important": Ibid., 307.

111 "If Roosevelt had not been there": Lindley, 160.

111 "In the estimation": H. C. Peterson and Gilbert C. Fite, *Opponents of War* (1957), 22.

111 "Every reform": Ray Stannard Baker, ed., *Woodrow Wilson: Life and Letters* (1927–39), 5:77.

111 "selection from a nation": Peterson and Fite, *Opponents of War*, 23.

112 "white heat": James R. Mock and Cedric Larson, *Words That Won the War* (1939), 124.

113 "Making the ten servants": *New York Times*, July 17, 1917.

113 "I am proud": To ER, July 18, 1917.

113 "I'd like to crawl away": From ER, July 20, 1917, FDRL.

121 "The bottom dropped out": ER to Lash, Oct. 25, 1943, in Lash, 220.

121 "Always remember": Teague, *Mrs. L*, 158.

122 "One can be": Sara Roosevelt to FDR and ER, Oct. 14, 1917.

122 The children . . . inferred: Cook, 1:232.

CHAPTER 11

123 "If you have approved": Wilson statement, Oct. 19, 1918, *Papers of Wilson*.

125 "a beautifully built young man": From Camp, July 25, 1917, FDRL.

125   "Very interesting": ER to Sara Roosevelt, Jan. 9, 1919.

125   "The old lion is dead": Brands, *TR*, 811.

125   "We were shocked": ER to Sara Roosevelt, Jan. 9, 1919.

125   "Hail the Champion . . . or superhuman": Thomas J. Knock, *To End All Wars: Woodrow Wilson and the Quest for a New World Order* (1992), 194–95.

126   "I never saw anything": ER to Sara Roosevelt, Jan. 11, 1919.

126   "a fait accompli": FDR to Sara Roosevelt, Jan. 18, 1919.

126   "This is a big success": ER to Sara Roosevelt, Jan. 14, 1919.

126   "The German people": Ward, *First-Class Temperament*, 427.

127   "The United States . . . to any man": ER, 1:289–90.

127   "Any man who resists": Wilson speech, Feb. 24, 1919, *Papers of Wilson*.

128   "Not on your life": Diary entry of Cary T. Grayson, July 10, 1919, *Papers of Wilson*.

129   "There will come some time": Wilson address, Sept. 5, 1919, *Papers of Wilson*.

129   "It seems a safe assertion": *New York Times*, Sept. 15, 1919.

129   "He looked as if he were dead": Irwin Hood (Ike) Hoover, *Forty-two Years in the White House* (1934), 99.

130   "Things have been so quiet": To Daniels, April 3, 1919, FDRL.

131   "I wish it were possible": To H. Morton Merriman, March 5, 1919, FDRL.

CHAPTER 12

134   "I went over to the Attorney General's": *New York Times*, June 3, 1919; *Washington Post*, June 3, 1919.

135   "although a Democrat": *New York Times*, July 5, 1917.

137   "As we came in sight": FDR quoted in letter from Claude Bowers to Cox, in *Personal Letters*, 2:496–97.

138   "Modern civilization": Acceptance speech, Aug. 9, 1920, *Personal Letters*, 2:500–08.

138   "It would have done": Daniels to ER, July 7, 1920, in ER, 1:310.

138   "I was glad . . . of little value": ER, 1:311–20.

141   "Thank the Lord": To Early, Dec. 21, 1920.

CHAPTER 13

142   Black and Fidelity threw a dinner: *New York Times*, Jan. 8, 1921.

143   "Never have I imagined": To Black, Jan. 13, 1921, FDRL.

143   "Lay Navy Scandal . . . dead history": *New York Times*, July 20, 1921; U.S. Senate, Committee on Naval Affairs, *Alleged Immoral Conditions at Newport Naval Training Station* (1921).

144   "I thought he looked quite tired": Missy LeHand to ER, Aug. 23, 1921, FDRL.

145   "I'd never felt anything so cold": Earle Looker, *This Man Roosevelt*, 111.

147   "We thought yesterday": ER to James R. Roosevelt, Aug. 18, 1921.

148   "He can do so much more": Lovett to Bennett, Sept. 2, 1921.

150   "Thank heavens": ER to James R. Roosevelt, Aug. 14, 1921.

150   "for $600!": ER to James R. Roosevelt, Aug. 18, 1921.

151   "Dearest Mama": ER to Sara Roosevelt, Aug. 27, 1921.

151   "He is a cripple": David M. Oshinsky, *Polio: An American Story* (2005), 32.

153   "I am glad you are back . . . hear them all laughing": Ward, *First-Class Temperament*, 594; Sara Roosevelt to Dora Delano Forbes, Sept. 3, 1921, FDRL.

153   "F. D. Roosevelt Ill": *New York Times*, Sept. 16, 1921.

154   Dr. Louis Harris, reported: Ibid., Sept. 18, 1921.

154   "Fellow Sufferer": From Elizabeth Carleton, Sept. 17, 1921.

154   "If I could feel assured": To Carleton, Sept. 23, 1921.

155 "This is just a line": From Walter Camp, Sept. 19, 1921.
155 "I can assure you": To Camp, Sept. 28, 1921.
156 "The psychological factor": Davis, 1:665.

CHAPTER 14

157 "He hauled off": Daniels, *Wilson Era: Years of Peace*, 131.
159 "dirty, ugly little man": Roosevelt and Shalett, 148.
159 "Granny, with a good insight": ER and Anna Roosevelt, 31.
159 "most trying . . . gone to pieces": ER, 1:338–39.
160 "I became conscious . . . injure someone": Ibid., 342–43.
161 "I had a very bad habit": Ibid., 352.
162 "The legs work wonderfully": Ward, *First-Class Temperament*, 645.
163 "A grand and glorious occasion": Ibid., 651–52.
164 "The old hotel": ER, 2:26.
164 "I spent over an hour": To Sara Roosevelt, undated (Oct. 1924), *Personal Letters*, 2:564–65.
165 "The doctor says": Ibid.
165 "We have gone motoring": To ER, undated (Oct. 1924), *Personal Letters*, 2:566.
165 "I remember the first house . . . to its owner": ER, 2:27–28.
166 "On Wednesday the people": To Sara Roosevelt, undated (Oct.–Nov. 1924), *Personal Letters*, 2:566.
167 This Logbook: Quoted in Roosevelt and Brough, 159–60.
167 "Resourcefulness and good humor": Ibid., 165.
168 "Where are your husbands?": Lash, 298.
169 "But aren't you girls silly? . . . Love Nest on the Val-Kill": Kenneth S. Davis, *Invincible Summer: An Intimate Portrait of the Roosevelts, Based on the Recollections of Marion Dickerman* (1974), 34–36, 50; Cook, 1:325. As Davis points out, there is some reason to believe that Dickerman remembered the date inaccurately and that the suggestion to build the cottage came earlier.
169 "She wanted to use methods . . . in a text book": ER, 2:33, 36.

CHAPTER 15

171 "I was *informed*": ER and Anna Roosevelt, 33.
171 "Sis was in a hurry": Roosevelt and Brough, 238.
172 "Eleanor dear": Lash, 301.
172 "In the summer of 1926": Roosevelt and Shalett, 176–77.
172 "I remember staying mad . . . and faults quiet": Ibid., 178–84.
173 "Last night we caught": *Larooco* log, March 22, 1924, *Personal Letters*.
175 "My own knees": To James R. Roosevelt, April 28, 1925.
176 "I had a nice visit": To Sara Roosevelt, March 7, 1926.
176 "I know how you love creative work": From ER, May 4, 1926.
176 "The first thing to be done": *Atlanta Constitution*, May 9, 1926.
177 "The waters of Warm Springs": Ibid., April 21, 1926.
178 "Mrs. Ford and I": From Edsel Ford, March 15, 1928.
178 "Roosevelt, the Reliever": *Atlanta Constitution*, Aug. 23, 1927.
178 "We'll grow no cotton": Bernard Asbell, *The F.D.R. Memoirs* (1973), 140.
179 "was treated as a simple fact of life . . . *impotentia coeundi*": Roosevelt and Brough, 198–205.
180 "It was way back in 1924": Remarks, March 8, 1937.
181 "So I went down to the station": Remarks, March 30, 1939.

CHAPTER 16

184   "making big money": *New York Times,* May 25, 1922.

184   "In every county": Ibid., Aug. 15, 1922.

185   "It appears": Freidel, 2:117.

185   "I had quite a tussle": Steve Neal, *Happy Days Are Here Again* (2004), 58.

186   "very successful summer": To James Cox, Dec. 8, 1922, FDRL.

188   "I stand four square": Lee N. Allen, "The McAdoo Campaign for the Presidential Nomination in 1924," *Journal of Southern History* 29 (1963), 218.

189   "I am not wholly convinced": To Cox, Dec. 8, 1922, FDRL.

189   "Society of Nations": Reprinted in ER, 2:353–66.

190   "Shall We Trust Japan?": *Asia* 23 (July 1923), 476–77, copy in FDRL.

191   "The paramount ambition": Maury Klein, *Rainbow's End: The Crash of 1929* (2001), 29.

192   "I have no trouble": *The Autobiography of William Allen White* (1946), 619.

194   "Go up and shake it": Roosevelt and Brough, 218.

194   "To meet again": *New York Times,* June 27, 1924.

195   "A noble utterance": Lindley, 223.

195   "the one man whose name . . . holds observers enchained": *New York Herald Tribune,* July 1, 1924, and *New York Evening World,* July 7, 1924, in *Personal Letters,* 2:562–63.

196   "I am here to make": *New York Times,* July 9, 1924.

197   "The most popular man in the convention": *New York Times,* July 10, 1924.

197   "I met your friend Franklin Roosevelt": Freidel, 2:180.

CHAPTER 17

198   "The Democracy must make it clear": To Thomas J. Walsh, Feb. 8, 1925, *New York Times,* March 9, 1925.

199   "throw away": *New York Times,* April 9, 1925.

199   "He was, at first, fearful": To William Oldfield, April 11, 1925, FDRL.

200   "God aimed at Darrow": Edward John Larson, *Summer for the Gods: The Scopes Trial and America's Continuing Debate over Science and Religion* (1997), 200.

201   "Strictly between ourselves": To Daniels, June 23, 1927, FDRL.

204   "not a war of revenge . . . which matters": "Our Foreign Policy: A Democratic View," *Foreign Affairs,* July 1928.

206   "It is that quality of soul": *New York Times,* June 28, 1928.

207   "Tammany is Tammany . . . to the people of this country": Christopher M. Finan, *Alfred E. Smith: The Happy Warrior* (2002), 206–13.

209   "They told me how much . . . I had not been calling": ER, 2:44–46.

210   "Damn the Foundation! . . . any more questions": Lindley, 19–20.

211   "Mess is no name for it": Davis, 2:29.

212   "Smith has burned his bridges": To Van Lear Black, July 25, 1928, FDRL.

212   "Somewhere in a pigeon-hole": Address of Oct. 20, 1928, *Public Papers,* 1:30–31.

213   "I have just come from the South": Address of Oct. 17, 1928, *Public Papers,* 1:19–21.

214   "One of the most oppressing things . . . your miserable soul": Addresses of Oct. 20 and 22, 1928, *Personal Papers,* 1:32–38, 43.

215   "Tell the candidate": Rosenman, 17.

215   "This is Franklin Roosevelt": Ibid., 26.

CHAPTER 18

219   "In the past, wish, want, and desire": William Leach, *Land of Desire: Merchants, Power, and the Rise of a New American Culture* (1993), 375.

219 "Advertising is the spark plug . . . of one year": Klein, *Rainbow's End*, 121–24.

220 "Wherever one went": Ibid., 190.

220 "Hardly a week now passes": *New York Times*, Aug. 11, 1929.

221 "Business is entering . . . prosperous coming year": Klein, *Rainbow's End*, 163.

221 "One of the oldest and perhaps the noblest": Frederick Lewis Allen, *Only Yesterday: An Informal History of the 1920s* (1957 ed.), 303.

221 "We have reached a higher degree": Hoover inaugural address, March 4, 1929.

222 "It looks like": To Archie Roosevelt, Nov. 19, 1928, FDRL.

222 "definitely remain in the people . . . reasonable and friendly": Annual message, Jan. 2, 1929, *Public Papers*, 1:80–86.

223 "Elections were won or lost": *New York Times*, Jan. 18, 1929.

224 "not a single move": Radio address, April 3, 1929, *Public Papers*, 1:541–46.

225 "The business community": To Herbert Pell, Jan. 28, 1929.

226 "You're sitting on a volcano": Klein, *Rainbow's End*, 193.

226 "A crash is coming": *New York Times*, Sept. 6, 1929.

226 "lunatic fringe of reckless speculation": Ibid., Oct. 24, 1929.

227 "Wild-eyed speculators": Ibid., Oct. 25, 1929.

227 "We believe that present conditions": Klein, *Rainbow's End*, 215.

227 "The fundamental business of the country": Hoover news conference, Oct. 25, 1929.

229 "East side, west side . . . unstable equilibrium": *New York Times*, Dec. 11, 1929.

230 "The stock market and business": Klein, *Rainbow's End*, 182.

230 "The very existence of the Federal Reserve System": John Steele Gordon, *Hamilton's Blessing: The Extraordinary Life and Times of Our National Debt* (1997), 116–17.

231 "I do not assume the rate structure": Hoover statement, June 16, 1930.

CHAPTER 19

232 "The tremendous vote for Governor Roosevelt": *New York Times*, Nov. 5, 1930.

233 "It is a joy to cooperate with him": From House, March 23, 1931.

233 "He has a wholesome breeziness of manner": Howe to House, Aug. 17, 1931, *Personal Letters*, 3:210.

234 "Bill was a canny politician": Farley, 1:83–85.

235 "He seemed glad to see me . . . damn fool friends": From Howell, Dec. 2, 1931.

237 "Though the people support the government": Richard E. Welch Jr., *The Presidencies of Grover Cleveland* (1988), 80.

237 "The economic depression . . . latitude and discretion": Message to legislature, Aug. 28, 1931, *Public Papers*.

238 "It is the simple duty": To F. W. McLean, Jan. 22, 1932, *Public Papers*.

238 "forgotten man . . . mobilize to meet it": Radio address, April 7, 1932, *Public Papers*.

239 "Two weeks ago . . . adjunct of manhood": Address, April 18, 1932, *Public Papers*.

240 "As you have viewed this world": Speech, May 22, 1932, *Public Papers*.

241 "The art of carrying water": Column, Jan. 8, 1932, in Walter Lippmann, *Interpretations, 1931–1932* (1932), 259–62.

242 "He became quite heated": Finan, *Alfred E. Smith*, 270.

242 "If the Democratic National Convention": *New York Times*, Feb. 8, 1932.

244 "Why in hell don't he speak out?": From Howell, Dec. 2, 1931.

244 "large source of additional revenue": *New York Times*, Feb. 21, 1932.

245 "In common with millions . . . American participation": Ibid., Feb. 3, 1932.

245 "Because I am at least an adopted Georgian": To *Atlanta Constitution*, Feb. 20, 1931.

247 "We'll vote for Jack Garner . . . one more national election": Freidel, 3:309–10.

CHAPTER 20

248 "Curiously unworn . . . anything else": Tugwell, 21–27.

250 "You ask what he is like . . . his visitor said": Moley, 3–11.

251 "sturdy and rugged character": *New York Times*, July 3, 1932.

251 "As Mr. Roosevelt advanced": Ibid.

252 "The Democratic party . . . its own people": Acceptance address, July 2, 1932.

254 "I have a streak of Dutch stubbornness": Farley, 1:164.

255 "Industrial prosperity": Speech, Sept. 14, 1932, *Public Papers*.

255 "the entire absence of national planning": Speech, Sept. 17, 1932, *Public Papers*.

256 "This principle of tariff by negotiation": Speech, Sept. 20, 1932, *Public Papers*.

256 "The question of power": Speech, Sept. 21, 1932, *Public Papers*.

257 "We are paying . . . can make to business": Campaign address, Oct. 19, 1932, *Public Papers*.

259 "He had no business . . . essence of revolution": Stephen E. Ambrose, *Eisenhower*, vol. 1 (1983), 98–99.

259 "A considerable part of those remaining": Hoover statements, July 28 and 29, 1932.

259 "Well, Felix": Donald J. Lisio, *The President and Protest: Hoover, Conspiracy, and the Bonus Riot* (1974), 285.

260 "God damn it, Frank! . . . his own way": Tugwell, 430–34.

261 "Give me a lift or I'll vote for Hoover": Richard Norton Smith, *An Uncommon Man: The Triumph of Herbert Hoover* (1984), 143.

262 "It is a catastrophe for us": Ibid., 143–44.

262 "labyrinth of inaccurate statements . . . to be preserved": Hoover statements, Oct. 4, 12, 22, and 31, 1932.

263 "As the campaign moved down the homestretch": Farley, 1:184.

264 "Our case has been stated . . . of its accomplishment": Campaign address, Nov. 5, 1932, *Public Papers*.

265 "Give my regards": Farley, 1:187.

CHAPTER 21

266 "I wish I knew what you are really thinking": ER, 2:69, 74.

267 "Before the end of our years": Ibid., 56.

267 "When we finally got home": Roosevelt and Shalett, 231–32.

268 "very simple religion": ER, 2:69.

269 "My education was that of an engineer": Smith, *Uncommon Man*, 153.

269 "I am loath to proceed": Hoover to Roosevelt, Nov. 12, 1932 (released Nov. 13, 1932).

269 "The President's telegram": Moley, 68.

269 "I have a number of things": Freidel, 4:27.

270 "When we arrived in Washington": Moley, 72–73.

272 "I'll be in the White House": Tugwell, 411.

273 "My chief fear": Stimson diary (Yale University microfilm), Nov. 22, 1932.

273 "My view is that the most convenient": *New York Times*, Nov. 24, 1932.

273 "very much excited": Stimson diary, Nov. 23, 1932.

274 "Serious problems": Hoover message to Congress, Dec. 19, 1932.

274 "It is my view": To Hoover, Dec. 19, 1932, *Public Papers*.

275 "The best reason": Tugwell, 297–98.

276 "In taking leave of you": Address, Jan. 2, 1933, *Public Papers*.

276 "from the mountains of Virginia": Extemporaneous remarks, Jan. 21, 1933, *Public Papers*.

277 "That means that among the other duties": Remarks, Feb. 15, 1933, *Public Papers*.

277 "Had you tried to kill in Italy?": "Sworn Statement of Joseph Zangara," Feb. 16, 1933, *Franklin D. Roosevelt Assassination Attempt* (FBI report released under Freedom of Information Act; available at University of Miami Libraries Web site).

277 to save $2,500: C. D. McKean to J. Edgar Hoover, Feb. 16, 1933, FBI report.

278 "I heard what I thought": *New York Times,* Feb. 17, 1933.

279 "Was anybody with you?": "Sworn Statement of Joseph Zangara," Feb. 16, 1933, FBI report.

279 "Roosevelt's nerve": Moley, 139.

280 "My client has insisted . . . to check crime": *New York Times,* Feb. 21, 1933.

281 "Damn fool, worthless shot": Letter from informant whose name was deleted upon declassification, March 21, 1933, FBI report.

281 "Lousy capitalists": *New York Times,* March 21, 1933.

282 "Mr. President, as you know": Roosevelt and Shalett, 252.

283 "Though the city was gay": *New York Times,* March 5, 1933.

283 "This is a day": Ibid.

CHAPTER 22

288 "all banking transactions shall be suspended": Proclamation, March 6, 1933.

289 "A common adversity": *Wall Street Journal,* March 4, 1933.

289 "I have been so occupied": Extemporaneous remarks, March 6, 1933.

290 "I got the sense": Moley, 112.

291 "I was really almost thunderstruck": Hull, 1:156.

291 "It's an open secret": Moley, 114.

292 "with fervent good wishes": Rixey Smith and Norman Beasley, *Carter Glass* (1939), 333.

292 "Prefer a wooden roof": Moley, 122.

293 "Which one of you is Ikes?": Freidel, 4:154–55.

293 "As you will eventually meet anyhow": Moley, 127.

293 "Generally speaking": *New York Times,* Feb. 26, 1933.

294 "So far as I was able to judge": Tully, 172–73.

296 "My hope is that these conferences": Press conference, March 8, 1933.

299 "Will you go to Congress": Ibid.

300 "Mr. Hoover always had a smile": Washington *Sunday Star,* March 4, 1934, excerpted in *Public Papers,* 2:45.

301 "I realize that if these declarations": Hoover to David Reed, Feb. 20, 1933, William Starr Myers and Walter H. Newton, eds., *The Hoover Administration: A Documented Narrative* (1936), 341.

301 "my friend Robey": Myers and Newton, *Hoover Administration,* 341.

303 "until further proclamation": Proclamation, March 9, 1933.

304 "I want to talk for a few minutes": Fireside Chat, March 12, 1933.

CHAPTER 23

306 "Granny endured it": Roosevelt and Shalett, 55.

306 "I shall leave my son . . . to be thankful for": Ibid., 271–73.

307 "I was lucky": ER, 2:90.

308 "I have great respect": Ibid., 104.

309 "What kind of a joint is this?": Roosevelt and Shalett, 265.

310 "This is my little boy . . . he offered me": Ibid., 230, 253–54.

310 "I guess I've worked myself out of a job": Alfred B. Rollins Jr., *Roosevelt and Howe* (1962), 454.

311 "Tell the president to go to hell": Ibid., 435.

311   "I hope to God you drown!": Roosevelt and Shalett, 226.

312   "She is one of the best groomed women . . . harder than anybody else": *Washington Post,* June 28, 1936, and Aug. 1, 1944.

313   "A little too large to be cozy": Perkins, 65–66.

314   "I'd love to, Mr. President": Tully, 311–12.

315   "I've never heard": Ibid., 23–25.

317   "It's a damn lie . . . what was she like?": Ibid., 79–87.

CHAPTER 24

319   "The president drove the moneychangers": Leuchtenburg, 44.

319   "Capitalism was saved in eight days": Moley, 155.

319   "With the utmost seriousness": Message to Congress, March 10, 1933.

320   "that great marble building": Campaign address, Oct. 19, 1932, *Public Papers.*

321   "If you don't support this bill . . . approval of Congress": Freidel, 4:245.

321   "shut the doors of the chambers . . . depression burden": *New York Times,* March 12, 1933.

321   "It will be exercised": Message, March 10, 1933.

322   "courageous . . . permanent recovery": Summary of editorials in *New York Times,* March 10, 1933.

322   "Last week marked an end": *Wall Street Journal,* March 13, 1933.

323   "I guess at your next election": Schlesinger, 2:13.

323   "If this currency results": *San Francisco Chronicle,* excerpted in *New York Times,* March 10, 1933.

324   "Pathetic letters . . . get one started first": Freidel, 4:84–85.

325   "I am going to call farmers' leaders together": Christiana McFadyen Campbell, *The Farm Bureau and the New Deal: A Study of the Making of National Farm Policy, 1933–40* (1962), 51.

325   "Things were complicated": Tugwell diary, Dec. 31, 1932, FDRL.

327   "No permanent relief is possible": Freidel, 4:315.

327   "Purely discretionary": Press conference, April 21, 1933.

327   "The chief purpose of the order": Statement, April 5, 1933.

327   "This order served to prevent": Note to Executive Order 6102, April 5, 1933.

328   "Congratulate me . . . instead of permissive": Freidel, 4:333; Moley, 159–60.

328   "designed for the purpose": Note to Executive Order 6111, April 20, 1933.

328   "When you send out this army . . . today to Hitler": *New York Times,* March 22 and 23, 1933.

CHAPTER 25

330   "You know": Press conference, May 19, 1933.

330   "I was rather surprised . . . Roosevelt sent his wife": ER, 2:112–13; Lash, 367.

331   "Instead, he began to describe": Moley, 173–74.

332   "The idea is to put people . . . Can't tell you": Press conference, March 15, 1933.

333   "The overwhelming majority": Message to Congress, March 21, 1933.

333   "of fascism, of Hitlerism": *New York Times,* March 25, 1933.

333   "No, because I might seem . . . no clothing": Press conference, March 22, 1933.

336   "The peace conference": Moley, 176.

336   "The big objective": Press conference, March 29, 1933.

337   "a tortuous dance": Moley, 183.

337   "This measure at last translates": Statement, May 27, 1933.

338   "the most wonderful real estate speculation": Richard Lewis Neuberger and Stephen Bertram Kahn, *Integrity: The Life of George W. Norris* (1937), 207.

338 "What are you going to say": Eric F. Goldman, *Rendezvous with Destiny* (1956 ed.), 263.

339 "It was a glorious fight": Freidel, 4:354.

CHAPTER 26

340 "You realize": Moley, 189.

341 "The country was dying": Fireside Chat, May 7, 1933.

344 "There was a certain little sweater factory": Press conference, April 12, 1933.

346 "slight but definite upturn . . . well-rounded national recovery": Address, May 4, 1933.

347 "We're fiddling along": Freidel, 4:437, 445.

348 "How much longer . . . expect it to be used": *New York Times,* June 1, 1933.

348 "There is a revolt in the air": Freidel, 4:447.

349 "by now a thorough hodge-podge": Moley, 190.

349 "In my Inaugural . . . of public disapproval": Message, June 16, 1933.

352 "sincere and whole-hearted cooperation": To Henry Rainey et al., June 16, 1933.

352 "Now that Congress has gone": *New York Times,* June 18, 1933.

353 "Ray, that fellow in there . . . confidence and power": Raymond B. Fosdick, *Chronicle of a Generation* (1958), 247.

353 "None of us close to F.D.R. . . . seemed to worry him": Moley, 191–92.

CHAPTER 27

357 "Last week": *Time,* Feb. 6, 1933.

360 "as everyone knew": Moley, 199.

360 "It was never the purpose": Joint statement by FDR and MacDonald, April 23, 1933, *FRUS: 1933,* 1:491.

361 "Pay as much as you can": Memo of conversation, April 27, 1933, *FRUS: 1933,* 1:497–99.

362 "first, the desire . . . ultimately blocked": Message, May 16, 1933.

363 "All problems at present . . . harm the world": *New York Times,* May 18, 1933.

365 "If we are to succeed": Hull address, June 13, 1933, *FRUS: 1933,* 1:637.

365 "I felt almost physically ill": Moley, 219, 227.

366 "Such reports cannot be founded in fact": Statement, June 15, 1933.

367 "absolutely off the record": Press conference, June 16, 1933.

368 "permanent lack of accord . . . of the New World": *Le Monde* and German papers excerpted in *New York Times,* June 21 and 22, 1933.

368 "If you love us at all": From Cox, June 22, 1933, *FRUS 1933,* 1:654.

369 "I want to ask you . . . to cooperate about": Moley, 234–36.

369 "liaison officer": *New York Times,* June 21 and 22, 1933.

370 "Moley's reception in London": Hull, 1:260.

371 "specious fallacy": Wireless message, July 3, 1933.

371 "A Manifesto of Anarchy": Schlesinger, 2:224.

371 "America is the bonfire boy": *Daily Express* excerpted in *New York Times,* July 5, 1933.

371 "All stated very clearly": From Hull via Phillips, July 4, 1933, *FRUS: 1933,* 1:683.

371 "I have rarely seen a man": Moley, 263.

372 "going on the rocks": Press conference, July 5, 1933.

372 "We have enough grousing": Press conference, Aug. 5, 1933.

372 "That piss-ant Moley . . . from Moley's back": Schlesinger, 2:230–32; Moley in Bingham to Phillips, July 4, 1933, *FRUS: 1933,* 1:680.

CHAPTER 28

373 "If public opinion . . . and immediate action": Hugh S. Johnson, *The Blue Eagle from Egg to Earth* (1935), 57, 68, 75, 93–94, 114, 123–25.

374 "I think he's a good number-three man": Perkins, 200–01.
374 "Stick with Hugh": Ibid., 202–03.
375 "It will be red fire at first": Johnson, *Blue Eagle*, 208.
376 "I am now asking": Statement, July 9, 1933.
377 "In war, in the gloom . . . the American people": Fireside Chat, July 24, 1933.
377 "There were, on both sides . . . by a professor": Johnson, *Blue Eagle*, 226–28.
378 "It must have been amusing": Press conference, Aug. 5, 1933.
379 "a pretty tough baby": *New York Times*, Sept. 19, 1933.
380 "If you do not give us price regulations": Daniel Yergin, *The Prize: The Epic Quest for Oil, Money, and Power* (1991), 256.
382 "General," the newsman asked: *New York Times*, Aug. 30, 1933.
382 "I don't think he has put it quite that way": Press conference, Aug. 30, 1933.
382 "Can you tell us anything": Press conference, Oct. 27, 1933.
383 "I want to avoid even the smallest semblance": Schlesinger, 2:110.
383 "Women do 80 percent . . . the whole situation": Johnson, *Blue Eagle*, 264–65.
384 "Swollen by streams of passengers": *New York Times*, Sept. 14, 1933.
385 "But it wasn't my arm": Johnson, *Blue Eagle*, 267.
385 "There have been more brilliant processions": *New York Times*, Sept. 15, 1933.
385 "This is off the record . . . third of the way back": Press conference, Sept. 13, 1933.
386 "I have been dissatisfied": Press conference, Sept. 16, 1933.
388 "From the standpoint of human welfare . . . union of his youth": Schlesinger, 2:138–43.
390 "I want *personally* to check on the location": John A. Salmond, *The Civilian Conservation Corps* (1967), 30.
390 "It is clearly impossible": Ibid., 35.
393 "I wish I could spend a couple of months here": *New York Times*, Aug. 13, 1933.

CHAPTER 29

394 "It was like being on top of the world": *New York Times*, April 21, 1933.
394 "No one is worth $500 a minute": *Time*, June 4, 1934.
395 "They predicted . . . *Never!*": Lorena A. Hickok, *Eleanor Roosevelt: Reluctant First Lady* (1962, 1980), 120, 161, 172–76.
396 "I've been wondering . . . feel very empty": Cook, 2:175, 190–200.
398 "the color of a sunburn coming on": A. J. Liebling, *The Earl of Louisiana* (1970), 8.
398 "It is here under this oak": Huey P. Long, *Every Man a King: The Autobiography of Huey P. Long* (1933; 1996 reprint), 99.
398 "I used to try to get things done . . . I'll be for him": Alan Brinkley, *Voices of Protest: Huey Long, Father Coughlin, and the Great Depression* (1982), 25, 28, 39, 46.
399 "Seven motor trucks": *Saturday Evening Post*, Oct. 15, 1932.
399 "I want to stay on good terms": Brinkley, *Voices*, 60.
400 "It was a morning appointment": Farley, 1:240–42.
400 "While you are at it": T. Harry Williams, *Huey Long* (1981 ed.), 639.
401 "God invited us all": Brinkley, *Voices*, 71–72.
402 "a voice of such mellow richness": Ibid., 92.
402 "The New Deal is Christ's deal": Leuchtenburg, 101.
403 "Dr. Townsend's error": Column, Jan. 3, 1935, in Lippmann, *Interpretations: 1933–1935* (1936), 374.
404 "My plan is too simple": *Time*, Jan. 14, 1935.
404 "The zeal of those promoting the plan . . . get back home": Ibid.
405 "Capitalism has served its time": *New York Times*, Aug. 30, 1934.

405 "When I got up at 7:30": Hickok to ER, Nov. 11 and 12, 1933, *One Third of a Nation*, 91–92.

407 "A few hundred funerals": Leuchtenburg, 113.

408 "Her quoted speed is 30 knots": *New York Times*, July 1, 1934.

408 "In the field of world policy": Inaugural address, March 4, 1933.

409 "the definite policy of the United States": Address, Dec. 28, 1933.

409 "They constitute an integral part": Address, July 28, 1934.

410 "It will put the president": Frances Perkins oral history (Columbia University microfilm), 6:311.

411 "both old friends of mine": Address, Aug. 9, 1934.

411 "No country, however rich": Radio address, Sept. 30, 1934.

411 "He has been all but crowned": *Time*, Nov. 19, 1934.

CHAPTER 30

412 "There is no reason": Perkins, 281–83.

413 "I felt sure that the political climate . . . are obliged to": Ibid.

414 "Unemployment insurance will be in the program": Address, Nov. 14, 1934.

415 "If the federal aspects of the law . . . insurance system": Perkins, 286–94.

416 "I guess you're right on the economics": Schlesinger, 2:308–09.

416 "You will hurt Bob Doughton's feelings": Perkins, 296.

416 "ultimate socialistic control . . . will be felt": Schlesinger, 2:311–12.

417 "We have tried to frame a law": Address, Aug. 14, 1935.

417 "You go first": Hickok report to Hopkins, Oct. 2–12, 1933, *One Third of a Nation*, 47–48.

418 "Action had to be immediate": Sherwood, 44–45.

418 "The half-billion dollars": *Washington Post*, May 23, 1933.

418 "they were young, thin": Hallie Flanagan, *Arena* (1940), 25.

419 "It takes a lot of nerve": Ibid., 26.

419 "There is not in the state": Hickok to Hopkins, Aug. 16–26, 1933, *One Third of a Nation*, 20.

419 "They are a curiously appealing people": Hickok to Hopkins, Aug. 31–Sept. 3, 1933, *One Third of a Nation*, 25–26.

420 "Everything I own": Hickok to Hopkins, Oct. 30, 1933, *One Third of a Nation*, 56–57.

421 "I worked every Sunday": U.S. Senate, *Nomination of Ebert K. Burlew: Hearings before the Committee on Public Lands and Surveys* (1938), 7.

421 "All day planning the work program": Hopkins diary, May 13, 1935, FDRL.

421 "It is becoming ever clearer": Ickes, 1:378.

421 "Ickes is a good administrator": Schlesinger, 3:344.

422 "Hopkins will fly off on tangents": Ickes, 1:352.

422 "He has a mind like a razor": Sherwood, 80.

422 "Hell," he said: Ibid., 57.

422 "We voted millions upon millions . . . Franklin D. Roosevelt": Ickes, 1:425–29, 589–94.

CHAPTER 31

424 "Oh, I've kidded myself": Hickok to Hopkins, April 11, 1934, *One Third of a Nation*, 217.

425 "absolute state socialism": Schlesinger, 2:121.

425 "The excessive centralization": Walter Lippmann, *Interpretations, 1933–1935*, 98–99.

425 "Men have died": Schlesinger, 2:120; Johnson, *Blue Eagle*, 265.

425 "hitting below the belt": Schlesinger, 2:153.

425 "complete and perfect buffer": *New York Times*, Sept. 28, 1934.

425 "You can treasure in your hearts": Ibid., Oct. 2, 1934.

426 "We must keep the NRA going . . . that ever was achieved": Schlesinger, 2:166.

426 "We must continue": Fireside Chat, April 28, 1935.

428 "The NRA law was enacted . . . under the Constitution": *New York Times*, May 4, 1935.

429 "Extraordinary conditions . . . legislative power": *Schechter Poultry Corp. v. United States*, 295 U.S. 495.

432 "The Bank, Mr. Van Buren . . . let him enforce it": H. W. Brands, *Andrew Jackson* (2005), 500, 493.

432 "His theory": Ickes, 1:373–74, 524.

433 "Wealth in the modern world": Message to Congress, June 19, 1935.

434 "burst on most of Congress": *New York Times*, June 23, 1935.

434 "I just want to say 'Amen' ": Schlesinger, 3:328.

434 "For the time being he has silenced Huey . . . to have his way": Summary of editorials, *New York Times*, June 21, 1935.

434 "Pat Harrison's going to be so surprised": Schlesinger, 3:327.

434 "I don't subscribe to the soak-the-rich idea . . . in the fall": *New York Times*, June 20–21, 1935.

435 "That certain elements of business": From Howard, Aug. 26, 1935; released by White House, Sept. 6, 1935.

436 "This basic program": Open letter to Howard, Sept. 2, 1935; released by White House, Sept. 6, 1935.

436 "The statement that his basic program": *New York Times*, Sept. 7, 1935.

437 "I always laughed Huey off": Ickes, 1:462.

CHAPTER 32

439 "The menace of Bolshevism": Leuchtenburg, 205–06.

439 "canonization of impudence": H. W. Brands, *Inside the Cold War: Loy Henderson and the Rise of the American Empire, 1918–1961* (1991), 39–42.

440 "His face lit up with a big smile": Dallek, 79; Morgenthau, 1:57.

440 "Litvinov and I continued to argue": From Bullitt, Nov. 15, 1933, *FRUS: Soviet Union, 1933–1939*, 25–26.

440 "I trust that the relations now established": To Litvinov, Nov. 16, 1933.

441 "Not even off the record": Press conference, March 29, 1933.

441 "The movement to make international justice practicable": Message, Jan. 16, 1935.

442 "I appeal to every solid American": *New York Times*, Jan. 28, 1935.

442 "From the strictly constitutional standpoint": Press conference, Jan. 23, 1935.

442 "I am speaking to you tonight": *New York Times*, Jan. 28, 1935.

443 "Any comment to make": Press conference, Jan. 30, 1935.

443 "As to the 36 gentlemen": *Franklin D. Roosevelt and Foreign Affairs*, 2:381.

444 "highly unethical, a discredit to American business": *Report of the Special Committee on Investigation of the Munitions Industry* (Nye Report), U.S. Senate, 74th Congress, 2nd sess., Feb. 24, 1936.

444 "Abolish the ROTC!": *New York Times*, April 13, 1935.

445 "These are without doubt": To Long, March 9, 1935, *Franklin D. Roosevelt and Foreign Affairs*, 2:437–38.

445 "No one today knows": From Pittman, Feb. 19, 1935, *Franklin D. Roosevelt and Foreign Affairs*, 2:423.

446 "We do want and ought to have": Press conference, July 19, 1935.

446 "I have approved this Joint Resolution": Signing statement, Aug. 31, 1935.

447 "It was a curious experience": Ickes, 1:477.

447 "either possess great wealth": *New York Times,* Dec. 5, 1935.

447 "Whether or not he read": Ickes, 1:480.

447 "In March 1933": Annual message, Jan. 3, 1936.

449 "I speak tonight to this Democratic meeting": Address, Jan. 8, 1936.

450 "The listeners in the dining room": *New York Times,* Jan. 26, 1936.

450 "I was born in the Democratic party": Ibid.

451 "Unless the Republican party is delivered": Ibid., Nov. 9, 1934.

452 "Our problems have been intensified . . . win the election": Schlesinger, 3:539–41.

452 "We cannot go back": *New York Times,* March 1, 1936.

453 "one of the most aggressive campaigns": Ibid., June 12, 1936.

453 "economic royalists": Acceptance speech, June 27, 1936.

453 "Of course we spent money": Address, Oct. 12, 1936.

454 "Nine crazy years": Address, Oct. 31, 1936.

454 "Betting commissioners recalled yesterday": *New York Times,* Nov. 1, 1936.

454 "I am sending you": Farley, 1:324–25.

455 "As Maine goes": Ibid., 1:326.

CHAPTER 33

456 "The President seemed very happy": Ickes, 1:703–05.

456 "If they can take it, I can": *New York Times,* Jan. 21, 1937.

457 "We have always known": Inaugural address, Jan. 20, 1937.

458 "Sometimes I say things . . . I have ever known": Lash, 363, 378, 424.

460 "The cost of the thing is shocking": Ickes, 1:152.

461 "Mr. Baruch has given me 'carte blanche' ": Cook, 2:141.

461 "Over in the school shop": *New York Times,* May 5, 1935.

461 "No hope beyond twenty-four hours . . . on his own now": Rollins, *Roosevelt and Howe,* 443–48.

462 "By assuring the employees": Statement, July 5, 1935.

464 "I'm not going down in history as Bloody Murphy!": Sidney Fine, *Sit-Down: The General Motors Strike of 1936–1937* (1969), 294.

464 "What law are they breaking?": Perkins, 321–22.

464 "Have you anything to say": Press conference, Jan. 22, 1937.

464 "I shall order the men": D. Kennedy, 313.

465 "I know you have been through a lot": Perkins, 323–34.

465 "another milestone . . . make automobiles": *New York Times,* Feb. 12, 1937.

466 "I think I can put it this way": Press conference, June 29, 1937.

466 "Though not as yet": *Nation,* July 31, 1937.

467 "It ill behooves one who has supped": *New York Times,* Sept. 4, 1937.

467 "All in . . . no discussion": Press conference, Feb. 5, 1937.

470 "disguise of sophistry . . . he will get it": Excerpts of editorial opinion in *New York Times,* Feb. 6, 1937.

471 "shortcut to dictatorship . . . of the country": Ibid., Feb. 6, 11, and 15, 1937; D. Kennedy, 331–32.

472 "frightful . . . of the government": *New York Times,* Feb. 14, 1937.

472 "I am reminded": Fireside Chat, March 9, 1937.

473 51 percent . . . 45 percent: *Washington Post,* May 24 and June 20, 1937.

474 "the greatest constitutional somersault": William E. Leuchtenburg, *The Supreme Court Reborn: The Constitutional Revolution in the Age of Roosevelt* (1995), 176.

CHAPTER 34

480   "Up with your spears!": *New York Times*, Oct. 4, 1935.

481   "I have seen war": Address, Aug. 14, 1936.

481   "At 2 A.M. today": *New York Times*, April 28, 1937.

481   "the unspeakable crime of war": Ibid., May 10, 1937.

482   "Here fascism presents to the world": Ibid., May 7, 1937.

483   "The present reign of terror": Address, Oct. 5, 1937.

483   "Japan will not easily be beaten . . . will be redoubled": Editorial summary in *New York Times*, Oct. 6, 1937.

484   "Do you care to amplify": Press conference, Oct. 6, 1937.

484   "It is a terrible thing": Rosenman, 167.

CHAPTER 35

485   "You have made yourself the trustee": From Keynes, Dec. 30, 1933, printed in *New York Times*, Dec. 31, 1933.

486   "Right in the midst of good business": *New York Times*, Oct. 19, 1937.

487   Uncertainty rules the tax situation": Robert Higgs, "Regime Uncertainty: Why the Great Depression Lasted So Long and Why Prosperity Resumed after the War," *Independent Review*, Spring 1997, 576.

487   "Practically no business group": Berle, 171.

487   "We are headed right": Morgenthau, 1:391–96.

489   "Businessmen have a different set of delusions": D. E. Moggridge, *Maynard Keynes: An Economist's Biography* (1992), 607.

490   "Most business men": Fireside Chat, Oct. 12, 1937.

490   "Capital is essential": Annual message, Jan. 3, 1938.

491   "The President told them": Morgenthau, 1:385.

491   "an hysteria resembling a mob . . . I don't": Ibid., 386–95.

492   "something terrible": Ibid., 398–400.

493   "strike . . . the cat steal it": *Washington Post*, Dec. 30, 1937.

493   "the sixty families": *New York Times*, Dec. 31, 1938.

493   "As I see it . . . heavyweight championship": Morgenthau, 1:414–15.

494   "They just stampeded him": Ibid., 421.

494   "definite additions to the purchasing power": Fireside Chat, April 14, 1938.

495   "Please tell the Japanese Ambassador": Memorandum, Dec. 13, 1937.

495   "This was the lamest of lame excuses": Hull, 1:562.

496   "profound apology": *FRUS: Japan, 1931–1941*, 1:521.

496   "wild, runaway, half-insane men": Dallek, 154.

496   "jingoism": *New York Times*, Dec. 14, 1937.

496   "After all": Morgenthau, 1:489.

497   "Within ninety days": Leuchtenburg, 261–62.

497   "That, my friends, is not right": Address, May 27, 1938.

498   "There will be many clashes": Fireside Chat, June 24, 1938.

499   "The Boss has stirred up . . . you're foolish": Farley, 2:122, 137.

499   "of enormous help to me": Address, July 9, 1938.

499   "He is, and I hope": Address, Aug. 11, 1938.

500   "It's time to stop feeling sorry": Farley, 2:121.

CHAPTER 36

501   "There were only two people": Lash, 505.

501   "Just before Christmas": Ibid., 504.

502 "This was pure spite": Sherwood, 90.

503 "And remember . . . assurances and hopes": Ibid., 93–97.

504 "We're here to implement a policy . . . I couldn't take it": Lash, 506.

505 "cripple any President": To William Bankhead, Jan. 6, 1938.

506 "international gangsters . . . serious concern": Dallek, 157; Berle, 168–69; Hull, 1:575.

507 "You cannot get news": Press conference, Sept. 6, 1938.

508 "force, militarism, and territorial aggression": Memo by Hull, July 7, 1938, *Peace and War*, 424.

508 "great tragedy of today": Hull, 1:588.

509 "immediate danger": Message, Sept. 26, 1938.

509 "It does not rest with the German Government": from Hitler, Sept. 27, 1938.

509 "The world asks of us": To Hitler, Sept. 27, 1938.

510 "The justified and understandable anger . . . German economic life": *New York Times*, Nov. 11–13, 1938.

510 "deeply shocked": Press conference, Nov. 15, 1938.

511 "I don't know . . . very difficult problem": Press conference, Nov. 18, 1938.

511 "A war which threatened to envelop": Address, Jan. 4, 1939.

512 "remotely intimate": Message, Jan. 12, 1939.

513 "No one here has any illusions": Berle, 201.

513 "Acts of wanton lawlessness": State Department statement, March 17, 1939.

513 "Mr. President": Press conference, March 17, 1939.

513 "madder and madder": Ickes, 2:597.

514 "Hundreds of millions": To Hitler and Mussolini, April 14, 1939.

514 "My friends of Warm Springs": Remarks, April 9, 1939.

515 "Mr. Roosevelt!" *New York Times*, April 29, 1939.

516 "Joe Robinson tells me": Walter White, *A Man Called White: The Autobiography of Walter White* (1948), 169–70.

516 "I'm sorry about the bill . . . obsession that he has": Lash, 518.

517 "I pointed out": Ickes, 54.

517 "The question is": "My Day," Feb. 27, 1939, in *My Day: The Best of Eleanor Roosevelt's Acclaimed Newspaper Columns, 1936–1962*, ed. David Emblidge (2001), 34.

517 "There are those": *New York Times*, April 10, 1939.

518 "She sang with her eyes closed": *Washington Post*, April 10, 1939.

518 "Thanks in large measure to you": Lash, 527.

CHAPTER 37

519 "Roosevelt wants to fight . . . eighteen bills": Dallek, 187.

519 "It was a desperate effort . . . all there is to it": Ibid., 192; Hull, 1:649–50.

521 "Today, August 7, 1939": Message, Aug. 7, 1939.

521 "I think it is very important": Press conference, Aug. 8, 1939.

522 "Don't, for Heaven's sake": Ibid.

524 "It is still too early to judge the implications": *New York Times*, Aug. 22, 1939.

524 "I am again addressing": To Hitler, Aug. 24, 1939.

525 "It is an eerie experience": J. Kennedy, 371.

526 "It is a terrible thing . . . their way homeward": Ibid., 365, 371.

526 "High Government officials": From Kennedy, Sept. 10, 1939, J. Kennedy, 372–74.

527 "With earnest best wishes": From Churchill, Oct. 8, 1933.

528 "It is because you and I": To Churchill, Sept. 11, 1939.

528 "I hope you will at all times": To Chamberlain, Sept. 11, 1939, FDRL.

528 "The only method": Telephone call from Churchill, Oct. 5, 1939.

529   "I do not believe at this particular time": Press conference, Sept. 1, 1939.
530   "hoped against hope": Fireside Chat, Sept. 3, 1939.
530   "I hope and believe": To Chamberlain, Sept. 11, 1939, FDRL.
531   "They are, in my opinion": Message to Congress, Sept. 21, 1939.
532   "In other words": *New York Times,* Oct. 22, 1939.
532   "a bond of race and not of political ideology": Ibid., Oct. 14, 1939.
532   "I certainly do not want to impose": Ibid., Oct. 24, 1939.
533   "You can't lick a steamroller": Ibid., Oct. 11, 1939.
533   "I am very glad": Ibid., Nov. 4, 1939.
533   The repeal of the arms embargo": From Chamberlain, Nov. 8, 1939, FDRL.
533   "Los Angeles aircraft manufacturers": *New York Times,* Nov. 3, 1939.

CHAPTER 38

537   "Hitler is taller": From Welles, March 2, 1940, FDRL.
537   "This visit is solely for the purpose": Press conference, Feb. 9, 1940.
538   "the greatest interest in the highest government circles": Kirk to Hull, Feb. 14, 1940, *FRUS: 1940,* 1:8.
538   "The Minister received me at the door": From Welles, March 2, 1940, FDRL.
540   "My car drove into a rectangular court": Ibid.
542   "The scene has darkened swiftly": From Churchill, May 15, 1940.
542   "Ever so many thanks": To Churchill, Feb. 1, 1940.
542   "Although I have changed my office": From Churchill, May 15, 1940.
543   "I am sure it is unnecessary": To Churchill, May 16, 1940.
544   "Our intention is whatever happens": From Churchill, May 20, 1940.
545   "Even though large tracts of Europe": Martin Gilbert, *Churchill: A Life* (1992), 656.
546   "The power of aviation": *New York Times,* May 20, 1940.
547   "further extension of the area of hostilities": To Mussolini, April 29, 1940, *Peace and War.*
547   "Italy has never concerned itself": From Mussolini, May 2, 1940, *Peace and War.*
547   "a realist": To Mussolini, May 14, 1940, *Peace and War.*
547   "There are two fundamental motives": From Mussolini, May 18, 1940, *Peace and War.*
547   "On this tenth day of June": Address, June 10, 1940.
548   "We all listened to you last night": From Churchill, June 11, 1940.
549   "For six days and six nights": From Reynaud, June 10, 1940, *Peace and War.*
550   "Our army is now cut into several parts": From Reynaud, June 14, 1940, *Peace and War.*

CHAPTER 39

551   "He needs this peace": From Churchill, June 14, 1940.
551   "This moment is supremely critical": From Churchill, June 15, 1940.
551   "I am doing everything possible": To Douglas, June 7, 1940.
552   "These are black days for the human race": Hull address, June 20, 1940, *Peace and War.*
552   "political miracle": *New York Times,* June 30, 1940.
552   "If a whore repented": Jonathan Daniels, *The Time between the Wars: Armistice to Pearl Harbor* (1966), 309.
553   "What I am against is power": *New York Times,* June 30, 1940.
553   "What's the Boss going to do?": Farley, 2:237.
554   "They did not support Roosevelt": Sherwood, 177–78.
554   "our beloved President—Franklin Delano Roosevelt": *New York Times,* July 16, 1940.
554   "The President's refusal to take anyone": Ickes, 3:240.
555   "Dear Will": Sherwood, 177.

555   "Apparently I am not the only one around here": *New York Times,* July 16, 1940.
556   "He goes about looking like an early Christian martyr": Ickes, 3:232.
556   "Just because the Republicans": Sherwood, 179.
557   "The party longs": Perkins oral history, 7:481.
557   "damned outrage": Farley, 2:297.
557   "I had luncheon today": Sherwood, 117–18.
558   "It might be very nice": ER, 2:215.
558   "The situation is not good": Farley, 2:283.
558   "Are you happy": *New York Times,* July 19, 1940.
559   "Eight years in the presidency": Radio address, July 19, 1940.
560   "The last three nights in London": Kennedy to Rose Kennedy, Sept. 10, 1940, J. Kennedy.
561   "It has now become most urgent": From Churchill, July 31, 1940.
561   "He was smoking a cigar": Kennedy diary, Aug. 14, 1940, J. Kennedy.
562   "I am beginning to feel very hopeful": From Churchill, July 31, 1940.
562   "It is my belief": To Churchill, Aug. 13, 1940.
564   "I need not tell you how cheered I am": From Churchill, Aug. 14, 1940.
564   "I had not contemplated": From Churchill, Aug. 22, 1940.
565   I told him the gist of the proposal": To Walsh, Aug. 22, 1940.
566   "This has nothing to do with destroyers": Press conference, Aug. 16, 1940.
567   "The right to bases in Newfoundland": Message, Sept. 3, 1940.

                              CHAPTER 40
569   "There is no more resemblance": Hull, 1:890.
569   "The American people": Hull memo, May 16, 1940, *Peace and War.*
569   "The United States has no aggressive designs": Hull to Grew, May 30, 1940, *Peace and War.*
569   "tantamount to an embargo": Japanese embassy to State Department, Aug. 3, 1940, *FRUS: Japan, 1931–1941,* 2:219.
569   "unfriendly act": Japanese embassy to State Department, Oct. 7, 1940, *FRUS: Japan, 1931–1941,* 2:224.
569   "There cannot be any doubt": Grew to Hull, Sept. 12, 1940, *Peace and War.*
570   "I should like to see this nation": Message, May 16, 1940.
570   "The one most obvious lesson": Message, May 31, 1940.
570   "The principal lesson of the war": Message, July 10, 1940.
571   "There is a very definite feeling": Press conference, Aug. 2, 1940.
571   "that smacks of totalitarianism": *New York Times,* Aug. 3, 1940.
571   "very antithesis of freedom": Ibid., Aug. 7, 1940.
571   A survey of papers . . . Gallup poll: Ibid., Aug. 4 and 11, 1940.
572   "This is the biggest day": Ibid., Aug. 11, 1940.
572   "He has no desire to cooperate": To Edward Taylor, Aug. 12, 1940.
572   "I am absolutely opposed to the postponement": Press conference, Aug. 23, 1940.
572   "America stands at the crossroads of its destiny": Proclamation, Sept. 16, 1940.
573   "If you elect him for a third term . . . they won't be sent": *New York Times,* Sept. 17 and 26, Oct. 9, 15, 18, 20, 26, 30, 1940.
574   "A lead of 53 percent": Ibid., Oct. 30, 1940.
574   "political shenanigans": Statement, Oct. 30, 1940.
574   "When that term is over": Address, Nov. 2, 1940.
574   "Did you definitely mean that?": Press conference, Nov. 8, 1940.
575   "I did not think it right for me as a foreigner": From Churchill, Nov. 6, 1940.
576   "Does anyone seriously believe": Fireside Chat, Dec. 29, 1940.

577   "Orders from Great Britain": Press conference, Dec. 17, 1940.

579   "In the future days": Annual message, Jan. 6, 1941.

580   "Make no mistake about it . . . every fourth American boy": *New York Times,* Jan. 13 and 15, Feb. 25, 1941; *Washington Post,* Feb. 23, 1941.

581   "the most dastardly, unpatriotic thing": Press conference, Jan. 14, 1941.

581   "Garner was there": Ickes, 3:409.

581   "So far as I know": Dallek, 258.

582   "In the last war": *New York Times,* Feb. 10, 1941.

582   "I think this verse applies": To Churchill, Jan. 20, 1941.

583   71 percent: *New York Times,* Jan. 26, 1941.

583   "Let not the dictators of Europe or Asia": Address, March 15, 1941.

CHAPTER 41

584   "I suppose you could say": Sherwood, 236.

584   "The extraordinary fact": Ibid., 212.

585   "You know": Ibid., 230.

585   "Does Mr. Hopkins have any special mission": Press conference, Jan. 3, 1941.

586   "I want to try to get an understanding . . . the future of democracy": Sherwood, 236–49.

588   "No power and no support . . . into the war": *Time,* March 24, 1941.

589   "the end of any attempts": Address, March 15, 1941.

589   "in the interest of national safety": Statement, April 21, 1941.

589   "Our problem is to see to it": Open letter to Knudsen and Hillman, April 30, 1941.

590   "Command of the air": Open letter to Frank Knox, May 5, 1941.

590   "Defense is a national task": Open letter to Doughton, May 1, 1941.

590   "Under the present circumstances": Announcement, April 10, 1941.

590   "I think some of you know": Press conference, April 25, 1941.

590   "What started as a European war": Fireside Chat, May 27, 1941.

592   "From every source at my disposal": From Churchill, June 14, 1941.

593   "The Russian danger": Churchill, 3:333.

593   "Any rallying of the forces": Welles statement, June 24, 1941, *Peace and War,* 684.

593   "It's a case of dog-eat-dog . . . prostrate Poland": *New York Times,* June 24, 1941.

594   "Is the defense of Russia the defense of the United States?": Ibid., June 25, 1941.

595   "I owed her that much": James Roosevelt, with Bill Libby, *My Parents* (1976), 108.

595   "though I do not know exactly what one's feelings are": from Lucy Mercer Rutherfurd, April 16, 1927, FDRL.

595   "Mrs. Johnson": Resa Willis, *FDR and Lucy* (2004), 97.

596   "There are two groups in Japan": Hull, 2:1003.

596   "de Gaullist French agents": Memo by Welles, July 23, 1941, *Peace and War,* 693.

596   "If these oil supplies": Memo of conversation, July 24, 1941, *Peace and War,* 699–703.

597   "I have had no answer yet": To Hopkins, July 26, 1941.

597   "to prevent the use of the financial facilities of the United States": Executive order, July 26, 1941.

CHAPTER 42

598   "The resistance of the Russian Army": Sherwood, 306–08.

599   "I ask you to treat Mr. Hopkins": To Stalin, July 26, 1941.

599   "It was monumental": Sherwood, 326.

599   "Mr. Stalin spoke of the necessity": Hopkins memo of meeting of July 30, 1941, *FRUS: 1941: Soviet Union,* 803–04.

600   "because then the troops learn . . . any other force": Hopkins memo of meeting of
       July 31, 1941, *FRUS: 1941: Soviet Union*, 804–14.
601   "Not once did he repeat himself": Sherwood, 343.
602   "Harry returned dead beat": From Churchill, Aug. 5, 1941.
603   "on board ship somewhere in the Atlantic": Hull to FDR, Aug. 6, 1941, FDRL.
603   "All that need be said": To Hull, Aug. 6, 1941, FDRL.
603   "I was faced with a practical problem": FDR memo, Aug. 23, 1941, FDRL.
606   "I saw Father in a new role": Elliott Roosevelt, *As He Saw It*, 10, 28–30.
607   "very remarkable religious service": Press conference, Aug. 16, 1941.
607   "would be compelled to take counter measures": Sherwood, 354.
607   "He did not think that there was much hope": Ibid.
608   "common principles in the national policies": Joint statement, Aug. 14, 1941.
609   "At the Atlantic meeting we had in mind": *The Churchill War Papers: The Ever Widen-*
       ing War, 1941, ed. Martin Gilbert (2001), 1186.
609   "Are we any closer to entering the war?": Press conference, Aug. 16, 1941.
609   "He would wage war": Dallek, 285.
610   "The danger today is infinitely greater": Message to Congress, July 21, 1941.
610   "She was carrying American mail to Iceland": Fireside Chat, Sept. 11, 1941.

                              CHAPTER 43
612   "I simply have not got enough navy": Ickes, 3:567.
613   68 percent of Americans: *New York Times*, Sept. 28, Oct. 3 and 5, 1941.
613   "After twenty years the American people": *Los Angeles Times*, Sept. 30, 1941.
613   "crippling provisions": Message to Congress, Oct. 9, 1941.
614   "The shooting has started": Address, Oct. 27, 1941.
615   Decades later a retired British agent claimed: Nicholas John Cull, *Selling War: The*
       British Propaganda Campaign against American "Neutrality" (1995), 171–73; Wesley K.
       Wark, *Espionage: Past, Present, Future?* (1994), 91, n. 26.
615   "If we take this one further step . . . theaters of this war": *New York Times*, Nov. 5, 1941.
616   "outrageous evidence . . . out of the fight": Ibid., Nov. 1, 1941.
616   "Lots of people who think": Press conference, Nov. 3, 1941.
617   "Failure to repeal": To Rayburn and McCormack, Nov. 13, 1941.
617   "Naturally, the President is pleased with the result": *New York Times*, Nov. 14, 1941.
617   "Japan and the United States": From Konoye, Aug. 27, 1941, *FRUS: Japan, 1931–1941*,
       2:572–73.
618   "of the efforts of a third country": Memo of conversation, Aug. 28, 1941, *FRUS: Japan,*
       1931–1941, 2:576.
618   "It is with great regret and disappointment": Konoye to Grew, Oct. 16, 1941, *FRUS:*
       Japan, 2:691.
618   "The Jap situation is definitely worse": To Churchill, Oct. 15, 1941.
619   "The Japanese menace": From Churchill, Oct. 18, 1941.
619   "that big ship you inspected": From Churchill, Nov. 2, 1941.
619   "Empire Approaches Its Greatest Crisis": Grew to Hull, Nov. 3, 1941, *FRUS: Japan*,
       2:701–4.
620   "This, to us, could mean only one thing": Hull, 2:1057.
620   "Relations are extremely critical": Ibid., 1058.
620   "We know that it was, in literal truth": Address, Nov. 11, 1941.
621   "Kurusu seemed to me the antithesis of Nomura": Hull, 2:1062–63.
621   "Nations must think one hundred years ahead": Memo by Hull, Nov. 10, 1941, *FRUS:*
       Japan, 2:718.

621   He jotted a note to Hull: William L. Langer and S. Everett Gleason, *The Undeclared War, 1940–1941: The World Crisis and American Foreign Policy* (1953), 872.

622   "All the way across the Pacific": Memo by Hull, Nov. 17, 1941, *FRUS: Japan*, 2:740.

622   "the restoration of peace between Japan and China": Japanese draft proposal, Nov. 20, 1941, *FRUS: Japan*, 2:755.

622   "of so preposterous a character": Hull, 2:1070.

622   "brought up entirely the relations with the Japanese": Stimson diary, Nov. 25, 1941.

623   "Any such expedition to the South": Ibid.

623   "He fairly blew up": Ibid., Nov. 26, 1941.

623   "The Government of Japan will withdraw": Hull to Nomura, Nov. 26, 1941, *FRUS: Japan*, 2:769.

624   "This seems to me a fair proposition": To Churchill, Nov. 24, 1941.

624   "We have been very patient": Memo by Hull, Nov. 27, 1941, *FRUS: Japan*, 2:771.

624   "It seems to me": From Churchill, Nov. 30, 1941.

625   "further aggression": Memo by Welles, Dec. 2, 1941, *FRUS: Japan*, 2:779.

625   "F.D.R.'s WAR PLANS!": *Chicago Tribune*, Dec. 4, 1941. Other papers picked up and repeated the story.

626   "They have never constituted an authorized program": *New York Times*, Dec. 6, 1941.

626   "If we had been at war": Ickes, 3:659.

626   "I refuse to believe": *New York Times*, Dec. 6, 1941.

626   "deep and far-reaching emergency": To Hirohito, Dec. 6, 1941.

                             CHAPTER 44

628   "It has been a hard two weeks": Lash, 643–44.

628   "I think she is failing fast": E. Roosevelt and A. Roosevelt, 135.

629   "The funeral was nice and simple": Ibid., 136.

629   "Pa has taken Granny's death": Ibid., 137.

629   "She had carefully saved": Tully, 105.

629   "He never looked toward the grave": *Washington Post*, Sept. 10, 1941.

630   "I just can't": E. Roosevelt and A. Roosevelt, 137.

630   "Hyde Park could be": Roosevelt and Shalett, 319.

630   "This son of man has just sent his final message": Ibid., 646.

631   "Sit down, Grace": Tully, 256.

632   "Yesterday, December 7, 1941": Address to Congress, Dec. 8, 1941.

633   "became engaged in a war against the United States": Sherwood, 441.

633   "The sudden criminal attacks": Fireside Chat, Dec. 9, 1941.

634   "Our patience is ended . . . place in the sun": *New York Times*, Dec. 12, 1941.

634   "The long known and the long expected": Message to Congress, Dec. 11, 1941.

635   "I've always heard things came in threes": *New York Times*, Dec. 12, 1941.

                             CHAPTER 45

636   "So we had won after all!": Churchill, 3:605–6.

636   "Now that we are": From Churchill, Dec. 9, 1941.

636   "In August it was easy to agree": Unsent draft to Churchill, Dec. 10, 1941.

637   "Delighted to have you here": To Churchill, Dec. 10, 1941.

637   "I clasped his strong hand": Churchill, 3:662–63.

639   "There was general agreement": Churchill to war cabinet, Dec. 23, 1941, Churchill 3:664.

640   "The Prime Minister of Great Britain": Sherwood, 442–43.

640   "Our view remains that Germany": Memo by U.S. and British chiefs of staff, Dec. 31, 1941, *FRUS: Conferences at Washington, 1941–1942, and Casablanca, 1943*.

640   "As a result of what I saw in France": U.S. minutes of meeting, Dec. 25, 1941, *FRUS: Washington and Casablanca,* 92–93.

641   "highest authority": Ibid.

641   "continuous line of battle": Minutes by Sexton, Dec. 26, 1941, *FRUS: Washington and Casablanca.*

641   "You should work on Churchill": Sherwood, 457.

641   "Don't be in a hurry . . . meet the American view": Churchill, 3:673–74.

643   "common program of purposes and principles": Declaration of United Nations, Jan. 1, 1942.

643   "Generals Arnold, Eisenhower, and Marshall": Stimson diary, Dec. 25, 1941.

644   "His view was that these reinforcements": Hollis to Smith, Dec. 24, 1941, *FRUS: Washington and Casablanca.*

644   "I then read to him extracts": Stimson diary, Dec. 25, 1941.

644   "We discussed various things": Ibid.

645   "This is a strange Christmas Eve": Churchill, 3:670.

645   "I wish indeed that my mother . . . and in peace": *New York Times,* Dec. 27, 1941.

646   "auspicious and impressive . . . less oratory and more action": Ibid.

647   "The last evening of Churchill's visit": Sherwood, 477–78.

CHAPTER 46

649   "In this year, 1942 . . . Italy and Japan": State of the Union address, Jan. 6, 1942.

651   "This is a new kind of war . . . freedom from fear": Fireside Chat, Feb. 23, 1942.

653   "This is not an impudent question, sir": Press conference, Dec. 9, 1941.

654   "subversive activities in the United States . . . those cocksuckers": Ronald Kessler, *The Bureau: The Secret History of the FBI* (2002), 52–53; Richard Gid Powers, *Broken: The Troubled Past and Uncertain Future of the FBI* (2004), 168.

655   "This task must be conducted": Statement, Sept. 6, 1939.

655   "With those aliens who are disloyal": Signing statement, June 29, 1940.

656   "There must not be permitted": Powers, *Broken,* 186.

656   "We're charged with wanting to get rid of the Japs": Greg Robinson, *By Order of the President: FDR and the Internment of Japanese Americans* (2001), 90.

656   "In view of the circumstances": *New York Times,* Feb. 12, 1942.

657   "The Fifth Column on the Coast": *Washington Post,* Feb. 12, 1942.

657   "We are so damned dumb": Ibid., Feb. 15, 1942.

657   "When it comes to suddenly mopping up": Morgenthau, 3:3.

657   "the Department of Justice would not under any circumstances": Francis Biddle, *In Brief Authority* (1962), 218.

657   "The second generation Japanese": Stimson diary, Feb. 10, 1942.

658   "There will probably be some repercussions": Robinson, *By Order of the President,* 106.

658   "the successful prosecution of the war": Executive Order 9066, Feb. 19, 1942.

659   "The Philippine theater is the locus of victory or defeat": H. W. Brands, *Bound to Empire: The United States and the Philippines* (1992), 190.

659   "The people of the United States": Message to Philippine people, Dec. 28, 1941.

660   "Our troops have been subsisted": Brands, *Bound to Empire,* 196.

660   "These people are depending on me now": Ibid., 197.

660   "The President of the United States ordered me": *New York Times,* March 21, 1942.

660   "When I reflect how I have longed and prayed": From Churchill, March 5, 1942.

662   "I reacted so strongly and at such length": Churchill, 4:209.

663   "I have given much thought": To Churchill, March 10, 1942.

663   "We must not on any account": From Churchill, March 4, 1942.

664 "disastrous effect": To Churchill, Aug. 11, 1942.

664 "Its proposed application to Asia and Africa": From Churchill, Aug. 9, 1942.

665 "I am sure you will have no objection": To Churchill, Aug. 13, 1942.

CHAPTER 47

666 "I realize how the fall of Singapore has affected you": To Churchill, Feb. 18, 1942.

667 "Thirteen B-25s effectively bombed . . . than we sent over": From Arnold, May 3, 1942, FDRL.

668 "How about the story about the bombing": Press conference, April 21, 1942.

671 "What Harry and Geo. Marshall will tell you": To Churchill, April 3, 1942.

671 "Marshall presented in broad outlines": Sherwood, 523.

671 "momentous proposal": Churchill, 4:317–20.

672 "I am delighted with the agreement": To Churchill, April 21, 1942.

672 "whole-hearted": From Churchill, April 17, 1942.

673 "I am very heartened at the prospect": To Churchill, April 21, 1942.

673 "I have a cordial message from Stalin": Ibid.

673 "I am looking forward": To Stalin, May 4, 1942.

674 "His style was cramped . . . second front this year": Sherwood, 561–63.

674 "Full understanding was reached": Roosevelt-Molotov statement, June 11, 1942.

675 "We know there will be two kinds . . . and possibly China": Sherwood, 572–73.

675 "May I very briefly recall": From Stimson, no date, *FRUS: Washington and Casablanca*, 458.

676 "You are familiar with my view": From Marshall, June 23, 1941, *FRUS: Washington and Casablanca*, 476.

677 "We are bound to persevere": From Churchill, June 20, 1942.

677 "This was one of the heaviest blows": Churchill, 4:383.

679 "extremely powerful bombs of a new type": From Einstein, Aug. 2, 1939, FDRL.

679 "Our talks took place after luncheon": Churchill, 4:379–80.

680 "One thing that might help win this war": Robert H. Ferrell, ed., *The Eisenhower Diaries* (1981), 48, 50.

680 "an integrated, general plan of operations" Memo from King, March 5, 1942, FDRL.

681 "Good for you": To Churchill, July 2, 1942.

681 "No responsible British General": From Churchill, July 8, 1942.

682 "You will proceed immediately to London": To Hopkins, Marshall, and King, July 16, 1942, Sherwood, 603–04.

682 "Marshall and King pushed very hard . . . full speed ahead": Sherwood, 611–12.

CHAPTER 48

683 "I should greatly like to have your aid": From Churchill, Aug. 4, 1942.

683 "Stalin took issue at every point": From Harriman, Aug. 10, 1942, *FRUS: 1942*, vol. 3.

684 "The Soviet Command built their plan": Stalin aide-mémoire, Aug. 13, 1942, *FRUS: 1942*, 3:621.

684 "I am sorry that I could not have joined with you": To Stalin, Aug. 18, 1942.

684 "Everything for us now turns on hastening Torch": Churchill, 4:494.

685 "The President has gone to Hyde Park": Ibid., 450–51.

685 "The attack should be launched": To Churchill, Aug. 30, 1942.

686 "as sharp a reproof . . . we needed him most": Sherwood, 635.

686 "They are almost prayerfully anxious": *New York Times*, Sept. 22, 1942.

686 "You did not know that was going on?": Press conference, Oct. 6, 1942.

686 "four main areas of combat": Fireside Chat, Sept. 14, 1942.

687 "You know . . . 'supposed to be secret' ": A. Merriman Smith, *Thank You, Mr. President* (1946), 54.

688 "Quite frankly I regard": To Early, Oct. 24, 1944, FDRL.

688 "to keep the cost of living": Message to Congress, April 27, 1942.

688 "stabilize the cost of living . . . of our own making": Message to Congress, Sept. 7, 1942.

689 "a comprehensive national economic policy": Executive Order 9250, Oct. 3, 1942.

690 "This whole nation of 130,000,000": Fireside Chat, Oct. 12, 1942.

690 "When I went in to see Roosevelt": Forrest C. Pogue, *George C. Marshall* (1966), 2:402.

691 "F.D.R. was on edge . . . We are striking back": Tully, 264.

691 "Upon the outcome depends": Burns, 2:292.

691 "I speak to you as one": Radio address, Nov. 7, 1942.

691 "My dear old friend . . . the Axis yoke": to Pétain, Nov. 8, 1942; Sherwood, 645–47; from Churchill, Nov. 2, 1942.

692 "You invoke pretexts which nothing justifies": Sherwood, 645.

693 "That man is Darlan": Ambrose, *Eisenhower,* 1:208.

693 "a nice old proverb of the Balkans": Press conference, Nov. 17, 1942.

693 "I have accepted General Eisenhower's political arrangements": Statement, Nov. 17, 1942.

693 "I appreciate fully the difficulties": Sherwood, 654.

694 "This is not the end": *New York Times,* Nov. 11, 1942.

694 "Darlan's murder": Churchill, 3:644.

CHAPTER 49

695 "We here are all highly gratified": From Stalin, Nov. 14, 1942.

695 "It seems to me that the Americans": Stalin to Churchill, Nov. 29, 1942, in Churchill to Roosevelt, Dec. 2, 1942.

695 "The more I consider our military situation": To Stalin, Dec. 2, 1942.

695 "I think I can tell you in advance": From Churchill, Nov. 26, 1942.

696 "It is impossible for me to leave the Soviet Union": From Stalin, Dec. 14, 1942.

696 "I prefer a comfortable oasis to the raft at Tilsit": To Churchill, Dec. 2, 1942.

696 "The aliases from this end": To Churchill, Jan. 2, 1943.

696 "Should you bring Willkie with you": From Churchill, Jan. 3, 1943.

696 "I'm not crazy about flying": To ER, Jan. 13, 1943.

696 "I dislike flying the more I do of it!": To John Roosevelt, Feb. 13, 1943.

697 "Inasmuch as I know that the Congressman": *Washington Post,* March 6, 1943.

698 "It was quite a place": Elliott Roosevelt, *As He Saw It,* 65–66.

698 "It gave me intense pleasure": Churchill, 3:675–76.

698 the Combined Chiefs produced a document: Final report of Combined Chiefs, Jan. 23, 1943, *FRUS: Washington and Casablanca.*

699 "At the time of France's surrender in 1940": Dwight D. Eisenhower, *Crusade in Europe* (1948), 84.

700 "I had continuous difficulties": Churchill, 3:682.

700 "De Gaulle is on his high horse . . . Get some sleep yourself, Elliott": Roosevelt, *As He Saw It,* 69–77.

703 "No distractions should be permitted . . . very slender reed": McCrea notes of Roosevelt-Giraud meeting, Jan. 19, 1943, Roosevelt, *As He Saw It,* 90–91.

703 "We delivered our bridegroom": To Hull, Jan. 18, 1943, *FRUS: Washington and Casablanca.*

704 "Roosevelt asked whether de Gaulle": Stimson diary, Feb. 3, 1943.

704 "the people realized that personal pride": John McCrea notes of Roosevelt–de Gaulle meeting, Jan. 22, 1943, *FRUS: Washington and Casablanca.*

704 "De Gaulle was a little bewildered": Hopkins notes, Jan. 24, 1943, *FRUS: Washington and Casablanca.*

705 "Another point": Press conference, Jan. 24, 1943.

705 "some feeling of surprise . . . our war effort": Churchill, 3:686–87.

706 "We have decided the operations": Roosevelt and Churchill to Stalin, Jan. 25, 1943.

706 "I thank you for the information": From Stalin, Jan. 30, 1943.

707 "When this is accomplished": Roosevelt and Churchill to Stalin, Feb. 9, 1943.

707 "In order to prevent the enemy from recovering": From Stalin, Feb. 16, 1943.

707 "unexpected heavy rains": To Stalin, Feb. 22, 1943.

707 "You will recall that you and Mr. Churchill": From Stalin, March 16, 1943.

CHAPTER 50

710 "The abolition of the extraterritorial system": Message to Senate, Feb. 1, 1943.

710 "Nations, like individuals, make mistakes": Message to Congress, Oct. 11, 1943.

711 "workers should not be discriminated against": Message to Congress, Sept. 13, 1940.

711 "the policy of the War Department": D. Kennedy, 766.

712 "I feel very strongly . . . Get it stopped": Lash, 534.

712 "I replied that there would be no violence": Jervis Anderson, *A. Philip Randolph: A Biographical Portrait* (1973), 255.

712 "Walter, how many people will *really* march?": Ibid., 257–58; White, *A Man Called White,* 190–92.

712 "I do hereby reaffirm the policy": Executive Order 8802, June 25, 1941.

714 "We'll destroy every zoot suit": *Los Angeles Times,* June 8 and 10, 1943.

714 "Anthony spent three evenings with me": To Churchill, March 17, 1943.

715 "a good deal of resistance . . . German public opinion": Hopkins memo, March 15, 1943, *FRUS: 1943,* vol. 3.

716 "This body should be world-wide . . . on our side": Hopkins memo, March 27, 1943, *FRUS: 1943,* vol. 3.

716 "I fear it will be the same story over again": Stimson diary, May 10, 1943.

716 "The United States accepts the strategic concept": Memo by Joint Chiefs, undated, *FRUS: Washington and Quebec,* 222.

717 "emphasis and priority . . . spring of 1944": Combined Chiefs of Staff minutes, May 12, 1943, *FRUS: Washington and Quebec.*

717 "invariably created a vacuum . . . until 1945 or 1946": Combined Chiefs of Staff minutes, May 13, 1943, *FRUS: Washington and Quebec.*

718 "every day a day in which we have toiled . . . hideous facts": *New York Times,* May 20, 1943.

720 "Mr. President, what is your reaction": Press conference, July 27, 1943.

721 "the moronic little king": *New York Times,* July 27, 1943.

721 "Neither of us": Press conference, July 27, 1943.

721 "The first crack in the Axis has come": Fireside Chat, July 28, 1943.

722 "We still have to knock out": Ibid.

723 "It seems highly probable": To Churchill, July 30, 1943.

723 "It is for their responsible government . . . on which to act:": From Churchill, July 29 and 30, 1943.

724 "I told the press today": To Churchill, July 30, 1943.

724 "My position is that once Mussolini": From Churchill, July 31, 1943.

724 "Poor Eisenhower is getting pretty harassed . . . than a master": Ambrose, *Eisenhower*, 1:254–55.

725 "Now is the time for every Italian": Joint statement by Roosevelt and Churchill, Sept. 10, 1943.

725 "We are in for some very tough fighting": Ambrose, *Eisenhower*, 1:263.

CHAPTER 51

726 "Heavy following seas" . . . 3806 miles": Log of President's Trip, Nov. 12–19, 1942, *FRUS: Conferences at Cairo and Tehran, 1943*.

729 "Peanut is really no dictator": Joseph W. Stilwell, *The Stilwell Papers*, ed. Theodore H. White (1991 ed.), 197.

729 "I was impressed by his calm": Churchill, 4:328.

730 "President Roosevelt expressed his view": Chinese summary of Nov. 23 meeting, *FRUS: Cairo and Tehran*.

731 "Let us make it a family affair . . . the President more gay": Churchill, 4:340–41.

732 "From the air we sighted train loads": Log, Nov. 27, 1943, *FRUS: Cairo and Tehran*.

732 "nervous time": Sherwood, 776.

732 "If anything like that were to happen": Churchill, 4:343–44.

733 "I am glad to see you": Charles Bohlen minutes of Roosevelt-Stalin meeting, Nov. 28, 1943, *FRUS: Cairo and Tehran*.

733 "I reflected on Stalin's fluency": Charles E. Bohlen, *Witness to History, 1929–1969* (1973), 142–43.

734 "The Chinese have fought very badly . . . would mean revolution": Bohlen minutes, Nov. 28, 1943, *FRUS: Cairo and Tehran*.

736 "We are sitting around this table . . . and northern France": Bohlen minutes and Combined Chiefs of Staff minutes of Roosevelt-Stalin-Churchill meeting, Nov. 28, 1943, *FRUS: Cairo and Tehran*.

737 "unbelievable quantity of food": Bohlen, *Witness to History*, 147.

738 "rotten to the core . . . of German capitulation": Bohlen minutes and supplementary memorandum of Roosevelt-Stalin-Churchill meeting, Nov. 28, 1943, *FRUS: Cairo and Tehran*.

739 "Roosevelt was about to say something else": Bohlen, *Witness to History*, 143–44.

740 "You know, the Russians are interesting people": Perkins, 83–84.

741 "The most notable feature of the dinner": Bohlen minutes of Roosevelt-Stalin-Churchill meeting, Nov. 29, 1943, *FRUS: Cairo and Tehran*.

742 "There are six to seven million Americans": Bohlen minutes of Roosevelt-Stalin meeting, Dec. 1, 1943, *FRUS: Cairo and Tehran*.

743 "Ike, you and I know who was the Chief of Staff": Sherwood, 770.

743 "We are engaged in a global war . . . if we keep him here": Pogue, *George C. Marshall*, 3:272–73.

744 "Hopkins came to see me . . . 'out of the country' ": Sherwood, 803.

745 "Who will command Overlord?": Bohlen minutes of Roosevelt-Churchill-Stalin meeting, Nov. 29, 1943, *FRUS: Cairo and Tehran*.

745 "Well, Ike": Eric Larabee, *Commander in Chief: Franklin Delano Roosevelt, His Lieutenants, and Their War* (1987), 438.

CHAPTER 52

746 "Resolved": *New York Times*, Nov. 6, 1943.

747 "the necessity of establishing": *Washington Post*, Nov. 2, 1943.

750   "William Bullitt, stand where you are . . . 'go *down there!*' ": Burns, 2:350; Benjamin Welles, *Sumner Welles: FDR's Global Strategist* (1997), 343–45.

750   "The President asked me to see him . . . more value than anyone": Welles, *Sumner Welles*, 347–49.

751   "Cut his throat": Ibid., 354.

751   "I do not remember ever seeing the President": Rosenman, 411.

752   "We had an awfully good time": Press conference, Dec. 17, 1943.

752   "Would you care to express any opinion": Press conference, Dec. 28, 1943.

753   "We have come to a clear realization . . . here at home": State of the Union address, Jan. 11, 1944.

754   "Within the past few weeks": Fireside Chat, Dec. 24, 1943.

756   "These are not mere strikes": Press conference, April 29, 1943.

757   "The action of the leaders of the United Mine Workers": Statement, June 23, 1943.

757   87 percent . . . "coal-black soul!": D. Kennedy, 643.

757   "For the entire year of 1942": Veto message, June 25, 1943.

758   "Railroad strikes by three brotherhoods": Executive Order 9412, Dec. 27, 1943.

758   "they and the organizations they represent": *Washington Post*, Dec. 30, 1943.

758   "I hereby charge that the responsibility": Ibid., Jan. 4, 1944.

CHAPTER 53

759   "We Jews of America": Henry Morgenthau, *All in a Lifetime* (1922), 404.

760   "Citizens, regardless of religious allegiance": *New York Times*, July 22, 1942.

760   "taken proportions and forms": Statement on Axis crimes, Aug. 21, 1942.

760   "Unless action is taken immediately": David S. Wyman, *The Abandonment of the Jews: America and the Holocaust, 1941–1945* (1984), 72–73.

760   "the President said that he was profoundly shocked": *New York Times*, Dec. 9, 1942.

760   "From all the occupied countries": *New York Times*, Dec. 18, 1942.

761   "cease to exist . . . we shall win the war": *New York Times*, July 15, 2000; Michael Beschloss, *The Conquerors: Roosevelt, Truman, and the Destruction of Hitler's Germany, 1941–1945* (2002), 40.

761   "One of the greatest crimes in history": "Personal Report to the President," Jan. 16, 1944, FDRL; Morgenthau memo, Jan. 16, 1944, FDRL.

761   "all measures within its power": Executive Order 9417, Jan. 22, 1944.

761   "In one of the blackest crimes of all history": Statement on war refugees, March 24, 1944.

763   "the Boss was not disposed to": *Washington Post*, April 17, 1983.

763   "We'll be accused of participating": Beschloss, *Conquerors*, 66.

763   "Yesterday, on June 4": Fireside Chat, June 5, 1944.

764   "My Lord! All smiles, all smiles!": Press conference, June 6, 1944.

765   "I think we have these Huns": Pogue, *George C. Marshall*, 3:391.

765   "an unheard-of achievement": Headnote to Stalin to Roosevelt, June 6, 1944.

766   "It rejoices all of us": From Stalin, June 7, 1944.

766   "It is remarkable": From Churchill, June 7, 1944.

766   "He may visit Washington": To Churchill, June 9, 1944.

766   "While I know that the chief interest tonight": Fireside Chat, June 12, 1944.

767   "Every one of our sons": To Robert Hannegan, July 11, 1944.

768   "The easiest way of putting it is this": To Jackson, July 14, 1944.

768   "very happy": *New York Times*, July 18, 1944.

769   "You have written me about Harry Truman": To Hannegan, July 19, 1944.

769 "Hell, I don't want to be president . . . in the first place?": David McCullough, *Truman* (1992), 308–14; Merle Miller, *Plain Speaking: An Oral Biography of Harry S. Truman* (1974), 181–82.

770 "You don't know how very much": *New York Times,* July 22, 1944.

770 "I shall not campaign, in the usual sense": Message to the Democratic convention, July 20, 1944.

772 "The humiliation of forcing me": Larabee, *Commander in Chief,* 342–43.

773 "One officer was conspicuously absent . . . worried to distraction": Rosenman, 456–59.

774 "Well, Douglas": Larabee, *Commander in Chief,* 343–44.

774 "Give me an aspirin": William Manchester, *American Caesar: Douglas MacArthur, 1880–1964* (1978), 427.

774 "When General MacArthur was about to leave": Press conference, July 29, 1944.

CHAPTER 54

776 "I was shocked by his appearance": Sherwood, 821.

778 "He appeared to be very tired": Howard G. Bruenn, "Clinical Notes on the Illness and Death of Franklin D. Roosevelt," *Annals of Internal Medicine* (1970), 579–91; Memo to Harper, undated, FDRL.

779 "This memorandum was rejected . . . and current events": Bruenn, "Clinical Notes."

780 "What would you think about our inviting": Goodwin, 517.

780 "They were occasions which I welcomed": Anna Roosevelt Halsted manuscript, undated, FDRL.

781 "I had really a grand time": Jean Edward Smith, *FDR* (2007), 606–07.

781 "He slept soundly and ate well": Bruenn, "Clinical Notes."

781 a low-fat diet: "Special Diet for the President," undated, FDRL.

781 "As usually happens . . . his normal, robust appearance": Bruenn, "Clinical Notes"; McIntire notes of FDR's vital signs, Sept. 20–Oct. 4, 1944, FDRL.

782 "You hear them everywhere you go": *Washington Post,* Oct. 28, 1944.

782 "good, very good": *New York Times,* Sept. 26, 1944.

782 "The President's health is perfectly O.K.": Ibid., Oct. 13, 1944.

782 "even more than the usual crop": Radio address, Nov. 2, 1944.

782 "You ought to hear him": Sherwood, 821.

783 "Imitation may be": Address, Sept. 23, 1944.

784 "Al Smith had qualities of heart": Statement, Oct. 4, 1944.

784 "doubly hypothetical surmise": Sherwood, 830.

784 "tremendous courage": Statement, Oct. 8, 1944.

785 "It's just a precaution . . . of righteous victory!": William B. Brewer, *Retaking the Philippines: America's Return to Corregidor and Bataan, July 1944–March 1945* (1986), 46–50; Douglas MacArthur, *A Soldier Speaks: Public Papers and Speeches of General of the Army, Douglas MacArthur,* ed. Vorin E. Whan Jr. (1965), 132–33.

785 "Please excuse this scribble": Douglas MacArthur, *Reminiscences* (1964), 216–18.

785 "The whole American nation today exults": Statement to MacArthur, Oct. 20, 1944.

786 "The power which this nation": Address, Oct. 21, 1944.

CHAPTER 55

787 "Dearest Franklin": Lash, 713.

787 "I offered a way": ER, 2:250.

787 "One feels": ER trip diary, Oct. 30, 1942, FDRL.

788 "Mrs. Roosevelt has been winning": From Churchill, Nov. 1, 1942.

788   "What would you do in China": ER, 2:284.
788   "Those delicate little petal-like fingers": Lash, 679.
788   "This trip will be attacked": Ibid., 682.
788   "This is the kind of thing": From ER, Sept. 6, 1943, FDRL.
788   "I've never been so hedged": Lash, 688.
789   "Wherever Mrs. Roosevelt went": *Christian Advocate,* Dec. 30, 1943.
789   "I wrote a column": ER to Joseph Lash, July 14, 1944, FDRL.
789   "I don't think Pa": Roosevelt and Shalett, 353.
789   "Mrs. Roosevelt urged the President": Sherwood, 831.
790   "Men and women": *New York Times,* Aug. 26, 1945.
790   "We rejoice with the gallant French people": Statement, Aug. 24, 1944.
791   "We should have sufficient material": Briefing paper by Groves, Dec. 30, 1944, *FRUS: Conferences at Malta and Yalta, 1945.*
792   "This was the first indication": Sherwood, 844–45.
792   "He says that if we had spent ten years": Log of Malta trip, Feb. 2, 1945, *FRUS: Malta and Yalta.*
794   "more bloodthirsty . . . only out of kindness": Bohlen notes of Roosevelt-Stalin meeting, Feb. 4, 1945, *FRUS: Malta and Yalta.*
794   "the whole map of Europe, in fact": Combined Chiefs of Staff minutes of Roosevelt-Stalin-Churchill meeting, Feb. 4, 1945, *FRUS: Malta and Yalta.*
795   "Marshal Stalin, the President, and the Prime Minister . . . wherefor they sang": Bohlen minutes of Roosevelt-Stalin-Churchill dinner meeting, Feb. 4, 1945, *FRUS: Malta and Yalta.*
796   "I would like to know, definitely . . . would be the limit": H. Freeman Matthews minutes, Feb. 5, 1945, *FRUS: Malta and Yalta.*
798   "in the Black Sea area": Joint communiqué, Feb. 7, 1945, *FRUS: Malta and Yalta.*
798   "in an excellent humor . . . from our grasp": Bohlen minutes, Feb. 8, 1945, *FRUS: Malta and Yalta.*
801   "I come from a great distance . . . they will be shot": Matthews minutes, Feb. 6, 1945, *FRUS: Malta and Yalta.*
802   "I am greatly disturbed": To Stalin, Feb. 6, 1945.
804   "Nazi Germany is doomed . . . and secret ballot": Yalta communiqué, Feb. 12, 1945, *FRUS: Malta and Yalta.*
804   "The leaders of the three Great Powers": Agreement, Feb. 11, 1945, *FRUS: Malta and Yalta.*

CHAPTER 56
805   "It was the best I could do": Berle, 477.
805   "Ten years from now": Bohlen minutes, Feb. 6, 1945, *FRUS: Malta and Yalta.*
806   "The President has lost ten pounds": Margaret Suckley, *Closest Companion: The Unknown Story of the Intimate Friendship between Franklin Roosevelt and Margaret Suckley,* ed. Geoffrey C. Ward (1995), 346.
806   "I had quite a talk with Anna": Ibid., 366–70.
806   "He was obviously greatly fatigued": Bruenn, "Clinical Notes."
807   "very tired": Churchill, 6:391, 397.
807   "Franklin feels his death very much": Suckley, *Closest Companion,* 397.
807   "I hope that you will pardon me . . . We cannot fail them again": Address to Congress, March 1, 1945.
809   "I did not think it": Hassett, 318.
809   "Tonight had another talk": Ibid., 327–28.

810   "The drive was too long": Suckley, *Closest Companion*, 413.

810   "His color was much better": Bruenn, "Clinical Notes."

810   "preceded by an Old-fashioned cocktail": Hassett, 332.

810   "His voice was wonderful": Smith, *Thank You, Mr. President*, 186.

810   "I have been offered": Morgenthau, 3:417.

811   "In the quiet beauty of the Georgia spring": Hassett, 333.

811   "He had slept well": Bruenn, "Clinical Notes."

811   "He came in, looking very fine": Suckley, *Closest Companion*, 417.

811   "He was in good spirits but did not look well": Hassett, 333.

811   "We have fifteen minutes . . . 'back of my head' ": Suckley, *Closest Companion*, 418.

812   "It was apparent that the President": Bruenn, "Clinical Notes"; Notes by Bruenn, April 12, 1945, FDRL.

CHAPTER 57

813   "I have a terrible announcement to make . . . miracle": *New York Times* and *Washington Post*, April 13–16, 1945.

815   "He should gain weight . . . in the question": Lash, 719–20.

816   "I did not even ask why": ER, 2:344.

816   "I am more sorry for the people . . . trouper to the last": Ibid.; *New York Times*, April 13, 1945; McCullough, *Truman*, 342.

817   She said that Lucy had been with the president: Lash, 722.

817   "I had schooled myself to believe": ER, 2:348–49.

820   "She would rather light a candle": *New York Times*, Nov. 8, 1962.

822   "Americans are gathered together": Posthumous message, April 13, 1945.

824   "You cannot go all this way": Churchill, 4:694.

824   "It's the most lovely spot": Charles McMoran Wilson Moran, *Churchill: The Struggle for Survival, 1940–1965, Taken from the Diaries of Lord Moran* (1966), 90.

824   "Come, Pendar, let's go home": Kenneth Pendar, *Adventure in Diplomacy: Our French Dilemma* (1945), 154.

Index